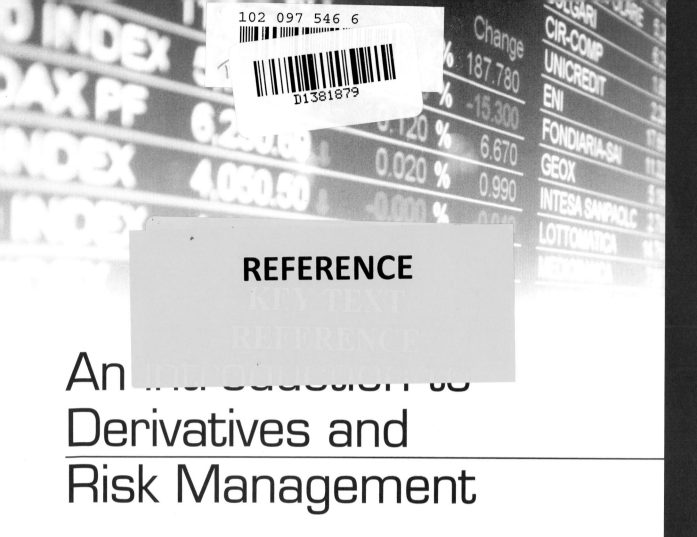

REFERENCE

An Introduction to Derivatives and Risk Management

An Introduction to Derivatives and Risk Management

9TH EDITION

DON M. CHANCE
Louisiana State University

ROBERT BROOKS
University of Alabama

SOUTH-WESTERN
CENGAGE Learning

Australia • Brazil • Japan • Korea • Mexico • Singapore • Spain • United Kingdom • United States

SOUTH-WESTERN
CENGAGE Learning

An Introduction to Derivatives and Risk Management, 9th International Edition
Don M. Chance, Robert Brooks

Vice President of Editorial, Business:
Jack W. Calhoun

Editor-in-Chief: Joe Sabatino

Executive Editor: Mike Reynolds

Developmental Editor: Ted Knight

Senior Editorial Assistant: Adele Scholtz

Marketing Manager: Nathan Anderson

Art Direction, Production Management, and Composition: PreMediaGlobal

Supervising Media Editor: Scott Fidler

Manufacturing Planner: Kevin Kluck

Senior Marketing Communications Manager: Jim Overly

Cover Designer: Patti Hudepohl

Cover Photo Credits:

   B/W Image: Ryan McVay/Getty Images

   Color Image: Shutterstock Images/ bioraven

Rights Acquisitions Specialist:
Amber Hosea

Library of Congress Control Number: 2011945841

International Edition:

ISBN-13: 978-1-133-19021-9

ISBN-10: 1-133-19021-9

Cengage Learning International Offices

Asia
www.cengageasia.com
tel: (65) 6410 1200

Australia/New Zealand
www.cengage.com.au
tel: (61) 3 9685 4111

Brazil
www.cengage.com.br
tel: (55) 11 3665 9900

India
www.cengage.co.in
tel: (91) 11 4364 1111

Latin America
www.cengage.com.mx
tel: (52) 55 1500 6000

UK/Europe/Middle East/Africa
www.cengage.co.uk
tel: (44) 0 1264 332 424

**Represented in Canada by
Nelson Education, Ltd.**
www.nelson.com
tel: (416) 752 9100 / (800) 668 0671

Cengage Learning is a leading provider of customized learning solutions with office locations around the globe, including Singapore, the United Kingdom, Australia, Mexico, Brazil, and Japan. Locate your local office at: **www.cengage.com/global**

For product information: **www.cengage.com/international**
Visit your local office: **www.cengage.com/global**
Visit our corporate website: **www.cengage.com**

Printed in Canada
1 2 3 4 5 6 7 16 15 14 13 12

Brief Contents

Contents

PART III   Advanced Topics

CHAPTER 13

Interest Rate Forwards and Options 456

Preface

DON CHANCE

As this book goes into its ninth edition, I continue to be amazed at how the derivatives and risk management world have evolved, even since the last edition. If there ever were a boring discipline, it is not this one. Perhaps it is because derivatives get so much of the blame and so little of the credit that we derivatives experts feel compelled to defend them against their critics. Warren Buffett, for example, called them "financial weapons of mass destruction," even though he uses them extensively. The Financial Crisis of 2008–2009 and the ensuing Dodd-Frank Act of 2010 took aim at certain derivatives while failing to note how well the overwhelming majority of firms managed their risks. Outside the misuse of credit default swaps by a handful of companies, most other derivatives resulted in little to no harm and indeed were highly beneficial to many. Yet, we advocates of derivatives have to remain vigilant, like the sentry on guard for the approaching enemy, the misuser of derivatives, who makes us all look bad.

In reading this book, I hope you become one of us: a vigilant defender of derivatives. And I hope you will become an intelligent and resourceful user of derivatives. When used properly with appropriate risk controls, they provide tremendous benefits. When misused, derivatives, like fire, chemicals, and electricity, can be extremely dangerous and indeed fatal to organizations. It is difficult to conceive of any product or service—indeed anything on the planet—that is not harmful if misused. Even water, the most vital element of life, can kill us. We simply resolve to use it properly. And we do not allow governments to ban swimming and boating just because someone drowned. There are no defenders of water, but the defenders of derivatives must be constantly on guard.

When I drafted the first proposal for this book many years ago, I was told by most publishers that there was no market for such a book. I tried to convince them that this was the future of finance. I hate to gloat, but I was right. Fortunately, a predecessor of Cengage had the foresight to create the future, not wait on it. Now we are in our ninth edition. To what Yogi Berra allegedly said, "the future ain't what it used to be," I would add that it's even better.

I would especially like to thank my wife Jan for numerous decades of support. Somewhere along the line I discovered that she had learned about derivatives just by being in love with me (Imagine that!). One day I was stuck on a crossword puzzle clue, a three-letter word meaning "option" that started with a "p." She then said, "Isn't there something called a put?" Needless to say it was embarrassing, but I have never been afraid to share that story, for it shows that derivatives knowledge is contagious. Hopefully you will pass some of it on to your loved ones.

ROBERT BROOKS

As we are now well into the twenty-first century and have experienced periods of financial calm as well as financial turmoil, the need for quality content on financial derivatives and risk management has never been greater. It is a privilege for me to collaborate with Don on such a successful book. My goal continues to be aiding students in understanding how to make financial derivatives theory work in practice. The financial derivatives and risk management subject area is a rapidly changing field that provides those who learn to navigate its complexities the opportunity for a rewarding career. By straddling the fence between the academic community and the practitioner community, I seek to continually enhance our book's quest to equip the next generation of financial risk managers.

I would like to encourage college students and others reading this book to consider a rewarding career in this field of study. From serving in a corporation, a financial services firm, or an investment management company, the ability to provide wise financial counsel inevitably leads to a fulfilling career. Knowing that you have contributed to protecting your firm from inappropriate financial risk or investing in an unsuitable strategy for your clients is both financially rewarding and personally gratifying.

I am deeply grateful to my wife Ann and my children: Joshua, Stephen, Paul, Rebekah, Phillips, and Rachael. At the time of this writing, two children are married and four children are teenagers, providing constant opportunities to refine teaching financial principles as well as applying risk management in practice. My family is a constant source of encouragement, and they are all very supportive of my activities related to this book.

DON AND BOB

We would like to thank Mike Reynolds, Executive Editor, Finance, for his continuing support over the years and for solving in a timely manner every problem that arose during the project. We would also like to thank Marketing Manager Nathan Anderson, to whose expertise we trust the future sales of the book.

Also, we would like to thank all those people who reviewed the 8th edition to make the 9th edition even stronger:

Karan Bhanot, University of Texas at San Antonio
David Enke, The University of Tulsa
Merlyn Foo, Athabasca University
Christine Jiang, University of Memphis
D.K. Malhotra, Philadelphia University
Gautam Vora, University of New Mexico

We would like to thank all of the people over the years who have both taught from this book and learned from it. They have, all along, generously provided constructive comments and corrections. After 20 years, this list of names is too long to print without leaving someone out. So to all of you unnamed heroes, we express our thanks.

We used to believe that the errors in a book should, through attrition over the years, disappear; however, we have learned otherwise. Although no one wants errors to remain, if you ever find a book in its ninth edition without any errors, you can be assured that the author is simply correcting old material and not keeping the book up to date. With a field as dynamic as derivatives, extensive changes are inevitable. Despite Herculean efforts to cleanse this work, there are ineluctably some errors that remain. We are fairly confident, however, that these are not errors of fact, but merely accidental oversights and perhaps typos that did not get caught as we read and reread the material.

Tell us what you like or don't like about the book. We would love to hear from you.

Don M. Chance, dchance@lsu.edu
James C. Flores Endowed Chair of MBA Studies & Professor of Finance
Department of Finance
2163 Patrick F. Taylor Hall
E. J. Ourso College of Business
Louisiana State University
Baton Rouge, LA 70803

Robert Brooks, rbrooks@cba.ua.edu
Wallace D. Malone, Jr. Endowed Chair of Financial Management
Department of Finance
The University of Alabama
200 Alston Hall, Box 870224
Tuscaloosa, AL 35487
March 2012

In life you just can't leave the future to chance. The best way to predict the future is to create the future.

Tim Ogunbiyi
Futures, February 2003, p. 90

An Introduction to Derivatives and Risk Management

CHAPTER 1

Introduction

Financial markets teach you humility. Two years ago, I made these related forecasts. First, I forecast the euro would strengthen as European economic recovery picked up and the U.S. economy slowed. Second, I forecast euro strength would be augmented over the next five years by a reduction of Europe's $100 billion to $150 billion of excess dollar reserves. Third, I forecast that the authorities would be less concerned over exchange rates, would only intervene after bigger exchange rate moves, and so exchange rate volatility would rise. Interestingly, people still ask for my opinion.

Avinash Persaud, Managing Director,
Global Markets Analysis, State Street Bank
Risk, October, 2000, p. 29

CHAPTER OBJECTIVES

- Provide brief introductions to the different types of derivatives: options, forward contracts, futures contracts, and swaps

- Reacquaint you with the concepts of risk preference, short selling, repurchase agreements, the risk-return relationship, and market efficiency

- Define the important concept of theoretical fair value, which will be used throughout the book

- Explain the relationship between spot and derivative markets through the mechanisms of arbitrage, storage, and delivery

- Identify the role that derivative markets play through their four main advantages

- Address some criticisms of derivatives

In the course of running a business, decisions are made in the presence of risk. A decision maker can confront one of two types of risk. Some risks are related to the underlying nature of the business and deal with such matters as the uncertainty of future sales or the cost of inputs. These risks are called **business risks**. Most businesses are accustomed to accepting business risks. Indeed, the acceptance of business risks and its potential rewards are the foundations of capitalism. Another class of risks deals with uncertainties such as interest rates, exchange rates, stock prices, and commodity prices. These are called **financial risks**.

Financial risks are a different matter. The paralyzing uncertainty of volatile interest rates can cripple the ability of a firm to acquire financing at a reasonable cost, which enable it to provide its products and services. Firms that operate in foreign markets can have excellent sales performance offset if their own currency is strong. Companies that use raw materials can find it difficult to obtain their basic inputs at a price that will permit profitability. Managers of stock portfolios deal on a day-to-day basis with wildly unpredictable and sometimes seemingly irrational financial markets.

Although our financial system is replete with risk, it also provides a means of dealing with risk in the form of derivatives. **Derivatives** are financial contracts whose returns are derived from those of other instruments. The word **instrument** is used here in the broadest possible way to include financial securities, financial contracts, and even items (e.g., temperature measurements). That is, derivatives performance depends on how other financial instruments perform. Derivatives serve a valuable purpose in providing a means of managing financial risk. By using derivatives, companies and individuals can transfer, for a price, any undesired risk to other parties who either have risks that offset or want to assume that risk.

Although derivatives have been around in some form for centuries, their growth has accelerated rapidly during the last several decades. They are now widely used by corporations, financial institutions, professional investors, and individuals. Certain types of derivatives are traded actively in public markets, similar to the stock exchanges with which you are probably already somewhat familiar. The vast majority of derivatives, however, are created in private transactions in over-the-counter markets. Just as a corporation may buy a tract of land for the purpose of ultimately putting up a factory, the company may also engage in a derivatives transaction. In neither case is the existence or amount of the transaction easy for outsiders to determine. Nonetheless, we have fairly accurate data on the amount of derivatives activity in public markets and reasonably accurate data, based on surveys, on the amount of derivatives activity in private markets. We shall explore the exchange-traded market data in the next section. If you need to be convinced that derivatives are worth studying, consider this fact: *The Bank for International Settlements of Basel, Switzerland, estimated that at the end of 2010, the notional amount of over-the-counter derivatives contracts outstanding worldwide is over $601 trillion. In comparison, gross domestic product in the United States at the end of 2010 was about $15 trillion.*

The **notional amount** is a measure of the size of a derivative contract, stated in units of currency, on which the payments are calculated. As we shall see later, measuring the derivatives market this way can give a false impression of the size of the market. Nonetheless, the market value of these contracts totals about $21 trillion, making the derivatives market a sizable force in the global economy. While notional amount reflects the size of the market on which derivatives are based, market value reflects the amount of actual money under exposure. By either measure, however, the derivatives market is extremely large.

Figure 1.1 illustrates the notional amounts of over-the-counter derivatives from 1998 through December 2010. Historically, the notional amounts have increased monotonically for many years. It is clear, however, that the financial crisis that emerged in 2008 had a significant impact on the size of the derivatives market.

FIGURE 1.1 Notional Amount of Over-the-Counter Derivatives Contracts

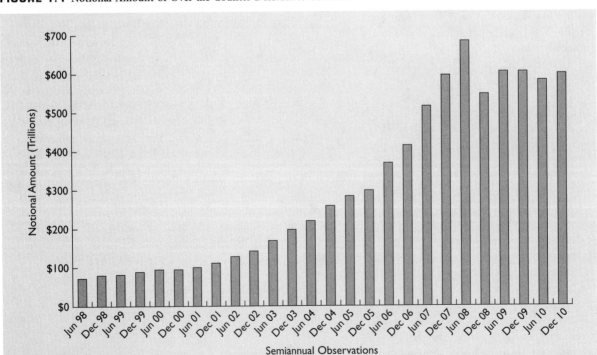

FIGURE 1.2 Market Value of Over-the-Counter Derivatives Contracts

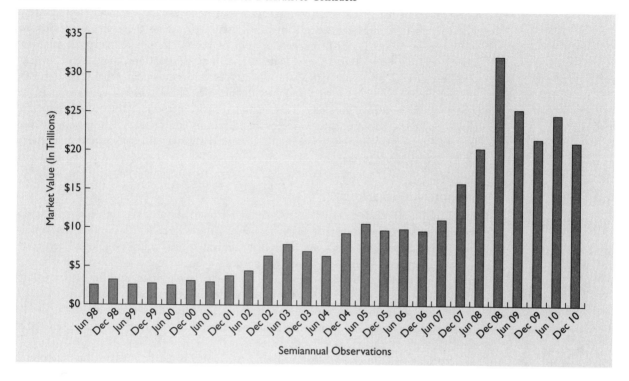

Interestingly, Figure 1.2 shows that as severe stress hit this market, the market value significantly increased, reaching over $32 trillion in December 2008. Clearly, these two measures of the size of the derivatives market capture different effects. Thus, in the fast-moving markets of 2008, the notional amount fell but the remaining market value rose.

This book is an introductory treatment of derivatives. Derivatives can be based on **real assets**, which are physical assets that include agricultural commodities, metals, and sources of energy. Although a few of these will come up from time to time in this book, our focus will be directed toward derivatives on **financial assets**, which are stocks, bonds/loans, and currencies. In this book, you will learn about the characteristics of the institutions and markets where these instruments trade, the manner in which derivative prices are determined, and the strategies in which they are used. Toward the end of the book, we will cover the way in which derivatives are used to manage the risk of a company.

This chapter welcomes you to the world of derivatives and provides an introduction to or a review of some financial concepts that you will need in order to understand derivatives. Let us begin by exploring the derivatives markets more closely and defining what we mean by these types of instruments.

DERIVATIVE MARKETS AND INSTRUMENTS

An asset is an item of ownership having positive monetary value. A liability is an item of ownership having negative monetary value. The term *instrument* is used to describe either assets or liabilities. Again, instrument is the more general term, vague enough to encompass the underlying asset or liability of derivative contracts. A contract is an enforceable legal agreement. A security is a tradable instrument representing a claim on a group of assets.

In the markets for assets, purchases and sales require that the underlying asset be delivered immediately or shortly thereafter. Payment usually is made immediately, although credit arrangements are sometimes used. Because of these characteristics, we refer to these markets as **cash markets** or **spot markets**. The sale is made, the payment is remitted, and the good or security is delivered. In other situations, the good or security is to be delivered at a later date. Still other types of arrangements allow the buyer or seller to choose whether to go through with the sale. These types of arrangements are conducted in derivative markets. This section briefly introduces the various types of derivative contracts: options, forward contracts, futures contracts, and swaps and related derivatives. We first, however, review the current derivatives markets where many derivatives contracts are traded.

Derivatives Markets

In contrast to the market for assets, derivative markets are markets for contractual instruments whose performance is determined by the way in which another instrument or asset performs. Notice that we referred to derivatives as contracts. Like all contracts, derivatives are agreements between two parties—a buyer and a seller—in which each party does something for the other. These contracts have a price, and buyers try to buy as cheaply as possible while sellers try to sell as dearly as possible.

Although an enormous number of derivatives transactions occur privately, in the over-the-counter market, there is still a vast number of derivatives transactions that occur on public exchanges.

According to *Futures Industry* magazine, the global listed derivatives trading volume in 2010 was 22.3 billion contracts that covered 78 derivatives exchanges worldwide. The trading volume was about equally split between options and futures contracts, with 11.2 billion futures and 11.1 billion options. The top five volume categories for 2010 were equity indices (7.4 billion), individual equities (6.3 billion), interest rate (3.2 billion), foreign currency (2.4 billion), and agriculture commodities (1.3 billion). The global listed derivatives volume by region for 2010 was 8.8 billion for Asia Pacific, 7.2 billion for North America, 4.4 billion for Europe, 1.5 billion for Latin America, and 0.3 billion for other smaller regions (Dubai, Israel, South Africa, and Turkey).

Table 1.1 provides statistics on the top ten derivatives exchanges worldwide measured by derivatives trading volume. The Korea Exchange had the largest volume at 3.75 billion contracts, or 16.8 percent of the worldwide derivatives exchange volume. The U.S.-based CME Group, which now includes both the Chicago Board of Trade and the New York Mercantile Exchange, was second with 13.8 percent of the worldwide volume. Now many exchanges have operations in multiple continents, and trading is conducted electronically. Notice that over 50 percent of the worldwide volume occurred on the top four exchanges in 2010, and over 80 percent occurred on the top nine exchanges. There are derivatives exchanges all over the world, and new ones are launched with regularity.

We now turn to introducing various types of derivative contracts.

Options

An **option** is a contract between two parties—a buyer and a seller—that gives the buyer the right, but not the obligation, to purchase or sell something at a later date at a price agreed upon today.

The option buyer pays the seller a sum of money called the price or premium. The option seller stands ready to sell or buy according to the contract terms if and when the buyer so desires. An option to buy something is referred to as a **call**; an option to sell something is called a **put**. Although options trade in organized markets, a large

TABLE 1.1 TOP TEN DERIVATIVES EXCHANGES WORLDWIDE TRADING VOLUME IN 2010 (IN BILLIONS)

RANK	EXCHANGE	VOLUME	PERCENTAGE	CUMULATIVE PERCENTAGE
1	Korea Exchange	3.75	16.8	16.8
2	CME Group (includes CBOT and Nymex)	3.08	13.8	30.6
3	Eurex (includes ISE)	2.64	11.8	42.5
4	NYSE Euronext (includes U.S. and EU markets)	2.15	9.6	52.1
5	National Stock Exchange of India	1.62	7.3	59.4
6	BM&FBovespa	1.42	6.4	65.7
7	CBOE Group (includes CFE and C2)	1.12	5.0	70.8
8	Nasdaq OMX (includes U.S. and Nordic markets)	1.10	4.9	75.7
9	Multi Commodity Exchange of India (includes MCX-5X)	1.08	4.8	80.5
10	Russian Trading Systems Stock Exchange	0.62	2.8	83.3
	Top Ten Total	18.58	83.3	

Source: Futures Industry magazine, March—April, 2011.

amount of option trading is conducted privately between two parties who find that contracting with each other may be preferable to a public transaction on the exchange. This type of market, called an over-the-counter market, was actually the first type of options market. The creation of an organized options exchange in the United States in 1973 reduced the interest in over-the-counter option markets; however, the over-the-counter market has been revived and is now very large and widely used, mostly by corporations and financial institutions.

Most of the options we shall focus on in this textbook are options that trade on organized options exchanges, but the principles of pricing and using options are very much the same, regardless of where the option trades. Many of the options of most interest to us are for the purchase or sale of financial assets, such as stocks and bonds. There are also options on futures contracts, metals, and foreign currencies. Many other types of financial arrangements, such as lines of credit, loan guarantees, and insurance, are forms of options. Moreover, stock itself is equivalent to an option on the firm's assets.

Forward Contracts

A **forward contract** is a contract between two parties—a buyer and a seller—to purchase or sell something at a later date at a price agreed upon today. A forward contract sounds a lot like an option, but an option carries the right, not the obligation, to go through with the transaction. If the price of the underlying good changes, the option holder may decide to forgo buying or selling at the fixed price. On the other hand, the two parties in a forward contract incur the obligation to ultimately buy and sell the good.

Although forward markets have existed for a long time, they are somewhat less familiar. Unlike options markets, they have no physical facilities for trading; there is no building or formal corporate body organized as the market. They trade strictly in an over-the-counter market consisting of direct communications among major financial institutions.

Forward markets for foreign exchange have existed for many years. With the rapid growth of derivative markets, we have seen an explosion of growth in forward markets for other instruments. It is now just as easy to enter into forward contracts for a stock index or oil as it is to trade foreign currencies. Forward contracts are also extremely useful in that they facilitate the understanding of futures contracts.

Futures Contracts

A **futures contract** is also a contract between two parties—a buyer and a seller—to buy or sell something at a future date at a price agreed upon today. The contract trades on a futures exchange and is subject to a daily settlement procedure. Futures contracts evolved out of forward contracts and possess many of the same characteristics. In essence, they are like liquid forward contracts. Unlike forward contracts, however, futures contracts trade on organized exchanges, called **futures markets**. For example, the buyer of a futures contract, who has the obligation to buy the good at the later date, can sell the contract in the futures market, which relieves her of the obligation to purchase the good. Likewise, the seller of a futures contract, who is obligated to sell the good at the later date, can buy the contract back in the futures market, relieving him of the obligation to sell the good.

Futures contracts also differ from forward contracts in that they are subject to a daily settlement procedure. In the daily settlement, investors who incur losses pay the losses every day to investors who make profits. Futures prices fluctuate from day to day, and contract buyers and sellers attempt to profit from these price changes and/or to lower the risk of transacting in the underlying goods. We shall learn more about this in Part II.

Options on futures, sometimes called *commodity options* or *futures options*, are an important synthesis of futures and options markets. An option on a futures contract gives the buyer the right to buy or sell a futures contract at a later date at a price agreed upon today. Options on futures trade on futures exchanges and are a rare case where the derivative contract and the instrument on which it is derived trade side by side in an open market. Although options on futures are quite similar to options on spot assets, there are a few important differences, which we shall explore later in this book.

Swaps and Other Derivatives

Although options, forwards, and futures compose the set of basic instruments in derivative markets, there are many more combinations and variations. One of the most popular is called a **swap**. A swap is a contract in which two parties agree to exchange cash flows. For example, one party is currently receiving cash from one investment but would prefer another type of investment in which the cash flows are different. The party contacts a swap dealer, a firm operating in the over-the-counter market, who takes the opposite side of the transaction. The firm and the dealer, in effect, swap cash flow streams. Depending on what later happens to prices or interest rates, one party might gain at the expense of the other. In another type of arrangement, a firm might elect to tie the payments it makes on the swap contract to the price of a commodity, called a commodity swap. Alternatively, a firm might buy an option to enter into a swap, called a **swaption**. As we shall show later, swaps can be viewed as a combination of forward contracts, and swaptions are special types of options.

Interest rate swaps make up more than 60 percent of the $601 trillion notional principal over-the-counter derivatives market in 2010. But interest rate swaps are only one of many types of contracts that combine elements of forwards, futures, and options. For example, a firm that borrows money at a floating rate is susceptible to rising interest rates. It can reduce that risk, however, by buying a cap, which is essentially an option that pays off whenever interest rates rise above a threshold. Another firm may choose to purchase an option whose performance depends not on how one asset performs, but rather on the better or worse performing of two (or even more than two) assets; this is called an alternative option.

Some of these types of contracts are referred to as **hybrids** because they combine the elements of several other types of contracts. All of them are indications of the ingenuity of participants in today's financial markets, who are constantly creating new and useful products to meet the diverse needs of investors. This process of creating new financial products is sometimes referred to as **financial engineering**. These hybrid instruments represent the effects of progress in our financial system. They are examples of change and innovation that have led to improved opportunities for risk management. Swaps, caps, and many other hybrid instruments are covered in Chapters 12, 13, and 14.

> The different types of derivatives include options, forwards, futures, options on futures, swaps, and hybrids.

THE UNDERLYING ASSET

All derivatives are based on the random performance of something. That is why the word *derivative* is appropriate. The derivative *derives* its value from the performance of something else. That "something else" is often referred to as the *underlying asset*. The term *underlying asset*, however, is somewhat confusing and misleading. For instance, the underlying asset might be a stock, bond, currency, or commodity, all of which are assets. The underlying "asset," however, might also be some other random element such as the weather, which is not an asset. It might even be another derivative, such as a futures contract or an option. Hence, to avoid saying that a derivative is on an "underlying something," we corrupt the word *underlying*, which is an adjective, and treat it as a noun. Thus, we say that the derivative is "on an underlying." This incorrect use of the word *underlying* serves a good purpose, however, because it enables us to avoid using the word *asset*.

IMPORTANT CONCEPTS IN FINANCIAL AND DERIVATIVE MARKETS

Before undertaking any further study of derivative markets, let us review some introductory concepts pertaining to investment opportunities and investors. Many of these ideas may already be familiar and are usually applied in the context of trading in stocks and bonds. These concepts also apply with slight modifications to trading in derivatives. Also important as you begin further study of derivative markets is a thorough mathematical review.

TECHNICAL NOTE: Mathematics
Review for Finance
go to www.cengagebrain.com

Presuppositions for Financial Markets

A presupposition is something that is assumed beforehand, often not clearly specified but tacitly understood. There are at least three presuppositions for well-functioning financial markets: clear rule of law, clean property rights, and a culture of trust. Complex and ambiguous laws and regulations may result in tyrannical enforcement where particular regulators arbitrarily bring enforcement actions. This lack of clarity impedes markets from functioning well. Well-defined and well-protected property rights are essential for efficient financial transactions. One cannot easily sell property if clean title cannot be produced. A culture of trust cannot be legislated; rather, it flourishes when nurtured from within. As in any business endeavor, trust makes financial transactions much more efficient. It is not surprising that economic development has been slow in countries where there is no culture of trust. Even though many people do not trust the global financial industry, all modern and successful economies are characterized by a high degree of honesty. Millions of financial transactions are successfully conducted without the slightest problem. It is only a small number of cases with dishonest participants that grab the headlines.

Risk Preference

Suppose you were faced with two equally likely outcomes. If the first outcome occurs, you receive $5. If the second outcome occurs, you receive $2. From elementary statistics, you know that the expected outcome is $5(0.5) + $2(0.5) = $3.50, which is the amount you would expect to receive on average after playing the game many times. How much would you be willing to pay to take this risk? If you say $3.50, you are not recognizing the risk inherent in the situation. You are simply saying that a fair trade would be for you to give up $3.50 for the chance to make $3.50 on average. You would be described as **risk neutral**, meaning that you are indifferent to the risk. Most individuals, however, would not find this a fair trade. They recognize that the $3.50 you pay is given up for certain, while the $3.50 you expect to receive is earned only on average. In fact, if you play twice, lose $1.50 once, and then gain it back, you will likely feel worse than if you had not played.

Thus, we say that most individuals are characterized by **risk aversion**. They would pay less than $3.50 to take this risk. How much less depends on how risk averse they are. People differ in their degrees of risk aversion. But let us say you would pay $3.25. Then the difference between $3.50 and $3.25 is considered the **risk premium**. This is the additional return you expect to earn on average to justify taking the risk.

Although most individuals are indeed risk averse, it may surprise you to find that in the world of derivative markets, we can actually value derivatives "as if" price-setting market makers are risk neutral. No, we are not making some heroic but unrealistic assumption. It turns out that we obtain the same valuations in a world of risk aversion as we do in a world of risk neutrality. Although this is a useful point in understanding derivative markets, we shall not explore it in much depth at the level of this book. Yet without realizing it, you will probably grow to accept and understand derivative models and the subtle implication of risk neutrality.

Short Selling

If you have already taken an investments course, you were probably exposed to the idea of short selling. Short selling is an important transaction related to making a market in derivatives. Therefore, the costs related to short selling have a direct impact on derivative pricing. Nonetheless, the concept is not very straightforward and a little review will be beneficial.

A typical transaction in the stock market involves one party buying stock from another party. It is possible, however, that the party selling the stock does not actually own the stock. That party could borrow the stock from a broker. That person is said to be **selling short**, or sometimes *shorting*.[1] She is doing so in anticipation of the price falling, at which time the short seller would then buy back the stock at a lower price, capturing a profit and repaying the shares to the broker. You may have heard the expression "Don't sell yourself short," which simply means not to view yourself as being less talented or less correct than someone else. Similarly, a short seller views the stock as being worth less than the market price.

Establishing a short position creates a liability. The short seller is obligated to someday buy back the stock and return it to the broker. Unlike an ordinary loan in which a borrower knows exactly how much he or she must pay back the lender, the short seller

---

[1]If the short seller fails to borrow shares, this is known as naked short selling. In this case, the buyer of the shares is also the lender of the shares. Naked short selling was widely tolerated prior to November 2009.

does not know how much he or she will have to pay to buy back the shares. This makes it a rather risky type of borrowing. Indeed, short selling is a very daring investment strategy.

Short selling, however, can be quite beneficial in that the risk of short positions can be useful in offsetting the risk of long positions. Alternatively, taking a short position in a derivative may be more efficient. Short selling of stocks can be quite complex and expensive relative to buying stocks, whereas taking a short position in a derivative is as simple as buying derivatives. Short selling of stocks requires finding someone willing to lend you the stock. The stock lender must also be willing to forgo his or her voting rights. At times, security lending can be expensive. Thus, it is common to find an investor holding a stock and protecting it by entering into a derivative.

We should note that anyone who has an obligation to purchase something at a later date has the equivalent of a short sale. It is not necessary to have borrowed stock from a broker. In either case, an increase in the price will be harmful.

The terminology of short selling can be confusing. In the context of financial securities, short selling, shorting, or going short are synonymous. In the context of derivative contracts, shorting or going short are synonymous. We do not refer to selling derivative contracts as short selling because the underlying security is not borrowed.

Repurchase Agreements

A **repurchase agreement** (known as a **repo**) is a legal contract between a seller and a buyer; the seller agrees to sell currently a specified asset to the buyer—as well as buy it back (usually) at a specified time in the future at an agreed future price. The seller is effectively borrowing money from the buyer at an implied interest rate. Typically, repos involve low-risk securities such as U.S. Treasury bills. Repos are useful because they provide a great deal of flexibility to both the borrower and lender.

Derivatives traders often need to be able to borrow and lend money in the most cost-effective manner possible. Repos are often a very low-cost way of borrowing money, particularly if the firm holds government securities. Repos are a way to earn interest on short-term funds with minimal risk (for buyers) as well as a way to borrow for short-term needs at a relatively low cost (for sellers).

As we will see in subsequent chapters, derivative market participants must often rely on the ability to borrow and lend money on a short-term basis. Many derivative valuation models are based on the assumption that the price-setting trader, often a dealer, has access to money or can lend money at the risk-free rate. The repo rate is an approximation of the dealer's marginal cost of funds and hence is a good approximation of the dealer's cost of borrowing and lending. Also, due to the strong collateral used in the repo market, the repo rate is roughly analogous to the government rate.

Return and Risk

Return is the numerical measure of investment performance. There are two main measures of return: dollar return and percentage return. **Dollar return** measures investment performance as total dollar profit or loss. For example, the dollar return for stocks is the dollar profit from the change in stock price plus any cash dividends paid. It represents the absolute performance. **Percentage return** measures investment performance per dollar invested. It represents the percentage increase in the investor's wealth that results from making the investment. In the case of stocks, the return is the percentage change in price plus the dividend yield. The concept of return also applies to options, but as we shall see later, the definition of the return on a futures or forward contract is somewhat unclear.

One fundamental characteristic of investors is their desire to increase in wealth. This translates into obtaining the highest return possible—but higher returns are accompanied by greater risk. **Risk** is the uncertainty of future returns. As we noted earlier, investors generally dislike risk, and they demonstrate this characteristic by avoiding risky situations when riskless ones that offer equivalent expected returns exist; however, they cannot always avoid uncertainty. Fortunately, the competitive nature of financial and derivative markets enables investors to identify investments by their degree of risk.

For example, the stock of a company that specializes in drilling wildcat oil wells will, all other things being equal, sell for less than the stock of a company that supplies health care.[2] The stock price is lower due to the drilling company's more uncertain line of business. Risk, of course, runs the spectrum from minimal to high. The prices of securities will reflect the differences in the companies' risk levels. The additional return one expects to earn from assuming risk is the risk premium, which we mentioned earlier.

What other factors influence a company's stock price and expected return? Consider a hypothetical company with no risk. Will people be willing to invest money in this company if they expect no return? Certainly not. They will require a minimum return, one sufficient to compensate them for giving up the opportunity to spend their money today. This return is called the **risk-free rate** and is the investment's opportunity cost.[3]

The return investors expect is composed of the risk-free rate and a risk premium. This relationship is illustrated in Figure 1.3, where $E(r_s)$ is the expected return on the spot asset, r is the risk-free rate, and $E(\varphi)$ is the risk premium—the excess of expected return over the risk-free rate.

Note that we have not identified how risk is measured. You might recall risk measures such as standard deviation and beta. At this point, we need not be concerned with the

FIGURE 1.3 **Risk-Return Trade-Off**

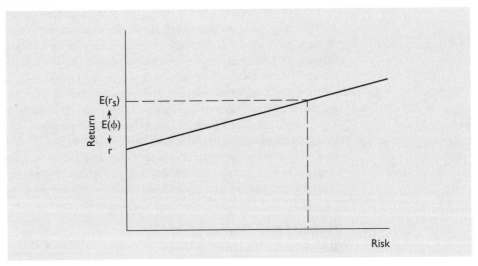

[2]In this context, "all other things being equal" means that the comparisons have not been distorted by differences in the number of shares outstanding or the amount of financial leverage.

[3]The concept of the risk-free rate and opportunity cost is well illustrated by the Biblical parable about the wealthy man who entrusted three servants to manage some of his money. Two of the servants earned 100-percent returns, while the third buried the money and returned only the principal sum. The wealthy man was infuriated that the third servant had not even earned the risk-free interest rate by putting the money in the bank, whereupon he reallocated the funds to one of the other servant's portfolios. The third servant, who was summarily discharged, evidently was not destined for a career as an investment manager (Matthew 25:14–30).

specific measure of risk. The important point is the positive relationship between risk and expected return, known as the **risk-return trade-off**. The risk-return trade-off arises because all investors seek to maximize expected return subject to a minimum level of risk. If a stock moves up the line into a higher risk level, some investors will find it too risky and will sell the stock, which will drive down its price. New investors in the stock will expect to earn higher returns by virtue of paying a lower price for the stock.

The financial markets are very effective at discriminating among firms with different risk levels. Firms with low risk will find capital plentiful and inexpensive. Firms with high risk may have trouble raising capital and will pay dearly. Markets that do a good job of pricing the instruments trading therein are said to be efficient, and the assets are said to be priced at their **theoretical fair values**.

Market Efficiency and Theoretical Fair Value

Market efficiency is the characteristic of a market in which the prices of the instruments trading therein reflect their true economic values to investors. In an efficient market, prices fluctuate randomly and investors cannot consistently earn returns above those that would compensate them for the level of risk they assume.

The idea that an asset has a "true economic value" is a particularly appealing concept. It suggests that there exists the *real* value of the asset. If we could determine this real value, we could perhaps make a lot of money buying when the asset is priced too low and selling when it is priced too high. But finding the true economic value requires a model of how the asset is priced.

In this book, we shall call the true economic value of the asset its *theoretical fair value*. There are many models that give the theoretical fair values of assets. You have probably already heard of the Capital Asset Pricing Model and perhaps the Arbitrage Pricing Theory. Derivatives also have theoretical fair values, and in this book, a great deal of emphasis is placed on determining the theoretical fair value of a derivative contract. Of course, these models and their respective values are correct only if the underlying market is efficient. Fortunately, there is considerable statistical evidence supporting the notion that financial markets are efficient. This is not surprising. Market efficiency is a natural consequence of rational and knowledgeable investor behavior in markets in which information spreads rapidly and inexpensively. We should be surprised if financial markets were highly inefficient.

Thus, as we weave our way through the world of derivatives, we should keep in mind that, by and large, the underlying financial markets are efficient. Although this book presents numerous strategies for using derivatives, all of them assume that the investor has already developed expectations about the direction of the underlying. Derivative strategies show how to profit if those expectations prove correct and how to minimize the risk of loss if they prove wrong. These strategies are methods for managing the level of risk and thus should be considered essential tools for survival in efficient markets.

Financial markets are the result of complex human interactions coupled with abstract estimates of potential future outcomes. It is important to remember that financial models are simplifications of reality. Equally important, our study of financial derivatives falls within the human sciences and not within the physical sciences. A physical model of gravity can easily be tested and its accuracy validated or rejected. Your belief in this model of gravity does not influence the actual behavior of a falling object. This independence between belief and physical observation may not hold in financial markets. Often widespread beliefs in an economic model will influence economic behavior, either validating or invalidating the model.[4] Thus, the discovery of a new financial valuation

---

[4]See Donald MacKenzie, *An Engine, Not a Camera: How Financial Models Shape Markets*, (Cambridge, MA: The MIT Press, 2006).

MAKING THE CONNECTION

Risk and Return and Arbitrage

One of the most human notions is that people like return and do not like risk. It follows that a rational person would not invest money without expecting to earn a return sufficient to compensate for the risk. The return one expects to earn, called the expected return, is the expected change in the value of an investment plus any cash flows relative to the amount invested. A portion of the expected return must compensate for the opportunity cost, as represented by the risk-free rate. The excess of the expected return over the risk-free rate is called the risk premium. In general, we say that

$$E(r_s) = r + E(\varphi),$$

where $E(r_s)$ is the expected return from some investment identified as "s" (often a stock is used to represent the investment, hence the "s"), r is the risk-free rate, and $E(\varphi)$ is the expected risk premium. There is no need to prove that the above statement is true. If it were not, people would be irrational.

But a part of the equation is somewhat vague. What does the expected risk premium consist of? How large is it? What makes it change? What risk is important, and what risk, if any, is not important? Financial economists have appealed to the Capital Asset Pricing Model, or CAPM, for answers. In the CAPM, the expected risk premium is replaced with something more specific. The expected return is written as follows:

$$E(r_s) = r + [E(r_m) - r]\beta_s,$$

where $E(r_m)$ is the expected return on the market portfolio, which is the combination of all risky assets, and β_s is called the asset's beta. The beta is a measure of the risk that an investor cannot avoid, which is the risk that the asset contributes to the market portfolio. The CAPM assumes that individuals diversify away as much risk as possible and hold the market portfolio. Thus, the only risk that matters is the risk that a given asset contributes to a diversified portfolio. As noted, investors hold the market portfolio and combine it with the risk-free asset or leverage it by borrowing at the risk-free rate so that the overall risk will be at the desired level. Hence, from the CAPM, we get our first look at what risk management means: to force the actual portfolio risk to equal the desired portfolio risk.

The CAPM is a controversial theory. Whether it holds true in practice cannot be verified. Nonetheless, it makes considerable sense. Variations of the CAPM and more complex models do exist, but understanding and accepting the CAPM is more than enough background to understanding derivatives. Yet understanding the CAPM is not completely necessary for understanding derivatives. It does indeed help to understand how risk is accounted for. But so much of what matters in understanding derivatives is grasping how they can be used to eliminate risk. With risk out of the picture, all one really needs to understand is arbitrage.

Arbitrage is a condition resulting from the fact that two identical combinations of assets are selling for different prices. An investor who spots such an opportunity will buy the lower-priced combination and sell the higher-priced combination. Because the combinations of assets perform identically, the performance of one combination hedges the performance of the other so that the risk is eliminated. Yet one was purchased for one price and the other was sold for a higher price. Some people refer to this as a money tree or money machine. In other words, you get money for doing nothing.

A world of rational investors is a world in which arbitrage opportunities do not exist. It is often said that in such a world, it would be impossible to walk down the street and find a $100 bill on the ground. If such a bill were ever there, someone would surely have already picked it up. Even good citizens and humanitarians would probably pick it up, hoping to find the owner or planning to give it to a charity. Of course, we know there is a possibility that we might find a $100 bill on the ground. But we do not expect to find one because people are not careless with large amounts of money, and if someone happens to be careless, it is unlikely the money will still be there by the time we arrive. And so it is in financial markets. People are not careless with their money. They are particularly careful, and they do not offer arbitrage opportunities. In fact, they work hard at understanding how to avoid offering arbitrage opportunities. And if anyone does offer an arbitrage opportunity, it will be snapped up quickly.

Studying this book will help you avoid offering arbitrage opportunities. And if someone carelessly offers an arbitrage opportunity, you will know how to benefit from it.

An efficient market is a market in which the price of an asset equals its true economic value, which is called the theoretical fair value. Spot and derivative markets are normally quite efficient.

model for a particular financial derivatives contract is never permanent. As the structure of financial markets changes and the understanding of financial market participants improves, then a particular model may no longer prove useful. Our understanding of financial markets will always be fluid. There are, however, fundamental models that aid in quickly gaining an understanding of the current financial landscape and indeed we will study many of these models

FUNDAMENTAL LINKAGES BETWEEN SPOT AND DERIVATIVE MARKETS

So far, we have not established a formal connection between spot and derivative markets. Instruments such as options, forwards, and futures are available for the purchase and sale of spot market assets such as stocks and bonds. The prices of the derivatives are related to those of the underlying spot market instruments through several important mechanisms. Chapters 3, 4, 5, and 9 examine these linkages in detail; nevertheless, a general overview of the process here will be beneficial.

Arbitrage and the Law of One Price

Arbitrage is a type of transaction in which an investor seeks to profit when the same good sells for two different prices. The individual engaging in the arbitrage, called the arbitrageur, buys the good at the lower price and immediately sells it at the higher price. Arbitrage is an attractive strategy for investors. Thousands of individuals devote their time to looking for arbitrage opportunities. If a stock sells on one exchange at one price and on another exchange at a different price, arbitrageurs will go to work buying at the low price and selling at the high price. The low price will be driven up and the high price driven down until the two prices are equal.

In your day-to-day life, you make many purchases and sales. Sometimes you encounter the same good selling for two different prices; for example, a computer from a mail-order discount house may cost less than the same computer at a local computer store. Why is there a difference? The store may offer longer warranties, localized service, and other conveniences not available through the discounter. Likewise, a pair of running shoes purchased at a local discounter may be less expensive than the same shoes purchased at a sporting goods store, where you pay extra for service and product knowledge. Where real differences exist between identical goods, the prices will differ.

But sometimes the differences appear real when they actually are not. For example, suppose there are two possible outcomes that might occur. We call these possible outcomes states. Look at the outcomes for two assets illustrated in Figure 1.4: A1 and A2. If state 1 occurs, asset A1 will be worth $100, while if state 2 occurs, asset A1 will be worth $80. In state 1, asset A2 will be worth $50, and in state 2, asset A2 will be worth $40. It should be obvious that asset A1 is equivalent to two shares of asset A2. Or in other words, by buying two shares of asset A2, you could obtain the same outcomes as buying one share of asset A1.

Now suppose asset A1 is selling for $85. What should be the price of asset A2? Suppose asset A2 is $41. Then you could buy two shares of asset A2, paying $82, and sell short one share of asset A1 by borrowing the share from your broker. The short sale of asset A1 means that you will receive its price, $85, up front, for a net cash flow of +$3 (= +$85 − $82). Then when the actual state is revealed, you can sell your two shares of asset A2 and generate exactly the amount of cash needed to cover your short sale position in asset A1. Thus, there is no risk to this transaction and yet you received a net cash

FIGURE 1.4 Arbitrage with Two Assets and Two States of the World

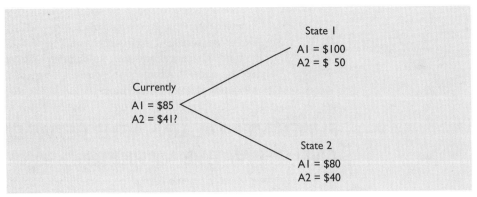

flow of $3 up front. This is like a loan in which you borrow $3 and do not have to pay back anything. Obviously, everyone would do this, which would push up the price of asset A2 and push down the price of asset A1 until the price of asset A1 was exactly equal to two times the price of asset A2.

The rule that states that these prices must be driven into line in this manner is called the **law of one price**. The law of one price does not mean that the price of asset A2 must equal the price of asset A1. Rather, it states that equivalent combinations of financial instruments must have a single price. Here the combination of two shares of asset A2 must have the same price as one share of asset A1.

Markets ruled by the law of one price have the following four characteristics:

- Investors always prefer more wealth to less.
- Given two investment opportunities, investors will always prefer one that performs at least as well as the other in all states and better in at least one state.
- If two investment opportunities offer equivalent outcomes, they must have equivalent prices.
- An investment opportunity that produces the same return in all states is risk-free and must earn the risk-free rate.

In later chapters, we shall see these rules in action.

In an efficient market, violations of the law of one price should never occur. But occasionally prices get out of line, perhaps through momentary oversight. Arbitrage is the mechanism that keeps prices in line. To make intelligent investment decisions, we need to learn how to identify appropriate arbitrage transactions, which we shall do in later chapters.

TECHNICAL NOTE: Arbitrage Principle
go to www.cengagebrain.com

The Storage Mechanism: Spreading Consumption across Time

> The law of one price requires that equivalent combinations of assets, meaning those that offer the same outcomes, must sell for a single price; otherwise, there would be an opportunity for profitable arbitrage that would quickly eliminate the price differential.

Storage is an important linkage between spot and derivative markets. Many types of assets can be purchased and stored. Holding a stock or bond is a form of storage. Even making a loan is a form of storage. One can also buy a commodity, such as wheat or corn, and store it in a grain elevator. Storage is a form of investment in which one defers selling the item today in anticipation of selling it at a later date. Storage spreads consumption across time.

Because prices constantly fluctuate, storage entails risk. Derivatives can be used to reduce that risk by providing a means of establishing today the item's future sale price. This suggests that the risk entailed in storing the item can be removed. In that case, the overall investment should offer the risk-free rate. Therefore, it is not surprising that the prices of the storable item, the derivative contract, and the risk-free rate are all related.

Delivery and Settlement

Another important linkage between spot and derivative markets is delivery and settlement. At expiration, a forward or futures contract calls for either immediate delivery of the item or a cash payment of the same value. Thus, an expiring forward or futures contract is equivalent to a spot transaction. The price of the expiring contract, therefore, must equal the spot price. Although options differ somewhat from forwards and futures at expiration, these instruments have an unambiguous value at expiration that is determined by the spot price.

Few derivative traders hold their positions until the contracts expire.[5] They use the market's liquidity to enter into offsetting transactions. Nonetheless, the fact that delivery or an equivalent cash payment will occur on positions open at expiration is an important consideration in pricing the spot and derivative instruments.

The foregoing properties play an important role in these markets' performance. Derivative and spot markets are inextricably linked. Nonetheless, we have not yet determined what role derivative markets play in the operations of spot markets.

ROLE OF DERIVATIVE MARKETS

Risk Management

Because derivative prices are related to the prices of the underlying spot market goods, they can be used to reduce or increase the risk of owning the spot items. Derivative market participants seeking to reduce their risk are called **hedgers**. Derivative market participants seeking to increase their risk are called **speculators**.

For example, buying the spot item and selling a futures contract or call option reduces the investor's risk. If the good's price falls, the price of the futures or call option contract will also fall. The investor can then repurchase the contract at the lower price, effecting a gain that can at least partially offset the loss on the spot item. This type of transaction is known as a hedge.

As we noted earlier, investors have different risk preferences. Some are more tolerant of risk than others. All investors, however, want to keep their investments at an acceptable risk level. Derivative markets enable those investors who want to reduce their risk to transfer it to those wanting to increase it. We call these latter investors speculators. Because these markets are so effective at reallocating risk among investors, no one need assume an uncomfortable level of risk. Consequently, investors are willing to supply more funds to the financial markets. This benefits the economy because it enables more firms to raise capital and keeps the cost of that capital as low as possible.

As noted, on the other side of hedging is speculation. Unless a hedger can find another hedger with opposite needs, the hedger's risk must be assumed by a speculator. Derivative markets provide an alternative and efficient means of speculating. Instead of trading the underlying stocks or bonds, an investor can trade a derivative contract. Many investors prefer to speculate with derivatives rather than with the underlying securities. In turn, the ease with which speculation can be done using derivatives makes it easier and less costly for hedgers.

We would be remiss if we left it at that, however, for speculation is controversial. Derivative markets have taken much criticism from outsiders, including accusations

---

[5]On derivative contracts that do not call for delivery at expiration but specify that an economically equivalent cash payment be made, positions are more likely to be held to expiration.

MAKING THE CONNECTION

Jet Fuel Risk Management at Southwest Airlines

The primary business objective of Southwest Airlines is to transport passengers and cargo in the continental United States at a low cost. While salaries are the largest expense for Southwest Airlines, the second largest is the cost of jet fuel. For many years, the company has aggressively managed its current and prospective jet fuel consumption. In its 2010 10-K Report, Section 10, "Derivative and Financial Instruments, Fuel Contracts," management partially explains its current financial derivatives positions:

"The Company has used financial derivative instruments for both short-term and long-term time frames, and typically uses a mixture of purchased call options, collar structures (which include both a purchased call option and a sold put option), call spreads (which include a purchased call option and a sold call option), and fixed price swap agreements in its portfolio.... For 2010, the Company had fuel derivatives in place related to approximately 40 percent of its fuel consumption. As of December 31, 2010, the Company had fuel derivative instruments in place to provide coverage on a large portion of its 2011 estimated fuel consumption...." Southwest also had significant hedging positions in place for 2011 through 2014.

Thus, Southwest Airlines appears to have a large fuel hedging program where it is attempting to hedge the risk of rising fuel prices. Notice that Southwest has hedged anticipated fuel consumption for many years to come.[6]

As we go through the material in this book, you will become familiar with the various instruments used by Southwest Airlines, such as options, collars, spreads, and swaps, and you will learn how companies and individuals can use these tools to manage risk.

[6]For more details on Southwest Airlines' fuel hedging program, see Robert Brooks, "The Life Cycle View of Enterprise Risk Management: The Case of Southwest Airlines Jet Fuel Hedging," *Journal of Financial Education*, forthcoming, 2012.

that their activities are tantamount to legalized gambling. We shall look at this point in a later section.

Price Discovery

Forward and futures markets are an important source of information about prices. Futures markets, in particular, are considered a primary means for determining the spot price of an asset. This should seem unusual because a spot market for the asset must exist. But for many assets on which futures trade, the spot market is large and fragmented. Gold, oil, and commodities trade at different places at different times. Within each asset's class, there are many varieties and quality grades. Hence, there are many potential candidates for the "spot" price of an asset. The futures market assembles that information into a type of consensus, reflecting the spot price of the particular asset on which the futures contract is based. The price of the futures contract that expires the earliest, referred to as the **nearby contract**, is often treated as the spot price.

Futures and forward prices also contain information about what people expect future spot prices to be. As we shall see later, spot prices contain this same information, but it may be harder to extract that information from the spot market than from the futures market. Moreover, in almost all cases, the futures market is more active; hence, information taken from it is often considered more reliable than is spot market information. While a futures or forward price should not be treated as an expected future spot price, a futures or forward price does reflect a price that a market participant could lock in today in lieu of accepting the uncertainty of the future spot price.

Hence, futures and forward markets are said to provide price discovery. Options markets do not directly provide forecasts of future spot prices. They do, however, provide valuable information about the volatility and hence the risk of the underlying spot asset.

Operational Advantages

Derivative markets offer several operational advantages. First, they entail lower transaction costs. This means that commissions and other trading costs are lower for traders in these markets. This makes it easy and attractive to use these markets in lieu of spot market transactions or as a complement to spot positions.

Second, derivative markets often have greater liquidity compared to the spot markets. Although spot markets generally are quite liquid for the securities of major companies, they cannot always absorb some of the large dollar transactions without substantial price changes. In some cases, one can obtain the same levels of expected return and risk by using derivative markets, which can more easily accommodate high-volume trades. This higher liquidity is at least partly due to the smaller amount of capital required for participation in derivative markets. Returns and risks can be adjusted to any level desired, but because less capital is required, these markets can absorb more trading.

Third, as noted earlier, derivative markets allow investors to sell short more easily. Securities markets impose several restrictions designed to limit or discourage short selling that are not applied to derivative transactions. Consequently, many investors sell short in these markets in lieu of selling short the underlying securities.

Market Efficiency

Spot markets for securities probably would be efficient even if there were no derivative markets. A few profitable arbitrage opportunities exist, however, even in markets that are usually efficient. The presence of these opportunities means that the prices of some assets are temporarily out of line with what they should be. Investors can earn returns that exceed what the market deems fair for the given risk level.

> Derivative markets provide a means of managing risk, discovering prices, reducing costs, improving liquidity, selling short, and making the market more efficient.

As noted earlier, there are important linkages between spot and derivative prices. The ease and low cost of transacting in these markets facilitate the arbitrage trading and rapid price adjustments that quickly eradicate these profit opportunities. Society benefits because the prices of the underlying goods more accurately reflect the goods' true economic values.

CRITICISMS OF DERIVATIVE MARKETS

As noted earlier, derivative markets allow the transfer of risk from those wanting to remove or decrease it to those wanting to assume or increase it. These markets require the presence of speculators willing to assume risk in order to accommodate the hedgers wanting to reduce it. Most speculators do not actually deal in the underlying goods and sometimes are alleged to know nothing about them. Consequently, these speculators have been characterized as little more than gamblers.

This view is a bit one-sided and ignores the many benefits of derivative markets. More important, it suggests that these markets siphon capital into wildly speculative schemes. Nothing could be further from the truth. Unlike financial markets, derivative markets neither create nor destroy wealth—they merely provide a means to transfer risk. For example, stock markets can create wealth. Consider a firm with a new idea that offers stock to the public. Investors buy the stock, and the firm uses the capital to develop and market the idea. Customers then buy the product or service, the firm earns a profit, the stock price increases, and everyone is better off. In contrast, in derivative markets, one party's gains are another's losses. These markets put no additional risk into the economy; they merely allow risk to be passed from one investor to another. More important, they allow the risk of transacting in real goods to be transferred from those not wanting it to those willing to accept it.

An important distinction between derivative markets and gambling is in the benefits provided to society. Gambling benefits only the participants and perhaps a few others who profit indirectly. The benefits of derivatives, however, extend far beyond the market participants. Derivatives help financial markets become more efficient and provide better opportunities for managing risk. These benefits spill over into society as a whole.

MISUSES OF DERIVATIVES

Derivatives have occasionally been criticized for having been the source of large losses by some corporations, investment funds, state and local governments, nonprofit investors, and individuals. Are derivatives really at fault? Is electricity to be blamed when someone with little knowledge of it mishandles it? Is fire to be blamed when someone using it becomes careless?

There is little question that derivatives are powerful instruments. They typically contain a high degree of leverage, meaning that small price changes can lead to large gains and losses. Although this would appear to be an undesirable feature of derivatives, it actually is what makes them most useful in providing the benefits discussed earlier. These are points we shall study later. At this time, however, you should recognize that to use derivatives without having the requisite knowledge is dangerous. That is all the more reason you should be glad you have chosen to study the subject.

Having acquired that knowledge, however, does not free you of the responsibility to act sensibly. To use derivatives in inappropriate situations is dangerous. The temptation to speculate when one should be hedging is a risk that even the knowledgeable often succumb to. Having excessive confidence in one's ability to forecast prices or interest rates and then acting on those forecasts by using derivatives can be extremely risky. You should never forget what we said about efficient markets. Regrettably, in recent years, many individuals have led their firms down the path of danger and destruction by forgetting these points, with the consequence that derivatives, not people, are often blamed.

For example, in the late 1990s, the U.S. economy, fueled by an expansionary Federal Reserve policy, experienced low interest rates and a housing boom. The demand by homeowners and speculators for mortgage contracts increased. Through the securitization process, mortgages were pooled together and derivative claims on these pools were sold to investors with a wide range of interests, a process called securitization that we will discuss in Chapter 14. Credit default swaps and other credit guarantees were used to strengthen the credit quality of these pools. Thus, many of these mortgage instruments enjoyed a perceived high credit quality and thus were in high demand. When interest rates rose in 2004, the housing market fell and home mortgage defaults began to increase. These losses were magnified due to the lack of liquidity and leveraged trading of some mortgage products. By 2008, a "death spiral" ensued where these losses triggered collateral calls and the prices of other financial instruments deteriorated. This financial trauma sent many investors to seek risk-free instruments; thus, short-term U.S. Treasury securities actually had a negative yield to maturity at times. In addition, many financial institutions sold what effectively amounted to credit insurance in the form of a derivative called credit default swaps, which we cover in Chapter 15, believing that credit risk, like casualty risk, was diversifiable. It wasn't, as defaults spread throughout the United States and the economies of other countries. The financial crisis of 2008, and indeed the ensuing recession that lingers even through 2011, was not caused by derivatives, but it was exacerbated by the misuse of some derivatives. Fortunately, derivatives are normally used by knowledgeable people in situations where the derivatives serve an appropriate purpose. We hear far too little about the firms and investors who saved money, avoided losses, and restructured their risks successfully.

DERIVATIVES AND ETHICS

Codes of ethics perform a vital role in governing the behavior of finance professionals. Every major finance practitioner association has adopted a code of ethics as well as standards of professional conduct. These moral principles provide essential guidance to professionals facing difficult and complex situations that often have conflicting economic interests. Before entering a profession, it is important to fully understand existing normative ethics and to consider your personal ability to abide by the expectations engendered by these codes of ethics.

We briefly introduce codes of ethics foundational to three leading professional organizations: Chartered Financial Analysts® Institute (www.cfainstitute.org), Global Association of Risk Professionals (www.garp.org), and Professional Risk Managers' International Association (www.prmia.org). When introducing their codes of ethics, these organizations clearly view this issue as foundational to everything they do. Consider the following quotes:

> The CFA Institute Code of Ethics and Standards of Professional Conduct are fundamental to the values of CFA Institute and essential to achieving its mission to lead the investment profession globally by setting high standards of education, integrity, and professional excellence.[7]
>
> The GARP Code of Conduct ("Code") sets forth principles of professional conduct for … [its members] … in support of the advancement of the financial risk management profession. These principles promote the highest levels of ethical conduct and disclosure and provide direction and support for both the individual practitioner and the risk management profession.[8]
>
> [The] standards of conduct for risk professionals … will promote the highest levels of ethical conduct and disclosure with respect to methods of analysis. The Board of PRMIA believes that these standards will provide direction and support for both the individual practitioner and for the risk management profession as a whole.[9]

The actual codes of ethics set a very high bar for professional conduct in investment management and financial risk management. For example, consider the following quotes taken from professional codes of ethics:

> Act with integrity, competence, diligence, respect, and in an ethical manner with the public, clients, prospective clients, employers, employees, colleagues in the investment management profession, and other participants in the global capital markets.[10]
>
> Shall act professionally, ethically and with integrity in all dealings with employers, existing or potential clients, the public, and other practitioners in the financial services industry.[11]
>
> PRMIA Member must act professionally, ethically and with integrity in all dealings with employers, existing or potential clients, the public, and other risk practitioners.

---

[7]See Preamble of *Code of Ethics and Standards of Professional Conduct* found at www.cfapubs.org/doi/pdf/10.2469/ccb.v2010.n14.1.

[8]See *GARP Code of Conduct*, Introductory Statement found at www.garp.org/media/59589/code of conduct0610.pdf.

[9]See Section 1 Purpose of Professional Standards, *Standards of Best Practice, Conduct & Ethics*, September 2009, found at http://prmia.org/pdf/ethicspdf/PRMIA_Standards_of_Best_Practice_Conduct_Ethics_4_2.pdf.

[10]See The Code of Ethics, *Code of Ethics and Standards of Professional Conduct* found at http://www.cfapubs.org/doi/pdf/10.2469/ccb.v2010.n14.1.

[11]See *GARP Code of Conduct*, Section III Rules of Conduct found at http://www.garp.org/media/59589/code of conduct0610.pdf.

Members should place the integrity of the risk management profession and users of risk management above their own personal interests.[12]

Note that professional associations hold their members to standards of conduct well in excess of the rule of law. Thus, a professional acting within her professional association's code of ethics is unlikely to violate existing laws as these codes also require upholding rules and laws governing their behavior.

DERIVATIVES AND YOUR CAREER

It is tempting to believe that derivatives are but an interesting subject for study. You might think that you will someday want to buy an option for your personal investment portfolio. You might think that you are unlikely to encounter derivatives in your career in business. That is simply not true.

As we noted earlier, the primary use of derivatives is in financial risk management. Businesses, by their very nature, face risks. Some of those risks are acceptable. In fact, a business must assume some type of risk; otherwise, there is no reason to be in business. But other types of risks are unacceptable and should be managed, if not eliminated. For example, a small furniture manufacturer may borrow money from a bank at a rate that will be adjusted periodically to reflect current interest rates. The furniture manufacturer is in the business of making money off the furniture market. It is not particularly suited to forecasting interest rates. Yet interest rate increases could severely hamper its ability to make a profit from its furniture business. If the firm sells its products in foreign countries, it may face significant foreign exchange risk. If the raw materials it purchases and the energy it consumes are subject to uncertain future prices, as they surely are, the firm faces additional risks, all having the potential to undermine its success in its main line of business.

It was but a few years ago that a small firm would not be expected to use derivatives to manage its interest rate or foreign exchange risk, nor would it be able to do so if it wanted. The minimum sizes of transactions were too large. Times have changed, and smaller firms are now more able to use derivatives.

If your career takes you into investment management, you will surely encounter derivatives. Those in public service who manage the assets of governments are finding numerous applications of derivatives. Those responsible for the commodities and energy purchased by firms will encounter situations where derivatives are or can be used. In short, derivatives are becoming commonplace and are likely to be even more so for the foreseeable future.

By taking a course and/or reading this book on derivatives, you are taking the first step toward obtaining the tools necessary to understand the nature and management of risk, a subject that lies at the very heart of a business.

SOURCES OF INFORMATION ON DERIVATIVES

The derivative markets have become so visible in today's financial system that virtually any publication that covers the stock and bond markets contains some coverage of derivatives. A number of companies and governmental agencies provide a variety of specialized trade publications, academic and professional journals, and Internet sites. The authors maintain a website containing many of these links as well as links to collections of links maintained by others. Access the site through the Author Updates link on the book's website: www.cengagebrain.com.

---

[12]See Section 4 Ethical Behaviour, *Standards of Best Practice, Conduct & Ethics*, September 2009, found at http://prmia.org/pdf/ethicspdf/PRMIA_Standards_of_Best_Practice_Conduct_Ethics_4_2.pdf.

BOOK OVERVIEW

We provide here a brief overview of the book, including the new features of this ninth edition.

Organization of the Book

This book is divided into three main parts. First, an introductory chapter gives an overview of the book's subject. Then Part I, consisting of Chapters 2–7, covers options. Chapter 2 introduces the basic characteristics of options and their markets. Chapter 3 presents the fundamental principles of pricing options. These principles are often called boundary conditions, and while we do tend to think of them as fundamental, they are nonetheless quite challenging. Chapter 4 presents the simple binomial model for pricing options. Chapter 5 covers the Black-Scholes-Merton model, which is the premier tool for pricing options and for which a Nobel Prize was awarded in 1997. Chapters 6 and 7 cover option trading strategies.

Part II covers forwards, futures, and swaps. It begins with Chapter 8, which introduces the basic characteristics of forward and futures markets. Chapter 9 presents the principles of pricing forwards, futures, and options on futures contracts. Chapter 10 covers futures arbitrage strategies, which is the primary determinant of futures prices. Chapter 11 covers various futures trading strategies. Chapter 12 is devoted to swaps, including interest rate, currency, and equity swaps.

Part III deals with various advanced topics, although one should not get the impression that the material is particularly complex. Chapter 13 deals with interest rate derivatives such as forward rate agreements, interest rate options, and swaptions. Chapter 14 covers some advanced derivatives and strategies, which are mostly extensions of previous topics and strategies. Chapters 15 and 16 deal with risk management. Chapter 15 covers quantitative risk management, emphasizing such topics as Value at Risk, delta hedging, and managing credit risk. Chapter 16 is more qualitative and focuses on the issues that must be addressed in an organization so that risk management is properly conducted. You will have the opportunity to learn how risk management is done well in organizations and how it is done poorly.

Key Features of the Book

Some key features of the book are as follows:

- An emphasis on practical application of theory; all ideas and concepts are presented with clear illustrations. You never lose touch with the real world.
- A minimal use of technical mathematics. While financial derivatives is unavoidably a technical subject, calculus is not necessary for learning the material at this level. (Note: Some calculus is used in appendices, but it is not essential for understanding that material.)
- A balanced emphasis on strategies and pricing.
- A liberal use of illustrations. The book contains over 120 figures and is supported with approximately 100 tables.
- Problems organized in two groups. In Concept Checks, the answers are provided at the end of the book. In Questions and Problems, the answers are available in *digital form on the publisher's website.* Additional problems have been added in each chapter.
- Over 80 concept checks questions and problems that allow you to test your skills. (Solutions keyed to chapter subheadings are provided in Appendix C so students can check their understanding.)

- Over 470 multiple choice questions and over 470 true/false questions are available to instructors who adopt the book.
- An additional 375 end-of-chapter questions and problems that allow you to test your skills. (Solutions keyed to chapter subheadings are available to adopting instructors.)
- Over 200 margin notes. These short summaries (a few sentences) of key points are found throughout the book.
- Key terms. At the end of each chapter is a list of important terms you should be able to define before you continue. This book contains approximately 400 key terms that correspond to the boldfaced words in the chapters. These important key terms will help build your vocabulary in this profession.
- Quotes that begin each chapter. While introductory students may not always catch the meaning behind these quotes, every quote has some meaning related to the topic of the chapter. Although the individual authors cited are a diverse group, most are practitioners in the field.
- Liberal use of boxed inserts, Making the Connection, which are designed to establish a better linkage between the theory of derivatives and risk management and the practice.
- Several Technical Notes, which are online derivations and proofs that take the material a step further than is covered in the book. These provide the instructor with the ability to easily assign more advanced material or allow certain students to take their study to a higher level. The number of these items has been increased from that in the eighth edition. Now with over 20 technical note references in the chapters, this feature allows more complex materials to be available to those faculty and students who want to explore the book's subject in more depth without distracting others.
- The Concept Checks feature for Chapter 3, which contains a question that directs readers to a detailed presentation of option pricing principles available on the book's website, www.cengagebrain.com. This presentation provides a visual and dynamic explanation of many of the important option pricing principles.
- Downloadable software. The product support website (www.cengagebrain.com) contains downloadable Excel spreadsheets. Throughout the book Software Demonstration sections contain illustrations of how to use the software.
- Appendices containing lists of formulas, references, and solutions to the Concept Checks.
- A glossary defining several hundred terms.
- A comprehensive index.
- A PowerPoint® presentation that is available for instructors adopting the book. Some of the other PowerPoint presentations that we have seen accompanying finance textbooks are mostly outlines; this book's presentations, however, contain much more detail and are available from the product support website.
- Solutions to the end-of-chapter questions and problems and answers to the true–false and multiple-choice tests. These items are available in digital form on the publisher's website.
- A website (www.cengagebrain.com) that contains PowerPoint slides, Excel spreadsheets, and links to relevant Internet sites. The site also provides restricted access to an electronic version of the solutions. Also contained in the site is updated information and errata. Yes, this book will probably have some errors, but at least we are willing to tell you about them.

Our focus in this book is on making theory work in practice. All points are illustrated as much as possible using practical situations. When strategies are covered, readers learn the theory, examine the algebraic equations that describe what is happening, and observe the results using a table or graph.

Specific New Features of the Ninth Edition

For those familiar with the previous editions, the following are new features:

- An update of contemporary market data references, websites, and regulatory agencies.
- A general updating of all material to reflect the rapidly changing nature of the field of derivatives and risk management.
- With the rapidly changing ownership structure of financial derivatives exchanges, updated references that reflect the present ownership structure.
- Approximately 50 new end-of-chapter questions and problems along with careful and detailed solutions in digital form.
- A thoroughly reviewed and updated test bank. Over 75 new multiple-choice questions and 75 new true false questions have been added.
- Additional figures have been added to Chapters 1, 2, 8, 12 and 13 providing a consistent overview of the size of the derivatives markets and various component parts of this market. The effects of the 2008–2009 credit crisis are clearly documented.
- A new section related to currencies in Chapters 4 and 5 as currencies are such an important part of financial risk management.
- Updated and improved spreadsheet software. For example, the binomial model now handles 5,000 time steps and up to 100 discrete dividends.
- A new section has been added to Chapter 1 on derivatives and ethics, emphasizing the important role of ethics in financial markets.
- A section has been added at the end of Chapter 5 discussing when the Black-Scholes-Merton option pricing model may or may not hold, introducing the important concept of performativity.
- Chapter 8 now has a section covering some of the recent advances in OTC central clearing.
- A new Making the Connection section is added to Chapter 12 stressing the importance of quality management of financial derivatives by municipalities.
- A new section was added at the end of Chapter 15 providing perspectives on financial risk management.

Use of the Book

The ideal way to use this book (and most finance textbooks) is in a two-semester course. A full academic year gives an excellent opportunity to cover the subject matter without flying at breakneck speed. Each semester can consist of eight chapters, leaving some time for quizzes, exams, and other in-class activities such as watching a video or engaging in a trading exercise. If, however, this book is used for only a one-semester course, instructors should find the material sufficiently flexible for picking and choosing chapters. There is a tendency, however, for one-semester courses to cover the chapters in the order in which they appear. Our recommendation is that a one-semester course should include swaps. The swap is the most widely used derivative and the one most likely to be encountered by those who enter the corporate world. Thus, the instructor might want to make a special effort to cover Chapter 12, which would probably not be covered if he or she just followed the sequence of chapters. In addition to swaps, a one-semester course should include interest rate options, which students are also likely to encounter in the corporate world. To make room for these topics, the instructor might need to de-emphasize futures and possibly even cut down on the coverage of option strategies. Chapters 14, 15, and 16, therefore, are the lowest priority chapters that should be forced into a one-semester course.

Although the primary audience is the university-level undergraduate, this book has been widely used at the MBA level, including MBA programs at some very prestigious universities. Instructors should not hesitate to adapt the book to an MBA course. The book has also been used in corporate training programs.

Summary

This chapter began by distinguishing between business and financial risk and by identifying the fact that financial risk results from uncertainty in interest rates, exchange rates, stock prices, and commodity prices. The chapter then introduced derivatives as a means of managing financial risk. It described the different types of derivatives and reviewed the concepts of presuppositions for financial markets, risk preference, short selling, return and risk, and market efficiency/theoretical fair value. It introduced the principles of arbitrage and the law of one price, the concept of storage, and the practice of delivery and settlement. It described the role of derivative markets in terms of helping to manage risk, discovering prices, lowering transaction costs and providing other operational advantages, and promoting a more efficient market. It identified and responded to criticisms of derivative markets and discussed the potential misuses of derivatives. It concluded by emphasizing the importance of this industry's codes of ethics.

Part I of this book consists of Chapters 2 through 7 and covers options markets. It introduces the instruments, examines pricing models, and illustrates strategies. Part II consists of Chapters 8 through 12 and covers forward, futures, and swap markets. In a similar manner, it introduces the instruments, examines pricing models, and illustrates strategies. Part III, Advanced Topics, takes the content a step further by examining the widely used interest rate derivatives (Chapter 13) and various advanced derivatives and strategies (Chapter 14) and ends with two chapters on risk management, one focusing on methods for managing risk and the other focusing on risk management in an organization.

Key Terms

Before continuing to Chapter 2, you should be able to give brief definitions of the following terms:

business risks, p. 1	futures markets, p. 6	percentage return, p. 9
financial risks, p. 1	options on futures, p. 6	risk, p. 10
derivatives, p. 1	swap, p. 6	risk-free rate, p. 10
instrument, p. 1	swaption, p. 6	risk-return trade-off, p. 11
notional amount, p. 2	hybrids, p. 7	theoretical fair values, p. 11
real assets, p. 3	financial engineering, p. 7	market efficiency, p. 11
financial assets, p. 3	risk neutral, p. 8	arbitrage, p. 13
cash markets/spot markets, p. 4	risk aversion, p. 8	law of one price, p. 14
option, p. 4	risk premium, p. 8	hedgers, p. 15
call, p. 4	selling short, p. 8	speculators, p. 15
put, p. 4	repurchase agreement (repo), p. 9	nearby contract, p. 16
forward contract, p. 5	return, p. 9	
futures contract, p. 6	dollar return, p. 9	

Further Reading

The following sources treat derivatives in a nontechnical manner or provide interesting insights into the world of derivatives:

Boyle, P., and F. Boyle. *Derivatives: The Tools That Changed Finance.* London: Risk Books, 2001.

Brooks, R. "The Life Cycle View of Enterprise Risk Management: The Case of Southwest Airlines Jet Fuel Hedging," *Journal of Financial Education,* forthcoming.

Chance, D. M. *Essays in Derivatives: Risk-Transfer Tools and Topics Made Easy.* Hoboken, NJ: John Wiley & Sons, 2008.

Derman, E. *My Life as a Quant: Reflections on Physics and Finance.* New York: Wiley, 2004.

Durbin, M. *All About Derivatives.* New York: McGraw-Hill, 2005.

Fenton-O'Creevy, M., N. Nicholson, E. Soane, and P. Willman. *Traders Risks, Decisions, and Management in Financial Markets.* Oxford: Oxford University Press, 2005.

Johnson, P. M. *Derivatives: A Manager's Guide to the World's Most Powerful Financial Instruments.* New York: McGraw-Hill, 1999.

Klein, R. A., and J. Lederman. *Derivatives Risk and Responsibility.* Chicago: Irwin, 1996.

Lindsey, R. R., and B. Schachter. *How I Became a Quant: Insights from 25 of Wall Street's Elite.* New York: Wiley, 2007.

MacKenzie, D. *An Engine, Not a Camera: How Financial Models Shape Markets.* Cambridge, MA: The MIT Press, 2006.

McLaughlin, R. M. *Over-the-Counter Derivative Products: A Guide to Business and Legal Risk Management and Documentation.* New York: McGraw-Hill, 1999.

Mehrling, P. *Fischer Black and the Revolutionary Idea of Finance.* New York: Wiley, 2005.

Modern Risk Management: A History. London: Risk Books, 2003.

Patterson, S. *The Quants: How a New Breed of Math Whizzes Conquered Wall Street and Nearly Destroyed It.* New York: Crown, 2010.

Schwager, J. D. *The New Market Wizards: Conversations with Americas Top Traders.* New York: Collins Business, 2005.

Taleb, N. N. *The Black Swan: The Impact of the Highly Improbable.* New York: Random House, 2007.

Taleb, N. N. *Fooled by Randomness: The Hidden Role of Chance in the Markets and in Life.* New York: Texere, 2001.

Concept Checks

1. Explain the concept of a risk-return trade-off.
2. What is the difference between an investor who is risk neutral and one who is risk averse?
3. What are the components of an expected return?
4. Distinguish between real assets and financial assets.
5. Distinguish between business risk and financial risk.

Questions and Problems

1. Assume that you have an opportunity to visit a civilization in outer space. Its society is at roughly the same stage of development as the U.S. society is now. Its economic system is virtually identical to that of the United States, but derivative trading is illegal. Compare and contrast this economy with the U.S. economy, emphasizing the differences due to the presence of derivative markets in the latter.
2. Contrast dollar return and percentage return. Be sure to identify which return is more useful when comparing investments.
3. What are the three ways in which derivatives can be misused?
4. An option dealer needs to finance the purchase of a security and holds an inventory of U.S. Treasury bills. Explain how the dealer can use the repo market for financing the security purchase.
5. What are the major functions of derivative markets in an economy?
6. Compare and contrast options and forward markets.
7. Why is speculation controversial? How does it differ from gambling?
8. All derivatives are based on the random performance of something. Identify and discuss this "something."
9. Why is delivery important if so few futures contracts end in delivery?
10. What contract would two parties utilize if they agreed to exchange cash flows? How might this transaction proceed?
11. What is storage? Why is it risky? What role does it play in the economy?
12. Assume that you are faced with an opportunity made up of three equally likely outcomes. If the first outcome occurs, you receive $10. If the second outcome occurs, you receive no money. If the third outcome occurs, you must pay out $1. Given that you can be characterized as risk neutral, how much would you pay to take this risk? Would you be willing to pay more or less for this opportunity? Explain.
13. Suppose you are shopping for a new automobile. You find the same car at two dealers but at different prices. Is the law of one price being violated? Why or why not?

14. If an individual anticipates the price of a stock falling, how would he go about shorting the stock in order to capture a profit? How does his short position create a liability?

15. Define arbitrage and the law of one price. What role do they play in the U.S. market system? What do we call the "one price" of an asset?

16. Explain three operational advantages offered by derivative markets.

17. What is an efficient market? Why do efficient markets benefit society?

18. What role do professional codes of ethics play in governing how people manage their financial careers?

19. Identify three presuppositions for well-functioning financial markets.

PART I

OPTIONS

Structure of Options Markets

There weren't many traders at the sharp end over thirty. Eyes flitting between flickering lines of information on four different screens, one ear on the phone, the other on the cries of the colleagues, twelve hours of split-second calculations, judging yourself and being judged on the score at the end of every day. These men and women lived and breathed the market.

Linda Davies
Into the Fire, 1999, p. 34

In Chapter 1 we introduced the concept of an option, a contract between two parties—a buyer and a seller, or writer—in which the buyer purchases from the writer the right to buy or sell an asset at a fixed price. As in any contract, each party grants something to the other. The buyer pays the seller a fee called the **premium,** which is the option's price. The writer grants the buyer the right to buy or sell the asset at a fixed price.

An option to buy an asset is a **call option**. An option to sell an asset is a **put option**. The fixed price at which the option buyer can either buy or sell the asset is called the **exercise price**, the **strike price**, or sometimes the **striking price**. In addition, the option has a definite life. The right to buy or sell the asset at a fixed price exists up to a specified **expiration date**.

Options are often encountered in everyday life. For example, a rain check offered by a store that allows you to return and purchase a sale item that is temporarily out of stock is an option. You return to the store and buy the item if it is worth the price, or you can throw the rain check away. You can even give (or sell) it to someone else. A coupon clipped from the newspaper that allows you to buy an item for a special price at any time up to an expiration date is also an option. Suppose you plan to purchase a deeply discounted airline ticket. You are afraid your plans might change, and the airline says that the ticket at that price is nonrefundable. For just $75 more, you can obtain the right to cancel the ticket at the last minute. If you pay the extra $75 for the right to cancel, you have just purchased an option. Finally, there is a good chance you are taking a college or university course right now, and you probably hold a valuable option: your right to drop the course up to a specific date. That right is paid for automatically with your tuition payment. On a certain date later in the term, you will decide whether to continue with the course or drop it. This is certainly a valuable option, but one we hope you will not use, at least not in this course.

In each example, you hold the right to do something. You will exercise that right if it turns out to be worthwhile to you. Although that is the essence of an option, options on securities and other assets do have a few more complicating features. First, let us take a look at how options markets developed.

DEVELOPMENT OF OPTIONS MARKETS

There are plenty of examples of options in everyday life. Historians and archaeologists have even discovered primitive options. Although these arrangements may resemble modern options, the current system of options markets traces its origins to the nineteenth century, when puts and calls were offered on shares of stock. Little is known about the options world of the 1800s other than that it was fraught with corruption.

Then in the early 1900s, a group of firms calling itself the Put and Call Brokers and Dealers Association created an options market. If someone wanted to buy an option, a member of the association would find a seller willing to write it. If the member firm could not find a writer, it would write the option itself. Thus, a member firm could be either a broker—one who matches buyer and seller—or a dealer—one who actually takes a position in the transaction.

Although this over-the-counter options market was viable, it suffered from several deficiencies. First, it did not provide the option holder the opportunity to sell the option to someone else before it expired. Options were designed to be held until expiration, whereupon they were either exercised or allowed to expire. Thus, an option contract had little or no liquidity. Second, the writer's performance was guaranteed only by the broker-dealer firm. If the writer or the Put and Call Brokers and Dealers Association member firm went bankrupt, the option holder suffered a credit loss.[1] Third, the cost of transacting was relatively high, due partly to the first two problems.

In 1973, a revolutionary change occurred in the options world. The Chicago Board of Trade, the world's oldest and largest exchange for the trading of commodity futures contracts, organized an exchange exclusively for trading options on stocks. The exchange was named the Chicago Board Options Exchange (CBOE). It opened its doors for call option trading on April 26, 1973, and the first puts were added in June 1977.

The CBOE created a central marketplace for options. By standardizing the terms and conditions of option contracts, it added liquidity. In other words, an investor who had previously bought or sold an option could go back into the market prior to the option's expiration and sell or buy it, thus offsetting the original position. Most importantly, however, the CBOE added a clearinghouse that guaranteed to the buyer that the writer would fulfill his or her end of the contract. Thus, unlike the over-the-counter market, option buyers no longer had to worry about the credit risk of the writer. This made options more attractive to the general public.

Since that time, several stock exchanges and almost all futures exchanges have begun trading options. Because exchanges that trade options also trade many other derivatives, we refer to them as derivatives exchanges. Fueled by the public's taste for options, the industry grew tremendously until the great stock market crash of 1987. Hit by the shock of the crash, many individual investors who had formerly used options stayed away, and volume recovered to its 1987 level in 1997 and has been rising. In 2004, total option contract volume exceeded 1 billion for the first time.

Although institutional trading on the derivatives exchanges remained fairly strong after the crash, a concurrent trend forced the exchanges to address a new competitive threat: the revival of the over-the-counter options markets. In the early 1980s, many corporations began to use currency and interest rate swaps to manage their risk. These contracts, which we briefly mentioned in Chapter 1 and shall cover in more detail in Chapter 12, are private transactions that are tailored to the specific needs of the two parties. They are subject to credit risk in that a party could default, leaving the opposite party holding a claim that had to be pursued in bankruptcy courts. As it turned out,

---

[1]The individual or firm could, of course, pursue costly legal remedies.

however, these claims were few and far between, and the market functioned exceptionally well. Soon thereafter, firms began to create other types of over-the-counter contracts, such as forwards, and as expected, options began to be used as well. Because of the large minimum size of each transaction and the credit risk, however, the general public is unable to participate in this new, revived over-the-counter market. The growth in this institutional over-the-counter market has placed severe pressures on the derivatives exchanges. By the early 1990s, the exchanges were trying to become more innovative to win back institutional trading and to stimulate the public's interest in options. These trends, however, should not suggest that options are fading in popularity; in fact, they are more popular than ever with corporations and financial institutions, but the growth is concentrated in the over-the-counter market. The exchanges have been very successful in the last 20 years and have enjoyed a competitive coexistence with the over-the-counter market. Indeed, both types of markets are large and healthy. The exchanges cater to smaller traders who want the assurance of market makers with whom they can trade and the credit guarantee that the exchanges provide what we will discuss later. Larger traders, while doing some exchange-listed options, often prefer the customization provided by over-the-counter options. We will return to our discussion of the over-the-counter markets later.

CALL OPTIONS

A call option is an option to buy an asset at a fixed price—the exercise price. Options are available on many types of assets, but for now we shall concentrate on stock options.[2] Consider the following example: On August 1, 2011, several exchanges offered options on the stock of Microsoft. One particular call option had an exercise price of $27.50 and an expiration date of September 16. Microsoft stock had a price of $27.27. The buyer of this option received the right to buy the stock at any time up through September 16 at $27.50 per share. The writer of that option therefore was obligated to sell the stock at $27.50 per share through September 16 whenever the buyer wanted it. For this privilege, the buyer paid the writer the premium, or price, of $0.125.

Why would either party have entered into the call option contract? The call option buyer would not have done so to immediately exercise the option because the stock could be bought in the market for $27.27, which was less than the exercise price of $27.50. The call option buyer must have expected the stock's price to rise above $27.50 before the option expired. Conversely, the call writer expected that the stock price would not get above $27.50 before the option expired. The call buyer and writer negotiated the premium of $0.125, which can be viewed as the call buyer's wager on the stock price going above $27.50 by September 16. Alternatively, either the call buyer or writer may have been using the option to protect a position in the stock—a strategy called hedging that we mentioned in Chapter 1.

Suppose that immediately after a call is purchased, the stock price increases. Because the exercise price is constant, the call option is now more valuable. New call options with the same terms will sell for higher premiums. Therefore, older call options with the same expiration date and exercise price must also sell for higher premiums. Similarly, if the stock price falls, the call's price also will decline. Clearly, the buyer of a call option has bullish expectations about the stock.

A call in which the stock price exceeds the exercise price is said to be **in-the-money**. As we shall see in Chapter 3, however, in-the-money calls should not necessarily be

---

[2]As we noted in Chapter 1, derivatives are created not only on assets, but also on futures contracts and the weather, neither of which would be considered an asset.

exercised prior to expiration. If the stock price is less than the exercise price, the call option is said to be **out-of-the-money**. Out-of-the-money calls should never be exercised. We shall explore these points more thoroughly in Chapter 3. If the stock price equals the exercise price, the option is **at-the-money**.

PUT OPTIONS

A put option is an option to sell an asset such as a stock. Consider the put option on Microsoft stock on August 1, 2011, with an exercise price of $27.50 per share and an expiration date of September 16. It allowed the put holder to sell the stock at $27.50 per share any time up through September 16. The stock currently was selling for $27.27. Therefore, the put holder could have elected to exercise the option, selling the stock to the writer for $27.50 per share. The put holder may, however, have preferred to wait and see if the stock price fell further below the exercise price. The put buyer expected the stock price to fall, while the writer expected it to remain the same or to rise.

The put option buyer and writer negotiated a premium of $1.70, which the buyer paid to the writer. The put option premium can be viewed as the buyer's wager that the stock price would not rise above $27.50 per share by September 16. The put writer accepted the premium because it was deemed to be fair compensation for the willingness to buy the stock for $27.50 any time up through September 16. As in the case of call options, either the put option buyer or the writer might have been using the put to hedge a position in the stock.

Because the put allows the holder to sell the stock for a fixed price, a decrease in the stock price will make the put more valuable. Conversely, if the stock price increases, the put will be less valuable. It should be apparent that the buyer of a put has bearish expectations for the stock.

If the stock price is less than the exercise price, the put is said to be in-the-money. In Chapter 3, we shall see that it is sometimes, but not always, optimal to exercise an in-the-money put prior to expiration. If the stock price is more than the exercise price, the put is out-of-the-money. An out-of-the-money put should never be exercised. When the stock price equals the exercise price, the put is at-the-money.

OVER-THE-COUNTER OPTIONS MARKET

As noted earlier, there is now a rather large over-the-counter (OTC) options market dominated by institutional investors. Chicago is no longer the center of the options industry. The scope of this market is worldwide. An option bought by an American corporation in Minnesota from the New York office of a Japanese bank, who in turn buys an offsetting option from the London office of a Swiss bank, would not be unusual. These contracts are entered into privately by large corporations, financial institutions, and sometimes even governments, and the option buyer is familiar with the creditworthiness of the writer or has had the credit risk reduced by some type of collateral guarantee or another credit enhancement or in some case, a clearing process. Nonetheless, the buyers of these options usually face some credit risk. There are, however, several major advantages of this type of option.

The first advantage is that the terms and conditions of the options can be tailored to the specific needs of the two parties. For example, suppose the manager of a pension fund would like to protect the profit in the fund's portfolio against a general decline in the market. As we shall discuss in great detail in Chapter 6, the purchase of a put in which the holder of the portfolio can sell it to the option writer for a specific value on a certain date can assure the manager of a minimum return. Unfortunately, this type of transaction cannot always be accomplished on the derivatives exchange. First, the options available on the exchange are based on certain stocks or stock indices. The manager would need an option on the specific portfolio, which might not match the indices on which options were available.[3] Second, the options on the exchange expire at specific dates, which might not match the manager's investment horizon. Third, even if options were available, there might not be enough liquidity to handle the large trades necessary to protect the entire portfolio. In the OTC market, the manager can specify precisely which combination of stocks the option should be written on and when it should be exercised.[4] Although unusually large transactions could take some time to arrange, it is likely that most pension fund managers could get the desired transactions accomplished. Fourth, in the OTC markets, options can be created on a wider range of instruments than just stocks. Options exist on bonds, interest rates, commodities, currencies, and many other types of assets as well as some instruments that are not even assets, such as the weather.

A second advantage is that the OTC market is a private market in which neither the general public nor other investors, including competitors, need know that the transactions were completed. This does not mean that the transactions are illegal or suspicious. On the derivatives exchange, a large order to buy puts could send a signal to the market that someone might have some bad news. This could send the market reeling as it worries about what impending information might soon come out.

Another advantage is that OTC trading is essentially unregulated. Its rules are those of commonsense business honesty and courtesy. Institutions that do not conform would find themselves unable to find counterparties with which to trade. This largely unregulated environment means that government approval is not needed to offer new types of options. The contracts are simply created by parties that see mutual gain in doing business with each other. There are no costly constraints or bureaucratic red tape to cut through.[5]

Clearly, there are some disadvantages to OTC trading, the primary one of which is that credit risk is higher and excludes many customers who are unable to establish their creditworthiness in this market. The credit risk problem is an important and highly visible contemporary issue in derivatives markets, and we shall discuss it more in later chapters. In addition to the credit risk problem, the sizes of the transactions in the OTC market are larger than many investors can handle. It is not clear, however, that OTC trading is any more or less costly than trading on the exchange.

The OTC market is quite large, but because of the private nature of the transactions, gauging its size is difficult. The Bank for International Settlements (BIS) conducts semiannual surveys that attempt to provide some data. These surveys, however, take a long time to complete and are published with a considerable lag. The BIS's latest survey estimated that in December 2010, the outstanding notional principal, which is the amount

---

[3]It would be wasteful to purchase an option on each security even if one were available; the purchase would protect the portfolio against risk that is already eliminated by the portfolio diversification.

[4]Because the specific combination of stocks is called a basket, these types of options are called basket options.

[5]At the time of this writing, the regulatory structure of the OTC derivatives market is undergoing change, a result of the Dodd-Frank Act of 2010. The bill was spurred, among other reasons, by a concern that the lack of regulatory oversight of the OTC market was contributing to market crashes. While it is unclear whether this connection is true, the Act requires that federal regulators extend their control into the OTC market. The writing of new rules designed to achieve that objective is a lengthy process and is subject to judicial review if challenged. Thus, there may or may not be significant regulatory overhaul that brings the OTC market under closer federal scrutiny.

FIGURE 2.1 Notional Amount of Over-the-Counter Options Contracts

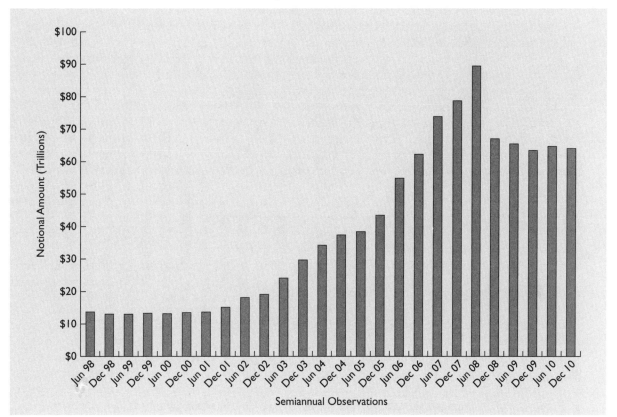

of the underlying instrument, of options on interest rates, currencies, equities, and commodities was $64 trillion, with a market value of about $2.2 trillion. Figure 2.1 illustrates the notional amounts of OTC option contracts from 1998 through December 2010. Historically, the options notional amounts have increased monotonically for many years. Again, as with the data from the overall derivatives markets shown in Chapter 1, it is clear that the financial crisis that emerged in 2008 had a significant impact on the size of the options market.

Interestingly, Figure 2.2 shows that as severe stress hit this market, the market value significantly increased, reaching over $3 trillion in December 2008. Again, in the fast-moving markets of 2008, the notional amount fell but the remaining market value rose. Once the crisis moved into 2009, however, firms liquidated their positions, lowering the notional amounts as well as the market values.

Most of the options created on the OTC market are not the traditional case of an option on an individual common stock. They tend to be options on bonds, interest rates, commodities, swaps, and foreign currencies and include many variations that combine options with other instruments. As noted earlier, a significant number are created on equity portfolios or indices. Many are on foreign stock indices. The principles behind pricing and using options, however, are fairly similar, whether the option is created on a derivatives exchange or on the OTC market. There are obvious variations to accommodate the different types of options. We shall cover many of these in later chapters. Most of the material on options, which comprises Chapters 2 through 7, however, will use

FIGURE 2.2 Market Value of Over-the-Counter Options Contracts

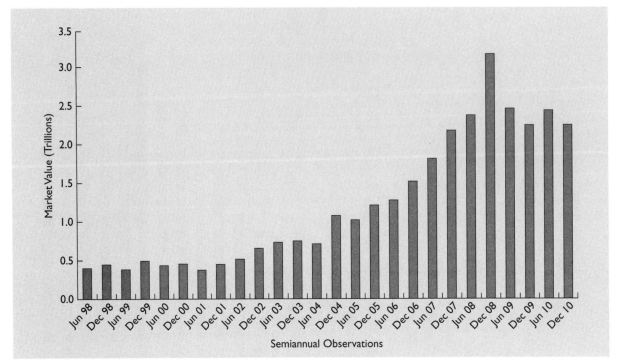

examples that come from organized markets. Now, let us take a look at how the organized options markets operate.

EXCHANGE-LISTED OPTION TRADING

An exchange is a legal corporate entity organized for the trading of securities, options, or futures. It provides the trading infrastructure and stipulates rules and regulations governing the transactions in the instruments trading thereon. In the options markets, organized exchanges evolved in response to the lack of standardization and liquidity of OTC options. OTC options were originally written for specific buyers by particular sellers. The terms and conditions of the contracts, such as the exercise price and expiration date, were tailored for the parties involved. As the OTC markets have developed, terms and conditions of contracts have been somewhat standardized but remain flexible for unique client needs.

Derivatives Exchanges

Organized exchanges filled the need for standardized option contracts wherein the exchange would specify the contracts' terms and conditions. Consequently, a secondary market for the option contracts was made possible. This made options more accessible and attractive to the general public.

As a result of providing a trading facility, specifying rules and regulations, and standardizing contracts, options became as marketable as stocks. If an option holder wanted to sell the option before the expiration date or an option writer wanted to get out of the obligation to buy or sell the stock, a closing transaction could be arranged at the derivatives exchange. We shall examine these procedures in more detail in a later section.

The Chicago Board Options Exchange (CBOE), the first organized options exchange, established the procedures that made options marketable. In addition, it paved the way for the American, Philadelphia, and Pacific Exchanges to begin option trading. The next several sections examine the CBOE's contract specifications.

According to data from *Futures Industry* magazine, of the 11.1 billion in exchange-listed options trading volume, about 1.12 billion derivative contracts were traded by the CBOE in 2010. Today's derivatives exchanges are no longer separated by type of contract and geographical location. For example, the CBOE now owns the CBOE Futures Exchange. Also, the New York Stock Exchange merged with Euronext in 2007, and this new entity owns the American Stock Exchange, which trades options, and the London International Financial Futures and Options Exchange, which trades both options and futures contracts. As of April 2011, *Futures Industry* tracks 78 different derivatives exchanges worldwide.

Listing Requirements

The derivatives exchange specifies the assets on which option trading is allowed. For stock options, the exchange's listing requirements prescribe the eligible stocks on which options can be traded. At one time, these requirements limited options listings to stocks of large firms; but these requirements have been relaxed, and more small firms' options are available for trading. The exchange also specifies minimum requirements that a stock must meet to maintain the listing of options on it. These requirements are similar to but slightly less stringent than those for the initial listing. In all cases, however, the exchange has the authority to make exceptions to the listing and delisting requirements.

All options of a particular type—call or put—on a given stock are referred to as an **option class**. For example, the Microsoft calls are one option class and the Microsoft puts are another. An **option series** is all the options of a given class with the same exercise price and expiration. For example, the Microsoft September 27.50 calls are a particular series, as are the Microsoft October 25 puts.

In recent years, many options have been listed on more than one exchange. A derivatives exchange determines whether options of a particular stock will be listed on its exchange. The company itself does not make this decision.

Contract Size

A standard exchange-traded stock option contract provides exposure to 100 individual stocks. Thus, if an investor purchases one contract, it actually represents options to buy 100 shares of stock. An exception to the standard contract size occurs when a stock splits or the company declares a stock dividend. In that case, the number of shares represented by a standard contract is adjusted to reflect the change in the company's capitalization. For example, if a company declares a 15 percent stock dividend, the number of shares represented by an outstanding contract changes from 100 to 115. In addition, the exercise price is adjusted to 0.8696 (= 1/1.15), rounded to the nearest eighth—or 0.875—of its former value. If a stock split or stock dividend results in the new number of shares being an even multiple of 100, holders of outstanding contracts are credited with additional contracts. For example, if the stock splits two-for-one, buyers and writers are credited with two contracts for every one formerly held and the exercise price is reduced to one-half of its previous value.

Contract sizes for options on indexes and certain other instruments are specified as a multiple. For example, an option on the S&P 100 index has a multiple of 100; an investor who buys one contract actually buys exposure to 100 times the index.

Exercise Prices

On derivatives exchanges, the exercise prices are standardized. Exchanges prescribe the exercise prices at which options can be written. Investors must be willing to trade options with the specified exercise prices. Of course, OTC transactions can have any exercise price the two participants agree on.

When establishing the exercise prices, the goal is to provide options that will attract trading volume. Most option trading is concentrated in options in which the stock price is close to the exercise price. Accordingly, exchange officials tend to list options in which the exercise prices surround and are close to the current stock price. They must use their judgment as to whether an exercise price is too far above or below the stock price to generate sufficient trading volume. If the stock price moves up or down, new exercise prices close to the stock price are added.

In establishing exercise prices of stock options, exchanges generally follow the rule that the exercise prices are in $2.50 intervals if the stock price is less than $25, in $5 intervals if the stock price is between $25 and $200, and in $10 intervals if the stock price is above $200. For index options, the exercise price intervals vary due to the wide range of the various indices. There are some exceptions to these rules; the very actively traded options have exercise prices closer together.

In 1993, the CBOE launched the FLEX (for flexible) option, a new type of option that represented a dramatic departure from the standardization of organized options markets. FLEX options can have any exercise price. In addition, there are other variations that we shall mention when we discuss expirations. FLEX options initially had a minimum face value of $10 million for index options and 250 contracts for options on individual stocks.

When a stock pays a dividend, the stock price typically falls by the present value of the dividend on the ex-dividend day, which is the day after the last day on which the purchaser of the stock is entitled to receive the upcoming dividend. Because call option holders do not receive dividends and benefit from increases in the stock price and put option holders benefit from stock price decreases, the ex-dividend decrease in the stock price would arbitrarily hurt call holders and help put holders. In the old OTC options market, options were dividend-protected. If the company declared a $1 dividend, the exercise price was reduced by $1. Because OTC options were not meant to be traded, the frequent dividend adjustments caused no problems. For exchange-listed options, however, such dividend adjustments would have generated many nonstandard exercise prices. Thus, the exchanges elected not to adjust the exercise price when a cash dividend was paid. This is also true in the current OTC market.

Expiration Dates

Expiration dates of OTC options are tailored to the buyers' and writers' needs. On the derivatives exchanges, each stock is classified in a particular expiration cycle. The expiration cycles are (1) January, April, July, and October; (2) February, May, August, and November; and (3) March, June, September, and December. These were called the *January*, *February*, and *March cycles*. The available expirations are the current month, the next month, and the next two months in the January, February, or March cycle to which the stock is assigned. For example, in early June, IBM, which is assigned to the January cycle, will have options expiring in June and July plus the next two months in the January cycle: October and the following January. When the June options expire, the August options will be added; when the July options expire, the September options will be added; and when the August options expire, the April options will be added. Index options typically have expirations of the current and next two months.

The maturities of options on individual stocks go out about nine months with a few exceptions. LEAPS (Long-Term Equity Anticipation Shares) are options on certain stocks and indices that have expirations of up to three years. LEAPS have proven to be very popular. Although LEAPS are available on index options, most of the trading volume is in LEAPS on individual stocks.

As noted above, FLEX options are available on stocks and indices and permit the investor to specify any exercise price. FLEX options can also have any desired expiration up to five years for index options and three years for options on individual stocks. FLEX options are a response on the part of the derivatives exchanges to the growing OTC market in which options have tailored exercise prices and expirations.

The expiration day of an exchange-traded option is the Saturday following the third Friday of the month. The last day on which the option trades is the third Friday of the month.

Position and Exercise Limits

In the United States, the Securities and Exchange Commission forces the derivatives exchanges to impose **position limits** that define the maximum number of options an investor can hold on one side of the market. For example, because both are bullish strategies, a long call and a short put on the same stock are transactions on the same side of the market. Likewise, both a short call and a long put are bearish strategies and thus are considered to be on the same side of the market. The derivatives exchange publishes the position limit for each stock, which varies widely depending on the stock's trading volume and number of outstanding shares. Index options also have position limits, but they are very wide due to the interest of large institutional managers. Certain traders called market makers have specific exemptions from these position limits.

Exercise limits are similar to position limits. An **exercise limit** is the maximum number of options that can be exercised on any five consecutive business days by any individual or group of individuals acting together. The figure for the exercise limit is the same as that for the position limit.

The purpose of position and exercise limits is to prevent a single individual or group from having a significant effect on the market. It is not clear, however, that such restrictions are necessary. But they do prevent many large investors from using exchange-traded options, and they reduce liquidity. They have probably hurt the derivatives exchanges by forcing institutional investors to take their business to the OTC markets.

Market Participants

In the OTC market, certain institutions, which may be banks or brokerage firms, stand ready to make markets in options. Exchange-listed options, of course, are created on an exchange, which is some form of legal corporate entity. Historically, the legal structure was a not-for-profit, non-stock corporation owned by members. Members were referred to as having a **seat** on the exchange. Now many derivatives exchanges are for-profit corporations with shareholders. Although the organizational structures of the various exchanges differ, access to the trading floor and the ability to trade options either on a physical exchange or electronically is restricted. We identify and discuss the types of market participants who have some form of direct access to the exchange's trading facility. We focus here on the current structure of the CBOE.[6] CBOE provides direct access through trading permits issued to either individuals or firms.

---

[6]On June 18, 2010, the CBOE became a stock corporation owned by CBOE Holdings, Inc. CBOE regular members (exchange seat holders) acquired 80,000 shares of Class A common stock. For more details, see CBOE Holding, Inc. 2010 annual report.

Liquidity Providers The main function of a derivatives exchange such as the CBOE is the execution of transactions in some form of market. Prior to 2000, exchange-traded options were transacted face-to-face in physical trading pits. Now, derivatives exchanges provide electronic access; therefore, geographical location is no longer essential. **Liquidity providers** have to provide both buy and sell prices for some subset of contracts offered on the exchange during some specified period of time. At the CBOE, trading permits are offered to market makers, lead market makers, floor brokers, designated primary market makers, and electronic designated primary market makers.

The **market maker** is responsible for meeting the public's demand for options. When someone from the public wants to buy (sell) an option and no other member of the public is willing to sell (buy) it, the market maker completes the trade. This type of system ensures that (1) if a private investor wants to buy a particular option, there will be a seller willing to make an offer and (2) if someone buys an option and later wants to sell it, a buyer will be available. The market maker offers the public the convenience of immediate execution of trades.

The market maker is essentially an entrepreneur. To survive, the market maker must profit by buying at one price and selling at a higher price. One way this is done is by quoting a bid price and an ask price. The **bid price** is the maximum price the market maker will pay for the option. The **ask price** is the minimum price the market maker will accept for the option. The ask price is set higher than the bid price. The difference between the ask price and the bid price is called the **bid-ask spread**.

The bid-ask spread is a significant transaction cost for those who must trade with a market maker. To the market maker, however, it represents the reward for the willingness to buy when the public is selling and sell when the public is buying. Bid-ask spreads are discussed further in the section on transaction costs.

Market makers use a variety of techniques to trade options intelligently and profitably. Many look at fundamentals such as interest rates, economic conditions, and company performance. Others rely on technical analysis, which purports to find signals of the direction of future stock prices in the behavior of past stock prices. Still others rely simply on intuition and experience. In addition, market makers tend to employ different trading styles. Some are **scalpers**, who try to buy at the bid and sell at the ask before the price moves downward or after the price moves just slightly upward. Scalpers seldom hold positions for more than a few minutes. In contrast, **position traders** have somewhat longer holding periods. Many option traders, including some scalpers and position traders, are also **spreaders**, who buy one option and sell another in the hope of earning small profits at low risk. Option spreading strategies are covered in more detail in Chapter 7. Given the importance of market making for a derivatives exchange, the specific responsibilities have been allocated to different participants.

At the CBOE, if physical "pit" trading exists, the **lead market maker** (LMM) must maintain a presence in specific trading areas consistent with their selected option classes. Often there are two LMMs quoting prices at all times. LMMs are used only in a few specific products and specific situations.

The **designated primary market maker** (DPM) is a firm chosen to provide both buy and sell prices like market makers but with greater responsibilities. They are not allowed to trade on behalf of customers and must trade solely for their own account. In return for these restrictions and other obligations, DPMs are allowed to hold a lower required margin and are allocated a minimum share of certain transactions.

The **electronic designated primary market maker** (eDPM) is similar to DPMs but operates only on the electronic exchange, not on the trading floor.

Floor Brokers   The **floor broker** is another type of trader on the exchange. The floor broker acts as an agent and executes trades for members of the public. If someone wants to buy or sell an option, that individual must first establish an account with a brokerage firm. That firm must either employ a floor broker or have an arrangement whereby it contracts with an independent floor broker or a floor broker of a competing firm.

The floor broker executes orders for nonmembers and earns either a flat salary or a commission on each order executed. The floor broker generally need not be concerned about whether the price is expected to go up or down; however, a good broker will work diligently to obtain the best price for the customer.

Order Book Official   Another position at the CBOE is the **order book official (OBO)** or **board broker**, an employee of the exchange. To see how an OBO works, suppose you place a *limit order*—an order specifying a maximum price to be paid on a purchase or a minimum acceptable price on a sale—to buy a call option at a maximum price of $3. The floor broker handling your order determines that the best quote offered by a market maker is 2.75 bid and 3.25 ask. This means that the lowest price at which a market maker will sell the call is 3.25. If your floor broker has other orders to execute, the OBO takes your limit order and enters it into the computer along with all of the other public limit orders. The market makers are informed of the best public limit orders. If conditions change such that at least one market maker is willing to quote an ask price of $3 or lower, the OBO will execute your limit order.

Public limit orders are always executed before market maker orders; however, the market makers, being aware of the best public limit orders, know the maximum and minimum prices at which they can trade. For example, if your limit order to buy at 3 is the highest bid and the market maker is quoting an ask price of 3.10, the market maker chooses between accepting your bid and selling the call at 3 or holding out for an offer of 3.05 or higher. If no one bids 3.05 within a reasonable time period, the market maker might choose to take your bid of 3.

The derivatives exchanges also have brought the benefits of modern technology to their order processing operations using a variety of electronic means for accelerating the rate at which orders are filled. For example, most CBOE traders now use handheld terminals instead of decks of handwritten cards and pieces of paper to submit and keep track of their trades.

Other Option Trading Systems

The CBOE uses the system of competing market makers. There are a variety of other approaches to facilitate trading. Historically, on stock exchanges, an individual called a **specialist** is responsible for making bids and offers on options. The specialist maintains and attempts to fill public limit orders but does not disclose them to others. In addition to the specialist are individuals called **registered option traders (ROTs)** who buy and sell options for themselves or act as brokers for others. Unlike the CBOE market makers, ROTs are not obligated to make a market in the options; market making is the specialist's task.

Most U.S. exchanges and many exchanges elsewhere have used pit trading in some form. Electronic trading systems do away with the pit and allow trading from electronic terminals, which can be placed anywhere, including offices and homes. There are a number of different electronic trading systems, but for the most part, they permit bids and offers to be entered into a computer that collects the information and makes it available to participants, who can then execute transactions with the stroke of a key. The International Securities Exchange, located in New York City, trades options electronically on many actively traded stocks. In addition, many foreign exchanges are fully automated, including EUREX, one of the world's largest exchanges.

Off-Floor Option Traders

The financial world consists of a vast number of institutions of all sizes, many of which participate in options trading. Some of these institutions are brokerage firms that execute orders for the public. Most brokerage firms employ individuals responsible for recommending profitable option trades to their brokers. Many, however, have specialized proprietary option-trading departments that search for mispriced options; trade in them; and, in so doing, contribute to their firms' profitability. Many large institutional investors such as pension funds, trusts, and mutual funds also trade options. In most cases, these types of investors write options on the stocks held in their portfolios. A growing contingent of foreign institutions also trade options. In addition to the large institutional investors, there are, of course, numerous individuals—some wealthy and some not—who trade options. Among those who trade options themselves are many wealthy people who turn over their financial affairs to specialized managers and thus participate in the options market without being personally involved. The dollar amounts required for trading exchange-listed options are so small that virtually anyone can afford to participate.

MECHANICS OF TRADING
Placing an Opening Order

An individual who wants to trade options must first open an account with a brokerage firm. The individual then instructs the broker to buy or sell a particular option. The broker sends the order to the firm's floor broker on the exchange on which the option trades. All orders must be executed during the normal trading hours, which vary by product. Historically, trading was performed in the trading pit designated for the particular option. The trading pit is a multilevel, octagonally shaped area within which the market makers and floor brokers stand. Now trading may be conducted at a physical location or electronically.

An investor can place several types of orders. A **market order** instructs the floor broker to obtain the best price. A **limit order**, as indicated earlier, specifies a maximum price to pay if buying or a minimum price to accept if selling. Limit orders can be either good-till-canceled orders or day orders. A **good-till-canceled order** remains in effect until canceled. A **day order** stays in effect for the remainder of the day. Finally, an investor holding a particular option might place a **stop order** at a price lower than the current price. If the market price falls to the specified price, the broker is instructed to sell the option at the best available price. There are a number of other types of orders designed to handle different contingencies.

In addition to specifying the option the investor wants to buy or sell, the order must indicate the number of contracts desired. The order might be a request to purchase ten contracts at the best possible price. The market maker's quote, however, need apply to only one contract. Therefore, if multiple contracts are needed, the market maker may offer a less favorable price. In that case, the order might be only partially filled. To avoid a partial fill, the investor can place an all or none order. An **all or none order** allows the broker to fill part of the order at one price and part at another price. Each derivatives exchange determines the set of permissible types of orders allowed on its exchange. These order types change as technology as well as traders' preferences change.

Role of the Clearinghouse

After the trade is consummated, the clearinghouse enters the process. The **clearinghouse** is an independent corporation that guarantees the writer's performance. The clearinghouse is the intermediary in each transaction. A buyer exercising an option looks not to the writer, but to the clearinghouse. The writer of an exercised option makes payment for or delivery of the stock to the clearinghouse. In the United States, the **Options Clearing Corporation (OCC)** is an independent corporation that guarantees the writer's performance. Several derivatives exchanges clear their trades through the OCC, including the CBOE, making it the largest options clearing organization in the world. In 2010, the OCC cleared 3.9 billion options contracts and 26.6 million futures contracts from over ten different derivatives exchanges. Of the 3.9 billion option contracts cleared by the OCC, 1.1 billion were from the CBOE. There are many other clearinghouses that serve various exchanges. For example, the CME Group clears trades through CME Clearing.

Each OCC member, known as a **clearing firm**, has an account with the OCC. Each market maker must clear all trades through a member firm, as must every brokerage firm, although in some cases a brokerage firm is also a clearing firm.

Figure 2.3 illustrates the flow of money and information as an option transaction is consummated and cleared. We shall illustrate how the clearinghouse, assumed to be the OCC here, operates by assuming that you bought the Microsoft September 27.50 call options we described earlier. You contacted your broker, who, through either his firm's floor broker or an independent floor broker, found a seller. You bought ten contracts at a price of $0.125 per option, which totals $125. The seller, whose identity you do not know, has an account with another brokerage firm. Your brokerage firm clears its trades through XYZ Trading Company, a clearing firm that is a member of the OCC. The seller's broker clears through ABC Options, another member of the OCC. You pay your broker the $125, and your broker pays XYZ Trading Company. XYZ pools the transactions

FIGURE 2.3 An Options Transaction on a Derivatives Exchange

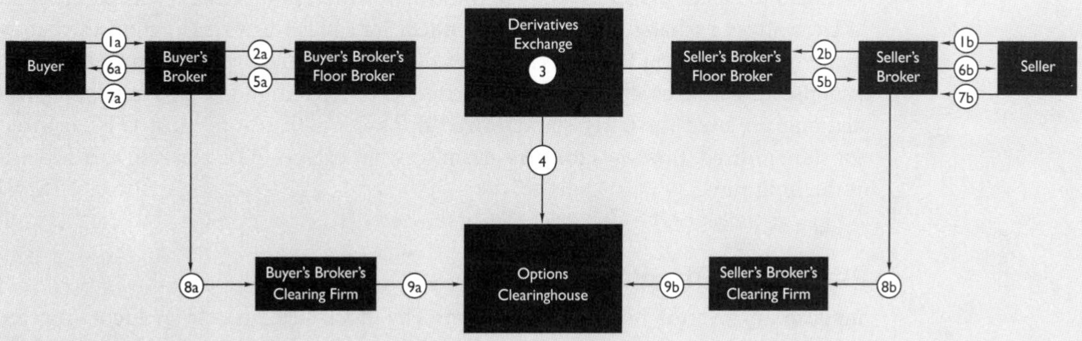

(1a)(1b)	Buyer and seller instruct their respective brokers to conduct an options transaction.
(2a)(2b)	Buyer's and seller's brokers request that their firms' floor brokers execute the transaction.
(3)	Both floor brokers meet in the pit on the floor of the options exchange and agree on a price.
(4)	Information on the trade is reported to the clearinghouse.
(5a)(5b)	Both floor brokers report the price obtained to the buyer's and seller's brokers.
(6a)(6b)	Buyer's and seller's brokers report the price obtained to the buyer and seller, respectively.
(7a)(7b)	Buyer deposits premium with buyer's broker. Seller deposits margin with seller's broker.
(8a)(8b)	Buyer's and seller's brokers deposit premium and margin with their clearing firms.
(9a)(9b)	Buyer's and seller's brokers' clearing firms deposit premium and margin with clearinghouse.

of all of its customers, and through a predetermined formula, it deposits a sum of money with the OCC.

Let us also assume that the seller does not already own the stock, so she will have to deposit some additional money, called **margin**, with ABC. The amount of margin required is discussed in Appendix 2.A; for now, however, just assume that the amount is 20 percent of the value of the stock, which comes to $(\$25.92)(100)(10)(0.2) = \$5,184$. The seller delivers $5,184 to the broker, who deposits it with ABC Options, which also keeps the $125 premium. ABC, in turn, is required to deposit with the OCC an amount of money determined according to a formula that takes its outstanding contracts into account.

TECHNICAL NOTE: Margin Trading and Short Selling
go to www.cengagebrain.com

The OCC guarantees the performance of ABC, the seller's clearing firm. Thus, you, the buyer, need not worry about whether the shares will be there if you decide to exercise your option. If the shares are not delivered by the seller, the OCC will look to ABC, which will look to the seller's brokerage firm, which will look to the seller's personal broker, who will look to the seller for payment or delivery of the shares.

The total number of option contracts outstanding at any given time is called the **open interest**. The open interest figure indicates the number of closing transactions that might be made before the option expires. In 2010, the average open interest in options cleared through the OCC was about 260 million contracts. About 93 percent of this is in options on individual stocks. Each contract covers 100 shares. Assuming an average stock priced at about $50, the underlying asset value is about $1.3 trillion. Seven percent of option open interest is index options and other options such as currency options.

The OCC thus fulfills the important responsibility of guaranteeing that option writers' obligations will be fulfilled. A call buyer need not examine the writer's credit; in fact, in the case of individuals and firms off the floor, the buyers do not even know the writers' identities.

Because the member clearing firms assume some risk, the OCC imposes minimum capital requirements on them. The OCC has a claim on their securities and margin deposits in the event of their default. As a further safeguard, the OCC maintains a special fund supported by its members. If that fund is depleted, the OCC can assess its other members to ensure its survival as well as that of the options market in general.

Derivatives exchanges outside the United States also use clearinghouses that operate similarly to the OCC. The OTC market does not generally provide for clearing, but in response to concerns about systemic crises, OTC clearinghouses have begun to be created and are used for fairly standardized transactions. Because most OTC contracts are not standardized, however, it is uncertain to what extend OTC clearing will be successful in the long run.

Placing an Offsetting Order

Suppose an investor holds a call option. The stock price has been increasing recently, and the call's price is now much higher than the original purchase price. The liquidity of the options market makes it possible for the investor to take the profit by selling the option in the market. This is called an **offsetting order**, or simply an **offset**. The order is executed in the same manner as an opening order. Continuing with our example in which you bought ten contracts of the Microsoft September 27.5 calls, suppose the price of the calls is now $0.50. You instruct your broker to sell the calls. Your broker orders his firm's floor broker to sell the calls. The floor broker finds a buyer who agrees to the price of $0.50. The buyer pays $500 to her broker, who passes the funds through to the company's clearing firm, which passes the funds through to the OCC. The OCC then credits the $500 to the account of your broker's clearing firm, XYZ Trading Company, which credits your broker's firm, which in turn credits your account. You now have $500 and no outstanding position in this option. The individual who bought these options from you may have been offsetting a previously established short position in the calls or may be establishing a new long position in them. About half of all opening stock option transactions are closed in this manner. In some cases, however, option traders may want to exercise the option, which we discuss in the next section.

In the OTC markets, there is no facility for selling back an option previously bought or buying back an option previously sold. These contracts are created with the objective of being held to expiration. As circumstances change, however, many holders or writers of OTC options find that they need to reverse their positions. This can be done by simply entering the market and attempting to construct an offsetting position. In other words, if you had previously bought an April 5400 call on London's Financial Times 100 index and now would like to reverse the transaction before expiration, you simply call a dealer and offer to sell the same option. In the over-the-counter market, however, no one is likely to be trying to do the exact offsetting trade at the same time. A dealer takes the opposite position, but there are many dealers willing to do the trade. The most important difference between offsetting in the over-the-counter market and offsetting in the exchange-listed market is that in the latter, the contracts cancel any obligations of the writer. In the former, both contracts remain on the books, so they are both subject to default risk. In some cases, a reversing trade with the same dealer with whom one did the original contract can be structured as an offset, thereby terminating both contracts.

Exercising an Option

An American option can be exercised any day up through the expiration date. European options, which have nothing to do with Europe, can be exercised only on the expiration date. Suppose you elect to **exercise** the Microsoft September 27.5 calls, which, like all options on stocks in the United States, are American options. You notify your brokerage firm, which in turn notifies the clearing firm through which the trade originally was cleared. The clearing firm then places an exercise order with the OCC, which randomly selects a clearing firm through which someone has written the same option. Using a procedure established and made known to its customers in advance, the clearing firm selects someone who has written that option. Procedures such as first-in, first-out or random selection are commonly used. The chosen writer is said to be **assigned**.

If the option is a call option on an individual stock, the writer must deliver the stock. You then pay the exercise price, which is passed on to the writer. If the option had been a put option on an individual stock, you would have had to deliver the stock. The writer pays the exercise price, which is passed on to you. For either type of option, however, the writer who originally wrote the contract might not be the one who is assigned the exercise.

Because an index represents a portfolio of stocks, exercise of the option ordinarily would require the delivery of the stocks weighted in the same proportions as they are in the index. This would be quite difficult and inconvenient. Instead, an alternative exercise procedure called **cash settlement** is used. With this method, if an index call option is exercised, the writer pays the buyer the contract multiple times the difference between the index level and the exercise price. For example, assume that you buy one index call option that has a multiple of 100. The index is at 1500, and the exercise price is 1495. If you exercise the option, the assigned writer pays you $100(1500 - 1495) = \$500$ in cash. No stock changes hands. A put option is exercised by the writer paying the buyer the multiple times the difference between the exercise price and the index level.

An order to exercise an index option during the day is executed after the close of trading. The index value *at the end of the day*, not the index value when the exercise was ordered, is used to determine the amount of the settlement. Thus, an investor is well advised to wait until the end of the day to order an exercise of an index option. In addition, certain index options are settled based on the index value at the opening of the next day.

For a call option on the expiration day, if you find that the stock price is less than the exercise price or, for a put, that the stock price is greater than the exercise price, you allow the option to expire by doing nothing. When the expiration day passes, the option contract is removed from the records of the clearing firm and the OCC.

About 10–20 percent of options on stocks are exercised, and about one-third expire with no value. In some cases, due to customer ignorance or lack of oversight, options that should have been exercised at expiration were not. Some brokerage firms have a policy of exercising options automatically when doing so is to the customer's advantage. Such a policy is usually stated in the agreement that the customer signs when opening the account. The OCC automatically exercises options that are at least slightly in-the-money at expiration.

OPTION PRICE QUOTATIONS

Option prices and other option-related information are available from a wide variety of sources, including *The Wall Street Journal* online and other data providers. This information originates from the derivatives exchanges. Often, the derivatives exchange limits access to real-time information, but most exchanges make options information available only on a delayed basis. Option trading information typically includes the last transaction price, the change from the prior day, the current bid and ask price, the daily volume, and the open interest.

One problem with option prices obtained online from newspapers and other data providers, however, is that by the time the prices are available, they are quite outdated. In addition, the price of an option is not necessarily synchronized with the indicated closing price of the underlying stock. The last transaction of the day for the option need not occur near the same time as the last transaction of the day for the stock. For one, the options market and the market where the stock trades may not even close at the same time. Also, for thinly traded options and/or stocks, the last trade for each can easily occur hours apart.

Another problem with option data providers is that they are transaction prices and not bid and ask prices. These are the prices at which the market maker will buy and sell to the public. Suppose the option bid price is 3.25 and the ask price is 3.30. If the last trade of the day is a public order to buy, the closing price will be 3.30. If the last trade of the day is a public order to sell, the closing price will be 3.25.

As a result of these problems and for numerous other obvious reasons, the best sources of option price information are the websites of the exchanges. Real-time price quotes are typically available on a fee-only basis; however, 15-minute-delayed quotes are available free. In addition, the derivatives exchanges show not only the last sale, but also the current bid and ask price. The latest stock price is also shown, but again, there is no guarantee that the indicated stock price is synchronized with the option quotes. That is, while the option bid and ask prices may be accurate and current (subject to the 15-minute delay), the indicated stock price will simply be the last trade, which may have occurred hours earlier. If one uses the stock price to help determine the value of an option, which is the focus of Chapters 4 and 5, the stock price may be stale and misleading. Nonetheless, having the bid and ask prices are better than having only the last trade

MAKING THE CONNECTION

Reading Option Price Quotations

The following example illustrates the price quotations for Microsoft® options during the trading day of August 11, 2011, around 10:50 A.M. Eastern time when Microsoft stock last traded at $24.87, up $0.67, or 2.77%, from the previous day. This observation was taken at a time of very high volatility in financial markets.

Option price quotations can be obtained from the websites of the derivatives exchanges. When accessing an option quote, you are typically given a choice of whether to enter the stock ticker symbol or the option symbol. Stock ticker symbols can found on the exchanges' websites, on other sites such as http://finance.yahoo.com, or in the stock quotation pages of *The Wall Street Journal*.

The ticker symbols of New York Stock Exchange-listed stocks are one, two, or three letters. The ticker symbols of NASDAQ-listed stocks are four letters. Microsoft is a NASDAQ stock, and its symbol is MSFT. To look up option quotations on Microsoft, go to www.cboe.com. From the menu, choose "Quotes & Data." Then select the free "Delayed Quotes" link.

From there, you can enter the stock ticker symbol in the "Get Quotes" box, then choose the "Options" tab. Next, you have a variety of choices, including the expiration month and year. You also can decide whether you want to see all option quotes and certain other restrictions that can make the amount of data returned to you very large or more limited. The websites of derivatives exchanges are constantly changing, so the exact sequence will likely vary over time and across derivatives exchanges.

On August 11, 2011, at 10:50 A.M. Eastern time, the quote was obtained for two Microsoft options illustrated below.

These are the options expiring in October 2011 with an exercise price of 25.00. The call's contract name is "MSFT\11J22\25.0," and the put's contract name is "MSFT\11V22\25.0." The first four letters denote the ticker symbol for the underlying instrument (Microsoft stock in this case). The next group of numbers and letters denote the expiration date: "11" denotes the year 2011, "22" denotes the day of the month, and "J" and "V" designate the month and whether it is a call or put. The table below provides the letters for each month for both calls and puts. Finally, the last set of numbers denotes the strike price ($25.0 in this case).

For calls, the last trade was at $1.28, which was up $0.14. The current bid is $1.33, and the current ask is $1.35. Clearly, the market price of these call options are rising on this day as the last trade was $1.28 but the current bid is $1.33. So far that day, 374 contracts had traded. Over the life of the contract, 19,728 contracts had been opened and not yet closed or exercised. Volume and open interest statistics include all exchanges.

For puts, the last trade was at $1.63, which was also up $0.07. The current bid is $1.62, and the current ask is $1.64. Both puts and calls were rising in response to increasing volatility during this period. So far that day, only 40 contracts had traded. Over the life of the contract, 43,856 contracts had been opened and not yet closed or exercised.

Contract Name	Last Trade	Calls Change	Bid	Ask	Volume	Interest	Strike Price	Contract Name	Last Trade	Puts Change	Bid	Ask	Volume	Interest	Strike Price
MSFT \11J22\ 25.0	1.28	0.14	1.33	1.35	374	19,728	25.00	MSFT \11V22\ 25.0	1.63	0.07	1.62	1.64	40	43,856	25.00

	Jan	Feb	Mar	Apr	May	Jun	Jul	Aug	Sep	Oct	Nov	Dec
Calls	A	B	C	D	E	F	G	H	I	J	K	L
Puts	M	N	O	P	Q	R	S	T	U	V	W	X

price. If the stock bid and ask prices and the time of the last stock trade are needed, they can usually be obtained from sites such as http://finance.yahoo.com or from a brokerage service website.

Both *The Wall Street Journal* and the exchange websites show volume and open interest for options on U.S. exchanges and the overall total for each exchange.

See Making the Connection for information on how to access and interpret this information.

TYPES OF OPTIONS

Two popular types of options are stock options and index options. We shall touch on these only briefly here, as they are the major focus of discussions through Chapter 7. We will also briefly review currency options, interest rate options, and real options, as well as many other types of options.

Stock Options

Options on individual stocks are sometimes called **stock options** or **equity options**. These options are available on several thousand individual stocks, although trading volume may be low for options on certain stocks. In addition, certain options on virtually every stock, such as options with long expirations and options that are either deep-in-the-money or deep-out-of-the-money, have very low trading volume. In the United States, the options of many stocks trade on more than one exchange.

Index Options

A stock index is a measure of the overall value of a designated group of stocks. As in any index, it is a relative measure, capturing value relative to a previous value. For **index options**, we interpret the quoted level as the market value of the stocks relative to a base level value, typically created many years ago when the index was initiated. The first option on a stock index was launched at the CBOE in 1983, and index options have been highly successful ever since. Since that time, a number of index options have been added and many, but not all, have been very actively traded. The option on the NASDAQ 100 stock index is typically the most active of all options in the United States. In most countries, there is an index option trading in which the underlying is a stock index representing the most actively traded stocks of that country's market. These are also usually among the most actively traded of all options in a given country.

Index options are available on broad-based indices such as the S&P 500 and NASDAQ 100 and on more narrowly defined indices. The widely followed Dow Jones Industrial Average consists of only 30 stocks, but its index options are very actively traded. In addition, there are index options on various industry indices (e.g., technology, telecommunications, and oil) and various market sectors (e.g., large-capitalization stocks, medium-capitalization stocks, and small-capitalization stocks).

Index options have been popular for two reasons. First, they are nearly always designed to be cash-settled at expiration, which enables investors to trade options without having to take or make delivery of stock. Cash settlement has, however, been both a blessing and a curse. Many institutional investors hold large portfolios of stocks that purport to replicate the index. They then write call options or sell futures against these portfolios. At other times, these investors sell short the stocks and buy call options or futures. When the options approach the expiration date, the institutional investors, not wanting to hold the stocks after the options expire, attempt to unwind their stock positions. Holders of stock sell the stock, and short sellers buy it back. As a result, many large stock transactions are made near expiration and are accompanied by increased volatility. The cash settlement feature of index options and futures has been blamed for this volatility, although it is not clear that it is the real cause.

The second reason for the popularity of index options is the fact that they are options on the market as a whole. Because there are so many stocks on which options trade, few investors have the time to screen that many opportunities. Many prefer to analyze the market as a whole and use index options (and futures) to act on their forecasts.

Currency Options

A foreign exchange rate is the price at which a party can exchange one currency for another currency. For example, if the exchange rate for euros (€) against dollars is $1.40 per €, one can give up $1.40 and receive €1. Alternatively, the exchange rate can be inverted to obtain €1/$1.40 = €0.7143. Thus, one could give up €0.7143 and receive $1. A currency can be viewed as an asset, much like a stock or bond. Like a stock or bond price, the currency price, which is the exchange rate, fluctuates in a market. One can buy the currency and deposit it in a foreign bank, during which time it will accrue interest at the foreign interest rate. The interest can be viewed like the interest on a bond or the dividends on a stock.

Call and put option terminology can be very confusing with foreign exchange. A call option to buy euros expressed in $/€ is equivalent to a put option to sell dollars expressed in €/$. Specifically, if the option is exercised, the call buyer delivers (or puts) dollars and receives (or calls) euros. For example, suppose the option contract is for 100,000€ and a call buyer exercises her option to buy euros for $1.40/€. In that case, the call buyer delivers $140,000 to the call writer and the call writer delivers 100,000€ to the call buyer.

Because many firms and investors have exposure to exchange rate risk, options and other currency derivatives are widely used. A currency option contract specifies an exercise price, expressed in terms of an exchange rate, an expiration, the identity of the underlying currency, the size of the contract, and various other specifications similar to those of stock and index options.

Exchange-listed currency options trade on the NASDAQ OMX PHLX (previously the Philadelphia Stock Exchange), although trading activity is very low. The more active market is the OTC currency options market. The Bank for International Settlements estimates that the notional amount of currency options at year-end 2010 was about $10.1 trillion, with a market value of about $362 billion.

Other Types of Options

The derivatives exchanges have experimented with a number of different types of options, including options on bonds, although these have attracted little interest. Options on bonds and related options, called *interest rate options*, are, however, extremely popular in the OTC markets. We shall explore these in Chapter 13. As previously noted, there are also options on futures, a topic we shall defer discussing until Chapter 8, when we cover futures.

Many financial institutions now offer securities on which they pay interest based on a minimum value plus the performance of the stock market above a specific level. This is like a call option plus a bond. Other innovative options include some that pay off based on how the price of a commodity, such as oil, performs. It is possible to trade an option that pays off based on which stock index (e.g., the S&P 500 or London's Financial Times 100) performs better. There are also options that expire if the stock price falls to a certain level; options that are based on the average, maximum, or minimum stock price during the life of the option; and an option that allows you to decide, after you buy it but before it expires, whether to make it a put or a call. These options, often called **exotics**, are but a sampling of the tremendous number of innovations that have developed in the OTC markets in recent years. We shall take a look at some of these kinds of instruments in Chapter 14.

A number of other common instruments are practically identical to options. For example, many corporations issue warrants, which are long-term options to buy the companies' stock. Warrants are often issued in conjunction with a public offering of debt or equity. Many corporations issue convertible bonds, which allow the holder to convert the bond into a certain number of shares of stock. The right to convert is itself a call option. Callable bonds, which give the issuing firm the right to repay the bonds early, contain an optionlike component. Stock itself is equivalent to a call option on the firm's assets written by the bondholders with an exercise price equal to the amount due on the debt. Executive stock options, which are nontraded call options written by a corporation and given to its executives, are used extensively as compensation and as a strong incentive for executives to engage in activities that maximize shareholder wealth.

Real Options

Real options are not options on real estate, nor does the name *real options* suggest that other options are somehow not real. Real options are options that are commonly found in corporate investment decisions, which are themselves often referred to as real investments.

Consider, for example, a firm that builds a new plant. Once the plant is built and operating, the company usually has the opportunity to expand it, contract it, temporarily shut it down, close, or sell it to another firm. These options are similar to ordinary options. They allow the owner, which is the firm, to decide at a future date whether to "exercise" the option, which can entail paying an additional sum of money and receiving something of greater value (as in a call)—or receiving a sum of money and giving up something of lesser value (as in a put). These examples are among the simplest of real options. Let us now consider a more complex real option.

Consider a pharmaceutical company that is considering whether or not to invest in research and development (R&D), clinical trials, government approval, and subsequent production and marketing of a new drug. Suppose the preliminary stages have the following times and costs:

Research and development	3 years	$100 million
Clinical trials	5 years	$200 million
Government approval	2 years	$20 million

If the firm elects to invest $100 million in three years of R&D and the R&D successfully results in developing a drug, the firm will subsequently face another decision: whether to invest $200 million in five years of clinical trials. At the end of five years, if the clinical trials are successful, the firm must then decide whether to invest two years and $20 million in obtaining governmental approval to manufacture and sell the drug. If governmental approval is obtained, let us assume that the firm would then need to decide whether to invest $500 million in manufacturing and marketing the drug.

Traditional capital investment analysis, such as net present value, is unable to adequately capture the value of the flexibility. Capital investment decisions are often made sequentially as additional information becomes available. For example, the firm will not decide whether to begin clinical trials until the results of the R&D period are in. It will not decide whether to seek governmental approval for the drug until the results of the clinical trials are in.

These decisions can be viewed as options. They are the choices the firm has to exercise by investing these sums of money, or not, at a future date conditional on the information available at those times. While the example given here is a relatively complex series of interrelated options, it should be easy to see that the company has a sequence of call options.

Real options have many of the characteristics of ordinary options. Yet in many ways, they are quite different. Real options have rights that clearly have value, but often the expirations and exercise prices of real options are not clearly known. For example, does the pharmaceutical company know today how long governmental approval will take or what it will cost? Real options are often based on vaguely specified underlying estimates of costs or benefits that either do not trade in a liquid market or do not trade at all. In the example mentioned earlier in the paragraph, the underlying includes the market value of the drug, which cannot be accurately assessed until it is marketed.

In spite of these and many other limitations, the use of option models for estimating the value of real options is a growing interest among academics and practitioners. While we cannot easily identify real options, we know that they are there and that they have value. You will have an opportunity to learn about them when you study the financial management of corporations. What you will learn in this book will be extremely helpful for understanding real options.

TRANSACTION COSTS IN OPTION TRADING

Option trading entails certain transaction costs. The costs depend on whether the trader is a member of the exchange, a nonmember institutional investor, or a member of the public who is trading through a broker. This section discusses the different types of transaction costs.

Floor Trading and Clearing Fees

Floor trading and clearing fees are the minimum charges assessed by the exchange, the clearing corporation, and the clearing firms for handling a transaction. For trades that go through a broker, these fees are included in the broker's commission, as discussed in the next section. For market makers, the fees are collected by the market maker's clearing firm.

The clearing firm enters into a contractual arrangement with a market maker to clear trades for a fee usually stated on a per contract basis.

The cost to a market maker is usually less than $1 per transaction, although this can vary based on the volume of trades. In addition, market makers incur a number of fixed costs.

For OTC options, these types of costs are not incurred; however, comparable, if not higher, costs are associated with a firm's trading operation and with the processing of these customized transactions.

Commissions

One of the main advantages of owning a seat on an exchange is that it lets a person avoid paying commissions on each trade. The market maker pays indirectly via the opportunity cost associated with the funds tied up in the seat price, the labor involved in trading, and the loss of earnings that would be realized in another line of work. The savings in commissions, however, are quite substantial.

Discount brokers offer the lowest commission rates, but frequent or large trades are sometimes necessary for taking advantage of discount brokers' prices. A discount brokerage firm does not provide the advice and research that is available from full-service brokers charging higher commission rates. One should not, however, automatically assume that a full-service broker is more costly.

Options commissions are fairly simple, based on a fixed minimum and a per contract charge. Internet rates of about $15 plus $1.25 per contract are available from major discount brokers. Some brokers may set charges based on the total dollar size of the transaction, and some offer discounts to more active customers.

When exercising a stock option, the investor must pay the commission for buying or selling the stock. (Stock commissions are discussed in a later section.) If an investor exercises a cash settlement option, the transaction entails only a bookkeeping entry. Some brokerage firms do not charge for exercising a cash settlement option. When any type of option expires unexercised, there is normally no commission.

For OTC options, commissions are not generally incurred because the option buyer or seller usually trades directly with the opposite party.

Bid-Ask Spread

The market maker's spread is a significant transaction cost. Suppose the market maker is quoting a bid price of 3 and an ask price of 3.25 on a call. An investor who buys the call immediately incurs a "cost" of the bid-ask spread, or a 0.25 point; that is, if the investor immediately sold the call, it would fetch only $3, the bid price, and the investor would immediately incur a 0.25 point, or $25, loss. This does not, however, mean that the investor cannot make a profit. The call price may well increase before the option is sold, but if the spread is constant, the bid price must increase by at least the amount of the bid-ask spread before a profit can be made.

The bid-ask spread is the cost of immediacy—the assurance that market makers are willing and able to buy and sell the options on demand. The cost is not explicitly observed, and the investor will not see it on the monthly statement from the broker. It is, however, a real cost and can be quite substantial, amounting to several percent of the option's price.

It may appear that market makers can avoid the bid-ask spread transaction cost. This is true in some cases. If, however, the market maker must buy or sell an option, there may be no public orders of the opposite position. In that case, the market maker would have to trade with another market maker and thus would incur the cost of the bid-ask spread.

In the OTC market, the buyer or seller trades directly with the opposite party. In many cases, one of the parties is a financial institution that makes markets in whatever options its clients want. Thus, the client will probably face a bid-ask spread that is quite significant; but of course, the client is free to shop around.

Other Transaction Costs

Option traders incur several other types of transaction costs. Costs such as margins and taxes are discussed in Appendix 2.A and Appendix 2.B, respectively. Most option traders also trade stocks. Thus, the transaction costs of stock trades are a factor in option trading costs.

Stock trading commissions vary widely among brokerage firms; however, 1–2 percent of the stock's value for a single purchase or sale transaction is a reasonable estimate. Market makers normally obtain more favorable rates from their clearing firms. Also, large institutional investors can usually negotiate volume discounts from their brokers.

Internet rates of $10 or less are sometimes seen. Stocks, however, also have bid-ask spreads; ultimately, 1–2 percent is probably a good estimate of stock trading costs for public investors.

All of the transaction costs discussed here are for single transactions. If the option or stock is subsequently purchased or sold in the market, the transaction cost is incurred again.

REGULATION OF OPTIONS MARKETS

In the United States, the exchange-traded options industry is regulated at several levels. Although federal and state regulations predominate, the industry also regulates itself according to rules and standards established by the exchanges and the Options Clearing Corporation.

The Securities and Exchange Commission (SEC) is the primary regulator of the options market in the United States. The SEC is a federal regulatory agency established in 1934 to oversee the securities industry, which includes stocks, bonds, options, and mutual funds. The SEC's general purpose is to ensure full disclosure of all pertinent information on publicly offered investments. It has the authority to establish certain rules and procedures and to investigate possible violations of federal securities laws. If the SEC observes a violation, it may seek injunctive relief, recommend that the Justice Department press charges, or impose some sanctions itself. For more information, go to www.sec.gov.

The exchanges establish rules and procedures that apply to all members as well as to individuals and firms participating in options transactions. Rule violations are punishable by fines and/or suspensions. The Options Clearing Corporation also regulates its members to help ensure that all activities in the options markets are proper and do not pose a risk to the market's viability.

The regulatory authority of an individual state extends to any securities or options trading occurring within that state. States with significant option trading, such as Illinois and New York, actively enforce their own laws on the propriety of transactions conducted therein. Many important issues in the options industry as a whole are sometimes settled in state courts in Illinois and New York.

Other levels of regulation are imposed by the Federal Reserve System, which regulates the extension of margin credit; the Securities Investor Protection Corporation, which provides insurance against the failure of brokerage firms; and the Financial Industry Regulatory Authority (FINRA), of which most firms involved in options trading are members. FINRA, created in July 2007, replaced the National Association of Securities Dealers and provides some of the regulatory functions of many U.S. exchanges. It is the largest self-regulator for security firms conducting business in the United States. For example, FINRA administers the Registered Options Principal (Series 4) exam that tests one's knowledge of the rules and regulations related to options trading and general knowledge of options. The Series 4 exam is required for options professionals that work with the public. For more information, go to www.finra.org. In addition, several regional and national organizations such as the CFA Institute indirectly regulate the industry by prescribing ethical standards for their members.

Outside the United States, the options industry is regulated by federal government regulatory agencies. In most countries, options and futures are regulated by the same federal agency. In the United States, these products are regulated by separate agencies, with the Commodity Futures Trading Commission (CFTC) regulating the futures industry.

Many new exchange-traded options products were introduced in the 1980s, including options on stock indices, options on foreign currencies, and options on futures. These products created some confusion as to whether the SEC or the CFTC had regulatory purview. The options on futures instrument caused the greatest confusion because it is similar to both an option and a futures. In an important step in resolving the matter, the then-chairmen of these agencies—John Shad of the SEC and Phillip McBride Johnson of the CFTC—reached an agreement. In what has come to be known as the **Johnson-Shad agreement,** or **CFTC-SEC accord,** it was decided that the SEC would regulate options on stocks, stock indices, and foreign currencies, whereas the CFTC would govern options on all futures contracts. Also, a CFTC-regulated contract cannot permit delivery of instruments regulated by the SEC. Although the Johnson-Shad agreement was a milestone in regulatory cooperation, continued disputes between the SEC and the CFTC characterized the regulatory environment of the early 1990s. We shall learn more about these issues when we cover futures.

The primary purpose of the exchange-traded regulatory system is to protect the public. Over the years, many controversial issues have been raised and discussed. In an industry as large as the options industry, some abuses will occur. In recent years, the options industry has been subjected to criticisms that it manipulated the stock market and abused the public's trust by charging exorbitant prices for options. There is no evidence, however, that any of these charges are true. There have even been a few defaults by writers, but thanks to the clearinghouse, in no case has any buyer lost money because of a writer's failure to perform. The options industry works hard to maintain the public's trust by operating in an environment of self-regulation. By policing itself and punishing wrongdoers, some of the cost of having federal regulation is offset for taxpayers.

MAKING THE CONNECTION

Suspicious Put Option Trading and Bear Stearns & Co., Inc. Implosion

The Bear Stearns Companies, Inc. (BSC) was founded in 1923 and grew into a large global investment bank. The market capitalization of its stock at fiscal year ending November 30, 2007, was approximately $13 billion ($100 share price, 130,000,000 shares outstanding). Due to the emerging global credit crisis, BSC stock price had fallen from an all-time high on January 18, 2007, of $172.61 to $100 by November 30, 2007, or a 58% decline. By March 11, 2008, BSC stock price had fallen to $63.8 due to the failure of hedge funds and the worsening of the credit crisis.

According to a Bloomberg.com article appearing on August 11, 2008, someone purchased put options on BSC on March 11, 2008, for 5.7 million shares with a strike price of $30 and 165,000 shares with a strike price of $25 maturing in nine days. Note again that the stock was at $63.8 and someone purchased puts to sell 5.7 million shares to sell the stock at $30 just nine days later! Six days later that person hit the jackpot as BSC reached an all-time low of $2.84 per share and was ultimately purchased by JP Morgan Chase for $10 per share. On March 20, 2008, when the options expired, BSC closed at $6 per share. The purchaser of these put options, if held to expiration, would have made $139,935,000 on an investment of approximately $1,700,000 in just nine days (an 8,131 percent rate of return).

How would anyone have had a suspicion that a stock worth over $60 might fall to below $30 in the next nine days? The only explanation is that this person had inside information. Based on SEC regulations, it is illegal to trade stock, stock options, or other stock-related derivatives based on material, nonpublic information, regardless of its source. Hence, SEC Chairman Christopher Cox indicated publicly that the SEC was investigating whether illegal trading occurred in BSC during this time.

Clearly, the option market makers bear significant risk related to trading with investors who have an informational advantage. Economists refer to this risk as *adverse selection*. The market maker has to trade with everyone and does not know which of his counterparties might have this kind of information. We will see in the coming chapters how option market makers attempt to mitigate their trading risk.

As noted earlier in the chapter, the OTC market is an unregulated market, bound loosely by customs and accepted procedures. The firms that participate, however, are often regulated by the FINRA, the Federal Reserve, or the Comptroller of the Currency. Of course, commercial laws always apply. The SEC and the CFTC, however, have no direct regulatory authority over the OTC options market.

Summary

This chapter provided the foundation for understanding the types of options, individuals, and institutions involved in the options markets. It examined contract specifications, the mechanics of trading, transaction costs, and regulations. This information is a prerequisite to the study of options trading strategies and the pricing of options.

Chapters 3, 4, and 5 focus on the principles and models that determine options prices. Chapters 6 and 7 concentrate on applying this knowledge to the implementation of options trading strategies.

Key Terms

Before continuing to Chapter 3, you should be able to give brief definitions of the following terms:

premium, p. 28
call option, p. 28
put option, p. 28
exercise price/strike price/ striking price, p. 28
expiration date, p. 28
in-the-money, p. 30
out-of-/at-the-money, p. 31
option class, p. 35
option series, p. 35
position limits, p. 37
exercise limit, p. 37
seat, p. 37
liquidity providers, p. 38
market maker, p. 38
bid price, p. 38
ask price, p. 38
bid-ask spread, p. 38
scalpers, p. 38

position traders, p. 38
spreaders, p. 38
lead market maker, 38
designated primary market maker, p. 38
electronic designated primary market maker, p. 38
floor broker, p. 39
order book official (OBO)/board broker, p. 39
specialist, p. 39
registered option traders (ROTs), p. 39
market order, p. 40
limit order, p. 40
good-till-canceled order, p. 40
day order, p. 40
stop order, p. 40
all or none order, p. 40

clearinghouse, p. 41
Options Clearing Corporation (OCC), p. 41
clearing firm, p. 41
margin, p. 42
open interest, p. 42
offsetting order/offset, p. 42
exercise, p. 43
assigned, p. 43
cash settlement, p. 43
stock options, p. 46
equity options, p. 46
index options, p. 46
exotics, p. 48
real options, p. 48
Johnson-Shad agreement/ CFTC-SEC accord, p. 52

Further Reading

The following provide good sources of information on options:

Boyle, P., and F. Boyle. *Derivatives: The Tools that Changed Finance.* London: Risk Books, 2001.

Levy, J. *Your Options Handbook: The Practical Reference and Strategy Guide to Trading Options.* Hoboken, NJ: John Wiley & Sons, 2011.

McMillan, L. G. *McMillan on Options.* New York: Wiley, 1996.

The Options Institute. *Options: Essential Concepts and Trading Strategies,* 3rd ed. New York: McGraw-Hill, 1999.

Shover, L. *Trading Options in Turbulent Markets: Master Uncertainty Through Active Volatility Management.* New York: Bloomberg Press, 2010.

Thomsett, M. C. *Getting Started in Options.* 8th ed. New York: Wiley, 2009.

Concept Checks

1. When an option exchange is trying to establish which exercise prices will be traded, what is the option exchange's goal?
2. Market makers can use a variety of trading styles. Identify and discuss three trading styles.
3. Explain the difference between an American option and a European option. What do they have in common?
4. Contrast option class and option series. Who determines the options that will be publicly traded?
5. Determine whether each of the following arrangements behaves like an option. If so, decide whether it is a call or a put and identify the premium.
   a. You purchase homeowner's insurance for your house.
   b. You are a high school senior evaluating possible college choices. One school promises that if you enroll, it will guarantee your tuition rate for the next four years.
   c. You enter into a noncancelable, long-term apartment lease.

Questions and Problems

1. Identify and discuss the different types of liquidity providers on the CBOE.
2. What is the primary purpose of option liquidity providers?
3. Compare and contrast the exercise procedure for stock options with that for index options. What major advantage does exercising an index option have over exercising a stock option?
4. Why is the procedure of cash settlement useful when exercising an index option? What index value is used to determine the amount of settlement?
5. Suppose you are an individual investor with an options account at a brokerage firm. You purchase 20 call contracts at a price of $2.25 each. Explain how your premium ends up at the clearinghouse.
6. What are some disadvantages associated with over-the-counter options markets that are not found in organized options exchanges?
7. Explain how the CBOE's order book official (OBO) handles public limit orders.
8. Distinguish between in-the-money and out-of-the money call options. Should an in-the-money call always be exercised prior to expiration? Are there situations in which an out-of-the money call should be exercised? Explain your answers.
9. Contrast the market maker system of exchange trading with the specialist system. What advantages and disadvantages do you see in each system?
10. Explain the major difference between the regulation of exchange-traded options and over-the-counter options.
11. Compare and contrast the roles of market maker and floor broker. Why do you think an individual cannot generally be both?
12. Identify and briefly discuss the various types of option transaction costs. How do these costs differ for market makers, floor brokers, and firms trading in the over-the-counter market?
13. Why are short puts and long calls grouped together when considering position limits?
14. Explain how real options are similar to but different from ordinary options.
15. Consider the January, February, and March stock option exercise cycles discussed in the chapter. For each of the following dates, indicate which expirations in each cycle would be listed for trading in stock options.
    a. February 1
    b. July 1
    c. December 1
16. Name and briefly describe at least two other instruments that are similar to options.
17. What adjustments to the contract terms of CBOE options would be made in the following situations?
    a. An option has an exercise price of 60. The company declares a 10 percent stock dividend.
    b. An option has an exercise price of 25. The company declares a two-for-one stock split.
    c. An option has an exercise price of 85. The company declares a four-for-three stock split.
    d. An option has an exercise price of 50. The company declares a cash dividend of $0.75.
18. Discuss the three ways in which an open option position can be terminated. Is your answer different if the option is created in the over-the-counter market? Explain.
19. Explain each of the terms in the following description of an option: AT&T January 65 call.
20. Discuss the limitations of prices obtained from newspapers such as *The Wall Street Journal* online and the advantages of quotes obtained from websites of the exchanges.

APPENDIX 2.A

Margin Requirements

Margin is the amount of money an individual commits when entering into an investment. The remainder is borrowed from the brokerage firm. The objective of a margin trade is to earn a higher return by virtue of investing less of one's own funds. This advantage is, however, accompanied by increased risk. If the value of the investment does not move sufficiently in the desired direction, the profit from the investment may not be enough to pay off the loan.

The **initial margin** is the minimum amount of funds the investor supplies on the day of the transaction. The difference between this amount and the full value of the transaction can be thought of as the amount advanced as credit. The **maintenance margin** is the minimum amount of funds required each day after the first day of the transaction. Also, on any day on which a trade is executed, the initial margin requirement must be met. Regulation T of the Federal Reserve Act authorizes the Federal Reserve to regulate the extension of credit in the United States, which means that the Federal Reserve regulates initial margins on both stocks and options. Maintenance margins are generally regulated by exchanges and the Financial Industry Regulatory Authority (FINRA). For options, however, the guaranty provided by the Options Clearing Corporation gives it some authority over margin requirements. In addition, the SEC's authority is typically relevant in cases of margin requirements.

Margin requirements on option transactions have traditionally been based on specific formulas that we will cover in the next section. In late 2006, however, the CBOE and New York Stock Exchange applied for and received permission from the SEC and OCC to institute a new system of margin requirements called portfolio margining, whereby combined positions of stock and options on that stock can be used to offset each other. Portfolio margining is based on a system of stress tests in which possible adverse movements in the overall position are evaluated and used as a basis for setting the margin as a function of potential losses. In most cases, portfolio margining results in lower margin requirements. Portfolio margining is not automatic, however, and is generally available only for large customers but is used by all U.S. derivatives exchanges. Because the stress testing involved in portfolio margining is a more advanced topic than we can cover at this point, we will present only the standard fixed margin requirements in this Appendix.

MARGIN REQUIREMENTS ON STOCK TRANSACTIONS

The minimum initial margin for stock purchases and short sales is 50 percent. The minimum maintenance margin is 25 percent. Many brokerage firms add an additional 5 percent or more to these requirements.

MARGIN REQUIREMENTS ON OPTION PURCHASES

Options with maturities of nine months or less must be paid for in full. That is, the margin requirement is 100 percent. Options with maturities of greater than nine months can, however, be margined. An investor can borrow up to 25 percent of the cost of these options.

MARGIN REQUIREMENTS ON THE UNCOVERED SALE OF OPTIONS

An **uncovered call** is a transaction in which an investor writes a call on stock not already owned. If the option is exercised, the writer must buy the stock in the market at the current price, which has no upper limit. Thus, the risk is quite high. Many brokerage firms do not allow their customers to write uncovered calls. Those that do usually restrict such trades to wealthy investors who can afford large losses; yet even these trades must meet the minimum margin requirements.

For an uncovered call, the investor must deposit the premium plus 20 percent of the stock's value. If the call is out-of-the-money, the requirement is reduced by the amount by which the call is out-of-the-money. The margin must be at least the option market value plus 10 percent of the value of the stock. Consider an investor who writes one call contract at an exercise price of $30 on a stock priced at $33 for a premium of $4.50. The required margin is 0.2($3,300) + $450 = $1,110. If the stock is priced at $28 and the call is at $0.50, the margin is 0.2($2,800) + $50 − $200 = $410. These amounts are greater than 10 percent of the value of the stock plus the option market value. The amount by which the call is out-of-the-money reduces the required margin.

The same rules apply for puts except that the 10 percent rule is applied to the aggregate exercise price. If a put is written at an exercise price of $30 when the stock price is $33 and the put price is $2.375, the required margin is 0.2($3,300) + $237.50 − $300 = $597.50. If the stock price is $29 and the put price is $3.25, the margin is 0.2($2,900) + $325 = $905. These amounts are greater than 10 percent of the aggregate exercise price of $3,000 plus the option value.

Broad-based index options are somewhat less volatile than options on individual stocks and, appropriately, have lower margin requirements. The required margin is 15 percent, instead of 20 percent, of the stock's value.

MARGIN REQUIREMENTS ON COVERED CALLS

A **covered call** is a transaction in which an investor writes an option against a stock already owned. If the option's exercise price is at least equal to the stock price, the investor need not deposit any additional margin beyond that required on the stock. Also, the premium on the option can be used to reduce the margin required on the stock. If, however, the exercise price is less than the stock price, the maximum amount the investor can borrow on the stock is based on the call's exercise price rather than on the stock price. For example, if the stock price is $40 and the exercise price is $35, the investor can borrow only 0.5($3,500) = $1,750, not 0.5($4,000) = $2,000, on the purchase of the stock.

Although it is possible to hold a portfolio of stocks that is identical to the index, current margin requirements do not recognize covered index call writing. Therefore, all short positions in index options must be margined according to the rules that apply to uncovered writing.

There are exceptions to many of these rules, particularly when spreads, straddles, and more complex option transactions are used. In these cases, the margin requirements often are complicated. Investors should consult a broker or some of the trade-oriented publications for additional information on margin requirements for more complex transactions.

Questions and Problems

1. Suppose a stock is currently priced at $50. The margin requirement is 20 percent on uncovered calls and 50 percent on stocks. Calculate the required margin, in dollars, for each of the following trades:
   a. Write 10 call contracts with an exercise price of 45 and a premium of 7.
   b. Write 10 call contracts with an exercise price of 55 and a premium of 3.
   c. Write 10 put contracts with an exercise price of 45 and a premium of 3.
   d. Write 10 put contracts with an exercise price of 55 and a premium of 7.
   e. Buy 1,000 shares of stock and write 10 call contracts with an exercise price of 45 and a premium of 7.
   f. Buy 20 put contracts with an exercise price of 50 and a premium of 5. The option matures in six months.

APPENDIX 2.B

Taxation of Option Transactions

Determining the applicable taxation of many investment transactions is a complex process that requires the advice of highly trained specialists. The rules covered in this Appendix outline most of the basic option transactions. There are many exceptions and loopholes, and the laws change frequently. In all cases, one should secure competent professional advice. Of course, these rules are based on U.S. tax law, which changes often, and the material presented here is based on 2010 law.

The ordinary income of most individuals is taxed at 10, 15, 25, 28, 33, or 35 percent. Long-term capital gains, defined as profits from positions held more than 12 months, are taxed at a maximum of 15 percent. Although there are some exceptions noted herein, most exchange-listed options profits are short-term.

In these examples, we ignore brokerage commissions; however, they are deductible. The commission on the purchase of the asset is added to the purchase price; the commission on its sale is subtracted from the sale price.

The deductibility of any losses is determined by offsetting them against other investment gains. If the losses exceed the gains, any excess up to $3,000 per year is deductible against the investor's ordinary income.

These rules apply to individual investors. Corporations and other institutions trading options, especially OTC options, may be subject to different tax rules and interpretations.

For the following examples, we shall assume that the investor is in the 28 percent tax bracket.

TAXATION OF LONG CALL TRANSACTIONS

If an investor purchases a call and sells it back at a later date at a higher price, there is a capital gain, which is either long-term or short-term, but usually short-term. Thus, the call is taxed at the ordinary income rate. If the investor sells the call at a loss or allows it to expire, the loss is deductible as previously described.

Consider an investor who purchases a call at $3.50 on a stock priced at $36 with an exercise price of $35. Less than 12 months later but before expiration, the investor sells the call at $4.75. The profit of $1.25 is taxed at 28 percent for a tax of $1.25(0.28) = $0.35. If the call were sold at a loss, the loss would be deductible as described earlier.

If the investor exercised the call, the call price plus the exercise price would be treated as the stock's purchase price and subsequently used to determine the taxable gain on the stock. For example, if the above call were exercised when the stock price was $38, the purchase price of the stock would be considered as the $35 exercise price plus the $3.50 call price for a total of $38.50. If the investor later sold the stock for $40, the taxable gain would be $1.50 and the tax $1.50(0.28) = $0.42. A tax liability or deduction arises only when the stock is subsequently sold.

TAXATION OF SHORT CALL TRANSACTIONS

If an investor sells a call and later repurchases it or allows it to expire, any profit is a short-term capital gain and is taxed at the ordinary income rate. If the call is exercised, the exercise price plus the call price is treated as the price at which the stock is sold. Then the difference between the price at which the stock is sold and the price at which it is purchased is the taxable gain.

For example, if the preceding investor writes the call at a price of $5.25 and subsequently buys it at $3.50 before expiration, the profit of $1.75 will be taxed at 28 percent for a tax of $1.75(0.28) = 0.49. A loss would be deductible as previously described. If the call were exercised, the writer would deliver the stock. Suppose the stock price was $38 and the writer did not already own the stock. Then the writer would purchase the stock for $38 and sell it to the buyer for $35. The sum of the exercise price plus the premium, $35 + $5.25 = 40.25, would be treated as the stock's sale price. The taxable gain to the writer would be $2.25, and the tax would be $2.25(0.28) = 0.63. Had the writer purchased the stock at an earlier date at $30, the taxable gain would have been $10.25 and the tax $10.25(0.28) = 2.87.

TAXATION OF LONG PUT TRANSACTIONS

If an investor purchases a put and sells it or allows it to expire less than 12 months later, the profit is a short-term capital gain and is taxed at the ordinary income rate. If the put is exercised, the exercise price minus the premium is treated as the stock's sale price. Then the profit from the stock is taxed at the ordinary income rate.

Consider an investor in the 28 percent tax bracket who purchases a put at $3 on a stock priced at $52 with an exercise price of $50. Later the investor sells the put for $4.25. The gain of $1.25 is taxed at 28 percent for a tax of $1.25(0.28) = 0.35. If the put is sold at a loss, the loss is deductible as previously described.

Suppose the investor exercises the put when the stock price is $46. The law would treat this as the sale of stock at $50 less the premium of $3 for a net gain of $47. If the investor purchases the stock at $46 and exercises the put, the taxable gain is $1 and the tax is $1(0.28) = 0.28. If the investor had previously purchased the stock at $40, the taxable gain would be $7 and the tax would be $7(0.28) = 1.96. Had the investor purchased the stock at a price higher than $47, the loss would have been deductible as described earlier.

Another possibility is that the investor uses the exercise of the put to sell short the stock. Recall from Chapter 1 that a short sale occurs when an investor borrows stock from the broker and sells it. If the stock price falls, the investor can buy back the stock at a lower price, repay the broker the shares, and capture a profit. A short sale is made in order to profit in a falling market. In our example, the stock is sold short at $47. When the investor later repurchases the stock, any gain on the stock is taxable or any loss is deductible.

TAXATION OF SHORT PUT TRANSACTIONS

If an investor writes a put and subsequently buys it back before expiration, any gain is considered a short-term capital gain and is taxed at the ordinary income rate and any loss is deductible. If the put is exercised, the put's exercise price minus the premium is considered to be the stock's purchase price. The taxable gain or loss on the stock is determined by the difference between the purchase and sale prices of the stock.

Consider the put with an exercise price of $50 written at $3 when the stock price is $52. Suppose the stock price goes to $46 and the put is exercised. The put writer is considered to have purchased the stock for $50 − $3, or $47. If the investor later sells the stock for $55, the taxable gain is $8 and the tax is $8(0.28) = 2.24.

TAXATION OF NON-EQUITY OPTIONS

Index options, debt options, and foreign currency options have a special tax status. At the end of the calendar year, all realized *and unrealized* gains are taxable. All losses are deductible as previously described. The profits are taxed at a blended rate in which

60 percent are taxed at the long-term capital gains rate and 40 percent are taxed at the short-term capital gains rate, which is the ordinary income rate. For an investor in the 28 percent bracket, this is an effective rate of $0.6(0.20) + 0.4(0.28) = 0.232$.

For example, assume that during the year, an investor in the 28 percent bracket had $1,250 of net profits (profits minus losses) on index options. At the end of the year, the investor holds 1,000 index options worth $2.25 that previously had been purchased for $1.75. The unrealized profit is thus $500. The total taxable profits are $1,250 + $500 = $1,750. The tax is $1,750(0.6)(0.20) + $1,750(0.4)(0.28) = $406.

WASH AND CONSTRUCTIVE SALES

Option traders should be aware of an important tax condition called the wash sale rule. A **wash sale** is a transaction in which an investor sells a security at a loss and replaces it with essentially the same security shortly thereafter. Tax laws disallow the deduction of the loss on the sale of the original security. The purpose of the wash sale rule is to prevent investors from taking losses at the end of a calendar year and then immediately replacing the securities. The time period within which the purchase of the security cannot occur is the 61-day period from 30 days before the sale of the stock through 30 days after.

The wash sale rule usually treats a call option as being the same security as the stock. Thus, if the investor sells the stock at a loss and buys a call within the applicable 61-day period, the loss on the stock is not deductible.

In addition, the sale of a call option on a stock owned can, under some circumstances, be treated as the investor effectively having sold the stock, thereby terminating the stock holding period. This is called a **constructive sale**.

Questions and Problems

1. Suppose a stock is priced at $30 and an eight-month call on the stock with an exercise price of $25 is priced at $6. Compute the taxable gain and tax due for each of the following cases, assuming that your tax bracket is 28 percent. Assume 100 shares and 100 calls.
   a. You buy the call. Four months later the stock is at $28 and the call is at $4.50. You then sell the call.
   b. You buy the call. Three months later the stock is at $31 and the call is at $6.50. You then sell the call.
   c. You buy the call. At expiration, the stock is at $32. You exercise the call and sell the stock a month later for $35.
   d. You buy the stock and write the call. You hold the position until expiration, whereupon the stock is at $28.
   e. You write the call. Two months later the stock is at $28 and the call is at $3.50. You buy back the call.
2. Consider an index option. The index is at 425.48, and a two-month call with an exercise price of 425 is priced at $15. You are in the 31 percent tax bracket. Compute the after-tax profit for the following cases. Assume 100 calls.
   a. You buy the call. One month later the index is at 428 and the call is at $12. You sell the call.
   b. You buy the call and hold it until expiration, whereupon the index is at 441.35. You exercise the call.
   c. You hold the call until expiration, when the index is at 417.15.
   d. How will your answers in parts a and b be affected if the option positions are not closed out by the end of the year?

3. Which of the following would be a wash sale? Explain.
    a. You buy a stock at $30. Three weeks later you sell the stock at $26. Two weeks later you buy a call on the stock.
    b. You buy a stock at $40. One month later you buy a call on the stock. One week later you sell the stock for $38.
    c. You buy a stock for $40. Three months later you sell the stock for $42 and buy a call on the stock.

CHAPTER 3

Principles of Option Pricing

Well, it helps to look at derivatives like atoms. Split them one way and you have heat and energy—useful stuff. Split them another way and you have a bomb. You have to understand the subtleties.

Kate Jennings
Moral Hazard, Fourth Estate, 2002, p. 8

This chapter identifies certain factors and shows why they affect an option's price. It examines option boundary conditions—rules that characterize rational option prices. Then it explores the relationship between options that differ by exercise price alone and options that differ only by time to expiration. Finally, the chapter discusses how put and call prices are related, as well as several other important principles. An overriding point throughout this chapter, and indeed throughout this entire book, is that arbitrage opportunities are quickly eliminated by investors.

Suppose an individual offers you the following proposition: You can play a game called Game I in which you draw a ball from a hat known to contain three red balls and three blue balls. If you draw a red ball, you receive nothing; if you draw a blue ball, you receive $10. Will you play? Because the individual did not mention an entry fee, most people will play. You incur no cash outlay up front and have the opportunity to earn $10. Of course, this opportunity is too good to be true and only an irrational person would make such an offer without charging an entry fee.

Now suppose a fair fee to play Game I is $4. Consider a new game called Game II. The person offers to pay you $20 if you draw a blue ball and nothing if you draw a red ball. Will the entry fee be higher or lower? If you draw a red ball, you receive the same payoff as in Game I; if you draw a blue ball, you receive a higher payoff than in Game I. You should be willing to pay more to play Game II because these payoffs dominate those of Game I.

From these simple games and opportunities, it is easy to see some of the basic principles of how rational people behave when faced with risky situations. The collective behavior of rational investors operates in an identical manner to determine the fundamental principles of option pricing. As you read the various examples in this chapter in which arbitrage is used to establish fundamental rules about option pricing, keep in mind the similarity of the investment situation to the games just described. In so doing, the rational result should become clear to you.

In this chapter, we do not derive the exact price of an option; rather, we confine the discussion to identifying upper and lower limits and factors that influence an option's price. Chapters 4 and 5 explain how the exact option price is determined.

CHAPTER OBJECTIVES

- Explain the role of arbitrage in option pricing, illustrating fundamental principles that determine an option's price, such as the minimum value, maximum value, value at expiration, and lower bound

- Identify and explain the rationale for factors that affect an option's price, including stock price, exercise price, time to expiration, risk-free rate, and volatility

- Explain the difference between American and European options and explain why early exercise may or may not occur

- Understand the very important relationship of put-call parity

BASIC NOTATION AND TERMINOLOGY

The following symbols are used throughout the book:

S_0 = stock price today (time 0 = today)
X = exercise price
T = time to expiration as defined below
r = risk-free rate as defined below
S_T = stock price at option's expiration
  (that is, after the passage of a period of time of length T)
$C(S_0, T, X)$ = price of a call option in which the stock price is S_0,
  the time to expiration is T, and the exercise price is X
$P(S_0, T, X)$ = price of a put option in which the stock price is S_0,
  the time to expiration is T, and the exercise price is X

In some situations, we may need to distinguish an American call from a European call. If so, the call price will be denoted as either $C_a(S_0, T, X)$ or $C_e(S_0, T, X)$ for the American and European calls, respectively. If there is no a or e subscript, the call can be either an American or a European call. In the case where two options differ only by exercise price, the notations $C(S_0, T, X_1)$ and $C(S_0, T, X_2)$ will identify the prices of the calls with X_1 less than X_2. A good way to remember this is to keep in mind that the subscript of the lower exercise price is smaller than that of the higher exercise price. In the case where two options differ only by time to expiration, the times to expiration will be T_1 and T_2, where $T_1 < T_2$. The options' prices will be $C(S_0, T_1, X)$ and $C(S_0, T_2, X)$. Identical adjustments will be made for put option prices.

For most of the examples, we shall assume that the stock pays no dividends. If, during the life of the option, the stock pays dividends of D_1, D_2, and so forth, we can make a simple adjustment and obtain similar results. To do so, we simply subtract the present value of the dividends, $\Sigma_{j=1}^{N} D_j (1 + r)^{-t_j}$ where there are N dividends and t_j is the time to each ex-dividend day, from the stock price. We assume that the dividends are known ahead of time.

The time to expiration is expressed as a decimal fraction of a year. For example, if the current date is April 9 and the option's expiration date is July 18, we simply count the number of days between these two dates: 21 days remaining in April, 31 in May, 30 in June, and 18 in July for a total of 100 days. The time to expiration therefore would be 100/365 = 0.274.

The risk-free rate, r, is the rate earned on a riskless investment assumed here to be compounded annually. An example of such an investment is a U.S. Treasury bill, or T-bill. A Treasury bill is a security issued by the U.S. government for purchase by investors. T-bills with original maturities of 91 and 182 days are auctioned by the Federal Reserve each week; T-bills with maturities of 365 days are auctioned every four weeks. All T-bills mature on a Thursday.[1] Because most exchange-traded options expire on a Friday, a T-bill is always maturing the day before expiration. For other options with maturities of six months or less, a T-bill is maturing within one week of the option's expiration. The rate of return on a T-bill of comparable maturity would be a proxy for the risk-free rate.[2]

---

[1]If Thursday is a holiday, such as Thanksgiving, the Treasury bill matures on Wednesday of that week.

[2]There is an ongoing debate regarding the appropriate discount rate to use with financial derivatives. Another possible rate to use is the London Interbank Offer Rate (LIBOR) because it is a good proxy for the marginal dealers' cost of funds. We will use the T-bill rate here because this is an introductory book and T-bills are familiar instruments to most students of finance. We will cover the use of LIBOR in later chapters.

TECHNICAL NOTE: Interest Rates
and Financial Derivatives
go to www.cengagebrain.com

T-bills pay interest not by using coupons, but by selling at a discount. The T-bill is purchased at less than face value. The difference between the purchase price and the face value is called the discount. If the investor holds the bill to maturity, it is redeemed at face value. Therefore, the discount is the profit earned by the bill holder.

Bid and ask discounts for several T-bills for the business day of May 14 of a particular year are as follows:

Maturity	Bid	Ask
5/20	4.45	4.37
6/17	4.41	4.37
7/15	4.47	4.43

The bid and ask figures are the discounts quoted by dealers trading in Treasury bills. The bid is the discount if one is selling to the dealer, and the ask is the discount if one is buying from the dealer. Bid and ask quotes are reported through a wide variety of outlets, including daily in *The Wall Street Journal.*

In the United States, most exchange-listed stock options expire on the third Friday of the month. In the preceding example, the third Friday of May was May 21. To find an estimate of the T-bill rate, we use the average of the bid and ask discounts, which is $(4.45 + 4.37)/2 = 4.41$. Then we find the discount from par value as $4.41(7/360) = 0.08575$, using the fact that the option has seven days until maturity. Thus, the price is

$$100 - 0.08575 = 99.91425.$$

Note that the price is determined by assuming a 360-day year. This is a long-standing tradition in the financial community, originating from the days before calculators, when bank loans often were for 60, 90, or 180 days. A banker could more easily calculate the discount using the fraction 60/360, 90/360, or 180/360. This tradition survives today.

The yield on our T-bill is based on the assumption of buying it at 99.91425 and holding it for seven days, at which time it will be worth 100.[3] This is a return of $(100 - 99.91425)/99.91425 = 0.000858$. If we repeated this transaction every seven days for a full year, the return would be

$$(1.000858)^{365/7} - 1 = 0.0457,$$

where 1.000858 is simply 100/99.91425, or one plus the seven-day return. Note that when we annualize the return, we use the full 365-day year. Thus, we would use 4.57 percent as our proxy for the risk-free rate for options expiring on May 21.

To illustrate the principles of option pricing, we shall use prices for options on DCRB, a fictional large, high-tech company traded on NASDAQ. These prices were assumed to be observed on May 14 and are presented in Table 3.1. The May options expire on May 21, the June options expire on June 18, and the July options expire on July 16.

In the U.S. markets, stock prices are quoted in units of $0.01 and option prices in units of $0.01 if the option price is below $3. For option prices above $3, the option prices are quoted in $0.05. The data illustrated in our examples assume that mid-market quotes implying option prices will be quoted in units of $0.01.

---

[3]Actually, the number of days is counted from the settlement day, which is the second business day after the purchase day. We shall disregard this point in the calculations in this book.

TABLE 3.1 DCRB OPTION DATA, MAY 14						
	CALLS			PUTS		
EXERCISE PRICE	**MAY**	**JUNE**	**JULY**	**MAY**	**JUNE**	**JULY**
120	8.75	15.40	20.90	2.75	9.25	13.65
125	5.75	13.50	18.60	4.60	11.50	16.60
130	3.60	11.35	16.40	7.35	14.25	19.65

Current stock price: 125.94
Expirations: May 21, June 18, July 16

Following the same procedure described for the May T-bill gives us risk-free rates of 4.56 and 4.63 for the June and July expirations, respectively. The times to expiration are 0.0192 (7 days/365) for the May options, 0.0959 (35 days/365) for the June options, and 0.1726 (63 days/365) for the July options.

PRINCIPLES OF CALL OPTION PRICING

In this section, we formulate rules that enable us to better understand how call options are priced. It is important to keep in mind that our objective is to determine the price of a call option *prior to* its expiration day.

Minimum Value of a Call

> Because a call option need not be exercised, its minimum value is zero.

A call option is an instrument with limited liability. If the call holder sees that it is advantageous to exercise the call, it will be exercised. If exercising it will decrease the call holder's wealth, the holder will not exercise it. The option cannot have negative value because the holder cannot be forced to exercise it. Therefore,

$$C(S_0,T,X) \geq 0.$$

For an American call, the statement that a call option has a minimum value of zero is dominated by a much stronger statement:

$$C_a(S_0,T,X) \geq Max(0,S_0 - X).$$

> The intrinsic value of an American call is the greater of zero or the difference between the stock price and the exercise price.

The expression $Max(0, S_0 - X)$ means "Take the maximum value of the two arguments, zero or $S_0 - X$."

The minimum value of an option is called its **intrinsic value**, sometimes referred to as **parity value**, **parity**, or **exercise value**. Intrinsic value, which is positive for in-the-money calls and zero for out-of-the-money calls, is the value the call holder receives from exercising the option and the value the call writer gives up when the option is exercised. Note that we are not concerned about the appropriateness of immediately exercising the option; we note only that one could do so if a profit opportunity were available.

To prove the intrinsic value rule, consider the DCRB June 120 call. The stock price is $125.94, and the exercise price is $120. Evaluating the expression gives $Max(0, 125.94 - 120) = 5.94$. Now consider what would happen if the call were priced at less than $5.94—say, $3. An option trader could buy the call for $3, exercise it—which would entail purchasing the stock for $120—and then sell the stock for $125.94. This arbitrage

TABLE 3.2	INTRINSIC VALUES AND TIME VALUES OF DCRB CALLS			
		TIME VALUE		
EXERCISE PRICE	INTRINSIC VALUE	MAY	JUNE	JULY
120	5.94	2.81	9.46	14.96
125	0.94	4.81	12.56	17.66
130	0.00	3.60	11.35	16.40

transaction would net an immediate riskless profit of $2.94 on each share.[4] All investors would do this, which would drive up the option's price. When the price of the option reached $5.94, the transaction would no longer be profitable. Thus, $5.94 is the minimum price of the call.

What if the exercise price exceeds the stock price, as do the options with an exercise price of $130? Then Max(0, 125.94 − 130) = 0, and the minimum value will be zero.

Now look at all of the DCRB calls. Those with an exercise price of $120 have a minimum value of Max(0, 125.94 − 120) = 5.94. All three calls with an exercise price of $120 indeed have prices of no less than $5.94. The calls with an exercise price of $125 have minimum values of Max(0, 125.94 − 125) = 0.94 and are priced at no less than 0.94. The calls with an exercise price of 130 have minimum values of Max(0, 125.94 − 130) = 0. All of those options obviously have nonnegative values. Thus, all of the DCRB call options conform to the intrinsic value rule. In fact, extensive empirical testing has revealed that options in general conform quite closely to the rule.

The intrinsic value concept applies only to an American call because a European call can be exercised only on the expiration day. If the price of a European call were less than Max(0, $S_0 − X$), the inability to exercise it would prevent traders from engaging in the aforementioned arbitrage that would drive up the call's price.

> The time value of an American call is the difference between the call price and the intrinsic value.

The price of an American call normally exceeds its intrinsic value. The difference between the price and the intrinsic value is called the **time value** or **speculative value** of the call, which is defined as $C_a(S_0,T,X) − $ Max(0, $S_0 − X$). The time value reflects what traders are willing to pay for the uncertainty of the underlying stock. Table 3.2 presents the intrinsic values and time values of the DCRB calls. Note that the time values increase with the time to expiration.

Figure 3.1 illustrates what we have established so far. The call price lies in the shaded area. Figure 3.1(a) illustrates that the European call price can lie in the entire area, whereas the American call price lies in a smaller area. This does not mean that the American call price is less than the European call price, but only that its range of possible values is narrower.

Maximum Value of a Call

A call option also has a maximum value:

$$C(S_0,T,X) \leq S_0.$$

---

[4]Actually, it would not be necessary to sell the stock. In the absence of transaction costs, it is immaterial whether one holds the stock—an asset valued at $125.94—or converts it to another asset—cash—worth $125.94. The wealth is the same, $125.94, in either case.

FIGURE 3.1 Minimum Values of European and American Calls

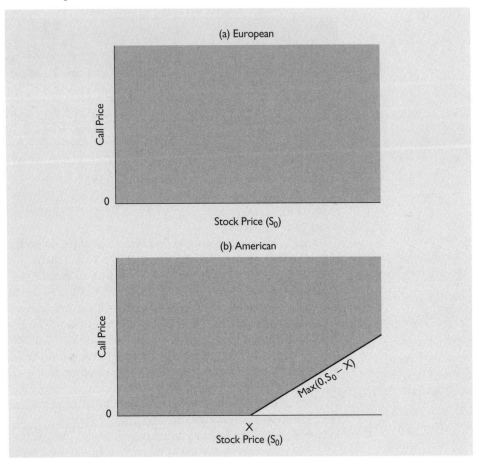

| The maximum value of a call is the price of the stock. |

The call is a conduit through which an investor can obtain the stock. The most one can expect to gain from the call is the stock's value less the exercise price. Even if the exercise price were zero, no one would pay more for the call than for the stock. One call, however, that is worth the stock price is a call with an infinite maturity. It is obvious that all of the DCRB calls are worth no more than the value of the stock.

Figure 3.2 adds the maximum value rule to Figure 3.1. Notice that the maximum value rule has significantly reduced the range of possible option values.

Value of a Call at Expiration

The price of a call at expiration is given as

$$C(S_T, 0, X) = Max(0, S_T - X).$$

| At expiration, a call option is worth the intrinsic value. |

Because no time remains in the option's life, the call price contains no time value. The prospect of future stock price increases is irrelevant to the price of the expiring option, which will be simply its intrinsic value.[5]

---

[5]Because of the transaction cost of exercising the option, it could be worth slightly less than the intrinsic value.

FIGURE 3.2 Minimum and Maximum Values of European and American Calls

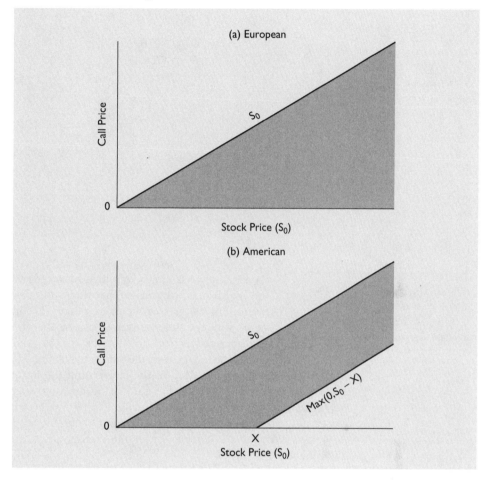

At expiration, an American option and a European option are identical instruments. Therefore, this rule holds for both types of options.

Figure 3.3 illustrates the value of the call at expiration. This is one situation in which the value of the call is unambiguous. But do not confuse this with our ultimate objective, which is to find the value of the call *prior to* expiration.

Effect of Time to Expiration

Consider two American calls that differ only in their times to expiration. One has a time to expiration of T_1 and a price of $C_a(S_0,T_1,X)$; the other has a time to expiration of T_2 and a price of $C_a(S_0,T_2,X)$. Remember that T_2 is greater than T_1. Which of these two options will have the greater value?

Suppose that today is the expiration day of the shorter-lived option. The stock price is S_{T_1}. The value of the expiring option is $\text{Max}(0, S_{T_1} - X)$. The second option has a time to expiration of $T_2 - T_1$. Its minimum value is $\text{Max}(0, S_{T_1} - X)$. Thus, when the shorter-lived option expires, its value is the minimum value of the longer-lived option. Therefore,

$$C_a(S_0,T_2,X) \geq C_a(S_0,T_1,X).$$

Normally the longer-lived call is worth more, but if it carries no time value when the shorter-lived option expires, the two options will have the same price. This can occur if

FIGURE 3.3 The Value of a Call at Expiration

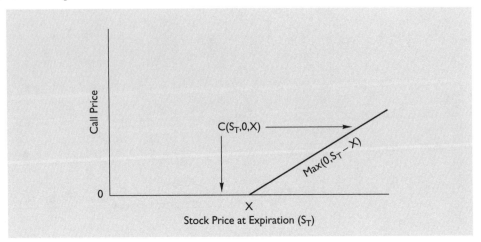

> A longer-lived American call must always be worth at least as much as a shorter-lived American call with the same terms.

the stock price is either very high or very low. Looking at the prices of the DCRB calls, we can see that this is the case. The longer the time to expiration, the greater the call's value. The time value of a call option varies with the time to expiration and the proximity of the stock price to the exercise price. Investors pay for the time value of the call based on the uncertainty of the future stock price. If the stock price is very high, the call is said to be **deep-in-the-money** and the time value will be low. If the stock price is very low, the call is said to be **deep-out-of-the-money** and the time value likewise will be low. The time value will be low because at these extremes, the uncertainty about the call expiring in- or out-of-the-money is lower. The uncertainty is greater when the stock price is near the exercise price, and it is at this point that the time value is higher.

A simple analogy is useful for understanding why the time value is highest when the stock price is close to the exercise price. Suppose you were watching an important basketball game between the New York Knicks and the Boston Celtics. Let us assume that you enjoy a good game but have no sentimental attachment to either team. It is now halftime. Suppose New York is ahead 65–38. How interesting is the game now? How probable is it that New York will win? Are you likely to keep watching if there is something more interesting to do with your time? But suppose, instead, that the score is tied at 55–55. Isn't the game much more interesting now? Aren't you more likely to watch the second half?

An option with the stock price near the exercise price is like a close game. A deep-in- or out-of-the-money option is like a game with one team well ahead. A close game and an option nearly at-the-money are situations to which people are more willing to allocate scarce resources—for example, time to watch the game or money to buy the option.

These properties of the time value and our previous results enable us to get a general idea of what the call price looks like relative to the stock price. Figure 3.4 illustrates this point for American calls. The curved line is the price of the call, which lies above the intrinsic value, $Max(0, S_0 - X)$. As expiration approaches, the call price loses its time value, a process called **time value decay**, and the curve moves gradually toward the intrinsic value. At expiration, the call price curve collapses onto the intrinsic value and the curve looks exactly like that in Figure 3.3.

FIGURE 3.4 The Price Curve for American Calls

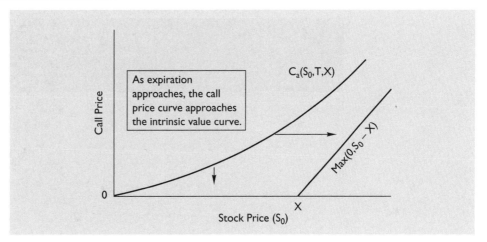

The time value effect is evident in the DCRB calls. Note that in Table 3.2, for a given exercise price, the time values increase with the time to expiration. For a given time to expiration, the time values are highest for the calls with an exercise price of 125, the exercise price closest to the stock price.

The relationship between time to expiration and option price also holds for European calls. Nevertheless, we cannot yet formally accept this as fact because we have not yet established a minimum value for a European call. That will come later.

Effect of Exercise Price

Effect on Option Value   Consider two European calls that are identical in all respects except that the exercise price of one is X_1 and that of the other is X_2. Recall that X_2 is greater than X_1. We want to know which price is greater: $C_e(S_0,T,X_1)$ or $C_e(S_0,T,X_2)$.

Now consider two portfolios, A and B. Portfolio A consists of a long position in the call with the exercise price of X_1 and a short position in the call with the exercise price of X_2. This type of portfolio is called a money spread and is discussed further in Chapter 7. Because we pay $C_e(S_0,T,X_1)$ and receive $C_e(S_0,T,X_2)$, this portfolio will have an initial value of $C_e(S_0,T,X_1) - C_e(S_0,T,X_2)$. We do not yet know whether the initial value is positive or negative; that will depend on which option price is higher.

Portfolio B consists simply of risk-free bonds with a face value of $X_2 - X_1$. These bonds should be considered as pure discount instruments, like Treasury bills, and as maturing at the options' expiration. Thus, the value of this portfolio is the present value of the bonds' face value, or simply $(X_2 - X_1)(1 + r)^{-T}$.[6]

For the time being, we shall concentrate on portfolio A. First, we need to determine the portfolio's value at expiration. The value of any portfolio will be its cash flow or payoff when the options expire, contingent on the stock price at expiration, S_T. The stock price at expiration has three possible ranges: (1) $S_T < X_1$, (2) $X_1 \leq S_T < X_2$, or (3) $X_1 < X_2 \leq S_T$. Table 3.3 illustrates the values of portfolios A and B at expiration.

---

[6]Note that the time to expiration can be denoted as T. Technically, it is the difference between time T and today, time 0; so we just use T − 0 = T. Also, we use annual compounding for ease of exposition. Any other form of rate quotation could be used, such as continuous compounding applied in Chapter 5.

TABLE 3.3 THE EFFECT OF EXERCISE PRICE ON CALL VALUE: PAYOFFS AT EXPIRATION OF PORTFOLIOS A AND B

PORTFOLIO	CURRENT VALUE	PAYOFFS FROM PORTFOLIO GIVEN STOCK PRICE AT EXPIRATION		
		$S_T < X_1$	$X_1 \leq S_T < X_2$	$X_1 < X_2 \leq S_T$
A	$+C_e(S_0,T,X_1)$	0	$S_T - X_1$	$S_T - X_1$
	$-C_e(S_0,T,X_2)$	0	0	$-S_T + X_2$
		0	$S_T - X_1 \geq 0$	$X_2 - X_1 > 0$
			$X_2 - X_1 > 0$	$X_2 - X_1 > 0$
B	$(X_2 - X_1)(1 + r)^{-T}$	$X_2 - X_1 > 0$	$X_2 - X_1 > 0$	$X_2 - X_1 > 0$

When S_T is greater than X_1, the call option with exercise price X_1 will be worth $S_T - X_1$. If S_T exceeds X_2, the call option with exercise price X_2 will be worth $S_T - X_2$. We are, however, short the option with exercise price X_2. Because the buyer receives a payoff of $S_T - X_2$ when this option expires in-the-money, the writer has a payoff of $-S_T + X_2$. Adding the payoffs from the two options shows that portfolio A will always produce a payoff of no less than zero and, in some cases, more than zero. Therefore,

$$C_e(S_0,T,X_1) \geq C_e(S_0,T,X_2).$$

> The price of a European call must be at least as high as the price of an otherwise identical European call with a higher exercise price.

Why is this so? The best way to understand this rule is to look at the contradiction. Suppose $C_e(S_0,T,X_1) < C_e(S_0,T,X_2)$. Because we pay $C_e(S_0,T,X_1)$ for the option bought and receive $C_e(S_0,T,X_2)$ for the option sold, we will have a net cash inflow at the beginning of the transaction. The payoffs at expiration were shown to be nonnegative. Anyone would jump at the opportunity to construct a portfolio with a positive cash inflow up front and no possibility of a cash outflow at expiration. There would be no way to lose money. Everyone would try to execute this transaction, which would drive up the price of the call with exercise price X_1 and drive down the price of the call with exercise price X_2. When the call with the lower exercise price is worth at least as much as the call with the higher exercise price, the portfolio will no longer offer a positive cash flow up front.

We have proven this result only for European calls. With American calls, the long call need not be exercised, so we need only consider what would happen if the short call were exercised early.

> The price of a American call must be at least as high as the price of an otherwise identical American call with a higher exercise price.

Suppose the stock price prior to expiration is S_t and exceeds X_2. For whatever reason, the short call is exercised. This produces a negative cash flow, $-(S_t - X_2)$. The trader then exercises the long call, which produces a positive cash flow of $S_t - X_1$. The sum of these two cash flows is $X_2 - X_1$, which is positive because $X_2 > X_1$.

Thus, early exercise will not generate a negative cash flow. Portfolio A therefore will never produce a negative cash flow at expiration even if the options are American calls. Thus, our result holds for American calls as well as for European calls.

Note that this result shows that the price of the call with the lower exercise price cannot be less than that of the call with the higher exercise price. The two call prices, however, conceivably could be equal. That could occur if the stock price were very low, in which case both calls would be deep-out-of-the-money. Neither would be expected to expire in-the-money, and both would have an intrinsic value of zero. Therefore, both prices could be approximately zero. With a very high stock price, however, the call with the lower exercise price would carry a greater intrinsic value; thus, its price would be higher than that of the call with the higher exercise price.

The prices of the DCRB calls adhere to the predicted relationships. The lower the exercise price, the higher the call option price.

> The difference in the prices of two European calls that differ only by exercise price cannot exceed the present value of the difference in their exercise prices.

Limits on the Difference in Premiums Now compare the results of portfolio A with those of portfolio B. Note that in Table 3.3, portfolio B's return is never less than portfolio A's. Therefore, investors would not pay less for portfolio B than for portfolio A. The price of portfolio A is $C_e(S_0,T,X_1) - C_e(S_0,T,X_2)$, the price of the option purchased minus the price of the option sold. The price of portfolio B is $(X_2 - X_1)(1 + r)^{-T}$, the present value of the bond's face value. Thus,

$$(X_2 - X_1)(1 + r)^{-T} \geq C_e(S_0,T,X_1) - C_e(S_0,T,X_2).$$

A related and useful statement is

$$X_2 - X_1 \geq C_e(S_0,T,X_1) - C_e(S_0,T,X_2).$$

This follows because the difference in the exercise prices is greater than the present value of the difference in the exercise prices. For two options differing only in exercise price, the difference in the premiums cannot exceed the difference in the exercise prices.

> **TECHNICAL NOTE: Cash Flow Approach to Option Boundary Conditions**
> go to www.cengagebrain.com

The intuition behind this result is simple: The advantage of buying an option with a lower exercise price over one with a higher exercise price will not be more than the difference in the exercise prices. For example, if you own the DCRB June 125 call and are considering replacing it with the June 120 call, the most you can gain by the switch is $5. Therefore, you would not pay more than an additional $5 for the 120 over the 125. This result will be useful in Chapter 7, where we discuss spread strategies.

For American calls, the call with the lower exercise price is worth at least as much as the call with the higher exercise price. The statement that the difference in premiums, however, cannot exceed the present value of the difference in exercise prices does not hold for the American call. If both calls are exercised at time t before expiration and the payoff of $X_2 - X_1$ is invested in risk-free bonds, portfolio A's return will be $(X_2 - X_1)(1 + r)^{(T-t)}$, which will exceed portfolio B's return of $X_2 - X_1$. Thus, portfolio B will not always outperform or match portfolio A.

If, however, the bonds purchased for portfolio B have a face value of $(X_2 - X_1)(1 + r)^{-T}$, and thus a present value of $X_2 - X_1$, portfolio B will always outperform portfolio A. In that case, the current value of portfolio A cannot exceed that of portfolio B. Accordingly, we can state that for American calls,

$$X_2 - X_1 \geq C_a(S_0,T,X_1) - C_a(S_0,T,X_2).$$

> The difference in the prices of two American calls that differ only by exercise price cannot exceed the difference in their exercise prices.

Table 3.4 presents the appropriate calculations for examining these properties on the DCRB calls. Consider the May 120 and 125 calls. The difference in their premiums is 3.

The present value of the difference in exercise prices is $5(1.0457)^{-0.0192}$ = 4.9957. The remaining combinations are calculated similarly using the appropriate risk-free rates and times to expiration for those options. Because these are American calls, the difference in their prices must be no greater than the difference in their exercise prices. As Table 3.4 shows, all of the calls conform to this

TABLE 3.4 THE RELATIONSHIP BETWEEN EXERCISE PRICE AND CALL PRICE FOR DCRB CALLS

EXERCISE PRICES	EXERCISE PRICE DIFFERENCE	DIFFERENCE BETWEEN CALL PRICES (PRESENT VALUE OF DIFFERENCE BETWEEN EXERCISE PRICES IN PARENTHESES)		
		MAY	JUNE	JULY
120, 125	5	3.00 (4.9957)	1.90 (4.9787)	2.30 (4.9611)
120, 130	10	5.15 (9.9914)	4.05 (9.9573)	4.50 (9.9222)
125, 130	5	2.15 (4.9957)	2.15 (4.9787)	2.20 (4.9611)

Note: Risk-free rates are 4.57% (May), 4.56% (June), and 4.63% (July); times to expiration are 0.0192 (May), 0.0959 (June), and 0.1726 (July).

condition. In addition, all of the differences in the call prices are less than the present value of the difference between the exercise prices. Remember that this result need not hold for American calls because they can be exercised early.

Lower Bound of a European Call

We know that for an American call,

$$C_a(S_0,T,X) \geq \text{Max}(0, S_0 - X).$$

Because of the requirement that immediate exercise be possible, we were unable to make such a statement for a European call. We can, however, develop a lower bound for a European call that will be higher than the intrinsic value of an American call.

Again, consider two portfolios, A and B. Portfolio A consists of a single share of stock currently priced at S_0, while portfolio B contains a European call priced at $C_e(S_0,T,X)$ and risk-free bonds with a face value of X and, therefore, a present value of $X(1 + r)^{-T}$. The current value of this portfolio is thus $C_e(S_0,T,X) + X(1 + r)^{-T}$. The payoffs from these two portfolios are shown in Table 3.5.

As the table shows, the return on portfolio B is always at least as large as that of portfolio A and sometimes larger. Investors will recognize this fact and price portfolio B at a value at least as great as portfolio A's; that is,

$$C_e(S_0,T,X) + X(1 + r)^{-T} \geq S_0.$$

Rearranging this expression gives

$$C_e(S_0,T,X) \geq S_0 - X(1 + r)^{-T}.$$

If $S_0 - X(1 + r)^{-T}$ is negative, we invoke the rule that the minimum value of a call is zero. Combining these results gives us a lower bound of

$$C_e(S_0,T,X) \geq \text{Max}[0,S_0 - X(1 + r)^{-T}].$$

The price of a European call must at least equal the greater of zero or the stock price minus the present value of the exercise price.

If the call price is less than the stock price minus the present value of the exercise price, we can construct an arbitrage portfolio. We buy the call

		PAYOFFS FROM PORTFOLIO GIVEN STOCK PRICE AT EXPIRATION	
PORTFOLIO	**CURRENT VALUE**	$S_T \leq X$	$S_T > X$
A	S_0	S_T	S_T
B	$C_e(S_0,T,X) + X(1 + r)^{-T}$	X	$(S_T - X) + X = S_T$

TABLE 3.5 THE LOWER BOUND OF A EUROPEAN CALL: PAYOFFS AT EXPIRATION OF PORTFOLIOS A AND B

and risk-free bonds and sell short the stock. This portfolio has a positive initial cash flow because the call price plus the bond price is less than the stock price. At expiration, the payoff is $X - S_T$ if $X > S_T$; otherwise, the payoff is zero. The portfolio has a positive cash flow today and either a zero or positive cash flow at expiration. Again, there is no way to lose money.

Figure 3.5 shows this result for European calls. The curved line is the call price, which must lie above the lower bound. As expiration approaches, the time to expiration decreases such that the lower bound moves to the right. The time value decreases on the option as well and follows the lower bound, with all eventually converging to the intrinsic value, $Max(0, S_0 - X)$, at expiration.

When we showed that the intrinsic value of an American call is $Max(0, S_0 - X)$, we noted that the inability to exercise early prevents this result from holding for a European call. Now we can see that this limitation is of no consequence. Because the present value of the exercise price is less than the exercise price itself, the lower bound of a European call is greater than the intrinsic value of an American call.

> For European calls, a longer-lived call will always be worth at least as much as a shorter-lived call with the same terms.

In the earlier description of how time to expiration affects the price of an American call, we could not draw the same relationship for a European call. Now we can. Consider two European calls that differ by their times to expiration, T_1 and T_2. Their prices are $C_e(S_0,T_1,X)$ and $C_e(S_0,T_2,X)$, respectively. At time T_1, the shorter-lived option expires and is worth $Max(0, S_{T_1} - X)$. The minimum value of the longer-lived option is $Max(0, S_{T_1} - X(1 + r)^{-(T_2 - T_1)})$. Thus, the value of the shorter-lived option is less than the lower bound of the longer-lived option. Therefore, the longer-lived call must be priced at least as high as the shorter-lived call.

FIGURE 3.5 The Price Curve for European Calls

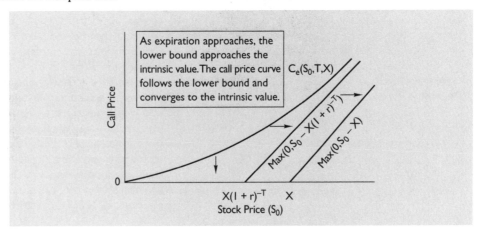

We should note that if the stock pays dividends such that the stock price minus the present value of the dividends is $S_0' = S_0 - \Sigma_{j=1}^{N} D_j(1 + r)^{-t_j}$, then the lower bound is restated as

$$C_e(S_0,T,X) \geq Max[0,S_0' - X(1 + r)^{-T}].$$

Suppose that instead of options on stock, the option is on a currency. The exchange rate is represented by S_0, but we must recognize that the currency pays interest at the discrete compounding rate of ρ. This is the foreign risk-free rate, which is obtained in the same manner we used for Treasury bills. If we buy one unit of the currency, it will grow to $(1 + \rho)^T$ units at time T. Let us redefine portfolio A to consist of $(1 + \rho)^{-T}$ units of the currency. Because of the accumulation of interest, the $(1 + \rho)^{-T}$ units of the currency will grow to $(1 + \rho)^{-T}(1 + \rho)^T = 1$ unit of the currency. Then, the payoffs are the same as those in Table 3.5. The only difference in this case is that the initial value of portfolio A is now defined as $S_0(1 + \rho)^{-T}$. The lower bound of the call then becomes

$$C_e(S_0,T,X) \geq Max[0,S_0(1 + \rho)^{-T} - X(1 + r)^{-T}].$$

The similarity between the interest paid on a currency and the dividends on a stock should be apparent. In each case, the asset makes payments to the holder. To establish the lower bound, we must remove these payments from the value of the asset.

MAKING THE CONNECTION

Asynchronous Closing Prices and Apparent Boundary Condition Violations

There are many apparent option boundary condition violations when you begin to explore actual market data. For example, the regular trading hours of both the New York Stock Exchange (NYSE) and the Chicago Board Options Exchange (CBOE) are 8:30 A.M. to 3:00 P.M. Central time (or 9:30 A.M. to 4:00 P.M. Eastern time). Both the CBOE and the NYSE report the closing option and stock prices that are roughly equivalent to the transaction prices of the last trades of the day.

Suppose you observe that the NYSE reports a given stock closing price of $100. The CBOE reports that the price of the last trade of a three-month option on the same stock with an exercise price of $95 is $5.90. Let us assume the option is European, there are no dividends, and transaction costs are zero. The appropriate annually compounded interest rate is 4.32 percent. Is there a boundary condition violation?

Although it appears there is, most likely there is not. Recall that the lower boundary condition is

$$C_e(S_0,T,X) \geq Max[0,S_0 - X(1 + r)^{-T}]$$

In this example, the lower bound is

$$C_e(S_0,T,X) \geq Max[0, 100 - 95(1 + 0.0432)^{-0.25}]$$
$$= 6.00$$

Because the last trade was reported at $5.90, there appears to be a boundary violation with $0.10 arbitrage profit available.

Most likely, this is not the case. The reported stock and option prices are asynchronous, meaning that they were not actually observed and available at the same time. The option price, which is the last trade of the day, may have occurred at 3:45 P.M. when the stock price was much lower (for example, $99.50) and the stock price was actively traded up to 4:00 P.M. and rose in those last 15 minutes to $100.

Therefore, because real-time (synchronous) prices are difficult to observe by those looking in from the outside, often there appear to be boundary condition violations that do not exist in practice. This point is very important in understanding derivatives markets because there is a market for the underlying asset and a market for the derivative, which are often in different time zones and often open and close at different times. This problem was more severe in the pre-Internet era, when option and stock prices were often taken from day-old newspapers. The Internet has enabled us to obtain nearly real-time prices for stock and option markets. But even real-time prices that are separated by only minutes are not necessarily synchronous. As traders will often say, "a few seconds is an eternity in this market."

We should note that some people view the lower bound for a European option as a kind of adjusted intrinsic value. The price of the stock or currency is, by definition, the present value of its value at expiration. The present value of the exercise price is obviously the exercise price discounted from the expiration. With that in mind, some people prefer to define an at-the-money option as the condition that the stock or currency price, adjusted for dividends or interest, equals the *present value* of the exercise price, instead of just the exercise price. Then the time value would be defined as the option price minus the lower bound. We do not use those definitions in this book, but do not be surprised to encounter them in other books.

American Call versus European Call

Many of the results presented so far apply only to European calls. For example, we restricted the derivation of the lower bound to European calls. That is because an early exercise of an American call can negate the cash flows expected from the portfolio at expiration.

| An American call will be at least as valuable as a European call with the same terms. |

In many cases, however, American calls behave exactly like European calls. In fact, an American call can be viewed as a European call with the added feature that it can be exercised early. Because exercising an option is never mandatory,

$$C_a(S_0,T,X) \geq C_e(S_0,T,X).$$

We already proved that the minimum value of an American call is $Max(0, S_0 - X)$ while the lower bound of a European call is $Max[0, S_0 - X(1 + r)^{-T}]$. Because $S_0 - X(1 + r)^{-T}$ is greater than $S_0 - X$, as shown in Figure 3.5, the lower bound value of the American call must also be $Max[0, S_0 - X(1 + r)^{-T}]$.

Let us now examine the DCRB options to determine whether their prices exceed the lower boundary. Table 3.6 presents the lower bound of each DCRB call. To see how the computations are performed, consider the May 120 call. The time to expiration is 0.0192, and the risk-free rate is 0.0457. Thus,

$$Max[0,S_0 - X(1 + r)^{-T}] = Max[0,125.94 - 120(1.0457)^{-0.0192}] = 6.0428.$$

From Table 3.1, the price of the call is $8.75. Thus, this option does meet the boundary condition. Tables 3.1 and 3.6 reveal that the remaining calls also conform to the lower boundary. In general, studies show that call prices conform closely to the lower bound rule.

| An American call on a non-dividend-paying stock will never be exercised early, and we can treat such a call as if it were European. |

With the lower bound of an American call established, we can now examine whether an American call should ever be exercised early. First, assume that the call is in-the-money; otherwise, we would not

TABLE 3.6 LOWER BOUNDS OF DCRB CALLS

	EXPIRATION		
EXERCISE PRICE	**MAY**	**JUNE**	**JULY**
120	6.0428	6.4520	6.8738
125	1.0471	1.4733	1.9127
130	0.0000	0.0000	0.0000

Note: Risk-free rates are 4.57% (May), 4.56% (June), and 4.63% (July); times to expiration are 0.0192 (May), 0.0959 (June), and 0.1726 (July).

even consider exercising it. If the stock price is S_0, exercising the call produces a cash flow of $S_0 - X$. The call's price, however, must be at least $S_0 - X(1 + r)^{-T}$. Because the cash flow from exercising, $S_0 - X$, can never exceed the call's lower bound, $S_0 - X(1 + r)^{-T}$, it will always be better to sell the call in the market. When the transaction cost of exercising is compared with the transaction cost of selling the call, the argument that a call should not be exercised early is strengthened. Thus, if the stock pays no dividends, Figure 3.5 is also the call price curve for American calls.

Although many people find it difficult to believe that an American option on a non-dividend-paying stock would never be exercised early, it is really quite easy to see by analogy. Have you ever subscribed to a magazine and, shortly afterward, received a renewal notice mentioning the attractive rate they could offer you? You have barely begun receiving the magazine, perhaps have not yet decided if you like it, and already you are granted an option to renew. Do you immediately renew? Few rational people would. Besides giving the magazine company the interest on your money, you would also be giving up the right to decide later if you wanted to renew. You usually still have the right to renew much later at the same rate. Likewise, exercising a call option early not only gives the writer the interest on your money, but also throws away the right to decide later if you want to own the stock.

If that argument is not convincing, consider this: You should suppress the urge to exercise a deep-in-the-money call simply because you think the stock has gone up as far as it will. If your views on the stock are correct, you will not be any more pleased to own a stock that is not increasing than you will to be holding the call option. The story changes, however, if the stock pays dividends.

Early Exercise of American Calls on Dividend-Paying Stocks

When a company declares a dividend, it specifies that the dividend is payable to all stock holders as of a certain date, called the holder-of-record date. Two business days before the holder-of-record date is the ex-dividend date. To be the stockholder of record by the holder-of-record date, one must buy the stock by the ex-dividend date. The stock price tends to fall by the amount of the dividend on the ex-dividend date.

When a stock goes ex-dividend, the call price drops along with it. The amount by which the call price falls cannot be determined at this point in our understanding of option pricing. Because the call is a means of obtaining the stock, however, its price could never change by more than the stock price change. Thus, the call price will fall by no more than the dividend. An investor could avoid this loss in value by exercising the option immediately before the stock goes ex-dividend. This is the only time the call should be exercised early.

> It may be optimal to exercise an American call early if the stock is about to go ex-dividend.

Another way to see that early exercise could occur is to recall that we stated that the lower bound of a European call on a dividend-paying stock is $\text{Max}[0, S_0' - X(1 + r)^{-T}]$, where S_0' is the stock price minus the present value of the dividends. To keep things simple, assume only one dividend of the amount D and the fact that the stock will go ex-dividend in the next instant. Then S_0' is approximately equal to $S_0 - D$ (because the present value of D is almost D). Because we would consider exercising only in-the-money calls, assume that S_0 exceeds X. Then it is easy to see that $S_0 - X$ could exceed S_0' minus the present value of X. By exercising the option, the call holder obtains the value $S_0 - X$. Suppose you were holding a European call whose value was only slightly above the lower bound. Then you might wish it were an American call because an American call could be exercised to capture the value $S_0 - X$. If you were holding a European call and wished it were an American call for at least that instant, then it should be obvious that the right to exercise early would have value. So an American call could be worth more than a European call. Note that this does not mean that exercise will definitely occur at the ex-dividend instant. It means only that exercise *could* occur. The value of the right to exercise early is what distinguishes an American call from a European call. That right is worth something only when there are dividends on the stock. A similar argument applies when the underlying is a currency, which pays interest.

There is one other situation in which you can determine that the right to exercise early has no value. If the present value of all of the dividends over the life of the option is less than $X(1 - (1 + r)^{-T})$, then the option would never be exercised early because the dividends are not large enough to offset the loss of interest from paying out the exercise price early.

In Chapters 4 and 5, we shall learn about option pricing models that will give us the exact price of the option. We will then be able to see the early exercise value more explicitly.

Effect of Interest Rates

The price of a call is directly related to interest rates.

Interest rates affect a call option's price in several ways. First, interest rates affect the lower bound. The lower the interest rate, the lower the lower bound. In the extreme case of a zero interest rate, the lower bound would be the same as the intrinsic value. Nothing special happens to the option price if the interest rate is zero. It will still have value that is limited by the lower bound/intrinsic value. But there are other more complex effects as well. Perhaps the easiest way to understand the effect of interest rates on calls is to think of a call as a way to purchase stock by paying an amount of money less than the face value of the stock. By paying the call premium, you save the difference between the call price and the exercise price, the price you are willing to pay for the stock. The higher the interest rate, the more interest you can earn on the money you saved by buying the call. Thus, when interest rates increase, calls are more attractive to buyers, so they will have higher prices.[7]

Effect of Stock Volatility

The price of a call is directly related to the volatility of the underlying stock.

One of the basic principles of investor behavior is that individuals prefer less risk to more. For holders of stocks, higher risk means lower value. But higher risk in a stock translates into greater value for a call option on it. This is because greater volatility increases the gains on the call if the stock price increases because the stock price can then exceed the exercise price by a larger amount. On the other hand, greater volatility means that if the stock price goes down, it can be much lower than the exercise price. To a call holder, however, this does not matter because the potential loss is limited; it is said to be truncated at the exercise price. For example, consider the DCRB July 125 call. Suppose the stock price is equally likely to be at 110, 120, 130, or 140 at expiration. The call, then, is equally likely to be worth 0, 0, 5, and 15 at expiration. Now suppose the stock's volatility increases so that it has an equal chance of being at 100, 120, 130, or 150. From a stockholder's point of view, the stock is far riskier, which is less desirable. From the option holder's perspective, the equally possible option prices at expiration are 0, 0, 5, and 25, which is more desirable.

---

[7]The exact relationship between interest rates and call prices is more involved than this, however, because the purchase of a call is actually more than just an option to defer purchase of the stock. Holding the call instead of the stock limits your loss to much less than if you had bought the stock. A call is said to have insurance value. Interest rates affect the insurance value of the call in a negative manner, but the overall effect on the call price is still positive. See D. M. Chance, "Translating the Greek: The Real Meaning of Call Option Derivatives," *Financial Analysts Journal* 50 (July–August 1994): 43–49.

In fact, the option holder will not care how low the stock can go. If the possibility of lower stock prices is accompanied by the possibility of higher stock prices, the option holder will benefit and the option will be priced higher when the volatility is higher.

Another way to understand the effect of volatility on the call price is to consider the extreme case of zero volatility.[8] If the stock price is less than the exercise price, the absence of volatility guarantees that the option will expire out-of-the-money. No one would pay anything for this option. If the stock price exceeds the exercise price and has zero volatility, it will expire in-the-money and will be worth $S_T - X$ at expiration, where S_T is the future value of S_0. In this case, the call will then simply be a risk-free asset worth S_0 minus the present value of X. Because volatility does not affect the lower bound, the call price and lower bound remain above the intrinsic value, reflecting the fact that the option will still not be exercised until expiration. On the other hand, high volatility is what makes call options attractive and investors are willing to pay higher premiums on options with greater volatility.

In Chapter 4, we shall begin to explore in more detail how volatility affects option prices. In Chapter 5, we shall look at volatility in more detail and see that volatility is captured by the standard deviation of the stock return.

PRINCIPLES OF PUT OPTION PRICING

Many of the rules applicable to call options apply in a straightforward manner to put options. There are, however, some significant differences.

Minimum Value of a Put

| Because a put option need not be exercised, its minimum value is zero. |

A put is an option to sell a stock. A put holder is not obligated to exercise it and will not do so if exercising will decrease wealth. Thus, a put can never have a negative value:

$$P(S_0,T,X) \geq 0.$$

An American put can be exercised early. Therefore,

$$P_a(S_0,T,X) \geq Max(0, X - S_0).$$

Suppose the DCRB June 130 put sells for less than $X - S_0$. Let the put sell for $3. Then, it would be worthwhile to buy the stock for $125.94, buy the put for $3, and exercise the put. This would net an immediate risk-free profit of $1.06. The combined actions of all investors conducting this arbitrage would force the put price up to at least $4.06, the difference between the exercise price and the stock price.

Figure 3.6 illustrates these points for puts. The European put price lies somewhere in the shaded area of graph a. The American put price lies somewhere in the shaded area of graph b.

| The intrinsic value of an American put is the greater of zero or the difference between the exercise price and the stock price. |

The value, $Max(0, X - S_0)$, is called the put's *intrinsic value*. An in-the-money put has a positive intrinsic value, while an out-of-the-money put has an intrinsic value of zero. The difference between the put price and the intrinsic value is the *time value* or *speculative value*. The time value is defined as $P_a(S_0,T,X) - Max(0, X - S_0)$. As with calls, the time value reflects what an investor is willing to pay for the uncertainty of the final outcome.

---

[8]To keep this discussion simple, we also assume a zero risk-free rate.

FIGURE 3.6 Minimum Value of European and American Puts

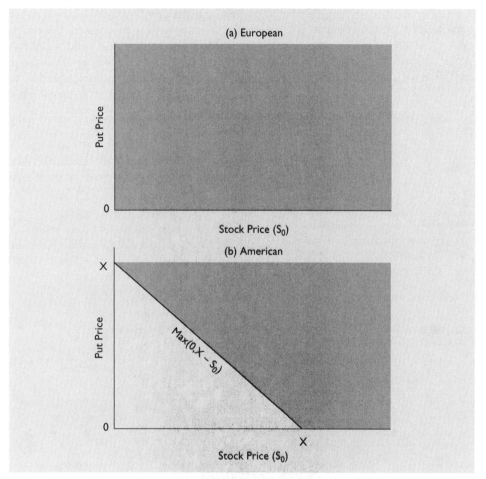

Table 3.7 presents the intrinsic values and time values of the DCRB puts. Note how the values increase with the time to expiration.

The intrinsic value specification, $Max(0, X - S_0)$, does not hold for European puts. That is because the option must be exercisable for an investor to execute the arbitrage transaction previously described. European puts indeed can sell for less than the intrinsic value. Later this will help us understand the early exercise of American puts.

> The time value of an American put is the difference between the put price and the intrinsic value.

TABLE 3.7   INTRINSIC VALUES AND TIME VALUES OF DCRB PUTS

EXERCISE PRICE	INTRINSIC VALUE	TIME VALUE		
		MAY	JUNE	JULY
120	0.00	2.75	9.25	13.65
125	0.00	4.60	11.50	16.60
130	4.06	3.29	10.19	15.59

Maximum Value of a Put

The maximum value of a European put is the present value of the exercise price. The maximum value of an American put is the exercise price.

At expiration, the payoff from a European put is $\text{Max}(0, X - S_T)$. The best outcome a put holder can expect is for the company to go bankrupt. In that case, the stock will be worthless and the put holder will be able to sell the shares to the put writer for X dollars. Thus, the present value of the exercise price is the European put's maximum possible value. Because an American put can be exercised at any time, its maximum value is the exercise price:

$$P_e(S_0, T, X) \leq X(1 + r)^{-T},$$
$$P_a(S_0, T, X) \leq X.$$

Figure 3.7 adds the maximum value rule to Figure 3.6. Although the range of possible values is reduced somewhat, there is still a broad range of possible values.

Value of a Put at Expiration

At expiration, a put option is worth the intrinsic value.

On the put's expiration date, no time value will remain. Expiring American puts therefore are the same as European puts. The value of either type of put must be the intrinsic value. Thus,

$$P(S_T, 0, X) = \text{Max}(0, X - S_T).$$

FIGURE 3.7 Minimum and Maximum Values of European and American Puts

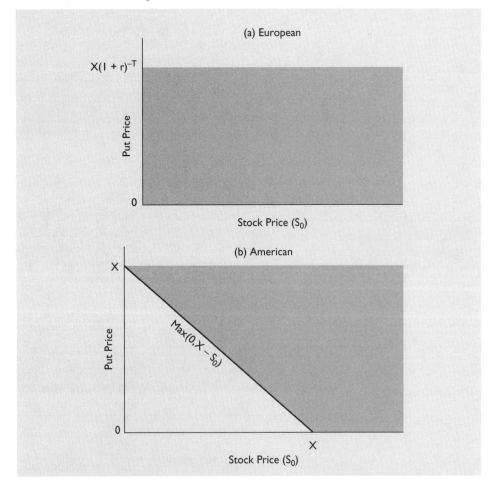

FIGURE 3.8 The Value of a Put at Expiration

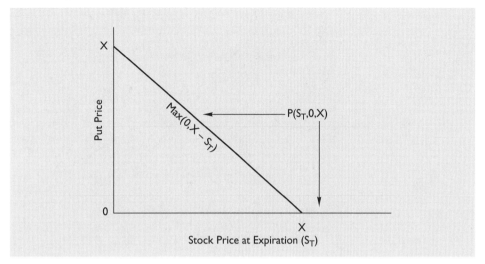

If $X > S_T$ and the put price is less than $X - S_T$, investors can buy the put and the stock and exercise the put for an immediate risk-free profit. If the put expires out-of-the-money ($X < S_T$), it will be worthless. Figure 3.8 illustrates the value of the put at expiration.

Effect of Time to Expiration

Consider two American puts, one with a time to expiration of T_1 and the other with a time to expiration of T_2, where $T_2 > T_1$. Now, assume that today is the expiration date of the shorter-lived put. The stock price is S_{T_1}. The expiring put is worth $Max(0, X - S_{T_1})$. The other put, which has a remaining time to expiration of $T_2 - T_1$, is worth at least $Max(0, X - S_{T_1})$. Consequently, it must be true that at time 0, we have

$$P_a(S_0, T_2, X) \geq P_a(S_0, T_1, X).$$

Note that the two puts could be worth the same; however, this would occur only if both puts were very deep-in-the-money or deep-out-of-the-money. Even then, the longer-lived put would likely be worth a little more than the shorter-lived put. The longer-lived put can do everything the shorter-lived put can do and has more time in which to increase in value.

A longer-lived American put must always be worth at least as much as a shorter-lived American put with the same terms.

The principles that underlie the time value of a put are the same as those that underlie the time value of a call. The time value is largest when the stock price is near the exercise price and smallest when the stock price is either very high or very low relative to the exercise price. With these points in mind, we can now see that the American put price would look like that shown in Figure 3.9. As expiration approaches, the put price curve approaches the intrinsic value, which is due to the time value decay. At expiration the put price equals the intrinsic value, as shown in Figure 3.8.

The relationship between time to expiration and put price is more complex for European puts. Think of buying a put as deferring the sale of stock at the exercise price, X. The further into the future the expiration date, the longer the put holder must wait to sell the stock and receive X dollars. This can make the longer-lived European put less valuable than the shorter-lived one. This does not hold for an American put because the holder can always exercise it and receive X dollars today. For a European put, the

FIGURE 3.9 The Price Curve for American Puts

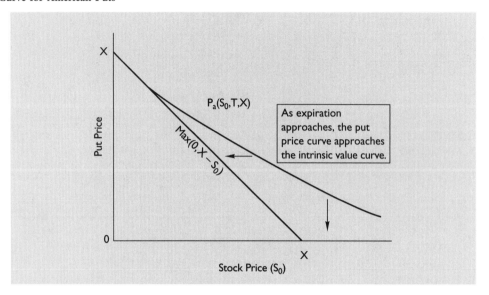

longer time to expiration is both an advantage—the greater time value—and a disadvantage—the longer wait to receive the exercise price. The time value effect tends to dominate, however, and in most cases, longer-lived puts will be more valuable than shorter-lived puts.

Because the DCRB puts are American options, the longer-term puts should be expected to show higher prices. A check of their premiums, shown in Table 3.1, confirms this point.

The Effect of Exercise Price

The Effect on Option Value Consider two European puts identical in all respects except exercise price. One put has an exercise price of X_1 and a premium of $P_e(S_0,T,X_1)$; the other has an exercise price of X_2 and a premium of $P_e(S_0,T,X_2)$. As before, $X_2 > X_1$. Which put will be more valuable?

Consider two portfolios. Portfolio A consists of a long position in the put priced at $P_e(S_0,T,X_2)$ and a short position in the put priced at $P_e(S_0,T,X_1)$. Portfolio B consists of a long position in risk-free bonds with a face value of $X_2 - X_1$ and a present value of $(X_2 - X_1)(1 + r)^{-T}$. Table 3.8 presents these portfolios' payoffs at expiration.

> The price of a European put must be at least as high as the price of an otherwise identical European put with a lower exercise price.

For portfolio A, all outcomes are nonnegative. Because this portfolio cannot produce a cash outflow for the holder, the price of the put purchased must be no less than the price of the put sold; that is,

$$P_e(S_0,T,X_2) \geq P_e(S_0,T,X_1).$$

To understand why this is so, consider what would happen if it were not. Suppose the price of the put sold was greater than the price of the put purchased. Then an investor would receive more for the put sold than would be paid for the put purchased. That would produce a net positive cash flow up front, and from Table 3.8, there would be no possibility of having to pay out any cash at expiration. This transaction would be like a loan that need not be paid back. Obviously, this portfolio would be very attractive and would draw the attention of other investors, who would buy the put with the

TABLE 3.8 THE EFFECT OF EXERCISE PRICE ON PUT VALUE: PAYOFFS AT EXPIRATION OF PORTFOLIOS A AND B

PORTFOLIO	CURRENT VALUE	PAYOFFS FROM PORTFOLIO GIVEN STOCK PRICE AT EXPIRATION		
		$S_T < X_1$	$X_1 \leq S_T < X_2$	$X_1 < X_2 \leq S_T$
A	$-P_e(S_0,T,X_1)$	$-X_1 + S_T$	0	0
	$+P_e(S_0,T,X_2)$	$X_2 - S_T$	$X_2 - S_T$	0
		$X_2 - X_1 > 0$	$X_2 - S_T > 0$	0
B	$(X_2 - X_1)(1 + r)^{-T}$	$X_2 - X_1 > 0$	$X_2 - X_1 > 0$	$X_2 - X_1 > 0$

higher exercise price and sell the put with the lower exercise price. This would tend to drive up the price of the former and drive down the price of the latter. The transaction would cease to be attractive when the put with the higher exercise price became at least as valuable as the put with the lower exercise price.

The intuition behind why a put with a higher exercise price is worth more than one with a lower exercise price is quite simple. A put is an option to sell stock at a fixed price. The higher the price at which the put holder can sell the stock, the more attractive the put.

> The price of an American put must be at least as high as the price of an otherwise identical American put with a lower exercise price.

Suppose these were American puts. In that case, the put with the lower exercise price could be exercised early. For example, let the stock price at time t prior to expiration be S_t, where $S_t < X_1$. Let the option with exercise price X_1 be exercised. Then the investor simply exercises the option with exercise price X_2. The cash flow from these two transactions is $-(X_1 - S_t) + (X_2 - S_t) = X_2 - X_1$, which is positive. Early exercise will not generate a negative cash flow. Thus, our result holds for American puts as well as for European puts.

Limits on the Difference in Premiums   Now let us compare the outcomes of portfolios A and B. We see that portfolio B's outcomes are never less than portfolio A's. Therefore, no one would pay more for portfolio A than for portfolio B; that is,

$$(X_2 - X_1)(1 + r)^{-T} \geq P_e(S_0,T,X_2) - P_e(S_0,T,X_1).$$

> The difference in the prices of two European puts that differ only by exercise price cannot exceed the present value of the difference in their exercise prices.

This result does not, however, hold for American puts. If the puts were American and both were exercised, the investor would receive $X_2 - X_1$ dollars. This amount would be invested in risk-free bonds and would earn interest over the options' remaining lives. At expiration, the investor would have more than $X_2 - X_1$, the payoff from portfolio B. Because the difference in exercise prices is greater than the present value of the difference in exercise prices, we can state that for European puts,

$$X_2 - X_1 \geq P_e(S_0,T,X_2) - P_e(S_0,T,X_1).$$

This means that the difference in premiums cannot exceed the difference in exercise prices. This result holds for American as well as European puts. To see this, let portfolio B's bonds have a face value of $(X_2 - X_1)(1 + r)^T$ and a present value of $X_2 - X_1$. If early exercise occurred at time t, the most the holder of portfolio A would have at expiration is $(X_2 - X_1)(1 + r)^{T-t}$. The holder of portfolio B would have a larger amount, $(X_2 - X_1)(1 + r)^T$. So again, portfolio A would never pay more at expiration than would portfolio B. Therefore, the current value of portfolio A, $P_a(S_0,T,X_2) - P_a(S_0,T,X_1)$, could not exceed the current value of portfolio B, $X_2 - X_1$. Thus,

$$X_2 - X_1 \geq P_a(S_0,T,X_2) - P_a(S_0,T,X_1).$$

> The difference in the prices of two American puts that differ only by exercise price cannot exceed the difference in their exercise prices.

Table 3.9 shows the differences between the put premiums and exercise prices for the DCRB puts. Because these are American puts, we would expect only that the difference in their put premiums will not exceed the difference in their exercise prices—which indeed is the case. In addition, the differences in premiums do not exceed the present values of the differences in exercise prices.

Lower Bound of a European Put

We showed that the minimum value of an American put is $\text{Max}(0, X - S_0)$. This statement does not hold for a European put because it cannot be exercised early. It is possible, however, to derive a positive lower bound for a European put.

Again, consider two portfolios, A and B. Portfolio A consists of a single share of stock. Portfolio B consists of a short position in a European put priced at $P_e(S_0,T,X)$ and a long position in risk-free bonds with a face value of X and a present value of $X(1 + r)^{-T}$. The payoffs at expiration from these portfolios are shown in Table 3.10.

Portfolio A's outcome is always at least as favorable as portfolio B's. Therefore, no one would be willing to pay more for portfolio B than for portfolio A. Portfolio A's current value must be no less than portfolio B's; that is,

$$S_0 \geq X(1 + r)^{-T} - P_e(S_0,T,X).$$

TABLE 3.9 THE RELATIONSHIP BETWEEN EXERCISE PRICE AND PUT PRICE FOR DCRB PUTS

EXERCISE PRICES	EXERCISE PRICE DIFFERENCE	DIFFERENCE BETWEEN PUT PRICES (PRESENT VALUE OF DIFFERENCE BETWEEN EXERCISE PRICES IN PARENTHESES)		
		MAY	JUNE	JULY
120, 125	5	1.85 (4.9957)	2.25 (4.9787)	2.95 (4.9611)
120, 130	10	4.60 (9.9914)	5.00 (9.9573)	6.00 (9.9222)
125, 130	5	2.75 (4.99571)	2.75 (4.97871)	3.05 (4.96111)

Note: Risk-free rates are 4.57% (May), 4.56% (June), and 4.63% (July); times to expiration are 0.0192 (May), 0.0959 (June), and 0.1726 (July).

TABLE 3.10	LOWER BOUND OF A EUROPEAN PUT: PAYOFFS AT EXPIRATION OF PORTFOLIOS A AND B		
		PAYOFFS FROM PORTFOLIO GIVEN STOCK PRICE AT EXPIRATION	
PORTFOLIO	**CURRENT VALUE**	$S_T < X$	$S_T \geq X$
A	S_0	S_T	S_T
B	$X(1 + r)^{-T} - P_e(S_0,T,X)$	$X - (X - S_T) = S_T$	X

Rearranging this statement gives

$$P_e(S_0,T,X) \geq X(1 + r)^{-T} - S_0.$$

If the present value of the exercise price is less than the stock price, this lower bound will be negative. Because we know that a put cannot be worth less than zero, we can say that

$$P_e(S_0,T,X) \geq \text{Max}[0, X(1 + r)^{-T} - S_0].$$

Figure 3.10 illustrates these results. The curved line is the European put price, which

> The price of a European put must at least equal the greater of zero or the present value of the exercise price minus the stock price.

must lie above the lower bound. As expiration approaches, the time to expiration gets smaller; so the lower bound moves to the right and at expiration converges to the intrinsic value. The put price curve moves down, a result of the loss of its time value as expiration approaches, but is still above the lower bound. At expiration, the put price, lower bound, and intrinsic value are all the same.

Now let us compare the minimum price of the American put, its intrinsic value of $\text{Max}(0, X - S_0)$, with the lower bound of the European put, $\text{Max}[0, X(1 + r)^{-T} - S_0]$. Because $X - S_0$ is greater than $X(1 + r)^{-T} - S_0$, the American put's intrinsic value is higher than the European put's lower bound. Therefore, the European put's lower

FIGURE 3.10 The Price Curve for European Puts

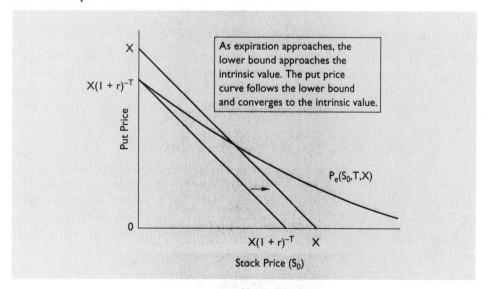

bound is irrelevant to the American put price because it is a lower minimum, as shown in Figure 3.10. $\text{Max}[0, X(1 + r)^{-T} - S_0]$ is, however, relevant to the European put's price.

Finally, we can use the lower bound of a European put to examine the effect of time to expiration on the option. Earlier we stated that the direction of this effect is uncertain. Consider two puts with times to expiration of T_1 and T_2, where $T_2 > T_1$. Suppose we are at time T_1, the stock price is S'_T, and the shorter-lived put is expiring and is worth $\text{Max}(0, X - S'_T)$. The longer-lived put has a remaining life of $T_2 - T_1$ and a lower bound of $\text{Max}[0, X(1 + r)^{-(T_2 - T_1)} - S'_T]$. Although the lower bound of the longer-lived put is less than the shorter-lived put's intrinsic value, the value of the additional time on the former, during which the stock price can move, can more than make up the difference. Therefore, we cannot unambiguously tell whether a longer- or shorter-lived European put will be worth more.

If the stock pays dividends such that $S'_0 = S_0 - \Sigma^N_{j=1} D_j (1 + r)^{-t_j}$ (that is, the stock price minus the present value of the dividends), the rule becomes

$$P_e(S_0, T, X) \geq \text{Max}[0, X(1 + r)^{-T} - S'_0].$$

As we did for a call, if the underlying is a currency, we adjust portfolio A to start off with $(1 + \rho)^{-T}$ units of the currency. This will grow to one unit at T, and the payoffs will be the same as those in Table 3.10. The net effect is that the lower bound for the put is

$$P_e(S_0, T, X) \geq \text{Max}[0, X(1 + r)^{-T} - S_0(1 + \rho)^{-T}].$$

American Put versus European Put

An American put will be at least as valuable as a European put with the same terms.

Everything that can be done with a European put can be done with an American put. In addition, an American put can be exercised any time prior to expiration. Therefore, the American put price must at least equal the European put price; that is,

$$P_a(S_0, T, X) \geq P_e(S_0, T, X).$$

Early Exercise of American Puts

Recall that it might be advisable to exercise an American call early if the stock is about to go ex-dividend. If the stock does not pay dividends, then the call will not be exercised early, and an American call will have the same value as a European call. The same cannot be said for American puts.

Let us suppose there are no dividends. Suppose you hold an American put and the company goes bankrupt, meaning that the stock price goes to zero. You are holding an option to sell it for X dollars. There is no reason to wait until expiration to exercise it and obtain your X dollars. You might as well exercise it now. Thus, bankruptcy is one obvious situation in which an American put would be exercised early, but *bankruptcy is not required to justify early exercise*. Look back at Figure 3.10. Note that the curved line representing the European put price crosses the straight line representing the intrinsic value of the American put. That means that at that stock price, the holder of the European put would prefer to have had an American put and would be willing to pay more to have one. This particular stock price, however, is not the one that would trigger early exercise of the American put because if the put were American, it would be optimal to hold it until the stock price dropped a little more.

If the stock price falls to a critical level, an American put might be exercised early. The likelihood of early exercise is reduced if the stock pays dividends.

If the stock pays dividends, it might still be worthwhile to exercise the stock early, but because dividends drive the stock price down, they make

American puts less likely to be exercised early. In fact, if the dividends are sufficiently large, it can sometimes be shown that the put would never be exercised early, thus making it effectively a European put. With currency options, the foreign interest has a similar effect.

At this point in our material, the exact situation at which an American put would be exercised early cannot be specified. We shall cover this topic in more detail in Chapter 4.

Put-Call Parity

The prices of European puts and calls on the same stock with identical exercise prices and expiration dates have a special relationship. The put price, call price, stock price, exercise price, time to expiration, and risk-free rate are all related by a formula called **put-call parity**. Let us see how this formula is derived.

> Put-call parity is the relationship among the call price, the put price, the stock price, the exercise price, the risk-free rate, and the time to expiration.

Imagine a portfolio, called portfolio A, consisting of one share of stock and a European put. This portfolio will require an investment of $S_0 + P_e(S_0,T,X)$. Now consider a second portfolio, called portfolio B, consisting of a European call with the same exercise price and risk-free pure discount bonds with a face value of X. That portfolio will require an investment of $C_e(S_0,T,X) + X(1 + r)^{-T}$. Now let us look at what happens at the expiration. Table 3.11 presents the outcomes.

The stock is worth S_T regardless of whether S_T is more or less than X. Likewise, the risk-free bonds are worth X regardless of the outcome. If S_T exceeds X, the call expires in-the-money and is worth $S_T - X$ and the put expires worthless. If S_T is less than or equal to X, the put expires in-the-money worth $X - S_T$ and the call expires worthless. The total values of portfolios A and B are equal. Recalling our law of one price from Chapter 1, the current values of the two portfolios must be equal. Thus, we require that

$$S_0 + P_e(S_0,T,X) = C_e(S_0,T,X) + X(1 + r)^{-T}.$$

This statement is referred to as put-call parity and it is probably one of the most important results in understanding options. It says that a share of stock plus a put is equivalent to a call plus risk-free bonds. It shows the relationship between the call and put prices, the stock price, the time to expiration, the risk-free rate, and the exercise price.

Suppose the combination of the put and the stock is worth less than the combination of the call and the bonds. Then you could buy the put and the stock and sell short the call and the bonds. Selling short the call just means to write the call, and selling short

TABLE 3.11 PUT-CALL PARITY

PAYOFF FROM	CURRENT VALUE	PAYOFFS FROM PORTFOLIO GIVEN STOCK PRICE AT EXPIRATION	
		$S_T \leq X$	$S_T > X$
A Stock	S_0	S_T	S_T
Put	$P_e(S_0,T,X)$	$X - S_T$	0
		X	S_T
B Call	$C_e(S_T,T,X)$	0	$S_T - X$
Bonds	$X(1 + r)^{-T}$	X	X
		X	S_T

the bonds simply means to borrow the present value of X and promise to pay back X at the options' expiration. The cash inflow of the value of the call and the bonds would exceed the cash outflow for the put and the stock. At expiration, there would be no cash inflow or outflow because you would have stock worth S_T and owe the principal on the bonds of X, but you would also have a put worth $X - S_T$ and a call worth zero or a call worth $-(S_T - X)$ and a put worth zero. All of this adds up to zero (check it). In other words, you would get some money up front but not have to pay any out at expiration. Because everyone would start doing this transaction, the prices would be forced back in line with the put-call parity equation.

By observing the signs in front of each term, we can easily determine which combinations replicate others. If the sign is positive, we should buy the option, stock, or bond. If the sign is negative, we should sell. For example, suppose we isolate the call price,

$$C_e(S_0,T,X) = P_e(S_0,T,X) + S_0 - X(1 + r)^{-T}.$$

Then owning a call is equivalent to owning a put, owning the stock, and selling short the bonds (borrowing). If we isolate the put price,

$$P_e(S_0,T,X) = C_e(S_0,T,X) - S_0 + X(1 + r)^{-T}.$$

This means that owning a put is equivalent to owning a call, selling short the stock, and buying the bonds. Likewise, we could isolate the stock or the bonds.

To convince yourself that these combinations on the right-hand side of the equation are equivalent to the combinations on the left-hand side, it would be helpful to set up a table like Table 3.11. By analyzing the outcomes at expiration, you will see that the various combinations on the right-hand side do indeed replicate the positions taken on the left-hand side.

If the stock pays dividends, once again, we simply insert S_0', which is the stock price minus the present value of the dividends, for the stock price S_0. If the underlying is a currency, then portfolio A is adjusted to start off with $(1 + \rho)^{-T}$ units of the currency. This will grow to one unit at T, and the payoffs will be the same as in Table 3.11. Then put-call parity for currency options will become

$$S_0(1 + \rho)^{-T} + P_e(S_0,T,X) = C_e(S_0,T,X) + X(1 + r)^{-T}.$$

While put-call parity is an extremely important and useful result, it does not hold so neatly if the options are American. The put-call parity rule for American options must be stated as inequalities,

$$C_a(S_0',T,X) + X + \Sigma_{j=1}^{N}D_j(1 + r)^{-t_j} \geq S_0 + P_a(S_0',T,X)$$
$$\geq C_a(S_0',T,X) + X(1 + r)^{-T},$$

where, again, S_0' is the stock price minus the present value of the dividends. Although we shall skip the formal proof of this statement, it is, nonetheless, easy to make the calculations to determine whether the rule is violated.

TECHNICAL NOTE: Proof of American Put-Call Parity
go to www.cengagebrain.com

Now let us look at whether put-call parity holds for the DCRB options. Because the stock does not pay dividends, the DCRB calls are effectively European calls. The puts, however, are strictly American. But first, let us apply the European put-call parity rule. Panel A of Table 3.12 shows the appropriate calculations. Each cell represents a combination of exercise price and expiration and contains two figures. The upper figure is the value of the stock plus the put, while the lower figure is the value of the call plus the bonds. If put-call parity holds, these two figures should be

TABLE 3.12 PUT-CALL PARITY FOR DCRB CALLS

A European Put-Call Parity

Top row of cell: $S_0 + P_e(S_0,T,X)$
Bottom row of cell: $C_e(S_0,T,X) + X(1 + r)^{-T}$

EXERCISE PRICE	MAY	JUNE	JULY
120	128.69	135.19	139.59
	128.6472	134.8880	139.9662
125	130.54	137.44	142.54
	130.6429	137.9667	142.6273
130	133.29	140.19	145.59
	133.4886	140.7953	145.3884

B American Put-Call Parity

Top row of cell: $C_a(S_0,T,X) + X$ (Note: No dividends, so $S_0' = S_0$.)
Middle row of cell: $S_0 + P_a(S_0,T,X)$
Bottom row of cell: $C_a(S_0,T,X) + X(1+r)^{-T}$

EXERCISE PRICE	MAY	JUNE	JULY
120	128.75	135.40	140.90
	128.69	135.19	139.59
	128.6472	134.8880	139.9662
125	130.75	138.50	143.60
	130.54	137.44	142.54
	130.6429	137.9667	142.6273
130	133.60	141.35	146.40
	133.29	140.19	145.59
	133.4886	140.7953	145.3884

Note: Risk-free rates are 4.57% (May), 4.56% (June), and 4.63% (July); times to expiration are 0.0192(May), 0.0959 (June), and 0.1726 (July).

identical. Of course, we might not expect it to hold perfectly because transaction costs may prevent some arbitrage opportunities from being worth exploiting. In most cases, the figures are very close.

Now we apply the American put-call parity rule. Panel B contains three figures for each cell. Recalling that there are no dividends, the top figure is $C_a(S_0,T,X) + X$, the middle figure is $S_0 + P_a(S_0,T,X)$, and the bottom figure is $C_a(S_0,T,X) + X(1 + r)^{-T}$. These figures should line up in descending order—that is, the top figure should be no lower than the middle figure, which should be no lower than the bottom figure in each cell. This is the case only for the May and June 120 options, although the discrepancies might not be large enough to justify an arbitrage transaction.

Put-call parity is the linkage between the call, put, underlying asset, and risk-free bond. Figure 3.11 illustrates these relationships. Throughout the book, we shall further develop this figure to show other important relationships between derivative contracts, the underlying asset, and the risk-free bond market.

FIGURE 3.11 The Linkage between Calls, Puts, and Underlying Asset and Risk-Free Bonds

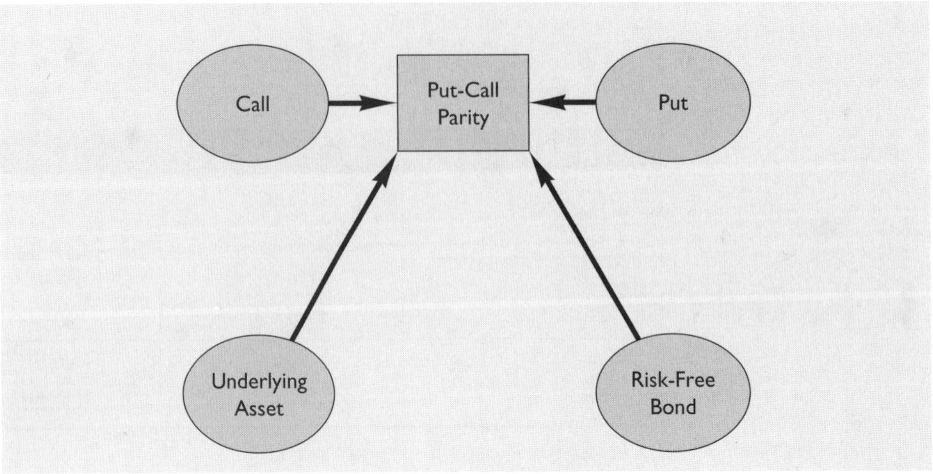

Effect of Interest Rates

> The price of a put is inversely related to interest rates.

Interest rates affect a put option in several ways. First, they affect the lower bound. The lower the interest rate, the higher the lower bound, reflecting the higher present value of the exercise price. In the extreme case of a zero interest rate, the lower bound is the same as the intrinsic value. Nonetheless, the put price will remain above the lower bound because there is nothing special about a put if the interest rate is zero. But there is another effect of interest rates on put prices. When you finally sell the stock by exercising the put, you receive X dollars. If interest rates are higher, the X dollars will have a lower present value. Thus, a put holder forgoes higher interest while waiting to exercise the option and receive the exercise price. So higher interest rates make puts less attractive to investors.

Effect of Stock Volatility

The effect of volatility on a put's price is the same as that for a call: Higher volatility increases the possible gains for a put holder. For example, in our discussion of the effect of volatility on a call, we considered four equally likely stock prices at expiration for DCRB: 110, 120, 130, and 140. The four possible put prices at expiration for a 125 put are 15, 5, 0, and 0. If the volatility increases so that the four possible stock prices at expiration are 100, 120, 130, and 150, the four possible put prices at expiration are 25, 5, 0, and 0. For the holder of a put, this increase in volatility is desirable because the put price now can rise much higher. It does not matter that the put can be even deeper out-of-the money when it expires because its lowest possible value is still zero. The put holder's loss thus is truncated. Therefore, the put will have a higher price if the volatility is higher.

> The price of a put is directly related to the volatility of the underlying stock.

Another approach to understanding the volatility effect is to consider a European put on a stock with zero volatility. If the put is currently in-the-money, it will be worth the present value of X minus the stock price S_0 because no further changes in the stock price other than the risk-free return will be expected. If the put is out-of-the-money, it will be worthless because it will have no chance of expiring in-the-money. Either of these cases would be like a risk-free asset and would have no use for either hedgers or speculators. In addition, the lower

MAKING THE CONNECTION

Put-Call Parity Arbitrage

The put-call parity equation states that

$$P(S_0,T,X) + S_0 = C(S_0,T,X) + X(1 + r)^{-T}.$$

The interpretation of the equation is that the left-hand side is a long put and long stock and that the right-hand side is a long call and long risk-free bond. Positive signs refer to long positions, and negative signs refer to short positions. There are a numerous other ways in which put-call parity can be rewritten:

$P(S_0,T,X) = C(S_0,T,X) - S_0 + X(1 + r)^{-T}$ (long put = long call, short stock, long bond)

$S_0 = C(S_0,T,X) - P(S_0,T,X) + X(1 + r)^{-T}$ (long stock = long call, short put, long bond)

$C(S_0,T,X) = P(S_0,T,X) + S_0 - X(1 + r)^{-T}$ (long call = long put, long stock, short bond)

$X(1 + r)^{-T} = P(S_0,T,X) + S_0 - C(S_0,T,X)$ (long bond = long put, long stock, short call)

$-P(S_0,T,X) = -C(S_0,T,X) + S_0 - X(1 + r)^{-T}$ (short put = short call, long stock, short bond)

$-S_0 = -C(S_0,T,X) + P(S_0,T,X) - X(1 + r)^{-T}$ (short stock = short call, long put, short bond)

$-C(S_0,T,X) = -P(S_0,T,X) - S_0 + X(1 + r)^{-T}$ (short call = short put, short stock, long bond)

$-X(1 + r)^{-T} = -P(S_0,T,X) - S_0 + C(S_0,T,X)$ (short bond = short put, short stock, long call)

There are even more combinations with two instruments on each side. Also, we can put all four instruments on one side of the equation. The important point is that if there is an arbitrage opportunity, then any one of these equations can be used to exploit it.

For example, put-call parity says that the put price should equal the call price minus the stock price plus the present value of the exercise price. Suppose we calculate $C(S_0,T,X) - S_0 + X(1 + r)^{-T}$. We then observe the put price in the market, which we shall label $P(S_0,T,X)^*$, and we find that $P(S_0,T,X)^*$ is too high. That is, $P(S_0,T,X)^* > C(S_0,T,X) - S_0 + X(1 + r)^{-T}$. So now what should we do?

Intuition says that because the put price is too high, we should sell it. The first equation in the preceding list

says that a put is equivalent to a combination of a long call, short stock, and long bond. Thus, this combination is equivalent to a put and is sometimes called a synthetic put. So if we sell the actual put and buy the synthetic put, we should be hedged; yet we receive more from the sale of the actual put than we paid for the synthetic put. Here are the outcomes:

	Value at Expiration	
Instrument	$S_T \leq X$	$S_T > X$
Short put	$-(X - S_T)$	0
Long call	0	$S_T - X$
Short stock	$-S_T$	$-S_T$
Long bond	X	X
Total	0	0

The absence of any positive or negative payoff means that this is a perfect hedge. But in fact, we could detect this mispricing using any of the preceding equations. Let us pick the second one, $S_0 = C(S_0,T,X) - P(S_0,T,X) + X(1 + r)^{-T}$. We use the market price of the put for $P(S_0,T,X)$ on the right-hand side. Because we know that $P(S_0,T,X)^*$ is too high, we will be subtracting too much from the right-hand side. Then the right-hand side will be too low relative to the left-hand side. So we should sell the left-hand side (meaning to sell short the stock) and buy the right-hand side (buy the call, sell the put, and buy the bond). Indeed, this is the strategy illustrated above.

It is even more important to see that it does not matter if the put is the mispriced instrument. We do not need to identify whether the put, call, bond, or stock is mispriced. In the preceding transaction, we see that we are short the put, long the call, and short the stock. This means that the same transaction would be done if the put were overpriced or the call were underpriced or the stock were overpriced. We do not need to determine which instrument is mispriced. We simply plug into the formula, and the equation will tell us what to do. All we need to do is remember to always sell overpriced instruments and buy underpriced instruments.

bound and put price would remain below the intrinsic value, reflecting the fact that a European put still cannot be exercised until expiration.

As we discussed in the section on calls, we shall take up the role and measurement of volatility in Chapters 4 and 5.

Summary

This chapter examined the basic principles of option pricing. It identified rules that impose upper and lower limits on put and call prices and examined the variables that affect an option's price. In addition, it demonstrated how put and call prices are related to each other by the put-call parity rule. Finally, the chapter examined the conditions that can induce an option trader to exercise an option prior to expiration.

We learned a number of principles that apply in some cases to European options only, in other cases to American options only, and in still other cases to both. Table 3.13 summarizes these principles.

An often confusing principle is the establishment of a minimum price. We started off by establishing a low minimum and then worked our way up until

we could establish the highest possible minimum. First, we developed the absolute minimum price of a call, which is zero. For American calls, the intrinsic value will provide a higher minimum if the option is in-the-money. Thus, it dominates the minimum of zero. It does not, however, apply to European calls because they cannot be exercised early. Nonetheless, there is a lower bound for European calls, which is the maximum of zero or the stock price minus the present value of the exercise price. This is at least as high as the intrinsic value of the American call. Because American calls must be worth at least as much as European calls, this lower bound applies to American calls as well. Thus, the ultimate minimum for both European and American calls on non-dividend-paying

TABLE 3.13 SUMMARY OF THE PRINCIPLES OF OPTION PRICING

	EUROPEAN CALLS	AMERICAN CALLS	EUROPEAN PUTS	AMERICAN PUTS
Assuming no dividends:				
Minimum value	≥ 0	≥ 0	≥ 0	≥ 0
Intrinsic value (IV)	NA	$Max(0, S_0 - X)$	NA	$Max(0, X - S_0)$
Time value	$C_e(S_0,T,X) - Max(0, S_0 - X)$	$C_a(S_0,T,X) - IV$	$P_e(S_0,T,X) - Max(0, X - S_0)$	$P_a(S_0,TX) - IV$
Maximum value	S_0	S_0	$X(1 + r)^{-T}$	X
Effect of time to expiration	$C_e(S_0,T_2,X)$ $\geq C_e(S_0,T_1,X)$	$C_a(S_0,T_2,X)$ $\geq C_a(S_0,T_1,X)$	$P_e(S_0,T_2,X)$ $\gtreqless P_e(S_0,T_1,X)$	$P_a(S_0,T_2,X)$ $\geq P_a(S_0,T_1,X)$
Effect of exercise price	$C_e(S_0,T,X_1)$ $\geq C_e(S_0,T,X_2)$	$C_a(S_0,T,X_1)$ $\geq C_a(S_0,T,X_2)$	$P_e(S_0,T,X_2)$ $\geq P_e(S_0,T,X_1)$	$P_a(S_0,T,X_2)$ $\geq P_a(S_0,T,X_1)$
Maximum difference in premiums	$(X_2 - X_1)(1 + r)^{-T}$	$X_2 - X_1$	$(X_2 - X_1)(1 + r)^{-T}$	$X_2 - X_1$
Lower bound	$Max[0, S_0 - X(1 + r)^{-T}]$	$Max[0, S_0 - X(1 + r)^{-T}]$	$Max[0, X(1 + r)^{-T} - S_0]$	$Max(0, X - S_0)$
Other results:				
American versus	$C_a(S_0,T,X) \geq C_e(S_0,T,X)$			
European option prices	$P_a(S_0,T,X) \geq P_e(S_0,T,X)$			
Put-call parity	$P_e(S_0,T,X) = C_e(S_0,T,X) - S_0 + X(1 + r)^{-T}$ (European) $C_a(S_0,T,X) + X \geq S_0 + P_a(S_0,T,X) \geq C_a(S_0,T,X) + X(1 + r)^{-T}$ (American)			
Effect of dividends	Replace S_0 with $S_0' = S_0 - \Sigma_{j=1}^N D_j(1 + r)^{-t_j}$, and for American put-call parity, add $\Sigma_{j=1}^N D_j(1 + r)^{-t_j}$ to the left-hand term. The middle S_0 does not have the dividend adjustment.			
Currency options	Replace S_0 with $S_0(1 + \rho)^{-T}$.			

stocks is the lower bound we established for European calls.

Both American and European puts have an absolute minimum value of zero. American puts have an intrinsic value, which is the maximum of zero or the exercise price minus the stock price. This minimum does not apply to European puts because they cannot be exercised early. European puts have a lower bound that is the maximum of zero or the present value of the exercise price minus the stock price. Because this lower bound is never greater than the intrinsic value of the American put, it does not help us raise the minimum for American puts. Thus, the lower bound is the minimum for European puts and the intrinsic value is the minimum for American puts (on non-dividend-paying stocks). Appendix 3 at the end of this chapter introduces an Excel spreadsheet that illustrates many of the principles in this chapter. It is highly recommended as a learning exercise.

Although we have identified the factors relevant to determining an option's price, we have not yet discussed how to determine the exact price. Although put-call parity appears to be a method of pricing options, it is only a relative option pricing model. To price the put, we need to know the call's price; to price the call, we must know the put's price. Therefore, we cannot use put-call parity to price one instrument without either accepting the market price of the other as correct or having a model that first gives us the price of the other.

In short, we need an option pricing model—a formula that gives the option's price as a function of the variables that should affect it. If the option pricing model is correct, it should give option prices that conform to these boundary conditions. Most important, it should establish the theoretically correct option price. If the market price is out of line with the model price, arbitrage should force it to move toward the model price. We are now ready to look at option pricing models.

Key Terms

Before continuing to Chapter 4, you should be able to give brief definitions of the following terms:

parity value/parity/
   exercise value, p. 64
time value/speculative value, p. 65

deep-in-the-money/
   deep-out-of-the-money/
   time value decay, p. 68

put-call parity, p. 87

Further Reading

Several excellent treatments of the rules covered in this chapter are found in the following sources:

Billingsley, R. S. *Understanding Arbitrage*. Upper Saddle River, NJ: Wharton School Publishing, 2006.

Hull, J. C. *Options, Futures, and Other Derivatives*, 8th ed. Upper Saddle River, NJ: Prentice Hall, 2012.

Jarrow, R., and S. Turnbull. *Derivative Securities*, 2nd ed. Cincinnati, OH: South-Western Publishing, 2000.

Stoll, H. R., and R. E. Whaley. *Futures and Options: Theory and Application*. Cincinnati, OH: South-Western Publishing, 1993.

The classic articles where the rules presented in this chapter were developed are as follows:

Merton, R. C. "The Relation between Put and Call Option Prices: Comment." *The Journal of Finance* 28 (1973): 183–184.

Merton, R. C. "Theory of Rational Option Pricing." *Bell Journal of Economics and Management Science* 4 (Spring 1973): 41–73.

Stoll, H. R. "The Relationship between Put and Call Option Prices." *The Journal of Finance* 31 (May 1969): 319–332.

Empirical studies on whether option prices conform to these rules are as follows:

Bhattacharya, M. "Transaction Data Tests of Efficiency of the Chicago Board Options Exchange." *Journal of Financial Economics* 12 (1983): 161–185.

Galai, D. "A Convexity Test for Traded Options." *Quarterly Review of Economics and Business* 19 (Summer 1979): 83–90.

Galai, D. "Empirical Tests of Boundary Conditions for CBOE Options." *Journal of Financial Economics* 6 (1978): 187–211.

Gould, J. P., and D. Galai. "Transaction Costs and the Relationship between Put and Call Prices." *Journal of Financial Economics* 1 (1974): 105–129.

Hemler, M. L., and T. W. Miller, Jr. "Box Spread Arbitrage Profits Following the 1987

Market Crash: Real or Illusory?" *Journal of Financial and Quantitative Analysis* 32 (March 1997): 71–90.

Klemkosky, R. C., and B. G. Resnick. "An Ex-Ante Analysis of Put-Call Parity." *Journal of Financial Economics* 8 (1980): 363–378.

Klemkosky, R. C., and B. G. Resnick. "Put-Call Parity and Market Efficiency." *The Journal of Finance* 34 (December 1979): 1141–1155.

Concept Checks

1. On the product support website, www.cengage brain.com, download the PowerPoint presentation titled Option Pricing Principles Tutorial 9e.ppt. It is designed to review most of the material in this chapter. Work through the presentation by going through each page and trying to anticipate what the next page will show.

2. Explain why a call option with zero exercise price is equivalent to the underlying stock, assuming no dividends on the stock during the life of the option.

3. Why might two calls or puts alike in all respects but exercise price have approximately the same price?

4. In this chapter, we did not learn how to obtain the exact price of a call without knowing the price of the put and using put-call parity. In one special case, however, we can obtain an exact price for a call. Assume that the option has an infinite maturity. Then use the maximum and minimum values we learned in this chapter to obtain the prices of European and American calls.

5. Assume that European call and put options exist on a stock. That stock, however, is the target of a takeover in which an acquiring firm offers a fixed price for the stock. The takeover is almost certain to occur shortly before the option expires. When it does, investors will tender their shares and receive the cash offer. Hence, the stock price is essentially frozen for the remainder of the life of the stock. Explain how the nature of in-the-money and out-of-the-money European calls and puts would change.

6. Suppose someone offers you the following gamble: You pay $7 and toss a coin. If the coin comes up heads, he pays you $10, and if tails comes up, he pays you $5. You in turn get the idea of offering another person a coin toss in which he pays you $7 and tosses another coin. You tell him that if heads comes up, you will pay him $9 and if tails comes up, you will pay him $5. You think you see an opportunity to earn an arbitrage profit by engaging in both transactions at the same time. Why is this not an arbitrage opportunity? How could you make it one assuming that you could get two people to engage in these gambles?

7. Why might two calls or puts alike in all respects but time to expiration have approximately the same price?

Questions and Problems

1. Critique the following statement made by an options investor: "My call option is very deep-in-the-money. I don't see how it can go any higher. I think I should exercise it."

2. Call prices are directly related to the stock's volatility, yet higher volatility means that the stock price can go lower. How would you resolve this apparent paradox?

3. Explain why an option's time value is greatest when the stock price is near the exercise price and why it nearly disappears when the option is deep-in- or out-of-the-money.

4. The value $\text{Max}[0, X(1 + r)^{-T} - S_0]$ was shown to be the lowest possible value of a European put. Why is this value irrelevant for an American put?

5. Suppose you observe a European call option that is priced at less than the value $\text{Max}[0, S_0 - X(1 + r)^{-T}]$. What type of transaction should you execute to achieve the maximum benefit? Demonstrate that your strategy is correct by constructing a payoff table showing the outcomes of expiration.

6. Why do higher interest rates lead to higher call option prices but lower put option prices?

7. What would happen in the options market if the price of an American call were less than the value Max(0, $S_0 - X$)? Would your answer differ if the option were European? Explain.

8. Why does the justification for exercising an American call early not hold up when considering an American put?

9. Consider an option that expires in 68 days. The bid and ask discounts on the Treasury bill maturing in 67 days are 8.20 and 8.24, respectively. Find the approximate risk-free rate.

10. Suppose a European put price exceeds the value predicted by put-call parity. How could an investor profit? Demonstrate that your strategy is correct by constructing a payoff table showing the outcomes at expiration.

The following option prices were observed for a stock on July 6 of a particular year. Use this information to solve problems 11 through 16. Unless otherwise indicated, ignore dividends on the stock. The stock is priced at 165.13. The expirations are July 17, August 21, and October 16. The risk-free rates are 0.0516, 0.0550, and 0.0588, respectively.

	CALLS			PUTS		
Strike	Jul	Aug	Oct	Jul	Aug	Oct
155	10.50	11.80	14.00	0.20	1.25	2.75
160	6.00	8.10	11.10	0.75	2.75	4.50
165	2.70	5.20	8.10	2.35	4.70	6.70
170	0.80	3.20	6.00	5.80	7.50	9.00

11. Compute the intrinsic values, time values, and lower bounds of the following puts. Identify any profit opportunities that may exist. Treat these as American options for purposes of determining the intrinsic values and time values and European options for the purpose of determining the lower bounds.
    a. July 165
    b. August 160
    c. October 170

12. Compute the intrinsic values, time values, and lower bounds of the following calls. Identify any profit opportunities that may exist. Treat these as American options for purposes of determining the intrinsic values and time values and European

options for the purpose of determining the lower bounds.
    a. July 160
    b. October 155
    c. August 170

13. Examine the following pairs of puts, which differ only by exercise price. Determine whether either of them violates the rules regarding relationships between American options that differ only by exercise price.
    a. August 155 and 160
    b. October 160 and 170

14. Examine the following pairs of calls, which differ only by exercise price. Determine whether either of them violates the rules regarding relationships between American options that differ only by exercise price.
    a. August 155 and 160
    b. October 160 and 165

15. Check the following combinations of puts and calls and determine whether they conform to the put-call parity rule for European options. If you see any violations, suggest a strategy.
    a. July 155
    b. August 160
    c. October 170

16. Repeat problem 15 using American put-call parity, but do not suggest a strategy.

17. A non-dividend-paying common stock is trading at $100. Suppose you are considering a European put option with a strike price of $110 and one year to expiration. What is the annually compounded risk-free interest rate where the boundary condition begins to be nonzero?

18. Suppose a European put has an exercise price of $110 on February 5. The put expires in 45 days. Suppose the appropriate discount rate on Treasury bills maturing in 44 days is 7.615. What is the maximum value of the European put? If the put were instead an American put, what would be its maximum value?

19. Suppose the annually compounded risk-free rate is 5% for all maturities. A non-dividend-paying common stock is trading at $100. Suppose you are considering a European call option with a strike price of $110. What is the time to maturity of this option where the boundary condition begins to be nonzero?

20. Suppose an American put is trading for $16.50 and an American call is trading for $15, where both options have identical terms. The underlying stock price is $99, and the exercise price is $100. The annual risk-free interest rate is 5 percent, and the time to expiration for both options is one year. Assuming that the stock pays no dividends, identify the appropriate arbitrage trading strategy.

21. Suppose the current stock price is $90, the exercise price is $100, the annually compounded interest rate is 5 percent, the stock pays a $1 dividend in the next instant, and the quoted put price is $6 for a one-year option. Identify the appropriate arbitrage opportunity and show the appropriate arbitrage strategy.

22. Suppose you observe options on Apple, Inc. stock trading such that the following condition is observed:

$$S_0 + P_a(S_0, T, X) < C_a(S_0, T, X) + X(1 + r)^{-T}$$

Explain how an arbitrageur would seek to capitalize on this observation and defend your answer.

23. Suppose the current stock price is $100, the exercise price is $100, the annually compounded interest rate is 5 percent, the stock pays a $1 dividend in the next instant, and the quoted call price is $3.50 for a one-year option. Identify the appropriate arbitrage opportunity and show the appropriate arbitrage strategy.

24. Consider a foreign exchange call option on Indian rupees (Rs). The current spot exchange rate is 70Rs/$, the Indian interest rate is 7 percent, and the U.S. interest rate is 5 percent (both annual compounding). If you observe a one-year at-the-money call option trading for 1.2Rs/$, what transaction would an arbitrageur pursue? (Assume that the call option is European.)

25. On December 9 of a particular year, a January Swiss franc call option with an exercise price of 46 had a price of 1.63.

The January 46 put was at 0.14. The spot rate was 47.28. All prices are in cents per Swiss franc.

The option expired on January 13. The U.S. risk-free rate was 7.1 percent, and the Swiss risk-free rate was 3.6 percent. Do the following:
a. Determine the intrinsic value of the call.
b. Determine the lower bound of the call.
c. Determine the time value of the call.
d. Determine the intrinsic value of the put.
e. Determine the lower bound of the put.
f. Determine the time value of the put.
g. Determine whether put-call parity holds.

26. (Concept Question) Suppose Congress decides that investors should not profit when stock prices go down, so it outlaws short selling. Congress has not figured out options, however, so there are no restrictions on option trading. Explain how to accomplish the equivalent of a short sale by using options.

27. (Concept Problem) Put-call parity is a powerful formula that can be used to create equivalent combinations of options, risk-free bonds, and stock. Suppose there are options available on the number of points LeBron James will score in his next game. For example, a call option with an exercise price of 32 would pay off Max(0, S_0 − 32), where S_0 is the number of points LeBron has recorded by the end of the game. Thus, if he scores 35, call holders receive $3 for each call. If he scores less than 32, call holders receive nothing. A put with an exercise price of 32 would pay off Max(0, 32 − S_0). If LeBron scores more than 32, put holders receive nothing. If he scores 28, put holders receive $4 for each put. Obviously there is no way to actually buy a position in the underlying asset, a point. Put-call parity shows, however, that the underlying asset can be re-created from a combination of puts, calls, and risk-free bonds. Show how this would be done and give the formula for the price of a point.

APPENDIX 3

Dynamics of Option Boundary Conditions: A Learning Exercise

As we have seen in this chapter, option prices are limited by various boundaries. We examined maximum prices and minimum prices, the latter of which can differ depending on whether the option is European or American. We also alluded to the fact that these boundaries change over time. This book comes with a Excel spreadsheet called BoundaryConditions9e.xls, which can be used to observe how these boundary conditions, as well as the option price, change with changes in various inputs.

The spreadsheet BoundaryConditions9e.xls is available as a download via the product support website. To access it:

1. Go to www.cengagebrain.com.
2. Click on Instructor Resources or Student Resources.
3. Click on the link for BoundaryConditions9e.xls.
4. Follow the instructions on the Web page to download and install the spreadsheet.

Download and access the spreadsheet to observe the sample case, a European call with exercise price of 100, risk-free rate of 8 percent, 200 days until expiration, and volatility of 50. At this point, we have not specifically studied how the volatility is measured. We mentioned that volatility is usually interpreted as the standard deviation of the stock return. In Chapters 4 and 5, we shall get into a more specific treatment of volatility. For this exercise, you should just be prepared to enter a value between 0 and 100 (%) for the volatility. Excel computes the option price based on the model we shall cover in Chapter 5.

Observe the graph, which shows four lines: the maximum price of a European call, the lower bound for a European call, the European option price, and the intrinsic value of an American call. Each input value is inserted into a cell. You can enter any reasonable value, but because the graph will print the results for a range of stock prices from 0 to 200, you should not choose an exercise price more than 200.

To observe how these lines change, you can slide the scroll bars left or right, which will automatically change the appropriate input value. Alternatively, you can click on the arrows at each end of the scroll bar for automatic incrementing of the appropriate input value. If you choose to slide the scroll bar, the graph will be redrawn only when you release the left mouse button. By dragging the scroll bar, you can observe the graph change.

Do the following exercise. You will be asked several questions. References to locations in the chapter where the answers can be found are provided.

- Select European Calls.
- Gradually drag the Days to Expiration from 200 down to zero. What happens?
  1. The call price converges to the lower bound. Do you know why? (pp. 72–73)
  2. The lower bound converges downward to the intrinsic value. Do you know why? (pp. 72–73)
- (With Days to Expiration at 200) Drag the volatility from 50 percent down to 0 percent. What happens?
  1. The call price converges to the lower bound. Do you know why? (pp. 77–78)
  2. The lower bound remains above the American intrinsic value. Do you know why? (p. 75)

- (With Days to Expiration at 200 and Volatility at 50 percent) Drag the risk-free rate from 8 percent down to zero. What happens?
    1. The lower bound converges downward to the intrinsic value. Do you know why? (pp. 77–78)
    2. The call price stays above the lower bound. Do you know why? (pp. 77–78)

Now do the same exercise for puts.

- Select European puts.
- Gradually drag the Days to Expiration from 200 down to zero. What happens?
    1. The put price converges to the lower bound. Do you know why? (pp. 85–86)
    2. The lower bound converges upward to the intrinsic value. Do you know why? (pp. 85–86)
- (With Days to Expiration at 200) Drag the volatility from 50 percent down to 0 percent. What happens?
    1. The put price converges to the lower bound. Do you know why? (pp. 85–86)
    2. The lower bound remains below the American intrinsic value. Do you know why? (pp. 85–86)
- (With Days to Expiration at 200 and Volatility at 50 percent) Drag the risk-free rate from 8 percent down to zero. What happens?
    1. The lower bound converges upward to the intrinsic value. Do you know why? (pp. 85–86)
    2. The put price stays above the lower bound. Do you know why? (pp. 85–86)

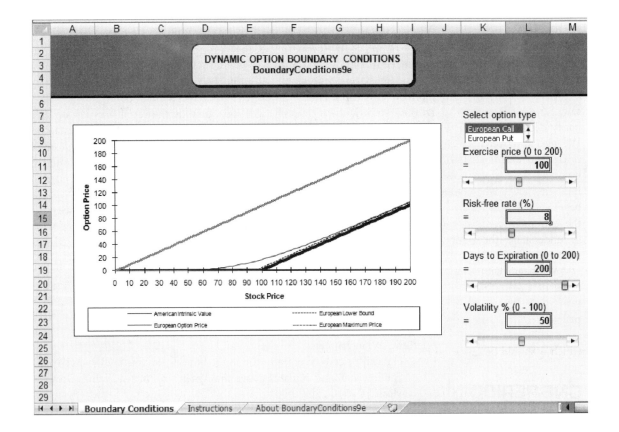

CHAPTER 4

Option Pricing Models

The Binomial Model

Options traders can get by with less math than you think. Tour de France cyclists don't need to know how to solve Newton's laws in order to bank around a curve. Indeed, thinking too much about physics while riding or playing tennis may prove a hindrance. But good traders do have to have the patience to understand the essential mechanism of replicating the factors they're trading.

Emanuel Derman
The Journal of Derivatives, Winter 2000, p. 62

This chapter examines the first of two general types of option pricing models. A **model** is a simplified representation of reality that uses certain inputs to produce an output, or result. An **option pricing model** is a mathematical formula or computational procedure that uses the factors determining the option's price as inputs. The output is the theoretical fair value of the option. If the model performs as it should, the option's market price will equal the theoretical fair value. Obtaining the theoretical fair value is a process called **option pricing**.

In Chapter 3, we examined some basic concepts in determining option prices. We saw, however, only how to price options relative to other options; for example, put-call parity demonstrates that given the price of a call, one can determine the price of a put. We also discovered relationships among the prices of options that differ by exercise prices and examined the upper and lower bounds on call and put prices. We did not, however, learn how to determine the exact option price directly from the factors that influence it. A large body of research on option pricing exists. Much of it goes far beyond the intended level of this book. The models range from the relatively simple to the extremely complex. All of the models have much in common, but it is necessary to understand the basic models before moving on to the more complex but more realistic ones.

We begin with a simple model called the **binomial option pricing model**, which is more of a computational procedure than a formula. After taking the binomial model through several stages, we move on to Chapter 5 and the **Black-Scholes-Merton option pricing model**, which is a mathematical formula. In both cases, however, we have the same objective: to obtain the theoretical fair value of the option, which is the price at which it should be trading.

ONE-PERIOD BINOMIAL MODEL

First, let us consider what we mean by a one-period world. An option has a defined life, typically expressed in days. Assume that the option's life is one unit of time. This time period can be as short or as long as necessary. If the time period is one day and the option has more than one day remaining, we will need a multiperiod model, which we shall examine later. For now, we will assume that the option's life is a single time period.

The model is called a **binomial** model. It allows the stock price to go either up or down, possibly at different rates. A binomial probability distribution is a distribution in which there are two outcomes or states. The probability of an up or down movement is governed by the binomial probability distribution. Because of this, the model is also called a **two-state model**.

In applying the binomial model to an underlying asset, however, it is immediately obvious that the range of possible outcomes is greater than the two states the binomial distribution can accommodate; however, that makes the model no less worthwhile. Its virtues are its simplicity and its ability to present the fundamental concepts of option pricing models clearly and concisely. In so doing, it establishes a foundation that facilitates an understanding of the Black-Scholes-Merton model.

Consider a world in which there is a stock priced at S on which call options are available.[1] The call has one period remaining before it expires. The beginning of the period is today and is referred to as time 0. The end of the period is referred to as time 1. When the call expires, the stock can take on one of two values: It can go up by a factor of u or down by a factor of d. If it goes up, the stock price will be uS. If it goes down, it will be dS.

For example, suppose the stock price is currently \$50 and it can go either up by 10 percent or down by 8 percent. Thus, u = 1.10 and d = 1 − 0.08 = 0.92. The variables u and d, therefore, are 1.0 plus the rates of return on the stock. When the call expires, the stock will be either 50(1.10) = 55 or 50(0.92) = 46.

Consider a call option on the stock with an exercise price of X and a current price of C. When the option expires, it will be worth either C_u or C_d. Because at expiration the call price is its intrinsic value, then

$$C_u = \text{Max}[0, uS - X]$$
$$C_d = \text{Max}[0, dS - X].$$

Figure 4.1 illustrates the paths of both the stock and the call prices. This diagram is simple, but it will become more complex when we introduce the two-period model.

If both stock prices resulted in the option expiring in-the-money, the option would not be very speculative; however, it would still be correctly priced by the model. The writer would receive a premium compensating for the future cash outflow expected upon exercising the option. To make things more interesting, however, we shall define our variables such that the option has a chance of expiring out-of-the-money. Assume that dS is less than X; that is, if the stock price goes down, the option will expire out-of-the-money. Also assume that uS is greater than X such that if the stock price goes up, the option will expire in-the-money.

Let the per period risk-free rate be identified by the symbol r. The risk-free rate is the interest earned on a riskless investment over a time period equal to the option's remaining life. The risk-free rate is between the rate of return if the stock goes up and the rate of return if the stock goes down. Thus, d < 1 + r < u.[2] We shall assume that all

---

[1] The model can also price put options. We shall see how this is done in a later section.

[2] This requirement is necessary, or there would be an arbitrage opportunity. If one could sell short the stock, one would then invest the proceeds in the risk-free bond, and (in the worst case) earn a return that would exceed the highest possible payout that would be owed to buy back the shorted stock. If one could borrow at the rate r, invest in the stock, and always earn more than the cost of the loan, then one could make unlimited amounts of money without committing any funds.

FIGURE 4.1 The One-Period Binomial Tree

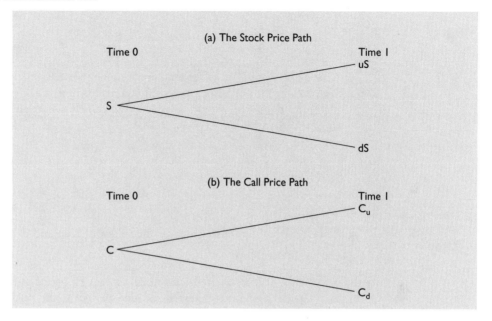

investors can borrow or lend at the risk-free rate. There are a wide variety of means to account for the interest rate. For example, in Chapter 5, we will be using an annualized, continuously compounded rate. Here we use a simple per period rate for ease of exposition. Be sure to pay close attention to how interest rates are quoted to appropriately compute present values.[3]

The objective of this model is to derive a formula for the theoretical fair value of the option, the variable C. The theoretical fair value is then compared to the actual price and reveals whether the option is overpriced, underpriced, or correctly priced. The formula for C is developed by constructing a riskless portfolio of stock and options. A riskless portfolio should earn the risk-free rate. Given the stock's values and the riskless return on the portfolio, the call's value can be inferred from the other variables.

This riskless portfolio, called a **hedge portfolio**, consists of h shares of stock and a single written call. The model provides the **hedge ratio**, h. The current value of the portfolio is the value of the h shares minus the value of the short call. We subtract the call's value from the value of the h shares because the shares are assets and the short call is a liability. Thus, the hedge portfolio value is assets minus liabilities, or simply net worth. The current hedge portfolio value is denoted as V, where $V = hS - C$. Alternatively, we can think of the hedge portfolio as requiring that we purchase h shares at S per share, but we offset some of this price by selling one call for C. Thus, $V = hS - C$ is the amount of our own money required to construct the hedge portfolio. Notice the investment perspective as opposed to the cash flow perspective for the hedge portfolio. A positive hedge ratio implies a positive investment in shares and hence a negative cash flow. The minus sign in front of the call indicates a negative investment or a positive cash flow; thus, the hedge portfolio requires selling the call option.

---

[3]See the Technical Note "Interest Rates and Financial Derivatives" in Chapter 3.

At expiration, the hedge portfolio value will be either V_u if the stock goes up or V_d if the stock goes down. Using the previously defined terms,

$$V_u = huS - C_u$$
$$V_d = hdS - C_d.$$

Think of V_u and V_d as the amount of money we can obtain by liquidating the hedge portfolio when the option expires. If the same outcome is achieved regardless of what the stock price does, the position is riskless. We can choose a value of h that will make this happen. We simply set $V_u = V_d$ so that

$$huS - C_u = hdS - C_d.$$

Solving for h,

$$h = \frac{C_u - C_d}{uS - dS}$$

> An option is priced by combining the stock and option in a risk-free hedge portfolio such that the option price can be inferred from other known values.

Because we know the values of S, u, and d, we can determine C_u, C_d, and h.

A riskless investment must earn a return equal to the risk-free rate. Thus, the hedge portfolio's value one period later should equal its current value compounded for one period at the risk-free rate. If it does not, the hedge portfolio will be incorrectly valued and represent a potential arbitrage opportunity. Later we shall see how the arbitrage would be executed.

If the hedge portfolio's initial value grows at the risk-free rate, its value at the option's expiration will be $(hS - C)(1 + r)$. The two values of the hedge portfolio at expiration, V_u and V_d, are equal, so we can select either one. Choosing V_u and setting it equal to the original value of the hedge portfolio compounded at the risk-free rate gives

$$V(1 + r) = V_u,$$
$$(hS - C)(1 + r) = huS - C_u.$$

Substituting the formula for h and solving this equation for C gives the option pricing formula,

$$C = \frac{pC_u + (1 - p)C_d}{1 + r},$$

where p is defined as $(1 + r - d)/(u - d)$ and is referred to as the binomial probability.

The formula gives the call option price as a function of the variables C_u, C_d, p, and r; however, C_u and C_d are determined by the variables S, u, d, and X. Thus, the variables affecting the call option price are the current stock price, S; the exercise price, X; the risk-free rate, r; and the parameters, u and d, which define the possible future stock prices at expiration. Notice how the call price is a weighted average of the two possible call prices the next period, discounted at the risk-free rate. Notice also that we never specified the actual probabilities of the two stock price movements; they do not enter into the model. The binomial probability above is not the actual probability assigned to the up move of the stock by a particular trader. The option is priced relative to the stock. Therefore, given the stock price, one can obtain the option price. The stock, however, is priced independently of the option; thus, the probabilities of the stock price movements would be a factor in pricing the stock. But pricing the stock is not our concern. We already have the stock price, S.

> The one-period binomial option pricing formula provides the option price as a weighted average of the two possible option prices at expiration, discounted at the risk-free rate.

TECHNICAL NOTE: Call Price Derivation Based on Hedged Portfolio
go to www.cengagebrain.com

In Chapter 1, we introduced the concept of risk neutrality and noted that we would be using it to price derivatives. The investors' feelings about risk play an important role in the pricing of securities, but in the risk neutral option pricing framework, investors' sensitivities to risk are of no consequence. This does not mean, however, that the model assumes that investors are risk- neutral. The stock price is determined by how investors feel about risk. If investors are risk-neutral and determine that a stock is worth $20, the model will use $20 and take no account of investors' feelings about risk. If investors are risk-averse and determine that a stock is worth $20, the model will use $20 and disregard investors' feelings about risk. This does not mean that the stock will be priced equally by risk-averse and risk-neutral investors; rather, the model will accept the stock price as given and pay no attention to how risk was used to obtain the stock price. In other words, given the stock price, both aggressive and conservative investors will assign the same price to an option on the stock.

Illustrative Example

Consider a stock currently priced at $100. One period later it can go up to $125, an increase of 25 percent, or down to $80, a decrease of 20 percent. Assume a call option with an exercise price of $100. The risk-free rate is 7 percent. The inputs are summarized as follows:

$$S = 100 \quad d = 0.80$$
$$X = 100 \quad r = 0.07$$
$$u = 1.25.$$

First, we find the values of C_u and C_d:

$$\begin{aligned} C_u &= \text{Max}[0, uS - X] \\ &= \text{Max}[0, 100(1.25) - 100] \\ &= 25 \\ C_d &= \text{Max}[0, dS - X] \\ &= \text{Max}[0, 100(0.80) - 100] \\ &= 0. \end{aligned}$$

The hedge ratio, h, is

$$h = \frac{25 - 0}{125 - 80} = 0.556.$$

The hedge requires 0.556 shares of stock for each call.[4] The value of p is

$$p = \frac{1 + r - d}{u - d} = \frac{1.07 - 0.80}{1.25 - 0.80} = 0.6.$$

Then

$$1 - p = 1 - 0.6 = 0.4.$$

Plugging into the formula for C gives

$$C = \frac{(0.6)25 + (0.4)0}{1.07} = 14.02.$$

Thus, the theoretical fair value of the call is $14.02.

---

[4]We assume that odd lots of stock can be purchased, but we do not permit the purchase of fractional shares.

Hedge Portfolio

Consider a hedge portfolio consisting of a short position in 1,000 calls and a long position in 556 shares of stock. The number of shares is determined by the hedge ratio of 0.556 shares per written call. The current value of the hedge portfolio is

$$556(100) - 1,000(14.02) = 41,580.$$

Thus, the investor buys 556 shares at $100 per share and writes 1,000 calls at $14.02. This requires a payment of 556($100) = $55,600 for the stock and receives payment of 1,000($14.02) = $14,020 for the calls. The net cash outlay is $55,600 - $14,020 = $41,580. This total represents the assets (the stock) minus the liabilities (the calls); thus, it is the net worth, or the amount the investor must commit to the transaction. Figure 4.2 illustrates the process.

If the stock goes up to $125, the call will be exercised for a value of $125 - $100 = $25. The stock will be worth 556($125) = $69,500. Thus, the hedge portfolio will be worth 556($125) - 1,000($125 - $100) = $44,500. If the stock goes down to $80, the call will expire out-of-the-money. The hedge portfolio will be worth 556($80) = $44,480. These two values of the hedge portfolio at expiration are essentially equal because the $20 difference is due only to rounding off the hedge ratio. The return on the hedge portfolio is

$$r_h = \left(\frac{\$44,500}{\$41,580}\right) - 1 \approx 0.07,$$

which is the risk-free rate. The original investment of $41,580 will have grown to $44,500—a return of about 7 percent, the risk-free rate.

If the call price were not $14.02, an arbitrage opportunity would exist. First, we will consider the case where the call is overpriced.

FIGURE 4.2 One-Period Binomial Example

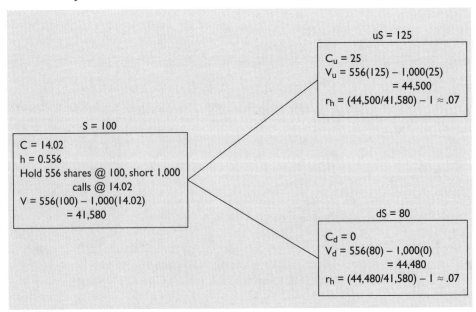

Overpriced Call

If the call were overpriced, a riskless hedge could generate a riskless return in excess of the risk-free rate. Suppose the market price of the call is $15. If you buy 556 shares and write 1,000 calls, the value of the investment today is

$$556(\$100) - 1,000(\$15) = \$40,600.$$

If the stock goes up to $125, at expiration, the call will be priced at $25 and the hedge portfolio will be worth 556($125) – 1,000($25) = $44,500. If the stock goes down to $80, the call will be worth nothing and the hedge portfolio will be worth 556($80) = $44,480. In either case, the hedge portfolio will be worth the same, the difference of $20 again due to rounding. The initial investment of $40,600 will have grown to $44,500, a riskless return of

$$r_h = \left(\frac{\$44,500}{\$40,600}\right) - 1 \approx 0.096,$$

which is considerably higher than the risk-free rate. In fact, the investor could have borrowed the $40,600 at the risk-free rate. Thus, the investor could have done this risk-free transaction without putting up any money.

A riskless portfolio that will earn more than the risk-free rate violates the law of one price. The risk-free bond and the hedge portfolio produce identical results but have different prices—$41,580 for the former and $40,600 for the latter. Obviously, this is a very attractive opportunity. All investors will recognize it and hurry to execute the transaction. This will increase the demand for the stock and the supply of the option. Consequently, the stock price will tend to increase and the option price will tend to decrease until the option is correctly priced. For illustrative purposes, assume that the stock price stays at $100. Then the option price must fall from $15 to $14.02. Only at an option price of $14.02 will this risk-free portfolio offer a return equal to the risk-free rate.

Now consider what happens if the option is underpriced.

Underpriced Call

If the option is underpriced, it is necessary to buy it. To hedge a long option position, the investor must sell the stock short. Suppose the call is priced at $13. Then the investor sells short 556 shares at $100, which generates a cash inflow of 556($100) = $55,600. Now the investor buys 1,000 calls at $13 each for a cost of $13,000. This produces a net cash inflow of $42,600.

If the stock goes to $125, the investor buys it back at 556($125) = $69,500. He exercises the calls for a gain of 1,000($125 – $100) = $25,000. The net cash flow is –$69,500 + $25,000 = –$44,500. If the stock goes down to $80, the investor buys it back, paying 556($80) = $44,480 while the calls expire worthless. The $20 difference is again due to rounding.

In both outcomes, the returns are essentially equivalent. The overall transaction is like a loan in which the investor receives $42,600 up front and pays back $44,500 later. This is equivalent to an interest rate of ($44,500/$42,600) – 1 = 0.0446. Because this transaction is the same as borrowing at a rate of 4.46 percent and the risk-free rate is 7 percent, it is an attractive borrowing opportunity. The investor could have lent the original $42,600 at the risk-free rate, thereby earning a profit at no risk and with no commitments of funds. All investors will recognize this and execute the transaction. This will tend to drive up the call price (or possibly drive down the stock price) until equilibrium is reached. If the price of the stock stays at $100, equilibrium will be reached when the call price rises to $14.02.

This model considered only a single period. In the next section, we extend the model to a two-period world.

TWO-PERIOD BINOMIAL MODEL

In the single-period world, the stock price goes either up or down. Thus, there are only two possible future stock prices. To increase the degree of realism, we will now add another period. This will increase the number of possible outcomes at expiration. Thus, our model has three time points: today or time 0, time 1, and time 2.

Suppose at the end of the first period the stock price has risen to uS. During the second period, it could go either up or down, in which case it would end up at either u^2S or udS. If the stock price has gone down in the first period to dS, during the second period, it will either go down again or go back up, in which case it will end up at either d^2S or duS. In this example, we let $d = 1/u$, which means that $udS = duS = S$. This is a convenient but not necessary assumption that is helpful when working with very basic versions of this model.

Figure 4.3 illustrates the paths of the stock price and the corresponding call prices. Viewed this way, we can see why the diagram is often called a binomial tree. The option prices at expiration are

$$C_{u^2} = Max[0, u^2S - X]$$
$$C_{ud} = Max[0, udS - X]$$
$$C_{d^2} = Max[0, d^2S - X].$$

The possible option prices at the end of the first period, C_u and C_d, initially are unknown; however, they can be found.

FIGURE 4.3 The Two-Period Binomial Tree

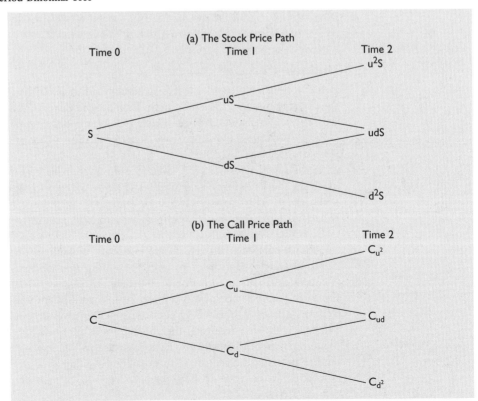

Suppose in the first period the stock price increases to uS. Because there will be only one period remaining with two possible outcomes, the one-period binomial model is appropriate for finding the option price, C_u. If at the end of the first period the stock price decreases to dS, we will again find ourselves facing a single-period world with two possible outcomes. Here we can again use the one-period binomial model to obtain the value of C_d. Using the one-period model, the option prices C_u and C_d are

$$C_u = \frac{pC_{u^2} + (1 - p)C_{ud}}{1 + r}$$

and

$$C_d = \frac{pC_{ud} + (1 - p)C_{d^2}}{1 + r}.$$

In a single-period world, a call option's value is a weighted average of the option's two possible values at the end of the next period. The call's value if the stock goes up in the next period is weighted by the factor p; its value if the stock goes down in the next period is weighted by the factor 1 − p. To obtain the call price at the start of the period, we discount the weighted average of the two possible future call prices at the risk-free rate for one period. The single-period binomial model is, thus, a general formula that can be used in any multiperiod world when there is but one period remaining.

Even if the call does not expire at the end of the next period, we can use the formula to find the current call price, the theoretical fair value, as a weighted average of the two possible call prices in the next period; that is,

$$C = \frac{pC_u + (1 - p)C_d}{1 + r}.$$

First, we find the values of C_u and C_d; then we substitute these into the above formula for C.

For a more direct approach, we can use

$$C = \frac{p^2 C_{u^2} + 2p(1 - p)C_{ud} + (1 - p)^2 C_{d^2}}{(1 + r)^2}.$$

This formula illustrates that the call's value is a weighted average of its three possible values at expiration two periods later. The denominator, $(1 + r)^2$, discounts this figure back two periods to the present.

Notice that we have not actually derived the formula by constructing a hedge portfolio. This is possible, however, and in a later section, we shall see how the hedge portfolio works. First, note that the hedge is constructed by initially holding h shares of stock for each call written. At the end of the first period, the stock price is either uS or dS. At that point, we must adjust the hedge ratio. If the stock is at uS, let the new hedge ratio be designated as h_u; if the stock is at dS, let the new ratio be h_d. The formulas for h_u and h_d are of the same general type as that of h in the single-period model. The numerator is the call's value if the stock goes up the next period minus the call's value if the stock goes down the next period. The denominator is the price of the stock if it goes up the next period minus its price if it goes down the next period. In equation form,

The two-period binomial option pricing formula provides the option price as a weighted average of the two possible option prices the next period, discounted at the risk-free rate. The two future option prices are obtained from the one-period binomial model.

$$h = \frac{C_u - C_d}{uS - dS}, \; h_u = \frac{C_{u^2} - C_{ud}}{u^2 S - udS}, \; h_d = \frac{C_{ud} - C_{d^2}}{duS - d^2 S}.$$

MAKING THE CONNECTION

Binomial Option Pricing, Risk Premiums, and Probabilities

You have observed that the binomial model does not require the actual probabilities of up and down moves. But what if we had the actual probabilities of the up and down moves? Would our binomial tree be inconsistent with this information? Let us take a look.

Go back to our example of the stock at 100 with u = 1.25, d = 0.80, and r = 0.07. Suppose we knew that the probability of an up move is 0.7 and the probability of a down move is 0.3. That means that the expected stock price at time 1 would be

$$(0.7)125 + (0.3)80 = 111.50.$$

If the current stock price is 100, then investors must be discounting the expected stock price at a rate of 11.5 percent. That is, 111.50/1.115 = 100. Thus, 11.5 percent is the required return on the stock. Because the risk-free rate is 7 percent, investors are requiring a risk premium of 4.5 percent for this stock.

Given that we know something about how investors value the stock, can we use that information to value the call option? Remember that we found that a one-period call with an exercise price of 100 is worth 14.02. The payoffs at time 1 were 25 and 0. Thus, the expected option price is

$$(0.7)25 + (0.3)0 = 17.50.$$

If we apply the same discount rate to the option as we did to the stock, we would obtain a current option price of

$$\frac{17.50}{1.115} = 15.70.$$

But if 15.70 is the price of the call option, we can easily earn an arbitrage profit. We demonstrated that this option, which should be worth 14.02, could be used to generate a riskless return of 9.6 percent if it is selling at 15. Hence, we could earn even more if the call were selling for 15.70. Clearly something is wrong.

What is wrong is that the required return on the option cannot be the same as that of the stock. To be priced at 14.02, the required return must be

$$\frac{17.50}{14.02} - 1 = 0.248.$$

In other words, the required return on the option must be almost 25 percent, which is more than twice that of the stock.

Options are riskier than stock; consequently, they must have higher required rates of return. We can determine how the required return on the call relates to the required return on the stock by using the binomial model.

Illustrative Example

Consider the example in a two-period world from the previous section. All input values remain the same. The possible stock prices at expiration are

$$u^2S = 100(1.25)^2$$
$$= 156.25$$
$$udS = 100(1.25)(0.80)$$
$$= 100$$
$$d^2S = 100(0.80)^2$$
$$= 64.$$

The call prices at expiration are

$$C_{u^2} = \text{Max}[0, u^2S - X]$$
$$= \text{Max}(0, 156.25 - 100)$$
$$= 56.25$$

Remember that if the stock goes up or down, the return on the hedge portfolio is the risk-free rate. So in either case, we have

$$\frac{V_u}{V} - 1 = \frac{huS - C_u}{hS - C} - 1 = r \text{ and}$$

$$\frac{V_d}{V} - 1 = \frac{hdS - C_d}{hS - C} - 1 = r.$$

The returns on the stock for the two outcomes are defined as

$$\frac{uS}{S} - 1 = r_s^u \text{ and } \frac{dS}{S} - 1 = r_s^d.$$

The returns on the call for the two outcomes are defined as

$$\frac{C_u}{C} - 1 = r_c^u \text{ and } \frac{C_d}{C} - 1 = r_c^d.$$

We shall need these in the form of $C(1 + r_c^u) = C_u$ and $C(1 + r_c^d) = C_d$. The initial value of the hedge portfolio of $hS - C$ should grow at the risk-free rate to equal the value if the hedge portfolio goes up, which is $huS - C_u$:

$$(1 + r)(hS - C) = huS - C_u.$$

Substituting $C(1 + r_c^u)$ for C_u and solving for r_c^u, we obtain the equation $r_c^u = r + (r_s^u - r)h(S/C)$.

If we do the same when the stock goes down, we obtain $r_c^d = r + (r_s^d - r)h(S/C)$.

By definition, the expected return on the call is a weighted average of the up and down returns, where the weights are the probabilities of the up and down returns, respectively:

$$E(r_c) = qr_c^u + (1 - q)r_c^d.$$

Substituting $r + (r_s^u - r)h(S/C)$ for r_c^u and $r + (r_s^d - r)h$ (S/C) for r_c^d and recognizing that $qr_s^u + (1 - q)r_s^d$ is the expected return on the stock, $E(r_s)$, we obtain the expected return on the call in terms of the expected return on the stock:

$$E(r_c) = r + [E(r_s) - r]h(S/C).$$

We see from this result that the expected return on the call is the risk-free rate plus a risk premium that is related to the risk premium on the stock, $E(r_s) - r$, and a factor, $h(S/C)$, that reflects the leverage on the call.

In our example, $h = 0.556$. Plugging in, we obtain

$$E(r_c) = 0.07 + [0.115 - 0.07]0.556(100/14.02)$$
$$= 0.248.$$

If an asset is correctly priced in the market, its expected return equals the return required by investors. Thus, the required return on the option is the risk-free rate and a premium related to the stock's risk premium and the option's leverage. We see here that the required and expected returns are 24.8 percent, which we found would have to be the option's required return to justify a price of 14.02.

But regardless of what the expected return on the stock and call are or what the true probabilities of the up and down moves are, we can price the call using the arbitrage approach presented in this chapter and be confident that nothing we have done is incompatible with the expected returns and true probabilities.

$$
\begin{aligned}
C_{ud} &= \text{Max}(0, udS - X) \\
&= \text{Max}(0, 100 - 100) \\
&= 0 \\
C_{d^2} &= \text{Max}[0, d^2S - X] \\
&= \text{Max}(0, 64 - 100) \\
&= 0.
\end{aligned}
$$

The value of p is the same, $(1 + r - d)/(u - d)$, regardless of the number of periods in the model.

We can find the call's value by either of the two methods discussed in the previous section. Let us first compute the values of C_u and C_d:

$$C_u = \frac{(0.6)56.25 + (0.4)0}{1.07} = 31.54$$

$$C_d = \frac{(0.6)0 + (0.4)0}{1.07} = 0.$$

Note why the value of the call is $0.00 at time 1 when the stock is at 80: The call cannot expire in-the-money at time 2; therefore, it must be worth nothing at time 1. The value of the call at time 0 is a weighted average of the two possible call values one period later:

$$C = \frac{(0.6)31.54 + (0.4)0}{1.07} = 17.69.$$

The same call analyzed in the one-period world is worth more in the two-period world. Why? Recall from Chapter 3 that a call option with a longer maturity is never worth less than one with a shorter maturity and usually is worth more. If this principle did not hold here, something would have been wrong with the model.

Hedge Portfolio

Now consider a hedge portfolio. Figure 4.4 illustrates this process. It would be very helpful to keep an eye on the figure as we move through the example. Let the call be trading in the market at its theoretical fair value of $17.69. The hedge will consist

FIGURE 4.4 Two-Period Binomial Example

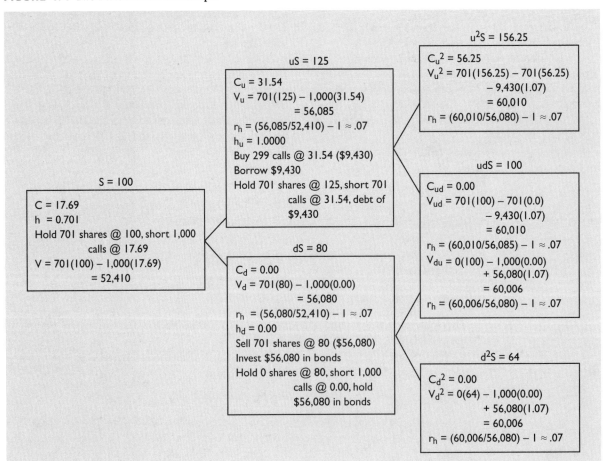

of 1,000 short calls. The number of shares purchased at time 0 is given by the formula for h,

$$h = \frac{31.54 - 0.00}{125 - 80} = 0.701.$$

Thus, we buy 701 shares of stock and write 1,000 calls. The transaction can be summarized as follows:

$$\text{Buy 701 shares at } \$100 = \$70,100 \text{ (assets)};$$
$$\text{write 1,000 calls at } \$17.69 = -\$17,690 \text{ (liabilities)};$$
$$\text{net investment} = \$52,410 \text{ (net worth).}$$

Stock Goes to 125 The hedge portfolio consists of 701 shares at $125 and 1,000 calls at $31.54. The value of the hedge portfolio is 701($125) − 1,000($31.54) = $56,085. Our investment has grown from $52,410 to $56,085. You should be able to verify that this is a 7 percent return, the risk-free rate. To maintain a hedge through the next period, we need to revise the hedge ratio. The new hedge ratio, h_u, is

$$h_u = \frac{56.25 - 0.00}{156.25 - 100} = 1.$$

The new hedge ratio will be one share of stock for each call.

To establish the new hedge ratio, we need either 701 calls or 1,000 shares of stock. We can either buy back 299 calls, leaving us with 701, or buy 299 shares, giving us 1,000 shares. Because it is less expensive to buy the calls, let us buy back 299 calls at $31.54 each for a total cost of $9,430. To avoid putting out more of our own funds, we borrow the money at the risk-free rate.

Stock Goes to 80 The hedge portfolio consists of 701 shares valued at $80 and 1,000 calls valued at $0.00. The hedge portfolio value is 701($80) − 1,000($0.00) = $56,080, which differs from the outcome at a stock price of $125 only by a round-off error. Because the return is the same regardless of the change in the stock price, the hedge portfolio is riskless. To maintain the hedge through the next period, we adjust the hedge ratio to

$$h_d = \frac{0.00 - 0.00}{100.00 - 64.00} = .000.$$

Thus, we need zero shares of stock for the 1,000 calls. We currently hold 701 shares, so we can sell off all of the shares at $80 and receive $56,080. Then we invest this money in riskless bonds paying the risk-free rate. At the end of the second period, the bonds will pay off $56,080 plus 7 percent interest.

Stock Goes from 125 to 156.25 We sell the 701 shares at $156.25, the calls are exercised at $56.25 each, and we repay the loan of $9,430 plus 7 percent interest. The value of the hedge portfolio is 701($156.25) − 701($56.25) − $9,430(1.07) = $60,010, a return of 7 percent from the previous period.

Stock Goes from 125 to 100 We have 701 shares valued at $100, 701 calls worth $0.00, and the repayment of the loan of $9,430 plus interest for a total hedge portfolio value of 701($100) − 701($0.00) − $9,430(1.07) = $60,010, a return of 7 percent from the previous period.

Stock Goes from 80 to 100 The hedge portfolio consists of no shares, 1,000 calls worth $0.00, and bonds worth $56,080 plus 7 percent interest. The total value of the hedge portfolio is 0($100) − 1000($0.00) + $56,080(1.07) = $60,006, a 7 percent return from the previous period.

Stock Goes from 80 to 64   We have no shares at $64, 1,000 calls expiring worthless, and principal and interest on the risk-free bonds. The value of this hedge portfolio is $0(\$64) + 1000(\$0.00) + \$56,080(1.07) = \$60,006$. This is essentially the same amount received as in the other cases; the difference is due only to a round-off error. Thus, regardless of which path the stock takes, the hedge will produce an increase in wealth of 7 percent in each period.

Now let us consider what happens if the call is mispriced.

Mispriced Call in the Two-Period World

If the call is mispriced at time 0, the law of one price is violated and an arbitrage opportunity exists. If the call is underpriced, we should purchase it and sell short h shares of stock. If the call is overpriced, we should write it and purchase h shares of stock. Whether we earn the arbitrage return over the first period, the second period, or both periods, however, will depend on whether the call price adjusts to its theoretical fair value at the end of the first period. If it does not, we may not earn a return in excess of the risk-free rate over the first period. The call must be correctly priced at the end of the second period, however, because it expires at that time. It is completely out of the question that an option could be mispriced at expiration.

The two-period return will be the geometric average of the two one-period returns; that is, if 6 percent is the first-period return and 9 percent is the second-period return, the two-period return will be $\sqrt{(1.06)(1.09)} - 1 = 0.0749$, or 7.49 percent. If one of the two returns equals the risk-free rate and the other exceeds it, the two-period return will exceed the risk-free rate. If one of the two returns is less than the risk-free rate and the other is greater, the overall return can still exceed the risk-free rate. The return earned over the full two periods will exceed the risk-free rate if the option is mispriced at time 0, the proper long or short position is taken, and the correct hedge ratio is maintained.

There are many possible outcomes of such a hedge, and it would take an entire chapter to illustrate them. We therefore shall discuss the possibilities only in general terms. In each case, we will assume that the proper hedge ratio is maintained and that the investor buys calls only when they are underpriced or correctly priced and sells calls only when they are overpriced or correctly priced.

Suppose the call originally was overpriced and is still overpriced at the end of the first period. Because the call has not fallen sufficiently to be correctly priced, the return over the first period actually can be less than the risk-free rate. Because the call must be correctly priced at the end of the second period, however, the return earned over the second period will more than make up for it. Overall, the return earned over the two periods will exceed the risk-free rate.

If the call originally is overpriced and becomes correctly priced at the end of the first period, the return earned over that period must exceed the risk-free rate. The return earned over the second period will equal the risk-free rate because the call was correctly priced at the beginning of the second period and is correctly priced at the end of it. Thus, the full two-period return will exceed the risk-free rate.

If the call is overpriced at the start and becomes underpriced at the end of the first period, the return earned over that period will exceed the risk-free rate. This is because the call will have fallen in price more than is justified and now is worth considerably less than it should be. At this point, we should close out the hedge and initiate a new hedge for the second period, consisting of a long position in the underpriced call and a short position in the stock. We can invest the excess proceeds in risk-free bonds. The second-period return will far exceed the risk-free rate. The overall two-period return obviously will be above the risk-free rate.

TABLE 4.1 HEDGE RESULTS IN THE TWO-PERIOD BINOMIAL MODEL

	RETURN FROM HEDGE COMPARED TO RISK-FREE RATE		
	PERIOD 1	PERIOD 2	TWO-PERIOD
Options Overpriced at Start of Period 1			
Status of option at start of period 2			
Overpriced	Indeterminate	Better	Better
Correctly priced	Better	Equal	Better
Underpriced	Better	Better	Better

Table 4.1 summarizes these results. Similar conclusions apply for an underpriced call, although the interpretation differs somewhat because the hedge portfolio is short.

EXTENSIONS OF THE BINOMIAL MODEL
Pricing Put Options

We can use the binomial model to price put options just as we can for call options. We use the same formulas, but instead of specifying the call payoffs at expiration, we use the put payoffs at expiration. To see the difference, look at Figure 4.3. Then we simply replace every C with a P; likewise, we substitute P for C in each formula. The relevant formulas are produced here for convenience.

$$P = \frac{p^2 P_{u^2} + 2p(1-p)P_{ud} + (1-p)^2 P_{d^2}}{(1+r)^2}$$

$$P_u = \frac{pP_{u^2} + (1-p)P_{ud}}{1+r}, \; P_d = \frac{pP_{ud} + (1-p)P_{d^2}}{1+r}, \; P = \frac{pP_u + (1-p)P_d}{1+r}$$

$$h_u = \frac{P_{u^2} - P_{ud}}{u^2 S - udS}, \; h_d = \frac{P_{ud} - P_{d^2}}{udS - d^2 S}, \; h = \frac{P_u - P_d}{uS - dS}.$$

Let us consider the same problem we have been working on, but we shall price the two-period European put that has an exercise price of 100. The values of the put at expiration are as follows:

$$P_{u^2} = Max(0,100 - 156.25) = 0.00$$
$$P_{ud} = Max(0,100 - 100) = 0.00$$
$$P_{d^2} = Max(0,100 - 64) = 36.$$

Note how we use the put intrinsic value formula at expiration, the greater of zero or X minus the stock price. Now we step back to time 1. Using the same formulas we used for calls,

$$P_u = \frac{(0.6)0 + (0.4)0}{1.07} = 0$$
$$P_d = \frac{(0.6)0 + (0.4)36}{1.07} = 13.46.$$

Pricing a put with the binomial model is the same procedure as pricing a call except that the expiration payoffs reflect the fact that the option is the right to sell the underlying stock.

Again, the option value is a weighted average of its two possible values in the next period, where the weights are p and 1 − p, discounted back one period at the risk-free rate. Now we find the time 0 value to be

$$P = \frac{(0.6)0 + (0.4)13.46}{1.07} = 5.03.$$

Now let us work through a hedge example. The principles are essentially the same as for hedging with calls, but instead of selling calls to hedge a long position in stock, we are buying puts. Calls move directly with the stock price; so to hedge, we have to sell calls. Puts, however, move inversely with the stock price; so to hedge stock, we buy puts.

The formula for the hedge ratio is the same as that for calls: the option price the next period if the stock goes up minus the option price the next period if the stock goes down divided by the stock price in the next period if the stock price goes up minus the stock price in the next period if the stock goes down. Thus, at time 0, the hedge ratio is

$$h = \frac{0 - 13.46}{125 - 80} = -0.299.$$

The negative sign seems to imply that we would be long stock and short puts, but because puts move opposite stock, that position makes no sense. It would mean that the puts gain or lose in value precisely when the stock is correspondingly increasing or decreasing, which would hardly constitute a hedge. The hedge ratio formula that we took from the call model assumed that we are long the stock and short the option. If we had actually set up the hedge portfolio using puts, we would be long the stock and long the put and the hedge ratio would be positive. We can, however, just use the hedge formula similar to the call and simply remember to change the sign. So we need to buy 299 shares for a long position in 1,000 puts. This will cost

299($100)	= $29,900 (in shares)
1,000($5.03)	= $5,030 (in puts)
Total	$34,930.

Stock Goes to 125   We now have 299 shares worth $125 and 1,000 puts worth $0.00 for a total value of 299($125) + 1,000($0.00) = $37,375. This is approximately 7 percent more than our initial investment of $34,930. Now the new hedge ratio will be

$$h_u = \frac{0 - 0}{156.25 - 100} = 0.$$

So we need no shares for our 1,000 puts. We sell the 299 shares, collecting 299($125) = $37,375 and invest this money in risk-free bonds that will earn 7 percent.

Stock Goes to 80   We now have 299 shares worth $80 and 1,000 puts worth $13.46 for a total value of 299($80) + 1,000($13.46) = $37,380. This is the same as when the stock went to 125 except for a round-off difference. Again, the return is 7 percent on our initial investment of $34,930. Now the hedge ratio will be

$$h_d = \frac{0 - 36}{100 - 64} = -1.0000.$$

Again, ignore the minus sign. So now we need 1,000 shares and 1,000 puts, or 299 shares and 299 puts. Let us buy 701 shares, which will give us 1,000 shares and 1,000 puts. This purchase of stock will cost money, so we borrow the funds at 7 percent. Now we have 1,000 shares worth $80, 1,000 puts worth $13.46, and a loan of $56,080.

Stock Goes from 125 to 156.25   We have only a bond worth $37,375(1.07) = $39,991, which is a return of 7 percent for the period.

Stock Goes from 125 to 100   Again, we have only a bond worth $37,375(1.07) = $39,991, which is a 7 percent return for the period.

Stock Goes from 80 to 100   Now we have 1,000 shares worth $100, we have 1,000 puts that are worthless, and we owe $56,080(1.07) = $60,006 on our loan. Thus, our total value is 1,000 ($100) + 1,000($0.00) − $60,006 = $39,994. This is the same total as the two outcomes above except for a small round-off error. Again, the return for the period is 7 percent.

Stock Goes from 80 to 64 Now we have 1,000 shares worth $64, we have 1,000 puts worth $36, and we owe $56,080(1.07) = $60,006 on our loan. Thus, our total value is 1,000($64) + 1,000($36) − $60,006 = $39,994, the same total and 7 percent return as above.

So we see that as long as the hedge is maintained properly, we earn the risk-free return over each period. If the put were mispriced, we would take the appropriate position and hedge it with the stock. For example, if the put were selling for less than the model price, we would consider it underpriced. We would then buy it and hedge by buying the proper number of shares of stock. If the put were overpriced, we would sell it, but to hedge, we would need to sell short the stock.

American Puts and Early Exercise

The two-period binomial model is an excellent opportunity to illustrate how American options can be exercised early. Let us use the same two-period put with an exercise price of 100, but make it an American put. This means that at any point in the life of the option, we can choose to exercise it early if it is best to do so. That means that at any point in the binomial tree when the put is in-the-money, we need to see if it is worth more to exercise it early.

For example, go back to the values calculated for the European put at time 1. Recall that they were

$$P_u = \frac{(0.6)0 - (0.4)0}{1.07} = 0.00 \text{ when the stock is at 125,}$$

$$P_d = \frac{(0.6)0 - (0.4)36}{1.07} = 13.46 \text{ when the stock is at 80.}$$

When the stock is at 125, the put is out-of-the-money; so we do not need to worry about exercising it. When the stock is at 80, however, the put is in-the-money and we have the right to exercise it. In fact, the put is in-the-money by $20[Max(0,100 − 80)], which is far more than its unexercised value of $13.46. So we exercise it, which means that we replace the calculated value P_d of 13.46 with 20. Thus, we now have $P_u = 0$ and $P_d = 20$. Then the value at time 0 is

$$P = \frac{(0.6)0 - (0.4)20}{1.07} = 7.48.$$

The binomial model can easily accommodate the early exercise of an American put when the computed value is replaced with the intrinsic value if the latter is greater.

We would also have to consider the possibility of exercising it immediately, but because it is at-the-money, there is no reason to exercise it today. Note that its value is considerably more than its value as a European put of 5.03.

Forming a hedge portfolio with American options follows the same procedure as forming a hedge portfolio for European options except that we use the American option values to compute the hedge portfolio values and hedge ratios.

Dividends, European Calls, American Calls, and Early Exercise

For call options on stocks without dividends, there will, of course, never be an early exercise. Let us now consider how early exercise will affect American calls in the binomial model. To do so, we must add a dividend.

There are a number of ways to incorporate dividends into the model. The simplest is to express the dividend as a yield of δ percent. Thus, when the stock price moves into the dividend period, it immediately declines by δ percent as it goes ex-dividend. We then use the ex-dividend stock prices in the binomial formulas. If the intrinsic value of the call before it goes ex-dividend exceeds the value of the call given by the binomial formula, the call should be exercised. Then the intrinsic value replaces the formula value.

Consider the same two-period problem we worked earlier in the chapter. Because we want to see a case where the call is exercised early, let us assume a fairly high dividend yield—say, 10 percent—and let the dividend be paid and the stock go ex-dividend at time 1. At time 1, if the stock goes to 125, it then pays a 12.50 dividend and falls to 112.50. If the stock goes down to 80, it pays a dividend of 8.00 and falls to 72. In the following period, its movement is based from values of either 112.50 or 72 and will be 140.625, 90, or 57.60. This process is shown in Figure 4.5. The corresponding call prices at expiration are

$$C_{u^2} = \text{Max}(0, 140.625 - 100) = 40.625$$

$$C_{ud} = C_{du} = \text{Max}(0, 90.00 - 100) = 0$$

$$C_{d^2} = \text{Max}(0, 57.60 - 100) = 0.$$

The European call prices after one period are

$$C_u = \frac{(0.6)40.625 + (0.4)0}{1.07} = 22.78$$

$$C_d = \frac{(0.6)0 + (0.4)0}{1.07} = 0.00.$$

Thus, the European call value at time 0 is

$$C = \frac{(0.6)22.78 + (0.4)0}{1.07} = 12.77.$$

FIGURE 4.5 Two-Period Stock Price Path with 10 Percent Dividend Yield at Time 1

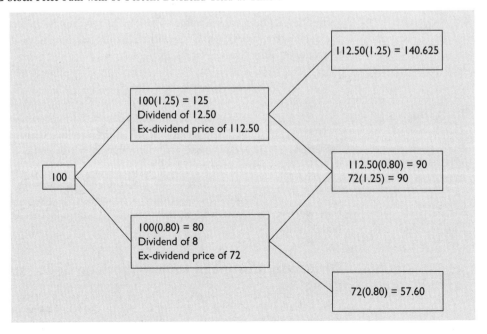

Note that this value is considerably less than its value without dividends of 17.69. Dividends always reduce the value of a European option because they represent a payout rather than a reinvestment of corporate cash flows for the purpose of generating growth in the stock price.

Now let the call be American. Let us move from time 0 to time 1 and let the stock move to 125. The firm is paying a dividend of 10 percent of 125, or 12.50, in just another instant. When that happens, the stock will fall to 112.50. Holding an American call, we have the right to exercise it before the stock goes ex-dividend, thereby paying 100 and receiving a stock worth 125. When the stock goes ex-dividend, its value drops to 112.50, but having acquired the stock before it goes ex-dividend, we are entitled to the dividend and have a net value of 25. Consequently, the option value at that point is 25. In other words, we simply choose to exercise the option before it goes ex-dividend and claim its intrinsic value of 25. Consequently, we, replace the binomial formula value of 22.78, previously computed in the European option example, with 25. Thus, we now have $C_u = 25$. In the time 1 outcome where the stock falls to 80, we cannot justify early exercise as the call is out-of-the-money.

Stepping back to time 0, we find that the value of the American call is, therefore,[5]

$$C = \frac{(0.6)25 + (0.4)0}{1.07} = 14.02.$$

As an alternative approach, suppose we simply have the firm pay a specific dollar dividend at time 1. Let us make it a dividend of 12. Now we run into a slight problem. As Figure 4.6 shows, at time 1, the stock goes ex-dividend to a value of either 113 or 68.

FIGURE 4.6 Two-Period Stock Price Path with Dividend of $12 at Time 1

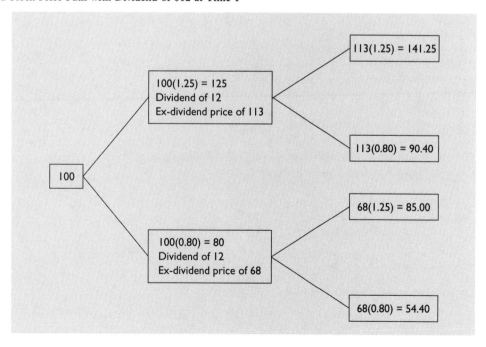

[5]You may recall that the value of 14.02 was also the value of the one-period call. There is no connection between the one-period European option value and the two-period American option value other than in the latter case, we exercised the option at time 1, thereby effectively making it a one-period option.

If the stock is at 113 and goes down at time 2, its new price will be 113(0.80) = 90.40. If the stock is at 68 and goes up at time 2, its new price will be 68(1.25) = 85. Consequently, the middle state at time 2 will not be the same regardless of where the stock was at time 1. In the example illustrated here, this is not really a problem: The option value can still be computed in the normal manner. When we expand the model to include a large number of periods, however, this problem greatly increases the computational requirements.

A binomial tree in which an up move followed by a down move puts you in the same location as a down move followed by an up move is called a **recombining tree**. When an up move followed by a down move does not put you in the same location as a down move followed by an up move, the tree is called **non-recombining tree**. For a tree with n time periods, a recombining tree will have n + 1 final stock prices. There will be 2^n distinct paths taken to reach the final stock prices, but some of the paths will leave you in the same location; consequently, we would not have to work our way through each path to identify the final outcome. This greatly simplifies and reduces the computations in a tree with a large number of time periods. A non-recombining tree will have 2^n distinct paths and therefore 2^n final outcomes. If n is large, this number becomes astronomical quite quickly and can pose severe computational difficulties, even for the fastest computers. Figure 4.7 illustrates a three-period recombining and non-recombining tree.

One special trick can greatly simplify the binomial computations in the case of an American option with dividends. Recall from Chapter 3 that in cases with dividends,

FIGURE 4.7 Recombining and Non-recombining Three-Period Binomial Trees

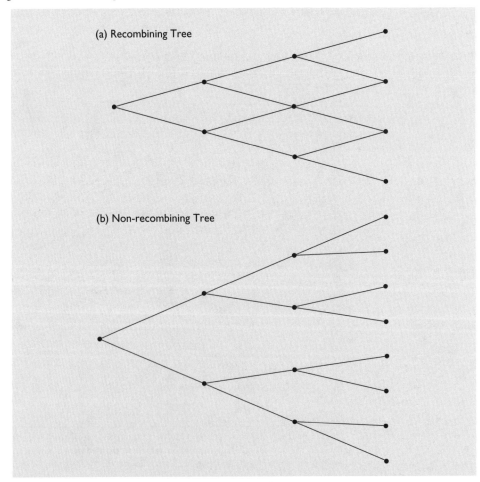

(a) Recombining Tree

(b) Non-recombining Tree

FIGURE 4.8 Two-Period Stock Price Path with Dividend of $12 at Time 1 and Stock Price Minus Present Value of Dividends Follows the Binomial Process

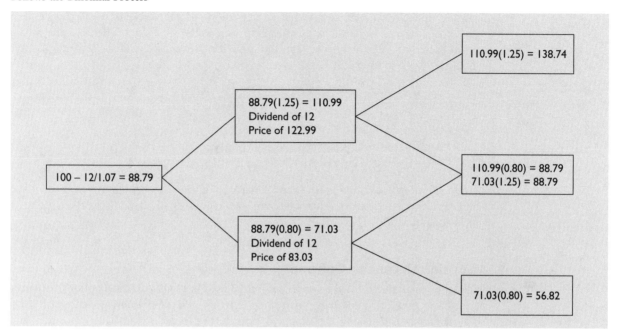

we subtracted the present value of the dividends from the stock price and used this adjusted value in our formulas. We can do the same here. We are simply assuming that the dividends are fully predictable and that it is the stock price minus the present value of the dividends that follows the binomial process.

Figure 4.8 illustrates this approach. The current stock price is $100, but we adjust that value to $100 - 12/1.07 = 88.79$. Then the value 88.79 goes up or down by the factor 1.25 or 0.80. Thus, at time 0, the stock is observed to be 100, which consists of a present value of the dividend of $12/1.07 = 11.21$ and the remainder of the price, 88.79, which reflects the stock's growth potential. At time 1, if the stock goes up, the adjusted stock price is $88.79(1.25) = 110.99$. Before the stock goes ex-dividend, its actual price is $110.99 + 12 = 122.99$. It then falls immediately to 110.99 as it goes ex-dividend. If at time 1, the stock goes down, the adjusted price will be $88.79(0.80) = 71.03$. Before it goes ex-dividend, it will be worth 83.03. Then it goes ex-dividend and will fall to 71.03. We then see in the figure that at time 2, the middle point will be the same, with the stock at 88.79 regardless of which path was taken to get there.

Now we can easily calculate the call value:

$$C_{u^2} = \text{Max}(0, 138.74 - 100) = 38.74$$

$$C_{ud} = \text{Max}(0, 88.79 - 100) = 0.00$$

$$C_{d^2} = \text{Max}(0, 56.82 - 100) = 0.00.$$

Now we step back to time 1. If the call is European, we calculate its values to be

$$C_u = \frac{(0.6)38.74 + (0.4)0}{1.07} = 21.72$$

$$C_d = \frac{(0.6)0 + (0.4)0}{1.07} = 0.$$

If the call is American, however, at time 1 when the stock is at 122.99, we have the opportunity to exercise the call just before the stock goes ex-dividend. In that case, we obtain a payoff of 22.99, resulting from acquisition of the stock for $100, collection of the dividend of $12, and the stock falling to a value of $110.99. Because the payoff from exercising 22.99 is greater than the value if not exercised, we use 22.99 for C_u. We then step back to time 1. The European option value would be

$$C = \frac{(0.6)21.72 + (0.4)0}{1.07} = 12.18.$$

The American option value would be

$$C = \frac{(0.6)22.99 + (0.4)0}{1.07} = 12.89.$$

The additional advantage of the American option in obtaining the dividend and avoiding the loss in value when the stock goes ex-dividend is worth a value of 0.71 today.

Foreign Currency Options

The binomial model can be extended to address foreign currency options. The key insight is that the underlying instrument in this case is the foreign currency itself. Thus, rather than having a position in a stock, the trader would have a position in a foreign currency. The foreign currency can be invested in a risk-free foreign debt instrument. Thus, the underlying will earn the foreign risk-free rate rather than the dividend yield in the case of common stock.

There are a number of ways to incorporate the foreign interest rate into the binomial model. The simplest is to express the foreign interest rate as a yield of ρ percent (ρ is the Greek symbol rho). The additional revenues from earning the foreign interest rate result in slight modifications of the binomial model. The binomial model for a call is still a weighted average of the possible option prices at expiration, discounted at the domestic risk-free rate. The only modification of the binomial probability of an up move is

$$p = \frac{\dfrac{1+r}{1+\rho} - d}{u - d}.$$

Thus, the higher the foreign interest rate, the lower the binomial probability of an up move.

Illustrative Example

Consider the euro currently trading at $1.40/€. One period later it can go up to $1.54/€, an increase of 10 percent, or down to $1.33/€, a decrease of 5 percent. Assume a call option with an exercise price of $1.41/€. The domestic risk-free rate is 2 percent, and the foreign (euro) risk-free rate is 1 percent. Compute the call price using a one-period binomial model. The inputs are summarized as follows:

$$S = 1.40 \quad d = 0.95$$

$$X = 1.41 \quad r = 0.02$$

$$u = 1.10 \quad \rho = 0.01.$$

First, we find the values of C_u and C_d:

$$C_u = Max[0, uS - X]$$
$$= Max[0, 1.40(1.10) - 1.41]$$
$$= 0.13$$
$$C_d = Max[0, dS - X]$$
$$= Max[0, 1.40(0.95) - 1.41] = 0.00.$$

The value of the binomial probability, p, is

$$p = \frac{\dfrac{1+r}{1+\rho} - d}{u - d} = \frac{\dfrac{1+0.02}{1+0.01} - 0.95}{1.10 - 0.95} = 0.399.$$

Then

$$1 - p = 1 - 0.399 = 0.601.$$

Plugging into the formula for C gives

$$C = \frac{pC_u + (1-p)C_d}{1+r} = \frac{0.399(0.13) + (1 - 0.399)0.00}{1 + 0.02} = 0.05085.$$

Thus, the theoretical fair value of the call is \$0.05085/€.

Extending the Binomial Model to n Periods

The binomial model is easily extended to any number of time periods. With n periods remaining until the option expires and no dividends, the European call price is given by the formula[6]

$$C = \frac{\displaystyle\sum_{j=0}^{n} \frac{n!}{j!(n-j)!} p^j (1-p)^{n-j} Max[0, u^j d^{n-j} S - X]}{(1+r)^n}.$$

This seemingly difficult formula actually is not nearly as complex as it appears. It simply captures all of the possible stock price paths over the n periods until the option expires. Consider the example from the text in a three-period world where j goes from 0 to 3. First, we find the summation of the following terms:

For j = 0,

$$\frac{3!}{0!3!}(.6)^0(.4)^3 Max[0, (1.25)^0(.80)^3 100 - 100] = 0.$$

For j = 1,

$$\frac{3!}{1!2!}(.6)^1(.4)^2 Max[0, (1.25)^1(.80)^2 100 - 100] = 0.$$

For j = 2,

$$\frac{3!}{2!1!}(.6)^2(.4)^1 Max[0, (1.25)^2(.80)^1 100 - 100] = 10.80.$$

For j = 3,

$$\frac{3!}{3!0!}(.6)^3(.4)^0 Max[0, (1.25)^3(.80)^0 100 - 100] = 20.59.$$

---

[6]The meaning of factorial or n! is n! = n(n − 1)(n − 2) ... 3(2)(1).

Adding these and dividing by $(1.07)^3$ gives

$$\frac{0 + 0 + 10.80 + 20.59}{(1.07)^3} = 25.62.$$

Because we did not hold the time to expiration fixed, the value of the call is higher in the three-period world than in the two-period world. This reflects the effect of a longer time to expiration.

Notice once again that the investor's subjective probability is not an input in the binomial model. Recall that the probability, p, used in the binomial model is based on the underlying asset growing at the risk-free interest rate.

The n-period binomial formula works because the factorial term n!/j!(n − j)! counts the number of ways a stock price could end up at a certain level. For example, when n = 3, the stock price at the end of the third period could be d^3S, ud^2S, u^2dS, or u^3S. There is only one path the stock could have taken to end up at d^3S: to go down three straight periods. There is only one path it could have taken to end up at u^3S: to go up three straight periods. For the stock price to end up at ud^2S, there are three possible routes: (1) up, down, down; (2) down, down, up; or (3) down, up, down. For the stock to end up at u^2dS, there are three paths: (1) up, down, up; (2) down, up, up; and (3) up, up, down. The factorial expression enumerates the routes that a stock can take to reach a certain level. The remaining terms in the formula then apply exactly as we have seen in the one- and two-period cases.

The three-period case is a good opportunity to observe one other aspect of the early exercise problem. Consider a three-period American put with an exercise price of 100. Figure 4.9 illustrates the tree. Below each stock price are two or more figures in parentheses. The first is the value of the European put expiring at time 3 with exercise price of 100, which we see is worth 7.26 today (check it for practice). The second figure in parentheses is the American put value. Notice that at time 2 when the stock price is 64, we show a value of 29.46 with a line drawn through it and replaced with 36. The value 29.46 is the value of the American put if not exercised at that point. It should, however, be exercised because it is $36 in-the-money. So we replace 29.46 with 36. Now we step back to time 2 and note what happens with the stock at 80. The European put value is

FIGURE 4.9 Three-Period Binomial Stock Price Path

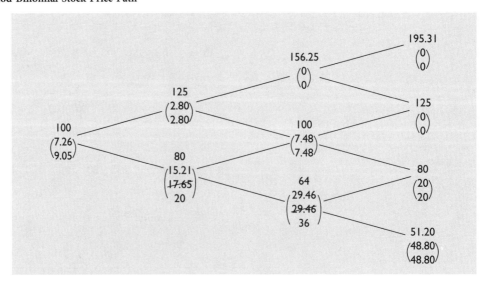

15.21 based on the next two possible values of 7.48 and 29.46. The American put value if not exercised is, however,

$$P_d = \frac{(0.6)7.48 + (0.4)36}{1.07} = 17.65.$$

It is \$20 in-the-money, however, so we would exercise it and replace the value of 17.65 with 20. The important point is that we can have early exercise at more than one location in the tree. Although it is optimal to exercise at time 3 if the stock is at 64, the stock would actually not get to 64 without having been at 80 at time 2 and having been exercised early. Yet the only way to determine if we should exercise at 80 at time 2 is to see what would happen if we do not exercise at that time. Thus, we must evaluate the possibility of being at 64 at time 3, not having exercised at 80 at time 2. In all cases, we should compare the American option value if not exercised at a given point with the intrinsic value and use the larger value for the value of the option at that point.

Behavior of the Binomial Model for Large n and Fixed Option Life

In the examples so far, when we added a time period, we simply extended the option's life. Naturally, we will get a larger option value. Suppose, however, that we keep the option's life the same and simply divide it into a larger number of increasingly smaller time periods. It turns out that when we do so, we need to make a few adjustments, but then we obtain an option value that increasingly reflects the realities of the world in which we live.

For example, let us again the June 125 DCRB call. Recall that the stock price is 125.94, the option has 35 days remaining, and the risk-free rate is 4.56 percent. The only information we have that could tell us something about the up and down factors is the volatility of the stock, a variable we briefly discussed in Chapter 3. Volatility is often measured by the statistical concept of standard deviation, which, more specifically, is the standard deviation of the return on the stock. This variable will become more meaningful to us in the next chapter, but for now, let us just take a value and use it. In the case of our DCRB stock, we shall use a volatility of 0.83, or 83 percent, a number we shall see how to obtain in Chapter 5.

To price this option in a binomial framework with the correct volatility, we need to know what to set the risk-free rate to and what to use as the up and down parameters. The risk-free rate is simple. We adjust it in the following manner:

$$\text{risk-free rate in binomial model} = (1 + r)^{T/n} - 1.$$

If the stock paid a dividend at a constant yield, it would be adjusted in an identical manner. There are several approaches to setting the up and down parameters. We shall initially use the following:

$$\text{binomial up parameter}: \quad u = e^{\sigma\sqrt{T/n}}$$
$$\text{binomial down parameter}: \quad d = 1/u,$$

where σ is the volatility. Of course, these adjustments will change the value of p. Let us do a one-period binomial model for the DCRB June 125 call. Our parameters are:

$$r = (1.0456)^{0.0959/1} - 1 = 0.004285$$
$$u = e^{0.83\sqrt{0.0959/1}} = 1.293087$$
$$d = 1/1.293087 = 0.773343.$$

Our stock prices at time 1 would be:

$$uS = 125.94(1.293087) = 162.8514$$

$$dS = 125.94(0.773343) = 97.3948.$$

Thus, the option values would be

$$C_u = Max(0,162.8514 - 125) = 37.85$$

$$C_d = Max(0,97.3948 - 125) = 0.00.$$

The value of p would be $(1.004285 - 0.773343)/(1.293087 - 0.773343) = 0.444$ and $1 - p = 0.556$. The value of the call today would, therefore, be

$$C = \frac{(0.444)37.85 + (0.556)0}{1.004285} = 16.74.$$

> The binomial model converges to a specific value of the option as the number of time periods increases.

The actual price of that option is 13.50, but, of course, we would not expect a one-period binomial model to accurately reflect reality. Notice in Table 4.2, however, what happens when we increase the number of time periods, each time adjusting the values of r, u, d, and p accordingly. We seem to be converging to the value of 13.56.

Using a binomial model to price an option is much like using a still camera to photograph an activity with fast action, such as a horse race. If we take a picture of the race at some point, we will not have a very good idea of what happened during the race. If we take several pictures, we begin to get a clearer view of how the race proceeded. If we take a large number of pictures, each at very short time intervals—meaning essentially to make a movie—we obtain a near-perfect reproduction of what happened from start to finish. In the binomial model, the process of making n large is like making a movie. If we take a large enough number of pictures, meaning to make n large enough, we obtain a very accurate depiction of what happens to the stock over the option's life. Consequently, we can be confident that our estimated option value is a fairly accurate reflection of the true value of the option.

The value of the option when n approaches infinity has a special name. It is the Black-Scholes-Merton value and is the subject of Chapter 5.

TABLE 4.2 BINOMIAL OPTION VALUES FOR DCRB JUNE 125 CALL WHEN N IS INCREASED

N	U	D	R	P	C
1	1.2931	0.7733	0.004285	0.4443	16.75
2	1.1993	0.8338	0.002140	0.4605	12.32
5	1.1218	0.8914	0.000856	0.4750	14.19
10	1.0847	0.9219	0.000428	0.4823	13.35
25	1.0528	0.9498	0.000171	0.4888	13.67
50	1.0370	0.9643	0.000086	0.4921	13.54
100	1.0260	0.9747	0.000043	0.4944	13.55
200	1.0183	0.9820	0.000021	0.4960	13.56

Note: S = 125.94, X = 125, r = 4.56%, T = 0.0959, σ = 0.83.

Alternative Specifications of the Binomial Model

In the preceding section, we saw that the binomial model can approximate a real-life scenario if we let the number of periods be large and adjust the up and down factors and the risk-free rate to reflect the volatility of the stock and the interest accrued per period. The formulas used in that section are not, however, the only ones that can be used. Although the adjustment for the risk-free rate is the same, the up and down parameters can be adjusted as follows:

$$u = e^{(\ln(1+r)-\sigma^2/2)(T/n)+\sigma\sqrt{T/n}}$$

$$d = e^{(\ln(1+r)-\sigma^2/2)(T/n)-\sigma\sqrt{T/n}},$$

where $\ln(1 + r)$ is the continuously compounded interest rate, which we shall cover in more detail in Chapter 5.

Recall that we have been using $p = (1 + r - d)/(u - d)$. Now, however, the formula for p is

$$p = \frac{e^{\sigma^2(T/n)/2} - e^{-\sigma\sqrt{T/n}}}{e^{\sigma\sqrt{T/n}} - e^{-\sigma\sqrt{T/n}}}.$$

As it turns out, however, the above formula for p tends to be very close to 0.5 and will approach 0.5 as the number of time periods, n, increases. So for all intents and purposes, we can use 0.5 for p and the above formulas for u and d.[7]

TECHNICAL NOTE: Derivation of Up Probability
go to www.cengagebrain.com

Let us make some comparisons between the two methods. Consider again the June 125 DCRB call. Let us first price the option using a two-period binomial model. The risk-free rate will be

$$r = (1.0456)^{0.0959/2} - 1 = 0.0021.$$

Although we do not have a dividend in this problem, if there were a dividend, the rate would be adjusted in the same manner.

First, we develop the model with the formulas for u and d used earlier in the chapter. We have

$$u = e^{0.83\sqrt{0.0959/2}} = 1.1993$$
$$d = 1/1.1993 = 0.8338.$$

The value of p is $(1.0021 - 0.8338)/(1.1993 - 0.8338) = 0.4605$. In Figure 4.10, part a shows the price of the option in the two-period binomial tree. The option value is shown in parentheses below the stock price. The option value today is 12.3235.

Now we develop the model with the formulas for u and d presented above in this section. We have

$$u = e^{\left(\ln(1.0456)-0.83^2/2\right)(0.0959/2)+0.83\sqrt{0.0959/2}} = 1.1822$$

$$d = e^{\left(\ln(1.0456)-0.83^2/2\right)(0.0959/2)-0.83\sqrt{0.0959/2}} = 0.8219.$$

The value of p is

$$p = \frac{e^{0.83^2(0.959/2)/2} - e^{-0.83\sqrt{0.0959/2}}}{e^{0.83(\sqrt{0.0959/2}} - e^{-0.83\sqrt{0.0959/2}}} = 0.500251.$$

---

[7]Turn back to Table 4.2 and observe the value of p using the model previously described. That value is also converging to 0.5.

FIGURE 4.10 Pricing the DCRB June 125 Call in a Two-Period World

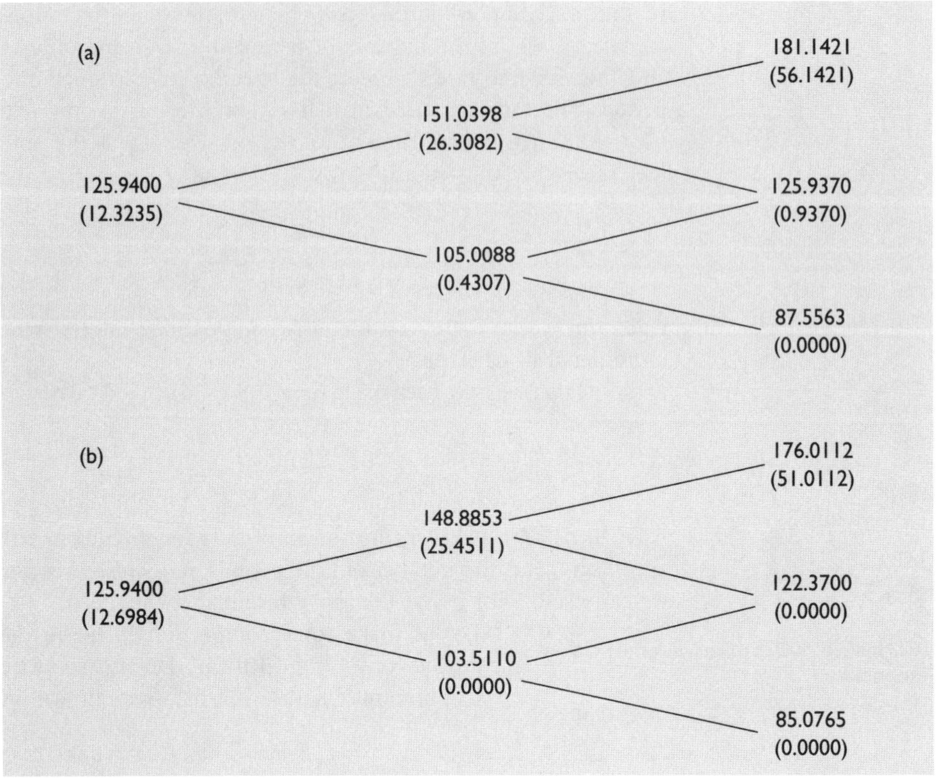

We shall just use 0.5. Part b of Figure 4.10 illustrates this option's price in the two-period binomial tree. The price today is $12.6984. The difference in what we are doing here and what we did previously is that the preceding formulas force the binomial model to replicate the behavior of the stock only in the limit, meaning when n is very large. These formulas force the binomial model to replicate the behavior of the stock regardless of the size of n. When we refer to replicating the behavior of the stock, we mean that the probability distribution of the stock will be of a particular form that we cover in the next chapter.

Obviously, there are significant differences in the option price using the two methods. So which is best? The binomial model has two primary purposes: (1) teaching the underlying principles of option pricing with a minimum of mathematics and (2) letting the number of time periods be sufficiently large to use in pricing options in real-world situations. In the case of a large number of time periods, these two methods will give nearly the same price. For example, with n = 200, we would find that the first method gives an option price of $13.56, while the second method gives a price of $13.55. Note from Table 3.1 that the actual price of the option is $13.50. Provided the correct inputs are used, the binomial model, in whatever version one chooses, will do a fairly good job of pricing options. For some types of options, specifically standard European calls and puts, there is an even better method—the Black-Scholes-Merton model, which is the subject of Chapter 5.

Obviously for a large number of time periods, a computer is necessary to perform the binomial option pricing calculations. There are a wide variety of ways to perform these calculations using computer programs, including Web-based applications, stand-alone programs, smartphone apps, and spreadsheets. This book provides Excel spreadsheets to do many of the computations. Software Demonstration 4.1 introduces you to the spreadsheet file BSMbin9e.xls, which computes binomial and Black-Scholes-Merton option prices.

Advantages of the Binomial Model

When you are first exploring option valuation models, the binomial model is very useful in illustrating important concepts. Perhaps the most valuable feature of the model is that it enables you to see how the construction of a dynamic risk-free hedge leads to a formula for the option price. You saw that if the option price in the market does not conform to the formula, someone could construct a dynamic hedge and earn better than the risk-free rate. Once we have the formula, we can see that the probability of stock price movements does not play a role in option pricing. While the probability that the stock will make a certain move does play an important role in the particular option strategy pursued, it does not appear anywhere in the formula and, hence, does not affect the option price. Because the probability of the stock price movement is irrelevant, the binomial model shows that option valuation is consistent with "risk neutrality." That is, the probability of an up jump and the size of the up jump are selected such that the expected

MAKING THE CONNECTION

Uses of the Binomial Option Pricing Framework in Practice

The actual practice of financial management will provide many instances when knowing how to deploy the binomial model will prove beneficial. For example, many projects faced by firms' management contain embedded options such as the option to expand a project, the option to terminate a project, the option to delay the start of a project, and various financing options. These kinds of choices are called real options. To properly analyze their value requires the ability to capture flexibility, meaning that a choice will be made and that such a choice has the potential of great value. The binomial framework is very flexible in capturing unique aspects related to managing projects that contain real options.

Many executives' incentive plans contain very complex options from both the firm's perspective and the manager's perspective. For example, executive stock option plans provide an incentive for senior management to seek better projects that should enhance stockholder value. Management, however, has the option to leave the firm, in which case the manager typically has about 90 days to exercise the options or lose them. The manager could also be terminated or die. Many executive stock options are very long-term, often expiring in ten years. There are vesting requirements that restrict the exercise of these options, often for several years. Many firms grant options to lower-level employees.

Hence, executive and employee stock options are very complex derivatives that require a flexible option valuation framework. The binomial option pricing framework is often used to value executive stock options both by management and the firm.

Debt securities often contain embedded options, making it more difficult to appraise their current market value. Examples of embedded options include the option to call the debt (callable bonds) and the option to convert the debt to equity (convertible bonds). The call feature essentially amounts to determining whether a bond is worth more to keep it alive, thereby paying the contracted interest rate, or to call it at the contracted call price, thereby paying it off. The conversion feature is one in which the value of the bond, if continued, is worth more or less than the value of the equity into which it would be converted. Both of these decisions are similar to exercising an option early. The binomial framework, through its ability to handle early exercise, provides a practical mechanism for determining the value of a call or conversion feature and assessing whether to exercise either of those options.

Thus, the binomial framework is an extremely useful tool for derivatives professionals called upon to estimate the fair market value of complex financial instruments.

SOFTWARE DEMONSTRATION 4.1

Calculating the Binomial Price with the Excel Spreadsheet BSMbin9e.xls

The Excel spreadsheet BSMbin9e.xls is saved in Excel 97-2003. It calculates both the binomial and Black-Scholes-Merton option pricing models. The binomial model provides European and American call and put prices, as well as the delta, gamma, and theta, known as the option "Greeks." These concepts are covered in Chapter 5, along with the Black-Scholes-Merton model. This spreadsheet is a read-only spreadsheet, meaning that it cannot be saved under the name BSMbin9e.xls, which preserves the original file. You may, however, load the spreadsheet without the read-only feature.

The spreadsheet BSMbin9e.xls is available as a download via the product support website. To use it:

1. Go to www.cengagebrain.com.
2. Click on Instructor Resources or Student Resources.
3. Click on the link for BSMbin9e.xls.
4. Follow the instructions on the Web page to download and install the spreadsheet.

Now let us calculate an option price. Assume that you want to find the binomial price of the option illustrated in this chapter, the DCRB June 125 call. The DCRB stock is at 125.94, the exercise price is 125,

the risk-free rate is 4.56 percent, the standard deviation is 0.83, and the time to expiration is 0.0959 (based on 35 days to expiration). There are no dividends on the stock.

The Excel screen below contains a section labeled **Inputs:** Each cell that will accept inputs has a double-line border, and the values are in blue. Output cells have a single-line border. Enter the values in the appropriate cells. For greater accuracy, enter the time to expiration as a formula: = 35/365. Leave the dividend yield and the discrete dividends blank or insert zeroes. For the risk-free rate, select "discrete" from the pull-down list. The risk-free rate can be entered with or without decimals, that is, as "0.0456" or "4.56". Volatility and the dividend yield can also be entered in this manner.

Near the right side of the screen is the section labeled **Binomial Model**. Enter the number of time steps, with a maximum of 5,000. Because the binomial calculation can be time-consuming, the spreadsheet does not automatically recalculate the binomial value. You must click on the button **Run Binomial Model**. While the program is running, Excel's status bar at the bottom of the screen will count down by displaying the line "Iterating through binomial tree at time step #xxx," where "xxx" is the number of the time step the program is on.

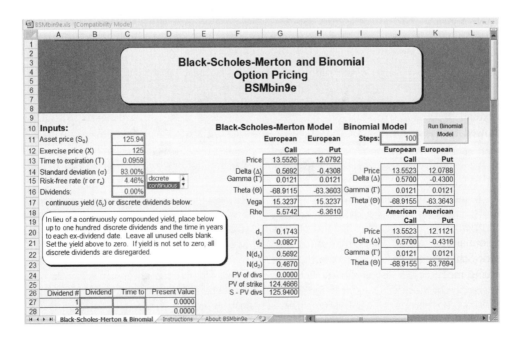

growth in the underlying asset is the risk-free interest rate even though, in reality, the stock does not grow at the risk-free rate. In short, the binomial model illustrates that options can be valued as the present value of the expected future payout, treating the underlying asset as though it grows at the risk-free interest rate. It is the ability to construct this dynamic risk-free hedge that enables the model to work in this manner.

In addition, there are several practical advantages of the binomial model. It is particularly useful in handling American options because investors may decide to exercise these options early. One can easily check if early exercise is advantageous at each location in the binomial tree. In addition, dividends can also easily be incorporated into the binomial model. As we will see later in the book, the binomial model can be very useful in valuing options far more complex than those shown here. The binomial model is a very useful tool to have in your toolbox when faced with an option-related problem.

Summary

This chapter introduced the concept of an option pricing model, which is a mathematical formula or computational procedure that produces the theoretical fair value of the option. This process is called option pricing. The theoretical fair value is the price at which the option should be trading. The chapter focuses on the binomial model, which is a computational procedure for pricing the option.

We began by developing the model in a one-period world, which means that one period later the option expires. A period is defined as a specific length of time over which the underlying stock can make one of two moves—up to a specific price or down to a specific price—and here is a given interest rate. We showed that it is possible to combine a long position in the stock with a short position in a call option to produce a risk-free portfolio. Given that the return on a risk-free portfolio should be the risk-free rate, it is then possible to solve for the theoretical option price, given the other input parameters. If the option is not selling for its theoretical price, it is possible to capture an arbitrage profit at no risk.

We then extended the model to a two-period world, where we showed that the combination of long stock and short calls must be adjusted over each period to maintain the risk-free nature of the hedge portfolio. Again, if the option is mispriced, it is possible to capture an arbitrage profit.

We examined how the binomial model will behave as the number of time periods is increased, and we showed that it seems to converge to a specific value. We also looked at how the binomial model can easily accommodate the problem of early exercise of American options. At a given time point, if the option is worth more exercised than not exercised, we simply replace the computed value of the option with the intrinsic value. We also saw that there are alternative specifications of the binomial model.

Although Chapter 4 focused only on the binomial model, we saw that as the number of time periods increased and the length of each time period decreased, we obtained a picture of a real world in which there are many possible prices over a given instant of time. This scenario, like the way in which a movie camera consolidates a collection of still photos to represent a more or less continuous view of time, leads us into Chapter 5, where we cover the Black-Scholes-Merton model.

Key Terms

Before continuing to Chapter 5, you should be able to give brief definitions of the following terms:

model/option pricing model/option pricing/binomial option pricing model/Black-Scholes-Merton option pricing model, p. 99

binomial/two-state model, p. 100

hedge portfolio/hedge ratio, p. 101

recombining tree/non-recombining tree, p. 118

Further Reading

The binomial option pricing model was developed in the following articles:

Cox, J. C., S. A. Ross, and M. Rubinstein. "Option Pricing: A Simplified Approach." *Journal of Financial Economics* 7 (1979): 229–263.

Rendleman, R. J., Jr., and B. J. Bartter. "Two-State Option Pricing." *The Journal of Finance* 34 (1979): 1093–1110.

Further advances are presented in the following articles:

Breen, R. "The Accelerated Binomial Option Pricing Model." *Journal of Financial and Quantitative Analysis* 25 (1991): 153–164.

Brennan, M. J. "The Pricing of Contingent Claims in Discrete Time Models." *The Journal of Finance* 34 (1979): 53–68.

Stapleton, R. C., and M. J. Subrahmanyam. "The Valuation of Options When Asset Returns Are Generated by a Binomial Process." *The Journal of Finance* 39 (1984): 1525–1539.

Other good references are as follows:

Chance, D. M. "A Synthesis of Binomial Option Pricing Models for Lognormally Distributed Assets." *Journal of Applied Finance* (2008): 38–56.

Chriss, N. *Black-Scholes and Beyond: Option Pricing Models.* Chicago: Irwin Professional Publishing, 1997.

Hsia, C. C. "On Binomial Option Pricing." *The Journal of Financial Research* 6 (1983): 41–46.

Nawalkha, S. K., and D. R. Chambers. "The Binomial Model and Risk Neutrality: Some Important Details." *The Financial Review* 30 (1995): 605–618.

Rendleman, R. J., Jr. *Applied Derivatives: Options, Futures, and Swaps.* Malden, MA: Blackwell, 2002.

Shreve, S. E. *Stochastic Calculus for Finance I: The Binomial Asset Pricing Model.* New York: Springer, 2005.

Concept Checks

1. Describe the components of a hedge portfolio in the binomial option pricing model where the instrument being hedged is (1) a call and (2) a put.
2. If the binomial model produces a call option price that is higher than the price at which the option is trading in the market, what strategy is suggested?
3. Explain the similarities and differences between pricing an option by its boundary conditions and using an exact option pricing formula.
4. Discuss how a binomial model accommodates the possibility of the early exercise of an option.
5. What is the principal benefit of a binomial option pricing model?

Questions and Problems

1. Find the value of an American put option using the binomial option pricing model. The parameters are S = 62, X = 70, r = 0.08, u = 1.10, and d = 0.95. There are no dividends. Use n = 2 periods.
2. Consider the following binomial option pricing problem involving an American call. This call has two periods to go before expiring. Its stock price is 30, and its exercise price is 25. The risk-free rate is .05, the value of u is 1.15, and the value of d is 0.90. The stock pays a dividend at the end of the first period at the rate of 0.06. Find the value of the call.
3. Consider a two-period, two-state world. Let the current stock price be 45 and the risk-free rate be 5 percent. Each period the stock price can go either up by 10 percent or down by 10 percent. A call option expiring at the end of the second period has an exercise price of 40.

   a. Find the stock price sequence.
   b. Determine the possible prices of the call at expiration.
   c. Find the possible prices of the call at the end of the first period.
   d. What is the current price of the call?
   e. What is the initial hedge ratio?
   f. What are the two possible hedge ratios at the end of the first period?
   g. Construct an example showing that the hedge works. Make sure the example illustrates how the hedge portfolio earns the risk-free rate over both periods.
   h. What would an investor do if the call were overpriced? if it were underpriced?

4. Consider a stock worth $25 that can go up or down by 15 percent per period. The risk-free rate is 10 percent. Use one binomial period.
   a. Determine the two possible stock prices for the next period.
   b. Determine the intrinsic values at expiration of a European call option with an exercise price of $25.
   c. Find the value of the option today.
   d. Construct a hedge by combining a position in stock with a position in the call. Show that the return on the hedge is the risk-free rate regardless of the outcome, assuming that the call sells for the value you obtained in part c.
   e. Determine the rate of return from a riskless hedge if the call is selling for $3.50 when the hedge is initiated.

5. Describe the three primary ways of incorporating dividends into the binomial model.

6. Why are the up and down parameters adjusted when the number of periods is extended? Recall that in introducing the binomial model, we illustrated one- and two-period examples, but we did not adjust the parameters. What is the difference in these two examples? Why did we adjust the parameters in one case and not in the other?

7. How is the volatility of the underlying stock reflected in the binomial model?

8. Explain the differences between a recombining and non-recombining tree. Why is the former more desirable?

9. Consider a stock currently priced at $80. In the next period, the stock can either increase by 30 percent or decrease by 15 percent. Assume a call option with an exercise price of $80 and a risk-free rate of 6 percent. Suppose the call option is currently trading at $12. If the option is mispriced, what amount of riskless return can be earned using a riskless hedge?

10. Why are the probabilities of stock price movements not used in the model for calculating an option's price? What variables are used?

11. (Concept Problem) In this chapter, we obtained the binomial option pricing formula by hedging a short position in the call option with a long position in stock. An alternative way to do this is to combine the stock and a risk-free bond to replicate the call option. Construct a one-period binomial option pricing model in which the stock and a risk-free bond are used to replicate a European call option. Then show that the option pricing formula is the same as the one developed in the text. Hint: Hold n_s shares of stock and issue B dollars of bonds paying r percent so that the value in both outcomes matches precisely the value of the option. Then solve for n_s and B and substitute back into the formula for the value of the hedge portfolio today to obtain the formula for C.

12. (Concept Problem) The binomial model can be used to price unusual features of options. Consider the following scenario: A stock priced at $75 can go up by 20 percent or down by 10 percent per period for three periods. The risk-free rate is 8 percent. A European call option expiring in three periods has an exercise price of $70. The parties to the option agree, however, that the maximum payout of this option is $40. Find the current value of the option. Then determine whether an American version of the option, also limited to a maximum payout of $40, would have any additional value over the European version. Compare your answers to the value of the option if there were no limitation on the payoff.

13. Suppose the spot exchange rate for Narnian currency is trading for $2/N and one year later it can go up to $2.5/N, an increase of 25 percent, or down to $1.80/N, a decrease of 10 percent. Assume a call option with an exercise price of $2.05/N. Assume initially that the U.S. interest rate is 1 percent and that the Narnian interest rate is 5 percent. Assume that the interest rate is based on annual compounding and round at the fifth decimal place.
   a. Compute the call price.
   b. Compute the put price.
   c. If the Narnian interest rate falls immediately, what happens to the call and put prices?

14. Why does the binomial model converge to a specific value of the option as the number of time periods increase? To what value does the option converge? When n approaches infinity, to what famous model does the binomial model converge?

15. Consider three call options identical in every respect except for the maturity of 0.5, 1, and 1.5 years. Specifically, the stock price is $100, the annually compounded risk-free rate is 5%, and the strike price is $100. Use a one-period binomial model with u = 4/3 and d = 3/4. Calculate the p and h. Explain.

16. Consider three call options identical in every respect except for the strike price of $90, $100, and $110. Specifically, the stock price is $100, the annually compounded risk-free rate is 5%, and time to maturity is one year. Use a one-period

binomial model with u = 4/3 and d = 3/4. Calculate the p and h. Explain.

17. Use the Excel spreadsheet BSMbin9e.xls and determine the value of a call option and a put option on a stock currently priced at 100, where the risk-free rate is 5 percent (compounded annually), the exercise price is 100, the volatility is 30 percent, the option expires in one year, and there are no dividends on the stock. Let the number of binomial periods be 25. Verify that put-call parity holds.

18. The binomial option pricing model has several advantages, particularly related to illustrating important concepts and practical applications. Identify and discuss three advantages related to illustrating important concepts and three advantages related to practical applications.

19. Use the binomial model and two time periods to determine the price of the DCRB June 130 American put. Use the appropriate parameters from the information given in the chapter (originally given in Chapter 3) and a volatility of 83 percent.

20. Use the Excel spreadsheet BSMbin9e.xls and determine the value of a call option on a stock currently priced at 165.13, where the risk-free rate is 5.875 percent (compounded annually), the exercise price is 165, the volatility is 21 percent, the option expires in 102 days, and there are no dividends on the stock. Let the number of binomial periods be 1, 5, 10, 25, and 50.

21. Construct a table containing the up and down factors for a one-year option with a stock volatility of 55 percent and a risk-free rate of 7 percent for n = 1, 5, 10, 50, and 100, where n is the number of binomial periods. Let u and d be defined as

$$u = e^{\sigma\sqrt{T/n}}$$
$$d = 1/u.$$

22. Consider a European call with an exercise price of 50 on a stock priced at 60. The stock can go up by 15 percent or down by 20 percent in each of two binomial periods. The risk-free rate is 10 percent. Determine the price today of the option. Then construct a risk-free hedge of long stock and short option. At each point in the binomial tree, show the composition and value of the hedge portfolio and demonstrate that the return is the same as the risk-free rate. On any revisions to the hedge portfolio, make the transactions (buying or selling) in stock and not options. You can borrow any additional funds required at the risk-free rate, and any excess funds should be invested at the risk-free rate.

CHAPTER 5

Option Pricing Models
The Black-Scholes-Merton Model

Good theories, like Black-Scholes, provide a theoretical laboratory in which you can explore the likely effect of possible causes. They give you a common language with which to quantify and communicate your feelings about value.

Emanuel Derman
The Journal of Derivatives, Winter, 2000, p. 64

ORIGINS OF THE BLACK-SCHOLES-MERTON FORMULA

The roots of the Black-Scholes-Merton formula go back to the nineteenth century. In the 1820s, a Scottish scientist, Robert Brown, observed the motion of pollen suspended in water and noticed that the movements followed no distinct pattern, moving randomly, independent of any current in the water. This phenomenon came to be known as Brownian motion. Similar versions of Brownian motion were subsequently discovered by other scientists studying other natural phenomena. In 1900, a French doctoral student, Louis Bachelier, wrote his dissertation on the pricing of options in the Paris market and developed a model strikingly similar to the Black-Scholes-Merton model. Unfortunately, his dissertation advisor was disappointed because Bachelier's work was oriented toward the practical issue of pricing a financial instrument. Although Bachelier received his degree, the less-than-enthusiastic support of his advisor damaged his career, and nothing further was heard from him.

In the early twentieth century, Albert Einstein, working on the foundations of his theories of relativity, used the principles of Brownian motion to explain movements of molecules. This work led to several research papers that earned Einstein the Nobel Prize and world renown. By that time, a fairly well-developed branch of mathematics, often attributed to American mathematician Norbert Wiener, proved useful for explaining the movements of random particles. Other contributions to the mathematics were made by Japanese mathematician Kiyoshi Itô. In 1951, Itô developed an extremely important result called Itô's Lemma that, 20 years later, made it possible to find an option's price. Keep in mind, however, that these people were working on complex problems in physics and mathematics, not finance.

The mathematics used to model random movements had now evolved into its own subdiscipline, which came to be known as stochastic calculus. While ordinary calculus defined the rates of change of known functions, stochastic calculus defined the rates of change of functions in which one or more terms were random but behaved according to well-defined rules of probability.

CHAPTER OBJECTIVES

- Present the Black-Scholes-Merton model and learn how to use it to price options

- Understand the relationship of the model's inputs to the option price

- Learn how to adjust the model to accommodate dividends and put options

- Understand how volatility is estimated, both historically and as the implied volatility

- Observe how an option position is delta-hedged and how the risk can be reduced by gamma hedging

In the late 1960s, Fischer Black finished his doctorate in mathematics at Harvard. Passing up a career as a mathematician, he went to work for Arthur Little, a management consulting firm in Boston. Black met a young MIT finance professor named Myron Scholes, and the two began an interchange of ideas on how financial markets worked. Soon Black joined the MIT finance faculty, where he made many contributions to our understanding of how assets other than options are priced. Black and Scholes then began studying options, which at that time were traded only on the over-the-counter market. They first reviewed the attempts of previous researchers to find the elusive option pricing formula.

Black and Scholes took two approaches to finding the price. One approach assumed that all assets were priced according to the Capital Asset Pricing Theory, a well-accepted model in finance. The other approach used the stochastic calculus. They obtained an equation using the first approach, but the second method left them with a differential equation they were unable to solve. This more mathematical approach was considered more important, so they continued to work on the problem, looking for a solution. Black eventually found that the differential equation could be transformed into the same equation that described the movement of heat as it traveled across an object. There was already a known solution, and Black and Scholes simply looked it up, applied it to their problem, and obtained the correct formula (which matched the formula they had obtained using the first method). Their paper reporting their findings was rejected by two academic journals before eventually being published in the *Journal of Political Economy*, which reconsidered an earlier decision to reject the paper.

At the same time, another young financial economist at MIT, Robert Merton, was also working on option pricing. Merton discovered many of the arbitrage rules that we covered in Chapter 3. In addition, Merton more or less simultaneously derived the formula. Merton's modesty, however, compelled him to ask a journal editor that his paper not be published before that of Black and Scholes. As it turned out, both papers were published, with Merton's paper appearing in the *Bell Journal of Economics and Management Science* at about the same time as Black and Scholes' paper. Merton, however, did not initially receive as much credit as Black and Scholes, whose names became permanently associated with the model. Fischer Black left academia in 1983 and went to work for the Wall Street firm of Goldman Sachs. Unfortunately, he died in 1995 at the age of 57. Scholes and Merton have remained in academia but have been extensively involved in real-world derivatives applications. In 1997, the Nobel Committee awarded the Nobel Prize for Economic Science to Myron Scholes and Robert Merton, while recognizing Black's contributions. You can read more about this important event at www.nobelprize.org/nobel_prizes/economics/laureates/1997.

The model has been one of the most significant developments in the history of the pricing of financial instruments. It has generated considerable research attempting to test the model and improve on it. A new industry of derivative products based on the Black-Scholes-Merton model has developed. Even if one does not agree with everything the model says, knowing something about it is important for surviving in the options markets.

BLACK-SCHOLES-MERTON MODEL AS THE LIMIT OF THE BINOMIAL MODEL

In Chapter 4, we developed the binomial model, which served two primary purposes. It enabled us to see the basic elements underlying the principles of pricing an option without resorting to advanced mathematics. We saw that an option is priced by combining it with the underlying asset in such a manner that the risk is eliminated, and as we move through time, the combination of stock and options must be adjusted. Because the return on a riskless portfolio is the risk-free rate, the value of that portfolio can be easily obtained by discounting its value at the option expiration by the risk-free rate. We saw that there is but a single value of the option that will result in the combined option-stock portfolio earning the risk-free rate. If the option is selling for any other price, the law of one price is violated and making an arbitrage profit is possible by selling an overpriced option and buying the stock or buying an underpriced option and selling short the stock. If the proper ratio of options to stock is maintained, the arbitrageur either has no risk and earns more than the risk-free rate or borrows at no risk and pays less than the risk-free rate. Another use of the binomial model is in pricing American options. The model can easily capture the value of exercising early.

In the last chapter, we worked through an example in which the DCRB June 125 call option was priced using the binomial model and an increasing number of time steps. We saw that its price was 13.56 with either 100 or 200 time steps. Figure 5.1 shows the behavior of the binomial option price in this problem as the number of time steps is increased in increments of 5, starting at n = 5 and ending at n = 200. We see that the option price bounces around and begins to stabilize at about 100 time steps. This behavior is what mathematicians call convergence. The binomial option pricing model converges to a specific value in the limit. It turns out that this value is the Black-Scholes-Merton price.

> The binomial model converges to the Black-Scholes-Merton model as the number of time periods increases.

The binomial model is one of two types of models called **discrete time** models. In such models, the life of the option is divided into a specific number of finite units of time. For example, if an option has a life of 100 days and we use binomial time steps, each time step represents one day. As time elapses, the stock price jumps from one level to either of the next two levels. The real world, however, is characterized by the continuous passage of time and the fact that the stock price generally moves only in very small increments. In fact, we might even characterize a stock's movements as being up the smallest possible increment, called an

FIGURE 5.1 Binomial Option Prices for Different n; DCRB June 125 call; S_0 = 125.94, r = 0.0456, T = 0.0959, σ = 0.83

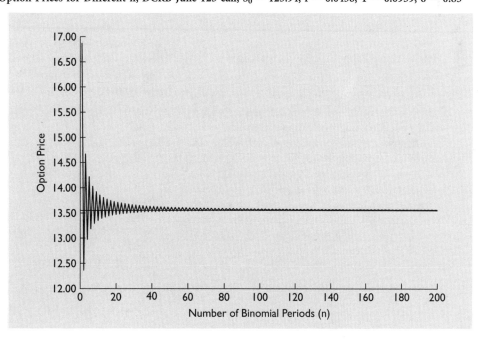

MAKING THE CONNECTION

Logarithms, Exponentials, and Finance

The Black-Scholes-Merton model requires the use of both the natural logarithm and the exponential function. Although this material is generally covered in secondary school math courses, you may find this review helpful.

A logarithm, often just called a log, is an exponent representing the power to which one number, called the base, must be raised to equal another number. The two most commonly used base numbers are 10 and e, where e is a special number approximately equal to 2.71828. Consider a number such as 25. Its logs are as follows:

$\log_{10} 25 = 1.3979$ (the log of the base 10 of 25)
$\log_e 25 = 3.2189$ (the log of the base e of 25).

We can verify these results as follows:

$$10^{1.3979} = 25$$
$$2.71828^{3.2189} = 25.$$

(Both numbers are subject to round-off error.) Logs using base 10 are referred to as common logs, while logs using base e are called natural logs. In finance, we use natural logs more often, a point we explain a few paragraphs down. Henceforth, when referring to logs, we mean natural logs.

Here are some important rules regarding logs:

- The log of a positive number is a positive number.
- The log of a negative number is undefined.
- The log of zero is undefined.
- The log of 1 is zero.
- The log of a number between zero and one is negative.

For shorthand notation, we tend to write $\log_e$ as simply ln.

In the financial world, logarithms are nearly always on the base e because e is the appropriate function for calculating continuously compounded interest. For example, consider the investment of $1 in a bank account for one year at 6 percent interest compounded annually. At the end of one year, you will have $1(1.06) = $1.06. If the interest is compounded semiannually, you will have $1(1 + (0.06/2))^2 = $1.0609. If the interest is compounded quarterly, you will have $1(1 + (0.06/4))^4 = $1.06136. If the interest is compounded daily, you will have $1(1 + (0.06/365))^{365} = $1.06183. If the rate is the same, the more frequent the compounding, the more money you will have. In general, if r is the rate, T is the number of years, and n is the number of compounding periods per year, the amount of money you will have per $1 invested after T years is

$$\left(1 + \left(\frac{r}{n}\right)\right)^{Tn}.$$

The table below shows the value of $1 invested for one year at 6% with various compounding frequencies.

Compounding Periods per Year	$1 Invested for One Year at 6%
1 (annually)	$1.06000000
2 (semiannually)	$1.06090000
4 (quarterly)	$1.06136355
12 (monthly)	$1.06167781
52 (weekly)	$1.06179982
365 (daily)	$1.06183131

It appears that we are converging to a little over $1.0618. Let us carry it further to verify:

1,000 (1000 times a year)	$1.06183464
10,000 (10,000 times a year)	$1.06183636
100,000 (100,000 times a year)	$1.06183653
1,000,000 (1,000,000 times a year)	$1.06183654

Indeed, the value is stabilizing.

The ultimate in compounding frequency is continuous compounding, in which the number of compounding periods is infinite. The formula for the continuous compounding factor must be written as a limit:

$$\lim_{n \to \infty} \left(1 + \left(\frac{r}{n}\right)\right)^{Tn}.$$

As it turns out, this is the definition of e:

$$\lim_{n \to \infty} \left(1 + \left(\frac{r}{n}\right)\right)^{Tn} = e^{rT},$$

where e is 2.71828.... In our example, $e^{0.06(1)} = $1.06183655. Because e captures the value of an investment compounded continuously, its role in finance is important.

The return on any asset over a period of time is usually expressed as either an annual return or a continuously compounded return. Consider a stock purchased for $100. Assume that a year later the stock is at

$110. Assume that there are no dividends, in which case we typically say that the stock earned a return of 10 percent. This is formally derived as

$$\frac{\$110}{\$100} - 1 = 0.10.$$

In other words, if we had put $100 in an investment that paid 10 percent interest, where the interest was added only at the end of the year, it would have grown to a value of $110. We can, however, obtain the same $110 at the end of the year if the $100 investment grows continuously at a rate of 9.531 percent. That is,

$$\$100e^{0.09531(1)} = \$110.$$

Where did we get 9.531 percent? It is simply the inverse of the exponential function, which is the natural logarithm function:

$$\ln(1.10) = 0.09531.$$

Thus, money invested at 9.531 percent compounded continuously for any number of years is the same as having invested that money at 10 percent, compounded only once per year. The same information is available in knowing that an asset earned 10 percent compounded annually or knowing that an asset earned 9.531 percent compounded continuously.

In general, for any exponent x, the function e^x is called the exponential function. For notational convenience and to avoid using a subscript, it is sometimes written as exp(x).

You will encounter continuous compounding (as well as discrete compounding) in many situations in this book as well as in other finance courses and books, and you should be very comfortable using either form of compounding and discounting, as well as expressing returns and interest rates as continuously compounded rates.

uptick, or down the smallest possible decrement, called a downtick. Such properties are captured much better with **continuous time** models. Although in a later section we shall see how discrete and continuous time come together, let us now proceed to identify and understand the characteristics of a continuous time model. It is this continuous time framework that the Black-Scholes-Merton model uses to price options.

ASSUMPTIONS OF THE BLACK-SCHOLES-MERTON MODEL

All models are based on a specific set of assumptions. In the binomial model, we assumed that the up and down factors were known and constant across time and that the risk-free rate was constant. More importantly, we made the critical assumption that the stock's movements can be characterized by the simplicity of the binomial model. We also implicitly made assumptions such as there are no transaction costs and taxes. Let us now look at the assumptions of the Black-Scholes-Merton model.

Stock Prices Behave Randomly and Evolve According to a Lognormal Distribution

The notion that stock prices are random is central for much of the body of knowledge of pricing assets and derivatives. Are stock prices really random, however? Look at Figure 5.2. We see two panels, each purporting to be the daily closing price of an actual stock for a period of one year. One panel is the actual sequence of stock prices. The other is a set of randomly generated stock prices that have statistical properties similar to those that DCRB had during that period. Can you identify which one is the actual sequence of stock prices?[1]

---

[1]Figure 5.2a is the imposter. It was randomly generated by the authors. If you got it right, you probably just made a lucky guess.

FIGURE 5.2a Simulated and Real Stock Prices of DCRB

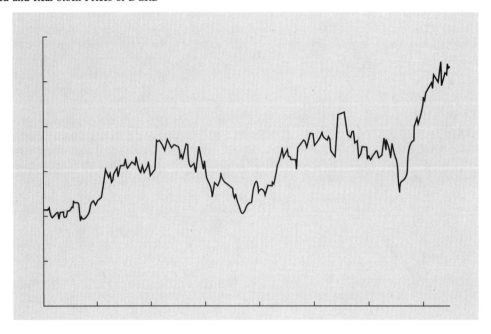

FIGURE 5.2b

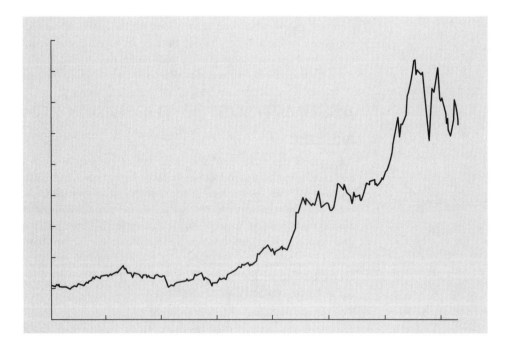

Many professional money managers claim to have the ability to predict stock prices. They observe a graph such as those shown in Figure 5.2 and claim that such a series is at least partially predictable. They see the upward trend and believe that it can be exploited to earn large gains. Consider, however, Figure 5.3, showing the daily returns, which are simply the daily percentage price changes, on the stock over that same period. It is the return series that determines how an investor will perform. Can anyone predict the movements in a series like this? Not likely. Although there may be very small elements

FIGURE 5.3 Daily Returns on DCRB

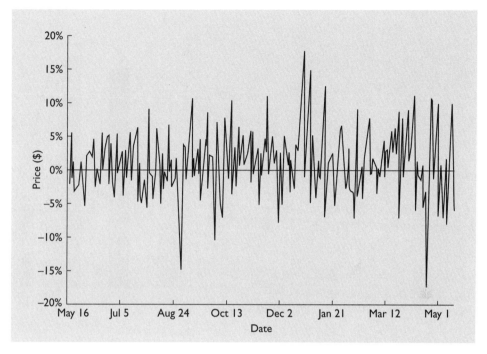

of predictability, particularly over very short time intervals, studies show that stock returns are largely unpredictable.

We also noted that stock returns are **lognormally distributed**. What do we mean by this? First, remember the normal, or bell-shaped, distribution. Are stock returns normally distributed? A look at the data would reveal that this is not the case. The return on a stock, however, can be expressed in a slightly different form, known as continuous compounding. Suppose we have a $100 stock. One year later that stock is at $120. We would say that its return is 20 percent. This is what we call the simple or discrete return. It compounds only once, at the end of the year. We can obtain the future value, $120, from the present value, $100, by the simple relationship $120 = $100(1.20), which involves no compounding. To express this return in continuous compounding, we take the natural logarithm of one plus the return.

Recall that the logarithm of a number is the power to which a base must be raised in order to equal that number. Typical bases for logarithms are 10, the base of common logarithms, and e, which is approximately 2.718 and is the base of natural logarithms. In financial models, the base is nearly always e.

The continuously compounded return, also called the log return, in our example is $\log(1.20) = 0.1823$, or 18.23 percent. The relationship between the end-of-year price and the beginning-of-year price is $120 = $100e^{0.1823}$. Obviously, we cannot change the prices; they were, after all, determined in a competitive market. But we can express the return in the form of log returns. It turns out that log returns tend to have properties that make them slightly closer to a normal distribution. Figure 5.4 shows a histogram of the log returns on the stock over the period indicated. Although we do not obtain a perfect representation of the normal distribution, we are probably not too far from it.

If the log of a variable is normally distributed, then that variable is said to be lognormally distributed. The distribution of the returns themselves has positive skewness, meaning that it has too many observations on the right side to be symmetric, as required

FIGURE 5.4 Histogram of Daily Log (Continuously Compounded) Returns of DCRB

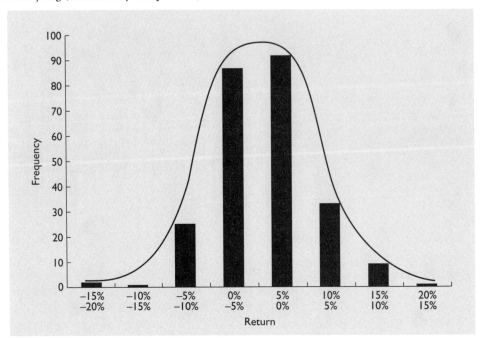

by the normal distribution. The assumption of a lognormal distribution is quite appealing. It is fairly consistent with reality and, more importantly, does not permit stock prices to be negative. Moreover, it lends itself nicely to the high-level mathematics that were required to develop the Black-Scholes-Merton model.

Risk-Free Rate and Volatility of the Log Return on the Stock Are Constant Throughout the Option's Life

The assumption that the risk-free rate is constant is tantamount to assuming that interest rates do not change. We know that is certainly not the case, and later in this book, we shall examine risk management problems that arise in a world of changing interest rates. For now, however, it is mostly a convenience to ignore interest rate uncertainty. As it turns out, we shall see later that interest rates do not have much effect on the prices of options on stocks and some other underlying assets; so this assumption is relatively harmless at this point and keeps the model as simple as possible.

The assumption that the volatility, which is the standard deviation, is constant is an important one. It turns out that this assumption is nearly always violated in the real world. In fact, it is virtually inconceivable that any risky asset will have the same level of volatility over a period of time such as a year. Later in this chapter, we learn how volatility is estimated, but for now, let us just note that estimates of the volatility of DCRB over this one-year period were as low as 37 percent and as high as 150 percent.

Because we fail to meet the assumption of constant volatility, should we throw out the Black-Scholes-Merton model in favor of one that assumes that the volatility can change? We could do that, but models with changing volatility are much more complicated. Also, it is not clear that such models are any better. Although changing volatility is a problem, we shall see that there are better ways to deal with it than to adopt a more complex model. Thus, we shall assume that we meet this requirement.

No Taxes or Transaction Costs

Option trading decisions are certainly affected by taxes and transaction costs, but these complexities will tend to cloud our understanding of the fundamentals of pricing options. The Black-Scholes-Merton option pricing model is based on the ability to actively trade stocks, risk-free instruments, and options. This active trading will trigger tax consequences and transaction costs. There are ways to relax these assumptions, but this is an advanced subject and not appropriate or necessary at this introductory level.

Stock Pays No Dividends

We have already made this assumption in previous chapters, and we saw how it can be relaxed. The same is true here, and we shall eventually learn how to incorporate dividends into the Black-Scholes-Merton model.

Options Are European

Unfortunately, the possibility of early exercise cannot be easily accommodated within the Black-Scholes-Merton framework. We shall see, however, that the **Black-Scholes-Merton model** can help us better understand what happens when a call is exercised early. For the most part, the binomial model remains the best way to price American options.

It is tempting to reject a model because its assumptions are not met. Perhaps surprisingly, the Black-Scholes-Merton model has been rejected by many experts who challenge whether its assumptions of constant volatility and the ability to dynamically trade in a near continuous manner are sufficiently realistic. Moreover, the existence of a volatility smile, which implies that the stock has more than one volatility, is inconsistent with the model. Other more sophisticated and complex models do exist and are used in practice. The Black-Scholes-Merton model should be viewed as the matriarch of a family of models that reflect a relaxation of the various assumptions. In choosing to use a model such as Black-Scholes-Merton, one must consider several issues: (1) Do the results obtained from the model conform to reality? (2) Is there a better model in the sense of being more accurate without being too much more costly and complex? (3) Is the model widely used in practice? The answers to those questions are not easy, but it is fairly safe to say that perhaps no other financial model, historically, had been so widely used in practice and had such an impact as the Black-Scholes-Merton model. At this level, we will go no further than this model, but be aware that the Black-Scholes-Merton model is not the end of the line of option pricing models;, it is only the beginning.

> The Black-Scholes-Merton option pricing model assumes that stock prices are random and lognormally distributed; that the risk-free rate and volatility are constant; that there are no taxes, transaction costs, or dividends; and that the options are European.

A NOBEL FORMULA

> The Black-Scholes-Merton call option pricing formula gives the call price in terms of the stock price, exercise price, risk-free rate, time to expiration, and variance of the stock return.

In Chapter 4, we saw that the binomial option pricing model is derived by forming a hedge portfolio consisting of a long position in shares and a short position in calls. We observed that in the two-period model, the relative number of shares to calls changes so that the investor must do some trading to maintain the riskless nature of the transaction. If this is done, the portfolio will earn the risk-free rate if and only if the option is priced by the formula we obtained. If the option trades at any other price, the law of one price is violated and the investor can earn an arbitrage profit. In the Black-Scholes-Merton model, trading occurs continuously, but the general idea is the same. A hedge portfolio is established and maintained by constantly adjusting the relative proportions of stock and options, a process called **dynamic trading**. The end result is obtained through complex mathematics, but the formula is straightforward.

The Black-Scholes-Merton formula is:

$$C = S_0 N(d_1) - X e^{-r_c T} N(d_2),$$

where

$$d_1 = \frac{\ln(S_0/X) + (r_c + \sigma^2/2)T}{\sigma\sqrt{T}}$$

$$d_2 = d_1 - \sigma\sqrt{T}.$$

$N(d_1), N(d_2)$ = cumulative normal probabilities
σ = annualized volatility (standard deviation) of the continuously compounded (log) return on the stock
r_c = continuously compounded risk-free rate.

All other variables are the same ones previously used.

Digression on Using the Normal Distribution

TECHNICAL NOTE: Deriving the Black-Scholes-Merton Model Using Stochastic Calculus
go to www.cengagebrain.com

Because computation of the Black-Scholes-Merton model requires the **normal probability** distribution, it will probably be helpful to review this concept. Figure 5.5 illustrates the normal, or bell-shaped, curve. Recall that the curve is symmetric and that everything we need to know about it is contained in the expected value, or mean, and the variance. Approximately 68 percent of the observations in a sample drawn from a normal distribution will occur within one standard deviation of the expected value. About 95 percent of the observations will lie within two standard deviations, and about 99 percent will lie within three standard deviations.

A standard normal random variable is called a **z statistic**. One can take any normally distributed random variable, convert it to a standard normal or z statistic, and use a table to determine the probability that an observed value of the random variable will be less than or equal to the value of interest.

Table 5.1 provides the cumulative probabilities of the standard normal distribution. Suppose we want to know the probability of observing a value of z less than or equal to 1.57. We go to the table and look down the first column for 1.5, then move to the right under the column labeled 0.07; that is, the 1.5 and 0.07 add up to the z value, 1.57. The entry in the 1.5 row/0.07 column is 0.9418, the probability in a normal distribution of observing a value of z less than or equal to 1.57.

FIGURE 5.5 **The Standard Normal Probability Distribution**

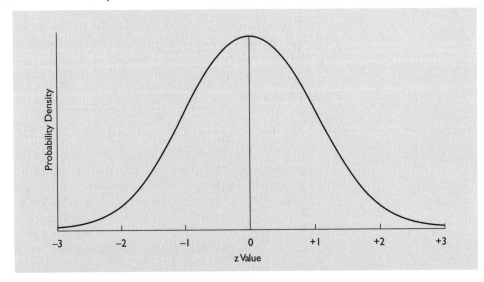

TABLE 5.1 STANDARD NORMAL PROBABILITIES

Z	0.00	0.01	0.02	0.03	0.04	0.05	0.06	0.07	0.08	0.09
0.0	0.5000	0.5040	0.5080	0.5120	0.5160	0.5199	0.5239	0.5279	0.5319	0.5359
0.1	0.5398	0.5438	0.5478	0.5517	0.5557	0.5596	0.5636	0.5675	0.5714	0.5753
0.2	0.5793	0.5832	0.5871	0.5910	0.5948	0.5987	0.6026	0.6064	0.6103	0.6141
0.3	0.6179	0.6217	0.6255	0.6293	0.6331	0.6368	0.6406	0.6443	0.6480	0.6517
0.4	0.6554	0.6591	0.6628	0.6664	0.6700	0.6736	0.6772	0.6808	0.6844	0.6879
0.5	0.6915	0.6950	0.6985	0.7019	0.7054	0.7088	0.7123	0.7157	0.7190	0.7224
0.6	0.7257	0.7291	0.7324	0.7357	0.7389	0.7422	0.7454	0.7486	0.7517	0.7549
0.7	0.7580	0.7611	0.7642	0.7673	0.7704	0.7734	0.7764	0.7794	0.7823	0.7852
0.8	0.7881	0.7910	0.7939	0.7967	0.7995	0.8023	0.8051	0.8078	0.8106	0.8133
0.9	0.8159	0.8186	0.8212	0.8238	0.8264	0.8289	0.8315	0.8340	0.8365	0.8389
1.0	0.8413	0.8438	0.8461	0.8485	0.8508	0.8531	0.8554	0.8577	0.8599	0.8621
1.1	0.8643	0.8665	0.8686	0.8708	0.8729	0.8749	0.8770	0.8790	0.8810	0.8830
1.2	0.8849	0.8860	0.8888	0.8907	0.8925	0.8943	0.8962	0.8980	0.8997	0.9015
1.3	0.9032	0.9049	0.9066	0.9082	0.9099	0.9115	0.9131	0.9147	0.9162	0.9177
1.4	0.9192	0.9207	0.9222	0.9236	0.9251	0.9265	0.9279	0.9292	0.9306	0.9319
1.5	0.9332	0.9345	0.9357	0.9370	0.9382	0.9394	0.9406	0.9418	0.9429	0.9441
1.6	0.9452	0.9463	0.9474	0.9484	0.9495	0.9505	0.9515	0.9525	0.9535	0.9545
1.7	0.9554	0.9564	0.9573	0.9582	0.9591	0.9599	0.9608	0.9616	0.9625	0.9633
1.8	0.9641	0.9649	0.9656	0.9664	0.9671	0.9678	0.9686	0.9693	0.9699	0.9706
1.9	0.9713	0.9719	0.9726	0.9732	0.9738	0.9744	0.9750	0.9756	0.9761	0.9767
2.0	0.9772	0.9778	0.9783	0.9788	0.9793	0.9798	0.9803	0.9808	0.9812	0.9817
2.1	0.9821	0.9826	0.9830	0.9834	0.9838	0.9842	0.9846	0.9850	0.9854	0.9857
2.2	0.9861	0.9864	0.9868	0.9871	0.9875	0.9878	0.9881	0.9884	0.9887	0.9890
2.3	0.9893	0.9896	0.9898	0.9901	0.9904	0.9906	0.9909	0.9911	0.9913	0.9916
2.4	0.9918	0.9920	0.9922	0.9925	0.9927	0.9929	0.9931	0.9932	0.9934	0.9936
2.5	0.9938	0.9940	0.9941	0.9943	0.9945	0.9946	0.9948	0.9949	0.9951	0.9952
2.6	0.9953	0.9955	0.9956	0.9957	0.9959	0.9960	0.9961	0.9962	0.9963	0.9964
2.7	0.9965	0.9966	0.9967	0.9968	0.9969	0.9970	0.9971	0.9972	0.9973	0.9974
2.8	0.9974	0.9975	0.9976	0.9977	0.9977	0.9978	0.9979	0.9979	0.9980	0.9981
2.9	0.9981	0.9982	0.9982	0.9983	0.9984	0.9984	0.9985	0.9985	0.9986	0.9986
3.0	0.9987	0.9987	0.9987	0.9988	0.9988	0.9989	0.9989	0.9989	0.9990	0.9990

Suppose the value of z is less than zero—say, −1.12. We then look for the appropriate value for a positive 1.12. In the 1.1 row/0.02 column is the value 0.8686. Then we subtract this number from 1. The answer is 0.1314. Because the table is symmetric, it is not necessary to show negative values. The probability of observing a value less than or equal to −1.12 is the same as that of observing a value greater than or equal to 1.12. The probability of observing a value greater than or equal to 1.12 is 1 minus the probability of observing a value less than or equal to 1.12. Note that we overlapped with the probability of observing a value exactly equal to 1.12. The probability of observing any single value is zero. This is so because we can observe an infinite number of possible values.

The normal probability can be accurately approximated using a polynomial equation instead of tables. There are several formulas that give good approximations for the normal probability. In addition, the mathematical function "=normsdist( )" in Excel is easy to use. In many applications in this book, we shall use values computed using Excel. Keep in mind, however, that Black-Scholes-Merton option values are highly sensitive to the normal probability calculation and can be off by several cents depending on which method is used.

Numerical Example

Let us use the Black-Scholes-Merton model to price the DCRB June 125 call. Recall that the inputs are a stock price of $125.94, an exercise price of $125, and a time to expiration of 0.0959. We gave the risk-free rate of 4.56 percent as the Treasury bill yield that corresponds to the option's expiration. In the Black-Scholes-Merton model, however, the risk-free rate must be expressed as a continuously compounded yield. The continuously compounded equivalent of 4.56 percent is $\ln(1.0456) = 4.46$. Later in this chapter, we shall take a closer look at the basis for this transformation and see how the volatility can be determined. For now, we will continue to use 0.83 as the standard deviation, which we used in Chapter 4.

The computation of the Black-Scholes-Merton price is a five-step process that is presented in Table 5.2. You first calculate the values of d_1 and d_2. Then you look up $N(d_1)$ and $N(d_2)$ in the normal probability table. Then you plug the values into the formula for C.

Here the theoretical fair value for the June 125 call is $13.21. The call's actual market price is $13.50. This suggests that the call is overpriced. Assuming no transaction costs, an investor should sell the call. The number of calls to sell to form a riskless hedge portfolio that will outperform the risk-free rate is discussed in a later section.

Unfortunately, the Black-Scholes-Merton model is especially sensitive to round-off error, most of which will occur in the normal probability figures. For example, consider the value of d_1 of 0.1743 and d_2 of -0.0827. To look up the d_1 and d_2 in the normal probability table, we were forced to round to two decimal places, obtaining $N(0.17) = 0.5675$ and $N(-0.08) = 0.4681$. Suppose we use Excel's = normsdist( ) function. We simply go to a clean spreadsheet and enter the formulas = normsdist(0.1743) and = normsdist(-0.0828). We obtain the following values:

$$N(0.1743) = 0.5692$$
$$N(-0.0827) = 0.4670.$$

TABLE 5.2 CALCULATING THE BLACK-SCHOLES-MERTON PRICE

$S_0 = 125.94$ $X = 125$ $r_c = 0.0446$ $\sigma = 0.83$ $T = 0.0959$

1 Compute d_1

$$d_1 = \frac{\ln(125.94/125) + (0.0446 + (0.83)^2/2)0.0959}{0.83\sqrt{0.0959}} = 0.1743$$

2 Compute d_2

$$d_2 = 0.1743 - 0.83\sqrt{0.0959} = -0.0827$$

3 Look up $N(d_1)$

$$N(0.17) = 0.5675$$

4 Look up $N(d_2)$

$$N(-0.08) = 1 - N(0.08) = 1 - 0.5319 = 0.4681$$

5 Plug into formula for C

$$C = 125.94(0.5675) - 125e^{-0.0446(0.0959)}(0.4681) = 13.21$$

The option price would then be

$$C = 125.94(0.5692) - 125e^{-0.0446(0.0959)}(0.4670) = 13.56,$$

which is substantially higher and quite close to the market price of $13.50. If anything, the option is now viewed as slightly underpriced in the market. Errors of this sort are common in Black-Scholes-Merton computations.

Although manual calculations are sometimes necessary, we should ultimately calculate option prices using a computer to obtain a more accurate measure for the normal probability. The accompanying Excel spreadsheet BSMbin9e.xls calculates the Black-Scholes-Merton price as well as the binomial price. Software Demonstration 5.1 illustrates how to use BSMbin9e.xls to obtain the Black-Scholes-Merton price.

Characteristics of the Black-Scholes-Merton Formula

Interpretation of the Formula   We see that the Black-Scholes-Merton formula has two main terms on the right-hand side. These terms have their own interpretation. In Chapter 4, we noted that pricing options is conducted as if investors were risk-neutral. A risk-neutral investor prices an asset by finding its expected future value and discounting it at the risk-free rate. For example, suppose you had the opportunity to participate in a coin toss in which you would receive $10 if it lands on heads and $5 if it lands on tails. How much would you pay for it? A risk-neutral investor would pay 0.5($10) + 0.5($5) = $7.50. Nearly all investors, however, are not risk-neutral; rather, they are risk-averse. They would recognize that half the time they would lose $2.50 and half the time they would make $2.50. A loss of $2.50 will hurt more than is offset by a profit of $2.50. Thus, a risk-averse investor would pay less than $7.50 (e.g., $6.75). The difference of $0.75 is the risk premium.

Risk-averse investors determine the prices of the primary assets, stocks and bonds, in the financial markets. They do not determine the prices of derivatives. Rather, the forces of arbitrage determine the prices of derivatives. Given the price of the stock, the price of an option on the stock is determined by combining the stock and option in a risk-free portfolio. The option price is then obtained as a function of the stock price and other variables. Consequently, we can price an option as if investors were risk-neutral—that is, by finding the expected future payoff of the option and discounting it at the risk-free rate.

When we did this in the binomial model, we needed the probabilities p, which was $(1 + r - d)/(u - d)$, and $1 - p$. These are called **risk-neutral probabilities**. We saw that they are not the actual probabilities of the up and down moves. They are what the probabilities would be if investors actually were risk-neutral. In the Black-Scholes-Merton model, the probability of ending up in the money is $N(d_2)$.

TECHNICAL NOTE: Deriving the Black-Scholes-Merton Model Using RiskNeutral Valuation
go to www.cengagebrain.com

Thus, to price this option, we first assume that investors are risk-neutral. Then we find the expected payoff and discount it at the risk-free rate. The expected payoff is the expected value of $Max(0, S_T - X)$, or, in other words, the expected value of:

$$\begin{array}{ll} 0 & \text{if } S_T \le X \\ S_T - X & \text{if } S_T > X. \end{array}$$

To ignore the outcomes where $S_T \le X$, we must calculate the expected value of $S_T - X$ given that S_T is greater than X.

Let us multiply the first term on the right-hand side of the Black-Scholes-Merton formula by $e^{r_c T}$,

$$S_0 N(d_1) e^{r_c T}.$$

This entire expression is the expected value of the stock price at expiration given that the stock price exceeds the exercise price times the probability that the stock price exceeds

SOFTWARE DEMONSTRATION 5.1

Calculating the Black-Scholes-Merton Price with the Excel Spreadsheet BSMbin9e.xls

The Excel spreadsheet BSMbin9e.xls is saved in Excel 97-2003. It calculates both the binomial and Black-Scholes-Merton option pricing models. The Black-Scholes-Merton model provides European call and put prices, as well as the delta, gamma, theta, vega, and rho, known as the option "Greeks."

This spreadsheet is a read-only spreadsheet, meaning that it cannot be saved under the name BSMbin9e.xls, which preserves the original file. You may, however, load the spreadsheet without the read-only feature. The spreadsheet BSMbin9e.xls is available as a download via the product support website. To access it:

1. Go to www.cengagebrain.com.
2. Click on Instructor Resources or Student Resources.
3. Click on the link BSMbin9e.xls.
4. Follow the instructions on the Web page to download and install the spreadsheet.

Now let us calculate an option price. Assume that you want to find the Black-Scholes-Merton price of the option illustrated in this chapter, the DCRB June 125 call. The DCRB stock is at 125.94, the exercise price is 125, the continuously compounded risk-free rate is 4.46%, the standard deviation is 0.83, and the time to expiration is 0.0959 based on 35 days to expiration. There are no dividends on the stock.

The Excel screen that follows contains a section labeled **Inputs:** Each cell that will accept inputs has a double-line border, and the values are in blue. Output cells have a single-line border. Enter the values in the appropriate cells. For greater accuracy, enter the time to expiration as a formula: = 35/365. Leave the dividend yield and the discrete dividends blank or insert zeroes. For the risk-free rate, select "continuous" from the pull-down list. The risk-free rate can be entered with or without decimals, that is, as "0.0446" or "4.46". Volatility and the dividend yield can also be entered in this manner. The spreadsheet automatically calculates the new values anytime an input is changed. Observe your answers in the section labeled **Black-Scholes-Merton Model**.

The software provided with this book contains another spreadsheet called BSMFunction9e.xls, which contains an Excel function for calculating the Black-Scholes-Merton price within a single cell. The instructions to that spreadsheet show you how to drag and drop the function into another spreadsheet where it will be available among your other Excel mathematical functions.

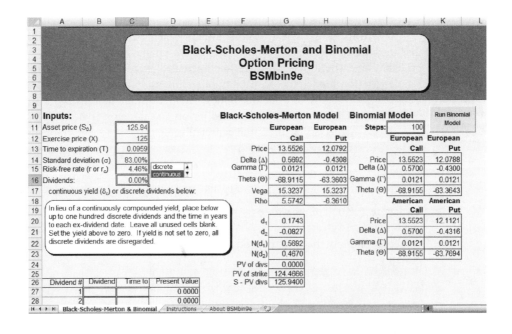

the exercise price at expiration; however, $N(d_1)$ is not that probability. It is just a component of the entire expression. After multiplying by the second term on the right-hand side of the Black-Scholes-Merton formula,

$$-XN(d_2),$$

TECHNICAL NOTE: Probability of Call Expiring in the Money
go to www.cengagebrain.com

is the expected value of the payment of the exercise price at expiration. Specifically, $N(d_2)$ is the probability for risk-neutral investors that X will be paid at expiration. Thus, $-XN(d_2)$ is the expected payout of the exercise price at expiration. Discounting these expressions at the continuously compounded risk-free rate—that is, multiplying by e^{-r_cT}—gives

$$(S_0N(d_1)e^{r_cT} - XN(d_2))e^{-r_cT} = S_0N(d_1) - Xe^{-r_cT}N(d_2),$$

which is the Black-Scholes-Merton formula.

Black-Scholes-Merton Formula and the Lower Bound of a European Call
Recall from Chapter 3 that we showed that the lower bound of a European call is

$$\text{Max}(0,S_0 - Xe^{-r_cT}).$$

For the Black-Scholes-Merton model to conform to this bound, it must always be no lower than this value. When S_0 is very high, d_1 and d_2 approach $+\infty$, which drives $N(d_1)$ and $N(d_2)$ to 1.0. Then the Black-Scholes-Merton formula becomes $S_0 - Xe^{-r_cT}$. When S_0 is very low, d_1 and d_2 approach $-\infty$ and $N(d_1)$ and $N(d_2)$ approach 0. Thus, the formula has a lower bound of $\text{Max}(0,S_0 - Xe^{-r_cT})$. The formula can never fall below this expression because the lowest it can get is zero. When S_0 is very high, the formula is precisely the lower bound.

Next we shall examine the Black-Scholes-Merton formula when some of the variables take on extreme values.

Black-Scholes-Merton Formula When T = 0
It is important to remember that the purpose of the Black-Scholes-Merton formula is to price an option prior to expiration. Yet, it would not be a correct formula if it did not price an option at its expiration as well. We know that at expiration, a call option should be worth $\text{Max}(0,S_T - X)$. Would the Black-Scholes-Merton formula give this value? Yes and no.

Let us move to expiration such that $T = 0$ and the stock price is S_T. First, look at d_1. Notice that we are dividing by zero. Let us write the formula as follows:

$$d_1 = \frac{\ln(S_T/X)}{\sigma\sqrt{T}} + \frac{(r_c + \sigma^2/2)T}{\sigma\sqrt{T}} = \frac{\ln(S_T/X)}{\sigma\sqrt{T}} + \frac{(r_c + \sigma^2/2)\sqrt{T}}{\sigma}.$$

When T goes to zero, the second term on the right-hand side disappears. What happens to the first term? It would appear to be infinite, but is it $1 + \infty$ or $2 - \infty$? That depends on whether S_T is greater than X. The natural log of a number greater than one is positive and the natural log of a number that is positive but less than one is negative. (Try it on your calculator.)

Thus, if $S_T > X$,

$$S_T/X > 1, \ln(S_T/X) > 0, \text{ and } d_1 \text{ approaches } +\infty.$$

If $S_T < X$,

$$S_T/X < 1, \ln(S_T/X) < 0, \text{ and } d_1 \text{ approaches } -\infty.$$

If $S_T = X$,

$$S_T/X = 1, \ln(S_T/X) = 0, \text{ and } d_1 \text{ approaches } -\infty.$$

The third situation can be handled only by application of a special mathematical case called L'Hôpital's rule, but we shall take this result for granted. As it turns out, it will not matter whether we let d_1 approach $+\infty$ or $-\infty$.

If d_1 approaches $+\infty$, then d_2 also approaches $+\infty$. If d_1 approaches $-\infty$, then d_2 also approaches $-\infty$. If d_1 or d_2 approaches $+\infty$, then $N(d_1)$ or $N(d_2)$ approach 1.0. If d_1 or d_2 approaches $-\infty$, then $N(d_1)$ and $N(d_2)$ approach zero. Thus, when T is zero, the Black-Scholes-Merton formula behaves as follows:

If $S_T > X$,

$$S_T/X > 1, \quad \ln(S_T/X) > 0, \quad d_1 \text{ approaches } +\infty, \quad d_2 \text{ approaches } +\infty,$$
$$N(d_1) \text{ approaches } 1.0, \quad N(d_2) \text{ approaches } 1.0,$$
$$\text{and because } e^{-r_c(0)} = 1, \text{ the formula becomes } S_T - X.$$

If $S_T \leq X$,

$$S_T/X > 1, \ln(S_T/X) \leq 0, \quad d_1 \text{ approaches } -\infty, \quad d_2 \text{ approaches } -\infty,$$
$$N(d_1) \text{ approaches } 1.0, \quad N(d_2) \text{ approaches } 0,$$
$$\text{and the formula becomes } 0 - 0 = 0.$$

Thus, the formula becomes $\text{Max}(0, S_T - X)$. Note, however, that if you program the formula on a computer, it will "blow up" upon division by zero. It would have to be coded to recognize the special case of $T = 0$ so that the formula becomes $\text{Max}(0, S_T - X)$.

Black-Scholes-Merton Formula When $S_0 = 0$ Now suppose that prior to expiration, the stock price goes to zero. What has happened to the underlying stock? It must be bankrupt with no chance of recovery, for if there were any chance of it recovering, a nonzero price for the option would imply an arbitrage opportunity. In other words, if there were any chance of the company recovering and the stock price were zero, everyone would want the stock. Thus, the case of $S_0 = 0$ must be reserved for the special situation of a completely dead company. A call option on it must have a value of zero.

Looking again at the preceding formula for d_1, we see that we must take the natural log of 0. There is no such number. We know, however, that when $S_0 < X$, the natural log of S_0/X is negative. As the stock is falling toward zero, the natural log of S_0/X approaches $-\infty$, and we can safely say that its limit is $-\infty$. Thus, we would have d_1 and d_2 approaching $-\infty$, meaning that $N(d_1)$ and $N(d_2)$ would approach 0. This would reduce the Black-Scholes-Merton formula to zero.

As in the case of $T = 0$, a computer program would require special coding to handle this case; otherwise, it would simply attempt to take $\ln(0/X)$, which is undefined, without recognizing that we really want the limit of this value.

Black-Scholes-Merton Formula When $\sigma = 0$ In Chapter 3 (p. 78), we gave an example of a case in which the volatility is zero. If the option is in-the-money, it would be like a zero coupon bond. It would pay off a positive value, and that value would not change. If the option is at- or out-of-the-money, it certainly would not pay off anything later and would have a value of zero today. Thus, when is zero, we need the formula to reflect the payoff of a sure positive amount at expiration or zero depending on whether S_0 is greater than, less than, or equal to zero.

Now let us write the formula for d_1 as follows:

$$d_1 = \frac{\ln(S_0/X)}{\sigma\sqrt{T}} + \frac{(r_c + \sigma^2/2)T}{\sigma\sqrt{T}} = \frac{\ln\left(\dfrac{S_0}{Xe^{-r_cT}}\right)}{\sigma\sqrt{T}} + \frac{(\sigma^2/2)T}{\sigma\sqrt{T}} = \frac{\ln\left(\dfrac{S_0}{Xe^{-r_cT}}\right)}{\sigma\sqrt{T}} + \frac{\sigma\sqrt{T}}{2}.$$

Now when we let σ go to zero, the second term goes to 0, but what happens to the first term? It depends on whether $S_0 > Xe^{-r_cT}$. If that is true, then we are taking the log of a number greater than 1.0, so the first term goes to $+\infty$. If it is not true, then we are taking the log of a number greater than zero and less than one, and the log will be negative. Then the term will go to $-\infty$. Thus, if $S_0 > Xe^{-r_cT}$,

 d_1 approaches $+\infty$, $N(d_1)$ and $N(d_2)$ approach 1.0, and the call price becomes $S_0 - Xe^{-r_cT}$. This means that at expiration, the call holder will pay X, which has a present value of Xe^{-r_cT}, and will receive stock that is currently worth S_0 and will have that value for sure at expiration. Thus, the call is now worth $S_0 - Xe^{-r_cT}$.

If $S_0 \le Xe^{-r_cT}$,

 d_1 approaches $-\infty$, $N(d_1)$ and $N(d_2)$ approach 0.0, and the call price become zero.

Note that it is not exactly the condition of being in-the-money that determines the value of the call when the volatility is zero. In other words, it is not that $S_0 > X$, but rather that $S_0 > Xe^{-r_cT}$. Also, note again that special coding would be required to accommodate this case in a computer program.

Black-Scholes-Merton Formula When X = 0   We saw in Chapter 3 that when $X = 0$, a call is equivalent to the stock. So the Black-Scholes-Merton formula should approach S_0 when that happens. It is easy to see that this will be the case. We would be taking $\ln(+\infty)$, which is $+\infty$. Thus, d_1 and d_2 would approach $+\infty$ and $N(d_1)$ and $N(d_2)$ would approach 1.0. Then with $X = 0$, the formula would become $S_0(1.0) - 0(1.0) = S_0$. Again, special coding would be required in a computer program.

Black-Scholes-Merton Formula When $r_c = 0$ A zero risk-free rate is no special case at all. It is not necessary to have a positive interest rate, and the Black-Scholes-Merton formula does not reduce to any special value.

VARIABLES IN THE BLACK-SCHOLES-MERTON MODEL[2]

We have already learned that there are five variables that affect the option's price: (1) the stock price, (2) the exercise price, (3) the risk-free rate, (4) the time to expiration, and (5) the volatility or standard deviation of the stock. With the Black-Scholes-Merton model, we can see the effects of different values of these variables on the option price. The sensitivities of some of the variables, in particular, are so important that they are quantified and given Greek names. Accordingly, they are referred to as *the Greeks*.

Stock Price

A higher stock price should lead to a higher call price. Suppose the stock price is $130 instead of $125.94. This gives values of $N(d_1)$ and $N(d_2)$ of 0.6171 and 0.5162, respectively, which gives a value of C of $15.96, which is higher than the previously obtained value of $13.55.

The value of our DCRB call for a broad range of stock prices is illustrated in Figure 5.6. Note that this graph is similar to Figure 3.5, where we showed what a European call price curve should look like.

---

[2]All of the calculations in this section were done using the spreadsheet BSMbin9e.xls. In addition, we start with a base value of the DCRB June 125 call of the Black-Scholes price of 13.55.

FIGURE 5.6 The Call Price as a Function of the Stock Price DCRB June 125; $r_c = 0.0446$, T = 0.0959, σ = 0.83

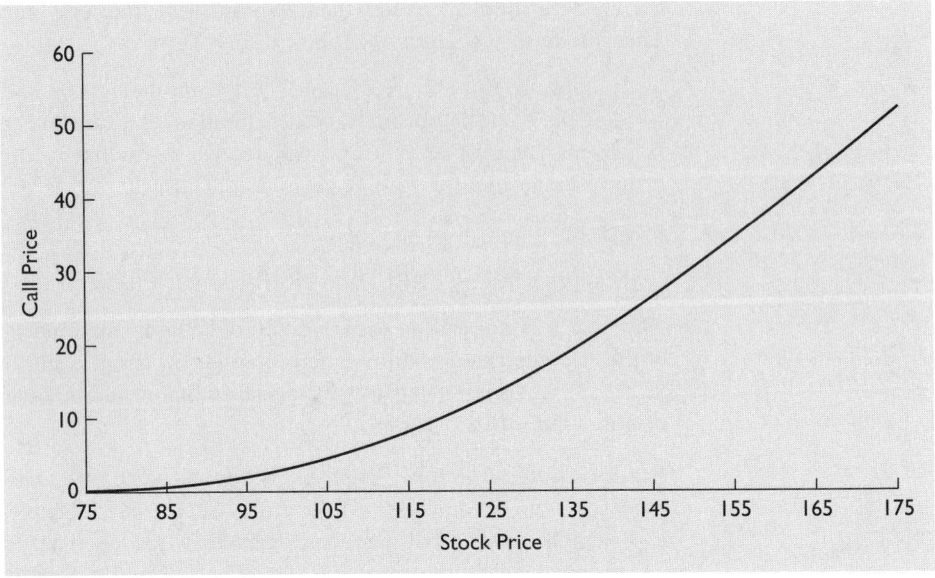

The relationship between the stock price and the call price is often expressed as a single value, referred to as its **delta**. The delta is obtained from the calculus procedure of differentiating the call price with respect to the stock price. The mathematical details of the procedure are a bit technical, but the result is quite simple:

> The delta is approximately the change in the option price for a small change in the stock price. It is obtained as $N(d_1)$ from the Black-Scholes-Merton model.

$$\text{Call } Delta = N(d_1).$$

Because $N(d_1)$ is a probability, the delta must range from zero to one.

Because of the assumptions behind the calculus, the delta is the change in the call price for a *very small* change in the stock price. Here our delta is 0.5692. This is somewhat loosely defined to mean that the option price moves 56.92 percent of the move in the stock price. Technically, this is correct only for a very small move in the stock price. For example, we noted previously that if the stock price were $130, a $4.06 move, the call price would be $15.96, a move of $2.41, which is about 59 percent of the stock price move. Thus, although delta is a very important measure of the option's sensitivity to the stock price, it is precise only if the stock price makes a very small move.

Recall that the delta ranges from zero to one. When the stock price is high relative to the exercise price, the delta is closer to one; when the stock price is low relative to the exercise price, the delta is closer to zero. The relationship between the delta and the level of the stock price for the DCRB June 125 call option is illustrated in Figure 5.7.

The delta also changes as the option evolves through its life. In other words, even if the stock price did not change, the delta would change. As the life of the option decreases, for in-the-money call options, the delta moves toward one; for out-of-the-money call options, the delta moves toward zero. This relationship appears in Figure 5.8, which illustrates how the deltas of two DCRB calls change as the option gets closer to its expiration, assuming that the stock price does not change. We look at the June 120, which is well in-the-money, and the June 130, which is well out-of-the-money. Notice how the deltas of these options change slowly until the last week of the options' lives, but then converge quickly toward 1.0 and 0.0.

FIGURE 5.7 The Delta of a Call as a Function of the Stock Price DCRB June 125; $S_0 = 125.94$, $r_c = 0.0446$, $\sigma = 0.83$

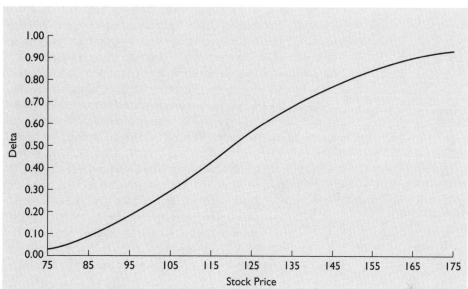

FIGURE 5.8 The Delta of a Call as a Function of the Time in Days to Expiration DCRB June 125; $S_0 = 125.94$, $r_c = 0.0446$, $\sigma = 0.83$

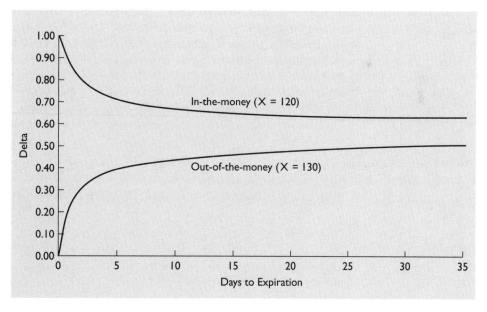

Recall from our discussion of the binomial model how we bought h shares of stock and sold one call. As long as we adjusted the number of options per share according to the formula for h, we maintained a risk-free hedge. In the Black-Scholes-Merton world, this is called a **delta hedge** and must be done continuously. A delta-hedged position is said to be **delta neutral**. For example, the stock price is \$125.94. Recall that the delta is 0.5692, so we construct a delta hedge by buying 569 shares and selling 1,000 calls. If the stock price falls by a small amount (for instance, $0.01), we shall lose $0.01(569) = $5.69 on the stock. The option price, however, will fall by approximately $0.01(0.569), or $0.00569. Because we have 1,000 calls, the options collectively will fall by $0.00569 (1,000) = $5.69. Because we are short the options, we gain $5.69, which offsets the loss on the stock. A similar result is obtained if the price goes up. Once the price changes or time elapses, however, which it does continuously, the delta changes, a new hedge ratio must be constructed, and shares or options must be purchased or sold. If this is done properly, then a risk-free return is earned, provided the call was correctly priced at the start. Of course, in practice, it is impossible to do a perfect delta hedge because one cannot trade continuously. We shall see this more explicitly later.

> The gamma is the change in the delta for a change in the stock price. Its value can be obtained from the Black-Scholes-Merton model.

An additional risk in delta hedging is that the stock price will not change by a very small amount. For example, suppose the stock went up to $130 and the call went to $15.96, as in our example. Then our 569 shares of stock would have gained $4.06 (569) = $2,310. Our 1,000 calls would have gone up by ($15.96 − $13.55)(1,000) = $2,410. Because we are short the calls, the overall position would have suffered a loss.

This type of risk is captured by the option's **gamma**. The gamma is the change in the delta for a very small change in the stock price. The formula for gamma is

$$Call\ Gamma = \frac{e^{-d_1^2/2}}{S_0\sigma\sqrt{2\pi T}}.$$

In our example with the stock at 125.94, the gamma is calculated as $e^{-(0.1742)^2/2}/$ $(125.94)(0.83)\sqrt{2(3.14159)(0.0959)} = 0.0123$. This suggests that if the stock increased to $130, the delta would go from 0.569 to 0.569 + (130 − 125.94)(0.0123) = 0.6189. If the stock goes to $130, the actual delta is 0.6171. Of course, the gamma provides only an estimate of the change in the delta, but in this case, the estimate is fairly accurate.

The larger the gamma is, the more sensitive the delta is to a stock price change and the harder it is to maintain a delta neutral position. The gamma is always positive and is largest when the stock price is near the exercise price. When the stock price is high or low relative to the exercise price, the gamma is near zero, as shown in Figure 5.9. The gamma changes as the option approaches expiration. If the option is approximately

FIGURE 5.9 The Gamma of a Call Price as a Function of the Stock Price DCRB June 125; $r_c = 0.0446$, T $= 0.0959$, $\sigma = 0.83$

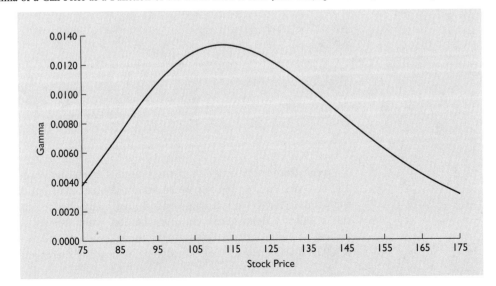

FIGURE 5.10 The Gamma of a Call Price as a Function of the Time in Days to Expiration DCRB June 125; $S_0 = 125.94$, $r_c = 0.0446$, $\sigma = 0.83$

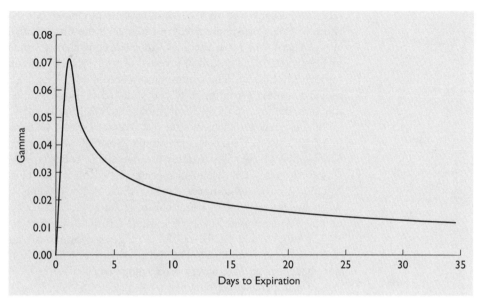

at-the-money, like our DCRB June 125 call, the uncertainly of whether it will finish in- or out-of-the-money causes the gamma to increase dramatically as expiration approaches, as shown in Figure 5.10.

Remember that the gamma represents the uncertainly of the delta. A large gamma makes it harder to delta hedge because the delta is changing more rapidly and is more sensitive to large stock price movements. In a later section of this chapter, we will illustrate more explicitly the nature and solution of this problem.

Exercise Price

Now let us change the exercise price to $130, which should decrease the call's value. Specifically, let us examine the June 130 call. We retain all of the other original values, including the stock price of $125.94. The values of d_1 and d_2 are 0.0217 and −0.2353, respectively. The normal probabilities are 0.5087 and 0.4070, and the resulting call price is $11.38, which is less than the original $13.55.

The change in the call price for a very small change in the exercise price is negative and is given by the formula $-e^{-r_c T} N(d_2)$. The exercise price of a given option does not change, however, so this concept is meaningful only in considering how much more or less a call with a different exercise price would be worth.[3] In that case, the difference in the exercise price would probably be too large to apply the preceding formula, which, as noted, holds only when X changes by a very small amount.

Risk-Free Rate

Chapter 3 showed how to identify the risk-free rate for the purpose of examining an option's boundary conditions. Within the Black-Scholes-Merton framework, the risk-free rate must be expressed as a continuously compounded rate.

Earlier in the chapter, we distinguished the simple or discrete return on a stock from the continuously compounded or log return on a stock. A similar distinction exists for

---

[3]It is possible to create an option in which the exercise price changes randomly, but we shall not cover this at this level.

interest rates. A simple or discrete risk-free rate assumes only annual compounding. A continuously compounded rate assumes that interest compounds continuously. A simple rate can be converted to a continuously compounded rate by taking the natural logarithm of 1 plus the simple rate. For example, if the simple rate is 6 percent, $100 invested at 6 percent for one year becomes $106. The equivalent continuously compounded rate is $\ln(1.06) = 0.0583$. Thus, $100 invested at 5.83 percent compounded continuously grows to $106 in one year. The continuously compounded rate is always less than the simple rate. To convert a continuously compounded rate to a simple rate, use the exponential function, the inverse of the logarithmic function (that is, $e^{0.0583} - 1 = 0.06$).

In our previous problem, the risk-free rate was 4.46 percent. We obtained this as $\ln(1.0456)$, where 0.0456 was the simple rate that we obtained in Chapter 3. The Black-Scholes-Merton formula requires the use of the continuously compounded rate, so we specify the rate as r_c where it appears in two places in the formula. Note that in the equation for C, we compute $Xe^{-r_c T}$, which is the present value of the exercise price when the interest rate is continuously compounded. The same value would have been obtained had we used $X(1 + r)^{-T}$, where r is the discrete rate.

The value of our DCRB call for a range of continuously compounded risk-free rates is illustrated in Figure 5.11. The call price is nearly linear in the risk-free rate and does not change much over a very broad range of risk-free rates. For example, at a risk-free rate of 4.46 percent, we obtained a call price of $13.55. If we raised the risk-free rate to 12 percent, a rather large change, the call price would increase to only $13.98. The sensitivity of the call price to the risk-free rate is called its **rho** and is given by the formula

$$Call\ Rho = TXe^{-r_c T}N(d_2).$$

The rho is the change in the option price for a change in the risk-free rate. It can be obtained from the Black-Scholes-Merton model.

In our original problem with the risk-free rate of 4.46 percent, the rho would be $(0.0959)125e^{-0.0446(0.0959)}(0.4670) = 5.57$. If we let the risk-free rate go from 0.0446 to 0.12, the rho would predict a change in the call price of $(0.12 - 0.0446)(5.57) = 0.42$. The actual change was $13.98 - 13.55 = \$0.43$. The nearly linear relationship between the

FIGURE 5.11   **The Call Price as a Function of the Risk-Free Rate DCRB June 125; $S_0 = 125.94$, $T = 0.0959$, $\sigma = 0.83$**

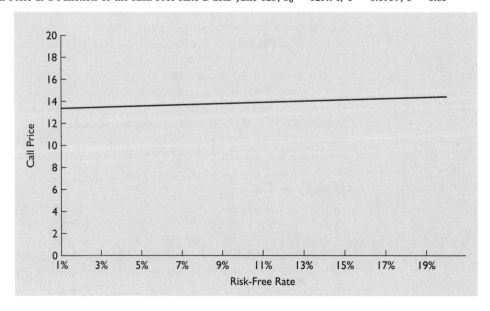

FIGURE 5.12 The Rho of a Call as a Function of the Stock Price DCRB June 125; $r_c = 0.0446$, T $= 0.0959$, $\sigma = 0.83$

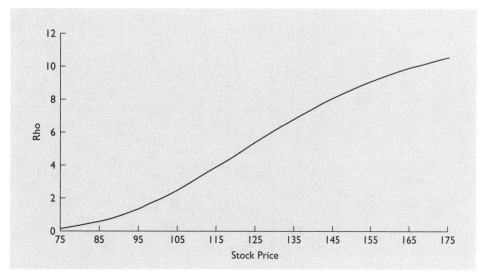

option price and the risk-free rate makes the rho a fairly accurate measure of the option's sensitivity to interest rate changes.

One should keep in mind, however, that the Black-Scholes-Merton model assumes that interest rates do not change during the life of the option. More sophisticated models are required to accurately capture the effects of changing interest rates.

The rho also changes with the level of the stock price, being higher the higher the stock price, as shown in Figure 5.12.

Volatility (or Standard Deviation)

As covered in Chapter 3, the volatility (or standard deviation) is a critical variable in valuing options. In the Black-Scholes-Merton model, the volatility is the standard deviation of the continuously compounded return on the stock. Because the volatility is the only unobservable variable, we devote an entire section later in the chapter to estimating its value.

Figure 5.13 shows the option price for a range of volatilities. Because in-, at-, and out-of-the-money calls behave somewhat differently with respect to volatility, we show the graph for options with exercise prices of 120, 125, and 130. Recall that our 125 call had a price of $13.55 when its volatility was 0.83. If we raise that volatility to 0.90, the call price is about $14.62. If we lower the volatility to 0.75, the call price is about $12.33. These are fairly large changes in the call price over a fairly small range of volatilities.

The sensitivity of the call price to a *very small* change in volatility is called its **vega** and is given as[4]

> The vega is the change in the option price for a change in the volatility. It can be obtained from the Black-Scholes-Merton model.

$$\text{Call } Vega = \frac{S_0 \sqrt{T} e^{-d_1^2/2}}{\sqrt{2\pi}}.$$

In our original problem, the vega is $125.94\sqrt{0.0959}e^{-(0.1743)^2/2}/\sqrt{2(3.14159)} = 15.32$. This suggests that if volatility changes by a very small amount (e.g., 0.01), the call price will change by $15.32(0.01) = 0.15$.

---

[4]Although vega is typically included as one of the option Greeks, the word *vega*, unlike delta, gamma, theta, and rho, is not actually Greek. Evidently, someone simply named the effect vega, associating the *v* with *volatility*. In order to make this effect truly a Greek word, it has also been called **kappa** and **lambda**.

FIGURE 5.13 The Call Price as a Function of the Volatility DCRB June 125; $S_0 = 125.94$, $r_c = 0.0446$, T = 0.0959

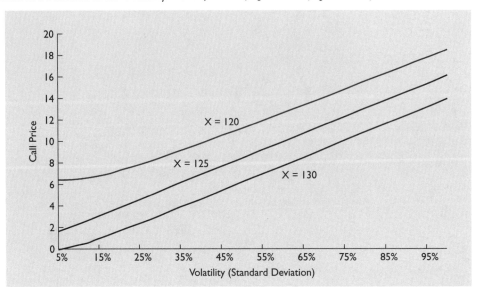

The actual call price change if volatility went to 0.84, an increase of 0.01, would be 0.16. If the volatility increased 0.12 to 0.95, the vega predicts that the call price would increase by 15.32(0.12) = 1.84, when the actual call price would go to $15.39, an increase of $15.39 − $13.55 = $1.84. This accuracy is due to the fact that, as Figure 5.13 illustrates, the volatility and the option price are nearly linear if the option is nearly at-the-money. This result will be useful in a later section. As Figure 5.13 shows, however, if the option is not at-the-money, the relationship is not quite linear and the vega will not capture all of the risk of a changing volatility.

Figure 5.14 illustrates how the vega changes with the level of the stock price for our DCRB June 125 call. Notice that when the stock price is near the exercise price, the vega is largest, meaning that the option price is more sensitive to changes in the volatility. When the stock price is large or small relative to the exercise price, the vega is smallest and the option price is less sensitive to changes in the volatility.

Regardless of the option's moneyness and whether the volatility change is large or small, the option is still quite sensitive to changes in the volatility. The Black-Scholes-Merton model does not actually permit the volatility to change while the option is alive. There are more complex models that account for this phenomenon. Nonetheless, the concept of changing volatility is still considered by option traders who use the Black-Scholes-Merton model. This vega risk can be hedged by using an offsetting position in another instrument, such as another call, based on its vega risk.

Time to Expiration

The relationship between the option price and the time to expiration is illustrated in Figure 5.15. The graph should be viewed from right to left. The decrease in the value of the call as time elapses is the time value decay, as we discussed in Chapter 3. The rate of time value decay is measured by the option's **theta**, which is given as

$$\text{Call } Theta = -\frac{S_0 \sigma e^{-d_1^2/2}}{2\sqrt{2\pi T}} - r_c X e^{-r_c T} N(d_2).$$

FIGURE 5.14 The Vega of a Call as a Function of the Stock Price DCRB June 125; $r_c = 0.0446$, $T = 0.0959$, $\sigma = 0.83$

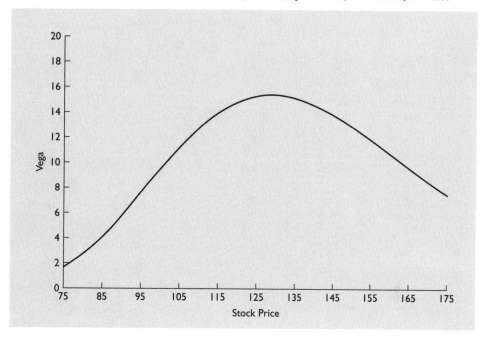

FIGURE 5.15 The Call Price as a Function of the Time in Days to Expiration DCRB June 125; $S_0 = 125.94$, $r_c = 0.0446$, $T = 0.0959$, $\sigma = 0.83$

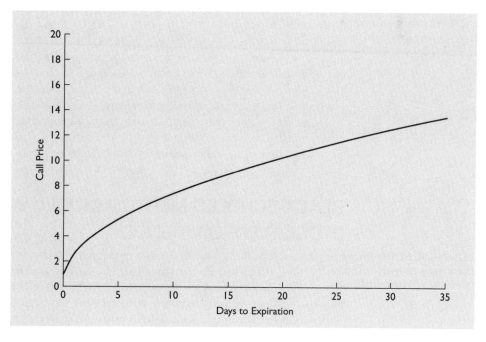

FIGURE 5.16 The Theta of a Call as a Function of the Stock Price DCRB June 125; $r_c = 0.0446$, $T = 0.0959$, $\sigma = 0.83$

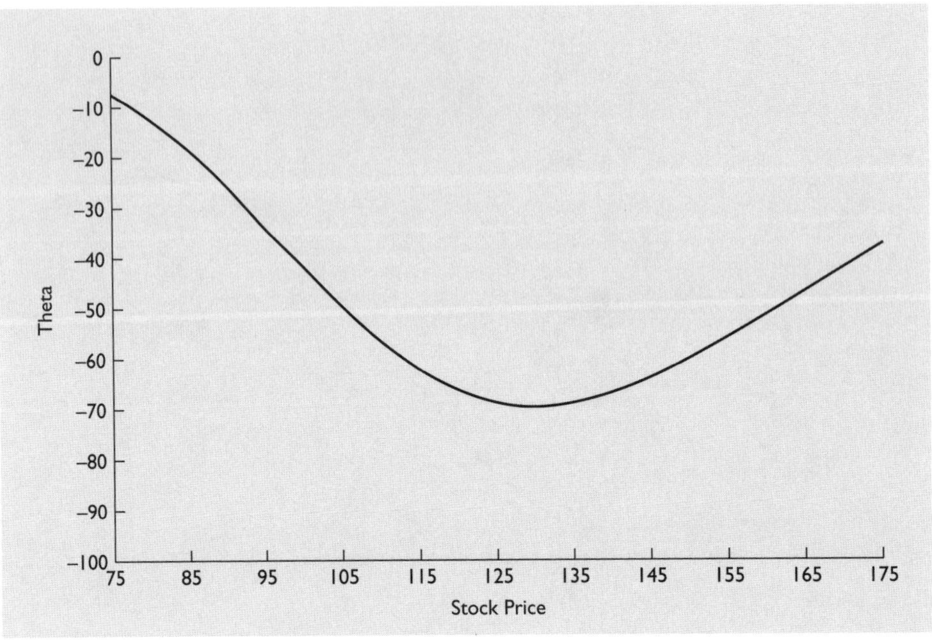

The theta is the change in the option price for a change in time. It measures the time value of decay and can be obtained from the Black-Scholes-Merton model.

For the June 125, d_1 is 0.1743, $N(d_2)$ is 0.4670, and theta is $-125.94(0.83)$ $e^{-(0.1743)^2/2}/2\sqrt{2(3.1459)(0.0959)}$ $-$ $(0.0446)125e^{-0.0446(0.0959)}(0.4670) =$ -68.91. Thus, in one week, the time to expiration goes from 0.0959 to $28/365 = 0.0767$ and the option price would be predicted to change by $(0.0959 - 0.0767)(-68.91) = -\$1.32$. The actual price changes to \$12.16, so the change is \$12.16 $-$ \$13.55 $= -\$1.39$. Of course, the theta is most accurate only for a very small change in time, but the predicted price change is still very close to the actual price change. Because time itself is not a source of risk, however, it makes no sense to worry about it, but, of course, that does not mean we do not need to know the rate of time value decay.

Figure 5.16 shows that the theta is a u-shaped function of the stock price, being directly related for out-of-the-money calls and inversely related for in-the-money calls. The rate of time value decay is greatest for at-the-money calls.

BLACK-SCHOLES-MERTON MODEL WHEN THE STOCK PAYS DIVIDENDS

TECHNICAL NOTE: Derivatives of the Black-Scholes-Merton Model
go to www.cengagebrain.com

The Black-Scholes-Merton model in the form we have seen so far applies to stocks that do not pay dividends, such as DCRB. As we saw in Chapter 3, dividends reduce the call option's price and may induce early exercise if the options are American. Incorporating dividends into the Black-Scholes-Merton model for European options is not difficult. There are several suggested approaches, none of which has proven superior to the others. We shall discuss two here.

Known Discrete Dividends

Suppose a stock pays a dividend of D_t at some time during the option's life. This dividend is payable after a time period t, which is defined by the ex-dividend date. The dividend is assumed to be known with certainly. If we make a small adjustment to the stock price, the Black-Scholes-Merton model will remain applicable to the pricing of this option.

> The Black-Scholes-Merton model can price European options on stocks with known discrete dividends by subtracting the present value of the dividends from the stock price.

The adjustment is one we have done several times before. We subtract the present value of the dividend from the stock price and use the adjusted stock price in the formula. Let the stock price in the Black-Scholes-Merton formula be S_0' defined as $S_0' = S_0 - D_t e^{-r_c t}$. If there were other dividends during the life of the option, their present values would be subtracted as well.

As noted earlier, the DCRB stock does not pay a dividend. For illustrative purposes, however, we will now assume that it pays a $2 dividend and has an ex-dividend date of June 4, 21 days later. All other variables are the same. The procedure for calculating the Black-Scholes-Merton price is laid out in Table 5.3. Note that now the call price is lower as we would expect.

The Excel spreadsheet BSMbin9e.xls, which is illustrated in Software Demonstration 5.1, lets you enter up to 100 known discrete dividends. You simply enter the dividend amount and the time in years to the ex-dividend date. Be sure that you do not enter a yield; if you do, the software will ignore the discrete dividends and use the yield. For the DCRB June 125 call with a $2 dividend, the spreadsheet gives the more accurate answer of $N(d_1) = 0.5447$, $N(d_2) = 0.4424$, and $C = \$12.44$.

Known Continuous Dividend Yield

Another approach to the problem of adjusting the Black-Scholes-Merton formula for dividends on the stock is to assume that the dividend is paid continuously at a known

---

TABLE 5.3 CALCULATING THE BLACK-SCHOLES-MERTON PRICE WHEN THERE ARE KNOWN DISCRETE DIVIDENDS

$S_0 = 125.94$ $\quad\quad$ $X = 125$ $\quad\quad$ $r_c = 0.0446$ $\quad\quad$ $\sigma = 0.83$ $\quad\quad$ $T = 0.0959$

One dividend of 2, ex-dividend in 21 days (May 14 to June 4)

1. Determine the amounts of the dividend(s).
$$D_t = \$2$$

2. Determine the time(s) to the ex-dividend date(s).
$$21 \text{ days, so } t = 21/365 = 0.0575$$

3. Subtract the present value of the dividend(s) from the stock price to obtain S_0'.
$$\$125.94 - 2e^{-0.0446(0.0575)} = \$123.9451$$

4. Compute d_1 using S_0' in place of S_0.
$$d_1 = \frac{\ln(123.9451/125) + (0.0446 + (0.83)^2/2)0.0959}{0.83\sqrt{0.0959}} = 0.1122$$

5. Compute d_2.
$$d_2 = 0.1122 - 0.83\sqrt{0.0959} = -0.1449$$

6. Look up $N(d_1)$.
$$N(0.11) = 0.5438$$

7. Look up $N(d_2)$.
$$N(-0.14) = 1 - N(0.14) = 1 - 0.5557 = 0.4443$$

8. Plug into formula for C, using S_0' in place of S_0.
$$C = 123.9451(0.5438) - 125e^{-0.0446(0.0959)}(0.4443) = 12.10$$

yield. This method assumes that the dividend accrues continuously, which means that a dividend is constantly being paid. We express the annual rate as a percentage, δ_c. For example, let the DCRB stock have an annual continuously compounded dividend yield of $\delta_c = 0.04$. Given the current stock price of $125.94, the annual dividend is $125.94(0.04) = $5.04. This dividend is not paid in four quarterly installments of $1.26 each; rather, it accrues continuously in very small increments that are reinvested and that accumulate over the year to $5.04.[5] Because the stock price fluctuates throughout the year, the actual dividend can change but the yield will remain constant. Thus, this model does not require the assumption that the dividend is known or is constant; it requires only that the dividend being paid at that instant be a constant percentage of the stock price.

The adjustment procedure requires substituting the value S_0' for S_0 in the Black-Scholes-Merton model, where $S_0' = S_0 e^{-\delta_c T}$. The expression $S_0(1 - e^{-\delta_c T})$ is the present value of the dividends. Subtracting this from S_0 gives S_0', as stated above. The adjustment removes the present value of the dividends during the option's life from the stock price. Table 5.4 illustrates the computation of the option price. Again, we see that the effect of dividends is to lower the option's price under what it would be if there were no dividends. There is, of course, no assurance that the discrete and continuous dividend adjustments will give equivalent option prices. Because the DCRB stock does not pay dividends, the dividend amount and the yield are merely assumptions made for illustration purposes and are not intended to be equivalent.

The assumption of a continuous dividend is unrealistic for most options on stocks; however, the convenience of using a single yield figure in lieu of obtaining the precise dividends could justify its use for many purposes. For options on stocks, however, only a few dividends are paid over the life of most options; thus, the discrete dividend adjustment is not especially difficult. For index options, however, the use of a yield may be

> The Black-Scholes-Merton model can price European options on stocks that pay dividends at a known continuous rate by discounting the stock price by that rate.

TABLE 5.4   CALCULATING THE BLACK-SCHOLES-MERTON PRICE WHEN THERE ARE CONTINUOUS DIVIDENDS

$S_0 = \$125.94$ $X = 125$ $r_c = 0.0446$ $\sigma = 0.83$ $T = 0.0959$ $\delta_c = 0.04$

1. Compute the stock price minus the present value of the dividends as $S_0' = S_0 e^{-\delta_c T}$.

$$\$125.94 e^{-0.04(0.0959)} = \$125.4578$$

2. Compute d_1 using S_0' in place of S_0

$$d_1 = \frac{\ln(125.4578/125) + (0.0446 + (0.83)^2/2)0.0959}{0.83\sqrt{0.0959}} = 0.1594$$

3. Compute d_2.

$$d_2 = 0.1594 - 0.83\sqrt{0.0959} = -0.0976$$

4. Look up $N(d_1)$.

$$N(0.16) = 0.5636$$

5. Look up $N(d_2)$.

$$N(-0.10) = 1 - N(0.10) = 1 - 0.5398 = 0.4602$$

6. Plug into formula for C, using S_0' in place of S_0.

$$C = 125.4578(0.5636) - 125 e^{-0.0446(0.0959)}(0.4602) = 13.43$$

---

[5]The quarterly dividend of $1.26 and the annual dividend of $5.04 are approximations and are not precisely equivalent to the continuously compounded yield of 4 percent due to differences in assumptions about the times and reinvestment of the dividends.

preferable. The dividends on the component stocks in the index would be paid more or less continuously; thus, it would be difficult to obtain an accurate day-by-day figure for the dividends.[6]

The Excel spreadsheet BSMbin9e.xls, which is illustrated in Software Demonstration 5.1, lets you enter a continuous dividend yield or a foreign interest rate when calculating an option price. Here the DCRB June 125 call with a dividend yield of 4 percent has a price of $13.28.

Black-Scholes-Merton Model and Currency Options

In Chapters 3 and 4, we observed that the case of a stock with a dividend is similar to a currency that pays interest. Consequently, option pricing models that incorporate dividends on the underlying stock can be easily adapted to price options on currencies. Under the assumption that the currency pays interest at the continuously compounded rate of ρ_c, the Black-Scholes-Merton model with continuous dividends can be used with ρ_c in place of δ_c. This model is sometimes referred to as the Garman-Kohlhagen model, named after the two people who first recognized that the Black-Scholes-Merton model could be adapted to currency options. An end-of-chapter problem will give you an opportunity to apply this result.

It is important to note that the foreign interest rate is not used for discounting future payments on the option; rather, it is used to account for the additional earnings potential from holding foreign currency. Thus, ρ_c is used only in place of δ_c.

BLACK-SCHOLES-MERTON MODEL AND SOME INSIGHTS INTO AMERICAN CALL OPTIONS

None of the adjustments here make the Black-Scholes-Merton model capable of pricing American options. Now having seen the Black-Scholes-Merton model, however, we can use it to gain a greater understanding of why call options might be exercised early.

Consider our DCRB options. Let us take an option that is well in-the-money, the June 120. Using the Black-Scholes-Merton model and the spreadsheet BSMbin9e.xls, we would find this option to be worth $16.03. Let us change things around a little. Suppose the stock is going to go ex-dividend in another instant. How large of a dividend would it take to justify exercising it before it goes ex-dividend? Let us assume that this is the last dividend the stock will pay during the option's life; so after the stock has gone ex-dividend, we can safely use the Black-Scholes-Merton model to price the option.

In Table 5.5, we try dividend levels of $5 to $25 in $5 increments. When the stock goes ex-dividend, it will fall by the amount of the dividend. Then we can compute again the option value using the Black-Scholes-Merton model, remembering that once the stock goes ex-dividend, the Black-Scholes-Merton model will correctly price the call because there are no more dividends during the option's remaining life. The value obtained if you exercise the option just before the stock goes ex-dividend is always the intrinsic value, here $5.94. The stock will then go ex-dividend and fall by the amount of the dividend. The third column shows the ex-dividend price of the call. You would exercise the option if the intrinsic value exceeded the ex-dividend option value. Here it would take a dividend of between $20 and $25 to justify early exercise. This would be an exceptionally large dividend, almost 20 percent of the stock price. Thus, if the DCRB option were American, it is unlikely that it would be exercised. A primary reason for this is that DCRB's volatility is so high that option holders would be throwing away a great deal of time value by exercising early.

---

[6]Dividends and ex-dividend dates are available from several data services for a fee. See, for example, www.ex-dividend.com.

TABLE 5.5 THE EARLY EXERCISE DECISION

$S_0 = 125.94$	$X = 120$	$r_c = 0.0446$	$\sigma = 0.83$	$T = 0.0959$
DIVIDEND	VALUE IF EXERCISED[1]	VALUE WHEN STOCK GOES EX-DIVIDEND[2]		EXERCISE?
0	5.94	16.03		No
5	5.94	13.03		No
10	5.94	10.35		No
15	5.94	7.99		No
20	5.94	5.98		No
25	5.94	4.32		Yes

[1]The intrinsic value before the stock goes ex-dividend.
[2]Computed using the Black-Scholes-Merton model, with an ex-dividend stock price of $125.94 − dividend.

Note that we never calculated the value of the option at any time before it went ex-dividend. This would require an American option pricing model. At that instant before the stock goes ex-dividend, if the dividend was not large enough to justify early exercise, the American call price would sell for the European call price. If the dividend was large enough to justify early exercise, the American call price would be $5.94, the intrinsic value. Well before the ex-dividend instant, however, it is much more difficult to price the option because the stock price at the ex-dividend instant is unknown. Thus, we would require an American option pricing model. In addition, if there were more than one dividend, we would need an American option pricing model to account for the remaining dividends. American option pricing models are generally beyond the scope of this book. Recall, however, that we covered the binomial model and demonstrated how it can be used to price American options. This is the preferred method used by professional option traders. As covered in Chapter 4, your Excel spreadsheet BSMbin9e.xls will calculate American call prices using the binomial model.

Estimating the Volatility

Obtaining a reliable estimate of the volatility (or standard deviation) is difficult. Moreover, the Black-Scholes-Merton model and option prices in general are extremely sensitive to that estimate. There are two approaches to estimating the volatility: the historical volatility and the implied volatility.

Historical Volatility

The **historical volatility** estimate is based on the assumption that the volatility that prevailed over the recent past will continue to hold in the future. First, we take a sample of returns on the stock over a recent period. We convert these returns to continuously compounded returns. Then we compute the standard deviation of the continuously compounded returns.

The returns can be daily, weekly, monthly, or any desired time interval. If we use daily returns, the result will be a daily standard deviation. To obtain the annualized standard deviation the model requires, we must multiply the variance by the number of trading days in a year, which is about 250, or multiply the standard deviation by $\sqrt{250}$. If we use monthly returns, the result will be a monthly variance (or standard deviation) and must be multiplied by 12 (or $\sqrt{12}$) to obtain an annualized figure.

There is no minimum number of observations; a sample size of about 60 is adequate in most cases. The trade-off in selecting a sample size is that the more observations one uses, the further back in time one must go. The further back one goes, the more likely the volatility will change. In the example used here, we do not use many historical observations, but this is primarily to keep the computations brief.

Assume that we have a series of J continuously compounded returns, where each return is identified as r_t^c, which equals $\ln(1 + r_t)$, and t goes from 1 to J. First, we calculate the mean return as

> The historical volatility is estimated from a sample of recent continuously compounded returns on the stock.

$$\bar{r}^c = \sum_{t=1}^{J} r_t^c / J.$$

Then the variance is

$$\sigma^2 = \frac{\sum_{t=1}^{J} (r_t^c - \bar{r}^c)^2}{J - 1} = \frac{\sum_{t=1}^{J} (r_t^c)^2 - (\sum_{t=1}^{J} r_t^c)^2 / J}{J - 1}.$$

Note that we divide the sum of the squared deviations around the mean by J − 1. This is the appropriate divisor if the observations are a sample taken from a larger population. This adjustment is necessary for the estimate of the sample variance to be an unbiased estimate of the population variance.

Table 5.6 illustrates this procedure for the DCRB stock using daily closing prices. The simple return, r_t, is computed and converted to a continuously compounded return, r_t^c.

TABLE 5.6 ESTIMATING THE HISTORICAL VOLATILITY OF DCRB

DATE	PRICE	r_t	r_t^c	$(r_t^c - \bar{r}^c)^2$
February 17	80.19	—	—	—
February 18	86.50	0.0787	0.0757	0.004650
February 19	88.00	0.0173	0.0172	0.000093
February 22	87.56	−0.0050	−0.0050	0.000158
February 23	87.19	−0.0042	−0.0042	0.000139
February 24	88.94	0.0201	0.0199	0.000152
February 25	89.56	0.0070	0.0069	0.000000
February 26	86.69	−0.0320	−0.0326	0.001610
March 1	87.06	0.0043	0.0043	0.000011
March 2	86.25	−0.0093	−0.0093	0.000286
March 3	86.94	0.0080	0.0080	0.000000
March 4	90.88	0.0453	0.0443	0.001352
March 5	90.13	−0.0083	−0.0083	0.000251
March 8	92.81	0.0297	0.0293	0.000473
March 9	95.81	0.0323	0.0318	0.000588
March 10	96.13	0.0033	0.0033	0.000018
March 11	102.00	0.0611	0.0593	0.002674
March 12	104.94	0.0288	0.0284	0.000435
March 15	109.06	0.0393	0.0385	0.000958
March 16	116.13	0.0648	0.0628	0.003053
March 17	119.25	0.0269	0.0265	0.000359
March 18	130.00	0.0901	0.0863	0.006202

(continued)

TABLE 5.6 (CONTINUED)				
DATE	PRICE	r_t	r_t^c	$(r_t^c - \bar{r}_t^c)^2$
March 19	121.00	−0.0692	−0.0717	0.006289
March 22	117.13	−0.0320	−0.0325	0.001605
March 23	126.50	0.0800	0.0770	0.004816
March 24	125.69	−0.0064	−0.0064	0.000195
March 25	132.38	0.0532	0.0519	0.001963
March 26	144.50	0.0916	0.0876	0.006407
March 29	147.00	0.0173	0.0172	0.000092
March 30	150.00	0.0204	0.0202	0.000160
March 31	166.94	0.1129	0.1070	0.009889
April 1	167.50	0.0034	0.0033	0.000018
April 5	158.00	−0.0567	−0.0584	0.004349
April 6	160.50	0.0158	0.0157	0.000066
April 7	159.94	−0.0035	−0.0035	0.000122
April 8	157.88	−0.0129	−0.0130	0.000421
April 9	159.31	0.0091	0.0090	0.000002
April 12	150.88	−0.0529	−0.0544	0.003835
April 13	143.88	−0.0464	−0.0475	0.003032
April 14	139.75	−0.0287	−0.0291	0.001346
April 15	115.88	−0.1708	−0.1873	0.037970
April 16	128.69	0.1105	0.1049	0.009466
April 19	142.75	0.1093	0.1037	0.009241
April 20	148.69	0.0416	0.0408	0.001103
April 21	147.00	−0.0114	−0.0114	0.000361
April 22	162.00	0.1020	0.0972	0.008029
April 23	153.00	−0.0556	−0.0572	0.004188
April 26	143.00	−0.0654	−0.0676	0.005648
April 27	141.38	−0.0113	−0.0114	0.000359
April 28	142.75	0.0097	0.0096	0.000004
April 29	133.13	−0.0674	−0.0698	0.005979
April 30	127.13	−0.0451	−0.0461	0.002881
May 3	129.75	0.0206	0.0204	0.000165
May 4	119.75	−0.0771	−0.0802	0.007702
May 5	118.19	−0.0130	−0.0131	0.000427
May 6	128.31	0.0856	0.0822	0.005565
May 7	141.44	0.1023	0.0974	0.008076
May 10	138.44	−0.0212	−0.0214	0.000841
May 11	132.63	−0.0420	−0.0429	0.002543
May 12	125.25	−0.0556	−0.0573	0.004200
Totals			0.4459	0.182817

$\bar{r}^c = \dfrac{0.4459}{59} = 0.0076 \quad \sigma = \sqrt{\dfrac{0.182817}{58}} = 0.056143 \text{ Annualized } \sigma = 0.056143\sqrt{250} = 0.8877$

Then the mean and variance of the series of continuously compounded returns are calculated. The variance is then converted to the standard deviation by taking the square root. The resulting figure is a daily volatility, so it must be multiplied by the square root of 250 to be converted to an annualized volatility, which is 0.8878.

The accompanying Excel spreadsheet Hisv9e.xls calculates the historical volatility. Software Demonstration 5.2 illustrates how to use Hisv9e.xls.

Implied Volatility

> The implied volatility is obtained by finding the standard deviation such that when it is used in the Black-Scholes-Merton model, it makes the model price equal the market price of the option.

The second approach to estimating the volatility is called the **implied volatility**, which we shall denote as $\hat{\sigma}$. This procedure assumes that the option's market price reflects the stock's current volatility. The Black-Scholes-Merton or any other acceptable option pricing model is used to infer a standard deviation. The implied volatility is the standard deviation that makes the Black-Scholes-Merton price equal the option's current market price.

The implied volatility approach would be simple if the Black-Scholes-Merton equation could be rearranged to solve for the standard deviation. Because that cannot be done, we obtain the solution by plugging in values of σ until we find the one that makes the Black-Scholes-Merton price equal the market price. The procedure is illustrated in Figure 5.17. Because it requires a trial-and-error search, it can be quite laborious; thus, it is helpful to use a computer to do the calculations.[7]

Let us estimate the implied volatility for the DCRB June 125 call. The input values are $S_0 = 125.94$, $X = 125$, $r_c = 0.0446$, and $T = 0.0959$. The market price of the call is $13.50. We need to find the value of σ that will make the Black-Scholes-Merton value come to $13.50. We must also be prepared to specify a certain degree of precision in our answer. (That is, how close should the model price come to the market price or

SOFTWARE DEMONSTRATION 5.2

Calculating the Historical Volatility with the Excel Spreadsheet Hisv9e.xls

The Excel spreadsheet Hisv9e.xls is saved in Excel 97-2003. It calculates the historical volatility (standard deviation) for a sample of stock prices.

This spreadsheet is a read-only spreadsheet, meaning that it cannot be saved under the name Hisv9e.xls, which preserves the original file. You may, however, load the spreadsheet without the read-only feature. The spreadsheet Hisv9e.xls is available as a download via the product support website. To access it:

1. Go to www.cengagebrain.com.
2. Click on Instructor Resources or Student Resources.
3. Click on the link Hisv9e.xls.

4. Follow the instructions on the Web page to download and install the spreadsheet.

Now let us assume that you want to calculate a historical volatility. In the accompanying example, already entered into the cells is a set of 26 weekly prices for DCRB stock. Each cell that will accept input has a double-line border, and the values are in blue. Output cells have a single-line border. In the section labeled **Inputs**, you should choose the data frequency. Directly below is a set of cells containing your data observations. Enter the prices in the column labeled "Asset Price."

To obtain the results, tap the F9 (manual recalculation) key. The output is shown in a section labeled **Results** The output consists of the variance, the standard deviation, and the mean return. The column

---

[7]A shortcut method is presented in Appendix 5, which also describes a spreadsheet included with this book that is used to compute the implied volatility.

labeled "Periodic" provides the results in terms of the data frequency you chose. The column labeled "Annualized" provides the figures annualized by multiplying by the appropriate factor. The variance and mean are annualized by multiplying by 250 (the approximate number of trading days in a year), 52, 12, or 1, depending on your data frequency. The annualized standard deviation is then the square root of the annualized variance, which is equivalent to multiplying the periodic standard deviation by the square root of 250, 52, 12, or 1.

In this example, there are 26 prices, which lead to 25 returns. Obviously, you may want to use this spreadsheet for a different number of prices. The spreadsheet is set as a read-only file, so you will need to save it under another name and then make sure the new file is not saved as a read-only file in the Save Options dialog box that is accessible through the Save As command. The file saved under a new name can then be edited. Enter or remove lines at the bottom by using the familiar Windows commands for adding rows and copying formulas or deleting rows. Always leave the double lines after the last row of cells, however, as the overall formulas look for those lines to determine the end of the data.

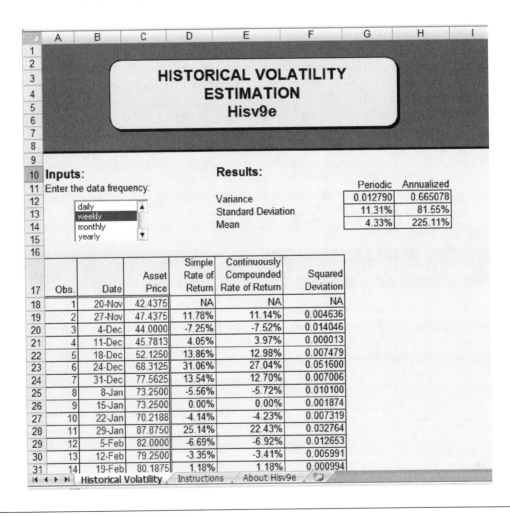

how many decimal places to the right of zero do we require in our implied volatility?) For illustrative purposes, we shall use two decimal places in the implied volatility and stop the trial-and-error process when we determine that the true implied volatility is within 0.01 of our answer.

FIGURE 5.17 Calculating the Implied Volatility

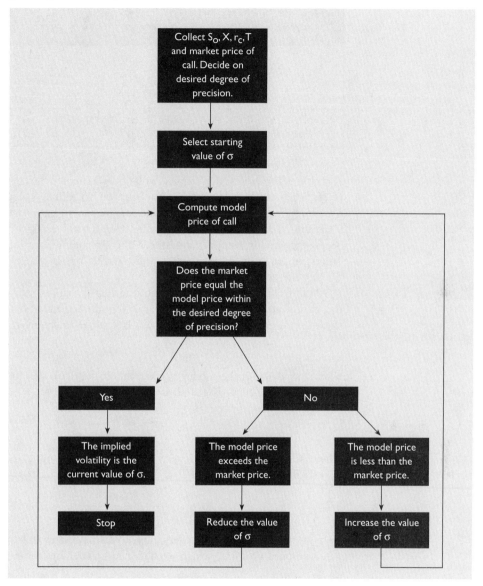

Deriving the implied volatility will involve repetitive Black-Scholes-Merton calculations, so we will use the Excel spreadsheet BSMbin9e.xls. Open the file BSMbin9e.xls and insert the appropriate values for the asset (stock) price, exercise price, risk-free rate, and time to expiration. Let us start with σ of 0.5. We see that the Black-Scholes-Merton call price is $8.48. Obviously this is too low, so let us try a σ of 0.6. The Black-Scholes-Merton call price is then $10.02, which is still too low. At a σ of 0.7, we get $11.56; a σ of 0.8 gives $13.09; a σ of 0.85 gives $13.86; and a σ of 0.83 gives $13.55. Thus, our answer is around 0.83.

Because σ is the stock's volatility, all options on a given stock with the same expiration should give the same implied volatility. For various reasons, including the possibility that the Black-Scholes-Merton model is deficient, different options on the same stock sometimes produce different implied volatilities.

TABLE 5.7 IMPLIED VOLATILITIES OF DCRB CALLS

	EXPIRATION		
EXERCISE PRICE	MAY	JUNE	JULY
120	0.76	0.79	0.85
125	0.75	0.83	0.85
130	0.76	0.83	0.85

$S_0 = 125.94$, $r_c = 0.0447$ (May), 0.0446 (June), 0.0453 (July)
$T = 0.0192$ (May), 0.0959 (June), 0.1726 (July)

Table 5.7 presents the implied volatilities obtained for the options whose exercise prices surround the stock price. The implied volatilities range from 75 to 85 percent. This forces us to choose a single value for the overall implied volatility.

Several methods have been suggested. Some involve taking a simple arithmetic average of the various implied volatilities. Others recommend using a weighted average. Still others simply select the implied volatility of the option whose exercise price is closest to the current stock price.

Recall from Figure 5.13 that we noticed that the call is nearly linear in the volatility if the call is at-the-money. Brenner and Subrahmanyam (1988) exploited this fact and showed that an at-the-money call price is approximately given as

$$C \approx (0.398)S_0\sigma\sqrt{T},$$

where they define at-the-money as when the stock price equals the present value of the exercise price, $S_0 = Xe^{-r_cT}$. The implied volatility of an at-the-money call can then be obtained as

$$\widehat{\sigma} \approx \frac{C}{(0.398)S_0\sqrt{T}},$$

where C is the market price of the call.[8] For example, our DCRB June 125 has $C = 13.50$, $S_0 = 125.94$, and $T = 0.0959$. Thus,

$$\widehat{\sigma} \approx \frac{13.50}{(0.398)125.94\sqrt{0.0959}} = 0.8697.$$

Because this particular call is very close to at-the-money, the answer is fairly close to its actual implied volatility, which we obtained by trial and error.

Interpreting the Implied Volatility   The concept of implied volatility is one of the most important ones in the world of options. Most investors consider the information in implied volatilities to be among the most valuable and accurate information that investors receive from the stock or options markets. In this section, we take a look at what we know and what we can learn from the implied volatility.

First, look back at Table 5.7 and observe that we obtain slightly different implied volatilities for different options on the same stock. If we think about the implication of this result, an inconsistency should immediately be apparent. How can these options tell us that the DCRB stock has different volatilities? There can be only one volatility for a stock. The implied volatilities tell us that the volatility of DCRB can range from 0.75 to 0.85, which is a fairly large range.

---

[8]For the curious, 0.398 is $\frac{1}{\sqrt{2\pi}}$ which is part of the mathematical formula that derives the normal probability.

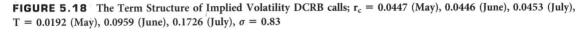

FIGURE 5.18 The Term Structure of Implied Volatility DCRB calls; r_c = 0.0447 (May), 0.0446 (June), 0.0453 (July), T = 0.0192 (May), 0.0959 (June), 0.1726 (July), σ = 0.83

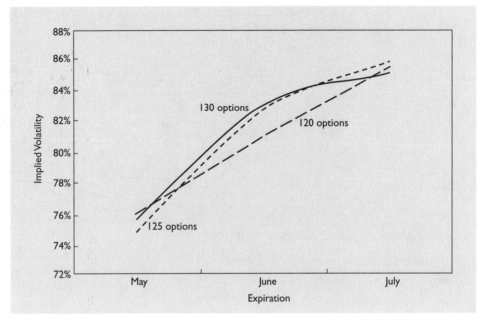

First, let us organize the information a little better. Let us hold the exercise price constant and look at the volatilities across maturities. For the 120 call, the implied volatilities range from 0.76 to 0.85. For the 125 call, they range from 0.75 to 0.85, and for the 130 call, they range from 0.76 to 0.85. For any given exercise price, the relationship between implied volatility and option expiration is called the **term structure of implied volatility**, which is depicted in Figure 5.18 for the DCRB options. Because the volatility is supposed to represent the volatility of the stock across the option expirations, it is quite possible that the volatilities could vary across different time horizons. In all cases here, we see that the longer the time to expiration, the greater the volatility, although this will not always be the case. In any case, there is nothing inherently wrong with different volatilities across different horizons.

> The pattern of implied volatility across expirations is often called the term structure of volatility, and the pattern of volatility across exercise prices is often called the volatility smile or skew.

For a given option expiration, however, the volatilities across different exercise prices are a bit disconcerting. For example, for options expiring in June, the call with exercise price of 120 tells us that the volatility of DCRB is 0.79, while the call with exercise price of 125 (as well as the 130) says that the volatility is 0.83. But how could the volatility of a stock over this period be 0.79 and 0.83? Clearly, something is amiss. As it turns out, this finding is a common occurrence. Quite often implied volatilities are lowest for at-the-money options and highest for deep-in- and out-of-the-money options. When the implied volatility is graphed against the exercise price, this relationship forms a u-shaped pattern that is referred to as the **volatility smile**. Oftentimes, the shape is more skewed, and the resulting pattern is called the **volatility skew**, which is the case for the DCRB options , as seen in Figure 5.19. Note that we used more strike prices to produce this figure than we had been working with in the preceding illustrations.

The volatility smile or skew tells us that the Black-Scholes-Merton model is not a perfect model. Options with higher implied volatilities are more expensive options than

FIGURE 5.19 The Implied Volatility Smile/Skew DCRB June and July Calls

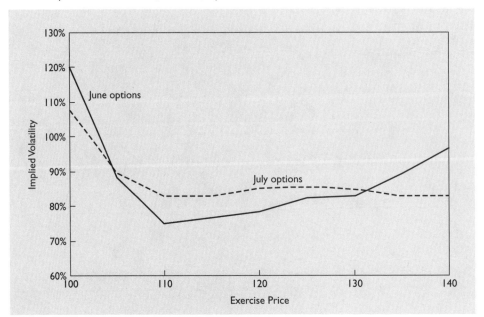

are options with lower implied volatilities. Whatever makes these options more or less expensive is not reflected in the Black-Scholes-Merton model. The source of these differences in implied volatilities is a subject of much interest to academic researchers and practitioners, but the answer is, so far, a mystery.

From a practical standpoint, however, the differences in implied volatilities are simply viewed as differences in the relative cost of these options. For whatever reason, some options will simply be more costly than others. This result is used by the options market in a manner that often simplifies the ability of a trader to obtain an accurate measure of how inexpensive or expensive certain options are. For example, following are the prices of the DCRB calls, information we have been using for several chapters.

Exercise price	May	June	July
120	8.75	15.40	20.90
125	5.75	13.50	18.60
130	3.60	11.35	16.40

Suppose we wanted to buy a June option. Which is the most expensive? We cannot say the June 120 is the most expensive simply because its premium is higher. We know that one reason its premium is higher is that it has the lowest exercise price. We found that its implied volatility is 0.79. The implied volatilities of the 125 and 130 are 0.83, so those options are actually more expensive than the June options, at least after taking into account the stock price, exercise price, risk-free rate, and time to expiration. We do not know why the June 120 is the least expensive June option, but at least we know that it is indeed the least expensive. Of course, we do not know if the market is using the Black-Scholes-Merton model.

MAKING THE CONNECTION

Smiles, Smirks, and Surfaces

The relationship between the implied volatility and option expiration for a given exercise price is known as the term structure of volatility. The relationship between the implied volatility and a set of exercise prices for a given option expiration is known as the implied volatility smile (or skew, smirk, and so forth). We can combine these two perspectives to create a three-dimensional implied volatility surface with strike and expiration on the horizontal axes and implied volatility on the vertical axis. For comparison purposes, the exercise price is converted to moneyness or S/X, as illustrated in the figure here.

According to the Black-Scholes-Merton option pricing model, the implied volatility surface should be flat. Prior to the 1987 stock market crash, the implied volatility surface was relatively flat. After the 1987 stock market crash, the implied volatility surface has become more skewed. In the time since 1987, a non-flat implied volatility surface has spread to most other options markets.

The non-flat implied volatility surface has important implications for estimating risk variables such as delta and gamma. Accurate risk variable estimates are required to adequately manage the risk of an options portfolio. Since the emergence of non-flat implied volatility surfaces, there has been a quest to improve the Black-Scholes-Merton option pricing model to achieve a more accurate depiction of market realities.

Although numerous more complex models have been explored, the fundamental question of how to modify the estimate of risk parameters such as delta and gamma in light of the non-flat implied volatility surface remains unanswered. Therefore, the task of managing the risks of a portfolio of options remains an intellectually challenging job.

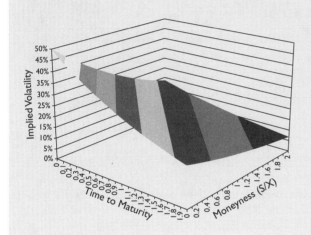

The options market often uses implied volatility to quote prices on options. For example, the June 125 option can be quoted at a volatility of 0.83, while the June 120 can be quoted at a volatility of 0.79. Of course, it must then be understood that a particular model, usually Black-Scholes-Merton, is used to obtain the actual price of the option. But by quoting the price as an implied volatility, an investor immediately knows that the June 120 is less expensive than the June 125. An investor can look at all of the options at once and immediately determine which is the most and least expensive, something that cannot be done just by looking at the prices themselves.

The implied volatility is an important piece of information that the options market reveals to us. For example, by observing the implied volatilities of index options, we can obtain some information on what investors believe is the volatility of the market. The Chicago Board Options Exchange has created two indices based on the implied volatilities of one-month at-the-money options. One index, called the VIX, represents the implied volatility of the S&P 500 Index, a very actively traded option on an index of large stocks. The other index, called the VXN, represents the implied volatility of the NASDAQ 100 Index, a very actively traded option on the NASDAQ Index of 100 leading over-the-counter stocks.

FIGURE 5.20 The Chicago Board Options Exchange's VIX Index (Implied Volatility of the S&P 500 Index)

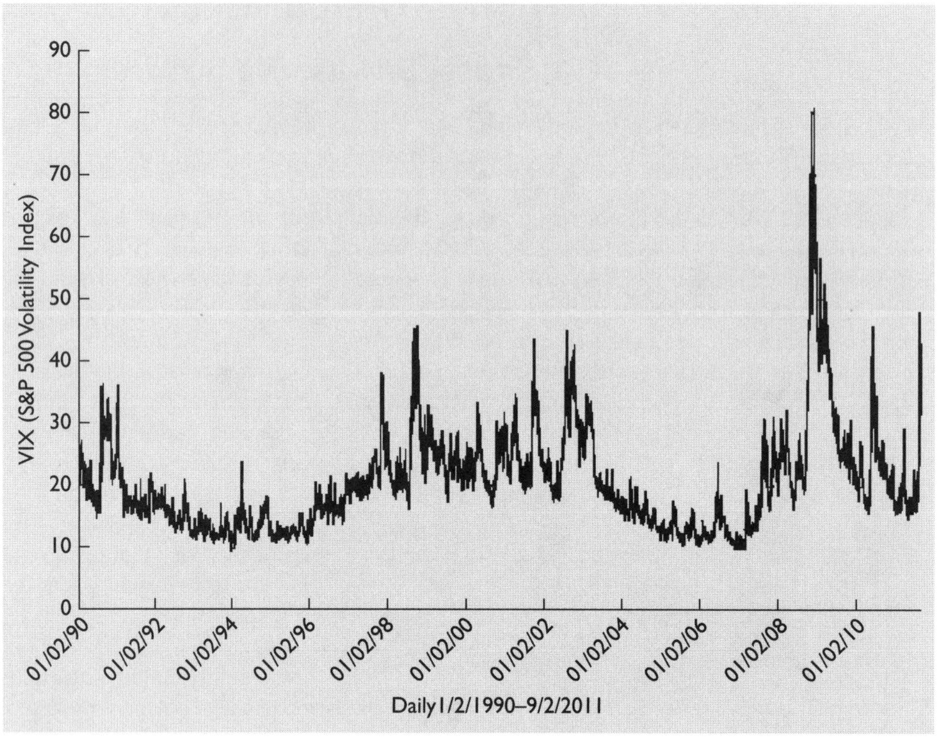

Data for the VIX and VXN are available on a daily basis from the CBOE's website, www.cboe.com. Figure 5.20 shows the VIX plotted on a daily basis from January 2, 1990, through September 2, 2011. Observe how the graph shows dramatic changes in the volatility of the S&P 500 index over this time period. The range has been from around 10 percent to over 80 percent and has averaged about 20 percent. Note also that the volatility moved up sharply in response to the market turmoil related to the recent credit crisis.

A number of studies have examined whether implied volatility is a good predictor of the future volatility of a stock. The results are inconclusive, but there is a general consensus that implied volatility is a better reflection of the appropriate volatility for pricing an option than is the historical volatility. There is, however, circularity in that line of reasoning. If we assume that the best estimate of the correct volatility is the implied volatility, then we throw the burden of determining the volatility on the options market. We simply look to the options market for the implied volatility and accept it as the true volatility. But all traders in the market cannot put the burden of estimating the volatility on the market. All traders, collectively, make up the market. Someone must estimate the appropriate volatility in order to price and trade the option.

Moreover, if we assume that the implied volatility is the best estimate of the market's volatility, then how do we use that information to trade? Suppose we find that a particular option has an unusually high implied volatility, making it undesirable for purchase. On what basis can we make the statement that its implied volatility is unusually high? We need a benchmark, that is, some measure of a reasonable value for volatility. In short, we cannot simply price an option using the implied volatility without considering whether that volatility is reasonable. And we cannot determine whether that volatility is reasonable without a benchmark. So we need some other source of information for volatility. As in the VIX case, when its volatility is over 40, we say that it is twice its historical level. Does that mean that the option is overpriced or that the market volatility is simply too high? Without a benchmark, we do not know.

But, of course, there is no clear-cut benchmark for an index's or stock's volatility. Investors cannot expect to find easy answers and a guarantee of trading success when using implied volatility. Indeed, investors are likely to disagree greatly over the implied volatility. But that is probably a good thing as it makes for more interesting and active markets.[9]

PUT OPTION PRICING MODELS

> The Black-Scholes-Merton call option pricing model can be turned into a put option pricing model by inserting it into put-call parity.

Recall that the put-call parity formula gives the relationship between a put price and a call price. Expressing the put price as a function of the call price with annually compounded interest rates, we have

$$P_e(S_0,T,X) = C_e(S_0,T,X) - S_0 + X(1 + r)^{-T}.$$

In the Black-Scholes-Merton world, it is customary to use continuously compounded interest rates for discounting. Restating put-call parity so that the present value of the exercise price is computed using continuously compounded rates for discounting gives

$$P_e(S_0,T,X) = C_e(S_0,T,X) - S_0 + Xe^{-r_cT},$$

where, as discussed earlier, r_c is the continuously compounded rate. Then we can substitute the Black-Scholes-Merton value for the call price. Letting P stand for $P_e(S_0,T,X)$ gives the Black-Scholes-Merton European put option pricing model:

$$P = Xe^{-r_cT}[1 - N(d_2)] - S_0[1 - N(d_1)],$$

where d_1 and d_2 are the same as in the call option pricing model. Based on the properties of the standard normal distribution, the put option can also be represented as:

$$P = Xe^{-r_cT}N(-d_2) - S_0N(-d_1).$$

In the example of the DCRB June 125 call, the values of $N(d_1)$ and $N(d_2)$ using the spreadsheet BSMbin9e.xls were 0.5692 and 0.4670, respectively. Plugging into the formula, we get

$$P = 125e^{-(0.0446)(0.0959)}(1 - 0.4670) - 125.94(1 - 0.5692) = 12.08.$$

The actual market price of the June 125 put was $11.50. Because this price must also include a premium for the additional benefit of early exercise and the Black-Scholes-Merton model does not reflect the early exercise premium, the difference between the market and model prices is actually greater than what we see here. In other words, if the put option pricing model reflected the early exercise premium, it would produce an even higher theoretical price.

The same variables that affect the call's price affect the put's price, although in some cases in a different manner. Table 5.8 summarizes these important concepts for puts.

---

[9]Mark Twain in *Pudd'nhead Wilson* (1894) expressed this point succinctly by saying, "It were not best that we should think alike; it is difference of opinion that makes horse races."

TABLE 5.8   THE EFFECTS OF VARIABLES ON THE BLACK-SCHOLES-MERTON PUT OPTION PRICE

The results for put options are obtained by using the put-call parity relationship, $P = C - S_0 + Xe^{-r_cT}$.

Stock Price

The relationship between the stock price and the put price is called the put **delta**.

$$\text{Put } Delta = N(d_1) - 1$$

Because $N(d_1)$ is between 0 and 1, the put delta is negative. This simply means that a put option moves in an opposite direction to the stock. A delta neutral position with stock and puts will require long positions in both stock and puts. The relationship between the put delta and the stock price is called the put **gamma**.

$$\text{Put } Gamma = \frac{e^{-d_1^2/2}}{S_0\sigma\sqrt{2\pi T}}$$

Notice that the put gamma is the same as the call gamma. Like a call, the gamma is highest when the put is at-the-money.

Exercise Price

For a difference in the exercise price, the put price will change by $e^{-r_cT}[1 - N(d_2)]$. Because both of the terms are positive, the overall expression is positive.

Risk-Free Rate

The relationship between the put price and the risk-free rate is called the put **rho**.

$$\text{Put } Rho = -T\,Xe^{-r_cT}[1 - N(d_2)]$$

This expression is always negative, meaning that the put price moves inversely to interest rates.

Volatility

The relationship between the put price and the volatility is called the **vega**.

$$\text{Put } Vega = \frac{S_0\sqrt{T}e^{-d_1^2/2}}{\sqrt{2\pi}}.$$

This is the same expression as the vega for a call. Like a call, a put is highly sensitive to the volatility.

Time to Expiration

The relationship between the put price and the time to expiration is called the **theta**.

$$\text{Put } Theta = -\frac{S_0\sigma e^{-d_1^2/2}}{2\sqrt{2\pi T}} + r_cXe^{-r_cT}(1 - N(d_2)).$$

This expression can be positive or negative, a point we covered in Chapter 3. A European put can either increase or decrease with time. The tendency to increase occurs because there is more time for the stock to move favorably. The tendency to decrease occurs because the additional time means waiting longer to receive the exercise price at expiration.

The Excel spreadsheet BSMbin9e.xls, which is illustrated in Software Demonstration 5.1, does the Black-Scholes-Merton calculations for puts as well as calls.

Without getting into some very advanced techniques, it is not possible to make the Black-Scholes-Merton model accommodate early exercise for American puts. If it is necessary to price an American put, we could use the binomial model with a large number of time periods. Thus, suppose we were attempting to price the DCRB June 125 put. Using the BSMbin9e.xls spreadsheet and selecting the binomial model with $n = 100$ time periods and inputs $S_0 = 125.94$, $X = 125$, $r_c = 0.0446$, $T = 0.0959$, and $\sigma = 0.83$, we would obtain an American put value of $12.11, which is only slightly higher than the European value of $12.08 obtained with the binomial model. This suggests that the premium for early exercise is not that great, a likely reflection of the fact that the volatility on DCRB is so high that exercising early throws away the time value. But when would such a put be exercised? We can tell by using the binomial model. If the American put value obtained using the binomial model equals the exercise value, the put should be exercised. In fact, the put would be selling for its intrinsic value and could be exercised or sold; either value is the same. Suppose that right now the stock is at $100. The intrinsic value would obviously be Max(0, 125 − 100) = 25. The American put value using the binomial model would be $27.72. So, the put is still worth more alive. Suppose the stock was at $90. Then the intrinsic value would be $35, and the American put value would be worth $35.99. The put is still worth slightly more alive. Not until a stock price around $71.38 is the put worth precisely its intrinsic value and at that point would be exercised early.

The critical stock price at which the put is worth exercising could be found by trial and error. As a rule, the critical stock price rises as expiration approaches, meaning that the stock does not have to get quite as low to justify exercising the put the closer to expiration. At expiration, the critical stock price is simply the exercise price.

MANAGING THE RISK OF OPTIONS

You may have gotten the impression that investors take option positions to establish the opportunity to make money when markets move in anticipated ways. Consider, however, that on the opposite side of each option transaction is a counterparty. The options market is characterized by counterparties who are in the market-making or dealer business. For exchange-listed options, these are individuals at the exchanges who offer to buy or sell options. For over-the-counter options, these are institutions that offer to buy or sell options with terms tailored to their customers' needs. We shall refer to both groups of counterparties as dealers. In general, they do not take option positions to speculate or hedge; their goal is to make money from bid-ask spreads. They have no desire to speculate, so they must neutralize the risk they acquire.

Earlier in the chapter we talked about delta hedging. We noted that to delta hedge an option, we must buy a certain number of shares of the underlying stock. In theory, a delta-hedged position must be adjusted continuously to reflect the fact that the delta changes with the level of the stock price and with time. Moreover, delta hedging neutralizes only the risk of small price changes. We noted that the option's gamma reflects the possibility of larger price changes. The dealer must be able to effectively hedge away this risk.

Let us begin by considering a dealer who sells 1,000 of the DCRB June 125 calls at the Black-Scholes-Merton price of 13.5533. The delta is 0.5692. From what we covered earlier in the chapter, we know that to hedge would require that we buy 1,000(0.5692), or approximately 569, shares. The dealer cannot adjust the delta continuously, so let us say that the dealer decides to adjust the hedge at the end of each day. Let the position be held for the full 35 days remaining in the option's life. Buying 569 shares at 125.94 and selling 1,000 calls at 13.5533 means that we must invest 569(125.94) − 1,000(13.5533) = 58,107. So we invest $58,107.

To obtain an idea of the risk involved, we can simulate the daily stock prices over the remaining life of the contract. Although generating prices by simulation is covered briefly later in this book, let us for now just assume that we have simulated the daily closing prices for DCRB for the next 35 days. At time 0, the time we put the delta hedge in place, DCRB is at 125.94. One day later it closes at 120.4020. Now there are 34 days until expiration, so the time remaining is $T = 34/365 = 0.0932$. We plug these values into the Black-Scholes-Merton spreadsheet, BSMbin9e.xls and find that the call would then be selling for $10.4078. How have we done on our hedge?

Stock worth	569($120.4020) =	$68,509, and
Options worth	−1,000($10.4078) =	−$10,408, for a
Total value of		$58,101

How much should we have? If we had invested $58,107 in risk-free bonds for one day at the rate of 4.46 percent, we should have $58,107e^{0.0446(1/365)} = $58,114.

How would we continue to do? Table 5.9 presents the outcomes based on a simulation of the remaining DCRB prices during the option's life. Day 0 is the day we put on the hedge. We start with no shares (column 2) or calls (column 3). We assume that we can trade only in whole numbers of shares and calls; so at the end of the day, we sell 1,000 calls (column 9) and buy 569 shares (column 11). In column 18, note that the portfolio delta is not actually zero but rather −0.1868. This comes from having 569 shares at a delta of 1.0 and 1,000 short calls at a delta of 0.5692, [569(1) − 1,000(0.5692)] = −0.2, or, more precisely, −0.1868. Because we cannot hold fractions of shares, we have a very slight negative delta.

At the end of day 1, as explained previously, our portfolio is worth $58,101 (column 7), whereas the target value is $58,114 (column 8). Now note the columns under the heading "End-of-Day Option Calculations" (columns 13–17). The new time to expiration is 34/365 = 0.0932. The new delta is the N(d_1) of 0.4981. Now we need 498 shares, as indicated in column 10. Column 11 shows that we must sell off 71 shares. With the stock price of $120.4020, this generates about 71($120.4020) = $8,549, which is then invested in bonds (column 12). Let us now move forward one more day.

At the end of day 2, the stock moves up to $126.2305 (column 5) and the call is $13.3358 (column 6). Our $8,549 of bonds accrued one day's interest to $8,550 (column 4). Thus, we have

Stock worth	498($126.2305) =	$62,863 and
Options worth	−1,000($13.3358) =	−13,336 and
Bonds worth		$ 8,550 for a
Total value of		$58,077 (column 7)

If we had been perfectly hedged through two days, we would have $58,107e^{0.0446(2/365)} = $58,121 (column 8). Thus, we are now short by $44.

This process continues, and on day 35, the expiration day of the option, we have a portfolio value of $59,762, while our target value is $58,356, an excess of $1,406. Clearly this is not a perfect hedge. In fact, we have gained more than 2 percent on our investment. What is the problem?

As we discussed earlier in the chapter, delta hedging works only if done continuously and only if the stock price changes are very small. The reason for this is as follows: The delta is based on the calculus concept of a first derivative. In the context here, the first derivative is the rate of change of the option price with respect to the stock price, under the assumption that the stock price change is extremely small. Look at Figure 5.6 again and note the curvature of the graph. The delta is simply the slope of the curve at a particular value of the stock price. But with a curve, as opposed to a straight line, the slope is different at every point. The slope at a given point can be accurately estimated only if we allow the stock to move by a very small amount.

TABLE 5.9 DAILY ADJUSTED DELTA HEDGE S_0 = 125.94, X = 125, r_c = 0.0446, T = 0.0959, σ = 0.83, 1000 SHORT CALLS

	BEGINNING-OF-DAY HOLDINGS		END-OF-DAY VALUES (BEFORE ADJUSTMENTS)					
DAY (1)	SHARES (2)	CALLS (3)	$ OF BONDS (4)	STOCK PRICE (5)	CALL PRICE (6)	PORTFOLIO VALUE (7)	TARGET PORTFOLIO VALUE (8)	NEW CALL TRADES (9)
0	0	0	0	125.9400	13.5533	0	58107	−1000
1	569	−1000	0	120.4020	10.4078	58101	58114	0
2	498	−1000	8550	126.2305	13.3358	58077	58121	0
3	572	−1000	−792	129.7259	15.2113	58200	58128	0
4	614	−1000	−6241	122.6991	11.0082	58088	58135	0
5	524	−1000	4803	116.8313	7.9826	58040	58142	0
6	441	−1000	14501	111.9864	5.8418	58046	58149	0
7	368	−1000	22679	104.3922	3.3160	57780	58156	0
8	257	−1000	34271	95.8023	1.4834	57409	58163	0
9	147	−1000	44815	97.6316	1.6663	57500	58170	0
10	161	−1000	43453	101.2905	2.2093	57552	58178	0
11	199	−1000	39609	107.7229	3.6022	57444	58185	0
12	281	−1000	30779	108.7139	3.7173	57611	58192	0
13	290	−1000	29805	100.3039	1.6632	57230	58199	0
14	167	−1000	42147	99.4745	1.4164	57343	58206	0
15	150	−1000	43844	106.1533	2.5476	57219	58213	0
16	232	−1000	35143	97.1141	0.9052	56769	58220	0
17	110	−1000	46997	94.3615	0.5666	56810	58227	0
18	78	−1000	50023	86.0927	0.1300	56608	58234	0
19	24	−1000	54678	88.4161	0.1625	56638	58242	0
20	29	−1000	54243	93.3283	0.3112	56638	58249	0
21	50	−1000	52289	90.6496	0.1604	56662	58256	0
22	30	−1000	54109	92.6696	0.1857	56703	58263	0
23	34	−1000	53745	92.2053	0.1325	56747	58270	0
24	26	−1000	54489	97.6458	0.2873	56741	58277	0
25	51	−1000	52054	101.2303	0.4257	56791	58284	0
26	73	−1000	49833	106.4213	0.7980	56804	58291	0
27	123	−1000	44518	110.5062	1.2135	56897	58299	0
28	175	−1000	38776	110.4197	0.9792	57120	58306	0
29	155	−1000	40990	108.7435	0.5619	57283	58313	0
30	106	−1000	46324	109.4487	0.4535	57472	58320	0
31	95	−1000	47533	111.5737	0.4654	57668	58327	0
32	104	−1000	46535	115.9403	0.7627	57830	58334	0
33	169	−1000	39004	122.7231	2.0457	57698	58341	0
34	396	−1000	11147	120.9295	0.6922	58343	58348	0
35	231	−1000	31104	124.0621	0.0002	59762	58356	0

(continued)

TABLE 5.9 (CONTINUED)

| | | | | END-OF-DAY OPTION CALCULATIONS | | | | |
ADJUSTED NO. OF SHARES (10)	NO. OF SHARES BOUGHT OR SOLD (11)	$ OF BONDS PURCHASED OR SOLD (12)	TIME TO EXPIRATION (13)	d_1 (14)	$N(d_1)$ (15)	d_2 (16)	$N(d_2)$ (17)	PORTFOLIO DELTA (18)
569	569	0	0.0959	0.1743	0.5692	−0.0827	0.4670	0.1868
498	−71	8549	0.0932	−0.0049	0.4981	−0.2582	0.3981	−0.0570
572	74	−9341	0.0904	0.1802	0.5715	−0.0694	0.4723	0.4981
614	42	−5448	0.0877	0.2898	0.6140	0.0440	0.5176	−0.0120
524	−90	11043	0.0849	0.0598	0.5238	−0.1821	0.4278	0.1536
441	−83	9697	0.0822	−0.1496	0.4405	−0.3876	0.3492	0.4638
368	−73	8175	0.0795	−0.3377	0.3678	−0.5717	0.2838	0.2222
257	−111	11588	0.0767	−0.6538	0.2566	−0.8837	0.1884	0.3818
147	−110	10538	0.0740	−1.0509	0.1467	−1.2766	0.1009	0.3436
161	14	−1367	0.0712	−0.9903	0.1610	−1.2119	0.1128	−0.0064
199	38	−3849	0.0685	−0.8455	0.1989	−1.0627	0.1440	0.0803
281	82	−8833	0.0658	−0.5787	0.2814	−0.7915	0.2143	−0.4097
290	9	−978	0.0630	−0.5523	0.2904	−0.7606	0.2234	−0.3815
167	−123	12337	0.0603	−0.9650	0.1673	−1.1688	0.1212	−0.2715
150	−17	1691	0.0575	−1.0348	0.1504	−1.2339	0.1086	−0.3890
232	82	−8705	0.0548	−0.7314	0.2323	−0.9257	0.1773	−0.2782
110	−122	11848	0.0521	−1.2259	0.1101	−1.4153	0.0785	−0.1154
78	−32	3020	0.0493	−1.4213	0.0776	−1.6056	0.0542	0.3802
24	−54	4649	0.0466	−1.9803	0.0238	−2.1595	0.0154	0.1674
29	5	−442	0.0438	−1.8942	0.0291	−2.0680	0.0193	−0.0998
50	21	−1960	0.0411	−1.6413	0.0504	−1.8096	0.0352	−0.3658
30	−20	1813	0.0384	−1.8846	0.0297	−2.0472	0.0203	0.2580
34	4	−371	0.0356	−1.8218	0.0342	−1.9785	0.0239	−0.2390
26	−8	738	0.0329	−1.9367	0.0264	−2.0872	0.0184	−0.3930
51	25	−2441	0.0301	−1.6323	0.0513	−1.7765	0.0378	−0.3037
73	22	−2227	0.0274	−1.4574	0.0725	−1.5948	0.0554	0.4937
123	50	−5321	0.0247	−1.1607	0.1229	−1.2911	0.0983	0.1260
175	52	−5746	0.0219	−0.9333	0.1753	−1.0562	0.1454	−0.3251
155	−20	2208	0.0192	−1.0138	0.1553	−1.1288	0.1295	−0.3333
106	−49	5328	0.0164	−1.2487	0.1059	−1.3552	0.0877	0.1158
95	−11	1204	0.0137	−1.3123	0.0947	−1.4095	0.0794	0.2860
104	9	−1004	0.0110	−1.2581	0.1042	−1.3450	0.0893	−0.1790
169	65	−7536	0.0082	−0.9568	0.1693	−1.0321	0.1510	−0.3413
396	227	−27858	0.0055	−0.2642	0.3958	−0.3257	0.3723	0.1939
231	−165	19953	0.0027	−0.7361	0.2308	−0.7796	0.2178	0.1717
2	−229	28410	0.0000	−2.9288	0.0017	−2.9314	0.0017	0.2986

Obviously the stock can move by much larger amounts, which is much more likely the less frequently trading can be done. When that happens, delta is not a good approximation of the risk of the option. This point was made earlier in the chapter. In such cases, factors known as second-order effects come into play. The second-order effect is the gamma, which we covered earlier. It turns out that using the gamma can enable us to get a better hedge.

Gamma hedging is a much more complex process, and we shall take only a brief and simple look at it. The objective of gamma hedging is to be both delta and gamma hedged, sometimes called delta neutral and gamma neutral, meaning that essentially any stock price move will be hedged. It will be impossible to be both delta and gamma hedged by holding only the stock and option. This is because the risk associated with the option's gamma must be eliminated by another instrument. The delta of a stock is 1.0, but its gamma is zero. Thus, the stock cannot hedge the option's gamma risk. What we require is an instrument that has a nonzero gamma—specifically, another option.

So let us add the June 130 call, whose Black-Scholes-Merton price is \$11.3792, whose delta is 0.5087, and whose gamma is 0.0123. The gamma of our June 125 call is 0.0121. In what follows, we use the Greek letter delta in the form of Δ_1 and Δ_2 to represent the deltas of our June 125 call (option 1) and the June 130 call (option 2), respectively. We use the Greek letter gamma—Γ_1 and Γ_2—to represent the gammas of our June 125 call and June 130 call, respectively. We shall hold a portfolio of h_S shares of stock, which have a delta of 1.0 and a gamma of 0.0, 1,000 short calls (the June 125), and h_c of the June 130 calls. To be delta hedged, we must meet the condition:

$$h_s(1) - 1{,}000\Delta_1 + h_c\Delta_2 = 0,$$

and to be gamma hedged, we must meet the condition,

$$-1{,}000\Gamma_1 + h_c\Gamma_2 = 0.$$

In other words, the combined gammas of the two options must equal zero. We now have two equations and two unknowns. We can solve the second one for h_c and obtain:

$$h_c = 1{,}000(\Gamma_1/\Gamma_2)$$

Once we have this value, we then solve the first equation for h_s:

$$h_s = 1{,}000[(\Delta_1 - (\Gamma_1/\Gamma_2)\Delta_2)].$$

Now, let us set up a gamma hedge and see how it performs. First, we have

$$\Delta_1 = 0.5692, \quad \Delta_2 = 0.5087, \quad \Gamma_1 = 0.0121, \quad \text{and} \quad \Gamma_2 = 0.0123.$$

Thus, the number of the second option we need, h_c, is

$$h_c = 1{,}000(0.0121/0.0123) = 984,$$

which we change to its spreadsheet-computed value of 985. The number of shares we need is

$$h_s = 1{,}000(0.5692 - (0.0121/0.0123)(0.5087)) = 68.$$

Thus, we buy 68 shares, sell 1,000 of the June 125 calls, and buy 985 of the June 130 calls. This will require that we invest funds of

$$68(125.94) - 1{,}000(13.5533) + 985(11.3792) = 6{,}219.$$

Now, at the end of the first day, the stock is at \$120.4020, the 125 call is at \$10.4078, and the 130 call would be worth \$8.5729. The portfolio is then worth

$$68(120.4020) - 1{,}000(10.4078) + 985(8.5729) = 6{,}224.$$

The portfolio should be worth $\$6,218e^{0.0446(1/365)} = \$6,220$.

The new deltas are $\Delta_1 = 0.4981$ and $\Delta_2 = 0.4366$. The new gammas are $\Gamma_1 = 0.0131$ and $\Gamma_2 = 0.0129$. Now the new number required of the 130 call is $1,000(0.0131/0.0129) = 1,016$. More precise spreadsheet calculations give us an answer of 1,013, so let us use 1,013. This means that we must buy $1,013 - 985 = 28$ of the 130 calls at the new price of $\$8.5729$. This will require $28(\$8.5729) = \$240$.

The number of shares we will need is

$$h_s = 1,000[0.4981 - (0.0131/0.0129)0.4366] = 54.73.$$

The more precise calculations of a spreadsheet give us 56. We must sell $68 - 56 = 12$ shares at $\$120.4020$. This raises $12(\$120.4020) = \$1,444$, leaving $\$1,444 - \$240 = \$1,204$ of new cash that we invest in risk-free bonds.

At the end of the next day, the stock is at $\$126.2305$, the 125 call is at $\$13.3358$, and the 130 call is at $\$11.1394$. Our bonds have earned a little interest but are still worth about $\$1,205$. Our portfolio is now worth

$$56(126.2305) - 1,000(13.3358) + 1,013(11.1394) + \$1,205 = \$6,222.$$

If our portfolio is hedged for two days, it should be worth $\$6,219e^{0.0446(2/365)} = \$6,221$. Thus, we are $\$1$ ahead.

Because of the large number of columns required to show the full details of this transaction, we shall omit them here. The final results are that for the set of stock prices in Table 5.9, the gamma hedge ends up with a value of $\$6,267$. The target ending value would be $\$6,246$. The difference is $\$21$ ahead.

Delta hedging is difficult because trading cannot be done continuously and because there are price changes that are too large to be captured by the delta. Gamma hedging can be used to partially deal with these problems.

Thus, gamma hedging can make the hedge better able to eliminate the risk caused by large price changes occurring over finite periods of time. Dealers have learned how to effectively delta and gamma hedge, but they also face the risk of the volatility changing. We identified this concept earlier as vega risk. We shall not cover it at this introductory level, but do be aware that vega risk can be hedged by introducing another instrument with a nonzero vega. This means that we would still need another option. Then we would have three equations and three unknowns, which are the number of shares, the number of the second call, and the number of the third call. The three equations would be solved to set the delta, gamma, and vega to zero.

When the Black-Scholes-Merton Model May and May Not Hold

As we have seen, delta hedging and delta-gamma hedging provide a compelling way for option market makers to manage the risk of options held in their portfolios. It should be clear, however, that this is not a perfect hedge and that this dynamic hedging is not exact. We review briefly here some of the issues that may influence the ability of the Black-Scholes-Merton model to be useful in the options marketplace.

One concern for option market makers is liquidity of both the options market and its underlying instrument. If it is costly to delta hedge, then that cost will be embedded in the market maker's bid-offer spread. If there is a risk that either the options market or the underlying instrument's market will become completely illiquid, then delta hedging is impossible.

The ability to short sell is important for market makers who need to acquire negative delta. If short selling is prohibited or highly restricted, then the ability to dynamically hedge is impaired. Often, regulators will provide option market makers with special exemptions from short-selling restrictions, such as having the ability to borrow the shares. Short selling without the ability to borrow the shares is known as naked short selling and was a significant problem leading up to, during, and after the credit crisis of 2008.

Another significant problem for option traders in general is the presence of market participants with significant informational advantages or information asymmetry. Clearly, if a company insider knows of a large pending merger or bankruptcy, then trading options with this person is disadvantageous. Remember, large jumps in stock prices are extremely difficult to manage for market makers.

Many options that are not "plain vanilla" have properties that make delta hedging virtually impossible. Plain vanilla options have deltas that range between –1 to 0 for puts and 0 to +1 for calls. Many exotic options, some of which are covered in Chapter 14, have deltas that range from $-\infty$ to 0 or 0 to $+\infty$. Clearly, when the delta has the potential for huge swings in value with small changes in the underlying instrument's value, then the Black-Scholes-Merton approach may not prove useful and other more advanced approaches should be pursued.

Finally, it is important to emphasize that the valuation research related to options falls within the human sciences. That is, finance is not physics. Here market makers' beliefs in a particular option valuation approach may actually influence the observed behavior of option prices so that they behave consistently with the option valuation approach. This phenomenon is known as **performativity**. For example, the empirical research supports the following observation about the Black-Scholes-Merton option pricing model. According to MacKenzie (2006), Fischer Black sold quote sheets to option market makers on the Chicago Board Option Exchange in the mid-1970s. The Black-Scholes-Merton option pricing model research papers were published in 1973. By mid-1976, option market markers believed in and used this model for their market-making activities. Interestingly, prior to 1973, the empirical evidence does not support the Black-Scholes-Merton option pricing model being a valid representation of observed option prices. Between mid-1976 and October 1987, observed option prices behaved as if the Black-Scholes-Merton model was valid. It seems that belief in the valuation model by market participants was self-fulfilling.

In the human sciences, performativity denotes when an observed economic activity is made more consistent with a particular economic model as economic participants increasingly believe in the model.

By mid-1980s, the Black-Scholes-Merton option pricing model was being used to promote "dynamic portfolio insurance." Without going into elaborate detail, dynamic portfolio insurance, based on Black-Scholes-Merton option pricing model, was counterperformative. Here, market participants' beliefs in a particular option valuation approach may actually influence the observed behavior of option prices so that they behave *inconsistently* with the particular option valuation approach. With the Black-Scholes-Merton model, investment professionals attempted to dynamically hedge their downside risk. The net result of this pursuit was that vast amounts of investable capital were following essentially a stop-loss strategy where a portion of the stock portfolio was sold whenever the stock market fell. As long as very few follow this strategy, there is no systemic problem. If a large portion of the market participants follow this strategy, then it is counterperformative or self-defeating. Interestingly, after the crash of October 1987, observed option prices no longer behaved consistently with the simple Black-Scholes-Merton model. A replacement model has yet to emerge that captivated so large a portion of the investment community.

In the human sciences, counterperformativity denotes when an observed economic activity is made less consistent with a particular economic model as economic participants increasingly believe in the model.

The Black-Scholes-Merton remains an important foundational model in understanding observed option markets. There will always be model uncertainty, due at least in part to the human science nature of finance and issues of performativity.

Summary

This chapter introduced the Black-Scholes-Merton option pricing model. We began by noting that the discovery of the Black-Scholes-Merton model was made possible by many developments in mathematics and the sciences.

We then observed that when the number of time steps increases, the binomial model converges to a specific value, which will be the Black-Scholes-Merton value.

We identified the assumptions of the Black-Scholes-Merton model, which are that (1) stock prices behave randomly according to a lognormal distribution, (2) the risk-free rate and volatility are constant over the option's life, (3) there are no taxes or transaction costs, (4) the stock pays no dividends, and (5) the options are European.

The Black-Scholes-Merton formula was presented and illustrated, and we observed that it employs risk-neutral probabilities, which are obtained from the normal probability distribution. We noted that the model conforms to the European lower bound and that it obtains the appropriate prices for extreme values such as a zero stock price, zero time to expiration, zero volatility, and zero exercise price.

We saw that the Black-Scholes-Merton call option formula and call options in general are directly related to the stock price, risk-free rate, time to expiration, and volatility and are inversely related to the exercise price.

We learned that the relationship between the call price and the stock price is the delta. The relationship between the delta and the stock price is the gamma. The relationship between the call price and the risk-free rate is the rho. The relationship between the call price and the volatility is the vega. The relationship between the call price and the time to expiration is the theta.

We saw that the Black-Scholes-Merton formula can be adjusted to accommodate dividends on the underlying stock by subtracting the present value of the dividends from the stock price under the assumption that the dividends over the option's life are known and discrete or under the assumption that the dividends are paid at a continuously compounded rate.

We found that the most critical input in the Black-Scholes-Merton model is the volatility, which must be estimated. Moreover, the model is highly sensitive to the volatility. The volatility is typically estimated using either a historical sample of stock returns or the implied volatility, which is inferred from the current prices of options.

We adapted the Black-Scholes-Merton model to price European puts by inserting the Black-Scholes-Merton call formula into put-call parity.

FIGURE 5.21   The Linkage between Calls, Puts, the Underlying Asset, and Risk-Free Bonds

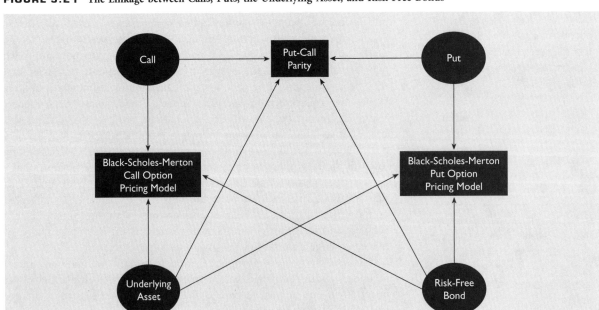

We concluded by examining how a dealer would manage an option position by delta hedging. We saw what the limitations of delta hedging are and how gamma hedging can reduce that risk. We also identified several weaknesses of the Black-Scholes-Merton option pricing model, including liquidity, short selling, information asymmetries, options with unusual delta behavior, and performativity.

In Chapter 3, we used put-call parity to find relative option prices. A put, call, and stock could be priced in relation to each other. But we had to have two of the three prices already. Now we have two option pricing models that do not rely on other option prices, the binomial and Black-Scholes-Merton. Figure 5.21 shows how the Black-Scholes-Merton models for puts and calls link the call and put with the underlying asset and risk-free bond.

Key Terms

Before continuing to Chapter 6, you should be able to give brief definitions of the following terms:

discrete time, p. 135	risk-neutral probabilities, p. 145	implied volatility, p. 165
continuous time, p. 137	delta, p. 150	term structure of implied
lognormally distributed,	delta hedge, p. 151	volatility, p. 169
p. 139	delta neutral, p. 151	volatility smile, p. 169
Black-Scholes-Merton	gamma, p. 152	volatility skew, p. 169
model, p. 141	rho, p. 154	gamma hedging, p. 179
dynamic trading, p. 141	vega, kappa, or lambda, p. 155	performativity, p. 181
normal probability, p. 142	theta, p. 156	
z statistic, p. 142	historical volatility, p. 162	

Further Reading

The original Black-Scholes and Merton papers are as follows:

Black, F., and M. Scholes. "The Pricing of Options and Corporate Liabilities." *Journal of Political Economy* 81 (1973): 637–659.

Merton, R. C. "Theory of Rational Call Option Pricing." *Bell Journal of Economics and Management Science* 4 (1973): 141–183.

The following sources provide empirical tests of the model:

Black, F., and M. Scholes. "The Valuation of Option Contracts and a Test of Market Efficiency." *Journal of Finance* 27 (1972): 399–418.

Galai, D. "A Survey of Empirical Tests of Option Pricing Models." In *Option Pricing*, edited by M. Brenner, 45–80. Lexington, MA: D. C. Heath, 1983.

Galai, D. "Tests of Market Efficiency of the Chicago Board Options Exchange." *Journal of Business* 50 (1977): 167–197.

MacBeth, J. D., and L. J. Merville. "An Empirical Examination of the Black-Scholes Call Option Pricing Model." *Journal of Finance* 34 (1979): 1173–1186.

Other significant papers involving the Black-Scholes-Merton option pricing model are as follows:

Cox, J. C., and S. A. Ross. "The Valuation of Options for Alternative Stochastic Processes." *Journal of Financial Economics* 3 (1976): 145–166.

Geske, R. "The Valuation of Compound Options." *Journal of Financial Economics* 7 (1979): 63–81.

Rubinstein, M. "The Valuation of Uncertain Income Streams and the Pricing of Options." *Bell Journal of Economics* 7 (1976): 407–425.

Several interesting and highly readable papers on the model by Fischer Black are as follows:

Black, F. "Fact and Fantasy in the Use of Options." *Financial Analysts Journal* 31 (July–August 1975): 36–41, 61–72.

Black, F. "How to Use the Holes in Black-Scholes." *Journal of Applied Corporate Finance* 1 (1989): 67–73.

Black, F. "How We Came Up with the Option Formula." *Journal of Portfolio Management* 15 (Winter 1989): 4–8.

You may benefit from the following coverage of the Black-Scholes-Merton model:

Alexander, G., and M. Stutzer. "A Graphical Note on European Put Thetas." *Journal of Futures Markets* 16 (1996): 201–209.

Boyle, P., and F. Boyle. *Derivatives: The Tools That Changed Finance*. London: Risk Books, 2001.

Chriss, N. *Black-Scholes and Beyond: Option Pricing Models*. Chicago: Irwin Professional Publishing, 1997.

Chung, S., and M. Schackleton. "The Binomial Black-Scholes Model and the Greeks." *Journal of Futures Markets* 22 (2002): 143–153.

Constantinides, G. M., J. C. Jackwerth, and S. Perrakis. "Mispricing of S&P 500 Index Options." *Review of Financial Studies* 22 (2009): 1247–1277.

MacKenzie, D. An Engine, Not a Camera: How Financial Models Shape Markets. Cambridge, MA: The MIT Press, 2006.

MacKenzie, D. "An Equation and Its Worlds: Bricolage, Exemplars, Disunity and Performativity in Financial Economics." *Social Studies of Science* 33 (December 2003): 831–868.

MacKenzie, D. "Physics and Finance: S-Terms and Modern Finance as a Topic for Science Studies." *Science, Technology, & Human Values* 26 (Spring 2001): 115–144.

Naib, F. A. "FX Option Theta and the 'Joker' Effect." *Derivatives Quarterly* 2 (Summer 1996): 56–58.

Pelsser, A., and T. Vorst. "The Binomial Model and the Greeks." *Journal of Derivatives* 1 (1994): 45–49.

Zimmermann, H., and Wolfgang H. "Amazing Discovery: Vincenz Bronzin's Option Pricing Models." *Journal of Banking and Finance* 31 (2007): 531–546.

Following are two other interesting books about some of the great people in option pricing are:

Derman, E. *My Life as a Quant: Reflections on Physics and Finance*. New York: Wiley, 2004.

Mehrling, P. G. *Fischer Black and the Revolutionary Idea of Finance*. New York: Wiley, 2005.

Concept Checks

1. Explain the difference between a normal and a lognormal distribution as it pertains to stock prices.
2. Which assumption in the Black-Scholes-Merton model did we drop in the chapter? What did we do in removing that assumption to ensure that the model would give the correct option price?
3. Explain what is meant by the following: The binomial model is a discrete time model, and the Black-Scholes-Merton model is a continuous time model.
4. What is the most critical variable in the Black-Scholes-Merton model? Explain.
5. Compare the variables in the binomial model with those in the Black-Scholes-Merton model. Note any differences and explain.

Questions and Problems

1. Suppose you subscribe to a service that gives you estimates of the theoretically correct volatilities of stocks. You note that the implied volatility of a particular option is substantially higher than the theoretical volatility. What action should you take? Why?
2. What factors contribute to the difficulty of making a delta hedge be truly risk-free?
3. A stock is priced at $50 with a volatility of 35 percent. A call option with an exercise price of $50 has an expiration in one year. The risk-free rate is 5 percent. Construct a table for stock prices of $5, 10, 15, …, 100. Compute the Black-Scholes-Merton price of the call and the European lower bound and verify that the former is at least as large as the latter. Use the spreadsheet BSMbin9e.xls.
4. Consider the right-hand side of the Black-Scholes-Merton formula as consisting of the sum of two terms. Explain what each of those terms represents.
5. Explain each of the following concepts as they relate to call options.
   a. Delta
   b. Gamma
   c. Rho
   d. Vega
   e. Theta
6. Answer the following questions as they relate to implied volatilities.
   a. Can implied volatilities be expected to vary for options on the same stock with the same exercise price but different expirations?
   b. Can implied volatilities be expected to vary for options on the same stock with the same expiration but different exercise prices?

c. Why and how are implied volatilities used to quote options prices?

The following option prices were observed for calls and puts on a stock for the trading day of July 6 of a particular year. Use this information in problems 7 through 14. The stock was priced at 165.13. The expirations were July 17, August 21, and October 16. The continuously compounded risk-free rates associated with the three expirations were 0.0503, 0.0535, and 0.0571, respectively. Unless otherwise indicated, assume that the options are European.

	Calls			Puts		
Strike	Jul	Aug	Oct	Jul	Aug	Oct
155	10.50	11.75	14.00	0.19	1.25	2.75
160	6.00	8.13	11.13	0.75	2.75	4.50
165	2.69	5.25	8.13	2.38	4.75	6.75
170	0.81	3.25	6.00	5.75	7.50	9.00

7. Suppose on July 7 the stock will go ex-dividend with a dividend of $2. Assuming that the options are American, determine whether the July 160 call would be exercised. Estimate the historical volatility of the stock for use in the Black-Scholes-Merton model. (Ignore dividends on the stock.)

8. Following is the sequence of daily prices on the stock for the preceding month of June:

Date	Price	Date	Price
6/1	159.88	6/16	162.00
6/2	157.25	6/17	161.38
6/3	160.25	6/18	160.88
6/4	161.38	6/19	161.38
6/5	160.00	6/22	163.25
6/8	161.25	6/23	164.88
6/9	159.88	6/24	166.13
6/10	157.75	6/25	167.88
6/11	157.63	6/26	166.50
6/12	156.63	6/29	165.38
6/15	159.63	6/30	162.50

9. Estimate the implied volatility of the August 165 call. Compare your answer with the one you obtained in problem 8. Use trial and error. Stop

when your answer is within 0.01 of the true implied volatility. Use the Excel spreadsheet BSMbin9e.xls.

10. Repeat the last problem using the approximation for an at-the-money call. Compare your answer with the one you obtained in problem 9. Is the approximation a good one? Why or why not?

11. Let the standard deviation of the continuously compounded return on the stock is 21 percent. Ignore dividends. Respond to the following:
    a. What is the theoretical fair value of the October 165 call? Calculate this answer by hand and then recalculate it using BSMbin9e.xls.
    b. Based on your answer in part a, recommend a riskless strategy.
    c. If the stock price decreases by $1, how will the option position offset the loss on the stock?

12. Use the Black-Scholes-Merton European put option pricing formula for the October 165 put option. Repeat parts a, b, and c of the previous problem with respect to the put.

13. Suppose the stock pays a $1.10 dividend with an ex-dividend date of September 10. Rework part a of problem 11 using an appropriate dividend-adjusted procedure. Calculate this answer by hand and then recalculate it using BSMbin9e.xls.

14. On July 6, the dividend yield on the stock is 2.7 percent. Rework part a of problem 11 using the yield-based dividend adjustment procedure. Calculate this answer by hand and then recalculate it using BSMbin9e.xls.

15. Using BSMbin9e.xls, compute the call and put prices for a stock option, The current stock price is $100, the exercise price is $100, the risk-free interest rate is 0 percent (continuously compounded), the volatility is 30 percent, and the time to expiration is one year. Explain the observed relationship between the call and put price. Further explain the relationship between your results here and in the previous question.

16. A stock has a current price of $115.83. A European call option on the stock expires in eight weeks and has $N(d_1) = 0.33$. If volatility changes by 0.03, approximate the amount the call price is expected to change.

17. Using BSMbin9e.xls, compute the call and put prices for a stock option. The current stock price is $100, the exercise price is $105.1271, the risk-free interest rate is 5 percent (continuously compounded), the volatility is 30 percent, and the time

to expiration is one year. Explain the observed relationship between the call and put price.

18. Consider a European put option that expires in four weeks with an exercise price of $120 trading on a stock currently priced at $126.30. Assuming an annualized volatility of the continuously compounded return on the stock of 0.78 and a continuously compounded risk-free rate of 0.0348, use the Black-Scholes-Merton model applied to European puts to price the option.

19. A stock has a current price of $132.43. For a particular European put option that expires in three weeks, the probability of the option expiring in-the-money is 63.68% and the annualized volatility of the continuously compounded return on the stock is 0.76. Assuming a continuously compounded risk-free rate of 0.0398 and an exercise price of $130, by what dollar amount would the option price be predicted to have changed in three days assuming no change in the underlying stock price (or any other inputs besides time)?

20. Using BSMbin9e.xls, compute the call and put prices for a stock option. The current stock price is $100, the exercise price is $100, the risk-free interest rate is 5 percent (continuously compounded), the volatility is 30 percent, and the time to expiration is one year. Now assume that in the next instant, the company announces an immediate 2-for-1 stock split. As expected, the stock price falls to $50. The options exchange rules call for dividing the exercise price by 2 and doubling the number of option contracts held. Verify that the option holders are unharmed by these stock split rules of the options exchange.

21. A financial institution offers a new over-the-counter option that pays 150% of the payoff of a standard European option. Demonstrate, using BSMbin9e.xls (or by hand), that the value of this option is simply 1.5 times the value of an ordinary option. Let the stock price be 82, the exercise price be 80, the risk-free rate (continuously compounded) be 4 percent, the volatility be 40 percent, and the option expire in one year.

22. A stock is selling for $100 with a volatility of 40 percent. Consider a call option on the stock with an exercise price of 100 and an expiration of one year. The risk-free rate is 4.5 percent. Let the call be selling for its Black-Scholes-Merton value. You construct a delta-hedged position involving the sale of 10,000 calls and the purchase of an appropriate number of shares. You can buy and sell shares and calls only in whole numbers. At the end of the next day, the stock is at $99. You then adjust your position accordingly to maintain the delta hedge. The following day the stock closes at $102. In all cases, use the spreadsheet BSMbin9e.xls to price the call.

    a. Compare the amount of money you end up with to the amount you would have had if you had invested the money in a risk-free bond. Explain why the target was or was not achieved.

    b. Now add another option, one on the same stock with an exercise price of 105 and the same expiration. Reconstruct the problem by delta and gamma hedging. Explain why the target was or was not achieved.

23. On December 9, a Swiss franc call option expiring on January 13 had an exercise price of $0.46. The spot exchange rate was $0.4728. The U.S. risk-free rate was 7.1 percent, and the Swiss risk-free rate was 3.6 percent. The volatility of the exchange rate was 0.145. Determine whether the call was correctly priced at $0.0163.

24. (Concept Problem) Suppose a stock is priced at 80 and has a volatility of 0.35. You buy a call option with an exercise price of 80 that expires in three months. The risk-free rate is 5 percent. Answer the following questions:

    a. Determine the theoretical value of the call. Use BSMbin9e.xls.

    b. Suppose the actual call is selling for $5. Suggest a strategy, but do not worry about hedging the risk. Simply buy or sell 100 calls.

    c. After purchasing the call, you investigate your possible profits. You expect to unwind the position one month later, at which time you expect the call to have converged to its Black-Scholes-Merton value. Of course, you do not know what the stock price will be, but you can calculate the profits for stock prices over a reasonable range. You expect that the stock will not vary beyond $60 and $100. Determine your profit in increments of $10 of the stock price. Comment on your results.

    Note: This problem will prepare you for Chapter 6.

25. (Concept Problem) Show how a delta hedge using a position in the stock and a long position in a put would be set up.

APPENDIX 5

A Shortcut to the Calculation of Implied Volatility

Solving for the implied volatility can be a tedious trial-and-error process. Manaster and Koehler (1982), however, provide a shortcut that can quickly lead to the solution. The technique employs a Newton-Raphson search procedure.

Suppose for a given standard deviation, σ^*, the Black-Scholes-Merton formula gives the call price as $C(\sigma^*)$. The true market price, however, is $C(\sigma)$, where σ is the true volatility. Manaster and Koehler recommend an initial guess of σ_1^*, where

$$\sigma_1^* = \sqrt{\left| \ln\left(\frac{S_0}{X}\right) + r_c T \right| \left(\frac{2}{T}\right)}.$$

Then compute the value of $C(\sigma_1^*)$ and compare it to the market price, $C(\sigma)$. If this is not close enough, the next guess should be

$$\sigma_2^* = \sigma_1^* - \frac{[C(\sigma_1^*) - C(\sigma)]e^{d_i^2/2}\sqrt{2\pi}}{S_0\sqrt{T}},$$

where d_1 is computed using σ_1^*. Then compute the value $C(\sigma_1^*)$ and compare it to the market price, $C(\sigma)$. If it is not close enough, the next guess should be

$$\sigma_3^* = \sigma_2^* - \frac{[C(\sigma_2^*) - C(\sigma)]e^{d_i^2/2}\sqrt{2\pi}}{S_0\sqrt{T}},$$

with d_1 computed using σ_2^*. Repeat the process until the model price is sufficiently close to the market price. In other words, given the ith guess of the implied volatility, the $(i + 1)$th guess should be

$$\sigma_{i+1}^* = \sigma_1^* - \frac{[C(\sigma_i^*) - C(\sigma)]e^{d_i^2/2}\sqrt{2\pi}}{S_0\sqrt{T}},$$

where d_1 is computed using σ_1^*.

Let us apply this procedure to the problem in the chapter. We have $S_0 = \$125.94$, $X = 125$, $r_c = 0.0446$, $T = 0.0959$, $\sigma = 0.83$, and $C(\sigma) = \$13.50$. The initial guess for the implied volatility is

$$\sigma_1^* = \sqrt{\left| \ln\left(\frac{125.94}{125}\right) + 0.0446(0.0959) \right| \left(\frac{2}{0.0959}\right)} = 0.4954.$$

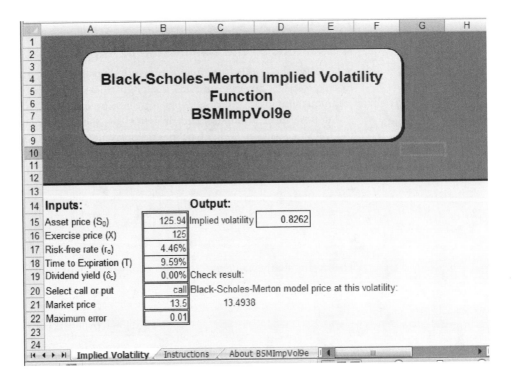

At a volatility of 0.4954, the Black-Scholes-Merton value is 8.41. The next guess should be

$$\sigma_2^* = 0.4954 - \frac{[8.41 - 13.50]e^{(0.1533)^2/2}(2.5066)}{125.94\sqrt{0.059}} = 0.8264$$

where 0.1533 is the value of d_1 computed from the Black-Scholes-Merton model using 0.4950 as the standard deviation. The value 2.5066 is $\sqrt{2\pi}$. The Black-Scholes-Merton price using 0.8260 as the volatility is 13.49, which is close enough.

Thus, we have found the solution in only two steps. In the chapter, we noted that the implied volatility was 0.83 with the slight difference being due to rounding off the answer.

The software included with this book contains a spreadsheet called BSMImpVol9e.xls that computes the implied volatility using the Manaster-Koehler technique. This procedure is written as an Excel function called = BlackScholesMertonImpliedVolatility (,,,,,,). Following the procedure described in the Instructions sheet, you can make this function available in any Excel spreadsheet, which would enable you to simply select Insert/Function and then select it from the User Defined functions. In the example provided here, the stock price is $125.94, the exercise price is 125, the risk-free rate is 4.46 percent, the time to expiration is 0.0959, the continuous dividend yield is 0.00 percent, the option is a call, and the market price is $13.50. The user specified that the option price using the implied volatility must be within 0.01 of the call price. As you can see, the function shows that the implied volatility is 0.8262. It also shows that the option price at a volatility of 0.8262 is 13.4937861, which is within 0.01 of the market price.

CHAPTER **6**

Basic Option Strategies

A good trader with a bad model can beat a bad trader with a good model.

William Margrabe
Derivatives Strategy, April, 1998, p. 27

One of the most interesting characteristics of an option is that it can be combined with stock or other options to produce a wide variety of alternative strategies. The profit possibilities are so diverse that virtually any investor can find an option strategy to suit his risk preference and market forecast.

In a world without options, the available strategies would be quite limited. If the market were expected to go up, one would buy stock; if the market were expected to go down, one would short sell stock. As noted in Chapter 1, however, short-selling stock requires an investor to meet certain requirements (such as having a minimum amount of capital to risk), selling short on an uptick or zero-plus tick, and maintaining minimum margins. Options make it simple to convert a forecast into a plan of action that will pay off if the plan is correct. Of course, any strategy will penalize one if the forecast is wrong. With the judicious use of options, however, the penalties can be relatively small and known in advance.

This and the next chapter examine some of the more popular option strategies. It is not possible to cover all of the strategies option traders could use. The ones we examine here should provide a basic understanding of the process of analyzing option strategies. Further study and analysis of the more advanced and complex strategies can be done using the framework presented here.

This chapter presents the basic option strategies. These strategies are the easiest to understand and involve the fewest transactions. Specifically, we shall cover the strategies of calls, puts, and stock and combining calls with stock and puts with stock. We shall see how calls and stock can be combined to form puts and how puts and stock can be combined to form calls. Chapter 7 will examine spread strategies, which involve one short option and one long option, and combination strategies, which entail both puts and calls.

The approach we use here to analyze option strategies is to determine the profit a strategy will produce for a broad range of stock prices when the position is closed. This methodology is simple yet powerful enough to demonstrate its strengths. One attractive feature is that there are actually three ways to present the strategy. Because reinforcement enhances learning, we shall utilize all three presentation methods.

The first method is to determine an equation that gives the profit from the strategy as a function of the stock price when the position is closed. You will find that the equations are quite simple and build on skills covered in Chapters 3, 4, and 5. The second method is a graphical analysis that uses the equations to construct graphs of the profit as a function of the stock price when the position is closed. The third approach is to use a specific

CHAPTER OBJECTIVES

- Introduce the three-way procedure for examining the risk and return of an option strategy: by equation, by graph, and by numerical example

- Examine the basic strategies of buying and selling stock, calls, and puts

- Examine the combination strategies of covered calls, protective puts, conversions, and reversals

- Explain how the choice of exercise price affects the possible outcomes of a strategy

- Explain how the length of the chosen holding period affects the outcomes of a strategy

- Illustrate the accompanying software for analyzing option strategies

numerical example to illustrate how the equations and graphs apply to real-world options. We continue with the same DCRB options previously examined.

Keep in mind that there are options on other types of assets, such as currencies, commodities and bonds, and there are also options on futures contracts and interest rates, which we shall encounter in later chapters. The basic principles covered in this chapter apply in a fairly straightforward manner to those cases. The end-of-chapter problems ask you to analyze some of the strategies in this chapter as applied to currency options.

As with our earlier analysis of options, we require several symbols. For convenience and because there are a few new notations, the following section presents the complete set of symbols.

TERMINOLOGY AND NOTATION

C = current call price
P = current put price
S_0 = current stock price
T = time to expiration as a fraction of a year
X = exercise price
S_T = stock price at option's expiration
Π = profit from the strategy

The following symbols indicate the number of calls, puts, or shares of stock:

N_C = number of calls
N_P = number of puts
N_S = number of shares of stock

As indicated in Chapter 2, the standard number of calls, puts, and shares is 100. For our purposes, it will not matter if we use a simple number such as 1 or 2. When working with the numerical examples, however, we shall assume a standard contract of options or block of stock, which, of course, means 100 options or shares.

Profit Equations

One of the powerful features of the N_C, N_P, and N_S notation is that these numbers' signs indicate whether the position is long or short. For example,

$N_C > (<)\ 0$, the investor is buying (writing) calls.
$N_P > (<)\ 0$, the investor is buying (writing) puts.
$N_S > (<)\ 0$, the investor is buying (selling short) stock.

To determine the profit from a particular strategy, we need only know how many calls, puts, and shares of stock are involved, whether the position is long or short, the prices at which the options or stock were purchased or written, and the prices at which the positions were closed. With calls held to the expiration date, we already know that the call will be worth its intrinsic value at expiration. Thus, the profit can be written as

$$\Pi = N_C[\text{Max}(0, S_T - X) - C].$$

Notice how the sign of N_C allows the equation to give the profit for both the call buyer and the call writer. For example, a buyer with one call, $N_C = 1$, has a profit of

$$\Pi = \text{Max}(0, S_T - X) - C.$$

For the writer with one call, $N_C = -1$, profit is

$$\Pi = -\text{Max}(0, S_T - X) + C.$$

For a put option, the profit can be written as

$$\Pi = N_P[\text{Max}(0, X - S_T) - P].$$

For a buyer with one put, $N_P = 1$,

$$\Pi = \text{Max}(0, X - S_T) - P.$$

For a writer with one put, $N_P = -1$,

$$\Pi = -\text{Max}(0, X - S_T) + P.$$

For a transaction involving only stock, the profit equation is simply

$$\Pi = N_S(S_T - S_0).$$

For a buyer of one share of stock, $N_S = 1$, profit is

$$\Pi = S_T - S_0.$$

For a short seller of one share of stock, $N_S = -1$, profit is

$$\Pi = -S_T + S_0.$$

These profit equations make it simple to determine the profit from any transaction. Consider, for example, the equations for the call buyer and the put buyer. In both cases, the profit per share is simply the dollar amount received from exercising the option minus the dollar amount paid for the option. The profit per share is then multiplied by the number of options to compute the profit. For the call writer and put writer, the profit per share is the amount received as the premium minus the amount paid out from exercising the option. The profit per share is then multiplied by the number of options written to compute the profit. Similarly, the profit per share for a stock buyer is simply the price at which the stock is sold minus the price paid for the stock. Again, the profit per share is then multiplied by the number of shares to compute the profit. For the short seller, the profit per share is the price received from the short sale minus the price paid for repurchasing the stock. The profit per share is then multiplied by the number of shares sold short to compute the profit. To keep the analysis as simple as possible, we shall ignore the interest foregone or implicitly earned on a long or short position in options or stock.

Finally, we shall often find ourselves using the terms **bull** and **bear**, which are part of the lingo of financial markets. A bull market is a market in which the price goes up. A bear market is a market in which the price goes down. A bullish investor believes that a bull market is coming, and a bearish investor believes that a bear market is coming.

Different Holding Periods

The cases described in the previous section are strategies in which the position is held until the option expires. Because the option has no time value remaining and sells for its intrinsic value, the profit is easy to determine. It is not necessary, however, that an option trader hold the position open until the option expires. The length of the investor's holding period can be any time interval desired. In the case of a position closed out prior to the option's expiration, it is necessary to determine at what price the option would sell. How would we go about doing this?

Remember that the available information would be the exercise price and the time remaining on the option. We would want to know at what price the option would sell given a certain stock price. If the risk-free rate and an estimate of the variance of the return on the stock were available, we could use the Black-Scholes-Merton model. Here we shall assume that this information is available, and we shall use the model to estimate the option's remaining time value to determine the profit from the strategy.

For illustrative purposes, we define three points in time: T_1, T_2, and T. We allow the investor to hold the position until either T_1, T_2, or all the way to expiration, T. The holding period from today until T_1 is the shortest. If an investor closes out the position at time T_1, the option will have a remaining time to expiration of $T - T_1$. The holding period from today until T_2 is of intermediate length. The investor who chooses it closes the option position with a remaining time to expiration of $T - T_2$. If the investor holds the position until expiration, the remaining time is $T - T = 0$.

Thus, the profit from a call position, if terminated at time T_1 before expiration and when the stock price is S_{T_1} is written as

$$\Pi = N_C[C(S_{T_1}, T - T_1, X) - C],$$

where $C(S_{T_1}, T - T_1, X)$ is the value obtained from the Black-Scholes-Merton or any other appropriate call option pricing model using a stock price of S_{T_1} and a time to expiration of $T - T_1$. C is, of course, the original price of the call. The expression for puts is the same except that we use a P instead of a C and employ the Black-Scholes-Merton or any other appropriate put option pricing model to calculate $P(S_{T_1}, T - T_1, X)$. Similar expressions obviously apply when the position is closed at T_2.

Although the examples in this chapter use exchange-traded options, they are equally applicable to over-the-counter options. Although there is no specific market for liquidating over-the-counter options before expiration, the equivalent result can be obtained by simply creating a new option that offsets the old option. This procedure, of course, assumes that the writer does not default.

Assumptions

Several important assumptions underlie the analysis of option strategies.

First, we assume the stock pays no dividends. As we saw in Chapters 3, 4, and 5, dividends can complicate option decisions. Although including them here would not be especially difficult, we will intentionally omit them to keep the analysis simple. Where it is especially important, we will discuss the effect of dividends.

Second, we assume that there are no taxes or transaction costs. These already have been covered and certainly are a consideration in option decisions, but they would add little to the analysis here. Where there are special tax and transaction cost factors, we provide an interpretation of their effects.

Recall that we have been analyzing the DCRB options in previous chapters. For convenience, Table 6.1 repeats those data.

TABLE 6.1 DCRB OPTION DATA, MAY 14

EXERCISE PRICE	CALLS			PUTS		
	MAY	JUNE	JULY	MAY	JUNE	JULY
120	8.75	15.40	20.90	2.75	9.25	13.65
125	5.75	13.50	18.60	4.60	11.50	16.60
130	3.60	11.35	16.40	7.35	14.25	19.65

Current stock price: 125.94
Expirations: May 21, June 18, July 16
Risk-free rates (continuously compounded): 0.0447 (May); 0.0446 (June); 0.0453 (July)

Now, let us move on to analyzing the strategies. The first group of strategies we shall examine are transactions involving stock.

STOCK TRANSACTIONS

Because combining stocks with options is sometimes an attractive strategy, it is important that we first establish the framework for stocks.

Buy Stock

The simplest transaction is the purchase of stock. The profit equation is

$$\Pi = N_S(S_T - S_0), \text{ given that } N_S > 0.$$

For illustrative purposes, let $N_S = 100$, a single round lot of stock. Figure 6.1 shows how the profit from this transaction varies with the stock price when the position is closed. The transaction is profitable if the DCRB stock ultimately is sold at a price higher than $125.94, the price paid for the stock. Dividends would lower this breakeven by the amount of the dividends, while transaction costs would raise it by the amount of those costs.

Short Sell Stock

The short sale of stock is the mirror image of the purchase of stock. The profit equation is

$$\Pi = N_S(S_T - S_0), \text{ given that } N_S < 0.$$

In this example, let $N_S = -100$, which means that 100 shares have been sold short. Figure 6.2 shows how the profit from the short sale varies with the price of the DCRB

FIGURE 6.1 Buy Stock

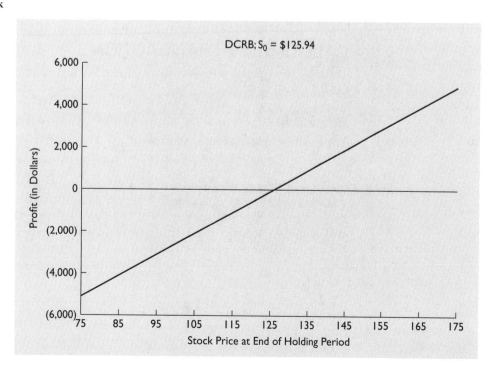

FIGURE 6.2 Sell Short Stock

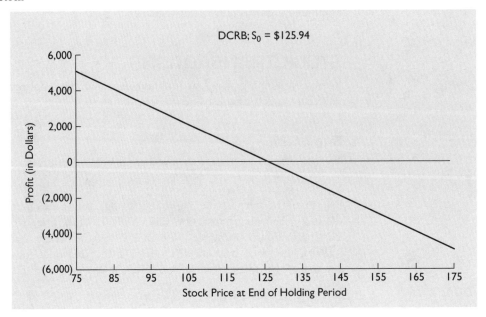

stock at the end of the investor's holding period. Short selling is a strategy undertaken in anticipation of a bear market. The investor borrows the stock from the broker, sells it at $125.94, and repurchases it at—it is hoped—a lower price.[1] If the shares are repurchased at less than $125.94, the transaction earns a profit. As Figure 6.2 shows, selling short has the potential for unlimited losses if the investor guesses wrong and the stock price rises. Now we turn to the first of the option strategies—the call transactions.

CALL OPTION TRANSACTIONS

There are two types of call option transactions. We first examine the strategy of buying a call.

Buy a Call

The profit from a call option purchase is

$$\Pi = N_C[\text{Max}(0, S_T - X) - C] \text{ given that } N_C > 0.$$

Consider the case where the number of calls purchased is simply 1 ($N_C = 1$). Suppose that the stock price at expiration is less than or equal to the exercise price so that the option expires out-of-the-money. What is the profit from the call? Because the call expires unexercised, the profit is simply $-C$. The call buyer incurs a loss equal to the premium paid for the call.

---

[1] Any dividends paid while the stock is sold short go to whoever purchased the stock from the short seller. In addition, the short seller must pay the broker the amount of the dividends. The lender of the shares also forfeits voting rights.

FIGURE 6.3 Buy Call

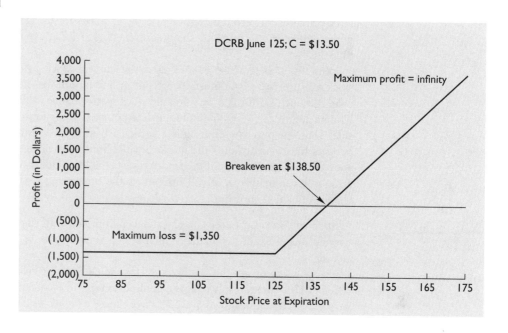

Suppose that the call option ends up in-the-money. Then the call buyer will exercise the call, buying the stock for X and selling it for S_T, which will net a profit of $S_T - X - C$.[2] These results are summarized as follows:

$$\Pi = S_T - X - C \qquad \text{if } S_T > X.$$
$$\Pi = -C \qquad \text{if } S_T \leq X.$$

Figure 6.3 illustrates this transaction for the DCRB June 125 call, which sells for $13.50. The call has limited downside risk. The maximum possible loss for a single contract is $1,350, which is the premium times 100. At any stock price at expiration less than the exercise price of 125, the call buyer loses the maximum amount. If the stock price is above 125, the loss will be less than $1,350. Losses, however, are incurred if the stock price is below a critical stock price, which we shall call the **breakeven stock price** at expiration.

Notice in Figure 6.3 that the breakeven stock price is above the exercise price and between $135 and $145. We can find the breakeven stock price at expiration by simply setting to zero the profit for the case where stock price exceeds exercise price. We then solve for the breakeven stock price, S_T^*. Thus,

$$\Pi = S_T^* - X - C = 0.$$

Solving for S_T^* gives

$$S_T^* = X + C.$$

Buying a call is a bullish strategy that has a limited loss (the call premium) and an unlimited potential gain.

The breakeven stock price at expiration, then, is the exercise price plus the call price. The call premium, C, is the amount already paid for the call. To break even, the call buyer must exercise the option at a price high enough to recover the option's costs. For every dollar by which the stock

---

[2]The stock need not be sold for this result to hold. The call buyer can retain the stock worth S_T or convert it to cash. An even better strategy would be to sell the call an instant before it expires. At that time, it should have little, if any, time value left. This would avoid the high transaction cost of taking delivery of the stock.

price at expiration exceeds the exercise price, the call buyer gains a dollar. Therefore, the stock price must exceed the exercise price by C dollars for the call buyer to recover the cost of the option. In this problem, the breakeven stock price at expiration is $125 + $13.50 = $138.50.

With the breakeven at $138.50 and the current stock price at $125.94, the DCRB stock must increase by almost 10 percent in one month for the transaction to be profitable. Although DCRB is a very volatile stock, performance of this sort would be unusual. Nonetheless, a call offers unlimited upside potential while limiting the loss on the downside. Thus, the purchase of a call is a particularly attractive strategy for those with limited budgets who want to "play the market" while limiting their losses to a level that will not wipe them out. Of course, if the trader invests the same dollar amount, as opposed to the same number of shares, in call options as the underlying stock, then there is a greater chance of being wiped out.

Choice of Exercise Price Usually, several options with the same expirations but different strike prices are available. Which option should we buy? There is no unambiguous answer.

Figure 6.4 compares the profit graphs for the DCRB June calls with strike prices of 120, 125, and 130. There are advantages and disadvantages to each. First, compare the 125, which we previously examined, with the 130. If we choose a higher strike price, the gain if the stock prices rises will be less. Because the call with the higher exercise price commands a lower premium, however, the loss if the stock price falls will be smaller. The breakeven for the 130 is X + C = 130 + 11.35 = 141.35, which is higher than that for the 125.

If we choose the 120 over the 125, we have the potential for a greater profit if the stock price at expiration is higher. Also, the breakeven is X + C = 120 + 15.40 = 135.40. If the market is down, however, the loss will be greater. The potential loss is the full premium of $1,540. This is because the call with the lower exercise price will command a greater premium.

> Buying a call with a lower exercise price has a greater maximum loss but greater upside gains.

Thus, the choice of which option to purchase is not easy and depends on how confident the call buyer is about the market outlook. If one

FIGURE 6.4 Buy Call: Different Exercise Prices

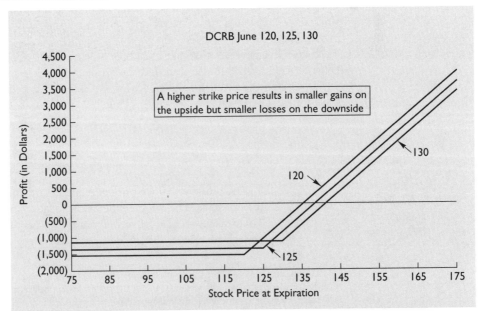

strongly believes that the stock price will increase, the call with the lowest exercise price is preferable. Otherwise, a higher exercise price will minimize the potential loss.

Choice of Holding Period The strategies previously examined assume the investor holds the option until the expiration date. Alternatively, the call buyer could sell the option prior to expiration. Let us look at what happens if a shorter holding period is chosen.

Recall that we plan to examine three holding periods. The shortest holding period involves the sale of the call at time T_1. The intermediate-length holding period is that in which the call is sold at time T_2. The longest holding period is that in which the option is held until expiration. If the option is sold at time T_1, the profit is the call price at the time of the sale minus the price originally paid for the option. We can use the Black-Scholes-Merton model with a time to expiration of $T - T_1$ to estimate the price of the call for a broad range of possible stock prices and thereby determine the profit graph. Using the July 125 call, the three holding periods are (1) sell the call on June 4, T_1; (2) sell the call on June 25, T_2; and (3) hold the call until it expires on July 16, T.

> For a given stock price, the longer a call is held, the more time value it loses and the lower the profit.

For the shortest holding period, in which the position is closed on June 4, the time remaining is 42 days; that is, there are 42 days between June 4 and July 16. Thus, the call price will be based on a remaining time to expiration of 42/365 = 0.1151. The call's time to expiration is $T - T_1 = 0.1151$. For the intermediate-length holding period, in which the position is held until June 25, the time remaining to expiration is 21 days. Thus, the time to expiration is 21/365 = 0.0575 and $T - T_2 = 0.0575$. For the longest holding period, the time remaining is, of course, zero. The parameters used in the model are X = 125, $\sigma = 0.83$, and $r_c = 0.0453$.

The results are shown in Table 6.2. As an example, note that on June 4, at a stock price of $110, the call would have a Black-Scholes-Merton value of $7.16. Because the investor paid $18.60 for the call, the profit per contract is 100($7.16 − $18.60) = −$1,144. If the

TABLE 6.2 ESTIMATION OF BLACK-SCHOLES-MERTON PRICES AND PROFITS FOR DCRB JULY 125 CALL

POSITION CLOSED AT: TIME TO EXPIRATION:	JUNE 4 0.1151		JUNE 25 0.0575	
STOCK PRICE AT END OF HOLDING PERIOD	BLACK-SCHOLES-MERTON CALL PRICE	PROFIT PER CONTRACT	BLACK-SCHOLES-MERTON CALL PRICE	PROFIT PER CONTRACT
105	$ 5.39	−$1,321	$ 2.44	−$1,616
110	$ 7.16	−$1,144	$ 3.74	−$1,486
115	$ 9.23	−$ 937	$ 5.43	−$1,317
120	$11.61	−$ 699	$ 7.54	−$1,106
125	$14.29	−$ 431	$10.06	−$ 854
130	$17.24	−$ 136	$12.98	−$ 562
135	$20.45	$ 185	$16.27	−$ 233
140	$23.90	$ 530	$19.88	$ 128
145	$27.57	$ 897	$23.77	$ 517
150	$31.43	$1,283	$27.91	$ 931
155	$35.47	$1,687	$32.24	$1,364

Note: Calculations were done on a spreadsheet, so they may differ slightly from calculations done by hand.

FIGURE 6.5 Buy Call: Different Holding Periods

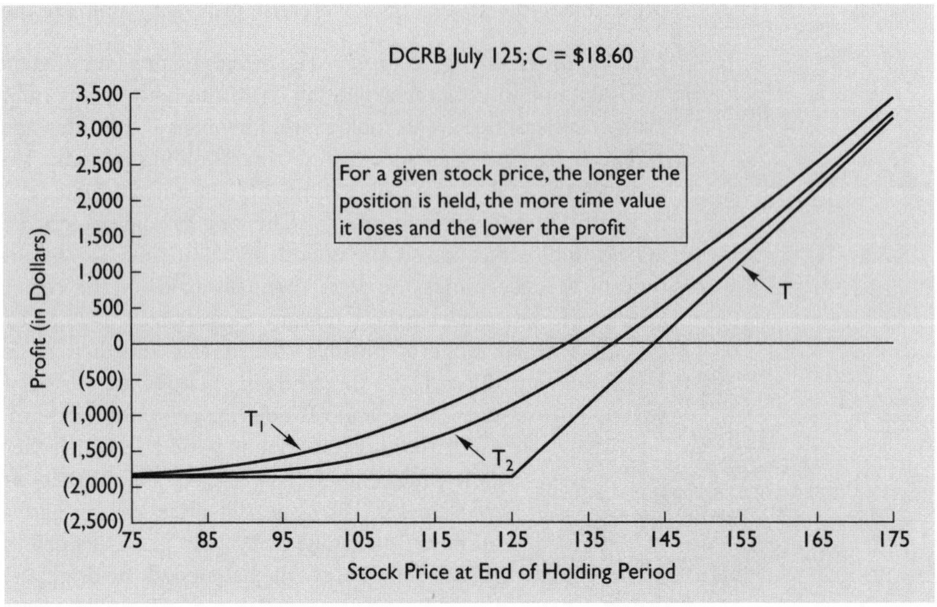

DCRB July 125; C = $18.60

For a given stock price, the longer the
position is held, the more time value
it loses and the lower the profit

stock price were $115, the call would be worth $9.23 and the profit would be 100($9.23 − $18.60) = −$937. On June 25, at a stock price of $110, the call would be worth $3.74 and the profit would be 100($3.74 − $18.60) = −$1,486. The remaining entries are computed in the same manner.

In Figure 6.5, the profit per contract is graphed as the dependent variable and the stock price at the end of the holding period is graphed as the independent variable.

The graph indicates that the shortest holding period provides a higher profit for all stock prices at expiration. It would appear that the shorter the holding period, the greater the potential profit. This is because with a shorter holding period, the call can be sold to recover some of its remaining time value. The longer the call is held, the greater is the time value lost.

This seems to present a paradox: It suggests that to maximize profits, one should hold the option for the shortest time possible. Obviously option traders do not always use such short holding periods. What is missing from the explanation?

The answer is that the shorter holding period provides superior profits *for a given stock price*. The profit graph does not indicate the likelihood that the stock price will end up high or low. In fact, with a shorter holding period, the possible range of stock prices is much lower because there is less time for the stock price to move. The longer holding period, on the other hand, gives the stock price more time to increase.

This completes our discussion of the strategy of buying a call. We now turn to the strategy of writing a call.

Write a Call

An option trader who writes a call without concurrently owning the stock is said to be writing an **uncovered** or **naked call**. The reason for this nomenclature is that the position is a high-risk strategy, one with the potential for unlimited losses. The uncovered call writer undertakes the obligation to sell stock not currently owned to the call buyer at the latter's request. The writer therefore may have to buy the stock at an unfavorable price. As a result, writing an uncovered call is a privilege restricted to those few traders with sufficient capital to risk. Because the brokerage firm must make up losses to the clearing-house, it, too, is at risk. Therefore, a trader's broker must agree to handle the transaction—and that is likely to be done only for the best and wealthiest customers. Of course, traders owning seats on the exchange or low-credit-risk institutions in the over-the-counter market are less restricted and can more easily write uncovered calls, but because of the high risk, even they do so infrequently. Moreover, with stocks that pay dividends, the writer faces the risk of early exercise if the calls are American, as discussed in Chapter 3.

If writing an uncovered call is such a risky strategy, why should we examine it? The reason is that writing an uncovered call can be combined with other strategies, such as buying stock or another option, to produce a strategy with very low risk. Therefore, it is necessary to establish the results for the short call before combining it with other strategies.

Because the buyer's and writer's profits are mirror images of each other, the profit equations and graphs are already familiar. The writer's profit is

$$\Pi = N_C[\text{Max}(0, S_T - X) - C] \text{ given that } N_C < 0.$$

Assume one call, $N_C = -1$. Then the profit is

$$
\begin{aligned}
\Pi &= C & &\text{if } S_T \leq X. \\
\Pi &= -S_T + X + C & &\text{if } S_T > X.
\end{aligned}
$$

> Selling a call is a bearish strategy that has a limited gain (the premium) and an unlimited loss.

Figure 6.6 illustrates the profit graph for the writer of 100 DCRB June 125 calls at a price of $13.50. Note that the breakeven stock price for the writer must be the breakeven stock price for the buyer, $X + C = \$138.50$. The maximum loss for the buyer is also the maximum gain for the writer, $1,350$. If the stock price ends up above the exercise price, the loss to the writer can be substantial—and as is obvious from the graph, there is no limit to the possible loss in a bull market.

> Selling a call with a lower exercise price has a greater maximum gain but greater upside losses.

Choice of Exercise Price Figure 6.7 compares the strategy of writing calls at different strike prices by showing the 120, 125, and 130 calls. Figure 6.7

FIGURE 6.6 Write Call

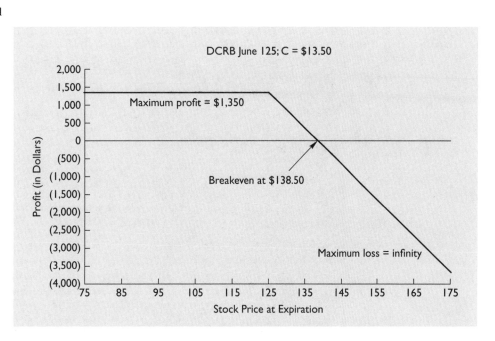

FIGURE 6.7 Write Call: Different Exercise Prices

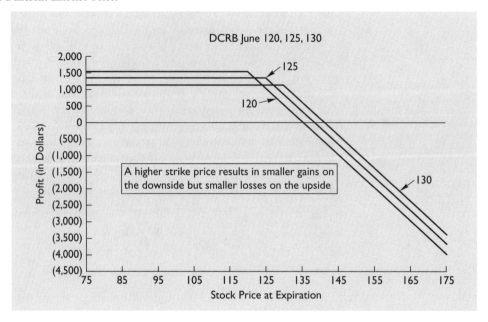

is the mirror image of Figure 6.4. The greatest profit potential is in the 120, which has the highest premium, $1,540, but is accompanied by the greatest loss potential and the lowest breakeven, X + C = 120 + 15.40 = 135.40. This would be the highest-risk strategy. The 130 would have the lowest risk of the three with the highest breakeven, X + C = 130 + 11.35 = 141.35, but also the lowest profit potential, the $1,135 premium.

Choice of Holding Period   Figure 6.8 illustrates the profit for the three possible holding periods previously described. These are the July 125 calls in which the holding period T_1 involves the repurchase of the call on June 4; T_2 assumes the call is

FIGURE 6.8 Write Call: Different Holding Periods

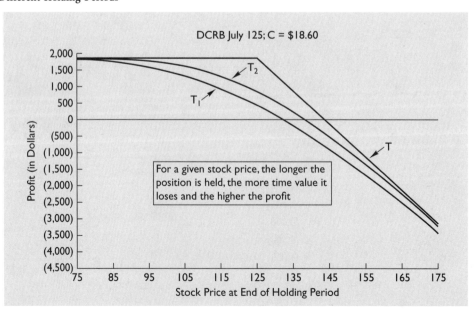

repurchased on June 25; and, T allows the call to be held until expiration, when it either is exercised or expires out-of-the-money.

Figure 6.8 is the mirror image of Figure 6.5. A writer repurchasing the call prior to expiration will have to pay for some of the remaining time value. Therefore, for the call writer, the profit is lowest with the shortest holding period *for a given stock price.*

This is because the time value repurchased is greater with the shorter holding period. With a shorter holding period, however, the stock price is less likely to move substantially; thus, the range of possible profits is far smaller. If the investor holds the position until expiration, the profit may be greater but the stock will have had more time to move—perhaps unfavorably. This completes our discussion of call buying and writing, which we see are mirror images of each other. We next turn to put option transactions.

> For a given stock price, the longer a short call is maintained, the more time value it loses and the greater the profit.

PUT OPTION TRANSACTIONS
Buy a Put

Buying a put is a strategy for a bear market. The potential loss is limited to the premium paid. The gain is also limited but can still be quite substantial. The profit from the purchase of a put is given by the equation

$$\Pi = N_P[\text{Max}(0, X - S_T) - P] \text{ given that } N_P > 0.$$

As in the example for calls, assume the purchase of a single put, $N_P = 1$. If the stock price at expiration ends up less than the exercise price, the put is in-the-money and is exercised. If the stock price at expiration is greater than or equal to the exercise price, the put ends up out-of-the-money. The profits are

$$\Pi = X - S_T - P \qquad \text{if } S_T < X.$$
$$\Pi = -P \qquad \text{if } S_T \geq X.$$

Figure 6.9 illustrates the profits from the put-buying strategy for the DCRB June 125 put with a premium of $11.50. The potential loss is limited to the premium paid, which

FIGURE 6.9 Buy Put

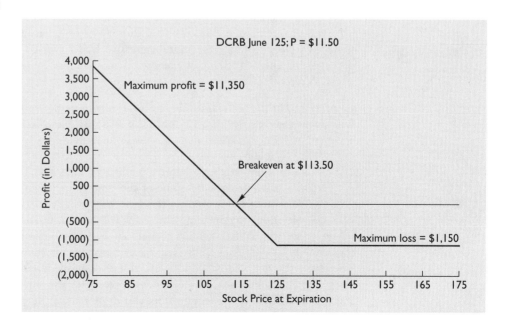

in this case is $1,150. The profit is also limited because there is a limit to how low the stock price can fall. The best outcome for a put buyer is for the company to go bankrupt. In that case, the stock would be worthless, $S_T = 0$, and the profit would be $X - P$. In this example, that would be $100(125 - 11.50) = 11,350$.

Notice that the breakeven occurs where the stock price is below the exercise price. Setting the profit equation for this case equal to zero gives

$$\Pi = X - S_T^* - P = 0.$$

Solving for the breakeven stock price, S_T^*, at expiration reveals that

$$S_T^* = X - P.$$

The put buyer must recover enough from the option's exercise to cover the premium already paid. For every dollar by which the option is in-the-money, the put buyer gains a dollar. Therefore, the stock price must fall below the exercise price by the amount of the premium. In this instance, this is $125 - 11.50 = 113.50$. For the investor to profit from this put, the stock price must fall to $113.50 or less by the expiration date. This is a decrease of almost 10 percent in one month, which is very large even for a volatile stock such as DCRB.

| Buying a put is a bearish strategy that has a limited loss (the put premium) and a large but limited potential gain. |

In any case, buying a put is an appropriate strategy when anticipating a bear market. The loss is limited to the premium paid, and the potential gain is quite high. Moreover, it is easier to execute a put transaction than a short sale. Puts need not be bought when the stock is on an uptick or zero-plus tick, and the amount paid for the put is far less than the margin on a short sale. More important, a put limits the loss while a short sale has an unlimited loss.

Choice of Exercise Price   Figure 6.10 compares the profit graphs for puts with different strike prices using the June 120, 125, and 130 puts. The highest exercise price, the 130, has the highest premium; thus, the potential loss is greatest—in this case, $1,425. Its profit potential is highest, however, with a maximum possible profit of $100(130 - 14.25) = 11,575$ if the stock price at expiration is zero. The breakeven is $130 - 14.25 = 115.75$. The 120 has the lowest potential profit, $100(120 - 9.25) = 11,075$, and the lowest breakeven stock price, $120 - 9.25 = 110.75$. It also has the lowest loss potential, however—its premium of $925. The put chosen will be determined by the risk the option trader is willing to take. The more aggressive trader will go for the maximum profit potential and choose the highest exercise price. The more conservative trader will choose a lower exercise price to limit the potential loss.

| Buying a put with a higher exercise price has a greater maximum loss but a greater downside gain. |

Choice of Holding Period   Figure 6.11 compares the profit potential of the three holding periods for the July 125 put. The Black-Scholes-Merton option pricing model for European puts was used to estimate the put prices for the shorter holding periods.

| For a given stock price, the longer a put is held, the more time value it loses and the lower the profit. For European puts, this effect is reversed when the stock price is low. |

By electing a shorter holding period—say, T_1—the put buyer can sell the put back for some of the time value originally purchased. If the put buyer holds until T_2, less time value will be recovered. If held until expiration, no remaining time value will be recaptured. As with the case for calls, the shorter holding periods show greater potential profit for *a given stock price*. They allow less time, however, for the stock price to go down. Therefore, shorter holding periods are not necessarily inferior or superior to longer ones. The choice depends on the trader's forecast for the stock price—specifically, how much it is expected to move, direction, and in how much time.

FIGURE 6.10 Buy Put: Different Exercise Prices

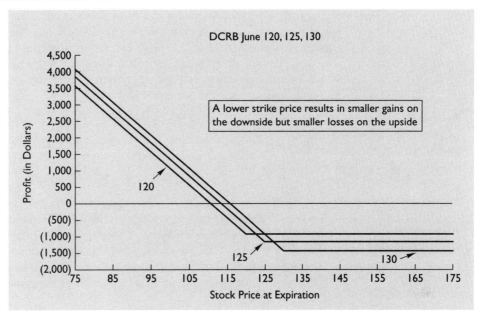

FIGURE 6.10 Buy Put: Different Exercise Prices

DCRB June 120, 125, 130

A lower strike price results in smaller gains on the downside but smaller losses on the upside

An exception to the pattern of time value decay can occur at very low stock prices. Recall that a European put can increase in value with a decrease in time.

With an understanding of the put buyer's profit potential, it should be simple to examine the case for the put writer. As you probably expect, the put writer's position is the mirror image of the put buyer's.

FIGURE 6.11 Buy Put: Different Holding Periods

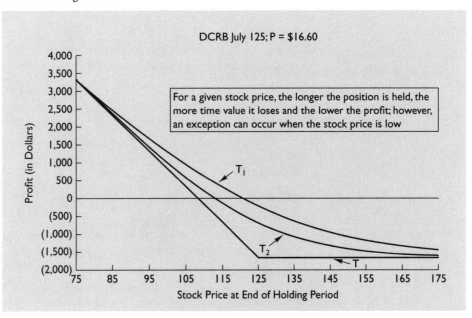

DCRB July 125; P = $16.60

For a given stock price, the longer the position is held, the more time value it loses and the lower the profit; however, an exception can occur when the stock price is low

Write a Put

The put writer is obligated to buy the stock from the put buyer at the exercise price. The put writer profits if the stock price goes up and the put therefore is not exercised, in which case the writer keeps the premium. If the stock price falls such that the put is exercised, the put writer is forced to buy the stock at a price greater than its market value. For an American put, this can, of course, occur prior to as well as at expiration. The profit equation for the put writer is

$$\Pi = N_P[\text{Max}(0, X - S_T) - P] \text{ given that } N_P < 0.$$

Selling a put is a bullish strategy that has a limited gain (the premium) and a large but limited potential loss.

Assume the simple case of a single short put, $N_P = -1$. The writer's profits are the mirror images of the buyer's:

$$\Pi = -X + S_T + P \qquad \text{if } S_T < X.$$
$$\Pi = P \qquad \text{if } S_T \geq X.$$

Figure 6.12 illustrates the put writer's profits using the June 125 put written at a premium of $11.50. The writer's maximum potential profit is the buyer's maximum potential loss—the amount of the premium, $1,150. The maximum potential loss for the writer is limited, but like the buyer's maximum potential gain, it is a very large amount: here $11,350. The breakeven stock price at expiration is the same as that for the buyer—$X - P$, or $113.50.

Selling a put with a higher exercise price has a greater maximum gain but a greater downside loss.

Choice of Exercise Price Figure 6.13 compares the put writer's profits for different strike prices using the June puts. The highest strike price, 130, offers the greatest premium income and therefore the greatest profit potential. The maximum profit is $1,425, and the breakeven is 130 − 14.25 = 115.75. The risk, however, is greatest because any losses will be larger in a bear market. The lowest strike price offers the lowest maximum profit—the premium income of $925—but also has the lowest breakeven—120 − 9.25 = 110.75—and the lowest loss if the market is down. Once again, the range of exercise prices offers the put writer several choices for assuming various degrees of risk and expected reward.

FIGURE 6.12 Write Put

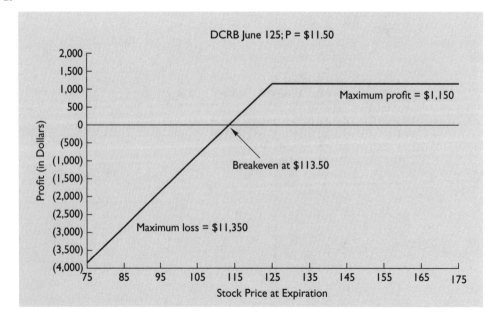

DCRB June 125; P = $11.50

Maximum profit = $1,150

Breakeven at $113.50

Maximum loss = $11,350

FIGURE 6.13 Write Put: Different Exercise Prices

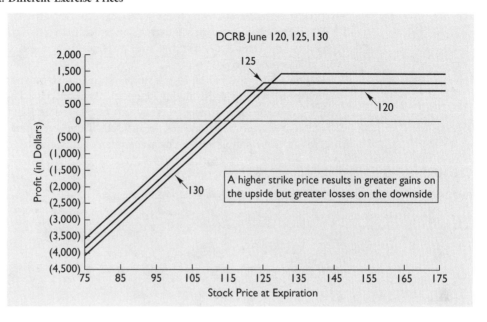

FIGURE 6.14 Write Put: Different Holding Periods

For a given stock price, the longer a short put is maintained, the more time value it loses and the greater the profit. For European puts, this effect is reversed when the stock price is low.

Choice of Holding Period Figure 6.14 compares the put writer's profits for different holding periods. Like the call writer, the put writer who chooses a shorter holding period makes a smaller profit or incurs a greater loss *for a given stock price*. This is because the writer buying back the put before expiration must pay for some of the remaining time value. The advantage to the writer, however, is that with a short holding period, there is a much smaller probability of a large, unfavorable stock price

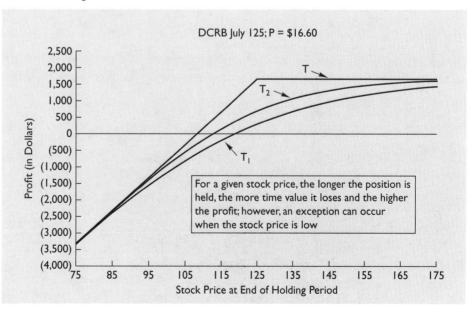

move. Again, the choice of holding period depends on the forecast for the market price and the time frame over which the writer expects that forecast to hold.

With European puts, we see that at low stock prices, the pattern of time value decay reverses itself. With American puts, the writer must be aware of the possibility that they will be exercised early.

We now have covered all of the simple strategies of buying stock, selling short stock, buying calls, writing calls, buying puts, and writing puts. Figure 6.15 summarizes the profit graphs of these strategies. They can be viewed as building blocks that are combined to produce other strategies. In fact, all of the remaining strategies are but combinations of these simple ones. The remainder of this chapter examines the strategies of

FIGURE 6.15 Summary of Profit Graphs for Positions Held to Expiration

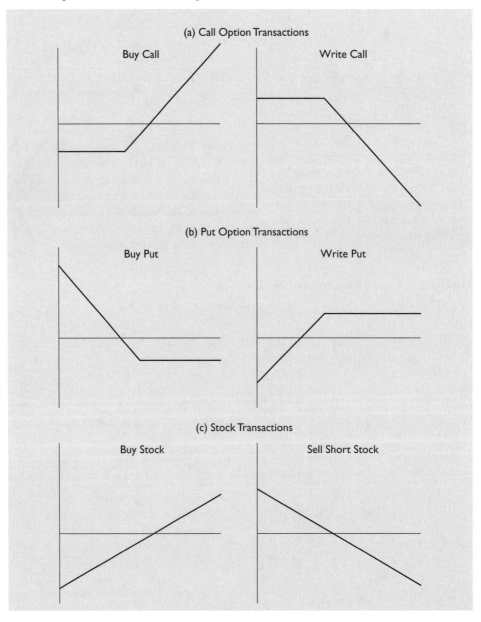

combining calls with stock, combining puts with stock, replicating puts with calls and stock, and replicating calls with puts and stock.

CALLS AND STOCK: THE COVERED CALL

Chapter 4 showed that it is possible to form a riskless hedge by buying stock and writing calls. The number of calls written must exceed the number of shares, and the appropriate hedge ratio must be maintained throughout the holding period. A simpler but nevertheless low-risk strategy involves writing one call for each share of stock owned. Although this strategy is not riskless, it does reduce the risk of holding the stock outright. It is also one of the most popular strategies among professional option traders. An investor executing this strategy is said to be writing a **covered call**.

Recall that we previously examined the uncovered call, in which the investor writes a call on a stock not owned. We found the risk to be unlimited. If the option writer also owns the stock, however, there is no risk of buying it in the market at a potentially high price. If the call is exercised, the investor simply delivers the stock. From another point of view, the holder of stock with no options written thereon is exposed to substantial risk of the stock price moving down. By writing a call against that stock, the investor reduces the downside risk. If the stock price falls substantially, the loss will be cushioned by the premium received for writing the call. Although in a bull market the call may be exercised and the stockholder will have to give up the stock, there are ways to minimize this possibility. We shall consider how to do this later.

Because we already examined the strategies of buying stock and writing calls, determining the profits from the covered call strategy is simple: we need only add the profit equations from these two strategies. Thus,

$$\Pi = N_S(S_T - S_0) + N_C[\text{Max}(0, S_T - X) - C]$$
$$\text{given that } N_S > 0, N_C < 0, \text{ and } N_S = -N_C.$$

The last requirement, $N_S = -N_C$, specifies that the number of calls written must equal the number of shares purchased. Consider the case of one share of stock and one short call, $N_S = 1$, $N_C = -1$.

The profit equation is

$$\Pi = S_T - S_0 - \text{Max}(0, S_T - X) + C.$$

If the option ends up out-of-the-money, the loss on the stock will be reduced by the call premium. If the option ends up in-the-money, it will be exercised and the stock will be delivered. This will reduce the gain on the stock. These results are summarized as follows:

$$\Pi = S_T - S_0 + C \qquad\qquad\qquad \text{if } S_T \le X.$$
$$\Pi = S_T - S_0 - S_T + X + C = X - S_0 + C \qquad \text{if } S_T > X.$$

Notice that in the case where the call ends up out-of-the-money, the profit increases for every dollar by which the stock price at expiration exceeds the original stock price. In the case where the call ends up in-the-money, the profit is unaffected by the stock price at expiration.

These results are illustrated in Figure 6.16 for the DCRB June 125 call written at a premium of $13.50. The dashed line is the profit from simply holding the stock. Notice that the covered call has a smaller loss on the downside but relinquishes the upside gain and has a lower breakeven. The maximum profit occurs when the stock price exceeds the exercise price; this profit is $X - S_0 + C$, which in this example is $100(125 - 125.94 + 13.50) = 1,256$. The maximum loss occurs if the stock price at expiration goes to zero. In that case, the profit will simply be $-S_0 + C$, which is $100(-125.94 + 13.50) = -11,244$.

A covered call reduces downside losses on the stock at the expense of upside gains.

FIGURE 6.16 Covered Call

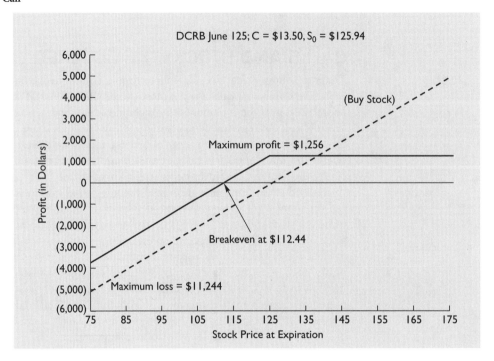

DCRB June 125; C = $13.50, S₀ = $125.94

Some investors would be concerned about the fact that the upside gain is limited. Consider, however, that if the maximum gain is achieved, the profit of $1,256 is a return of over 11 percent relative to the initial value of the position (the stock price of $125.94 minus the call premium of $13.50). This return occurs over a one-month period. Of course, any return beyond a stock price of $125 is lost, but an 11 percent maximum return in one month would generally be considered excellent performance, especially given that the risk of the position is less than the risk of the stock position alone.

The breakeven stock price occurs where the profit is zero. This happens when the call ends up out-of-the-money. Setting the profit equal to zero for the case where the call is out-of-the-money,

$$\Pi = S_T^* - S_0 + C = 0,$$

and solving for S_T^* gives a breakeven of

$$S_T^* = S_0 - C.$$

Here the breakeven is $125.94 - 13.50 = 112.44$. At any stock price above $112.44, this covered call is profitable. Another way to view this is that the covered call provides a profit at any stock price at expiration down to $112.44. Thus, the covered call is profitable down to a stock price decrease of almost 11 percent. Ownership of the stock without the protection of the call provides a profit only at a stock price above $125.94, the current stock price.

> A covered call with a lower exercise price provides greater downside protection but a lower maximum gain on the upside.

Choice of Exercise Price The covered call writer has a choice of calls at different strike prices. Figure 6.17 illustrates the profit graphs for the covered call using the DCRB June calls with strike prices of 120, 125, and 130. Because the highest strike price, the 130, has the lowest premium with which to cushion a stock price decrease, it offers the least amount of

FIGURE 6.17 Covered Call: Different Exercise Prices

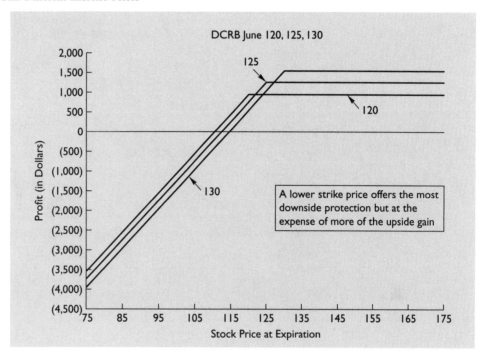

protection for the covered call writer. It offers the maximum profit potential, however, because the high strike price allows the writer to receive a greater amount for the stock if the call is exercised. In this example, the 130 call has a maximum profit of $100(130 - 125.94 + 11.35) = 1,541$. The breakeven is $125.94 - 11.35 = 114.59$. The minimum profit, which occurs if the stock price at expiration is zero, is $100(-125.94 + 11.35) = -11,459$.

In contrast, the lowest exercise price, the 120, offers the most protection. Because it has the highest premium, the cushion on the downside is greater. If the stock moves up and the call is exercised, however, the writer will receive a lower price for the stock. The maximum profit is $100(120 - 125.94 + 15.40) = 946$. The breakeven stock price is $125.94 - 15.40 = 110.54$. The minimum profit, which occurs at a stock price at expiration of zero, is $100(-125.94 + 15.40) = -11,054$.

Writing a covered call at the lowest exercise price is the most conservative choice because the loss on the downside is lower; however, the gain on the upside is also lower. Writing a covered call at the highest exercise price is a riskier strategy because the upside profit potential is greater but the downside protection is less. Regardless of the exercise price chosen, writing a covered call is far less risky than owning the stock outright. The premium on the call, no matter how large or small, cushions the stockholder against a loss on the stock in a falling market.

> For a given stock price, the longer a covered call is maintained, the more time value is lost and the greater the profit.

Choice of Holding Period   Figure 6.18 illustrates the July 125 covered call in which the position is closed out prior to expiration. Again, the Black-Scholes-Merton model was used to estimate the call's value in the manner described earlier in the chapter. The shortest holding period, T_1, which corresponds to closing out the position on June 4, gives the smallest profit *for a given stock price*. This is because the writer closes out the position by buying back the call. If there is time remaining, the writer must buy back some of the remaining time value. If a longer holding period is used, the remaining time value,

FIGURE 6.18 Covered Call: Different Holding Periods

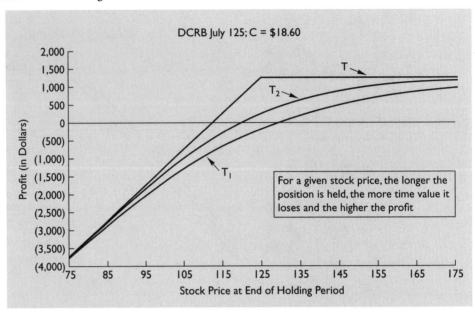

which must be bought back, is less. If held to expiration, there is no time value remaining for repurchase.

Does this suggest that covered call writers should use long holding periods? Not necessarily. Again, it depends on the covered call writer's forecast for the stock price and the time frame over which it applies. The investor might earn a larger profit by holding the position until expiration, but such a long holding period will also give the stock price more time to move down. A short holding period increases the likelihood that the stock price will not move much, and this could be more profitable for the covered call writer.

Some General Considerations with Covered Calls

As indicated earlier, covered call writing is a very popular strategy among professional option traders. This is because it is a low-risk strategy—much less risky than buying stock or options outright. Some studies also show that covered call writing is more profitable than simply buying options. This should make one wonder why everyone does not simply write covered calls. Obviously, if that occurred, the prices of the calls would fall so low that the strategy would no longer be attractive. This superior performance of covered call writing is most likely attributable to the fact that the studies covered years in which listed options were new. Veterans of those early years widely agree that the public avidly purchased these new instruments as an inexpensive and exciting way to play the market. Little regard was paid to whether the calls were fairly priced. In fact, option pricing theory itself was in its infancy, and little was known about pricing options. Public demand, coupled with ignorance, most likely kept call prices artificially high and led to substantial profits for clever call writers in those years. Although there have been no similar studies recently, it seems unlikely that such superior performance could be sustained.

It is commonly believed that writing covered calls is a way to pick up extra income from a stock. Writing a call, however, imposes on the stockholder the possibility of having to sell the stock at an inconvenient or unsuitable time. If the stock price goes up, the covered call writer will be unable to participate in the resulting gains and the stock will

---

MAKING THE CONNECTION

Alpha and Covered Calls

The covered call strategy of writing call options along with purchasing a stock can be extended to a portfolio of stocks, such as the S&P 500 index. Many portfolio managers are measured by their performance relative to broad market measures such as the S&P 500 index. As we will see in Chapter 11, the unsystematic return that reflects investment performance over and above the risk associated with the systematic or market-wide factor is called alpha.

One way to attempt to generate alpha is by writing call options. As discussed in the chapter, writing call options lowers the risk of the underlying stock portfolio. It is also possible that it increases the return, thus generating positive alpha.

In theory, the current call price is determined by arbitrage considerations and there are no market imperfections. In practice, the price of a call option may be influenced by a variety of factors, including investor preferences for certain payoffs as well as investors' expectations of stock volatility. As demand for the payoffs of a long call increases, the call price increases and the call writer receives a higher premium. Thus, there is a direct link between investor preferences for payoffs from a long call position and the earnings generated from writing covered call options.

The price of the call option is also driven by the expected level of volatility. The higher is the volatility, the higher the cost of the call option. The expected level of volatility, however, is not the actual level of volatility. If investors overestimate the volatility, then they will overpay for purchasing the call option. Therefore, the call writer will benefit from overestimates of volatility.

Thus, the additional returns generated by the covered call strategy can easily change over time as investor preferences for particular payoffs change, as well as investor estimates of volatility.

---

likely be called away by exercise. If, however, the call is exercised early, the writer will be no worse off from a financial perspective. The profit will still be $X - S_0 + C$, the maximum expected profit at expiration. In fact, the writer actually will be better off because this amount will be available before expiration.

Suppose that the covered writer does not want to lose the stock by exercise. One way to minimize the likelihood of exercise is to write calls at a high exercise price so that the call is deep-out-of-the-money. This reduces the chance of the call ending up in-the-money. Suppose that the stock price starts upward and it appears that the out-of-the-money call will move in-the-money and thus increase the chance of exercise. The writer can then buy back the call and write a new call at a higher exercise price, a strategy called *rolling up*. If the stock price continues to rise, the writer can buy back the new call and write another one at an even higher exercise price. In this manner, the covered call writer establishes a position in which the exercise price will always stay well ahead of the stock price. The purpose of this strategy is to avoid exercise and keep the stock in the portfolio. This may be important to someone who likes to hold on to certain stocks for various reasons. The disadvantage of this strategy is that the high exercise price means a lower premium and less downside protection. Also, transaction costs from the frequent rollovers will be higher. These factors can be weighed against the inconvenience of exercise and the investor's willingness to give up the stock.

Many institutional investors also use covered call writing strategies. Those holding large portfolios of stocks that are expected to gain little value often believe that the performance of their portfolios will improve if they write calls against the stock they own. But covered call writing—or any other strategy—cannot be the gate to unlimited wealth. In fact, it is more likely to *reduce* the portfolio's expected return because it decreases the risk. It therefore should be viewed as a risk-reducing rather than return-enhancing strategy.

As one might imagine, the opposite of a long-stock/short-call position is to buy a call to protect a short-stock position. The results obtained from this strategy are the mirror image of the covered call results. We explore this strategy in an end-of-chapter problem.

Another option strategy that can be used to reduce the risk of holding stock is the protective put, which is the topic of the next section.

PUTS AND STOCK: THE PROTECTIVE PUT

As discussed in the previous section, a stockholder who wants protection against falling stock prices may elect to write a call. In a strong bull market, the stock is likely to be called away by exercise. One way to obtain protection against a bear market and still be able to participate in a bull market is to buy a **protective put**; that is, the investor simply buys stock and buys a put. The put provides a minimum selling price for the stock.

The profit equation for the protective put is found by simply adding the profit equations for the strategies of buying stock and buying a put. From this we get

$$\Pi = N_S(S_T - S_0) + N_P[\text{Max}(0, X - S_T) - P]$$
$$\text{given that } N_S > 0, N_P > 0, \text{ and } N_S = N_P.$$

As in previous examples, assume that one share of stock and one put, $N_S = 1$, $N_P = 1$. If the stock price ends up above the exercise price, the put will expire out-of-the-money. If the stock price ends up less than the exercise price, the put will be exercised. The results are as follows:

$$\Pi = S_T - S_0 - P \qquad\qquad \text{if } S_T \geq X.$$
$$\Pi = S_T - S_0 + X - S_T - P = X - S_0 - P \qquad \text{if } S_T < X.$$

The protective put works like an insurance policy. When you buy insurance for an asset such as a house, you pay a premium that assures you that in the event of a loss, the insurance policy will cover at least some of the loss. If the loss does not occur during the policy's life, you simply lose the premium. Similarly, the protective put is insurance for a stock. In a bear market, a loss on the stock is somewhat offset by the put's exercise. This is like filing a claim on the insurance policy. In a bull market, the insurance is not needed and the gain on the upside is reduced by the premium paid.

From the above equations, it is clear that the profit in a bull market varies directly with the stock price at expiration. The higher S_T is, the higher is the profit, Π. In a bear market, the profit is not affected by the stock price at expiration. Whatever losses are incurred on the stock are offset by gains on the put. The profit graph for a protective put is illustrated in Figure 6.19 for the DCRB June 125 put purchased at a premium of $11.50. The dashed line is the profit from simply holding the stock. Notice that the protective put has a smaller downside loss and smaller upside gain as well as a higher breakeven.

The maximum loss on a protective put is found as the profit if the stock price at expiration ends up below the exercise price. Because the profit equation shows that this is $X - S_0 - P$, the DCRB protective put has a minimum of $100(125 - 125.94 - 11.50) = -1,244$. This is a loss of about 9 percent relative to the initial value of the position (the stock price of 125.94 plus the put price of 11.50). Clearly, there is no maximum gain because the investor profits dollar for dollar with the excess of the stock price over the exercise price. Notice how the graph of the protective put is the same shape as that of a long call. This is due to put-call parity.

FIGURE 6.19 Protective Put

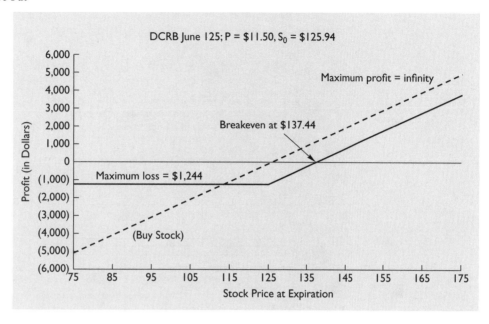

The breakeven stock price at expiration occurs when the stock price at expiration exceeds the exercise price. Setting this profit to zero and solving for the breakeven stock price, S_T^*, gives

$$\Pi = S_T^* - S_0 - P = 0,$$
$$S_T^* = P + S_0.$$

A protective put sets a maximum downside loss at the expense of some of the upside gain. It is equivalent to an insurance policy on the asset.

Thus, breakeven occurs at a stock price at expiration equal to the original stock price plus the premium. This should be apparent because the stock price must rise above the original stock price by an amount sufficient to cover the premium paid for the put. In this example, the breakeven stock price at expiration is $11.50 + 125.94 = 137.44$. Thus, to reach breakeven, the stock price must increase by about 9.1 percent. The cost of protection has, thus, put the investor in a significant hole at the start, but the upside is unlimited.

> A protective put with a higher exercise price provides greater downside protection but lower upside gains.

Choice of Exercise Price: The Deductible Decision The amount of coverage the protective put provides is affected by the chosen exercise price. This is equivalent to the insurance problem of deciding on the deductible. A higher deductible means that the insured bears more of the risk and thus pays a lower premium. With a lower deductible, the insurer bears more of the risk and charges a higher premium. With a protective put, a higher exercise price is equivalent to a lower deductible.

Figure 6.20 illustrates the comparative performances of DCRB protective puts at different exercise prices. The 130 put gives the stockholder the right to sell the stock at $130 per share. The breakeven on this strategy is $125.94 + 14.25 = 140.19$. This will be the most expensive insurance but will provide the greatest coverage, with a minimum profit of $100(130 - 125.94 - 14.25) = -1,019$. If the stock price rises and the put is not needed, the gain from the stock will be lower than it would be with a lower exercise price. This is because the more expensive premium was paid, but the insurance was not needed.

FIGURE 6.20 Protective Put: Different Exercise Prices

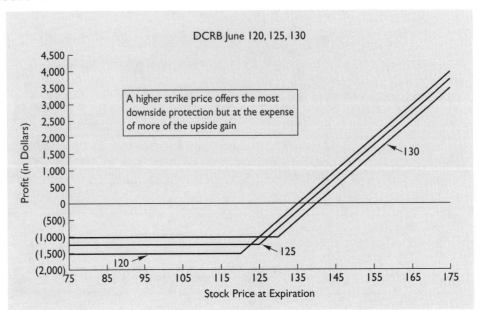

The lowest exercise price, the 120, provides the least coverage. The breakeven is 125.94 + 9.25 = 135.19. The minimum profit is 100(120 − 125.94 − 9.25) = −1,519. If the market rises, the less expensive insurance will reduce the gain by a smaller amount.

As you can see, selecting an exercise price is like choosing a deductible: The investor must balance the willingness to assume some of the risk against the ability to pay for the coverage.

> For a given stock price, the longer a protective put is held, the more time value is lost and the lower the profit. For European puts, this effect is reversed when the stock price is low.

Choice of Holding Period Figure 6.21 illustrates the profit for different holding periods for the DCRB July 125 protective put. The shorter holding period provides more coverage *for a given stock price.* This is because with a shorter holding period, the investor can sell back the put before expiration and recover some of the time value previously purchased. With a longer holding period, there will be less time value to recover. Again, however, we see an exception to this rule when the stock price is low. By holding all the way to expiration, there will be no time value to recover.

The choice of holding period depends on the investor's view of the probable stock price moves and the period over which they are likely to occur. If a large stock price move is needed to provide a profit, a longer holding period will allow more time for the stock price to move. A shorter holding period is preferable if the stock price is not expected to move much. The stock price must increase by at least the amount of the premium, however, for the investor to break even. Therefore, the investor must weigh the likelihood of this occurring over the holding period.

The protective put strategy can also be turned around so that a short sale of stock is protected by a short put, or vice versa. The results would be the mirror image of those presented here. We examine this strategy as an end-of-chapter problem.

We have seen that investors holding stock can use both the covered call and the protective put to reduce risk. Which strategy is preferable? The answer depends on the investor's outlook for the market. If a bull market is believed to be more likely

MAKING THE CONNECTION

Using the Black-Scholes-Merton Model to Analyze the Attractiveness of a Strategy

In this chapter and the next, we look at a number of option strategies. We examine the performance of a strategy given a range of possible values of the underlying stock at expiration. Although the possible outcomes might be satisfactory to an investor, is the strategy attractively priced? Using the Black- Scholes-Merton model, or some other appropriate model such as the binomial), we can determine if the prices offered for the strategy are fair.

Consider the following scenario: An investor holds a position in an S&P 500 index fund. The index is at 1,200. The investor is considering protecting the position by either buying a put or selling a call using European-style put and call options available on the CBOE. The options of interest have an exercise price of 1,200 and expire in 74 days. The call can be sold for $31, and the put can be purchased for $28. The investor is aware of the differences in the performance of a covered call versus a protective put, but is more concerned that the two strategies might not be priced attractively. The investor would be willing to use either strategy, but will decide based on which has the better price.

The investor knows that the Black-Scholes-Merton model is an appropriate model for determining whether a European option is mispriced. He gathers the necessary information, which is as follows:

Stock price = 1,200

Exercise price = 1,200

Risk-free rate = 4.0%

Time to expiration = 74/365 = 0.2027

Volatility of the S&P 500 = 0.15

Dividend yield = 1.7%.

The risk-free rate is based on the continuously compounded yield on the U.S. Treasury bill maturing closest to the option expiration. The dividend yield is estimated to be 1.7 percent discretely compounded. Therefore, we convert it to the continuously compounded equivalent of $\ln(1.017) = 0.016857$.

As described in Chapter 5, the volatility is the most difficult information to obtain. The investor uses the implied volatility of the nearby options and takes into account his beliefs and those of others that the volatility may change over the life of the option. He knows that the estimate of 0.15 is quite low by historical standards, but the market is currently experiencing unusually low volatility and most experts do not expect that to change over the next few months.

Of course, the investor realizes he will be in a dilemma if he finds that the call is underpriced and the put is overpriced because these strategies require selling the call or buying the put. If the call is under-priced, he would not want to sell it. If the put is overpriced, he would not want to buy it. He hopes that at least one option will be fairly priced. Of course, he does not expect the options to trade for exactly their theoretical values, but he hopes their prices will be close to their theoretical fair values.

Using a computer program (you can use BSMbin9e.xls), the investor obtains the following values for the Black-Scholes-Merton prices of the call and put:

Black-Scholes-Marton call value = $35.02
Black-Scholes-Merton put value = $29.42.

As noted, the call can be sold at its bid price of $31 and the put can be bought at its ask price of $28. The call appears to be substantially underpriced, because the model says it should be sold for $35.02. The put, however, appears to be slightly underpriced, because the model says it is worth $29.42. Because the covered call requires selling the call and the protective put requires buying the put, the protective put would appear to be the better strategy. The investor sees an opportunity and knows he must act quickly before the put price rises. He also knows that he could be wrong about the volatility. If the volatility is lower than what he thinks, the Black-Scholes-Merton put and call values will come down. If the theoretical value of the call were lower and closer to its market price, selling the call would become more attractive. If the theoretical value of the put were lower, perhaps lower than the market price, then buying the put would become less attractive.

FIGURE 6.21 Protective Put: Different Holding Periods

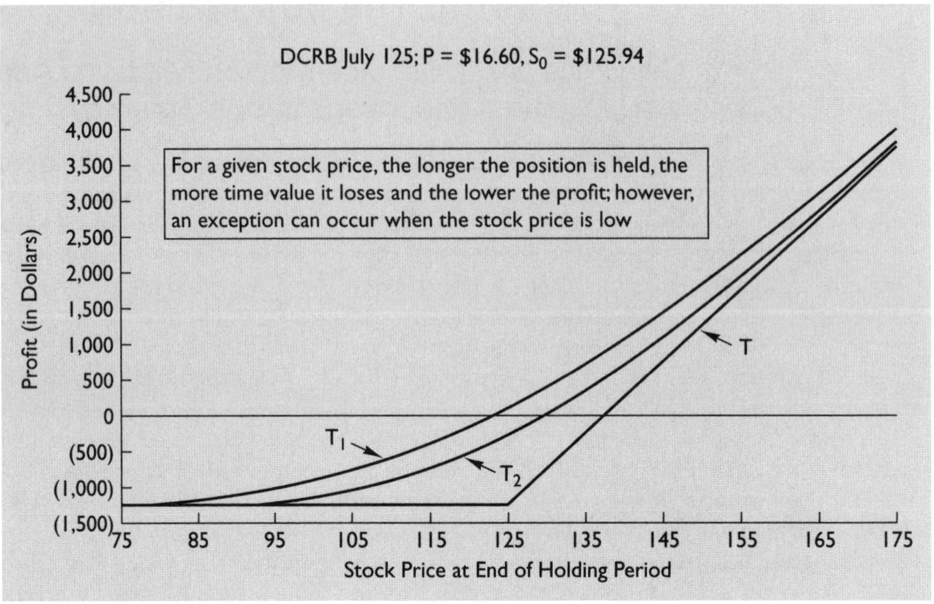

to occur, the protective put will allow the investor to participate in it. The protective put will be more expensive, however, because the investor must pay for it. The covered call writer actually receives money for writing the call. Thus, there are advantages and disadvantages to each strategy that one must carefully weigh before making a decision.

The role of put options in providing insurance is explored more thoroughly in Chapter 14. That material will show how puts, calls, Treasury bills, and futures can be used to create portfolio insurance.

The following section examines some strategies in which puts can be created from calls and in which calls can be created from puts. For this reason, these strategies are called **synthetic puts** and **synthetic calls**.

SYNTHETIC PUTS AND CALLS

In Chapters 3 and 5, we discussed put-call parity, the relationship between call prices and put prices:

$$P + S_0 = C + Xe^{-r_cT}.$$

The left-hand side of the equation is the value of a put and the stock; the right-hand side is the value of a call and a risk-free bond. We can rearrange put-call parity such that

$$P = C - S_0 + Xe^{-r_cT},$$

where the left-hand side is the value of a put and the right-hand side is the value of a portfolio that behaves like a put. That portfolio consists of a long call, a short sale of stock, and the purchase of a pure discount bond, or making of a loan, with a face value equal to the exercise price. Note that the signs in front of the prices in the equations indicate whether we are long or short in puts, calls, or stocks. Long positions are represented by plus (+) signs and short positions by minus (−) signs.

We actually need not buy a bond to replicate a put. The term representing the present value of the exercise price is simply a constant value that does not affect the shape of the profit graph. For example, consider a synthetic put, which consists of long calls and the short sale of an equal number of shares of stock. The profit is simply

$$\Pi = N_C[\text{Max}(0, S_T - X) - C] + N_S(S_T - S_0)$$
$$\text{given that } N_C > 0, N_S < 0, \text{ and } N_C = -N_S.$$

Letting the number of shares and the number of calls both be 1, the profits for the two possible ranges of stock prices at expiration are:

$$\Pi = -C - S_T + S_0 \qquad\qquad \text{if } S_T \leq X.$$
$$\Pi = S_T - X - C - S_T + S_0 = S_0 - X - C \qquad \text{if } S_T > X.$$

If the stock price at expiration is equal to or below the exercise price, the profit will vary inversely with the stock price at expiration. If the stock price at expiration is above the exercise price, the profit will not be affected by the stock price at expiration. This is the same general outcome provided by a put, hence the name synthetic put.

We can see the difference between the actual put and the synthetic put from the put-call parity formula. In put-call parity, one replicates the put by buying a call, selling short a stock, and buying a pure discount bond with a face value equal to the exercise price. To replicate a put precisely, we need to buy that pure discount bond. In practice, however, most traders simply buy the call and sell short the stock.

Figure 6.22 compares the synthetic put and its actual counterpart using the DCRB July 125 options. The synthetic put has a profit of

$$-C - S_T + S_0 \qquad \text{if } S_T \leq X.$$
$$S_0 - X - C \qquad \text{if } S_T > X.$$

The actual put has a profit of

$$X - S_T - P \qquad \text{if } S_T \leq X.$$
$$-P \qquad\qquad \text{if } S_T > X.$$

FIGURE 6.22 Synthetic and Actual Put

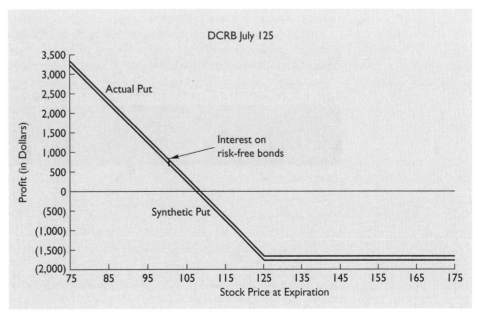

The difference is the profit of the actual put minus the profit of the synthetic put, $X - P + C - S_0$, in either case. From put-call parity, we can substitute $C - S_0 + Xe^{-r_cT}$ for P. The difference is then

$$X(1 - e^{-r_cT}),$$

which is the interest lost by not buying the pure discount bond.

There are two reasons why someone would want to use a synthetic put. First, there once were restrictions on the listing of puts on the exchanges; puts were phased in slowly. There was also a moratorium on new option listings that started soon after the first few puts were listed in 1977. This prevented more puts from being listed until the moratorium was lifted in 1980. During the period, an investor could have created a synthetic put to use in lieu of the actual put.

Second, one can use a synthetic put to take advantage of mispricing in the relationship between puts and calls. For example, the difference between the actual put price, P, and the value of the synthetic put, $C - S_0$, should be Xe^{-r_cT}; however, if $P - (C - S_0)$ is greater than Xe^{-r_cT}, either the actual put is overpriced or the synthetic put is underpriced. The investor should sell the actual put and buy the synthetic put by purchasing the call and selling short the stock. This strategy often is called a **reverse conversion**, or simply **reversal**. It will generate a cash outflow at expiration of X, as shown in Table 6.3.

> Synthetic puts and calls can be constructed from options and stock.

This property makes the reverse conversion resemble a risk-free loan. The money received when the position is opened is (1) S_0 (from the short sale of the stock), (2) P (from the sale of the put), and (3) $-C$ (from the purchase of the call). If, as we assumed, this exceeds the present value of the exercise price, we can invest the amount $S_0 + P - C$ at the risk-free rate, r_c, until the options expire. The accumulated future value of this investment will then exceed X. This means that we can repay the loan and have money left over.[3] Of course, investing this money at the risk-free rate is equivalent to buying the risk-free bonds.

We can also create synthetic calls by buying stock and an equal number of puts. It should be apparent that this strategy is like a call because it is nothing more than a protective put. The graph for the protective put is, as we saw earlier, the same type of graph as that for a call.

Many investors buy the synthetic call and write the actual call when the latter is overpriced. This strategy is called a **conversion** and is used to exploit mispricing in the relationship between put and call prices.

The accompanying Excel spreadsheet Stratlyz9e.xls calculates and graphs the profits from any combination of positions in the asset and up to six different options on the same asset. Positions can be held to expiration or closed out prior to expiration.

TABLE 6.3 PAYOFFS FROM REVERSE CONVERSION

POSITION	PAYOFFS FROM PORTFOLIO GIVEN STOCK PRICE AT EXPIRATION	
	$S_T \leq X$	$S_T > X$
Long call	0	$S_T - X$
Short stock	$-S_T$	$-S_T$
Short put	$-X + S_T$	0
	$-X$	$-X$

[3]If the options are American and the short put is exercised early, however, we will have to pay out X dollars prior to expiration. Thus, it is possible that the interest earned on the cash inflow will be insufficient to make the required payout.

SOFTWARE DEMONSTRATION 6.1

Analyzing Option Strategies with the Excel Spreadsheet Stratlyz9e.xls

The Excel spreadsheet Stratlyz9e.xls is saved in Excel 97-2003 form. It calculates and graphs the profits from option strategies with up to six options and a position in the underlying asset. The graphical output can be viewed as the overall graph of the combined position (Overall Graph tab) or the combined position alone with its components (Component Graph tab). This spreadsheet is a read-only spreadsheet, meaning that it cannot be saved under the name Stratlyz9e.xls, which preserves the original file. You may, however, load the spreadsheet without the read-only feature. The spreadsheet Stratlyz9e.xls is available as a download via the product support website. To access it:

1. Go to www.cengagebrain.com.
2. Click on Instructor Resources or Student Resources.
3. Click on the link Stratlyz9e.xls.
4. Follow the instructions on the Web page to download and install the spreadsheet.

Now let us do an example. Assume you wish to find the results for a simple strategy of buying one DCRB June 125 call. The call is priced at $13.50. The DCRB stock is at $125.94. First, let us examine the strategy of holding the position until expiration, and then we shall close the position prior to expiration.

Observe the section labeled **General Inputs** in the accompanying figure. It requests five pieces of information. Each cell that will accept input has a double-line border, and the values are in blue. The first input item is the asset price when the transaction is initiated, but this is required only if your strategy includes buying or selling short the asset. Insert a blank for our example. The next input is the number of units of the asset, with a positive number for buying and a negative number for selling. Insert a zero or leave it blank. The next input is the asset price at expiration. This information is required in order to center the graph. Although you obviously do not know where the asset will be at expiration, you can choose any price. Let us choose the exercise price of 125. The graph will be centered around this price, and the overall profit of the strategy for this particular price will be calculated and shown in the section below. The next two required inputs are the lowest and highest asset prices to graph. This simply defines a range over which the graph will be drawn. Let us arbitrarily choose a range of $40 on either side; so the minimum is 85 and the maximum is 165.

The next section is called **Option-Specific Inputs**. Here you can enter information on up to six options that differ by either time to expiration or exercise price and can be either calls or puts. Insert blanks or zeros for options not used. All options must be on the same underlying asset. In the first row, use the pulldown list to select "Call," "Put," or "No option." For this strategy, select "Call." The next row should contain the exercise price (125 in our case). The next

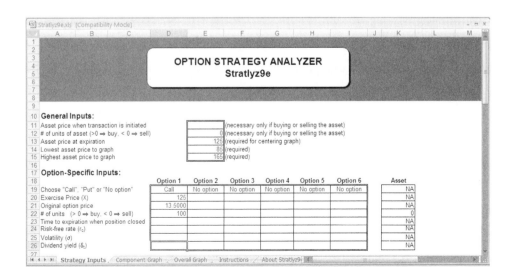

row should contain the original option price. This is the price at which the option is either purchased or sold when the transaction is initiated—$13.50 in this example. The next line contains the number of options with a positive number for buying and a negative number for selling. Let us insert "100" for a standard long contract. The next four input cells contain information that is necessary only if the position is closed prior to expiration. If the position is held to expiration, the "Time remaining to expiration when position is closed"

will be blank or zero and the last three lines can be left blank. Leave it blank for our example. If the position is closed prior to expiration, insert the remaining time in years (i.e., days/365); then insert the risk-free rate, volatility, and dividend yield in the next three cells below. This lets the program use the Black-Scholes-Merton model to calculate the option's value when the position is terminated for a given asset price. We shall leave this information blank. Hit the F9 (manual recalculation) key.

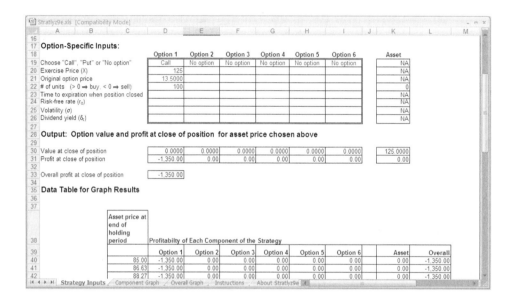

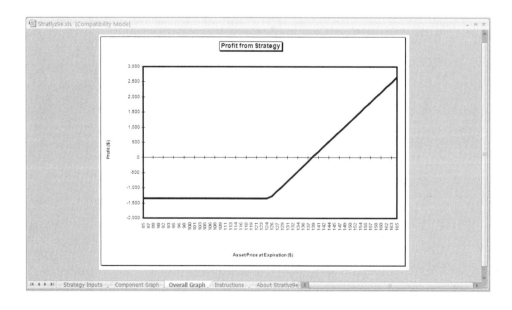

The section labeled **Output: Option value and profit at close of position for asset price chosen above** shows for each option the value of the option at the close of the position, the profit on the option transaction, and the overall profit on the transaction, which includes option(s) and potential positions in the asset, for the asset price you specified above. Note that output cells have a single-line border. These answers, of course, represent only one point on the profit graph. In our example, the profit is –$1,350 because we specified an asset price at expiration of 125, which is the exercise price. The next section, **Data Table for Graphic Results**, shows the overall profit for the strategy for 50 possible asset prices at the end of the holding period, running from the minimum to maximum price you specified, centered around the asset price at expiration you specified. The graphs are provided on a different spreadsheets, which you can access by clicking on the tab labeled either **Component Graph** or **Overall Graph** near the bottom of your screen. Note that if only one position is being graphed, then the overall and component graphs are identical.

As noted above, for positions closed out prior to expiration, the program automatically calculates Black-Scholes-Merton prices for the options for each possible asset price in the range specified, provided you supply the necessary information on the time remaining, the volatility, the interest rate, and the dividend yield, if any. For example, if there are 15 days remaining until expiration (time = 15/365), the risk-free rate is 4.53 percent, the volatility is 0.83, the dividend yield is zero, the call value is $8.4898, and the profit is –$501.02. We present this result from the Component Graph tab below.

Although Stratlyz9e.xls will correctly graph any strategy you choose, it is possible that the graph will not look exactly as you expect it will. The various possible combinations of inputs and outputs, along with the fixed parameters used to generate the graph, such as 50 asset prices, will not always produce visually appealing graphs the first time. This often happens because the graph's tick marks are not located on the exercise price. If anything looks unusual, experiment with different maximum and minimum prices until your graph looks as expected.

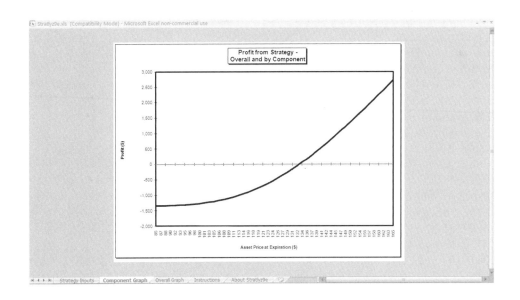

Summary

This chapter examined the basic option strategies. Designing the profit equations and graphs is a simple extension of material learned in previous chapters. For positions held to expiration, it is necessary only to determine the intrinsic values of puts and calls. If we elect not to hold the options until expiration, we can use the Black-Scholes-Merton model to estimate their prices. The material in this chapter, however, is basic. Option investors should always be aware of the factors that lead to early exercise, as well as tax and dividend implications. Moreover, transaction costs will lower profits, increase losses, and make breakevens higher for bullish strategies and lower for bearish strategies. The more options and stocks employed, the greater the transaction costs. Understanding how option transactions produce payoffs is only the first step toward using options. Unfortunately, there are no simple or even complex formulas for predicting the future. We have seen, however, that options can be used to modify risk—to increase or decrease it as needed.

The strategies examined here form the building blocks for exploring more exotic strategies. Chapter 7 looks at these advanced strategies, which combine many of the strategies discussed here to produce a much more diverse set of opportunities.

Key Terms

Before continuing to Chapter 7, you should be able to give brief definitions of the following terms:

bull/bear, p. 191
breakeven stock price, p. 195
uncovered/naked call, p. 198

covered call, p. 207
protective put, p. 212
synthetic puts/calls, p. 216

reverse conversion/
reversal/conversion, p. 218

Further Reading

Augen, J. *Trading Options at Expiration: Strategies and Models for Winning the Endgame.* Upper Saddle River, NJ: Pearson Education, 2009.

Austin, M. "Index Option Overwriting: Strategies and Results." *Derivatives Quarterly* 1 (Summer 1995): 77–84.

Constantinides, G. M., M. Czerwonko, J. C. Jackwerth, and S. Perrakis, "Are Options on Index Futures Profitable for Risk-Averse Investors? Empirical Evidence." *The Journal of Finance* 66(2011): 1407–1437.

Ferguson, R. "Some Formulas for Evaluating Two Popular Option Strategies." *Financial Analysts Journal* 49 (September–October 1993): 71–76.

Figelman, I. "Expected Return and Risk of Covered Call Strategies." *The Journal of Portfolio Management* 34 (Summer 2008): 81–97.

Grube, R. C., D. B. Panton, and J. M. Terrell. "Risks and Rewards in Covered Call Positions." *The Journal of Portfolio Management* 5 (Winter 1979): 64–68.

McIntyre, M. L., and D. Jackson. "Great in Practice, Not in Theory: An Empirical Examination of

Covered Call Writing." *Journal of Derivatives & Hedge Funds* 13(2007): 66–79.

Mueller, P. A. "Covered Call Options: An Alternative Investment Strategy." *Financial Management* 10 (Winter 1981): 64–71.

Mullaney, M. *The Complete Guide to Option Strategies: Advanced and Basic Strategies on Stocks, ETFs, Indexes and Stock Index Futures.* New York: Wiley Trading, 2009.

Pounds, H. M. "Covered Call Option Writing: Strategies and Results." *The Journal of Portfolio Management* 5 (Winter 1978): 31–42.

Rendleman, R. "Covered Call Writing Strategies From an Expected Utility Perspective." *The Journal of Derivatives* 9 (Spring 2001): 63–75.

Singleton, J. C., and R. Grieves. "Synthetic Puts and Portfolio Insurance Strategies." *The Journal of Portfolio Management* 10 (Spring 1984): 63–69.

Concept Checks

1. Explain how a protective put is like purchasing insurance on a stock.
2. Why is choosing an exercise price on a protective put like deciding which deductible to take on an insurance policy?
3. Discuss and compare the two bullish strategies of buying a call and writing a put. Why would one strategy be preferable to the other?
4. Suppose that one is considering buying a call at a particular exercise price. What reasons could

be given for the alternative of buying a call at a higher exercise price? at a lower exercise price?

Questions and Problems

1. The three fundamental profit equations for call, puts, and stock are identified symbolically in this chapter as

$$\Pi = N_C[\text{Max}(0, S_T - X) - C]$$
$$\Pi = N_P[\text{Max}(0, X - S_T) - P]$$
$$\Pi = S_T - S_0.$$

   Prepare a single graph showing both the long and short for each profit equation above. Assume the positions are held to maturity. Therefore, you need to produce a total of three graphs. Describe the relationship between the long and short for each profit equation. Also describe the relationship between the call graph and the put graph.

2. You have inherited some stock from a wealthy relative. The stock had poor performance recently, and analysts believe it has little growth potential. You would like to write calls against the stock; however, the will stipulates that you must agree not to sell it unless you need the funds for a personal financial emergency. How can you write covered calls and minimize the likelihood of exercise?

3. Explain the considerations facing a covered call writer regarding the choice of exercise prices.

4. Explain the advantages and disadvantages to a covered call writer of closing out the position prior to expiration.

5. A short stock can be protected by selling a put. Determine the profit equations for this position and identify the breakeven stock price at expiration and maximum and minimum profits.

6. Suppose that you wish to buy stock and protect yourself against a downside movement in its price. You consider both a covered call and a protective put. What factors will affect your decision?

7. *Buying an at-the-money put has a greater return potential than buying an out-of-the-money put because it is more likely to be in-the-money.* Appraise this statement.

8. A short position in stock can be protected by holding a call option. Determine the profit equations for this position and identify the breakeven stock price at expiration and maximum and minimum profits.

9. We briefly mentioned the synthetic call, which consists of stock and an equal number of puts. Assume that the combined value of the puts and stock exceeds the value of the actual call by less than the present value of the exercise price. Show how an

arbitrage profit can be made. Note: Do not use the data from the chapter. Show your point as it was illustrated in the text for the synthetic put.

The following option prices were observed for a stock for July 6 of a particular year. Use this information in problems 10 through 15. Ignore dividends on the stock. The stock is priced at 165.13. The expirations are July 17, August 21, and October 16. The continuously compounded risk-free rates are 0.0503, 0.0535, and 0.0571, respectively. The standard deviation is 0.21. Assume that the options are European.

	Calls			Puts		
Strike	Jul	Aug	Oct	Jul	Aug	Oct
165	2.70	5.25	8.10	2.40	4.75	6.75
170	0.80	3.25	6.00	5.75	7.50	9.00

In problems 10 through 15, determine the profits for possible stock prices of 150, 155, 160, 165, 170, 175, and 180. Answer any other questions as requested. Note: Your Excel spreadsheet Stratlyz9e.xls will be useful here for obtaining graphs as requested, but it does not allow you to calculate the profits for several user-specified asset prices. It permits you to specify one asset price and a maximum and minimum. Use Stratlyz9e.xls to produce the graph for the range of prices from 150 to 180, but determine the profits for the prices of 150, 160, …, 180 by hand for positions held to expiration. For positions closed prior to expiration, use the spreadsheet BSMbin9e.xls to determine the option price when the position is closed; then calculate the profit by hand.

10. Buy 100 shares of stock and write one October 170 call contract. Hold the position until expiration. Determine the profits and graph the results. Identify the breakeven stock price at expiration, the maximum profit, and the maximum loss.

11. Repeat the previous problem, but close the position on September 1. Use the spreadsheet to find the profits for the possible stock prices on September 1. Generate a graph and use it to approximate the breakeven stock price.

12. Buy 100 shares of stock and buy one August 165 put contract. Hold the position until expiration. Determine the profits and graph the results.

Determine the breakeven stock price at expiration, the maximum profit, and the maximum loss.

13. Buy one October 165 put contract. Hold it until the options expire. Determine the profits and graph the results. Identify the breakeven stock price at expiration. What are the maximum possible gain and loss on this transaction?

14. Buy one August 165 call contract. Hold it until the options expire. Determine the profits and graph the results. Then identify the breakeven stock price at expiration. What is the maximum possible loss on this transaction?

15. Repeat problem 14, but close the position on August 1. Use the spreadsheet to find the profits for the possible stock prices on August 1. Generate a graph and use it to identify the approximate breakeven stock price.

For problems 16, 17, and 18, determine the profit from the following basic foreign currency option transactions for each of the following spot rates at expiration: $0.90, $0.95, $1.00, $1.05, and $1.10. Construct a profit graph. Find the breakeven spot rate at expiration. Assume that each contract covers 100,000 euros.

16. A call option on the euro expiring in six months has an exercise price of $1.00 and is priced at $0.0385. Construct a simple long position in the call.

17. A euro put with an exercise price of $1.00 is priced at $0.0435. Construct a simple long position in the put.

18. Use the information in problem 16 to construct a euro covered call. Assume that the spot rate at the start is $0.9825.

19. Suppose the call price is $14.20 and the put price is $9.30 for stock options where the exercise price is $100, the risk-free interest rate is 5 percent (continuously compounded), and the time to expiration is one year. Explain how you would create a synthetic stock position and identify the cost. Suppose you observe a $100 stock price; identify any arbitrage opportunities.

20. The Black-Scholes-Merton option pricing model assumes that stock price changes are lognormally distributed. Show graphically how this distribution changes when an investor is long the stock and long the put.

21. The Black-Scholes-Merton option pricing model assumes that stock price changes are lognormally distributed. Show graphically how this distribution

changes when an investor is long the stock and short the call.

22. Using BSMbin9e.xls, compute the call and put prices for a stock option, where the current stock price is $100, the exercise price is $100, the risk-free interest rate is 5 percent (continuously compounded), the volatility is 30 percent, and the time to expiration is one year. Explain how you would create a synthetic call option and identify the cost.

23. (Concept Problem) Another consideration in evaluating option strategies is the effect of transaction costs. Suppose that purchases and sales of an option incur a brokerage commission of 1 percent of the option's value. Purchases and sales of a share of stock incur a brokerage commission of 0.5 percent of the stock's value. If the option is exercised, there is a transaction cost on the purchase or sale of the stock. Determine the profit equations for the following strategies assuming that the options are held to expiration and exercised if in-the-money rather than sold back. Assume that one option and/or share is used and that any shares left in the portfolio are sold.
    a. Long call
    b. Long put
    c. Covered call
    d. Protective put

24. (Concept Problem) Suppose an investor is considering buying one of two call options on a particular stock with the same maturity. The only difference between the two call options is the strike prices. The rate of return on a call option is its profit divided by the investment (the call price here). Identify the terminal stock price where the profits on the two long call positions are the same. Also identify the terminal stock price where the rates of return on the two long call positions are the same (but are not both −100%). Discuss the difference in these two terminal stock prices.

25. (Concept Problem) In each case examined in this chapter and in the preceding problems, we did not account for the interest on funds invested. One useful way to observe the effect of interest is to look at a conversion or a reverse conversion. Evaluate the August 165 puts and calls and recommend a conversion or a reverse conversion. Determine the profit from the transaction if the options are held to expiration. Make sure that the profit properly accounts for the interest that accrues over the holding period.

CHAPTER 7

Advanced Option Strategies

Read every book by traders to study where they lost money. You will learn nothing relevant from their profits (the markets adjust). You will learn from their losses.

Nassim Taleb
Derivatives Strategy, April, 1997, p. 25

Chapter 6 provided a foundation for the basic option strategies. We can now move on to some of the more advanced strategies. As often noted, options can be combined in some interesting and unusual ways. In this chapter, we look at two types of advanced option strategies: spreads and combinations.

OPTION SPREADS: BASIC CONCEPTS

A **spread** is the purchase of one option and the sale of another. There are two general types of spreads. One is the **vertical**, **strike**, or **money spread**. This strategy involves the purchase of an option with a particular exercise price and the sale of another option differing only by exercise price. For example, one might purchase an option on DCRB expiring in June with an exercise price of 120 and sell an option on DCRB also expiring in June but with an exercise price of 125; hence the terms *strike* and *money spread*. Because exercise prices were formerly arranged vertically in the option pages of newspapers, this also became known as a *vertical spread*.

Another type of spread is a **horizontal**, **time**, or **calendar spread**. In this spread, the investor purchases an option with an expiration of a given month and sells an otherwise identical option with a different expiration month. For example, one might purchase a DCRB June 120 call and sell a DCRB July 120 call. The term *horizontal spread* comes from the horizontal arrangement of expiration months in newspaper option pages, a practice since discontinued.

Sometimes spreads are identified by a special notation. The aforementioned DCRB money spread is referred to as the June 120/125 spread. The month is given first; the exercise price before the slash (/) is the option purchased, and the exercise price after the slash is the option sold. If the investor buys the June 125 and sells the June 120, the result is a June 125/120 spread. The calendar spread described in the previous paragraph is identified as the June/July 120 spread. The month preceding the slash is the option purchased, while the month following the slash identifies the option sold.

Spreads can be executed using either calls or puts. A July 120/125 call spread is a net long position. This is because the 120 call costs more than the 125 call; that is, the cash outflow from buying the 120 exceeds the inflow received for selling the 125.

CHAPTER OBJECTIVES

- Present and analyze the option spread strategies, including money spreads, collars, calendar spreads, and ratio spreads

- Present and analyze the option combination strategies, including straddles and box spreads

This transaction is called **buying the spread** and is sometimes referred to as a **debit spread** for the type of accounting entry associated with it. In the July 120/125 put spread, the cash inflow received from selling the 125 put is more than the cash outflow paid in buying the 120 put. This transaction is known as **selling the spread** or a **credit spread** and results in a net short position.

For calendar spreads, the June/July 120 call spread would be net short and selling the spread because an investor would receive more for the July call than he or she would pay for the June call. The July/June 120 call spread would be net long and buying the spread because the July call would cost more than the June call. The terms *debit* and *credit spread* are also used here. With calendar spreads, the terminology is similar for both calls and puts because the premiums for both are greater the longer the time to expiration.

Why Investors Use Option Spreads

Spreads offer the potential for a small profit while limiting the risk. Of course, they are not, of course, the sure route to riches; we already have seen that no such strategy exists. But spreads can be very useful in modifying risk while allowing profits if market forecasts prove accurate.

Risk reduction is achieved by being long in one option and short in another. If the stock price decreases, the loss on a long call will be somewhat offset by a gain on a short call. Whether the gain outweighs the loss depends on the volatility of each call. We shall illustrate this effect later. For now, consider a money spread held to expiration. Assume that we buy the call with the low strike price and sell the call with the high strike price. In a bull market, we will make money because the low-exercise-price call will bring a higher payoff at expiration than will the high-exercise-price call. In a bear market, both calls will probably expire worthless and we will lose money. For that reason, the spread involving the purchase of the low-exercise-price call is referred to as a **bull spread**. Similarly, in a bear market, we make money if we are long the high-exercise-price call and short the low-exercise-price call. This is called a **bear spread**. Opposite rules apply for puts: A position of long (short) the low-exercise-price put and short (long) the high-exercise-price put is a bull (bear) spread. In general, a bull spread should profit in a bull market and a bear spread should profit in a bear market.

Time spreads are not classified into bull and bear spreads. They profit by either increased or decreased volatility. We shall reserve further discussion of time spreads for a later section.

Transaction costs are an important practical consideration in spread trading. These costs can represent a significant portion of invested funds, especially for small traders. Spreads involve several option positions, and the transaction costs can quickly become prohibitive for all but floor traders and large institutional investors. As in Chapter 6, we will not build transaction costs directly into the analyses here, but will discuss their special relevance where appropriate.

Notation

The notation here is the same as that used in previous chapters. We must add some distinguishing symbols, however, for the spreads' different strike prices and expirations. For a money spread, we will use subscripts to distinguish options differing by strike price. For example,

X_1, X_2, X_3 = exercise prices of calls where $X_1 < X_2 < X_3$

C_1, C_2, C_3 = prices of calls with exercise prices X_1, X_2, X_3

N_1, N_2, N_3 = quantity held of each option.

TABLE 7.1 DCRB OPTION DATA, MAY 14						
	CALLS			PUTS		
EXERCISE PRICE	**MAY**	**JUNE**	**JULY**	**MAY**	**JUNE**	**JULY**
120	8.75	15.40	20.90	2.75	9.25	13.65
125	5.75	13.50	18.60	4.60	11.50	16.60
130	3.60	11.35	16.40	7.35	14.25	19.65

Current stock price: 125.94
Expirations: May 21, June 18, July 16
Risk-free rates (continuously compounded): 0.0447 (May); 0.0446 (June); 0.0453 (July)

The N notation indicates the number of options where a positive N is a long position and a negative N is a short position. In time spreads,

T_1, T_2 = time to expiration where $T_1 < T_2$

C_1, C_2 = prices of calls with times to expiration of T_1, T_2

N_1, N_2 = quantity held of each option.

The numerical illustrations will use the DCRB options presented in earlier chapters. For convenience, Table 7.1 repeats the data. Unless otherwise stated, assume that an option contract for 100 shares of stock is employed.

Your Excel spreadsheet Stratlyz9e.xls can be very useful for analyzing spreads and, indeed, all of the transactions in this chapter.

MONEY SPREADS

As indicated earlier, money spreads can be designed to profit in either a bull or a bear market. The former is called a bull spread.

Bull Spreads

Consider two call options differing only by exercise price—X_1 and X_2, where $X_1 < X_2$. Their premiums are C_1 and C_2, and we know that $C_1 > C_2$. A bull spread consists of the purchase of the option with the lower exercise price and the sale of the option with the higher exercise price. Assuming one option of each, $N_1 = 1$ and $N_2 = -1$, the profit equations are

$$\Pi = \text{Max}(0, S_T - X_1) - C_1 - \text{Max}(0, S_T - X_2) + C_2.$$

The stock price at expiration can fall into one of three ranges: less than or equal to X_1, greater than X_1 but less than or equal to X_2, or greater than X_2. The profits for these three ranges are as follows:

$$\Pi = -C_1 + C_2 \qquad \text{if } S_T \le X_1 < X_2.$$
$$\Pi = S_T - X_1 - C_1 + C_2 \qquad \text{if } X_1 < S_T \le X_2.$$
$$\Pi = S_T - X_1 - C_1 - S_T + X_2 + C_2$$
$$= X_2 - X_1 - C_1 + C_2 \qquad \text{if } X_1 < X_2 < S_T.$$

In the case where the stock price ends up equal to or below the lower exercise price, both options expire out-of-the-money. The spreader loses the premium on the long call and retains the premium on the short call. The profit is the same regardless of how far below the lower exercise price the stock price is. Because the premium on the long call is greater than the premium on the short call, however, this profit is actually a loss.

In the third case, where both options end up in-the-money, the short call is exercised on the spreader, who exercises the long call and then delivers the stock. The effect of the stock price cancels and the profit is constant for any stock price above the higher exercise price. Is this profit positive? The profit is $(X_2 - X_1) - (C_1 - C_2)$, or the difference between the exercise prices minus the difference between the premiums. Recall from Chapter 3 that the difference in premiums cannot exceed the difference in exercise prices. The spreader paid a premium of C_1, received a premium of C_2, and thus obtained the spread for a net investment of $C_1 - C_2$. The maximum payoff from the spread is $X_2 - X_1$. No one would pay more than the maximum payoff from an investment. Therefore, the profit is positive.

Only in the second case, where the long call ends up in-the-money and the short call is out-of-the-money, is there any uncertainty. The equation shows that the profit increases dollar for dollar with the stock price at expiration.

Figure 7.1 illustrates the profits from the bull spread strategy for the DCRB June 125 and 130 calls with premiums of $13.50 and $11.35, respectively. The dashed line is the profit graph had we simply purchased the 125 call. The maximum loss is the net premium of $1,350 − $1,135, or $215, which occurs at any stock price at expiration at or below $125. The maximum gain is the difference in strike prices minus the difference in premiums, $100(130 − 125 − 2.15) = 285$, which occurs at any stock price at expiration above 130. Note that even though the gain is limited, the maximum is reached at a stock price of 130, which is only 3.2 percent higher than the current stock price. The maximum profit of $285 is 135 percent of the initial value of the position of $215. On the downside, however, the maximum loss, 100 percent of the net premium, is reached with only a downward move of 0.7 percent.

> A call bull spread has a limited gain, which occurs in a bull market, and a limited loss, which occurs in a bear market.

From the graph, it is apparent that the breakeven stock price at expiration is between the two exercise prices. To find this breakeven—call it

FIGURE 7.1 Call Bull Spread

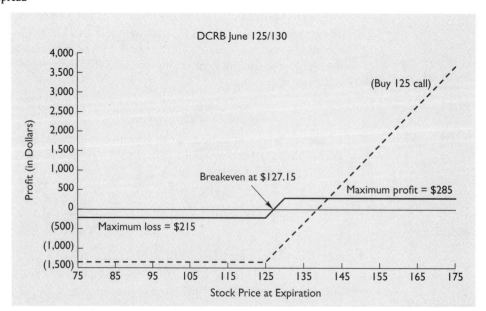

S_T^*—take the profit equation for the second case, where the stock price is between both exercise prices, and set it equal to zero:

$$\Pi = S_T^* - X_1 - C_1 + C_2 = 0.$$

Then solve for S_T^*:

$$S_T^* = X_1 + C_1 - C_2.$$

The stock price must exceed the lower exercise price by the difference in the premiums. This makes sense. The spreader exercises the call with exercise price X_1. The higher the stock price, the greater the amount received from the exercise. To break even, the spreader must receive enough to recover the net premium, $C_1 - C_2$. In this problem, the breakeven stock price at expiration is $125 + 13.50 - 11.35 = 127.15$, which is about 1 percent higher than the original stock price.

Note that in comparison to simply buying the 125 call, as indicated by the dashed line, the spreader reduces the maximum loss by the premium on the short 130 call and lowers the breakeven, but gives up the chance for large gains if the stock moves up substantially.

Early exercise poses no problem with the bull spread. Suppose that the stock price prior to expiration is S_t. If the short call is exercised, the stock price must be greater than X_2. This means that the stock price is also greater than X_1, and the long call can be exercised for a net payoff of $(S_T - X_1) - (S_T - X_2) = X_2 - X_1$. This is the best outcome one could obtain by holding the spread all the way to expiration.

Choice of Holding Period As with any option strategy, it is possible to hold the position for a period shorter than the option's entire life. Recall that in Chapter 6, we made assumptions about closing out the option positions prior to expiration. We used short holding periods of T_1, which meant closing the position on June 4, and T_2, in which we closed the position on June 25. When a position is closed prior to expiration, we estimate the option price for a range of stock prices and use those estimates to generate the profit graph. We illustrated the general procedure in Chapter 6. Using the same methodology here, we obtain the graph in Figure 7.2, the bull spread under the assumption of three different holding periods.

FIGURE 7.2 Call Bull Spread: Different Holding Periods

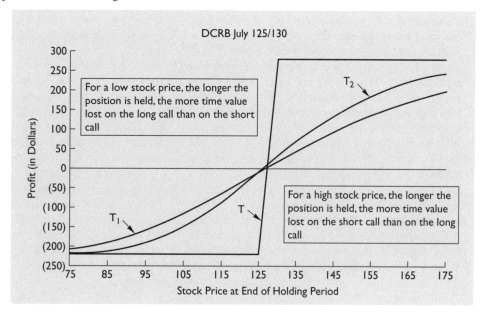

For a given stock price, the profit of a call bull spread increases as expiration approaches if the stock price is on the high side and decreases if the stock price is on the low side.

Recall that T_1 is the shortest holding period, T_2 is slightly longer, and T represents holding all the way to expiration. The graph indicates that the short holding period has the lowest range of profits. If the stock price is low, the shortest holding period produces the smallest loss while the longest holding period produces the largest loss. If the stock price is high, the shortest holding period produces the smallest gain and the longest holding period produces the largest gain.

The logic behind these results is simple. First, recall that the low-exercise-price call will always be worth more than the high-exercise-price call; however, their relative time values will differ. An option's time value is greatest when the stock price is near the exercise price. Therefore, when stock prices are high, the high-exercise-price call will have the greater time value, and when they are low, the low-exercise-price call will have the greater time value.

When we close out the spread prior to expiration, we can always expect the long call to sell for more than the short call because the long call has the lower exercise price. The excess of the long call's price over the short call's price will, however, decrease at high stock prices. This is because the time value will be greater on the short call because the stock price is closer to the exercise price. The long call will still sell for a higher price because it has more intrinsic value, but the difference will be smaller at high stock prices.

MAKING THE CONNECTION

Spreads and Option Margin Requirements

Many option strategies are inherently risky, and option traders face the risk of default from their trading counterparts. Exchange-traded options have the significant advantage of an intermediary that manages credit risk, typically some sort of clearinghouse. In return for the mitigation of counterparty credit risk, clearinghouses require option traders to post margin requirements.

In the past, the margin requirements were based on the specific strategy followed by the trader. For complex positions where many risks are offset, the strategy-based margin requirement would remain very high. Now clearinghouses take a portfolio approach and seek to measure market risk exposures based on the cumulative portfolio risk exposure. The net effect is that option margin positions are considerably lower than in the past.

For example, the margin requirements for a protective put strategy (long stock and long put) could result in a decrease in the margin requirements dramatically. The strategy-based approach would calculate margin based on the 50 percent margin requirement for holding common stock and the 100 percent margin requirement for purchasing puts. We know, however, that protective put buying sets a floor on the portfolio's losses; hence, the portfolio-based approach margin requirement would be dramatically lower. In other words, viewed separately, individual risks of these two positions are quite large, but they have an offsetting, or hedging, element that lowers their combined risks. Fortunately, margin requirements take the combined risk into account.

As we consider numerous other complex option strategies, such as spreads, collars, and other complex combinations, it is important to know that there are margin implications for the trader. An example of the new portfolio margin requirements can be found on the Chicago Board of Options Exchange website (currently www.cboe.com/tradtool/MarginReq.aspx).

With the combination of lower margin requirements for complex option positions along with an understanding that a call option can be viewed as a leveraged position in stock, the option trader can achieve an extremely high degree of implied leverage in a trading position. While leverage is beneficial if the position moves in your favor, it can prove disastrous if the position moves against you.

Conversely, at low stock prices, the long call will have a greater time value because its exercise price is closer to the stock price.

The result of all of this is that when we close the bull spread well before expiration, the profit will be lower at high stock prices and higher at low stock prices than if we did so closer to expiration. If we hold the position longer, but not all the way to expiration, we will obtain the same effect, but the impact will be smaller because the time value will be less.

Which holding period should an investor choose? There is no consistently right or wrong answer. An investor who is strongly bullish should realize that the longer the position is held, the greater the profit that can be made if the forecast is correct. In addition, a long holding period allows more time for the stock price to move upward. If the forecast proves incorrect, the loss will be lower the shorter the holding period. With short holding periods, however, there is less time for a large stock price change.

The following section examines a put bear spread. We shall see that a bear spread is, in many respects, the opposite of a bull spread.

Bear Spreads

A bear spread is the mirror image of a bull spread: The trader is long the high-exercise-price put and short the low-exercise-price put. Since $N_1 = -1$ and $N_2 = +1$ and the profit equation is

$$\Pi = -\text{Max}(0, X_1 - S_T) + P_1 + \text{Max}(0, X_2 - S_T) - P_2.$$

The outcomes are as follows:

$$\Pi = -X_1 + S_T + P_1 + X_2 - S_T - P_2 \qquad \text{if } S_T \leq X_1 < X_2.$$
$$= X_2 - X_1 + P_1 - P_2$$
$$\Pi = P_1 + X_2 - S_T - P_2 \qquad \text{if } X_1 < S_T < X_2.$$
$$\Pi = P_1 - P_2 \qquad \text{if } X_1 < X_2 \leq S_T.$$

> A put bear spread has a limited gain, which occurs in a bear market, and a limited loss, which occurs in a bull market.

Figure 7.3 illustrates the put bear spread for the DCRB June 125 and 130 puts with premiums of $11.50 and $14.25, respectively. The dashed line is a long position in the 130 put. The maximum gain is the difference

FIGURE 7.3 Put Bear Spread

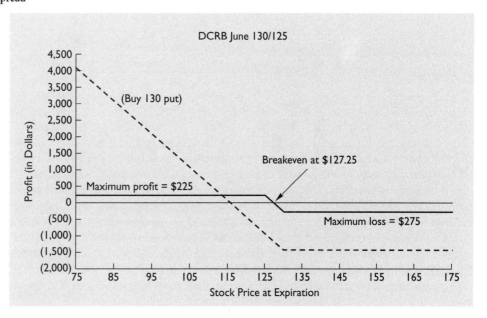

232 Part I Options

in the strike prices minus the difference in the premiums, $100(130 - 125 + 11.50 - 14.25) = 225$, which occurs at any stock price at expiration below 125. The maximum loss is the net premium of $\$1,425 - \$1,150 = \$275$, which occurs at any stock price at expiration above 130.

As with the call bull spread, the breakeven stock price at expiration is between the two exercise prices. To find this breakeven, S_T, take the profit equation for the second case, where the stock price is between both exercise prices, and set it equal to zero:

$$\Pi = P_1 + X_2 - S_T^* - P_2 = 0.$$

Then solve for

$$S_T^* = P_1 + X_2 - P_2.$$

Here the breakeven stock price is $\$130 + \$11.50 - \$14.25 = \$127.25$.

Note that the maximum gain is a return of almost 82 percent on an investment of $275 and requires a downward move of only about 1 percent (from 125.94 to 125). This would seem to make the bear spread an exceptionally tempting strategy. But note also that a slight upward move of just a little more than 1 percent would put the stock past the break-even and generate a loss. An upward move of only about 3.2 percent would take the stock to the upper exercise price, and the entire investment of $275 would be lost.

Relative to the long put, as shown by the dashed line, the bear spread has a lower maximum profit (which is limited to $225), a higher breakeven, and a lower loss on the upside by the amount of the premium from the written put.

Early exercise is not an issue for the put bear spread. This is because the put bear spread will have the long put in-the-money whenever the short put is in-the-money. If the short put is exercised, the long put can be exercised for an overall cash flow of $X_2 - X_1$, which is the maximum payoff obtainable if held to expiration.

> For a given stock price, the profit of a put bear spread increases as expiration approaches if the stock price is on the low side and decreases if the stock price is on the high side.

Choice of Holding Period Figure 7.4 illustrates a bear spread when different holding periods are used. The longer holding period produces higher profits in a bear market and larger losses in a bull market. Again,

FIGURE 7.4 Put Bear Spread: Different Holding Periods

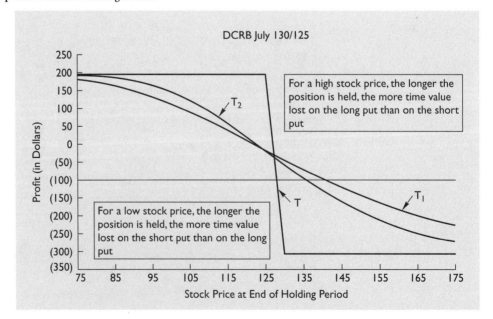

this is because of the time value effect. The spread trader closing the position prior to expiration buys back the time value of the short put and sells the long put's remaining time value. For high stock prices, the long put has more time value than the short put; thus, our long position loses faster than our short position. As time goes by, we lose from this effect. At low stock prices, the short put has more time value than our long put; thus, our short position loses faster than our long position. As time goes by, we gain from this effect.

We should repeat, however, that these statements do not advocate a short or long holding period because the length of the holding period affects the range of possible stock prices.

A Note about Call Bear Spreads and Put Bull Spreads

As we have seen, it is possible to design a call money spread that will profit in a bull market. It is also possible to construct a call money spread that will profit in a bear market. There is, however, a risk of early exercise. The short call can be sufficiently in-the-money to justify early exercise, while the long call is still out-of-the-money. Even if the long call is in-the-money, the cash flow from early exercise will be negative.

For example, suppose that S_t is the stock price prior to expiration. The cash flow from the exercise of the short call is $-(S_t - X_1)$, while the cash flow from the exercise of the long call is $S_t - X_2$. This gives a total cash flow of $X_1 - X_2$, which is negative. Early exercise ensures that the bear spreader will incur a cash outflow. Because the loss occurs prior to expiration, it is greater in present value terms than if it had occurred at expiration. Thus, the call bear spread entails a risk not associated with the bull spread.

Just as we can construct bear money spreads with calls, we can also construct bull money spreads with puts. Here we would buy the low exercise price put and sell the high exercise price put. The pattern of payoffs would be similar to those of the call bull money spread, but as with call bear money spreads, early exercise would pose a risk.

Collars

Now we shall look at a popular strategy often used by professional money managers that is referred to as a **collar**. A collar is very similar to a bull spread. In fact, the relationship between the two can be seen by applying what we learned about put-call parity.

Suppose that you buy a stock. You wish to protect it against a loss but participate in any gains. An obvious strategy is one we covered in Chapter 6, the protective put. If you buy the put, you will have to pay out cash for the price of the put. The collar reduces the cost of the put by adding a short position in a call, where the exercise price is higher than the exercise price of the put. Although a call with any exercise price can be chosen, there is in fact one particular call that tends to be preferred: the one whose price is the same as that of the put you are buying.

Thus, let us buy the stock and buy a put with an exercise price of X_1 at a price of P_1. Now let us sell a call at an exercise price of X_2 with a premium of C_2. With $N_P = 1$ and $N_C = -1$, the profit equation is

$$\Pi = S_T - S_0 + \text{Max}(0, X_1 - S_T) - P_1 - \text{Max}(0, S_T - X_2) + C_2.$$

The profits for the three ranges are as follows:

$$\Pi = S_T - S_0 + X_1 - S_T - P_1 + C_2 \qquad \text{if } S_T \leq X_1 < X_2.$$
$$= X_1 - S_0 - P_1 + C_2$$
$$\Pi = S_T - S_0 - P_1 + C_2 \qquad \text{if } X_1 < S_T < X_2.$$
$$\Pi = S_T - S_0 - P_1 - S_T + X_2 + C_2 \qquad \text{if } X_1 < X_2 \leq S_T.$$
$$= X_2 - S_0 - P_1 + C_2.$$

Because X_1 is below the current stock price, S_0, and X_2 is above it, the profit on the stock is either $X_1 - S_0$, which is negative, when S_T is at X_1 or below or $X_2 - S_0$, which is positive, when S_T is at X_2 or above. Thus, the potential loss and gain on the stock are fixed and limited. Only in the middle range, where S_T is essentially between the two exercise prices, is there any uncertainty. As noted above, it is common to set X_2 such that $C_2 = P_1$, so these terms drop out of the above profit equations. It is not necessary, however, that we choose the call such that its price offsets the price paid for the put. In such a case, we must add $-P_1 + C_2$ to the stock profit, as indicated in the above equations.

When the call and put premiums do offset each other, the collar is sometimes referred to as a zero-cost collar, but this term is somewhat misleading. While there is no cash outlay for the options, the cost is in the willingness to give up all gains beyond X_2. In other words, the investor will be selling the stock at a maximum price of X_2, in exchange for which the investor receives the assurance that the stock will be sold for no worse than X_1.

> A collar is a strategy in which the holder of a position in a stock buys a put with an exercise price lower than the current stock price and sells a call with an exercise price higher than the current stock price. The call premium is intended to reduce the cost of the put premium. The call exercise price is often set to make the call premium completely offset the put premium.

Although collars are normally used with index options in conjunction with diversified portfolios, we shall stay with the example here of the single stock, DCRB. Figure 7.5 illustrates the collar for the DCRB July 120/136.165. The stock is bought at 125.94. Let us say that we buy the put with an exercise price of 120, which costs 13.65. Now, we need to sell a call with an exercise price such that its premium is 13.65. For the July options, we see that none of the calls have a price of 13.65. The 130 has a price of 16.40, so we will need a call with an exercise price greater than $130. We can use the Black-Scholes-Merton model to figure out what the exercise price should be. We use the following inputs: $S_0 = 125.94$, $X = 136.165$, $r_c = 0.0453$, $\sigma = 0.83$, and $T = 0.1726$. We find that this call has a Black-Scholes-Merton price of 13.65.

Now we are faced with a problem we have not yet seen. If we use exchange-listed options, we cannot normally designate the exercise price, for this is set by the exchange. We could sell the 135 or the 140, but there is no 136.165. We have two

FIGURE 7.5 Collar

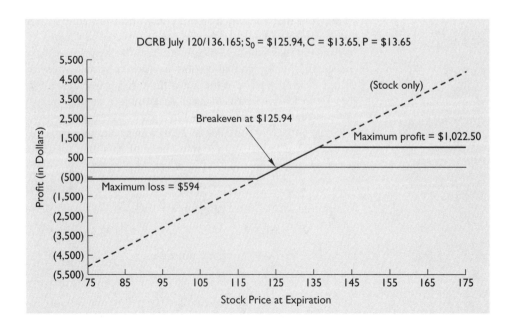

choices. We can use an over-the-counter option, as discussed in Chapter 2, which can be customized to any exercise price. We go to an options dealer and request this specific option. Alternatively, if we trade in sufficient volume, we can use FLEX options, also mentioned in Chapter 2, which trade on the exchanges and permit us to set the exercise price. Let us assume that we do one or the other. For illustrative purposes, it does not matter.

Thus, we buy the 120 put for $13.65 and sell the 136.165 call for $13.65. We do 100 of each and buy 100 shares of the DCRB stock. Note that the maximum profit is capped at 100 $(X_2 - S_0) = 100(136.165 - 125.94) = 1,022.50$ and that the maximum loss is $100(S_0 - X_1) = 100(125.94 - 120) = 594$. The breakeven is found by setting the middle equation to zero:

$$\Pi = S_T^* - S_0 = 0,$$

which we see is obviously

$$S_T^* = S_0,$$

and in our problem, $S_T^* = 125.94$, the original stock price. Note in Figure 7.5 that the line for the stock profit passes right through the middle range of profit for the collar. So the investor effectively buys the stock and establishes a maximum loss of $594 and a maximum gain of $1,022.50. Note that the maximum profit is earned with an upward move of about 8.1 percent. The maximum loss is incurred with a downward move of about 4.7 percent.

This strategy looks a lot like a bull spread. Let us examine the difference. For the three ranges of S_T, the profit equations for the bull spread and collar are given below. For the collar, we substitute from put-call parity, $C_1 - S_0 + X_1(1 + r)^{-T}$ for P_1.

$S_T \leq X_1 < X_2$

    Bull spread: $-C_1 + C_2$

    Collar: $X_1 - S_0 - P_1 + C_2$

                $= X_1 - X_1(1 + r)^{-T} - C_1 + C_2$

$X_1 < S_T < X_2$

    Bull spread: $S_T - X_1 - C_1 + C_2$

    Collar: $S_T - S_0 - P_1 + C_2$

                $= S_T - X_1(1 + r)^{-T} - C_1 + C_2$

$X_1 < X_2 \leq S_T$

    Bull spread: $X_2 - X_1 - C_1 + C_2$

    Collar: $X_2 - S_0 - P_1 + C_2$

                $= X_2 - X_1(1 + r)^{-T} - C_1 + C_2$

Thus, in all cases, the collar is more profitable by the difference between X_1 and the present value of X_1.

Thus, the bull spread and the collar are similar but not identical. Note that the range of profits for the bull spread is $X_2 - X_1 - C_1 + C_2 - (-C_1 + C_2) = X_2 - X_1$. The range of profits for the collar is $X_2 - X_1(1 + r)^{-T} - C_1 + C_2 - (X_1 - X_1(1 + r)^{-T} - C_1 + C_2) = X_2 - X_1$. So the two strategies have the same range of profits. The initial outlay for the bull spread is $C_1 - C_2$. The initial outlay for the collar is $S_0 + P_1 - C_2$. Substituting from put-call parity for P_1, this is $X_1(1 + r)^{-T} + C_1 - C_2$. The collar is equivalent to a bull spread plus a risk-free bond paying X_1 at expiration.

Choice of Holding Period In Figure 7.6, we see what the profit would look like if the position were closed early. On the downside, by closing the position at T_1, we recoup more of the time value on the long put than we pay to buy back the short call. The longer

FIGURE 7.6 Collar: Different Holding Periods

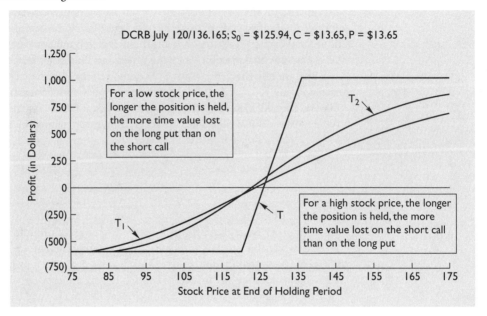

DCRB July 120/136.165; $S_0 = \$125.94$, $C = \$13.65$, $P = \$13.65$

For a low stock price, the longer the position is held, the more time value lost on the long put than on the short call

For a high stock price, the longer the position is held, the more time value lost on the short call than on the long put

we hold the position on the downside, the less this works to our advantage. On the upside, if we close the position early, the more time value we must buy back on the short call than we receive from selling the long put. The longer we hold the position, the more this works to our advantage. Remember that these statements are true because the time value is greater where the stock price is close to the exercise price. On the downside, the time value is greater on the long put; on the upside, the time value is greater on the short call.

Butterfly Spreads

A **butterfly spread**, sometimes called a **sandwich spread**, is a combination of a bull spread and a bear spread. This transaction, however, involves three exercise prices: X_1, X_2, and X_3, where X_2 is halfway between X_1 and X_3. Suppose we construct a call bull spread by purchasing the call with the low exercise price, X_1, and writing the call with the middle exercise price, X_2. Then we also construct a call bear spread by purchasing the call with the high exercise price, X_3, and writing the call with the middle exercise price, X_2. Combining these positions shows that we are long one each of the low- and high-exercise-price options and short two middle-exercise-price options. Because $N_1 = 1$, $N_2 = -2$, and $N_3 = 1$, the profit equation is

$$\Pi = \text{Max}(0, S_T - X_1) - C_1 - 2\text{Max}(0, S_T - X_2) + 2C_2 + \text{Max}(0, S_T - X_3) - C_3.$$

To analyze the behavior of the profit equation, we must examine four ranges of the stock price at expiration:

$$\Pi = -C_1 + 2C_2 - C_3 \qquad\qquad\qquad \text{if } S_T \le X_1 < X_2 < X_3.$$

$$\Pi = S_T - X_1 - C_1 + 2C_2 - C_3 \qquad\qquad \text{if } X_1 < S_T \le X_2 < X_3.$$

$$\Pi = S_T - X_1 - C_1 - 2S_T + 2X_2 + 2C_2 - C_3$$
$$= -S_T + 2X_2 - X_1 - C_1 + 2C_2 - C_3 \qquad \text{if } X_1 < X_2 < S_T \le X_3.$$

$$\Pi = S_T - X_1 - C_1 - 2S_T + 2X_2 + 2C_2 + S_T - X_3 - C_3$$
$$= -X_1 + 2X_2 - X_3 - C_1 + 2C_2 - C_3 \qquad \text{if } X_1 < X_2 < X_3 < S_T.$$

MAKING THE CONNECTION

Designing a Collar for an Investment Portfolio

Avalon Asset Management (AAM) is a (fictional) small investment management company with $50 million of assets under management. Its performance is measured at the end of the calendar year. Through nine months this year, AAM has earned outstanding returns for its clients, with its overall portfolio up about 21 percent. AAM is, however, concerned about the fourth quarter. AAM management has worked hard for this performance year to date and would not want to see it evaporate.

A partner has learned of the collar strategy, which would enable the company to purchase insurance against downside losses, in the form of puts, by selling off some of its upside gains, in the form of calls. AAM has never used options before, but believes that it understands the risks and rewards. It is not authorized, however, to use options for any of its client accounts. The partners decide to experiment with the collar strategy using $500,000 from the company's pension fund. The partners know that the collar is a conservative strategy and will not jeopardize the pension fund.

The partners approach First National Dealer Bank (FNDB) with a request to purchase a collar covering $500,000 of the portfolio. FNDB knows that this is a small derivatives transaction, which it would ordinarily not do, but it knows that if AAM is satisfied with this strategy, it will likely do larger transactions later. The bank knows that it can do the transaction and hedge the risk in the stock index options market. It also believes that it can buy and sell the options at slightly better prices than it would give AAM, thereby covering its costs and generating a small profit.

FNDB asks AAM about the amount of downside risk it is willing to bear. AAM feels it can tolerate a loss of about 6 percent in the fourth quarter so that its overall annual return would be about 15 percent. The S&P 500 is currently at 1250, so a 6 percent loss from that would put it at 1250(1 − 0.06) = 1,175. Thus, the put option would have an exercise price of 1,175. The expiration is three months, so T = 3/12 = 0.25. The S&P 500 dividend yield is 1.5 percent, the estimated volatility is 0.2, and the risk-free rate is 4 percent.

Given these inputs, a put with an exercise price of 1,175 would have a price of $17.74. An exercise price of 1,352 would produce a call premium of $17.76. FNDB agrees to round the call premium to $17.74. So the call will be struck at 1,352 and the put at 1,175. Thus, on the upside, the index can increase by 8.16 percent before the gain is lost. On the downside, the index can fall by 6 percent before

the put stops the loss. Because the S&P 500 is at 1,250 and the transaction covers a $500,000 portfolio, there will be 400 individual options.

FNDB is concerned about one point. What if AAM's portfolio does not perform identically to the S&P 500? It discusses this with AAM, which says that its portfolio sensitivity to the S&P 500 is about 101 percent. In technical terms, the beta is 1.01. AAM is satisfied that this is a close enough match to the S&P 500. FNDB is not so sure, but believes that the risk is worth taking. So the collar is executed.

During the final three months of the year, the market surprisingly continues to perform well. The portfolio rises 7.5 percent to $537,500. The S&P 500, however, outperforms the portfolio, increasing at a 10 percent rate to 1375. The call options expire in-the-money, and AAM must pay 400Max(0,1375 − 1352) = $9,200. This effectively reduces the value of the overall position to $537,500 − $9,200 = $528,300. The rate of return is, therefore,

$$\frac{\$528,300}{\$500,000} - 1 = 0.0566.$$

This is an overall return of a little over three-fourths of what the portfolio earned. The partners are confused. They believed they had room on the upside to earn the full return up to about 8 percent. With their portfolio slightly more volatile than the market, they believed that if they lost anything, it would be the excess of the portfolio's performance relative to the S&P 500. So what happened?

The portfolio underperformed the S&P 500. Even though the portfolio was thought to be more volatile than the S&P 500, measuring a portfolio's volatility is difficult. With the portfolio underperforming the S&P 500, the short call expired in-the-money without a corresponding gain on the portfolio to offset. Had the portfolio grown by 10 percent, the performance of the S&P 500, its value would have been $550,000. Deducting the $9,200 payoff on the call, the total value would have been $550,000 − $9,200 = $540,800, a gain of 8.16 percent, which is the precise upside margin built into the collar.

AAM attempted to protect a portfolio using options in which the underlying was not identical to the portfolio. Whether it uses the collar strategy again will depend on its tolerance for small discrepancies in performance from its target. AAM is, however, generally pleased because its annual performance was enhanced through its fourth-quarter performance, although not as much as its performance would otherwise have been.

Now look at the first profit equation, $-C_1 + 2C_2 - C_3$. This can be separated into $-C_1 + C_2$ and $C_2 - C_3$. We already know that a low-exercise-price call is worth more than a high-exercise-price call. Thus, the first pair of terms is negative and the second pair is positive. Which pair will be greater in an absolute sense? The first pair will. The advantage of a low-exercise-price call over a high-exercise-price call is smaller at higher exercise prices because there the likelihood of both calls expiring out-of-the-money is greater. If that happens, neither call will be of any value to the trader. Because $-C_1 + C_2$ is larger in an absolute sense than $C_2 - C_3$ the profit for the lowest range of stock prices at expiration is negative.

For the second range, the profit is $S_T - X_1 - C_1 + 2C_2 - C_3$. The last three terms, $-C_1 + 2C_2 - C_3$, represent the net price paid for the butterfly spread. Because the stock price at expiration has a direct effect on the profit, a graph would show the profit varying dollar for dollar in a positive manner with the stock price at expiration. The profit in this range of stock prices can, however, be either positive or negative. This implies that there is a breakeven stock price at expiration. To find that stock price, S_T^* set this profit equal to zero:

$$S_T^* - X_1 - C_1 + 2C_2 - C_3 = 0.$$

Solving for S_T^* gives

$$S_T^* = X_1 + C_1 - 2C_2 + C_3.$$

The breakeven equation indicates that a butterfly spread is profitable if the stock price at expiration exceeds the low exercise price by an amount large enough to cover the net price paid for the spread.

Now look at the third profit equation. Because the profit varies inversely dollar for dollar with the stock price at expiration, a graph would show the profit decreasing one for one with the stock price at expiration. The profit can be either positive or negative; hence, there is a second breakeven stock price. To find it, set the profit equal to zero:

$$-S_T^* + 2X_2 - X_1 - C_1 + 2C_2 - C_3 = 0.$$

Solving for S_T^* gives

$$S_T^* = 2X_2 - X_1 - C_1 + 2C_2 - C_3.$$

Recall that in this range of stock prices, the profit declines with higher stock prices. Profit will disappear completely if the stock price is so high that it exceeds the cash flow received from the exercise of the middle-exercise-price call, $2X_2$, minus the cash flow paid for the exercise of the low-exercise-price call, X_1, minus the net premiums on the calls.

In the final range of the stock price at expiration, profit is the net premiums paid plus the difference in the exercise prices. Because X_2 is halfway between X_1 and X_3, then $X_2 - X_1$ is the same as $X_3 - X_2$. Therefore, $- X_1 + 2X_2 - X_3 = 0$. This means that the profit in this range is the same as that in the first range and is simply the difference in the premiums.

Now that we have a good idea of what a butterfly spread looks like, consider the DCRB June 120, 125, and 130 calls. In this example, a plot of the results would reveal that the butterfly spread would profit at any stock price. Upon further inspection of the prices, we would see that the cost of buying the butterfly spread is less than the lowest possible value of the spread at expiration. Therefore, one or more of the options must be mispriced. To avoid any confusion about the performance of the butterfly spread, we should use theoretically correct prices, which can be obtained from the Black-Scholes-Merton model. Using the volatility of 83 percent, we would see that at a market

FIGURE 7.7 Call Butterfly Spread

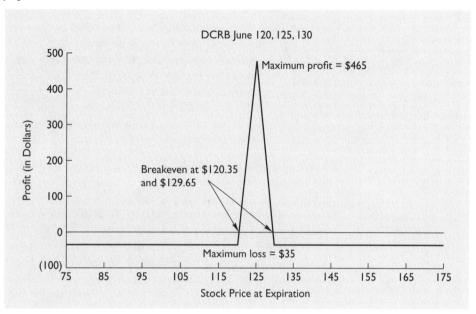

price of $15.40, the 120 call is significantly lower than its Black-Scholes-Merton value of about $16. Thus, let us use $16 as its price.

Figure 7.7 illustrates the butterfly spread for the June 120, 125, and 130 calls with premiums of $16.00, $13.50, and $11.35, respectively. The worst outcome is simply the net premiums, or $100[-16.00 + 2(13.50) - 11.35] = -35$. This is obtained for any stock price less than $120 or greater than $130. The maximum profit is obtained when the stock price at expiration is at the middle exercise price. Using the second profit equation and letting $S_T = X_2$, the maximum profit is

$$\Pi = X_2 - X_1 - C_1 + 2C_2 - C_3,$$

which in this example is $100[125 - 120 - 16.00 + 2(13.50) - 11.35] = 465$. The lower breakeven is $X_1 + C_1 - 2C_2 + C_3$, which in this case is $120 + 16.00 - 2(13.50) + 11.35 = 120.35$. The upper breakeven is $2X_2 - X_1 - C_1 + 2C_2 - C_3$, which in this example is $2(125) - 120 - 16.00 + 2(13.50) - 11.35 = 129.65$.

The butterfly spread strategy assumes that the stock price will fluctuate very little. In this example, the trader is betting that the stock price will stay within the range of $120.35, a downward move of 4.4 percent, to $129.65, an upward move of 2.9 percent. If this prediction of low stock price volatility proves incorrect, however, the potential loss will be limited—in this case, to $35. Thus, the butterfly spread is a low-risk transaction.

A trader who believes that the stock price will be extremely volatile and will fall outside of the two breakeven stock prices might want to write a butterfly spread. This will involve one short position in each of the X_1 and X_3 calls and two long positions in the X_2 call. We shall leave it as an end-of-chapter problem to explore the short butterfly spread.

Early exercise can pose a problem for holders of butterfly spreads. Suppose the stock price prior to expiration is S_t, where S_t is greater than or equal to X_2 and less than or equal to X_3. Assume that the short calls are exercised shortly before the stock goes ex-dividend. The spreader then exercises the long call with exercise price X_1. The cash flow from the short calls is $-(2S_t - 2X_2)$, and the cash flow from the long call is $S_t - X_1$. This gives a total cash flow of $-S_t + X_2 + X_2 - X_1$. The minimum value of this expression is $-X_2 + X_2 + X_2 - X_1 = X_2 - X_1$, which is positive. If S_t exceeds X_3 and the two short calls are exercised, they will be offset by the exercise of both long calls and the overall cash flow will be zero.

Thus, early exercise does not result in a cash outflow, but that does not mean that it poses no risk. If the options are exercised early, there is no possibility of achieving the maximum profit obtainable at expiration when $S_T = X_2$. If the spread were reversed and the X_1 and X_3 calls were sold while two of the X_2 calls were bought, early exercise could generate a negative cash flow.

> A butterfly spread has a limited loss, which occurs on large stock price moves, either up or down, and a limited gain, which occurs if the stock price ends up at the middle exercise price.

Choice of Holding Period   As with any option strategy, the investor might wish to close the position prior to expiration. Consider the June 120, 125, and 130 calls. Let us continue to use the same prices used in the preceding example: $16.00, $13.50, and $11.35, respectively. Let holding period T_1 involve closing the position on June 1 and holding period T_2 close the position on June 11.[1] The graph is shown in Figure 7.8.

For a given stock price, the profit of a butterfly spread increases as expiration approaches if the stock price is near the middle exercise price and decreases if the stock price is on the low or high side.

At high stock prices, time value will be greatest on the call with the highest exercise price. Because we are long that call, we gain the advantage of being able to sell it back early and recapture some of the time value. This advantage, however, erodes with a longer holding period because the time value decreases.

At low stock prices, the time value will be greatest on the call with the lowest exercise price. Because we are also long that call, we can sell it back early and recapture some of its remaining time value. This advantage also decreases, however, as we hold the position longer and time value decays.

FIGURE 7.8 Call Butterfly Spread: Different Holding Periods

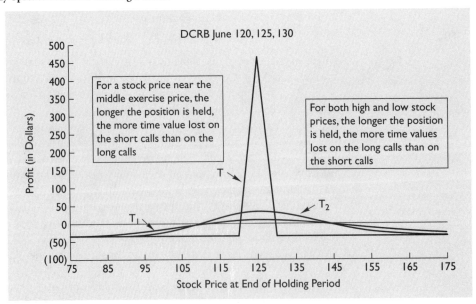

DCRB June 120, 125, 130

For a stock price near the middle exercise price, the longer the position is held, the more time value lost on the short calls than on the long calls

For both high and low stock prices, the longer the position is held, the more time values lost on the long calls than on the short calls

---

[1]The holding period was changed in this example because the time value decay does not show up as clearly for the holding periods we have previously used.

In the middle range of stock prices, the time value will be very high on the two short calls. For short holding periods, this is a disadvantage because we have to buy back these calls, which means that we must pay for the remaining time value. This disadvantage turns to an advantage, however, as the holding period lengthens and time value begins to disappear. At expiration, no time value remains; thus, profit is maximized in this range.

The breakeven stock prices are substantially further away with shorter holding periods. This is advantageous because it will then take a much larger stock price change to produce a loss.

As always, we cannot specifically identify an optimal holding period. Because the butterfly spread is a spread in which the trader expects the stock price to stay within a narrow range, profit is maximized with a long holding period. The disadvantage of a long holding period, however, is that it gives the stock price more time to move outside of the profitable range.

All of the above spreads are money spreads. We now turn to an examination of calendar spreads.

CALENDAR SPREADS

A **calendar spread**, also known as a **time spread** or **horizontal spread**, involves the purchase of an option with one expiration date and the sale of an otherwise identical option with a different expiration date. Because it is not possible to hold both options until expiration, analyzing a calendar spread is more complicated than analyzing a money spread. Because one option expires before the other, the longest possible holding period would be to hold the position until the expiration of the shorter maturity option. Then the other option would have some remaining time value that must be estimated.

Because both options have the same exercise prices, they will have the same intrinsic values; thus, the profitability of the calendar spread will be determined solely by the difference in their time values. The longer-term call will have more time value. This does not, however, necessarily mean that one should always buy the longer-term call and sell the shorter-term call. As with most option strategies, which option is purchased and which one is sold depends on the investor's outlook for the stock.

To best understand the calendar spread, we will again illustrate with the DCRB calls. This spread consists of the purchase of the July 125 call at $18.60 and the sale of the June 125 call at $13.50. This position is net long because you pay more for the July than you receive for the June. Consider two possible holding periods. One, T_1, will involve the spread's termination on June 1; the other, T_2, will have the spread held until June 18, the date of the June call's expiration. Using the Black-Scholes-Merton model to estimate the remaining time values produces the graph in Figure 7.9.

Like the butterfly spread, the calendar spread is one in which the stock's volatility is the major factor in its performance. The investor obtains the greatest profit if the stock has low volatility and thus trades within a narrow range. If the stock price moves substantially, the investor will likely incur a loss.

How does the calendar spread work? Recall that we are short the June call and long the July call. When closing out the position, we buy back the June call and sell the July call. If the stock price is around the exercise price, both calls will have more time value remaining than if the stock price were at the extremes. The June call will always have less time value, however, than the July call on any given date. Thus, when we close out the position, the time value repurchased on the June call will be low relative to the remaining time value received from the sale of the July call. As we hold the position closer and

FIGURE 7.9 Call Calendar Spread

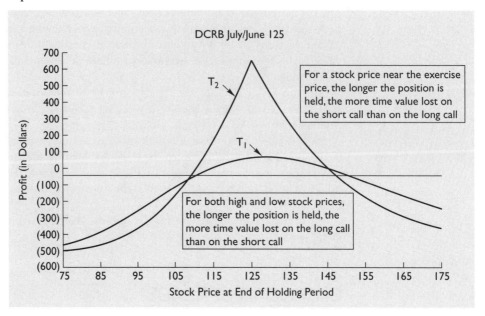

DCRB July/June 125

For a stock price near the exercise price, the longer the position is held, the more time value lost on the short call than on the long call

For both high and low stock prices, the longer the position is held, the more time value lost on the long call than on the short call

closer to the June call's expiration, the remaining time value we must repurchase on that option will get lower and lower.

If the stock price is at the high or low extreme, the time values of both options will be low. If the stock price is high enough or low enough, there may be little, if any, time value on either option. Thus, when closing out the position, there may be little time value to recover from the July option. Because the July call is more expensive, we will end up losing money on the overall transaction.

The breakeven stock prices can be obtained only by visual examination.[2] In this example, the shorter holding period has a slightly wider range between its two breakeven stock prices—about $110 and $150. For the longer holding period, the lower breakeven is about $109 and the higher breakeven is still around $147.

An investor who expected the stock price to move into the extremes could execute a reverse calendar spread. This would require purchasing the June call and selling the July

For a given stock price, a long calendar spread gains as expiration approaches if the stock price is near the exercise price and loses if the stock price is on the low or high side.

call. If the stock price became extremely low or high, there would be little time value remaining to be repurchased on the July call. Because the spreader received more money from the sale of the July call than was paid for the purchase of the June call, a profit would be made. If the stock price ended up around the exercise price, however, the trader could incur a potentially large loss. This is because the July call would possibly have a large time value that would have to be repurchased.

Time Value Decay

Because a calendar spread is completely influenced by the behavior of the two calls' time value decay, it provides a good opportunity to examine how time values decay. Using the Black-Scholes-Merton model, we can compute the week-by-week time values for each call during the spread's life, holding the stock price constant at $125.94. Keep in mind,

---

[2]It is possible, however, to use a computer search routine with the Black-Scholes-Merton model to find the precise breakeven.

TABLE 7.2 TIME VALUE DECAY, JUNE AND JULY 125 AND CALENDAR SPREAD

DATE	TIME	JUNE 125 TIME VALUE	THETA	TIME	JULY 125 TIME VALUE	THETA	SPREAD TIME VALUE	THETA
May 14	0.0959	12.61	−68.91	0.1726	17.14	−51.54	4.53	17.37
May 21	0.0767	11.22	−76.92	0.1534	16.12	−54.65	4.91	22.27
May 28	0.0575	9.64	−88.63	0.1342	15.04	−58.39	5.40	30.24
June 4	0.0384	7.77	−108.19	0.1151	13.88	−63.02	6.11	45.17
June 11	0.0192	5.35	−152.11	0.0959	12.62	−68.95	7.27	83.16
June 18	0.0000	0.00	0.00	0.0767	11.22	−76.96	11.22	−76.96

$\sigma = 0.83$, $S_0 = 125.94$, $r_c(\text{June}) = 0.0446$, $r_c(\text{July}) = 0.0453$
The spread time value and theta equal the time value and theta on the long July call minus the time value and theta on the short June call. The time value of each option is obtained as the Black-Scholes-Merton value, which is the intrinsic value plus the time value minus the intrinsic value of 0.94.

of course, that time values will change if the stock price changes. Because time values are greatest for at-the-money options, we use the June and July 125 calls. The pattern of time values at various points during the options' lives is presented in Table 7.2. The table also presents the thetas, which we learned from Chapter 5 are the changes in the option prices for a very small change in time. Negative thetas imply that the option price will fall as we move forward in time.

Notice what happens as expiration approaches. Because of the June call's earlier expiration, its theta is more negative, and its time value decays more rapidly than does that of the July call. Because we are long the July call and short the June call, the spread's time value—the time value of the long call minus the time value of the short call—increases, as indicated by its positive theta. Once the June call expires, however, we are left with a long position in the July call, which leaves us with a negative theta. Time value will then begin decaying.

Figure 7.10 illustrates the pattern of time value decay. As expiration approaches, the time value of the June call rapidly decreases and the overall time value of the spread increases. At expiration of the June call, the spread's time value is composed entirely of the July call's time value.

Time value decay would appear to make it easy to profit with a time spread. One would simply buy the longer-term option and write the shorter-term option. As the time values decayed, the spread would gain value. In reality, however, it seldom works out like this. The pattern of time value decay illustrated here was obtained by holding the stock price constant. In actuality, the stock price will almost surely change. Thus, there is indeed risk to a calendar spread. This risk is mitigated somewhat by the fact that the investor is long one option and short the other. Nonetheless, the calendar spread, in which one buys the long-term option and writes the short-term option, is a good strategy if one expects the stock price to remain fairly stable.

> Time value decays more rapidly as expiration approaches.

The degree of risk of early exercise on a calendar spread depends on which call is bought and which is sold. Because both calls have the same exercise price, the extent to which they are in-the-money is the same. As discussed in Chapter 3, however, the time to expiration is a factor in encouraging early exercise. We saw that if everything else is equal, the shorter-term option is the one more likely to be exercised early. Thus, if we write the shorter-term option, it could be exercised early. We always, however, have the

FIGURE 7.10 Time Value Decay

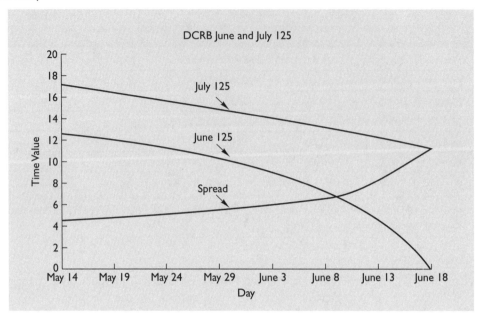

choice of exercising the longer-term option early. It will certainly be in-the-money if the shorter-term option is in-the-money. If S_t is the stock price prior to expiration and the shorter-term call is exercised, the cash flow will be $-(S_t - X)$, while the cash flow from exercising the longer-term option will be $S_t - X$. Thus, the total cash flow will be zero. This means that in the event of early exercise, there will be no negative cash flow. It does not mean that there will be no overall loss on the transaction.

The longer-term call is more expensive than the shorter-term call. This means that early exercise would ensure a loss by preventing us from waiting to capture the time value decay.

Calendar spreads can also be constructed with puts. By using the Black-Scholes-Merton model to determine the time value on the puts, similar results can be obtained. Like money spreads, put calendar spreads should not be overlooked. The puts could be mispriced, in which case a spread might offer the most profitable opportunity.

The butterfly spread and calendar spread are two of several transactions called **volatility strategies**. We shall look at the others later in this chapter. For now, however, note that all of the strategies covered so far are risky. Some option traders prefer riskless strategies because if the options are mispriced, it may be possible to construct a riskless portfolio that will earn a return in excess of the risk-free rate.

RATIO SPREADS

Chapter 5 examined the Black-Scholes-Merton model. It showed that when an option is mispriced, an investor can construct a riskless hedge by buying an underpriced call and selling short the stock or by buying stock and selling an overpriced call. Because of margin requirements and other regulations, selling short stock can be complicated. By using spreads, however, the investor can buy an underpriced call and sell an overpriced or correctly priced call, producing a ratio of one call to the other that creates a riskless position. This transaction is called a **ratio spread**.

The ratio spread can be either a money spread or a calendar spread. Consider two calls priced at C_1 and C_2. Initially, we need not be concerned with which one is purchased and which one is sold, nor do we need to determine whether the two calls differ by time to expiration or by exercise price. The approach presented here can accommodate all cases.

Let the investor hold N_1 units of the call priced at C_1 and N_2 units of the call priced at C_2. The value of the portfolio is

$$V = N_1C_1 + N_2C_2.$$

Recall that the delta of a call is the change in the call price over the change in the stock price, assuming that the change in the stock price is very small. Let us use the symbols Δ_1 and Δ_2 as the deltas of the two calls. Remember that the deltas are the values of $N(d_1)$ from the Black-Scholes-Merton model. If the stock price changes, the first call generates a total price change of $N_1\Delta_1$ and the second call generates a total price change of $N_2\Delta_2$. Thus, when the stock price changes, the portfolio will change in value by the sum of these two values. A hedged position is one in which the portfolio value will not change when the stock price changes. Thus, we set $N_1\Delta_1 + N_2\Delta_2$ to zero and solve for the ratio N_1/N_2.

$$\frac{N_1}{N_2} = -\frac{\Delta_2}{\Delta_1}.$$

A riskless position is established if the ratio of the quantity of the first call to the quantity of the second call equals minus the inverse ratio of their deltas. The transaction would then be delta neutral.

Consider an example using the DCRB June 120 and June 125 calls. Using $S_0 = 125.94$, $r_c = 0.0446$, and $T = 0.0959$ in the Black-Scholes-Merton model gives a value of $N(d_1)$ of 0.630 for the June 120 and 0.569 for the June 125. Thus, the ratio of the number of June 120s to June 125s should be $-(0.569/0.630) = -0.903$. Hence, the investor would buy 903 of the June 120s and sell 1,000 of the June 125s.

Note that the investor could have purchased 1,000 of the June 125s and sold 903 of the June 120s. The negative sign in the formula is a reminder to be long one option and short the other. An investor should, of course, always buy underpriced or correctly priced calls and sell overpriced or correctly priced calls.

If the stock price decreases by $1, the June 120 should decrease by 0.630 and the June 125 by 0.569. The investor is long 903 of the June 120s and therefore loses $0.630(903) \approx 569$. Likewise, the investor is short 1,000 of the June 125s and thus gains $0.569(1,000) \approx 569$. The gain on one call offsets the loss on the other.

The ratio spread, of course, does not remain riskless unless the ratio is continuously adjusted. Because this is somewhat impractical, no truly riskless hedge can be constructed. Moreover, the values of $N(d_1)$ are simply approximations of the change in the call price for a change in the stock price. They apply for only very small changes in the stock price. For larger changes in the stock price, the hedger would need to consider the gamma, which we discussed in Chapter 5. Nonetheless, spreads of this type are frequently done by option traders attempting to replicate riskless positions. Although the positions may not always be exactly riskless, they will come very close to being so as long as the ratio does not deviate too far from the optimum.

This completes our coverage of option spread strategies. The next group of strategies is called **combinations** because they involve combined positions in puts and calls. We previously covered some combination strategies, namely conversions and reversals, which we used to illustrate put-call parity. The strategies covered in the remainder of this chapter are straddles and box spreads. We will use the same approach as before; the notation should be quite familiar to you by now.

A ratio spread is a risk-free transaction involving two options weighted according to their deltas.

STRADDLES

Straddles, like calendar and butterfly spreads, are volatility strategies because they are based on the expectation of high or low volatility rather than the direction of the stock.

A **straddle** is the purchase of a call and a put that have the same exercise price and expiration date. By holding both a call and a put, the trader can capitalize on stock price movements in either direction.

Consider the purchase of a straddle with the call and put having an exercise price of X and an expiration of T. Then $N_C = 1$ and $N_P = 1$ and the profit from this transaction if held to expiration is

$$\Pi = \text{Max}(0, S_T - X) - C + \text{Max}(0, X - S_T) - P.$$

Because only one exercise price is involved, there are only two ranges of the stock price at expiration. The profits are as follows:

$$\Pi = S_T - X - C - P \qquad \text{if } S_T \geq X.$$
$$\Pi = X - S_T - C - P \qquad \text{if } S_T < X.$$

For the first case, in which the stock price equals or exceeds the exercise price, the call expires in-the-money.[3] It is exercised for a gain of $S_T - X$, while the put expires out-of-the-money. The profit is the gain on the call minus the premiums paid on the call and the put. For the second case, in which the stock price is less than the exercise price, the put expires in-the-money and is exercised for a gain of $X - S_T$. The profit is the gain on the put minus the premiums paid for the put and the call.

For the range of stock prices above the exercise price, the profit increases dollar for dollar with the stock price at expiration. For the range of stock prices below the exercise price, the profit decreases dollar for dollar with the stock price at expiration. When the options expire with the stock price at the exercise price, both options are at-the-money and essentially expire worthless. The profit then equals the premiums paid, which, of course, makes it a loss. These results suggest that the graph is V-shaped. Figure 7.11 illustrates the straddle for the DCRB June 125 options. The dashed lines are the strategies of buying the call and the put separately.

As noted, the straddle is designed to capitalize on high stock price volatility. To create a profit, the stock price must move substantially in either direction. It is not necessary to know which way the stock will go; it is necessary only that it make a significant move. How much must it move? Look at the two breakeven points.

For the case in which the stock price exceeds the exercise price, set the profit equal to zero:

$$S_T^* - X - C - P = 0.$$

Solving for S_T^* gives a breakeven of

$$S_T^* = X + C + P.$$

The upside breakeven is simply the exercise price plus the premiums paid for the options. For the case in which the stock price is below the exercise price, set the profit equal to zero:

$$X - S_T^* - C - P = 0.$$

Solving for S_T^* gives a breakeven of

$$S_T^* = X - C - P.$$

---

[3]The case in which $S_T = X$ is included in this range. Even though $S_T = X$ means that the call is at-the-money, it can still be exercised for a gain of $S_T - X = 0$.

FIGURE 7.11 Straddle

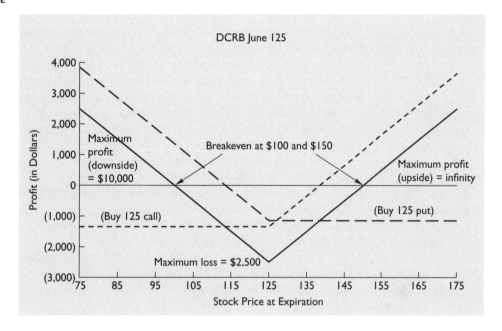

The downside breakeven is the exercise price minus the premiums paid on the options.

Thus, the breakeven stock prices are simply the exercise price plus or minus the premiums paid for the call and the put. This makes sense. On the upside, the call is exercised for a gain equal to the difference between the stock price and the exercise price. For the investor to profit, the stock price must exceed the exercise price by enough that the gain from exercising the call will cover the premiums paid for the call and the put. On the downside, the put is exercised for a gain equal to the difference between the exercise price and the stock price. To generate a profit, the stock price must be sufficiently below the exercise price that the gain on the put will cover the premiums on the call and the put.

In this example, the premiums are $13.50 for the call and $11.50 for the put, for a total of $25. Thus, the breakeven stock prices at expiration are $125 plus or minus $25, or $100 and $150. The stock price currently is at $125.94. To generate a profit, the stock price must increase by $24.06 or decrease by $25.94 in the remaining 35 days until the options expire.

The worst-case outcome for a straddle is for the stock price to end up equal to the exercise price where neither the call nor the put can be exercised for a gain.[4] The option trader will lose the premiums on the call and the put, which in this example total $100(13.50 + 11.50) = 2,500$.

The profit potential on a straddle is unlimited. The stock price can rise infinitely, and the straddle will earn profits dollar for dollar with the stock price in excess of the exercise price. On the downside, the profit is limited simply because the stock price can go no lower than zero. The downside maximum profit is found by setting the stock price at expiration equal to zero for the case in which the stock price is below the exercise price. This gives a profit of $X - C - P$, which here is $100(125 - 13.50 - 11.50) = 10,000$.

---

[4]The put, the call, or both could be exercised, but the gain on either would be zero. Transaction costs associated with exercise would suggest that neither the call nor the put would be exercised when $S_T = X$.

The potentially large profits on a straddle can be a temptation too hard to resist. One should be aware that the straddle normally requires a fairly large stock price move to be profitable. Even to a novice investor, stock prices always seem highly volatile, but that volatility may be misleading. In this example, it would require about a 19 percent increase or a 21 percent decrease in the stock price in one month to make a profit, which would be a rare event. An investor considering a straddle is advised to carefully assess the probability that the stock price will move into the profitable range.

Because both the call and the put are owned, the problem of early exercise does not exist with a straddle. The early-exercise decision is up to the straddle holder. Transaction costs also need to be considered.

When the straddle is established, there is a commission on both the call and the put. At exercise, there will be a commission only on either the call or the put, whichever is in-the-money. Suppose the stock price ends up slightly higher than the exercise price. Because of the commission on the exercise of the call, it might be inadvisable to exercise the call even though it is in-the-money. A similar argument can be made for the case against exercising the put when the stock price ends up slightly less than the exercise price. This means that, as with any option strategy, the maximum loss is slightly more than the analysis indicates because of the commission. Moreover, the stock price at which such a loss occurs is actually a range around the exercise price.

Choice of Holding Period   Now consider what happens upon closing the position prior to expiration. Figure 7.12 illustrates the outcomes for the DCRB July 125 straddle using the same three holding periods employed in examining the other strategies;[5] that is, the shortest holding period involves closing the position on June 4, the intermediate-

FIGURE 7.12 Straddle: Different Holding Periods

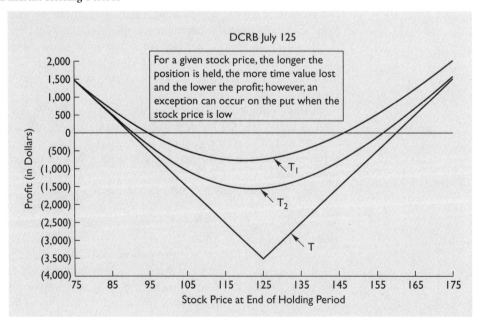

---

[5]Specifically, the holding period T_1 means that the remaining maturity is 0.1151 based on 42 days remaining, T_2 means that the remaining maturity is 0.0575 based on 21 days remaining, and $T = 0$ assumes holding all the way to expiration.

length holding period closes the position on June 25, and the long holding period closes the position at expiration. The profit graphs are curves that collapse onto the straight line for the case in which the position is held to expiration. The highest curve is the shortest holding period.

We should keep in mind that this graph does not imply that the shortest holding period is the best strategy. For a given stock price, the shortest holding period indeed provides the highest profit. The uncertainty of the stock price at expiration prevents the short holding period from dominating the longer holding periods. Because a straddle is designed to permit profiting from large stock price fluctuations, the short holding period leaves less time for the stock price to make a significant move.

When the straddle is closed out prior to expiration, both the call and the put will contain some remaining time value. If the stock price is extremely high or low, neither option will have much time value, but either the call or the put will have a high intrinsic value. If the stock price is close to the exercise price, both options will have a fair amount of time value. When closing out the position, the investor sells the options back and recovers this time value. As the holding period is extended closer to the expiration date, there is less time value to recover and the profit declines. The profit curve gradually decreases until, at expiration, it becomes the curve for the case in which the straddle is held to expiration. Thus, the higher profits from shorter holding periods come from recapturing the time value of the put and the call.

Figure 7.12 shows that the shorter holding period leads to a lower upside and higher downside breakeven. This reduces the risk to the trader because the range of stock prices in which a loss can be incurred is smaller. In this example, the shortest holding period has breakeven stock prices of about $93 and $146, and the intermediate-term holding period has breakeven stock prices of about $90 and $156.

> For a given stock price, a straddle, being long two options, loses value as expiration approaches.

Applications of Straddles   A straddle is an appropriate strategy for situations in which one suspects that the stock price will move substantially but does not know in which direction it will go. An example of this occurs when a major bank or corporation is about to fail.

Suppose that a failing bank applies for a bailout from the government.[6] During the period in which the request is under consideration, a straddle will be a potentially profitable strategy. If the request is denied, the bank probably will fail and the stock will become worthless. If the bailout is granted, the bank may be able to turn itself around, in which case the stock price will rise substantially.

A similar scenario exists when a major corporation applies for federal loan guaranties. A straddle is also an appropriate strategy for situations in which important news is about to be released and it is expected that the news will be either very favorable or very unfavorable. The weekly money supply announcements present opportunities that could be exploited with index options. Corporate earnings announcements are other examples of situations in which uncertain information will be released on a specific date.

The straddle certainly is not without risk. If investors already know or expect the information, the stock price may move very little when the announcement is made. If this happens, the investor might be tempted to hold on to the straddle in the faint hope that some other unanticipated news will be released before the options expire. In all likelihood, however, the stock price will move very little and the straddle will produce

---

[6]Bailouts frequently take the form of loan guaranties but can also involve sale of unproductive assets, or sale of new equity or hybrid securities.

a loss. The trader might wish to cut the loss quickly by closing the position if the expected move does not materialize.

The most important thing to remember when evaluating a straddle is to note that the greater uncertainty associated with the examples described here is recognized by everyone. Thus, the options would be priced according to a higher stock volatility, making the straddle more expensive. The most attractive straddles will be those in which the investor is confident that the stock will be more volatile than everyone else believes.

Short Straddle   An investor who expects the market to stay within a narrow trading range might consider writing a straddle. This would involve the sale of a put and a call with the same exercise price and expiration date. From the previous analysis, it should be obvious that the profit graph would be an inverted V. A short straddle would be a high-risk strategy because of the potential for large losses if the stock price moved substantially, particularly upward. Also, there would be the risk of early exercise of either the put or the call.

BOX SPREADS

A **box spread** is a combination of a bull call money spread and a bear put money spread. In contrast to the volatility strategies, the box spread is a low-risk—in fact, riskless—strategy.

Consider a group of options with two exercise prices, X_1 and X_2, and the same expiration. A bull call spread would involve the purchase of the call with exercise price X_1 at a premium of C_1 and the sale of the call with exercise price X_2 at a premium of C_2. A bear put spread would require the purchase of the put with exercise price X_2 at a premium of P_2 and the sale of the put with exercise price X_1 at a premium of P_1. Under the rules for the effect of exercise price on put and call prices, both the call and put spread would involve an initial cash outflow because $C_1 > C_2$ and $P_2 > P_1$. Thus, the box spread would have a net cash outflow at the initiation of the strategy.

The profit at expiration is

$$\Pi = \text{Max}(0, S_T - X_1) - C_1 - \text{Max}(0, S_T - X_2) + C_2$$
$$+ \text{Max}(0, X_2 - S_T) - P_2 - \text{Max}(0, X_1 - S_T) + P_1.$$

Because there are two exercise prices, we must examine three ranges of the stock price at expiration. The profits are

$$\Pi = -C_1 + C_2 + X_2 - S_T - P_2 - X_1 + S_T + P_1$$
$$= X_2 - X_1 - C_1 + C_2 - P_2 + P_1 \qquad \text{if } S_T \leq X_1 < X_2.$$

$$\Pi = S_T - X_1 - C_1 + C_2 + X_2 - S_T - P_2 + P_1$$
$$= X_2 - X_1 - C_1 + C_2 - P_2 + P_1 \qquad \text{if } X_1 < S_T \leq X_2.$$

$$\Pi = S_T - X_1 - C_1 + X_2 - S_T + C_2 - P_2 + P_1$$
$$= X_2 - X_1 - C_1 + C_2 - P_2 + P_1 \qquad \text{if } X_1 < X_2 < S_T.$$

Notice that the profit is the same in each case: The box spread will be worth $X_2 - X_1$ at expiration, and the profit will be $X_2 - X_1$ minus the premiums paid, $C_1 - C_2 + P_2 - P_1$. The box spread is thus a riskless strategy. Why would anyone want to execute a box spread if one can more easily earn the risk-free rate by purchasing Treasury bills? The reason is that the box spread may prove to be incorrectly priced, as a valuation analysis can reveal.

Because the box spread is a riskless transaction that pays off the difference in the exercise prices at expiration, it should be easy to determine whether it is correctly priced. The payoff can be discounted at the risk-free rate. The present value of this amount is then compared to the cost of obtaining the box spread, which is the net premiums paid. This procedure is like analyzing a capital budgeting problem. The present value of the payoff at expiration minus the net premiums is a net present value (NPV). Because the objective of any investment decision is to maximize NPV, an investor should undertake all box spreads in which the NPV is positive. On those spreads with a negative NPV, one should execute a reverse box spread.

The net present value of a box spread is

$$NPV = (X_2 - X_1)(1 + r)^{-T} - C_1 + C_2 - P_2 + P_1,$$

where r is the risk-free rate and T is the time to expiration.[7] If NPV is positive, the present value of the payoff at expiration will exceed the net premiums paid. If NPV is negative, the total amount of the premiums paid will exceed the present value of the payoff at expiration. The process is illustrated in Figure 7.13.

An alternative way to view the box spread is as the difference between two put-call parities. For example, for the options with exercise price X_1, put-call parity is

$$P_1 = C_1 - S_0 + X_1(1 + r)^{-T},$$

and for the options with exercise price X_2, put-call parity is

$$P_2 = C_2 - S_0 + X_2(1 + r)^{-T}.$$

Rearranging both equations to isolate the stock price gives

$$S_0 = C_1 - P_1 + X_1(1 + r)^{-T}.$$
$$S_0 = C_2 - P_2 + X_2(1 + r)^{-T}.$$

Because the left-hand sides are equal, the right-hand sides must also be equal; therefore,

$$C_1 - P_1 + X_1(1 + r)^{-T} = C_2 - P_2 + X_2(1 + r)^{-T}.$$

Rearranging this equation gives

$$0 = (X_2 - X_1)(1 + r)^{-T} - C_1 + C_2 - P_2 + P_1.$$

FIGURE 7.13 The Box Spread

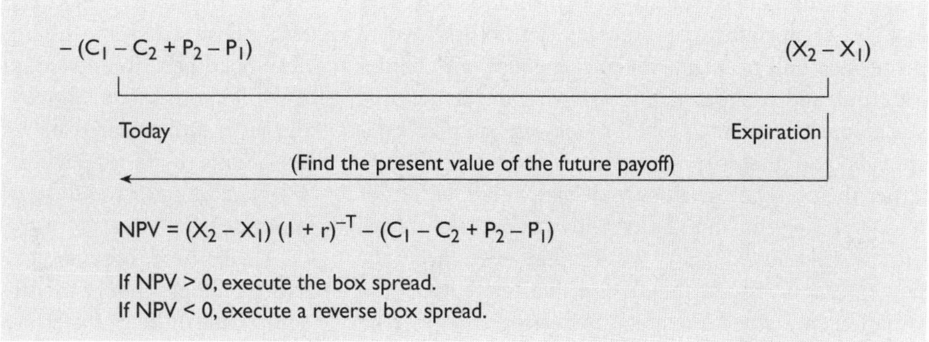

$-(C_1 - C_2 + P_2 - P_1)$ $(X_2 - X_1)$

Today   Expiration

(Find the present value of the future payoff)

$NPV = (X_2 - X_1)(1 + r)^{-T} - (C_1 - C_2 + P_2 - P_1)$

If NPV > 0, execute the box spread.
If NPV < 0, execute a reverse box spread.

---

[7]Alternately, one could compute the present value of $X_2 - X_1$ as $(X_2 - X_1)e^{-r_cT}$ and obtain the same result.

This is our put-call parity equation when the NPV is zero, which results if all puts and calls are correctly priced relative to one another.

Let us examine the DCRB June box spread using the 125 and 130 options. Consider the following transaction: Buy the 125 call at $13.50, buy the 130 put at $14.25, write the 130 call at $11.35, and write the 125 put at $11.50. The premiums paid for the 125 call and 130 put minus the premiums received for the 130 call and 125 put net out to $4.90. Thus, it will cost $490 to buy the box spread.

The payoff at expiration is $X_2 - X_1$. The net present value is

$$\text{NPV} = 100[(130 - 125)(1.0456)^{-0.0959} - 4.90] = \$7.85,$$

where 0.0456 is the discrete risk-free rate for June as determined in Chapter 3, and 0.0959 is the time to expiration from May 14 to June 18. Thus, the spread is underpriced and should be purchased. Had the NPV been negative, the box spread would have been overpriced and should have been sold. In that case, an investor would buy the 130 call and 125 put and sell the 125 call and 130 put. This would generate a positive cash flow up front that exceeded the present value of the cash outflow of $X_2 - X_1$ at expiration.

If the investor is holding a long box spread, the risk of early exercise is unimportant. Suppose the short call is exercised. Because the short call is in-the-money, the long call will be even deeper in-the-money. The investor can then exercise the long call. If the short put is exercised, the investor can, in turn, exercise the long put, which will be even deeper in-the-money than the short put. The net effect is a cash inflow of $X_2 - X_1$, the maximum payoff at expiration. For the short box spread, however, early exercise will result in a cash outflow of $X_2 - X_1$. Thus, the early exercise problem is an important consideration for short box spreads.

Transaction costs on a box spread will be high because four options are involved. At least two of the four options, however, will expire out-of-the-money. Nonetheless, the high transaction costs will make the box spread costly to execute for all but those who own seats on the exchange.

> A box spread is a risk-free transaction in which the value can be easily calculated as the present value of a future payoff minus the initial outlay.

Summary

This chapter showed how some of the basic option strategies introduced in Chapter 6 can be combined to produce more complex strategies, such as spreads and combinations. Spreads were shown to be relatively low-risk strategies. Money spreads can be designed to profit in a bull or a bear market. A collar uses both a long put and a short call, along with the underlying stock, and is similar to a bull money spread. Calendar spreads and butterfly spreads are used to profit in either the presence or absence of high volatility. Straddles were also shown to be attractive in periods of high or low volatility. Finally, the chapter introduced the box spread, a riskless transaction that lends itself to a variation of a standard capital budgeting analysis with the end result being a net present value, a concept often encountered elsewhere in finance.

The strategies covered in this and the preceding chapter are but a few of the many possible option strategies. Those interested in furthering their knowledge of option strategies can explore the many excellent books cited in the references. The framework developed here should be sufficient to get you started. At this point, you should be capable of assessing the risks and rewards of a few simple option strategies. This book is an introduction and hopefully will encourage you to explore option strategies in more depth.

At one time, options, forward, and futures markets existed almost independently of each other. Now it is sometimes difficult to tell where one market ends and the other begins. Although we shall leave the world of options for a while, we will return to it in time.

Key Terms

Before continuing to Chapter 8, you should be able to give brief definitions of the following terms:

spread/vertical/strike/money
   spread/horizontal/time/
   calendar spread, p. 225
buying the spread/debit spread/
   selling the spread/credit spread/
   bull spread/bear spread, p. 226

collar, p. 233
butterfly/sandwich spread, p. 236
calendar/time/
   horizontal spread, p. 241
volatility strategies/
   ratio spread, p. 244

combinations, p. 245
straddle, p. 246
box spread, p. 250

Further Reading

More advanced analysis and option strategies can be found in the following:

Billingsley, R. S., and D. M. Chance. "Options Market Efficiency and the Box Spread Strategy." *The Financial Review* 20 (November 1985): 287–301.

Cohen, G. *The Bible of Option Strategies: The Definitive Guide for Practical Trading Strategies.* Upper Saddle River, NJ: Financial Times Prentice Hall, 2005.

Gombola, M. J., R. L. Roenfeldt, and P. L. Cooley. "Spreading Strategies in CBOE Options: Evidence on Market Performance." *The Journal of Financial Research* 1 (Winter 1978): 35–44.

Jabbour, G., and P. H. Budwick. *The Option Trader Handbook: Strategies and Trade Adjustments.* Hoboken, NJ: John Wiley & Sons, 2010.

Johnson, K. E., *Option Spread Strategies: Trading Up, Down, and Sideways Markets.* New York: Bloomberg Financial, 2009.

The Options Institute. *Options: Essential Concepts and Trading Strategies*, 3rd ed. New York: McGraw-Hill, 1999.

Slivka, R. T., "Call Option Spreading." *The Journal of Portfolio Management* 7 (Spring 1981): 71–76.

Slivka, R. T., "Risk and Return for Option Investment Strategies." *Financial Analysts Journal* 36 (September–October 1980): 67–73.

Concept Checks

1. Explain why option traders often use spreads instead of simple long or short options and combined positions of options and stock.

2. Suppose that an option trader has a call bull spread. The stock price has risen substantially, and the trader is considering closing the position early. What factors should the trader consider with regard to closing the transaction before the options expire?

3. Suppose that you are following the stock of a firm that has been experiencing severe problems. Failure is imminent unless the firm is granted government guaranteed loans. If the firm fails, its stock will, of course, fall substantially. If the loans are granted, it is expected that the stock will rise substantially. Identify two strategies that would be appropriate for this situation. Justify your answers.

4. Explain how a short call added to a protective put forms a collar and how it changes the payoff and up-front cost.

5. Explain the process by which the profit of a short straddle closed out prior to expiration is influenced by the time values of the put and call.

Questions and Problems

1. Derive the profit equations for a put bull spread. Determine the maximum and minimum profits and the breakeven stock price at expiration.

2. Explain why a straddle is not necessarily a good strategy when the underlying event is well known to everyone.

3. The chapter showed how analyzing a box spread is like a capital budgeting problem using the net present value approach. Consider the internal rate of return method of examining capital budgeting problems and analyze the box spread in that context.

4. One way to create a bull spread positions is by purchasing a low strike call option and selling a high strike call option. Identify a strategy with put options that creates a similar bull spread-shaped profit profile.

5. One way to create a bear spread positions is by purchasing a high strike put option and selling a low strike put option. Identify a strategy with call options that creates a similar bear spread-shaped profit profile.

The following option prices were observed for calls and puts on a stock on July 6 of a particular year. Use this information for problems 6 through 24. The stock was priced at 165.13. The expirations are July 17, August 21, and October 16. The continuously compounded risk-free rates associated with the three expirations are 0.0503, 0.0535, and 0.0571, respectively. The standard deviation is 0.21.

	Calls			Puts		
Strike	Jul	Aug	Oct	Jul	Aug	Oct
160	6.00	8.10	11.10	0.75	2.75	4.50
165	2.70	5.25	8.10	2.40	4.75	6.75
170	0.80	3.25	6.00	5.75	7.50	9.00

For problems 6 through 10 and 13 through 16, determine the profits for the holding period indicated for possible stock prices of 150, 155, 160, 165, 170, 175, and 180 at the end of the holding period. Answer any other questions as indicated. Note: Your Excel spreadsheet Stratlyz9e.xls will be useful here for obtaining graphs as requested, but it does not allow you to calculate the profits for several user-specified asset prices. It lets you specify one asset price and a maximum and minimum. Use Stratlyz9e.xls to produce the graph for the range of prices from 150 to 180, but determine the profits for the prices of 150, 155,…, 180 by hand for positions held to expiration. For positions closed prior to expiration, use the spreadsheet BSMbin9e.xls to determine the option price when the position is closed; then calculate the profit by hand.

6. Construct a bear money spread using the October 165 and 170 calls. Hold the position until the options expire. Determine the profits and graph the results. Identify the breakeven stock price at expiration and the maximum and minimum profits.

Discuss any special considerations associated with this strategy.

7. Repeat problem 6, but close the position on September 20. Use the spreadsheet to find the profits for the possible stock prices on September 20. Generate a graph and use it to identify the approximate breakeven stock price.

8. Construct a collar using the October 160 put. First, use the Black-Scholes-Merton model to identify a call that will make the collar have zero up-front cost. Then close the position on September 20. Use the spreadsheet to find the profits for the possible stock prices on September 20. Generate a graph and use it to identify the approximate breakeven stock price. Determine the maximum and minimum profits.

9. Suppose you are expecting the stock price to move substantially over the next three months. You are considering a butterfly spread. Construct an appropriate butterfly spread using the October 160, 165, and 170 calls. Hold the position until expiration. Determine the profits and graph the results. Identify the two breakeven stock prices and the maximum and minimum profits.

10. Construct a calendar spread using the August and October 170 calls that will profit from high volatility. Close the position on August 1. Use the spreadsheet to find the profits for the possible stock prices on August 1. Generate a graph and use it to estimate the maximum and minimum profits and the breakeven stock prices.

11. Using the Black-Scholes-Merton model, compute and graph the time value decay of the October 165 call on the following dates: July 15, July 31, August 15, August 31, September 15, September 30, and October 16. Assume that the stock price remains constant. Use the spreadsheet to find the time value in all of the cases.

12. Consider a riskless spread with a long position in the August 160 call and a short position in the October 160 call. Determine the appropriate hedge ratio. Then show how a $1 stock price increase would have a neutral effect on the spread value. Discuss any limitations of this procedure.

13. Construct a long straddle using the October 165 options. Hold until the options expire. Determine the profits and graph the results. Identify the breakeven stock prices at expiration and the minimum profit.

14. Repeat the previous problem, but close the positions on September 20. Use the spreadsheet to find the profits for the possible stock prices on September 20. Generate a graph and use it to identify the approximate breakeven stock prices.
15. A slight variation of a straddle is a strap, which uses two calls and one put. Construct a long strap using the October 165 options. Hold the position until expiration. Determine the profits and graph the results. Identify the breakeven stock prices at expiration and the minimum profit. Compare the results with the October 165 straddle.
16. A strip is a variation of a straddle involving two puts and one call. Construct a short strip using the August 170 options. Hold the position until the options expire. Determine the profits and graph the results. Identify the breakeven stock prices at expiration and the minimum profit.
17. Analyze the August 160/170 box spread. Determine whether a profit opportunity exists. If it does, explain how to exploit it.
18. Complete the following table with the correct formula related to various spread strategies.

Item	Bull Spread with Calls	Bear Spread with Puts	Butterfly Spread with Calls
Value at expiration			
Profit			
Maximum profit			
Maximum loss			
Breakeven			and

19. Complete the following table with the correct formula related to various spread strategies.

Item	Collar Strategies with Calls and Puts	Straddle with Calls and Puts
Value at expiration		
Profit		
Maximum profit		
Maximum loss		
Breakeven		and

20. Explain conceptually the choice of strike prices when it comes to designing a call-based bull spread. Specifically, address the costs and benefits of two bull spread strategies. One strategy has the call strike prices further from the current stock price than the second strategy.
21. Explain conceptually the choice of strike prices when it comes to designing a zero-cost collar. Specifically, address the costs and benefits of two strategies. One strategy has a higher put strike price than the second strategy.
22. Pear, Inc., is presently trading at $100 per share; at-the-money one-month calls are trading at $5.43, and puts are trading at $5.01; and at-the-money two-month calls are trading at $7.72, and puts are trading at $6.89. At present, these option prices reflect a Black-Scholes-Merton implied volatility of 45 percent for all options. You believe, however, that the volatility over the next month will be lower than 45 percent and the volatility in the second month will be higher than 45 percent because you think Pear, Inc., will publicly scheduled an earnings announcement in 45 days and there will be an information blackout period leading up to the announcement. A blackout period occurs when a company does not provide any information to the public for a stated period of time. The earnings announcement will cause higher volatility, and the blackout period will result in lower volatility. Design an option strategy using all four options that will profit if you are correct in your volatility belief, the company publicly schedules the announcement within the next few days, and option prices immediately adjust to these beliefs.
23. (Concept Problem) Another variation of the straddle is called a *strangle*. A strangle is the purchase of a call with a higher exercise price and a put with a lower exercise price. Evaluate the strangle strategy by examining the purchase of the August 165 put and 170 call. As in the problems above, determine the profits for stock prices of 150, 155, 160, 165, 170, 175, and 180. Hold the position until expiration and graph the results. Find the breakeven stock prices at expiration. Explain why one would want to use a strangle.
24. (Concept Problem) Many option traders use a combination of a money spread and a calendar spread called a *diagonal spread*. This transaction involves the purchase of a call with a lower exercise price and longer time to expiration and the sale of a call with a higher exercise price and shorter time to expiration. Evaluate the diagonal spread that

involves the purchase of the October 165 call and the sale of the August 170 call. Determine the profits for the same stock prices you previously examined under the assumption that the position is closed on August 1. Use the spreadsheet to find the profits for the possible stock prices on August 1. Generate a graph and use it to estimate the break-even stock price at the end of the holding period.

25. (Case) Professors Don Chance of Louisiana State University and Michael Hemler of the University of Notre Dame have authored an options trading case that corresponds to the material in Chapters 6 and 7. Go to the product website at www.cengagebrain. com and download the Second City Options case.

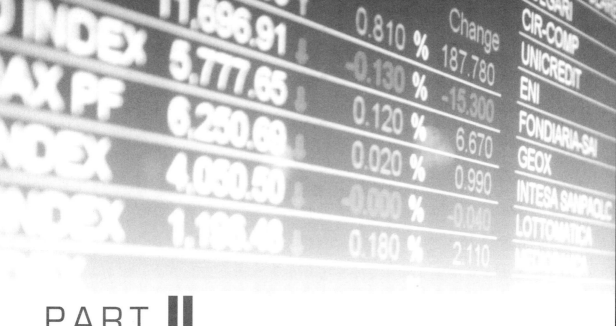

PART II

FORWARDS, FUTURES, AND SWAPS

CHAPTER 8

The Structure of Forward and Futures Markets

Futures traders tend to be superstitious—when on a good run they are reluctant to change their mojo, this includes washing their jackets. Traders will wear their lucky jackets until they fall apart or their luck runs out. Some traders have even been buried in their lucky jackets, reflecting a hope that the good luck their jackets provided in the trading pits on Earth could be retained for eternity in that Great Trading Pit in the sky.

Jim Overdahl
Futures Fall Special Issue 2005, p. 14

Part I explored the world of options markets. The next five chapters look at forward, futures, and swap markets. In this chapter, we focus on forward and futures markets. A **forward contract**, sometimes called a **forward commitment**, is an agreement between two parties (a buyer and a seller) that calls for the delivery of an asset at a future point in time with a price agreed upon today. A **futures contract** is a forward contract that has standardized terms, is traded on an organized exchange, and follows a daily settlement procedure in which the losses of one party to the contract are paid to the other party.

Forward and futures contracts have many of the characteristics of option contracts. Both provide for the sale and delivery of an asset on a later date at a price agreed upon today. An option—more specifically, a call option—gives the holder the right to forgo the future purchase of the asset. This is done, as we have seen, when the asset's price is below the exercise price. A forward or futures contract does not offer the right to forgo purchase of the asset. Like an exchange-listed option, however, a futures contract can be sold in the market prior to expiration. Like an over-the-counter option, a forward contract can be offset by creating a new forward contract.

Forward contracts are common in everyday life. For example, an apartment lease is a series of forward contracts. The current month's use of the apartment is a spot transaction, but the two parties also have agreed to usage of the apartment for future months at a rate agreed upon today. Near and dear to the hearts of most college students (and many others) is your basic pizza delivery order, which is also a forward contract. The customer and the restaurant agree that the customer will buy the pizza at a specific price at a future point in time ("30 minutes or less"). Upon delivery, the customer must accept and pay for the pizza, even though in the interim the customer might have seen an ad or a coupon for an identical pizza that costs less.

Any type of contractual arrangement calling for the delivery of a good or service at a future date at a price agreed upon today is a forward contract. Neither party can legally get out of the commitment. Nonetheless, either party can enter into a new, offsetting forward contract with someone else. For example, suppose after ordering the pizza, you decide that you would prefer Chinese food. You know, however, that your neighbor next door is practically addicted to pizza; so you offer to sell the pizza to your neighbor when it is delivered. You might even be able to negotiate a better price, depending on how hungry your neighbor is. In that case, you contracted to deliver the pizza to your neighbor and you agreed upon a price. You are long a forward contract with the restaurant and short a forward contract with your neighbor. In the case of the apartment lease, subleasing your apartment is a way of offsetting your forward contract with the landlord.

Of course, all of these transactions are subject to a degree of uncertainty about whether a party will perform as promised. For example, suppose the pizza delivery person shows up at your door and finds no one there because you changed your mind and went out for Chinese food. Alternatively, perhaps you accepted delivery of your pizza, but your neighbor refused to accept the pizza because he changed his mind. This potential for default is quite similar to that of the over-the-counter options market. There the buyer faced the potential default of the writer. In a forward contract, however, each party is subject to the default of the other. The pizza restaurant faces the potential that you will default. Do you face the potential that the restaurant will default by not delivering your pizza? The risk is slight but still there. Here the pizza delivery order is an example of a forward contract between an extremely creditworthy customer, the restaurant, and one with lower credit quality, yourself.

These examples are but small-scale, familiar cases of forward contracting. If we substitute agricultural products, precious metals, securities, or currencies for pizza, apartments, magazines, and airline tickets, we have the real world of big-time forward contracting. To mitigate the risk of default, many forward markets evolved into futures markets. Futures markets permit organized trading in standardized versions of these forward contracts. To reduce the risk of default, futures contracts require a daily settling of gains and losses. As we move through the chapter, we shall look at these characteristics in more detail. But first, let us see how these markets evolved.

DEVELOPMENT OF FORWARD AND FUTURES MARKETS

As noted above, forward contracts are common in everyday life. Quite naturally, such contracts go back to the beginnings of commerce. For example, at medieval trade fairs, merchants often contracted for deferred delivery of goods at a price agreed to in advance. Over the next few hundred years, organized spot markets for commodities began to develop in major European cities. Meanwhile, a similar market for rice developed in Japan. The characteristics of these markets were not too unlike those of today's futures markets. Modern futures markets, however, generally trace back to the formation of the Chicago Board of Trade in 1848.

Chicago Futures Markets

In the 1840s, Chicago was rapidly becoming the transportation and distribution center of the Midwest. Farmers shipped their grain from the farm belt to Chicago for sale and subsequent distribution eastward along rail lines and the Great Lakes. Due to the seasonal nature of grain production, however, large quantities of grain were shipped to Chicago in the late summer and fall. The city's storage facilities were inadequate for accommodating this temporary increase in supply. Prices fell drastically at harvest time as supplies increased and then rose steadily as supplies were consumed.

In 1848, a group of businessmen took the first step toward alleviating this problem by forming the Chicago Board of Trade (CBOT). The CBOT initially was organized for the purpose of standardizing the quantities and qualities of the grains. A few years later the first forward contract was developed. Called a *to-arrive* contract, it provided that a farmer could agree to deliver the grain at a future date at a price determined in advance. This meant that the farmer would not ship the grain to Chicago at harvest time but could fix the price and the date at which the grain subsequently would be sold.

These to-arrive contracts proved to be a curious instrument. Speculators soon found that rather than buy and sell the grain itself, they could buy and sell the contracts. In that way, they could speculate on the price of grain to be delivered at a future date and not have to worry about taking delivery of and storing the grain. Soon thereafter, the exchange established a set of rules and regulations for governing these transactions. In the 1920s, the clearinghouse was established to provide a means of offsetting or unwinding positions and guaranteeing to each party that the other would perform. By that time, most of the essential ingredients of futures contracts were in place.

In 1874, the Chicago Produce Exchange was formed and later became the Chicago Butter and Egg Board. In 1898, it was reorganized as the Chicago Mercantile Exchange and grew to be one of the largest futures exchanges in the world. In fact, in 2007, it acquired its major and older competitor, the Chicago Board of Trade, the two keeping their separate names but merging their operations into a single firm, the Chicago Mercantile Exchange Group. The 1990s saw an explosion in the development of futures exchanges around the world, and mergers were frequent, resulting in some other very large exchanges.

Development of Financial Futures

For the first 120 years, futures exchanges offered trading in contracts on commodities such as agricultural goods and metals. Then in 1971, the major Western economies began to allow their currency exchange rates to fluctuate. This opened the way for the formation in 1972 of the International Monetary Market (IMM), a subsidiary of the Chicago Mercantile Exchange that specializes in the trading of futures contracts on foreign currencies. These were the first futures contracts that could be called **financial futures**. The first interest rate futures contract appeared in 1975, when the Chicago Board of Trade originated its GNMA futures, a contract on Government National Mortgage Association pass-through certificates, whose yields reflect mortgage interest rates.

In 1976, the International Monetary Market introduced the first futures contract on a government security and a short-term financial instrument—90-day U.S. Treasury bills. This contract was actively traded for many years, but its popularity has declined somewhat, at least partly due to the remarkable success of a competing contract, the Eurodollar futures, which was launched in 1981.

In 1977, the Chicago Board of Trade started what became one of the most successful contracts of all time—U.S. Treasury bond futures. In just a few years, this instrument became the most actively traded contract, surpassing many grain futures that had traded for more than 100 years. In the 1990s, however, the Eurodollar contract surpassed the bond contract as the most actively traded futures contract in the United States.

The 1980s brought the highly successful stock index futures contract. This instrument, sometimes referred to as "pin-stripe pork bellies," has helped bridge the long-standing gap between New York's stock traders and Chicago's futures traders. Interestingly, however, the first stock index futures contract appeared not in New York or Chicago, but in Kansas City. The Kansas City Board of Trade completed the formal registration process ahead of its New York and Chicago counterparts, and on February 16, 1982, it launched the Value Line Index futures. The Index and Option Market, a division of the Chicago Mercantile Exchange, followed on April 21 with its S&P 500 futures contract. The New York Futures Exchange entered the game on May 6 with its New York Stock Exchange Index futures. Today, however, the Value Line and NYSE Index futures have little trading volume.

Interestingly, in the United States, the Dow Jones Industrial Average, the most well-known measure of stock market activity, has had a futures contract on it only since 2001. Shortly after the first stock index futures contracts appeared in 1982, the Chicago Board of Trade attempted to start a contract on the Average, but was rebuffed in a lengthy legal process started by the Dow Jones Company. Dow Jones stated that it did not want its name associated with speculative trading and believed that the CBOT and traders were profiting from its name. Standard and Poor's, on the other hand, has eagerly licensed its name to futures exchanges for contracts and has even developed new indices with an eye toward having futures contracts traded on them. Rebuffed by Dow Jones, the CBOT then created a similar contract, called the Major Market Index, which traded successfully for a number of years but eventually died. It was not until the late 1990s, however, that Dow Jones decided that it should enter the index futures business and licensed its famous Average to the Chicago Board of Trade for futures trading and the Chicago Board Options Exchange for options trading. Dow Jones also began licensing other averages and creating new market averages, including a number for foreign markets, with the intention of encouraging futures trading on them. Today futures contracts on Dow Jones averages based on stocks, commodities, and other underlyings are found on various derivatives exchanges.

Stock index futures contracts have been extremely successful worldwide. Almost every major country has its own derivatives exchange with a successful stock index contract. Countries in which stock index futures are extremely popular include the United Kingdom, France, Japan, Germany, Korea, Spain, and China (Hong Kong).

In Part I, we studied both options on individual stocks and stock index options. Individual stock futures, often called single stock futures, are a fairly new instrument. These instruments trade actively in a number of countries outside the United States but until 2001, U.S. futures markets could not offer single stock futures because of regulatory restrictions. In Chapter 2, we noted that the Securities and Exchange Commission (SEC), which regulates stocks, and the Commodity Futures Trading Commission (CFTC), which regulates futures, had reached an agreement in 1982 on how to divide their regulatory responsibilities. The CFTC regulates the stock index futures market, and the SEC regulates the securities and stock and stock index options markets. Single stock futures were prohibited because the regulatory authority was not clear. As futures contracts, single stock futures would ordinarily be regulated by the CFTC, but the SEC claimed that these instruments would be close substitutes for securities and single stock options. Finally, in 2001, a new law permitted these instruments and defined a joint regulatory structure. Single stock futures were then introduced in the United States in November 2002.

Over the years, there has been a tremendous degree of competition between the derivatives exchanges to introduce new contracts that would generate significant trading volume. Barely a month passes without at least one new futures contract being introduced. A few of these contracts, such as municipal bond futures, were moderately successful. Some, such as oil futures, were highly successful. Most of the contracts (e.g., inflation futures, commercial paper futures, and corporate bond index futures) failed to attract much trading volume. Even the original GNMA futures contract died and attempts to modify and revive it failed. You should note, however, that such failures are not a sign of weakness, but rather a sign of a healthy and highly competitive business in which only those contracts that truly meet a need will survive.

Development of Options on Futures Markets

The futures markets offer not only futures contracts, but also option contracts. In 1982, the first option contracts in which the underlying is a futures contract were created in the United States. This was a five-year experimental program that was deemed a tremendous success, and the instrument was permanently authorized in the United States in 1987. Options on futures have since been offered on many markets around the world, and most have been relatively successful.

Options on futures are also sometimes called **commodity options** and, more commonly, **futures options**. An option on futures permits the holder to buy for a call, or to sell for a put, a specific underlying futures contract at a fixed price up to a specific expiration day. The buyer of the option pays a premium and receives the call or put, which permits exercise into the underlying futures contract. Note that in this case, the option is a derivative on a derivative. That is, the underlying itself is a derivative. Thus, there are two expirations—the option's expiration and the futures' expiration. For some contracts, the option and futures expire simultaneously, effectively making the option on the futures equivalent to an option on the underlying spot asset. For example, the E-mini S&P 500 index futures options as well as the E-mini S&P 500 index futures contract both expire at 8:30 A.M. on the third Friday of the contract month.[1] For all other contracts, the option expires before but relatively close to the expiration of the futures.

As noted, options on futures contracts have been very successful. This success was primarily a result of the success of options on futures in the United States, where regulations had prohibited the trading of options in the same markets in which the underlying asset would be traded. That is, options on stocks trade in one market, but the underlying stocks trade elsewhere. When options on futures were introduced, the option would trade on the same exchange on which the underlying futures traded. The parallel trading of the option and the underlying created a strong demand for arbitrage trading between these two instruments and led to highly active and efficient markets.

Parallel Development of Over-the-Counter Markets

The most active early forward market was the market for foreign exchange, called the **interbank market**. This market grew tremendously in response to the floating of currencies in the early 1970s, as mentioned above. It consists of hundreds of banks worldwide that make forward and spot commitments with each other, representing themselves or their clients. The market is quite large, although the exact size is difficult to estimate because the transactions are essentially private and unregulated. The transaction sizes are quite large as well, and it would be unusual for individual investors to be able to participate in this market.

Forward markets for various financial instruments and commodities have also developed in recent years. The decade of the 1980s saw a tremendous jump in the level of understanding and appreciation for derivative instruments. While futures and options markets were growing, forward markets began to grow as well. The primary stimulant for forward market growth was the development of swaps. A swap is an agreement between two parties to exchange a series of payments. There are quite a few variations on this basic theme, but in general, swaps are similar to forward contracts. We shall cover swaps in detail in Chapter 12. For now, however, let us note that the growing

---

[1]E-mini denotes electronic trading on GLOBEX and mini denote a small contract size, attractive to retail traders.

acceptance of swaps stimulated the development of other over-the-counter transactions, such as options noted in Chapter 2, and a variety of other forward contracts. For example, one can enter into a forward contract, called a forward rate agreement, or FRA, that is simply an arrangement for one party to pay a certain fixed amount of cash while the other party pays an amount of cash determined by the interest rate at a predetermined future date. This contract can be used to hedge or speculate on interest rates. It does not actually require delivery of a security or commodity as it is settled by simply exchanging cash.

It is also possible to arrange for forward delivery of almost any security or commodity at a price agreed upon today. The forward market is a large and healthy market that competes with and yet complements the futures market.

OVER-THE-COUNTER FORWARD MARKET

In Chapter 2, we discussed how over-the-counter options differ from exchange-traded options. Now we shall do the same for forward and futures contracts. The forward market is large and worldwide. Its main participants are banks, corporations, and governments. The two parties to a forward contract must agree to do business with each other, which means that each party accepts credit risk from the other. That is, unlike in options markets where the writer does not assume any credit risk from the buyer, in forward markets, each party accepts the credit risk of the other. In spite of the credit risk, however, forward contracts offer many advantages.

The primary advantage is that the terms and conditions are tailored to the specific needs of the two parties. Suppose that a firm would like to secure the future purchase price of 400,000 bushels of sorghum, a grain similar in use to corn. As we shall see later, the futures markets permit trading only in contracts on specific commodities and with certain expiration dates. There is no sorghum futures contract that would permit the company to lock in the future purchase price of the sorghum. If the firm could substitute corn, however, there is a corn futures contract available, although its expiration might not match the horizon date of the firm. Moreover, it might permit the seller of the futures to deliver any of several grades of corn at any of several locations. The firm would perhaps prefer to arrange a specific contract with the terms tailored to meet its needs. Similar arguments can be made with respect to financial contracts. A portfolio manager might wish to lock in the market value of a specific portfolio on a certain date. If the futures market does not have such a contract, the manager might look to the forward market.

As noted about the over-the-counter options market, the forward market also has the advantage of being a private market in which the general public does not know that the transaction was done. This prevents other traders from interpreting the size of various trades as perhaps false signals of information.

The over-the-counter market is also an unregulated market. Although there is now much debate about whether this market should be regulated, and we shall bring this topic up again later in this chapter, most governments view these contracts as private arrangements. This gives participants considerably more flexibility, saves money, and allows the market to quickly respond to changing needs and circumstances by developing new variations of old contracts.

Of course, all of this comes at the expense of assuming credit risk and the requirement that the transactions be of a rather large size—several million dollars or more. It is not clear which is more costly, forwards or futures, but since the markets coexist, they must be serving their clientele in an efficient manner.

FIGURE 8.1 Notional Amount of Over-the-Counter Forward Contracts

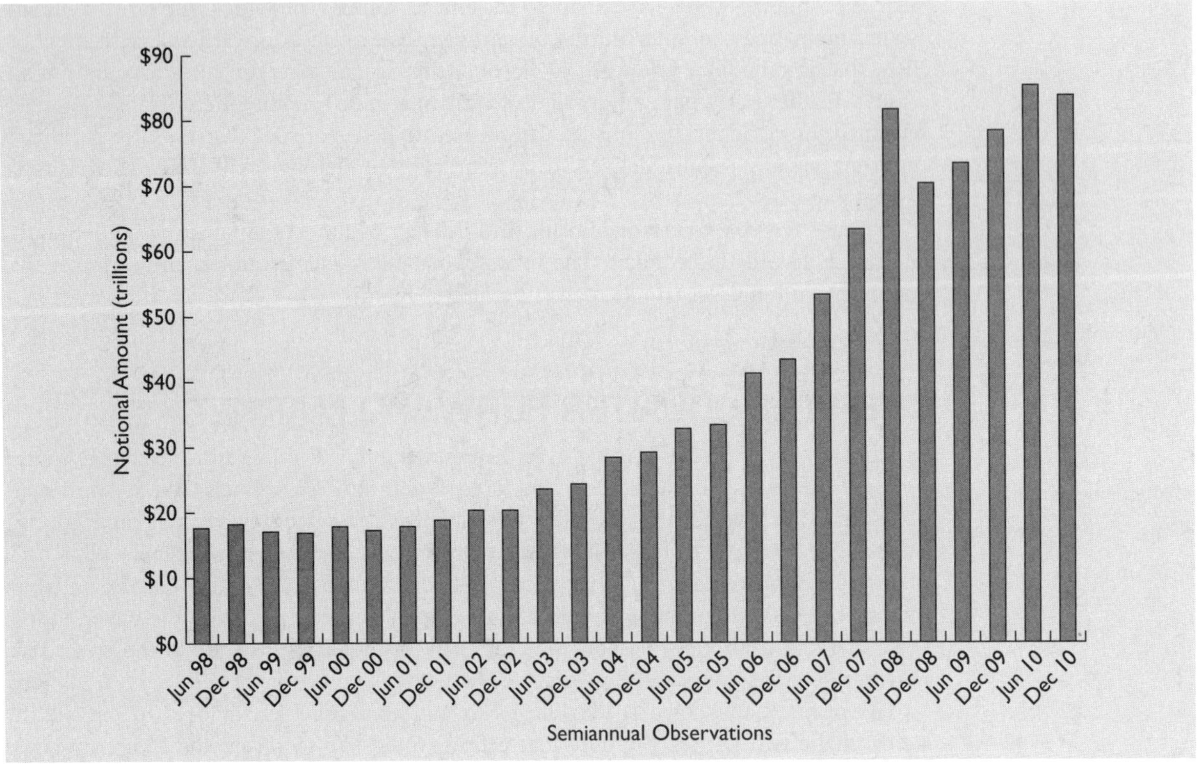

The OTC forward market is quite large, but because of the private nature of the transactions, gauging its size is difficult. The Bank for International Settlements (BIS) conducts semiannual surveys that attempt to provide some data. These surveys, however, take a long time to complete and are published with a considerable lag. The BIS's latest survey estimated that in December 2010, the outstanding notional principal, which is the amount of the underlying instrument, of all forward contracts was $84 trillion, with a market value of about $1,259 billion.[2] Figure 8.1 illustrates the notional amounts of OTC forward contracts from June 1998 through December 2010. Historically, the forward notional amounts have increased monotonically for many years. Again, as with the data from the overall derivatives markets shown in Chapter 1 and options in Chapter 2, it is clear that the financial crisis that emerged in 2008 had a significant impact on the size of the options market. For forwards, however, the notional amount quickly resumed its upward climb.

Interestingly, as shown in Figure 8.2, as severe stress hit this market, the market value jumped to over $2.3 trillion in December 2008. Again, in the fast-moving markets of 2008, the notional amount fell but the remaining market value rose. Once the crisis moved into 2009, however, firms appeared to again add to their positions, increasing the notional amounts, but the market values remained relatively flat.

---

[2]Our measure of the forward markets includes the following categories from the BIS survey data: forwards and forex swaps (not currency swaps), forward rate agreements (FRAs), equity forwards and swaps, and commodity forwards and swaps. Forex and FRAs comprise the vast majority of forward contracts (94 percent in 2010).

FIGURE 8.2 Market Value of Over-the-Counter Forward Contracts

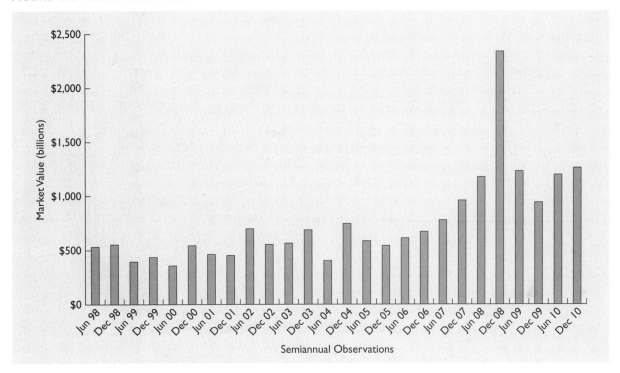

ORGANIZED FUTURES TRADING

Futures trading is organized around the concept of a futures exchange. The exchange is probably the most important component of a futures market and distinguishes it from forward markets.

A **futures exchange** is a corporate entity comprised of members. Although some exchanges allow corporate memberships, most members are individuals. The members elect a board of directors, which, in turn, selects individuals to manage the exchange. The exchange has a corporate hierarchy consisting of officers, employees, and committees. The exchange establishes rules for its members and may impose sanctions on violators.

Historically, most futures exchanges were nonprofit corporations owned by their member traders; today many exchanges are profit-making corporations with publicly traded stock. For example, the common stock of the CME Group, which includes the Chicago Mercantile Exchange and Chicago Board of Trade, trades on the New York Stock Exchange under the ticker symbol CME. It is interesting to also note that the Chicago Board Options Exchange, which we covered extensively in Chapter 2, has launched a futures exchange within itself. This exchange, called CBOE Futures, trades futures contracts on volatility. As we saw in previous chapters, volatility is a critical factor in options. These CBOE futures products permit futures trading on measures of volatility, allowing option traders to hedge the risk of changing volatility. Figure 8.3 illustrates the daily volume of volatility index futures contracts. Clearly, it took awhile for this contract to attract trading volume. As the financial crisis unfolded, many market participants apparently decided to either hedge or speculate on volatility, resulting in a sharp rise in trading volume.

FIGURE 8.3 Daily Volume of Volatility Index Futures Trading on CBOE Futures Exchange

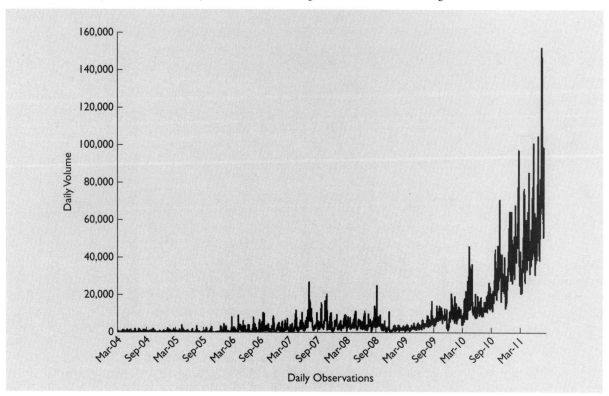

Contract Development

One of the exchange's important ongoing activities is identifying new and useful futures contracts. Most exchanges maintain research staffs that continuously examine the feasibility of new contracts. In the United States, when the exchange determines that a contract is likely to be successful, it writes a proposal specifying the terms and conditions and applies to the Commodity Futures Trading Commission (CFTC), the regulatory authority, to initiate trading.[3] Similar procedures are followed in other countries.

It is becoming increasingly difficult to determine the characteristics of an asset that make it a likely candidate for a successful futures contract. At one time, it was thought that the asset had to be storable, but there are now futures contracts on nonstorable assets such as electricity and even such factors as the weather, which is not a specific asset at all. What does seem to be a common thread is the existence of an identifiable, volatile spot price and a group of potential users who face a risk of loss if prices move in a certain direction. It is not necessary that the spot price be the price of an asset that one can actually buy and hold.

Thus, it is conceivable that virtually anything can have a futures contract traded on it. Whether the contract will be actively traded depends on whether it fills the needs of hedgers and whether speculators are interested enough to take risks in it. The business of creating, launching, and making futures contracts succeed is a highly competitive

---

[3]Since 2000, the CFTC has permitted exchanges to self-certify contract proposals. Thus, an exchange need only attest that a new contract complies with all applicable laws. In that sense, the exchange does not apply for and receive permission to trade a contract, but the CFTC must, nonetheless, be fully apprised of all new contracts and their terms.

business, and success is a difficult achievement. The derivatives exchanges are in the business of facilitating trading, and they collect fees for each transaction. Thus, there is an incentive to launch successful futures contracts. A study of the successes and failures of futures contracts launched in the United States finds that almost 60 percent of all contracts launched ultimately fail. The most successful exchange has been the New York Commodity Exchange, where about 66 percent of its contracts have succeeded. The New York Mercantile Exchange is second with about 61 percent. The Chicago Mercantile Exchange has succeeded on about 42 percent of its contracts, and the Chicago Board of Trade has been successful on about 28 percent of its contracts.

Contract Terms and Conditions

The contract's terms and conditions are determined by the exchange subject to regulatory approval. The specifications for each contract are the size, quotation unit, minimum price fluctuation, grade, and trading hours. In addition, the contract specifies delivery terms and daily price limits as well as delivery procedures, which are discussed in separate sections. Complete contract specifications can be found on the websites of the exchanges.

Contract size means that one contract covers a specific number of units of the underlying asset. This might be a designated number of bushels of a grain or dollars of face value of a financial instrument. Contract size is an important decision. If too small, speculators will find it more costly to trade because there is a cost for trading each contract. The contracts are not divisible; thus, if they are too large, hedgers may be unable to get a matching number of contracts. For example, if the Chicago Board of Trade had established $1 million as the Treasury bond contract, a hedger with $500,000 of bonds to hedge probably would be unable to use it.[4]

The quotation unit is simply the unit in which the price is specified. For example, corn is quoted in fourths of a cent and Treasury bonds are quoted in percentage points and thirty-seconds of a point of par value. In most cases, the spot market quotation unit is used.

Closely related to the quotation unit is the minimum price fluctuation. This is usually the smallest unit of quotation. For example, Treasury bonds are quoted in a minimum unit of thirty-seconds. Thus, the minimum price change on a Treasury bond futures contract is 1/32 of 1 percent of the contract price, or 0.0003125. Because the contract has a face value (contract size) of $100,000, the minimum price change is $0.0003125 \times (\$100,000) = \$31.25$.

The exchange also establishes the contract grade. In the case of agricultural commodities, there may be numerous grades, each of which would command a quality price differential in the spot market. The contract must specify the grades that are acceptable for delivery. Financial futures contracts must indicate exactly which financial instrument or instruments are eligible for delivery. If multiple instruments are deliverable, the seller of the contract holds a potentially valuable option, which we shall discuss in Chapter 10.

The exchange also specifies the hours during which the contract trades. Most agricultural futures trade for four to five hours during the day. Most financial futures trade for about six hours. In most U.S. markets, this trading occurs on the floor of the exchange, as described in a later section, but many exchanges have been migrating to electronic trading systems, whereby trading occurs at terminals that can be placed in offices and even in homes. Electronic trading initially occurred during hours the exchange was not open for floor trading, which in some cases meant throughout the night. This practice is part of the exchange's attempt to keep pit trading alive in this age in which so much

---

[4]We say "probably" because if the bonds being hedged were twice as volatile as the futures contract, one contract would be the correct number. Chapter 11 explains this point.

economic activity is conducted electronically. There are some contracts, however, that are designated solely for electronic trading and others that trade simultaneously with floor trading. Some exchanges, such as the highly successful EUREX (originally formed as a combined German-Swiss futures exchange) and NYSE-Euronext (a family of exchanges located in multiple countries), have exclusively electronic trading, and trading hours are usually longer than a standard business day.

Delivery Terms

The contract must also indicate a specific delivery date or dates, the delivery procedure, and a set of expiration months. In the case of harvestable commodities, the exchange usually establishes expiration months to correspond with harvest months. In nonharvestable commodities such as financial futures, the exchange usually follows the pattern of allowing expirations in March, June, September, and December. There are some exceptions, however.

The exchange also decides how far into the future the expiration dates will be set. For some contracts, the expirations extend only a year or two, while the Eurodollar contract extends about ten years.

Once the expiration month has been set, the exchange determines a final trading day. This may be any day in the month, but the most common ones are the third Friday of the month and the business day prior to the last business day of the month. The first delivery day also must be set. Most contracts allow delivery on any day of the month following a particular day. Usually, the first eligible delivery day is the first business day of the month, but for certain contracts, other days may be specified. In the case of stock index futures and other cash-settled contracts, the settlement occurs on the last trading day or on the day after the last trading day.

For non-cash-settled contracts, the delivery procedure must be specified. The deliverable spot commodity must be sent to any of several eligible locations. Financial adjustments to the price received upon delivery are required when an acceptable but lower-grade commodity is delivered. We shall say more about the delivery procedure later.

Daily Price Limits and Trading Halts

During the course of a trading day, prices fluctuate continuously, but many contracts have limits on the maximum daily price change. If a contract price hits the upper limit, the market is said to be **limit up**. If the price moves to the lower limit, the market is said to be **limit down**. Any such move, up or down, is called a **limit move**. Normally, no transactions above or below the limit price are allowed. Some contracts have limits only during the opening minutes; others have limits that can be expanded according to prescribed rules if prices remain at the limits for extended periods.

In conjunction with price limits, some futures contracts—notably stock index futures—contain built-in trading halts sometimes called **circuit breakers**. When prices move rapidly, trading can be stopped for predetermined periods. These halts can be accompanied by similar halts in the spot market. Such cessations of trading were installed after the stock market crash of 1987 in response to concern that extremely volatile markets might need a cooling-off period. Although it is not clear that trading halts are necessarily effective, it seems likely that they will continue to be used in futures markets.

Other Exchange Responsibilities

The exchange also specifies that members meet minimum financial responsibility requirements. In some contracts, it may establish position limits, which, like those in options markets, restrict the number of contracts that an individual trader can hold. The exchange establishes rules governing activities on the trading floor and maintains a department responsible for monitoring trading to determine whether anyone is attempting to manipulate the market. In some extreme cases, the exchange may elect to suspend trading if unusual events occur.[5]

Derivatives Exchanges

Futures trading takes place on numerous derivatives exchanges around the world. One advantage of such global futures trading, particularly when it is fully automated, is the potential it offers for linkages between exchanges. For example, the Chicago Mercantile Exchange and the Singapore International Monetary Exchange (SIMEX) are linked so that a trader opening a position in Eurodollars on one exchange can close the position on the other. Linkages among derivatives exchanges around the world are becoming increasingly common.

As previously noted, a trend in futures trading worldwide is the use of electronic trading systems. For a fee, computer terminals are placed in trading rooms of institutions and individuals. These terminals permit traders to submit bids and offers and to consummate trades by simply moving the computer's mouse over the bid or offer the trader wants to accept and then clicking. Alternative systems match up bids and offers automatically. The Chicago Mercantile Exchange (CME) began the process with a system called GLOBEX, which eventually included access to trading not only in the CME's contracts, but also in contracts of certain other exchanges. Several U.S. and foreign exchanges have developed their own electronic trading systems, and some are merging their systems or working on joint ventures to combine their systems.

According to data provided by *Futures Industry* magazine (March/April 2011 issue), approximately 3.7 billion futures and options contracts were traded at the Korea Exchange in 2010, the busiest derivatives exchange in the world. The CME Group traded 3.1 billion futures and options contracts, and EUREX traded about 2.6 billion contracts. *Futures Industry* estimates that worldwide futures volume in 2010 was almost 11.2 billion contracts, with about 43 percent from the Asia-Pacific region and 13 percent from North America.

FUTURES TRADERS

The members of the derivatives exchange are individuals who physically go on the exchange floor or, on electronic systems, sit at designated terminals and trade futures contracts. There are several ways to characterize these futures traders.

General Classes of Futures Traders

All traders on the futures exchange are either commission brokers or locals.

Commission brokers simply execute transactions for other people. A commission broker can be an independent businessperson who executes trades for individuals or institutions or a representative of a major brokerage firm. In the futures industry, these brokerage firms are called **futures commission merchants (FCMs)**. The commission broker simply executes trades for the FCM's customers. Commission brokers make their money by charging a commission for each trade.

Locals are individuals in business for themselves who trade from their own accounts. They attempt to profit by buying contracts at a given price and selling them at a higher

---

[5]The 1980 grain embargo against the Soviet Union and the 1987 stock market crash were two such cases.

price. Their trading provides liquidity for the public. Locals assume the risk and reap the rewards from their skill at futures trading. It has been said that locals represent the purest form of capitalism and entrepreneurship.

Because a futures trader can be a local or an FCM, a conflict occasionally arises between traders' loyalty to themselves and their customers' interests. For example, some traders engage in **dual trading**, in which they trade for themselves and also trade as brokers for others. Dual trading has become very controversial in recent years. To illustrate the conflict that might arise, suppose that a trader holds a set of orders that includes a large order for a customer. Knowing that the price may move substantially when the customer's order is placed, the trader executes a purchase for his or her own account prior to placing the customer's order. There are a number of other ways in which dual trading can be profitable to the trader at the expense of the customer. For this to occur, however, the trader must act unscrupulously. The exchanges argue that abuses of dual trading are rare. Moreover, they claim that dual trading provides liquidity to the market. Some limitations on dual trading have been enacted.

Classification by Trading Strategy

Futures traders can be further classified by the strategies they employ.

Recall that in Chapter 1, we briefly discussed hedging. A **hedger** holds a position in the spot market. This might involve owning a commodity, or it may simply mean that the individual plans or is committed to the future purchase or sale of the commodity. Taking a futures contract that is opposite to the position in the spot market reduces the risk. For example, if you hold a portfolio of stocks, you can hedge that portfolio's value by selling a stock index futures contract. If the stocks' prices fall, the portfolio will lose value, but the price of the futures contract is also likely to fall. Because you are short the futures contract, you can repurchase it at a lower price, thus making a profit. The gain from the futures position will at least partially offset the loss on the portfolio.

Hedging is an important activity in any futures or derivatives market. This section has given only a cursory overview of it. Chapter 11 devotes a lot of attention to hedging.

Speculators attempt to profit from guessing the direction of the market. Speculators include locals as well as the thousands of individuals and institutions off the exchange floor. They play an important role in the market by providing the liquidity that makes hedging possible and assuming the risk that hedgers are trying to eliminate. Speculating is discussed in more detail in Chapter 11.

Spreaders use futures spreads to speculate at a low level of risk. Like an option spread, a futures spread involves a long position in one contract and a short position in another contract. Spreads may be intracommodity or intercommodity. An intracommodity spread is like a time spread in options. The spreader buys a contract with one expiration month and sells an otherwise identical contract with a different expiration month. An intercommodity spread, which normally is not used in options, consists of a long position in a futures contract on one commodity and a short position in a contract on another commodity. In some cases, the two commodities even trade on different exchanges. The rationale for this type of spread rests on a perceived "normal" difference between the prices of the two futures contracts. When the prices move out of line, traders employ intercommodity spreads to take advantage of the expected price realignment.

Futures spreads work much like option time spreads in that the long position in one contract is somewhat offset by the short position in the other contract. There actually is no real difference between this type of spread and a hedge. For example, suppose the contract is on U.S. Treasury bonds; the current month is October; and the available futures expirations are December, March, and June. A hedger holds Treasury bonds and sells a December contract. A spreader holds a December contract and sells a March contract. Each holds a long position in a spot or nearby futures contract and a short position in a deferred futures contract. Each is attempting to profit from one position while expecting a loss on the other. Neither knows which position will make a profit and which will create a loss.

Arbitrageurs attempt to profit from differences in the prices of otherwise identical spot and futures positions. An analogous type of arbitrage that we already covered is the execution of conversions and reversals to take advantage of option prices that fail to conform to put-call parity. In futures markets, there are some important theoretical relationships, which we shall study in Chapters 9 and 10. When prices get out of line with these theoretical predictions, arbitrageurs enter the market and execute trades that bring prices back in line. Because arbitrage is designed to be riskless, it resembles hedging and spreading. One way to identify an arbitrage transaction is that it can be structured so that it does not require any investment and it does not contain any risk. An easy way to remember this is to say that an arbitrageur operates by two rules: (1) Do not take any risk, and (2) do not spend any money. In many cases, however, it is difficult to determine whether a given strategy is arbitrage, hedging, or spreading.

Classification by Trading Style

Futures traders can also be classified by the style of trading they practice. There are three distinct trading styles: scalping, day trading, and position trading.

Scalpers attempt to profit from small changes in the contract price. Scalpers seldom hold their positions for more than a few minutes. They trade by using their skill at sensing the market's short-term direction and by buying from the public at the bid price and selling to the public at the ask price. They are constantly alert for large inflows of orders and short-term trends. Because they operate with very low transaction costs, they can profit from small moves in contract prices. The practice of making a large number of quick, small profits is referred to as scalping.

Day traders hold their positions for no longer than the duration of the trading day. Like scalpers, they attempt to profit from short-term market movements; however, they hold their positions much longer than do scalpers. Nonetheless, they are unwilling to assume the risk of adverse news that might occur overnight or on weekends.[6]

Position traders hold their transactions open for much longer periods than do scalpers and day traders. Position traders believe they can make profits by waiting for a major market movement. This may take as much as several weeks or may not come at all.

Scalpers, day traders, and position traders are not mutually exclusive. A speculator may employ any or all of these techniques in transactions.

In addition to those who trade on the derivatives exchange, there are many individuals who trade off the derivatives exchange and employ some of the same techniques.

Off-Floor Futures Traders

Participants in the futures markets also include thousands of individuals and institutions. Institutions include banks and financial intermediaries, investment banking firms, mutual funds, pension funds, hedge funds, and other corporations. In addition, some

---

[6]Day trading in this context should be distinguished from the trading of securities and derivatives on the Internet.

farmers and numerous individuals actively trade futures contracts, particularly today, with increasing access and low cost through the Internet.

In addition to those who directly participate in trading, U.S. federal law recognizes and regulates certain other participants. An **introducing broker (IB)** is an individual who solicits orders from public customers to trade futures contracts. IBs do not execute orders themselves, nor do their firms; rather, they subcontract with FCMs to do this. The IB and the FCM divide the commission.

A **commodity trading advisor (CTA)** is an individual or a firm that analyzes futures markets and issues reports, gives advice, and makes recommendations on the purchase and sale of contracts. CTAs earn fees for their services but do not necessarily trade contracts themselves.

A **commodity pool operator (CPO)** is an individual or a firm that solicits funds from the public, pools them, and uses them to trade futures contracts. The CPO profits by collecting a percentage of the assets in the fund and sometimes by earning sales commissions. A CPO essentially is the operator of a futures fund, a topic discussed later in this chapter. Some commodity pools are privately operated, however, and are not open for public participation.

An **associated person (AP)** is an individual associated with any of the above individuals or institutions or any other firm engaged in the futures business. APs include directors, partners, officers, and employees, but not clerical personnel.

Forward Market Traders

The forward market is dominated by large institutions such as banks and corporations. A typical forward market trader is an individual sitting at a desk with a telephone and a computer terminal. Using the computer or telephone, the trader finds the current prices available in the market. The trader can then agree on a price with another trader at another firm. The trader may represent his or her own firm or may execute a trade for a client such as a corporation or hedge fund. The trade may be a hedge, a spread, or an arbitrage. In fact, it is the thousands of traders off the floor whose arbitrage activities play a crucial role in making the market so efficient.

It would be remiss to suggest that the forward and futures markets are not linked. In a formal sense, forward contracts cannot be reversed by futures contracts. It is common, however, for a trader to do a forward contract and then immediately do a futures contract to hedge the forward market risk. In fact, the trader might even combine these positions with an option or a swap. Why a trader might do this is a subject we shall get into later when we look at hedging, relationships between the prices in these markets, and risk management.

MECHANICS OF FUTURES TRADING

Before placing an order to trade futures contracts, an individual must open an account with a broker. Because the risk of futures trading can be quite high, the individual must make a minimum deposit—usually at least $5,000—and sign a disclosure statement acknowledging the possible risks.

Placing an Order

One can place several types of orders. These are essentially the same as the option orders covered in Chapter 2. Stop orders and limit orders are used as are good-till-canceled and day orders.

Under a pit trading system, when an investor places an order, the broker phones the firm's trading desk on the exchange floor and relays the order to the firm's floor broker. The floor broker goes to the pit in which the contract trades. The pit is an octagonal- or polygonal-shaped ring with steps descending to the center. Hand signals and a considerable amount of verbal activity are used to place bids and make offers. This process is called **open outcry**. When the order is filled, the information is relayed back, ultimately to the broker's office, whereupon the broker telephones, faxes, or emails the customer to confirm the trade.

The process of placing and executing an order through the open-outcry system is a 140-year-old tradition that is slowly becoming outdated. As noted earlier, most derivatives exchanges outside the U.S. are fully automated so that bids and offers are submitted through a computer and trades are executed off the floor. Some systems even match buyer and seller. Automated systems are gradually gaining favor in the United States, but pit trading is unlikely to die for many more years.

Role of the Clearinghouse

At this point in the process, the clearinghouse intervenes. Most derivatives exchanges operate their own independent clearinghouses. The clearinghouse in futures markets works like that in options markets, so its basic operations should be familiar to you from Chapter 2.

The concept of a clearinghouse as an intermediary and a guarantor to every trade is not nearly as old as the futures markets themselves. The first such clearinghouse was organized in 1925 at the Chicago Board of Trade. Historically, the clearinghouse was an independent corporation serving only one derivatives exchange, and its stockholders are typically that exchange's member clearing firms. With the mergers of several derivatives exchanges, clearing services are now being offered by derivatives exchanges. For example, in 2011, the CME Group operated a clearinghouse known as CME Clearing. Also, in 2011, LCH.Clearnet was an independent international clearinghouse serving multiple derivatives exchanges as well as providing support for some OTC derivatives products. Each firm maintains a margin account with the clearinghouse and must meet minimum standards of financial responsibility.

For each transaction, obviously, there is both a buyer, usually called the **long**, and a seller, typically called the **short**. In the absence of a clearinghouse, each party would be responsible to the other. If one party defaulted, the other would be left with a worthless claim. The clearinghouse assumes the role of intermediary to each transaction. It guarantees the buyer that the seller will perform and guarantees the seller that the buyer will perform. The clearinghouse's financial accounts contain separate records of contracts owned, the respective clearing firms and contracts sold, and the respective clearing firms. Note that the clearinghouse keeps track only of its member firms. The clearing firms, in turn, monitor the long and short positions of individual traders and firms. All parties to futures transactions must have an account with a clearing firm or with a firm that has an account with a clearing firm.

Figure 8.4 illustrates the flow of money and information as a futures transaction is consummated and cleared. Let us illustrate how the clearinghouse operates by assuming that you sell a U.S. Treasury bond futures contract at a price of 97 27/32, which is $97,843.75. You have contacted your broker, who is an FCM or who contracts with an FCM, whose commission broker finds a buyer in the U.S. Treasury bond futures pit of the Chicago Board of Trade. The buyer might be a local, or a commission broker, representing a customer off the floor.

FIGURE 8.4 A Futures Transaction on the Derivatives Exchange

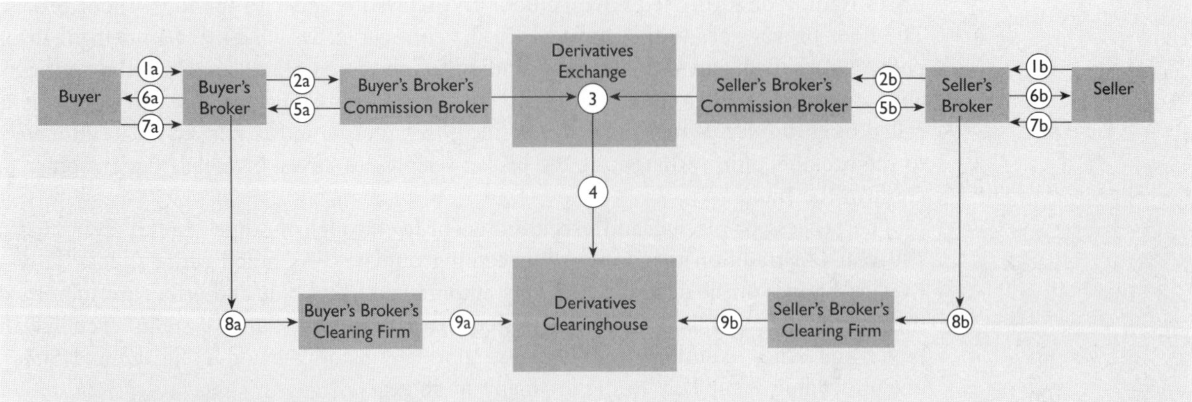

(1a)(1b) Buyer and seller instruct their respective brokers to conduct a futures transaction.
(2a)(2b) Buyer's and seller's brokers request that their firms' commission brokers execute the transaction.
(3) Both commission brokers meet in the bit on the floor of the derivatives exchange and agree on a price.
(4) Information on the trade is reported to the clearinghouse.
(5a)(5b) Both commission brokers report the price obtained to the buyer's and seller's brokers.
(6a)(6b) Buyer's and seller's brokers report the price obtained to the buyer and seller.
(7a)(7b) Buyer and seller deposit margin with their brokers.
(8a)(8b) Buyer's and seller's brokers deposit margin with their clearing firms.
(9a)(9b) Buyer's and seller's brokers' clearing firms deposit margin with clearinghouse.

Note: Buyer or seller (or both) could be a floor trader, eliminating the broker and the commission broker.

Your brokerage firm clears its trades through ABC Futures, a member firm of The Clearing Corporation, a company that clears trades for the Chicago Board of Trade (TCC). The buyer's FCM clears through ACME Trading Company, a clearing firm that is also a member of TCC. The required margin changes often on these contracts; we shall assume it is $2,500. You deposit this amount with ABC. ABC pools the transactions of all of its customers and deposits an amount required in its account with TCC. The buyer deposits the same amount with ACME, which also deposits a sum of money, based on its customers' open positions, with TCC.

TCC guarantees the performance of you and the buyer. Thus, neither of you has to worry about whether the other will be able to make up the losses. TCC will look to the clearing firms, ABC and ACME, for payment, and they in turn will look to you and the buyer.

Of course, the forward market is an over-the-counter market. The parties to the contract deal directly with each other. There is currently no clearinghouse to guarantee to each party that the other will perform, although there are plans under way to begin a type of clearinghouse for certain over-the-counter transactions.

Daily Settlement

One way in which the clearinghouse helps ensure its survival is by using margins and the daily settlement of accounts. For each contract, there is both an **initial margin**, the amount that must be deposited on the day the transaction is opened, and a **maintenance margin**, the amount that must be maintained every day thereafter. There are also initial and maintenance margins for spread and hedge transactions, which usually are lower than those for purely speculative positions.

The margin deposit is not quite like the margin on a stock trade. In stock trading, the investor deposits margin money and borrows the remainder of the stock price from the

MAKING THE CONNECTION

How Clearinghouses Reduce Credit Risk

Suppose there are four participants in a futures market: investors A, B, C, and D. Investor A owes B $100, B owes C $50, C owes D $40, and D owes A $30, as illustrated in the following diagram.

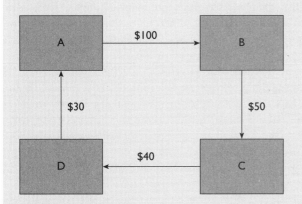

Suppose A defaults to B. B, however, desperately needs the $100 due from A and is, therefore, forced to default to C. C, likewise, needs the $50 from B and has to default to D, which in turn has to default to A. This chain of defaults on a much larger scale in the market as a whole is sometimes referred to as systemic risk.

Clearinghouses can greatly reduce this risk. Let us inject a clearinghouse into this picture. The clearinghouse, which we will call CLH, is set up such that all cash flows owed are payable to the clearinghouse and all cash flows due will come from the clearinghouse, as in the following manner.

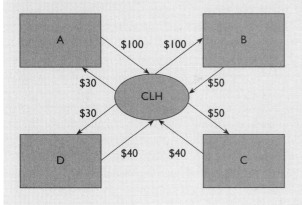

The clearinghouse consolidates all of these positions, resulting in the following net amounts owed and due from.

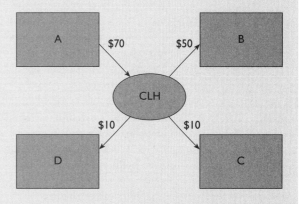

The position of the clearinghouse is balanced. It is due $70 from A and owes $50 to B, $10 to C, and $10 to D. Note that B, C, and D cannot default because they do not owe money to another of these parties.

Of course, no clearinghouse can provide complete insurance against default. If A defaults to the clearinghouse, it might be unable to pay B, C, and D. In that case, B, C, and D can default to another party outside the clearinghouse. But a clearinghouse is a multilateral organization that can significantly reduce credit risk *within the transactions conducted through the clearinghouse*. In the example here, without the clearinghouse, four parties could default to each other. With the clearinghouse, only one can default. There is obviously much less credit risk with the clearinghouse.

broker. In futures trading, not only is the margin requirement much smaller, but the remainder of the funds are not borrowed. The margin deposit is more like a good-faith security deposit. In fact, some prefer to call them **performance bonds** rather than margins so that the distinction is clear. In any case, some large and actively trading investors are able to deposit Treasury bills for margins. Others are required to deposit cash.

At the end of each day, a committee composed of clearinghouse officials establishes a **settlement price**. This usually is an average of the prices of the last few trades of the day. Using the settlement price, each account is **marked to market**. The difference in the current settlement price and the previous day's settlement price is determined. If the difference is positive because the settlement price increased, the dollar amount is credited to the margin accounts of those holding long positions. Where does the money come from? It is charged to the accounts of those holding short positions. If the difference is negative because the settlement price decreased, the dollar amount is credited to the holders of short positions and charged to those holding long positions.

This process, sometimes called the **daily settlement**, is an important feature of futures markets and a major difference between futures and forward markets. In forward markets, the gains and losses are normally incurred at the end of the contract's life, when delivery is made. Futures markets credit and charge the price changes on a daily basis. This helps ensure the markets' integrity because large losses are covered a little at a time rather than all at expiration, by which time the holder of the losing position may be unable to cover the loss.

To illustrate the daily settlement procedure, let us consider the transaction we previously described. We assume that it was initiated on Friday, August 1, of a given year. You sold one Treasury bond futures contract on the Chicago Board of Trade at that day's opening price of 116 27/32. One such contract is for a face value of $100,000, so the price is 1.1684375($100,000) = $116,843.75. We shall assume that the initial margin requirement was $5,940 and that the maintenance margin requirement was $4,400. You maintain the position until repurchasing the contract on August 18 at the opening price of 120 16/32, or $120,500. Table 8.1 illustrates the transactions to the account while the position was open.

Note that the account is first marked to market on the day of the trade and you made a profit of $437.50 on the first day. Each day thereafter you must maintain $4,400 in the account so that on any given day when the balance is greater than $4,400, the excess over the initial margin can be withdrawn. We shall assume, however, that you do not withdraw the excess. If the balance falls below the $4,400 maintenance margin requirement, you receive a margin call and must deposit enough funds to bring the balance back up to the initial margin requirement. The additional funds deposited are called the **variation margin**. They are officially due within a few days but usually are required to be deposited immediately; we shall assume that the money is deposited before trading begins on the day you receive the margin call. By the end of the day on Friday, August 8, the account shows a balance of $3,111.88. On Monday morning, you receive a margin call for $2,828.13, which is immediately deposited. Another margin call, for $2,718.75, follows on August 14. Undaunted and still confident of ultimately turning things around, you make the deposit on August 14. When you finally buy back the contract on August 18, the account balance withdrawn is $7,830.63. In all, you have made deposits of $5,940, $2,828.13, and $2,718.75 for a total of $11,486.88. Thus, the overall loss on the trade is $3,656.25.

The preceding example is not at all unusual. It was selected at random. You, the seller of this contract, quickly incurred a substantial loss. For every dollar lost, however, there is a dollar gained by someone else. Traders who were bullish on Treasury bond futures from August 1 to 18 did quite well. Nonetheless, the large dollar flows

TABLE 8.1 DAILY SETTLEMENT EXAMPLE

Assume that on Friday, August 1, you sell one Chicago Board of Trade September Treasury bond futures contract at the opening price of 116 27/32 ($116,843.75). The initial margin requirement is $5,940, and the maintenance margin requirement is $4,400. You maintain your position every day through Friday, August 15, and then buy back the contract at the opening price on Monday, August 18. The example below illustrates the daily price changes and the flows in and out of the margin account. The settlement prices are rounded to the nearest penny, but the mark-to-market amounts are first computed based on actual settlement prices (not rounded) and then the final result is rounded. Thus, there may appear to be slight errors in mark-to-market amounts if computed based on rounded settlement prices.

DATE	SETTLEMENT PRICE	SETTLEMENT PRICE ($)	MARK TO MARKET	OTHER ENTRIES	ACCOUNT BALANCE	EXPLANATION
8/1	116–13	$116,406.25	+$437.50	+$5,940.00	+$6,377.50	Initial margin deposit of $5,940. Price fell by 14/32, leaving profit by day-end of $437.50.
8/4	116–25	116,781.25	−375.00		6,002.50	Price rose by 12/32, giving loss of $375. Balance exceeds maintenance requirement.
8/5	115–185	115,578.13	+1,203.13		7,205.63	Price fell by 1 6.5/32, giving profit of $1,203.13. Balance well above maintenance requirement.
8/6	115–07	115,218.75	+359.38		7,565.00	Price fell by 11.5/32, giving profit of $359.38. Balance well above maintenance requirement.
8/7	116–05	116,156.25	−937.50		6,627.50	Price rose by 30/32, giving loss of $937.50. Balance still above maintenance requirement.
8/8	119–215	119,671.88	−3,515.63		3,111.88	Price rose by 3 16.5/32, giving loss of $3,515.63. Balance short by $1,288.12.
8/11	121–01	121,031.25	−1,359.38	+2,828.13	4,580.63	$2,828.13 deposited. Price rose 1 11.5/32, giving loss of $1,359.38. Balance exceeds maintenance requirements.
8/12	119–25	119,781.25	+1,250.00		5,830.63	Price fell 1 8/32, giving profit of $1,250. Balance well above maintenance requirement.
8/13	122–125	122,390.63	−2,609.38		3,221.25	Price rose by 2 19.5/32, giving loss of $2,609.38. Balance short by $1,178.75. $2,718.75 deposited.
8/14	120–25	120,781.25	+1,609.38	+2,718.75	7,549.38	Price fell by 1 19.5/32, giving profit of $1,609.38. Balance above maintenance requirement.
8/15	120–255	120,796.88	−15.63		7,533.75	Price rose by 1/2 of 32nd for a loss of $15.63.
8/18	120–16	120,500.00	+296.88	−7,830.63	0.00	Bought contract back at gain of 9.5/32, or $296.88. Withdrew remaining balance.

from day to day serve as a stern reminder of the substantial leverage component that futures contracts offer.

It is also important to note that with futures contracts, it is possible to lose more money than one has invested. For example, assume that the market makes a substantial move against the investor. The account balance is depleted, and the broker asks the investor to deposit additional funds. If the investor does not have the funds, the broker will attempt to close out the position. Now assume that the market moves quickly before the contracts can be closed. Ultimately, the contracts are sold out, but not before the investor has incurred additional losses. Those losses must be covered in cash. In the limit, a long position can ultimately lose the full price of the contract. This would occur if the price went to zero. On a short position, however, there is no upper limit on the price. Therefore, the loss theoretically is infinite.

One method that derivatives exchanges use to limit the losses incurred on any given day is the daily price limit, which we briefly discussed earlier. Also, the clearinghouse can request that additional margin funds be deposited during a trading session rather than waiting until the end of the day.

Of course, in forward markets, there is no clearinghouse, price limits, or daily settlement. There may or may not be margins required; this would depend on the creditworthiness of the party. In many cases, credit is established by posting a letter of credit provided by a bank, which, in effect, stands ready to lend money to cover losses.[7]

The total number of futures contracts outstanding at any one time is called the **open interest**. The concept is the same as it is for options markets. Each contract has both a long and short position and counts as one unit of open interest.

Most futures traders do not hold their positions to expiration; rather, they simply reenter the market and execute an offsetting transaction. In other words, if one held a long position in a contract, one might elect to simply sell that contract in the market. The clearinghouse would properly note that the trader's positions were offsetting. If the position were not offset before the expiration month, delivery would become likely.

Delivery and Cash Settlement

All contracts eventually expire. As noted earlier, each contract has a delivery month. The delivery procedure varies among contracts. Some contracts can be delivered on any business day of the delivery month. Others permit delivery only after the contract has traded for the last day—a day that also varies from contract to contract. Still others are cash-settled; thus, there is no delivery at all.

Most non-cash-settled financial futures contracts permit delivery any business day of the delivery month. Delivery usually is a three-day sequence beginning two business days prior to the first possible delivery day. The clearing member firms report to the clearinghouse those of their customers who hold long positions. Two business days before the intended delivery day, the holder of a short position who intends to make delivery notifies the clearinghouse of its desire to deliver. This day is called the **position day**. On the next business day, called the **notice of intention day**, the exchange selects the holder of the oldest long position to receive delivery. On the third day, the **delivery day**, delivery takes place and the long pays the short. For most financial futures, delivery is consummated by wire transfer.

Most futures contracts allow for more than one deliverable instrument. The contract usually specifies that the price paid by the long to the short be adjusted to reflect a

---

[7]Some swaps and other over-the-counter contracts periodically settle gains and losses, but to date, this is the exception and not the rule.

difference in the quality of the deliverable good. We shall look at this more closely in Chapter 10.

On cash-settled contracts such as stock index futures, the settlement price on the last trading day is fixed at the closing spot price of the underlying instrument, such as the stock index. All contracts are marked to market on that day, and the positions are deemed to be closed. One exception to this procedure is the Chicago Mercantile Exchange's S&P 500 futures contract, which closes open-outcry trading on the Thursday before the third Friday of the expiration month but bases the final settlement price on the opening stock price on Friday morning. This procedure was installed to avoid some problems created when a contract settles at the closing prices.

The fact that all futures contracts can be delivered or cash settled is critical to their pricing. About 99 percent of all futures contracts are not delivered or cash settled. Most traders close out their positions prior to expiration, a process called **offsetting**. The futures market is not the best route to acquiring the underlying asset because the long contract holder is at the mercy of the short contract holder. The short can deliver on any of several delivery days and can choose to deliver any of several related but slightly different assets. The long must accept whatever the short offers. Thus, the long usually closes out the position early. Therefore, if one needs the underlying asset, one often will do better to purchase it in the spot market.

Despite the flexibility sellers have in determining the delivery terms, some contracts actually are delivered through a process called **exchange for physicals (EFP)**, also known as **against actuals** or **versus cash**. This is, in fact, the only type of permissible futures transaction that occurs off the floor of the exchange (or outside its electronic trading platform if it has one). In an EFP transaction, the holders of long and short positions get together and agree on a cash transaction that would close out their futures positions. For example, farmer A holds a short position in a wheat contract and firm B holds a long position in the same contract. Firm B wants to buy farmer A's wheat, but either the wheat is not one of the grades acceptable for delivery on the contract or the farmer would find it prohibitively expensive to deliver at Chicago or Toledo as the contract requires. In either case, farmer A and firm B could arrange for A to deliver the wheat at some other acceptable location and B to pay A for the wheat at an agreed-upon price. Then A and B would be permitted to report this transaction to the CBOT as though each had offset its futures contract with a trade with the other party. Thus, the EFP market simply gives the parties additional flexibility in making delivery, choosing the terms, and conducting such business when the exchanges are closed. EFPs can also be used in cash settlement contracts. EFPs are used in several futures markets and compose almost 100 percent of deliveries made in oil futures markets.

Because forward contracts do not have standard terms and conditions like futures contracts, it is not as simple to offset them the way one can futures. If an institution has purchased a forward contract obligating it to purchase a commodity at a future date, however, it can generally sell a new forward contract obligating it to deliver the commodity on that date. Of course, the price negotiated may lead to a profit or a loss. While this type of transaction is basically an offsetting transaction, the liquidity of the forward market may be such that it might be somewhat more difficult to find someone to do the precise transaction the institution wants. In addition, the new transaction also entails some credit risk. In the most liquid forward, offsetting is a fairly simple procedure, as noted above, and is subject to essentially no credit risk. In some cases, however, a forward contract can be offset by entering into the opposite transaction with the same party with which one contracted originally. By mutual agreement, the parties can treat the contracts as offsetting, thereby terminating both contracts and eliminating the credit risk.

When a forward contract is written, the intention is generally to hold it to the expiration day and take delivery. Some contracts, however, do stipulate a cash settlement. Thus, an expiring forward contract works much like an expiring futures contract.

FUTURES PRICE QUOTATIONS

Futures prices for selected underlying instruments are available daily in *The Wall Street Journal* and in many newspapers in large cities. The information provided is usually the open, high, low, and settlement prices; the change in the settlement price; the highest and lowest prices during the life of the contract; and the open interest. The volume is provided for all contracts of the same underlying, but not for each individual contract expiration. The print version of *The Wall Street Journal* covers selected futures contracts; information on many other futures contracts is available on the newspaper's website, www.wsj.com.

Like option prices obtained from newspapers, futures prices are outdated by the time they are available. In addition, the prices are not synchronized with the price of the underlying. For better information without paying a fee, the Internet is the best source. The website of *The Wall Street Journal* provides free quotes on all futures contracts, showing the last trade price, the open, the high, the low, the volume, and open interest. In addition, the site shows the time of the last transaction. Probably the best sources of price information are the websites of the derivatives exchanges. Although these sites typically do not provide bid and ask prices, they do provide the most current information, such as the last trade, and the volume and open interest figures. This information is nearly always provided with a short delay. Some of the exchanges allow you to download historical data for free, which can include a complete list of every transaction, the price, and the time it took place. Real-time quotes require payment of a fee. There are a few other services on the Internet that provide futures price information, which is obtained from the exchanges, but the information is formatted differently and can be more useful.

See "Making the Connection" on pp. 283–284 for information on how to access and interpret this information.

TYPES OF FUTURES CONTRACTS

Many types of futures contracts trade on derivatives exchanges around the world. Some of these contracts are essentially the same underlying commodity. Many of those listed are not actively traded; some have not been traded at all for some time. Keep in mind that new contracts are frequently introduced and old contracts are sometimes delisted. A brief discussion of some of the characteristics of each major group of contracts follows.

Agricultural Commodities

This category is the oldest group of futures contracts. It includes widely used grains such as wheat, corn, oats, soybeans, and rice. In addition, futures are actively traded on livestock such as cattle and hogs and on various food products such as coffee, cocoa, orange juice, and sugar. Also, futures are traded on cotton, wool, and wood.

Most of the volume of trading in these contracts is in U.S. markets, but there is also some activity in Canada and a few other countries. Participants in these markets include farmers and firms that use these raw materials as vital inputs.

An important characteristic of these types of futures contracts is that buying and holding these assets typically incurs significant costs. Moreover, the spot markets for these assets are usually quite dispersed. In other words, there is often no central spot market. Hence, it is difficult to refer to a single spot price. A grain harvested in Iowa will be a different product if delivered in Chicago due to the costs of transporting it and any losses involved when the product is shipped. In addition, the delivery of these assets at expiration of a futures contract will also incur significant costs.

Many of these products are characterized by seasonal production cycles. Hence, the supply of the asset tends to be augmented at certain times of the year. Shortages and surpluses are common.

Natural Resources

Futures contracts are actively traded on two types of natural resources: metals and energy products. The primary metals on which futures are traded are gold, silver, and copper, with lighter trading on platinum and palladium. Because these products are primarily used in manufacturing, market participants often include companies that buy and sell these products and the products into which they are made. Gold and silver, however, have a special status as popular precious metals that people often use as a store of value. Some futures trading in these instruments is based on views about such factors as inflation, international politics, and the world economy, whereby gold and silver are seen as defensive investments against political and economic instability.

Miscellaneous Commodities

This category includes contracts that have mostly traded very lightly, and many are no longer listed. They include futures on fertilizer, shrimp, electricity, rubber, glass, cement, potatoes, peanuts, sunflower seeds, inflation, peas, flax, kerosene, yarn, and shipping freight rates. There have also been futures on various measures of weather, including weather-related insurance claims. These futures have not been actively traded, but weather derivatives have found a home in the over-the-counter markets; we cover this type of product in Chapter 14.

In addition, futures have been traded on indices that reflect the average of the prices of a combination of other futures contracts.

Foreign Currencies

As noted earlier in this chapter, there is a very large forward market in foreign currencies. Futures contracts on foreign currencies are also traded, but these are not as active as are forward contracts. Foreign currency futures, however, have an important historical legacy in that they were the first financial futures contracts. Launched in 1972 in response to a move on the part of nations to allow their currencies to freely float in relation to each other, they were the first futures contracts on money, which some view as the ultimate commodity.

Although there are about 50 currencies with at least a moderately active interbank market, the futures contracts with much volume are those involving the U.S. dollar, the euro, the Japanese yen, the British pound, the Swiss franc, the Canadian dollar, and the Mexican peso. Even those contracts have almost relatively small volume compared to the forward market for those currencies.

Federal Funds and Eurodollars

Federal funds contracts trade on the Chicago Board of Trade and Eurodollar contracts trade on the International Monetary Market of the Chicago Mercantile Exchange. In the United States, the Eurodollar contract is the most actively traded futures contract. We shall explore these contracts in great detail in later chapters.

Treasury Notes and Bonds

Treasury note and bond contracts, which are traded on the Chicago Board of Trade, are virtually identical except that there are three T-note contracts that are based on two-year, five-year, and ten-year maturities, while the T-bond contract is based on Treasury bonds with maturities of at least 15 years that are not callable for at least 15 years. Thus, the T-note contracts are intermediate-term interest rate futures contracts and the T-bond contract is a long-term interest rate futures contract. The T-note contracts are traded quite actively, but the T-bond contract is one of the most active of all futures contracts. Other than the difference in maturity of the underlying instruments and the margin requirements, the contract terms are essentially identical. We shall use these contracts extensively in later chapters.

Swap Futures

Swap futures contracts trade on the Chicago Mercantile Exchange. Futures contracts are offered for two-year, five-year, and ten-year interest rate swaps. We will cover interest rate swaps in detail in Chapter 12. Presently, swap futures have very low trading volume.

Equities

Stock index futures have been one of the spectacular success stories of the financial markets in recent years. These cash-settled contracts are indices of combinations of stocks. Investors use them to hedge positions in stock, speculate on the direction of the stock market in general, and arbitrage the contracts against comparable combinations of stocks.

Stock index futures contracts are based on indices of common stocks. One of the most widely traded contracts is the E-mini S&P 500 futures at the CME Group. The futures price is quoted in the same manner as the index. The original S&P 500 futures contract has a multiplier of $250, and the E-mini has a multiplier of $50. Thus, if the S&P 500 futures price is 1500, the actual price is 1500($250) = $375,000 for the original contract and 1500($50) = $75,000 for the E-mini. At expiration, the settlement price is set at the price of the S&P 500 index and the contract is settled in cash. The expirations are March, June, September, and December. The last trading day is the Thursday before the third Friday of the expiration month for the original contract and Friday morning at 8:30 A.M. for the E-mini (the same time as the futures expiration).

As described earlier in this chapter, futures on individual stocks have been actively traded in some countries and began trading in the United States on November 8, 2002. These contracts are generally available only on the most actively traded stocks. Specifications for the U.S. contracts call for each futures to cover 100 shares of stock. The contracts are settled at expiration by actual delivery of the shares, although some contracts in other markets are settled in cash.

Somewhat closely related to single stock futures are futures on relatively narrow indices of stocks. In the U.S., a narrow index contains nine or fewer securities, one in which a single component security comprises more than 30 percent of the index, one in which the five highest-weighted component securities comprise more than 60 percent of the index, or one in which the lowest weighted component securities comprising 25 percent of the index have an average daily trading volume of less than $50 million. Many of these indices will have only about five stocks.

In the U.S., single stock futures are traded by several consortia of exchanges. The Chicago Board of Trade, the Chicago Mercantile Exchange, and the Chicago Board Options Exchange have formed a joint venture called OneChicago (www.onechicago.com)

for the trading of single stock futures. It is interesting to note the participation of the CBOE in this new futures market. It had formerly been involved only in the trading of options. The NASDAQ Stock Market has formed a joint venture with the London International Financial Futures Exchange (LIFFE) called NASDAQ/LIFFE Markets, which joins the highly successful NASDAQ markets with LIFFE in Europe for the trading of single stock futures (now part of NYSE Euronext). OneChicago appears to be the market leader in single stock futures. In May 2006, OneChicago offered markets for over 196 single stock futures contracts. Trading volume, however, remains relatively low. For example, on Wednesday, August 24, 2011, OneChicago reported the total contract volume for single stock futures was 1,628 contracts and open interest of 341,289 (volume data available at www.onechicago.com).

MAKING THE CONNECTION

Reading Futures Price Quotations

Current (ten-minute delay) futures prices quotations can be obtained from several sources. The website of *The Wall Street Journal* contains quotes that can be accessed by choosing (from the menu on the top) "Markets," then "Market Data," and finally "Commodities & Futures." Scroll below "Commodities & Futures Overview" and select the contract group. A pull-down menu will enable you to select the specific contracts. You can also access quotes for options on futures from this menu.

Suppose we are interested in a quote for the E-mini S&P 500 futures contract (symbol ES). The following information was obtained around 2 P.M. on August 25, 2011. The first column identifies the futures contract as the E-mini S&P 500. The *E* denotes electronic trading on GLOBEX. The *mini* denotes that the multiplier is 50 and not 250 for the standard contract. The profits and losses are computed by multiplying the unit change in the futures price by $50 for the E-mini and $250 for the standard S&P 500 futures contract. Interestingly, the E-mini is now much more popular than the standard

contract. The second column indicates the month and year of the contract. The third column gives the time of the last trade. Note that the fourth row contains the June 2012 contract, which had not yet traded on August 25. It had last traded on August 24 at 20:21:17. The fourth column gives the last trade, which is in bold (y indicates that the contract has not yet traded this day). The next column gives the change in the last price from the prior day's settlement price. The next three columns give the open, high, and low price for the day. Volume is a measure of the current day's trading volume, and open interest represents the current existing contracts. The exchange is the Chicago Merchantile Exchange (electronic). The time is given in Greenwich mean time (GMT) or Universal time to facilitate trade observations from other global locations. Eastern U. S. time (ET) is four hours before GMT; thus, 18:56 GMT is 14:56 ET, or 2:56 P.M.[8]

Contract	Month	Last	Chg	Open	High	Low	Volume	OpenInt	Exchange	Date	Time
E-MINI S&P 500	Sep '11	1160.00	−12.00	1171.50	1188.50	1153.25	2631320	3395461	CMEE	08/25/11	18:55:17
E-MINI S&P 500	Dec '11	1154.25	−12.00	1166.00	1183.00	1147.50	15315	68753	CMEE	08/25/11	18:55:18
E-MINI S&P 500	Mar '12	1152.25	−8.50	1175.00	1175.00	1152.25	19	597	CMEE	08/25/11	18:40:09
E-MINI S&P 500	Jun '12	1155.25y					0	102	CMEE	08/24/11	20:21:17
...	...	...	...	...	...	...	...	...	...	...	...

[8]The treatment of daylight saving time varies, so this difference may be off by five hours during other times of the year.

The fifth data row contains ellipses. The actual screen may show additional available contracts even if they did not trade, such as the June '12 contract shown above.

At the end of the day, the last trade is replaced with the settlement price.

The Chicago Mercantile Exchange's website can be used to obtain similar information. Go to www.cmegroup.com. Highlight "Equity Index" and then select "E-mini S&P 500 (Dollar)." You now should be able to view the list of contracts. Consider the quotes below for the E-mini S&P 500 electronic futures, which were taken around 2 P.M. on August 24, 2011.

The CME's page includes both the last trade and the prior settlement price. The value of –12.00 means –12.00 points. Thus, the loss per long contract is $600 (–12.00 [multiplication symbol] $50). The volume is shown as 2,630,581 contracts for the September 2012 contract and 15,314 contracts for the December 2012 contract. The time is given in Central standard time, which is five hours before GMT as the quote was taken in the summer with daylight saving time. The table on the CME's website shows all contracts, even those that have not traded.

Bid and ask prices are not generally available for free, nor are prices more current than a ten-minute delay.

Month	Last	Change	Prior Settle	Open	High	Low	Volume	Time
Sep 2011	1160.00	–12.00	1172.00	1171.50	1188.50	1153.25	2,630,581	1:54:49 PM CST 8/25/2011
Dec 2011	1154.00	–12.25	1166.25	1166.00	1183.00	1147.50	15,314	1:54:16 PM CST 8/25/2011
Mar 2012	1149.50a	–11.25	1160.75	1175.00	1176.50b	1152.25	19	1:54:17 PM CST 8/25/2011
Jun 2012	1148.25a	–9.00	1155.25	—	1163.50b	1146.25a	0	1:30:01 PM CST 8/25/2011
...								

Managed Funds

Recent years have witnessed the growth of the **managed funds** industry. *Managed funds* refers to the arrangement by which an investor hires a professional futures trader to conduct transactions on his or her behalf. The futures manager is a commodity trading advisor (CTA), which we discussed earlier. Managed funds can exist in one of four forms: futures funds, private pools, a specialized contract with one or more CTAs, or hedge funds.[9]

Futures funds, sometimes called **commodity funds**, are essentially mutual funds that pool investors' money and trade futures. Most funds invest only about 20 percent of their money in margin positions. The remainder is kept in interest-earning assets. Futures funds offer the public a way of participating in the futures market with a very low financial commitment. Often a fund will accept deposits of $1,000 or less. In some cases, the organizers of a fund guarantee that the investor will not lose more than the original investment.

In spite of the apparent attractiveness of funds, they have been quite controversial—and with just cause. Their performance has been highly volatile, and their costs are quite high, often running to 20 percent of the value of the fund in a given year.

Commodity pools, mentioned earlier in the context of the pool operator, or CPO, are private arrangements that operate much like futures funds. The latter, however, are open

---

[9]In addition to futures, these funds also use options and spot market instruments.

to the general public, while pools normally solicit funds from specific investors. When the fund reaches a certain size, the pool is closed to other investors. Pools generally require at least a $10,000 investment. Pools have suffered some of the same problems as funds, namely inconsistent performance and heavy costs.

An increasingly popular form of managed futures is the private contractual arrangement with one or more CTAs. A typical arrangement involves a large institutional investor agreeing to allocate a portion of its funds to a group of CTAs. In some cases, the CTAs are supervised by a consultant or an introducing broker. Because these arrangements are negotiated between the institutional investor and the introducing broker and the CTAs, the costs are usually significantly lower. Often a rather large number of CTAs, sometimes 20 to 30, is used, leading to diversified and somewhat stable performance. These arrangements are growing in popularity, particularly among pension funds.

Hedge Funds

The hedge fund industry is technically part of the managed funds industry, but hedge funds have become such a large and powerful force in the market that we put them in their own category. A hedge fund is a privately organized pool of money that is invested in literally any financial instruments on any markets of the world. Although hedge funds actively use futures contracts, they also use options; spot instruments such as stocks and bonds; and over-the-counter instruments such as swaps, structured notes, and forward contracts. A hedge fund typically uses a high degree of leverage and takes short positions as willingly as long positions. In addition, a hedge fund frequently borrows heavily. It should be apparent that a hedge fund is a very risky form of investment. These funds normally take in only investors who have large amounts of money and a willingness to take high risks. Also, hedge funds tend to be quite secretive, often registering their legal status in offshore locations such as the Cayman Islands. Many hedge funds even maintain a great deal of secrecy from their investors, who trust that the fund organizers will invest their money wisely and manage the risk carefully. This has not always been the case.

The term *hedge fund* is probably a misnomer. The general idea of calling this type of company a hedge fund is that the fund would take short positions, which in some sense hedge long positions. That was the original design of a hedge fund. Today, however, these funds are probably as far from the practice of hedging as one can get. That does not mean they are not legitimate investment outlets because their success and popularity are well established in the financial system. Hedge funds are major providers of liquidity and employ astute traders whose arbitrage transactions help make the market more efficient.

Options on Futures

As described earlier in this chapter, options on futures trade on many derivatives exchanges. In most cases throughout the world, the most actively traded futures contracts also have options available on the futures contracts. Of course, many also have options trading on the underlying asset itself.

TRANSACTION COSTS IN FORWARD AND FUTURES TRADING

In Chapter 2, we discussed the different types of option trading costs that the public and professional traders incur. In this section, we shall do the same for forwards and futures. There is, however, less material available on the trading costs in these markets. One reason is that futures markets have very low trading costs—indeed, that is one of their major advantages. In addition, the costs of trading futures contracts are less documented than the costs of trading options and stocks. Also, forward markets are private and the costs are less publicized; however, forward contracting, being tailored to the specific needs of the parties, can be quite costly.

Commissions

Commissions paid by the public to brokers are assessed on the basis of a dollar charge per contract. The commission is paid at the order's initiation and includes both the opening and closing commissions; that is, a round-trip commission is charged regardless of whether the trader ultimately closes out the contract, makes or takes delivery, or makes a cash settlement. There is no typical commission rate, but rates of less than $10 for a round-trip are common.

All traders, whether on or off the exchange floor, incur a minimum charge that is paid to the clearing firm and includes the exchange fee and a fee assessed by the National Futures Association, an organization we shall discuss in a later section. These fees are usually less than $2 per contract.

In the forward market, transactions are usually conducted directly with dealers, so there is typically no commission. There are, however, significant costs associated with processing the paperwork.

Bid-Ask Spread

A second type of trading cost is the bid-ask spread. Chapter 2 explained the concept of the spread for options. Unlike options and stock markets, however, there is no real market maker. Many floor traders, particularly spreaders and scalpers, quote prices at which they are willing to simultaneously buy at the bid price and sell at the ask price. The bid-ask spread is the cost to the public of liquidity—the ability to buy and sell quickly without a large price concession. Because the spread is not captured and reported electronically, there is little statistical evidence about its size. The spread usually is the value of a minimum price fluctuation, called a **tick**, but occasionally equals a few more ticks for less liquid markets.

In the forward markets, bid-ask spreads are set by dealers in much the same way they are on the exchange. These spreads can be quite large depending on how eager the dealer and its competitors are to make a trade.

Delivery Costs

A futures trader who holds a position to delivery faces the potential for incurring a substantial delivery cost. In the case of most financial instruments, this cost is rather small. For commodities, however, it is necessary to arrange for the commodity's physical transportation, delivery, and storage. Although the proverbial story of the careless futures trader who woke up to find thousands of pounds of pork bellies dumped on the front lawn certainly is an exaggeration, anyone holding a long position in the delivery month must be aware of the delivery possibility. This no doubt explains part of the popularity of cash settlement contracts.

In forward markets, transactions are tailored to the needs of the parties. Consequently, the terms are usually set to keep delivery costs at a minimum. Cash settlement is frequently used.

REGULATION OF FUTURES AND FORWARD MARKETS

Throughout history, some regulators and legislators have taken a dim view of futures trading, likening it to gambling. In the nineteenth century, there were numerous attempts to outlaw futures trading. In virtually all countries, futures markets are permitted but heavily regulated at the federal level.

In the United Kingdom, the regulatory agency is the Financial Services Authority. In Canada, futures regulation is done at the provincial level, so there are several provincial regulatory agencies. In Japan, the regulatory agency is called the Financial Services Agency. Similar agencies exist in other countries.

The structure of regulation in the United States is somewhat different from the structure in other countries. As noted in Chapter 2, the financial markets are regulated by several different agencies. The Securities and Exchange Commission, or SEC, (www.sec.gov) regulates the securities markets. With the introduction of single stock futures, the SEC regulates a small segment of the futures markets. The CFTC (www.cftc.gov) is a completely separate regulatory body that is the primary regulator of futures markets in the United States.

The objective of most federal regulatory agencies is to authorize derivatives exchanges to operate, approve new contracts and modifications of existing contracts, ensure that price information is made available to the public, authorize individuals to provide services related to futures trading, and oversee the markets to prevent manipulation. In carrying out their mandate, these agencies monitor the market by observing prices, requiring **reportable positions**, which document large-size positions held by traders, and establishing **position limits**, which are restrictions on the number of contracts a given trader can hold. In authorizing new contracts, the regulatory agencies evaluate proposals to determine if the contracts serve an "economic purpose," which is generally considered to be whether the contract can be used for hedging.

One important role of government in the futures industry is in adjudicating disputes. For example, a customer may believe that he has a legal claim against a broker. Ordinarily, the customer would file a lawsuit, but this action is costly for all parties. In most countries, the federal regulatory agency is generally authorized to provide a means of settling such disputes. In the U.S., these disputes are handled by a professional trade organization called the National Futures Association, or NFA (www.nfa.futures.org). The NFA is authorized to license personnel who will engage in services related to futures markets, monitor and regulate trading rule violations, and impose fines and sanctions. Perhaps its most important role is to provide a means of settling disputes outside the courtroom. Similar organizations exist in some other countries. Groups such as the NFA are referred to as industry self-regulatory organizations.

Banking regulators also indirectly regulate the futures markets by virtue of their regulatory authority over the banking industry, which is a major participant in the futures markets. In addition, regional governments such as the states in the U.S., have some regulatory authority. Various professional organizations and trade associations also impose standards on their members.

The over-the-counter market for forward contracts, as well as swaps and options, historically was not highly regulated. In 2010, the Dodd-Frank Wall Street Reform and Consumer Protection Act (DFA) was signed into law. The DFA provides for a dramatic increase in regulation of OTC derivatives, including hundreds of new rules and numerous studies. Although the details are still being worked out, OTC derivatives markets will have much more regulatory oversight. Most of the participating institutions, however, were already subject to some form of regulation based on their other activities, such as banking and securities. Hence, banking and securities regulators do exert some indirect regulation over the over-the-counter derivative markets. Of course, forward market transactions are always subject to ordinary commercial and criminal laws.

Futures markets participants have often complained that the heavy regulation they are subject to and the light regulation that forward markets are subject to has led to an "uneven playing field." Futures markets and forward markets are indeed competitors, offering similar transactions, but futures markets are guaranteed against credit losses and are more open to the public. Forward markets are essentially private transactions. Hence, most governments have taken the view that futures markets must be regulated for the sake of the general public, while forward markets are private transactions in which any parties should be able to engage, provided they do not violate any other laws.

OTC CENTRAL CLEARING

Even prior to the financial crisis in 2008, the derivatives industry was working to develop OTC central clearing. The DFA, in its effort to create more transparency and accountability for participants in the OTC derivatives markets, helped stimulate these efforts further. Although the dust has not yet settled, one avenue for providing more transparency is central clearing of OTC derivatives transactions. There are now several clearing corporations competing for OTC derivatives transactions. In the United States, there is the Intercontinential Exchange Trust, CME Clearing, and the International Derivatives Clearing Group. In Europe, there is LCH.Clearnet, ICE Clear Europe, CME Clearing Europe, and Eurex Clearing AG. There are other clearing corporations around the world and many other organizations considering entering this line of business.

OTC derivatives transactions are still negotiated privately between the interested counterparties. The resultant contract is given up, or novated, to the central counterparty. That is, the original derivatives contract is replaced with two new derivatives contracts where each counterparty to the original contract is now solely exposed to the central counterparty (CCP). The CCP acts like an exchange-traded derivatives clearinghouse by collecting appropriate margin from both OTC counterparties and managing the resultant risk exposure. Specifically, the CCP will operate in a similar fashion to exchange-traded clearinghouses and require some form of margins and daily settlement.

A centrally cleared market is similar to the way some airlines route traffic. The hub-and-spoke method of routing air passengers works well in routing a wide variety of smaller airports to a central hub. For example, Hartsfield-Jackson Atlanta International Airport acts as a primary hub for several airlines. Clearly, the hub-and-spoke method is more efficient than trying to route direct flights to and from multiple small locations. The OTC derivatives market, historically, was a bilateral market. That is, each OTC derivatives transaction was negotiated between the counterparties without any consideration of other existing positions, similar to the direct flights approach. In response to the financial crisis and the DFA, components of the OTC derivatives markets are migrating to centrally cleared markets. What should be obvious is that just as a major storm at Hartsfield-Jackson causes havoc in the hub-and-spoke system of managing air traffic; so a major financial crisis at a clearing corporation would cause significant havoc in the OTC derivatives markets. In an effort to minimize the likelihood of major financial problems at a clearing corporation, typically clearing members agree in advance to mutually share in any subsequent default. It appears that central clearing will increase in the OTC derivatives markets.

Summary

This chapter provided the descriptive material necessary for understanding how the forward and futures markets operate. We learned the definition of a futures contract, the general types of contracts that trade, the characteristics of the markets and traders, the role of the exchange, and the mechanics of trading. We also examined the nature of transaction costs and the structure of regulation. We learned what forward contracts are and how they differ from futures contracts.

The next three chapters deal with specific aspects of futures and forward trading. Chapter 9 explains the concepts of pricing forward and futures contracts as well as options on futures. Chapter 10 examines futures arbitrage strategies. Chapter 11 addresses various hedging strategies and provides illustrations of hedge transactions. Chapter 11 also introduces spread strategies, and various target strategies, including target duration and target beta.

Key Terms

Before continuing to Chapter 9, you should be able to give brief definitions of the following terms:

forward contract/forward commitment/futures contract, p. 258

financial futures, p. 260

commodity options/futures options/interbank market, p. 262

futures exchange, p. 265

limit up/limit down/limit move/circuit breakers, p. 268

futures commission merchants (FCMs)/Locals, p. 269

dual trading/hedger/Speculators/Spreaders, p. 270

Arbitrageurs/Scalpers/Day traders/Position traders, p. 271

introducing broker (IB)/commodity trading advisor (CTA)/commodity pool operator (CPO)/associated person (AP), p. 272

open outcry/long/short, p. 273

initial margin/maintenance margin, p. 274

performance bonds/settlement price/marked to market/daily settlement/variation margin, p. 276

open interest/position day/notice of intention day/delivery day, p. 278

offsetting/exchange for physicals (EFP)/against actuals/versus cash, p. 279

managed funds/Futures funds/commodity funds/Commodity pools, p. 284

tick, p. 286

reportable positions/position limits, p. 287

Further Reading

Three articles on the existence and role of futures markets are as follows:

Chance, D. M. "Competition and Innovation in U.S. Futures Markets." *The Journal of Alternative Investments* 11 (Summer, 2008): 97–109.

Telser, L. G. "Why There Are Organized Futures Markets." *Journal of Law and Economics* 24 (1981): 1–22.

Telser, L. G., and H. N. Higinbotham. "Organized Futures Markets: Costs and Benefits." *Journal of Political Economy* 85 (1977): 969–1000.

Studies of the performance and profitability of futures trading are as follows:

Hartzmark, M. L. "Luck versus Forecasting Ability: Determinants of Trader Performance in Futures Markets." *Journal of Business* 64 (1991): 49–74.

Hartzmark, M. L. "Returns to Individual Traders of Futures: Aggregate Results." *Journal of Political Economy* 95 (1987): 1292–1306.

Hieronymus, T. A. *The Economics of Futures Trading.* New York: Commodity Research Bureau, 1977.

Jones, T., and R. Brooks. "An Analysis of Single-Stock Futures Trading in the U.S." *Financial Services Review* 14 (June 2005): 85–96.

Kuserk, G. J., and P. R. Locke. "Scalper Behavior in Futures Markets: An Empirical Examination." *The Journal of Futures Markets* 13 (June 1993): 409–431.

Moran, M. T. "Taking a Ride on the Volatile Side." *Journal of Indexes* (October/November 2004): 16–19.

Silber, W. L. "Marketmaker Behavior in an Auction Market: An Analysis of Scalpers in Futures Markets." *The Journal of Finance* 39 (September 1984): 937–953.

Studies of trading on derivatives exchanges include the following:

Kuserk, G. J., and P. R. Locke. "Market Maker Competition on Futures Exchanges." *The Journal of Derivatives* 1 (Summer 1994): 56–66.

Kuserk, G. J., and P. R. Locke. "Market Making with Price Limits." *The Journal of Futures Markets* 16 (September 1996): 677–696.

Lambert, E. *The Futures: The Rise of the Speculator and the Origins of the World's Biggest Markets.* New York: Basic Books, 2011.

Manaster, S., and S. C. Mann. "Life in the Pits: Competitive Market Making and Inventory Control." *Review of Financial Studies* 9 (Fall 1996): 953–975.

Melamed, L. *For Crying Out Loud.* Hoboken, NJ: John Wiley & Sons, 2009.

Olson, E. S. *Zero-Sum Game: The Rise of the World's Largest Derivatives Exchange.* Hoboken, NJ: John Wiley & Sons, 2011.

Pirrong, C. "The Clearinghouse Cure." *Regulation* (Winter 2008–2009): 44–51.

Pirrong, C. "Market Liquidity and Depth on Computerized and Open Outcry Trading Systems." *The Journal of Futures Markets* 16 (August 1996): 519–543.

Concepts Checks

1. Explain the difference between a forward contract and an option.
2. What factors distinguish a forward contract from a futures contract? What do forward and futures contracts have in common? What advantages does each have over the other?
3. How do options on futures differ from options on the asset underlying the futures?
4. The open interest in a futures contract changes from day to day. Suppose investors holding long positions are divided into two groups: A is an individual investor, and OL represents other investors. Investors holding short positions are denoted as S. Currently, A holds 1,000 contracts and OL holds 4,200; thus, S is short 5,200 contracts. Determine the holdings of A, OL, and S after each of the following transactions.
   a. A sells 500 contracts; OL buys 500 contracts.
   b. A buys 700 contracts; OL sells 700 contracts.
   c. A buys 200 contracts; S sells 200 contracts.
   d. A sells 800 contracts; S buys 800 contracts.
      What determines whether volume increases or decreases open interest?
5. List and briefly explain the important contributions provided by derivatives exchanges.

Questions and Problems

1. What exchange-determined specifications are set upon the inception of a futures contract?
2. What is the difference between an initial margin and a maintenance margin?
3. Describe the process of daily settlements in a clearinghouse.
4. How does the practice of daily settlements distinguish futures and forward markets from each another?
5. Explain several ways in which investors utilize stock index futures. On what types of stock are stock index futures generally available?
6. How do locals differ from commission brokers? How do commission brokers differ from futures commission merchants?
7. Explain the basic differences between open-outcry and electronic trading systems.
8. What factors would determine whether a particular strategy is a hedge or a speculative strategy?
9. How are spread and arbitrage strategies forms of speculation? How can they be interpreted as hedges?
10. What are the differences among scalpers, day traders, and position traders?
11. What are the various ways in which an individual may obtain the right to go on to the floor of an exchange and trade futures?
12. What are daily price limits? Why are they used?
13. What are circuit breakers? What are their advantages and disadvantages?
14. Explain how the clearinghouse operates to protect the futures market.
15. Explain the differences among the three means of terminating a futures contract: an offsetting trade, cash settlement, and delivery. How is a forward contract terminated?
16. Suppose you buy a stock index futures contract at the opening price of 452.25 on July 1. The multiplier on the contract is 500, so the price is

$500 (452.25) = $226,125. You hold the position open until selling it on July 16 at the opening price of 435.50. The initial margin requirement is $9,000, and the maintenance margin requirement is $6,000. Assume that you deposit the initial margin and do not withdraw the excess on any given day. Construct a table showing the charges and credits to the margin account. The daily prices on the intervening days are as follows:

Day	Settlement Price 1
7/1	453.95
7/2	454.50
7/3	452.00
7/7	443.55
7/8	441.65
7/9	442.85
7/10	444.15
7/11	442.25
7/14	438.30
7/15	435.05
7/16	435.50

17. The crude oil futures contract on the New York Mercantile Exchange covers 1,000 barrels of crude oil. The contract is quoted in dollars and cents per barrel (e.g., $27.42), and the minimum price change is $0.01. The initial margin requirement is $3,375, and the maintenance margin requirement is $2,500. Suppose you bought a contract at $27.42, putting up the initial margin. At what price would you get a margin call?

18. Explain the difference between hedge funds and futures funds.

19. What are the objectives of federal regulation of future markets?

20. What is the objective of an industry self-regulatory organization?

21. Compare and contrast three types of futures trading costs.

22. Compare and contrast cash settlement with physical settlement.

23. U.S. federal law regulates some futures market participants even though they do not directly participate in trading. Explain the difference between an introducing broker, a commodity trading advisor, a commodity pool operator, and an associated person.

24. Identify the typical characteristics of a forward market trader.

APPENDIX 8

Taxation of Futures Transactions in the United States

Investors' and traders' profits from most futures contracts as well as index options are considered to be 60 percent capital gains and 40 percent ordinary income. Capital gains are taxed at the ordinary income rate but are subject to a maximum of 20 percent. Thus, an investor in the 31 percent tax bracket would have futures profits taxed at a blended rate of $0.6(0.20) + 0.4(0.31) = 0.244$.

In addition, all futures and index options profits are subject to a mark to market rule in which accumulated profits are taxable in the current year even if the contract has not been closed out. For example, assume that you bought a futures contract on October 15 at a price of $1,000. Your account was, of course, marked to market daily. At the end of the year, the accumulated profit in the account was $400, meaning that the futures price at the end of the year was $1,400. Then you would have to pay the tax that year on $400 even though you had not closed out the contract. In other words, realized and unrealized profits are taxed and losses are recognized.

These rules apply only to speculative transactions. Taxation of hedge transactions is more complex and will be examined in Chapter 11.

Consider the following example. Suppose an investor in the 31 percent tax bracket purchases a futures contract at $1,000 on October 15 and ultimately sells it at $1,300 on January 20 of the next year. Assume that the contract price was $1,400 at the end of the year. The first year the tax liability is on $400, so the tax is $400(0.6)(0.20) + $400(0.40)(0.31) = $97.60, an effective rate of 24.4 percent. In the second year, there is a taxable loss of $1,400 − $1,300 = $100. This can be used to offset taxable gains; thus, it will save the trader 0.244 ($100) = $24.40 in taxes on profitable futures trades in that year. Losses can be used to offset gains but not more than the total amount of taxable gains. Any losses not used can be carried back to offset prior trading profits for up to three years.

Suppose the contract expired in February and the investor took delivery of the commodity. Let the price at expiration be $1,500. Then it would be assumed that the commodity was purchased at $1,500. The investor would have paid tax on the $400 profit at the end of the year in which the contract was bought; the investor would owe tax on the $100 profit that accrued between the end of the year and the expiration.

The new futures contracts on individual stocks will be taxed the same way as individual stocks. Gains and losses from offsetting a position can be either long-term or short-term, but most will be short-term because of the short lives of most contracts. If the investor takes delivery of the stock, the futures holding period is added to the stock holding period, which is generally beneficial to the investor.

Although recent tax laws have greatly simplified the taxation of futures contracts, many complexities remain. Competent tax advice is necessary to keep up with the many changes and to ensure compliance with the various rules.

Questions and Problems

1. On October 1, you purchase one March stock index futures contract at the opening price of 410.30. The contract multiplier is $500, so the price of 410.30 is really $500(410.30) = $205,150. You hold the position open until February 20, whereupon you sell the contract at the opening price of 427.30. The settlement price on December 31 was 422.40. You are in the 31 percent tax bracket. Compute your tax liability.

2. In November, you buy a futures contract on a commodity at a price of $10,000. At the end of the year, the futures price is $10,500. You hold your position open until January 20, at which time the commodity price is $11,200, the contract expires, and you take delivery. You are in the 31 percent tax bracket. Compute your tax liability in both years.

CHAPTER 9

Principles of Pricing Forwards, Futures, and Options on Futures

Futures markets are an accurate representation of consensus opinion, but if we pool all our ignorance, we do not get wisdom from it.

Jim Bianco
The Wall Street Journal, March 11, 2006, p. B3

We are now ready to move directly into the pricing of forward and futures contracts. The very nature of the word *futures* suggests that futures prices concern prices in the future. Likewise, the notion of a forward price suggests looking ahead to a later date. But as we shall learn, futures and forward prices are not definitive statements of prices in the future. In fact, they are not even necessarily predictions of the future. But they are important pieces of information about the current state of a market, and futures and forward contracts are powerful tools for managing risk. In this chapter, we shall see how futures prices, forward prices, spot prices, expectations, and the costs of holding positions in the asset are interrelated. As with options, our objective is to link the price of the futures or forward contract to the price of the underlying instrument and to identify factors that influence the relationship between these prices.

In Chapter 1, we noted that there are options in which the underlying is a futures. When we covered options in which the underlying is an asset, we could not cover options on futures because we had not yet covered futures. Because this chapter covers the pricing of futures contracts, we can also cover the pricing of options on futures, as we do later in this chapter.

In the early part of this chapter, we shall treat forward and futures contracts as though they are entirely separate instruments. Recall that a forward contract is an agreement between two parties to exchange an asset for a fixed price at a future date. No money changes hands, and the agreement is binding. In order to reverse the transaction, it is necessary to find someone willing to take the opposite side of a new, offsetting forward contract calling for delivery of the asset at the same time as the original contract. A forward contract is created in the over-the-counter market and is subject to default risk. A futures contract is also an agreement between two parties to exchange an asset for a fixed price at a future date. The agreement is made on a futures exchange, however, and is regulated by that exchange. The contract requires that the parties make margin deposits, and their accounts are marked to market every day. The contracts are standardized and can be bought and sold during regular trading hours. These differences between forward and futures contracts, particularly the marking to market, create some differences in their

CHAPTER OBJECTIVES

- Introduce the basic concepts of price and value for futures and forward contracts

- Show the conditions under which futures and forward prices are equivalent and when they are different

- Show how the spot price of an asset is determined from the cost of storage, the net interest, and the risk premium

- Present the cost of carry formula for the theoretical fair price of futures and forward contracts

- Introduce the concepts of contango, backwardation, and convenience yield

- Present the two opposing views to the question of whether futures prices reward speculators with a risk premium

- Illustrate how intermediate cash flows such as dividends affect the cost of carry model

- Present put-call-forward/ futures parity

- Present the principles of pricing options on futures

prices and values. As we shall see later, these differences may prove quite minor; for now, we shall proceed as though forward and futures contracts were entirely different instruments.

GENERIC CARRY ARBITRAGE

In this section, our goal is to illustrate the basic principles of pricing forward and futures contracts without reference to any specific type of contract. Unique contract characteristics lead to complexities that are best deferred until the fundamental principles of pricing are understood. Thus, in this section, the underlying asset is not identified. It is simply a generic asset.

Concept of Price versus Value

In Chapter 1, we discussed how an efficient market means that the price of an asset equals its true economic value. The holder of an asset has money tied up in the asset. If the holder is willing to retain the asset, the asset must have a value at least equal to its price. If the asset's value were less than its price, the owner would sell it. The value is the present value of the future cash flows, with the discount rate reflecting the opportunity cost of money and a premium for the risk assumed.

Although this line of reasoning is sound in securities markets, it can get one into trouble in forward and futures markets. A forward or futures contract is not an asset. You can buy a futures contract, but do you actually pay for it? A futures contract requires a small margin deposit, but is this really the price? You can buy 100 shares of a $20 stock by placing $1,000 in a margin account and borrowing $1,000 from a broker. Does that make the stock worth $10 per share? Certainly not. The stock is worth $20 per share: You have $10 per share invested and $10 per share borrowed.

The margin requirement on a futures contract is not really a margin in the same sense as the margin on a stock. You might deposit, for example, 3 percent of the price of the futures contract in a margin account, but you do not borrow the remainder. The margin is only a type of security deposit. Thus, the buyer of a futures contract does not actually "pay" for it, and, of course, the seller really receives no money for it. As long as the price does not change, neither party can execute an offsetting trade that would generate a profit. As noted previously, a forward contract may or may not require a margin deposit or some type of credit enhancement, but if it does, the principle is still the same: The forward price is not the margin.

When dealing with forward and futures contracts, we must be careful to distinguish between the **forward or futures price** and the **forward or futures value**. The price is an observable number. The value is less obvious. But fortunately, the value of a forward or futures contract at the start is easy to determine. That value is simply zero. This is because neither party pays anything and neither party receives anything of monetary value. That does not imply, however, that neither party will pay or receive money at a later date. The values of futures and forward contracts during their lives, however, are not necessarily equal to each other or to zero.

The confusion over price and value could perhaps be avoided if we thought of the forward or futures price as a concept more akin to the exercise price of an option. We know that the exercise price does not equal an option's value. It simply represents the figure that the two parties agreed will be the price paid by the call buyer or received by the put buyer if the option is ultimately exercised. In a similar sense, the futures or forward price is simply the figure that the two parties have agreed will be paid by the buyer to the seller at expiration in exchange for the underlying asset. This price is sometimes called the "delivery price." Although we could call the forward price or the futures price the "exercise price" of the contract, the use of the terms *forward price* and *futures price* or *delivery price* is so traditional that it would be unwise not to use them.

Let us now proceed to understand how the values and prices of forward and futures contracts are determined. First, we need some notation. We let $V_t(0,T)$ and $v_t(T)$ represent the values of forward and futures contracts at time t that were created at time 0 and expire at time T. Similarly, $F(0,T)$ and $f_t(T)$ are the prices at time t of forward and futures contracts created at time 0 that expire at time T. Because a forward price is fixed at a given time, conditional on the expiration date, the price does not change and, therefore, does not require a time subscript. Also, because a futures price does change, it does not matter when the contract was established.

> The value of a futures contract when written is zero.

Value of a Forward Contract

> The value of a forward contract when written is zero.

Given our statement above that the value of each contract is zero when established, we can initially say that $V_0(0,T) = 0$ and $v_0(T) = 0$.

Forward Price at Expiration The first and most important principle is that the price of a forward contract that is created at expiration must be the spot price. Such a contract will call for delivery, an instant later, of the asset. Thus, the contract is equivalent to a spot transaction, and its price must, therefore, equal the spot price. Thus, we can say that

$$F(T,T) = S_T.$$

> The price of a forward contract that expires immediately is the spot price.

If this statement were not true, it would be possible to make an immediate arbitrage profit by either buying the asset and selling an expiring forward contract or selling the asset and buying an expiring forward contract.

Value of a Forward Contract at Expiration At expiration, the value of a forward contract is easily found. Ignoring delivery costs, the value of a forward contract at expiration, $V_T(0,T)$, is the profit on the forward contract. The profit is the spot price minus the original forward price. Thus,

$$V_T(0,T) = S_T - F(0,T).$$

> The value of a forward contract at expiration is the spot price minus the original forward price.

When you enter into a long forward contract with a price of $F(0,T)$, you agree to buy the asset at T, paying the price $F(0,T)$. Thus, your profit will be $S_T - F(0,T)$. This is the value of owning the forward contract. At the time the contract was written, the contract had zero value. At expiration, however, anyone owning a contract permitting him or her to buy an asset worth S_T by paying a price $F(0,T)$ has a guaranteed profit of $S_T - F(0,T)$. Thus, the contract has a value of $S_T - F(0,T)$. Of course, this value can be either positive or negative. The value to the holder of the short position is simply minus one times the value to the holder of the long position.

Value of a Forward Contract Prior to Expiration Before we begin, let us take note of why it is important to place a value on the forward contract. If a firm enters into a forward contract, the contract does not initially appear on the balance sheet. Although it may appear in a footnote, the contract is not an asset or a liability; so there is no place to put it on the balance sheet. During the life of the forward contract,

TABLE 9.1   VALUING A FORWARD CONTRACT PRIOR TO EXPIRATION

PORTFOLIO	COMPOSITION	VALUE AT 0	VALUE AT t	VALUE AT T
A	Long forward contract established at 0 at price of F(0,T)	0	$V_t(0,T)$	$S_T - F(0,T)$
B	Long position in asset and loan of $F(0,T)(1 + r)^{-(T-t)}$ established at t	N/A	$S_t - F(0,T)(1 + r)^{-(T-t)}$	$S_T - F(0,T)$

Conclusion: The value of portfolio A at t must equal the value of portfolio B at t.
$$V_t(0, T) = S_t - F(0, T)(1 + r)^{-(T-t)}$$

however, value can be created or destroyed as a result of changing market conditions. For example, we already saw that the forward contract has a value at expiration of $S_T - F(0,T)$, which can be positive or negative. To give a fair assessment of the assets and liabilities of the company, it is important to determine the value of the contract before expiration. If that value is positive, the contract can be properly viewed and recorded as an asset; if that value is negative, the contract should be viewed and recorded as a liability. Investors should be informed about the values of forward contracts and, indeed, all derivatives so that they can make informed decisions about the impact of derivative transactions on the overall value of the firm.

> The value of a forward contract prior to expiration is the spot price minus the present value of the forward price.

Table 9.1 illustrates how we determine the value. As we did in valuing options, we construct two portfolios that obtain the same value at expiration. Portfolio A is a forward contract constructed at time 0 at the price F(0,T). It will pay off $S_T - F(0,T)$ at expiration, time T. To construct portfolio B, we do nothing at time 0. At time t, we know that the spot price is S_t and that a forward contract that was established at time 0 for delivery of the asset at T was created at a price of F(0,T). We buy the asset and borrow the present value of F(0,T), with the loan to be paid back at T. Thus, the value of our position is $S_t - F(0,T)(1 + r)^{-(T-t)}$. At T, we sell the asset for S_T and pay back the loan amount, F(0,T). Thus, the total value at T is $S_T - F(0,T)$. This is the same as the value of portfolio A, which is the forward contract. Thus, the value of portfolio B at t must equal the value of the forward contract, portfolio A, at t. Hence,

$$V_t(0,T) = S_t - F(0,T)(1 + r)^{-(T-t)}.$$

It is intuitive and easy to see why this is the value of the forward contract at t. If you enter into the contract at time 0, when you get to time t, you have a position that will require you to pay F(0,T) at time T and will entitle you to receive the value of the asset at T. The present value of your obligation is $F(0,T)(1 + r)^{-(T-t)}$. The present value of your claim is the present value of the asset, which is its current price of S_t.

Numerical Example   Suppose you buy a forward contract today at a price of $100. The contract expires in 45 days. The risk-free rate is 10 percent. The forward contract is an agreement to buy the asset at $100 in 45 days. Now 20 days later, the spot price of the asset is $102. The value of the forward contract with 25 days remaining is then

$$102 - 100(1.10)^{-25/365} = 2.65.$$

In other words, at time T, we are obligated to pay $100 in 25 days, but we shall receive the asset, which has a current value of $102.

Price of a Forward Contract

In this section, we consider the initial price of a forward contract. As noted previously, we use the notation F(0,T) for the forward price. We have already noted that the price of a forward contract when originally written is zero; hence, we can set the forward contract price equation at time 0 equal to 0,

$$V_0(0,T) = S_0 - F(0,T)(1 + r)^{-T} = 0.$$

Solving for the forward price, we have

$$F(0,T) = S_0(1 + r)^T.$$

Therefore, the price of a forward contract on a generic asset is simply the future price of the current spot price of the asset, where the future price is obtained by grossing up the spot price by the risk-free interest rate. The forward price is seen as the price that forces the contract price to equal zero at the start. This valuation method is known as the **carry arbitrage model** or **cost of carry model** because the forward price depends only on the carrying costs related to the underlying asset. In this case, the forward price depends on the finance carrying costs. In subsequent sections, we will examine unique aspects of forward pricing for different forward contracts such as stock indices, currencies, and commodities.

> The price of a forward contract is the spot price compounded to the expiration at the risk-free rate. It is the price that guarantees that the forward contract has a price at the start of zero.

Value of a Futures Contract

In this section, we shall consider the valuation of futures contracts. As noted previously, we shall use $f_t(T)$ for the futures price and $v_t(T)$ for the value of a futures contract. Let us recall that a futures contract is marked to market each day. We have already established that the value of a futures contract when originally written is zero.

Futures Price at Expiration   The instant at which a futures contract is expiring, its price must be the spot price. In other words, if you enter into a long futures contract that will expire an instant later, you have agreed to buy the asset an instant later, paying the futures price. This is the same as a spot transaction. Thus,

$$f_T(T) = S_T.$$

> The price of a futures contract that expires immediately is the spot price.

If this statement were not true, buying the spot and selling the futures or selling the spot and buying the futures would generate an arbitrage profit.

Value of a Futures Contract during the Trading Day but before Being Marked to Market   When we looked at forward contracts, the second result we obtained was the value of a forward contract at expiration. In the case of futures contracts, it is more useful to look at how one values a futures contract before it is marked to market. In other words, what is a futures contract worth during the trading day?

Suppose we arbitrarily let the time period between settlements be one day. Suppose you purchase a futures contract at $t - 1$ when the futures price is $f_{t-1}(T)$. Let us assume that this is the opening price of the day and that it equals the settlement price the previous day. Now let us assume that we are at the end of the day, but the market is not yet closed. The price is $f_t(T)$. What is the value of the contract? If you sell the contract, it

> The value of a futures contract during a trading day but before it is marked to market is the amount by which the price changed since the contract was opened or last marked to market, whichever comes later.

MAKING THE CONNECTION

When Forward and Futures Contracts Are the Same

Assuming no possibility of default, there are several conditions under which forward and futures contracts produce the same results at expiration and, therefore, would have the same prices. First, recall that forward contracts settle their payoffs at expiration. Given the price of the underlying at expiration of S_T and the price entered into when the contract is established, the holder of a long position would have a payoff of

$$S_T - F(0,T).$$

This, as we noted, is the value of the forward contract at expiration. A futures contract is written at a price that changes every day. Thus, if a futures expiring at time T is established at time 0 at a price of $f_0(T)$, the price at the end of the next day will be $f_1(T)$. The following day the price is $f_2(T)$, and this continues until it settles at expiration at $f_T(T)$, which is the spot price, S_T. The last mark to market profit is $f_T(T) - f_{T-1}(T)$. We see that these contracts clearly have different cash flow patterns as summarized below:

Day	Futures Cash Flow	Forward Cash Flow
0	0	0
1	$f_1(T) - f_0(T)$	0
2	$f_2(T) - f_1(T)$	0
3	$f_3(T) - f_2(T)$	0
...		
T − 2	$f_{T-2}(T) - f_{T-3}(T)$	0
T − 1	$f_{T-1}(T) - f_{T-2}(T)$	0
T	$f_T(T) - f_{T-1}(T) = S_T - f_{T-1}(T)$	$S_T - F(0,T)$

We want to know whether the original futures price, $f_0(T)$, would equal the original forward price, $F(0,T)$. Thus, we now look at the conditions under which they will be equal.

The futures price will equal the forward price one day prior to expiration. This should be obvious. Look at the table of cash flows for futures and forward contracts created one day prior to expiration.

Day	Futures Cash Flow	Forward Cash Flow
T − 1	0	0
T	$f_T(T) - f_{T-1}(T) = S_T - f_{T-1}(T)$	$S_T - F(T-1,T)$

The futures price, $f_{T-1}(T)$, would have to equal the forward price, $F(T-1,T)$, because neither contract requires an outlay at the start, day T−1. Both contracts require the payment of an amount of cash, $f_{T-1}(T)$ for the futures and $F(T-1, T)$ for the forward, at time T, and both contracts produce the amount, S_T, at T. These amounts paid at T would have to be the same; otherwise, one could sell the contract requiring the higher payment and buy the contract requiring the lower payment to generate a sure positive payoff without paying anything.

The futures price will equal the forward price two days (or more) prior to expiration if the interest rate one day ahead is known in advance. Suppose we initiate futures and forward contracts at the end of day T − 2. We hold the position through the end of day T−1 and then to the end of day T. Let r_1 be the interest rate one day prior to expiration, which is assumed to be known two days prior to expiration. We assume that these are daily rates; so to obtain one day's interest, we just multiply by 1 − r, that is, without using an exponent. Let us do the following transactions two days prior to expiration:

Go long one forward contract at the price $F_{T-2}(T)$.
Sell $1/(1 - r_1)$ futures contracts at the price $f_{T-2}(T)$

Now move forward to the end of day T − 1:

The forward contract will have no cash flow. Buy back the futures for a gain or loss of $-(f_{T-1}(T) - f_{T-2}(T))$. Multiplying by the number of contracts gives an amount of $-[1/(1 + r_1)][f_{T-1}(T) - f_{T-2}(T)]$. Compound this value forward for one day, which means reinvesting at r_1 if this is a gain or financing at r_1 if this is a loss. Then sell one new futures at a price of $f_{T-1}(T)$.

Now, at expiration, we have the following results:

The forward contract will pay off $S_T - F(0,T)$.

The value of the previous day's gain or loss reinvested for one day is

$$-[1/1(1 + r_1)][f_{T-1}(T) - f_{T-2}(T)][1 + r_1]$$
$$= -(f_{T-1}(T) - f_{T-2}(T)).$$

The mark to market profit or loss from the single futures contract is

$$-(f_T(T) - f_{T-1}(T)) = -(S_T - f_{T-1}(T)).$$

The total is

$$S_T - F(0, T) - (f_{T-1}(T) - f_{T-2}(T)) - (S_T - f_{T-1}(T))$$
$$= f_{T-2}(T) - F(0, T).$$

When the contracts were first established, these two prices were known because they were the prices at which the contracts were entered. Thus, this strategy will produce a known amount at expiration. Because there were no initial cash flows, this cash flow at expiration has to be zero. Otherwise, one could sell the higher-priced contract and buy the lower-priced contract. This would require no cash outlay at the start but would produce a positive cash flow at expiration. Thus, the futures price would have to equal the forward price.

If the interest rate one day ahead is not known, this strategy will not be feasible. In that case, the correlation between futures prices and interest rates can tell us which price will be higher, although it will not tell us by how much one price will exceed the other. This point is discussed in this chapter.

generates a gain of $f_t(T) - f_{t-1}(T)$. Thus, we can say that the value of the futures contract is

$$v_t(T) = f_t(T) - f_{t-1}(T) \text{ before the contract is marked to market.}$$

The value of the futures contract is simply the price change since the time the contract was opened or, if it was opened on a previous day, the last price change since marking to market. Note, of course, that the value could be negative. If we were considering the value of the futures to the holder of the short position, we would simply change the sign.

As soon as a futures contract is marked to market, its value is zero.

Value of a Futures Contract Immediately after Being Marked to Market   When a futures contract is marked to market, the price change since the last marking to market or, if the contract was opened during the day, the price change since it was opened is distributed to the party in whose favor the price moved and is charged to the party whom the price moved against. This, of course, is the mark to market procedure. As soon as the contract is marked to market, the value of the contract reverts to zero. Thus,

$$v_t(T) = 0 \text{ as soon as the contract is marked to market.}$$

If the futures price was still at the last settlement price and the futures trader then tried to sell the contract to capture its value, it would generate no profit, which is consistent with its zero value.

Thus, to summarize these two results, we find that the value of a long futures contract at any point in time is the profit that would be generated if the contract were sold. Because of the daily marking to market, the value of a futures contract reverts to zero as soon as it is marked to market. The value for the holder of a short futures contract is minus one times the value for the holder of the long futures contract. For a long futures contract, value is created by positive price changes; for a short futures contract, value is created by negative price changes.

Price of a Futures Contract

In this section, we consider the initial price of a futures contract. As noted previously, we use $f_t(T)$ for the futures price. We have already noted that the value of a futures contract when originally written is zero. Assuming that the mark to market feature of futures contracts does not impact its current price, then

$$f_t(T) = F(0,T) = S_0(1 + r)^T.$$

> The price of a futures contract is the spot price compounded to the expiration at the risk-free rate and, therefore, is the same as the forward price.

Therefore, the price of a generic futures contract is the same as that of a generic forward contract. It is important to note, however, that this result assumes no marking to market. In the next section, we explore the implications of marking to market on pricing futures contracts.

Forward versus Futures Prices

At expiration, forward and futures prices equal the spot price, but there are also a few other conditions under which they are equal. First, however, let us assume that there is no default risk. Now consider the case of one day prior to expiration. A futures contract that has only one day remaining will be marked to market the next day, which is at the expiration. The forward contract will be settled at expiration. Thus, the forward and futures contracts have the same cash flows and are, effectively, the same contract.

If we back up two days prior to expiration, the comparison is more difficult. Suppose that we make the assumption that the risk-free interest rate is either the same on both days or that we know one day what the rate will be the next day. Hence, we effectively rule out any interest rate uncertainly. In that case, it can be shown that the forward price will equal the futures price.

> Forward and futures prices will be equal at expiration, one day before expiration, and they will be equal prior to expiration if interest rates are certain or if futures prices and interest rates are uncorrelated.

If we do not assume interest rate certainty, we can argue heuristically which price will be higher. If interest rates are positively correlated with futures prices, an investor holding a long position will prefer futures contracts over forward contracts, because futures contracts will generate mark to market profits during periods of rising interest rates and incur mark to market losses during periods of falling interest rates. This means that gains will be reinvested at higher rates and losses will be incurred when the opportunity cost is falling. Futures contracts would, therefore, carry higher prices than forward contracts. If interest rates are negatively correlated with futures prices, an investor holding a long position will prefer forward contracts over futures contracts because the marking to market of futures contracts will be disadvantageous. Then forward contracts would carry higher prices. If interest rates and futures prices are uncorrected, forward and futures contracts will have the same prices.

Of course, as we have previously noted, forward contracts are subject to default and futures contracts are guaranteed against default by the clearinghouse. Default risk can also affect the difference between forward and futures prices. It would seem that if forward contract buyers (sellers) faces more risk of default than forward contract sellers (buyers), the forward price would be pushed down (up). The forward market, however, does not typically incorporate credit risk into the price. As we shall cover in Chapter 15, virtually all qualifying participants in over-the-counter markets pay/receive the same price. Parties with greater credit risk pay in the form of collateral or other credit-enhancing measures. Hence, we are not likely to observe differences in forward and futures prices due to credit issues.

By not observing any notable differences in forward and futures prices, we can reasonably assume that forward prices are the same as futures prices. Thus, the remaining material in this chapter, while generally expressed in terms of futures prices, will also apply quite reasonably to forward prices.

CARRY ARBITRAGE WHEN UNDERLYING GENERATES CASH FLOWS

Until now, we have avoided any consideration of how intermediate cash flows such as interest and dividends affect forward and futures prices. We did note earlier in this chapter that these cash payments would have an effect on the cost of carry, possibly making it negative. Now we shall look more closely at how they affect forward and futures prices. The examples will be developed in the context of futures contracts. Note also that, in this section, we are no longer focusing on a generic asset. We will be examining contracts on specific types of assets, the characteristics of which give rise to cash flows to the holder of the asset.

Stock Indices and Dividends

We shall start here by assuming that our futures contract is a single stock futures, although the general principles are the same for stock index futures. For example, we could consider a portfolio that contains only one stock. In either case, assume that this stock pays a sure dividend of D_T on the expiration date. Now suppose that an investor buys the stock at a spot price of S_0 and sells a futures contract at a price of $f_0(T)$.

At expiration, the stock is sold at S_T, the dividend D_T is collected, and the futures contract generates a cash flow of $-(f_T(T) - f_0(T))$, which equals $-(S_T - f_0(T))$. Thus, the total cash flow at expiration is $D_T + f_0(T) = -(S_T - f_0(T)) + S_T + D_T$. This amount is known in advance; therefore, the current value of the portfolio must equal the present value of $D_T + f_0(T)$. The current portfolio value is simply the amount paid for the stock, S_0. Putting these results together gives

$$S_0 = (f_0(T) + D_T)(1 + r)^{-T},$$

or

$$f_0(T) = S_0(1 + r)^T - D_T.$$

Here we see that the futures price is the spot price compounded at the risk-free rate minus the dividend. Note that a sufficiently large dividend could bring the futures price down below the spot price.

To take our model one step closer to reality, let us assume that the stock pays several dividends. In fact, our underlying could actually be a portfolio of stocks that is identical to an index such as the S&P 500. Suppose that N dividends will be paid during the life of the futures. Each dividend is denoted as D_j and is paid t_j years from today. Now suppose we buy the stock and sell the futures. During the life of the futures, we collect each dividend and reinvest it in risk-free bonds earning the rate r. Thus, dividend D_1 will grow to a value of $D_1(1 + r)^{T-t_j}$ at expiration. By the expiration day, all dividends will have grown to a value of

$$\sum_{j=1}^{N} D_j(1 + r)^{T-t_j},$$

which we shall write compactly as D_T. Thus, now we let D_T be the accumulated value at T of all dividends over the life of the futures plus the interest earned on them. In the previous example, we had only one dividend, but D_T was still the same concept, the accumulated future value of the dividends. At expiration, the stock is sold for S_T and the futures is settled and generates a cash flow of $-(f_T(T) - f_0(T))$, which equals $-(S_t - f_0(T))$. Thus, the total cash flow at expiration is

$$S_T - (S_T - f_0(T)) + D_T,$$

or

$$f_0(T) + D_T.$$

This amount is also known in advance; so its present value, discounted at the risk-free rate, must equal the current value of the portfolio, which is the value of the stock, S_0. Setting these terms equal and solving for $f_0(T)$ gives

$$f_0(T) = S_0(1 + r)^T - D_T.$$

Thus, the futures price is the spot price compounded at the risk-free rate minus the compound future value of the dividends. The entire process of buying the stock, selling a futures, and collecting and reinvesting dividends to produce a risk-free transaction is illustrated in Figure 9.1 for a stock that pays two dividends during the life of the futures. The total value accumulated at expiration is set equal to the total value today.

As an alternative to compounding the dividends, we can instead find the present value of the dividends and subtract this amount from the stock price before compounding it at the risk-free rate. In other words, the present value of the dividends over the life of the contract would be

$$D_0 = \sum_{j=1}^{N} D_j(1 + r)^{-t_j}.$$

The futures pricing formula would then be

$$f_0(T) = (S_0 - D_0)(1 + r)^T.$$

This approach is the one we took when pricing options. In fact, we encountered the concept of the present value of the dividends in Chapters 3, 4, and 5. We subtracted the

FIGURE 9.1 The Cost of Carry Model with Stock Index Futures

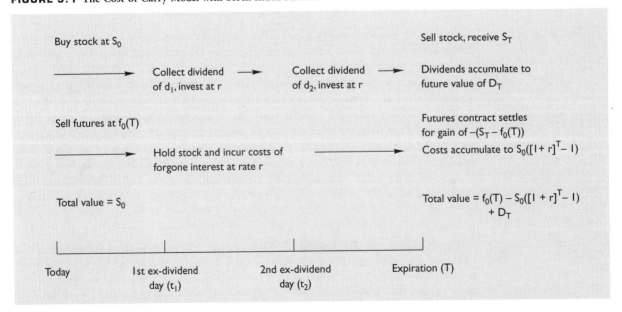

present value of the dividends from the stock price and used the stock price in the options pricing model. We do the same here: subtract the present value of the dividends and insert this adjusted stock price into the futures pricing model.

A stock index is a weighted combination of securities, most of which pay dividends. In reality, the dividend flow is more or less continuous, although not of a constant amount. As we did with options, however, we can fairly safely assume a continuous flow of dividends at a constant yield, δ_c. Using r_c as the continuously compounded risk-free rate and S_0 as the spot price of the index, the model is written as

$$f_0(T) = S_0 e^{(r_c - \delta_c)T}.$$

It is worth noting that this formula is precisely what one would obtain if all of the assumptions of the Black-Scholes-Merton model were applied to futures.

> A stock index futures price is the stock price compounded to expiration at the risk-free rate minus the future value of the dividends. Alternatively, it can be viewed as the dividend-adjusted stock price compounded to expiration at the risk-free rate.

This format makes an interpretation somewhat easier. Suppose an investor is considering speculating on the stock market. There are two ways to do this: buy the stock index portfolio or buy the futures contract. If the portfolio is purchased, the investor receives dividends at a rate of δ_c. If the futures contract is purchased, the investor receives no dividends. The dividend yield enters the model as the factor $e^{\delta_c T}$, which is less than 1. Thus, the effect of dividends is to make the futures price lower than it would be without them. Note that the futures price will exceed (be less than) the spot price if the risk-free rate is higher (lower) than the dividend yield. Alternatively, the formula can be written as $f_0(T) = (S_0 e^{-\delta_c T}) e^{r_c T}$, which can be interpreted as the dividend-adjusted stock price compounded at the risk-free rate.

Numerical Example Consider the following problem: A stock index is at 50, the continuously compounded risk-free rate is 8 percent, the continuously compounded dividend yield is 6 percent, and the time to expiration is 60 days; so T is 60/365 = 0.164. Then the futures price is

$$f_0(T) = 50 e^{(0.08 - 0.06)(0.164)} = 50.16.$$

If the risk-free rate were 5 percent, the futures price would be

$$f_0(T) = 50 e^{(0.05 - 0.06)(0.164)} = 49.92.$$

In Chapter 10, we shall see how arbitrage forces the market to adjust when the price does not equal the price given by the cost of carry model.

Most of the volume in futures contracts on equities is in stock index futures. There are, however, futures contracts on certain individual stocks. These contracts have traded outside the United States for several years and began trading in the United States in the fall of 2002. In the United States, most individual stocks pay dividends on a quarterly basis. Outside the United States, individual stocks tend to pay dividends once or twice a year. In either case, pricing futures on individual stocks would typically be done by incorporating the value of the individual dividends into the calculation. In other words, the same general approach presented here for pricing futures on stock indices would apply for pricing futures on individual stocks, but the use of discrete dividends would be more appropriate for futures on individual stocks.

Earlier in the chapter, we learned that the valuation of a forward contract is determined by subtracting the present value of the forward price that was established when the contract was originated from the spot price. We then learned how to price forward contracts on assets that make cash payments. To value a forward contract on an asset that pays cash dividends, we must make an adjustment. If the spot asset makes cash payments such as discrete dividends, we simply adjust the spot price to eliminate the present value of the cash payments.

$$V_t(0,T) = S_t - D_{t,T} - F(0,T)(1 + r)^{-(T-t)},$$

where $D_{t,T}$ is the present value from t to T of any remaining dividends. For a continuous dividend yield, we have

$$V_t(0,T) = S_t e^{-\delta_c(T-t)} - F(0,T)e^{-r_c(T-t)},$$

The value of a stock index futures contract is the stock price minus the present value of the dividends minus the present value of the forward price.

where we observe that all of the discounting is done using the continuous form.

The basic idea behind pricing futures on a stock or stock index is generally applicable to pricing futures on bonds that pay coupons. But in practice, futures contracts based on bonds have certain features that complicate pricing beyond what we intend to cover in this chapter. These instruments are, however, covered in great detail in Chapter 10.

Foreign Currencies and Foreign Interest Rates: Interest Rate Parity

Interest rate parity is an important fundamental relationship between the spot and forward exchange rates and the interest rates in two countries. It is the foreign currency market's version of the carry arbitrage forward and futures pricing model. A helpful way to understand interest rate parity is to consider the position of someone who believes that a higher risk-free return can be earned by converting to a currency that pays a higher interest rate. For example, suppose that a French corporate treasurer wants to earn more than the euro interest rate and believes that he can convert euros to dollars and earn the higher U.S. rate. If the treasurer does so but fails to arrange a forward or futures contract to guarantee the rate at which the dollars will be converted back to euros, he runs the risk not only of not earning the U.S. rate, but also of earning less than the euro rate. If the dollar weakens while he is holding dollars, the conversion back to euros will be costly. This type of transaction is similar to going to a foreign country but not buying your ticket home until after you have been there a while. You are subject to whatever rates and conditions exist at the time you purchase the return ticket. Buying a round-trip ticket locks in the return price and conditions. Hence, the corporate treasurer might want to lock in the rate at which the dollars can be converted back to euros by selling a forward or futures contract on the dollar. But forward and futures prices will adjust so that the overall transaction will earn no more in euros than the euro interest rate. In effect, the cost of the return ticket will offset any interest rate gains while in the foreign currency. If it does not, there are arbitrage profits to be earned that will force prices to adjust appropriately. Consider the following situation involving euros and U.S. dollars, observed from the perspective of a European.

The spot exchange rate is S_0. This quote is in euros per U.S. dollar. The U.S. risk-free interest rate is ρ, and the holding period is T. You take $S_0(1 + \rho)^{-T}$ euros and buy $(1 + \rho)^{-T}$ dollars. Simultaneously, you sell one forward contract expiring at time T. The forward exchange rate is F_0, which is also in euros per dollar. You take your $(1 + \rho)^{-T}$ dollars and invest them in U.S. T-bills that have a return of ρ.

When the forward contract expires, you will have one dollar. This is because your $(1 + \rho)^{-T}$ dollars will have grown by the factor $(1 + \rho)^T$, so $(1 + \rho)^{-T}(1 + \rho)^T = 1$. Your forward contract obligates you to deliver the dollar, for which you receive $F(0,T)$

euros. In effect, you have invested $S_0(1 + \rho)^{-T}$ and received $F(0,T)$ euros. Because the transaction is riskless, your return should be the euro rate, r; that is,

$$F(0,T) = S_0(1 + r)^{-T}(1 + r)^T.$$

Interest rate parity, the relationship between futures or forward and spot exchange rates, is determined by the relationship between the risk-free interest rates in the two countries.

This relationship is called *interest rate parity*.[1] It is sometimes expressed as

$$F(0,T) = S_0(1 + r)^T / (1 + \rho)^T.$$

Numerical Example Consider the following example from a European perspective. On June 9 of a particular year, the spot rate for dollars was 0.7908 euros. The U.S. interest rate was 5.84 percent, while the euro interest rate was 3.59 percent. The time to expiration was $90/365 = 0.2466$. Recall that we have

$$F(0,T) = €0.7908(1.0584)^{-0.2466}(1.0359)^{0.2466} = 0.7866 \text{ euros}.$$

Thus, the forward rate should be about 0.7866 euros.

Interest rate parity can be confusing to some people because of the difference in the way the rates can be quoted. You may also see interest rate parity stated as $F(0,T) = S_0(1 + \rho)^T (1 + r)^{-T}$. This is correct if the spot rate is quoted in units of the foreign currency. In our euro example, we could have stated the spot rate as $1/€ 0.7908 = 1.2645$ dollars per euro. In that case, the forward rate would be stated in dollars per euro and the formula would be correctly given as $F(0,T) = S_0(1 + \rho)^T (1 + r)^{-T}$, with ρ being the foreign rate and r being the domestic rate. An easy way to remember this is that the factor for the interest rate for a given country multiplies by the spot quote stated in that country's currency. The other interest rate factor then appears with the $-T$ in the exponent or simply in the denominator to the power T.

As we noted earlier in the chapter, when a forward rate is quoted in units of the domestic currency (e.g., the dollar quoted per euros), when the forward rate is higher than the spot rate, the forward rate is said to be at a premium. Because the word *premium* tends to imply something higher, we have another reason to quote the currency in terms of the domestic currency. Had we quoted it the other way, a higher forward rate would have implied a discount.

It has become common in discussions of international finance to interpret a forward premium (discount) as implying that the currency is expected to strengthen (weaken). Unfortunately, this is a mistaken belief. The principle of arbitrage is what gives rise to a forward premium or discount. If a person could convert his or her domestic currency to a foreign currency, lock in a higher risk-free return, and convert back with the currency risk hedged, everyone would do this, which would erase any possibility of being able to earn a return better than the domestic risk-free rate. Any forward premium or discount is caused strictly by a difference in the interest rates of the two countries. If the domestic rate is lower and one forgoes the domestic risk-free return to earn the higher foreign risk-free return, the currency must sell at a forward rate proportional to the relative interest earned and given up. This has nothing to do with what people expect the spot rate to do in the future. People may have quite different beliefs about what might happen to spot rates, but we know they would agree that the forward rate must align with the spot rate by the proportional interest factors—or, in other words, by interest rate parity.

---

[1] There are also several common variations of this formula. It is sometimes approximated as $F(0,T) = S_0(1 + r - \rho)^T$ and sometimes as $F(0,T) = S_0(1 + rT)/(1 + \rho T)$, where T is days/360 or 365. The latter formula would be the case if r and ρ were in the form of LIBOR as discussed in previous chapters. Interest is added to the principal in the form of $1 + r(180/360)$. If the interest rates are continuously compounded, the formula would be $F(0,T) = S_0 e^{(r_c - \rho_c)T}$.

Although currency futures contracts are not traded as heavily as currency forwards, interest rate parity is also applicable to pricing those instruments, at least under the assumptions we have made here. Therefore,

$$f_0(T) = S_0(1 + r)^T / (1 + \rho)^T.$$

The value of currency forward contracts, following the same approach used with stock index forwards, is

> The value of a foreign currency forward contract is the spot exchange rate discounted at the foreign interest rate minus the present value of the forward exchange rate.

$$V_t(0,T) = S_t(1 + \rho)^{-(T-t)} - F(0, T)(1 + r)^{-(T-t)},$$

where ρ is the foreign interest rate.

Commodities and Storage Costs

In this section, we consider commodity futures contracts and the impact of storage costs. For simplicity, assume that the storage cost for holding the underlying commodity, s, is paid at the end of the period. Now suppose that an investor buys the commodity at a spot price of S_0 and sells a futures contract at a price of $f_0(T)$.

At expiration, the commodity is sold at S_T; the storage cost, s, is paid; and the futures contract generates a cash flow of $-(f_T(T) - f_0(T))$, which equals $-(S_T - f_0(T))$. Thus, the total cash flow at expiration is $-s + f_0(T)$. This amount is known in advance; therefore, the current value of the portfolio must equal the present value of $-s + f_0(T)$. The current portfolio value is simply the amount paid for the commodity, S_0. Putting these results together gives

$$S_0 = (f_0(T) - s)(1 + r)^{-T},$$

> The price of a commodity futures contract is the spot price compounded to expiration at the risk-free rate plus the storage costs.

or

$$f_0(T) = S_0(1 + r)^T + s.$$

TECHNICAL NOTE: Generalizing the Cost of Carry Model
go to www.cengagebrain.com

Here we see that the futures price is the spot price compounded at the risk-free rate plus the storage costs. We will explore commodity futures in more detail when risk premiums are discussed next.

PRICING MODELS AND RISK PREMIUMS

In this section, we make the connection between forward or futures contract pricing and risk premiums. Recall from Chapter 1 (and other courses you may have taken) that a risk premium is the additional return expected in order to justify taking on the risk. You may already be familiar with asset pricing models, such as the famous Capital Asset Pricing Model, which give the relationship between expected return and risk. In this section, we want to determine whether futures and forward contracts provide risk premiums to parties that take positions in these contracts.

In the previous section, we saw that forward and futures prices can differ but that the differences are usually quite small. To make things sound a little smoother, we shall stop referring to these contracts as both forward and futures contracts and simply refer to them as futures contracts. We shall assume that marking to market is done only on the expiration day, thus making a futures contract essentially a forward contract.

Before exploring risk premiums with futures contracts, let us review a few principles for determining spot prices from risk premiums and carry arbitrage.

Spot Prices, Risk Premiums, and Carry Arbitrage for Generic Assets

Let us first establish a simple framework for valuing generic spot assets. Let S_0 be the spot price, s be the cost of storing the asset over a period of time from 0 to T, and iS_0 be the interest forgone on S_0 dollars invested in the asset over that period of time.

Let us assume that there is no uncertainly of the future asset price. Then, we can say with certainty that S_T will be the asset price at T. Thus, the current price of the asset would have to be

$$S_0 = S_T - s - iS_0.$$

Under certainty, today's spot price equals the future spot price minus the cost of storage and the interest forgone.	In other words, the asset price today would simply be the future price less the cost of storage and interest. No one would pay more than this amount because storage and interest costs would wipe out any profit from holding it. No one would sell it for less than this amount because someone would always be willing to pay more, up to the amount given in the above formula.

If we relax the assumption of a certain future asset price, then we must use the expected future asset price, $E(S_T)$. If investors are risk neutral, however, they will be willing to hold the asset without any expectation of receiving a reward for bearing risk. In that case,

$$S_0 = E(S_T) - s - iS_0.$$

Under uncertainty and risk neutrality, today's spot price equals the expected future spot price minus the cost of storage and the interest forgone.	In other words, the price today is the expected future price less the storage and interest costs.

Most investors, however, are risk averse and consequently would not pay this much for the asset. They would pay a smaller amount, the difference being the risk premium. Let us denote that risk premium by $E(\phi)$. Then the current price would be |

$$S_0 = E(S_T) - s - iS_0 - E(\phi).$$

Under uncertainty and risk aversion, today's spot price equals the expected future spot price minus the storage costs minus the interest forgone minus the risk premium.	In other words, in the real world of risk-averse investors, the current spot price is the expected future spot price less any storage costs less the interest forgone less the risk premium.

This statement is quite general and does not tell us anything about how the risk premium is determined. For financial assets, there are few, if any, storage costs, but in that case, we just set s = 0. The above statement is a powerful reminder that asset prices must reflect expectations, the costs of ownership—both explicit and implicit—and a reward for bearing risk. |

Let us make one final refinement. Recall that we discussed futures and forward contracts in which the underlying pays a cash return. Now let us make that assumption again, this time with the cash return being in the form of interest or a dividend. Let us capture this effect by reducing the interest opportunity cost by any such cash flows paid by the asset. So from now on, let us remember that iS_0 is the interest forgone less any cash flow—interest or dividends—received. We shall call this the **net interest**. Note that if the dividend or coupon interest rate is high enough, it can exceed the interest opportunity cost, making i negative. This is not a problem and is, in fact, not all that rare. When a bond with a high coupon rate is held in an environment in which rates are low, the net interest can easily be negative.

The cost of carry is the storage cost and the net interest and represents the cost incurred in storing an asset.	The combination of storage costs and net interest, $s + iS_0$, is referred to as the **cost of carry** and is denoted with the Greek symbol θ (theta). The cost of carry is positive if the cost of storage exceeds the net interest and negative if the net interest is negative and large enough to offset the cost of

storing. Sometimes, however, this concept is referred to as the **carry**. An asset that has a negative cost of carry, meaning that the net interest is a net inflow and exceeds the cost of storage, is said to have positive carry. An asset that has a positive cost of carry is said to have negative carry. For our purposes in this book, we shall refer to the concept as strictly the cost of carry.

For nonstorable goods such as electricity, there would not necessarily be a relationship between today's spot price and the expected future spot price. Supply and demand conditions today and in the future would be independent. The risk of uncertain future supplies could not be reduced by storing some of the good currently owned. Large price fluctuations likely would occur. The cost of carry would be a meaningless concept.

At the other extreme, a commodity might be indefinitely storable. Stocks, metals, and some natural resources such as oil are indefinitely or almost indefinitely storable. Their spot prices would be set in accordance with current supply and demand conditions, the cost of carry, investors' expected risk premia, and expected future supply and demand conditions.

For many agricultural commodities, limited storability is the rule. Grains have a fairly long storage life, while frozen concentrated orange juice has a more limited life. In the financial markets, Treasury bills, which mature in less than a year, have a short storage life. Treasury bonds, with their longer maturities, have a much longer storage life.

For any storable assets, the spot price is related to the expected future spot price by the cost of carry and the expected risk premium. We shall use this relationship to help explain forward and futures pricing.

Forward/Futures Pricing Revisited

Based on this chapter's previous discussions, we expand now our examination of forward and futures pricing. In particular, we explore some practical considerations such as the margin or other collateral requirements and the notion of convenience yield. Consider the following transaction: You buy the spot asset at a price of S_0 and sell a futures contract at a price of $f_0(T)$. At expiration, the spot price is S_T and the futures price is $f_T(T)$, which equals S_T. At expiration, you deliver the asset. The profit on the transaction is $f_0(T) - S_0$ minus the storage costs incurred and the opportunity cost of the funds tied up:

$$\Pi = f_0(T) - S_0 - s - iS_0 = f_0(T) - S_0 - \theta.$$

Because the expression $f_0(T) - S_0 - \theta$ involves no unknown terms, the profit is riskless, meaning the transaction should not generate a risk premium. The amount invested is S_0, the original price of the spot asset. The profit from the transaction is $f_0(T) - S_0 - \theta$, which should equal zero. Thus,

$$f_0(T) = S_0 + \theta.$$

The futures price equals the spot price plus the cost of carry. The cost of carry, therefore, is the difference between the futures price and the spot price and is related to the basis.[2] We shall say much more about the basis in Chapter 11.

> In equilibrium, the futures price equals the spot price plus the cost of carry.

An alternative interpretation of this transaction is shown in Figure 9.2. The value of the position when initiated is S_0; the value at expiration is $f_0(T) - \theta$. Because $f_0(T) - \theta$ is known when the transaction is initiated, the transaction is risk-free. So S_0

---

[2]The basis is usually defined as the spot price minus the futures price, and we shall use this definition in Chapter 11.

FIGURE 9.2 Buy Asset, Sell Futures, and Store Asset

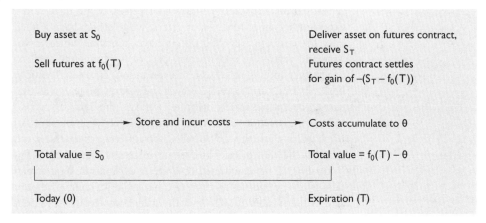

should equal the present value of $f_0(T) - \theta$ using the risk-free rate. But the present value adjustment has already been made because θ includes the interest lost on S_0 over the holding period. Thus,

$$f_0(T) = S_0 + \theta.$$

What makes this relationship hold? Assume that the futures price is higher than the spot price plus the cost of carry:

$$f_0(T) > S_0 + \theta.$$

Arbitrageurs will then buy the spot asset and sell the futures contract. This will generate a positive profit equal to $f_0(T) - S_0 - \theta$. Many arbitrageurs will execute the same transaction, which will put downward pressure on the futures price. When $f_0(T) = S_0 + \theta$, the opportunity to earn this profit will be gone.

Now suppose the futures price is less than the spot price plus the cost of carry; that is,

$$f_0(T) < S_0 + \theta.$$

First, let us assume that the asset is a financial instrument. Then arbitrageurs will sell short the asset and buy the futures. When the instrument is sold short, the short seller will not incur the storage costs. Instead of incurring the opportunity cost of funds tied up in the asset, the short seller can earn interest on the funds received from the short sale. We shall examine arbitrage transactions in more detail in Chapter 10.

Thus, the cost of carry is not paid but received. The profit thus is $S_0 + \theta - f_0(T)$, which is positive. The combined actions of arbitrageurs will put downward pressure on the spot price and upward pressure on the futures price until the profit is eradicated. At that point, $f_0(T) = S_0 + \theta$.

Short selling may not actually be necessary for inducing the arbitrage activity. Consider an investor who holds the asset unhedged. That person could sell the asset and buy a futures contract. While the asset is not owned, the arbitrageur avoids the storage costs and earns interest on the funds received from its sale. At expiration, the arbitrageur takes delivery and again owns the asset unhedged. The profit from the transaction is $S_0 + \theta - f_0(T)$, which is positive. Thus, the transaction temporarily removes the asset from the investor's total assets, earns a risk-free profit, and then replaces the asset in the investor's total assets. Because many arbitrageurs will do this, it will force the spot price down and the futures price up until no further opportunities exist. This transaction is called **quasi arbitrage**.

There has been some confusion, even among experts, over whether futures prices reflect expectations about future spot prices. Some have said that futures prices provide expectations about future spot prices, while others have argued that futures prices reflect only the cost of carry. Still others have said that futures reveal expectations part of the time and reveal the cost of carry part of the time. We shall more fully address the issue of whether futures prices reveal expectations in a later section; here we should note that both positions are correct. Because the futures price equals the spot price plus the cost of carry, the futures price definitely reflects the cost of carry. The spot price, however, reflects expectations. This is a fundamental tenet of spot pricing. Because the futures price will include the spot price, it too reflects expectations; however, it does so indirectly through the spot price. The overall process is illustrated in Figure 9.3.

So far, we have assumed that the small margin requirement imposed on futures traders is zero. Suppose now in the transaction involving the purchase of the asset at S_0 and sale of the futures at $f_0(T)$ that the trader was required to deposit M dollars in a margin account. Let us assume that the M dollars will earn interest at the risk-free rate. Then at expiration, the trader will have delivered the asset and received an effective price of $f_0(T)$ and have incurred the cost of carry of θ. In addition, the trader will be able to release the

FIGURE 9.3 How Futures Prices Are Determined

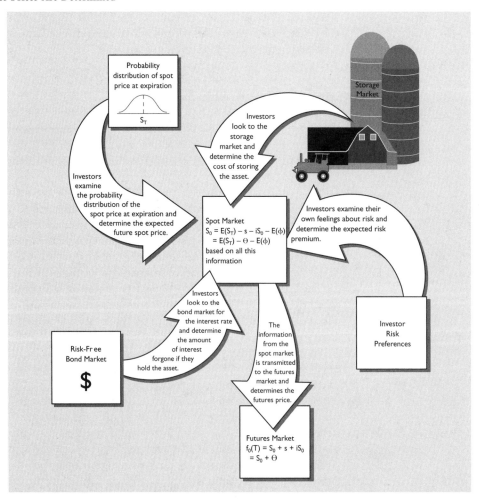

Probability distribution of spot price at expiration

S_T

Investors examine the probability distribution of the spot price at expiration and determine the expected future spot price.

Investors look to the storage market and determine the cost of storing the asset.

Storage Market

Spot Market
$S_0 = E(S_T) - s - iS_0 - E(\phi)$
$= E(S_T) - \theta - E(\phi)$
based on all this information

Investors examine their own feelings about risk and determine the expected risk premium.

Investors look to the bond market for the interest rate and determine the amount of interest forgone if they hold the asset.

Risk-Free Bond Market

$

The information from the spot market is transmitted to the futures market and determines the futures price.

Investor Risk Preferences

Futures Market
$f_0(T) = S_0 + s + iS_0$
$= S_0 + \theta$

TABLE 9.2 AN EXAMPLE OF A CONTANGO MARKET

COTTON (NEW YORK COTTON EXCHANGE)

EXPIRATION	SETTLEMENT PRICE (CENTS PER POUND)
Spot (September 26)	36.75
October	41.60
December	42.05
March	42.77
May	43.50
July	43.80
October	45.20
December	45.85

margin deposit of M dollars plus the interest on it. Because the total value at expiration, $f_0(T) - \theta + M +$ interest on M, is known in advance, the overall transaction remains risk-free. On the front end, however, the trader put up S_0 dollars to buy the asset and M dollars for the margin account. The present value of the total value at expiration should, therefore, equal $S_0 + M$. Obviously, the present value of M plus the interest on M equals M. This means that S_0 must still equal $f_0(T) - \theta$, giving us our cost of carry model, $f_0(T) = S_0 + \theta$. If, however, interest is not paid on the margin deposit, the futures price can be affected by the loss of interest on the margin account. How the futures price is affected is not clear because the trader who does the reverse arbitrage, selling or selling short the asset and buying the futures, also faces the same margin requirement. Does it really matter? Probably not. Large traders typically are able to deposit interest-bearing securities. The price we observe is almost surely being determined by large traders. So it seems reasonable to assume that the margin deposit is irrelevant to the pricing of futures.

For storable assets as well as for securities that do not pay interest or dividends, the cost of carry normally is positive. This would cause the futures price to lie above the current spot price. A market of this type is referred to as a **contango**.

In a contango market, the futures price exceeds the spot price.

Table 9.2 presents some spot and futures prices from a contango market. The example is for cotton traded on the New York Cotton Exchange. The cost of carry implied for the October contract is $41.60 - 36.75 = 4.85$.

Remember that this figure includes the interest forgone on the investment of 36.75 cents for a pound of cotton and the actual physical costs of storing the cotton from late September until the contract's expiration in October.

It would be convenient if fact always conformed to theory. If that were the case, we would never observe the spot price in excess of the futures price. In reality, spot prices sometimes exceed futures prices. A possible explanation is the convenience yield.

Convenience Yield We are seeking an explanation for the case in which the futures price is less than the spot price. If $f_0(T) = S_0 + \theta$ and $f_0(T) < S_0$, then $\theta < 0$. What type of market condition might produce a negative cost of carry?

Suppose the commodity is in short supply; current consumption is unusually high relative to supplies of the good. This is producing an abnormally high spot price. The current tight market conditions discourage individuals from storing the commodity. If the situation is severe enough, the current spot price could be above the expected future spot price. If the spot price is sufficiently high, the futures price may lie below it. The relationship between the futures price and the spot price is then given as

$$f_0(T) = S_0 + \theta - \chi,$$

The convenience yield is the additional return earned by holding a commodity in short supply or a nonpecuniary gain from an asset.

where χ (chi) is simply a positive value that accounts for the difference between $f_0(T)$ and $S_0 + \theta$. If χ is sufficiently large, the futures price will lie below the spot price. This need not be the case, however, because χ can be small.

The value χ often is referred to as the **convenience yield**. It is the premium earned by those who hold inventories of a commodity that is in short supply. By holding inventories of a good in short supply, one could earn an additional return, the convenience yield. Note that we are not saying that the commodity is stored for future sale or consumption. Indeed, when the spot price is sufficiently high, the return from storage is negative. There is no incentive to store the good. In fact, there is an incentive to borrow as much of the good as possible and sell short.

For some assets, a convenience yield can be viewed as a type of nonpecuniary return. For example, consider a person who owns a house, which usually offers some potential for price appreciation but the expected gain is rarely sufficient to compensate for the risk involved. In some cases, the expected gain may be no more or even less than the risk-free rate. The house, however, provides a nonpecuniary yield, which is the utility from living in the house. The buyer of the house is normally willing to pay more, thereby reducing the expected return, for the right to live in the house.

When the commodity has a convenience yield, the futures price may be less than the spot price plus the cost of carry. In that case, the futures is said to be at **less than full carry**.

In a backwardation market, the spot price exceeds the futures price.

A market in which the futures price lies below the current spot price is referred to as **backwardation** or sometimes an **inverted market**. An example of a backwardation market is presented in Table 9.3.

This example is taken from a day in the month of November. Because there is a November futures contract, the price of this contract is a good proxy for the spot price. Note that the November futures price of 563.25 is higher than all of the other futures prices. Clearly in this case, there is a convenience yield associated with the spot price. Soybeans are probably in short supply, but this shortage is likely to be alleviated over the next year because all of the futures prices are clearly below the spot price and the cost of carry.

TABLE 9.3 AN EXAMPLE OF A BACKWARDATION MARKET

SOYBEANS (CHICAGO BOARD OF TRADE)	
EXPIRATION	**PRICE (CENTS PER BUSHEL)**
November	563.25
January	558.50
March	552.75
May	545.75
July	543.25
August	536.50
September	520.50
November	502.25

TABLE 9.4 AN EXAMPLE OF A SIMULTANEOUS BACKWARDATION AND CONTANGO MARKET

SOYBEAN MEAL (CHICAGO BOARD OF TRADE)	
EXPIRATION	**PRICE (CENTS PER BUSHEL)**
Spot (November 8)	159.50
December	163.50
January	164.40
March	164.80
May	163.00
July	162.40
August	161.10
September	158.30
October	154.90
December	155.10
January	154.10

It is not uncommon to see characteristics of both backwardation and contango in a market at the same time. Table 9.4 shows this case for soybean meal from an example taken in November. Note that the spot price is lower than the December contract price, which is lower than the January contract price. Note, however, that the May contract price is lower than the March contract price. This downward pattern continues, and the prices of all contracts expiring in September of the following year or later are lower than the spot price.

Another factor that can produce backwardation in commodity markets is the inability to sell the commodity short and the reluctance on the part of holders of the commodity to sell it when its price is higher than it should be and replace it with an underpriced long futures contract. In the previous section, we referred to this as quasi arbitrage. If quasi arbitrage is not executed in sufficient volume to bring the futures price to its theoretical fair price, then we could see backwardation. The spot price becomes too high, and no one is willing to sell the asset and replace it with a futures contract or no one is able to sell short the asset.

Of course for financial assets, the cost of storage is negligible and the supply of the commodity is fairly constant. Yet we still often observe an inverted market. For interest-sensitive assets such as Eurodollars and Treasury bonds, either backwardation or contango can be observed. Later in this chapter, we shall look at some other reasons financial futures prices can be below spot prices.

With these concepts in mind, we now turn to an important and highly controversial issue in futures markets: Do futures prices contain a risk premium?

Futures Prices and Risk Premia

We have already discussed the concept of a risk premium in spot prices. No one would hold the spot commodity for purely speculative reasons unless a risk premium was expected. Although investors do not always earn a risk premium, they must expect to do so on average. Is there a risk premium in futures prices? Are speculators in futures contracts rewarded, on average, with a risk premium? There are two schools of thought on the subject.

No Risk Premium Hypothesis Consider a simple futures market in which there are only speculators. The underlying commodity is the total amount of snowfall in inches in Vail, Colorado, in a given week. The contracts are cash settled at expiration. Individuals can buy or sell contracts at whatever price they agree on. Similar derivatives exist on the over-the-counter market.

For example, suppose two individuals make a contract at a price of 30. If the total snowfall is above 30 at expiration, the trader holding the short position pays the holder of the long position a sum equal to the total snowfall minus 30. Although the ski resorts and merchants have exposures highly correlated with the level of snowfall, no one can actually "hold" the commodity; so there is no hedging or arbitrage.

Now suppose that after a period of several weeks, it is obvious that the longs are consistently beating the shorts. The shorts conclude that it is a good winter for skiing. Determined to improve their lot, those individuals who have been going short begin to go long. Of course, those who have been going long have no desire to go short. Now everyone wants to go long, and no one will go short. This drives up the futures price to a level at which someone finds it so high that it looks good to go short. Now suppose the price has been driven up so high that the opposite occurs: The shorts begin to consistently beat the longs. This causes the longs to turn around and go short. Ultimately, an equilibrium must be reached in which neither the longs nor the shorts consistently beat the other side. In such a market, there is no risk premium. Neither side wins at the expense of the other.

> If the futures price does not contain a risk premium, then speculators are not rewarded for taking on risk. Futures prices will then be unbiased expectations of future spot prices.

In futures markets, this argument means that on average, the futures price today equals the expected price of the futures contract at expiration; that is, $f_0(T) = E(f_T(T))$. Because the expected futures price at expiration equals the expected spot price at expiration, $E(f_T(T)) = E(S_T)$, we obtain the following result:

$$f_0(T) = E(S_T).$$

This is an extremely important and powerful statement. It says that *the futures price is the market's expectation of the future spot price.* If one wants to obtain a forecast of the future spot price, one need only observe the futures price. In the language of economists, *futures prices are unbiased expectations of future spot prices.*

As an example, on September 26 of a particular year, the spot price of silver was $5.58 per troy ounce. The December futures price was $5.64 per troy ounce. If futures prices contain no risk premium, the market is forecasting that the spot price of silver in December will be $5.64. Futures traders who buy the contract at $5.64 expect to sell it at $5.64.

Figure 9.4 illustrates a situation that is reasonably consistent with this view. The May wheat futures contract is shown, along with the spot price for a period of 20 weeks prior to expiration. Both prices fluctuate, and the spot price exhibits a small risk premium, as suggested by the slight upward trend.[3] The futures price, however, follows no apparent trend.

We must caution, of course, that this is just an isolated case. The question of whether futures prices contain a risk premium must be answered by empirical studies. First, however, let us turn to the arguments supporting the view that futures prices do contain a risk premium.

Asset Risk Premium Hypothesis If a risk premium were observed, we would see that

$$E(f_T(T)) > f_0(T).$$

---

[3]The upward drift, however, could also be due to the risk-free rate or possibly the storage costs.

FIGURE 9.4 An Example of No Risk Premium: May Wheat

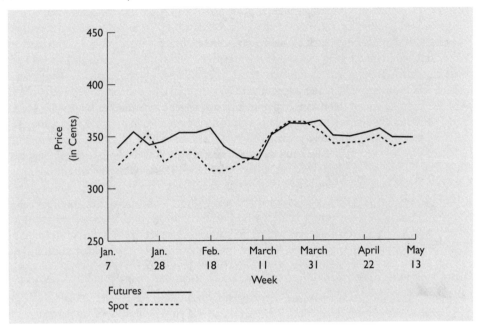

The futures price would be expected to increase. Buyers of futures contracts at price $f_0(T)$ would expect to sell them at $E(f_T(T))$. Because futures and spot prices should converge at expiration, $E(f_T(T)) = E(S_T)$,

$$E(f_T(T)) = E(S_T) > f_0(T).$$

From this, we conclude that the futures price is a low estimate of the expected future spot price.

Consider a contango market in which the cost of carry is positive. Holders of the commodity expect to earn a risk premium, $E(\phi)$, given by the following formula covered earlier in this chapter:

$$E(S_T) = S_0 + \theta + E(\phi),$$

where θ is the cost of carry and $E(\phi)$ is the risk premium. Because $f_0(T) = S_0 + \theta$, then $S_0 = f_0(T) - \theta$. Substituting for S_0 in the formula for $E(S_T)$, we get

$$E(S_T) = f_0(T) - \theta + \theta + E(\phi),$$

or simply

$$E(S_T) = f_0(T) + E(\phi) = E(f_T(T)).$$

The expected futures price at expiration is higher than the current futures price by the amount of the risk premium. This means that buyers of futures contracts expect to earn a risk premium. They do not, however, earn a risk premium because the futures contract is risky. They earn the risk premium that existed in the spot market; it was merely transferred to the futures market.

Now consider the silver example in the previous section. The spot price is $5.58, and the December futures price is $5.64. The interest lost on $5.58 for two months is about $0.05. Let us assume that the cost of storing silver for two months is $0.01.

Let us also suppose that buyers of silver expect to earn a $0.02 risk premium. Thus, the variables are

$$S_0 = 5.58$$
$$f_0(T) = 5.64$$
$$\theta = 0.05 + 0.01 = 0.06$$
$$E(\phi) = 0.02.$$

The expected spot price of silver in December is

$$E(S_T) = S_0 + \theta + E(\phi) = 5.58 + 0.06 + 0.02 = 5.66.$$

Because the expected spot price of silver in December equals the expected futures price in December, $E(f_T(T)) = 5.66$. This can also be found as

$$E(f_T(T)) = f_0(T) + E(\phi) = 5.64 + 0.02 = 5.66.$$

Futures traders who buy the contract at 5.64 expect to sell it at 5.66 and earn a risk premium of 0.02. The futures price of 5.64 is an understatement of the expected spot price in December by the amount of the risk premium. The process is illustrated as follows:

Spot:	Buy silver $5.58	Store and incur costs + $0.06	Expected risk premium + $0.02	Expected selling price = $5.66
Futures:	Buy silver futures $5.64		Expected risk premium + $0.02	Expected selling price = $5.66

> If the futures price contains a risk premium, then speculators will be rewarded for taking on risk. Futures prices will then be biased expectations of future spot prices.

The idea that futures prices contain a risk premium was proposed by two famous economists: Keynes (1930) and Hicks (1939). They argued that futures and spot markets are dominated by individuals who hold long positions in the underlying commodities. These individuals want the protection afforded by selling futures contracts. That means that they need traders who are willing to take long positions in futures. To induce speculators to take long positions in futures, the futures price must be below the expected price of the contract at expiration, which is the expected future spot price. Keynes and Hicks argued, therefore, that *futures prices are biased expectations of future spot prices*, with the bias attributable to the risk premium. This perspective is known as the **risk premium hypothesis**. Based on the carry arbitrage model, the risk premium in futures prices exists only because it is transferred from the spot market.

An example of such a case is shown in Figure 9.5, which illustrates a June S&P 500 futures contract. Both the spot and futures prices exhibit an upward trend.[4] Again, however, we must caution that this is only an isolated case.

How can we explain the existence of a risk premium when we argued earlier that neither longs nor shorts would consistently win at the expense of the other? The major difference in the two examples is the nature of the spot market. In the first example in which the futures contract was on snowfall, there was no opportunity to take a "position" in the spot market. In fact, there was no spot market; futures traders were simply competing with one another in a pure gambling situation. When we allow for a spot

---

[4]Again the upward drift in the spot price could be due to the risk-free rate.

FIGURE 9.5 An Example of a Risk Premium: S&P 500 Futures and Spot

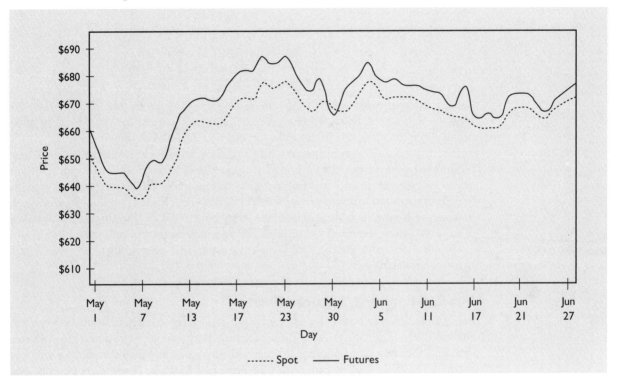

market, we introduce individuals who hold speculative long positions in commodities. If the positions are unhedged, these individuals expect to earn a risk premium. If they are unwilling to accept the risk, they sell futures contracts. They are, in effect, purchasing insurance from the futures traders, and in so doing, they transfer the risk and the risk premium to the futures markets.

This explanation is useful in seeing why futures markets should not be viewed as a form of legalized gambling. There are probably no greater risk takers in our society than farmers. They risk nearly all of their wealth on the output of their farms, which are subject to the uncertainties of weather, government interference, and foreign competition, not to mention the normal fluctuations of supply and demand. Farmers can lay off some or all of that risk by hedging in the futures markets. In so doing, they transfer the risk to parties willing to bear it. Yet no one would call farming legalized gambling. Nor would anyone criticize pension fund portfolio managers for gambling when they purchase stocks. Futures markets, and indeed all derivative markets, serve a purpose in facilitating risk transfer from parties not wanting it to parties willing to take it—for a price.

What about situations in which the hedgers buy futures? This would occur if hedgers were predominantly short the commodity. This would drive up futures prices, and futures prices would, on average, exhibit a downward trend as contracts approached expiration. Futures prices would overestimate future spot prices. Speculators who sold futures would earn a risk premium.

A market in which the futures price is below the expected future spot price is called **normal backwardation**, and a market in which the futures price is above the expected future spot price is called **normal contango**. The choice of names for these markets is a bit confusing, and they must be distinguished from simply contango and backwardation.

$$\text{Contango: } S_0 < f_0(T)$$
$$\text{Backwardation: } f_0(T) < S_0$$
$$\text{Normal Contango: } E(S_T) < f_0(T)$$
$$\text{Normal Backwardation : } f_0(T) < E(S_T)$$

Because the spot price can lie below the futures price, which in turn can lie below the expected future spot price, we can have contango and normal backwardation simultaneously. We can also have backwardation and normal contango simultaneously.

Which view on the existence of a risk premium is correct? Because there is almost certainly a risk premium in spot prices, the existence of hedgers who hold spot positions means that the risk premium is transferred to futures traders. Thus, there would seem to be a risk premium in futures prices. If there are not enough spot positions being hedged, however, or if most hedging is being done by investors who are short in the spot market, there may be no observable risk premium in futures prices. Empirical studies have given us no clear-cut answer and suggest that the issue is still unresolved.

TECHNICAL NOTE: Futures Risk Premium

go to www.cengagebrain.com

Put-Call-Forward/Futures Parity

Recall from Chapter 3 that we examined put-call parity: the relationship between put and call prices and the price of the underlying stock, the exercise price, the risk-free rate, and the time to expiration. We derived the equation by constructing a risk-free portfolio. Now we shall examine **put-call-forward/futures parity** with puts, calls, and forward or futures contracts. To keep things as simple as possible, we shall assume that the risk-free rate is constant. This allows us to ignore marking to market and treat futures contracts as forward contracts. We assume that the options are European.

The first step in constructing a risk-free portfolio is to recognize that if the exercise price is set to the futures price, a combination of a long call and a short put is equivalent to a (long) futures contract. In fact, a long-call/short-put combination is called a **synthetic futures contract**. A risk-free portfolio would consist of a long futures contract and a short synthetic futures contract. Selling the synthetic futures contract requires selling a call and buying a put.

Consider the portfolios illustrated in Table 9.5. We construct two portfolios, A and B. Examining the payoffs at expiration reveals that a long futures and a long put is equivalent to a long call and long risk-free bonds with a face value of the difference between the exercise price (X) and the futures price ($f_0(T)$). If $f_0(T)$ is greater than X, as it could

TABLE 9.5 PUT-CALL-FORWARD/FUTURES PARITY

PORTFOLIO	CURRENT VALUE	PAYOFFS FROM PORTFOLIO GIVEN STOCK PRICE AT EXPIRATION	
		$S_T \leq X$	$S_T > X$
A. Futures	0	$S_T - f_0(T)$	$S_T - f_0(T)$
Put	$P_e(S_0,T,X)$	$\dfrac{X - S_T}{X - f_0(T)}$	$\dfrac{0}{S_T - f_0(T)}$
B. Call	$C_e(S_0,T,X)$	0	$S_T - X$
Bonds	$(X - f_0(T))(1 + r)^{-T}$	$\dfrac{X - f_0(T)}{X - f_0(T)}$	$\dfrac{X - f_0(T)}{S_T - f_0(T)}$

easily be, then instead of long bonds, you will take out a loan for the present value of $f_0(T) - X$, promising to pay back $f_0(T) - X$ when the loan matures at the options' expiration. With equivalent payoffs, the value of portfolio A today must equal the value of portfolio B today. Thus,

$$P_e(S_0,T,X) = C_e(S_0,T,X) + (X - f_0(T))(1 + r)^{-T}.$$

We can, of course, write this several other ways, such as

$$C_e(S_0,T,X) - P_e(S_0,T,X) = (f_0(T) - X)(1 + r)^{-T}.$$

Notice that whether the put price exceeds the call price depends on whether the exercise price exceeds the futures price. If the parity is violated, it may be possible to earn an arbitrage profit. Of course, futures can be replaced with forwards under our assumptions.

> Put-call-futures parity is the relationship between the prices of puts, calls, and futures on an asset. With minimal assumptions, futures can be replaced by forwards.

Numerical Example   A good instrument for examining put-call-forward/futures parity is the S&P 500 index options and futures. The options are European and trade on the CBOE, while the futures trade on the Chicago Mercantile Exchange. Suppose on May 14 the S&P 500 index was 1337.80 and the June futures was at 1339.30. The June 1340 call was at 40, and the put was at 39. The expiration date was June 18, and the risk-free rate was 4.56 percent.

Because there are 35 days between May 14 and June 18, the time to expiration is $35/365 = 0.0959$. The left-hand side of the first put-call-futures parity equation is

$$P_e(S_0,T,X) = 39.$$

The right-hand side is

$$C_e(S_0,T,X) + (X - f_0(T))(1 + r)^{-T}$$
$$= 40 + (1340 - 1339.30)(1.0456)^{-0.0959}$$
$$= 40.70.$$

Thus, if you bought the put and futures, paying 39, and sold the call and the bond, receiving 40.70, the two portfolios would offset at expiration. So there is no risk and yet you earn a net gain of $40.70 - 39 = 1.70$. Of course, transaction costs might consume the difference.

PRICING OPTIONS ON FUTURES

In this section, we shall look at some principles of pricing options on futures. These principles are closely related to the principles of pricing ordinary options that were established in Chapters 3, 4, and 5 but also tie in with the principles of pricing futures contracts, as covered in this chapter. We will make the assumptions that the options and the futures contracts expire simultaneously and that the futures price equals the forward price.

Intrinsic Value of an American Option on Futures

The minimum value of an American call on a futures is its intrinsic value. We can formally state this as

$$C_a(f_0(T),T,X) \geq \text{Max}(0, f_0(T) - X),$$

where $\text{Max}(0, f_0(T) - X)$ is the intrinsic value. It is easy to see that this statement must hold for options on futures in the same way as options on the spot. If the call price is

> The intrinsic value of an American call option on a futures is the greater of zero or the difference between the futures price and the exercise price.

less than the intrinsic value, the call can be bought and exercised. This establishes a long position in a futures contract at the price of X. The futures is immediately sold at the price of $f_0(T)$, and a risk-free profit is made.

Consider a March 1390 S&P 500 option on futures. The underlying futures price is 1401. The intrinsic value is $Max(0, 1401 - 1390) = 11$. The call is actually worth 49.20. The difference of $49.20 - 11 = 38.20$ is the time value. Like the time value on an option on the spot, the time value here decreases as expiration approaches. At expiration, the call must sell for its intrinsic value.

The intrinsic value of an American put option on futures establishes its minimum value. This is stated as

$$P_a(f_0(T),T,X) \geq Max(0, X - f_0(T)),$$

> The intrinsic value of an American put option on a futures is the greater of zero or the difference between the exercise price and the futures price.

where $Max(0, X - f_0(T))$ is the intrinsic value. Again, if this is not true, the arbitrageur can purchase the futures contract and the put, immediately exercise the put, and earn a risk-free profit.

The March 1405 S&P 500 put option on futures was priced at 44.60. The futures price was 1401. The minimum value is $Max(0, 1405 - 1401) = 4$. The difference between the put price, 44.60, and the intrinsic value, 4, is the time value, 40.60. The time value, of course, erodes as expiration approaches. At expiration, the put is worth the intrinsic value.

Lower Bound of a European Option on Futures

The intrinsic values apply only to American options on futures. This is because early exercise is necessary to execute the arbitrage. As you should recall from our study of options on stocks, we can establish a lower bound for a European option.

Let us first look at the call option on futures. We construct two portfolios, A and B. Portfolio A consists of a single long position in a European call. Portfolio B consists of a long position in the futures contract and a long position in risk-free bonds with a face value of $f_0(T) - X$. Note that if X is greater than $f_0(T)$, this is actually a short position in bonds and thus constitutes a loan in which we pay back $X - f_0(T)$ at expiration. We do not really care whether we are borrowing or lending. As long as we keep the signs correct, we will obtain the desired result in either case. Table 9.6 presents the outcomes of these portfolios.

If $f_T(T) \leq X$, the call expires worthless. The futures contract is worth $f_T(T) - f_0(T)$, and the bonds are worth $f_0(T) - X$; thus, portfolio B is worth $f_T(T) - X$. If $f_T(T) > X$, the call is worth $f_T(T) - X$, the intrinsic value, and portfolio B is still worth $f_T(T) - X$.

TABLE 9.6 THE LOWER BOUND OF A EUROPEAN CALL OPTION ON FUTURES: PAYOFFS AT EXPIRATION OF PORTFOLIOS A AND B

PORTFOLIO	INSTRUMENT	CURRENT VALUE	PAYOFFS FROM PORTFOLIO GIVEN FUTURES PRICE AT EXPIRATION	
			$f_T(T) \leq X$	$f_T(T) > X$
A	Long call	$C_e(f_0(T),T,X)$	0	$f_T(T) - X$
B	Long futures	0	$f_T(T) - f_0(T)$	$f_T(T) - f_0(T)$
	Bond	$(f_0(T) - X)(1 + r)^{-T}$	$\dfrac{+f_0(T) - X}{f_T(T) - X}$	$\dfrac{+f_0(T) - X}{f_T(T) - X}$

As you can see, portfolio A does at least as well as portfolio B in all cases; therefore, its current value should be at least as high as portfolio B's. We can state this as

$$C_e(f_0(T),T,X) \geq (f_0(T) - X)(1 + r)^{-T}.$$

Because an option cannot have negative value,

$$C_e(f_0(T),T,X) \geq Max[0, (f_0(T) - X)(1 + r)^{-T}].$$

The price of a European call option on a futures contract must at least equal the greater of zero or the present value of the difference between the futures price and the exercise price.

Note that we used an important result from earlier in this chapter: The value of a futures contract when initially established is zero. Thus, portfolio B's value is simply the value of the risk-free bonds.

This result establishes the lower bound for a European call on the futures. Remember that a European call on the spot has a lower bound of

$$C_e(S_0,T,X) \geq Max[0, S_0 - X(1 + r)^{-T}].$$

As we saw earlier in this chapter, in the absence of dividends on the spot instrument, the futures price is

$$f_0(T) = S_0(1 + r)^T.$$

Making this substitution for $f_0(T)$, we see that these two lower bounds are equivalent. In fact, if the option and futures expire simultaneously, a European call on a futures is equivalent to a European call on the spot. This is because a European call can be exercised only at expiration, at which time the futures and spot prices are equivalent.

As an example of the lower bound, let us look at the March 1390 S&P 500 call option on futures on January 31 of a leap year. The option expires on March 16; thus, there are 45 days remaining and $T = 45/365 = 0.1233$. The futures price is 1401. The risk-free rate is 5.58 percent. The lower bound is

$$C_e(f_0,T,X) \geq Max[0, (1401 - 1390)(1.0558)^{-0.1233}] = 10.93.$$

The actual call price is 49.20.

Note, however, that the lower bound established here is slightly less than the intrinsic value of 11. This should seem unusual. For ordinary equity options, the lower bound of $Max[0, S_0 - X(1 + r)^{-T}]$ exceeds the intrinsic value of $Max(0, S_0 - X)$. For options on futures, however, this is not necessarily so. As we shall see in a later section, this explains why some American call (and put) options on futures are exercised early.

Now let us look at the lower bound for a European put option on a futures. Again, we shall establish two portfolios, A and B. Portfolio A consists of a long position in the put. Portfolio B consists of a short position in the futures contract and a long position in risk-free bonds with a face value of $X - f_0(T)$. Again, if $f_0(T)$ is greater than X, this is actually a short position in bonds, or taking out a loan. Table 9.7 illustrates the current value and future payoff of each portfolio.

By now, you should be able to explain each outcome. If $f_T(T) < X$, the put is exercised; so portfolio A is worth $X - f_T(T)$. If $f_T(T) \geq X$, the put expires worthless. In both cases, the futures contract in portfolio B is worth $-(f_T(T) - f_0(T))$ and the bonds are worth $X - f_0(T)$, for a total of $X - f_T(T)$. Portfolio A does at least as well as portfolio B. Thus, the current value of A should be at least as great as the current value of B,

$$P_e(f_0(T),T,X) \geq (X - f_0(T))(1 + r)^{-T}.$$

The price of a European put option on a futures must at least equal the greater of zero or the present value of the difference between the exercise price and the futures price.

Because the option cannot have a negative value,

$$P_e(f_0(T),T,X) \geq Max[0, (X - f_0(T))(1 + r)^{-T}].$$

TABLE 9.7   THE LOWER BOUND OF A EUROPEAN PUT OPTION ON FUTURES: PAYOFFS AT EXPIRATION OF PORTFOLIOS A AND B

PORTFOLIO	INSTRUMENT	CURRENT VALUE	PAYOFFS FROM PORTFOLIO GIVEN FUTURES PRICE AT EXPIRATION	
			$f_T(T) < X$	$f_T(T) \geq X$
A	Long put	$P_e(f_0(T),T,X)$	$X - f_T(T)$	0
B	Short futures	0	$-(f_T(T) - f_0(T))$	$-(f_T(T) - f_0(T))$
	Bond	$+(X - f_0(T))(1 + r)^{-T}$	$\dfrac{+X - f_0(T)}{X - f_T(T)}$	$\dfrac{+X - f_0(T)}{X - f_T(T)}$

As we saw with calls, we can substitute S_0 for $f_0(T)(1 - r)^{-T}$ and see that the lower bound for a put option on a futures is the same as that for a put option on the spot. As is true for calls, European put options on futures in which the put and the futures expire simultaneously are equivalent to options on the spot.

As an example, let us look at the March 1405 S&P 500 put option on futures on January 31, 2000. The futures price is 1401, the time to expiration is 0.1233, and the risk-free rate is 5.58 percent. The lower bound is

$$P_e(f_0(T),T,X) \geq \text{Max}[0, (1405 - 1401)(1.0558)^{-0.1233}] = 3.97.$$

The actual price of the put is 44.60. As we saw for equity puts, the European lower bound will be less than the American intrinsic value. Thus, the actual minimum price of this American put is its intrinsic value of $1405 - 1401 = 4$.

Put-Call Parity of Options on Futures

We have looked at put-call parity for options on stocks. We can also establish a put-call parity rule for options on futures.

First, let us construct two portfolios, A and B. Portfolio A will consist of a long futures and a long put on the futures. This can be thought of as a protective put. Portfolio B will consist of a long call and a long bond with a face value of the exercise price minus the futures price. If X is greater than $f_0(T)$, this is indeed a long position in a bond. If $f_0(T)$ is greater than X, then we are simply issuing bonds with a face value of $f_0(T) - X$. In either case, the cash flow of the bond will be $X - f_0(T)$ when it matures on the option expiration day. The payoffs are illustrated in Table 9.8.

As we can see, the two portfolios produce the same result. If the futures price ends up less than the exercise price, both portfolios end up worth $X - f_0(T)$. If the futures price ends up greater than the exercise price, both portfolios end up worth $f_T(T) - f_0(T)$. Thus,

TABLE 9.8   PUT-CALL PARITY OF OPTIONS ON FUTURES

PORTFOLIO	INSTRUMENT	CURRENT VALUE	PAYOFFS FROM PORTFOLIO GIVEN FUTURES PRICE AT EXPIRATION	
			$f_T(T) \leq X$	$f_T(T) > X$
A	Long Futures	0	$f_T(T) - f_0(T)$	$f_T(T) - f_0(T)$
	Long Put	$P_e(f_0(T),T,X)$	$\dfrac{X - f_T(T)}{X - f_0(T)}$	$\dfrac{0}{f_T(T) - f_0(T)}$
B	Long Call	$C_e(f_0(T),T,X)$	0	$f_T(T) - X$
	Bonds	$(X - f_0(T))(1 + r)^{-T}$	$\dfrac{X - f_0(T)}{X - f_0(T)}$	$\dfrac{X - f_0(T)}{f_T(T) - f_0(T)}$

portfolio B is also like a protective put and its current value must equal the current value of portfolio A. Because the value of the long futures in portfolio A is zero, we conclude that

$$P_e(f_0(T),T,X) = C_e(f_0(T),T,X) + (X - f_0(T))(1 + r)^{-T}.$$

As with put-call parity for options on spot assets, we can write this several different ways isolating the various terms. Note the similarity between put-call parity for options on futures and put-call parity for options on the spot:

> Put-call parity of options on futures is the relationship among the call price, the put price, the futures price, the exercise price, the risk-free rate, and the time to expiration.

$$P_e(f_0(T),T,X) = C_e(f_0(T),T,X) - S_0 + X(1 + r)^{-T}.$$

Because the futures price must equal $S_0(1 + r)^T$, these two versions of put-call parity are equivalent. As we stated earlier, in many ways, the options themselves are equivalent.

Let us look at the March 1400 puts and calls on the S&P 500 futures on January 31. As we saw in Chapter 3, we can calculate the put price and compare it with the actual market price or calculate the call price and compare it with the actual market price. Here we shall calculate the put price. The call price is \$43.40. The other input values given earlier are $f_0 = 1401$, $r = 0.0558$, and $T = 0.1233$. The put price should be

$$P_e(f_0(T),T,X) = 43.40 + (1400 - 1401)(1.0558)^{-0.1233} = 42.41.$$

The actual put price was 42.40. This is very close, but we should expect a difference because these are American options and the formula is for European options. The formula price should be less than the market price, but in this case, it is not. The effect of transaction costs, however, might explain the difference.

Early Exercise of Call and Put Options on Futures

Recall that in the absence of dividends on a stock, a call option on the stock would not be exercised early; however, a put option might be. With an option on a futures contract, either a call or a put might be exercised early. Let us look at the call.

Consider a deep-in-the-money American call. If the call is on the spot instrument, it may have some time value remaining. If it is sufficiently deep-in-the-money, it will have little time value. That does not, however, mean it should be exercised early. Disregarding transaction costs, early exercise would be equivalent to selling the call. If the call is on the futures, however, early exercise may be the better choice. The logic behind this is that a deep-in-the-money call behaves almost identically to the underlying instrument. If the call is on the spot instrument, it will move one for one with the spot price. If the call is on the futures, it will move nearly one for one with the futures price. Thus, the call on the futures will act almost exactly like a long position in a futures contract. The investor, however, has money tied up in the call, but because the margin can be met by depositing interest-earning T-bills, there is no money tied up in the futures. By exercising the call and replacing it with a long position in the futures, the investor obtains the same opportunity to profit but frees up the funds tied up in the call. If the call were on the spot instrument, we could not make the same argument. The call may behave in virtually the same manner as the spot instrument, but the latter also requires the commitment of funds.

From an algebraic standpoint, the early-exercise problem is seen by noting that the minimum value of an in-the-money European call, $(f_0(T) - X)(1 + r)^{-T}$, is less than the value of the call if it could be exercised, $f_0(T) - X$. The European call cannot be exercised, but if it were an American call, it could be.

These points are illustrated in panel A of Figure 9.6. The European call option on futures approaches its lower bound of $(f_0(T) - X)(1 + r)^{-T}$. The American call option

FIGURE 9.6 American and European Calls and Puts on Futures

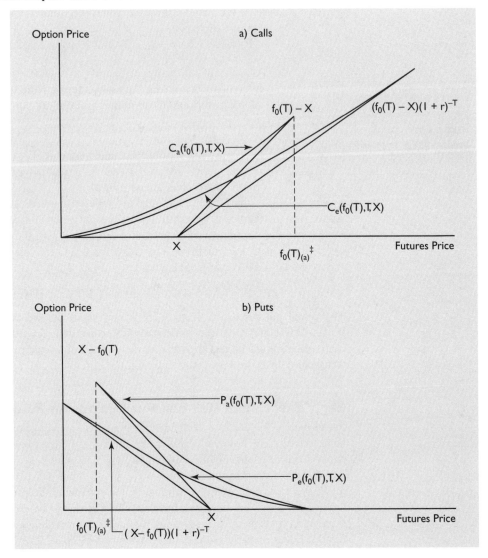

on futures approaches its minimum value, its intrinsic value of $f_0(T) - X$, which is greater than the European lower bound. There is a futures price, $f_0(T)_{(a)}^{\ddagger}$, at which the American call will equal its intrinsic value. Above that price, the American call will be exercised early. Recall that for calls on spot instruments, the European lower bound was higher than the intrinsic value. Thus, there was no early exercise premium—provided, of course, that the underlying asset paid no dividends.

For put options on futures, the intuitive and algebraic arguments work similarly. Deep-in-the-money American puts on futures tend to be exercised early. Panel B of Figure 9.6 illustrates the case for puts. The price of European put options on futures approaches its lower bound of $(X - f_0(T))(1 + r)^{-T}$, while the price of the American put option on futures approaches its intrinsic value of $X - f_0(T)$. The American intrinsic value is greater than the European lower bound. There is a price, $f_0(T)_{(a)}^{\ddagger}$, at which the American put option

> It may be optimal to exercise early either an American call on a futures or an American put on a futures.

on futures would equal its intrinsic value. Below this price, the American put would be exercised early.

Although these instruments are options on futures, it is conceivable that one would be interested in an option on a forward contract. Interestingly, these options would not be exercised early. This is because when exercised, a forward contract is established at the price of X. A forward contract is not marked to market, however, so the holder of a call does not receive an immediate cash flow of $F(0,T) - X$. Instead, that person receives only a position with a value, as we learned earlier in this chapter, of $(F(0,T) - X)(1 + r)^{-T}$. This amount, however, is the lower bound of a European call on a forward contract. Early exercise cannot capture a gain over the European call value; thus, it offers no advantage. Similar arguments hold for early exercise of a European put on a forward contract.

Black Futures Option Pricing Model

Fischer Black (1976) developed a variation of his own Black-Scholes-Merton model for pricing European options on futures. Using the assumption that the option and the futures expire simultaneously, the **Black model** gives the option price as follows:

$$C = e^{-r_cT}[f_0(T)N(d_1) - XN(d_2)],$$

where

$$d_1 = \frac{\ln(f_0(T)/X) - (\sigma^2/2)T}{\sigma\sqrt{T}}$$

$$d_2 = d_1 - \sigma\sqrt{T}.$$

The Black call option on futures pricing model gives the call price in terms of the futures price, exercise price, risk-free rate, time to expiration, and volatility of the futures.

Here σ is the volatility of the futures. Note that the expression for d_1 does not contain the continuously compounded risk-free rate, r_c, as it does in the Black-Scholes-Merton model. That is because the risk-free rate captures the opportunity cost of funds tied up in the underlying asset. If the option is on a futures contract, no funds are invested in the futures, and therefore there is no opportunity cost. The price of the call on the futures, however, will be the same as the price of the call on the spot. This is because when the call on the futures expires, it is exercisable into a futures position, which is immediately expiring. Thus, the call on the futures, when exercised, establishes a long position in the spot asset.

To prove that the Black futures option pricing model gives the same price as the Black-Scholes-Merton model for an option on the spot, notice that in the Black model, $N(d_1)$ is multiplied by $f_0(T)e^{-r_cT}$, while in the Black-Scholes-Merton model, it is multiplied by S_0. We learned earlier in this chapter that with no dividends on the underlying asset, the futures price will equal $S_0e^{r_cT}$. Thus, if we substitute $S_0e^{-r_cT}$ for $f_0(T)$ in the Black model, the formula will be the same as the Black-Scholes-Merton formula.[5]

---

[5]This may not be obvious in the formula for d_1. If we substitute $S_0e^{r_cT}$ for $f_0(T)$ in the above formula for d_1, we obtain

$$d_1 = \frac{\ln(S_0e^{r_cT}/X + (\sigma^2/2)T}{\sigma\sqrt{T}}.$$

The expression $(S_0e^{r_cT}/X)$ is equivalent to $\ln S_0 + \ln e^{r_cT} - \ln X$. Now $\ln e^{r_cT} = r_cT$, so d_1 becomes

$$d_1 = \frac{\ln(S_0/X) + (r_c + \sigma^2/2)T}{\sigma\sqrt{T}},$$

which is d_1 from the Black-Scholes-Merton formula.

We know that in the presence of dividends, the futures price is given by the formula $f_0(T) = S_0 e^{(r_c - \delta_c)T}$. Thus, $S_0 = f_0(T)e^{-(r_c - \delta_c)T}$. If we substitute this expression for S_0 into the Black-Scholes-Merton model, we obtain the Black futures option pricing model if the underlying spot asset—in this case, a stock—pays dividends. The dividends do not show up in the Black model, however, so we need not distinguish the Black model with and without dividends. Dividends do affect the call price, but only indirectly, as the futures price captures all of the effects of the dividends.

Another useful comparison of the Black and Black-Scholes-Merton models is to consider how the Black-Scholes-Merton model might be used as a substitute for the Black model. Suppose that we have available only a computer program for the Black-Scholes-Merton model, but we want to price an option on a futures contract. We can do this easily by using the version of the Black-Scholes-Merton model in Chapter 5 that had a continuous dividend yield and inserting the risk-free rate for the dividend yield and the futures price for the spot price. The risk-free rate minus the dividend yield is the cost of carry, so it will equal zero. The Black-Scholes-Merton formula will then be pricing an option on an instrument that has a price of $f_0(T)$ and a cost of carry of zero. This is precisely what the Black model prices: an option on an instrument—in this case, a futures contract—with a price of $f_0(T)$ and a cost of carry of zero. Remember that the futures price reflects the cost of carry on the underlying spot asset, but the futures itself does not have a cost of carry because there are no funds tied up and no storage costs.

Let us now use the Black model to price the March 1400 call option on the S&P 500 futures. Recall that the futures price is 1401, the exercise price is 1400, the time to expiration is 0.1233, and the risk-free rate is $\ln(1.0558) = 0.0543$. We now need only the standard deviation of the continuously compounded percentage change in the futures price. For illustrative purposes, we shall use 21 percent as the standard deviation. Table 9.9 presents the calculations.

The actual value of the call is $43.40. Thus, the call would appear to be underpriced. As we showed in Chapter 5, an arbitrageur could create a risk-free portfolio by selling the underlying instrument and buying the call. The hedge ratio would be $e^{-r_c T}N(d_1)$ futures contracts for each call. Remember, however, that the model gives the European option price; so we expect it to be less than the actual American option price.

Your software, BSMbin9e.xls, introduced in Chapter 5, can be used to obtain prices of options on futures for the Black model. Simply insert the value you used for the risk-free rate for the continuously compounded dividend yield and insert the futures price for the underlying asset price.

When we studied the Black-Scholes-Merton model in Chapter 5, we carefully examined how the model changes when any of the five underlying variables changes. Many of these effects were referred to with the Greek names delta, gamma, theta, vega, and rho. Because the Black model produces the same price as the Black-Scholes-Merton model,

TABLE 9.9 CALCULATING THE BLACK OPTION ON FUTURES PRICE

$f_0(T)=1401$ $X = 1400$ $r_c = 0.0543$ $\sigma = 0.21$ $T = 0.1233$

1. Compute d_1 $d_1 = \dfrac{\ln(1401/1400) + ((0.21)^2/2)0.1233}{0.21\sqrt{0.1233}} = 0.0466$

2. Compute d_2 $d_2 = 0.0466 - 0.21\sqrt{0.1233} = -0.0271$

3. Look up $N(d_1)$ $N(0.05) = 0.5199$

4. Look up $N(d_2)$ $N(-0.03) = 0.4880$

5. Plug into formula for C $C = e^{-(0.0543)(0.1233)}[1401(0.5199) - 1400(0.4880)] = 44.88$

we will get the same effects here. The only difference is that with the Black model, we express these results in terms of the futures price rather than the spot or stock price. For any of the formulas in which S_0 appears, such as the gamma, vega, and theta, we simply replace S_0 with $f_0(T)e^{-r_cT}$. In the case of the delta, we must redefine delta as the change in the call price for a change in the futures price. For an option on a stock, we saw that the delta is $N(d_1)$. For an option on a futures, the delta is $e^{-r_cT}N(d_1)$.

We can easily develop a pricing model for European put options on futures from the Black model and put-call parity. Using the continuously compounded version, put-call parity is expressed as $C - P = \left(f_0(T) - X\right)e^{-r_cT}$. Rearranging this expression to isolate the put price gives

$$P = C - (f_0(T) - X)e^{-r_cT}.$$

Now we can substitute the Black European call option on futures pricing model for C in put-call parity and rearrange the terms to obtain the Black European put option on futures pricing model,

$$P = Xe^{-r_cT}[1 - N(d_2)] - f_0(T)e^{-r_cT}[1 - N(d_1)].$$

> The Black call option on futures pricing model can be turned into a put option on futures pricing model by using put-call parity for options on futures.

Some end-of-chapter problems will allow us to use this model and examine it further.

Earlier we noted that even in the absence of dividends, American calls on futures might be exercised early. Like options on the spot, American puts on futures might be exercised early. The Black model does not price American options, and we cannot appeal to the absence of dividends, as we could for some stocks, to allow us to use the European model to price an American option. Unfortunately, American option on futures pricing models are fairly complex and beyond the scope of this book. It is possible, however, to price American options on futures using the binomial model. We would fit the binomial tree to the spot price, derive the corresponding futures price for each spot price, and then price the option using the futures prices in the tree.

In addition to the problem of using a European option pricing model to price American options, the Black model has difficulty pricing the most actively traded options on futures, Treasury bond options on futures. That problem is related to the interest rate component. The Black model, like the Black-Scholes-Merton model, makes the assumption of a constant interest rate. This generally is considered an acceptable assumption for pricing options on commodities and sometimes even stock indices. It is far less palatable for pricing options on bonds. There is a fundamental inconsistency in assuming a constant interest rate while attempting to price an option on a futures that is on an underlying Treasury bond, whose price changes because of changing interest rates. More appropriate models are available but this is an advanced topic that we do not address in this book.

Summary

This chapter presented the principles of pricing forward and futures contracts and options on futures. It first established the distinction between the price and value of a forward or futures contract. The value of both contracts is zero the contract. The forward or futures price is obtained as the spot price increased by the cost of carry. Cash flows paid by the asset or a convenience yield on the asset reduce the cost of carry and the forward or futures price. We also looked at the controversy over whether futures prices contain a risk premium. We discussed the factors that determine whether futures and forward prices are equal. We showed how the prices of puts, calls, and forward or futures contracts are related. Finally, using material we learned in Chapters 3 and 5 on the pricing of options, we determined how options on futures are priced.

Throughout this book, we have examined linkages between spot and derivative markets. In the chapters on options, we saw that puts and calls are related (along with risk-free bonds and the underlying asset) by put-call parity and that options are related to the underlying asset and risk-free bonds by the Black-Scholes-Merton model. In this chapter, we added more elements to those relationships. We saw how the forward price is related to the price of the underlying asset and the risk-free bond through the cost of carry model. We saw how options on the asset and forward or futures contracts are related to each other by put-call-forward/futures parity. We saw how puts and calls on futures are related to the underlying asset by the

Black model. We illustrate these interrelationships in Figure 9.7. Table 9.10 provides a summary of the valuation and pricing equations presented in this chapter.

As we move into Chapter 10, we should keep a few points in mind. We can reasonably accept the fact that forward and futures prices and spot prices are described by the cost of carry relationship. We do not know whether forward and futures prices are unbiased, but it seems logical to believe that holders of spot

---

TABLE 9.10   SUMMARY OF THE PRINCIPLES OF FORWARD/FUTURES VALUE AND PRICING

	FORWARD CONTRACTS	FUTURES CONTRACTS
Pricing Equations:		
At expiration	$F(T,T) = S_T$	$f_T(T) = S_T$
Prior to expiration	$F(0,T) = S_0 + \theta - \chi$	$f_0(T) = S_0 + \theta - \chi$
Risk premium	$F(0,T) = E(S_T) - E(\phi)$	$f_0(T) = E(S_T) - E(\phi)$
Dividends (discrete)	$F(0,T) = S_0(1+r)^T - D_T$ $F(0,T) = (S_0 - D_0)(1+r)^T$	$f_0(T) = S_0(1+r)^T - D_T$ $f_0(T) = (S_0 - D_0)(1+r)^T$
Dividends (continuous)	$F(0,T) = S_0 e^{(r_c - \delta_c)T}$	$f_0(T) = S_0 e^{(r_c - \delta_c)T}$
Foreign Exchange	$F(0,T) = S_0(1+r)^T/(1+\rho)^T$	$f_0(T) = S_0(1+r)^T/(1+\rho)^T$
Value Equations:		
At expiration	$V_T(0,T) = S_T - F(0,T)$	$v_t(T) = 0$ (after M2M)
Prior to expiration	$V_t(0,T) = S_t - F(0,T)(1+r)^{-(T-t)}$	$v_t(T) = 0$ (after M2M)
Dividends (discrete)	$V_t(0,T) = S_t - D_{t,T} - F(0,T)(1+r)^{-(T-t)}$	$v_t(T) = 0$ (after M2M)
Dividends (continuous)	$V_t(0,T) = S_t e^{-\delta_c(T-t)} - F(0,T)e^{-r_c(T-t)}$	$v_t(T) = 0$ (after M2M)
Foreign Exchange	$V_t(0,T) = S_t(1+\rho)^{-(T-t)} - F(0,T)(1+r)^{-(T-t)}$	$v_t(T) = 0$ (after M2M)

OPTIONS ON FUTURES	CALL OPTIONS	PUT OPTIONS
Minimum value	≥ 0	≥ 0
Intrinsic value	$C_a(f_0(T),T,X) \geq \text{Max}(0, f_0(T) - X)$	$P_a(f_0(T),T,X) \geq \text{Max}(0, X - f_0(T))$
Lower bound	$C_e(f_0(T),T,X) \geq \text{Max}\left[0,(f_0(T) - X)(1+r)^{-T}\right]$ $C_a(f_0(T),T,X) \geq \text{Max}(0, f_0(T) - X)$	$P_e(f_0(T),T,X) \geq \text{Max}\left[0,(X - f_0(T))(1+r)^{-T}\right]$ $P_a(f_0(T),T,X) \geq \text{Max}(0, X - f_0(T))$
Other Results:		
Black OPM	$C = e^{-r_c T}\left[f_0(T)N(d_1) - XN(d_2)\right]$	$P = Xe^{-r_c T}[1 - N(d_2)] - f_0(T)e^{-r_c T}[1 - N(d_1)]$
	$d_1 = \dfrac{\ln(f_0(T)/X) + (\sigma^2/2)T}{\sigma\sqrt{T}}$	
	$d_2 = d_1 - \sigma\sqrt{T}$	
Put-call parity	$C_e(f_0(T),T,X) = P_e(f_0(T),T,X)$ $\quad - (X - f_0(T))(1+r)^{-T}$	$P_e(f_0(T),T,X) = C_e(f_0(T),T,X)$ $\quad + (X - f_0(T))(1+r)^{-T}$
Effect of dividends	No direct effect, forward price lowered when dividends increase	No direct effect, futures price lowered when dividends increase
Currency options	No direct effect, forward price lowered when foreign interest rates increase	No direct effect, futures price lowered when foreign interest rates increase

FIGURE 9.7 The Linkage between Forwards/Futures, Stock, Bonds, Options on the Underlying Asset, and Options on the Futures

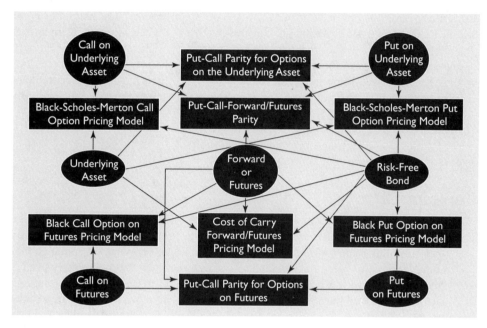

positions expect to earn a risk premium. When they hedge, they transfer the risk to forward and futures traders. It is, therefore, reasonable to expect forward and futures traders to demand a risk premium. Finally, although we have good reason to believe that forward prices are not precisely equal to futures prices, we see little reason to give much weight to the effect of marking to market on the performance of trading strategies. Accordingly, we shall ignore its effects in Chapter 10, which covers arbitrage strategies, and in Chapter 11, which presents hedging strategies, spread strategies, and target strategies.

Key Terms

Before continuing to Chapter 10, you should be able to give brief definitions of the following terms:

forward or futures price/forward or futures value, p. 294
carry arbitrage model/cost of carry model, p. 297
Interest rate parity, p. 304
net interest/cost of carry, p. 307

carry, p. 308
quasi arbitrage, p. 309
contango, p. 311
convenience yield/less than full carry/backwardation/inverted market, p. 312

risk premium hypothesis, p. 316
normal backwardation/normal contango, p. 317
put-call-forward/futures parity/ synthetic futures contract, p. 318
Black model, p. 325

Further Reading

Excellent explanations of forward and futures pricing are as follows:

Duffie, D. *Futures Markets.* Englewood Cliffs, NJ: Prentice Hall, 1989.

French, K. C. "Pricing Financial Futures Contracts: An Introduction." *The Journal of Applied Corporate Finance* 1(1989): 59–66.

The relationships between futures and forward prices were first derived in the following articles:

Cox, J. C., J. E. Ingersoll, Jr., and S. A. Ross. "The Relation between Forward Prices and Futures Prices." *Journal of Financial Economics* 9(1981): 321–346.

Jarrow, R. A., and G. S. Oldfield. "Forward Contracts and Futures Contracts." *Journal of Financial Economics* 9(1981): 373–382.

Empirical studies on several of the pricing relationships studied in this chapter are found in the following articles:

Bell, A. R., C. Brooks, and P. Dryburgh. "Interest Rates and Efficiency in Medieval Wool Forward Contracts." *Journal of Banking and Finance* 31(2007): 361–380.

Brooks, R. "Samuelson Hypothesis and Carry Arbitrage" (November 11, 2010). Available at SSRN: http://ssrn.com/abstract=1568969.

Clements, S., A. J. Ziobrowski, and M. Holder. "Lumber Futures and Timberland Investments." *Journal of Real Estate Research* 33(2011): 49–71.

Cornell, B., and M. Reinganum. "Forward and Futures Prices: Evidence from the Foreign Exchange Markets." *The Journal of Finance* 36(1981): 1035–1046.

French, K. R. "A Comparison of Futures and Forward Prices." *Journal of Financial Economics* 12(1983): 311–342.

French, K. R. "Detecting Spot Price Forecasts in Futures Prices." *The Journal of Business* 59(1986): S39–S54.

Concept Checks

1. Why is the value of a futures or forward contract at the time it is purchased equal to zero? Contrast this with the value of the corresponding spot commodity.

2. Identify and provide a brief explanation of the factors that affect the spot price of a storable asset.

3. If futures prices are less than spot prices, the explanation usually given is the convenience yield. Explain the convenience yield. Then identify certain assets on which convenience yields are more likely to exist and other assets on which they are not likely to be found.

4. What is a contango market? How do we interpret the cost of carry in a contango market? What is a backwardation market? How do we explain the cost of carry in a backwardation market?

5. On September 26, the spot price of wheat was $3.5225 per bushel and the price of a December wheat futures was $3.64 per bushel. How do you interpret the futures price if there is no risk premium in the futures market?

Questions and Problems

1. Solve for the price of a forward contract on a generic asset that expires on September 10 whose spot price as of June 10 is $45, assuming that the annually compounded risk-free rate is 6.01 percent.

2. Given an investor holding a long position two days prior to expiration, when will he prefer futures contracts to forward contracts? (Do not assume interest rate certainty.)

3. Calculate the net effect that a change in the annually compounded risk-free rate from 6.83 percent to 6.60 percent would make on the price of a commodity futures contract whose spot price as of March 30 was $49.90, assuming that there is a $5.60 storage cost and the futures contract expires on November 30.

4. Compare and contrast the characteristics of contango, backwardation, normal contango, and normal backwardation markets.

5. On July 10, a farmer observes that the spot price of corn is $2.735 per bushel and the September futures price is $2.76. The farmer would like a prediction of the spot price in September but believes the market is dominated by hedgers holding long positions in corn. Explain how the farmer would use this information in a forecast of the future price of corn.

6. Explain why American call options on futures could be exercised early when call options on the spot are not. Assume that there are no dividends.

7. Describe two problems in using the Black option on futures pricing model for pricing options on Eurodollar futures.

8. Explain why the Black option on futures pricing model is simply a pricing model for options on instruments with a zero cost of carry.

9. Assume that there is a forward market for a commodity. The forward price of the commodity is $45. The contract expires in one year. The risk-free rate is 10 percent. Now six months later, the spot price is $52. What is the forward contract worth at this time? Explain why this is the correct value of the forward contract in six months even though the contract does not have a liquid market as a futures contract does.

10. On a particular day, the S&P 500 futures settlement price was 899.30. You buy one contract at the settlement price at around the close of the market. The next day the contract opens at 899.70, and the settlement price at the close of the day is 899.10. Determine the value of the futures contract at the opening, an instant before the close, and after the close. Remember that the S&P futures contract has a $250 multiplier.

11. Construct an arbitrage example involving an asset that can be sold short and use it to explain the cost of carry model for pricing futures.

12. On September 26, the spot price of wheat was $3.5225 per bushel and the price of a December wheat futures was $3.64 per bushel. The interest forgone on money tied up in a bushel until expiration is 0.03, and the cost of storing the wheat is 0.0875 per bushel. The risk premium is 0.035 per bushel.
    a. What is the expected price of wheat on the spot market in December?
    b. Show how the futures price is related to the spot price.
    c. Show how the expected spot price at expiration, your answer in part a, is related to the futures price today.
    d. Show how the expected futures price at expiration is related to the futures price today.
    e. Explain who earns the risk premium and why.

13. On a particular day, the September S&P 500 stock index futures was priced at 960.50. The S&P 500 index was at 956.49. The contract expires 73 days later.
    a. Assuming continuous compounding, suppose the risk-free rate is 5.96 percent and the dividend yield on the index is 2.75 percent. Is the futures overpriced or underpriced?
    b. Assuming annual compounding, suppose the risk-free rate is 5.96 percent and the future value of dividends on the index is $5.27. Is the futures overpriced or underpriced?

14. Suppose there is a commodity in which the expected future spot price is $60. To induce investors to buy futures contracts, a risk premium of $4 is required. To store the commodity for the life of the futures contract would cost $5.50. Find the futures price.

15. The following information was available: Spot rate for Japanese yen: $0.009313; 730-day forward rate for Japanese yen: $0.010475 (assume a 365-day year); U.S. risk-free rate: 7.0 percent; Japanese risk-free rate: 1.0 percent
    a. Assuming annual compounding, determine whether interest rate parity holds and, if not, suggest a strategy.
    b. Assuming continuous compounding, determine whether interest rate parity holds and, if not, suggest a strategy.

16. On September 12, a stock index futures contract was at 423.70. The December 400 call was at 26.25, and the put was at 3.25. The index was at 420.55. The futures and options expire on December 21. The discrete risk-free rate was 2.75 percent. Determine whether the futures and options are priced correctly in relation to each other. If they are not, construct a risk-free portfolio and show how it will earn a rate better than the risk-free rate.

17. Use the following data from January 31 of a particular year for a group of March 480 options on futures contracts to answer parts a through g.

Futures price: 483.10

Expiration: March 13

Risk-free rate: 0.0284 percent (simple)

Call price: 6.95

Put price: 5.25

---

    a. Determine the intrinsic value of the call.
    b. Determine the time value of the call.
    c. Determine the lower bound of the call.
    d. Determine the intrinsic value of the put.
    e. Determine the time value of the put.
    f. Determine the lower bound of the put.
    g. Determine whether put-call parity holds.

18. The put-call parity rule can be expressed as $C - P = (f_0(T) - X)(1 + r)^{-T}$. Consider the following data: $f_0(T) = 102$, $X = 100$, $r = 0.1$, $T = 0.25$, $C = 4$, and $P = 1.75$. A few calculations will show that the prices do not conform to the rule. Suggest an arbitrage strategy and show how it can be used to capture a risk-free profit. Assume that there are no transaction costs. Be sure your answer shows the payoffs at expiration and proves that these payoffs are riskless.

19. Assume a standard deviation of 8 percent and use the Black model to determine whether the call option in problem 17 is correctly priced. If not, suggest a riskless hedge strategy.

20. Using the information in the previous problem, calculate the price of the put described in problem 17, using the Black model for pricing puts.

21. Suppose the U.S. interest rate for the next six months is 1.5 percent (annual compounding). The foreign interest rate is 2 percent (annual compounding). The spot price of the foreign currency in dollars is $1,665. The forward price is $1,664. Determine the correct forward price and recommend an arbitrage strategy.

22. Suppose you observe a one-year futures price of $100, the futures option strike price of $90, and a 5 percent interest rate (annual compounding). If the futures option call price is quoted at $9.40, identify any arbitrage and explain how it would be captured.

23. Identify and define three versions of put-call parity.

24. Using the Black-Scholes-Merton option pricing model and the generic carry formula for forward contracts (using continuous compounding), demonstrate that $C_e(S_0,T,X) = C_e(f_0(T),T,X)$.

25. (Concept Problem) Suppose there is a futures contract on a portfolio of stocks that currently are worth $100. The futures has a life of 90 days, and during that time, the stocks will pay dividends of $0.75 in 30 days, $0.85 in 60 days, and $0.90 in 90 days. The simple interest rate is 12 percent.
    a. Find the price of the futures contract assuming that no arbitrage opportunities are present.
    b. Find the value of 9, the cost of carry in dollars.

26. (Concept Problem) Suppose that a futures margin account pays interest but at a rate that is less than the risk-free rate. Consider a trader who buys the asset and sells a futures to form a risk-free hedge. Would the trader believe that the futures price should be lower or higher than if the margin account paid interest at the risk-free rate?

CHAPTER 10

Futures Arbitrage Strategies

Often Jadwin had noted the scene, and unimaginative though he was, had long since conceived the notion of some great, some resistless force within the Board of Trade Building that held the tide of the streets within its grip, alternately drawing it in and throwing it forth. Within there, a great whirlpool, a pit of roaring water spun and thundered, sucking in the life tides of the city, sucking them in as into the mouth of some tremendous cloaca, the maw of some colossal sewer; then vomiting them forth again, spewing them up and out, only to catch them in the return eddy and suck them in afresh.

Frank Norris
The Pit, 1902, 1994 edition, Penguin Books, p. 72

This chapter examines arbitrage futures trading strategies. We discussed arbitrage frequently in previous chapters. Arbitrage is one of the mechanisms that links derivative prices to spot prices. Without arbitrage, the markets would be far less efficient. Derivative and spot prices, however, do not always conform to their theoretical relationships. When this happens, arbitrageurs step in and execute profitable transactions that quickly drive prices back to their theoretical levels. This chapter illustrates some of the arbitrage transactions important to the proper functioning and efficiency of the futures markets. It should be noted that while we sometimes ignore transaction costs in these examples, in practice, any arbitrage opportunities must be evaluated by considering whether the profits cover the transaction costs.

Our approach here is to examine four groups of contracts: short-term interest rate futures contracts, intermediate- and long-term interest rate futures contracts, stock index futures contracts, and foreign exchange futures contracts. Within each group of contracts, we shall examine the unique challenges of arbitrage trading with these instruments.

CHAPTER OBJECTIVES

- Illustrate arbitrage strategies using short-term interest rate futures, intermediate- and long-term interest rate futures, stock index futures, and foreign exchange futures

- Illustrate how to determine the cheapest-to-deliver bond on the Treasury bond futures contract

- Examine delivery options on the Treasury bond futures contract

SHORT-TERM INTEREST RATE ARBITRAGE

In the category of short-term interest rate futures, we shall look at federal funds and Eurodollar futures strategies. But before we start looking at specific strategies, let us examine some basic concepts that are used in understanding the arbitrage transactions that lead to the prices of these types of futures contracts. We begin by looking at the notion of carry arbitrage and a related concept, the implied repo rate.

Carry Arbitrage and the Implied Repo Rate

In Chapter 9, we saw that the futures price is determined by the spot price and the cost of carry. The basic arbitrage transaction that determines this relationship often is referred to as a **cash-and-carry arbitrage**, or the shortened name **carry arbitrage**. The investor purchases the security in the spot market and sells a futures contract. If the futures contract is held to expiration, the security's sale price is guaranteed.[1] Because the transaction is riskless, it should offer a return sufficient to cover the cost of carry or the financing charge from the purchase of the security, assuming that the position is financed completely by borrowing. Because there is no risk, the investor will not earn a risk premium.

Another way to approach this problem is to focus on the rate at which the security's purchase can be financed. Often the financing is obtained by means of a repurchase agreement. A **repurchase agreement**, or **repo**, is an arrangement with a financial institution in which the owner of a security sells that security to the financial institution with an agreement to buy it back, usually a day later. This transaction is referred to as an overnight repo. The repo thus is a form of a secured loan. The investor obtains the use of the funds to buy the security by pledging it as collateral. The interest charged on a repo is usually quoted and calculated as if there were 360 days in a year, but here we shall use the assumption of a full 365-day year.

Repurchase agreements are frequently used in transactions involving government securities. Overnight repos are more common, but longer-term arrangements, called term repos, of up to two weeks are sometimes employed. In cash-and-carry transactions, the security is considered as being financed by using a repo. If the return from the transaction is greater than the repo rate, the arbitrage will be profitable.

From Chapter 9, the futures-spot price relationship is

$$f_0(T) = S_0 + \theta.$$

Because we are focusing on securities here, there is no significant storage cost; thus, the cost of carry, θ, is strictly the interest, iS_0. Now let us define the implicit interest cost as

$$\theta = f_0(T) - S_0.$$

> The implied repo rate is the return implied by the carry arbitrage relationship between spot and futures prices and reflects the return to a cash-and-carry position.

Thus, θ is the implied cost of financing expressed in dollars. Suppose we express it as a percentage of the spot price, θ/S_0, and denote this as $\hat{r}$. Then $\hat{r}$ is the **implied repo rate**. If the cost of financing the position—the actual repo rate—is less than the implied repo rate, the arbitrage will be profitable.

Readers familiar with the concept of internal rate of return (IRR) will find that it is analogous to the implied repo rate. If the arbitrage brings no profit, the cost of financing is the implied repo rate. In a capital budgeting problem, a zero net present value (NPV) defines the internal rate of return. If the opportunity cost is less than the IRR, the project is attractive and produces a positive NPV. Likewise, an arbitrage is profitable if it can be financed at a rate lower than the implied repo rate.

For example, suppose there is a security that matures at time T and an otherwise identical security that matures at an earlier time, t. There is also a futures contract that expires at time t. You buy the longer-term security at a price of S_0, finance it at the rate r (an annualized rate), and sell a futures contract. At time t, the futures expires and you deliver the security. You have effectively sold the security at t for a price of $f_0(t)$. The profit from the transaction is

$$\Pi = f_0(t) - S_0(1 + r)^t.$$

---

[1]Recall that this is true because the spot price at expiration equals the futures price at expiration. The profit on the spot transaction is $S_T - S_0$, and the profit on the futures transaction is $-(f_T(T) - f_0(T))$. The total profit is $f_0(T) - S_0$. Thus, $f_0(T)$ is the effective sale price of the underlying asset.

The term $S_0(1 + r)^t$ reflects what you paid for the security factored up by the cost of financing over period t. The implied repo rate, $\hat{r}$, is the cost of financing that produces no arbitrage profit; therefore, solving for the rate, we have

$$\hat{r} = \left(\frac{f_0(t)}{S_0}\right)^{1/t} - 1.$$

The exponent 1/t can be easily interpreted as 365/days, where "days" is the number of days that the transaction is held in place. Raising $f_0(t)/S_0$ to this power just annualizes the rate.

There is yet another approach to understanding the basic carry arbitrage. Suppose we buy the security that matures at time T and simultaneously sell the futures contract that expires at time t (t < T). When the futures contract expires, we deliver the security, which has a remaining maturity of T − t. The net effect is that we have taken a security that matures at T and shortened its maturity to t. Thus, we have created a synthetic t-period instrument. If the return from the synthetic t-period instrument is greater than the return from an actual security maturing at t, prices are out of line and an arbitrage profit is possible.

Federal Funds Futures Carry Arbitrage and the Implied Repo Rate

Banks keep reserves at Federal Reserve Banks to fulfill their capital reserve requirements. Reserve balances in excess of reserve requirements held by one bank can be loaned to other banks with reserve balance deficiencies. These loans are typically very short-term, usually overnight. Federal funds (also known as fed funds) are reserve balances held at Federal Reserve Banks that can be loaned to other banks. Federal funds can be held by commercial banks, thrift institutions, Federal agencies, branches of foreign banks in the U.S., and government securities dealers. Federal funds rates are highly correlated with Treasury bill rates, LIBOR, and commercial paper rates and are somewhat correlated with longer-term corporate and treasury rates. For example, the correlation coefficient between overnight effective federal funds rate and one-month LIBOR is estimated to be more than 0.98. Hence, arbitrageurs can use other interest rate instruments in their trading activities rather than just federal funds. Federal funds are quoted on an add-on interest basis using an actual day count and a 360-day year.

The federal funds futures contract covers $5,000,000 of federal funds. Hence, one basis point is worth $41.67 (=$5,000,000 × 0.0001 × (30/360)). Prices are quoted as 100 minus the average daily federal funds overnight rate for the delivery month. If the average daily federal funds overnight rate is 5 percent, then the futures contract is quoted as 95.00. If a trader believes that short-term interest rates will rise, she could sell federal funds futures contracts.

We shall use federal funds futures contracts to illustrate a potential arbitrage strategy. The following strategy is based on the assumption that LIBOR and federal funds rate are perfect substitutes; that is, there is no basis risk. We shall say more about this assumption after the illustration. Suppose we lend based on the two-month LIBOR rate and sell a fed funds futures contract expiring in one month. This transaction creates a synthetic one-month LIBOR-based loan, with a rate that should equal the rate on an actual one-month LIBOR rate. If it does not, arbitrageurs will be attracted to the strategy and their transactions will drive down the two-month LIBOR rate and drive down the fed funds futures price, or vice versa, until the synthetic LIBOR-based loan and the actual LIBOR have the same rates.

An Example Table 10.1 illustrates the carry arbitrage transaction with federal funds futures contracts and LIBOR. This is an example of a situation in which lending based

---

TABLE 10.1 FEDERAL FUNDS CARRY ARBITRAGE

Scenario: On March 1, the one-month LIBOR rate is 5.50 percent and the two-month LIBOR rate is 6.00 percent. The April fed funds futures is quoted at 93.75. An arbitrage opportunity is available. Contract size is $5,000,000, and this example illustrates the arbitrage strategy for one contract.

DATE	SPOT MARKET	FUTURES MARKET
March 1	Borrow present value of $5,000,000 at one-month LIBOR ($4,977,187.89); lend same amount at two-month LIBOR.	Sell one April fed funds futures contract at 93.75.
April 1	Repay borrowing (−$5,000,000). Pay off present value of loan.	Buy one April fed funds futures contract to offset initial futures position.

Analysis: The key insight is that the payoff required on April 1 of the two-month LIBOR loan depends on the one-month LIBOR rate observed on April 1. Also, we assume no basis risk between one-month LIBOR rates and fed funds futures implied rates as long as we are not in the delivery month. The loan balance due on May 1 is

$$LB_2 = LB_0\left(1 + r_2\left(\frac{60}{360}\right)\right) = \$4,977,187.89\left(1 + 0.06\left(\frac{60}{360}\right)\right) = \$5,026,959.77.$$

Assuming that the one-month LIBOR rate observed on April 1 is 7.25 percent, then the present value of the initial two-month loan after one month is

$$PV_1(LB_2) = \frac{LB_2}{\left(1 + r_{1,1}\left(\frac{30}{360}\right)\right)} = \frac{\$5,026,959.77}{\left(1 + 0.0725\left(\frac{30}{360}\right)\right)} = \$4,996,770.94.$$

Assuming no basis risk, the fed funds futures price in one month is 92.75 (=100 − 7.25). Therefore, the gain on the fed funds futures contract is $4,166.67(=(93.75 − 92.75) × ($5,000,000) × (30/360)/100). Adding the gain on the futures contract with the proceeds from the present value of the two-month loan, we have $5,000,937.61. Paying off the one-month loan provides arbitrage profits of $937.61. The implied one-month repo rate, therefore, is

$$\left(\frac{\$5,000,937.61}{\$4,977,187.89} - 1\right)\frac{360}{30} = 0.0573,$$

or 5.73 percent. The one-month LIBOR rate is 5.50 percent, indicating the potential arbitrage opportunity.

---

on longer-term LIBOR, the selling of a fed funds futures contract that expires before the LIBOR loan matures, and borrowing based on the fed funds rate when the futures expires creates a synthetic shorter-term LIBOR loan. The return on this synthetic LIBOR loan is about 23 basis points higher than the return on an actual LIBOR loan with the same maturity.

There are, however, several limitations to the effectiveness of this strategy. The effectiveness of this strategy hinges critically on the assumption of no basis risk between one-month LIBOR and fed funds rates. Although the fed funds rate is a rather volatile interest rate, historically, the difference between fed funds on short-term LIBOR rates is only a few basis points. Recall that historical data confirms that the correlation coefficient between fed funds and one-month LIBOR is extremely high. This makes sense because banks decide where to lend their excess reserves—either to other banks through the Federal Reserve Bank or to other banks through the interbank market (LIBOR). Federal funds futures contracts are cash settled based on the average daily effective rate observed during the delivery month. Hence, within the delivery month, there are considerable differences between short-term LIBOR rates and the implied federal funds futures rate.[2] Another limitation to the carry arbitrage is that the repo rate is not fixed for the

---

[2]The arbitrage described here has other subtle risks. See Footnote 3 for an issue related to the Eurodollar futures contract that also applies to the fed funds futures contract.

full time period. As noted earlier, some term repos for up to two weeks are available, but most repo financing is overnight. In either case, the financing rate on this strategy is unknown when the arbitrage is executed. Each time a repo matures, new financing must be arranged, and the rate may well be much higher than originally expected. A number of other limitations, such as transaction costs, come into play when determining the implied repo rate from other futures instruments. There are several other very technical limitations that are beyond the scope of this introductory book.

Eurodollar Arbitrage

The Eurodollar deposit and Eurodollar derivatives markets are large markets in which foreign banks and foreign branches of U.S. banks issue dollar-denominated deposits and often commit to forward and futures transactions. The Eurodollar futures contract was introduced by the Chicago Mercantile Exchange (CME) in 1981 and represents the offer interest rate on an interbank three-month deposit of $1 million. Since their introduction on December 9, 1981, Eurodollar futures have developed into one of the most widely traded money market futures contract in the world. The contracts are cash settled on the second London bank business day immediately preceding the third Wednesday of the contract month. Each Eurodollar futures contract is based on three-month LIBOR settings and represents the interest paid on a three-month interbank time deposit of dollars held outside the United States beginning two days after settlement of the contract. Thus, the interest rate underlying the Eurodollar futures contract is the LIBOR deposit rate applicable to a 90-day period beginning on the third Wednesday of the delivery month. Although the Eurodollar market is highly efficient, there may be occasional arbitrage opportunities resulting from violations of the carry arbitrage relationship between spot and futures or forward prices.

An Example Table 10.2 illustrates a situation in which a London bank, needing to issue a 180-day Eurodollar time deposit, finds that it can get a better rate by issuing a 90-day time deposit and selling a futures expiring in 90 days. By stringing the 90-day time deposit to the futures contract, the bank creates a synthetic 180-day time deposit with a better rate.

It might appear that the result was contingent on the rate on the time deposit issued on December 16—a rate that was not known back in September. In fact, the result of this transaction was known when it was executed. The 90-day time deposit was issued at a rate of $0.0825(90/360) = 0.020625$ for the 90 days. The Eurodollar futures was sold at a rate of $0.0863(90/360) = 0.021575$. Thus, if the bank issued a 90-day time deposit at 0.020625 and followed that with a 90-day time deposit at 0.021575, the overall rate for 180 days would be

$$(1.020625)(1.021575) - 1 = 0.042645.$$

Annualizing this rate gives

$$(1.042645)^{(365/180)} - 1 = 0.0884,$$

which is the rate obtained by the bank.[3]

---

[3]The arbitrage described here is not a perfect transaction in that the outcome is not without a small amount of risk. Because the Eurodollar futures contract settles at expiration as a discount instrument (that is, by subtracting rate × days/360 from par) and spot Eurodollars are priced as add-on instruments (that is, by multiplying par by 1 + rate × days/360), the spot and futures prices do not precisely converge. This characteristic of the Eurodollar market will prevent the arbitrage from being risk free. Arbitrageurs would consider the potential for small variations in the outcome that may or may not be material to the overall success of the strategy.

TABLE 10.2 EURODOLLAR ARBITRAGE

Scenario: On September 16, a London bank needs to issue $10 million of 180-day Eurodollar time deposits. The current rate on such time deposits is 8.75. The bank is considering the alternative of issuing a 90-day time deposit at its current rate of 8.25 and selling a Eurodollar futures contract. If the 180-day time deposit is issued, the bank will have to pay back

$$\$10,000,000[1 + 0.0875(180/360)] = \$10,437,500,$$

which is an effective rate of

$$\left(\frac{\$10,437,500}{\$10,000,000}\right)^{365/180} - 1 = 0.0907.$$

The rates available in the spot and futures market are such that the bank can obtain a better rate by doing the following:

DATE	SPOT MARKET	FUTURES MARKET
September 16	The 90-day time deposit rate is 8.25.	December Eurodollar IMM Index is at 91.37. Price per $100 face value:
		$100 - (100 - 91.37)(90/360) = 97.8425$.
	Issue 90-day time deposit for $10,000,000	Price per contract: $978,425. **Sell 10 contracts**
December 16	The 90-day time deposit matures and the bank owes $10,000,000 $(1 + 0.0825(90/360)) = \$10,206,250$.	December Eurodollar IMM Index is at 92.04. Price per $100 face value:
		$100 - (100 - 92.04)(90/360) = 98.01$.
	The rate on new 90-day time deposits is 7.96.	Price per contract: $980,100.
	Issue new 90-day time deposit for $10,223,000	**Buy 10 contracts**

Analysis: On September 16, the bank received $10,000,000 from the newly issued 90-day time deposit. On December 16, it bought back its ten futures contracts at a loss of 10($980,100 − $978,425) = $16,750. It issued $10,223,000 of new time deposits using $16,750 to cover the loss in the futures account and the remaining $10,206,250 to pay off the maturing 90-day time deposit. On March 16, it paid off the new time deposit, owing

$$\$10,223,000[1 + 0.0769(90/360)] = \$10,426,438.$$

Thus, on September 16, it received $10,000,000 and on March 16, it paid out $10,426,438. It had no other cash flows in the interim. Thus, its effective borrowing cost for 180 days was

$$\left(\frac{\$10,426,438}{\$10,000,000}\right)^{365/180} - 1 = 0.0884,$$

which is 23 basis points less than the cost of a 180-day Eurodollar time deposit.

INTERMEDIATE- AND LONG-TERM INTEREST RATE ARBITRAGE

Intermediate- and long-term interest rate futures include Treasury notes, Treasury bond futures, and the Ultra Treasury bond futures. As we noted in earlier chapters, these instruments are virtually identical, except for eligible maturity U.S. Treasury instruments. Here we shall concentrate on the Treasury bond contract. The U.S. Treasury bond contract is based on the assumption that the underlying bond has a 6 percent coupon rate and a maturity or call date of not less than 15 years and not more than 25 years measured from the first day of the delivery month.[4]

---

[4]The Ultra Treasury bond contract includes bonds not less than 25 years to maturity on the first business day of the delivery month, and the Treasury note contract includes Treasury instruments of at least 6.5 years but not more than 10 years to maturity on the first business day of the delivery month. Because the details of contracts change often, see www.cmegroup.com for current contract specifications.

Suppose you are short the March 2012 contract. As the holder of the short position, you have the choice of which day during the delivery month to make delivery and which bond from among the eligible bonds you will deliver.

Let us assume that you have decided to deliver the bonds with a coupon of 5 1/2 percent and that the bonds mature on August 15, 2028. Suppose delivery in this particular example will be made on Thursday, March 8, 2012. There are two important days when managing the delivery of the underlying bond of a U.S. Treasury bond futures contract. First, there is the day of intention when the short notifies the clearinghouse of its intention to deliver the bonds and the futures settlement price is determined. Second, there is the day of delivery when the delivered bond's accrued interest is computed (two business days later). On the day of delivery, the long taking delivery of the bond must make the funds available at the clearinghouse and the short must make the bonds available.

Because the contract assumes delivery of a bond with a 6 percent coupon, the delivery of the 5 1/2 requires an adjustment to the price paid by the long to the short.

> The conversion factor is the price of a $1 bond with a coupon and maturity equal to that of the deliverable bond on the bond futures contract and a coupon of 6 percent. The conversion factor makes it possible for more than one bond to be eligible for delivery.

The adjustment is based on the CBOT's conversion factor system. The **conversion factor (CF)** is defined for each eligible bond for a given contract. The CF is the price of a bond with a face value of $1, coupon and maturity equal to that of the deliverable bond, and yield of 6 percent. The maturity is defined as the maturity of the bond on the first day of the delivery month. If the bond is callable, the call date is substituted for the maturity date. The CF for the 5 1/2 of 2028 would be the price of a bond with a face value of $1; coupon of 5 1/2 percent; maturity equal to the time remaining from March 1, 2012, the first day of the month, to August 15, 2028, the maturity date of the bond; and yield of 6 percent. That same bond delivered on the June 2012 contract would have a different CF because it would have a different maturity—June 2012 rather than March 2012. A different bond delivered on the March 2012 contract would have a different conversion factor.

The conversion factor system is designed to place all bonds on an equivalent basis for delivery purposes, which is designed to reduce the possibility that a single bond will be in excessive demand for delivery. If the holder of the short position delivers a bond with a coupon greater than 6 percent, the CF will be greater than 1. The short will then receive more than the futures price in payment for the bond. If the coupon is less than 6 percent, the CF will be less than 1 and the short will receive less than the futures price in payment for the bond.

Tables of conversion factors are available, and there is a specific formula for determining the conversion factor, which is provided in Appendix 10. Your software includes the Excel spreadsheet CF9e.xls that calculates the conversion factor, and both the spreadsheet and the conversion factor are explained in the appendix. In this problem, the CF for the 5 1/2 of 2028 delivered on the March 2012 contract would be 0.9485. To determine the invoice price—the amount the long pays to the short for the bond—multiply the CF by the settlement price on the day of intention. Then the accrued interest from the last coupon payment date until the day of delivery is added.[5]

---

[5]The accrued interest is the amount of interest that has built up since the last coupon date. Most bonds pay interest semiannually on the maturity day and six months hence. Thus, a bond maturing on February 15, 2021, would pay interest every year on February 15 and August 15. The accrued interest is the semiannual coupon times the number of days since the last coupon date divided by the number of days between the last coupon date and the next coupon date. It is simply a proration of the next coupon. The buyer of a bond will receive the full next coupon, but because she is not entitled to all of it, must pay the seller the accrued interest. The actual correct bond price will accurately include the accrued interest, although the quoted price will not.

> Invoice price = (Settlement price on the day of intention)
> (Conversion factor) + Accrued interest on day of delivery.

In this problem, assume that the settlement price on Tuesday, March 6, which is called the day of intention, was 140, or $140,000. The bond has coupon payment dates of February 15 and August 15. Thus, the last coupon payment date was February 15, 2012. The number of days from February 15 to the day of delivery of March 8 is 22 days (recall that 2012 is a leap year), and the number of days between coupon payment dates of February 15, 2012, and August 15, 2012, is 182. Thus, the accrued interest is

$$\$100,000(0.055/2)(22/182) = \$332.42.$$

The invoice price therefore is

$$\$140,000(0.9485) + \$332.42 = \$133,122.42.$$

On the day of delivery, Thursday, March 8, the holder of the long position receives an invoice of $133,122.42 and must pay this amount and accept the bond. Table 10.3 indicates 133,116, and this difference is due to rounding.

Table 10.3 presents the conversion factors, accrued interest, and invoice prices for other bonds deliverable on the March 2012 contract. Note how the conversion factors vary directly with the level of the coupon.

Determining the Cheapest-to-Deliver Bond on the Treasury Bond Futures Contract

As previously explained, the specifications on the Treasury bond contract allow delivery of many different bonds subject to the minimum 15-year maturity or call date and a maximum of 25-year maturity. As we noted, the conversion factor system is designed to place all bonds on an equivalent basis for delivery purposes. If the conversion factor

TABLE 10.3 CONVERSION FACTORS AND INVOICE PRICES FOR DELIVERABLE BONDS (MARCH 2012 T-BOND FUTURES CONTRACT)

Contract price: 140
Delivery date: March 8, 2012

COUPON	MATURITY DATE	CF	ACCRUED INTEREST	INVOICE PRICE
6.375%	August 15, 2027	1.0370	385	145,567
6.250%	May 15, 2030	1.0273	1,957	145,778
6.125%	November 15, 2027	1.0125	1,918	143,668
6.125%	August 15, 2029	1.0132	370	142,219
5.500%	August 15, 2028	0.9485	332	133,116
5.375%	February 15, 2031	0.9301	325	130,541
5.250%	November 15, 2028	0.9221	1,644	130,742
5.250%	February 15, 2029	0.9213	317	129,305
4.750%	February 15, 2037	0.8398	287	117,860
4.500%	February 15, 2036	0.8113	272	113,856

Note: These calculations were done on a computer and can vary from the amounts obtained if done by hand.

system were perfect, all bonds would be equally desirable for delivery. But the conversion factor system is not perfect, and all bonds are not equally desirable for delivery. At any given time prior to expiration, it is impossible to determine which bond will be delivered. It is, however, possible to identify the bond that is most likely to be delivered. That bond is referred to as the **cheapest-to-deliver (CTD)**.

Suppose it is Thursday, September 15, 2011, and you are interested in determining the bond that is most likely to be delivered on the upcoming March 2012 contract. The procedure involves a series of calculations that we shall now illustrate for one particular bond—the 6 1/4s that mature on May 15, 2030.

If the holder of a long position in this bond also holds a short position in the Treasury bond futures contract, that trader can elect to maintain the position until expiration and deliver this particular bond. Even if another bond would be cheaper to deliver, the trader always has the option to deliver the bond already held. The cost of delivering the particular bond is the net profit or loss from buying the bond, selling a futures, holding the position until expiration, and then delivering the bond. Thus, the trader incurs the cost of carry on the bond held. Remember that this cost is somewhat offset by the coupons received on the bond.

For evaluating at time t the best bond to deliver at time T, the general expression for the cost of delivering a bond is

$$f_0(T)(CF) + AI_T - [(B + AI_t)(1 + r)^{(T-t)} - CI_{t,T}],$$

where AI_T is the accrued interest on the bond at T, the delivery date (formally the day of delivery); AI_t is the accrued interest on the bond at t, today; r is the risk-free rate that represents the interest lost on the funds invested in the bond; and $CI_{t,T}$ is the value at time T of the coupons received and reinvested over the period of t to T. The term inside the brackets is the spot price of the bond (quoted price plus accrued interest) factored up by the cost of carry and reduced by the compound future value of any coupons received while the position is held. These coupons, of course, help offset the cost of carry, and by subtracting them, we are simply reflecting the net cost of carry. The bracketed term is, thus, the forward price of the bond. The first two terms are the amount the trader would receive from delivering the bond, which is the invoice price.

An Example Suppose the futures price is again 140, but assume it is now September 15, 2011, and the conversion factor for our bond is 1.0273 (the 6 1/4s that mature on May 15, 2030). The accrued interest on September 15, 2011, is 2.0890, and the accrued interest on March 8, 2012, the day we shall assume delivery, is 1.9574. The price quoted for the bond is 148:17, or 148.53125. The reinvestment rate is 1.0 percent. There are 114 days between November 15, 2011, and March 8, 2012. The invoice price for the futures is

$$140(1.0273) + 1.9574 = 145.7794.$$

There is one interim coupon paid on November 15. Thus, the forward price of the bond is

$$(148.53125 + 2.0890)(1.01)^{(175/365)} - 3.125(1.01)^{(114/365)} = 148.2058.$$

Hence, the 6 1/4s maturing on May 15, 2030 bond would cost 2.43 (=148.2058 − 145.7794) more than it would return.

This conclusion by itself does not enable us to make a decision. We can only compare this figure for one bond to that for another bond. Let us consider a second bond, the 6 1/8s maturing on November 15, 2027. Its conversion factor is 1.0125, and its price is 144 5/32, or 144.15625. The accrued interest is 2.0472 on September 15, 2011, and

1.9183 on March 8, 2012. The coupon of 3.0625 received on November 15 is reinvested at 1.0 percent for 114 days and grows to a value of

$$3.0625(1.01)^{(114/365)} = 3.0720.$$

Thus, the forward price of the bond is

$$(144.15625 + 2.0472)(1.01)^{(175/365)} - 3.0720 = 143.8306.$$

The invoice price is

$$140(1.0125) + 1.9183 = 143.6683.$$

Thus, the 6 1/8s maturing on November 15, 2027 bond would cost 0.16 (=143.8306 − 143.6683) more than it would return.

Therefore, it is clear that the 6 1/8 percent, November 15, 2027 bond is better to deliver than the 6 1/4 percent, May 15, 2030 bond. Of course, this calculation should be done for all bonds that are eligible for delivery. The cheapest bond to deliver is the bond for which the difference between the amount received and the amount paid is the maximum.

> The cheapest-to-deliver bond is the bond for which the difference between the revenue received from delivery of the bond and the cost incurred to buy and hold the bond is maximized.

Table 10.4 presents these calculations for the March 2012 contract evaluated on September 15, 2011. Ten eligible bonds are shown. The column labeled "Difference" is the difference between the invoice price and the forward price. In real time, all of these "Difference" values should all be negative; otherwise, one could earn an easy arbitrage profit. The cheapest bond to deliver is the one in which "Difference" is the largest. In this case, it is the 6 3/8 of August 15, 2027. The Excel spreadsheet CTD9e.xls will automatically do these calculations for you. Software Demonstration 10.1 illustrates how to use CTD9e.xls.

TABLE 10.4   THE CHEAPEST-TO-DELIVER BOND ON THE TREASURY BOND FUTURES CONTRACT

Current date: September 15, 2011
Delivery date: March 8, 2012
Reinvestment rate: 1.0%
Futures price: 140

COUPON	MATURITY DATE	ASK PRICE	FORWARD PRICE	INVOICE PRICE	DIFFE-RENCE	ACCRUED INTEREST AT t	ACCRUED INTEREST AT T	FUTURE VALUE OF COUPONS	CF
6.375%	August 15, 2027	147 9/16	145.6183	145.5668	−0.0515	0.5370	0.3853	3.1894	1.0370
6.250%	May 15, 2030	148 17/32	148.2058	145.7781	−2.4277	2.0890	1.9574	3.1347	1.0273
6.125%	November 15, 2027	144 5/32	143.8306	143.6683	−0.1623	2.0472	1.9183	3.0720	1.0125
6.125%	August 15, 2029	145 7/8	144.0267	142.2190	−1.8076	0.5160	0.3702	3.0643	1.0132
5.500%	August 15, 2028	136 1/4	134.6154	133.1157	−1.4998	0.4633	0.3324	2.7516	0.9485
5.375%	February 15, 2031	136 3/32	134.5104	130.5411	−3.9693	0.4528	0.3249	2.6891	0.9301
5.250%	November 15, 2028	132 25/32	132.5462	130.7422	−1.8040	1.7548	1.6442	2.6332	0.9221
5.250%	February 15, 2029	132 7/8	131.3282	129,3049	−2.0233	0.4423	0.3173	2.6266	0.9213
4.750%	February 15, 2037	126 5/8	125.2562	117,8603	−7.3958	0.4001	0.2871	2.3764	0.8398
4.500%	February 15, 2036	122 1/4	120.9642	113.8564	−7.1077	0.3791	0.2720	2.2513	0.8113

The cheapest bond to deliver is important for several reasons. Any futures contract must reflect the behavior of the spot price. In the case of Treasury bond and note futures, the so-called "spot price" is not easy to determine. The cheapest bond to deliver is the bond that represents the spot instrument that the futures contract is tracking. Therefore, the cost of carry model examined in Chapter 9 would apply only to the cheapest bond to deliver.

Delivery Options

The characteristics of the Treasury bond futures contract create some interesting opportunities for alert investors. Specifically, the contract contains several imbedded options. While these **delivery options** are not formally traded in the same way stock options are, they have many of the characteristics of the options we studied in earlier chapters. We shall examine some of these options here.

Wild Card Option The **wild card option** results from a difference in the closing times of the spot and futures markets. The Treasury bond futures contract stops trading at 3:00 P.M. Eastern time. The spot market for Treasury bonds operates until 5:00 P.M. Eastern time. During the delivery month, the holder of a short position knows the settlement price for that day at 3:00 P.M. Multiplying the settlement price by the conversion factor gives the invoice price the holder would receive if a given bond were delivered. This figure is locked in until the next day's trading starts.

During the two-hour period after the futures market closes, the spot market continues to trade. If the spot price declines during those two hours, the holder of a short futures position may find it attractive to buy a bond and deliver it. Because the futures market is closed and the invoice price is fixed, the futures market is unable to react to the new information that drove the spot price down. Moreover, the short has until about 9:00 P.M. to make the decision to deliver.

Let us use the following symbols:

$$f_3 = \text{futures price at 3:00 P.M.}$$
$$B_3 = \text{spot price at 3:00 P.M.}$$
$$CF = \text{conversion factor of bond under consideration}$$

You hold a short position in the futures contract that is expiring during the current month. Assume that you own 1/CF bonds. Why this unusual amount? If you do not own any bonds, your position will be quite risky. Also, the bond under consideration should be the cheapest bond to deliver. That way your risk is quite low. Unexpected changes in the futures price will be approximately matched by changes in the value of the 1/CF bonds. We require the case that CF > 1.0.

The wild card option is the opportunity the holder of the short futures contract has to lock in the invoice price at 3:00 P.M. and make delivery if the spot price falls below the established invoice price between 3:00 P.M. and 5:00 P.M. The option exists only during the delivery month.

If you make delivery that day, you will be required to deliver one bond per contract. You own only 1/CF bonds, so you will have to buy $1 - 1/CF$ additional bonds. If the bonds' spot price declines sufficiently between 3:00 P.M. and 5:00 P.M., you may be able to buy the additional bonds at a price low enough to make a profit. These additional bonds are called the *tail*.

Now suppose at 5:00 P.M. the bond price is B_5. If you buy the additional $1 - 1/CF$ bonds at the price of B_5 and deliver them, your profit will be

$$\Pi = f_3(CF) - \left[\left(\frac{1}{CF}\right)B_5 + \left(1 - \frac{1}{CF}\right)B_5\right] = f_3(CF) - B_5.$$

The first term, $f_3(CF)$, is the invoice price. This is simply the 3:00 P.M. settlement price on the futures contract times the conversion factor on the bond. The invoice price is the amount you receive upon delivery. The terms in brackets denote values of the bonds you are delivering. The first term, $(1/CF)B_5$, is the 5:00 P.M. value of the $1/CF$ bonds you already owned. The second term is the cost of the $1 - 1/CF$ bonds bought at the 5:00 P.M. price. As indicated above, the expression simplifies to $f_3(CF) - B_5$. Note that the 3:00 P.M. bond price does not enter into the decision to deliver because the delivery decision is made at 5:00 P.M. By that time, the $1/CF$ bonds are worth $(1/CF)B_5$ and can be sold for that amount.

If the transaction is profitable, $\Pi > 0$. This requires that

$$B_5 < f_3(CF).$$

A trader can observe the spot price at 5:00 P.M. If the price is sufficiently low, the trader should buy the remaining $1 - 1/CF$ bonds and make delivery. The wild card option thus will be profitable if the spot price at 5:00 P.M. falls below the invoice price established at 3:00 P.M.

As an example, suppose that on March 2 the March futures contract has a settlement price at 3:00 P.M. of 101.8125. The cheapest bonds to deliver were the 12 1/2s maturing in about 22 years, which have a conversion factor of 1.464. We do not have the 3:00 P.M. spot price, but let us assume it is 149.65. Suppose we are short 100 contracts, which obligates us to deliver bonds with a face value of $100(\$100,000) = \$10,000,000$. Assume each bond has a face value of $1,000. Thus, we will have to deliver 10,000 bonds. To begin this strategy, we must have a position in the spot Treasury bonds; otherwise, our risk will be quite high. We weight that position by the conversion factor; that is, we hold bonds with a face value of $\$10,000,000(1/1.464) = \$6,830,601$—in other words, about 6,831 bonds. To make delivery, we will need to buy 3,169 bonds. For us to make a profit, the 5:00 P.M. price must decline to

$$B_5 < 101.8125(1.464) = 149.05$$

or less. Thus, if the spot price declined by at least 0.60 by 5:00 P.M., it would pay to buy the remaining 3,169 bonds and make delivery.

The alternative to delivery is holding the position until the next day. In fact, that will always be the better choice if the conversion factor is less than 1.0. Note that if $CF < 1.0$, the hedged position will include $1/CF$ bonds, which exceeds 1.0. Thus, the hedger will hold more bonds than futures and there will be no tail, or additional bonds, to purchase at the lower 5:00 P.M. price. In that case, the wild card option is worthless. Moreover, if the price does not fall sufficiently by 5:00 P.M., holding the position is preferred over delivery. Of course, it is possible that the wild card option will never be worth exercising, meaning simply that it ends up, like many other options, out-of-the-money.

Quality Option The holder of the short position has the right to deliver any of a number of acceptable bonds. Sometimes the holder of the short position will be holding a bond that is not the best to deliver. A profit is sometimes possible by switching to another bond. This is called the **quality option** because the deliverable bonds are considered to be of different quality; it is also sometimes called the switching option.

The value of this option arises because of changes in the term structure of interest rates. You may be holding a hedged position in Treasury bonds and futures, anticipating that you will make delivery of the bond that you hold on the futures contract. Then if the term structure changes, another bond may become the cheapest to deliver. Although you could always deliver the bond you hold, the right to switch to a more favorably priced bond has value.

The quality option exists not only in Treasury bond and note markets, but also in the markets for many commodity futures. For example, the wheat futures contract of the Chicago Board of Trade (owned by the CME Group) specifies that the holder of the short position can deliver any of four different grades of wheat. Other agricultural contracts have similar options. In fact, agricultural contracts usually grant the right to deliver at one of several locations. This feature, called the location option, has essentially the same economic effect as the quality option.

> The quality option is the opportunity the holder of the short futures contract has to switch to another deliverable bond if it becomes more favorably priced. The option exists on any futures contract that permits delivery of one of several underlying assets, with the decision made by the holder of the short position.

The quality option conveys a right to the holder of the short position. Because this right has value, the futures price will tend to be lower by the value of this option. In other words, the seller of a futures receives a lower price that reflects the valuable option attached to the contract. Likewise, the buyer pays a lower price for granting the seller this valuable right.

End-of-the-Month Option The last day for trading a Treasury bond futures contract is the eighth-to-last business day of the delivery month. Delivery can take place during the remaining business days. The invoice price during those final delivery days is based on the settlement price on the last trading day. Thus, during the last seven delivery days, the holder of the short position has full knowledge of the price that would be received for delivery of the bonds. This gives the holder of the short position the opportunity to watch the spot market for a fall in bond prices. The trader can continue to wait for spot prices to fall until the second-to-last business day because delivery must occur by the last business day.

> The end-of-the-month option is the opportunity the holder of the short futures contract has to deliver during the final business days of the month. The futures contract no longer trades; so the invoice price is locked in, and the option can be profitable if the spot price falls during the last few trading days of the month.

The **end-of-the-month option**, thus, is similar to the wild card option. There is a period during which spot prices can change while the delivery price is fixed. It is also related to the quality option, for the holder of the short position can also switch to another bond.

The timing option is the opportunity the holder of the short futures contract has to deliver anytime during the expiration month. Early delivery is made if the cost of financing exceeds the coupon on the bond, and later delivery is made if the coupon exceeds the cost of financing.

Timing Option Because the short is often permitted to make delivery on any day during the delivery month, he holds another valuable option. Suppose the Treasury bond pays a coupon that exceeds the cost of financing the position, which is the repo rate. Then the short should hold the long bond-short futures position as long as possible because it pays more than it costs. If the repo rate exceeds the bond coupon, then the position costs more to hold than it yields; thus, an early delivery is advised. Ignoring all other delivery options, this **timing option** would suggest that all deliveries would occur early or late in the month. As we have already noted, however, there are many other options that are in effect and early delivery would preclude the right to take advantage of some of these other options.

Determining the values of these delivery options is very difficult. Most contracts contain more than one option, and as noted earlier, the Treasury bond futures contract contains several delivery options. Thus, it is difficult to isolate them and observe their separate effects. There have been numerous studies, which are reviewed in Chance and Hemler (1993). Most of them found that the value of delivery options is fairly small. That does not mean they should be dismissed as insignificant. To the holder of one or more of these options, the value may at times be quite large. For our purposes, however, we can safely conclude that the economic effects are minor in comparison to the more important factors that determine the futures price.

Implied Repo, Carry Arbitrage, and Treasury Bond Futures

Earlier in this chapter, we examined the concept of the implied repo rate in the context of the carry arbitrage model for federal funds futures. The concept is equally applicable to Treasury bond futures.

First, we must identify the cheapest bond to deliver. If we buy that bond today (time 0), we pay the spot price plus the accrued interest. The sale of a repo finances the bond's purchase. This means that we borrow the funds by selling the bond and agreeing to buy it back at a specified later date. We simultaneously sell a futures contract expiring at T. During the period of 0 to T, we may receive coupons, which would be reinvested at some appropriate rate and accrue to some value at T. Let us denote this value of reinvested coupons as $CI_{0,T}$. Thus, we hold the position from 0 to T, collecting and reinvesting the coupons. At expiration, we deliver the bond and effectively receive $(CF)(f_0(T))$, the futures price times the conversion factor plus accrued interest for it. In an efficient market, there should be no arbitrage profit. Therefore, the amount we receive for the bond must equal the amount we paid for it plus the cost of carry:

$$(CF)(f_0(T)) - AI_T + CI_{0,T} = (B_0 + AI_0)(1 + \hat{r})^T,$$

where B_0 is the bond price when it is bought, AI_T is the accrued interest on the bond at expiration, AI_0 is the accrued interest when the bond is bought, and $\hat{r}$ is the implied repo rate. The left-hand side of the formula is the amount we receive upon delivery. The right-hand side is the amount paid for the bond, $B_0 + AI_0$, factored up by the cost of financing over the holding period, 0 to T. Solving for $\hat{r}$,

$$\hat{r} = \left[\frac{(CF)(f_0(T)) + AI_T + CI_{0,T}}{B_0 + AI_0} \right]^{(1/T)} - 1.$$

SOFTWARE DEMONSTRATION 10.1

Identifying the Cheapest-to-Deliver Bond with the Excel Spreadsheet CTD9e.xlsc

The Excel spreadsheet CTD9e.xls is written in Excel. It identifies the cheapest-to-deliver bond from among a set of bonds for the Chicago Board of Trade bond futures contract. The spreadsheet is available as a download via the product support website. To access it:

1. Go to www.cengagebrain.com.
2. Click on Instructor Resources or Student Resources.
3. Click on the link CTD9e.xls.
4. Follow the instructions on the Web page to download and install the spreadsheet.

This spreadsheet is a read-only spreadsheet, meaning that it cannot be saved under the name CTD9e.xls, which preserves the original file.

Now let us work an example. Consider the problem in the text in which on September 15, 2011, you want to identify the cheapest-to-deliver bond on the March 2012 contract. The current repo rate is 1.0 percent, and the futures price is 142. You have identified ten bonds that meet the maturity requirement and are eligible for delivery.

Observe on the spreadsheet a section labeled **Inputs:** Each cell that will accept inputs has a double-line border, and the values are in blue. Enter the current date in the form mm/dd/yyyy. Insert "9/15/2011" in the appropriate box. Then enter the delivery date "3/8/2012" in its box. The repo rate can be entered as either "1.0" or "0.01" in the appropriate box. The futures price should be entered as points and thirty-seconds. For example 142 3/32 should be entered as "142.03". The trailing zero can be omitted for values such as "142.2" for 142 20/32. List the individual bonds in the section below. Consider the first bond. Let it have a coupon rate of 6.375 percent; a maturity date of August 15, 2027; and an ask price of 147 18/32. For the coupon rate, enter "6.375" or "0.06375". Enter the maturity date as "8/15/2027". Enter the ask price the same way you did the futures price. Thus, 147 18/32 is entered as "147.18". Tap F9 to recalculate, and the values will appear for each bond in the section labeled **Results:** Output cells have a single-line border.

The calculations shown are the forward price; the invoice price; the difference between the invoice price and forward price; the decimal price, which is simply the ask price converted from thirty-seconds to decimals; the accrued interest on the current date; the

accrued interest on the delivery date; and the value of the coupons at delivery. The last figure is the value of the coupons paid between the current date and the delivery date plus any interest paid on their reinvestment. To the right of each row are additional columns used to perform the calculations. These columns include the conversion factor and various other figures used in the calculations. The column labeled "Difference" is the value you are looking for. The bond with the largest difference, which will be the one with the least negative value, is the cheapest bond to deliver.

The number of bonds you want to analyze may differ. To accommodate additional bonds, copy all of the formulas from columns D through AE into new rows.

TREASURY BOND FUTURES
CHEAPEST TO DELIVER
Ctd9e

Inputs:

Current Date (mm/dd/yyyy): September 15, 2011

Delivery Date (mm/dd/yyyy): March 8, 2012

Repo rate (decimal or percent): 1.0000%

Futures price (points and 32nds after the decimal): 140

Results:

Coupon Rate	Maturity Date (mm/dd/yyyy)	Ask Price (pts & 32nds)	Forward Price	Invoice Price	Difference	Decimal Price	Accrued Interest Today	Accrued Interest at Delivery	Value of Coupons at Delivery
6.3750%	August 15, 2027	147.18	145.6183	145.5668	-0.0515	147.5625	0.5370	0.3853	3.1894
6.2500%	May 15, 2030	148.17	148.2058	145.7781	-2.4277	148.5313	2.0890	1.9574	3.1347
6.1250%	November 15, 2027	144.05	143.8306	143.6683	-0.1623	144.1563	2.0472	1.9183	3.0720
6.1250%	August 15, 2029	145.28	144.0267	142.2190	-1.8076	145.8750	0.5160	0.3702	3.0643
5.5000%	August 15, 2028	136.08	134.6154	133.1157	-1.4998	136.2500	0.4633	0.3324	2.7516
5.3750%	February 15, 2031	136.03	134.5104	130.5411	-3.9693	136.0938	0.4528	0.3249	2.6891
5.2500%	November 15, 2028	132.25	132.5462	130.7422	-1.8040	132.7813	1.7548	1.6442	2.6332
5.2500%	February 15, 2029	132.28	131.3282	129.3049	-2.0233	132.8750	0.4423	0.3173	2.6266
4.7500%	February 15, 2037	126.20	125.2562	117.8603	-7.3958	126.6250	0.4001	0.2871	2.3764
4.5000%	February 15, 2036	122.08	120.9642	113.8564	-7.1077	122.2500	0.3791	0.2720	2.2513

The exponent $1/T$ is just 365/days, where "days" is the number of days the position is held. This factor simply annualizes the calculation to obtain the rate $\hat{r}$. If the bond can be financed in the repo market at a rate of less than $\hat{r}$, profitable arbitrage is possible.

An Example On September 15, 2011, the cheapest bond to deliver on the upcoming March contract is the 6 3/8 maturing on August 15, 2027. We shall assume delivery on March 8 for this particular example. The spot price is 147 18/32, the accrued interest is 0.5370, the conversion factor is 1.0370, and the futures price is 140. From September 15 to March 8 is 175 days, so $T = 175/365 = 0.47945$. There is one interest payment made during this period; hence, $CI_{0,T} = 3.1894$ ($= (6.375/2)(1.01)^{(22/365)}$). The accrued interest as of March 8, 2011, is 0.3853. The implied repo rate is, therefore,

$$\hat{r} = \left[\frac{140(1.0370) + 0.3853 + 3.1894}{147.5625 + 0.5370} \right]^{1/0.47945} - 1 = 0.00925.$$

If the bond can be financed in the repo market for less than the implied repo rate, the arbitrage would will be profitable. Note that the implied repo rate is higher than the actual repo rate, meaning that there appears to be profitable arbitrage. There are several microstructure issues that could easily account for this observation, such as asynchronous prices.

Treasury Bond Futures Spreads and the Implied Repo Rate

In Chapter 7, we learned about option spreads, which are transactions that are long one option and short another. Spreads are also widely used in futures trading, especially in the Treasury bond contracts. Suppose a trader takes a long position in a futures contract. If this is the only transaction, the risk is quite high. One way to modify the risk is to sell short a Treasury bond, but short selling requires that the trader execute a transaction in the spot market. In addition, there are margin requirements on short sales. An alternative that is easy to execute is to simply sell another Treasury bond futures contract. That transaction could be executed in the same trading pit. In addition, the margin requirement on a spread is much lower than the margin requirement on either a long or short position.

Suppose there is a futures contract expiring at time t and another expiring at time T with t coming before T. Suppose today (time 0) we sell the longer-term contract and buy the shorter-term contract. At time t, the shorter-term contract expires. We take delivery of the bond, financing it at the repo rate, r, and hold it until time T, when the longer-term contract expires. Because we are short that contract, we simply deliver the bond. Assume we can identify today the cheapest bond to be delivered on the shorter-term contract.

Consider the following notation:

$$CF(t) = \text{conversion factor for bond delivered at t}$$
$$CF(T) = \text{conversion factor for same bond delivered at T}$$
$$f_0(t) = \text{today's futures price for contract expiring at t}$$
$$f_0(T) = \text{today's futures price for contract expiring at T}$$
$$AI_t = \text{accrued interest on bond as of time t}$$
$$AI_T = \text{accrued interest on bond as of time T}$$

At time t, we take delivery of the bond and pay the invoice price,

$$(CF(t))f_0(t) + AI_t.$$

To finance the acceptance and holding of this bond, we borrow this amount at the rate r. Then at time T, we deliver the bond and receive the invoice price plus coupons received and reinvested from t to T,

$$(CF(T))f_0(T) + AI_T + CI_{t,T}.$$

Because this transaction is riskless, the profit from it should be zero. Therefore,

$$[(CF(t))f_0(t) + AI_t](1 + \hat{r})^{T-t} = (CF(T))f_0(T) + AI_T + CI_{t,T}.$$

The bracketed term on the left-hand side is the amount we paid for the bond at t. Because we borrowed this amount, we must factor it up by the interest rate compounded over the period T − t. The right-hand side is the amount received from delivering the bond at T. We can now solve for $\hat{r}$, the implied repo rate:

$$\hat{r} = \left[\frac{(CF(T))f_0(T) + AI_T + CI_{t,T}}{(CF(t))f_0(t) + AI_t} \right]^{1/(T-t)} - 1.$$

The numerator is the amount received for the bond, and the denominator is the amount paid for it. Dividing these two numbers gives the rate of return over the period T − t. Raising this term to the power 1/(T − t) annualizes the rate. The implied repo thus is the return we could earn over the period $T - t$. If the bond can be financed at less than this rate, the transaction will be profitable.

The implied repo rate on a spread is the implied cost of establishing a cash-and-carry position at the expiration of the earlier futures contract of the spread.

An Example Assume that on September 15, 2011, the cheapest bond to deliver was the 6 3/8s maturing on August 15, 2027. Let us examine the March-June Treasury bond futures spread. For this particular example, we assume a March delivery date of the 8th and we assume a June delivery date of the 8th. The March contract is priced at 140, and the conversion factor is 1.0370. The June futures price is 139. There are 92 days from March 8 to June 8, so $T - t = 92/365 = 0.2521$. The conversion factor for the 6 3/8s maturing on August 15, 2027, delivered on the June contract is 1.0368. The accrued interest on the bond on March 8 is 0.3853, and the accrued interest on June 8 is 1.9966. There are no coupons between the two futures expiration dates, so $CI_{t,T} = 0$. Because the time from March 8 to June 8 is 92 days, the implied repo rate is

$$\hat{r} = \left[\frac{1.0368(139) + 1.9966}{1.0370(140) + 0.3853} \right]^{1/0.2521} - 1 = 0.0150.$$

The implied repo rate thus is 1.50 percent. Note that this is a forward rate because it reflects the repo rate over the future period from March 8 to June 8. If the bond could be financed at a rate of less than 1.50 percent from March 8 to June 8, the transaction would be profitable.

One way traders determine whether the implied repo rate on the spread is attractive is to evaluate what is called a turtle trade. The implied repo rate of 1.48 percent is an implied forward rate. It can be compared to the implied rate in the fed funds futures market. If the fed funds futures rate is lower, the trader sells the fed funds futures and buys the Treasury bond spread. This creates a risk-free position and earns the difference between the implied repo rate on the Treasury bond spread and the implied rate on the fed funds futures. If the implied rate on the fed funds futures is higher, the investor reverses the Treasury bond spread and buys the fed funds futures.

STOCK INDEX ARBITRAGE

We discussed carry arbitrage with federal funds, Eurodollars, and Treasury bond futures. The concept is equally applicable to stock index futures. In fact, this type of transaction is one of the most widely used in the futures markets. It is called **stock index arbitrage**.

Recall that the model for the stock index futures price when interest and dividends are expressed in continuously compounded form is

$$f_0(T) = S_0 e^{(r_c - \delta_c)T},$$

where r_c is the continuously compounded risk-free rate and δ_c is the continuously compounded dividend yield. Consider the following example of a futures contract that has 40 days to go until expiration. The S&P 500 index is at 1305, the risk-free rate is 5.2 percent, and the dividend yield is 3 percent. The time to expiration will be $40/365 = 0.1096$. Thus, the futures should be priced at

$$f_0(T) = 1305 e^{(0.052 - 0.03)(0.1096)} = 1{,}308.15.$$

Now suppose the actual futures price is 1309.66. Thus, the futures contract is slightly overpriced. We would sell the futures and buy the stocks in the S&P 500 index in the same proportions as in the index. At expiration, the futures price would equal the spot price of the S&P 500 index. We then would sell the stocks. The transaction is theoretically riskless and would earn a return in excess of the risk-free rate.

Now suppose at expiration the index closes at 1,300.30. The profit on the futures contract is $1,309.66 - 1,300.30 = 9.36$. We bought the stocks for 1305; however, over the life of the futures, this investment lost interest at a rate of 5.2 percent and accumulated dividends at a rate of 3 percent. Thus, the effective cost of the stock was $1,305e^{(0.052-0.03)(0.1096)} = 1,308.15$, which, by no coincidence, is the theoretical futures price. The stock is sold at 1,300.30 for a profit of $1,300.30 - 1,308.15 = -7.85$. Thus, the overall profit is $9.36 - 7.85 = 1.51$. This is the difference between the theoretical futures price and the actual futures price. Because the actual futures price was higher than the theoretical price, we were able to execute an arbitrage involving the purchase of stocks and sale of futures to capture the 1.51 differential. Had the actual futures price been less than the theoretical price, then we would have executed a reverse carry arbitrage involving the purchase of futures and short sale of stock, which would have created a synthetic loan that would have cost less than the risk-free rate.

> Stock index arbitrage is the purchase or sale of a portfolio of stock that replicates a stock index and the sale or purchase of a futures contract on the index. Stock index arbitrage occurs when the futures price does not conform to the cost of carry model and, if properly executed, will earn, at no risk, the difference between the futures price and the theoretical futures price.

Let us now determine the implied repo rate. Given the pricing formula, $f_0(T) = S_0e^{(r_c-\delta_c)T}$, suppose the futures price is equal to its theoretical fair price. Then we solve this equation for the implied interest rate, $\hat{r}_c$, and obtain

$$\hat{r}_c = \frac{\ln(f_0(T)/S_0)}{T} + \delta_c.$$

In this example, we have

$$\hat{r}_c = \frac{\ln(1,309.66/1305)}{0.1096} + 0.03 = 0.0625.$$

If this transaction were undertaken, it would provide a risk-free return of 6.25 percent. With the risk-free rate at 5 percent, the transaction is an attractive opportunity. Also, if an arbitrageur could not borrow at 5 percent but could borrow at any rate less than 6.25 percent, the transaction would still be worth doing.

Stock index arbitrage has proven to be particularly popular. It turns out, however, that there are a number of serious practical considerations that can limit its profitability.

Some Practical Considerations There are several problems in implementing stock index arbitrage. We referred to the arbitrageur as buying the stock index at 1305. In reality, the arbitrageur would have to purchase all 500 stocks in the appropriate proportions as the index and immediately execute all of the trades. The New York Stock Exchange has established a computerized order processing system, called the Designated Order Turnaround, or DOT, that expedites trades. Nonetheless, it is still difficult to get all of the trades in before the price of any single stock changes. Thus, most arbitrageurs do not duplicate the index, but use a smaller subset of the stocks. Naturally, this introduces some risk into what is supposed to be a riskless transaction.[6]

Let us assume, however, that the trades can be executed simultaneously. Let the index be 1305. Now assume that an arbitrageur has $20 million to use. Then the arbitrageur will buy the appropriately weighted 500 stocks with that amount. Because of the $250 multiplier on the futures, the S&P 500 is actually priced at $1,305(250) = \$326,250$, so

---

[6]As an alternative, the arbitrageur could use exchange-traded funds, which are securities that represent claims on a portfolio identical to an underlying index. Many exchange-traded funds are very actively traded.

the arbitrageur will need to buy \$20,000,000/\$326,250 = 61.30 futures contracts. Because one cannot buy fractional contracts, the transaction will not be weighted precisely.

In addition, there are transaction costs of about 0.5 percent of the market value of the stocks. Would this consume the profit in this example? If the index is 1,305 and the net profit is 1.51, the profit is approximately 0.0012 percent of the index and clearly would be absorbed by the transaction costs.

In addition, there are problems involved in simultaneously selling all of the stocks in the index at expiration. These transactions must be executed such that the portfolio will be liquidated at the closing values of each stock. This is very difficult to do and frequently causes unusual stock price movements at expiration.

Nonetheless, many large financial institutions execute this type of arbitrage transaction. Every day billions of dollars trade on the basis of this futures pricing model. This trading of large blocks of stock simultaneously is called **program trading**.[7] The New York Stock Exchange defines a program trade as "the simultaneous or near simultaneous purchase or sale of at least 15 stocks with a total market value of at least \$1 million." The NYSE requires that these program trades be reported to it, and all index arbitrage trades must also be reported.

Program trading is the execution on a stock market of a large number of simultaneous buy or sell orders. It is normally triggered by a computer program that detects an arbitrage opportunity or suggests some other reason for quickly establishing a large portfolio of stock.

In this type of trading, the model is programmed into a computer, which continuously monitors the futures price and the individual stock prices. When the computer identifies a deviation from the model, it sends a signal to the user. Many large institutions have established procedures for immediately executing the many simultaneous transactions, usually sending the orders through the DOT system. Table 10.5 illustrates a successful index arbitrage trade using the same example as before, but with a more significantly overpriced futures.

Are stock index futures contracts correctly priced? Is it truly possible to profit from index arbitrage? This question has been studied at great length. In the early days of stock index futures trading, there was considerable evidence that stock index futures prices were too low (Figlewski, 1984). In time, prices began to conform more closely to the model, as shown by Cornell (1985). Deviations from the model remain, however, and some can be exploited by traders with sufficiently low transaction costs. MacKinlay and Ramaswamy (1988) revealed that (1) mispricing is more common the longer the remaining time to expiration and (2) when a contract becomes overpriced or underpriced, it tends to stay overpriced or underpriced rather than reversing from overpriced to underpriced or vice versa. Sofianos (1993) found that it was very difficult to profit from index arbitrage after accounting for the problem of simultaneously executing all trades.

One consequence of program trading is that large stock price movements often occur quickly and without an apparent flow of new information. For example, when the index or futures price becomes out of line with the carry model, many investors recognize this event simultaneously and react by buying and selling large quantities of stock and futures. Such actions have attracted considerable attention from the media. Critics have charged that program trading has led to increased volatility in the spot markets. Regulators and legislators have called for restrictions on such trading in the form of circuit breakers and reduced access to the DOT system for rapidly executing orders. Others have argued for imposing higher margins on futures trading. These issues continue to generate a lot of debate.

[7]Index arbitrage is but one form of program trading. Another is portfolio insurance, which is covered in Chapter 14. See Hill and Jones (1988) for a discussion of the different forms of program trading.

TABLE 10.5 STOCK INDEX ARBITRAGE

Scenario: On November 8, the S&P 500 index is at 1,305, the continuously compounded dividend yield is 3 percent, and the continuously compounded risk-free rate is 5.2 percent. The December futures contract, which expires in 40 days, is priced at 1316.30. Its theoretical price is

$$f = 1,305e^{(0.052-0.03)(0.1096)} = 1,308.15,$$

where T = 40/365 = 0.1096. Thus, the futures contract is overpriced and the carry arbitrage transaction will be executed using $20 million. Transaction costs are 0.5 percent of the dollars invested.

DATE	SPOT MARKET	FUTURES MARKET
November 8	The S&P 500 is at 1,305. The stocks have a dividend yield of 3 percent. The risk-free rate is 5 2 percent. **Buy $20 million of stock in the same proportions as make up the S&P 500**	The S&P 500 futures, expiring on December 18, is at 1,316.30. The appropriate number of futures is $20 million/[(1,305)(250)] = 61.30.* **Sell 61 contracts**
December 18	The S&P 500 is at 1,300.36. The stocks will be worth (1,300.36/1305)($20 million) = $19.928889 million. The $20 million invested in the stocks effectively costs ($20 million)e^{(0.052-0.03)(0.1096)} = $20.048242 million. Transactions costs are $20 million (0.005) = $100,000 (includes futures costs). **Sell stocks**	Futures expires at the S&P 500 price of 1,300.36. **Close out futures at expiration**

Analysis
Profit on stocks

$19,928,889 (received from sale of stocks)
−$20,048,282 (invested in stocks)
  −$119,393

Profit on futures

61(250)(1,316.30) (sale price of futures)
−61(250)(1,300.36) (purchase price of futures)
  $243,085

Overall profit

$243,085 (from futures)
−$119,393 (from stock)
−$100,000 (transaction costs)
  $23,692

*The appropriate number of futures contracts to match $20 million of stock is $20 million divided by the index price, *not the futures price*, times the multiplier. Even though the $20 million is allocated across 500 different stocks, it is equivalent to buying $20 million/ 1,305 = 15,326 "shares" of the S&P 500. The appropriate number of futures is one for each equivalent "share" of the S&P 500. Each futures, of course, has a $250 multiplier.

FOREIGN EXCHANGE ARBITRAGE

We have discussed carry arbitrage with federal funds, Eurodollars, Treasury bond futures, and stock indices so far. The arbitrage concept is also applicable to foreign exchange futures. Recall that the model for the foreign exchange futures price is[8]

---

[8]In Chapter 9, we introduced foreign exchange forward contracts. We ignore any differences related to forwards and futures here.

$$f_0(T) = S_0(1 + r)^T / (1 + \rho)^T,$$

where S_0 is the spot foreign exchange rate expressed in local currency per unit of foreign currency, r denotes the domestic risk-free interest rate (annually compounded), and ρ denotes the foreign risk-free interest rate (annually compounded). The continuously compounded equivalent is expressed as

$$f_0(T) = S_0 e^{(r_c - \rho_c)T},$$

where r_c is the continuously compounded risk-free rate and ρ_c is the continuously compounded foreign interest rate. Recall that this relationship between the spot foreign exchange rate and the forward/futures price is known as interest rate parity. Interest rate parity is based on four transactions: a spot currency transaction, a domestic bank borrowing or lending transaction, a foreign bank borrowing or lending transaction, and a forward foreign exchange transaction. If we omit the forward foreign exchange transaction, we have a transaction known as the carry trade. It is often undertaken for the purpose of exporting one's currency into a foreign country in order to earn a higher rate of interest. But without the forward contract, the carry trade bears a great deal of risk. If the foreign currency weakens while the trade is in place, the conversion back into the domestic currency will result in a potentially large loss. Thus, what might be gained from the higher interest rate of the foreign currency could be more than lost on the unfavorable exchange rate movement. Adding the forward contract locks in the rate at which the foreign currency will be converted back into the domestic currency, thereby making the transaction free of exchange rate risk. Because arbitrage transactions are supposed to be risk-free, the forward foreign exchange transaction is a vital part of foreign exchange arbitrage.

Numerical Example Consider again (p. 305) the following example from a European perspective. On June 9 of a particular year, the spot rate for dollars was 0.7908 euros. The U.S. interest rate was 5.84 percent, while the euro interest rate was 3.59 percent. The time to expiration was 90/365 = 0.2466. Recall that we have

Foreign exchange arbitrage is the purchase or sale of a foreign exchange and the sale or purchase of a futures contract on foreign exchange. Foreign exchange arbitrage occurs when the futures price does not conform to the carry arbitrage model and, if properly executed, will earn, at no risk, the difference between the futures price and the theoretical futures price.

$$f_0(T) = €0.7908(1.0584)^{-0.2466}(1.0359)^{0.2466} = 0.7866 \text{ euros.}$$

Again, the forward rate should be about 0.7866 euros.

Now suppose that the observed market forward rate is 0.80 euros. Then, an arbitrage opportunity is available. An arbitrageur buys $(1.0584)^{-0.2466} = 0.9861$ dollars for $0.9861 (€0.7908) = 0.7798$ euros and sells one forward contract at a forward rate of 0.80 euros. The 0.9861 dollars are invested at the U.S. risk-free rate. When the contract expires, the arbitrageur will have 1 dollar, which is delivered on the forward contract and for which 0.80 euros is received. Thus, the arbitrageur has invested 0.7798 euros and received 0.80 euros in 90 days. The annualized return is

$$\left(\frac{0.80}{0.7798}\right)^{365/90} - 1 = 0.1093,$$

TECHNICAL NOTE: More on Interest Rate Parity
go to www.cengagebrain.com

which exceeds the euro risk-free rate of 3.59 percent. This transaction is called **covered interest arbitrage.** The combined effects of numerous arbitrageurs would push the spot rate up and/or the forward rate down until the spot and forward rates were properly aligned with the relative interest rates in the two countries.[9] Of course, some transaction costs and the dealer bid-ask spread would prevent the relationship from holding precisely.

MAKING THE CONNECTION

Currency-Hedged Cross-Border Index Arbitrage

We have now covered how to engage in covered interest arbitrage, in which a trader buys a currency and hedges its conversion back to the trader's currency using a forward or futures contract. We have also covered how to engage in stock index arbitrage, in which the trader buys a portfolio of stock and sells a futures on an index that matches the portfolio. Now, we shall take a look at combining these two strategies.

Suppose you are a Swiss equity trader who follows equities in the various European countries. The Dow Jones Euro STOXX 50, in particular, is a euro-denominated index of 50 leading European stocks. A futures contract, also denominated in euros, trades on EUREX, a European derivatives exchange. The trader observes that the futures seems to be overpriced. A stock index arbitrage transaction could be executed using an exchange-traded fund, or ETF, which is a portfolio representing claims on a given index. To undertake this transaction, however, the trader would need to convert his own currency (Swiss francs) to euros, do the stock index arbitrage, and then convert the euros back to Swiss francs. Thus, the transaction is exposed to the risk of the euro-Swiss franc exchange rate. The trader knows, however, that he can hedge the conversion of euros back into Swiss francs, but the details are more complex than a straightforward conversion of euros to Swiss francs. The trader will have to take into account the value of the hedged portfolio when deciding on the size of the forward contract.

Suppose that the Dow Jones Euro STOXX index is at 2,664. A futures contract on the index is at 2,680. Both numbers are in euros. The euro interest rate is 3 percent, and the Swiss franc interest rate is 2.5 percent. These rates were based on LIBOR-type interest but have been converted to continuous compounding equivalents. The continuously compounded dividend yield on the index is 1.2 percent. The exchange rate is SF1.4726 per euro. The futures expires in exactly three months, and each futures contract covers €10. That is, the quoted futures price is multiplied by 10 to obtain the actual futures price. ETFs on the index trade at 1/10 the price of the index. Thus, the ETF is at 266.40.

First, the trader calculates the theoretical price of the futures:

$$2,664e^{(0.03-0.012)(0.25)} = 2,676.$$

Observing the futures price of 2,680, the trader knows that the futures is overpriced. He decides to sell 1,000 contracts. Accounting for the multiplier, this would be like selling futures to cover $1,000(10) = 10,000$ shares. He must take into account, however, that if he purchases ETFs, the price is set at 1/10 of the index. Thus, he must purchase 100,000 ETF shares. In addition, if he purchases the shares, he will accrue dividends at the rate of 1.2 percent per year. He can reinvest these dividends into new shares. Because he wants the equivalent of 100,000 ETF shares after three months, he should purchase

$$100,000e^{-0.012(0.25)} = 99,700$$

shares of the ETF. He then sells 1,000 futures at 2,680. He will also need to engage in a forward contract to convert a specific amount of euros into Swiss francs. Because he will be effectively selling 10,000 shares of the index at 2,680, the amount of euros he should receive is $10,000(2,680) = 26,800,000$. Thus, the forward contract should be

---

[9]Arbitrage could also put pressure on interest rates in the two countries. The U.S. rate could decrease, while the euro rate could increase. Interest rates are, however, so heavily influenced by other effects, such as inflation, government borrowing, and central bank policy, that it is unlikely that arbitrageurs could influence rates.

written to cover €26,800,000. The forward price would be

$$1.4726e^{(0.025-0.03)(0.25)} = 1.4708.$$

The forward contract is assumed to be correctly priced, so the trader has entered into a commitment to deliver €26,800,000 at SF1.4708 per euro.

Thus, the trader buys the stock in the form of 99,700 ETF shares. This will require 99,700(€266.40) = €26,560,080, so he will have to commit €26,560,080 (SF1.4726/€) = SF39,112,374. Remember that the trader could earn 2.5 percent on this money by keeping it invested risk free in Switzerland. He sells 1,000 futures at 2,680 and sells a forward contract on €26,800,000 at SF1.4708.

At expiration, the index is at S_T and the ETF is at $(1/10)S_T$. Due to the reinvestment of dividends, he now holds

$$99,700e^{0.012(0.25)} = 100,000$$

shares of the ETF, which are worth

$$100,000(1/10)S_T.$$

The futures payoff, ignoring the mark-to-market effect, is

$$-1,000(10)(S_T - 2,680).$$

Thus, the total payoff is

$$100,000(1/10)S_T - 1,000(10)(S_T - 2,680)$$
$$= 26,800,000$$

euros. Using forward contracts, he converts this amount back into Swiss francs at the rate of SF1.4708 to obtain

$$€26,800,000(SF1.4708/€) = SF39,417,440.$$

Now let us see how well he has done. He invested SF39,112,374 and ended up with SF39,417,440. This is a return per Swiss franc invested of 39,417,440/ 39,112,374 = 1.00779973. The annualized continuously compounded rate of return can be found in the following manner:

$$\frac{39,417,440}{39,112,374} = e^{k(0.25)}.$$

Then

$$\ln\left(\frac{39,417,440}{39,112,374}\right) = k(0.25),$$

and k will be 3.11 percent, which is earned risk free. This is better than the 2.5 percent rate he could have gotten by investing risk free in Switzerland. Of course, the trader must execute the transactions quickly and cover all costs.

Summary

Building on the basic principles established in Chapter 9, this chapter examined the application of arbitrage strategies. It looked at how fed funds, Eurodollar, Treasury bond, stock index, and foreign exchange futures can be used if market prices do not conform to the formulas that assume no arbitrage profits are available. For Treasury bond contracts, the chapter also examined how these contracts permit delivery of any bond chosen from a group of eligible bonds and how the price paid or received is adjusted to reflect differences in the deliverable bonds. It also examined how the cheapest deliverable bond is identified. This chapter also introduced the important concept of the implied repo rate, which is seen to be the equivalent of the internal rate of return.

The main focus of this chapter has been on arbitrage trading strategies. In Chapter 11, we will examine a wide variety of other futures trading strategies.

Key Terms

Before continuing to Chapter 11, you should be able to give brief definitions of the following terms:

cash-and-carry arbitrage/carry arbitrage/repurchase agreement/ repo/implied repo rate, p. 334
conversion factor (CF), p. 339
cheapest-to-deliver (CTD), p. 341

delivery options/wild card option, p. 343
quality option, p. 344
end-of-the-month option/timing option, p. 345

stock index arbitrage, p. 349
program trading, p. 351
covered interest arbitrage, p. 353

Further Reading

A survey of the literature on delivery options is found in the following article:

Chance, D. M., and M. L. Hemler. "The Impact of Delivery Options on Futures Prices: A Survey." *The Journal of Futures Markets* 13 (1993): 127–155.

The following articles contain empirical tests of arbitrage opportunities in futures markets:

Elton, E. J., M. J. Gruber, and J. Rentzler. "Intra-Day Tests of Efficiency of the Treasury Bill Futures Market." *Review of Economics and Statistics* 66 (1984): 129–137.

MacKinlay, A. C., and K. Ramaswamy. "Index-Futures Arbitrage and the Behavior of Stock Index Futures Prices." *The Review of Financial Studies* 1 (1988): 137–158.

Neal, R. "Direct Tests of Index Arbitrage Models." *Journal of Financial and Quantitative Analysis* 31 (1996): 541–562.

Rendleman, R. J., Jr., and C. Carabini. "The Efficiency of the Treasury Bill Futures Market." *The Journal of Finance* 44 (1979): 895–914.

Program trading and stock index arbitrage are examined in the following:

Furbush, D. "Program Trading and Price Movement: Evidence from the October 1987 Market Crash." *Financial Management* 18 (1989): 68–83.

Stoll, H. R., and R. E. Whaley, Jr. "Program Trading and Expiration Day Effects." *Financial Analysts Journal* 43 (March–April, 1987): 16–28.

In addition, the websites of the derivatives exchanges provide many excellent examples of how futures contracts can be used.

Concept Checks

1. Explain how the repurchase agreement plays a role in the pricing of futures contracts. What is the implied repo rate?
2. Identify and explain some factors that make the execution of stock index futures arbitrage difficult in practice.
3. What is program trading? Why is it so controversial?
4. Explain the relationship between carry arbitrage and the implied repo rate.
5. Define the conversion factor. Why are U.S. Treasury bond futures contracts designed with conversion factors?

Questions and Problems

1. Identify and discuss four nontraded delivery options related to U.S. Treasury bond futures contracts.
2. Explain the implied repo rate on a U.S. Treasury bond futures spread position.
3. Identify two ways to express interest rate parity based on how interest rates are quoted. Explain why, in practice, they contain the same information.
4. What are some potential dangers posed by program trading?
5. Why does a market participant not earn a risk premium on a carry arbitrage transaction?
6. The S&P 500 index is at 1,371.00, the continuously compounded risk-free rate is 5.12 percent, time to expiration is 55 days, and the futures price is 1,376.42. Assuming the futures price is equal to its theoretical fair price and the underlying has a continuously compounded dividend yield, solve for the implied dividend yield.

7. On February 4 of a particular year, the spot rate for U.S. dollars ($) expressed in euros (€) was $0.7873/€. The U.S. interest rate (compounded semiannually) was 5.36 percent, while the euro interest rate (compounded semiannually) was 3.11 percent. From a European perspective, what should be the forward rate of a contract that expires September 4? (Assume that each month is one-twelfth of a year.)

8. Again, like the previous problem, on February 4 of a particular year, the spot rate for U.S. dollars ($) expressed in euros (€) was $0.7873/€. The U.S. interest rate (compounded annually) was 5.36 percent, while the euro interest rate (compounded annually) was 3.11 percent. From a European perspective, what should be the forward rate of a

contract that expires September 4? (Assume that each month is one-twelfth of a year.) How does your answer here differ from that of the previous problem?

9. On November 1, the one-month LIBOR rate is 4.0 percent and the two-month LIBOR rate is 5.0 percent. Assume that fed funds futures contracts trades at a 25 basis point rate under one-month LIBOR at the start of the delivery month. The December fed funds futures is quoted at 94.75. Assuming no basis risk between fed funds and one-month LIBOR at the start of the delivery month, identify whether an arbitrage opportunity is available. Contract size is $5,000,000. Be sure to illustrate the arbitrage strategy for one contract. To show the dollar arbitrage, assume that the one-month LIBOR rate on December 1 was 7 percent.

10. Repeat the previous problem, but now assume that the one-month LIBOR rate on December 1 was 5.5 percent.

11. A corporate cash manager who often invests her firm's excess cash in the Eurodollar market is considering the possibility of investing $20 million for 180 days directly in a Eurodollar CD at 6.15 percent. As an alternative, she considers the fact that the 90-day rate is 6 percent and the price of a Eurodollar futures expiring in 90 days is 93.75 (the IMM index). She believes that the combination of the 90-day CD plus the futures contract would be a better way of lending $20 million for 180 days. Suppose she executes this strategy and the rate on 90-day Eurodollar CDs 90 days later is 5.9 percent. Determine the annualized rate of return she earns over 180 days and compare it to the annualized rate of return on the 180-day CD.

12. On September 26 of a particular year, the March Treasury bond futures contract settlement price as 94-22. Compare the following two bonds and determine which is the cheaper bond to deliver. Assume that delivery will be made on March 1. Use 5.3 percent as the repo rate.
    a. Bond A: A 12 3/4 percent bond callable in about 19 years and maturing in about 24 years with a price of 148 9/32 and a CF of 1.4433. Coupons are paid on November 15 and May 15. The accrued interest is 4.64 on September 26 and 3.73 on March 1.
    b. Bond B: A 13 7/8 percent bond callable in about 20 years and maturing in about 25 years with a price of 159 27/32 and a CF of 1.5689. Coupons

are paid on November 15 and May 15. The accrued interest is 5.05 on September 26 and 4.06 on March 1.

13. It is August 20, and you are trying to determine which of two bonds is the cheaper bond to deliver on the December Treasury bond futures contract. The futures price is 89 12/32. Assume that delivery will be made on December 14 and use 7.9 percent as the repo rate. Find the cheaper bond to deliver.
    a. Bond X: A 9 percent noncallable bond maturing in about 28 years with a price of 100 14/32 and a CF of 1.1106. Coupons are paid on November 15 and May 15. The accrued interest is 2.37 on August 20 and 0.72 on December 14.
    b. Bond Z: An 11 1/4 percent noncallable bond maturing in about 25 years with a price of 121 14/32 and a CF of 1.3444. Coupons are paid on February 15 and August 15. The accrued interest is 0.15 on August 20 and 3.7 on December 14.

14. Assume that on March 16, the cheapest bond to deliver on the June Treasury bond futures contract is the 14s, callable in about 19 years and maturing in about 24 years. Coupons are paid on November 15 and May 15. The price of the bond is 161 23/32, and the CF is 1.584. The June futures price is 100 17/32. Assume a 5.5 percent reinvestment rate. Determine the implied repo rate on the contract. Interpret your result. Note that you will need to determine the accrued interest. Assume delivery on June 1.

15. On July 5, a stock index futures contract was at 394.85. The index was at 392.54, the risk-free rate was 2.83 percent, the dividend yield was 2.08 percent, and the contract expired on September 20. Determine whether an arbitrage opportunity was available and explain what transactions were executed.

16. Rework the last problem assuming that the index was at 388.14 at expiration. Determine the profit from the arbitrage trade and express it in terms of the profit from the spot and futures sides of the transaction. How does your answer relate to that in problem 15?

17. On August 20, a stock index futures, which expires on September 20, was priced at 429.70. The index was at 428.51. The dividend yield was 2.7 percent. Discuss the concept of the implied repo rate on an index arbitrage trade. Determine the implied repo rate on this trade and explain how you would evaluate it.

18. On March 16, the March Treasury bond futures settlement price was 101 21/32. Assume that the 12 1/2 percent bond maturing in about 22 years is the cheapest bond to deliver. The CF is 1.4639. Assume that the price at 3:00 P.M. was 150 15/32. Determine the price at 5:00 P.M. that would be necessary to justify delivery.

19. On September 12, the cheapest-to-deliver bond on the December Treasury bond futures contract is the 9s of November 2018. The bond pays interest semiannually on May 15 and November 15. Its price is 125 12/32. The December futures price is 112 24/32. The bond has a conversion factor of 1.1002. Its accrued interest on September 12 is 2.91 and its accrued interest on December 1 is 4.92, which reflects the payment of the coupon on November 15. Assuming delivery on December 1, determine the implied repo rate. Then write an interpretation of your result.

20. On March 16, the June Treasury bond futures contract was priced at 100 17/32 and the September contract was at 99 17/32. Determine the implied repo rate on the spread. Assume that the cheapest bond to deliver on both contracts is the 11 1/4 maturing in 28 years and currently priced at 140 21/32. The CF for delivery in June was 1.3593, and the CF for delivery in September was 1.3581. Delivery is on the first of the month, and the coupons are paid on February 15 and August 15. The accrued interest is 3.29 on June 1 and 6.16 on September 1.

21. Explain the impact on the implied repo rate of changing from the bid to the offer futures price of the longer-dated futures contract.

22. Assume that on December 2, 2010, the cheapest bond to deliver was the 6 1/4s maturing on August 15, 2028. The March contract is priced at 112, and the conversion factor is 1.0269. The June futures price is 111.75. The conversion factor for the 6 1/4s delivered on the June contract is 1.0265. The accrued interest on the bond on March 7, the assumed delivery date, is 0.35, and the accrued interest on June 5 is 1.90. There are no coupons between the two futures expiration dates. Calculate the implied repo rate for the March–June 2011 Treasury bond futures spread. If the actual forward repo rate is 4 percent, what do you recommend?

23. (Concept Problem) In this chapter, there are two equations presented for the implied repo rate related to bond futures contracts shown below. Explain these equations and discuss the differences between them.

$$\hat{r} = \left[\frac{(CF)(f_0(T)) + AI_T + CI_{0,T}}{B_0 + AI_0} \right]^{(1/T)} - 1 \quad \text{and}$$

$$\hat{r} = \left[\frac{(CF(t))f_0(t) + AI_t + CI_{t,T}}{(CF(t))f_0(t) + AI_t} \right]^{1/(T-t)} - 1$$

24. (Concept Problem) Referring to problem 15, suppose transaction costs amounted to 0.5 percent of the value of the stock index. Explain how these costs would affect the profitability and the incidence of index arbitrage. Then calculate the range of possible futures prices within which no arbitrage would take place.

APPENDIX 10

Determining the CBOT Treasury Bond Conversion Factor

Step 1 Determine the maturity of the bond in years, months, and days as of the first day of the expiration month. If the bond is callable, use the first call date instead of the maturity date. Let YRS be the number of years and MOS the number of months. Ignore the number of days. Let c be the coupon rate on the bond.

Step 2 Round the number of months down to 0, 3, 6, or 9. Call this MOS*.

Step 3 If MOS* = 0,

$$CF_0 = \frac{c}{2}\left[\frac{1 - (1.03)^{-2\cdot YRS}}{0.03}\right] + (1.03)^{-2\cdot YRS}.$$

If MOS* = 6,

$$CF_3 = (CF_0 + c/2)(1.03)^{-0.5} - c/4.$$

If MOS* = 6,

$$CF_6 = \frac{c}{2}\left[\frac{1 - (1.03)^{-(2\cdot YRS+1)}}{0.03}\right] + (1.03)^{-(2\cdot YRS+1)}.$$

If MOS* = 9,

$$CF_9 = (CF_6 + c/2)(1.03)^{-0.5} - c/4.$$

Example: Determine the CF for delivery of the 5 1/4s of February 15, 2029, on the March 2012 Treasury bond futures contract.

On March 1, 2012, the bond's remaining life is 16 years, 11 months, and 14 days. Thus, YRS = 16 and MOS = 11. Rounding down gives MOS* = 9. First, we must find CF_6:

$$CF_6 = \frac{0.0525}{2}\left[\frac{1 - (1.03)^{-(2(16)+1)}}{0.03}\right] + (1.03)^{-(2(16)+1)} = 0.922128.$$

Then we find CF_9 as

$$CF_9 = (0.922128 + 0.0525/2)(1.03)^{-0.5} - 0.0525/4 = 0.9213,$$

which is shown in Table 10.3 in the chapter.

The Excel spreadsheet CF9e.xls will automatically calculate the conversion factor for you. Software Demonstration 10.2 illustrates how to use CF9e.xls.

SOFTWARE DEMONSTRATION 10.2

Determining the CBOT Conversion Factor with the Excel Spreadsheet CF9e.xls

The Excel spreadsheet CF9e.xls is saved in Excel 97-2003. It calculates the conversion factor for a bond delivered on the Chicago Board of Trade Treasury bond futures contract. The spreadsheet is available as a download via the product support website. To access it:

1. Go to www.cengagebrain.com.
2. Click on Instructor Resources or Student Resources.
3. Click on the link for CF9e.xls.
4. Follow the instructions on the Web page to download and install the spreadsheet.

This spreadsheet is a read-only spreadsheet, meaning that it cannot be saved under the name CF9e.xls, which preserves the original file.

Now let us work an example. Suppose we want to deliver the 5 1/4 of February 15, 2029 on the March 2012 contract. Each cell that will accept input has a double-line border, and the values are in blue. In the section labeled **Inputs:** you should enter the delivery date. This will always be simply a month and a year. Enter it in the form mm/yyyy. Thus, you should insert "3/2012" in the cell. Several rows below, you should enter the coupon rate and maturity date. Enter the coupon rate as a percentage or decimal. For example, our bond's coupon is 5.25, so enter "5.25" or "0.0525". Enter the maturity date in the format mm/dd/yyyy. Thus, in this case, you would enter "2/15/2029". The spreadsheet displays both of these dates in Excel's date format. Tap F9 (manual recalculation).

The results are then calculated and appear in the section labeled **Results:** Output values have a single-line border. The conversion factor here is 0.9138. The spreadsheet also shows the maturity in years (here, 19), months (11), and days based on the first day of the expiration month (14). This enables you to see whether the bond has a sufficiently long maturity to be eligible for delivery on the bond or note contract.

TREASURY BOND FUTURES CONVERSION FACTOR Cf9e

Inputs:

Delivery Date (mm/yyyy)

Mar-12

Coupon Rate	Maturity Date (mm/dd/yyyy)
5.250%	February 15, 2029

Results:

Conversion Factor

0.9213

Maturity on Delivery Date

Years	Months	Days
16	11	14

CHAPTER 11

Forward and Futures Hedging, Spread, and Target Strategies

The beauty of finance and speculation was that they could be different things to different men. To some: poetry or high drama; to others, physics, scientific and immutable; to still others, politics or philosophy. And to still others, war.

Michael M. Thomas
Hanover Place, 1990, p. 37

Hedging is a type of transaction designed to reduce or, in some cases, eliminate risk. Our material on options presented numerous examples of hedges, the most obvious being the covered call and protective put. Now we shall find that it is also possible, in some cases preferable, to use forwards or futures to hedge.

Until now, we have emphasized that there are many similarities and differences between forward and futures contracts. Both can be used for hedging. When choosing a forward or futures hedge over an option hedge, the hedger agrees to give up future gains and losses. No up-front cost is incurred. In contrast, an option hedge such as a protective put preserves future gains but at the expense of an up-front cost, the option premium. Forward contracting, as we previously noted, involves some credit risk and is generally available only in very large transaction sizes. Forward contracting, however, allows the user to customize the terms of the transaction to get a near-perfect hedge. Certain types of business situations are more suited to forward hedges. Others are more suited to futures hedges. In others, options are more appropriately used. While the choice of instrument is often a trade-off between the advantages and disadvantages of each, it is also sometimes true that the instrument chosen is a function of the extent to which the hedger is familiar with the type of instrument, what competing firms do, and the efforts made by futures exchanges and over-the-counter dealers to convince hedgers to use their products.

In this chapter, we shall see a number of examples of various types of hedges. These include hedges with foreign currency forwards and futures, futures on bonds and notes, and stock index futures.

In this chapter, we also explore various spread strategies. Spread strategies are usually pursued when a trader has a particular view on the future direction of various futures contracts. In addition, we cover target strategies wherein investors use futures contracts to target their desired durations and betas.

In spite of all of the material we cover in this chapter, our treatment will be incomplete. A considerable number of hedge strategies utilize swaps and interest rate

CHAPTER OBJECTIVES

- Explain some of the reasons for and against hedging

- Present the basic concepts associated with hedging, such as the basis, short and long hedging, and the risks of hedging

- Identify the factors that are involved in deciding to undertake a hedge

- Illustrate the different methods (price sensitivity, minimum variance) of determining the number of futures contracts to use in a hedge

- Illustrate examples of intramarket and intermarket spread strategies

- Review selected target strategies, including targeted duration, alpha capture, targeted beta, and tactical asset allocation

derivatives, topics we cover in Chapters 12 and 13. Accordingly, we shall return to the topic of hedging in those chapters.

We start this chapter with a discussion of several general issues involved in the process of hedging. For example, why should anyone hedge in the first place?

WHY HEDGE?

Before we begin with the technical aspects of hedging, it is worthwhile to ask two questions: (1) Why do firms hedge? and (2) Should they hedge? Hedging is done to reduce risk, but is this desirable? If everyone hedged, would we not simply end up with an economy in which no one takes risks? This would surely lead to economic stagnancy. Moreover, we must wonder whether hedging can actually increase shareholder wealth.[1]

If the famous Modigliani-Miller propositions are correct, then the value of the firm is independent of any financial decisions, which include hedging. Hedging, however, may be desired by the shareholders simply to find a more acceptable combination of expected return and risk. It can be argued, however, that firms need not hedge because shareholders, if they wanted hedging, could do it themselves. But this ignores several important points. It assumes that shareholders can correctly assess all of the firm's risks that can be hedged. If a company is exposed to the risk associated with volatile raw materials prices, can the shareholders properly determine the degree of risk? Can they determine the periods over which that risk is greatest? Can they determine the correct number of futures contracts necessary to hedge their share of the total risk? Do they even qualify to open a futures brokerage account? Will their transaction costs be equal to or less than their proportional share of the transaction costs incurred if the firm did the hedging? The answer to each of these questions is "maybe not." It should be obvious that hedging is not something that shareholders can always do as effectively as firms.

Corporate hedging activities may be related to the relative cost of internal and external financing. Froot, Scharfstein, and Stein suggest that corporate hedging is motivated by a desire to ensure lower cost financing internally when attractive investment opportunities are available.

> Firms hedge to save taxes, reduce bankruptcy costs, and, in some cases, because managers want to reduce the risk of their own wealth, which is tied to their firms' performance. Hedging is also done in the course of offering risk management services for clients and possibly because shareholders cannot hedge as effectively as firms can.

In addition, there may be other reasons why firms hedge, such as tax advantages. Low-income firms, for example those that are below the highest corporate tax rate, can particularly benefit from the interaction between hedging and the progressive corporate income tax structure.[2] Hedging also reduces the probability of bankruptcy. This is not necessarily valuable to the shareholders except that it can reduce the expected costs that are incurred if the firm does go bankrupt.

A firm may choose to hedge because its managers' livelihoods may be heavily tied to the performance of the firm. The managers may then benefit from reducing the firm's risk. This may not be in the shareholders' best interests, but it can at least explain why some firms hedge. Finally, hedging may send a signal to potential creditors that the firm is making a concerted effort to protect the value of the underlying assets. This can result in more favorable credit terms and less costly restrictive covenants.

---

[1]The material in this section draws heavily from C. W. Smith and R. M. Stulz, "The Determinants of Firms' Hedging Policies," *Journal of Financial and Quantitative Analysis* 20 (1985): 391–405; D. Duffie, "Corporate Risk Management 101: Why Hedge?" *Corporate Risk Management* 3 (May 1991): 22–25; D. R. Nance, C. W. Smith Jr., and C. W. Smithson, "On the Determinants of Corporate Hedging," *The Journal of Finance* 48 (March 1993): 267–284; and K. A. Froot, D. S. Scharfstein, and J. C Stein, "Risk Management: Coordinating Corporate Investment and Financing Policies," *The Journal of Finance* 48 (December 1993): 1629–1658.

[2]See Appendix 11 for more on hedging and taxes.

Many firms such as financial institutions are constantly trading over-the-counter financial products such as swaps and forwards on behalf of their clients. They offer these services to help their clients manage their risks. These financial institutions then turn around and hedge the risk they have assumed on behalf of their clients. How do they make money? They quote rates and prices to their clients that reflect a spread sufficient to cover their hedging costs and include a profit. In this manner, they become retailers of hedging services.

Lest we give a one-sided view of hedging, it is important to consider some reasons not to hedge. One reason is that hedging can give a misleading impression of the amount of risk reduced. There is an old saying in derivatives: "The only perfect hedge is in a Japanese garden." Hedges nearly always leave some risk, and some hedges leave a surprising amount of risk that was supposed to have been eliminated. Hedging should always be viewed as risk reducing but not eliminating, thus requiring that the remaining risk be identified and monitored.

Another problem with hedging is that it eliminates the opportunity to take advantage of favorable market conditions. In other words, hedging reduces the gain potential as well as the loss potential. Carried to an extreme, hedging can nearly eliminate any reason for being in business in the first place. The creation of wealth does not come about by indiscriminate hedging. Hedging should be selective—that is, reducing certain risks while maintaining exposures where an advantage is perceived.

Finally, we should add that *there is really no such thing as a hedge.* As surprising as that sounds, consider this. When an investor moves all funds from stock to cash, he may think he is hedging, but he is really taking a position that the market will go down. When a corporation hedges away the risk associated with borrowing at a floating rate, it is taking a position that interest rates will go up. In either case, the elimination of risk is taking a position based on a view that an unfavorable event will occur in the market. This is as much of a speculative action as is investing all of one's money in the stock market or borrowing at a floating rate. In other words, reducing risk is a bet that bad things will happen in the market.

> Hedging is a component of a more general process called risk management, the alignment of the actual level of risk with the desired level of risk.

With all of this talk about hedging, however, we would be remiss not to note that hedging is just a part of an overall process called *risk management*. Hedging is a specific example of managing risk for the purpose of reducing it. In a broader sense, however, there is much more to managing risk than just hedging. In some situations, risk will be lower than desired, calling for an increase in risk. Is this the opposite of hedging? Some would indeed call it *speculation*, but in fact, it is just part of the overall process of risk management, the alignment of the actual level of risk with the desired level of risk. While the focus of this chapter is on hedging, we shall discuss the bigger picture of managing risk in Chapters 15 and 16.

HEDGING CONCEPTS

Before we can understand why a certain hedge is placed or how it works, we must become acquainted with a few basic hedging concepts. We have mentioned some of these points before but have not specifically applied them to hedging strategies. In the discussion below, we shall primarily refer to futures, but the ideas are nearly always applicable to forward contracts as well.

> A short hedge means to hedge by taking a short position in a futures contract. A long hedge means to hedge by taking a long position in a futures contract.

Short Hedge and Long Hedge

The terms **short hedge** and **long hedge** distinguish hedges that involve short and long positions in the futures contract, respectively. A hedger who holds an asset and is concerned about a decrease in its price, such as a grain elevator operator owning a large inventory of wheat, might consider hedging it with a short position in futures. If the spot price and futures price move together, the hedge will reduce some of the risk. For example, if the spot price decreases, the futures price also will decrease. Because the hedger is short the futures contract, the futures transaction produces a profit that at least partially offsets the loss on the spot position. This is called a *short hedge* because the hedger is short futures. The grain elevator operator is able to hedge price risk with a short wheat futures position.

Another type of hedge situation is faced when a party plans to purchase an asset at a later date, such as a cereal producer. Fearing an increase in wheat prices, the cereal producer might buy futures contracts. Then if the price of wheat increases, the wheat futures price also will increase and produce a profit on the futures position. That profit will at least partially offset the higher cost of purchasing wheat. This is a *long hedge* because the hedger, the cereal producer in this example, is long in the futures market. Because it involves an anticipated transaction, it is sometimes called an **anticipatory hedge**.

Another type of long hedge might be placed when one is short an asset. Although this hedge is less common, it would be appropriate for someone who has sold short a stock and is concerned that the market will go up. Rather than close out the short position, one might buy a futures contract and earn a profit on the long position in futures that will at least partially offset the loss on the short position in the stock.

In each of these cases, the hedger held a position in the spot market that was subject to risk. The futures transaction served as a temporary substitute for a spot transaction. Thus, when one holds the asset and is concerned about a price decrease but does not want to sell it, one can execute a short futures trade. Selling the futures contract would substitute for selling the commodity. Table 11.1 summarizes these various hedging situations.

The Basis

The basis is the difference between the spot price and the futures price.

The **basis** is one of the most important concepts in futures markets because it aids in understanding the process of hedging. The basis usually is defined as the spot price minus the futures price. Some books and articles, however, define it as the futures price minus the spot price. In this book, we shall use the former definition:

$$\text{Basis} = \text{Spot price} - \text{Futures price}.$$

Hedging and the Basis   Here we will look at the concept of hedging and how the basis affects the performance of a hedge. Ultimately, we need to understand the factors that influence the basis.

Let us define the following terms:

T = time point of expiration (e.g., a particular month, day, and year)

t = time point prior to expiration ($t = 0$ implies "today")

TABLE 11.1   SUMMARY OF HEDGING SITUATIONS

CONDITION TODAY	RISK	APPROPRIATE HEDGE
Hold asset	Asset price may fall	Short hedge
Plan to buy asset	Asset price may rise	Long hedge
Sold short asset	Asset price may rise	Long hedge

Note: *Short hedge* means long spot, short futures; *long hedge* means short spot, long futures. Hedging situations involving loans are examined in Chapters 12 and 13.

S_0 = spot price today

f_0 = futures price today

S_t = spot price at time t prior to expiration

f_t = futures price at time t prior to expiration

S_T = spot price at expiration

f_T = futures price at expiration

Π = profit from a given strategy

For the time being, we shall ignore marking to market, any costs of storing the asset, and other transaction costs.

The concept of a hedge is not new. When we looked at options, we constructed several types of hedges, some of which were riskless. By taking a position in a stock and an opposite position in an option, gains (losses) on the stock are offset by losses (gains) on the option. We can do the same thing with futures: hold a long (short) position in the spot market and a short (long) position in the futures market. For a long position in the spot market, the profit from a hedge held to expiration is

$$\Pi(\text{short hedge}) = (S_T - S_0) \text{ (spot market profit)} + (f_0 - f_T) \text{ (futures market profit)}.$$

Recall that profit is always the selling price minus the purchase price. The futures market profit from a short position is $(f_0 - f_T)$ or $-(f_T - f_0)$. For a short position in the spot market and a long position in the futures market, the sign of each term in the above equation is reversed; that is,

$$\Pi(\text{long hedge}) = (S_0 - S_T)(\text{spot market profit}) + (f_T - f_0)(\text{futures market profit}).$$

In some cases, we might want to close out the position at time t, that is, before expiration. Then the profits from a short hedge and a long hedge are

$$\Pi\ (\text{short hedge}) = (S_t - S_0) + (f_0 - f_t)$$
$$\Pi\ (\text{long hedge}) = (S_0 - S_t) + (f_t - f_0).$$

At expiration, a person buying a futures contract can expect to receive immediate delivery of the good. Thus, an expiring futures contract is the same as the purchase of the spot commodity; therefore, $S_T = f_T$. Thus, the profit if the short hedge is held to expiration is simply $f_0 - S_0$. That means that the hedge is equivalent to buying the asset at price S_0 and immediately guaranteeing a sale price of f_0. Also, the profit if the long hedge is held to expiration is $S_0 - f_0$, which is equivalent to selling the asset at price S_0 and immediately guaranteeing the purchase price of f_0.

As an example, suppose you buy an asset for $100 and sell a futures contract on the asset at $103. Therefore, you have a short hedge. At expiration, the spot and futures prices are both $96. You sell the asset for $96, taking a $4 loss, and close your futures contract at $96, making a $7 gain, for a net profit of $3. Alternatively, you could deliver the asset on your futures contract, receiving $96, and collect the $7 that has accumulated in your futures account, making the effective sale price of the asset $103. In either case, the transaction is equivalent to selling the asset for $103, the original futures price.

Now suppose instead you short sell an asset for $100 and buy a futures contract on the asset at $103. Therefore, you have a long hedge. At expiration, the spot and futures prices are both $96. You buy back the asset for $96, receiving a $4 gain, and close your futures contract at $96, taking a $7 loss, for a net loss of $3. Alternatively, you could purchase the asset on your futures contract, paying $96, and with the $7 loss that has accumulated in your futures account, the effective purchase price of the asset is $103. In either case, the transaction is equivalent to purchasing the asset for $103, the original futures price.

Because the basis is defined as the spot price minus the futures price, we can write it as a variable, b, where

$$b_0 = S_0 - f_0 \text{(initial basis)}$$
$$b_t = S_t - f_t \text{(basis at time t)}$$
$$b_T = S_T - f_T \text{(basis at expiration)}.$$

Thus, for positions closed out at time t,

$$\Pi \text{ (short hedge)} = (S_t - f_t) - (S_0 - f_0),$$
$$\Pi \text{ (short hedge)} = b_t - b_0.$$
$$\Pi \text{ (long hedge)} = (S_0 - f_0) - (S_t - f_t),$$
$$\Pi \text{ (long hedge)} = b_0 - b_t.$$

> Hedging entails the assumption of basis risk, which is the uncertainty of the basis over the hedge period. The hedge profit is the change in the basis.

The profits from the hedges are simply the change in the basis. The uncertainty regarding how the basis will change is called **basis risk**. A hedge substitutes the change in the basis for the change in the spot price. The basis change usually is far less variable than the spot price change; hence, the hedged position is less risky than the unhedged position. Because basis risk results from the uncertainty over the change in the basis, hedging is a speculative activity that produces a risk level much lower than that of an unhedged position.

Hedging can also be viewed as a transaction that attempts to establish the expected future price of an asset. A short (long) hedge establishes the expected future sales (purchase) price. For example, the equation for the profit on a short hedge can be written as $f_0 + (S_t - f_t) - S_0$. Because the short hedger paid S_0 dollars to purchase the asset, then the effective sale price of the asset can be viewed as $f_0 + (S_t - f_t)$, which can be written as $f_0 + b_t$. In other words, a short hedge establishes the future sale price of the asset as the current futures price plus the basis. Because f_0 is known, the effective future sale price is uncertain only to the extent that the basis is uncertain. If the short hedge is held to expiration, the effective sale price becomes $f_0 + b_T$, which is simply f_0 because the basis at expiration is zero. Thus, the sale price of the asset is established as f_0 when the transaction is initiated. The short hedger would be sure that she would be able to effectively sell the asset for the futures price. This would be a "perfect" short hedge. Most hedges are imperfect for a variety of reasons but often because the hedger does not typically hold the position to expiration.

If the spot price increases by more than the futures price, the basis will increase. This is said to be a strengthening basis, and it improves (reduces) the performance of the short (long) hedge. If the futures price increases by more than the spot price, the basis will decrease, reducing (improving) the performance on the short (long) hedge. In that case, the basis is said to be weakening. These relationships between hedging profitability and the basis are summarized in Table 11.2.

As noted above, if a hedge is held all the way to expiration, the basis goes to zero. In that case, the profit is simply $-b_0$ from a short hedge and $+b_0$ from a long hedge.

Finally, we should remember that hedging incurs costs such as the transaction costs of the futures. In addition, if the asset is held, it will incur costs of storage. These will reduce the profit, but their effects are generally known in advance and thus do not impose any additional risk.

Hedging Example   Let us consider an example using gold. On March 30, the price of a gold futures expiring in June was $1,388.60 per troy ounce. The spot price of gold

TABLE 11.2 HEDGING PROFITABILITY AND THE BASIS

TYPE OF HEDGE	BENEFITS FROM	WHICH OCCURS IF
Short hedge	Strengthening basis	Spot price rises more than futures price rises or Spot price falls less than futures price falls or Spot price rises and futures price falls
Long hedge	Weakening basis	Spot price rises less than futures price rises or Spot price falls more than futures price falls or Spot price falls and futures price rises

Note: *Short hedge* means long spot, short futures; *long hedge* means short spot, long futures.

was $1,387.15. Suppose a gold dealer held 100 troy ounces of gold worth $100(1,387.15) = 138,715$. We shall disregard the storage costs because they are reasonably certain. To protect against a decrease in the price of gold, the dealer might sell one futures contract on 100 troy ounces; hence, he has entered a short hedge. In our notation,

$$S_0 = 1,387.15$$
$$f_0 = 1,388.60$$
$$b_0 = 1,387.15 - 1,388.60 = -1.45.$$

If the hedge is held to expiration, the basis should converge to zero. It might not go precisely to zero, however, and we shall see why later. If it does, the profit should be -1 times the original basis times the number of ounces:

$$\Pi = -1(-1.45)(100) = 145.$$

Suppose that at expiration the spot price of gold is $1,408.50. Then the dealer sells the gold in the spot market for a profit of $100(1,408.50 - 1,387.15) = 2,135$. The short futures contract is offset by purchasing it in the futures market for a profit of $-100(1,408.50 - 1,388.60) = -1,990$. The overall profit therefore is $-1,990 + 2,135 = 145$, as we predicted.

Now suppose we close the position prior to expiration. For example, on May 5, the spot price of gold was $1,377.52 and the June futures price was $1,378.63. In our notation, $S_t = 1,377.52$ and $f_t = 1,378.63$. If the gold is sold in the spot market, the profit is $100(1,377.52 - 1,387.15) = -963$. The futures contract is bought back at 1,378.63 for a profit of $-100(1,378.63 - 1,388.60) = 997$. The net gain is $-963 + 997 = 34$. As we said earlier, this should equal the change in the basis, $b_t - b_0$. The original basis was -1.45. The basis when the position is closed is $S_t - f_t$, or $1,377.52 - 1,378.63 = -1.11$. The profit, therefore, is

$$-1.11 - (-1.45) = 0.34,$$

which is the gain on the hedge per ounce of gold.

Behavior of the Basis Figure 11.1 shows the basis on a September S&P 500 index futures contract for a two-year period prior to expiration. Notice that the basis is quite volatile but finally converges to zero as maturity approaches. The volatility of the basis can be attributed to changing interest rates, changing expectations about dividend payments, and asynchronous prices. Asynchronous pricing refers to pricing being set at different points in time. The S&P 500 index closing value is set based on the closing prices

FIGURE 11.1 The September S&P 500 Index Basis, September 22, 2006–September 18, 2008

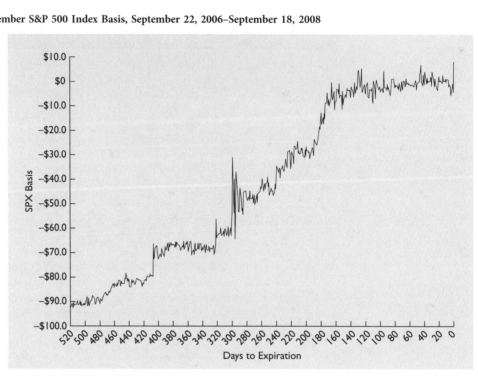

of the 500 stocks in the index. The stock markets close at 3:00 P.M. EST. The S&P 500 index futures markets close at 3:15 P.M. EST; hence, there is a slight timing difference.

The basis does not always converge exactly to zero. In the case of gold, for example, an investor who purchased gold on the spot market and immediately sold a futures contract that is about to expire would have to deliver the gold. There is a potentially significant delivery cost that could leave the futures price slightly above the spot price. For some commodities, there are several acceptable grades that can be delivered, so there are multiple spot prices. The short has control over the delivery and will choose to deliver the most economical grade. The futures price will tend to converge to the spot price of the commodity that is most likely to be delivered.

Of course, in forward markets, the basis is rarely an issue. The hedge is customized so that the basis risk can be eliminated.

Some Risks of Hedging

> Cross hedging involves an additional source of basis risk arising from the fact that the asset being hedged is not the same as the asset underlying the futures.

Sometimes the asset being hedged and the asset underlying the futures contract differ. A typical example, which we shall illustrate later, is the hedging of a corporate bond with a Treasury bond futures contract. This is referred to as a **cross hedge** and is a type of basis risk much greater than that encountered by hedging government bonds with Treasury bond futures. Corporate and government bond prices tend to move together, but the relationship is weaker than that of two government bonds. In addition, bonds with higher ratings would be more highly correlated with government bonds. Thus, lower-quality corporate bonds would carry some additional basis risk, and hedges would tend to be less effective.

In some cases, the price of the asset being hedged and that of the futures contract move in opposite directions. Then a hedge will produce either a profit or a loss on

> Quantity risk is the uncertainty of the amount of the underlying at risk. It typically arises when the hedger does not know how many units of the underlying he will own or owe at a future date.

both the spot and the futures positions. If one chooses the correct futures contract, this is unlikely to occur. If it occurs frequently, the hedger should find a different contract.

Hedging also entails another form of risk called **quantity risk**. For instance, suppose a farmer wants to lock in the selling price of the crop that has not yet been harvested. The farmer might sell a futures contract and thereby establish the future selling price of the crop. Yet what the farmer does not know and cannot hedge is the uncertainty over the size of the crop. This is the farmer's quantity risk. The farmer's total revenue is the product of the crop's price and its size. In a highly competitive market, the farmer's crop is too small to influence the price, but there are systematic factors, such as weather, that could influence everyone's crop. Thus, the crop size could be small when prices are high and large when prices are low. This situation creates its own natural hedge. When the farmer hedges, the price volatility no longer offsets the uncertainy of the crop size. Thus, the hedge actually can *increase* the overall risk. Quantity uncertainty is common in farming but is by no means restricted to it. Many corporations and financial institutions do not know the sizes of future cash flows and thus must contend with quantity risk.

In the ideal hedge, the so-called perfect hedge, the hedger knows the horizon date on which he will enter into the spot transaction that he is trying to hedge. He would use a futures or another derivative that expires on that exact date. In some cases, however, the hedger does not know the horizon date for the hedge. For example, the owner of an asset might know for sure that he will need to sell the asset at a future date, but he might not know the exact date on which the sale will take place. In another situation, a party might know that she will receive some cash at a future date and will use the cash to purchase a particular asset. But she may not know the exact date on which the cash will be received. When the hedger does not know the horizon date, it will be more difficult to align the expiration date of the futures or forward contract with the hedge horizon date. Then the effectiveness of the hedge will be lower.

Contract Choice

When using futures to hedge, the choice of contract actually consists of four decisions: (1) which futures underlying asset, (2) which expiration month, (3) whether to be long or short, and (4) the number of contracts. The number of contracts is so important that we defer it to the next main section.

> The futures contract used for hedging should be liquid and should be on an asset that is highly correlated with the asset being hedged.

Which Futures Underlying Asset? From the previous section, we can see that it is important to select a futures contract on an asset that is highly correlated with the underlying asset being hedged. In many cases, the choice is obvious, but in some cases, it is not.

For example, suppose that a party wants to hedge the value of a highly diversified portfolio of mid-cap stocks. There is a futures contract on the S&P Mid-Cap Index, a measure of the performance of 400 medium-sized stocks. But the portfolio at risk does not perfectly match the S&P MidCap Index. Moreover, the futures contract on this index is not all that actively traded. Thus, it is possible that the hedger would want to use a futures contract on a more actively traded large- or small-cap index. Of course, if the hedger wanted a perfect match between the portfolio and the index underlying the hedging contract, he would choose a forward contract customized to match his portfolio, but the higher costs might be a factor in choosing the standardized futures contract.

Another factor one should consider is whether the contract is correctly priced. A short hedger will be selling futures contracts and therefore should look for contracts that are overpriced or, in the worst case, correctly priced. A long hedger should hedge by buying underpriced contracts or, in the worst case, correctly priced contracts.

Sometimes the best hedge can be obtained by using more than one futures commodity. For example, a hedge of a jet fuel position might be more effective if both heating oil futures *and* crude oil futures are used.

Which Expiration?   Once one has selected the futures commodity, one must decide on the expiration month. As we know, only certain expiration months trade at a given time. For example, in September, the Treasury bond futures contract has expirations of December of the current year; March, June, September, and December of the following year; and March, June, and September of the year after that. If the Treasury bond futures contract is the appropriate hedging vehicle, the contract used must come from this group of expirations.

> The hedger should choose a contract that expires as close as possible to but after the hedge termination date.

In most cases, the hedger knows the time horizon over which the hedge must remain in effect. To obtain the maximum reduction in basis risk, a hedger should hold the futures position until as close as possible to that date. Thus, an appropriate contract expiration would be one that corresponded as closely as possible to the horizon date. The general rule of thumb, however, is to avoid holding a futures position in the expiration month. This is because unusual price movements sometimes are observed in the expiration month, which would pose an additional risk to hedgers. Thus, the hedger should choose an expiration month that is as close as possible to but after the month in which the hedge is terminated.[3]

Table 11.3 lists possible hedge termination dates for a Treasury bond futures hedge and the appropriate contracts for use. Consider, however, that *the longer the time to expiration, the less liquid the contract*. Therefore, the selection of a contract according to this criterion may need to be overruled by the necessity of using a liquid contract. If this happens, one should use a contract with a shorter expiration. When the contract moves into its expiration month, the futures position is closed out and a new position is opened in the next expiration month. This process, called *rolling the hedge forward*, generates some additional risk but can still be quite effective.

TABLE 11.3   CONTRACT EXPIRATIONS FOR PLANNED HEDGE TERMINATION DATES (TREASURY BOND FUTURES HEDGE INITIATED ON SEPTEMBER 30, 2012)

HEDGE TERMINATION DATE	APPROPRIATE CONTRACT
10/1/12–11/30/12	Dec 12
12/1/12–2/28/13	Mar 13
3/1/13–5/31/13	Jun 13
6/1/13–8/31/13	Sep 13
9/1/13–11/30/13	Dec 13
12/1/13–2/28/14	Mar 14
3/1/14–5/31/14	Jun 14
6/1/14–8/31/14	Sep 14
9/1/14–11/30/14	Dec 14

Note: The appropriate contract is based on the rule that the expiration date should be as soon as possible after the hedge termination date, subject to no contract being held in its expiration month. Liquidity considerations may make some more distant contracts inappropriate.

---

[3]Not all contracts exhibit unusual price behavior in the expiration month. Thus, this rule need not always be strictly followed.

Of course, the time horizon problem can be handled perfectly by using a forward contract from the over-the-counter market. In fact, some hedgers have horizons of longer than ten years, which can be hedged only by using forward contracts or swaps.

Long or Short? Regardless of whether one uses forwards or futures, the most important decision is whether to be long or short. There is absolutely no room for a mistake here. If a hedger goes long (or short) when she should have been short (or long), she has doubled the risk. The end result will be a gain or loss twice the amount of the gain or loss of the unhedged position.

> The decision of whether to go long or short forwards or futures is critical and can be made by determining whether a spot market move will help or hurt the spot position and how the forward or futures market can be used to offset that risk.

The decision of whether to go long or short requires a determination of which type of market move will result in a loss in the spot market. It then requires establishing a forward or futures position that will be profitable while the spot position is losing. Table 11.4 summarizes three methods that will correctly identify the appropriate transaction. The first method requires that the hedger identify the worst-case scenario and then establish a forward/futures position that will profit if the worst case does occur. The second method requires taking a forward/ futures position that is opposite that of the current spot position. This is a simple method, but in some cases, it is difficult to identify the current spot position. The third method identifies the spot transaction that will be conducted when the hedge is terminated. The forward/ futures transaction that will be conducted when the hedge is terminated should be the opposite of this spot transaction. The forward/futures transaction that should be done

---

TABLE 11.4 HOW TO DETERMINE WHETHER TO BUY OR SELL FORWARDS/FUTURES WHEN HEDGING

Worst-Case Scenario Method

1. Assuming that the spot and forward/futures markets move together, determine whether long and short positions in forward/ futures will be profitable if the market goes up or down.
2. What is the worst that could happen in the spot market?
   a. The spot market goes up.
   b. The spot market goes down.
3. Given your answer in 2, assume that the worst that *can* happen *will* happen.
4. Given your answer in 3 and using your answer in 1, take a forward/futures position that will be profitable.

Current Spot Position Method

1. Determine whether your current position in the spot market is long or short.
   a. If you own an asset, your current position is long.
   b. If you are short an asset, your current position is short.
   c. If you are committed to buying an asset in the future, your current position is short.
2. Take a forward/futures position that is opposite the position given by your answer in 1.

Anticipated Future Spot Transaction Method

1. Determine what type of spot transaction you will be making when the hedge is terminated.
   a. Sell an asset.
   b. Buy an asset.
2. Given your answer in 1, you will need to terminate a forward/futures position at the horizon date by doing the opposite transaction to the one in 1 (e.g., if your answer in 1 is "sell," your answer here is "buy a forward/futures").
3. Given your answer in 2, you will need to open a forward/futures contract today by doing the opposite (e.g., if your answer in 2 is "buy a forward/futures," your answer here should be "sell a forward/futures")

today should be the opposite of the forward/futures transaction that should be done at the termination of the hedge.

Margin Requirements and Marking to Market

Two other considerations in hedging with futures contracts are the margin requirement and the effect of marking to market. We discussed these factors earlier, but now we need to consider their implications for hedging.

Margin requirements, as we know, are very small and virtually insignificant in relation to the size of the position being hedged. Moreover, margin requirements for hedges are even smaller than speculative margins. In addition, margins can sometimes be posted with risk-free securities; thus, interest on the money can still be earned. Therefore, the initial amount of margin posted is really not a major factor in hedging.

What is important, however, is the effect of marking to market and the potential for margin calls. Remember that the profit on a futures transaction is supposed to offset the loss on the spot asset. At least part of the time, there will be profits on the spot asset and losses on the futures contract. On a given day when the futures contract generates a loss, the hedger must deposit additional margin money to cover that loss. Even if the spot position has generated a profit in excess of the loss on the futures contract, it may be impossible, or at least inconvenient, to withdraw the profit on the spot position to cover the loss on the futures.

This is one of the major obstacles to more widespread use of futures. Because futures profits and losses are realized immediately and spot profits and losses do not occur until the hedge is terminated, many potential hedgers tend to weigh the losses on the futures position more heavily than the gains on the spot. They also tend to think of hedges on an ex post rather than ex ante basis. If the hedge produced a profit on the spot position and a loss on the futures position, it would be apparent *after the fact* that the hedge was not the best that could have been done. But this would not be known *before the fact*.

Thus, a hedger must be aware that hedging will produce both gains and losses on futures transactions and will require periodic margin calls. The alternative to not meeting a margin call is closing the futures position. It is tempting to do this after a streak of losses and margin calls. If the futures position is closed, however, the hedge will no longer be in effect and the individual or firm will be exposed to the risk in the spot market, which is greater than the risk of the hedge.

In Chapter 9, we examined the effect of marking to market on the futures price. We concluded that the impact is fairly small. If, however, the interest earned or paid on the variation margin is not insignificant, it is possible to take it into account when establishing the optimal number of contracts. We shall cover this topic in a later section.

Of course, forward contracts do not entail margin requirements and marking to market, but they are subject to credit risk. Indeed, margin requirements and marking to market are primarily used by futures markets to reduce, if not effectively eliminate, credit risk.

These are several of the most important factors one must consider before initiating a hedge. As we noted earlier, another important consideration is the size of the hedge transaction. With forward hedges, it is a fairly simple matter to determine the appropriate size. For example, if a position of $10 million in an asset with a horizon date in exactly 60 days is to be hedged with a forward contract, the hedger simply specifies that he wants a forward contract covering $10 million of an asset with an expiration in 60 days. For futures contracts, the decision is not that simple. First, as noted, the asset underlying the futures may not match the asset being hedged. Second, even if the asset underlying the futures contract does match the asset being hedged, futures contracts may not be available in denominations that, in multiples, would equal $10 million. For example, the standard size could be $3 million. Third, the hedge horizon date may not correspond to the expiration date of any of the available futures contracts. Assuming that the hedger has chosen the underlying contract, he will need to carefully decide how many futures contracts to use to balance the risk being added by the futures contract with the risk that he is trying to hedge. The appropriate number of futures contracts is called the hedge ratio.

DETERMINATION OF THE HEDGE RATIO

The hedge ratio is the number of futures contracts needed to offset the spot market risk.

The **hedge ratio** is the number of futures contracts one should use to hedge a particular exposure in the spot market.[4] The hedge ratio should be the one in which the futures profit or loss matches the spot profit or loss. There is no exact method of determining the hedge ratio before performing the hedge. There are, however, several ways to estimate it.

The most elementary method is to take a position in the futures market equivalent in size to the position in the spot market. For example, if you hold $10 million of the asset, you should hold futures contracts covering $10 million. If each futures contract has a price of $80,000, you should sell 125 contracts. This approach is relatively naive because it fails to consider that the futures and spot prices might not change in the same proportions. In some cases, however, particularly when the asset being hedged is the same as the asset underlying the futures contract, such a hedge ratio will be appropriate.

Nevertheless, in most other cases, the futures and spot prices will change by different percentages. Suppose we write the profit from a hedge as follows:

$$\Pi = \Delta S + \Delta f N_f,$$

where the symbol Δ means "change in." Thus, the profit is the change in the spot price (ΔS) plus the change in the futures price (Δf) multiplied by the number of futures contracts (N_f). A positive N_f means a long position, and a negative N_f means a short position. For the futures profit or loss to completely offset the spot loss or profit, we set $\Pi = 0$ and find the value of N_f as

$$N_f = -\frac{\Delta S}{\Delta f}.$$

Because we assume that the futures and spot prices will move in the same direction, ΔS and Δf have the same sign; thus, N_f is negative. This example therefore is a short hedge, but the concept is equally applicable to a long hedge, where $\Pi = -\Delta S + \Delta f N_f$ and N_f would be positive.

Now we need to know the ratio $\Delta S/\Delta f$. There are several approaches to estimating this value.

Minimum Variance Hedge Ratio

The objective of a hedge—indeed, of any investment decision—is to maximize the investor's expected utility. In this book, however, we do not develop the principles of expected utility maximization. Therefore, we shall take a much simpler approach to the hedging problem and focus on risk minimization. The model used here comes from the work of Johnson (1960) and Stein (1961).

---

[4]Technically, the hedge ratio is the dollar value of the futures position relative to the dollar value of the spot position. It is then used to determine the number of futures contracts necessary. In this book, we shall let the hedge ratio refer to the number of futures contracts.

The profit from the short hedge is[5]

$$\Pi = \Delta S + \Delta f N_f.$$

The variance of the profit is

$$\sigma_{\Pi}^2 = \sigma_{\Delta S}^2 + \sigma_{\Delta f}^2 N_f^2 + 2\text{Cov}_{\Delta S,\Delta f} N_f,$$

where

> The minimum variance hedge ratio gives the optimal number of futures when the objective is to minimize risk.

$$\sigma_{\Pi}^2 = \text{variance of hedged profit}$$
$$\sigma_{\Delta S}^2 = \text{variance of change in the spot price}$$
$$\sigma_{\Delta f}^2 = \text{variance of change in the futures price}$$
$$\text{Cov}_{\Delta S,\Delta f} = \text{covariance of change in the spot price and change in the futures price}$$
$$\rho_{\Delta S,\Delta f} = \text{correlation of the change in the spot price and change in the futures price.}$$

Recall that $\text{Cov}_{\Delta S,\Delta f} = \sigma_{\Delta S}\sigma_{\Delta f}\rho_{\Delta S,\Delta f}$; hence, there is a direct relationship between covariance and correlation. The objective is to find the value of N_f that gives the minimum value σ_{Π}^2.[6] The formula for the optimal number of futures contracts, N_f^*, is

$$N_f^* = -\frac{\sigma_{\Delta S,\Delta f}}{\sigma_{\Delta f}^2} = -\rho_{\Delta S,\Delta f}\frac{\sigma_{\Delta S}}{\sigma_{\Delta f}}.$$

This formula gives the number of futures contracts that will produce the lowest possible variance. In nearly all cases, the covariance/correlation is positive; so the negative sign means that the hedger should sell futures. If the problem were formulated as a long hedge, the sign would be positive.

TECHNICAL NOTE:
Hedge Ratios and Futures Contracts
go to www.cengagebrain.com

You may recognize that the formula for N_f is very similar to that for beta (β) from a least squares regression. In fact, we can estimate N_f by running a regression with ΔS as the dependent variable and Δf as the independent variable. Of course, this can give us the correct value of N_f only for a historical set of data. We cannot know the actual value of N_f over an upcoming period. Extrapolating the future from the past is risky, but at least it is a starting point.

The effectiveness of the minimum variance hedge can be estimated by examining the percentage of the risk reduced. Suppose we define **hedging effectiveness** as

$$e^* = \frac{\text{Risk of unhedged postion} - \text{Risk of hedged position}}{\text{Risk of unhedged position}}.$$

This can be written as

$$e^* = \frac{\sigma_{\Delta S}^2 - \sigma_{\Pi}^2}{\sigma_{\Delta S}^2}.$$

Thus, e^* gives the percentage of the unhedged risk that the hedge eliminates. By substituting the formulas for σ_{Π}^2 and N_f^* in the formula for e^* and rearranging terms, we get

$$e^* = \frac{N_f^{*2}\sigma_{\Delta f}^2}{\sigma_{\Delta S}^2} = \rho_{\Delta S,\Delta f}^2.$$

---

[5]The problem as formulated here is in terms of the profit. An alternative, and in some ways preferable, formulation is in terms of the rate of return on the hedger's wealth. We shall use the profit formulation here because it is more frequently seen in the literature.

[6]See Hedge Ratios and Futures Contracts Technical Note, in the section "Derivation of Minimum Variance Hedge Ratio."

This happens to be the formula for the coefficient of determination for the regression, which is the square of the correlation coefficient. It indicates the percentage of the variance in the dependent variable, ΔS, that is explained by the independent variable, Δf.

We shall see an example of the minimum variance hedge ratio in a hedging situation we examine later in this chapter.

Price Sensitivity Hedge Ratio

The price sensitivity hedge ratio comes from the work of Kolb and Chiang (1981). The objective here is to determine the value of N_f^* that will result in minimum change in the bond portfolio's value for a small change in interest rates. Because the strategy is designed for interest rate futures, we will illustrate it with reference to a bond and a bond futures contract.

In order to understand the price sensitivity formula, we must first review the concept of a bond's **duration**. Duration has several specific definitions, but generally is used as a measure of price sensitivity. The bond price, B, is the sum of the present values of each of its cash payments—coupon interest and principal. These present values can be found by discounting each cash payment at a single interest rate, which is known as the yield or sometimes yield to maturity (y_B). Formally, we have

$$B = \sum_{t=1}^{T} \frac{CP_t}{(1 + y_B)^t},$$

where CP_t is the cash payment made at time t and will be either the coupon interest or principal. If the yield changes, we know that the price changes inversely. An approximation to the change in price as it relates to the change in yield is given by the formula

$$\Delta B \approx -B \frac{DUR_B(\Delta y_B)}{1 + y_B},$$

where DUR_B represents the bond's duration and A represents the change in B or y_B. Formally, the duration is a weighted average of the time to each cash payment date and is specified in units of time. There are several versions of the concept of duration. This particular one, though often just called duration, is more precisely identified as **Macaulay's duration**, named after one of the first economists to derive it.

Macaulay's duration measures the timing and size of a bond's cash flows. Bonds with high coupons and short maturities have short durations, whereas bonds with low coupons and long maturity have long durations. A zero coupon bond has a duration equal to its maturity, whereas a 30-year bond might have a duration of 8 to 14 years. From the above equation, we see that duration is a measure of a bond's price sensitivity, with longer duration bonds being more sensitive. For comparative purposes, we can say that, for example, a 10-year zero coupon bond has the same price sensitivity as a 30-year bond with a duration of 10.

One important variation of Macaulay's duration is called modified duration, which measures the bond price change, adjusted for the level of yield (the yield per compounding period). Specifically, **modified duration** is expressed as

$$MD_B = \frac{DUR_B}{1 + y_B} \approx -\frac{\Delta B/B}{\Delta y_B}.$$

In all material that follows, we shall use modified duration. Although modified duration has some limitations, it is a very useful concept in hedging. Knowing the modified duration of a bond, we can hedge the bond's price sensitivity by using knowledge of the modified duration of an appropriate futures contract and trading enough futures to offset the risk of the bond.[7] Now let us look at how a hedge can be designed.

Suppose changes in interest rates on all bonds are caused by a change in a single interest rate, r, which can be viewed as a default-free government bond rate. Thus, when r changes, all other bond yields change. Let B be the price of the bond held in the spot market and y_B be its yield. We will assume that the bond futures contract is based on a single government bond. The futures contract has a price of f. Based upon that price, the remaining life of the deliverable bond at the expiration of the futures, and the coupon of the deliverable bond, we can infer that the deliverable bond at expiration would have a yield of y_f and a modified duration of MD_f. We shall refer to these as the **implied yield** and the **implied modified duration** of the futures.

The profit from a hedge is the change in value of the hedger's position as a result of a change in the rate, r. If we are hedged, this change in value is should be zero.[8] The formula for N_f^* is

$$N_f^* = -\left(\frac{\Delta B}{\Delta f}\right)\left(\frac{\Delta y_f}{\Delta y_B}\right).$$

| The price sensitivity hedge ratio gives the optimal number of futures to hedge against interest rate changes. |

This expression can be considerably simplified. Recall from the formula above that we can express modified duration as

$$MD_B \approx -\frac{\Delta B/B}{\Delta y_B}.$$

The implied modified duration of a futures contract can be expressed in a similar manner as

$$MD_f \approx -\frac{\Delta f/f}{\Delta y_f}.$$

Letting $\Delta y_f = \Delta y_B$ and substituting in the expression for N_f gives

$$N_f^* = -\left(\frac{MD_B}{MD_f}\right)\left(\frac{B}{f}\right).$$

Yet another version of the price sensitivity hedge ratio is often used in practice. It is given as

$$N_f^* = -(\text{Yield beta})\frac{PVBP_B}{PVBP_f},$$

where $PVBP_B$ is the present value of a basis point change for the bond and is specifically defined as $\Delta B/\Delta y_B$, which we know is $-MD_B B$. $PVBP_f$ is the present value of a basis point change for the futures and is defined as $\Delta f/\Delta y_f$, which is $-MD_f f$. These variables are, in effect, the change in the price of the bond or futures for a change in the yield of Δy_B or Δy_f.

[7]Another potential duration measure is effective duration. The effective duration is a cash-flow-adjusted measure of risk based on estimates of the percentage change in bond price for a given change in yield, incorporating any cash flow effects of the given change in yield. For example, a callable bond may be called if interest rates fall, thus shortening the duration to zero when it is called.

[8]See Hedge Ratios and Futures Contracts Technical Note, in the section "Derivation of Price Sensitivity Hedge Ratio."

The **yield beta** is the coefficient from a regression of the bond yield on the implied yield of the futures. In the price sensitivity formula, we assumed that the bond yield changes one for one with the implied yield on the futures. This makes the yield beta 1. The yield beta, however, is not always equal to one and the preceding equation becomes

$$N_f^* = -\left(\frac{MD_B}{MD_f}\right)\left(\frac{B}{f}\right)\beta_y,$$

which is the yield-beta-adjusted price sensitivity formula. If the hedger does not believe that the bond and futures prices will change in a one-to-one ratio, however, the yield beta actually should be estimated. In the examples used in this chapter, we shall assume that the yield beta is 1.

The price sensitivity formula takes into account the volatility of the bond and futures prices. Thus, it incorporates information from current prices rather than regressing past bond prices on past futures prices. There are merits to both approaches, and in practice, one approach sometimes may be more practical than the other. We shall illustrate both methods in some hedging examples later in the chapter.

There is another consideration in using the price sensitivity formula. Because it is derived from calculus, the formula hedges against only very small changes in interest rates. These changes must occur over a very short period of time. Once the interest rate changes and/or a period of time elapses, the modified durations of the bond and futures change and a new hedge ratio is required. This problem is much like the delta hedging we covered earlier in the Black-Scholes-Merton model. It is possible that many of our bond hedges, which are over periods of a few months at most, would not require major changes in the hedge ratio. Regardless, for our purposes here, we shall maintain the hedge ratio at the same value as obtained from the formula under the initial conditions, keeping in mind that the hedge will be less than perfect. If we want a perfect hedge in practice, we must make adjustments.

In the example developed here, the instrument being hedged is an individual bond. In practice, it is often the case that the instrument being hedged will be a bond portfolio. Thus, the value of the underlying, B, will be the sum of the values of the component bonds. The modified duration, MD_B, will be the overall modified duration of the portfolio, which is a weighted average of the modified durations of the component bonds with each bond's weight given by its market value relative to the overall market value of the portfolio. The overall yield, y_B, is the overall discount rate for the portfolio that equates the present value of all of the cash flows for the portfolio to the market value of the portfolio. It is a complex weighted average of the yields of the component bonds. We shall not deal with how the overall yield is obtained. Any bond portfolio management software can easily obtain this number, so we shall assume that it is known. Although the price sensitivity formula will often be used at the portfolio level, the principles underlying it are exactly the same as we learned here for individual bonds, and its effectiveness will be just as great, if not greater.

Stock Index Futures Hedging

Because the price sensitivity hedge is not applicable to stock index futures, the minimum variance hedge usually is employed. Suppose we define ΔS as Sr_s, where r_s is the return on the stock, which is the percentage change in price. Then we define Δf as fr_f, where r_f is the percentage change in the price of the futures contract. Note that this is not the return on the futures contract. Because there is no initial outlay, there is no return on a futures contract. If we substitute Sr_s and fr_f for ΔS and Δf, respectively, in the minimum variance formula for N_f^*, we get

$$N_f^* = -\left(\frac{S}{f}\right)\left(\frac{\text{Cov}_{r_s,r_f}}{\sigma_{r_f}^2}\right),$$

The minimum variance hedge ratio for stock index futures takes into account the stock portfolio's beta.

where Cov_{r_s,r_f} is the covariance between r_s and r_f and $\sigma_{r_f}^2$ is the variance of r_f. If we run a regression of the percentage change in the spot price on the percentage change in the futures price, we obtain a regression coefficient we can denote as β_S. You may recognize this concept as similar to the beta from the Capital Asset Pricing Model. Is this the same beta? Not exactly, but because the futures contract is based on a market index, the beta should be somewhat close. In that case,

$$N_f = -\left(\frac{\beta_S}{\beta_f}\right)\left(\frac{S}{f}\right)$$

is the minimum variance hedge ratio for a stock index futures contract where β_S is the beta of the stock portfolio and β_f is the beta of the futures contract.

The beta of the stock portfolio is always measured relative to some broad-based index. It is often assumed that if the index underlying the futures is a broad-based index, the futures beta in the above equation would be close to 1.0 and could be effectively ignored. In that case, the futures beta will indeed be close to one; it differs by only a small interest and dividend-related adjustment. But many portfolios are not based on broad-based market indices even though their betas are measured relative to broad-based indices. If the hedger used a futures contract that would be a good hedging instrument for this portfolio, he would need to know the beta of this futures contract relative to the broad-based index. Thus, for example, a portfolio might consist of slightly higher than average risk stocks and have a beta of 1.15. A futures contract on a portfolio of over-the-counter stocks might make a good hedge. Its beta might be 1.10. Thus, the ratio 1.15/1.10 = 1.045 would play a role in the calculation of the hedge ratio and would be quite different from the result that would be obtained by assuming a beta of 1.0 for the futures. Throughout this chapter, we shall assume a futures beta of 1.0.

In addition, the hedging approach described here does not take into account dividends on the stocks in the portfolio. Dividends will affect the overall outcome of the transaction, but the uncertainly of dividends over most hedge horizons is fairly small and is not a risk most portfolio managers would worry about having to hedge.

We shall see some examples of stock index futures hedging later in the chapter.

HEDGING STRATEGIES

So far, we have examined some basic principles underlying the practice of hedging. The next step is to illustrate how these hedges are executed. We shall look at some examples developed from a variety of economic and financial environments that illustrate several hedging principles.

The examples are divided into three groups: foreign currency hedging, intermediate- and long-term interest rate risk hedging, and stock hedging. One category is conspicuously absent from our list: hedging short-term interest rates. Indeed, the risk associated with short-term interest rates is one of the most visible risks in the financial markets. Short-term interest rate futures contracts do exist for the purpose of hedging this type of risk, which is largely faced by corporations in the course of borrowing and lending and by banks as they borrow, lend, and engage in their dealership activities in over-the-counter derivatives. But in reality, the actual use of short-term interest rate futures for hedging purposes is relatively minimal. In the United States, futures contracts on Federal funds and one-month LIBOR have relatively low trading volume.

Eurodollar futures are widely traded but rarely used by corporations for hedging interest rate risk. Corporations prefer the use of swaps and customized interest rate derivatives for this purpose. Banks are heavy users of Eurodollar futures, but they do so largely to hedge the swaps and other interest rate derivatives they use in their activities as dealers. We shall cover in Chapters 12 and 13 these instruments and their use by corporations in hedging and by banks in managing their over-the-counter positions.

Foreign Currency Hedges

Before getting into the details of foreign currency hedging, let us review a few concepts of foreign currency futures and forward contracts. Futures contracts are available in given sizes, indicated by the amount of the foreign currency. For example, in the United States, three of the most actively traded foreign currency futures contracts are the euro, available with a size of 125,000; the British pound, available in units of £62,500; and the Japanese yen, available in contracts covering ¥12,500,000. Of course, a hedger can transact in only a whole number of futures contracts; thus, some hedges will cover slightly more or slightly less than the size of the position being hedged.

Foreign currency futures prices are stated in the currency of the home country. Thus, in the United States, the euro futures price might be quoted as $1.05 and the British pound futures price might be $1.58. For a single contract, this would mean that the aggregate price is 125,000($1.05) = $131,250 for the euro contract and 62,500($1.58) = $98,750 for the pound contract. Because of the large number of Japanese yen in a dollar (typically over 100), the price is usually quoted without the two leading zeroes. Thus, a price of 0.8310 is really $0.008310, which is equivalent to about 120.34 yen per dollar. The aggregate contract price would be 12,500,000 ($0.008310) = $103,875.

Long Hedge with Foreign Currency Futures   Recall that a long hedge with futures involves the purchase of a futures contract. In the case of foreign currencies, a long hedger is concerned that the value of the foreign currency will rise. An example is presented in Table 11.5.

Here an American car dealer plans to buy 20 British sports cars. Each car costs 35,000 pounds, which will have to be paid in the British currency. Based on the current forward rate of the pound, the dealer's current cost is $914,200. If, however, the pound increases in value, the cars will end up costing more. The dealer hedges by buying futures on the pound. As the table indicates, this was a good decision because the pound did appreciate; the cars ended up costing $1,009,400, which is $95,200 more, but the futures contracts generated a profit of $109,656.25, which more than covered the increased cost of the cars.

As long as the pound spot and futures rates move in the same direction, the hedge will be successful in reducing some of the loss in the spot market. Had the pound weakened, there would have been a loss in the futures market that would have offset some or all of the gain in the spot market.

This transaction was executed in the futures market. Remember that futures contracts have standardized terms and provide a guarantee against default on the part of the other party. Forward contracts permit the parties to customize the terms of the contract. This transaction, however, would not be large enough to justify a forward contract. In the next example, we shall execute the hedge in the forward market.

TABLE 11.5 A LONG HEDGE WITH FOREIGN CURRENCY FUTURES

Scenario: On July 1, an American auto dealer enters into a contract to purchase 20 British sports cars with payment to be made in British pounds on November 1. Each car will cost 35,000 pounds. The dealer is concerned that the pound will strengthen over the next few months, causing the cars to cost more in dollars.

DATE	SPOT MARKET	FUTURES MARKET
July 1	The current exchange rate is $1.3190 per pound. The forward rate of the pound is $1.3060. Forward cost of 20 cars: 20(35,000)($1.3060) = $914,200.	December pound contract is at $1.278. Price per contract: 62,500($1.278) = $79,875. The appropriate number of contracts is $$\frac{20(35,000)}{62,500} = 11.2.$$ **Buy 11 contracts**
November 1	The spot rate is $1.442. Buy the 700,000 pounds to purchase 20 cars. Cost in dollars: 700,000($1.442) = $1,009,400.	December pound contract is at $1.4375. Price per contract: 62,500($1.4375) = $89,843.75. **Sell 11 contracts**

Analysis: The cars ended up costing $1,009,400 − $914,200 = $95,200 more. The profit on the futures transaction is

$$
\begin{array}{ll}
11(\$89,843.75) & \text{(sale price of futures)} \\
-11(\$79,875.00) & \text{(purchase price of futures)} \\
\hline
\$109,656.25 & \text{(profit on futures)}.
\end{array}
$$

The profit on the futures more than offsets the higher cost of the cars, leaving a net gain of $109,656.25 − $95,200 = $14,456.25. The dealer effectively paid $1,009,400 − $109,656.25 = $899,743.75 for the 20 cars.

Short Hedge with Foreign Currency Forwards   A short hedge is a commitment to sell a currency using futures or forwards and is designed to protect against a decrease in the foreign currency's value. In Table 11.6, we have a situation in which a multinational firm has 10 million pounds that it will convert at a later date. A transaction of this size can often be better executed with a customized forward contract. In addition, when the amount of exposure is large, the basis risk of a futures contract may be a risk not worth

---

TABLE 11.6 A SHORT HEDGE WITH FOREIGN CURRENCY FORWARDS

Scenario: On June 29, a multinational firm with a British subsidiary decides it will need to transfer 10 million pounds from an account in London to an account with a New York bank. Transfer will be made on September 28. The firm is concerned that over the next two months, the pound will weaken.

DATE	SPOT MARKET	FORWARD MARKET
June 29	The current exchange rate is $1.362 per pound. The forward rate of the pound is $1.357. Forward value of funds: 10,000,000($1.357) = $13,570,000.	Sell pounds forward for delivery on September 28 at $1.357.
September 28	The spot rate is $1.2375.	Deliver pounds and receive 10,000,000($1.357) = $13,570,000.

Analysis: The pounds end up worth $13,570,000 − $12,375,000 = $1,195,000 less but are delivered on the forward contract for $13,570,000, thus completely eliminating the risk. Had the transaction not been done, the firm would have converted the pounds at the spot rate of $1.2375.

bearing. In this example, the customer is long pounds and is exposed to the risk of the pound weakening. To protect against this risk, it sells a forward contract on the exact number of pounds it will convert, with the contract expiring on the day of conversion. This allows the firm to convert the pounds to dollars by simply delivering them to the dealer on the opposite side of the forward contract. As the table indicates, the pound did depreciate, which would have caused a loss of $1,195,000. Instead, the firm locked in the rate on the day it entered into the forward contract.

In Chapter 12, we shall return to the subject of foreign currency hedging when we learn about currency swaps. For now, let us turn to the hedging of intermediate- and long-term interest rate risk.

Intermediate- and Long-Term Interest Rate Hedges

The risk associated with intermediate- and long-term interest rates is typically faced by bond portfolio managers, who are responsible for current and anticipated positions in bonds. These bonds can be issued by governments or corporations. The interest rate futures markets in most countries are extremely active and are widely used by bond portfolio managers to hedge the risk associated with interest rate changes. Most of these futures contracts are based on federal government bonds, which are usually more actively traded than are corporate or non-federal government bonds. We should note that many risks related to corporate, state, and non-federal government bonds are a function of changes in perceptions of credit quality. The hedging of credit risk is addressed in Chapter 15.

We now turn to some examples of bond portfolio hedging, employing the U.S. Treasury note and bond contracts of the Chicago Board of Trade (CBOT). Treasury note and bond contracts on the CBOT are virtually identical except that there are three T-note contracts that are based on 2-year, 5-year, and 10-year maturities, whereas the T-bond contract is based on Treasury bonds with maturities of at least 15 years that are not callable for at least 15 years and mature in less than 25 years. The Ultra Treasury bond contract is for bonds maturing in not less than 25 years. Thus, the T-note contracts are intermediate-term interest rate futures contracts and the T-bond contracts are a long-term interest rate futures contract. Other than the difference in maturity of the underlying instruments and the margin requirements, the contract terms are essentially identical.

As discussed in Chapter 10, the T-bond contract is based on the assumption that the underlying bond has a coupon rate of 6 percent and, as mentioned, a maturity or call date of at least 15 years and less than 25 years. The specific coupon requirement is not restrictive, however; the CBOT permits delivery of bonds with other coupon rates, with an appropriate adjustment (recall the conversion factor) made to the price received for the bonds. There are many different bond issues eligible for delivery on a given contract.

Recall that T-bond futures prices are quoted in dollars and half thirty-seconds of par value of $100. For example, a futures price of 93-14.5 is 93 14.5/32, or 93.453125. The face value of T-bonds underlying the contract is $100,000; therefore, a price of 93.453125 is $93,453,125. Expiration months are March, June, September, and December, extending out about two years. The last trading day is the business day prior to the last seven days of the expiration month. The first delivery day is the first business day of the month.

Hedging a Long Position in a Government Bond Portfolio managers constantly face decisions about when to buy and sell securities. In some cases, such decisions are automatic. Securities are sold at certain times to generate cash for meeting obligations such as pension payments. Consider the following example.

MAKING THE CONNECTION

Hedging Contingent Foreign Currency Risk

In this chapter, we are learning how to use forward and futures contracts to hedge. If the hedger wants to receive the benefits of favorable movements in the underlying, options can be used. We saw an example of this type of strategy in Chapter 6 with the use of covered calls and protective puts.

There is one particular situation in which currency options can be particularly valuable: the hedging of contingent foreign currency risk. This scenario occurs when a party anticipates the possibility—but is not certain—of a future position in a foreign currency.

For example, suppose an American firm is bidding for a contract to construct a sports complex in London. The bid must be submitted in British pounds. The firm plans to make a bid of £25 million. At the forward exchange rate of $1.437, the bid in dollars is equivalent to £25,000,000 ($1.437) = $35,925,000. Once the bid is submitted, the firm must be prepared to accept £25 million if the bid is successful. Because it is an American firm, it will convert the pounds into dollars at whatever rate prevails on the date payment is made. If the pound weakens, the firm will effectively receive fewer dollars. To simplify the example somewhat, we shall assume that the payment will be made as soon as the decision is made as to which firm is awarded the construction contract.

Consider the possibility of a forward or futures hedge in comparison to the purchase of a put on the pound. For discussion purposes, we shall refer only to the forward and put hedges.

If the bid is successful and the pound increases, the firm will receive the pounds, which now are valued at more dollars per pound. The forward hedge will, however, reduce this gain because the hedge will be a short position. If the option is used, the put will expire worthless.

If the bid is successful and the pound decreases, the forward hedge will reduce the loss caused by the decline in the pound's value. The option will, however, also reduce the loss on the pound.

If the bid is unsuccessful and the pound increases, the forward hedge will result in a potentially large speculative loss. This is because the firm will not receive the pounds if the bid fails but will have a short position in a forward contract. If the option hedge is used, the put will expire worthless. The firm will have lost money—the premium on the put—but the amount lost is likely to be less than it would have been with the forward hedge.

If the bid is unsuccessful and the pound decreases, the forward hedge will result in a potentially large speculative profit because the firm will be short forward and will not receive the pounds as a result of the failure to win the bid. If the option hedge is used, the put's exercise will also result in a potentially large profit on the put.

The option hedge is most beneficial when the bid is unsuccessful. Because the firm does not receive the pounds, the forward position generates a potentially large profit or loss. The option, however, can generate a large profit if the pound declines; if the pound rises, the loss will be limited to the premium. Of course, the option hedge requires payment of the option premium, while the forward hedge might require collateral. Neither type of hedge dominates the other, but each has its merits.

Let us now look at this specific hedge. The firm needs to hedge the anticipated receipt of £25 million. We shall assume it uses either forwards or over-the-counter put options. The forward price is $1.424, and the option premium is $0.025. Thus, the option will cost £25,000,000 ($0.025) = $625,000. The forward contract locks in £25,000,000($1.424) = $35,600,000. We can assume that the option or forward expires on the date on which the outcome of the bid is determined and that on that date the firm either receives the cash payment of £25 million or not.

For the case in which the bid is successful, either hedge works fairly well. The option hedge is like a protective put, which benefits from a strong pound and which has limited losses from a weak pound. The forward hedge locks in $35,600,000 regardless of the value of the pound. Note that if the firm does not hedge, the overall value will move one-for-one with the value of the pound.

For the case in which the bid is unsuccessful, the forward hedge leaves the firm highly exposed, with the potential for a rather substantial loss. In the option hedge, the most the firm can lose is the option premium of $625,000, but it can gain if the pound decreases, even though it did not win the bid.

Of course, the firm could choose not to bid, but this is unlikely because bidding on contracts is the nature of the construction business. The firm could choose not to hedge, but it could win the bid and earn a much smaller profit or even a loss if the pound falls significantly. The option hedge provides an alternative that will be attractive to some firms, while the forward hedge will be better for others. The differences in their expectations and willingness to take exchange rate risk will determine whether they use options or forwards.

TABLE 11.7 HEDGING A LONG POSITION IN A GOVERNMENT BOND

Scenario: On February 25, a portfolio manager holds $1 million face value of a government bond, the 11 7/8s, which mature in about 25 years. The bond is currently priced at 101 and has a modified duration of 7.83. The manager will sell the bond on March 28 to generate cash to meet an obligation.

DATE	SPOT MARKET	FUTURES MARKET
February 25	The current price of the bonds is 101. Value of position: $1,010,000. The short end of the term structure is flat, so this is the forward price of the bonds in March.	June T-bond futures is at 70 16/32. Price per contract: $70,500. The futures price and the characteristics of the deliverable bond imply a modified duration of 7.20. Appropriate number of contracts: $$N_f = -\left(\frac{7.83}{7.20}\right)\left(\frac{1,010,000}{70,500}\right)$$ $$= -15.6.$$ **Sell 16 contracts**
March 28	The bonds are sold at the current price of 95 22/32. This is a price of $956.875 per bond. Value of position: $956,875.	June T-bond futures is at 66 22/32. Price per contract: $66,718.75. **Buy 16 contracts**

Analysis: When the $1 million face value bonds are sold on March 28, they are worth $956,875, a loss in value of $1,010,000 − $956,875 = $53,125.

The profit on the futures transaction is

$$\begin{array}{ll} 16(\$70,500) & \text{(sale price of futures)} \\ \underline{-16(\$66,718.75)} & \text{(purchase price of futures)} \\ \$60,500 & \text{(profit on futures).} \end{array}$$

Thus, the hedge eliminated the entire loss in value and resulted in an overall gain in value of $60,500 − $53,125 = $7,375.

On February 25, a portfolio manager holds $1 million face value of government bonds with a coupon of 11 7/8 percent and maturing in about 25 years. The bond currently is priced at 101 per $100 par value, and the yield is 11.74 percent. The modified duration is 7.83 years. The bond will be sold on March 28 to generate cash to meet an obligation.[9]

The portfolio manager is concerned that interest rates will increase, resulting in a lower bond price and the possibility that the proceeds from the bond's sale will be inadequate for meeting the obligation. The manager knows that if interest rates increase, a short futures position will yield a profit that can offset at least part of any decrease in the bond's value. Because this is a government bond, the Treasury bond futures contract should be used.[10]

Table 11.7 presents the results of the hedge. The manager will use the June T-bond futures contract. Using the price sensitivity hedge ratio, the manager determines that he should sell 16 contracts. When the bonds were sold on March 28, they generated a loss of over $53,000. The futures transaction produced a profit of over $60,000. Thus, the hedge eliminated all of the loss and even produced a gain. Had bond prices moved up,

---

[9]In actual situations, a portfolio manager would hold a diversified portfolio of bonds. If the intention were to hedge the entire portfolio, the hedge ratio would be based on the overall portfolio value, yield, and duration. We assume that the manager needs approximately $1 million of cash on March 28 and will sell only this bond to generate the cash.

[10]Technically, the accrued interest would be a component of the outcome of this strategy; but it is not subject to any uncertainty, so we leave it out of the hedging examples.

the futures price would have increased and the futures transaction would have generated a loss that would have reduced or perhaps eliminated all of the increase in the value of the bonds.

This short hedge represents one of the most common hedging applications, and we shall see a slight variation of it later when we examine stock index futures hedging. This hedge is applicable to many firms and institutions, such as banks, insurance companies, pension funds, and mutual funds.

Anticipatory Hedge of a Future Purchase of a Treasury Note Previously, we saw how one could hedge the future purchase of a Treasury bond. In this example, we do the same with a Treasury note.

Suppose that on March 29, a portfolio manager determines that approximately $1 million will be available on July 15. The manager decides to purchase the 11 5/8 Treasury notes maturing in about nine years. The forward price of the notes is 97 28/32, or $978,750, for $1 million face value. This price implies a forward yield of 12.02 percent. If yields decline, the notes' price will increase and the manager may be unable to make the purchase. If this happens, a profit could have been made by purchasing futures contracts. Because the Treasury note futures contract is quite liquid, the manager decides to buy T-note futures. Because the hedge is to be terminated on July 15, the September contract is appropriate. The results are presented in Table 11.8.

When the bonds are ultimately purchased, they end up costing over $97,000 more, but the futures transaction generated a profit of over $82,000. Thus, the effective

---

TABLE 11.8 ANTICIPATORY HEDGE OF A FUTURE PURCHASE OF A TREASURY NOTE

Scenario: On March 29, a portfolio manager determines that approximately $1 million will be available for investment on July 15. The manager plans to purchase the 11 5/8s Treasury notes maturing in about nine years, which have a modified duration of 5.6.

DATE	SPOT MARKET	FUTURES MARKET
March 29	The forward price of notes is 97 28/32. Current forward value of notes: $978,750. This implies a yield of 12.02 percent.	September T-note futures are at 78 21/32. Price per contract: $78,656.25. The futures price and the characteristics of the deliverable bond imply a modified duration of 6.2. Appropriate number of contracts: $$N_f = -\left(\frac{\$978,750}{\$78,656.25}\right)\left(\frac{5.6}{6.2}\right) = 11.24.$$ **Buy 11 contracts**
July 15	The notes are purchased at their current price of 107 19/32. This is a price of $1,075.9375 per note. Value of position: $1,075,937.50.	September T-note futures is at 86 6/32. Price per contract: $86,187.50. **Sell 11 contracts**

Analysis: When the $1 million face value notes are purchased on July 15, they cost $1,075,937.50, an increased cost of $1,075,937.50 − $978,750 = $97,187.50. The yield at this price is 10.31 percent.

The profit on the futures transaction is

$$
\begin{array}{ll}
11(\$86,187.50) & \text{(sale price of futures)} \\
-11(\$78,656.25) & \text{(purchase price of futures)} \\
\hline
\$82,843.75 & \text{(profit on futures).}
\end{array}
$$

Thus, the hedge offset about 85 percent of the increased cost. The effective purchase price of the notes is $1,075,937.50 − $82,843.75 = $993,093.75, which is an effective yield of 11.75 percent.

purchase price is actually about $15,000 higher and gives an effective yield of 11.75 percent, which is reasonably close to the target forward yield of 12.02 percent.

Had bond prices moved down, the hedger would have regretted doing the hedge. The notes would have cost less, but this would have been offset by a loss on the futures contract. Once again, this is the price of hedging—forgoing gains to limit losses.

Hedging a Corporate Bond Issue One interesting application of an interest rate futures hedge occurs when a firm decides to issue bonds at a future date. There is an interim period during which the firm prepares the necessary paperwork and works out an underwriting arrangement for distributing the bonds. During that period, interest rates could increase so that when the bonds ultimately are issued, they will command a higher yield. This will be more costly to the issuer.

Consider the following example. On February 24, a corporation decides to issue $5 million face value of bonds on May 24. As a standard of comparison, the firm currently has a bond issue outstanding with a coupon of 9 3/8 percent, a yield of 13.76 percent, and a maturity of about 21 years. Any new bonds issued will require a similar yield. Thus, the firm expects that when the bonds are issued in May, the coupon would be set at 13.76 percent, so the bonds would will go out at par.

If rates increase, the firm will have to discount the bonds or adjust the coupon upward to the new market yield. We shall assume that the coupon is fixed so that the price will decrease. In either case, the firm will incur a loss. The firm realizes that if rates increase, it can make a profit from a short transaction in futures. Thus, it decides to hedge the issue by selling futures contracts.

There is no corporate bond futures contract, so the hedger chooses the Treasury bond futures contract. Because the hedge will be closed on May 24, the June contract is chosen.

The hedge is illustrated in Table 11.9. Using the price sensitivity hedge ratio, the firm sells 67 futures contracts. When the bonds are ultimately issued, the yield is 15.25 percent. This results in a loss of over $460,000 on the bonds, but the futures transaction made over $500,000. The firm made a net gain of about $44,000. The futures profit can be added to the proceeds from the bond of about $4.5 million so as to infer an effective issue price of slightly more than $5 million. This sets the effective yield on the bonds at 13.63 percent, which is quite close to the target of 13.76 percent.

Had interest rates declined, the firm would have obtained a higher price for the bonds; however, this would have been at least partially offset by a loss on the futures transaction. By executing the hedge, the firm was able to protect itself against an interest rate change while preparing the issue. In a similar vein, investment bankers might do this type of hedge. An investment banker purchases the bonds from the firm and then resells them to investors. Between the time the bonds are purchased and resold, the investment banker is exposed to the risk that bond yields will increase.[11] Therefore, a short hedge such as this would be appropriate. Many investment banking firms have been able to protect themselves against large losses by hedging with interest rate futures.

Forward contracts are less commonly used than futures to hedge the risk associated with intermediate- and long-term securities. The futures markets have developed a niche in meeting the hedging needs of parties bearing this kind of risk.

---

[11]Investment bankers do employ other means of minimizing their risk exposure. The use of a syndicate, in which a large number of investment bankers individually take a small portion of the issue, spreads out the risk. Many issues are taken on a "best efforts" basis. This allows the investment banker to return the securities to the issuing firm if market conditions make the sale of the securities impossible without substantial price concessions.

TABLE 11.9 HEDGING A CORPORATE BOND ISSUE

Scenario: On February 24, a corporation decides to issue $5 million of bonds on May 24. The firm currently has outstanding comparable bonds with a coupon of 9 3/8, a yield of 13.76 percent, and a maturity of about 21 years. The firm anticipates that if conditions do not change, the bonds when issued in May will be issued with a 13.76 percent coupon and be priced at par with a 20-year maturity and a modified duration of 7.22.

DATE	SPOT MARKET	FUTURES MARKET
February 24	If issued in May, it is expected that the bonds would offer a coupon of 13.76 percent and be priced at par with a modified duration of 7.22. Value of position: $5,000,000.	June T-bond futures are at 68 11/32. Price per contract: $68,343.75. The futures price and the characteristics of the deliverable bond imply a modified duration of 7.88 and a yield of 13.60 percent. Appropriate number of contracts: $$N_f = -\left(\frac{7.22}{7.88}\right)\left(\frac{5,000,000}{68,343.75}\right)$$ $$= -67.0.$$ **Sell 67 contracts**
May 24	The yield on comparable bonds is 15.25 percent. The bonds are issued with a 13.76 percent coupon at a price of 90.74638. Price per bond: $907.46. Value of bonds: $4,537,319.	June T-bond futures is at 60 25/32. Price per contract: $60,781.25. **Buy 67 contracts**

Analysis: When the $5 million face value bonds are issued on May 24, they are worth $4,537,319, a loss in value of $5,000,000 − $4,537,319 = $462,681. The yield at this price is 15.25 percent. (Note: Alternatively, if the bonds actually were issued at par with the coupon set at the yield on May 24 of 15.25 percent, the firm would receive the full $5,000,000 but the present value of its increased interest cost would be $462,681.)

The profit on the futures transaction is

$$
\begin{array}{ll}
67(\$68,343.75) & \text{(sale price of futures)} \\
\underline{-67(\$60,781.25)} & \text{(purchase price of futures)} \\
\$506,687.50 & \text{(profit on futures)}.
\end{array}
$$

Thus, the hedge offset more than all of the increased cost and left a net gain of $506,687.50 − $462,681 = $44,006.50. The effective issue price of the bonds is $4,537,319 + $506,687.50 = $5,044,006.50, which is an effective yield of 13.63 percent.

Stock Market Hedges Stock index futures have been one of the spectacular success stories of the financial markets. These cash-settled contracts are based on stocks. Investors use them to hedge positions in stock, speculate on the direction of the stock market in general, and arbitrage the contracts against comparable combinations of stocks.

Stock index futures contracts are based on indices of common stocks. The most widely traded index futures contract in the United States is the E-mini S&P 500 futures at the Chicago Mercantile Exchange.[12] The futures price is quoted in the same manner as the index. The E-mini S&P 500 futures contract has an implicit multiplier of $50, and the standard S&P 500 futures contract has an implicit multiplier of $250. Thus, if the E-mini futures price is 1,300, the actual price is 1,300($50) = $65,000. At expiration, the settlement price is set at the price of the S&P 500 index and the contract is settled in cash. The expirations are March, June, September, and December. The last trading day is the Thursday before the third Friday of the expiration month.

---

[12]Based on statistics reported in *Futures Industry*, March 2011 issue.

Several of the hedging examples illustrated with T-note and T-bond futures are similar to stock index futures hedges where a firm attempts to hedge a long position in a security or portfolio. The first example we shall consider is the hedge of a stock portfolio.

Stock Portfolio Hedge A central tenet of modern investment theory is that diversification eliminates unsystematic risk, leaving only systematic risk. Until the creation of stock index futures, investors had to accept the fact that systematic risk could not be eliminated. Now investors can use stock index futures to hedge the systematic risk. But should they do that? If all systematic and unsystematic risk is eliminated, the portfolio can expect to earn only the risk-free return. Why not just buy risk-free bonds? The answer is that investors occasionally want to change or eliminate systematic risk for brief periods. During times of unusual volatility in the market, they can use stock index futures to adjust or eliminate the systematic risk. This is much easier and less costly than adjusting the relative proportions invested in each stock. Later the portfolio manager can close out the futures position, and the portfolio systematic risk will be back at its original level.

Consider a portfolio manager who on March 31 is concerned about the market over the period ending July 27. The portfolio has accumulated an impressive profit, and the manager would like to protect the portfolio value over this time period. The manager knows that the portfolio is exposed to a loss in value resulting from a decline in the market as a whole, the systematic risk effect, as well as losses resulting from the unsystematic risk of the individual stocks. Although the portfolio contains only eight stocks, the manager is not particularly worried about the unsystematic risk. The manager knows that the systematic risk can be hedged by using S&P 500 stock index futures, specifically the September contract, which we shall assume has a beta of 1.0.

The results are shown in Table 11.10. The portfolio beta, which reflects the influence of the market as a whole on a stock or portfolio, is a weighted average of the betas of the component stocks, where each weight of a given stock is the market value of that stock divided by the total market value of the portfolio. This gives a portfolio beta of 1.06. Using the minimum variance hedge ratio results in the sale of 25 contracts. On July 27, the portfolio has declined in value by over $200,000, a loss of 2.68 percent. The futures transaction, however, generated a profit of $60,000, which reduced the effective loss to only 1.90 percent.

The objective of the hedge was to eliminate systematic risk. Clearly, systematic risk was reduced but not eliminated. The stock portfolio value declined about 2.68 percent while the futures price decreased a little over 1 percent. The hedge certainly helped but was far from perfect. There are several possible explanations for this result. One is that the betas are an estimate taken from a popular investment advisory service. Beta estimates over the recent past have not necessarily been stable. It is also possible that the portfolio was not sufficiently diversified and some unsystematic risk contributed to the loss. Some of the stocks may have paid dividends during the hedge period. We did not account for these dividends in illustrating the hedge results. Dividends would have reduced the loss on the portfolio and made the hedge more effective.

Had the market moved up, the portfolio would have shown a profit, but this would have been at least partially offset by a loss on the futures transaction. In either outcome, however, the portfolio manager would have been reasonably successful in capturing at least some of the accumulated profit on the portfolio.

Anticipatory Hedge of a Takeover or Acquisition The exciting world of takeovers and acquisitions offers an excellent opportunity to apply hedging concepts. The

TABLE 11.10 STOCK PORTFOLIO HEDGE

Scenario: On March 31, a portfolio manager is concerned about the market over the next four months. The portfolio has accumulated an impressive profit, which the manager wants to protect over the period ending July 27 using the standard S&P 500 futures contract. The prices, number of shares, and betas are given below.

STOCK	PRICE (3/31)	NUMBER OF SHARES	MARKET VALUE	WEIGHT	BETA
Federal Mogul	18.875	18,000	$ 339,750	0.044	1.00
Lockheed Martin	73.500	16,000	1,176,000	0.152	0.80
IBM	50.875	7,000	356,125	0.046	0.50
US West	43.625	10,800	471,150	0.061	0.70
Bausch & Lomb	54.250	21,000	1,139,250	0.147	1.10
First Union	47.750	28,800	1,375,200	0.178	1.10
Walt Disney	44.500	25,000	1,112,500	0.144	1.40
Tesoro	52.875	33,200	<u>1,755,450</u>	<u>0.227</u>	1.20
			$7,725,425	1.000	

Portfolio beta:

$0.044(1.00) + 0.152(0.80) + 0.046(0.50) + 0.061(0.70) + 0.147(1.10) + 0.178(1.10) + 0.144(1.40) + 0.227(1.20) = 1.06.$

S&P 500 September futures contract (assumed to have a beta of 1.0):

  Price on March 31: 1305

  Multiplier: $250

  Price of one contract: $250(1305) = $326,250$

Optimal number of futures contracts:

$$N_f = -1.06\left(\frac{7,725,425}{326,250}\right) = -25.10.$$

SELL 25 CONTRACTS

STOCK	PRICE (7/27)	MARKET VALUE
Federal Mogul	21.625	$ 389,250
Lockheed Martin	81.500	1,304,000
IBM	43.875	307,125
US West	47.125	508,950
Bausch & Lomb	45.875	963,375
First Union	48.125	1,386,000
Walt Disney	40.000	1,000,000
Tesoro	50.000	<u>1,660,000</u>
		$7,518,700

Results: The values of the stocks on July 27 are shown below:

S&P 500 September futures contract:

  Price on July 27: 1,295.40

  Multiplier: $250

  Price of one contract: $250(1,295.40) = $323,850$

Buy 25 contracts

Analysis: The market value of the stocks declined by $7,725,425 − $7,518,700 = $206,725, a loss of 2.68 percent. The futures profit was

      $25($326,250)$ (sale price of futures)

    <u>$-25($323,850)$</u> (purchase price of futures)

       $60,000$ (profit on futures).

Thus, the overall loss on the stocks was effectively reduced to $206,725 − $60,000 = $146,725, a loss of 1.90 percent.

acquiring firm identifies a target firm and intends to make a bid for the latter's stock. Typically, the acquiring firm plans to purchase enough stock to obtain control. Because of the large amount of stock usually involved and the speed with which takeover rumors travel, the acquiring firm frequently makes a series of smaller purchases until it has accumulated sufficient shares to obtain control. During the period in which the acquiring firm is slowly and quietly buying the stock, it is exposed to the risk that stock prices in general will increase. This means that either the shares will cost more or fewer shares can be purchased.

Consider the following situation: On July 15, a firm has identified Felix Corporation as a potential acquisition. Felix stock currently is selling for $26.50 and has a beta of 1.80. The acquiring firm plans to buy 100,000 shares, which will cost $2.65 million. The purchase will be made on August 15. This could be viewed as one purchase in a series of purchases designed to ultimately acquire controlling interest in the target firm. The acquiring firm realizes that if stock prices as a whole increase, the shares will be more expensive. If the firm purchases stock index futures, however, any general increase in stock prices will lead to a profit in the futures market.

Because the hedge will be terminated on August 15, the acquiring firm chooses to buy September S&P 500 futures. Table 11.11 shows the results of the hedge. On August 15,

---

MAKING THE CONNECTION

Using Derivatives in Takeovers

Most people think of Porsche as a German company that makes fast cars. In the summer of 2008, Porsche revealed to the world that it also makes derivatives. That is, it uses derivatives, evidently quite successfully. During a period in which U. S. automakers were teetering on the brink of bankruptcy, Porsche announced record profits, almost all of which came from buying options on none other than one of its leading competitors, Volkswagen.

In 2005, Porsche announced that it was going to try to take over VW, a company that makes 60 times as many cars per year as Porsche. As described in the chapter, a firm that plans to buy another firm is exposed to the risk of the target firm's stock increasing. As described, stock index futures can hedge the effect of the market increasing and pulling up the price of the target, but it cannot hedge the unsystematic effect that the target firm's stock will move independently of the market. To hedge that possibility or perhaps to speculate on a rising price of VW, Porsche began buying over-the-counter cash-settled call options on VW. Upon exercise, it would receive the difference between the price of the VW stock and the chosen exercise price. If VW's stock fell below the exercise price, Porsche would simply let the options expire, absorbing the loss from the premiums paid. By purchasing privately negotiated over-the-counter options, Porsche could somewhat disguise its exposure in VW, although it did begin buying VW shares as it exercised the options.

Over the next two years, Porsche accumulated a very large position in VW in both stock and options. Between the shares held by the banks that were hedging the options sold to Porsche and the shares held by Porsche, the market had been effectively cornered. Short sellers, primarily hedge funds, had to come up with VW shares, but there were few to be had. Desperate for shares, short sellers bid up the VW stock to a very high price, bringing Porsche greater profits on its stock and options.

Such strategies look great in hindsight, but they are fraught with risk. If VW's stock had fallen, Porsche would have taken large losses given its huge exposure. Moreover, what Porsche did is often looked upon badly by observers of the market and regulators. In some countries, it might have even been illegal. On the other hand, had the stock risen and Porsche not bought the options, it would have had to invest much more money as it pursued its takeover objective.

TABLE 11.11 ANTICIPATORY HEDGE OF A TAKEOVER

Scenario: On July 15, a firm has decided to begin buying up shares of Felix Corporation with the ultimate objective of obtaining controlling interest. The acquisition will be made by purchasing lots of about 100,000 shares until sufficient control is obtained. The first purchase of 100,000 shares will take place on August 15. The stock is currently worth $26.50 and has a beta of 1.80.

DATE	SPOT MARKET	FUTURES MARKET
July 15	Current price of the stock is 26.50. Current cost of shares: 100,000($26.50) = $2,650,000. The beta is 1.80.	September S&P 500 futures is at 1,260.50. Price per contract: $315,125. Approximate number of contracts: $$N_f = -1.8\left(\frac{-2,650,000}{315,125}\right) = 15.14.$$ Therefore, it should buy futures. **Buy 15 contracts**
August 15	The stock is purchased at its current price of 28.75. Cost of shares: 100,000($28.75) = $2,875,000.	September S&P 500 futures is at 1,327.20. Price per contract: $331,800. **Sell 15 contracts**

Analysis: When the 100,000 shares are purchased on August 15, they cost $2,875,000, an additional $225,000. The profit on the futures transaction is

$$
\begin{array}{ll}
15(\$331,800) & \text{(sale price of futures)} \\
\underline{-15(\$315,125)} & \text{(purchase price of futures)} \\
\$250,125 & \text{(profit on futures).}
\end{array}
$$

Thus, the hedge eliminated all of the additional cost and left a small gain. The shares end up effectively costing ($2,875,000 − $250,125)/100,000 = 26.25.

the Felix stock price is $28.75. The shares thus cost an additional $225,000.[13] The profit on the futures transaction, however, was $250,125. Thus, the effective cost of the shares is $26.25.

The hedge was successful in reducing some of the additional cost of the shares; however, the unsystematic risk cannot be hedged. In takeover situations, the unsystematic risk is likely to be very high. For example, if word leaks out that someone is buying up the stock, the price will tend to rise substantially. This can occur even if the market as a whole is going down. Also, federal regulations require that certain takeover attempts be announced beforehand. If there were options or futures on the target firm's stock, however, the acquiring firm could use these to hedge the unsystematic risk.

The takeover game is intense and exciting, with high risk and the potential for large profits. Stock index futures can play an important role, but the extent to which futures are used to hedge this kind of risk is not known because much of this kind of activity is done with a minimum of publicity.

The takeover example is but one type of situation wherein a firm can use a long hedge with stock index futures. Any time someone is considering buying a stock, there is the risk that the stock price will increase before the purchase is made. Stock index futures cannot hedge the risk that factors specific to the company will drive up the stock price, but they can be used to protect against increases in the market as a whole.

Forward markets for stocks and stock indices are not widely used. As we shall see in Chapter 12, however, swaps, which are closely related to forward contracts, are popular

---

[13]It is unlikely that all of the 100,000 shares could have been purchased at the same price. Therefore, we should treat $28.75 as the average price at which the shares were acquired.

tools for controlling stock market risk. We turn now to explore various spread strategies. Hedging strategies are focused on risk reduction, whereas spread strategies are typically focused on revenue enhancement with some incremental increase in risk.

SPREAD STRATEGIES

> Intramarket spread consists of a long position in one futures contract and a short position on a futures contract on the same underlying with a different expiration.

We turn now to selected spread strategies. Spread strategies are similar to hedge strategies in that there are two positions with one intended to offset or partially offset the risk of the other. In the case of a hedge, one position is in the underlying and one is in futures. In the case of a spread, both positions are in the futures. Two forms of spread strategies are reviewed: intramarket spreads and intermarket spreads. **Intramarket spreads** involve going long and short futures contracts on the same underlying instruments, whereas **intermarket spreads** involve going long and short futures contracts on different underlying instruments.

> Intermarket spread consists of a long position in one futures contract and a short position on a futures contract on a different underlying.

Spread strategies are very important to the liquidity of various futures contracts. Hedgers often have specific contracts and specific maturities required to achieve their hedging objectives. When arbitrage is feasible, arbitrage traders can provide the necessary liquidity to support hedging demand. Recall that arbitrage trading requires that the risk acquired is to be be offset in a related instrument, often the underlying. Arbitrageurs may not be able to execute transactions in the underlying with sufficient volume. Arbitrages may be able to achieve their desired result with other futures contracts, resulting in spread strategies. Speculative traders and other market participants often use spread strategies to achieve their desired objectives. This additional trading activity often provides liquidity to support hedging demand. Speculators are very careful in their assessment of relative value, and for a sufficient risk premium, they will be induced to take positions. We explore, first, selected intramarket spreads and then turn our attention to selected intermarket spreads.

Intramarket Spreads

Intramarket spread trading activities add liquidity to the market, thereby making hedging activities less costly. We focus first on generic futures spreads using the carry arbitrage model and then illustrate intramarket spreads using Treasury bond futures contracts and stock index futures contracts.

Generic Intramarket Futures Spreads We explore first the behavior of generic futures contracts. Recall from Chapter 9 that the futures price was established as the spot price plus the cost of carry. Now consider two futures contracts with different expirations, times T_1 and T_2. The longer-term contract has a futures price of $f_0(2)$, equal to $S_0 + \theta_{0,2}$, and the shorter-term contract has a futures price of $f_0(1)$, equal to $S_0 + \theta_{0,1}$. Subtracting the two, we obtain

$$f_0(2) - f_0(1) = \theta_{0,2} - \theta_{0,1}.$$

This equation defines the spread between futures prices. The spread between the nearby and deferred contracts is the difference in their respective costs of carry. The term $\theta_{0,2} - \theta_{0,1}$ is the cost of the carry for the time interval between T_1 and T_2, observed at time 0, based on the carry arbitrage relationship, $f_0(T_i) = S_0 + \theta_{0,i} = 1,2$. Therefore, the profit from a spread trade can be expressed as the profit on the two positions. Assuming that we are long the T_2 contract and short the T_1 contract, the profit is

$$\Pi = [f_t(2) - f_0(2)] - [f_t(1) - f_0(1)]$$
$$= [\theta_{t,2} - \theta_{0,2}] - [\theta_{t,1} - \theta_{0,1}] = [\theta_{t,2} - \theta_{t,1}] - [\theta_{0,2} - \theta_{0,1}]$$

which is the difference between the change in carry costs of contracts 2 and 1. Based on this result, the risk and opportunities related to spread trading depend solely on changes in carry costs over time.

> The performance of intramarket spreads depends on changes in the cost of carry for each contract over the life of the contract.

Successful spread trading will depend on successfully predicting changes in carry costs. Figure 11.2 illustrates the change in the spread based on a simulation of changes in carry costs.[14] Two cases are presented—one where carry costs are simulated to increase and the other where carry costs are simulated to decrease. We see that profitable spread trading strategies exist if one can reasonably predict changes in carry costs.

If carry costs are expected to increase, then the trader should go long the more distant futures contract, T_2, and go short the nearby futures contract, T_1. If carry costs are expected to decrease, then the trader should go short the more distant futures contract, T_2, and go long the nearby futures contract, T_1.

Treasury Bond Futures Spreads Recall that Treasury bond futures contracts had several complicating issues, including the application of conversion factors and the question of which bond is the cheapest to deliver. Therefore, Treasury bond spread trading has some additional risks.

Treasury bond futures contracts are quoted in half 32nds; hence, the prices will exhibit jumps for each half 32nd difference. Figure 11.3 illustrates the spread between

FIGURE 11.2 Changes in Spread Based on Carry Costs Changes

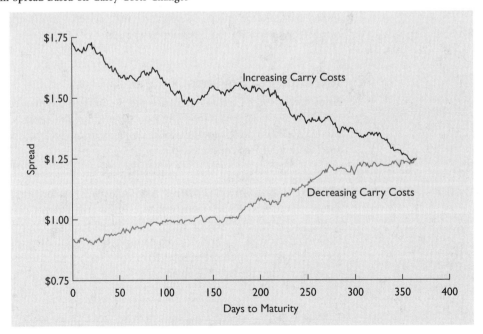

---

[14]A generic carry arbitrage model is assumed with carry costs following geometric Brownian motion with mean of plus or minus 25 percent and a standard deviation of 10 percent.

FIGURE 11.3 Changes in Spread U.S. Treasury Bond Futures Contracts

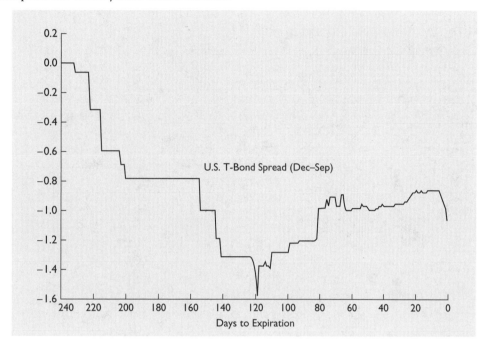

the December and September futures contract. At the time this graph was produced, short-term interest rates were mostly lower than the yield on U.S. Treasury bonds; therefore, U.S. Treasury bond futures contracts exhibited negative carry, and hence the spread was negative. Figure 11.4 illustrates short-term interest rates for this same period, indicating that interest rates are an important component of carrying costs. A general relationship appears between short-term interest rates and Treasury bond futures spreads.

Table 11.12 presents an example of a simple spread taken in anticipation of changes in interest rates in the T-bond market. The trader goes short the September contract and long the December in the hope that a small gain will be made. If the trader's forecast is wrong, the loss is not likely to be large. This example involves a simple position of one contract long and one contract short. In practice, many traders use weighted positions, taking more of either the long or short contract so as to balance their different volatilities. The proper number of each contract to provide a risk-free position is obtained by using their modified durations in the same manner that we did when we constructed long spot and short futures positions. In this example, the trader's expectations were not at all realized. Rates fell and bond futures prices rose. The September contract was not profitable, but the long December contract was profitable and the overall loss was negligible.

Stock Index Futures Spreads The factors determining the carry costs for stock index futures contracts are interest rates and dividends. Dividends are usually more predictable than interest rates, although somewhat tedious; hence, the driving force determining changes in spreads should be interest rates.

Figure 11.5 illustrates the intramarket spread for the S&P 500 index futures contracts of September and December. A rough relationship clearly exists between short-term interest rates and equity futures spreads.

FIGURE 11.4 Short-Term LIBOR Interest Rates

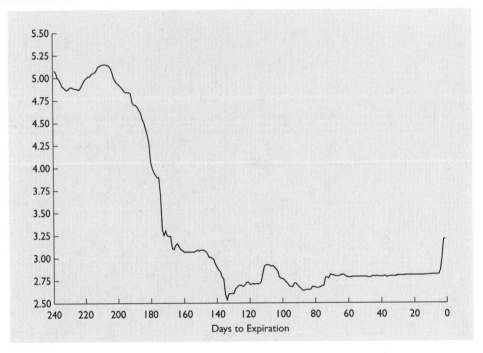

Intermarket Spreads

In the previous section, we discussed three forms of intramarket spreads. There are also a number of intermarket spreads or intercommodity spreads. These are transactions in which the two futures contracts are on different underlying instruments. There are a vast number of different intermarket spreads. We first review the generic futures case, highlighting the difference from intramarket spread strategies, and then only briefly review bond and stock strategies.

Generic Intermarket Futures Spreads Intermarket spreads tend to be riskier because the two positions do not share a common underlying instrument. Thus, intermarket spreads not only change in value due to changes in the carry costs, but also change due to changes in the value of the underlying instrument, as can be seen in the following identity:

$$f_0(C2) - f_0(C1) = S_{0,C2} + \theta_{0,C2} - [S_{0,C1} + \theta_{0,C1}].$$

This equation defines the spread between futures prices involving two different underlying instruments (denoted CI and C2), where we assume that you are long the C2 futures contract and short the CI futures contract. Recall that S_0 denotes the underlying price at time 0 and that θ_0 denotes the carrying costs at time 0. Therefore, the profit from a spread trade can be expressed as the profit on the two positions:

$$\begin{aligned}
\Pi &= [f_t(C2) - f_0(C2)] - [f_t(C1) - f_0(C1)] \\
&= [S_{t,C2} + \theta_{t,C2} - S_{0,C2} - \theta_{0,C2}] - [S_{t,C1} + \theta_{t,C1} - S_{0,C1} - \theta_{0,C1}] \\
&= \{[S_{t,C2} - S_{t,C1}] - [S_{0,C2} - S_{0,C1}]\} + \{[\theta_{t,C2} - \theta_{t,C1}] - [\theta_{0,C2} - \theta_{0,C1}]\},
\end{aligned}$$

which is two sets of differences, one being the difference between the change in price of the underlying instrument of contracts 2 and 1 and the other being the difference between the change in the carry costs of contract 2 and 1. Therefore, the predictions

TABLE 11.12 A TREASURY BOND FUTURES SPREAD

Scenario: It is July 6. Interest rates have steadily risen over the last six months. The yield on long-term government bonds is 13.54 percent. A Treasury bond futures floor trader anticipates that rates will continue upward; however, the economy remains healthy, and there are no indications that the Fed will tighten the money supply, which would drive rates further upward. Thus, while the trader is bearish, she is encouraged by other economic factors. She wants to take a speculative short position in T-bond futures but is concerned that rates will fall, generating a potentially large loss. She believes that if rates have not changed by late August, they will not change at all. Thus, she shorts the September contract and buys the December contract.

DATE	FUTURES MARKET
July 6	The September T-bond futures price is 60 22/32, or 60.6875. Price per contract: $60,687.50. **Sell one contract** The December T-bond futures price is 60 2/32, or 60.0625. Price per contract: $60,062.50. **Buy one contract**
August 31	The September T-bond futures price is 65 27/32, or 65.84375. Price per contract: $65,843.75. **Buy one contract** The December T-bond futures price is 65 5/32, or 65.15625. Price per contract: $65,156.25. **Sell one contract**

Analysis: The profit on the September contract was

$$\$60,687.50 - \$65,843.75 = -\$5,156.25.$$

The profit on the December contract was

$$\$65,156.25 - \$60,062.50 = \$5,093.75.$$

Thus, the overall profit was

$$-\$5,156.25 + \$5,093.75 = -\$62.50.$$

FIGURE 11.5 S&P 500 Index Futures Spread and Short-Term Interest Rates

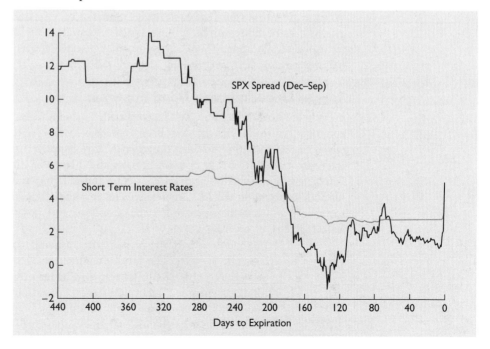

are more complex. Often the volatility of changes in the underlying instruments is much higher than the volatility of carry costs. Hence, the spread trader's main task relates to predicting changes in the prices and carrying costs of the underlying instruments.

> The performance of intermarket spreads depends on changes in the prices and carrying costs of the two underlying assets over the life of the contract.

Note and Bond Futures There are a variety of intermarket spread strategies within the debt market. We examine here the NOB, or notes over bonds, spread. This spread involves comparing T-note futures and T-bond futures.

The NOB trade would be used to capitalize on shifts in the yield curve. For example, if a trader believes that rates on the 7-to-10-year range of the yield curve will fall and rates on the 15-plus-year range will either rise or fall by less, a long position in the NOB spread might be warranted. If the investor's expectations prove correct, a profit could be made because the T-note futures price will rise and the T-bond futures price will either fall or rise by a smaller amount. Of course, if yields on the long-term end of the market fall, the trader could end up losing money because long-term bond prices will be expected to rise by a greater amount for a given yield change. So the trader might prefer to take a weighted position in which the ratio of T-note futures to T-bond futures is something other than one-to-one. In general, however, the NOB spread is designed to capitalize on changes in the relationship between Treasury note and Treasury bond futures prices.

Stock Index Futures Intermarket spread trading can also be performed with stock index futures contracts. Spread traders may have a view on the relative performance of one equity sector when compared to another. With the addition of single stock futures contracts, spread trading with futures contracts can now involve two individual stocks or one individual stock and an equity index. As with other intermarket spread trading activities, the success of the spread trader is directly related to forecasting skill.

TARGET STRATEGIES

We now turn to various target strategies. Specifically, we explore target duration strategies with bond futures, alpha capture, target beta strategies with stock index futures, and tactical asset allocation. There are many other possible target strategies to consider, but the ones covered here will give an adequate overview of target strategies.

Target Duration with Bond Futures

We showed how hedge ratios can be constructed using futures. The procedure essentially combines futures so that the overall investment is insensitive to interest rate changes. In effect, this changes the modified duration to zero. Suppose a market timer believes that interest rates will move in one direction or the other, but the timer does not want to completely eliminate the exposure by taking the modified duration to zero. If interest rates are expected to fall, the timer may want to increase the modified duration; if rates are expected to rise, the timer may want to decrease the modified duration but not necessarily reduce it to zero.

> Buying or selling futures provides a simple way of increasing or decreasing a bond's modified duration to engage in target duration strategies.

Suppose a portfolio of bonds has a market value of B and a modified duration of MD_B. The futures contract has a modified duration of MD_f and a price of f. The timer wants to increase the spot modified duration to MD_T, which we shall call the **target duration**. One way to do this is to put more money in high modified duration bonds and less money in low modified duration bonds, but this would incur transaction costs on the purchase and sale of at least two bonds. Futures can be used to easily adjust the modified duration. Also, by doing the transaction with futures rather than buying and selling the spot instruments, there are significant savings in transaction costs.

The number of futures needed to change the modified duration to MD_T is[15]

$$N_f = \left(\frac{MD_T - MD_B}{MD_f}\right)\left(\frac{B}{f}\right).$$

Notice how similar this formula is to the one given earlier in this chapter. That formula was

$$N_f^* = \left(\frac{MD_B}{MD_f}\right)\left(\frac{B}{f}\right),$$

which reduces the interest sensitivity and modified duration to zero.[16] N_f^* denotes the optimal hedge ratio where the objective is to minimize price volatility. Here we will not use the asterisk, *, when seeking to change modified duration to a nonzero target. If the target duration were zero in our new formula, we would obtain the old formula. Thus, the new formula is a much more general restatement of the optimal hedge ratio covered earlier in this chapter because it permits the modified duration to be adjusted to any chosen value. If the investor expected falling interest rates and wanted to increase the modified duration, MD_T would be larger than MD_B. Then N_f would be positive and futures would be bought. This makes sense because adding futures to a long spot position should increase the risk. If the trader is bearish and wants to reduce the modified duration, MD_T would be less than MD_B and N_f would be negative, meaning that futures would be sold. This is so because an opposite position in futures should be required to reduce the risk.

An Example Let us rework the T-bond hedging example that appeared in Table 11.7. In that problem, on February 25, the portfolio manager held $1 million face value of the 11 7/8s bond maturing in about 25 years. The bond price is 101, and the bond will be sold on March 28. In that example, we feared an increase in interest rates and lowered the modified duration to zero by selling 16 futures contracts. Suppose, however, that we wanted to lower the modified duration from its present level of 7.83 to 4. This would make the portfolio less sensitive to interest rates, but not completely unaffected by them. In that way, if the forecast proved incorrect, the positive modified duration would still leave room to profit.

The example is presented in Table 11.13. The bond ends up losing 2.26 percent. To determine how close the outcome was to the desired outcome, we need to know the change in the yield on the bonds. On February 25, the yield on the spot bond was 11.74 percent; on March 28, the yield that corresponded to a price of 95 22/32 was 12.50 percent. Recall that the following formula expresses the relationship between the change in the yield and the percentage change in the bond price:

$$\frac{\Delta B}{B} \approx -MD(\Delta y),$$

---

[15]See Hedge Ratios and Futures Contracts Technical Note in the section "Derivation of Price Sensitivity Hedge Ratio."

[16]As noted above, both of these formulas apply only to extremely short holding periods. Any increment of time or change in yield will require recalculation of the number of futures contracts, so the number of contracts will need adjustment throughout the holding period.

TABLE 11.13 TARGET DURATION WITH BOND FUTURES

Scenario: On February 25, a portfolio manager holds $1 million face value of a government bond, the 11 7/8s, which matures in about 25 years. The bond is currently priced at 101, has a modified duration of 7.83, and has a yield of 11.74 percent. The manager plans to sell the bond on March 28. The manager is worried about rising interest rates and would like to reduce the bond's sensitivity to interest rates by lowering its modified duration to 4. This would reduce its interest sensitivity, which would help if rates increase, but would not eliminate the possibility of gains from falling rates.

DATE	SPOT MARKET	FUTURES MARKET
February 25	The current price of the bonds is 101. Value of position: $1,010,000. The short end of the term structure is flat, so this is the forward sale price of the bonds in March.	June T-bond futures is at 70 16/32. Price per contract: $70,500. The futures price and the characteristics of the deliverable bond imply a modified duration of 7.20 and a yield of 14.92 percent. Appropriate number of contracts: $$N_f = \left(\frac{4 - 7.83}{7.20}\right)\left(\frac{1,010,000}{70,500}\right) = -7.62.$$ **Sell 8 contracts**
March 28	The bonds are sold at their current price of 95 22/32. This is a price of $956.875 per bond. Value of position: $956,875.	June T-bond futures is at 66 22/32. Price per contract: $66,718.75. **Buy 8 contracts**

Analysis: When the $1 million face value bonds are sold on March 28, they are worth $956,875, a loss in value of $1,010,000 − $956,875 = $53,125.

The profit on the futures transaction is

8(70,500)	(sale price of futures)
−8($66,718.75)	(purchase price of futures)
$30,250	(profit on futures).

Thus, the overall transaction resulted in a loss in value of $53,125 − $30,250 = $22,875, which is a 2.26 percent decline in overall value.

where B represents the bond price. With a modified duration reset to 4, the formula predicts that for a yield change of 0.1250 − 0.1174 = 0.0076, the percentage price change would be

$$\frac{\Delta B}{B} \approx -4(0.0076) = -0.0304,$$

or 3.04 percent. The actual change was 2.26 percent. Without the futures position, the modified duration still would have been 7.83. Plugging into the formula gives a predicted percentage change in the bond price of

$$\frac{\Delta B}{B} \approx -7.83(0.0076) = -0.0595,$$

or a loss of 5.95 percent. The actual change without the hedge would have been −$53,125/$1,010,000 = −0.0526, or a 5.26 percent loss.

Alpha Capture

Recall that the systematic risk of a diversified portfolio can be hedged by using stock index futures. Because the portfolio is diversified, there is no unsystematic risk; therefore, the portfolio is riskless. In some cases, however, an investor might want to hedge the systematic risk and retain the unsystematic risk.

The unsystematic return that reflects investment performance over and above the risk associated with the systematic or marketwide factor is called *alpha*. In an efficient market, investors cannot expect to earn positive alpha. Professional financial analysts, however, do not believe this is true. Thousands of analysts devote all of their time to identifying overpriced and underpriced stocks. An analyst who thinks a stock is underpriced normally recommends it for purchase. If the stock is purchased and the market goes down, the stock's overall performance can be hurt. For example, a drug firm might announce an important new drug that can help cure diabetes. If that announcement occurs during a strong bear market, the stock can be pulled down by the market effect. The extent of the stock's movement with the market is measured by its beta. In this section, we shall look at how alpha can be captured by using stock index futures to eliminate the systematic component of performance, leaving the unsystematic performance, the alpha. In this sense, the strategy is based on a target beta of zero.

We will use the following notation:

$$S = \text{stock price}$$
$$M = \text{value of market portfolio of all risky assets}$$
$$r_S = \Delta S/S = \text{rate of return on stock}$$
$$r_M = \Delta M/M = \text{rate of return on market}$$
$$\beta = \text{beta of the stock}$$

The stock's return consists of its systematic return, βr_M, and its unsystematic return or alpha, denoted as α. Thus,

$$r_S = \beta r_M + \alpha.$$

If we multiply both sides of the equation by S, we have

$$S r_S = S \beta r_M + S\alpha,$$

which is equivalent to

$$\Delta S = S\beta(\Delta M/M) + S\alpha.$$

This is the return on the stock expressed in dollars. The objective of the transaction is to capture a profit equal to the dollar alpha, $S\alpha$.

The profit from a transaction consisting of the stock and N_f futures contracts is

$$\Pi = \Delta S + N_f^* \Delta f.$$

Stock index futures can be used to eliminate the systematic risk to enable an investor to capture an alpha from identifying on underpriced security.

Recall that the formula for N_f^* in an ordinary stock index futures hedge is $-\beta(S/f)$. Let us substitute this for N_f^*:

$$\Pi = \Delta S - \beta\left(\frac{S}{f}\right)\Delta f.$$

Now we need to substitute $S\beta(\Delta M/M) + S\alpha$ for ΔS and assume that the futures price change will match the index price change. In that case, $\Delta M/M = \Delta f/f$. Making these substitutions gives

$$\Pi = S\alpha.$$

Thus, if we use N_f^* futures contracts where N_f^* is the ordinary hedge ratio for stock index futures, we will eliminate systematic risk and the profit will be the dollar alpha.

An Example   Table 11.14 illustrates an application of this result. In this example, you have identified what you believe to be an underpriced stock. You are worried, however, that the market as a whole will decline and drag the stock down. To hedge the market effect, you sell stock index futures.

This transaction should not be considered riskless. Suppose your analysis is incorrect and the company announces some bad news during a bull market. Selling the futures contract would eliminate the effect of the bull market while retaining the effect of the bad news announcement. Moreover, this type of trade depends not only on the correctness of the analysis, but also on the beta's stability.

TABLE 11.14 ALPHA CAPTURE

Scenario: On July 1, you are following the stock of Helene Curtis, which has a price of 17.38 and a beta of 1.10. Barring any change in the general level of stock prices, you expect the stock to appreciate by about 10 percent by the end of September. Your analysis of the market as a whole calls for about an 8 percent decline in stock prices in general over the same period. Because the stock has a beta of 1.10, this would bring the stock down by 1.10(.08) = 0.088, or 8.8 percent, which will almost completely offset the expected 10 percent unsystematic increase in the stock price. You decide to hedge the market effect by selling a particular stock index futures contract with a multiplier of 500.

DATE	SPOT MARKET	FUTURES MARKET
July 1	Own 150,000 shares of Helene Curtis stock at 17.38. Value of stock: 150,000($17.38) = $2,607,000.	December stock index futures price is 444.60. Price of one contract: 444.60($500) = $222,300. Appropriate number of contracts $$N_f = -1.10\left(\frac{\$2,607,000}{\$222,300}\right) = -12.90.$$ **Sell 13 contracts**
September 30	Stock price is 17.75. Value of stock: 150,000($17.75) = $2,662,500.	December stock index futures price is 411.30. Price of one contract: 411.30($500) = $205,650. **Buy 13 contracts**

Analysis

Profit on stock:

$$\begin{array}{r} \$2,662,500 \\ -\$2,607,000 \\ \hline \$55,500 \end{array}$$

Profit on futures:

$$\begin{array}{r} 13(\$222,300) \\ -13(\$205,650) \\ \hline \$216,450 \end{array}$$

Overall profit:

$$\begin{array}{r} \$55,500 \\ +\$216,450 \\ \hline \$271,950 \end{array}$$

Overall rate of return:

$$\frac{\$271,950}{\$2,607,300} = 0.1043$$

Target Beta with Stock Index Futures

Recall in the hedging discussion above that we considered a portfolio manager who sold stock index futures to eliminate the systematic risk. At a later date, the futures contracts were repurchased and the portfolio was returned to its previous level of systematic risk. Assuming that the beta of the futures is 1, the number of futures contracts was given by the formula

$$N_f^* = -\beta_S \frac{S}{f}.$$

In some cases, a portfolio manager may want to change the systematic risk but not eliminate it altogether. For example, if a portfolio manager believes that the market is highly volatile, the portfolio beta could be lowered but not reduced to zero. This would enable the portfolio to profit if the market did move upward but would produce a smaller loss if the market moved down. At more optimistic times, the portfolio beta could be increased. In the absence of stock index futures (or options), changing the portfolio beta would require costly transactions in the individual stocks.

Assume that we have a portfolio containing stock valued at S and N_f futures contracts. We drop the asterisk, *, because we are not focused on the minimum risk solution now. The return on the portfolio is given as r_{Sf}, where

$$r_{Sf} = \frac{\Delta S + N_f \Delta f}{S}.$$

The first term in the numerator, ΔS, is the change in the price of the stock. The second term, $N_f \Delta f$, is the number of contracts times the change in the price of the futures contract. The denominator, S, is the amount of money invested in the stock. The expected return on the portfolio, $E(r_{Sf})$, is

$$E(r_{Sf}) = \frac{E(\Delta S)}{S} + N_f \frac{E(\Delta f)}{S} = E(r_S) + \frac{N_f}{S} E(\Delta f),$$

where $E(r_S)$ is the expected return on the stock defined as $E(\Delta S)/S$ and $E(\Delta f)$ is the expected change in the price of the futures contract.

From modern portfolio theory, the Capital Asset Pricing Model (CAPM) gives the expected return on a stock as $r + [E(r_M) - r]\beta$, where the beta is the systematic risk and reflects the influence of the market as a whole on the stock. If the market is efficient, the investor's required return will equal the expected return. If the CAPM holds for stocks, it should also hold for stock index futures; however, it would be written as

$$\frac{E(\Delta f)}{f} = [E(r_M) - r]\beta_f = E(r_M) - r,$$

where β_f is the beta of the futures contract, assumed to be 1. Although in reality β_f will not be precisely equal to 1, it is sufficiently close that we shall assume it to keep the example simple. Note that this CAPM equation seems to be missing the term r from the right-hand side. The risk-free rate reflects the opportunity cost of money invested in the asset. Because the futures contract requires no initial outlay, there is no opportunity cost; thus, the r term is omitted. Thus, a long position in a stock index futures contract would be expected to return the market risk premium, and a short position in a stock index futures contract would be expected to lose the market risk premium.

The objective is to adjust the portfolio beta, β_S, and expected return, $E(r_{Sf})$, to a more preferred level. Because the CAPM holds for the portfolio, we can write the relationship between expected return and beta as

$$E(r_{Sf}) = r + [E(r_M) - r]\beta_T,$$

where β_T is the **target beta**, the desired risk level. Now we substitute for $E(r_s)$ and $E(\Delta f)$ and get

$$E(r_{Sf}) = r + [E(r_M) - r]\beta_S + N_f(f/S)[E(r_M) - r].$$

Setting this equal to $r + [E(r_M) - r]\,\beta_T$ and solving for N_f gives

$$N_f = (\beta_T - \beta_S)\left(\tfrac{S}{f}\right).$$

> Buying or selling futures provides a simple way of increasing or decreasing a stock portfolio's beta to engage in target beta strategies.

This formula differs only slightly from the previous formula of N_f^*, which was covered in our hedging material earlier in this chapter. In fact, the N_f^* formula is but a special case of this one. For example, if the target beta is zero, the above formula reduces to $-\beta_S\left(\tfrac{S}{f}\right)$, where the negative sign means that you would sell N_f futures. This is the same formula we used in the hedging discussion above to eliminate systematic risk.

When the manager wants to increase the beta, β_T will be greater than β_S and N_f will be positive. In that case, the manager will buy futures contracts. That makes sense because the risk will increase. When the beta needs to be reduced, β_T will be less than β_S, and the manager should sell futures to reduce the risk.

An Example Table 11.15 presents an example in which the manager of a portfolio that has a beta of 0.95 would like to temporarily increase the beta to 1.25. The manager buys stock index futures, which results in an overall gain of almost 12 percent when the stocks themselves gained only 10 percent.

Tactical Asset Allocation Using Stock and Bond Futures

A typical investment portfolio often consists of money allocated to certain classes of assets. Stock is one general class, while bonds are another. Some portfolios contain additional asset classes such as real estate, hedge funds, venture capital, or commodities. Within a given asset class, there may be subdivisions into more specific classes. For example, the stock asset class could be divided into domestic stock and international stock or perhaps large-cap stock, mid-cap stock, and small-cap stock[17]. Portfolio managers then usually try to adjust the allocation of funds among the asset classes in such a manner that the most attractive classes receive the highest weights. This form of portfolio management is usually called *asset allocation*.

Over the long run, a portfolio typically has a specified set of target weights for each asset class. These weights are usually called the *strategic asset allocation*. In the short run, the portfolio manager can deviate from these weights by allocating more funds to the classes expected to provide the best performance. These short run deviations from the strategic asset allocation make up a process called *tactical asset allocation*. Of course, such a strategy is just a variation of target strategies, as we discussed with respect to both stock and bond futures.

The execution of tactical asset allocation strategies can be done by buying and selling assets within the various classes. When futures are available on underlyings that are sufficiently similar to the asset classes, they are often used to execute these strategies in a more efficient, less costly manner. Let us see how this can be done.

Consider a portfolio with just two asset classes, stock and bonds. The stock asset class has a specific beta, and the bond asset class has a specific modified duration. If the manager wants to decrease the allocation to stock and increase the allocation to bonds, she can do so by selling stocks and buying bonds. Alternatively, she may be able to sell stock

---

[17]Cap is an abbreviation for market capitalization, or the current market value of outstanding common stock.

TABLE 11.15 TARGET BETA STRATEGIES WITH STOCK INDEX FUTURES

Scenario: On August 29, a portfolio manager is holding a portfolio of stocks worth $3,783,210. The portfolio beta is 0.95. The manager expects the stock market as a whole to appreciate substantially over the next three months and wants to increase the portfolio beta to 1.25. The manager could buy and sell shares in the portfolio, but this would incur high transaction costs and later the portfolio beta would have to be adjusted back to 0.95. The manager decides to buy stock index futures to temporarily increase the portfolio's systematic risk. The prices, number of shares, and betas are given below. The target date for evaluating the portfolio is November 29.

STOCK	PRICE (8/29)	NUMBER OF SHARES	MARKET VALUE	WEIGHT	BETA
Beneficial Corp.	40.50	11,350	$ 459,675	0.122	0.95
Cummins Engine	64.50	10,950	706,275	0.187	1.10
Gillette	62.00	12,400	768,800	0.203	0.85
Kmart	33.00	5,500	181,500	0.048	1.15
Boeing	49.00	4,600	225,400	0.059	1.15
W. R. Grace	42.62	6,750	287,685	0.076	1.00
Eli Lilly	87.38	11,400	996,132	0.263	0.85
Parker Pen	20.62	7,650	157,743	0.042	0.75
			$3,783,210	1.000	

Portfolio beta:

$0.122(0.95) + 0.187(1.10) + 0.203(0.85) + 0.048(1.15) + 0.059(1.15) + 0.076(1.00) + 0.263(0.85) + 0.042(0.75) = 0.95.$

December stock index futures contract:

Price on August 29: 759.60

Multiplier: $250

Price of one contract: $250(759.60) = $189,900

Required number of futures contracts:

$$N_f = (1.25 - 0.95)\left(\frac{3,783,210}{189,900}\right) = 5.98.$$

Buy 6 contracts

Results: The values of the stocks on November 29 are shown below.

STOCK	PRICE (11/29)	MARKET VALUE
Beneficial Corp.	45.13	$ 512,226
Cummins Engine	66.75	730,913
Gillette	69.87	866,388
Kmart	35.12	193,160
Boeing	49.12	225,952
W. R. Grace	40.75	275,062
Eli Lilly	103.75	1,182,750
Parker Pen	22.88	175,032
		$4,161,483

December stock index futures contract:

Price on November 29: 809.60

Multiplier: $250

Price of one contract: $250(809.60) = $202,400

Sell 6 contracts

Analysis: The market value of the stocks increased by $4,161,483 − 3,783,210 = $378,273, a gain of about 10 percent. The futures profit was

6($202,400)	(sale price of futures)
−6($189,900)	(purchase price of futures)
$75,000	(profit on futures).

Thus, the overall gain on the portfolio was effectively increased to $378,273 + $75,000 = $453,273, a return of about 12 percent.

futures and buy bond futures to achieve the desired result. Of course, whether futures are an acceptable substitute for transactions in the actual securities depends on whether the stock index underlying the stock index futures is similar enough to the stock component of her portfolio and whether the bond underlying the bond futures is similar enough to the bond component of her portfolio. Because practitioners use these instruments so often to make asset allocation changes, we can safely assume that these conditions hold so that stock and bond futures can be used for this purpose.

Suppose she wants to sell a certain dollar amount of stock and buy an equivalent dollar amount of bonds. Using the formula we previously showed for target beta strategies with stock index futures, she will sell the number of futures contracts to adjust the beta on that given amount of stock from its current level to zero. This transaction has the effect of selling the stock and converting it to cash. Now she wants to convert this synthetically created cash to bonds. She will then buy bond futures to adjust the modified duration on this synthetic cash from zero to its desired level, which is the modified duration of the existing bond component of the portfolio.

Note that the securities in the portfolio have not changed, but the allocation between stock and bonds has been synthetically altered by the addition of a short position in stock index futures and a long position in bond futures. Now suppose she also would like to change the risk characteristics of the existing stock and bond asset classes. She can then adjust the beta on the stock by buying or selling more stock index futures contracts, and she can adjust the modified duration on the bonds by buying or selling more bond futures contracts.

> Stock index and bond futures can be used to efficiently execute asset allocation strategies involving stock and bond asset classes.

An Example Table 11.16 illustrates this type of strategy. Here the portfolio manager wants to reduce the allocation from two-thirds stock, one-third bonds to half stock, half bonds. In addition, the manager wants to lower the risk exposure on the stock and raise the risk exposure on the bonds.

TABLE 11.16 TACTICAL ASSET ALLOCATION USING STOCK AND BOND FUTURES

Scenario: A $30 million portfolio consists of $20 million of stock at a beta of 1.15 and $10 million of bonds at a modified duration of 6.25 with a yield of 7.15 percent. The manager would like to change the allocation to $15 million of stock and $15 million of bonds. In addition, the manager would like to adjust the beta on the stock to 1.05 and the modified duration on the bonds to 7. A stock index futures contract has a price of $225,000, and we can assume that its beta is 1.0. A bond futures contract is priced at $92,000 with an implied modified duration of 5.9 and an implied yield of 5.65 percent. The manager will use futures to synthetically sell $5 million of stock, reduce the beta on the remaining stock, synthetically buy $5 million of bonds, and increase the modified duration on the remaining bonds. The horizon date is three months.

Step 1. Synthetically sell $5 million of stock
This transaction will effectively reduce the beta on $5 million of stock to zero, thereby synthetically converting the stock to cash. The number of stock futures, which we denote as N_{sf}, will be

$$N_{sf} = (0 - 1.15)\left(\frac{5,000,000}{225,000}\right) = -25.56.$$

This rounds off to selling 26 contracts. After executing this transaction, the portfolio effectively consists of $15 million of stock at a beta of 1.15, $10 million of bonds at a modified duration of 6.25, and $5 million of synthetic cash. Of course, the actual portfolio consists of $20 million of stock at a beta of 1.15, $10 million of bonds at a modified duration of 6.25, and $5 million of short stock index futures.

TABLE 11.16 (CONTINUED)

Step 2. Synthetically buy $5 million of bonds

This transaction will effectively convert the $5 million of synthetic cash, which can be treated as a bond with a modified duration of zero, to $5 million of synthetic bonds with a modified duration of 6.25. The number of bond futures, which we denote as N_{bf} will be

$$N_{bf} = \left(\frac{6.25 - 0}{5.9}\right)\left(\frac{5,000,000}{92,000}\right) = 56.6.$$

This rounds off to buying 57 contracts. After executing this transaction, the portfolio effectively consists of $15 million of stock at a beta of 1.15 and $15 million of bonds at a modified duration of 6.25. Of course, the actual portfolio consists of $20 million of stock at a beta of 1.15, $10 million of bonds at a modified duration of 6.25, $5 million of short stock index futures, and $5 million of long bond futures.

Step 3. Lower the beta on the stock from 1.15 to 1.05

Now the manager wants to lower the beta from 1.15 to 1.05 on $15 million of stock. This will require

$$N_{sf} = (1.05 - 1.15)\left(\frac{15,000,000}{225,000}\right) = -6.67$$

contracts. Rounding off, the manager would sell 7 contracts. In the aggregate, the manager would sell 33 stock index futures contracts.

Step 4. Raise the modified duration on the bonds from 6.25 to 7

Now the manager wants to raise the modified duration from 6.25 to 7 on $15 million of bonds. This will require

$$N_{bf} = \left(\frac{7 - 6.25}{5.9}\right)\left(\frac{15,000,000}{92,000}\right) = 20.73$$

contracts. Rounding off, the manager would buy 21 contracts. In the aggregate, the manager would buy 78 bond futures contracts.

It is important to know that the same results would be obtained if the transactions were carried out in a different order. The manager could first reduce the beta on the $20 million of stock and then synthetically sell $5 million of stock. The manager could then increase the modified duration on the $10 million of bonds and then synthetically buy $5 million of bonds.

Results

Three months later the stock is worth $19,300,000 and the bonds are worth $10,100,000. The stock index futures price falls to $217,800, and the bond futures price rises to $92,878. The profit on the stock index futures transaction is

$$-33(\$217,800 - \$225,000) = \$237,600.$$

The profit on the bond futures transaction is

$$78(\$92,878 - \$92,000) = \$68,484.$$

The overall value of the portfolio is

Stock	$19,300,000
Stock index futures profit	237,600
Bonds	10,100,000
Bond futures profit	68,484
Total	$29,706,084.

Had the transactions not been executed, the portfolio would have been worth

Stock	$19,300,000
Bonds	10,100,000
Total	$29,400,000.

Of course, this transaction is speculative. The reduction of the stock allocation and reduction of the stock beta, combined with the increase in the bond allocation and the increase in the bond beta, was a good move, but it could have been a bad one. In any case, however, derivatives allowed these transactions to be executed synthetically and less expensively.

Summary

This chapter looked at managing currency, interest rate, and stock market risk. It began by examining some basic concepts necessary for understanding and formulating hedge strategies. It explored the concepts of long and short hedging and basis risk and identified rules that help determine which contract to select, including the choice of commodity, expiration month, and whether to be long or short. The chapter also examined techniques for determining the optimal number of futures contracts for providing the volatility needed to offset the spot market risk.

The hedge examples were grouped by type of contract—foreign currency hedges, intermediate- and long-term interest rate futures hedges, and stock index futures hedges. While these examples span a broad range of applications, there are numerous similar situations in which virtually the same type of hedge would apply. This chapter's emphasis was on understanding the concept of hedging by observing it in practical situations.

Spread strategies with futures contracts were also reviewed in this chapter. Intramarket spreads focus on one underlying, whereas intermarket spreads focus on two underlyings. The risk related to intramarket spreads stems from changes in carry costs. Intermarket spreads' risk also contains the risk of changes in the underlying relative value.

Targeted strategies reviewed here included managing risk with duration and beta. Target strategies are pursued when the investor has a well-defined preferred risk profile. We saw that futures can be used to alter the risk profit from where it currently is to where the investor wants it to be.

Table 11.17 contains capsule descriptions of the various trading situations that are likely to be encountered, with an identification of the nature of the risk and a prescription for a potential trading strategy.

In several chapters, we have made many references to managing interest rate risk. One of the most popular tools for managing interest rate risk is the swap. In Chapter 12, we shall learn about swaps and not only how they can be used to manage interest rate risk, but also how they can be used to manage currency and equity risk. Looking past Chapter 12, we shall learn even more about interest rate risk management in Chapter 13, when we introduce interest rate forwards and options.

TABLE 11.17 HEDGE SITUATIONS

THE SCENARIO	THE RISK	THE APPROPRIATE ACTION
Plan to purchase a foreign currency with domestic currency.	The foreign currency will increase in value.	Buy forwards or futures.
Plan to convert a foreign currency into domestic currency.	The foreign currency will decrease in value.	Sell forwards or futures.
Hold a bond or bond portfolio.	Interest rates will increase, decreasing the value of the bond.	Sell futures on notes or bonds.
Plan to purchase a bond.	Interest rates will decrease, increasing the value of the bond.	Buy futures on notes or bonds.
Plan to issue a bond.	Interest rates will increase, decreasing the value of the bond.	Sell futures on notes or bonds.
Hold stock portfolio.	Stock prices will fall, decreasing the value of the portfolio.	Sell stock index futures.
Plan to purchase a stock.	Stock prices will increase, increasing the cost to purchase.	Buy stock index futures.
Expect changes in futures prices with the same underlying.	Futures prices fail to comply with expectations.	Intramarket spread.
Expect changes in futures prices with different underlying.	Futures prices fail to comply with expectations.	Intermarket spread.
Alter interest rate risk of bond portfolio.	Interest rates move in unexpected way.	Target duration.
Capture excess return within an actively managed portfolio.	Active management fails to generate excess returns.	Alpha capture.
Alter equity risk of stock portfolio.	Stock prices move in unexpected way.	Target beta.
Alter both interest rate risk and equity risk in portfolio.	Rates and prices move in unexpected ways.	Tactical asset allocation.

Key Terms

Before continuing to Chapter 12, you should be able to give brief definitions of the following terms:

short hedge/long hedge, p. 363
anticipatory hedge/basis, p. 364
basis risk, p. 366
cross hedge, p. 368
quantity risk, p. 369
hedge ratio, p. 373

hedging effectiveness, p. 374
duration/Macaulay's duration/
  modified duration, p. 375
implied yield/implied modified
  duration, p. 376

yield beta, p. 377
Intramarket spreads/intermarket
  spreads, p. 391
target duration, p. 396
target beta, p. 402

Further Reading

The theory underlying some of the hedging models in this chapter can be found in the following articles:

Johnson, L. L. "The Theory of Hedging and Speculation in Commodity Futures Markets." *Review of Economic Studies* 27(1960): 139–151.

Stein, J. L. "The Simultaneous Determination of Spot and Futures Prices." *The American Economic Review* 51(1961): 1012–1025.

Empirical research on hedging effectiveness can be found in these articles:

Ederington, L. H. "The Hedging Performance of the New Futures Market." *The Journal of Finance* 34(1979): 157–170.

Figlewski, S. "Hedging Performance and Basis Risk in Stock Index Futures." *The Journal of Finance* 39(1984): 657–669.

Figlewski, S. "Hedging with Stock Index Futures: Theory and Application in a New Market." *The Journal of Futures Markets* 5(1985): 183–199.

The following articles provide the rationale for and evidence of the hedging and risk management activities of corporations:

Froot, K. A., D. S. Scharfstein, and J. C. Stein, "Risk Management: Coordinating Corporate Investment and Financing Policies," *The Journal of Finance* 48 (December 1993): 1629–1658.

Nance, D. R., C. W. Smith, Jr., and C. W. Smithson. "On the Determinants of Corporate Hedging." *The Journal of Finance* 48(1993): 267–284.

Smith, C. W., and R. M. Stulz. "The Determinants of Firms' Hedging Policies." *Journal of Financial and Quantitative Analysis* 20(1985): 391–405.

Concept Checks

1. Explain the difference between a short hedge and a long hedge.
2. a. What is the basis?
   b. How is the basis expected to change over the life of a futures contract?
   c. Explain why a strengthening basis benefits a short hedge and hurts a long hedge.
3. What factors must one consider when deciding on the appropriate underlying asset for a hedge?
4. For each of the following hedge termination dates, identify the appropriate contract expiration. Assume that the available expiration months are March, June, September, and December.
   a. August 10
   b. December 15
   c. February 20
   d. June 14
5. State and explain two reasons why firms hedge.

Questions and Problems

1. A major bread maker is planning to purchase wheat in the near future. Identify and explain the appropriate hedging strategy.
2. Explain how the implied repo rate on a spread transaction differs from that on a nearby futures contract.
3. Suppose you are a dealer in sugar. It is September 26, and you hold 112,000 pounds of sugar worth

$0.0479 per pound. The price of a futures contract expiring in January is $0.0550 per pound. Each contract is for 112,000 pounds.
   a. Determine the original basis. Then calculate the profit from a hedge if it is held to expiration and the basis converges to zero. Show how the profit is explained by movements in the basis alone.

b. Rework this problem, but assume that the hedge is closed on December 10, when the spot price is $0.0574 and the January futures price is $0.0590.

4. a. Define the minimum variance hedge ratio and the measure of hedging effectiveness. What do these two values tell you?

   b. What is the price sensitivity hedge ratio? How are the price sensitivity and minimum variance hedge ratios alike? How are they different?

5. Explain how to determine whether to buy or sell futures when hedging.

6. For each of the following situations, determine whether a long or short hedge is appropriate. Justify your answers.

   a. A firm anticipates issuing stock in three months.

   b. An investor plans to buy a bond in 30 days.

   c. A firm plans to sell some foreign currency denominated assets and convert the proceeds to domestic currency.

7. On June 17 of a particular year, an American watch dealer decided to import 100,000 Swiss watches. Each watch costs SF225. The dealer would like to hedge against a change in the dollar/Swiss franc exchange rate. The forward rate was $0.3881. Determine the outcome from the hedge if it was closed on August 16, when the spot rate was $0.4434.

8. On January 2 of a particular year, an American firm decided to close out its account at a Canadian bank on February 28. The firm is expected to have 5 million Canadian dollars in the account at the time of the withdrawal. It would convert the funds to U.S. dollars and transfer them to a New York bank. The relevant forward exchange rate was $0.7564. The March Canadian dollar futures contract was priced at $0.7541. Determine the outcome of a futures hedge if on February 28 the spot rate was $0.7207 and the futures rate was $0.7220. All prices are in U.S. dollars per Canadian dollar. The Canadian dollar futures contract covers CD 100,000.

9. On January 31, a firm learns that it will have additional funds available on May 31. It will use the funds to purchase $5,000,000 par value of the APCO 9 1/2 percent bonds maturing in about 21 years. Interest is paid semiannually on March 1 and September 1. The bonds are rated A2 by Moody's and are selling for 78 7/8 per 100 and yielding 12.32 percent. The modified duration is 7.81.

The firm is considering hedging the anticipated purchase with September T-bond futures. The futures price is 71 8/32. The firm believes that the futures contract is tracking the Treasury bond with a coupon of 12 3/4 percent and maturing in about 25 years. It has determined that the implied yield on the futures contract is 11.40 percent and the modified duration of the contract is 8.32.

The firm believes that the APCO bond yield will change 1 point for every 1-point change in the yield on the bond underlying the futures contract.

   a. Determine the transaction the firm should conduct on January 31 to set up the hedge.

   b. On May 31, the APCO bonds were priced at 82 3/4. The September futures price was 76 14/32. Determine the outcome of the hedge.

10. On July 1, a portfolio manager holds $1 million face value of Treasury bonds, the 11 1/4s maturing in about 29 years. The price is 107 14/32. The bond will need to be sold on August 30. The manager is concerned about rising interest rates and believes that a hedge would be appropriate. The September T-bond futures price is 77 15/32. The price sensitivity hedge ratio suggests that the firm should use 13 contracts.

   a. What transaction should the firm make on July 1?

   b. On August 30, the bond was selling for 101 12/32 and the futures price was 77 5/32. Determine the outcome of the hedge.

11. Suppose you are concerned about your firm's jet fuel exposure. Further, your analysis suggests the best futures contract to hedge jet fuel is unleaded gasoline. The fuel volatility (standard deviation of changes in your firm's entire jet fuel exposure) is $17,347,281, and the unleaded gasoline futures contract volatility (standard deviation of price changes in one unleaded gasoline futures contract) is $14,490. Suppose the correlation coefficient between fuel volatility and unleaded gasoline futures contract volatility is 0.71. Calculate the minimum variance hedge ratio. Defend whether this is a perfect hedge.

12. Based on the jet fuel exposure information in the previous problem, calculate the hedging effectiveness. Explain how to interpret this number.

13. The price sensitivity hedge ratio, including yield beta, was shown in this chapter to be

$$N_f^* = -\left(\frac{MD_B}{MD_f}\right)\left(\frac{B}{f}\right)\beta_y.$$

Discuss how changing each of the five input parameters will influence the hedge ratio (assume that all input parameters are positive).

14. You are the manager of a stock portfolio. On October 1, your holdings consist of the eight stocks listed in the following table, which you intend to sell on December 31. You are concerned about a market decline over the next three months. The number of shares, their prices, and the betas are shown, as well as the prices on December 31.

Stock	Number of Shares	Beta	10/1 Price	12/31 Price
R.R. Donnelley	10,000	1.00	19.63	27.38
B.F Goodrich	6,200	1.05	31.38	32.88
Raytheon	15,800	1.15	49.38	53.63
Maytag	8,900	0.90	55.38	77.88
Kroger	11,000	0.85	42.13	47.88
Comdisco	14,500	1.45	19.38	28.63
Cessna	9,900	1.20	29.75	30.13
Foxboro	4,500	0.95	24.75	26.00

On October 1, you decide to execute a hedge using a particular stock index futures contract, which has a $500 multiplier. The March contract price is 376.20. On December 31, the March contract price is 424.90. Determine the outcome of the hedge.

15. On March 1, a securities analyst recommended General Cinema stock as a good purchase in the early summer. The portfolio manager plans to buy 20,000 shares of the stock on June 1 but is concerned that the market as a whole will be bullish over the next three months. General Cinema's stock currently is at 32.88, and the beta is 1.10.

Construct a hedge that will protect against movements in the stock market as a whole. Use the September stock index futures, which is priced at 375.30 on March 1 and has a $500 multiplier. Evaluate the outcome of the hedge if on June 1 the futures price is 387.30 and General Cinema's stock price is 38.63.

16. During the first six months of the year, yields on long-term government debt have fallen about 100 basis points. You believe that the decline in rates is over, and you are interested in speculating on a rise in rates. You are, however, unwilling to assume much risk, so you decide to do an intramarket spread. Use the following information to construct a T-bond futures spread on July 15 and determine the profit when the position is closed on November 15.

July 15
December futures price: 76 9/32
March futures price: 75 9/32

November 15
December futures price: 79 13/32
March futures price: 78 9/32

17. On November 1, an analyst who has been studying a firm called Computer Sciences believes that the company will make a major announcement before the end of the year. Computer Sciences currently is priced at 27.63 and has a beta of 0.95. The analyst believes that the stock can advance about 10 percent if the market does not move. The analyst thinks the market might decline by as much as 5 percent, leaving the stock with a return of $0.10 + (-0.05 \times 0.95) = 0.0525$. To capture the full 10 percent alpha, the analyst recommends the sale of a particular stock index futures. The March contract currently is priced at 393. Assume that the investor owns 100,000 shares of the stock. Set up a transaction by determining the appropriate number of futures contracts. Then determine the effective return on the stock if, on December 31, the stock is sold at 28.88, the futures contract is at 432.30, and the multiplier is 500. Explain your results.

18. You are the manager of a bond portfolio of $10 million face value of bonds worth $9,448,456. The portfolio has a yield of 12.25 percent and a duration of 8.33. You plan to liquidate the portfolio in six months and are concerned about an increase in interest rates that would produce a loss on the portfolio. You would like to lower its duration to 5 years. A T-bond futures contract with the appropriate expiration is priced at 72 3/32 with a face value of $100,000, an implied yield of 12 percent, and an implied duration of 8.43 years.

a. Should you buy or sell futures? How many contracts should you use?

b. In six months, the portfolio has fallen in value to $8,952,597. The futures price is 68 16/32. Determine the profit from the transaction.

19. You are the manager of a stock portfolio worth $10,500,000. It has a beta of 1.15. During the next three months, you expect a correction in the market that will take the market down about 5 percent; thus, your portfolio is expected to fall about 5.75 percent (5 percent times a beta of 1.15). You want to lower the beta to 1. A particular stock index futures contract with the appropriate expiration is priced at 425.75 with a multiplier of $500.

a. Should you buy or sell futures? How many contracts should you use?

b. In three months, the portfolio has fallen in value to $9,870,000. The futures has fallen to 402.35. Determine the profit and portfolio return over the quarter. How close did you come to the desired result?

20. The manager of a $20 million portfolio of domestic stocks with a beta of 1.10 would like to begin diversifying internationally. He would like to sell $5 million of domestic stock and purchase $5 million of foreign stock. He learns that he can do this using a futures contract on a foreign stock index. The index is denominated in dollars, thereby eliminating any currency risk. He would like the beta of the new foreign asset class to be 1.05. The domestic stock index futures contract is priced at $250,000 and can be assumed to have a beta of 1.0. The foreign stock index futures contract is priced at $150,000 and can also be assumed to have a beta of 1.0.

a. Determine the number of contracts he would need to trade of each type of futures in order to achieve this objective.

b. Determine the value of the portfolio if the domestic stock increases by 2 percent, the domestic stock futures contract increases by 1.8 percent, the foreign stock increases by 1.2 percent, and the foreign stock futures contract increases by 1.4 percent.

21. (Concept Problem) As we discussed in the chapter, futures can be used to eliminate systematic risk in a stock portfolio, leaving it essentially a risk-free portfolio. A portfolio manager can achieve the same result, however, by selling the stocks and replacing them with T-bills. Consider the following stock portfolio.

Stock	Number of Shares	Price	Beta
Northrop Grumman	14,870	18.13	1.10
H.J. Heinz	8,755	36.13	1.05
Washington Post	1,245	264.00	1.05
Disney	8,750	134.50	1.25
Wang Labs	33,995	4.25	1.20
Wisconsin Energy	12,480	29.00	0.65
General Motors	14,750	48.75	0.95
Union Pacific	12,900	71.50	1.20
Royal Dutch Shell	7,500	78.75	0.75
Illinois Power	3,550	15.50	0.60

Suppose the portfolio manager wants to convert this portfolio to a riskless portfolio for a period of one month. The price of a particular stock index futures with a $500 multiplier is 369.45. To sell each share would cost $20 per order plus $0.03 per share. Each company's shares would constitute a separate order. The futures contract would entail a cost of $27.50 per contract, round-trip. T-bill purchases cost $25 per trade for any number of T-bills. Determine the most cost-effective way to accomplish the manager's goal of converting the portfolio to a risk-free position for one month and then converting it back.

22. (Concept Problem) You plan to buy 1,000 shares of Swiss International Airlines stock. The current price is SF950. The current exchange rate is $0.7254/SF. You are interested in speculating on the stock but do not want to assume any currency risk. You plan to hold the position for six months. The appropriate futures contract currently is trading at $0.7250. Construct a hedge and evaluate how your investment will do if in six months the stock is at SF926.50, the spot exchange rate is $0.7301, and the futures price is $0.7295. The Swiss franc futures contract size is SF125,000. Determine the overall profit from the transaction. Then break down the profit into the amount earned solely from the

performance of the stock, the loss or gain from the currency change while holding the stock, and the loss or gain on the futures transaction.

23. (Concept Problem) Recall from the chapters on options that we learned about bull and bear spreads. Intramarket futures spreads also are considered bull and bear spreads. Describe what you think might be a bull spread with T-bonds futures. Be sure to explain your reasoning.

APPENDIX 11

Taxation of Hedging

The tax treatment of hedging was originally established in a 1936 IRS ruling that stated that using futures contracts to reduce business risk generates ordinary income or loss. The ruling was reaffirmed in a 1955 Supreme Court case involving the firm Corn Products Refining Company. Corn Products had purchased futures contracts to hedge the future purchase of corn it expected to need. The futures price went up, and Corn Products reported the profits as capital gains, which at that time were treated more favorably for tax purposes. The IRS disagreed, and the case ultimately ended up in the Supreme Court, which ruled that the purchase of the corn futures was related to the everyday operations of the firm and, thus, should be considered ordinary income for tax purposes. From that point on, the taxation of futures hedges was determined by what came to be known as the *business motive test*. Put simply, was the hedge designed to reduce the firm's business risk? If so, then any profits or losses would be treated as ordinary income.

This interpretation held for 33 years until a shocking ruling occurred on a case that had nothing to do with hedging. Arkansas Best, a holding company, sold shares of the National Bank of Commerce of Dallas at a substantial loss, which it reported as an ordinary loss. Ordinary losses are more attractive to the taxpaying entity because capital losses are limited to the total of capital gains. So capital losses can potentially be unusable as tax credits, while ordinary losses are fully deductible against ordinary income. In 1988, the Supreme Court ruled that Best's losses were capital losses. It argued that the shares did not constitute a sufficient exception to the established definition of a capital asset. In other words, the shares were not part of Arkansas Best's inventory. Because Best was a holding company, it believed that the shares were a part of its inventory.

The IRS then began using the Arkansas Best case to argue that certain futures hedges could be treated as capital transactions, thus calling into question the millions of routine hedging transactions executed by businesses. It used the case to argue that the Federal National Mortgage Association (FNMA), a firm that buys and sells mortgages, must treat over $120 million in interest rate futures and options losses as capital. Furthermore, it ruled that while long futures and options to purchase (calls) could be viewed as substitutes for inventory positions and, thus, taxable as ordinary income, short positions and put options could never be used as substitutes for inventory because they represent contracts to sell.

Such an interpretation implied that a business holding an inventory could not reduce its risk by agreeing to sell some of the inventory in advance, at least not without potentially serious tax consequences. In other words, the IRS ruling discourages conservative business practices. The implications for the futures markets and for businesses that had routinely hedged for years were far-reaching. The futures markets could be effectively shut down, and millions of back taxes might be owed.

The futures exchanges and many businesses lobbied Treasury Secretary Lloyd Bentsen. Finally on October 18, 1993, the IRS reversed its ruling on the FNMA case. The IRS did argue that hedgers would need to be able to prove that futures and options transactions to protect inventory were indeed hedges. In addition, the taxation of liability hedges (such as the selling of futures in anticipation of a future issuing of liabilities), of hedges to protect the cost of raw materials purchases, and of many over-the-counter market hedges (such as the use of swaps) is still somewhat unclear.

CHAPTER 12

Swaps

Let us not forget there were plenty of financial disasters before quants showed up on Wall Street, and the subsequent disasters (including the current one) had plenty of help from the non-quants.

Aaron Brown
Risk Professional, April 2010, p. 18

In the last four chapters, we discussed forward and futures contracts, which are commitments for one party to buy something from another at a fixed price at a future date. In some cases, a party would like to make a series of purchases, instead of a single purchase, from the other at a fixed price at various future dates. The parties could agree to a series of forward or futures contracts, each expiring at different dates. If each contract were priced according to the standard cost of carry formula, the contracts would each have a different price so that each would have a zero value at the start. A better way to construct this type of strategy, however, is to enter into a single agreement for one party to make a series of equal payments to the other party at specific dates and to receive a payment from the other party. This type of transaction, specifically characterized by a series of regularly scheduled payments, is called a **swap**. The parties are said to be swapping payments or assets.

Over the years, many varieties of swaps have evolved. The more common types of swaps involve one party making a series of fixed payments and receiving a series of variable payments. In addition, there are swaps in which both parties make variable payments. There are swaps in which both parties make fixed payments, but one payment is in one currency and the other is in another currency. Hence, the payments can be fixed but their values are effectively variable, given exchange rate fluctuations. The number of varieties of swaps makes it difficult to give a good all-encompassing definition, but in general, *a swap is a financial derivative in which two parties make a series of payments to each other at specific dates.*

There are four primary types of swaps, based on the nature of the underlying variable. These are **currency swaps**, **interest rate swaps**, **equity swaps**, and **commodity swaps**. In a currency swap, the parties make either fixed or variable interest payments to each other in different currencies. There may or may not be a notional amount payment, a point we shall cover in more detail later. In an interest rate swap, the two parties make a series of interest payments to each other, with both payments in the same currency. One payment is variable, and the other payment can be variable or fixed. The notional amount on which the payments are based is not exchanged. In an equity swap, at least one of the two parties makes payments determined by the price of a stock, the value of a stock portfolio, or the level of a stock index. The

CHAPTER OBJECTIVES

- Introduce the concept of a swap, which is a transaction to exchange a series of cash flows

- Understand the three different types of swaps based on the underlying: currency, interest rate, and equity

- Determine how to price and value the three different types of swaps

- Illustrate strategies using the three different types of swaps

A swap is a transaction in which two parties agree to pay each other a series of cash flows over a specified period of time. The four types of swaps are currency swaps, interest rate swaps, equity swaps, and commodity swaps.

TECHNICAL NOTE: Commodity Swaps
go to www.cengagebrain.com

other payment can be determined by another stock, portfolio, or index or by an interest rate, or it can be fixed. In a commodity swap, at least one set of payments is determined by the price of a commodity, such as oil or gold. The other payment is typically fixed, but there is no reason why it cannot be determined by some other variable. Because this book focuses on financial instruments, we shall not cover commodity swaps. For commodity swaps, see the Technical Note.

Swaps have an initiation date; a termination date; and, of course, the dates on which the payments are to be made. Like forward and futures contracts, swaps do not typically involve a cash up-front payment from one party to another. Thus, swaps have zero value at the start, which means that the present values of the two streams of payments are the same. The date on which a payment occurs is called the **settlement date**, and the period between settlement dates is called the **settlement period**. Swaps are exclusively customized over-the-counter instruments. Thus, the two parties are usually a dealer, which is a financial institution that makes markets in swaps, and an end user, which is usually a customer of the dealer and might be a corporation, a pension fund, a hedge fund, or some other organization. Of course, swaps between dealers are common as well.

Swap dealers quote prices and rates at which they will enter into either side of a swap transaction. When they do a transaction with a counterparty, they assume some risk from the counterparty. The dealers then typically hedge that risk with some other type of transaction, which could involve trading in the underlying or using futures, forwards, or options. Interestingly, swap dealers are a major contributor to trading volume in Eurodollar futures, as they use the contract to hedge many of their interest rate swaps as well as other interest rate derivatives, which we shall cover in Chapter 13. In fact, this is the most common use of Eurodollar futures.

Like forward contracts, swaps are subject to the risk that a given party could default. Wherever possible the payments are netted, so that only a single amount is paid from one party to the other. This procedure reduces the credit risk by reducing the amount of money flowing between the parties. We shall cover credit risk in more detail in Chapter 15.

Each swap is characterized by an amount of money called the **notional amount**. Because currency swaps and interest rate swaps both involve making interest payments, the payments are based on the multiplication of an interest rate times a notional amount. In interest rate swaps, this notional amount is never exchanged.[1] For that reason, it is not called principal, but rather notional amount.[2]

Swaps have been one of the greatest success stories in the financial markets of the 1980s and 1990s. Interest rate swaps, for example, are widely used by corporations to manage interest rate risk. As we shall see, corporations often convert floating-rate loans to fixed-rate loans using interest rate swaps. Currency and equity swaps are used far less than interest rate swaps, but they are still important tools for managing currency and equity risk, respectively.

Figure 12.1 shows the notional amount of interest rate and currency swaps from 1998 through December 2010, taken from the semiannual surveys of the Bank for International Settlements (www.bis.org). There had been steady growth in the use of interest rate swaps through December 2007. With the onset of the credit crisis in 2008, the use of interest rate swaps fell for a period of time. The notional amount at the end of December 2010,

---

[1]In addition, notional amount is not exchanged in an equity swap. In a currency swap, notional amount may or may not be exchanged. We shall cover this point later in this chapter.

[2]In this context, the *notional amount* is not considered to be real. As noted, the notional amount is never paid in an interest rate or equity swap, and for that reason, the notional amount is considered not to be real. In some currency swaps, the notional amount is paid, but the term *notional* is still used.

FIGURE 12.1 Notional Amount of Interest Rate and Currency Swaps

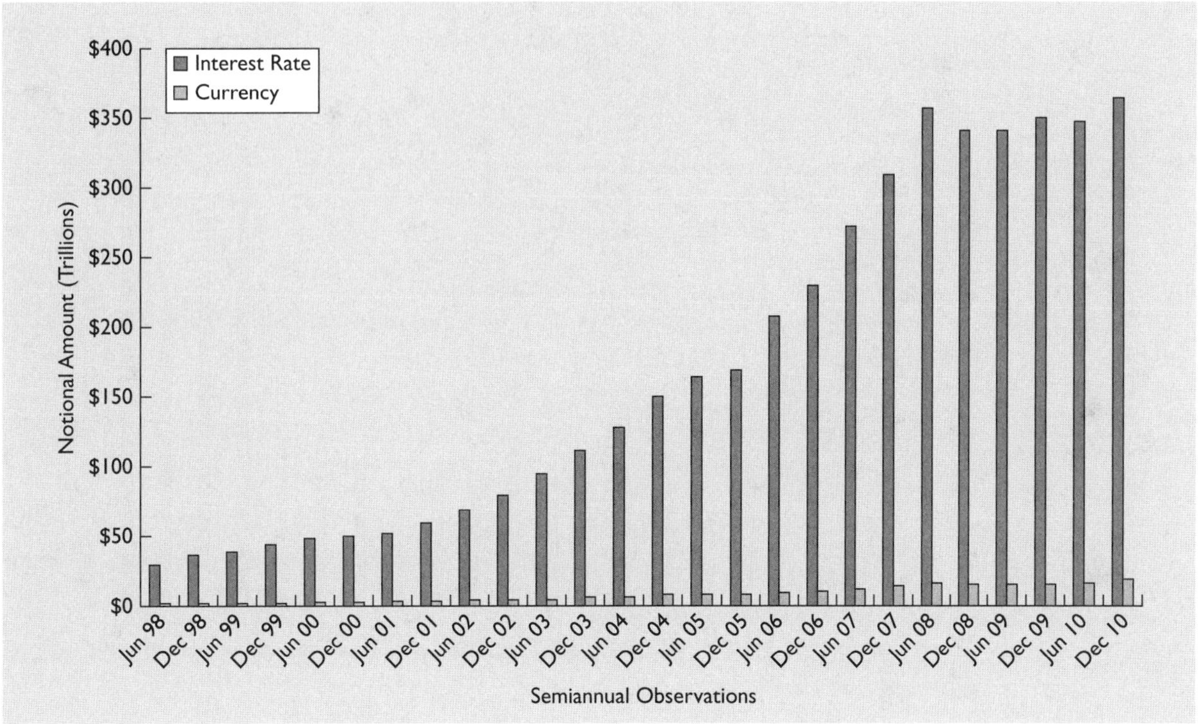

Source: Bank for International Settlements, www.bis.org

however, was over $360 trillion. Currency swaps have not experienced as much growth. Their notional amount at the end of December 2010 was about $19 trillion.[3]

Figure 12.2 shows the gross market values of interest rate and currency swaps from 1998 through December 2010. Historically, the growth in market value has been more erratic. Note that during the credit crisis, however, the significant spike in gross market value in December 2008. The gross market value declined significantly in 2009 and 2010, but remained rather erratic.

The reason that interest rate swaps are more widely used than currency swaps is that virtually every business borrows money and is, therefore, exposed to some form of interest rate risk. Even if a business borrows at a fixed rate, changes in interest rates create opportunity costs. Many businesses are exposed to currency risk, either through their international operations, their international customers or suppliers, or from foreign competitors who offer similar products and services and sell those services in the business's home market. Nonetheless, far more firms are exposed to and understand the implications of interest rate risk than currency risk. Hence, interest rate swaps are more widely used than currency swaps in managing risk.

This chapter is divided into three main sections, each based on the three different types of swaps characterized by the underlying. For each type of swap, we shall examine the basic characteristics of the instruments, learn how to set the terms of the swap

---

[3]Equity swaps are not shown because the market is so small relative to even currency swaps. In addition, the Bank for International Settlements combines forwards with swaps in reporting the figures for the equity markets. The notional amount of equity swaps and forwards in December 2010 was only about 9 percent of currency swaps.

FIGURE 12.2 Gross Market Value of Interest Rate and Currency Swaps

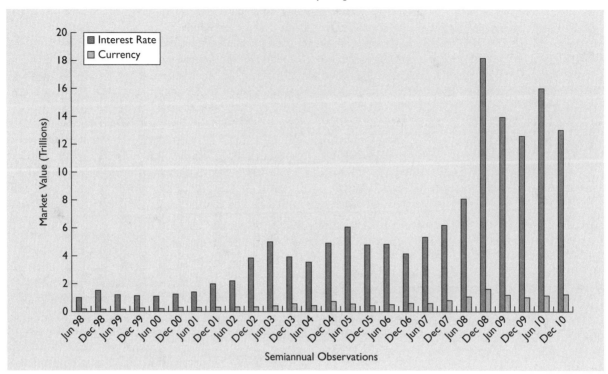

Source: Bank for International Settlements, www.bis.org

(a process called pricing), learn how to find the market value of the swap, and examine some strategies using the swap.

INTEREST RATE SWAPS

As we previously described, an interest rate swap is a series of interest payments between two parties. Each set of payments is based on either a fixed or a floating rate. If the rate is floating and the swap is in dollars, the rate usually employed is dollar LIBOR. Swaps in other currencies use comparable rates in those currencies. The two parties agree to exchange a series of interest payments in the same currency at the various settlement dates. The payments are based on a specified notional amount, but the parties do not exchange the notional amount because this would involve each party giving the other party the same amount of money.

The most common type of interest rate swap, indeed the most common type of all swaps, is a swap in which one party pays a fixed rate and the other pays a floating rate. This instrument is called a **plain vanilla swap**, and sometimes just a vanilla swap. Let us look at an example of a plain vanilla swap. At this point, however, we shall not concern ourselves with the reason a company enters into a swap. Our goal right now is to understand the basic characteristics of the transaction.

Structure of a Typical Interest Rate Swap

Consider a firm called XYZ that enters into a $50 million notional amount swap with a dealer called ABSwaps. The initiation date is December 15. The swap calls for

An interest rate swap is a swap in which the two parties agree to exchange a series of interest payments. A plain vanilla swap is an interest rate swap in which one party agrees to make a series of fixed interest payments and the other agrees to make a series of floating (variable) interest payments.

ABSwaps to make payments to XYZ based on 90-day LIBOR on the 15th of March, June, September, and December for one year. The payment is determined by three-month LIBOR at the beginning of the settlement period. Payment is then made at the end of the settlement period. Thus, the payment on March 15 is based on LIBOR on the previous December 15, and the payment on June 15 is based on LIBOR on the previous March 15, and so forth. This rate setting and settlement procedure is known as advanced set, settled in arrears.[4] XYZ will pay ABSwaps fixed payments at a rate of 7.5 percent per year. The interest payments can be based on the exact day count between payment dates, or the parties could assume 30 days in a month. Here we assume they use the exact day count. In addition, the parties could base the payment on a 360- or 365-day year. We assume that they use 360 days. In the general case, the party paying a fixed rate and receiving a floating rate will have a cash flow at each interest payment date of

$$(\text{Notional Amount})(\text{LIBOR} - \text{fixed rate})\left(\frac{\text{Days}}{360 \text{ or } 365}\right),$$

where it is understood that LIBOR is determined on the previous settlement date (advanced set, settled in arrears).

The fraction of the year calculation is known as the accrual period. There are many different ways to compute the accrual period. You can compute the actual number of days between two dates or use a method known as "30/360" day count method. The treatment of weekends and holidays also varies. The number of days in a year also can vary, including 360 days, 365 days, actual number of days, and so forth. Whether the swap is advanced set, advanced settled, or advanced set, settled in arrears—as well as the way in which the accrual period is computed—are important considerations when designing and valuing interest rate swaps. These technical aspects of swap design are a combination of elements: the convention within a particular market for the underlying instrument, the manner in which the dealer customarily quotes swaps, and the needs or preferences of the end user.

Throughout this chapter, we will assume advanced set, settled in arrears and that the accrual period is the actual number of days divided by 360. From the perspective of XYZ, the payments are

$$\$50,000,000(\text{LIBOR} - 0.075)\left(\frac{\text{Days}}{360}\right).$$

So if LIBOR exceeds 7.5 percent, XYZ will receive a payment in the above amount from ABSwaps. If LIBOR is less than 7.5 percent, XYZ will make a payment to ABSwaps. As we previously mentioned, to reduce the flow of money, which reduces the credit risk, the two parties agree to net the payments. Thus, one party makes a net payment to the other.

Figure 12.3 shows the cash flows on the swap from the perspective of XYZ. Note that LIBOR on the previous date determines the payment. Hence, when the swap is initiated, LIBOR on December 15 determines the floating payment on March 15. Then on March 15, LIBOR on that day determines the payment on June 15. In this manner,

---

[4]An alternative rate setting and settlement procedure is known as advanced set, advanced settled, where payment is determined by LIBOR at the beginning of the settlement period and payment is also made at the beginning of the settlement period. This type of settlement helps to lower credit risk.

FIGURE 12.3 Cash Flows in Plain Vanilla Interest Rate Swap from Point of View of XYZ Company

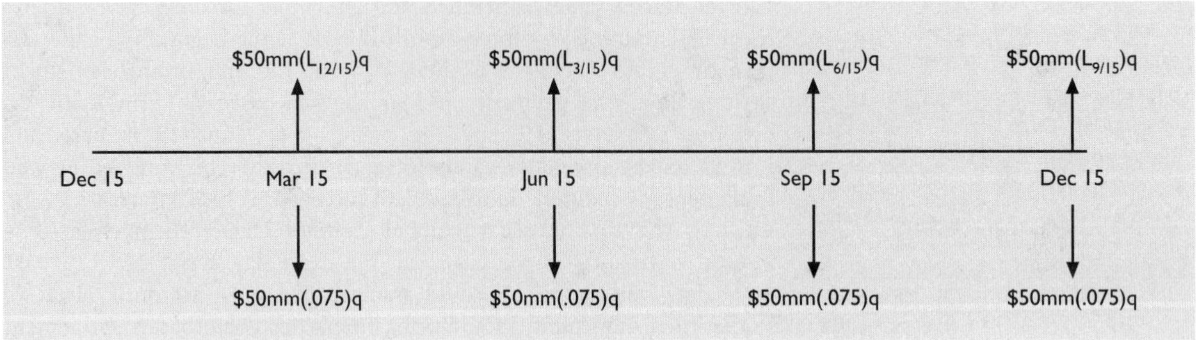

Note: $L_{mon/dd}$ represents LIBOR on month mon, day dd, and q represents the factor (days/360).

the parties always know the upcoming floating payment, but they do not know any floating payments beyond the next one.

Now let us make an assumption about the interest rates that prevail over the life of the swap in order to calculate the payments in the swap. Suppose LIBOR on December 15 is 7.68 percent. The first payment occurs on March 15. Assuming that there is no leap year, there are 90 days between December 15 and March 15. Thus, on March 15, ABSwaps will owe

$$\$50,000,000(0.0768)\left(\frac{90}{360}\right) = \$960,000.$$

XYZ will owe

$$\$50,000,000(0.075)\left(\frac{90}{360}\right) = \$937,500.$$

Because the two parties agree to net the payments, only the difference of $22,500 is paid by ABSwaps to XYZ. Now let us assume that LIBOR on March 15 is 7.50 percent, on June 15 is 7.06 percent, and on September 15 is 6.06 percent. Table 12.1 illustrates the payments in this swap. Remember, however, that the floating payments on June 15, September 15, and December 15 were not known when the swap was initiated, and we merely assumed a series of interest rates over the life of the swap for illustrative purposes. The actual interest rates and payments could be quite different from these. Note also that the parties never exchange the notional amount, because this would be unnecessary.

On some occasions, the parties could specify that both payments be floating. Suppose that instead of paying 7.5 percent fixed, XYZ would prefer to pay a floating rate based on the Treasury bill rate. Of course, XYZ receives a floating rate based on LIBOR. Because LIBOR is the rate paid by a London bank, which is a private borrower, and the Treasury bill rate is the rate paid by the U.S. government, LIBOR will always be more than the Treasury bill rate. Obviously, XYZ would prefer to receive a higher rate, but ABSwaps would not agree to such a transaction because it would always lose money. ABSwaps would be willing to do the transaction, however, by adding a spread to the Treasury bill rate or deducting a spread from LIBOR. This type of swap is called a **basis swap**, because the underlying is the basis risk in the relationship between LIBOR and the Treasury bill rate. In order to determine an appropriate spread, we must learn how to determine the prices and values of swaps.

TABLE 12.1 AFTER-THE-FACT PAYMENTS IN PLAIN VANILLA INTEREST RATE SWAP

Notional amount: $50,000,000
Fixed rate: 7.5%
Accrual period: Actual day count and 360-day year
Settlement: Advanced set, settled in arrears

DATE	LIBOR (%)	DAYS IN PERIOD	ABSWAPS OWES	XYZ OWES	NET TO XYZ
Dec 15	7.68				
Mar 15	7.50	90	$960,000	$937,500	$22,500
Jun 15	7.06	92	958,833	958,833	0
Sep 15	6.06	92	902,111	958,833	−56,222
Dec 15		91	765,917	947,917	−182,000

Note: This combination of LIBORs on the above dates represents only one of an infinite number of possible outcomes to the swap. They are used only to illustrate how the payments are determined and not the likely results.

Pricing and Valuation of Interest Rate Swaps

In the example of the plain vanilla swap in the previous section, we assumed a fixed rate of 7.5 percent. This is not an arbitrary rate. The dealer, ABSwaps, determined this rate by taking into account current interest rates and its ability to hedge the risk associated with this transaction. Just as we priced options, forwards, and futures by eliminating the opportunity to earn an arbitrage profit, we must do similarly with swaps. For plain vanilla swaps, we must determine the fixed rate in a process called pricing the swap. We do this in such a manner that there is no opportunity to earn an arbitrage profit. Recalling that a swap has zero value at the start, we determine the fixed rate so that the present value of the stream of fixed payments is the same as the present value of the stream of floating payments at the start of the transaction. Thus, the obligations of one party have the same value as the obligations of the other at the start of the transaction.

In order to understand interest rate swap pricing, we must first take a slight digression and look at floating-rate bonds. A floating-rate bond is one in which the coupons change at specific dates with the market rate of interest. Typically, the coupon is set at the beginning of the interest payment period, interest then accrues at that rate, and the interest is paid at the end of the period. The coupon is then reset for the next period. The coupon is usually determined by a formula that defines it as a specific market rate, such as LIBOR, plus a spread to reflect the credit risk. Because we are not addressing credit risk at this stage of the book, we shall assume a zero credit spread.

Suppose we are given a term structure of interest rates of $L_0(t_1)$, $L_0(t_2)$, ..., $L_0(t_n)$ where the Ls represent LIBOR for maturities of t_1 days, t_2 days, and so forth, up to t_n days. Thus, if we are looking out two years at quarterly intervals, t_1 might be 90, t_2 might be 180, and t_8 might be 720. Let $B_0(t_1)$ be the price of a $1 discount (zero coupon) bond based on the rate $L_0(t_1)$; a similar pattern applies for other discount bond prices. Thus,

$$B_0(t_1) = \frac{1}{1 + L_0(t_1)\left(\frac{t_1}{360}\right)}, B_0(t_2) = \frac{1}{1 + L_0(t_2)\left(\frac{t_2}{360}\right)}, ..., B_0(t_n) = \frac{1}{1 + L_0(t_n)\left(\frac{t_n}{360}\right)}.$$

FIGURE 12.4 Cash Flows in One-Year Floating-Rate Bond with Quarterly Payments at LIBOR

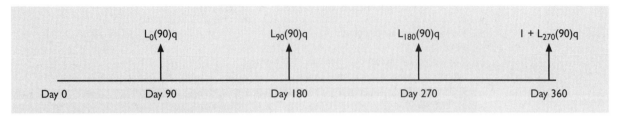

Note: $L_0(90)$, for example, is 90-day LIBOR on day 0, and q represents the factor (days/360).

In other words, the bond price for a maturity of t_1 days is the present value of \$1 in t_1 days, using the LIBOR method of discounting, which is based on a bond with add-on interest. Thus, these zero coupon bond prices can be viewed as present value factors, so we can use them to discount future payments.

Consider a one-year floating-rate bond, with interest paid quarterly at LIBOR, assuming 90 days in each quarter. Assume a par value of 1. Thus, at time 0, 90-day LIBOR is denoted as $L_0(90)$. Ninety days later, 90-day LIBOR is denoted as $L_{90}(90)$, and $L_{180}(90)$ and $L_{270}(90)$ are the 90-day LIBORs over the remainder of the life of the loan. Of course, only $L_0(90)$ is known at the start. The party buying this floating-rate bond receives the payments shown in Figure 12.4, where q = 90/360.

Note the payment at the maturity date, day 360, of the principal plus the interest of $L_{270}(90)(90/360)$. Now look back to day 270 and determine the value of this upcoming payment. To determine this value, we would discount $1 + L_{270}(90)(90/360)$ using an appropriate one-period discount rate, which is $L_{270}(90)$. Let us denote the value of this floating-rate bond on day 270 as $FLRB_{270}$, which is obtained as

$$FLRB_{270} = \frac{1 + L_{270}(90)(90/360)}{1 + L_{270}(90)(90/360)} = 1.$$

Hence, the value of the floating-rate bond on day 270 is its par value of 1. Now step back to day 180 and determine the value of the floating-rate bond. From day 180 looking ahead to day 270, the holder of the bond knows that he will receive a coupon of $L_{180}(90)(90/360)$ and will hold a bond worth $FLRB_{270} = 1$, which the equation above tells us is equal to 1. He will then discount these two values at the appropriate one-period rate $L_{180}(90)$. Thus,

$$FLRB_{180} = \frac{1 + L_{180}(90)(90/360)}{1 + L_{180}(90)(90/360)} = 1.$$

Continuing this procedure back to day 0 shows that the value of the floating-rate bond at any payment date, as well as on the initial date, is 1, its par value. This will always be the case if the coupon does not contain a spread over LIBOR. A floating-rate bond is designed such that its price will stay at or near par value. Between the interest payment dates, its price can stray from par value, but it would take a very large interest rate change for it to deviate much from par value. *The result that the value of a floating-rate bond is par at its payment date is an extremely important one, and one upon which we shall rely heavily when pricing and valuing interest rate swaps.*[5]

---

[5]Clearly, credit risk changes may cause floating-rate bonds not to trade at par. Credit risk changes and other technical nuances are beyond the scope of this introductory book.

FIGURE 12.5 Cash Flows in One-Year Quarterly Plain Vanilla Interest Rate Swap Decomposed into Fixed- and Floating-Rate Bonds

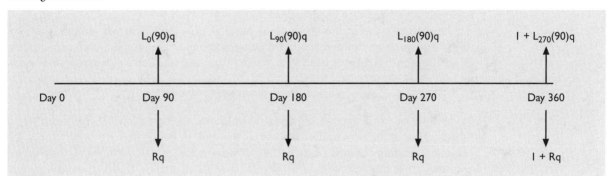

Note: $L_0(90)$, for example, is 90-day LIBOR on day 0, R is the fixed rate, and q represents the factor (days/360).

Now let us consider what we mean by the value of a swap. Look back at Figure 12.3. A plain vanilla swap is a stream of fixed interest payments and a stream of floating interest payments. The fixed interest payments are similar to those of a fixed-rate bond, except that a fixed-rate bond would pay back its principal at maturity. Likewise, the floating interest payments are similar to those of a floating-rate bond, except that the floating-rate bond would pay back its principal at maturity. An interest rate swap, of course, does not involve principal or notional amount payments. Suppose, however, that we add and subtract the notional amount at the termination date of the swap. The cash flows would still be the same as those on a swap, but now we could view the fixed payments as though they were the cash flows on a fixed-rate bond and the floating payments as though they were the cash flows on a floating-rate bond.

Consider Figure 12.5, which depicts the cash flows on the one-year quarterly swap, assuming a general fixed rate of R and a floating rate of 90-day LIBOR. The notional amount is 1. Note that the payment of a notional amount of 1 offsets the receipt of a notional amount of 1 on day 360. Thus, these cash flows are identical to those on a plain vanilla swap. Note that the fixed cash flows, including the notional amount, are identical to those of a fixed-rate bond with coupon R and that the floating cash flows, including the notional amount, are identical to those of a floating-rate bond with the coupon at LIBOR. The inclusion of the notional amounts on both the fixed and floating sides is critical, because otherwise the fixed and floating cash flows would not be identical to those of fixed- and floating-rate bonds.

It should now be apparent that a pay-fixed, receive-floating swap is equivalent to issuing a fixed-rate bond and using the proceeds to purchase a floating-rate bond. Thus, the value of a swap to pay a fixed rate and receive a floating rate is equal to the value of the floating-rate bond minus the value of the fixed-rate bond.

To make these results a little more general, let us consider a swap with n payments, made on days t_1, t_2, …, t_n. The value of the corresponding fixed-rate bond, V_{FXRB}, with coupon R is easy to determine:

$$V_{FXRB} = \sum_{i=1}^{n} R\left(\frac{t_i - t_{i-1}}{360}\right)B_0(t_i) + B_0(t_n),$$

where $B_0(t_i)$ is the discount factor, as discussed above, for the period 0 to day t_i. In other words, it is the value of an m-day zero coupon bond with maturity on day t_i. Each coupon $R((t_i - t_{i-1})/360)$ is multiplied by the discount factor. In addition, the final notional amount of 1 (omitted in the equation above) is multiplied by the discount factor for day t_n. The above expression is simply the present value of the interest and notional amount payments on a fixed-rate bond.

The present value of the floating-rate bond at time 0 is extremely simple. Now, we must recall what we learned about a floating-rate bond. That value at any coupon date as well as at the start is the par value, here 1. Thus, the value of the floating-rate bond is

$$V_{FLRB} = 1 \text{ (at time 0 or a payment date).}$$

Suppose we are at a date such as time t, which we shall position between time 0 and time t_1. How would we value the swap at this point? Recall that we would know the upcoming floating payment, $L_0(t_1)(t_1/360)$, because this rate was known at time 0. We also know that the floating-rate bond will be worth 1 at time t_1. Thus, we can simply discount $1 + L_0(t_1)((t_1 - t)/360)$ by the rate $L_t(t_1 - t)$:

$$V_{FLRB} = \frac{1 + L_0(t_1)(t_1/360)}{1 + L_t(t_1 - t)((t_1 - t)/360)} \text{ (between payment dates 0 and 1).}$$

Although this formula is written for the case of t between 0 and t_1, it is easily adapted to any pair of dates. In fact, the previous payment date can always be viewed as time 0 and the next one as time 1, meaning the first payment to come.

Thus, the value of the plain vanilla swap to receive a floating rate and pay a fixed rate is

$$VS = V_{FLRB} - V_{FXRB}.$$

The value of a pay-fixed, receive-floating interest rate swap is found as the value of a floating-rate bond minus the value of a fixed-rate bond. Changing the sign of this value produces the value of the swap from the opposite perspective.

This result is based on a notional amount of 1. For any other notional amount, simply multiply VS by the notional amount. Also note that from the counterparty's perspective, the value is found by subtracting V_{FLRB} from V_{FXRB}. This, of course, would be the value of the plain vanilla swap for paying a floating rate and receiving a fixed rate.

This formulation takes the fixed rate, R, as already known. At the beginning of the life of the swap, the fixed rate is set such that the value of the swap is zero. In this manner, each party's obligation to the other is the same. Hence, the swap has zero value to both parties, and neither pays the other anything at the start. To establish the value of R at the start, we must solve for R such that the present value of the stream of fixed payments plus the hypothetical notional amount equals 1, which is the present value of the stream of floating payments plus the hypothetical notional amount. Thus, R is the coupon rate on a par value bond. We find R by setting VS to zero and solving for R to obtain (where $q = ((t_i - t_{i-1})/360)$, which we assume is constant for all i):

$$R = \left(\frac{1}{q}\right)\left(\frac{1 - B_0(t_n)}{\sum\limits_{i=1}^{n} B_0(t_i)}\right).$$

This is a simple calculation to perform. An example is illustrated in Table 12.2.

Swap dealers perform this calculation to determine the fixed rate, but they typically quote the rate to their customers in a different manner. To make money, dealers must pay a lower fixed rate when they enter into a pay-fixed, receive-floating swap and receive a higher fixed

---

TABLE 12.2 PRICING A PLAIN VANILLA INTEREST RATE SWAP

Scenario: Quantum Electronics enters into a two-year $20 million notional amount interest rate swap in which it promises to pay a fixed rate and receive payments at LIBOR. The payments are made every six months based on the assumption of 30 days per month and 360 days in a year. The term structure of LIBOR interest rates and the zero coupon bond prices based on those rates are given as follows:

TERM	RATE	DISCOUNT BOND PRICE
180 days	$L_0(180) = 3.00\%$	$B_0(180) = 1/(1 + 0.03(180/360)) = 0.9852$
360 days	$L_0(360) = 3.75\%$	$B_0(360) = 1/(1 + 0.0375(360/360)) = 0.9639$
540 days	$L_0(540) = 4.20\%$	$B_0(540) = 1/(1 + 0.0420(540/360)) = 0.9407$
720 days	$L_0(720) = 4.50\%$	$B_0(720) = 1/(1 + 0.0450(720/360)) = 0.9174$

With $q = 180/360$, then $1/q = 360/180$ and the fixed rate would, therefore, be

$$R = \left(\frac{360}{180}\right)\left(\frac{1 - 0.9174}{0.9852 + 0.9639 + 0.9407 + 0.9174}\right) = 0.0434.$$

Thus, the rate would be 4.34 percent. The swap fixed payments would be

$$\$20,000,000(0.0434)(180/360) = \$434,000.$$

> Pricing a swap means to find the fixed rate on the swap at the start of the transaction. The fixed rate is obtained by finding the fixed payment that sets the market value of the swap to zero at the start. This fixed rate is quoted as a spread over the rate on a Treasury security of equivalent maturity.

rate when they enter into a pay-floating, receive-fixed swap. For example, the dealer might quote a rate of 4.38 percent for a swap in which the dealer receives a fixed rate and 4.30 percent for a swap in which the dealer pays a fixed rate.

Many dealers quote their rates electronically and make them available through various data service providers. Sometimes, however, the dealer does not quote the receive fixed or receive floating swap rates in this form. For example, to quote either rate on a two-year swap, the dealer determines the rate on a two-year government security, such as a U.S. Treasury note. Suppose this rate is 4.19 percent. Then 4.38 percent would be quoted as the 2-year Treasury rate plus 19, and 4.30 percent would be quoted as the 2-year Treasury rate plus 11. This procedure enables the dealer to make a quote that will hold up for a period of time. If interest rates make a quick move, the Treasury rate will move and the quoted swap rate will still be aligned at a fixed spread over the Treasury rate.

The spread of the swap rate over the corresponding Treasury rate is referred to as the **swap spread** and reflects the general level of credit risk in the global economy. That is, LIBOR is a borrowing rate that reflects the credit risk of London-based banks. The Treasury note rate reflects the default-free borrowing rate of the U.S. government as well as several other unique features such as being exempt from state and local taxes. When the economy weakens, credit risk becomes greater and the spread between LIBOR and the Treasury rate widens, leading to a larger swap spread.

As we discussed, the swap would have a value of zero at the start. As soon as interest rates change or time elapses, however, the swap will move to a nonzero value. In other words, its value to one party will be positive, and its value to the other will be negative.

Table 12.3 illustrates how the Quantum Electronics swap is valued three months into its life, or halfway between the initiation date and the first payment date.

Valuation of a swap is extremely important. If a firm enters into a swap, it knows that, ignoring the dealer's spread, the swap has a zero value at the start. It is neither an asset nor a liability. Once time elapses or interest rates change, however, the value of

MAKING THE CONNECTION

LIBOR and the British Bankers' Association

The London Interbank Offer Rate, or LIBOR, is the most popular reference floating rate for interest rate swaps. LIBOR has become a global benchmark interest rate governing the interest cost of debt for major corporations, car loans, home mortgages, and a wide array of other financial instruments. LIBOR represents the key interbank lending rate. U.S. dollar-denominated LIBOR historically tracks the federal funds rate quite closely. During times of financial stress, however, LIBOR can deviate dramatically from the federal funds rate.

For example, in late 2008 during the height of the credit crisis, the LIBOR rate was over 300 basis points above the comparable federal funds rate. Historically, the LIBOR rate is about 15 basis points above the comparable federal funds rate.

LIBOR reflects an average of the borrowing costs for large banks with AA credit rating. The British Bankers' Association in London is responsible for collecting the appropriate rates by using a daily survey. Because LIBOR is based on a survey and not on actual transactions, during times of financial distress, the accuracy of this survey data has been suspect.

For example, consider a bank that is under financial stress, which will make it have higher borrowing costs. If this strain is not well-known, then the act of reporting higher borrowing costs has the effect of publicly acknowledging the financial stress. Thus, there is concern that banks in this situation could understate their borrowing rates when they respond to the surveys.

Therefore, if these survey results are not carefully monitored and misreporting occurs, then LIBOR will be underestimated. This bias has a host of implications for financial markets worldwide. First, all loans tied to LIBOR would have a lower cost. Second, financial derivatives, such as interest rate swaps covered here, would have inaccurate payment requirements. For example, a receive-fixed, pay-floating interest rate swap counterparty will receive more than what is appropriate because LIBOR, the floating rate, is too low. Third, as the financial condition of the reporting bank deteriorates, then LIBOR no longer reflects the anticipated AA credit rated bank.

During times of financial strain, the British Bankers' Association is particularly focused on constantly overseeing the survey process to ensure the integrity of the reported number. In 2008, it undertook an intense investigation of the manner in which LIBOR data are collected and processed, but it ultimately chose not to change anything.

Historical information on LIBOR rates for many currencies is available from the British Bankers' Association website, www.bba.org.uk.

the swap will move to a positive value for one party and a negative value for the other. If the swap has a positive value, it is an asset. If it has a negative value, it is a liability. Proper accounting practice requires that swaps be valued, their gains and losses shown on the balance sheet.[6] Moreover, any financial officer responsible for a firm's swaps would want to know the values of its swap to determine how well the transaction is performing. Another reason why valuation is important is that it is a measure of the credit risk in a transaction. Suppose your firm holds a swap worth $100,000. Because the obligations of the counterparty exceed the obligations of your firm by $100,000, you are susceptible to losing $100,000 if the counterparty defaults.[7] Yet another reason why we would want to know the value of the swap is that we might want to terminate the swap position. We could do this by selling it back to the counterparty if it has a positive value or buying it back from the counterparty if it has a negative value. We shall discuss this procedure later in this chapter.

Thus, having a position in a swap and determining its value is, in principal, no different from owing a stock, looking into the market, and seeing what its price is. More

---

[6]We shall cover derivatives accounting in Chapter 16.

[7]We shall cover credit risk in more detail in Chapter 15.

TABLE 12.3 VALUING A PLAIN VANILLA INTEREST RATE SWAP DURING ITS LIFE

When the Quantum Electronics swap was first established, the first floating payment was set at the 180-day rate of 3 percent. For a $1 notional amount, the payment would be $0.03(180/360) = 0.015$. The fixed payment is at 4.34 percent, so it would be $0.0434(180/360) = 0.0217$. To value the swap 90 days into its life, we need the new term structure of interest rates as follows:

TERM	RATE	DISCOUNT BOND PRICE
90 days	$L_{90}(90) = 3.125\%$	$B_{90}(90) = 1/(1 + 0.03125(90/360)) = 0.9922$
270 days	$L_{90}(270) = 4.000\%$	$B_{90}(270) = 1/(1 + 0.04(270/360)) = 0.9709$
450 days	$L_{90}(450) = 4.375\%$	$B_{90}(450) = 1/(1 + 0.04375(450/360)) = 0.9481$
630 days	$L_{90}(630) = 4.625\%$	$B_{90}(630) = 1/(1 + 0.04625(630/360)) = 0.9251$

The value of the fixed payments, including the hypothetical notional amount, is

$$V_{FXRB} = 0.0217(0.9922 + 0.9709 + 0.9481 + 0.9251) + 1.0(0.9251) = 1.00837259.$$

The value of the floating payments, including the hypothetical notional amount, is based on discounting the next floating payment of 0.0415 and the market value of the floating-rate bond on the next payment date, which is 1:

$$V_{FLRB} = (0.015 + 1.0)(0.9922) = 1.00713178.$$

Thus, the value of the swap per $1 notional amount is

$$VS = 1.00713178 - 1.00837259 = -0.00124081.$$

Taking into account the $20 million notional amount, the value of the swap is

$$\$20,000,000(-0.00124081) = -\$24,816.$$

To the counterparty, the value of the swap is $24,816.

calculations are required with swaps, because unlike stock, a swap is a customized instrument that does not trade in an open market where its value can be read off a computer screen. Nonetheless, the information necessary for valuing the swap can be observed in the market, and the calculations can be easily made. Alternatively, an end user can simply ask the dealer counterparty for a valuation at any time during the life of the swap.

We have been discussing the pricing and valuation of plain vanilla interest rate swaps. Recall that we also briefly discussed the basis swap, which is a swap in which both sides make floating payments. One common type of basis swap is where one side pays the Treasury rate and the other pays LIBOR. As we noted, the side paying LIBOR would always be paying the higher rate, so it would need to be compensated with a fixed spread. To price this swap, let us make the present value of the payments at the Treasury bill rate equal the present value of the payments at LIBOR by incorporating a spread. Consider the following:

> A basis swap is priced by adding a spread to the higher rate or subtracting a spread from the lower rate. This spread is found as the difference between the fixed rate on a plain vanilla swap based on one of the rates and the fixed rate on a plain vanilla swap based on the other rate.

A swap to
    pay the T-bill rate
    receive a fixed rate derived from the T-bill term structure
Plus,
A swap to
    pay a fixed rate derived from the LIBOR term structure
    receive LIBOR
Equals
    a swap to pay the T-bill rate and receive LIBOR and pay the difference between the LIBOR fixed rate and the T-bill fixed rate.

TABLE 12.4 PRICING A BASIS SWAP

Consider a one-year swap with semiannual payments to pay the T-bill rate and receive LIBOR minus a spread with payments based on days/360, assuming 30 days in a month. The notional amount is $50 million. The term structures are as follows:

TERM	LIBOR	DISCOUNT BOND PRICE
180 days	7.01%	$B_0(180) = 1/(1 + 0.0701(180/360)) = 0.9661$
360 days	7.21%	$B_0(360) = 1/(1 + 0.0721(360/360)) = 0.9327$

TERM	T-BILL RATE	DISCOUNT BOND PRICE
180 days	5.05%	$B_0(180) = 1 - 0.0505(180/360) = 0.9748$
360 days	5.95%	$B_0(360) = 1 - 0.0595(360/360) = 0.9405$

Note that the T-bill discount factor is determined using the discount method, while the LIBOR discount factor is determined using the add-on method. This is the convention in the two markets, as we have seen in previous chapters. Solving for the LIBOR fixed rate, we obtain

$$R = \left(\frac{360}{180}\right)\left(\frac{1 - 0.9327}{0.9661 + 0.9327}\right) = 0.0709.$$

Solving for the T-bill fixed rate, we obtain

$$R = \left(\frac{360}{180}\right)\left(\frac{1 - 0.9405}{0.9748 + 0.9405}\right) = 0.0621.$$

The spread is, thus, $0.0709 - 0.0621 = 0.0088$. Thus, in this swap, the party paying the T-bill rate would pay 88 basis points more or the party paying LIBOR would pay 88 basis points less. We shall assume that the party paying LIBOR pays LIBOR minus 88 basis points.

> The value of a basis swap is obtained by determining the difference in the two floating streams of payments, recognizing that both of the next floating payments are known and that the value of the remaining floating payments and the hypothetical notional amount is the par value on the next payment date.

Thus, a basis swap to pay the T-bill rate and receive LIBOR will also involve paying the difference between the LIBOR fixed rate and the T-bill fixed rate. This should make sense from a logical point of view: LIBOR is greater than the T-bill rate, so the party receiving LIBOR would have to give up something. Table 12.4 illustrates the pricing of this swap. In it, we price a swap using both the T-bill term structure and the LIBOR term structure. The spread between these fixed rates is the spread on a basis swap.

Now suppose we move three months into the life of the swap and want to obtain its value. Table 12.5 shows how to value the basis swap during its life.

Interest Rate Swap Strategies

Now let us return to the example we used at the beginning of the chapter. Recall that a firm called XYZ entered into a swap to pay a fixed rate and receive a floating rate. Now, we want to understand why XYZ would do this transaction. Suppose the current date is December 15. XYZ has a one-year floating-rate loan at LIBOR plus 100 basis points. The payments are on the 15th of March, June, September, and December, and the interest is calculated based on the actual number of days in the period divided by 360. If XYZ would prefer a fixed-rate loan, it can easily convert the floating-rate loan into a fixed-rate loan by engaging in the swap we described. Recall that in that swap, XYZ pays a fixed rate of 7.5 percent and receives LIBOR. Figure 12.6 shows that the swap has the effect of leaving XYZ paying a fixed rate of 8.5 percent, reflecting the 7.5 percent fixed rate on the swap, plus the 100 basis point spread it pays over LIBOR on the floating-rate loan.

> Plain vanilla interest rate swaps are primarily used to convert floating-rate loans to fixed-rate loans and fixed-rate loans to floating-rate loans.

TABLE 12.5 VALUING A BASIS SWAP DURING ITS LIFE

Consider the swap described in Table 12.4. Now it is 90 days into the life of the swap. The new term structures are as follows:

TERM	LIBOR	DISCOUNT BOND PRICE
90 days	7.20%	$B_{90}(90) = 1/(1 = 0.072(90/360)) = 0.9823$
270 days	7.35%	$B_{90}(270) = 1/(1 = 0.0735(270/360)) = 0.9478$
TERM	**T-BILL RATE**	**DISCOUNT BOND PRICE**
90 days	5.30%	$B_{90}(90) = 1 - 0.053(90/360) = 0.9868$
270 days	6.20%	$B_{90}(270) = 1 - 0.062(270/360) = 0.9535$

The present value of the floating T-bill payments can be found by discounting the upcoming payment plus the par value of the payments on the next payment date, which as we saw is the market value of the floating-rate bond on the next payment date. The next payment will be at the rate of 5.05% because this was the 180-day rate when the swap was initiated:

$$(1 + 0.0505(180/360))(0.9868) = 1.0117167.$$

The upcoming LIBOR payment will be at 7.01% minus the spread of $0.0088 = 0.0613$. Then the present value of the LIBOR payments will be

$$(1 + 0.0613(180/360))(0.9823) = 1.0124075.$$

Then the value of the swap to pay the T-bill rate and receive LIBOR for a $1 notional amount will be

$$1.0124075 - 1.0117167 = 0.0006908.$$

Based on the $50 million notional amount, the value of the swap will be

$$\$50,000,000(0.0006908) = \$34,540.$$

Of course, you may be wondering why XYZ did not just take a fixed-rate loan in the first place. One reason is that because they tend to borrow at floating rates, banks prefer to make floating-rate loans. They tend to charge a slight premium for fixed-rate loans. In addition, if XYZ takes a floating-rate loan and swaps it into a fixed-rate loan, it will assume some credit risk from the possibility that the ABSwaps will default. If XYZ had taken out a fixed-rate loan it would assume no credit risk, because it would not have a claim on any payments. The assumption of credit risk can result in some savings. Of course, ABSwaps could default, and XYZ would still have to make its floating interest payments to its lender. The savings come at the expense of assuming the risk of ABSwaps defaulting.

FIGURE 12.6 Conversion of Floating-Rate Loan into Fixed-Rate Loan Using Plain Vanilla Interest Rate Swap

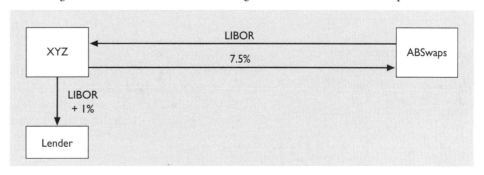

This example is the most common application of interest rate swaps, particularly by corporations. Indeed it is probably one of the most common of all financial transactions. It should be easy to see that a swap can alternatively be used to convert a fixed-rate loan to a floating-rate loan. Corporations often do these types of transactions to alter their mix of fixed- to floating-rate borrowing to a more desirable level. Some, if not most, of these transactions are done in anticipation of interest rate changes. But regardless of the reason, the plain vanilla interest rate swap combined with a position in a fixed- or floating-rate bond or loan is a widely used financial strategy.

Basis swaps are frequently used in speculative situations. Considering the example above, the spread between the LIBOR and T-bill swap rates is 88 basis points. A party might believe that the spread would widen or narrow due to changes in the perception of credit risk in the global economy. A basis swap could be used to speculate on such an occurrence. Likewise, a basis swap could be used to hedge changes in the general level of credit risk in the global economy. Such a strategy might be useful to a party holding a portfolio of credit risky bonds, who is concerned about the effects of a deterioration of credit quality in the global economy. As we shall see in Chapter 15, however, there are credit derivatives that work much better in managing credit risk.

Index Amortizing Swaps An **index amortizing swap** is one in which the notional amount is reduced as one moves through time. A typical application of this type of swap would be where the party holds another position in which the notional amount is designed to decline through time. The most common example of this is the mortgage loan. When a homeowner takes out a mortgage, the loan balance reduces through time according to a fixed schedule. Homeowners, however, nearly always have the option to prepay and refinance their mortgages. When interest rates fall, more homeowners exercise their options. The holders of mortgages thus suffer losses by having their income streams reduced to zero and having to reinvest the prepaid principal at lower rates. In an index amortizing swap, the notional amount declines according to a schedule that specifies an acceleration of the amortization rate if interest rates fall. This results in the swap notional amount behaving much like the mortgage notional amount. There are numerous variations of this type of swap.

> An index amortizing swap is one in which the notional amount is reduced through time. The amortization accelerates as interest rates decrease. This feature is designed to reflect the prepayments that might occur on a mortgage or another similar loan being hedged with the swap.

Securities based on mortgages have become popular instruments and are often classified as derivatives. We discuss them later in Chapter 14.

Diff Swaps A **diff swap** is an interest rate swap based on the interest rates in two countries but where the payments are made in a single currency. For example, a U.S. firm might be concerned that German interest rates will increase relative to U.S. rates. It could hedge this position by purchasing a euro-denominated floating-rate note and selling a dollar-denominated floating-rate note. This would, however, be assuming unwanted currency risk. Alternatively, it could enter into a diff swap in which it receives the German interest rate and pays the U.S. interest rate, with all payments made in dollars. Thus, if German interest rates rise relative to U.S. interest rates, the swap will result in a net payment in dollars to the firm. Obviously, the dealer in such a swap would incur the currency

> A diff swap is a swap in which each party makes an interest payment based on the difference between interest rates in different countries but both payments are made in the same currency. This enables the parties to speculate or hedge on relative interest rate changes of different countries without the currency risk.

risk and would probably pass on to the party the cost of hedging that risk, but presumably the dealer could do it much cheaper.

It should be apparent that this swap is simply a currency-hedged basis swap. If the interest rates of one country are consistently higher than those in the other country, there would be a spread similar to that in a basis swap negotiated up front.

> A constant maturity swap is a swap in which one party pays a fixed rate or short-term floating rate and the other pays a floating rate tied to the yield on a treasury security of intermediate-term maturity. This security is usually called the Constant Maturity Treasury. Its maturity is typically longer than the swap settlement period.

Constant Maturity Swaps A **constant maturity swap** is similar to a plain vanilla swap or a basis swap. One party pays a floating rate such as LIBOR, and the other party pays another floating rate represented by the yield on a security with a maturity longer than the reset period. In other words, if the swap settles every six months, one party pays a rate on a security with longer than six months' maturity. Typically, this is the yield on a security with a maturity in the range of two to five years. In dollar-denominated swaps, that rate is often referred to as the Constant Maturity Treasury (CMT) rate. The **CMT rate** is the yield on a U.S. Treasury note with a maturity closest to the maturity of interest. Naturally, there is not always a Treasury note with precisely the desired maturity. In that case, however, the parties agree that the CMT rate will be interpolated from the rates on securities with maturities slightly above and below the desired maturity. Also, the Federal Reserve publishes its own estimate of the CMT rate, which is often used.

As an example, consider a three-year swap with semiannual payments in which one party pays the six-month LIBOR and the other pays the CMT on a five-year U.S. Treasury note. This is just a variation of a basis swap because both rates are floating. Depending on the shape of the term structure, a spread might also be paid by the party paying the lower rate. Constant maturity swaps can also have one party paying a fixed rate, with the other paying the CMT rate. It should be apparent that this is just a variation of a plain vanilla swap where the floating rate has a longer maturity than the standard LIBOR-based plain vanilla swap.

This observation gives rise to an important arbitrage relationship. If a party enters into a swap paying LIBOR and receiving the CMT and another swap paying the CMT and receiving the fixed rate, the net result is a plain vanilla swap paying LIBOR and receiving fixed. The fixed rate would reflect the fixed rate on the CMT-versus-fixed swap and the spread on the CMT-versus-LIBOR swap.

The parties to a constant maturity swap are obviously concerned about a change in the shape of the term structure. For example, if a party will be hurt short-term rates increase more or decrease less than intermediate-term rates, it could engage in a swap to receive LIBOR and pay the CMT.

As LIBOR is widely used as an indicator of short-term interest rates, the CMT rate is also widely used as an indicator of intermediate-term interest rates. Consequently, the CMT rate is found as the underlying rate in many other types of derivatives, including caps and floors.

These examples are designed to give you a basic familiarity with the most popular variations of the plain vanilla swap. The number of variations actually seen in practice is much greater than we can show here. Moreover, many of these variations of interest rate swaps can also be used with commodity, currency, and equity swaps. If you have a good understanding of what we have covered so far, you should be ready to deal with the other types of swaps you may someday encounter.

Although interest rate swaps are more widely used than currency swaps, currency swaps are actually much more general instruments. This means that, as we shall see, an interest rate swap is just a special case of a currency swap.

MAKING THE CONNECTION

United States Municipal Finance and Interest Rate Swaps

Municipal finance has several very unique and challenging aspects. Municipalities in the United States are often able to borrow at the tax-exempt interest rate. That is, municipal bond investors do not have to pay income tax on interest paid on qualified municipal bond issues. The net effect is that municipalities can borrow at an interest rate significantly below prevailing taxable rates. This tax exemption, combined with the political preference for deferring expenditures into the future, has led to the development of a $3 trillion municipal bond market as of the end of 2010.

For a variety of reasons, municipalities were induced into a structured finance strategy where they borrowed at the short-term, tax-exempt variable rate (based on a spread over the AAA-rated SIFMA swap index, a seven-day, tax-exempt interest rate) and entered into an interest rate swap where the municipality received 67 percent of the three-month LIBOR rate and paid a fixed rate. The 67 percent was an estimate of the implied income tax rate from these markets of 33 percent. Thus, the price setting marginal investors appeared to be indifferent between the tax exempt SIFMA swap index rate and 67 percent of three-month LIBOR rate (after-tax).

The idea is that this structured finance transaction would result in a lower all-in fixed rate for the municipality. It should be apparent that this structure has numerous problems. First, the SIFMA swap index-based variable rate was based on a seven-day variable rate demand obligation. Investors in these bonds could demand their money back every seven days. Thus, in a crisis, investors would flee, requiring the municipality to immediately raise the money during a time of distress or to prepay a liquidity provider to be willing to step in and lend money. The liquidity providers often had contractual terms and conditions that enabled them to avoid having to lend the money in many stress situation.

Second, there is basis risk between the SIFMA swap index rate and 67 percent of three-month LIBOR. The SIFMA swap index rate is based on seven days and the reference LIBOR rate was often three months, introducing term risk. Also, in stress markets, the individual municipality's borrowing rate will spike significantly above the benchmark AAA-rated SIFMA swap index rate.

Third, there is potential credit exposure to the liquidity provider and the swap provider. During the credit crisis of 2008, some liquidity providers failed to honor their obligations due to credit distress of their own. Also, municipalities learned that the liquidity provider would not have to meet their obligations due to a variety of contractual covenants. For example, one covenant was based on the credit rating of the municipality. If the municipality's credit rating fell below, say BB, then the liquidity provider did not have to lend the municipality the funds even though it had been paid a premium for this service for years.

Finally, this particular structure often caused an expensive mismatch between the rate-sensitive municipal assets (usually very short term) and rate-sensitive municipal liabilities (this structure was very long term). The yield curve is historically much steeper in the municipal market. Hence, this interest rate-sensitive mismatch is particularly expensive for municipalities.

For the right young professional, serving the municipal finance community is very rewarding, particularly if she successfully helps municipalities navigate through these complexities. The skills required include strong quantitative abilities coupled with being politically astute as well as having a strong and accurate ethical compass. For example, the failure to have the right municipal finance professionals serving the best interest of Jefferson County, Alabama, between 1997 and 2008 resulted in over 20 felony convictions, billions of dollars lost by municipal investors, and an adverse economic impact in and around Jefferson County, Alabama, for many years to come.

CURRENCY SWAPS

> A currency swap is a swap in which the two parties agree to exchange a series of interest payments in different currencies. Either or both sets of payments can be fixed or floating.

As we previously described, a currency swap is a series of payments between two parties in which the two sets of payments are in different currencies.[8] The payments are effectively equivalent to interest payments because they are calculated as though interest were being paid on a specific notional amount. In a currency swap, however, there are two notional amounts, one in each of the two currencies. In addition, in a currency swap, the notional amount can be exchanged at the beginning and at the end of the life of the swap, depending on the parties' desires. Because currency swap payments are in different currencies, they are typically not netted. Thus, the first party pays the second the amount owed, and the second party pays the first the amount owed.[9]

Structure of a Typical Currency Swap

Let us take a look at a currency swap between a hypothetical U.S. firm, Reston Technology, and a hypothetical dealer, Global Swaps, Inc. (GSI). For now, let us not concern ourselves with why Reston wants to enter into this swap. We shall address the motivation for currency swaps in a later section. So let us assume that Reston enters into a currency swap with GSI in which it will make a series of semiannual interest payments in euros to GSI at a rate of 4.35 percent per year, based on a notional amount of €10 million. GSI will pay Reston semiannual interest in dollars at a rate of 6.1 percent for two years, based on a notional amount of $9.804 million. The two parties will exchange the notional amount at the beginning and at the end of the transaction. Thus, the following transactions take place:

At the initiation date of the swap

- Reston pays GSI $9.804 million
- GSI pays Reston €10 million

Semiannually for two years

- Reston pays GSI 0.0435(180/360)€10,000,000 = €217,500
- GSI pays Reston 0.061(180/360)$9,804,000 = $299,022

At the termination date of the swap

- Reston pays GSI €10 million
- GSI pays Reston $9.804 million

Figure 12.7 illustrates these cash flows from the point of view of Reston. Note that the series of cash flows looks as though Reston has issued a euro-denominated bond for €10 million, taken the funds, and purchased a dollar-denominated bond for $9.804 million. During the two years, Reston makes payments in euros and receives payments in dollars. At the end of the two years, Reston pays back the principal of €10 million and receives the principal of $9.804 million. Of course, Reston does not actually issue a

---

[8]It is important to clear up some potential confusion over another similarly named transaction. In the foreign currency markets, a long position in one forward contract and a short position in a forward contract on the same currency but with a different expiration date is called an FX swap. This type of transaction is, therefore, similar to what we referred to as a spread when using futures. FX swaps and currency swaps are completely different transactions, but have similar names. We shall not cover FX swaps, but given that we covered futures spreads, the similarity should be obvious.

[9]In 2002, the CLS Bank International began operating as a currency clearinghouse bank, with the objective of allowing parties to net payments on all types of currency transactions. If this bank is successful in attracting users, netting will become commonplace on currency swaps, thereby reducing credit risk.

FIGURE 12.7 Cash Flows in a Currency Swap from the Point of View of Reston Technology

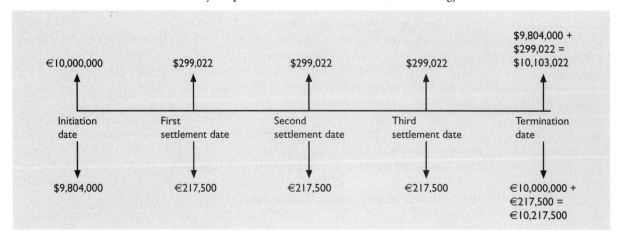

dollar-denominated bond or purchase a euro-denominated bond. It enters into a swap, but the payments are the same as if it had done the transactions in bonds. This is an important point in understanding how currency swaps are priced.

Note that the initial exchange of notional amounts is €10 million for $9.804 million. Because we said that swaps normally have zero value at the start, the exchange rate at the time the swap is initiated is $0.9804 per euro. Of course, at the end of the life of the transaction, the same €10 million is exchanged for $9.804 million, but at that time, the exchange rate will almost surely be different from $0.9804. This exchange rate risk gives rise to gains and losses for the two parties, which is an important factor in determining the value of the swap.

In this swap, both sets of payments are at a fixed rate, but both could be at a floating rate or either could be fixed and the other be floating. If a floating rate were used, the dollar floating rate would probably be LIBOR. The euro floating rate would probably be Euribor, which is the rate at which banks lend euros to each other in Frankfurt, Germany, the financial center of the European Union.

There are some important relationships between interest rate and currency swaps that we must understand. Recall that there are four types of currency swaps: (1) paying both currencies at fixed rates, (2) paying both at floating rates, (3) paying the first currency at a floating rate and the second at a fixed rate, and (4) paying the second currency at a floating rate and the first at a fixed rate. Using our example of dollars and euros as the two currencies, Figure 12.8 illustrates how currency swaps can be combined to equal interest rate swaps. We can combine two currency swaps to produce a plain vanilla interest rate swap. Likewise, we could combine a currency swap and an interest rate swap to produce another currency swap. For example, consider the first combination in Figure 12.8. Suppose we combine the swap to pay € fixed and receive $ fixed with the interest rate swap to pay $ fixed and receive $ floating. This will produce a currency swap to pay € fixed and receive $ floating. The relationships illustrated in Figure 12.8 are like an algebraic equation. The terms can be rearranged by changing "pay" to "receive" and vice versa when moving a transaction to the other side of the equality.

Perhaps the most important relationship between interest rate and currency swaps, however, is the simple fact that an interest rate swap is just a currency swap involving one side paying floating and the other paying fixed, but where both currencies are the same. Thus, the currency swap is far more general than the interest rate swap. The currency swap contains the interest rate swap as a special case.

FIGURE 12.8 Creating Interest Rate Swaps out of Currency Swaps

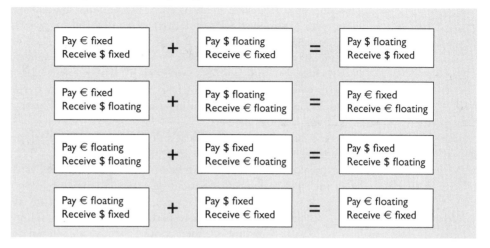

Pricing and Valuation of Currency Swaps

A currency swap is a transaction with two streams of cash flows, one in one currency and one in another currency. Each cash flow stream is based on a different amount of notional amount, and each can be at a fixed or a floating rate. To determine the value of a currency swap, we must find the present values of the two streams of cash flows, with both expressed in a common currency. We subtract the value of the outflow stream from the value of the inflow stream.

Let us start by considering a currency swap with payments in dollars and euros. Let the dollar notional amount be $NP^\$ = 1$ and the euro notional amount be expressed as $NP^\euro$, but the amount is initially unspecified. Because the value of the swap should be zero at the start, $NP^\euro$ will be related to $NP^\$$ by the current exchange rate. Let S_0 be the exchange rate, expressed as dollars per euro. Then

$$NP^\euro = 1/S_0$$

for every dollar of notional amount.

In plain vanilla interest rate swaps, we do not exchange the notional amount.[10] In a currency swap, the exchange of notional amounts is perfectly normal. The two parties exchange $NP^\$$ and $NP^\euro$ at the start. This exchange has no value as the two amounts are equivalent. At the end of the life of the swap, the parties reverse the original exchange. At that point, however, the exchange rate is not likely to be S_0, so the exchange is not for equivalent value. In some currency swaps, the notional amounts are not exchanged. In the examples here, we shall assume that the notional amounts are exchanged. Later, we shall discuss a situation in which it would be preferable to not exchange the notional amounts.

For our swap with fixed payments in dollars and euros, we first need to determine the fixed rate in dollars that will make the present value of the payments equal the notional amount of $1. Fortunately, we already know that rate, because we determined it when pricing the plain vanilla interest rate swap. It is simply the fixed rate on a plain vanilla swap using the term structure in dollars. Let us denote that rate as $R^\$$.

---

[10]Remember, however, that we assumed a *hypothetical* exchange of equivalent notional amounts so that the two streams of cash flows would be equivalent to those of fixed- and floating-rate bonds, thereby permitting us to value the swap as though it were a long position in one bond and short position in the other.

Now we need to determine the fixed rate in euros that will make the present value of the fixed payments in euros equal the notional amount of NP^{ϵ}. Of course, we have not yet determined NP^{ϵ}. But first let us note that if we constructed a plain vanilla swap in euros with a notional amount of €1, the fixed rate would be found the same way we found the fixed rate in dollars. We would simply use the euro term structure. Let this rate be denoted as R^{ϵ}. The present value of the fixed payments in euros at this rate would be €1. The value of the euro payments for the actual swap would be found by discounting them at a rate of R^{ϵ} and then multiplying by the notional amount of NP^{ϵ}.

If either set of payments is at a floating rate, we can find their present value using the same method we used for plain vanilla interest rate swaps. We discount the next floating payment, which will be known because it has already been established, and also the value of the swap at the next payment date, which is known to be the notional amount of 1 (either dollars or euros). After obtaining the values of both sets of payments in their respective currencies and multiplying each by the notional amount, we then convert them to a common currency.

> Pricing a currency swap means to find the fixed rates in the two currencies. These fixed rates are the same as the fixed rates on plain vanilla swaps in the respective currencies. In addition, the notional amounts must be set equal, which is done by finding the value of one notional amount in the other currency using the current exchange rate.

Let us now work a problem. Recall the Reston-GSI swap that we previously discussed. Table 12.6 presents the term structures in dollars and euros and solves for the fixed rate on plain vanilla swaps in both currencies. Recall that we are interested in a currency swap involving semiannual payments for two years.

We see in Table 12.6 that a plain vanilla interest rate swap in dollars would be at a rate of 6.1 percent, while a plain vanilla interest rate swap in euros would be at a rate of 4.35 percent. Thus, the present value of a stream of dollar payments with a hypothetical notional amount of $1 at

TABLE 12.6 SOLVING FOR THE FIXED RATE IN TWO CURRENCIES

The following term structures, discount bond prices, and resulting swap fixed rates are given below.

TERM	DOLLAR RATE	DISCOUNT BOND PRICE
180 days	5.5%	$B_0^{\$}(180) = 1/(1 + 0.055(180/360)) = 0.9732$
360 days	5.5%	$B_0^{\$}(360) = 1/(1 + 0.055(360/360)) = 0.9479$
540 days	6.2%	$B_0^{\$}(540) = 1/(1 + 0.062(540/360)) = 0.9149$
720 days	6.4%	$B_0^{\$}(720) = 1/(1 + 0.064(720/360)) = 0.8865$

The fixed rate on a dollar plain vanilla interest rate swap would be

$$R^{\$} = \left(\frac{360}{180}\right)\left(\frac{1 - 0.8865}{0.9732 + 0.9479 + 0.9149 + 0.8865}\right) = 0.061.$$

TERM	EURO RATE	DISCOUNT BOND PRICE
180 days	3.8%	$B_0^{\epsilon}(180) = 1/(1 + 0.038(180/360)) = 0.9814$
360 days	4.2%	$B_0^{\epsilon}(360) = 1/(1 + 0.042(360/360)) = 0.9597$
540 days	4.4%	$B_0^{\epsilon}(540) = 1/(1 + 0.044(540/360)) = 0.9381$
720 days	4.5%	$B_0^{\epsilon}(720) = 1/(1 + 0.045(720/360)) = 0.9174$

The fixed rate on a euro plain vanilla interest rate swap would be

$$R^{\epsilon} = \left(\frac{360}{180}\right)\left(\frac{1 - 0.9174}{0.9814 + 0.9597 + 0.9381 + 0.9174}\right) = 0.0435.$$

a rate of 6.1 percent is $1. The present value of a stream of euro payments with a hypothetical notional amount of €1 at a rate of 4.35 percent is €1. These are the rates we have been using in the Reston-GSI swap.

Recall that the Reston-GSI swap has notional amounts of $9.804 million and €10 million. Thus, the current exchange rate must be $0.9804. Because the present value of the dollar payments at 6.1 percent per $1 notional amount is $1, the present value of the dollar payments at 6.1 percent for a notional amount of $9.804 million would be $9.804 million. The present value of the euro payments at 4.35 percent for a notional amount of €1 is €1, so the present value of the euro payments at 4.35 percent for a notional amount of €10 million would be €10 million. Converting €10 million to dollars gives €10,000,000($0.9804) = $9,804,000, which is the dollar notional amount. Thus, these two interest rates, the exchange rate, and the two notional amounts equate the present values of the two streams of payments at the start of the transaction.

If either set of payments is at a floating rate, we do not have to solve for a fixed rate and can be assured that the present value of the payments equals one unit of notional amount in the given currency. We know that because we know from studying interest rate swaps that the present value of the stream of floating payments is equivalent to the present value of the stream of fixed payments, provided the appropriate fixed rate is used.

> The value of a currency swap is found by determining the value of each set of payments in their respective currencies, taking into account the different notional amounts, and converting to a common currency.

Although the swap value is zero at the start, after the swap begins, its value will change. Valuation of the currency swap is obtained by finding the present value of the two streams of payments per unit of notional amount. This is precisely what we did when valuing an interest rate swap. We then adjust the value of the foreign stream of payments by the actual foreign notional amount and then convert it to the domestic currency using the new exchange rate. Let us illustrate this in Table 12.7, three months into the life of the swap with the new exchange rate being $0.9790. In addition to finding the present value of the fixed payments, as in this actual swap, we shall also determine the present value of the payments as if they were floating so that we can examine the valuation of the swap if it had been designed with floating payments.

The values computed in Table 12.7 are the values of the streams of payments per notional amount of either $1 or €1. Consider this the standard case. Now we must determine the values for the actual notional amounts in the swap.

The value of the dollar fixed payments for a notional amount of $9,804 million is

$$\$9,804,000(1.01132335) = \$9,915,014.$$

If the payments had been floating, their value for a notional amount of $9.804 million would be

$$\$9,804,000(1.013115) = \$9,932,579.$$

The value of the euro fixed payments for a notional amount of €10 million is

$$€10,000,000(1.00883078) = €10,088,308.$$

If the euro payments had been floating, their value for a notional amount of €10 million would be

$$€10,000,000(1.0091157) = €10,091,157.$$

To determine the value of the currency swap, we must do two final things. We must first convert the values of the two streams of cash flows into a common currency and then net the two amounts. Typically, we would prefer to convert to the home currency

TABLE 12.7 VALUING A CURRENCY SWAP DURING ITS LIFE

Three months into the Reston-GSI swap, the new term structures and zero coupon bond prices for dollars are as follows:

TERM	DOLLAR RATE	DISCOUNT BOND PRICE
90 days	5.7%	$B_{90}^{\$}(90) = 1/(1 + 0.057(90/360)) = 0.9860$
270 days	6.1%	$B_{90}^{\$}(270) = 1/(1 + 0.061(270/360)) = 0.9563$
450 days	6.4%	$B_{90}^{\$}(450) = 1/(1 + 0.064(450/360)) = 0.9259$
630 days	6.6%	$B_{90}^{\$}(630) = 1/(1 + 0.066(630/360)) = 0.8965$

The present value of the dollar fixed payments of 0.061(180/360) plus a $1 notional amount is

$$0.061\left(\frac{180}{360}\right)(0.9860 + 0.9563 + 0.9259 + 0.8965) + 1.0(0.8965) = 1.01132335.$$

If the swap had been designed with floating payments, the present value of the dollar floating payments would be found by discounting the next floating payment, which is at the original 180-day floating rate of 5.5%, plus the market value of the floating-rate bond on the next payment date:

$$\left(1.0 + 0.055\left(\frac{180}{360}\right)\right)0.9860 = 1.013115.$$

The new term structure and discount bond prices for the euro are as follows:

TERM	EURO RATE	DISCOUNT BOND PRICE
90 days	3.9%	$B_{90}^{\euro}(90) = 1/(1 + 0.039(90/360)) = 0.9903$
270 days	4.3%	$B_{90}^{\euro}(270) = 1/(1 + 0.043(270/360)) = 0.9688$
450 days	4.5%	$B_{90}^{\euro}(450) = 1/(1 + 0.045(450/360)) = 0.9467$
630 days	4.6%	$B_{90}^{\euro}(630) = 1/(1 + 0.046(630/360)) = 0.9255$

The present value of the euro fixed payments of 0.0435(180/360) plus a €1 notional amount is

$$0.0435\left(\frac{180}{360}\right)(0.9903 + 0.9688 + 0.9467 + 0.9255) + 1.0(0.9255) = 1.00883078.$$

If the payments were floating, the present value of the euro payments would be found by discounting the next floating payment, which is at the original 180-day floating rate of 3.8%, plus the market value of the floating-rate bond on the next payment date:

$$\left(1.0 + 0.038\left(\frac{180}{360}\right)\right)0.9903 = 1.0091157.$$

of the party from whose perspective we are valuing the swap. The actual swap was for Reston to pay euros fixed and receive dollars fixed. With an exchange rate of $0.9790, the value of the swap in dollars would be

$$\$9,915,014 - \euro10,088,308(0.9790/\euro) = \$38,560.$$

Because we have the necessary information, let us determine the values of the other possible swaps Reston could have arranged. The value if the swap had involved paying euros fixed and receiving dollars floating would be

$$\$9,932,579 - \euro10,088,308(0.9790/\euro) = \$56,125.$$

The value if the swap had involved paying euros floating and receiving dollars fixed would be

$$\$9,915,014 - \euro10,091,157(0.9790/\euro) = \$35,771.$$

The value if the swap had involved paying euros floating and receiving dollars floating would be

$$\$9,932,579 - €10,091,157(0.9790/€) = \$53,336.$$

Note that the value of a currency swap is driven by changes in interest rates between the two countries and the change in the exchange rate. But regardless of the determinants, the value of a currency swap is simply the present value of one stream of payments minus the present value of the other stream of payments, accounting for the notional amounts, and converting the payments to a common currency.

Currency Swap Strategies

We discussed the Reston-GSI swap without explaining why Reston might want to enter into the swap. Now let us take a look at the possible motivation for Reston to do this transaction.

Reston Technology is an established Internet company in Northern Virginia's technology corridor. It is planning to expand its operations into Europe. To do so, it needs to borrow €10 million. It would like to issue bonds at a fixed rate and pay them back semiannually over two years. At the current exchange rate of $0.9804 per euro, Reston could borrow $9,804,000 and convert this amount to euros. Its expanded operations, however, will generate cash flow in euros, so it would prefer to make its interest payments in euros.

Currency swaps are primarily used to convert a loan in one currency into a loan in another currency. Currency swaps can also be used for any situation in which a party has to convert a series of future payments in one currency into another currency.

While Reston considers borrowing in euros, its primary bank has a subsidiary, Global Swaps, Inc. (GSI), which is a large global derivatives dealer. GSI suggests that Reston borrow in U.S. dollars and engage in a currency swap to convert its loan to euros. Specifically, Reston would borrow $9,804,000 in the U.S. market and enter into a currency swap with GSI in which GSI pays Reston 10 million up front and Reston pays GSI $9,804,000 up front. Of course, Reston would get this $9,804,000 from the loan it takes out in dollars. As we know from previously examining the swap, GSI will pay Reston interest in dollars at 6.1 percent semiannually for two years, and Reston will pay GSI interest at 4.35 percent in euros semiannually for two years. During this two-year period, Reston will make semiannual interest payments to its creditor at the rate it borrows in dollars. After two years, GSI will pay Reston $9,804,000, which it will use to pay off its loan. Reston will pay GSI €10 million. The net effect is that Reston has issued a loan in dollars, but converted it to a loan in euros.

Reston is not likely to be able to borrow in dollars at the swap dollar fixed rate of 6.1 percent. That rate applies to high-quality London-based banks. Let us assume that Reston borrows at 6.5 percent. Thus, its loan interest payment will be $9,804,000 (0.065(180/360)) = $318,630. The overall transaction, consisting of the swap and the loan, is illustrated in Figure 12.9.

While Reston could have borrowed in euros, it would not likely have obtained terms as favorable as it gets by borrowing in dollars and using its relationship with GSI to save some money on the conversion of dollars to euros. GSI is a subsidiary of a large global bank and can use its contacts, reputation, and expertise to operate on behalf of Reston in the international markets. GSI will hedge whatever risk it assumes.

Another reason why Reston might get better terms by borrowing in dollars and swapping into euros rather than borrowing in euros is that it assumes some credit risk resulting from the possibility that GSI might default. If GSI defaults, Reston would still have to make the dollar payments on its loan. If Reston borrowed in euros, it would have no

MAKING THE CONNECTION

Valuing a Currency Swap as a Series of Currency Forward Contracts

In Chapters 8 and 10, we learned about currency forward contracts, in which one party agrees to pay a certain amount of money in one currency at a future date, while the other agrees to pay a certain amount of money in another currency on that same date. Thus, the two parties have implicitly agreed to exchange a given amount of two currencies at a fixed rate at a future date. A currency swap is similar to a currency forward contract, but there are important differences. First, there is a *series* of exchanges of currency as opposed to a single exchange. Thus, a currency swap can be viewed as a combination of several currency forward contracts. Second, a currency forward contract is priced using the interest rates in the two countries and the exchange rate such that the contract will have zero value at the start. A currency swap is a series of payments in which the *overall* value is zero. Some of the component payments do not, however, have zero value.

Let us take a look at how a currency swap can be viewed as a series of currency forward contracts using the Reston-GSI currency swap we discuss in this chapter. Recall that the swap calls for Reston to pay euros to GSI and receive dollars from GSI. The notional amount is $9,804,000 and €10,000,000, which is based on the exchange rate of $0.9804. The term structures and associated information are repeated in the table below. Recall that we found the dollar rate as 6.1 percent and the euro rate as 4.35 percent. The payments were obtained as follows:

Dollar payments:

$$9,804,000(0.061)\left(\frac{180}{360}\right) = 299,022.$$

Euro payments:

$$10,000,000(0.0435)\left(\frac{180}{360}\right) = 217,500.$$

Term	Dollar Rate	Discount Bond Price
180 days	5.5%	$B_0^\$(180) = 1/(1 - 0.055(180/360)) = 0.9732$
360 days	5.5%	$B_0^\$(360) = 1/(1 - 0.055(360/360)) = 0.9479$
540 days	6.2%	$B_0^\$(540) = 1/(1 - 0.062(540/360)) = 0.9149$
720 days	6.4%	$B_0^\$(720) = 1/(1 - 0.064(720/360)) = 0.8865$

Term	Euro Rate	Discount Bond Price
180 days	3.8%	$B_0^{€}(180) = 1/(1 - 0.038(180/360)) = 0.9814$
360 days	4.2%	$B_0^{€}(360) = 1/(1 - 0.042(360/360)) = 0.9597$
540 days	4.4%	$B_0^{€}(540) = 1/(1 - 0.044(540/360)) = 0.9381$
720 days	4.5%	$B_0^{€}(720) = 1/(1 - 0.045(720/360)) = 0.9174$

credit risk, because it would not be receiving any payments from another party. For assuming this credit risk, Reston may be able to obtain a better rate.

Another possible use of a currency swap is in hedging a stream of foreign cash flows. Suppose that a firm expects to receive a stream of equivalent cash flows from its foreign operations. As we have discussed in previous chapters, it could use options, forwards, or futures to hedge the conversion of that stream into its domestic currency. But swaps can also be used. In this case, however, the firm would prefer a currency swap that does not involve the payment of notional amount.

For example, consider a firm called FXI with a Swiss subsidiary that generates annual cash flows of SF20 million, which are converted into dollars on the last day of the year.

Thus, the streams of payments for Reston are as follows:

Four payments at 180, 360, 540, and 720 days:
  Pay €217,500
  Receive $299,022
One payment at 720 days:
  Pay €10,000,000
  Receive $9,804,000

Let us treat these payments as forward contracts and find their market values. We shall, however, need to know the forward rates for the euro in terms of dollars. In Chapter 9, we learned how interest rate parity provides the forward rate based on the spot rate compounded at the domestic interest rate and discounted at the foreign interest rate. These forward rates are as follows:

180-day forward rate:

$$\$0.9804\left(\frac{1+0.055(180/360)}{1+0.038(180/360)}\right) = \$0.9886.$$

360-day forward rate:

$$\$0.9804\left(\frac{1+0.055(360/360)}{1+0.042(360/360)}\right) = \$0.9926.$$

540-day forward rate:

$$\$0.9804\left(\frac{1+0.062(540/360)}{1+0.044(540/360)}\right) = \$1.0052.$$

720-day forward rate:

$$\$0.9804\left(\frac{1+0.064(720/360)}{1+0.045(720/360)}\right) = \$1.0146.$$

Now we can find the market values of the forward contracts that are implicitly contained within the swap. The swap consists of either four or five payments, depending on how one views the last payment. Recall that the last payment is an interest payment and a notional amount payment. These

could be combined, but here we shall treat them as separate payments.

The values of the implicit forward contracts contained within the swap are as follows:

First forward contract, expiring in 180 days:

($299,022 – €217,500($0.9886))0.9732
  = $81,750.

Second forward contract, expiring in 360 days:

($299,022 – €217,500($0.9926))0.9479
  = $78,800.

Third forward contract, expiring in 540 days:

($299,022 – €217,500($1.0052))0.9149
  = $73,550.

Fourth forward contract, expiring in 720 days:

($299,022 – €217,500($1.0146))0.8865
  = $69,455.

Fifth forward contract, expiring in 720 days:

($9,804,000 – €10,000,000($1.0146))0.8865
  = –$303,183.

The sum of these values is $372, which is effectively zero (only 0.004% of the notional amount) but is not precisely zero only because of rounding many of these input values. Thus, the swap consists of five implicit forward contracts, the first four having positive value and the last having negative value that offsets and effectively makes the overall transaction have a value of zero. Ordinarily, if a party constructed five currency forwards, the rates on these contracts would be set individually according to the term structure and the forward exchange rates. In a currency swap, the implicit forward contracts are treated as a package with the payments made at the same rate. A currency swap is more efficient than a group of individual currency forward contracts, because it combines into a single transaction what would otherwise take five transactions.

FXI would like to hedge the conversion of these cash flows into dollars for the next five years. In our previous treatment of currency swaps, we did not cover the pricing of currency swaps that do not involve the exchange of notional amounts. This procedure is only slightly harder and simply requires the omission of the notional amount and the calculation of forward rates. Let us just assume that the fixed rate for such a swap is 5 percent for Swiss francs and 6 percent for dollars. The exchange rate is $0.65. The swap will consist of annual payments.

To generate an annual swap payment of SF20 million if the fixed rate is 5 percent would require a notional amount of SF20,000,000/(0.05) = SF400 million. This notional

FIGURE 12.9 **Example of a Currency Swap**
Scenario: Reston issues a loan of $9.804 million at 6.5 percent with interest paid semiannually for two years. Reston prefers to borrow in euros so it enters into a currency swap with GSI for £10 million and $9.804 million. Payments are made semiannually at 6.1 percent in dollars and 4.35 percent in euros. Notional amount payments are exchanged up front and at the termination date of the swap.

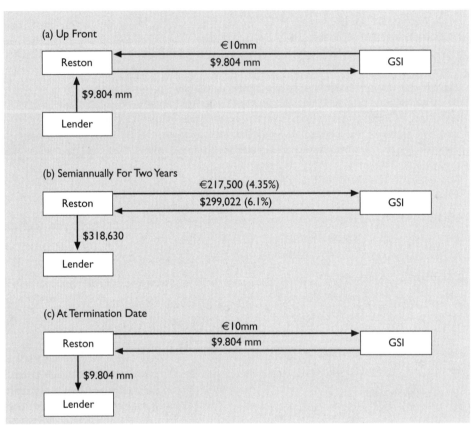

amount converts to a dollar notional amount of SF400,000,000($0.65) = $260 million. The dollar swap payments would, therefore, be $260,000,000(0.06) = $15,600,000.

Thus, FXI enters into a swap with notional amount of SF400 million and $260 million. The swap will require FXI to pay the counterparty SF400,000,000(0.05) = SF20 million, which will come from its subsidiary's cash flows. The counterparty will pay FXI $260,000,000(0.06) = $15,600,000. Thus, FXI has locked in the conversion of its Swiss franc cash flows to dollars. Of course, FXI bears the risk that its cash flows will deviate from SF20 million, but of course, it would face that risk whether it uses swaps, options, forwards, or futures.

The third type of swap we study in this chapter is the equity swap.

EQUITY SWAPS

In an equity swap, at least one of the two streams of cash flows is determined by a stock price, the value of a stock portfolio, or the level of a stock index. The other stream of cash flows can be a fixed rate or a floating rate such as LIBOR, or it can be determined by the value of another stock, stock portfolio, or stock index. In this manner, an equity

An equity swap is a swap in which the two parties agree to exchange a series of payments, at least one of which is determined by the return on a stock, stock portfolio, or stock index.

swap can substitute for trading in an individual stock, stock portfolio, or stock index. In this section, we shall just refer to the underlying equity as a stock, which could represent an individual stock, a stock portfolio, or a stock index.

Equity swaps are certainly similar to interest rate and currency swaps, but they also differ notably. One difference is that the swap payment is determined by the return on the stock. Because stock returns can be negative, the swap payment can be negative. That is, suppose party A agrees to pay party B the return on the underlying stock. Suppose that at a given payment date, the return on the stock is negative. Then party A effectively owes a negative return. This means that party B would have to pay the return to party A. Unless party B also owes a negative return, party B will end up making both payments.

Another way in which equity swaps differ from interest rate and currency swaps is the fact that the upcoming equity payment is never known. The upcoming floating payment in an interest rate or currency swap is always known, and of course, a fixed payment would always be known. In an equity swap, however, the equity return is not determined until the end of the settlement period, which of course is when the payment is due.

Finally, we should note that there is no adjustment such as days/360 for the equity payment on an equity swap.[11] It is determined strictly as the return on the stock over a given period, and no such adjustment is required.

Structure of a Typical Equity Swap

For an equity swap in which a party pays the return on the stock and receives a fixed rate, the cash flow will be

$$(\text{Notional Amount})((\text{Fixed rate})q - \text{Return on stock over settlement period}).$$

Consider an investment management company called IVM. It wants to enter into an equity swap to pay the return on the Standard & Poor's 500 Total Return Index and receive a fixed rate. This index includes the effect of reinvesting dividends.[12] On the day the swap is arranged, the index is at 2,710.55. The swap will call for payments every 90 days for a 360-day period. Financial Swaps (FNS), the dealer, offers IVM a fixed rate of 3.45 percent with payments calculated on the basis of 90 days divided by 360. The notional amount will be $25 million. Let us treat the payment dates as day 90, day 180, day 270, and day 360. The initial day is day 0. Let S_0, S_{90}, etc., be the S&P 500 Total Return Index on day 0, day 90, and so forth. The cash flow to IVM on the settlement date will be

$$\$25,000,000 \left(0.0345 \left(\frac{90}{360} \right) - \text{Return on stock over settlement period} \right).$$

Obviously the fixed component of the payment will be

$$\$25,000,000(0.0345) \left(\frac{90}{360} \right) = \$215,625.$$

Table 12.8 contains an example of the payments that might occur on such a swap. Keep in mind that these are hypothetical results, based on assumptions about the course of the

---

[11]Of course, if the other side of the transaction makes a fixed or floating interest payment, the (days/360 or 365) adjustment is required.

[12]The concept of a total return means that it includes capital gains and dividends. Most standard stock indices reflect only the prices of the component stocks, and, thus, incorporate only capital gains.

TABLE 12.8 AFTER-THE-FACT PAYMENTS IN EQUITY SWAP TO PAY S&P 500 TOTAL RETURN INDEX AND RECEIVE A FIXED RATE OF 3.45 PERCENT

DAY	FIXED INTEREST PAYMENT	S&P TOTAL RETURN INDEX	S&P PAYMENT	NET PAYMENT
0		2,710.55		
90	$215,625	2,764.90	$501,282	−$285,657
180	215,625	2,653.65	−1,005,913	1,221,538
270	215,625	2,805.20	1,427,750	−1,212,125
360	215,625	2,705.95	−864,518	1,100,143

Note: This combination of outcomes on the above dates represents only one of an infinite number of possible outcomes to the swap. They are used only to illustrate how the payments are determined and not the likely results.

S&P 500 Total Return Index. The parties to the swap do not know what these payments will be when the swap is initiated.

Let us determine the first equity payment. When the swap is initiated on day 0, the S&P 500 Total Return Index is at 2,710.55. On day 90, the index is at 2,764.90. The equity payment would, therefore, be

$$\$25,000,000 \left(\frac{2,764.90}{2,710.55} - 1 \right) = \$501,282.$$

In other words, the rate of return on the Index is $(2,764.90/2,710.55) - 1 = 0.02005$, or about 2 percent. Multiplied by $25,000,000 (retaining full decimal accuracy) gives a payment of $501,282. Thus, for the first payment, IVM owes $501,282 and is due $215,625, for a net payment of −$285,657. So IVM pays the dealer $285,657.

For the second payment, IVM still receives $215,625. Note that the S&P 500 Total Return Index fell to 2,653.65, a return of $(2,653.65/2,764.90) - 1 = -0.0402$, or −4.02 percent, which amounts to $1,005,913. Now, IVM owes a negative return on the stock, which means that the counterparty pays IVM. So IVM is due a cash flow of $215,625 − (−$1,005,913) = $1,221,538.

Of course, IVM could have constructed the swap so that it received a floating payment based on LIBOR. In that case, the calculations would be similar to those above, except that LIBOR on day 0 would determine the interest payment on day 90, LIBOR on day 90 would determine the interest payment on day 180, etc. The payoff formula would be

(Notional Amount) ((LIBOR)q − Return on stock over settlement period).

Alternatively, IVM could have constructed the swap to involve payment of the return on the S&P 500 Total Return Index and receipt of the return on some other stock index.

(Notional Amount) (Return on one stock index − Return on other stock index).

Suppose for example, that IVM wanted to receive the return on the NASDAQ Index. Then the interest payment it receives in the example above would be replaced with the return on the NASDAQ Index, which would be computed in the same manner as the return on the S&P 500 Total Return Index. When we examine equity swap strategies, we shall take a look at why these different types of swaps would be used.

Pricing and Valuation of Equity Swaps

We shall now look at the pricing and valuation of the three types of equity swaps: a swap involving an equity return vs. a fixed rate, a swap involving an equity return vs. a floating rate, and a swap involving one equity return vs. another equity return.

We start with the swap to pay a fixed rate and receive the equity return. The fixed rate is denoted as R, and the notional amount is $1. To determine the value of the swap, we need to construct a strategy that will replicate the payments on the equity swap. We can do this quite easily.

- Invest $1 in the stock.
- Issue a $1 face value loan with an interest rate of R. Pay interest on each of the swap settlement dates and repay the notional amount at the swap termination date. Interest payments will be calculated on the basis of days/360.

We shall use the symbol q for (days/360).

Let us now see why this strategy works. Suppose we execute the above transactions for the purpose of replicating a one-year swap with semiannual payments on days 180 and 360. Then,

on day 180, we would have stock worth S_{180}/S_0, and
we would owe Rq.

Suppose we sell the stock and withdraw only the return, $S_{180}/S_0 - 1$, which can be positive or negative. If the return is positive, we have a cash inflow. If it is negative, we have a cash outflow. Combined with the interest payment, the overall net cash flow is $S_{180}/S_0 - 1 - Rq$. This is precisely the payment on the swap. Because we withdrew only the return from the stock sale, we have $1 left over, which we reinvest in the stock. Now let us proceed to the next period.

On day 360, the stock would be worth S_{360}/S_{180}. We pay back the loan principal of $1 and the interest of Rq. We liquidate the stock. Then the net cash flow would be $S_{360}/S_{180} - 1 - Rq$. This is precisely the cash flow on the swap. Thus, this strategy replicates the equity swap. In general, for a swap with n payments, the strategy will cost $1 to buy the stock, which is offset by the cash flow from the loan. The overall cost to establish the position is the value of the position when it is established.

$$1 - B_0(t_n) - Rq\sum_{i=1}^{n} B_0(t_i).$$

The first term, 1, is the $1 invested in the stock. The second term, $-B_0(t_n)$, is the loan principal due on day t_n. The term with the summation is the present value of the series of loan interest payments of Rq on each swap payment date.

Because the swap is established so that its value at the start is zero, we set the above equation to zero and solve for R:

Pricing an equity swap means finding the fixed rate that will be paid against the equity return. The fixed rate is found using a strategy consisting of a stock and a loan that replicates the equity swap payments. This fixed rate is the same as the fixed rate on a plain vanilla swap.

$$R = \left(\frac{1}{q}\right)\left(\frac{1 - B_0(t_n)}{\sum_{i=1}^{n} B_0(t_i)}\right).$$

Interestingly, this rate is the same rate as the fixed rate on a plain vanilla swap. This should make sense. The swap is designed to equate the present value of the equity payments with the present value of the fixed interest payments. Because we start off by investing $1 in the stock, the present value of the equity payments is $1. To make the present

---

TABLE 12.9 PRICING AN EQUITY SWAP

IVM enters into an equity swap to receive a fixed rate and pay the return on the S&P 500 Total Return Index. The payments will be quarterly for one year with interest calculated using the adjustment factor 90/360. The term structure is as follows:

TERM	RATE	DISCOUNT BOND PRICE
90 days	$L_0(90) = 3\%$	$B_0(90) = 1/(1 + 0.03(90/360)) = 0.9926$
180 days	$L_0(180) = 3.2\%$	$B_0(180) = 1/(1 + 0.032(180/360)) = 0.9843$
270 days	$L_0(270) = 3.3\%$	$B_0(270) = 1/(1 + 0.033(270/360)) = 0.9758$
360 days	$L_0(360) = 3.5\%$	$B_0(360) = 1/(1 + 0.035(360/360)) = 0.9662$

With $q = 90/360$, then $1/q = 360/90$, and the fixed rate would, therefore, be

$$R = \left(\frac{360}{90}\right)\left(\frac{1-0.9622}{0.9926 + 0.9843 + 0.9758 + 0.9662}\right) = 0.0345.$$

Thus, the rate would be 3.45 percent.

---

value of the fixed interest payments equal $1, we need only set the payments at the fixed rate on a plain vanilla swap. Table 12.9 shows how the IVM swap is valued.

Now let us consider a time during the life of the swap at which we want to determine the value of the swap. Assume that this is before the first payment date. The problem will be a little simpler if we look at it from the standpoint of the party receiving the equity return and paying the fixed rate. On the first payment day, we shall receive an equity payment of $S_{90}/S_0 - 1$. We could replicate this payment by purchasing $1/S_0$ shares, currently at S_t, which will cost $(1/S_0)S_t$. At the next payment date, we will have stock worth $(1/S_0)S_{90}$.[13] We sell this stock, generating a cash flow of $(1/S_0)S_t - 1$, which could be positive or negative, plus the $1 left over, which we reinvest into the stock. This will replicate the stock payment the next period. This procedure continues throughout the life of the swap and will leave $1 at the end. Thus, to replicate the cash flows, we do the following:

- Invest $(1/S_0)S_t$, which equals S_t/S_0, in the stock. Liquidate and reinvest as described.
- Issue a $1 loan at an interest rate of R, with interest to be paid on each of the swap settlement dates and the notional amount to be repaid at the swap termination date. Interest payments will be calculated on the basis of $q =$ days/360.

This strategy will replicate the payments on the swap. The cost to establish this strategy is

$$\left(\frac{S_t}{S_0}\right) - B_t(t_n) - Rq\sum_{i=1}^{n} B_t(t_i).$$

> The value of an equity swap can be found by finding the value of a portfolio of a stock and a loan that replicates the payments on the swap.

The first term is the investment in stock necessary to replicate the equity cash flows. The second is the present value of the repayment of the loan principal at the swap termination date, and third is the present value of the set of payments of Rq on each of the swap settlement dates.

Let us apply the formula to our example of the IVM swap. Suppose it is 60 days into the life of the swap. Table 12.10 presents a set of new interest rates and the value of the equity swap at this time.

---

[13]This expression is $1/S_0$ shares worth S_{90} per share.

TABLE 12.10 VALUING AN EQUITY SWAP DURING ITS LIFE

We are now 60 days into the life of the IVM swap. The new term structure is as follows:

TERM	RATE	DISCOUNT BOND PRICE
30 days	$L_{60}(30) = 3.50\%$	$B_{60}(30) = 1/(1 + 0.035(30/360)) = 0.9971$
120 days	$L_{60}(120) = 3.75\%$	$B_{60}(120) = 1/(1 + 0.0375(120/360)) = 0.9877$
210 days	$L_{60}(210) = 3.90\%$	$B_{60}(210) = 1/(1 + 0.039(210/360)) = 0.9778$
300 days	$L_{60}(300) = 4.00\%$	$B_{60}(300) = 1/(1 + 0.04(300/360)) = 0.9677$

The stock index is at 2,739.60. Thus, the value of the swap per $1 notional amount is

$$\left(\frac{2{,}739.60}{2{,}710.55}\right) - 0.9677 - 0.0345\left(\frac{90}{360}\right)(0.9971 + 0.9877 + 0.9788 + 0.9677) = 0.00911854.$$

This formulation, however, is from the perspective of the party paying the fixed rate and receiving the equity return. So to IVM, the value is actually -0.00911854 per $1 notional amount. Thus, for a notional amount of $25 million, the value of the swap is

$$\$25{,}000{,}000(-0.00911854) = -227{,}964.$$

Now suppose we are interested in an equity swap with floating payments. We know that at the start, the present value of the fixed payments (including a notional amount of 1) at the rate R is 1 and that this equals the present value if the payments were floating (including the notional amount). Thus, the value of a swap involving the payment of the equity return against floating payments is zero at the start, as it should be. To value the swap during its life, notice that we can replicate the equity swap involving floating payments by doing the following:

- Enter into an equity swap to pay the equity return and receive a fixed rate.
- Enter into a plain vanilla swap to pay a fixed rate and receive a floating rate.

The fixed payments would cancel, and this would net out to an equity swap to pay the equity return and receive a floating rate. We have already valued the equity swap to pay the equity return and receive a fixed rate and obtained a value of $-\$227{,}964$. We now need only value a plain vanilla swap to pay a fixed rate and receive the floating rate. Recall that we learned this earlier in the chapter. Using the information in Table 12.10, the value of the fixed payments, plus hypothetical notional amount, is

$$0.0345\left(\frac{90}{360}\right)(0.9971 + 0.9877 + 0.9778 + 0.9677) + 1.0(0.9677) = 1.00159884.$$

Recall from our examination of interest rate swaps that we value the floating payments as the present value of the upcoming floating payment plus the par value of 1. The upcoming floating payment is at 3 percent. Thus, the value of the floating payments plus hypothetical notional amount is

$$\left(1 + 0.03\left(\frac{90}{360}\right)\right)0.9971 = 1.00457825.$$

Thus, the value of a plain vanilla swap to pay fixed and receive floating is

$$1.00457825 - 1.00159884 = 0.00297941.$$

For a $25 million notional amount, this value is

$$\$25,000,000(0.00297941) = \$74,485.$$

So the value of the equity swap to pay the equity return and receive a floating payment is

$$-\$227,964 + \$74,485 = -\$153,479.$$

If the swap involves the payment of one equity return for another, we must develop a new strategy for replicating the payments. Let $S_0(1)$ be the value of stock index 1 on day 0 and $S_0(2)$ be the value of stock index 2 on day 0. We then change the subscript to reflect later days in the life of the swap. Assume that we pay the return on stock index 2 and receive the return on stock index 1 with payments on days 180, 360, etc. The first cash flow on the swap will be $(S_{180}(1)/S_0(1)) - 1 - (S_{180}(2)/S_0(2)) - 1) = S_{180}(1)/S_0(1) - S_{180}(2)/S_0(2)$. The remaining cash flows will be done in a similar manner, changing the time subscripts to 360 from 180 and so forth.

To replicate the swap, we sell short $1 of stock index 2, take the proceeds, and buy $1 of stock index 1. This will require no money of our own. At time 1, we sell stock index 1, generating cash of $S_{180}(1)/S_0(1)$. We withdraw the cash return, $(S_{180}(1)/S_0(1)) - 1$ and reinvest $1 in stock index 1. We cover the short sale of stock index 2 by buying back the stock. This will require an outlay of $S_{180}(2)/S_0(2)$. We then sell short $1 of stock index 2, so our net flow from the transaction in stock index 2 is $-(S_{180}(2)/S_0(2) - 1)$. The overall net cash flow is $S_{180}(1)/S_0(1) - S_{180}(2)/S_0(2)$, which is the cash flow from the swap. We now move forward with $1 invested in stock index 1 and $1 sold short of stock index 2. If we proceed in this manner, we will generate the cash flows on the swap. Because there is no cost to establishing the position, the value of the swap is zero at the start, as it should be.

It is very simple to value this type of swap during its life. We value it as a position of being long in one stock and short the other. Suppose in the IVM example that we change the fixed payment that IVM will receive to be the return on the NASDAQ stock index. Let the index be 1,835.24 at the start of the transaction. Sixty days later, the index is at 1,915.71. Then the value of the swap is easily found as

$$\left(\frac{1,915.71}{1,835.24}\right) - \left(\frac{2,739.60}{2,710.55}\right) = 0.03312974.$$

For a $25 million notional amount swap, the value is

$$\$25,000,000(0.03312974) = \$828,244.$$

Equity Swap Strategies

Equity swaps are useful strategies for equity investors. An equity swap to pay a fixed rate and receive the equity return is essentially equivalent to issuing a fixed-rate bond and using the proceeds to buy stock. An equity swap to pay a floating rate and receive the equity return is essentially the same as issuing a floating-rate bond and using the proceeds to buy stock. An equity swap to pay the return on one stock index and receive the return on another is essentially the same as selling short one stock and using the proceeds to buy another. Of course, certain transactions are required at the payment dates, so these swap strategies are not identical to buying and holding stock. In addition, the payments required on equity swaps make them a form of buying stocks using leverage. Nonetheless, equity swaps are very similar to stock transactions and can serve as valuable substitutes for stock transactions, as is the case for virtually any equity derivative.

Equity swaps are primarily used to execute synthetic transactions in equity. Instead of buying or selling stock, a party can engage in an equity swap, thereby effectively buying or selling the stock without actually doing a transaction in the stock itself.

Going back to the IVM strategy, recall that IVM is an asset management company. It holds a portfolio of stock. In some cases, it needs to make adjustments to its portfolio. These adjustments typically involve buying and selling stock. As we have seen throughout this book, assets can be bought and sold synthetically using derivatives. In this case, a company such as IVM could use an equity swap to synthetically replicate the sale of stock and purchase of another asset. Suppose IVM wants to sell some domestic large-cap stock and buy a fixed-rate bond. Then it might enter into an equity swap to pay the return on an index of domestic large-cap stock, such as the S&P 500 Total Return Index, and receive a fixed return. The swap we described earlier is precisely this type of transaction. A diagram of the overall transaction is shown in Figure 12.10. In doing the transaction, IVM effectively sells domestic large-cap stock, as represented by the S&P 500 Total Return Index, and converts to a fixed-rate bond paying 3.45 percent.

You should be aware, however, that IVM assumes some risk in this transaction. Besides the aforementioned fact that the swap dealer could default, there are two other important risks. One is that the performance of the domestic, large-cap stock portfolio will not precisely match the performance of the S&P 500 Total Return Index. This is a form of basis risk, similar to the risk we discussed in using futures. In the investment management field, this risk is usually referred to as **tracking error**, meaning the risk that the index on which the derivative is based will not track the underlying portfolio. Obviously, this risk is not new to us. It applies anytime a derivative on an index is used with a portfolio that does not precisely match the index.

Another risk is that if the swap generates net cash outflows, the firm must produce the cash to make the swap payments. While the portfolio could be earning a sufficiently high return, that return is likely to include some unrealized capital gains. If there is not sufficient cash to make the swap payment, the firm could be forced to sell some stock to generate the cash. This would then defeat the purpose of using the swap, which was to avoid selling the stock in the first place. Thus, to use an equity swap, a firm would need to take into account the potential for cash outflows and would need to set aside a liquidity pool.

As we have noted, variations of this strategy include having the interest payment be at a floating rate. In that case, the strategy would be approximately equivalent to selling

FIGURE 12.10 Equity Swap of IVM to Exchange the Return on Domestic Large-Cap Stock for a Fixed Return

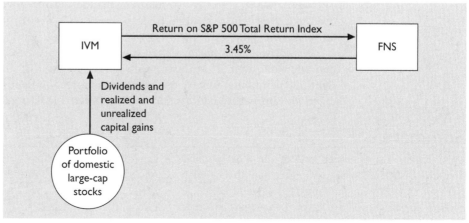

stock and investing the proceeds in a floating-rate bond. If the firm wanted to sell the stock and buy a floating-rate bond, this type of equity swap would be a good substitute.

Alternatively, if the firm did a swap in which it pays the return on the S&P 500 and the dealer pays it the return on another index, such as the NASDAQ index, the firm would be synthetically selling stock as represented by the S&P 500 and buying stock as represented by the NASDAQ index.

SOME FINAL WORDS ABOUT SWAPS

We began the chapter by mentioning that swaps are like combinations of forward contracts. This is an important analogy, but it applies only to swaps that involve fixed payments, as in forward contracts. For swaps with strictly floating payments, the analogy breaks down. Moreover, for swaps with fixed payments, the analogy is only partial. For example, if a party engaged in a series of currency forward contracts, the forward rate would be different for each expiration. After all, forward prices and rates nearly always differ by maturity. A currency swap with fixed payments would involve payments at the same rate.

Because swaps are similar to forward contracts, swaps will also be similar to futures contracts. In addition, swaps can be shown to be similar to combinations of options. In the next chapter, we shall look at interest rate options and show how they can be combined to replicate interest rate swaps.

Swaps are nearly always designed with the intention of holding the position until the termination date. In some cases, a party changes its mind and wants out of the swap. There are a number of ways it can exit a swap. The primary way is to go back to the dealer and ask to terminate the swap or enter an offsetting swap. In effect, the parties would do the opposite swap and cancel the original swap. For example, recall the Quantum Electronics plain vanilla swap in which it paid a fixed rate and received LIBOR. Ninety days into its life, the market value to Quantum was −$24,816. If Quantum wanted to terminate the swap, it could go back to the dealer and ask for an offset. The dealer would do so if Quantum would pay the market value of $24,816. The swap would then be eliminated. Alternatively, Quantum could go to another dealer and ask for a quote on a swap to pay floating and receive fixed. If Quantum executed this transaction, it would have two swaps in place, with one paying LIBOR and the other receiving LIBOR. The LIBOR effects would offset, although both swaps would remain in force. Quantum would be paying one fixed rate and receiving another. The present value of the difference in these two swaps would be −$24,816, which is precisely the market value of the original swap. With both swaps in force, however, credit risk would remain, and Quantum would be better off (unless it wanted the credit risk) to go back to the original dealer, pay the market value, and terminate the swap.

Another way to terminate a swap is with either a forward contract on the swap or an option on the swap. These instruments give a party either a firm commitment or the right to enter into an offsetting swap at terms agreed to in advance. These instruments, called forward swaps and swaptions, will be covered in Chapter 13.

Summary

This chapter has examined one of the most popular financial instruments, the swap. We saw that a swap is a transaction in which two parties agree to exchange a series of cash flows. We learned that there are four general types of swaps, based on the nature of the underlying: currency, interest rate, equity, and commodity. In this book, we cover only currency, interest rate, and equity swaps.

We examined the basic characteristics of these swaps. We then covered how to price the swap and how to determine its market value. We saw that pricing a swap entails identifying a strategy using other instruments that replicate the cash flows from the swap. The value of the swap is then equivalent to the value of the replicating transaction. The price of the swap, which refers to the fixed rate for swaps involving a fixed payment, is found by forcing the value to equal zero at the start of the transaction. For swaps that do not involve a fixed payment, there is no initial pricing, but we must verify that the values of the two streams of payments are the same.

We also examined some strategies using these types of swaps. As with all derivatives, swaps are used to adjust a position by taking on or eliminating risk. They substitute for transactions in the underlying and do so at much lower cost. For all we have seen, however, we have taken only a brief look at the ways in which swaps can be used.

The most widely used swap is the interest rate swap, specifically the plain vanilla interest rate swap. The reason for the popularity of interest rate swaps is that interest rate risk is faced by all businesses, whereas currency risk is directly faced only by businesses with multinational operations or whose operations are affected by foreign competition. Equity risk is faced only by equity portfolio managers and by organizations with direct exposure in equity markets.

As widely used as interest rate swaps are, however, they are not the only instruments that can be used to manage interest rate risk. In Chapter 13, we examine some other types of derivatives based on interest rates. Interestingly, however, these new derivatives will still be just forwards and options, which are instruments we have already seen, but their characteristics are somewhat different from the forwards and options we have covered. In addition, we have not seen all we shall see of swaps. In Chapter 13, we shall examine options and forwards on swaps.

Key Terms

Before continuing to Chapter 13, you should be able to give brief definitions of the following terms:

swap/currency swaps/interest rate swaps/equity swaps/commodity swaps, p. 413
settlement date/settlement period/ notional amount, p. 414

plain vanilla swap, p. 416
basis swap, p. 418
swap spread, p. 423
index amortizing swap/diff swap, p. 428

constant maturity swap/CMT rate, p. 429
tracking error, p. 447

Further Reading

Swaps are widely covered in the following books:

Buetow, G. W., and F. J. Fabozzi. *Valuation of Interest Rate Swaps and Swaptions.* New Hope, PA: Frank J. Fabozzi Associates, 2001.

Burghardt, G., T. Belton, M. Lane, G. Luce, and R. McVey. *Eurodollar Futures and Options: Controlling Money Market Risk.* Chicago: Probus Publishing, 1991.

Flavell, R. *Swaps and Other Instruments,* 2nd ed. New York: Wiley, 2010.

Ludwig, M. S. *Understanding Interest Rate Swaps.* New York: McGraw-Hill, 1993.

Smithson, C. W. *Managing Financial Risk: A Guide to Derivative Products, Financial Engineering, and Value Maximization,* 3rd ed. New York: McGraw-Hill, 1998.

Important swap topics are also addressed in the following articles:

Brooks, R. "Approaches to Valuation Illustrated with Interest Rate Swaps." *Derivatives Quarterly* 4 (1998): 51–62.

Ching, J. "A Market Perspective on Interest Rate Swap Clearing and Execution." *Futures Industry* (June 2011): 28–34.

Cooper, I., and A. Mello. "The Default Risk of Swaps." *Journal of Finance* 46 (1991): 597–620.

Finnerty, J. D., and P. Kishlaya. "A Review of Recent Derivatives Litigation." *Fordham Journal of Corporate & Financial Law* 16 (2011): 73–123.

Hodgson, R. "The Birth of the Swap." *Financial Analysts Journal* 65 (2009): 32–35.

Concept Checks

1. Explain why interest rate swaps are more widely used than currency and equity swaps.
2. Why is notional amount often exchanged in a currency swap but not in an interest rate or equity swap? Why would the parties to a currency swap choose not to exchange the notional amount?
3. Explain how the following types of swaps are analogous to transactions in bonds.
   a. Interest rate swaps
   b. Currency swaps
4. Explain how swaps are similar to and different from forward contracts.
5. Suppose that a party engages in a swap, but before the expiration date of the swap, the party decides that it would like to terminate the position. Explain how it can do so.

Questions and Problems

1. An interest rate swap has two primary risks associated with it. Identify and explain each risk.
2. Define and explain a constant maturity swap.
3. Consider a $30 million notional amount interest rate swap with a fixed rate of 7 percent, paid quarterly on the basis of 90 days in the quarter and 360 days in the year. The first floating payment is set at 7.2 percent. Calculate the first net payment and identify which party, the party paying fixed or the party paying floating, pays.
4. Consider a currency swap for $10 million and SF_{15} million. One party pays dollars at a fixed rate of 9 percent, and the other pays Swiss francs at a fixed rate of 8 percent. The payments are made semiannually based on the exact day count and 360 days in a year. The current period has 181 days. Calculate the next payment each party makes.
5. Consider a $100 million equity swap with semiannual payments. When the swap is established, the underlying stock is at 1,215.52. One party pays a fixed rate of 5.5 percent based on the assumption of 30 days per month and 360 days in a year. If the stock index is at 1,275.89 on the first payment date, calculate the net swap payment, indicating which party pays it.
6. A swap dealer quotes that the rate on a plain vanilla swap, for it to pay fixed, is the five-year Treasury rate plus 10. To receive fixed, the dealer quotes the rate as the five-year Treasury rate plus 15. Assuming the five-year Treasury rate is 7.60 percent, explain what these quotes mean.
7. Explain how an interest rate swap is a special case of a currency swap.
8. Show how to combine a currency swap paying Swiss francs at a floating rate and receiving Japanese yen at a floating rate with another currency swap to obtain a plain vanilla swap paying Swiss francs at a floating rate and receiving Swiss francs at a fixed rate.
9. A bank currently holds a loan with a principal of $12 million. The loan generates quarterly interest payments at a rate of LIBOR plus 300 basis points, with the payments made on the 15th of February, May, August, and November on the basis of the actual day count divided by 360. The bank has begun to believe that interest rates will fall. It would like to use a swap to synthetically alter the payments on the loan it holds. The rate it could obtain on a plain vanilla swap is 7.25 percent. Explain how the bank would use a swap to achieve this objective.
10. Suppose a trader has entered two $50 million notional amount interest rate swaps both with a fixed rate of 3 percent, paid quarterly on the basis of 90 days in the quarter and 360 days in the year. The first swap is a receive fixed and pay three-month LIBOR swap. The second swap is a receive three-month U.S. Treasury bill + 35 basis points and pay fixed swap. Explain the net cash flows from this portfolio as well as identify the market risk.
11. Suppose a trader has entered two $15 million notional amount equity swaps both with a fixed rate of 6 percent, paid quarterly on the basis of 90 days in the quarter and 360 days in the year. The first swap is a receive fixed and pay three-month total return on Apple, Inc. The second swap is a receive three-month total return on Microsoft, Inc., and pay fixed swap. Explain the net cash flows from this portfolio as well as identify the market risk.

12. Suppose you are a municipal finance director for a large metropolitan city. Based on your asset-liability analysis, you determine that your rate-sensitive assets are equivalent to a one-year LIBOR deposit and your rate-sensitive liabilities are equivalent to a ten-year LIBOR deposit. Also, the assets earn the fully taxable interest rate, whereas the liabilities are all tax exempt. At the moment, based on differences in interest rates, you expect to lose about 1 percent. That is, the assets will earn about 1 percent below the liabilities. How might interest rate swaps assist in lowering the interest rate risk and decrease the expected losses?

13. The U.K. manager of an international bond portfolio would like to synthetically sell a large position in a French government bond, denominated in euros. The bond is selling at its par value of €46.15 million, which is equivalent to £30 million at the current exchange rate of £0.65. The bond pays interest at a fixed rate of 5.2 percent annually for ten years. The manager would like to sell the bond and invest the proceeds in a pound-denominated floating-rate bond. Design a currency swap strategy that would achieve the desired objective and identify the payments that would occur on the overall position, which includes both the French bond and the swap. The fixed rates on the currency swap are 4.9 percent in pounds and 5.7 percent in euros.

14. The CEO of a large corporation holds a position of 25 million shares in her company's stock, which is currently priced at $20 and pays no dividends. She is concerned that because of her large shareholdings and the fact that her compensation is tied to the performance of the stock, she is very poorly diversified. She does not think it is wise to sell a significant amount of stock, because she knows that she needs to be heavily invested in the stock to satisfy the shareholders, and she values the voting rights she has from owning so many shares. Nonetheless, she would be interested in synthetically selling about five million shares using an equity swap. Assume the role of a swap dealer and present three possible equity swap proposals based on the three different types of cash flows that could be paid against payment of the return on the stock.

15. A corporation enters into a $35 million notional amount interest rate swap. The swap calls for the corporation to pay a fixed rate and receive a floating rate of LIBOR. The payments will be made every 90 days for one year and will be based on the adjustment factor 90/360. The term structure of LIBOR when the swap is initiated is as follows:

Days	Rate
90	7.00%
180	7.25
270	7.45
360	7.55

a. Determine the fixed rate on the swap.
b. Calculate the first net payment on the swap.
c. Assume that it is now 30 days into the life of the swap. The new term structure of LIBOR is as follows:

Days	Rate
60	6.80%
150	7.05
240	7.15
330	7.20

Calculate the value of the swap.

16. A U.S. corporation is considering entering into a currency swap that will call for the firm to pay dollars and receive British pounds. The dollar notional amount will be $35 million. The swap will call for semiannual payments using the adjustment 180/360. The exchange rate is $1.60. The term structures of dollar LIBOR and pound LIBOR are as follows:

Days	Dollar LIBOR	Pound LIBOR
180	7.00%	6.50%
360	7.25	7.10
540	7.45	7.50
720	7.55	8.00

Answer the following questions.

a. Determine the appropriate pound notional amount. Use this result in each of the remaining questions.

b. Determine the fixed rates in dollars and in pounds.

c. For each of the following cases, determine the first payment on the swap:
   i.   Dollars fixed, pounds fixed
   ii. Dollars fixed, pounds floating
   iii. Dollars floating, pounds floating
   iv. Dollars floating, pounds fixed

d. Now assume it is 120 days into the life of the swap. The new exchange rate is $1.42. The new term structures are as follows:

Days	Dollar LIBOR	Pound LIBOR
60	6.80%	6.40%
240	7.05	6.90
420	7.15	7.30
600	7.20	7.45

Determine the value of the swap for each of the following cases:
   i.   Dollars fixed, pounds fixed
   ii. Dollars fixed, pounds floating
   iii. Dollars floating, pounds floating
   iv. Dollars floating, pounds fixed

17. A pension fund wants to enter into a six-month equity swap with a notional amount of $60 million. Payments will occur in 90 and 180 days. The swap will allow the fund to receive the return on a stock index, currently at 5,514.67. The fund is considering three different types of swaps—one of which would require it to pay a fixed rate; another that would require it to pay floating rate; and another that would require it to pay the return on another stock index, which is currently at 1,212.98. Refer to these as swaps 1, 2, and 3. The term structure is as follows:

Term	Rate	Discount Bond Price
90 days	9%	$B_0(90) = 1/(1 + 0.09(90/360)) = 0.9780$
180 days	10	$B_0(180) = 1/(1 + 0.10(180/360)) = 0.9524$

a. Find the fixed rate for swap 1.

b. Find the payments on day 90 for swaps 1, 2, and 3. For swap 3, assume that on day 90, stock index 1 is at 5,609.81 and stock index 2 is at 1,231.94. Be sure to indicate the net payment.

c. Assume it is 30 days into the life of the swap. Stock index 1 is at 5,499.62, and stock index 2 is at 1,201.45. The new term structure is as follows:

Term	Rate	Discount Bond Price
60	6.80%	$B_{30}(90) = 1/(1 + 0.068(60/360)) = 0.9888$
150	7.05	$B_{30}(180) = 1/(1 + 0.0705(150/360)) = 0.9715$

Find the values of swaps 1, 2, and 3.

18. You are a pension fund manager who anticipates having to pay out 8 percent (paid semiannually) on $100 million for the next seven years. You currently hold $100 million of a floating-rate note that pays LIBOR + 2 1/2 percent. You view this as an attractive investment but realize that if LIBOR falls below 5 1/2 percent, you will not have enough cash to make your fixed payments. You arrange a swap with a dealer who agrees to pay you 6 percent fixed, while you pay it LIBOR. Determine your cash flow as a percent of the notional amount at each payment date under this arrangement. Assume for simplicity that each period is 180 days and that there are 360 days in the year.

19. A hedge fund is currently engaged in a plain vanilla euro swap in which it pays euros at the euro floating rate of Euribor and receives euros fixed. It would like to convert this position into one in which it pays the return on the S&P 500 and receives euros at a fixed rate. Show how it can use currency and equity swaps to maintain its position in the plain vanilla euro swap and convert its overall position to the one desired.

20. (Concept Problem) An asset management firm has a $300 million portfolio consisting of all stock. It would like to divest 10 percent of its stock and invest in bonds. It considers the possibility of synthetically selling some stock using equity swaps. It does not, however, want to receive a fixed or

floating rate. If it actually sold the stock, it would invest in a broadly diversified portfolio of bonds. In fact, there are bond indices that are quite representative of the universe of bonds in which it would invest. Design a strategy using swaps that would enable it to achieve its objective.

21. (Concept Problem) Consider a currency swap with but two payment dates, which are one year apart, and no exchange of notional amounts. On the first date, the party pays U.S. dollars at a rate of 4 percent and receives British pounds at a rate of 3.5 percent. Because the payments are annual, no adjustment, such as days/360, is necessary. The notional amounts are $10 million and £6.25 million. Explain from an American's perspective how this transaction is like a series of forward contracts on the pound. Also, explain how the transaction can be fairly priced, which you can assume it is, even though the implied forward rate is the same for both maturities.

PART III

ADVANCED TOPICS

CHAPTER 13

Interest Rate Forwards and Options

As with a second-hand car, you never really know what an OTC option is worth until you actually sell it or buy it. Placing a value on it in the interim is, in some ways, only a more sophisticated version of pinning the tail on the donkey.

Richard Thomson
Apocalypse Roulette, 1998, p. 149

CHAPTER OBJECTIVES

- Introduce the concept of a derivative on an interest rate, in contrast to a derivative on an asset

- Understand the pricing, valuation, and use of forward rate agreements (FRAs), interest rate options, swaptions, and forward swaps

While this chapter deals with certain **interest rate derivatives**, we have already covered the most widely used interest rate derivative, the plain vanilla interest rate swap. In addition, we have already covered Eurodollar futures, which are also appropriately called interest rate derivatives. In some cases, futures on such instruments as Treasury bonds and notes are also called interest rate derivatives. But we need to make an important distinction between derivative contracts on interest rates and derivative contracts on fixed-income securities.

Consider a Eurodollar time deposit that pays $1 in 90 days. At a current rate of 8 percent, this Eurodollar has a value of $1/(1 + 0.08(90/360)) = $0.9804. Suppose that a forward contract had been created on this Eurodollar and that contract is expiring right now. The payoff of a long position would be $0.9804 minus the forward price agreed to when the contract was initiated. The payoff of a forward contract on the Eurodollar interest rate, LIBOR, would be 0.08(90/360) minus the forward rate agreed to when the contract was initiated. Forward contracts on interest rates and forward contracts on Eurodollars are related but different contracts.

Recall that Eurodollars are priced based on the add-on interest method. Hence, we found the price of the Eurodollar above as $1/(1+0.08(90/360)). Treasury bills are based on the discount interest method. For a rate of 8 percent, a Treasury bill price would be $1(1 − 0.08(90/360)) = $0.98. A long position in a forward contract on a Treasury bill would pay off 1 minus 0.08(90/360) minus the forward price. A short position in a forward contract on the rate would pay off the forward rate minus 0.08 times 90/360. It should be easy to see that a long position in a forward contract on a discount instrument is equal to a short position in a forward contract on a rate with the forward rate based on one minus the forward price. Similar comments can be made for options.

Thus, in some cases, derivatives on interest rates are essentially the same as derivatives on bonds. For others, this is not the case. In this chapter, we shall focus on derivative on interest rates. In some cases, we shall gain some advantage by noting the equivalence with derivatives on bonds. But in most cases, we shall just focus on the fact that the underlying is an interest rate and that its payoff formula is based directly on the underlying interest rate rather than the price of a bond.

This chapter is called "Interest Rate Forwards and Options" and will cover four primary types of instruments. The first is the interest rate forward, more commonly known as a **forward rate agreement**, or **FRA**. This instrument is a forward contract in which the two parties agree to make interest payments to each other at futures dates. One party makes a payment at a rate agreed to in advance. The other party makes a payment at a rate to be determined later. The second type of instrument is the **interest rate option**, in which one party pays the other a premium today and receives the right to either make a known interest payment and receive an unknown interest payment at a future date or receive a known interest payment and make an unknown interest payment at a future date. The right to make a known payment is an **interest rate call**. The right to receive a known payment is an **interest rate put**.

In addition to standard interest rate forwards and options, we shall cover two other types of forward and option contracts involving interest rates. The third instrument we cover in this chapter is an option to enter into a swap, which is commonly referred to as a swap option, or **swaption**. The buyer of a swaption in which the underlying is an interest rate swap pays a premium and receives the right to enter into a swap to pay the fixed rate and receive the floating rate or pay the floating rate and receive the fixed rate. These instruments may seem like calls and puts, but these terms are not commonly used in the world of swaptions. We shall cover this point in more detail later. The fourth instrument we cover is the **forward swap**, which is a forward contract to enter into a swap. Obviously, a forward swap commits the two parties to enter into a swap, whereas a swaption gives one party the right to enter into a swap.

These types of instruments exist with underlyings other than interest rates, but we have already covered such instruments as forwards and options on currencies and equities. The interest rate derivatives market is much larger than the market for currency and equity derivatives. Interest rate derivatives are also different from currency and equity derivatives and, thus, merit special consideration. Of course, we have already covered the most important interest rate derivative, the swap. While currency and equity swaptions and forward swaps exist, the market is quite small relative to the market for interest rate swaptions and forward swaps, and we do not cover equity and currency versions of these instruments in this book.

Data are not available on the size of the market for swaptions and forward swaps, but Figure 13.1 shows the notional amount of interest rate options and FRAs as estimated by the

FIGURE 13.1 Notional Amount of Interest Rate Options and Forward Rate Agreements (FRAs)

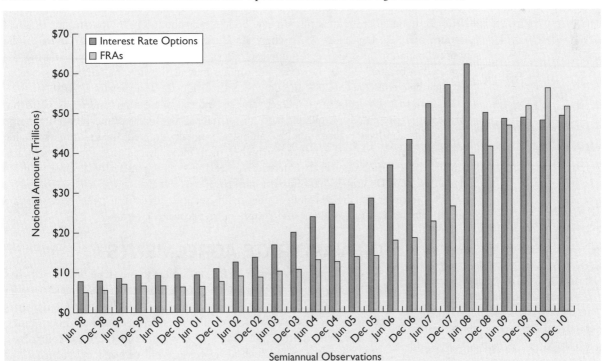

FIGURE 13.2 Gross Market Value of Interest Rate Options and Forward Rate Agreements

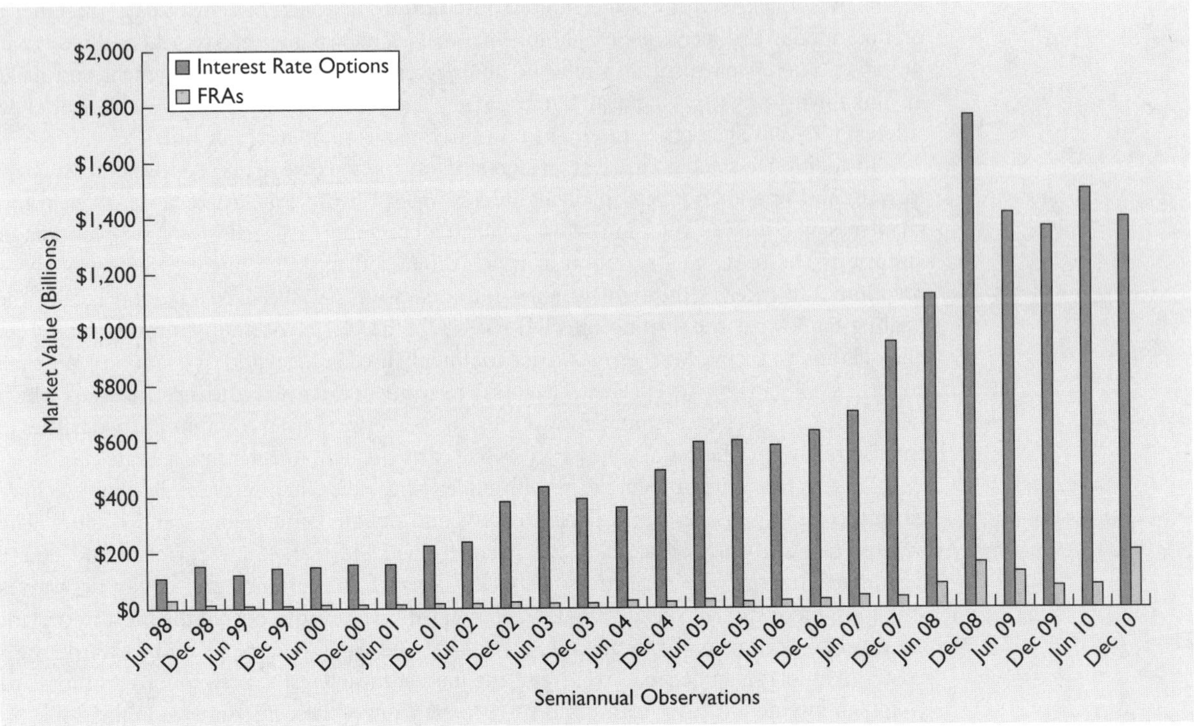

Source: Bank for International Settlements, www.bis.org

Bank for International Settlements (www.bis.org) in its semiannual survey. As of December 2010, the notional amount of interest rate options was about $49 trillion and the notional amount of FRAs was about $52 trillion. As we have seen before in other markets, the notional amount outstanding for interest rate options dropped significantly during the credit crisis of 2008. FRAs, however, are unique in that the notional amounts increased through the credit crisis of 2008 and only recently dropped off in December 2010.

Figure 13.2 shows the gross market value for interest rate options and FRAs. Note that this data is presented in billions and not trillions. Because options are asymmetric instruments and have positive market value when initially entered, the gross market value of interest rate options is significantly higher than FRAs. Recall that forward contracts typically have zero value when entered. We see the typical pattern of a spike in gross market value in December 2008 in both markets.

This chapter is divided into three main sections that deal with forward rate agreements, interest rate options, and swaptions and forward swaps.

FORWARD RATE AGREEMENTS

A forward rate agreement, or FRA, is a forward contract in which the underlying is an interest rate. One party agrees to make a payment at a fixed interest rate, while the other agrees to make a payment at a floating interest rate, which is determined at the expiration date.

A forward rate agreement, or FRA, is similar to any type of forward contract, but the payoff is based on an interest rate, rather than the price of an asset. For example, suppose a financial manager believed that interest rates were going up and wanted to lock in a specific rate to be paid on a future loan. She could do that by taking a short position in a forward contract on a fixed-income security such as a Treasury bill or bond. If rates rose, the security price would fall, the forward price would also fall, and the short position would be profitable, offsetting some of the effect of the higher borrowing rate. Alternatively, she could get a similar result using futures contracts.

An FRA is another means of obtaining this result, and in many situations, an FRA is better suited for managing this type of risk. The payoff of a forward contract on a bond is determined directly by the price of the bond, but only indirectly by the underlying interest rate. The payoff of an FRA, however, is determined *directly* by the underlying interest rate.

Structure and Use of a Typical FRA

As with swaps, FRAs are typically based on rates such as LIBOR and Euribor, quoted as an annual rate. The underlying rate is for a specific term, such as 90-day LIBOR, 180-day Euribor, and so forth. Thus, the payoff is prorated by using a days/360 factor, as we did with swaps.[1] The payoff is based on the difference between the underlying rate and the rate agreed upon when the contract is established, adjusted for the number of days and multiplied by a notional amount.

In addition, there is another important factor in the payoff of an FRA that we must examine carefully. Consider an FRA based on 90-day LIBOR and assume that this FRA is expiring today. As such, the parties look in the London Eurodollar market and determine the rate on a 90-day spot LIBOR instrument. Let us assume that rate is 5 percent. Remember that the rate is on a Eurodollar interbank time deposit, a loan made by one London bank to another for 90 days. When the borrowing bank takes out this loan today, it promises to pay back the principal plus 5 percent interest 90 days later. Thus, when the rate of 5 percent is determined in the London Eurodollar market, the assumption is that the interest on such a loan is paid back 90 days later.

The FRA market uses the London interbank Eurodollar market as its source of the underlying rate. Yet when the FRA expires and LIBOR is 5 percent, the FRA pays off at the 5 percent rate *today*. The Eurodollar deposit itself, which is the source of the 5 percent rate, pays off 90 days later. Consequently, to use LIBOR to determine the FRA payoff, an adjustment is required. This adjustment is to discount the FRA payment for 90 days at the 90-day rate. Because their payoffs are deferred for 90 days, interest rate swaps and options do not require this adjustment. Recall that when LIBOR is determined at the beginning of the settlement period, the swap payment based on that rate occurs at the end of the settlement period. In Chapter 12, we called this advanced set, settled in arrears. As we shall see later in this chapter, a similar procedure occurs for interest rate options. Yet, the FRA market works differently for reasons that no one seems to know[2]. So in general, an FRA on an m-day interest rate pays off at expiration, but the payoff is discounted for m days at the m-day rate, which is the settlement procedure known as advanced set, advanced settled that we briefly mentioned in Chapter 12.

Using LIBOR as the underlying rate, the general payoff of a receive floating or long FRA is

$$(\text{Notional Amount})\left(\frac{(\text{LIBOR} - \text{Agreed upon rate})\frac{m}{360}}{1 + \text{LIBOR}\frac{m}{360}}\right),$$

---

[1]It is possible to use a 365-day year assumption, but FRAs are nearly always based on LIBOR, Euribor, or a similar rate, which are always based on a 360-day year assumption.

[2]It is likely that the first FRAs were created in the same departments that were trading currency forwards at dealer banks. Because currency forwards make their payoffs at expiration, FRAs were probably structured in the same manner. Evidently, interest rate swaps and options were not created in this manner. They were structured much more like floating-rate loans, in which the rate is determined at one point in time, and the interest accrues for a period and is paid at the end of the period, the procedure known as advanced set, settled in arrears.

where the reference to "LIBOR" is the underlying LIBOR when the contract expires. The "Agreed upon rate" is the rate the two parties agree on when the contract is established. Note that LIBOR appears in both the numerator and the denominator. Recall that "m/360" denotes the accrual period which in this case is actual days divided by 360.

Suppose a party takes a long position (receive floating) in an FRA based on 90-day LIBOR that expires in 30 days. The notional amount is $20 million. Let the rate agreed upon by the two parties be 5 percent. Thus, in 30 days, the payoff to the holder of the long position will be

$$\$20,000,000 \left(\frac{(\text{LIBOR} - 0.05)\left(\dfrac{90}{360}\right)}{1 + \text{LIBOR}\left(\dfrac{90}{360}\right)} \right).$$

Now let us consider some possible payoffs to the holder of this FRA. Suppose LIBOR at expiration is 4 percent. Then the payoff is

$$\$20,000,000 \left(\frac{(0.04 - 0.05)\left(\dfrac{90}{360}\right)}{1 + 0.04\left(\dfrac{90}{360}\right)} \right) = -\$49,505.$$

This means that the party who is long has to pay $49,505 to the party who is short. If LIBOR at expiration is 6 percent, the payoff is

$$\$20,000,000 \left(\frac{(0.06 - 0.05)\left(\dfrac{90}{360}\right)}{1 + 0.06\left(\dfrac{90}{360}\right)} \right) = \$49,261.$$

Hence, the party who is long receives $49,261 from the party who is short. When LIBOR at expiration is above (below) 5 percent, the holder of the long (short) position receives a positive payoff, to be paid by the counterparty. The payoff of the holder of the short position is found by changing the sign of the payoff of the holder of the long position.

The FRA market uses a distinct terminology to describe its contracts. It refers to an FRA in the form of "A × B," where A refers to the number of months until the FRA expires and B refers to the number of months, as of the contract initiation date, in the Eurodollar time deposit underlying the FRA. For example, a 6 × 9 FRA (pronounced "6 by 9") is an FRA that expires in six months with the underlying 90-day LIBOR. That is, the underlying Eurodollar time deposit matures in nine months, which is three months, or 90 days, after the FRA expiration. A 12 × 18 FRA expires in 12 months, and the underlying is 180-day Eurodollar time deposit, which has 18 months to go before maturity when the contract is initiated.

Pricing and Valuation of FRAs

In the example above, we assume that the parties agreed on a rate of 10 percent. In this section, we shall learn how that rate is determined. In addition, we shall learn how to determine the value of the FRA at a point during its life before expiration. Let F be the rate the parties agree on at the start. Let $L_0(h)$ be the spot rate for a maturity of h days, which we shall assume is the maturity date of the FRA. The underlying is m-day LIBOR. Then $L_0(h + m)$ is the spot rate for a maturity of $h + m$ days. We assume a notional amount of $1.

One way to determine the fixed rate on an FRA is to do another set of transactions that will replicate the payoff of the FRA. Let us do the following to replicate a long position in an FRA:

- Go short a Eurodollar time deposit maturing in h + m days that pays 1 + F(m/360). Assume that we can pay off this loan at any time prior to maturity or pay another party to take over this obligation.
- Go long a Eurodollar time deposit maturing in h days that pays $1.

In other words, we borrow 1 + F(m/360) for h + m days. We lend $1 to be paid back in h days.

Now move forward to day h. The loan we owe is not due, but it has a market value of

$$-\frac{1 + F\left(\dfrac{m}{360}\right)}{1 + L_h(m)\left(\dfrac{m}{360}\right)},$$

which reflects the discounting of the payoff 1 + F(m/360) at the LIBOR rate at the expiration, which is $L_h(m)$. The minus sign reflects the fact that we owe this amount. We shall now go ahead and pay off the loan early. Because this is the value of this loan, we could technically pay it off. The loan we hold is due, so we receive $1. Thus, the cash flow at this point is

$$1 - \frac{1 + F\left(\dfrac{m}{360}\right)}{1 + L_h(m)\left(\dfrac{m}{360}\right)}.$$

Algebraic rearrangement of this equation gives

$$\frac{\left(1 + L_h\left(\dfrac{m}{360}\right)\right) - \left(1 + F\left(\dfrac{m}{360}\right)\right)}{1 + L_h(m)\left(\dfrac{m}{360}\right)} = \frac{(L_h(m) - F)\left(\dfrac{m}{360}\right)}{1 + L_h(m)\left(\dfrac{m}{360}\right)}.$$

This is the payoff of the FRA, so this strategy replicates an FRA. Thus, it must have the same value as the FRA at the start. The value of the FRA at the start is the value of the loan we made minus the value of the loan we took out, which is

$$\frac{1}{1 + L_0(h)\left(\dfrac{h}{360}\right)} - \left(\frac{1 + F\left(\dfrac{m}{360}\right)}{1 + L_0(h + m)\left(\dfrac{h + m}{360}\right)}\right),$$

which must equal zero. Setting this to zero and solving for F gives

$$F = \left(\frac{1 + L_0(h + m)\left(\dfrac{h + m}{360}\right)}{1 + L_0(h)\left(\dfrac{h}{360}\right)} - 1\right)\left(\frac{360}{m}\right).$$

An FRA is priced by finding the forward rate in the term structure of the underlying rate.

This looks like a complex formula, but it is actually just the formula for the forward rate using the LIBOR term structure. A typical forward rate calculation would have 1 + the longer term rate raised to a power in the numerator and 1 + the shorter term rate raised to a power in the denominator. This is more or less what we see here, but there are no exponents because compounding and discounting in the Eurodollar market is done using rate × days/360, rather than raising 1 + the

> **TABLE 13.1 SOLVING FOR THE RATE ON A FORWARD RATE AGREEMENT**
>
> To solve for the rate on a 30-day FRA in which the underlying is 90-day LIBOR, we have h = 30 and m = 90. Thus, we need $L_0(30)$ and $L_0(120)$, the 30- and 120-day LIBOR spot rates, which are as follows:
>
> | TERM | RATE |
> |------|------|
> | 30 days | 5.5% |
> | 120 days | 5.14% |
>
> The forward rate is found as follows:
>
> $$F = \left(\frac{1 + 0.0514\left(\dfrac{120}{360}\right)}{1 + 0.055\left(\dfrac{30}{360}\right)} - 1 \right)\left(\frac{360}{90}\right) = 0.05$$

rate to a power. Also, in the above formula, subtracting 1 and multiplying by 360/m annualizes the rate.

Table 13.1 illustrates how this formula is used to solve for the rate on an FRA. A firm enters into an FRA that expires in 30 days. The underlying is 90-day LIBOR. The term structure of interest rates is 5.5 percent for 30 days and 5.14 percent for 120 days.

> The value of an FRA is obtained by determining the value of a strategy of long a long-term underlying and short a short-term underlying.

Recall that in examining swaps, the value of the contract is zero at the start. Later during its life—after the swap was initiated but before it expires—we needed to determine the value of the swap. We need to do the same for the FRA. To do so, let us position ourselves at a future day g, which is after day 0 but before the expiration, day h. We hold an FRA set at the rate F that will pay off in h − g days. The relevant term structure is LIBOR for h − g days and h + m − g days.

Recall the transactions that we set up on day 0 to replicate the payoff of the FRA. The value of that combination of Eurodollar time deposits on day g will give us the value of the FRA on day g. Remember that the combination consists of a time deposit that we owe paying 1 + F(m/360) on day h + m and one that we hold paying $1 on day h. The value of this combination on day g is the value of the FRA, which we denote as VFRA,

$$\text{VFRA} = \left(\frac{1}{1 + L_g(h-g)\left(\dfrac{h-g}{360}\right)} \right) - \left(\frac{1 + F\left(\dfrac{m}{360}\right)}{1 + L_g(h+m-g)\left(\dfrac{h+m-g}{360}\right)} \right).$$

The first term in the large parentheses is the value of the Eurodollar time deposit that we hold. Its value is based on discounting the payoff of $1 at the rate for h − g days. The second term in large parentheses is the value of the time deposit we owe, in which we pay 1 + F(m/360) in h + m − g days, discounted at the rate for h + m − g days.

An alternative expression for the value of an FRA on day g is (note we introduce a subscript to denote when the forward rate is set)

$$\text{VFRA} = \frac{(F_g - F_0)\left(\dfrac{m}{360}\right)}{1 + L_g(h+m-g)\left(\dfrac{h+m-g}{360}\right)}.$$

> ┌───┐
> │ **TABLE 13.2 VALUING A FORWARD RATE AGREEMENT**   │
> │ **DURING ITS LIFE**   │
> └───┘

Consider the FRA we priced in Table 13.1. It is now 20 days into its life, with 10 days remaining. Thus, $g = 20$, $h = 30$, and $h + m = 120$. We shall need the term structure for $h - g = 10$ days and $h + m - g = 100$ days. These rates are as follows:

TERM	RATE
10 days	5.25%
100 days	5.10%

The value of the FRA is found as follows:

$$20,000,000 \left[\left(\frac{1}{1 + 0.0525 \left(\frac{10}{360} \right)} \right) - \left(\frac{1 + 0.05 \left(\frac{90}{360} \right)}{1 + 0.0510 \left(\frac{100}{360} \right)} \right) \right] = \$3,744$$

The value of the FRA is the present value of the change in the forward rate.

Table 13.2 illustrates this result. We see that changes in market conditions over this 20-day period of time have resulted in an increase in the value of the FRA from zero to over $3,000.

Applications of FRAs

In the example we have been working with, the buyer of the FRA could well have been a pure speculator, using the instrument to profit from an expectation of higher interest rates. In most cases, however, users of FRAs are borrowers and lenders who want protection against interest rate changes. FRAs are ideal for parties who anticipate the need to borrow money at a future date. The most appropriate type of loan for an FRA is a loan equivalent to a zero coupon bond. The borrower receives the proceeds from the loan and makes a single payment at maturity of principal plus interest. Of course, for the best match, the interest on the loan should be calculated in the same manner in which it is calculated on the FRA.

Continuing with our example, consider a firm that needs to borrow $20 million in 30 days. The rate will be set at LIBOR plus 100 basis points. The firm is concerned with the risk associated with LIBOR over this 30-day period, so it believes that the purchase of an FRA would be a good way to protect against a possible increase in LIBOR. Of course, the FRA would also prevent the firm from benefiting from a decrease in LIBOR. The firm decides that a long position in an FRA is an appropriate response to this risk that it does not want to bear. There are, however, a few technical details that must be considered.

Recall that the FRA will pay off in 30 days. The loan, however, will be taken out at that time and will be paid back, with interest, 90 days later. Thus, the FRA payoff is designed to protect against interest that is paid 90 days after the FRA expires. To appropriately analyze the effectiveness of the FRA, we might consider the FRA payoff as reducing or increasing the amount borrowed. Alternatively, we could take the FRA payoff, compound it for 90 days, and incorporate it into the amount paid back on the loan. In other words, if the FRA pays a positive amount, we reinvest this amount at LIBOR for

---

TABLE 13.3 HEDGING AN ANTICIPATED LOAN WITH A FORWARD RATE AGREEMENT

Scenario: A firm plans to borrow $20 million in 30 days at 90-day LIBOR plus 100 basis points. The loan will be paid back with principal and interest 90 days later. Concerned about the possibility of rising interest rates, the firm would like to lock in the rate it pays by going long an FRA. The rate on 30-day FRAs based on 90-day LIBOR is 5 percent. Interest on the loan and the FRA is based on the factor 90/360. The outcomes for a range of LIBORs are shown below.

LIBOR ON DAY 30	FRA PAYOFF ON DAY 30	FRA PAYOFF COMPOUNDED TO DAY 120	AMOUNT DUE ON LOAN ON DAY 120	TOTAL AMOUNT PAID ON DAY 120	EFFECTIVE RATE ON LOAN	EFFECTIVE RATE WITHOUT FRA
1.00%	−$199,501	−$200,000	$20,100,000	$20,300,000	6.22%	2.04%
1.50	−174,346	−175,000	20,125,000	20,300,000	6.22	2.56
2.00	−149,253	−150,000	20,150,000	20,300,000	6.22	3.08
2.50	−124,223	−125,000	20,175,000	20,300,000	6.22	3.60
3.00	−99,255	−100,000	20,200,200	20,300,000	6.22	4.12
3.50	−74,349	−75,000	20,225,000	20,300,000	6.22	4.64
4.00	−49,504	−50,000	20,250,000	20,300,000	6.22	5.17
4.50	−24,721	−25,000	20,275,000	20,300,000	6.22	5.69
5.00	0	0	20,300,000	20,300,000	6.22	6.22
5.50	24,661	25,000	20,325,000	20,300,000	6.22	6.76
6.00	49,262	50,000	20,350,000	20,300,000	6.22	7.29
6.50	73,801	75,000	20,375,000	20,300,000	6.22	7.82
7.00	98,281	100,000	20,400,000	20,300,000	6.22	8.36
7.50	122,700	125,000	20,425,000	20,300,000	6.22	8.90
8.00	147,059	150,000	20,450,000	20,300,000	6.22	9.44
8.50	171,359	175,000	20,475,000	20,300,000	6.22	9.99
9.00	195,600	200,000	20,500,000	20,300,000	6.22	10.53

90 days. If it pays a negative amount, we borrow this amount at LIBOR for 90 days. This is the approach we shall take here: we borrow the $20 million in 30 days and compound the FRA payoff 90 days, adding it to or subtracting it from the interest.[3] The results are shown in Table 13.3.

Let us verify one of the outcomes. Let LIBOR be 6 percent. The calculation of the FRA payoff of $49,261 was covered earlier. Compounding this amount for 90 days at 6 percent gives

$$\$49,261\left(1 + 0.06\left(\frac{90}{360}\right)\right) = \$50,000,$$

---

[3]It is possible, if not likely, that we might not be able to borrow or invest the payoff at LIBOR, but we shall ignore this point to keep the illustration as simple as possible.

subject to round-off error. The amount due on the loan is the principal compounded at 6 percent plus the 100 basis point premium for 90 days:

$$\$20,000,000\left(1 + (0.06 + 0.01)\left(\frac{90}{360}\right)\right) = \$20,350,000.$$

The total amount due is $20,350,000 minus the payoff on the FRA of $50,000 for $20,300,000. Thus, the firm borrowed $20 million and 90 days later paid back $20,300,000. The effective rate is found as follows:

$$\left(\frac{\$20,300,000}{\$20,000,000}\right)^{365/90} - 1 = 0.0622.$$

Had the firm not done the FRA, it would have paid back $20,350,000. The effective rate without the FRA would then be

$$\left(\frac{\$20,350,000}{\$20,000,000}\right)^{365/90} - 1 = 0.0729.$$

We see that the effective rate using the FRA is always 6.22 percent, which is illustrated in Figure 13.3. The higher LIBOR is, the higher the effective rate without the FRA. If LIBOR were below 5 percent, the FRA payoff would be negative and the amount paid back would be larger as a result of the loss on the FRA. But overall, the total amount due would be the same, $20,300,000, and the effective rate would be 6.22 percent.

FIGURE 13.3 Cost of Loan with or without FRA

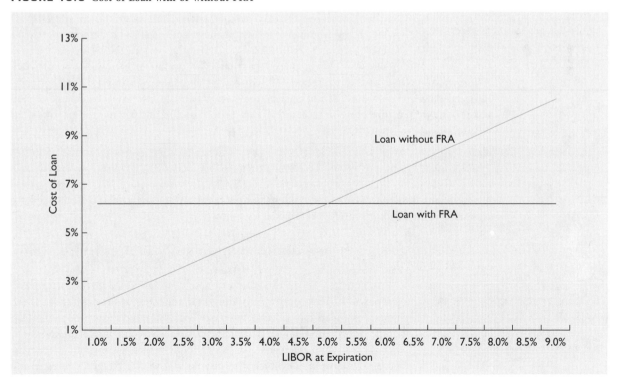

FRAs have fairly limited uses, being mostly restricted to the situation described here. As noted, they can be used to speculate on interest rates. A series of FRAs with different expirations could be combined to hedge the risk on a floating-rate loan. Because the term structure would not likely be flat, however, each FRA would probably be at a different rate. Thus, the firm would lock in a series of different fixed rates for each of the floating interest payments on its loan. Most firms prefer to lock in the same fixed rate for each of its loan payments. This result is easily achieved with a swap. Indeed a swap is a series of FRAs, but with each FRA at the same rate. Of course if each FRA were priced at the same rate, some of the FRAs would be worth more than zero and some would be worth less than zero at the start, but collectively they would add up to a value of zero. An FRA that is not worth zero at the start is called an **off-market FRA**. Thus, a swap is a series of off-market FRAs.

INTEREST RATE OPTIONS

Interest rate options are a lot like forward rate agreements. Instead of being *a firm commitment* to make a fixed interest payment and receive a floating interest payment, they represent the *right* to make a fixed interest payment and receive a floating interest payment or to make a floating interest payment and receive a fixed interest payment. Unlike the options we have already covered, interest rate options have an **exercise rate** or strike rate, rather than an exercise price or strike price. While European and American versions are available, interest rate options are more often than not of the European variety. This is because they are normally used to hedge an interest rate exposure on a specific date.

Structure and Use of a Typical Interest Rate Option

> An interest rate call option gives the holder the right to make an interest payment at a fixed rate and receive an interest payment at a floating rate.

Like most options, interest rate options come in the form of calls and puts. An interest rate call gives the holder the right to make a known interest payment, based on the exercise rate, and receive an unknown interest payment. This unknown interest payment will usually be determined by an interest rate such as LIBOR. To acquire the option, the buyer pays a premium, the option price, up front. The option expires at a specific date known, of course, as the expiration. As with swaps and FRAs, an interest rate option is based on a given amount of notional amount on which the interest is calculated. Using the symbol X as the exercise rate and m-day LIBOR as the underlying, the payoff of an interest rate call is as follows:

$$(\text{Notional Amount})\left(\text{Max}(0, \text{LIBOR} - X)\left(\frac{m}{360}\right)\right).$$

An interest rate put permits the holder the right to pay a floating rate and receive a fixed rate. The payoff of an interest rate put is as follows:

$$(\text{Notional Amount})\left(\text{Max}(0, X - \text{LIBOR})\left(\frac{m}{360}\right)\right).$$

> An interest rate put option gives the holder the right to make an interest payment at a floating rate and receive an interest payment at a fixed rate.

As noted earlier in this chapter, in contrast to the payment on an FRA, the payoff of an interest rate option does not occur at the expiration. If the underlying is m-day LIBOR, the payoff occurs m days after the expiration of the option. Remember that in an FRA, the payoff is made at expiration, but is based on a rate such as m-day LIBOR, which assumes that payment occurs m days later. Hence, the discounting of the payoff is appropriate for an FRA. For an interest rate option (as well as an interest rate swap), the payoff is deferred, so no discounting is required.

Consider interest rate call and put options with notional amounts of $20 million, expiring in 30 days; an underlying of 90-day LIBOR; and exercise rates of 5 percent. Let us look at how the payoffs are calculated. Suppose that at expiration, LIBOR is 1 percent. The call payoff would be

$$\$20,000,000\left(\text{Max}(0,0.01 - 0.05)\left(\frac{90}{360}\right)\right) = \$0,$$

and the put payoff would be

$$\$20,000,000\left(\text{Max}(0,0.05 - 0.01)\left(\frac{90}{360}\right)\right) = \$200,000.$$

If LIBOR at expiration is 9 percent, the call payoff would be

$$\$20,000,000\left(\text{Max}(0,0.09 - 0.05)\left(\frac{90}{360}\right)\right) = \$200,000,$$

and the payoff on the put would be

$$\$20,000,000\left(\text{Max}(0,0.05 - 0.09)\left(\frac{90}{360}\right)\right) = \$0.$$

These payoffs are made 90 days after the expiration of the options.

Pricing and Valuation of Interest Rate Options

In Part 1 of this book, we devoted a great deal of effort to pricing options. We discussed the binomial model and the Black-Scholes-Merton model for pricing options on assets and the Black model for pricing options on futures. Pricing interest rate options, however, is much more complicated. To obtain the most accurate interest rate, option pricing requires the development of a fairly sophisticated model that will capture movements in the term structure. To capture movements in the term structure, the model must simultaneously reflect movements in all bonds in the market and do so without permitting any arbitrage opportunities. Binomial models of the term structure are commonly used for this purpose, but they are quite sophisticated. We shall approach interest rate option pricing from an alternative and less complex angle. In fact, many interest rate option dealers use this simple approach.

The method we use is the Black model. Remember from Chapter 9 that the Black model is designed for pricing options on futures contracts. Likewise, it can be used for pricing options on forward contracts. The Black model is commonly used in pricing interest rate options by noting that in an interest rate option, the underlying is the current value of the interest rate at expiration. The current value of this rate would be the forward rate. That is, suppose the underlying is 90-day LIBOR and the option expires in 30 days. Then the forward rate for a 90-day Eurodollar time deposit to start in 30 days is the underlying when the option is initiated. That rate evolves over the 30-day life of the option into the 90-day LIBOR at the expiration of the option. Thus, we start by taking the forward rate as the underlying in the Black model. The exercise rate of the option is used as the exercise price in the model. The time to expiration is easily defined as the number of days to expiration of the option divided by 365. The volatility is the volatility of the forward rate. We shall not spend much time on the volatility, relying primarily on our understanding of the general notion of volatility from Chapter 5. Note, however, that we are referring to the volatility of the relative change in a rate, rather than a price. The risk-free rate is the risk-free rate for the period to the option's expiration. It is important to note, however, that the forward rate and risk-free rate should be in continuously compounded form. Technically, the exercise rate should also be viewed as a continuously compounded rate, but we shall just leave it in discrete form. The Black model is not a perfect fit for the situation of pricing an interest rate option, but it provides a reasonable approximation.

The interest rate call option that we shall examine has 30 days until expiration. Thus, T = 30/365 = 0.0822. The exercise rate is 5 percent. The continuously compounded forward rate is obtained as the continuously compounded equivalent of the forward rate based on the term structure. The problem we are working here is the same one we worked when examining FRAs. In Table 13.1, we saw that the 30-day LIBOR is 5.5 percent and the 120-day LIBOR is 5.14 percent. Using this information, we calculate the continuously forward rate as follows:

$$\ln\left(\frac{1 + 0.0514\left(\frac{120}{360}\right)}{1 + 0.05\left(\frac{30}{360}\right)}\right)\left(\frac{365}{90}\right) = 0.0520.$$

The numerator inside the log function is the compound value of $1 invested at 5.14 percent for 120 days. The denominator is the compound value of $1 invested at 5 percent for 30 days. This ratio is one plus the forward rate for 30 days. Taking the log converts it to continuous compounding, and multiplying by 365/90 annualizes it.

> Pricing an interest rate option is a complex process, but a simple approach can be taken by applying the Black model for pricing options on futures, with the forward rate serving as the underlying.

Finally, we need the continuously compounded risk-free rate for 30 days. We know that $1 invested for 30 days grows to $1(1 + 0.05(30/360)) = 1.0041667. We take the log of this and multiply by 365/30 to obtain r = 0.0506.

Now, suppose we plug these values into the Black model. The result we obtain reflects the assumption that the option payoff occurs at expiration. With interest rate options, the payoff is deferred. Thus, when the underlying is an m-day rate, we need to discount the payoff m days (90 in this problem) at the continuously compounded forward rate, denoted as F. Letting C be the Black call option price:

$$\text{Interest rate option price} = e^{-F(m/365)}C.$$

Finally, we must note that the result we obtain is stated in terms of an annual interest rate. This is an acceptable way to quote the option price, but to obtain the contract premium (the actual amount paid), we must multiply by m/360 and the notional amount:

$$\text{Contract premium} = (\text{Notional Amount})\left(\frac{\text{days}}{360}\right)(\text{Interest rate options price}).$$

Table 13.4 illustrates the calculation of the interest rate option price and the contract premium.

Interest Rate Option Strategies

Recall the interest rate call example that we used previously. We purchased a call on 90-day LIBOR expiring in 30 days. The exercise rate was 10 percent. In the previous section, we showed that the price of this call, using a computer for the calculations, would be $14,866. It is easy to consider a scenario in which we might want to buy this call. In fact, this call was created to show an alternative to the FRA as a solution for the problem we discussed earlier in this chapter. Recall that a company was planning to borrow $20 million in 30 days at 90-day LIBOR plus 100 basis points. The loan would involve a single repayment of interest and principal 90 days later. When using an option, however,

---

TABLE 13.4 CALCULATING AN INTEREST RATE OPTION PRICE AND CONTRACT PREMIUM USING THE BLACK MODEL

$F = 0.0520$ $\qquad$ $X = 0.05$ $\qquad$ $r_c = 0.0506$ $\qquad$ $\sigma = 0.3$ $\qquad$ $T = 0.0822$ $\qquad$ $m = 90$

1. Compute d_1:

$$d_1 = \frac{\ln(0.0520/0.05) + (0.3^2/2)0.0822}{0.3\sqrt{0.0822}} = 0.4990$$

2. Compute d_2:

$$d_2 = 0.4990 - 0.3\sqrt{0.0822} = 0.4130$$

3. Look up $N(d_1)$: $\qquad\qquad\qquad\qquad\qquad\qquad$ $N(0.50) = 0.6915$

4. Look up $N(d_2)$: $\qquad\qquad\qquad\qquad\qquad\qquad$ $N(0.41) = 0.6591$

5. Calculate the Black call option price and discount at the risk-free rate for the life of the option to obtain the interest rate option price:

$$C = e^{-0.0506(0.0822)}[0.0520(0.6915) - 0.05(0.6591)] = 0.00299054$$

$$\text{Interest rate option price} = 0.00299054e^{-0.0520(90/365)} = 0.00295244$$

6. Multiply the interest rate option price by the notional amount times $m/360$:

$$\text{Contract price} = 20,000,000\left(\frac{90}{360}\right)0.00295244 = \$14,762$$

Note: Using a computer for a more precise result gives a premium of $14,866, which we shall use.

---

there is one additional aspect of the problem we must consider. Remember that we pay the option premium today. Thirty days later, the option expires and its payoff is determined. We borrow the money at that point. Ninety days later, we receive the option payout, if any, and pay back the loan. When using FRAs, we had cash flows on day 30 and 90 days later on day 120. When using options, we have cash flows on day 0, day 30, and day 120. To determine the effective rate on the loan, we must somehow incorporate the option premium into the cash flows on the loan. We do this by compounding it from day 0 to day 30 at the 30-day rate.[4] This amounts to

$$\$14,866\left(1 + 0.05\left(\frac{30}{360}\right)\right) = \$14,928.$$

When the loan is taken out, the proceeds of $20 million are effectively only $20,000,000 − $14,928 = $19,985,072, reflecting the fact that the option was purchased in conjunction with the loan. Table 13.5 presents the results of this strategy of hedging a loan with an interest rate call. Let us do a sample calculation.

Suppose LIBOR at expiration is 3 percent. The option payoff is

$$\$20,000,000\,\text{Max}(0, 0.03 - 0.05)\left(\frac{90}{360}\right) = \$0.$$

---

[4]An argument can be made for the fact that the rate used in this calculation should be the 30-day rate plus the 1 percent premium. If the company borrowed this money, then it would have to pay the 30-day LIBOR plus the 1 percent premium. Alternatively, if the company used its own cash to buy the option, we should compound the premium at its opportunity cost or the lending rate, which is probably less than LIBOR. For FRAs, this problem is not an issue because no premium is paid up front. There is no clear-cut answer to this question, so we shall just compound it at LIBOR.

TABLE 13.5 HEDGING AN ANTICIPATED LOAN WITH AN INTEREST RATE CALL

Scenario: A firm plans to borrow $20 million in 30 days at 90-day LIBOR plus 100 basis points. The loan will be paid back with principal and interest 90 days later. Concerned about the possibility of an increase in interest rates before the loan is taken out, the firm would like to protect against an increase in interest rates while preserving the flexibility to benefit from a decrease in interest rates. An interest rate call is appropriate for this objective. Interest on the loan and the call is based on the factor 90/360. The call will have an exercise rate of 10 percent and cost $14,866. The cost of the call is compounded for 30 days at the 30-day rate of 5 percent to obtain $14,928, which is the effective cost of the call at the time the loan is taken out. The proceeds from the loan are $20,000,000 − $17,528 = $19,985,072. The outcomes for a range of LIBORs are shown below.

LIBOR ON DAY 30	CALL PAY-OFF ON DAY 120	AMOUNT DUE ON LOAN ON DAY 120	TOTAL AMOUNT PAID ON DAY 120	EFFECTIVE RATE ON LOAN	EFFECTIVE RATE WITHOUT CALL
1.00%	$0	$20,100,000	$20,100,000	2.35%	2.04%
1.50%	$0	$20,125,000	$20,125,000	2.87%	2.56%
2.00%	$0	$20,150,000	$20,150,000	3.39%	3.08%
2.50%	$0	$20,175,000	$20,175,000	3.91%	3.60%
3.00%	$0	$20,200,200	$20,200,200	4.43%	4.12%
3.50%	$0	$20,225,000	$20,225,000	4.96%	4.64%
4.00%	$0	$20,250,000	$20,250,000	5.49%	5.17%
4.50%	$0	$20,275,000	$20,275,000	6.02%	5.69%
5.00%	$0	$20,300,000	$20,300,000	6.55%	6.22%
5.50%	$25,000	$20,325,000	$20,300,000	6.55%	6.76%
6.00%	$50,000	$20,350,000	$20,300,000	6.55%	7.29%
6.50%	$75,000	$20,375,000	$20,300,000	6.55%	7.82%
7.00%	$100,000	$20,400,000	$20,300,000	6.55%	8.36%
7.50%	$125,000	$20,425,000	$20,300,000	6.55%	8.90%
8.00%	$150,000	$20,450,000	$20,300,000	6.55%	9.44%
8.50%	$175,000	$20,475,000	$20,300,000	6.55%	9.99%
9.00%	$200,000	$20,500,000	$20,300,000	6.55%	10.53%

The amount due on the loan 90 days later is

$$\$20{,}000{,}000\left(1 + (0.03 + 0.01)\left(\frac{90}{360}\right)\right) = \$20{,}200{,}000.$$

Thus, the total amount due is $20,200,000. The effective rate on the loan is

$$\left(\frac{\$20{,}200{,}000}{\$19{,}985{,}072}\right)^{365/90} - 1 = 0.0443.$$

Without the call, the full loan proceeds of $20 million would be received on day 30. Then the effective rate on the loan would be

$$\left(\frac{\$20{,}200{,}000}{\$20{,}000{,}000}\right)^{365/90} - 1 = 0.0412.$$

Now, suppose LIBOR at expiration is 7 percent. The option payoff is

$$\$20,000,000 \text{Max}(0, 0.07 - 0.05)\left(\frac{90}{360}\right) = \$100,000.$$

The amount due on the loan 90 days later is

$$\$20,000,000\left(1 + (0.07 + 0.01)\left(\frac{90}{360}\right)\right) = \$20,400,000.$$

Thus, the total amount due is $20,400,000 less the option payoff of $100,000 for a total of $20,300,000. The effective rate on the loan is

$$\left(\frac{\$20,300,000}{\$19,985,072}\right)^{365/90} - 1 = 0.0655.$$

Without the call, the full loan proceeds of $20 million would be received on day 30. Then the effective rate on the loan would be

$$\left(\frac{\$20,400,000}{\$20,000,000}\right)^{365/90} - 1 = 0.0836.$$

Figure 13.4 illustrates the effective rate on the loan with and without the call. Observe how the effective rate increases without limit in the absence of the call. The call limits the effective rate. If the 30-day LIBOR at expiration is below the exercise rate of 5 percent, however, the call is not exercised and the cost of the call raises the effective rate on the loan.

Let us look at an interest rate put in a much higher interest rate scenario. Consider a bank that plans to make a $10 million floating-rate loan in 90 days. The loan will be for

FIGURE 13.4 Cost of Loan with and without Interest Rate Call

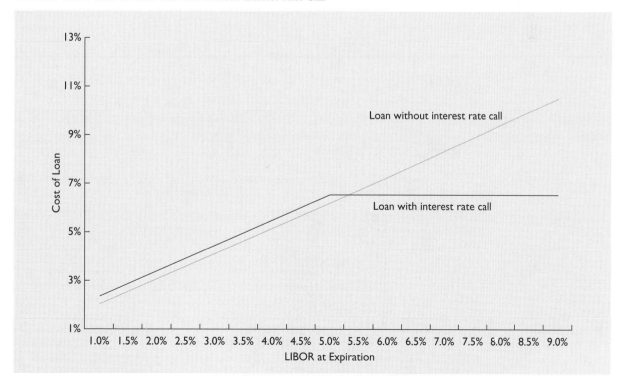

180 days, and the rate will be 180-day LIBOR plus 150 basis points. The current 90-day LIBOR is 10.5 percent. The bank is worried about falling interest rates over the period from now until the loan starts. Thus, an interest rate put option would be appropriate. An interest rate put option with an exercise rate of 9 percent is priced at $5,023 for this contract.[5] This premium would then be compounded for 90 days at the 90-day rate of 10.5 percent to obtain a value of

$$\$5,023\left(1 + 0.105\left(\frac{90}{360}\right)\right) = \$5,155.$$

Even though the option is purchased on day 0, this is the effective cost of the option on the day the loan is taken out, 90 days later. Thus, when the bank makes the loan, it effectively pays out $10,000,000 + $5,155 = $10,005,155. The results are presented in Table 13.6.

Suppose LIBOR at expiration is 5 percent. Then the payoff of the put is

$$\$10,000,000\text{Max}(0,0.09 - 0.05)\left(\frac{180}{360}\right) = \$200,000.$$

The amount due on the loan is

$$\$10,000,000\left(1 + (0.05 + 0.015)\left(\frac{180}{360}\right)\right) = \$10,325,000.$$

So the bank receives $10,325,000 on the loan plus $200,000 on the put for a total amount due of $10,525,000. As we noted, the effective outlay on the loan is $10,005,155. Thus, the effective rate on the loan is

$$\left(\frac{\$10,525,000}{\$10,005,155}\right)^{365/180} - 1 = 0.1082.$$

Without the put, the outlay on the loan is only $10,000,000, but the effective rate on the loan is

$$\left(\frac{\$10,325,000}{\$10,000,000}\right)^{365/180} - 1 = 0.067.$$

Suppose LIBOR at expiration is 13 percent. Then the payoff of the put is

$$\$10,000,000\text{Max}(0,0.09 - 0.13)\left(\frac{180}{360}\right) = \$0.$$

The amount due on the loan is

$$\$10,000,000\left(1 + (0.13 + 0.015)\left(\frac{180}{360}\right)\right) = \$10,725,000.$$

So the bank receives $10,725,000 on the loan, but nothing on the put. Given the effective outlay on the loan of $10,005,155, the effective rate on the loan is

$$\left(\frac{\$10,725,000}{\$10,005,155}\right)^{365/180} - 1 = 0.1513.$$

---

[5]You can verify this result using the Black model for an interest rate put and the following information. The continuously compounded forward rate is 9.45 percent, the exercise rate is 9 percent, the continuously compounded risk free rate is 10.51 percent, the time to expiration is 90/365 = 0.2466, and the volatility is 0.15. The answer of $5,023 was obtained on a computer. Your answer computed by hand should be about $4,323.

TABLE 13.6 HEDGING AN ANTICIPATED LOAN WITH AN INTEREST RATE PUT

Scenario: A bank plans to lend $10 million in 90 days at 180-day LIBOR plus 150 basis points. The loan will be paid back with principal and interest 180 days later. Concerned about the possibility of falling interest rates before the loan is taken out, the bank would like to protect against a decrease in interest rates while preserving the flexibility to benefit from an increase in interest rates. An interest rate put is appropriate for this objective. Interest on the loan and the put is based on the factor 180/360. The put will have an exercise rate of 9 percent and will cost $5,023. The cost of the put is compounded for 90 days at the 90-day rate of 10.5 percent to obtain $5,155, which is the effective cost of the put at the time the loan is taken out. The effective amount lent is $10,000,000 + $5,155 = $10,005,155. The outcomes for a range of LIBORs are shown below.

LIBOR ON DAY 90	PUT PAYOFF ON DAY 270	AMOUNT RECEIVED ON LOAN ON DAY 270	TOTAL AMOUNT RECEIVED ON DAY 270	EFFECTIVE RATE ON LOAN	EFFECTIVE RATE WITHOUT PUT
5.0%	$200,000	$10,325,000	$10,525,000	10.82%	6.70%
5.5	175,000	10,350,000	10,525,000	10.82	7.22
6.0	150,000	10,375,000	10,525,000	10.82	7.75
6.5	125,000	10,400,000	10,525,000	10.82	8.28
7.0	100,000	10,425,000	10,525,000	10.82	8.81
7.5	75,000	10,450,000	10,525,000	10.82	9.34
8.0	50,000	10,475,000	10,525,000	10.82	9.87
8.5	25,000	10,500,000	10,525,000	10.82	10.40
9.0	0	10,525,000	10,525,000	10.82	10.93
9.5	0	10,550,000	10,550,000	11.35	11.47
10.0	0	10,575,000	10,575,000	11.89	12.00
10.5	0	10,600,000	10,600,000	12.42	12.54
11.0	0	10,625,000	10,625,000	12.96	13.08
11.5	0	10,650,000	10,650,000	13.50	13.62
12.0	0	10,675,000	10,675,000	14.04	14.16
12.5	0	10,700,000	10,700,000	14.59	14.71
13.0	0	10,725,000	10,725,000	15.13	15.25

Without the put, the effective rate on the loan is

$$\left(\frac{\$10,725,000}{\$10,000,000}\right)^{365/180} - 1 = 0.1525.$$

A graph of the results is in Figure 13.5. Note how the loan without the put has considerable downside risk. The loan with the put participates in the benefits from high interest rates but is protected against low interest rates. If interest rates are higher, however, the loan generates a lower return, due to the put premium, than the loan without the put.

Interest Rate Caps, Floors, and Collars

What we have covered so far with respect to interest rate options does not include the majority of the situations in which interest rate options are used. Recall from Chapter 12 how we showed that swaps are widely used in conjunction with floating-rate loans. In this

FIGURE 13.5 Return on Loan with and without Interest Rate Put

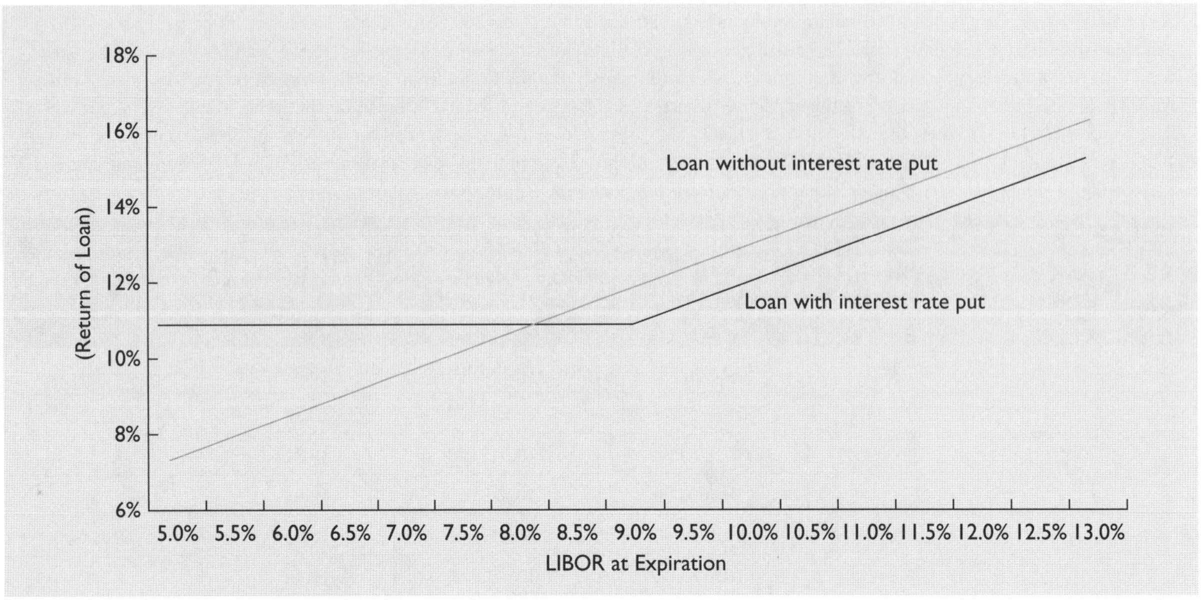

chapter so far, we have examined only loans involving one payment. FRAs, interest rate calls, and interest rate puts are not useful for loans involving more than one payment, at least not in the form we have seen them here. Interest rate calls and puts can, however, be combined into a series of options that can effectively protect floating-rate loans. The analogy is that a swap, which is effectively a combination of FRAs, can protect a floating-rate loan, as we saw in Chapter 12. Of course, swaps and FRAs are commitments. In some cases, an option is preferred. Options provide flexibility to benefit from rate movements in one direction while not being hurt by rate movements in another direction.

A combination of interest rate calls designed to protect a borrower in a floating-rate loan against increases in interest rates is called an **interest rate cap**. Each component call is referred to as a **caplet**. A combination of interest rate puts designed to protect a lender in a floating-rate loan against decreases in interest rates is called an **interest rate floor**. Each component put is referred to as a **floorlet**. A combination of a long cap and short floor is called an **interest rate collar**, which is similar to but still different from the collars we discussed in Chapter 7. A collar is most often used by a borrower and consists of a long position in a cap, financed by selling a short position in a floor.

Interest Rate Caps   Let us first look at an example of a cap. On January 2, a firm borrows $25 million over one year. It will make payments on April 2, July 2, October 2, and next January 2. On each of these dates starting with January 2, LIBOR in effect on that date will be the interest rate paid over the next three months. The current LIBOR is 10 percent. The firm wants to fix the rate on each payment at no more than 10 percent, so it buys a cap for an up-front payment of $70,000 with an exercise rate of 10 percent. The payoffs are based on the exact number of days in the settlement period and a 360-day year. At each interest payment date, the cap will be worth

> An interest rate cap is a combination of interest rate calls designed to protect a borrower in a floating-rate loan against increases in interest rates.

$$\$25,000,000\,\text{Max}(0,\text{LIBOR} - 0.010)\left(\frac{\text{days}}{360}\right),$$

where LIBOR is understood to be set on the previous settlement date and "days" is the number of days in the period. LIBOR for the first payment is

TABLE 13.7 AFTER-THE-FACT PAYMENTS FOR LOAN WITH INTEREST RATE CAP

Scenario: On January 2, a company takes out a $25 million one-year loan with interest paid quarterly at LIBOR. To protect against rising interest rates, the company buys an interest rate cap with an exercise rate of 10 percent for a premium of $70,000. The interest payments on the loan and the payoffs of the cap are based on the exact number of days and a 360-day year.

DATE	DAYS IN PERIOD	LIBOR (%)	INTEREST DUE	CAP PAYMENT	PRINCIPAL REPAYMENT	NET CASH FLOW	NET CASH FLOW WITHOUT CAP
Jan 2		10.000		−$70,000	$0	$24,930,000	$25,000,000
Apr 2	90	9.750	$625,000	–	0	−625,000	−625,000
Jul 2	91	12.375	616,146	0	0	−616,146	−616,146
Oct 2	92	11.500	790,625	151,736	0	−638,889	−790,625
Jan 2	92		734,722	95,833	25,000,000	−25,638,889	−25,734,722

Effective annual rate

   Without cap: 11.50%

   With cap: 10.78%

Note: This combination of LIBORs on the above dates represents only one of an infinite number of possible outcomes. They are used only to illustrate how the payments are determined and not the likely results.

set when the loan is initiated. Thus, as we previously discussed for interest rate options, the decision to exercise is made at the beginning of the settlement period, which is the date on which the rate is set, but the payoff occurs at the end of the settlement period. If LIBOR exceeds 10 percent, the firm will exercise the option and receive an amount as given by this equation. This payoff helps offset the higher interest rate on the loan. Table 13.7 illustrates a set of possible payments that might occur on this loan. Of course, these payments represent only one of an infinite number of possible LIBORs on the various settlement dates.

For the first quarter, the firm will pay LIBOR of 10 percent in effect on January 2. Thus, on April 2, it will owe $25,000,000(0.10)(90360) = $625,000$, based on 90 days from January 2 to April 2.[6] Then on April 2, LIBOR is 9.75 percent, and the caplet expires out-of-the-money. On July 2, LIBOR is 12.375 percent. Because this rate exceeds the exercise rate of 10 percent, the caplet expires in-the-money. Thus, on October 2, the company will receive a payment of

$$\$25,000,000 \text{Max}(0, 0.12375 - 0.10)\left(\frac{92}{360}\right) = \$151,736.$$

This payment will help offset the interest of $790,625, based on a rate of 12.375 percent for 92 days from July 2 to October 2. LIBOR on October 2 is 11.5 percent, so a caplet will also pay off on January 2. The net effect of these cash flows is seen in Column 7 of Table 13.7. On January 2, the firm received $25 million from the lender but paid out $70,000 for the cap, for a net cash inflow of $24,930,000. It made periodic payments as

---

[6]There is no caplet that pays off on April 2, because the rate on April 2 is set on January 2, the day the loan is taken out and the cap is purchased. There is no uncertainty associated with that rate. If the cap were purchased in advance of the day on which the loan is taken out, the firm might add a caplet that would expire on January 2 and pay off on April 2.

shown and on the next January 2 repaid the principal and made the final interest payment less the cap payoff. Note that because of the cap, the net interest payments differ only because of the different number of days during each settlement period and not because of the rate. The interest rate is effectively capped at the exercise rate of 10 percent.

If we want to know the annualized rate the firm actually paid, we must solve for the internal rate of return, which requires a computer or financial calculator. We are solving for the rate that equates the present value of the four payouts to the initial receipt:

$$\$24{,}930{,}000 = \frac{\$625{,}000}{(1+y)^1} + \frac{\$616{,}146}{(1+y)^2} + \frac{\$638{,}889}{(1+y)^3} + \frac{\$25{,}638{,}889}{(1+y)^4}.$$

The solution is $y = 0.025927$. Annualizing this result gives a rate of $(1.025927)^4 - 1 = 0.1078$. The last column in Table 13.7 shows the cash flows if the cap had not been purchased. Solving for the internal rate of return using those numbers and annualizing this result gives a rate of 0.115. Thus, the cap saved the firm 72 basis points, because during the life of the loan, interest rates were higher than they were at the time the loan was initiated. Of course, if rates had fallen, the firm probably would have paid a higher effective rate with the cap, because the caplets would have been out-of-the-money but the premium was expended. Pricing caps proceeds in the same manner as pricing interest rate calls. Each caplet is a separate interest rate call, but with a different expiration and a potentially different forward rate, risk-free rate, and volatility. The total price of the cap is the sum of the prices of the component caplets.

Interest Rate Floors An interest rate floor is typically used by a lender in a floating-rate loan who wants protection against falling rates. As noted above, a floor contains a series of interest rate put options, each of which is called a floorlet. At each interest payment date, the payoff of an interest rate floor tied to LIBOR with an exercise rate of, say, 8 percent, payoffs based on the exact number of days and a 360-day year, and a notional amount of $15 million will be

$$\$15{,}000{,}000 \, \text{Max}(0, 0.08 - \text{LIBOR})\left(\frac{\text{days}}{360}\right),$$

where as previously noted, LIBOR is set at the beginning of the settlement period.

Suppose on December 16 a bank makes a one-year $15 million loan with payments at LIBOR on March 16, June 16, September 15, and next December 16. LIBOR is currently 7.875 percent. Thus, on March 16, the bank will receive $15,000,000 [0.07875(90/360)] = $295,313 in interest, which is based on 90 days between December 16 and March 16. The bank purchases a floor for $30,000 at an exercise rate of 8 percent. The new rate on March 16 is 8.25 percent, so the first floorlet expires out-of-the-money. LIBOR on June 16 is 7.125 percent, however, so the floorlet expires in-the-money and pays off

$$\$15{,}000{,}000 \, \text{Max}(0, 0.08 - 0.07125)\left(\frac{91}{360}\right) = \$33{,}177$$

on the next interest payment date of September 15. This payoff will add to the interest received of $270,156, which is lower because of the fall in interest rates. The complete results for this one-year loan under a series of assumed LIBORs over the life of the loan are shown in Table 13.8.

> An interest rate floor is a combination of interest rate puts designed to protect a lender in a floating-rate loan against interest rate decreases.

The bank paid out $15,000,000 up front to the borrower and another $30,000 for the floor. Column 7 in Table 13.8 indicates the periodic cash flows associated with the loan combined with the floor. Following the same procedure as in the cap, we can solve for the periodic rate that equates the present value of the inflows to the outflow. This rate turns

TABLE 13.8 AFTER-THE-FACT PAYMENTS FOR LOAN WITH INTEREST RATE FLOOR

Scenario: On December 16, a bank makes a $15 million one-year loan with interest paid quarterly at LIBOR. To protect against falling interest rates, the bank buys an interest rate floor with an exercise rate of 8 percent for a premium of $30,000. The interest payments on the loan and the payoffs of the floor are based on the exact number of days and a 360-day year.

DATE	DAYS IN PERIOD	LIBOR (%)	INTEREST DUE	FLOOR PAYMENT	PRINCIPAL REPAYMENT	NET CASH FLOW	NET CASH FLOW WITHOUT FLOOR
Dec 16		7.875		−$30,000	$0	−$15,030,000	−$15,000,000
Mar 16	90	8.250	$295,313	–	0	295,313	295,313
Jun 16	92	7.125	316,250	0	0	316,250	316,250
Sep 15	91	6.000	270,156	33,177	0	303,333	270,156
Dec 16	92		230,000	76,667	$15,000,000	15,306,667	15,230,000

Effective annual rate

    Without cap: 7.64%

    With cap: 8.17%

Note: This combination of LIBORs on the above dates represents only one of an infinite number of possible outcomes. They are used only to illustrate how the payments are determined and not the likely results.

out to be about 1.9831 percent. Annualizing gives a rate of $(1.019831)^4 − 1 = 0.0817$. The last column shows the cash flows if the floor had not been used. The annualized return without the floor is 7.64 percent. Thus, the floor boosted the bank's return by 76 basis points. Of course, in a period of rising rates, the bank will gain less from the increase in interest rates because the floor premium is lost, but the floorlets will tend to not be exercised, in which case the bank might have been better off without the floor.

As with caps, the price of a floor is found by pricing each of the component floorlets and adding up their prices.

Interest Rate Collars In Chapter 7, we discussed how an investor could use a collar to protect a portfolio of stock. The investor owns the portfolio and purchases a put for downside protection. To finance the purchase of the put, the investor sells a call in which the exercise price of the call is set at a level that will produce a premium level on the call that will offset the premium paid for the put. This transaction creates a range for the value of the stock. The value of the position will not fall below the exercise price of the long put, nor will it rise above the exercise price of the short call. In a similar manner, a borrower can use a collar to create a range of interest rates, ensuring that the borrower will pay no more than a given rate or any less than another rate.

> An interest rate collar is a long position in an interest rate cap and a short position in an interest rate floor designed to protect a borrower in a floating-rate loan against higher interest rates. The premium on the floor is designed to reduce or offset the premium on the cap. The net result is that maximum and minimum rates are established on the loan.

Consider a firm planning to borrow money that decides to purchase an interest rate cap. In doing so, the firm is trying to place a ceiling (cap) on the rate it will pay on the loan. If rates fall, it can gain by paying a lower rate. In some cases, however, a firm will find it more advantageous to give up the right to gain from falling rates in order to lower the cost of the cap. One way to do this is to sell a floor. The combination of a long interest rate cap and short interest rate floor is called an *interest rate collar*, or sometimes just a collar. While it is not necessary that the premium from selling the floor be exactly equal to the premium from buying the cap, in most situations, that is what borrowers prefer.

This type of collar is called a **zero-cost collar**. This term is somewhat misleading, however, because nothing comes at zero cost. The cost to the borrower is in its willingness to give up the benefits from a decrease in interest rates below the exercise price of the floor. A collar establishes a range of rates within which there is interest rate uncertainty, but the maximum and minimum rates are locked in.

Table 13.9 illustrates a zero-cost collar in which a firm borrowing $50 million over two years buys a cap for $250,000 with an exercise rate of 10 percent and sells a floor for $250,000 with an exercise rate of 8.5 percent. The loan begins on March 15 and will require payments at approximately 91-day intervals at LIBOR.

By now you should be able to verify the numbers in the table. The interest paid on June 15 is based on LIBOR on March 15 of 10.5 and 92 days during the period. The cap pays off on September 14 and December 14 because those are the ends of the settlement periods in which LIBOR at the beginning of the period was greater than 10 percent. The floor pays off on September 14 and December 15 of the next year and on March 14 of the following year, the due date on the loan. Note that when the floor pays off, the firm makes rather than receives the payment.

Column 8 of Table 13.9 shows the cash flows associated with the collar. Following the procedure previously described to solve for the internal rate of return gives an annualized rate of 9.83 percent for the loan with the collar. Column 9 shows the cash flows had the firm done only the loan with the cap. The rate associated with this strategy would have been 9.93 percent. The last column indicates the cash flows had the firm done neither the cap nor the floor. The borrowing rate associated with that strategy would have been 10.10 percent.

The cap by itself would have helped lower the firm's cost of borrowing. By selling the floor, and thus creating a collar, the cost of the loan was lowered from 9.93 percent to 9.83 percent. Other outcomes, of course, would lead to different results, and it is possible that the loan without the cap or collar would end up best.

Collars are most often used by borrowers, but they could certainly be used by lenders. A lender could buy a floor to protect against falling rates below the floor exercise rate and sell a cap that would give up the gains from rising rates above the cap exercise rate.

Interest Rate Options, FRAs, and Swaps

Before we leave interest rate options, it is important for us to take a look at the relationships between the three most important interest rate derivatives: swaps, FRAs, and options. Recall that in this chapter, we first introduced the FRA, which is a forward contract on an interest rate. A party agrees to pay a fixed rate and receive a floating rate. We showed that the fixed rate is the forward rate in the term structure. A swap is like a series of FRAs, but where all fixed payments are at the same rate. In other words, it is a series of FRAs, but each FRA is priced at the swap fixed rate. That means that some of the component FRAs will be priced at a fixed rate higher than they would have if priced individually. Some will have a lower fixed rate. As we mentioned earlier, when an FRA is not priced at the forward rate, it is called an off-market FRA. Thus, a swap is a series of off-market FRAs.

A combination of interest rate calls and puts can also be shown to reproduce the payments on a swap. Assume that we buy a call (in this context, also known as a caplet) and sell a put (floorlet). Let R be the fixed rate on a swap and let X be the exercise rate on both a call and a put. Let the underlying rate be LIBOR. Suppose that we are at a settlement date. The long call payoff is

$$0 \quad \text{if} \quad \text{LIBOR} \leq X$$
$$\text{LIBOR} - X \quad \text{if} \quad \text{LIBOR} > X.$$

TABLE 13.9 AFTER-THE-FACT PAYMENTS FOR LOAN WITH INTEREST RATE COLLAR

Scenario: On March 15, a company takes out a $50 million two-year loan with interest paid quarterly at LIBOR. To protect against rising interest rates, the company buys an interest rate cap with an exercise rate of 10 percent for a premium of $250,000. To offset the cost of the cap, the company sells an interest rate floor with an exercise rate of 8.5 percent for $250,000. The interest payments on the loan and the payoffs of the cap and floor are based on the exact number of days and a 360-day year.

DATE	DAYS IN PERIOD	LIBOR (%)	INTEREST DUE	CAP PAYMENT	FLOOR PAYMENT	PRINCIPAL REPAYMENT	NET CASH FLOW WITH COLLAR	NET CASH FLOW WITH CAP ONLY	NET CASH FLOW WITHOUT CAP OR FLOOR
Mar 15		10.500		−$250,000	$250,000	$0	$50,000,000	$49,750,000	$50,000,000
Jun 15	92	11.500	$1,341,667	–	–	0	−1,341,667	−1,341,667	−1,341,667
Sep 14	91	11.750	1,453,472	189,583	0	0	−1,263,889	−1,263,889	−1,453,472
Dec 14	91	9.125	1,485,069	221,181	0	0	−1,263,889	−1,263,889	−1,485,069
Mar 15	91	9.500	1,153,299	0	0	0	−1,153,299	−1,153,299	−1,153,299
Jun 14	91	7.625	1,200,694	0	0	0	−1,200,694	−1,200,694	−1,200,694
Sep 14	92	8.375	974,306	0	−111,806	0	−1,086,111	−974,306	−974,306
Dec 15	92	8.000	1,070,139	0	−15,972	0	−1,086,111	−1,070,139	−1,070,139
Mar 14	89		988,889	0	−61,806	50,000,000	−51,050,694	−50,988,889	−50,988,889

Effective annual rate

Without collar:	10.10%
With collar:	9.83%
With cap only:	9.93%

Note: This combination of LIBORs on the above dates represents only one of an infinite number of possible outcomes. They are used only to illustrate how the payments are determined and not the likely results.

The short put payoff is

$$
\begin{array}{ll}
(\text{X} - \text{LIBOR}) & \text{if} \quad \text{LIBOR} \leq \text{X} \\
0 & \text{if} \quad \text{LIBOR} > \text{X}.
\end{array}
$$

Thus, the combined payoff of the long call and short put is

$$
\begin{array}{lll}
\text{LIBOR} - \text{X} & \text{if} & \text{LIBOR} \leq \text{X} \\
\text{LIBOR} - \text{X} & \text{if} & \text{LIBOR} > \text{X}
\end{array}
$$

This result can be simplified to

$$
\text{LIBOR} - \text{X},
$$

which will occur on the next settlement date. This result applies to each settlement date.

Now let us examine the payoffs of a swap to pay a fixed rate R and receive a floating rate. The payoff is

$$
\text{LIBOR} - \text{R},
$$

which will occur on the next settlement date. This result applies to each settlement date.

> A long position in a series of interest rate calls and a short position in a series of interest rate floors is equivalent to a swap when the exercise rate on the calls and puts is the same as the fixed rate on the swap.

The swap and long call/short put results are similar. Whether they are the same depends on whether X = R. Remember from Chapter 12 that we found R by pricing the swap, using the information in the term structure. The exercise rate on a call or put is chosen by the parties to the contract. Thus, X is arbitrary and can be any rate. When X is chosen to equal R, the long call/short put produces the same payoffs as the pay-fixed, receive-floating swap. Recall that a swap requires no initial outlay. Thus, the value of the swap is zero at the start. Hence, when X is chosen to equal R, the long call/short put must also have a zero value at the start. This means that the premium on the call must equal the premium on the put. Otherwise, there would be an arbitrage opportunity.

TECHNICAL NOTE: Put-Call Parity of Interest Rate Options
go to www.cengagebrain.com

Because a swap has multiple payments, there would have to be a series of calls and puts. It is important to note, however, that the option strategy we have just described is not a zero-cost collar. We noted that in a zero-cost collar, the call and put premiums are the same but the exercise prices are different. In fact, it is not a collar at all because the options have the same exercise prices.

INTEREST RATE SWAPTIONS AND FORWARD SWAPS

Earlier in this chapter, we mentioned that a firm that had entered into a swap could exit the swap before it terminates if the firm had previously purchased an option on the swap. Options on swaps are called swap options, or *swaptions*. A swaption is an option in which the buyer pays a premium up front and acquires the right to enter into a swap. Although swaptions exist on interest rate, currency, equity, and commodity swaps, we shall focus exclusively on swaptions on interest rate swaps, where it is understood that the underlying is a plain vanilla swap. In an interest rate swaption, the buyer receives the right to enter into a swap as either a fixed-rate payer, floating-rate receiver or a floating-rate payer, fixed-rate receiver. The former is called a **payer swaption**, while the latter is called a **receiver swaption**.

> A swaption is an option to enter into a swap. It provides the holder with the right to enter into a swap at a fixed rate, which is the exercise rate, or better. The right to enter into a swap paying a fixed rate is called a payer swaption, and the right to enter into a swap receiving a fixed rate is called a receiver swaption.

A swaption can be viewed as a variation of an interest rate option, but there are several important differences. Like an interest rate option, the

MAKING THE CONNECTION

Binomial Pricing of Interest Rate Options

We noted in this chapter that the Black model provides a simple approximation for interest rate option prices. A better approach is to build a model of the term structure that eliminates the possibility of earning arbitrage profits by trading bonds or derivatives with prices driven by interest rates. Binomial models are commonly used to price interest rate options. Here we look at a simple binomial model of the term structure and use it to price an interest rate option. Consider the term structure of LIBORs below.

Term	Rate	Discount Bond Price
360 days	8.0%	$B_0(360) = 1/(1 + 0.08(360/360)) = 0.9259$
720 days	8.5%	$B_0(720) = 1/(1 + 0.085(720/360)) = 0.8547$

Let us define a one-period binomial period as 360 days. The information above will be sufficient to build a two-period binomial model. At time zero, we have the prices of a one-period bond (0.9259) and a two-period bond (0.8547). At time 1 in either outcome, the original one-period will mature to its face value of 1. At time 1, the original two-period bond will be worth a price denoted as $B_1(2)^+$ in the up state or $B_1(2)^-$ in the down state. Thus, the binomial term structure will look like this:

$$B_1(1)^+ = 1$$
$$B_1(2)^+ = ?$$

$$B_0(1) = 0.9259$$
$$B_0(2) = 0.8547$$

$$B_1(1)^- = 1$$
$$B_1(2)^- = ?$$

We need to find the missing bond prices and convert them to interest rates. It is very important to note that the bond prices in the higher states are bond prices in higher interest rate states. Thus, $B_1(2)^+$ is less than $B_1(2)^-$, which may seem a little counterintuitive. That is, the plus (1) state at time 1 is a higher interest rate but lower bond price than the minus (−) state.

To eliminate arbitrage opportunities, we must impose the following restrictions:

- It is not possible to make an arbitrage profit by buying a one-period bond, financing it by selling short a two-period bond.
- It is not possible to make an arbitrage profit by buying a two-period bond, financing it by selling short a one-period bond.

For the first strategy, an arbitrage profit would occur if

$$\frac{1}{B_0(1)} > \frac{B_1(2)^-}{B_0(2)}.$$

An arbitrage profit would occur if the return from investing $1 in a one-period bond, the left-hand side above, is higher than the highest return one would owe from shorting a two-period bond, the right-hand side above. For the second strategy, an arbitrage profit would occur if

$$\frac{1}{B_0(1)} < \frac{B_1(2)^+}{B_0(2)}.$$

An arbitrage profit would occur if the financing cost from shorting a one-period bond, the left-hand side above, were less than the worst outcome from buying a two-period bond, the right-hand side above. To prevent both conditions from holding, we require that

$$\frac{B_1(2)^+}{B_0(2)} < \frac{1}{B_0(1)} < \frac{B_1(2)^-}{B_0(2)}.$$

Although there are many ways to meet this condition, a simple one is to apply weights of 0.5 and 0.5 to the two expressions on the ends of the inequality, giving us

$$0.5B_1(2)^+ + B_1(2) = \frac{B_0(2)}{B_0(1)}.$$

The right-hand side is the forward price from the term structure of one- and two-period bonds. The left-hand side can be interpreted as the expected price of the two-period bond at time 1 for a probability of 0.5.

This requirement is a single equation with two unknowns, $B_1(2)^+$ and $B_1(2)^-$, so we cannot solve it. We can, however, solve it by adding the constraint that the volatility of the interest rate is a particular known value, σ. Now, we have two equations and two unknowns. Let r^+ and r^- be the two possible continuously compounded one-period rates at time 1. The volatility of the interest rate in a binomial model is found as follows:

$$\sigma = \frac{r^+ + r^-}{2}.$$

These two rates determine the prices, $B_1(2)^+$ and $B_1(2)^-$. Although solving these two equations for the bond prices is not simple, it can be done. The results are

$$r^+ = 0.0901 \quad r^- = 0.0701,$$

which correspond to zero coupon bond prices of

$$B_1(2)^+ = e^{-0.0901} = 0.9138$$
$$B_1(2)^- = e^{-0.0701} = 0.9323.$$

The LIBORs that produce these prices are 9.43 percent and 7.26 percent as verified in the following:

$$B_1(2)^+ = \frac{1}{1 + 0.0943\left(\frac{360}{360}\right)} = 0.9138$$

$$B_1(2)^- = \frac{1}{1 + 0.0726\left(\frac{360}{360}\right)} = 0.9323$$

Thus, the one-period rates at time 1 are 9.43 percent and 7.26 percent.

As an example of how this model would be used, the payoff of a call option payoff expiring at time 1 with an exercise rate of 8 percent would be

$$C^+ = \text{Max}(0, 0.0943 - 0.08)0.9138 = 0.0131$$
$$C^- = \text{Max}(0, 0.0726 - 0.08)0.9323 = 0.0,$$

where we multiply by the one-period bond price to discount for the delay in the payoff. The option price at time 0 based on a $1 notional amount is, therefore,

$$C = (0.5(0.0131) + 0.5(0.0))0.9323 = 0.0061,$$

where we see that the weighted average of the next two prices is discounted using the one-period discount factor.

To price options with longer expirations, we would need information on the prices of longer-term zero coupon bonds and the volatilities of other interest rates.

exercise rate is stated in terms of an interest rate. A swaption is based on an underlying swap and has a fixed maturity. A swaption can be American- or European-style. The parties agree up front that exercise will be accomplished by entering into the underlying swap or by an equivalent cash settlement.

Structure of a Typical Interest Rate Swaption

Consider the following situation. A company called MPK Resources is considering the possibility that it will need to engage in an interest rate swap two years from now with a notional amount of $10 million. It expects that the swap would be a three-year pay fixed-receive floating swap. The firm is concerned about rising interest rates over the next two years that would force it to pay a higher fixed rate if it entered into the swap at that time. It thus decides to purchase a two-year European-style payer swaption where the underlying is a three-year, pay fixed-receive floating swap. Naturally, the underlying swap should be identical to the one MPK expects to take out in two years. MPK specifies an exercise rate of 11.5 percent. MPK pays a premium up front, the amount of which we do not need to know at this point. To keep the illustration as simple as possible, assume that the underlying swap calls for annual interest payments.

Now let us consider what happens when the swaption expires in two years. At that time, we observe a term structure of LIBOR as follows:

Term	Rate	Discount Bond Price
360 days	12.00%	$B_0(360) = 1/(1 + 0.12(360/360)) = 0.8929$
720 days	13.28%	$B_0(720) = 1/(1 + 0.1328(720/360)) = 0.7901$
1080 days	14.51%	$B_0(1080) = 1/(1 + 0.1451(1080/360)) = 0.6967$

Based on this information, what would be the rate in the market for three-year swaps? This result is easily found using what we learned in Chapter 12:

$$R = \left(\frac{1 - 0.6967}{0.8929 + 0.7901 + 0.6967}\right)\left(\frac{360}{360}\right) = 0.1275.$$

Thus, MPK, or any party, could enter into a pay-fixed, receive-floating swap at a fixed rate of 12.75 percent. As it turns out, however, MPK holds a payer swaption that allows it to enter into a pay-fixed, receive-floating swap paying a fixed rate of 11.5 percent. It should be obvious that the swaption is expiring with a positive value. MPK can enter into a swap to pay 11.5 percent fixed and receive LIBOR, whereas without the swap, it would have to pay 12.75 percent fixed to receive LIBOR. Clearly, the swap has value, but how much?

Suppose that MPK exercises the swaption, resulting in the entry into a swap to pay a fixed rate of 11.5 percent and receive LIBOR. Now suppose that it enters into the opposite swap in the market at the rate of 12.75 percent. Thus, it has the following positions:

A swap to pay 11.5 percent and receive LIBOR, plus
A swap to pay LIBOR and receive 12.75 percent.
The effect of LIBOR offsets on both swaps, leaving the following:
A position to pay 11.5 percent and receive 12.75 percent.

The net effect is that this position becomes a three-year annuity that pays 12.75% − 11.5% = 1.25%. It is a simple matter to determine the value of this annuity. The payments will be $10,000,000(0.0125) = \$125,000$. We find their present value using the discount factors for LIBOR obtained above:

$$\$125,000(0.8929 + 0.7901 + 0.6967) = \$297,463.$$

Thus, the swaption is worth $297,463 at expiration. In general, the payoff of a payer swaption at expiration is

$$(\text{Notional Amount})\text{Max}(0, R - X)\left(\frac{\text{days}}{360}\right)\sum_{i=1}^{n} B_0(t_i).$$

where R is the swap rate at the swaption expiration, X is the exercise rate of the swaption, and the summation term captures the present value factors over the life of the swap. The payoff of a receiver swaption is

$$(\text{Notional Amount})\text{Max}(0, X - R)\left(\frac{\text{days}}{360}\right)\sum_{i=1}^{n} B_0(t_i).$$

Returning to our example, MPK would exercise the swaption. MPK would then be engaged in a swap with a market value of $297,463. MPK could also choose to enter into a pay-floating, receive-fixed swap at the market rate of 12.75 percent. The net effect of these two swaps would be to create the annuity as described above, which has a market value of $297,463. Alternatively, MPK could just leave in place the swap created by exercise of the swaption. Its market value would be $297,463 instead of the normal zero market value when a swap is initiated. Had the swaption been structured to settle in cash, the short would have simply paid MPK $297,463. Of course, had the rate on swaps in the market been less than 11.5 percent, the swaption would have expired with no value. It should be apparent that when interest rates are high (at least high enough that the swap rate is above the swaption exercise rate), payer swaptions expire in-the-money and are, thus, somewhat like interest rate calls. When rates are low (at least low enough that the swap rate is below the swaption exercise rate), receiver swaptions expire in-the-money and are, thus, somewhat like interest rate puts.

Equivalence of Swaptions and Options on Bonds

Although swaptions may seem like complex instruments, it is actually quite easy to show that a swaption is identical to an option on a bond. Consider the MPK payer swaption. When it expires, it will have the same value as that of a put option on a bond whose maturity corresponds to the maturity of the swap and whose coupon rate is the exercise rate of the swap. To simplify the problem, let us assume a notional amount of $1. Recall that we calculated its payoff value in the following manner:

$$\text{Max}(0, 0.1275 - 0.115)\left(\frac{360}{360}\right)(0.8929 + 0.7901 + 0.6967).$$

Recall that we found the value of 0.1275 in the following manner:

$$\left(\frac{1 - 0.6967}{0.8929 + 0.7901 + 0.6967}\right)\left(\frac{360}{360}\right) = 0.1275.$$

If we substitute the second equation into the first, we can write the payoff value of the swaption as

$$\text{Max}(0, 1 - 0.6967 - 0.115(0.8929 + 0.7901 + 0.6967)).$$

Now suppose that instead of the swaption, we purchase a put option with an exercise price of $1 on a bond that will have a three-year maturity when the option expires, annual interest payments of 11.5 percent, and a face value of $1. The value of this bond when the option expires would be the present value of three coupons of 0.115 and the present value of the principal of 1:

$$0.115(0.8929 + 0.7901 + 0.6967) + 1(0.6967).$$

The payoff of a put on this bond would be

$$\text{Max}(0, 1 - 0.6967 - 0.115(0.8929 + 0.7901 + 0.6967)),$$

which is the same as the payoff of the payer swaption. Thus, a payer swaption is the same as a put option on a bond. Similarly, a receiver swaption can be shown to be equivalent to a call option on a bond.

Pricing Swaptions

Pricing swaptions is a somewhat advanced and complex topic that we cannot take up in detail at this level. We can, however, appeal to the result of the previous section and gain some understanding of this process. As we showed, a swaption can be shown to be equivalent to an option on a bond. Thus, if we can price options on bonds, we can price swaptions. We have not taken up the pricing of options on bonds because this is a relatively advanced topic requiring the construction of an arbitrage-free model of the evolution of the term structure. As an alternative, the Black-Scholes-Merton model can be adapted to pricing bonds, with considerable care and a number of caveats.

> An interest rate swaption can be shown to be equivalent to an option on a bond and, therefore, can be priced like an option on a bond.

Forward Swaps

Throughout this book, we have covered options and forward contracts. Because there are options on swaps, there will also be forward contracts on swaps. These instruments are called *forward swaps*. A forward swap commits the two parties to enter into a swap at a specific fixed rate. One party, the long, commits to enter into the swap to pay the fixed rate; the

> A forward swap is a contract that obligates the two parties to enter into a swap at a later date at a fixed rate agreed to in advance.

Solving for the fixed rate on a forward swap is equivalent to pricing a swap using the forward rates instead of the spot rates in the term structure.

other commits to enter into the swap to receive the fixed rate. Because it is a forward contract, there is no cash flow up front.

Going back to our MPK example, suppose that instead of using a swaption, it wants to lock in the rate on the swap. Recall that when pricing a swap, we showed that a pay-fixed, receive-floating swap is equivalent to issuing a fixed-rate bond and using the proceeds to buy a floating-rate bond. In a similar manner, entering into a forward contract on a pay-fixed, receive-floating swap is equivalent to entering into a forward contract to issue a fixed-rate bond and buy a floating-rate bond. Entering into a forward contact to buy a floating-rate bond is trivial. Because the bond will be issued at par value, there is no uncertainly over its value when issued. Two parties simply agree that on a later date, one party will pay par value and receive a bond selling at par. Entering into a forward contract to issue a fixed-rate bond, however, does require solving for a given rate. The bond will need to be issued at par so that its value will equal that of the floating-rate bond. Thus, its coupon will be adjusted so that it sells at par. When entering into a forward contract on this bond, the parties would need to solve for the appropriate coupon rate to make a forward contract on this bond be fairly priced.

This problem reduces to the simple problem of solving for the coupon rate on a par value bond to be issued at a later date. Going back to the MPK problem, suppose that at the time the forward swap is created, MPK faces the following term structure:

Term	Rate	Discount Bond Price
360 days	9.00%	$B_0(360) = 1/(1 + 0.09(360/360)) = 0.9174$
720 days	10.06%	$B_0(720) = 1/(1 + 0.1006(720/360)) = 0.8325$
1080 days	11.03%	$B_0(1080) = 1/(1 + 0.1103(1080/360)) = 0.7514$
1440 days	12.00%	$B_0(1440) = 1/(1 + 0.12(1440/360)) = 0.6757$
1800 days	12.95%	$B_0(1800) = 1/(1 + 0.1295(1800/360)) = 0.6070$

MPK is interested in a forward contract expiring in two years on a swap that will last three years. To find the appropriate fixed rate, we need the forward rates two years ahead for periods of one, two, and three years. These are found in the following manner.

The forward rates two years ahead are

$$\text{One year} = \left(\frac{1 + 0.1103\left(\dfrac{1080}{360}\right)}{1 + 0.1006\left(\dfrac{720}{360}\right)} - 1 \right) \left(\frac{360}{360} \right) = 0.1080$$

$$\text{Two years} = \left(\frac{1 + 0.12\left(\dfrac{1440}{360}\right)}{1 + 0.1006\left(\dfrac{720}{360}\right)} - 1 \right) \left(\frac{360}{720} \right) = 0.1161$$

$$\text{Three years} = \left(\frac{1 + 0.1295\left(\dfrac{1440}{360}\right)}{1 + 0.1006\left(\dfrac{720}{360}\right)} - 1 \right) \left(\frac{360}{1080} \right) = 0.1238.$$

The discount factors using the forward rates would be[7]

$$B_0(720,1080) = \frac{1}{1 + 0.1080\left(\dfrac{360}{360}\right)} = 0.9025$$

$$B_0(720,1440) = \frac{1}{1 + 0.1161\left(\dfrac{720}{360}\right)} = 0.8116$$

$$B_0(720,1800) = \frac{1}{1 + 0.1238\left(\dfrac{1080}{360}\right)} = 0.7292.$$

The rate on the forward swap would then be

$$\frac{1 - 0.7292}{0.9025 + 0.8116 + 0.7292} = 0.1108.$$

Applications of Swaptions and Forward Swaps

The most obvious application of a swaption is when a company anticipates that it will need to enter into a swap at a later date and would like to establish a swap rate in advance. A swaption would permit the company to benefit from a favorable interest rate move while protecting it against an unfavorable move. Of course, a swaption would require the payment of cash up front.

Consider a company that has already entered into a pay-fixed, receive-floating swap. If the company anticipates that it might want to terminate the swap, a receiver swaption would give it the right to do so by allowing it to enter into a pay-floating, receive-fixed swap at favorable terms. If the firm exercised the swaption, it would have two swaps with equivalent streams of floating cash flows that are opposite in sign. It would also have two fixed streams at different rates. Of course, with both swaps in place, there would be some credit risk. Alternatively, if the counterparty to the swaption is the same counterparty to the original swap, then exercise of the swaption can be achieved by canceling the original swap and replacing it with a lump sum cash payment of the market value or by leaving in place a stream of the net of the fixed rates on the two swaps. Because the firm might not know when it would want to terminate the swap, an American-style swaption would be preferred. In this manner, the company is using a swaption to give it flexibility to exit a swap.

Swaptions can also be used as a substitute for an option on a bond. When firms issue bonds and consider the possibility of wanting to change them from fixed rate to floating rate (or vice versa) at a later date, a swaption can provide that flexibility.

Another application of a swaption is in creating synthetic callable debt. A callable bond is a bond in which the issuing firm has the right to call or retire it early. If a non-callable bond is issued but the firm would like to add the right to call it, the firm can purchase a receiver swaption. If properly structured, this swaption gives the firm the economic equivalent of an option to retire the bond early. Likewise, if the firm has

---

[7]Here we must make a slight clarification in our notation. Using the first case as an example, the factor $B_0(720,1080)$ is the discount factor based on the forward rate established on day 0 that is based on a transaction to start on day 720 and end on day 1080.

issued a callable bond and no longer wants the right to call it, the firm can sell a receiver swaption, which effectively offsets the right to call the bond. Figure 13.6 presents a graphical depiction of a callable bond, a swaption, and the net position. The up arrows indicate receiving cash, and the down arrows indicate paying cash.

FIGURE 13.6 Illustration of Synthetic Fixed-Rate Bond with Swaption

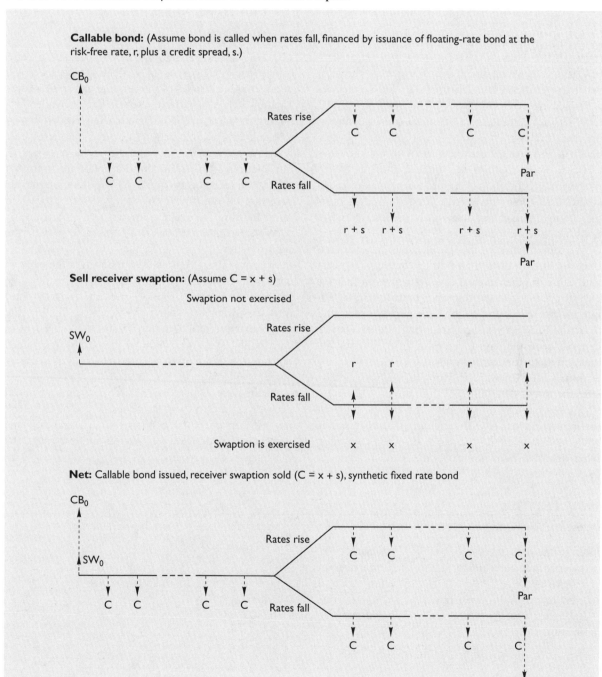

A puttable bond is a bond that the holder of the bond has the right to sell back to the issuer early, thereby forcing the issuer to pay off the bond before its maturity. A bond that is not puttable can be effectively made puttable by selling a payer swaption. A bond that is puttable can be made nonputtable by buying a payer swaption.

In all of these situations, a forward swap can be used instead of a swaption. A forward swap would have the advantage of not having an initial cash outlay but would have the disadvantage of locking in the terms of the underlying swap, rather than permitting the holder flexibility.

Summary

In Chapter 12, we examined swaps, which are the most widely used interest rate derivatives. In this chapter, we examined two general classes of interest rate derivatives: forward contracts and options. Forward contracts on interest rates are known as forward rate agreements, or FRAs, and forward contracts on swaps are known as forward swaps. Options on interest rates are called interest rate options, and options on swaps are called swaptions. These derivatives trade in the over-the-counter market and are widely used by corporations facing interest rate risk.

We found that even though FRAs are forward contracts on interest rates, their payoffs contrast somewhat with those of other interest rate derivatives in that the payoffs are made at the time the contract expires. For interest rate swaps and options, the payoffs occur after a certain number of days following the expiration, depending on the days to maturity of the instrument that defines the underlying rate. Thus, if the underlying is m-day LIBOR, swaps and options pay off m days after the rate is determined at expiration.

Interest rate call options pay off when the underlying interest rate is above the exercise rate at expiration, while interest rate put options pay off when the underlying interest rate is below the exercise rate at expiration. A borrower in a floating-rate loan will often combine a series of interest rate calls into a combination known as an interest rate cap. A lender in a floating-rate loan will often combine a series of interest rate puts into a combination known as an interest rate floor. A borrower will sometimes combine a long position in a cap with a short position in a floor to form a collar, whereby the premium on the floor offsets the premium on the cap. A collar provides an upper and lower limit on the effective interest rate on a loan.

We saw that swaptions can be used to provide the right to enter into a swap or they can be used to effectively exit a swap. A payer swaption gives the right to enter into a swap as a fixed-rate payer, floating-rate receiver. A receiver swaption gives the right to enter into the swap as a fixed-rate receiver, floating-rate payer. Exercise of a swaption creates the equivalent of an annuity. We also examined forward swaps, which obligate the two parties to enter into a swap at a rate agreed to in advance.

In the next chapter, we shall look at some advanced derivative contracts and strategies. Many of these will involve derivatives on equities, but we shall see one more type of derivative based on interest rates: the mortgage-backed security.

Key Terms

Before continuing to Chapter 14, you should be able to give brief definitions of the following terms:

interest rate derivatives/
   forward rate agreement
   (FRA), p. 456
interest rate option/interest rate
   call/interest rate put/swaption/
   forward swap, p. 457

off-market FRA/
   exercise rate, p. 466
interest rate cap/caplet/
   interest rate floor/floorlet/
   interest rate collar, p. 474

zero-cost collar, p. 478
payer swaption/receiver
   swaption, p. 480

Further Reading

Good overview materials on interest rate derivatives include the following:

Abken, P. A. "Interest Rate Caps, Collars, and Floors." *Federal Reserve Bank of Atlanta Economic Review* 72 (November/December, 1989): 2–24.

Jha, S. *Interest Rate Markets: A Practical Approach to Fixed Income.* New York: Wiley Finance, 2011.

Sadr, A. *Interest Rate Swaps and Their Derivatives.* New York: Wiley Finance, 2009.

More advanced treatments of the pricing and modeling of interest rate derivatives are given in the following books:

Buetow, G. W., and F. J. Fabozzi. *Valuation of Interest Rate Swaps and Swaptions.* New Hope, PA: Frank J. Fabozzi Associates, 2001.

James, J., and N. Webber. *Interest Rate Modelling.* Chichester, UK: John Wiley, 2000.

Jarrow, R. A. *Modeling Fixed-Income Securities and Interest Rate Options,* 2nd ed. Stanford, CA: Stanford University Press, 2002.

Concept Checks

1. How are the payment terms of an FRA different from those of most other interest rate derivatives?
2. Explain how FRAs are like swaps and how they are different.
3. Compare the use of interest rate options with forward rate agreements. Explain why a financial manager might prefer one type of contract over another.
4. Show how a combination of interest rate caps and floors can be equivalent to an interest rate swap.
5. What are the advantages and disadvantages of an interest rate collar over an interest rate cap?

Questions and Problems

1. Explain how the Black model, which is designed for pricing options on futures contracts, can be used for pricing interest rate options.
2. Explain how a swaption can be terminated at expiration by either exercising it or settling it in cash. Why are these procedures financially equivalent?
3. Explain how the two types of swaptions are like interest rate options and how they are different.
4. Explain how a bank could use a swaption to hedge the possibility that it will enter into a pay-floating, receive-fixed swap at a later date.
5. Explain how a forward swap is like a swaption and how it is different.
6. Suppose you are long a 90-day LIBOR-based FRA (receive floating) with notional amount of $50,000,000. At expiration, LIBOR is 4 percent and the strike rate (the agreed upon rate) is 3 percent. Assuming a 360-day year, what is the dollar profit or loss on this FRA? How would your answer change if you were short (receive fixed)?
7. Suppose you are long a 180-day LIBOR-based FRA (receive floating) with notional amount of $50,000,000. At expiration, LIBOR is 4 percent and the strike rate (the agreed upon rate) is 3 percent. Assuming a 360-day year, what is the dollar profit or loss on this FRA? How would your answer change if you were short (receive fixed)? Is your answer to this question twice the amount of the previous question? Why or why not?
8. Suppose you work on an interest rate derivatives trading desk and observe the following market quotes. Long (short) $100,000,000 interest rate cap, 90/360 day count, 4 percent strike rate priced at $4,950,000 ($4,925,000). Long (short) $100,000,000 interest rate floor, 90/360 day count, 4 percent strike rate priced at $5,000,000 ($4,975,000). An at-market receive floating interest rate swap with identical terms of the caps and floors above is quoted at 4.0 percent (3.95 percent for receive fixed). Identify an arbitrage strategy and identify any new risks introduced by pursuing the arbitrage.

9. Suppose a firm plans to borrow $5 million in 180 days. The loan will be taken out at whatever LIBOR is on the day the loan begins and will be repaid in one lump sum 90 days later. The firm would like to lock in the rate it pays, so it enters into a forward rate agreement with its bank. The bank agrees to lock in a rate of 12 percent. Determine the annualized cost of the loan for each of the following outcomes. Interest is based on 90 days and a 360-day year.
   a. LIBOR in 180 days is 14 percent.
   b. LIBOR in 180 days is 8 percent.
10. The following term structure of LIBOR is given.

Term	Rate
90 days	6.00%
180 days	6.20%
270 days	6.30%
360 days	6.35%

   a. Find the rate on a new 6 × 9 FRA.
   b. Consider an FRA that was established previously at a rate of 5.2 percent with a notional amount of $30 million. The FRA expires in 180 days, and the underlying is 180-day LIBOR. Find the value of the FRA from the perspective of the party paying fixed and receiving floating as of the point in time at which the above term structure applies.
11. You are the treasurer of a firm that will need to borrow $10 million at LIBOR plus 2.5 points in 45 days. The loan will have a maturity of 180 days, at which time all the interest and principal will be repaid. The interest will be determined by LIBOR on the day the loan is taken out. To hedge the uncertainty of this future rate, you purchase a call on LIBOR with a strike of 9 percent for a premium of $32,000. Determine the amount you will pay back and the annualized cost of borrowing for LIBORs of 6 percent and 12 percent. Assume the payoff is based on 180 days and a 360-day year. The current LIBOR is 9 percent.
12. A large, multinational bank has committed to lend a firm $25 million in 30 days at LIBOR plus 100 bps. The loan will have a maturity of 90 days, at which time the principal and all interest will be repaid. The bank is concerned about falling interest rates and decides to buy a put on LIBOR with a strike of 9.5 percent and a premium of $60,000.

Determine the annualized loan rate for LIBORs of 6.5 percent and 12.5 percent. Assume the payoff is based on 90 days and a 360-day year. The current LIBOR is 9.5 percent.
13. As the assistant treasurer of a large corporation, your job is to look for ways your company can lock in its cost of borrowing in the financial markets. The date is June 28. Your firm is taking out a loan of $20 million, with interest to be paid on September 28, December 31, March 31, and June 29. You will pay the LIBOR in effect at the beginning of the interest payment period. The current LIBOR is 10 percent. You recommend that the firm buy an interest rate cap with a strike of 10 percent and a premium of $70,000. Determine the cash flows over the life of this loan if LIBOR turns out to be 11 percent on September 28, 11.65 percent on December 31, and 12.04 percent on March 31. The payoff is based on the exact number of days and a 360-day year. If you have a financial calculator or a spreadsheet with an IRR function, solve for the internal rate of return and annualize it to determine the effective cost of borrowing.
14. You are a funds manager for a large bank. On April 15, your bank lends a corporation $35 million, with interest payments to be made on July 16, October 15, January 16, and next April 16. The amount of interest will be determined by LIBOR at the beginning of the interest payment period. On April 15, LIBOR is 8.0 percent. Your forecast is for declining interest rates, so you anticipate lower loan interest revenues. You decide to buy an interest rate floor with a strike set at 8 percent and a premium of $60,000. Determine the cash flows associated with the loan if LIBOR turns out to be 7.9 percent on July 16, 7.7 percent on October 15, and 8.1 percent next January 16. The payoff is based on the exact number of days and a 360-day year. If you have a financial calculator or spreadsheet with an IRR function, determine the internal rate of return and annualize it to determine your annualized return on the loan.
15. On January 15, a firm takes out a loan of $30 million, with interest payments to be made on April 16, July 15, October 14, and the following January 15, when the principal will be repaid. Interest will be paid at LIBOR based on the rate at the beginning of the interest payment period, using the exact number of days and a 360-day year. The firm wants to buy a cap with an exercise rate of 10 percent and a premium of $125,000 but is

concerned about the cost. Its bank suggests that the firm sell a floor with an exercise rate of 9 percent for the same premium. The current LIBOR is 10 percent. Determine the firm's cash flows on the loan if LIBOR turns out to be 11.35 percent on April 16, 10.2 percent on July 15, and 8.86 percent on October 14. If you have a financial calculator or spreadsheet, determine the internal rate of return and annualize it to determine the cost of borrowing.

16. A bank is offering an interest rate call with an expiration of 45 days. The call pays off based on 180-day LIBOR. The volatility of forward rates is 17 percent. The 45-day forward rate for 180-day LIBOR is 0.1322, and the exercise rate is 12 percent. The risk-free rate for 45 days is 11.28 percent. All rates are continuously compounded. Use the Black model to determine how much the bank should receive for selling this call for every $1 million of notional amount.

17. A firm is interested in purchasing an interest rate cap from a bank. It has received an offer price from the bank but would like to determine if the price is fair. The cap will consist of two caplets, one expiring in 91 days and the other in 182 days. They will both have strikes of 7 percent. The forward rate applicable to the first caplet is 8 percent, and the forward rate applicable to the second caplet is 8.2 percent. The 91-day risk-free rate is 7.1 percent, and the 182-day risk-free rate is 7.3 percent. All rates are continuously compounded. The firm's best estimate of the volatility of forward rates is 16.6 percent. The notional amount is $10 million, and the payoff is based on 90-day LIBOR. Use the Black model to determine a fair price for the cap.

18. Consider a three-year receiver swaption with an exercise rate of 11.75 percent in which the underlying swap is a $20 million notional amount four-year swap. The underlying rate is LIBOR. At the expiration of the swaption, the LIBOR rates are 10 percent (360 days), 10.5 percent (720 days), 10.9 percent (1,080 days), and 11.2 percent (1,440 days). Assume 360 days in a year. Determine the payoff value of the swaption.

19. A company wants to enter into a commitment to initiate a swap in 90 days. The swap would consist of four payments 90 days apart with the underlying being LIBOR. Use the term structure of LIBOR as given below to solve for the rate on this forward swap.

Term	Rate
90 days	10.2%
180 days	11.0%
270 days	11.6%
360 days	11.9%
450 days	12.2%

20. Suppose your firm had issued a 12 percent annual coupon, 15-year bond, callable at par at the eighth year. It is now two years later, so the bonds are not callable for another six years. At this time, new bonds could be issued at 8 percent, which is historically quite low, especially relative to the 12 percent coupon on the bond you issued two years ago. To provide a better matching of the interest sensitivities of your assets and liabilities, you want to lengthen the duration of the bonds. How could you use swaptions to restructure the debt? Explain what happens assuming two subsequent future possibilities: rates going up and rates going down.

21. A firm has previously issued fixed-rate non-callable debt. Because interest rates are perceived to be temporarily high, the firm would like to have the flexibility of calling the debt later when rates are expected to fall and replacing it with floating-rate debt. Explain how a firm can use swaptions to achieve this desired result. Also identify and compare an alternative method that can be used to convert fixed-rate debt to floating-rate debt.

22. Assume the 30-day LIBOR is 5 percent and the 120-day LIBOR is also 5 percent. This implies a continuously compounded 90-day forward rate of 5.0172 percent. Verify this result and explain what happens to the continuously compounded 90-day forward rate as the 120-day LIBOR rate increases.

23. Assume the 30-day LIBOR is 5 percent and the 120-day LIBOR is 6 percent. This implies a continuously compounded 90-day forward rate of 6.3448 percent. Verify this result and explain what happens to the continuously compounded forward rate as the number of days in the forward contract increases and the more distant spot rate remains at 6 percent.

24. (Concept Problem) Use the Black model to determine a fair price for an interest rate put that expires in 74 days. The forward rate is 9.79 percent, and the exercise rate is 10 percent. The appropriate risk-free rate is 8.38 percent. All rates are continuously compounded. The volatility of forward rates

is 14.65 percent. The put is based on a $22 million notional amount and pays off based on 90-day LIBOR.

25. (Concept Problem) Consider a call option with an exercise rate of x on an interest rate, which we shall denote as simply L. The underlying rate is an m-day rate and pays off based on 360 days in a year. Now consider a put option on a $1 face value zero coupon bond that pays interest in the add-on manner (as in Eurodollars) based on the rate L. The exercise rate is X. Show that the interest rate call option with a notional amount of $1 provides the same payoffs as the interest rate put option if the notional amount on the put is $1(1 + x(m/360)) and its exercise price, X, is $1/(1 + x(m/360)). If these two options have the same payoffs, what does that tell us about how to price the options?

CHAPTER 14

Advanced Derivatives and Strategies

Blinded by greed and wishful thinking we often seem to believe that huge and growing market momentum is a strong signal that a pattern will continue. In fact, such momentum often creates the very conditions that produce a painful correction—so-called self-referential risk. The growth and eventual unraveling of the sub-prime mortgage market is just the latest example.

David Rowe
Risk, December 2008, p. 93

In this chapter, we examine some advanced derivatives and strategies. Although it may seem like we are taking a leap forward, that is not necessarily the case. While some of these derivatives are complex, others are fairly simple and some are constructed by combining derivatives we have already covered.

We shall begin the chapter with a group called equity derivatives. Although these types of derivatives have been written primarily on stocks and stock portfolios, some of them are also written on bonds, interest rates, currencies, and commodities. The second group of derivatives we cover are structured notes and mortgage derivatives, which are related to interest rates. The third group is called *exotic* options. This is a term used to classify the most advanced types of options. Some of them hardly seem exotic, but they are typically referred to that way.

ADVANCED EQUITY DERIVATIVES AND STRATEGIES

An **equity derivative** is a derivative on a stock or stock index. While the over-the-counter market is much larger for interest rate derivatives, the over-the-counter equity derivatives market is growing rapidly. Recall that we have already studied at great length exchange-traded equity derivatives such as options on stocks and stock indices, futures on stock indices, and options on stock index futures. While these contracts meet the needs of many investors, the specialization afforded by customized over-the-counter contracts can be increasingly worth the cost.

For example, many investors need derivatives that match specific portfolios. Exchange-traded derivatives are based on well-known indices such as the S&P 500. To use a derivative on the S&P 500 to hedge a position in a portfolio that does not match the index induces some basis risk. While that risk may be acceptable for some investors, others would prefer to avoid it by using derivatives customized to their particular holdings. Such derivatives, called **baskets**, can be constructed by simply showing a derivatives dealer the composition of the portfolio. The dealer then constructs a derivative based on that specific portfolio.

CHAPTER OBJECTIVES

- Build on our previous coverage of the basics of derivatives by examining several new derivatives and strategies, some of which are combinations of previously studied derivatives and others of which are entirely new

- Understand the strategy of portfolio insurance, see how it enables a portfolio to achieve a target minimum return, and illustrate how it can be implemented

- Examine equity forwards, warrants, and equity-linked debt

- Examine structured notes so as to understand how they are constructed and to gain an appreciation for their volatility

- Understand mortgage securities, including pass-throughs, IOs, POs, and CMOs, and gain an understanding of how their values change as interest rates change

- Examine various exotic options, including digital and chooser options, path-dependent options, and miscellaneous exotic options, and use the binomial model to price several of them

- Be aware of new derivatives on electricity and weather

Equity derivatives are especially useful in international investing. Equity derivatives on international stocks or indices allow an investor to capture the gains from investing in foreign securities without actually having to incur the additional transaction cost of acquiring those securities directly. In addition, there are often costly foreign regulations to deal with and many countries impose a dividend withholding tax, which requires that some of the dividends be left in the foreign country to cover any future tax liabilities. Equity derivatives are often structured to pay off both capital gains and dividends, but because no money leaves the country, the dividend withholding tax is avoided. While investing directly in foreign securities imposes exchange rate risk, many equity derivatives are structured with a fixed exchange rate, which thereby avoids that risk.

Equity derivatives also permit fast, low-cost realignment of domestic portfolios. For example, an investor holding primarily large cap stocks and wanting to increase the allocation to small cap stocks can do so using derivatives on those two groups of stocks. This is much like our description of adjusting the risk of an equity portfolio in Chapter 11.

Naturally, these features come at a cost that is incurred by the dealer and passed on to the end user. Fortunately, the large size and sophisticated operations of most dealers result in efficiency and low costs, which benefit the end user.

Of course, we have seen many of these benefits in previous chapters, but most of those instruments were exchange-traded equity derivatives. While we did cover equity swaps in Chapter 12, we take a look here at some specialized equity derivatives and strategies that meet needs not met by the instruments we have already covered.

Portfolio Insurance

The concept of insurance has been around for hundreds of years. Individuals and business firms routinely insure their lives and property against risk of loss. The concept extends easily to portfolios. In fact, we touched on the subject in Chapter 6 when we covered protective puts.

Suppose we initially own an uninsured portfolio consisting solely of N_S^U shares of stock with an initial stock price of S_0 (the superscript "U" denotes Uninsured). We are considering insuring the portfolio by selling some shares to purchase put options. In the insured portfolio, we own N_S shares of stock and N_P puts. We denote the put price as P and the exercise price as X, the puts are European, and we assume no dividends on the stock. The value of the uninsured and insured portfolio can be expressed as

$$V = N_S^U S_0 = N_S S_0 + N_P P.$$

Letting $N_S = N_P$ and calling this N, we have

$$N = \frac{V}{S_0 + P}.$$

This tells us how many shares of stock and how many puts we can buy. Note that $N < N_S^U$ due to the positive cost of purchasing put options. At expiration, the insured portfolio's value is

$$V_T = N S_T \qquad\qquad\qquad\quad \text{if } S_T > X$$
$$V_T = N S_T + N(X - S_T) = NX \quad \text{if } S_T \leq X,$$

where S_T is the stock price when the put expires. The uninsured portfolio's value is

$$V_T^U = N_S^U S_T.$$

The worst possible outcome is that in which $S_T = 0$. In this case, the uninsured portfolio value is zero. Suppose we define V_{min} as the minimum value of V_T for the insured portfolio, which occurs when $S_T = 0$. Then with the insured portfolio $V_{min} = NX$ and, because N must also equal $V/(S_0 + P)$,

$$V_{min} = \frac{XV}{S_0 + P}.$$

This formula establishes the minimum value of the portfolio at expiration. Note that it occurs not only when $S_T = 0$ but also whenever $S_T \leq X$.

The decision to insure the portfolio will involve trade-offs. If the stock price declines, then the insured portfolio will outperform the uninsured portfolio. If the stock price rises, then the uninsured portfolio will outperform the insured portfolio. These trade-offs should be carefully evaluated by the portfolio manager.

Let us illustrate how this works. Suppose that on September 26, the market index is at 445.75 and the December 485 put option on the index is priced at $38.57. The option expires on December 19, which is 84 days away; so the time to expiration is 84/365 = 0.2301. The risk-free rate is 3.04 percent stated as a simple annual rate or 2.99 percent continuously compounded. The standard deviation is 15.5 percent.

Suppose we hold a diversified portfolio of stocks that replicates the index. The portfolio is worth $44,575,000 ($V_T^U$), which is equivalent to 100,000 units of the index (N_S^U). In other words, we hold a portfolio that is weighted exactly like the index and is worth 100,000 times the index level.

The minimum level of the insured portfolio is

$$V_{min} = \frac{XV}{S_0 + P} = \frac{(485)(44,575,000)}{445.75 + 38.57} = 44,637,585.$$

Thus, the minimum level at which we can insure the portfolio is $44,637,585. This means that if we own N shares and N puts, where

$$N = \frac{V}{S_0 + P} = \frac{44,575,000}{445.75 + 38.57} = 92,036,$$

the minimum value of the portfolio on December 19 is $44,637,585. Note that to insure this portfolio, the portfolio manager had to sell 7,964 units of the index to purchase 92,036 put options (ignoring rounding error). This is a guaranteed return of 0.0014 for 84 days, or $(1.0014)^{(365/84)} - 1 = 0.0061$ per year. This figure must be below the risk-free rate or an arbitrage opportunity would be possible. After all, how could we guarantee a minimum return on a risky portfolio greater than the risk-free rate?

We buy 92,036 shares and 92,036 puts. Suppose that at expiration, the index is at 510:

Value of stock = 92,036($510) = $46,938,360

+ Value of puts = 92,036($0) =   0

Total   = $46,938,360

> An appropriate combination of stock and puts establishes an insured portfolio.

This exceeds the minimum value. If at expiration the index is at 450,

Value of stock = 92,036($485) = $44,637,460 (by exercising the puts).

While this amount appears to be slightly below the minimum, it is actually the same due to rounding off some of the previously computed values. The error is less than 1/1,000th of 1 percent.

Figure 14.1 shows the value of the insured stock-put portfolio when the put expires. The exact minimum cannot be read from the graph but is mathematically equal to $44,637,585. The graph should look familiar. It is essentially the same as that of the

FIGURE 14.1 Insured Portfolio: Stock-Put

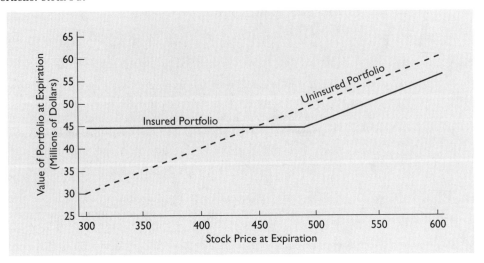

protective put covered in Chapter 6. In this example, however, we are looking only at the value of the investor's position at expiration and not at the profit. The dotted line shows the value of the portfolio if it were uninsured.

Like any form of insurance, **portfolio insurance** entails an opportunity cost. By *opportunity cost*, we are not referring to commissions, bid-ask spreads, and so on. These trading costs certainly are important, but the opportunity cost of portfolio insurance is the difference in the value of the insured portfolio and the value of the uninsured portfolio when the market goes up. In other words, it is the dollar value that is given up in bull markets, in which the insurance was not needed. This opportunity cost varies with the uninsured future value of the portfolio.

For example, when the index ended up at 510, the insured portfolio was worth $46,938,360 ($= NS_T$). Had the portfolio not been insured, it would have consisted of 100,000 shares valued at $510 each for a total value of $51,000,000 ($= N_S^U S_T$). The opportunity cost thus is $4,061,640 ($= 51,000,000 - 46,938,360$), or about 9.1 percent ($= 4,061,640/44,575,000$) of the uninsured portfolio's initial value. Note that the rate of return of the uninsured portfolio was 14.4 percent ($= 51,000,000/44,575,000 - 1$). Thus, the opportunity cost was 63.2 percent ($= 9.1/14.4$) of the uninsured portfolio's return. Thus, one significant economic consideration of portfolio insurance is opportunity cost.

Another measure of the economic consequences of portfolio insurance is known as the **upside capture**, the percentage of the uninsured portfolio value that is represented by the insured portfolio value. In our example above where the index ends up at 510, the upside capture is 92 percent ($= 46,938,360/51,000,000$).

TECHNICAL NOTE: Portfolio Insurance When Beta Is Not One go to www.cengagebrain.com

Because of put-call parity, an identical result is obtained with calls and risk-free debt, a strategy referred to as a **fiduciary call**. Let B be the price of a risk-free debt instrument and B_T be its face value when it matures. Suppose we own a portfolio of N_C calls and N_B debt. At expiration, the portfolio will be worth $V_T = N_B B_T$ if $S_T \leq X$ and $N_C(S_T - X) + N_B B_T$ if $S_T > X$. Again, the worst case is S_T going to zero. We define this outcome as V_{min}, which will be the value of the debt at maturity (i.e., $V_{min} = N_B B_T$). Thus,

$$N_B = \frac{V_{min}}{B_T}.$$

FIGURE 14.2 Insured Portfolio: Call-Risk-Free Debt

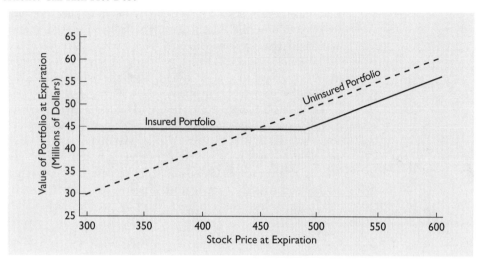

If we buy N_B debt, we can buy $N_C = (V - N_B B)/C$ calls. The number of calls can be shown to equal the number of shares and puts from the stock-put example. Thus, we also have

$$N_C = \frac{V}{S_0 + P}.$$

Continuing with our numerical example, the call is worth $2.65 and the debt has a face value of $100. Thus, we would want $44,637,585/$100 = 446,376$ of debt and 92,036 calls. At expiration, if the index is at 510, the calls will expire $25 in-the-money. With 92,036 calls worth $25 and 446,376 debt worth $100 each, the total portfolio value is $46,938,500. If the index goes to 450, there will be 92,036 worthless calls and 446,376 debt worth $100 each for a total of $44,637,600, which is the same minimum in the stock-put case, subject to a round-off error. The example is illustrated in Figure 14.2. It is important to note that most stock portfolios do not match an exchange-traded index option contract. Also, the customized portfolio option contracts are often very expensive due to the additional costs borne by the derivatives dealers. There is another alternative that we discuss now.

> An appropriate combination of calls and risk-free debt establishes an insured portfolio.

A European put (or call) with the appropriate terms and conditions would obviously be a means of insuring a portfolio. While such options generally are not available on the options exchanges, it is possible to replicate the behavior of the stock-put or call-debt insured portfolio by continuously adjusting a portfolio of stocks and index futures or stocks and risk-free debt. This technique is referred to as **dynamic hedging**. When using stock index futures, dynamic hedging involves selling a number of futures contracts such that the portfolio responds to stock price movements the same way the stock-put or call-debt insured portfolio would respond. The hedge ratio for stock index futures contracts is

$$N_f = \left[\left(\frac{V_{min}}{X} \right) N(d_1) - \left(\frac{V}{S_0} \right) \right] e^{-r_c t}.$$

This gives the number of futures contracts. Because most futures contracts have a multiplier, this number should be divided by the multiplier. For example, if using the E-mini S&P 500 futures, the contract size is actually 50 times the quoted price. The above formula should then be divided by 50. Because futures require no outlay, the hedger can put all the funds in stock. The hedger must be sure to continuously adjust the number of futures contracts so that it always equals the value of N_f. Because the delta and T will change, this necessitates frequent review.

An alternative approach to the use of futures in dynamic hedging is the use of risk-free debt. It is possible to combine stock and risk-free debt so that the portfolio behaves like the protective put or fiduciary call. The key assumption behind this result is that the risk-free debt price changes only as a result of time. It is not directly influenced by the stock price. This is a fairly reasonable assumption because the long-run correlation between stock returns and risk-free debt returns is nearly zero. The appropriate combination of stocks and risk-free debt results in the number of risk-free debt securities of:

$$N_B = \frac{V - N_S S_0}{B}.$$

The number of shares of stock is

$$N_f = \left(\frac{V_{min}}{X}\right) N(d_1).$$

TECHNICAL NOTE: Derivation of the Dynamic Hedge Ratio for Portfolio Insurance
go to www.cengagebrain.com

Dynamic hedging is the use of stock and either stock index futures or risk-free debt to achieve portfolio insurance by setting the delta of the stock-futures or stock-debt combination to the delta of a combination of stock and puts.

As with the use of futures, these values will change continuously.

Both of these approaches work by equating the deltas of the dynamically hedged portfolios to the delta of the hypothetical portfolio of stock and puts. For example, for the December 485 call, the delta is 0.1574. This means that the put delta is $0.1574 - 1 = -0.8426$. A combination of one unit of stock and one put would have a delta of 1 (the stock's delta) plus -0.8426 (the put's delta), which equals 0.1574, the call's delta. When using stock index futures for dynamic hedging, the combination of all $44,575,000 in stock along with N_f futures has a delta of 0.1574, the same delta as would have been obtained if the hedger had owned 92,036 shares and 92,036 puts. When using the combination of stock and risk-free debt, the combination of N_S shares and N_B debt also has a delta of 0.1574.

Table 14.1 illustrates the appropriate calculations using stock and futures in a dynamic hedge, stock and risk-free debt in a dynamic hedge, and the exact hedge that would result if the necessary puts were available.[1]

The lower panel shows that the differences in the three methods are very small. These differences can be explained by a combination of round-off error and the fact that a strategy equating deltas is only approximately correct if there is a non-infinitesimal change in the stock price, a point we introduced as the gamma effect in Chapter 5 and reexamine in Chapter 15. Moreover, dynamic hedging, or any delta-matching strategy, will require that the hedge ratio be adjusted continuously, which obviously cannot be done in the presence of transaction costs.

The dynamic hedging version of portfolio insurance was a widely used strategy in the mid-1980s. Its efficacy depends on the stock market having only small price changes within a short time interval. During the stock market crash of October 1987, however, stock prices experienced enormous jumps over short time intervals. While

---

[1]The old and new options and futures prices were calculated using the Black-Scholes-Merton model, as covered in Chapter 5, and the cost of carry model with continuous compounding, as covered in Chapter 9.

TABLE 14.1 DYNAMIC HEDGE PORTFOLIO INSURANCE

BASIC INFORMATION		CONTRACT INFORMATION	
Current day	September 26	Futures price	448.83
Horizon day	December 19	Futures delta	1.0069
Time to horizon	0.2301	Futures multiplier	50
Stock price	445.75	Exercise price	485
Number of shares held	100,000	Put price	38.57
Market value of portfolio	$44,575,000	Call price	2.65
Risk-free rate	2.99%	Call delta	0.1574
Volatility of stock	15.5%	Put delta	−0.8426
Price of risk-free debt	99.31		
Minimum portfolio value (V_{min})	$44,637,585		

Dynamic hedge with futures

Number of contracts needed:

$$N_f = \left[\left(\frac{44,637,585}{485} \right)(0.1574) - \left(\frac{44,575,000}{445.75} \right) \right] e^{-(0.0299)(0.2301)}/50 \approx -1,700$$

Dynamic hedge with risk-free debt

Number of shares held:

$$N_S = \left(\frac{44,637,585}{485} \right)(0.1574) \approx 14,786$$

Amount of debt needed:

$$N_B = \frac{44,575,000 - 14,486(445.75)}{99.31} \approx 383,827$$

EFFECTS OF A $1 DECREASE IN THE STOCK PRICE

New derivative prices:

Put	$39.42	
Futures	447.82	
Stock plus put:		
Gain on stock	−$92,036	(92,036 shares × −$1)
Gain on put	78,230	(92,036 puts × ($39.42 − $38.57))
Net gain	−$13,806	(0.03% of value of portfolio)
Stock plus futures dynamic hedge:		
Gain on stock	−$100,000	(100,000 shares × −$1)
Gain on futures	85,850	(−1,700 contracts × (447.82 − 448.83) × 50)
Net gain	−$14,150	
Stock plus debt dynamic hedge:		
Gain on stock	−$14,486	(14,486 shares × −$1)
Gain on debt	0	(debt price does not change due to stock price change)
Net gain	−$14,486	

portfolios that were insured did better than those that were not, they failed to achieve their targets. The massive volume of selling done by portfolio insurers adjusting their hedge ratios was, probably wrongly, blamed for exacerbating the crash. Investors then became disillusioned with portfolio insurance. In response, however, it was not too long afterward that many new, customized equity products began to appear.

Equity Forwards

An **equity forward** contract is simply a forward contract on a stock, stock index, or portfolio. The principles are the same as those we studied previously in Chapter 9. An investor buying an equity forward simply enters into a contract with a counterparty, the seller, in which the buyer agrees to buy the stock, stock index, or portfolio from the seller at a future date at a price agreed upon today. In many cases, the equity instrument is a stock index or a portfolio of stocks. Rather than have the seller deliver stock to the buyer at expiration, the contract frequently specifies that it will be cash settled.

> An equity forward is simply a forward contract on a stock, stock index, or portfolio. It is an agreement for one party to buy the stock, stock index, or portfolio from another party at a fixed price. It is usually settled in cash.

The price agreed upon by the two parties, called the forward price, was covered in Chapter 9. Recall that the price of a forward (or futures) contract on a stock is the current stock price, compounded at the risk-free rate minus the compound future value of the dividends. Because we have covered pricing at great length, we shall not repeat it here, but it may be useful for the reader to review the relevant parts of Chapter 9.

An interesting variation of a forward contract is the break forward. A **break forward** is a combination of spot and derivative positions that replicates the outcome of an ordinary call with one exception—the positions are structured such that the overall position costs nothing up front. This instrument is like a zero-cost call, except that it would be impossible to have an instrument that costs nothing up front and returns either zero or a positive amount, like an ordinary call. The break forward achieves this result by penalizing the investor if the option ends up out-of-the-money. An ordinary call pays off $Max(0, S_T - X)$. A break forward is a call that pays off if it expires in-the-money and incurs a charge if it expires out-of-the-money. Even the in-the-money payoff, however, can be negative.

To illustrate the break forward and to keep the explanation simple, we assume no dividends on the stock. A break forward will pay off $S_T - K$ if $S_T > F$ and $F - K$ if $S_T \leq F$. The value K is the sum of the compound future value of an ordinary call on the stock with exercise price F plus the compound future value of the stock. The latter term, you know, is the forward price. Thus, K will exceed F; so when $S_T \leq F$, the payoff, $F - K$, is definitely negative. It is also possible that $S_T - K$ can be negative. If the break forward were structured as a put, the exercise price would be the forward price plus the compound value of the put price.

> A break forward is similar to an ordinary call in that it has a limited loss and unlimited gain; however, it requires no premium up front. Unlike an ordinary call, its value at expiration can be negative.

A break forward contract is identical to an ordinary long call with an exercise price of F and a loan in which the investor receives the present value of K − F and promises to pay back K − F. Table 14.2 illustrates this result. Recall from Chapters 2–7 that we examined some results for DCRB options. We shall use the same DCRB options for many of the examples in this chapter.[2] The value of the break forward at expiration is illustrated in Figure 14.3.

---

[2]In practice, many of these types of contracts are based on the S&P 500 or a specific portfolio. We use the DCRB examples for convenience and because you should by now be quite familiar with these options.

TABLE 14.2 PAYOFFS FROM BREAK FORWARD

| INSTRUMENT | CURRENT VALUE | PAYOFFS FROM PORTFOLIO GIVEN STOCK PRICE AT EXPIRATION | |
		$S_T \leq F$	$S_T > F$
Long Call	$C_e(S_0,T,F)$	0	$S_T - F$
Loan	$-(K - F)e^{-r_c t}$	$-(K - F)$	$-(K - F)$
	0	$F - K$	$S_T - K$

FIGURE 14.3 Break Forward

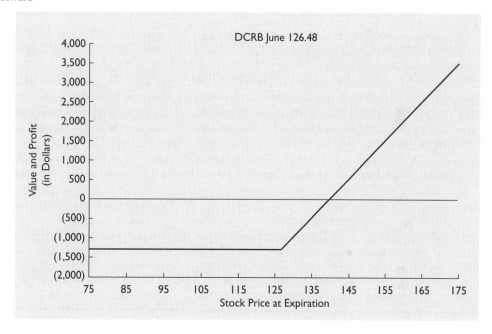

The example is based on a stock price of 125.94, a time to expiration of 0.0959 (35 days/365), a risk-free rate of 4.46 percent continuously compounded, a volatility of 83 percent, and 100 units of the break forward. The forward price of DCRB is $125.94e^{0.0446(0.0959)} = 126.48$. This value is the exercise price of the break forward. As noted above, the break forward is equivalent to a loan and a call with exercise price of F; so we need the price of a call expiring in 35 days with an exercise price of 126.48. Using the Black-Scholes-Merton model, that call price would be 12.88. Next, we need to know the value of K. This will equal the forward price plus the compound future value of the call price. This is $126.48 - 12.88e^{0.0446(0.0959)} = 139.41$. Thus, the break forward will be worth $126.48 - 139.41 = -12.93$ if $S_T \leq 126.48$ and $S_T - 139.41$ if $S_T > 126.48$. In the figure, all values are multiplied by \$100.

Because the up-front cost is zero, the value at expiration is also the profit. While this figure looks exactly like a call, it is important to remember that a break forward incurs a payment if it expires out-of-the-money. This is the penalty for having to pay nothing for it up front.

It should be apparent that a break forward is similar to a forward contract and a call option. Like a forward contract, a break forward requires no initial outlay but can have negative value at expiration. Like a call, it has a limited loss. Due to the parity

MAKING THE CONNECTION

Portfolio Insurance in a Crashing Market

On October 19, 1987, the Dow Jones Industrial Average fell over 22 percent in one day. Many factors were blamed for the crash, but none took more criticism than portfolio insurance.

As discussed in this chapter, portfolio insurance is a strategy in which a portfolio is protected by buying puts, combining calls with risk-free bonds, or replicating a protective put using a dynamic hedging strategy. Exchange-listed puts with the necessary terms are not available for the customized portfolios of many institutional investors; hence, portfolio insurance is typically implemented using dynamic hedging.

As we have discussed in this chapter, dynamic hedging attempts to replicate a position combining an asset with a put. Futures contracts can be combined with the portfolio to obtain the same sensitivity of the portfolio combined with a put. Because it is based on calculus, the formula is correct only for a small change in the underlying. Thus, portfolio insurance works well only when the market makes small moves and only if the market is liquid.

One of the primary vendors of portfolio insurance was the California-based Leland O'Brien Rubinstein, known as LOR, which had been formed in 1982. Hayne Leland and Mark Rubinstein are finance professors at the University of California at Berkeley who had developed the theory underlying portfolio insurance. John O'Brien, an investment practitioner, brought marketing skills to the firm. LOR successfully implemented this strategy for numerous clients. Because the product was simple and required no specialized trade secrets, it was quickly copied. Soon portfolio insurance strategies were associated with billions of dollars of money in the U.S. stock market.

But on October 19, 1987, the Dow dropped about 200 points in the first two hours and about 200 points in the last two hours. Although the Dow made a 100-point move upward during mid-day, it was largely a day of declines. The Dow was at its highest at the opening and its lowest at the close. It was a day unheard of in stock market history.

Following large market movements, portfolio insurers must make rapid adjustments to their positions. Consider a portfolio insured with a specific number of short positions in futures. If the market makes a large downward move, the portfolio would then require more short futures contracts. The portfolio insurer then attempts to sell more futures contracts, and these transactions must be executed before another large move. If the portfolio insurer needs to sell a large number of contracts, the market could mistakenly infer that the portfolio insurer believes the market is going down further, a negative but misleading signal. The transaction is not based on a belief that the market is going down further. Even if the portfolio insurer believes the market is going up, the same transaction—selling more futures contracts—would be required. In addition, there is the possibility that the large number of futures contracts would strain the capacity of the market and liquidity would suffer. Prices would rapidly fall further. Portfolio insurance models would then dictate further selling, leading to an endless spiral. Of course, if prices rose rapidly, portfolio insurance models would dictate rapid buying, but this was not the case that day. To make matters worse, many markets were shut down at various times, effectively prohibiting anyone from getting in or out.

At the end of the day, portfolio insurance took considerable blame for the bloodbath. In fact, the portfolio insurance strategy and many portfolio insurance firms would never be the same. This criticism was unjust. While it is probably true that portfolio insurance strategies were responsible for some of the decline, much of the problem lay in the fact that the market panicked, misinterpreted signals, and then shut itself down.

In fact, portfolio insurance resulted in significant savings to investors who had it. It did not live up to its promises, however, because it could not operate well in rapidly moving markets. Clients were dissatisfied and terminated their relationships with portfolio insurance firms. Most (including LOR) did not survive. Since that time, the market has developed a variety of alternative and successful derivative instruments and strategies. For that, we can thank portfolio insurance and companies such as LOR. Financial products that succeed could never be developed without knowing that products such as portfolio insurance worked well in some circumstances and badly in others.

relationships that exist between puts, calls, and forwards, a break forward can also be constructed by entering into a long forward contract at the price F, borrowing the present value of K − F and buying a put with an exercise price of F.

Like a forward contract or a swap, a break forward has a value of zero at the start. Later during its life, the value will change to positive or negative. Thus, we need to know how to determine its value during its life. This is a simple procedure. Because we know that a break forward is like an ordinary call and a loan, we can value it by valuing the ordinary call and the loan. Thus, suppose we are at time t prior to expiration. The call is worth $C_e(S_t, T − t, F)$, and the loan is worth $-(K − F)e^{-r_c(T-t)}$. The latter is the loan payoff, the amount that would be owed if the loan were repaid now. In the example we worked here, suppose we are 15 days into the life of the break forward, and DCRB is at 115.75. The other inputs are F = 126.48 (the exercise price), $r_c = 0.0446$, K = 139.41, $\sigma = 0.83$, and T − t = 20/365 = 0.0548. Using a spreadsheet for greater precision, we obtain a Black-Scholes-Merton value for the call of 5.05. The loan value is $-(139.41 − 126.48)e^{-0.0446(0.0548)} = 12.90$. Thus, the value of the break forward is 5.05 − 12.90 = −7.85. Because the break forward can have a negative payoff at expiration, it can obviously have a negative value during its life.

A more general version of a break forward is a **pay-later option**. In this case, the buyer of the option simply borrows the premium. Using a European call as an example, this is an ordinary call with a premium of $C_e(S_0, T, X)$ that also includes a loan in the amount of $C_e(S_0, T, X)$. At expiration, the borrower either exercises the call or not but is required to pay back the amount $C_e(S_0, T, X)e^{r_c T}$. This instrument is, in effect, an option in which the premium does not have to be paid until expiration. With an option of this type, any exercise price can be chosen. A break forward is a special case in which the exercise price is the forward price. Later in this chapter, we look at an option in which the premium is not paid until expiration and is paid only if the option expires in-the-money.

> A pay-later option is an option in which the premium is paid at expiration. It is essentially an ordinary option in which the seller lends the buyer the premium.

Equity Warrants

Warrants have been around much longer than exchange-listed options. A warrant is an option written by a firm on its own stock and usually offered with a bond issue. Anyone purchasing the bond receives one or more warrants, which give the bondholders the right to buy the stock later. The original life of a warrant is usually three to ten years. Warrants can be priced similarly to ordinary options except that their exercise dilutes the value of the stock, and this must be taken into account. Many warrants trade on stock exchanges.

From time to time, warrants are written by a financial institution, offered for sale to the public, and typically based on a stock index. Many of these warrants on foreign indices offer the interesting feature that even though the underlying index is stated in units of the foreign currency, the payoff is fixed in U.S. dollars. For example, suppose there is a call warrant on the Japanese index, the Nikkei 225 with a fixed exchange rate of ¥100 per dollar. Let the exercise price be ¥19,000. At expiration, let the Nikkei be ¥19,950. Thus, the call warrant expires in-the-money by ¥950.

Because the index value is based on prices quoted in yen, the warrant ends up worth ¥950. This figure is automatically converted to dollars at ¥100 per dollar, so the warrant pays off $9.50. This type of fixed exchange rate derivative is called a **quanto**.

Quantos are particularly attractive because they permit investors to earn returns in foreign markets without exchange rate risk.

Equity-Linked Debt

Equity-linked debt is a combination of a call option and a bond that guarantees a return of principal and no interest, a small amount of interest, or a guarantee of returning a given fraction of the principal. In addition, it provides an extra payment based on how a stock or stock index performed. Instruments of this sort were first offered in 1987 in the form of bank certificates of deposit and were available to the general public. These original market-indexed CDs did not prove to be very popular, and they were abandoned. In the last few years, they have resurfaced with some alterations.

Suppose a bank or an investment banking firm makes the following offer: Purchase a one-year zero coupon bond paying 1 percent interest and receive 50 percent of any upside gain on the S&P 500. Each unit is sold with a principal amount of $10. Currently, a one-year zero coupon bond without the S&P feature would pay 5 percent compounded annually. The S&P 500 is at 1500, its standard deviation is 12 percent, and its dividend yield is 1.5 percent. Is this a good deal?

If you invest $10, you are guaranteed to receive $10(1.01) = $10.10. Because the opportunity cost is 5 percent, the present value of this amount is $10.10/1.05 = $9.62. This means that you are implicitly paying $10.00 − $9.62 = $0.38 for 50 percent of the S&P 500 upside gain. Obviously, the upside gain feature is like a call option. We can easily determine its value.

> Equity-linked debt offers a guaranteed return of a fraction of the principal, the full principal, or the principal and a below-market interest rate, plus a percentage of the return on a market index.

Because the option payoff cannot be earned early, it is a European call and the Black-Scholes-Merton model applies with a slight twist. The payoff is $10(0.5)Max(0, (S_T − 1500)/1500)$ where S_T is the S&P 500 at expiration. This can be written as $(5/1500)Max(0, S_T − 1500)$, making it equivalent to 5/1500th of an at-the-money call. The option value will, therefore, be 5/1500th of the Black-Scholes-Merton value. The inputs to the Black-Scholes-Merton calculation are $S = 1500$, $X = 1500$, $r = \ln(1.05) = 0.0488$, $T = 1$, $\sigma = 0.12$, and $\delta = 0.015$. Plugging into the Black-Scholes-Merton model gives $C = \$96.81$. Thus, the option value to the holder of this security is $(5/1500)(\$96.81) = \$0.32$. This is slightly less than the implied cost of the option of $0.38, which is not surprising given that the firm offering the deal must cover its costs and make a profit.

These equity-linked securities sometimes have other features. Some pay off based on the average price over the last ten days or so before expiration. Others pay no interest or even implicitly a negative interest rate by promising to return a given percentage but less than 100 percent of the amount invested. The holder then gets a greater percentage of the gain in the S&P 500. Some of the securities make their minimum interest payments quarterly or semiannually. Others pay off based on any depreciation in the index, which makes the option feature like a put.

ADVANCED INTEREST RATE DERIVATIVES

In Chapter 12, we covered interest rate swaps. In Chapter 13, we encountered some other derivatives on interest rates. These consisted of forward rate agreements, options, and swaptions. In this section, we look at some other widely used interest rate instruments that are not technically derivatives but are generally considered as such.

Structured Notes

Corporations routinely issue debt obligations with maturities in the range of two to ten years. These instruments are usually called notes. Sometimes the notes carry fixed rates. Other times the notes have variable rates, such as those tied to LIBOR. In the early

1990s, many corporations began issuing notes with derivative transactions attached so as to change the return pattern from the standard fixed or LIBOR-floating type. These instruments have come to be known as **structured notes**.

Most structured notes are issued by corporations of extremely high credit quality. Consequently, there is very little credit risk. The notes are typically designed with a specific user in mind. The user wants a particular exposure and normally plans to hold the notes until maturity. Thus, these tend to be fairly illiquid instruments.

> A structured note is an intermediate-term debt security issued by a corporation with a good credit rating and tailored to a particular investor's needs. The coupon is altered by the use of a derivative transaction to provide an exposure not found in most other securities with similar characteristics.

Some of these notes have coupons indexed to the CMT rate. Recall that we discussed the CMT, or constant maturity treasury, rate in Chapter 12. It is the rate on a government security of a fixed maturity. If there is no government bond outstanding with the desired maturity, the CMT rate is obtained by interpolating the rates on bonds with surrounding maturities.

For example, the coupon could be the CMT rate plus 50 basis points. Some structured notes have leveraged coupons, meaning that, for example, the coupon might be 1.5 times the CMT rate. Let us say the CMT rate is currently 5.5 percent. Then the coupon would be $5.5(1.5) = 8.25$ percent. Suppose that the CMT rate went up 100 basis points to 6.5. Then the structured note coupon would go up to $6.5(1.5) = 9.75$, a 150-basis-point increase.

One interesting type of structured note is the **range floater**. This instrument pays interest only if a specified interest rate, such as LIBOR, stays within a given range. The ranges are sometimes different for each year of the note's life. As an example, consider a two-year note in which the coupon is LIBOR + 3 percent provided that:

> For the first year, LIBOR is between 0 and 6 percent, and
>
> For the second year, LIBOR is between 0 and 7 percent.

> A range floater is a type of structured note in which a higher coupon is paid but only if a particular interest rate is within a specified range of rates.

In other words, if LIBOR is outside the specified range, the coupon is zero. Otherwise, the coupon is LIBOR + 3 percent, which would be considered above normal for a two-year note. You can see that this is a bet on LIBOR staying within a range. To the investor, this transaction would be like a standard floating-rate note and the sale of an interest rate cap. If rates rise above a certain threshold, the investor gives up all the interest.

A popular and controversial type of structured note is the **inverse floater**, sometimes called the **reverse floater**. Whereas a standard floating-rate note pays interest at a rate that changes directly with interest rates in the market, an inverse floater pays interest that changes in an opposite manner to rates in the market. In other words, as interest rates go up, the coupon on an inverse floater goes down. This is usually established by setting the coupon at a formula such as Y − LIBOR, where Y is a specified fixed rate. Sometimes it is simply a multiple of the fixed rate on a plain vanilla swap.

Suppose Y is 12 percent and LIBOR is currently 5.5 percent. Then the coupon will be 6.5 percent. If LIBOR moves up to 7 percent, the coupon will be 5 percent. If LIBOR moves down to 3 percent, the coupon will be 9 percent. It should be obvious that if LIBOR exceeds 12 percent, the coupon is negative, meaning that the lender rather than the borrower would pay the interest! In practice, however, most inverse floaters specify that the minimum interest rate will be zero or perhaps a very small positive rate.

> An inverse floating-rate note is an intermediate-term security in which the coupon moves opposite to market interest rates.

The issuer of an inverse floater could hedge its position with a plain vanilla swap paying LIBOR and receiving a fixed rate. For the case of LIBOR < 12 percent, the issuer's payment would be 12 minus LIBOR on the structured note and + LIBOR minus the fixed rate on the swap for a total payment of 12 minus the fixed rate. The issuer would have created a synthetic fixed-rate loan at this rate. If LIBOR exceeds 12 percent, the issuer's payment would be the same as a pay floating-receive fixed swap. If the issuer does not want such a position, it might want to buy a cap with a strike rate of 12, which would pay it LIBOR minus 12 if LIBOR exceeds 12 percent. In that case, for LIBOR of more than 12, the issuer's total payment would be $-(LIBOR - 12)$ from the cap and LIBOR minus the fixed rate on the swap for a total payment of 12 minus the fixed rate. In cases where the inverse floater payment is twice the fixed rate minus LIBOR, the net payment of the issuer after the swap will be twice the fixed rate minus the fixed rate or simply once the fixed rate. In that case, the issuer has offered an inverse floater but effectively pays only the fixed rate.

Some inverse floaters are leveraged with formulas such as three times the fixed-rate minus twice LIBOR. Many inverse floaters have caps on the maximum rate. Some are de-levered by using formulas such as $Y - 0.75LIBOR$, where the floating coupon moves less than the movement in LIBOR.

There are many variations found in structured notes. Some have coupons determined by the difference between two interest rates, such as the TED spread, and others have coupons tied to foreign interest rates but with payments made in the domestic currency. Structured notes have also been based on complex formulas reflecting differences in rates and bond prices at different ends of the term structure.

The success of structured notes is attributed to the fact that they offer return possibilities tailored to specific investors. Unfortunately, structured notes have also been aggressively marketed in some cases to investors who were not well suited for them. Large interest rate changes coupled with high leverage resulted in large losses for investors who were not aware they had so much exposure.

Mortgage-Backed Securities

The fixed-rate home mortgage is the primary means by which individuals purchase houses. Most homeowners pay off their mortgages over a period of 15 to 30 years with fixed and equal monthly payments consisting of interest on the remaining balance and a contribution to the principal. Nearly every mortgage also provides the homeowner the right to prepay the mortgage, which will frequently be done if interest rates decline sufficiently to cover the transaction cost of refinancing. A certain number of prepayments occur due to demographic factors, such as a family moving to another city. Mortgage lenders are primarily banks, savings and loan associations, and mortgage companies. These financial institutions that originate mortgage loans are exposed to the risk of interest rate changes. If interest rates increase, the value of a mortgage decreases. If interest rates decrease, the value of a mortgage increases, but the increase is limited by the fact that lower interest rates encourage homeowners to refinance. If that happens, the mortgage holder receives the principal early and is forced to reinvest it at a lower rate. This is referred to as **prepayment risk**.

> A mortgage-backed security is a security issued by a party who makes payments based on the payments it receives from a portfolio of underlying mortgages.

Many mortgages are combined into portfolios; claims on the portfolio are sold to investors in the form of **mortgage-backed securities**. The process of combining loans into portfolios and selling claims on the portfolio is called **securitization**. Not all securitized portfolios are mortgages. Credit card receipts and other types of loans are also securitized, but the mortgage securitization market is one of the largest and most complex. The process of securitization provides depth to the market because lenders know that they can sell the loans they hold and receive immediate cash. This increases the number of willing lenders and provides individual and institutional investors access to investment opportunities in markets that would otherwise be accessible only to financial institutions. Securitized mortgages are nearly always guaranteed against default by the purchase of credit insurance, often from a federal agency such as the Government National Mortgage Association (GNMA).

Securities that are issued based on mortgage portfolios are generally considered to be derivatives because they derive their values from the values of the underlying mortgages. They are, however, somewhat different from traditional derivatives. Although most mortgages have imbedded prepayment options, mortgage securities are more like mutual funds. They are investments in a security that represents holdings of another security. Nonetheless, we shall cover them here because it is important to know something about them and in practice, nearly everyone, rightly or wrongly, thinks of them as derivatives.

> A mortgage pass-through is a mortgage-backed security in which the holder receives the principal and interest payments on a portfolio of mortgages, less a servicing fee.

Mortgage Pass-Throughs and Strips Portfolios of mortgages on which claims are sold are called **mortgage pass-throughs**. An investor who purchases a mortgage pass-through receives a monthly check consisting of a proportional share of interest and principal on the portfolio of mortgages, less a servicing fee. Mortgage pass-throughs, however, are still subject to the risk of interest rate changes, which, as we noted above, result in changes to the values of the securities and affect the frequency with which homeowners refinance their mortgages. Consequently, mortgage pass-through values can change dramatically with changes in interest rates.

> Interest-only (IO) and principal-only (PO) strips are mortgage-backed securities entitling their holders to the interest and principal payments, respectively, of a portfolio of underlying mortgages.

Some mortgage pass-throughs are decomposed into **mortgage strips**, each consisting of an interest or principal stream, which are sold separately. An investor can purchase either or both strips. The **interest-only strip**, called an **IO**, provides the investor with the interest payments on the portfolio of underlying mortgages. The **principal-only strip**, called a **PO**, provides the investor with the principal payments on the portfolio of underlying mortgages. If interest rates decrease and prepayments accelerate, the holder of an IO will find the value of his position decreasing, perhaps quite dramatically. Thus, it sounds as if the holder of an IO would prefer interest rates to increase. That will be the case to a limited extent. Beyond a point, however, increases in interest rates will reduce the present value of the interest-only stream.

Understanding the mechanics of mortgage-backed securities is difficult. At this introductory level, our objective is just to grasp the fundamentals. We shall do this by looking at a simple mortgage portfolio, one consisting of a single mortgage. Let that mortgage be a $100,000 loan at 9.75 percent for 30 years. Although most mortgages have monthly payments, we shall use annual payments in this example. This enables us to show the entire amortization schedule, which is in Table 14.3.

First, let us determine the annual payment, a simple problem in the mathematics of compound interest. The payment will equal the loan amount divided by the discount factor for an annuity:

$$\text{Payment} = \frac{\$100,000}{(1 - (1.0975)^{-30})/0.0975} = 10,387.$$

Each payment consists of interest, which is 0.0975 times the balance owed, plus the contribution to the principal, which is $10,387 minus the interest. For example, the tenth payment of $10,387 consists of interest of $91,436(0.0975) = $8,915$ and the contribution to principal of $1,472, which leaves a balance of $91,436 - $1,472 = $89,964.[3]

---

[3]The figures in the table reflect more precise calculations, so they occasionally differ slightly from manually calculated figures.

TABLE 14.3   AMORTIZATION SCHEDULE FOR A 30-YEAR, $100,000 MORTGAGE AT 9.75 PERCENT

| | ANNUAL PAYMENTS | | | |
PAYMENT NO.	BALANCE BEFORE PAYMENT	PAYMENT	INTEREST	PRINCIPAL	BALANCE AFTER PAYMENT
1	$100,000	$10,387	$9,750	$637	$99,363
2	99,363	10,387	9,688	699	98,663
3	98,663	10,387	9,620	768	97,896
4	97,896	10,387	9,545	843	97,053
5	97,053	10,387	9,463	925	96,128
6	96,128	10,387	9,373	1,015	95,113
7	95,113	10,387	9,274	1,114	94,000
8	94,000	10,387	9,165	1,222	92,777
9	92,777	10,387	9,046	1,342	91,436
10	91,436	10,387	8,915	1,472	89,963
11	89,963	10,387	8,771	1,616	88,348
12	88,348	10,387	8,614	1,773	86,574
13	86,574	10,387	8,441	1,946	84,628
14	84,628	10,387	8,251	2,136	82,492
15	82,494	10,387	8,043	2,344	80,147
16	80,147	10,387	7,814	2,573	77,574
17	77,574	10,387	7,563	2,824	74,750
18	74,750	10,387	7,288	3,099	71,651
19	71,651	10,387	6,986	3,401	68,250
20	68,250	10,387	6,654	3,733	64,517
21	64,517	10,387	6,290	4,097	60,420
22	60,420	10,387	5,891	4,496	55,924
23	55,924	10,387	5,453	4,935	50,989
24	50,989	10,387	4,971	5,416	45,573
25	45,573	10,387	4,443	5,944	39,629
26	39,629	10,387	3,864	6,524	33,105
27	33,105	10,387	3,228	7,160	25,946
28	25,946	10,387	2,530	7,858	18,088
29	18,088	10,387	1,764	8,624	9,465
30	9,465	10,387	923	9,465	0

Note: Annual payments are used as an approximation. Most mortgages have monthly payments.

Now let us examine the values of IOs and POs. The value of the IO strip will be the present value of the column of numbers representing the interest. The value of the PO strip will be the present value of the column of numbers representing the principal.

To determine these values, we need two pieces of information. One is the rate at which to discount the cash flows. Assuming the payments are guaranteed by a federal agency, we can discount these at a rate appropriate for a Treasury security. So at the present, let us assume a rate of 7 percent. We also have to make an assumption about when the loan will be paid off. Although it is a 30-year loan, it has a good chance of being paid off early. We shall assume that it is paid off in its twelfth year, which is considered to be an average payoff date for 30-year mortgages.

At the current interest rate of 7 percent with the mortgage prepaid in the twelfth year, the value of the IO strip is found by discounting the 12 interest payments at 7 percent:

Value of IO strip at 7 percent interest and prepayment in year 12

$$= \$9{,}750(1.07)^{-1} + \$9{,}688(1.07)^{-2} + \cdots + \$8{,}614(1.07)^{-12} = \$74{,}254.$$

The value of the PO strip is found by discounting the 12 principal payments, taking into account that the final principal payment will include the full payoff of $86,574:

Value of PO strip at 7 percent interest and prepayment in year 12

$$= \$637(1.07)^{-1} + \$699(1.07)^{-2} + \cdots + (\$1{,}773 + \$86{,}574)(1.07)^{-12} = \$46{,}690.$$

The overall pass-through would be worth the sum of these two, or

$$\text{Value of pass-through} = \$74{,}254 + \$46{,}690 = \$120{,}944.$$

Now assume the interest rate falls to 6 percent and assume the homeowner prepays in two years. Then we have

Value of IO strip at 6 percent interest and prepayment in year 2

$$= \$9{,}750(1.06)^{-1} + \$9{,}688(1.06)^{-2} = \$17{,}820,$$

which is a loss of 76 percent.

Value of PO strip at 6 percent interest and prepayment in year 2

$$\$637(1.06)^{-1} + (\$699 + \$98{,}663)(1.06)^{-2} = \$89{,}034,$$

which is a gain of 91 percent. The overall pass-through is worth

$$\text{Value of pass-through} = 17{,}820 + 89{,}034 = 106{,}854,$$

a loss of almost 12 percent.

Assume that the interest rate is at 8 percent and prepayment still occurs in year 12. Then we have the following:

Value of IO strip at 8 percent interest and prepayment in year 12

$$= \$9{,}750(1.08)^{-1} + \$9{,}688(1.08)^{-2} + \cdots + \$8{,}614(1.08)^{-12} = \$70{,}532,$$

a loss of 5 percent.

Value of PO strip at 8 percent interest and prepayment in year 12

$$= \$637(1.08)^{-1} + \$699(1.08)^{-2} + \cdots + (\$1{,}773 + \$86{,}574)(1.08)^{-12} = \$42{,}128,$$

a loss of almost 10 percent. The overall pass-through is worth

$$\text{Value of pass-through} = \$70{,}532 + \$42{,}128 = \$112{,}660,$$

a loss of almost 7 percent.

It would appear that IO holders lose either way, but that is not exactly how it works in practice. IO and PO strips represent portfolios of mortgages. Each mortgage will not prepay at the same time. Any increase in interest rates is likely to push the average prepayment date further out. If in our example the interest rate change to 8 percent pushes the prepayment to year 14, we have

Value of IO strip at 8 percent interest and prepayment in year 14

$$= \$9{,}750(1.08)^{-1} + \$9{,}688(1.08)^{-2} + \cdots + \$8{,}251(1.08)^{-14} = \$76{,}445,$$

which is a gain of about 3 percent.

Value of PO strip at 8 percent interest and prepayment in year 14

$$= \$637(1.08)^{-1} + \$699(1.08)^{-2} + \cdots + (\$2{,}136 + \$82{,}492)(1.08)^{-14} = \$37{,}276,$$

which is a loss of about 20 percent. The overall pass-through is worth

$$\text{Value of pass-through} = \$76{,}445 + \$37{,}276 = \$113{,}721,$$

a loss of about 6 percent.

A mortgage pass-through decreases in value with increases in interest rates. When rates decrease, however, the gains on the pass-through are limited because of the increased prepayment rate. The pass-through is not as volatile as the IO or PO individually, but it can still be fairly volatile and has limited gains because of the prepayment risk.[4]

The main point from this demonstration is that mortgage securities are complex and that POs and IOs can be extremely volatile. Not only are they affected by the discounting effect of interest rates but they are extremely sensitive to the effect that interest rate changes have on prepayments. As you might well imagine, it is difficult to predict prepayments, making it all the more difficult to get a firm grasp on the risk of these securities. This does not mean that investors should avoid them. They are priced fairly for their risk.

Collateralized Mortgage Obligations (CMOs) Another type of mortgage security is the **collateralized mortgage obligation (CMO)**. CMOs, like mortgage pass-throughs, are debt securities whose payoffs are based on a portfolio of mortgages. CMOs, however, have risks and rewards that differ substantially from standard pass-throughs and IO and PO strips. In fact, some CMOs have considerably more risk and others have considerably less risk than pass-throughs and strips. This is accomplished by structuring the different types of CMO securities, called **tranches**, to have different priorities on the payments made on the underlying mortgages. In addition, some CMOs serve as equity, providing support to the liabilities and being paid after all other tranches are paid. This is called the residual tranche.

CMOs can be extremely complex securities, but we can understand the basics with a few simple examples. In the mortgage pass-through described above, the combined value of the IO and PO is $120,944. Suppose we hold this mortgage and issue debt tranches with a total value of $100,000, leaving a residual or equity tranche of $20,944, which has the lowest priority of claims on the underlying mortgages. There are numerous variations of tranches in CMOs, distinguished by the different coupon rates and prepayment provisions. One type of tranche, called a planned amortization class, or PAC, is characterized by a nearly fixed amortization schedule. In other words, it is designed to not be subject to prepayment risk. If, however, prepayments are dramatically above or below a specified reasonable range, some prepayments may be applied to the

---

[4]The limited downside gain is often referred to as the negative convexity, a concept also associated with callable bonds.

PAC tranche. Nonetheless, its substantially reduced prepayment risk results in a lower coupon.

> A collateralized mortgage obligation, or CMO, is a mortgage-backed security in which different types of CMOs, called tranches, have different risks and returns resulting from different priorities of claims on the payments generated by the underlying mortgages.

With the PAC tranche protected against prepayment risk, obviously other tranches must bear more of that risk. The other tranches are arranged in priority according to which bears the greater prepayment risk. The tranches with higher coupons will receive larger percentages of any prepayments. In some cases, the tranche bearing the greatest prepayment risk must be fully paid off before the other tranches begin receiving prepayments. All tranches generally accrue interest, however, while higher-priority tranches are being paid off. In that manner, the tranches accrue interest and are retired sequentially. Some tranches are called Z-bonds. They accrue interest at a given rate, but no principal is paid until all other tranches are paid off.

All tranches tend to gain in value as interest rates decrease, but the tranches bearing the greater prepayment risk gain less and the Z-bond gains more. It continues to accrue interest while the other tranches start receiving more prepayments. When interest rates increase, the securities bearing the greater prepayment risk do better because their prepayments are invested at higher rates. Although their values tend to fall, they fall less. The Z-bond value will then fall more.

When all tranches are paid off, there may be value left over, which is paid to the holders of the residual tranche. Any gain in value from the amount paid for the residual tranche will result from unexpected changes in interest rates and their effect on deviations in the prepayment rate from the assumptions built into the original structure.

Collateralized mortgage obligations are some of the most complicated and volatile financial instruments. Like mortgage pass-throughs, they have been aggressively marketed, sometimes to investors who had little understanding of the risks. Unfortunately, considerable misunderstanding occurred because many mortgage-backed securities were referred to as "government guaranteed." Of course, the guarantee is only that if a homeowner defaults, the payments will be made by the government agency, usually GNMA. Thus, this is only a credit guarantee; it does not guarantee against losses arising from interest rate changes and changes in the rate of prepayments. The volatility and illiquidity often seen in the market for mortgage-backed securities suggests that they be used only with caution and then only by investors who fully understand them.

The concept of securitizing mortgages has been extended to securitizing many other types of instruments, such as bonds and loans. In Chapter 15, we discuss credit derivatives, which can be combined with some of these other securitized debt instruments to create more opportunities for managing risk.

EXOTIC OPTIONS

In recent years, the proliferation of option products has led to a new class of options called **exotic options**. Although it is difficult to identify exactly where ordinary options end and exotic options begin, it is becoming common to refer to almost any option that is not traded on an exchange or not essentially identical to one traded on an exchange as an exotic option. In some cases, these options are simple; in other cases, they are quite complex. What distinguishes them from what we have previously covered, however, is the fact that they offer different types of payoffs. What makes them like what we previously covered is that their final payoffs are determined by whether a value exceeds or is less than an exercise price.

Exotic options typically have unique features that make the option market maker's task of hedging its book of business much more difficult. Each exotic option market has its own unique set of risk management difficulties. Because the

Black-Scholes-Merton framework has become the language of communicating market option prices, it is not uncommon to have exotic options quoted based on their implied volatilities taken from the strict Black-Scholes-Merton model. The novice quantitative analyst should not interpret this quotation convention as an indication that option market makers rely on the Black-Scholes-Merton model for dynamically hedging their positions. Most financial institutions have several different models that they consider, and they keep proprietary the particular models that given them a comparative advantage.

Digital and Chooser Options

Digital Options   **Digital options**, which are sometimes called **binary options**, are actually very simple options and are of two types. An **asset-or-nothing option** pays the holder the asset or its equivalent cash value if the asset price at expiration exceeds the exercise price and nothing if the asset price at expiration is less than the exercise price. A **cash-or-nothing option** pays the holder a fixed amount of cash at expiration if the asset price at expiration exceeds the exercise price and nothing if the asset price at expiration is less than the exercise price. These descriptions apply to call versions, but put versions also exist. These options can be useful for hedging positions in standard European calls. In fact, there is a simple relationship between digital options and a standard European option.

Table 14.4 illustrates the payoffs to the holder of an asset-or-nothing option paying one share of stock who also sells X cash-or-nothing options, each paying \$1 if $S_T > X$. Notice that the payoffs are $S_T - X$ if $S_T > X$ and zero otherwise. Does this look familiar? It should because it is the payoff of a standard European call. This gives us some insights into how to price digital options. Recall that the Black-Scholes-Merton price is $S_0 N(d_1) - Xe^{-r_cT}N(d_2)$. The first term is the price of the asset-or-nothing digital call option. The second term, ignoring the minus sign, is the price of X cash-or-nothing digital call options that pay off \$1 if they expire in-the-money. In other words, an asset-or-nothing digital call option price is given as

$$DC_{aon} = S_0 N(d_1).$$

A standard cash-or-nothing digital call option price that pays off \$1 is given as

$$DC_{con} = e^{-r_cT}N(d_2);$$

Two types of digital options are an asset-or-nothing option, which pays the asset value if it expires in-the-money and nothing otherwise, and a cash-or-nothing option, which pays a fixed cash value if it expires in-the-money and nothing otherwise.

so X cash-or-nothing digital call options are worth $Xe^{-r_cT}N(d_2)$. Thus, a portfolio of long a one share asset-or-nothing digital call option and short \$X cash-or-nothing digital call option is equivalent to being long one standard call option.

Similarly, a portfolio of long \$X cash-or-nothing digital put option and short a one share asset-or-nothing digital put option is equivalent to being long one standard put option. Thus, an asset-or-nothing digital put option price is given as

$$DP_{aon} = S_0[1 - N(d_1)].$$

A standard cash-or-nothing digital put option price that pays off \$1 is given as

$$DP_{con} = e^{-r_cT}[1 - N(d_2)].$$

Clearly, standard call and put options can be viewed as specific portfolios of digital options.

TABLE 14.4 PAYOFFS TO A POSITION LONG AN ASSET-OR-NOTHING OPTION AND SHORT A CASH-OR-NOTHING OPTION

PAYOFF FROM	PAYOFFS FROM PORTFOLIO GIVEN ASSET PRICE AT EXPIRATION	
	$S_T \leq X$	$S_T > X$
Long asset-or-nothing option	0	S_T
Short X cash-or-nothing options	0	$-X$
Total	0	$S_T - X$

Note that long one asset-or-nothing digital call and long one asset-or-nothing digital put is equivalent to owning the underlying instrument.

$$DC_{aon} + DP_{aon} = S_0 N(d_1) + S_0[1 - N(d_1)] = S_0$$

Also note that long one cash-or-nothing digital call and long one cash-or-nothing digital put is equivalent to owning a zero coupon bond paying \$1.

$$DC_{con} + DP_{con} = e^{-r_c T}N(d_2) + e^{-r_c T}[1 - N(d_2)] = e^{-r_c T}$$

Thus, as shown above, that portfolio is worth the present value of \$1.

As an example, consider an asset-or-nothing option written on the S&P 500 Total Return Index, which is at 1,440. At expiration, the option pays the full cash value of the S&P 500. The exercise price is 1,440. The risk-free rate is 4.88 percent continuously compounded, the standard deviation is 11 percent, and the option expires in exactly one-half year. Because the option is written on the Total Return Index, which includes the dividends, we need not adjust for dividends when pricing the option. Substituting these values into d_1 for the Black-Scholes-Merton model gives $d_1 = 0.3526$. Using Table 5.1, we have $N(0.35) = 0.6368$. Then the asset-or-nothing option is worth $1,440(0.6368) = 917.00$. If this option had been 1,440 cash-or-nothing options with an exercise price of 1,440, we would need d_2, which would be 0.2748. The $N(0.27) = 0.6064$ and the cash-or-nothing options would be worth $1440e^{-0.0488(0.5)}(0.6064) = 852.17$. The difference in these two values, 64.83, is the value of a standard European call.

Recall that earlier in the chapter, we looked at pay-later options, in which the buyer of the option pays the premium at expiration. This result is achieved by effectively borrowing the option premium. Thus, the option premium is paid not at the start, but at expiration, where it is increased by the interest accrued over the life of the contract. A variation of this type of contract is the **contingent-pay option**. In this type of option, the premium is paid at expiration but only if the option expires in-the-money. To see how this option is identical to instruments we already know, consider the following combination. Buy an ordinary call expiring at T with exercise price X and sell C_{cp} cash-or-nothing calls, each paying \$1 at expiration. Of course, we do not yet know the value of C_{cp}, which represents the premium of the contingent-pay option, but we can determine it. Table 14.5 shows the payoff of this combination at expiration, using a stock as the underlying.

TABLE 14.5 PAYOFFS FROM CONTINGENT-PAY OPTION

| INSTRUMENT | CURRENT VALUE | PAYOFFS FROM PORTFOLIO GIVEN STOCK PRICE AT EXPIRATION | |
		$S_T \leq X$	$S_T > X$
Long call	$C_e(S_0,T,X)$	0	$S_T - X$
Short C_{cp} cash-or-nothing calls	$-C_{cp}DC_{con}$	0	$-C_{cp}$
	$C_e(S_0,T,X) - C_{cp}DC_{con}$	0	$S_T - X - C_{cp}$

A contingent-pay option is an option in which the holder pays the premium at expiration only if the option expires in-the-money. It is equivalent to an ordinary call and a specific number of cash-or-nothing calls.

We see that this combination of a long call and C_{cp} cash-or-nothing calls each paying \$1 at expiration replicates a contingent-pay option. Therefore, the value of the contingent pay option should equal the value of this combination at any time. We know, however, that at the start, the value of a contingent-pay option is zero, because there is no payment up front. Recall that the value of a cash-or-nothing option paying \$1 at expiration is $e^{-r_c T}N(d_2)$. Therefore, let us set the value of this combination at the start to zero:

$$C_e(S_0,T,X) - C_{cp}e^{-r_c T}N(d_2) = 0$$

and solve for C_{cp}:

$$C_{cp} = \frac{C_e(S_0,T,X)}{e^{-r_c T}N(d_2)}.$$

This is the premium of the contingent-pay option that would be paid at expiration but only if the option expires in-the-money.

Let us work an example using the same digital option we looked at in the previous section. This option was based on the S&P 500 Total Return Index. Recall that the index is at 1,440 and the exercise price is also 1,440, the risk-free rate is 4.88 percent continuously compounded, the standard deviation is 11 percent, and the option expires in one-half year. We determined that the value of a standard European call is 64.83. The value of $N(d_2)$ is 0.6064. The premium of the contingent-pay option would be

$$C_{cp} = \frac{64.83}{e^{-(0.0488)(0.5)}0.6064} = 109.55.$$

Note that the contingent-pay premium is considerably higher than the premium of an ordinary European call. This is because the contingent-pay premium is deferred and may never have to be paid at all.

Like a forward contract and a swap, the contingent-pay option has zero value at the start. During its life, however, its value changes and can be either positive or negative. Thus, we need a formula to determine its value. Suppose we are at a time t during the life of the option. Because the premium, C_{cp}, was set at the start, we know the payoff will be either $S_T - X - C_{cp}$ or zero. We can then value the contingent-pay option as a combination of an ordinary call and C_{cp} cash-or-nothing calls that pay \$1 at expiration. In other words, we simply value it the same as the portfolio we constructed to solve for C_{cp}.

For example, suppose that two months into the life of this contingent-pay option, the index is at 1400. We using the following values for inputs: $S_t = 1,400$, $X = 1,440$,

$r_c = 0.0488$, $T - t = 0.333$ (based on four months remaining), $\sigma = 0.11$, and $C_{cp} = 109.55$. Using a spreadsheet for greater accuracy, we find that $d_1 = -0.1561$, $N(d_1) = 0.4380$, $d_2 = -0.2195$, and $N(d_2) = 0.4131$. The value of a standard European call would be 27.89. The value of 109.55 cash-or-nothing calls that each pay \$1 at expiration is $109.55e^{-0.0488(0.333)}(0.4131) = 44.53$. Thus, the value of the contingent-pay call is $27.89 - 44.53 = -16.64$. As we noted, this type of option can have a negative payoff; hence, it can clearly have a negative value prior to its expiration.

Chooser Options   A **chooser option** permits the investor to decide at a specific point during the life of the option whether it should be a call or a put. For example, suppose an investor believes the market will make a strong move but does not know which direction it will go. As we studied in Chapter 7, an investor can purchase a straddle, which is a call and a put. A cheaper alternative is to purchase a chooser option. The chooser

A chooser option allows the holder to designate at a specific time prior to expiration whether the option will be a call or a put.

allows the investor to decide at time t, which is prior to expiration, whether to make it a call or a put. A chooser option is also called an **as-you-like-it option**.

Suppose at time t, an investor decides to make it a call. Then at expiration, the call pays off $S_T - X$ if $S_T > X$ and zero otherwise. If the investor had chosen the put, it would have paid off $X - S_T$ if $S_T \leq X$ and zero otherwise. Note that unless $S_T = X$, a straddle will always pay off through either the call or the put, but it is possible that a chooser will not pay off at all.

Pricing a chooser option is quite simple. At time t, the investor will make it a call if the value of the call exceeds the value of the put. At t, the call price can be expressed as $C(S_t, T - t, X)$ and the put price can be expressed as $P(S_t, T - t, X)$. A little algebra using put-call parity shows that the call is worth more and would be chosen if $S_t > X(1 + r)^{-(T-t)}$. The chooser can be replicated by simply holding an ordinary call expiring at T with exercise price of X and a put expiring at t with exercise price of $X(1 + r)^{-(T-t)}$. An end-of-chapter problem asks you to verify this statement.

Let us consider a chooser option on the DCRB stock. Recall that the stock price is 125.94, the exercise price is 125, the risk-free rate is 4.56 percent discrete (4.46 percent continuous), the time to expiration is 0.0959 (35 days), and the volatility is 83 percent. Let us assume the choice must be made in 20 days. First, let us price an ordinary straddle. From Chapter 5, we used the Black-Scholes-Merton model and found the call to be worth 13.55 and the put to be worth 12.08. Therefore, the straddle would cost 25.63. The chooser would be worth the value of an ordinary call (13.55) and the value of a put expiring in 20 days (t = 20/365 = 0.0548, so $T - t = 0.0959 - 0.0548 = 0.0411$) with an exercise price of $125(1.0456)^{-0.0411} = 124.77$ and a volatility of 83 percent. Plugging into the Black-Scholes-Merton model gives a put value of 7.80. Thus, the chooser would cost $13.21 + 7.80 = 21.01$. The lower cost of the chooser over the straddle comes from the possibility that the payoff at expiration will be zero.

A chooser option that allows the holder to designate at *any* time before expiration whether it will be a call or a put is called a complex chooser. It is much more difficult to evaluate, and we do not cover it here.

Path-Dependent Options

Path-dependent options are those in which the path followed by the asset during the life of the option has an effect on the option's price. Path-independent options are those in which only the asset price at expiration and not the path followed affects the options' values.

An important distinction among options is whether the path followed by the underlying asset price matters to the price of the option. For standard European options, the path taken does not matter. They can be exercised only at expiration, so it does not matter how the asset reached a certain price. Standard European options are said to be path-independent. For some options, however, the path taken does matter. American options are a classic case in point. Certain paths lead to early exercise. Although we did not refer to them this way in Chapters 4 and 5, we can certainly now call them **path-dependent options**.[5]

In recent years, a family of new options, however, has become better known for its property of path-dependency. Some of these options are based on the average price or the maximum or minimum prices of the underlying asset during the option's life. Others have the property that they can expire worthless before expiration or can expire worthless even if they apparently are in-the-money at expiration. Today when one hears of path-dependent options, the reference is nearly always to these types of options, although these are certainly not all of the path-dependent types.

The binomial model provides a good framework within which to see how path-dependent options work. Table 14.6 presents a simple three-period binomial model where the current asset price is 50 and each period it can go up 25 percent or down 20 percent. The risk-free rate is 5 percent. We shall use an exercise price of 50. The table shows the binomial tree with the asset moving from 50 at time 0 to 97.66, 62.50, 40, or 25.60 at time 3.

Also shown in the table is a listing of each of the eight paths the asset could take. Notice that it could go up-up-up, up-up-down, or any of six other possible paths. Recalling from our binomial model material in Chapter 4, the probability factor, p, is $(1 + r - d)/(u - d)$, which the table shows is 0.556. The probability of a given path is $p^{\# \text{ of times price goes up}}(1 - p)^{\# \text{ of times price goes down}}$. For example, the probability of going up, down, and then up is $0.552^2 0.444^1 = 0.137$. Also keep in mind that this is not the true probability, but only the risk-neutral probability, as discussed in Chapter 4. It is important not to combine paths, such as the fact that the stock can reach 62.50 at expiration three different ways. Each path can lead to different values of path-dependent options, so we must keep the paths separate.

The table also shows the sequence of asset prices for each path: S_0, S_1, S_2, and S_3. The eighth column shows the average price over the path, counting the original asset price. Thus, for path 1, the average is $(50.00 + 62.50 + 78.13 + 97.66)/4 = 72.07$. The next two columns show the maximum and minimum prices attained over the given path.

The last two columns show the payoffs at expiration for standard European calls. The value for a given path is $Max(0, S_3 - 50)$ for calls and $Max(0, 50 - S_3)$ for puts, which reflects those options' dependencies on only the final asset price, S_3. To find the price of those options, we simply multiply each option payoff by the probability of that payoff occurring, sum the payoffs, and divide by $(1.05)^3$, which is simply discounting the total to the present. This is the same procedure we used in previous applications of the binomial model in Chapter 4. The European call price is 11.50, and the European put price is 4.69.[6] We now look at several types of path-dependent options.

Asian Options An **Asian option** is an option where the payoff is based on the average price attained by the underlying asset during the life of the option or over a specified period of time, which does not have to correspond to the life of the option. An Asian option can take the form of either a call or a put. The average price can be used in

---

[5]The concept of path-independence versus path-dependence is illustrated by considering the following situation encountered in traveling. Suppose you are in Baltimore and need to fly to San Francisco. There are numerous ways to get from Baltimore to San Francisco, including direct flights and many possible connecting flights. If your objective is only to get from Baltimore to San Francisco, it does not matter what route you take. This would be consistent with path independence. If your objective is to get from Baltimore to San Francisco in the least amount of time and/or at the lowest cost, then certain routings, especially direct flights, are preferred. This would be consistent with path dependence.

[6]As an example, the call price is found as $(0.171(47.66) + 0.137(12.50) + \cdots + 0.088(0))/(1.05)^3 = 11.50$.

TABLE 14.6 PATH-DEPENDENT OPTIONS INFORMATION

		TIME 0	TIME 1	TIME 2	TIME 3
S_0:	50	S_0	S_1	S_2	S_3
u:	1.25				97.66
d:	0.80			78.13	
r:	0.05		62.50		62.50
X:	50	50.00		50.00	
p:	0.556[1]		40.00		40.00
1 – p:	0.444			32.00	
					25.60

PATH NO.	PATH	PROBABILITY[2]	S_0	S_1	S_2	S_3	AVERAGE PRICE	S_{MAX}	S_{MIN}	EUROPEAN CALL PAYOFFS	EUROPEAN PUT PAYOFFS
1	uuu	0.171	50.00	62.50	78.13	97.66	72.07	97.66	50.00	47.66	0.00
2	uud	0.137	50.00	62.50	78.13	62.50	63.28	78.13	50.00	12.50	0.00
3	udu	0.137	50.00	62.50	50.00	62.50	56.25	62.50	50.00	12.50	0.00
4	duu	0.137	50.00	40.00	50.00	62.50	50.63	62.50	40.00	12.50	0.00
5	udd	0.110	50.00	62.50	50.00	40.00	50.63	62.50	40.00	0.00	10.00
6	dud	0.110	50.00	40.00	50.00	40.00	45.00	50.00	40.00	0.00	10.00
7	ddu	0.110	50.00	40.00	32.00	40.00	40.50	50.00	32.00	0.00	10.00
8	ddd	0.088	50.00	40.00	32.00	25.60	36.90	50.00	25.60	0.00	24.40

European call price: 11.50
European put price: 4.69

[1]Computed as $(1 + r - d)/(u - d)$.
[2]Probability of a given path is $p^{\text{\# of times price goes up}}(1 - p)^{\text{\# of times price goes down}}$. For example, for path 5 (udd), the probability is $0.556^1 0.444^2 = 0.110$.

place of either the expiration price of the asset or the exercise price. The former are called **average price options**, while the latter are called **average strike options**. For the three-period case, the payoffs at expiration are as follows:

$$\text{Average price call: } Max(0, S_{avg} - X)$$
$$\text{Average put price: } Max(0, X - S_{avg})$$
$$\text{Average strike call: } Max(0, S_3 - S_{avg})$$
$$\text{Average strike put: } Max(0, S_{avg} - S_3).$$

An Asian option is an option in which either the final asset price or the exercise price is replaced by the average price of the asset over the option's life.

Table 14.7 illustrates how to price an Asian option. Look at the fifth column, which shows the payoffs for the average price call. For path 1, at expiration, the average price is 72.07, which makes the option be in-the-money by 22.07. The remaining payoff values are computed similarly using the first formula above. Then the values in the payoff column are multiplied by their respective probabilities (column 3). The sum of these probability-weighted outcomes is then discounted over three periods to the present. We see that both types of Asian options are considerably less valuable than their European counterparts. There are several reasons for this, but the most obvious one is that the volatility of an average of a series of numbers is less than the volatility of the series itself.

TABLE 14.7 PRICING AN ASIAN OPTION

PATH NO.	PATH	PROBABILITY	AVERAGE PRICE (S_{AVG})	AVERAGE PRICE CALL PAYOFF[1]	AVERAGE PRICE PUT PAYOFF[2]	AVERAGE STRIKE CALL PAYOFF[3]	AVERAGE STRIKE PUT PAYOFF[4]
1	uuu	0.171	72.07	22.07	0.00	25.59	0.00
2	uud	0.137	63.28	13.28	0.00	0.00	0.78
3	udu	0.137	56.25	6.25	0.00	6.25	0.00
4	duu	0.137	50.63	0.63	0.00	11.88	0.00
5	udd	0.110	50.63	0.63	0.00	0.00	10.63
6	dud	0.110	45.00	0.00	5.00	0.00	5.00
7	ddu	0.110	40.50	0.00	9.50	0.00	0.50
8	ddd	0.088	36.90	0.00	13.10	0.00	11.30
			Value of Option[5]	5.72	2.37	5.94	2.48

[1]$\text{Max}(0, S_{avg} - 50)$.
[2]$\text{Max}(0, 50 - S_{avg})$.
[3]$\text{Max}(0, S_3 - S_{avg})$.
[4]$\text{Max}(0, S_{avg} - S_3)$.
[5]Value of Option is found as the sum of the product of the payoffs of the option (column 5, 6, 7, or 8) by the respective probability of that payoff (column 3) discounted at the risk-free rate (i.e., divided by 1.05^3).

The lower prices of Asian options relative to European options make them useful for situations in which the user wants to hedge or speculate on the price series but is unwilling to spend the full price required by European options. In some cases, a hedge of only an average price is satisfactory. Asian options are also used in markets where prices are unusually volatile and may be susceptible to distortion or manipulation. The averaging process results in the option payoff not being completely dependent on the price at expiration.

As we discussed in Chapter 4, the binomial model requires a large number of time steps to give an accurate approximation to the Black-Scholes-Merton price for standard European options. Unfortunately, there is no formula like the Black-Scholes-Merton for Asian options.[7] The binomial model is useful for illustrative purposes, but applying it in practice with a large number of time steps is impractical for Asian options. The computer must keep track of 2^n paths, where n is the number of time periods. For our three-period model, the number of paths is $2^3 = 8$. For a realistic situation, we would require at least 50 time steps, in which case the computer must keep track of 1,125,900,000,000,000 paths! There are some Asian option approximation formulas used in practice, but a convenient method of pricing Asian options is by **Monte Carlo simulation**. We illustrate the Monte Carlo simulation procedure in Appendix 14.

Lookback Options Another interesting path-dependent option is the **lookback option**.

A lookback call allows you to buy the asset at the lowest price and a lookback put allows you to sell it at the highest price attained during the life of the option. It is said

---

[7]An exception is that if the average is a geometric average, then a formula does exist. Geometric average Asian options, however, are rarely used in practice.

that lookback options allow you to "buy low, sell high." Because you never have to miss in timing the market, a lookback option is also called a **no-regrets option**.

For the three-period binomial example, the standard lookback option has payoffs at expiration as follows:

$$\text{Lookback call: } \text{Max}(0, S_3 - S_{min})$$
$$\text{Lookback put: } \text{Max}(0, S_{max} - S_3).$$

In other words, the lookback call sets the exercise price at the lowest price the asset attained during the option's life. A lookback put sets the exercise price at the highest price it attained during the life of the option. In the worst case, a lookback option expires at-the-money.

Another class of lookback options, which are sometimes called **modified lookback options**, has the exercise price fixed but replaces the terminal asset price with the maximum price for a call and minimum price for a put. Thus, their payoffs are:

> Lookback options base their expiration payoffs on the maximum or minimum price reached by the asset during the option's life. They allow the user to buy at the low price or sell at the high price.

$$\text{Fixed strike lookback call: } \text{Max}(0, S_{max} - X)$$
$$\text{First strike lookback put: } \text{Max}(0, X - S_{min}).$$

Table 14.8 illustrates the pricing of lookback options. Consider the standard lookback call, whose payoffs are listed in column 6. If path 1 occurs, the asset ends up at 97.66. The minimum price along that path is 50. Thus, it expires in-the-money worth 47.66. Notice particularly path 7. From Table 14.6, we see that the asset price ended up at 40 but it went as low as 32, so the call ends up worth 8. Similarly, the basic lookback put in path 2 pays off 15.63 because the asset ended up at 62.50 but went as high as 78.13. The remaining payoffs are determined in a similar manner using the appropriate formulas shown above. The value of each option is once again found by multiplying each option

TABLE 14.8 PRICING A LOOKBACK OPTION

PATH NO.	PATH	PROBABILITY	MAXIMUM PRICE (S_{MAX})	MINIMUM PRICE (S_{MIN})	LOOKBACK CALL PAYOFF[1]	LOOKBACK PUT PAYOFF[2]	FIXED STRIKE LOOKBACK CALL PAYOFF[3]	FIXED STRIKE LOOKBACK PUT PAYOFF[4]
1	uuu	0.171	97.66	50.00	47.66	0.00	47.66	0.00
2	uud	0.137	78.13	50.00	12.50	15.63	28.13	0.00
3	udu	0.137	62.50	50.00	12.50	0.00	12.50	0.00
4	duu	0.137	62.50	40.00	22.50	0.00	12.50	10.00
5	udd	0.110	62.50	40.00	0.00	22.50	12.50	10.00
6	dud	0.110	50.00	40.00	0.00	10.00	0.00	10.00
7	ddu	0.110	50.00	32.00	8.00	10.00	0.00	18.00
8	ddd	0.088	50.00	25.60	0.00	24.40	0.00	24.40
				Value of Option[5]	13.45	7.73	14.54	6.64

[1]$\text{Max}(0, S_3 - S_{min})$.
[2]$\text{Max}(0, S_{max} - S_3)$.
[3]$\text{Max}(0, S_{max} - 50)$.
[4]$\text{Max}(0, 50 - S_{min})$.
[5]Value of Option is found as the sum of the product of the payoffs of the option (column 6, 7, 8, or 9) multiplied by the respective probability of that payoff (column 3) discounted at the risk-free rate (i.e., divided by 1.05^3).

payoff by the appropriate probability (column 3), summing these probability-weighted payoffs, and discounting at 5 percent over three periods.

Because lookback options allow their holders to achieve higher payoffs for some outcomes and positive payoffs for some outcomes where European options would have zero payoffs, they are worth substantially more. Is the additional price worth it? That depends on the investor. An investor who experiences anguish over failing to buy when the price is low or sell when the price is high would probably find the extra cost worth it.

Formulas for the prices of most lookback options have been derived. Using these formulas in practice, however, is complicated by the fact that many lookback options do not provide for continuous monitoring of the asset price. Instead, they consider only the closing price of the asset in determining the maximum or minimum. Because of the aforementioned large number of paths that must be followed in the binomial model, Monte Carlo methods are often used.

Barrier Options The final type of path-dependent option we examine is the **barrier option**. While lookback options have positive payoffs for more outcomes than do standard European options, barrier options have fewer positive payoffs than European options. This makes them less expensive than standard European options. Investors who want to save a little money and do not want to pay for outcomes they do not believe are likely to occur will be attracted to barrier options.

In one type of barrier option, the holder specifies a level of the asset price that, if touched by the asset before the option expires, causes the option to terminate. In the other type of barrier option, the holder specifies a level of the asset price that must be hit by the asset to activate the option. If the asset never hits the barrier during the option's life, the option cannot be exercised even if it expires in-the-money at expiration. Options that can terminate early are called **out-options** and sometimes **knock-out options**. Options that will be unexercisable if they fail to touch the barrier are called **in-options** or sometimes **knock-in options**. Out-options, thus, can expire prematurely with no value if the barrier is hit. In-options must be activated by hitting the barrier. If they are never activated, they automatically expire worthless. If the barrier is set above the current asset price, both in- and out-options are referred to as **up-options**. If the barrier is set below the current asset price, in- and out-options are referred to as **down-options**.

Table 14.9 illustrates the pricing of barrier options. The table shows the payoffs at expiration of all eight types of barrier options. We first look at down-and-out and down-and-in options. The bold zero values are outcomes in which out-options hit the barrier and, thus, were knocked out with no value. The italicized values are outcomes in which in-options failed to hit the barrier and, thus, were never activated.

Consider the down-and-out call illustrated in column 4, where the barrier is set at 45. This means that if the asset ever hits 45, the option terminates with no value. This will occur in paths 4, 6, 7, and 8, where in each path, the asset hit 40 at time 1. In path 5, the option hits the barrier but expires worthless anyway. Now move one column over to the down-and-in call. This option will never activate if the asset does not fall to 45 during the option's life. This occurs in paths 1, 2, and 3.

The values of the options are shown in the bottom row of the table and are computed the same way as in the previous examples. Notice a very interesting result. If one combines the payoffs from the down-and-out call with those of the down-and-in call, one obtains the same payoffs of a standard European call. This should make sense. When one holds both options, if the out-option knocks out, the in-option immediately knocks in. Thus, the value of the two options combined is $10.02 + 1.48 = 11.50$, which is

Barrier options are options that either terminate early without value if the asset price hits a pre-specified barrier or must be activated by the asset price hitting a pre-specified barrier. The former are called out-options, and the latter are called in-options.

TABLE 14.9 PRICING A BARRIER OPTION

PATH NO.	PATH	PROBABILITY	DOWN-AND-OUT AND DOWN-AND-IN OPTIONS (H = BARRIER)				UP-AND-OUT AND UP-AND-IN OPTIONS (H = BARRIER)			
			OUT CALL PAYOFF (H = 45)	IN CALL PAYOFF (H = 45)	OUT PUT PAYOFF (H = 35)	IN PUT PAYOFF (H = 35)	OUT CALL PAYOFF (H = 70)	IN CALL PAYOFF (H = 70)	OUT PUT PAYOFF (H = 55)	IN PUT PAYOFF (H = 55)
1	uuu	0.171	47.66	*0.00*	0.00	*0.00*	**0.00**	47.66	**0.00**	0.00
2	uud	0.137	12.50	*0.00*	0.00	*0.00*	**0.00**	12.50	**0.00**	0.00
3	udu	0.137	12.50	*0.00*	0.00	*0.00*	12.50	*0.00*	**0.00**	0.00
4	duu	0.137	**0.00**	12.50	0.00	*0.00*	12.50	*0.00*	**0.00**	0.00
5	udd	0.110	0.00	0.00	10.00	*0.00*	0.00	*0.00*	**0.00**	10.00
6	dud	0.110	**0.00**	0.00	10.00	*0.00*	0.00	*0.00*	10.00	*0.00*
7	ddu	0.110	**0.00**	0.00	**0.00**	10.00	0.00	*0.00*	10.00	*0.00*
8	ddd	0.088	**0.00**	0.00	**0.00**	24.40	0.00	*0.00*	24.40	*0.00*
	Value of Option[1]		10.02	1.48	1.90	2.80	2.96	8.54	3.75	0.95

[1]Value of Option is found as the sum of the product of the payoffs of the option (columns 4, 5, 6, 7, 8, 9, 10, and 11) by the respective probability of that payoff (column 3) discounted at the risk-free rate (i.e., divided by 1.05^3).

Note: Bold values for out-options are outcomes in which the option hit the barrier and, thus, was knocked out. Italicized values for in-options are outcomes in which the option failed to hit the barrier and, thus, was not exercisable at expiration.

the price we previously obtained for the standard European call. Likewise the value of the down-and-out put and down-and-in put add up to the value of the standard European put, subject to a round-off error. Similar results hold for the up-options.

Some barrier options have an additional feature called a rebate. If a knock-out barrier option provides for a rebate, the holder is paid a fixed sum of cash whenever the option knocks out. If a knock-in option provides for a rebate, the holder is paid a fixed sum of cash at expiration if the option never crosses the barrier. When a barrier option has a rebate, the values of the complementary out- and in-options will add up to more than the standard European option price.

As noted above, barrier options allow investors to avoid paying a price for states they do not believe will occur. As an example of the use of a barrier option, consider a protective put. A standard European put would cost 4.69. To save a little money, an investor might purchase an up-and-out protective put with a barrier of 55 for 3.75. This option would knock out if the asset goes to 55. The holder would in effect be saying that if the asset price rises quickly, he does not expect to need the insurance. Thus, his willingness to terminate the insurance early allows him to save money. Note, however, that this does not guarantee a better result. It simply eliminates the payoff in path 5. The knocked-out put will not pay off if the asset goes up, down, and then down because it knocked out at time 1, even though at expiration the asset price is below the exercise price. Similarly, an investor interested in holding a call might consider purchasing a down-and-out call. The standard call will cost 11.50, while the down-and-out with the barrier at 45 will cost 10.02. The barrier option will not pay off in path 4 where the asset goes down, up, and up, whereas the standard call would pay off if that occurred.

There are many variations of path-dependent options, including some that are American-style, that is, with early exercise. Barrier options in particular can have many types of twists, including barriers both above and below the current price and requirements that the barrier be hit more than once. Another type of barrier option allows the holder to reset the exercise price if the barrier is hit. A more common and somewhat complicating factor is that often only the closing price is considered when determining whether the barrier was touched. This necessitates the use of the binomial model with a large number of time steps and special care to position the barrier on the nodes. Monte Carlo methods, as described in Appendix 14, are also required.

Other Exotic Options

Most of the exotic options described above are reasonably simple to understand. There are many others that are quite complex, and we will not attempt to tackle the pricing of these instruments. It is useful to examine the basic characteristics of these instruments so that you will be aware of them and perhaps recognize them when you encounter them in the future.

Compound options are options on options. For example, you can buy a call option that gives you the right to buy another call option. This is a call on a call. Likewise, there are calls on puts, puts on calls, and puts on puts. The latter two give you the right to sell a call or a put. Compound options would be useful if an investor thought he might need an option later and wanted to establish a price at which the option could be bought or sold. A variation of the compound option is the **installment option**, which permits the premium to be paid in equal installments over the life of the option. At each payment date, the holder of the option decides whether it is worth paying the next installment. This is equivalent to deciding whether it is worth exercising the compound option to acquire another option.

Multi-asset options consist of a family of options whose payoffs depend on the prices of more than one asset. A simple type of multi-asset option is the **exchange option**. This option allows the holder to acquire one asset by giving up another. This kind of option is actually a special case of an ordinary European call. In a European call, the call holder has the right to give up one asset, cash, and acquire another asset, the stock. Exchange options are not commonly traded in the over-the-counter market, but they have proven to be useful in valuing many other types of options, such as the quality option in the Treasury bond futures contract that we covered in Chapter 10.

Another type of multi-asset option is the **min-max option**. This is an option that pays off according to the better or worse performing of two assets. For example, consider a call on two assets, stocks X and Y, in which at expiration, we determine which asset has the higher price and then calculate the payoff based on that asset. This is an option on the maximum of two assets. In an option on the minimum of two assets, the payoff is calculated based on the asset with the lower price at expiration. These options can be puts or calls, and they are sometimes called **rainbow options**. A slight and more common variation determines the better- or worse-performing asset, not on the basis of how high or low its price is, but according to the rate of return on the asset during the option's life. This is also called an **alternative option**. Another variation of this is the **out-performance option**, whose payoff is determined by the difference in the prices or rates of return on two assets or indices relative to an exercise price or rate.

Shout options permit the holder at any time during the life of the option to establish a minimum payoff that will occur at expiration. For example, suppose the stock price is very high relative to the exercise price. The investor, holding such an option and fearing that the stock price will fall, can establish the minimum payoff as the amount by which it is currently in-the-money. A slight variation of this is a **cliquet option**, in which the exercise price can periodically increase as the stock price rises. Still another variation, the **lock-in option**, permits establishment of the exact payoff, as opposed to just the minimum, prior to expiration. A **deferred strike option** is one in which the exercise price is not set until a specific date prior to expiration.

MAKING THE CONNECTION

Accumulator Contracts

Investors often search far and wide to find a good deal. Many financial derivative contracts appear as a very good deal on the surface, but once you read the fine print, the deal is sometimes not as good as it looks. One example popular in Asia is known as an accumulator contract.

The general idea of an accumulator contract is that the contract buyer agrees to purchase a predetermined number of shares of a particular common stock at a predetermined price on a series of future dates. Initially, it appears that the accumulator contract is really just a series of forward contracts, making it somewhat like an equity swap, as we covered in Chapter 12. Assuming no cash dividends and positive interest rates, we know that due to carry arbitrage, the forward price should be above the current stock price. Often, however, the predetermined price is set below the current stock price, making the accumulator contract appear to be a very good deal indeed.

Accumulator contracts tend to be popular when stock prices are believed to be in a prolonged upward trend and the downside risk is diminished in the minds of investors. Clearly, if you purchase accumulator contracts at a discount to current stock prices, you can still lose if the stock price falls dramatically and you are obligated to purchase the stock at the higher predetermined price. By now, we know that we could hedge this

risk by short selling the stock and purchasing the accumulator contract at a discount to lock in a profit, assuming the securities lending fees did not completely offset the discount.

Now enter the fine print. Accumulator contracts became known as "I kill you later" contracts in the global market downturn of 2008. Many accumulator contracts have a knockout provision that terminates the contract if the stock rises by a pre-specified amount. The knockout provision makes the simple short-selling hedge more difficult due to losses on the short position when the accumulator is knocked out, resulting in no gain on the accumulator contract. Also, many accumulator contracts have a double down provision that requires the buyer to purchase more shares at the predetermined price if the stock price falls by a specified amount. These contingency clauses in the fine print can easily be overlooked.

None of these characteristics of accumulator contracts should be taken to mean that they or other derivatives are inherently bad instruments. As long as these factors are explicitly stated in the contract, an investor is free to choose whether to buy or sell the contract. But when scouring the globe for a good investment deal, investors should read contracts carefully and consider the wide array of risks associated with complex financial instruments.

Forward-start options are options whose lives do not begin until a later date. The premium is paid up front and the purchaser specifies a desired degree of moneyness, such as at-the-money, 5 percent out-of-the-money, and so forth. Once the option begins, it is like an ordinary option. This type of option is similar to the types of executive and employee stock option plans used by firms. The firm makes a commitment that will result in its awarding options at various future dates. When the options are structured so that as one expires another begins, the combination is called a **tandem option**.

The exotic options described here are the primary ones that are used in today's markets, but there are many more. A few years ago, most of these options did not exist. The pace of creativity is quite rapid. As your career in the financial world evolves, you will likely encounter new ones quite often.

SOME UNUSUAL DERIVATIVES

In most of this book, we have examined derivatives based only on stocks, bonds, and currencies. On occasion, we have made reference to derivatives on certain commodities such as metals and oil. In recent years, derivatives have emerged on some most unusual underlyings. We take a look at two of these here.

Electricity Derivatives

Derivatives on electricity can be used to manage the risk of electricity prices, but they are more difficult to price than most derivatives because the underlying is not storable.

Most of the energy consumed on the earth derives from three primary sources: fossil fuels, nuclear reaction, and the sun. Fossil fuels in the form of oil, coal, and natural gas are the primary sources of energy. We have already mentioned derivatives on oil, and derivatives on natural gas exist as well. Derivatives on coal have not, however, developed to any great extent. These sources of energy are also converted into other sources of energy, the primary one of which is electricity, which is obviously quite widely used in businesses and by consumers. Until recent years, electricity was largely regulated by the various states in the U.S. and foreign countries, but these governments have begun to relax this regulation, thereby allowing electricity prices to fluctuate and giving consumers the choice of where to buy their electricity. In response to this new-found price volatility, the energy industry created spot and derivative markets on electricity. These markets have proven to be useful by large-volume electricity users and public utilities for managing the volatility of electricity prices.

On the surface, it would seem that one could use standard models for pricing forwards, futures, and options on electricity, but that is not the case. Electricity is quite unlike any asset we have studied so far in that it cannot be stored. Stocks, bonds, currencies, and most commodities can be purchased and held, but electricity is manufactured, sent along lines to where it is needed, and almost immediately consumed. All of the models we have learned are based on the idea that the underlying asset can be held for a finite period of time. Hence, we have reason to believe that the cost of carry model and the Black-Scholes-Merton model cannot be used to price electricity derivatives. Indeed, the industry generally does not use these models. Unfortunately there is little agreement on a better alternative. These issues are quite advanced for this level of the subject, and we are not covering them here. In spite of the lack of agreement on pricing electricity derivatives, the market for **electricity derivatives** continues to grow. Confusion over pricing clearly does not stop a market in which the product serves an important need. In fact, confusion over pricing could even stimulate trading if some investors believe they know the proper way to price these instruments before everyone else knows.

Weather Derivatives

Weather derivatives permit parties to manage the risk driven by uncertainty of the weather. These derivatives can take the form of derivatives where the underlying is temperature or precipitation or where the underlying is financial loss caused by the weather.

All of the underlyings we have covered can be owned. Even electricity can be owned, even though as we noted, it is consumed immediately. But in general, the most important feature of an underlying is not that it can be owned, but that it is a source of risk. One important source of risk is the weather. There are few companies whose operations are completely unaffected by the weather. Some entities' fortunes are tied almost completely to the weather. For example, the profitability and survival of orange juice growers in central Florida are highly affected by temperatures, primarily the potential for freezes. Farmers in general are highly exposed to weather. But so are airlines, ski resorts, various tourist attractions, and recreational services. Retail establishments and public utilities are likewise affected by the weather.

To manage these risks, an array of options, forwards, futures, and swaps on the weather have been created in recent years. Weather has many excellent properties that make it appropriate for having derivatives created thereon. One important justification for **weather derivatives** is that weather is highly measurable, and there is a long history of data on the weather. There are three primary ways to measure the weather. One is by temperature, one by precipitation, and the one by the financial damage caused by the weather.

Information on temperature is widely available. The weather derivatives industry has created a standard measure used in derivative contracts called the heating degree day and cooling degree day. In the U.S., a benchmark of 65 degrees Fahrenheit is considered to be a normal level of comfort. On a cool (<65 degrees) day, energy is considered to be consumed in providing heat. A quantity of one heating degree day (HDD) is the difference between 65 degrees and the average temperature of that day. On a warm (>65 degrees) day, energy is considered to be consumed in providing air conditioning. A quantity of one cooling degree day (CDD) is the difference between the average temperature of that day and 65 degrees. Over a period of time, such as the life of a derivative contract, the number of heating degree days or cooling degree days is accumulated and compared to the exercise price of an option, the price of a forward or futures contract, or the fixed price of a swap.

Another measure of the weather is the quantity of precipitation. Suppose, for example, that a ski resort knows that unless it receives at least 10 feet of snow during the December through March period, it will not achieve its target cash flow. It might buy a put option on the amount of snowfall. The option pays off based on the difference between 10 feet and the actual amount of snow received. If the quantity of snow received exceeds 10 feet, the option would expire out-of-the-money. Of course, the ski resort could sell a forward contract, which would not require a payment up front, but would require the resort to pay off based on the difference between the actual amount of snowfall and the benchmark amount, which would not necessarily be 10 feet.

A third measure of weather is the amount of financial loss incurred from weather damage. Hurricanes, earthquakes, tornadoes, and floods are the primary forms of weather damage. The insurance industry tabulates losses based on its claims. Derivative contracts are based on these financial loss figures. The insurance industry itself is particularly attracted to these types of derivatives, because it gives the industry a means of shedding some of its risk.

Pricing weather derivatives, like pricing electricity derivatives, is particularly challenging. Weather cannot be stored, but storable assets are influenced by the weather and the effects of weather can be measured. Suppose that the aforementioned ski resort can predict with relative certainty the number of skiers it will have for various amounts of snow over the season. It might determine that if it receives only 10 feet of snow, it will generate sufficient cash to earn a risk-free return. Thus, a forward contract priced at 10 would earn a risk-free return. This would form the basis for pricing the contract. A similar, although slightly more complex, analysis would be used to price an option. Of course, not all weather derivatives can be priced easily, but as noted, weather data are available in large quantities over long periods of time, which facilitates measuring its effects on the cash flows of a business.

The weather derivatives industry has grown slowly but steadily. Interestingly, it has offered many new job opportunities to meteorologists. No longer are they primarily limited to employment at local television stations. Many of these weather experts now work for financial institutions and commodity trading companies.

Summary

This chapter carried our treatment of derivatives one step further by examining some advanced derivatives and strategies. We learned how portfolio insurance works and saw several different ways of implementing it. We also examined various equity derivatives that trade in the over-the-counter market, including forwards, break forwards, and equity-linked debt.

Picking up where we left off with our treatment of interest rate derivatives in the previous chapter, we examined two other types of interest-sensitive instruments, structured notes and mortgage-backed securities, that are not strictly derivatives, but, for better or for worse, are usually viewed as such. We saw that these instruments can have extremely volatile prices and require careful analysis.

We also looked at several types of exotic options, including digital options, chooser options, and path-dependent options. In the latter category, we examined Asian options, lookback options, and barrier options and observed how their prices are derived in a binomial framework. All of the options classified as exotics have payoffs structured quite differently from those of standard European and American options.

We also looked at derivatives in which the underlying is electricity or weather. We saw that these derivatives are far more complex because the underlying is not a storable asset.

Nearly all of the standard derivative instruments can be used with slight modifications in equity, currency,

commodity, and interest rate markets. Firms with significant exposures to oil price risk are major users of derivatives. Indeed, derivatives are applicable to risk management problems throughout an organization. In fact, the widespread use of derivatives has spawned a new profession, risk management.

In the first 14 chapters of this book, you have gained exposure to a broad range of derivative contracts. While the coverage here is only introductory, it sets the stage for further study and eventual application of these instruments to solving risk management problems. Accordingly, we devote the final two chapters to gaining an understanding of the process of risk management, the problems that risk managers must address, some techniques used by risk managers, and the consequences of good and bad risk management.

Key Terms

Before continuing to Chapter 15, you should be able to give brief definitions of the following terms:

equity derivative/baskets, p. 493
portfolio insurance/upside capture/ fiduciary call, p. 496
dynamic hedging, p. 497
equity forward/break forward, p. 500
pay-later option/Warrants/quanto, p. 503
structured notes/range floater/ inverse floater/reverse floater, p. 505
prepayment risk/mortgage-backed securities/securitization, p. 506
mortgage pass-throughs/mortgage strips/interest-only strip/IO/ principal-only strip/ PO, p. 507

collateralized mortgage obligation (CMO)/tranches, p. 510
exotic options/Digital options/ binary options/asset-or-nothing option/cash-or-nothing option, p. 512
contingent-pay option/chooser option/as-you-like-it option, p. 515
path-dependent options/Asian option, p. 516
average price options/average strike options, p. 517
Monte Carlo simulation/lookback option, p. 518
no-regrets option/modified lookback options, p. 519

barrier option/out-options/ knock-out options/in-options/ knock-in options/up-options/ down-options, p. 520
Compound options/installment option/Multi-asset options/ exchange option/min-max option/rainbow options/ alternative option/out-performance option/Shout options/cliquet option/lock-in option/deferred strike option, p. 522
Forward-start options/tandem option, p. 523
electricity derivatives/weather derivatives, p. 524

Further Reading

The following books and articles are good treatments of the topics covered here:

Portfolio Insurance:

Abken, P. A. "An Introduction to Portfolio Insurance." *Federal Reserve Bank of Atlanta Economic Review* 72 (1987): 2–25.
Garcia, C. B., and F. J. Gould. "An Empirical Study of Portfolio Insurance." *Financial Analysts Journal* 43 (July–August 1987): 44–54.
O'Brien, T. J. "Portfolio Insurance Mechanics." *Journal of Portfolio Management* 14 (1988): 40–47.

Rubinstein, M. "Alternative Paths to Portfolio Insurance." *Financial Analysts Journal* 41 (July–August 1985): 42–52.

Equity Derivatives:

Beder, T. S. "Equity Derivatives for Investors." *The Journal of Financial Engineering* 1 (1992): 174–195.
Equity Derivatives: Applications in Risk Management and Investment. London: Risk Publications, Ltd., 1997.

Kat, H. M. *Structured Equity Derivatives.* Chichester, UK: Wiley, 2001.

Structured Notes:

Bluemke, A. *How to Invest in Structured Products: A Guide for Investors and Asset Managers.* West Sussex, UK: John Wiley & Sons, 2009.

Crabbe, L. E., and J. D. Argilagos. "Anatomy of the Structured Note Market." *Journal of Applied Corporate Finance* 7 (1994): 85–98.

Goodman, L. S. "Anatomy of the Secondary Structured Note Market." *Derivatives Quarterly* 2 (1995): 39–43.

Kawaller, I. G. "Understanding Structured Notes." *Derivatives Quarterly* 1 (1995): 29–32.

Mortgage-Backed Securities:

Becketti, S. "The Prepayment Risk of Mortgage-Backed Securities." *Federal Reserve Bank of Kansas City Economic Review* 74 (1989): 43–57.

Fabozzi, F. J., A. K. Bhattacharya, and W. S. Berliner. *Mortgage-Backed Securities: Products, Structuring, and Analytical Techniques.* Hoboken, NJ: John Wiley & Sons, 2007.

Midanek, D. H., and J. I. Midanek. "Understanding Mortgage-Based Securities." *Derivatives Quarterly* 2 (1996): 39–46.

Smith, S. D. "Analyzing Risk and Return for Mortgage-Backed Securities." *Federal Reserve Bank of Atlanta Economic Review* 76 (1991): 2–13.

Stone, C. A., and A. Zissu. "The Risk of Mortgage-Backed Securities and Their Derivatives." *Journal of Applied Corporate Finance* 7 (1994): 99–111.

Exotic Options:

Bouzoubaa, M., and A. Osseiran. *Exotic Options and Hybrids: A Guide to Structuring, Pricing and Trading.* West Sussex, UK: John Wiley & Sons, 2010.

Clewlow, L., and C. Strickland, eds. *Exotic Options: State of the Art.* London: International Thomson, 1997.

Haug, E. G. *The Complete Guide to Option Pricing Formulas,* 2nd ed. New York: McGraw-Hill, 2007.

Nelken, I., ed. *The Handbook of Exotic Options: Instruments, Analysis, and Applications.* Chicago: Irwin, 1996.

Tan, C. *Demystifying Exotic Products: Interest Rates, Equities and Foreign Exchange.* West Sussex, UK: John Wiley & Sons, 2010.

Concepts Checks

1. Explain the advantages and disadvantages of implementing portfolio insurance using stock and puts in comparison to using stock and futures in a dynamic hedge strategy.

2. Explain how a portfolio manager might justify the purchase of an inverse floating-rate note.

3. Explain why an interest-only (IO) mortgage strip has a value that is extremely volatile with respect to interest rates. What two factors determine its value?

4. Explain the difference between path-dependent options and path-independent options and give examples of each.

5. Give an example of a situation in which someone might want to use a barrier option.

Questions and Problems

1. Explain the advantages and disadvantages of implementing portfolio insurance using stock and puts in comparison to using a fiduciary call.

2. Contrast lookback options and barrier options and explain the difference between in- and out-options.

3. Demonstrate that the payoffs of a chooser option with an exercise price of X and a time to expiration of T that permits the user to designate it as a call or a put at t can be replicated with two transactions. Specifically, by (1) buying a call with an exercise price of X and time to expiration of T and (2) buying a put with an exercise price equal to $X(1 + r)^{-(T-t)}$ and time to expiration of t. This proof will require that you consider two possible outcomes

at t (user designates it as a call or user designates it as a put according to the rule given in this chapter). For each outcome at t, there are two possible outcomes at T, $S_T > X$ or $S_T < X$. Explain why a chooser option is less expensive than a straddle.

4. Explain how weather derivatives could be used by an electric utility to manage the risk associated with power consumption as affected by the weather.

5. In modern financial derivatives markets, there are many exotic options. Briefly explain compound options, multi-asset options, shout options, and forward start options.

6. On July 5, a market index is at 492.54. You hold a portfolio that duplicates the index and is worth 20,500

times the index. You want to insure the portfolio at a particular value over the period until September 20. You can buy risk-free debt maturing on September 20 with a face value of $100 for $98.78.

a. You plan to use puts, which are selling for $23.72 and have an exercise price of 510. Determine the appropriate number of puts and shares to hold. What is the insured value of the portfolio?

b. Determine the value of the portfolio if the index on September 20 is at 507.35.

c. Determine the value of the portfolio if the index on September 20 is at 515.75. Compute the upside capture and the cost of the insurance.

7. Use the information in problem 9 to set up a dynamic hedge using stock index futures. Assume a multiplier of 500. The futures price is 496.29. The volatility is 17.5 percent. The continuously compounded risk-free rate is 3.6 percent, and the call delta is 0.3826. Let the stock price increase by $1 and show that the change in the portfolio value is almost the same as it would have been had a put been used.

For the next three problems, use a two-period binomial model on a stock worth 100 that can go up 20 percent or down 15 percent. The risk-free rate is 6 percent each period.

8. Determine the price of an average price Asian call option. Use an exercise price of 95. Count the current price in determining the average. Comment on whether you would expect a standard European call to have a lower or higher price.

9. Determine the prices of lookback and modified lookback calls and puts. For the modified lookbacks, use an exercise price of 95.

10. Determine the prices of the following barrier options.

a. A down-and-out call with the barrier at 90 and the exercise price at 95

b. An up-and-out put with the barrier at 110 and the exercise price at 105

c. Select any other barrier option but base your selection on the following instructions: Calculate the value of your selected barrier option and use it with the results you obtained in part a or b to determine the price of a standard European call or put. Then calculate the actual value of the European call or put and compare that answer with the answer you obtained from the barrier options. Explain why this result is obtained.

11. A portfolio manager is interested in purchasing an instrument with a call option-like payoff but does not want to have to pay money up front. The manager learns from a banker that one can do this

by entering into a break forward contract. The manager wants to learn if the banker is quoting a fair price. The stock price is 437.55. The contract expires in 270 days. The volatility is 18 percent, and the continuously compounded risk-free rate is 3.75 percent. The exercise price will be set at the forward price of the stock.

a. Determine the exercise price.

b. The loan implicit in the break forward contract will have a face value of 40.19. Determine if this is a fair amount by using your answer in part a and computing the value of K.

c. Regardless of whether the break forward is found to be fairly priced, determine the value of the position if the stock price ends up at 465 and at 425.

12. Consider a stock priced at 100 with a volatility of 25 percent. The continuously compounded risk-free rate is 5 percent. Answer the following questions about various options, all of which have an original maturity of one year.

a. Find the premium on an at-the-money pay-later call option. Then determine the market value of the option nine months later if the stock is at 110.

b. Find the value of F and K on a break forward contract. Then determine the market value of the break forward nine months later if the stock is at 110.

c. Find the premium on an at-the-money contingent-pay call option. Then determine the market value of the option nine months later if the stock is at 110.

13. A stock is priced at 125.37, the continuously compounded risk-free rate is 4.4 percent, and the volatility is 21 percent. There are no dividends. Answer the following questions.

a. Determine a fair price for a two-year asset-or-nothing option with exercise price of 120.

b. Assuming you purchased the asset-or-nothing option at the price you determined in part a, calculate your profit if the asset price at expiration is (1) 138 and (2) 114.

c. Determine a fair price for a two-year cash-or-nothing option with exercise price of 120 that pays 120 if it expires in-the-money.

d. Assuming you purchased the cash-or-nothing option at the price you determined in part c, calculate your profit if the asset price at expiration is (1) 138 and (2) 114.

14. Consider a ten-year, fixed-rate mortgage of $500,000 that has an interest rate of 12 percent. For simplification, assume that payments are made annually.

a. Determine the amortization schedule.

b. Using your answer in part a, determine the value of both IO and PO strips with a discount rate of 10 percent under the assumption that the mortgage will not be prepaid.

c. Now recompute the values of the IO and PO under the assumption that interest rates immediately fall to 8 percent and the mortgage is prepaid in year 6.

d. Explain the risk characteristics of IO and PO strips.

15. An investment manager expects a stock to be quite volatile and is considering the purchase of either a straddle or a chooser option. The stock is priced at 44, the exercise price is 40, the continuously compounded risk-free rate is 5.2 percent, and the volatility is 51 percent. The options expire in 194 days. The chooser option must be declared a call or a put exactly 90 days before expiration.

a. Determine the prices of the straddle and the chooser.

b. Suppose at 90 days before expiration, the stock is at 28. Find the value of the chooser option at expiration if the stock price ends up at 50 and at 30.

c. Suppose at 90 days before expiration, the stock is at 60. Find the value of the chooser option at expiration if the stock price ends up at 50 and at 30.

d. Compare your answers in parts c and d to the performance of the straddle.

16. Suppose FRM, Inc., issued a zero-coupon, equity index-linked note with a five-year maturity. The par value is $1,000, and the coupon payment is stated as 75% of the equity index return or as zero. Calculate the cash flow at maturity assuming the equity index appreciates by 30 percent over this five-year period.

17. Suppose an investor owns 1,000 shares of Pear, Inc. stock that is trading at $100 per share. Design a portfolio insurance strategy assuming a strike price of $100, time to maturity of one year, and a put price of $9.35 per share. Compute the number of puts to purchase and the minimum level of the portfolio. Compute the upside capture if the stock is trading at $120 per share in one year and if the stock is trading at $80 per share in one year.

18. Derive the terminal stock price of a portfolio insurance strategy with put options such that the upside capture exactly equals 100 percent.

19. Suppose you observe a one year cash-or-nothing digital call option trading for $0.48 and an equivalent cash-or-nothing digital put option trading for $0.45. Calculate the implied interest rate (annualized, continuously compounded).

20. (Concept Problem) Suppose you are asked to assist in the design of an equity-linked security. The instrument is a five-year zero coupon bond with a guaranteed return of 1 percent, compounded annually. At the end of five years, the bond will pay an additional return based on any appreciation of the Nikkei 300 stock index, a measure of the performance of 300 Japanese stocks. The risk-free rate is 5.5 percent, compounded annually, and the volatility of the index is 15 percent. In addition, the index pays a dividend of 1.7 percent continuously compounded. Presently, the index is at 315.55 and the additional return is based on appreciation above the current level of the index. You expect to sell these bonds in minimum increments of $100. Overall you expect to sell $10 million of these securities. Your firm has determined that it needs a margin of $175,000 in cash today to cover costs and earn a reasonable profit. Determine the percentage of the Nikkei return that your firm should offer to cover its costs. Your firm would then set the percentage offered at less than this. Assuming that your firm sells this security, comment on the risk it creates for itself and suggest how it might deal with that risk.

21. (Concept Problem) A convertible bond is a bond that permits the holder to turn in the bond and convert it into a certain number of shares of stock. Conversion would, thus, occur only when the stock does well. As a result of the option to convert the bond to stock, the coupon rate on the bond is lower than it otherwise would be. A new type of financial instrument, the reverse convertible, pays a higher-than-normal coupon, but the principal payoff can be reduced if the stock falls. Let us specify that the principal payoff of the reverse convertible is FV, the face value, if $S_T > S_0$, where S_0 is the stock price when the bond is issued. If $S_T \leq S_0$, the principal payoff is FV(S_T/S_0). Thus, for example, if the stock falls by 10 percent, S_T/S_0, the principal payoff, is 0.9FV. Show that this payoff (FV if $S_T > S_0$ and FV(S_T/S_0) if $S_T \leq S_0$) is equivalent to a combination of an ordinary bond and a certain number of European puts with an exercise price of S_0. Determine how many puts you would need.

APPENDIX 14

Monte Carlo Simulation

Simulation is a procedure in which random numbers are generated according to probabilities assumed to be associated with a source of uncertainty, such as a new product's sales or, more appropriately for our purposes, stock prices, interest rates, exchange rates, or commodity prices. Outcomes associated with these random drawings are then analyzed to determine the likely results and the associated risk. Often this technique is called *Monte Carlo simulation*, being named for the city of Monte Carlo, which is noted for its casinos.

The gambling analogy notwithstanding, Monte Carlo simulation is a legitimate and widely used technique for dealing with uncertainty in many aspects of business operations. For our purposes, it has been shown to be an accurate method of pricing options and particularly useful for path-dependent options and others for which no known formula exists.

To facilitate an understanding of the technique, we shall look at how Monte Carlo simulation has been used to price standard European options. Of course, we know that the Black-Scholes-Merton model is the correct method of pricing these options; so Monte Carlo simulation is not really needed. It is useful, however, to conduct this experiment because it demonstrates the accuracy of the technique for a simple option of which the exact price is easily obtained from a known formula.

The assumptions of the Black-Scholes-Merton model imply that for a given stock price at time t, simulated changes in the stock price at a future time can be generated by the following formula:

$$\Delta S = S r_c \Delta t + S \sigma \varepsilon \sqrt{\Delta t},$$

where S is the current stock price, S is the change in the stock price, r_c is the continuously compounded risk-free rate, σ is the volatility of the stock, and Δt is the length of the time interval over which the stock price change occurs. The variable ε is a random number generated from a standard normal probability distribution. Remember from Chapter 5 that the standard normal random variable has a mean of zero and a standard deviation of 1.0 and occurs with a frequency corresponding to that associated with the famous bell-shaped curve.

Generating future stock prices according to the above formula is actually quite easy. A standard normal random variable can be approximated with a slight adjustment to Microsoft Excel's Rand() function. The Rand() function produces a uniform random number between 0 and 1, meaning that it generates numbers between 0 and 1 with equal probability. A good approximation for a standard normal variable is obtained by the Excel formula "= Rand() + Rand() + Rand() + Rand() + Rand() + Rand() + Rand() + Rand() + Rand() + Rand() + Rand() + Rand() − 6.0," or simply 12 uniform random numbers minus 6.0.[*] Alternatively, a normal random number generator is available in Excel's Data Analysis tool pack.

After generating one standard normal random variable, you then simply insert it into the right-hand side of the above formula for ΔS. This gives the price change over the life

---

[*]This approximation is based on the fact that the distribution of the sum of 12 uniformly distributed random numbers between 0 and 1 will have a mean of six and a standard deviation of 1. By subtracting 6.0, we adjust the mean to zero without changing the standard deviation. What we obtain is technically not normally distributed but is symmetric with a mean of zero and a standard deviation of 1.0, which are three properties associated with the normal distribution. The procedure is widely accepted as a quick and reasonable approximation but would not pass the most demanding tests for normality.

of the option, which is then added to the current price to obtain the price of the asset at expiration. You then compute the price of the option at expiration according to the standard formulas, Max(0, S_T − X) for a call or Max(0, X − S_T) for a put. This produces one possible option value at expiration. You then repeat this procedure many thousands of times, take the average value of the option at expiration, and discount that value at the risk-free rate. Some users compute the standard deviation of the call prices in order to obtain a feel for the possible error in estimating the price.

Let us price the DCRB June 125 call that we first encountered in Chapter 3. The DCRB stock price is 125.94, the exercise price is 125, the risk-free rate is 4.46 percent, the volatility is 83 percent, and the time to expiration is 0.0959 years. Inserting the above approximation formula for a standard normal random variable in any cell in an Excel spreadsheet produces a random number. Suppose that number is 0.733449. Inserting into the formula for ΔS gives $125.94(0.0446)(0.0959) + 125.94(0.83)(0.733449)\sqrt{0.0959} = 24.28$. Thus, the simulated value of the stock at expiration is $125.94 + 24.28 = 150.22$. At that price, the option will be worth Max(0, 150.22 − 125) = 25.22 at expiration. We then draw another random number. Suppose we get −0.18985. Inserting into the formula for ΔS, we obtain $125.94(0.0446)(0.0959) + 125.94(0.83)(-0.18985)\sqrt{0.0959} = -5.61$, which gives us a stock price at expiration of 125.94 − 5.61 = 120.33, leading to an option price of Max(0,120.33 − 125) = 0. We repeat this procedure several thousand times, after which we take an average of the simulated option prices and then discount that average to the present using the present value formula $e^{-0.0446(0.0959)}$.

Naturally, every simulation is different because each set of random numbers is different. A Monte Carlo procedure written in Excel's Visual Basic produced the following values for this call, whose actual Black-Scholes-Merton price is 13.55:

Number of Random Drawings	Call Price
1,000	12.64
10,000	13.73
50,000	13.69
100,000	13.67

It would appear that at least 100,000 random drawings are required for the simplest case of a standard European option.

Applying the Monte Carlo technique to more complicated options such as path-dependent options requires a partitioning of the option's life into time periods, as in the binomial model. For example, suppose you wanted to price an Asian call option in which the average price would be computed by collecting the daily closing price over the life of the option. Ignoring holidays and weekends, let us say that the option has a 90-day life. Then a run would consist of 90 random drawings, each used to simulate the stock price at the end of each of the 90 days. The formula for each ΔS would be based on the previous day's closing price. The value of Δt would be 1/365. Then the average of the 90 stock prices would determine the call payoff at expiration as described in this chapter. You would then need to repeat the procedure a large number of times.

This may seem like a formidable task, but that is what computers are for. More than likely computations such as these would be written in a fast and efficient language such as C++. In addition, there is a considerable amount of research going on for ways to make Monte Carlo simulations run more efficiently.

For your purposes here, the important thing is to gain an understanding of the principles of option pricing with Monte Carlo simulation. For example, consider a Monte Carlo simulation of a European option. Each run generates a possible outcome. Provided enough runs are made, the outcomes will occur with the same relative frequency implied by the probabilities assumed by the Black-Scholes-Merton model. The option price will then become what we have so often described throughout this book—a probability-weighted average of the expiration values of the option, discounted at the risk-free rate. More complex options will naturally require modifications to the procedure.

CHAPTER 15

Financial Risk Management Techniques and Applications

Risk managers need to be perceived like good goalkeepers, always in the game and occasional at the heart of it, like in a penalty shoot-out.

Anonymous
"Confessions of a Risk Manager," *The Economist*,
August 7, 2008

In the first 14 chapters, we studied the use of many different types of derivatives in a variety of situations. In the financial markets in recent years, derivatives have been playing a major part in the decision-making process of corporations, financial institutions, and investment funds. Derivatives have been embraced not only as tools for hedging but also as means of controlling risk; that is, reducing risk when one wants to reduce risk and increasing risk when one wants to increase it. The low transaction costs and the ease of using derivatives have given firms flexibility to make adjustments to the risk of a firm or portfolio. Corporations have been particularly avid users of derivatives for managing interest rate and foreign exchange risks.

As we have seen throughout this book, derivatives generally carry a high degree of leverage. When used improperly, they can increase the risk dramatically, sometimes putting the survival of a firm in jeopardy. In fact, in Chapter 16, we shall take a look at a few stories of how derivatives were used improperly—and in some cases were fatal.

The critical importance of using derivatives properly has created a whole new activity called **risk management**. Risk management is the practice of defining the risk level a firm desires, identifying the risk level a firm currently has, and using derivatives or other financial instruments to adjust the actual level of risk to the desired level of risk. Risk management has also spawned an entirely new industry of financial institutions that offer to take positions in derivatives opposite the end users, which are corporations or investment funds. These financial institutions, which we previously identified as dealers, profit off of the spread between their buying and selling prices and generally hedge the underlying risks of their portfolios of derivatives.

CHAPTER OBJECTIVES

- Understand the concept and practice of risk management
- Know the benefits of risk management
- Know the difference between market and credit risks
- Understand how market risk is managed using delta, gamma, and vega
- Understand how to calculate and use Value at Risk
- Understand how credit risk is determined and how firms control credit risk
- Introduce credit derivatives
- Be aware of risks other than market and credit risk

> Risk management is the practice of defining the risk level a firm desires, identifying the risk level it currently has, and using derivative or other financial instruments to adjust the actual risk level to the desired risk level.

WHY PRACTICE RISK MANAGEMENT?

Impetus for Risk Management

Growth in the use of derivatives for managing risk did not occur simply because people became enamored with them. In fact, there has always been a great deal of suspicion, distrust, and outright fear of derivatives. Eventually, firms began to realize that derivatives were the best tool for coping with markets that had become increasingly volatile and over which most businesses believed were beyond their means to forecast and control.

The primary sources of these risks are interest rates, exchange rates, commodity prices, and stock prices. These are risks over which most businesses have little expertise. Obviously, businesses must take some risks or there would be no reason to be in business. Acceptable risks are those related to the industries and products in which a business operates. These risks, which are often called strategic risks, are those in which a business should have some expertise. Risks driven by factors external to an industry or products, such as interest rates, exchanges rates, commodity prices, and stock prices, are those over which a typical business has little strategic advantage. It makes sense, therefore, for a business to manage and largely eliminate these risks.

For example, consider an airline. Its strategic expertise is in transporting people safely from one destination to another. Yet, airlines assume a number of risks over which they have little control or expertise. The cost of fuel, borrowing costs, and exchange rates exert an enormous influence on airlines' performance. While some airlines merely accept all of these risks as a part of doing business, others choose to actively manage these risks. An increasing number of businesses have begun to recognize the benefits of this strategy of accepting risks over which they have some control and expertise while actively managing the other risks.

Another reason many firms have begun to practice risk management is simply that they have learned a lesson by watching other firms. Seeing other companies fail to practice risk management and watching them suffer painful and embarrassing lessons—or hearing of another company that has successfully developed a risk management system—can be a powerful motivator.

Naturally derivatives have emerged as a popular tool for managing risks, and companies have shown an increasing tendency to use derivatives. Financial institutions have made this growth possible by creating an environment that is conducive to the efficient use of derivatives. This environment depended heavily on the explosion in information technology witnessed in the 1980s and 1990s. Without enormous developments in computing power, it would not have been possible to do the numerous and complex calculations necessary for pricing derivatives quickly and efficiently and for keeping track of positions taken.[1]

Another factor that has fueled the growth of derivatives was the favorable regulatory environment. In the U.S., the CFTC adopted a pro-market position in the early 1980s, which paved the way for an increasing number of innovative futures contracts such as Eurodollars and stock index futures. These contracts established a momentum that led to more innovation in the global exchange-listed and over-the-counter markets. Perhaps one of the most important steps taken by the CFTC was a non-step: its decision not to regulate over-the-counter derivatives transactions.

We should note that the derivatives industry has gone through a significant evolution in what it calls itself. In its early stages, it was known as *commodities*. As exchange-listed

---

[1]In fact, one could argue that the development of the personal computer was one of the single most important events for derivatives.

options and financial futures were created, it began to call itself *futures and options*. When over-the-counter products such as swaps and forwards were added, it began to be known as *derivatives*. Now the focus has shifted away from the instruments toward the process, leaving us with the term *risk management* and sometimes **financial risk management**.

Benefits of Risk Management

In Chapter 11, we identified several reasons why firms hedge. At this point, however, we are focusing not on the simple process of hedging, but on the more general process of managing risk. Let us restate our Chapter 11 reasons for hedging in the context of risk management.

In the Modigliani-Miller world in which there are no taxes or transaction costs and information is costless and available to everyone, financial decisions have no relevance for shareholders. Financial decisions, such as how much debt a firm issues, how large a dividend it pays, or how much risk it takes, merely determine how the pie is sliced. The size of the pie, as determined by the quality of a firm's investments in its assets, is what determines shareholder value. Modigliani and Miller argue that shareholders can do these financial transactions just as well by buying and selling stocks and bonds in their personal portfolios. Risk management is also a financial decision. Thus, risk management can, in theory, be practiced by shareholders by adjusting their personal portfolios; consequently, there is no need for firms to practice risk management.

This argument ignores the fact that most firms can practice risk management more effectively and at lower cost than shareholders. Their size and investment in information systems give firms an advantage over their shareholders. Firms can also gain from managing risk if their income fluctuates across numerous tax brackets. With a progressive tax system, they will end up with lower taxes by stabilizing their income. Risk management can also reduce the probability of bankruptcy, a costly process in which the legal system becomes a partial claimant on the firm's value. Risk management can also be done because managers, whose wealth is heavily tied to the firm's performance, are simply managing their own risk.

Firms manage risk with derivatives to reduce taxes, lower bankruptcy costs, protect their personal wealth, avoid underinvesting, take speculative positions, earn arbitrage profits, and lower borrowing costs.

Firms that are in a near-bankrupt state will find that they have little incentive to invest in seemingly attractive projects that will merely help their creditors by increasing the chance that the firm will be able to pay off its debts. This is called the underinvestment problem and is more thoroughly explored in corporate finance books. Managing risk helps avoid getting into situations like that and, as such, increases the chance that firms will always invest in attractive projects, which is good for society as a whole. Risk management also allows firms to generate the cash flow necessary to carry out their investment projects. If internal funds are insufficient, they may have to look toward external funds. Some firms would cut investment rather than raise new capital.

As described in an earlier section, when a firm goes into a particular line of business, it knowingly accepts risks. Airlines, for example, accept the risks of competition in the market for transporting people from one place to another. The risk associated with volatile oil prices is an entirely different type of risk, one that airlines often prefer to eliminate. Hence, many airlines hedge oil prices, which allows them to concentrate on their main line of business. On occasion, however, they may believe that oil prices are heading downward, suggesting that they lift their hedges. Thus, they are not just hedging, but rather practicing risk management by setting the current level of risk to the desired level of risk.

Some firms use risk management as an excuse to speculate in areas in which they have less expertise than they think. As we shall see in Chapter 16, when a consumer products company speculates on foreign interest rates, it is no longer just a consumer products company. It becomes a financial trading company, and it must be prepared to suffer the consequences if its forecasts are wrong. Some firms practice risk management because they truly believe that they can time movements in the underlying source of a risk. When that source of risk is unrelated to the firm's basic line of business, the consequences of bad forecasting combined with highly leveraged derivatives can be dire.

Other firms manage risk because they believe that arbitrage opportunities are possible. For example, suppose a firm could borrow at a floating rate of LIBOR plus 110 basis points or at a fixed rate of 10.5 percent. It can enter into a swap paying a fixed rate of 9.25 percent and receiving LIBOR. Simple arithmetic shows that it would get a lower rate by issuing floating-rate debt and entering into a pay fixed-receive floating swap. The net effect is to pay LIBOR plus 110 on the floating-rate debt, receive LIBOR, and pay 9.25 on the swap, which adds up to a fixed rate of $9.25 + 1.10 = 10.35$, or 15 basis points cheaper than straight fixed-rate debt. Yet if the firm had simply issued fixed-rate debt at 10.5 percent, it would have assumed no credit risk. Now it assumes the credit risk of the swap counterparty and is compensated to the tune of a 15 basis point reduction in the interest rate. Is this worth it? In the early days of the market, the savings were probably large enough to be worth it, but as the market has become more efficient, the savings have decreased and are likely just fair compensation for the assumption of credit risk. Nonetheless, the credit risk may be worth taking in order to lower borrowing costs.

It is important to emphasize that reducing risk is not in and of itself a sufficient reason to hedge or manage risk. Firms that accept lower risks will in the long run earn lower returns. Moreover, if their shareholders truly wanted lower risks, they could easily realign their portfolios, substituting lower-risk securities for higher-risk securities. Managing risk must create value for shareholders, giving them something they cannot get themselves. To the extent that risk management reduces the costly process of bankruptcy, saves taxes, and makes it easier for firms to take on profitable investment projects, value is clearly created.

In the next section, we take a close look at how to manage the most important type of risk: market risk.

MANAGING MARKET RISK

Market risk is the uncertainty and potential for loss associated with movements in interest rates, foreign exchange rates, stock prices, or commodity prices.

Market risk is the uncertainty of a firm's value or cash flow that is associated with movements in an underlying source of risk. For example, a firm might be concerned about movements in interest rates, foreign exchange rates, stock prices, or commodity prices.

When considering interest rate risk, there is the risk of short-, intermediate-, and long-term interest rates. Within short-term interest rate risk, there is the risk of LIBOR changing, the risk of the Treasury bill rate changing, the risk of the commercial paper rate changing, and numerous other risks associated with specific interest rates. A risk manager responsible for positions in LIBOR-based instruments and instruments tied to the commercial paper rate would have to take into account the extent to which those rates are correlated. A long position in LIBOR and a short position in commercial paper would be a partial hedge because LIBOR is correlated with the commercial paper rate. Thus, the combined effects of all sources of risk must be considered.

The effects of changes in the underlying source of risk will show up in movements in the values of spot and derivative positions. You should recall that in Chapter 5, we introduced the concept of an option's delta, which was the change in the option's price divided by the change in the underlying stock's price. We noted that a delta-hedged option would move perfectly with and be offset by an appropriately weighted position in the stock. A delta-hedged portfolio would be neutral with respect to stock price movements, but only for very small stock price changes. For large stock price changes, the delta may move too quickly. We noted that the risk of the delta changing too quickly is captured by the option's gamma. We also saw that if the volatility of the underlying stock changes, the option price can change quite significantly, even without a movement in the stock price. This risk is captured by the option's vega. These delta, gamma, and vega risk measures are equally applicable to many instruments other than options and stocks. They are some of the tools used by risk managers to control market risk.

Let us consider a situation in which, to accommodate a customer, a derivatives dealer has taken a position in a $10 million notional amount four-year interest rate swap that pays a fixed rate and receives a floating rate. In addition, the dealer has sold a three-year $8 million notional amount interest rate call with an exercise rate of 12 percent. We assume that for both instruments, the underlying is LIBOR. To keep things as simple as possible, we shall let the payments on the swap occur once a year. The current term structure of LIBOR and the implied forward rates are shown at the top of Table 15.1.

Let us first price the interest rate swap. Using the procedure we learned in Chapter 12, we see in Table 15.1 that the rate is 11.85 percent. Now let us price the three-year interest rate call. Table 15.1 uses the Black model we learned about in Chapter 13 and shows that the premium on this option would be $73,745. Now let us look at how to delta hedge this combination of a swap and an option.

TABLE 15.1 CURRENT TERM STRUCTURE AND FORWARD RATES

TERM (DAYS)	LIBOR	DISCOUNT FACTOR
360	10.00%	0.9091
720	11.61%	0.8116
1080	13.00%	0.7195
1440	14.34%	0.6355

Determination of the rate on a four-year swap with annual payments:

$$\frac{1 - 0.6355}{0.9091 + 0.8116 + 0.7195 + 0.6355} = 0.1185.$$

Inputs for the Black model to price a three-year call option on the one-year forward rate:
Continuously compounded one-year forward rate three years ahead:

$$\ln\left(\frac{1}{(0.6355/0.7195)}\right) = 0.1241.$$

Continuously compounded three-year risk-free rate:

$$\frac{\ln\left(\frac{1}{0.7195}\right)}{3} = 0.1098.$$

Other inputs: X = 0.12, T = 3, σ = 0.147

Plugging into the Black model (using a spreadsheet) gives an option price of 0.01043587. Recall that we must discount this value to reflect the delayed payoff. Discounting for one year at 12.41 percent gives 0.00921815. Multiplying by the notional amount of $8 million gives a premium of $73,745.

Delta Hedging

In order to delta hedge, we must make the portfolio be unaffected by small movements in interest rates. To do this, we need the delta of the swap and the option. Either can be obtained by taking the mathematical first derivative of the swap or option value with respect to interest rates. In this example, however, we shall estimate the delta by repricing both instruments when the one-period spot rate and the remaining forward rates move up and down one basis point. Then we shall average the movement in the derivative's price, which will be a good approximation of the delta.[2]

If all forward rates move up one basis point, the new one-period spot rate will be 10.01 percent and the new forward rates will be 12.02 percent, 12.82 percent, and 13.22 percent. This necessitates recalculating the spot rates, which will be 11.01 percent, 11.61 percent, and 12.01 percent.[3] Using the procedure we learned in Chapter 12, we determine that the new market value of the swap, if rates increase by 0.0001, would be $2,130. If rates decrease by −0.0001, the swap market value will be −$2,131. Averaging these results gives a swap delta of $2,130.5, which we round to $2,131. This result is shown in Table 15.2.

We also need to estimate the delta of the option. Recall that it is an $8 million notional amount call with a strike rate of 12 percent. Although the Black model will give us the delta, we shall recalculate the model price and estimate the delta based on the average change from a one basis point move in either direction. Table 15.2 also provides this information for the option. The original price was $73,745. The new price if LIBOR moves up one basis point is $73,989, a gain of $244. If LIBOR moves down one basis point, the option is worth $73,501, a loss of $244. The average is obviously $244.

Recall that we pay the fixed rate and receive the floating rate on the swap so that we are long the swap. That means we have a positive delta of $2,131. We are short the

TABLE 15.2 ESTIMATION OF SWAP AND OPTION DELTAS

	DERIVATIVE INSTRUMENT			
	4-YEAR SWAP, FIXED RATE = 0.1185		**3-YEAR CALL OPTION AT EXERCISE RATE OF 0.12**	
LIBOR change	+0.0001	−0.0001	+0.0001	−0.0001
New value	$2,130	−$2,131	$73,989	$73,501
Gain or loss*	same as new value		($73,989 − $73,745) = $244	($73,501 − $73,745) = −$244
Estimated delta	[$2,130 − (−$2,131)]/2 = $2,130.5. Round to $2,131.		[$244 − (−244)]/2 = $244	

*The original value of the swap is zero. The original value of the option is $73,745. For a swap, the gain or loss is the new value because the old value of the swap was zero.

[2]The price change for a one basis point move up is slightly different from that for a one basis point move down. This is why we take the average price change. This effect results from the convexity of the price curve and plays a role in gamma hedging.

[3]It appears as if the new spot rates are just one basis point above the old spot rates. This is not precisely the case, as would be indicated if we let the forward rates shift by a much larger amount or if we carried our results out to more significant digits.

option, so we have a delta of −$244. This makes the overall position delta $2,131 − $244 = $1,887. This means that if rates move up one basis point, we gain $1,887. If rates move down one basis point, we lose $1,887. Because we want to be hedged, we must find an instrument that loses $1,887 if rates move up and gains $1,887 if rates move down.

Naturally, we could hedge each derivative with a completely offsetting transaction in the opposite direction. In other words, we could execute a four-year swap, paying floating and receiving fixed, and buy a three-year call with a strike of 12 percent. That is not, however, how dealers normally hedge. They would rarely have a customer wanting the exact opposite transaction at that point in time, and they would not be willing to take the risk of waiting until their next customer calls. The most typical hedge transaction they would execute is to trade Eurodollar futures. Recall that we studied these instruments in Chapters 8 through 11. The futures are based on a $1,000,000 Eurodollar deposit, and their prices move opposite to interest rates. The delta is −$25, which is based on the calculation −$1,000,000(0.0001)(90/360), with 0.0001 representing a one basis point change. Note, however, that if rates move up, a long position loses, and if rates move down, a long position gains. In other words, Eurodollar futures are like bonds: Their values move opposite to interest rates. Eurodollar futures are particularly attractive for dealers to hedge with, because they are extremely liquid. Also, being futures contracts and not options, they require that no cash be paid up front; their margin requirements are very low.

> A delta-hedged position is one in which the combined spot and derivatives positions have a delta of zero. The portfolio would then have no gain or loss in value from a very small change in the underlying source of risk.

To offset our risk, we need a position that will both gain $1,887 if rates move down and lose $1,887 if rates move up, or, in other words, a delta of −$1,887. A long position in Eurodollar futures could provide this delta. The number of contracts would be −$1,887/(−$25) = 75.48. Because fractional contracts are not allowed, we round to 75. This would mean our overall delta is

$$
\begin{aligned}
+\$2,131 \quad &\text{(from the swap)} \\
-\$244 \quad &\text{(from the option)} \\
75(-\$25) \quad &\text{(from the futures)} \\
= \$12.
\end{aligned}
$$

This means that the portfolio value will go up $12 if rates move up one basis point. This is basically a perfect hedge.

In practice, some minor technical problems would make this hedge less than precise. The 90-day LIBOR that the futures is based on and the one-year LIBOR that the swap and option are based on would not both be likely to move exactly one basis point. They would, however, almost always move in the same direction at the same time and certainly be highly correlated. A few minor adjustments could take care of any risk in the hedge resulting from differences in the magnitudes of their respective movements.

As we discussed in Chapter 5, a delta hedge takes care of small movements in the underlying. Larger movements, however, can bring about additional risk. This is called gamma risk. To deal with it requires a gamma hedge.

Gamma Hedging

Our estimates of the delta are based on a one basis point change. If rates move by a much larger amount, there will be an additional risk caused by the fact that the values of the derivatives do not move equally in both directions. For example, if rates move 50 basis points down, the swap value will change to −$107,914. A 50 basis point increase will cause the swap value to move to $105,127. Recall that a one basis point move caused the swap value to change by virtually the same amount. For the option, a one basis point move in either direction caused a virtually equal value change. A 50 basis point move up would cause the option value to move to \$89,269, a loss of \$15,524. A 50 basis point decrease would cause the option value to move to \$61,919, a gain of \$11,826.[4]

As we learned in Chapter 5, the risk associated with larger price moves in which the delta does not fully capture the risk is called gamma risk. It is the risk of the delta changing. To be fully hedged, a dealer would have to be delta hedged at all times. If rates move sharply, the effective delta would not equal the actual delta until the dealer could put on another transaction that would reset its delta to the appropriate value. This could be too late. This risk can be hedged, however, by combining transactions so that the delta and gamma are both zero. First, however, we must estimate the gamma. Table 15.3 illustrates the calculation of the gammas of the swap and the option. The gammas are −\$12,500 for the swap and \$5,000 for the option. This means that as LIBOR increases, the swap delta decreases in value by \$12,500(0.0001) = \$1.25 and the option delta increases in value by \$5,000(0.0001) = \$0.50. Because we are short the option, its gamma is actually −\$5,000. Thus, our overall gamma is −\$17,500.

TABLE 15.3 ESTIMATION OF SWAP AND OPTION GAMMAS

BASIS POINT CHANGE	SWAP VALUE	AVERAGE CHANGE IN SWAP VALUE[1]	SWAP GAMMA[2]	OPTION VALUE	AVERAGE CHANGE IN OPTION VALUE[3]	OPTION GAMMA[4]
−0.0002	−\$4,263			\$73,258		
−0.0001	−2,131	\$2,131.50		73,501	\$243.50	
0.0000	0	2,130.50	−\$12,500	73,745	244.00	\$5,000
+0.0001	2,130	2,129.00		73,989	244.50	
+0.0002	4,258			74,234		

[1]The average change in the swap value is estimated as follows:

From a basis point change of 0.0000: $\dfrac{(0 - (-2,131)) + (2,130 - 0)}{2} = 2,130.50.$

From a basis point change of 0.0001: $\dfrac{(2,130 - 0) + (4,258 - 2,130)}{2} = 2,129.00.$

From a basis point change of −0.0001: $\dfrac{(-2,131 - (-4,263)) + (0 - (2,131))}{2} = 2,131.50.$

These calculations are the deltas at these points.

[2]The swap gamma is estimated as follows: $\dfrac{(-2,130.50 - 2,131.50) + (2,129.00 - 2,130.50)}{2} = -1.25.$

A change in the delta of −1.25 for a one basis point move implies a gamma of −1.25/0.0001 = −\$12,500.

[3]The average change in the option value is estimated as follows:

From a basis point change of 0.0000: $\dfrac{(73,745 - 73,501) + (73,989 - 73,745)}{2} = 244.00.$

From a basis point change of 0.0001: $\dfrac{(73,989 - 73,757) + (74,234 - 73,989)}{2} = 244.50.$

From a basis point change of −0.0001: $\dfrac{(73,501 - 73,258) + (73,745 - 73,501)}{2} = 243.50.$

[4]The option gamma is estimated as follows: $\dfrac{(244.00 - 243.50) + (244.50 - 244.00)}{2} = 0.50.$

A change in the delta of 0.50 for a one basis point move is a gamma of 0.50/0.0001 = \$5,000.

---

[4]Recall that we are short the option, so gains occur on rate decreases and losses occur on rate increases.

Assuming that we have delta hedged the swap and option with the Eurodollar futures, our gamma will still be −$17,500 because the gamma of the futures is zero. We are delta hedged but not gamma hedged. To become gamma hedged, we will need another instrument. Let us assume that the instrument chosen is a one-year call option with an exercise rate of 11 percent whose delta is $43 and whose gamma is $2,500, both figures under the assumption of a $1 million notional amount. The problem is to determine the appropriate notional amount of this new option so that we will be delta hedged and gamma hedged. This is a simple problem answered by solving simultaneous equations.

Let us assume that we take x_1 Eurodollar futures, which have a delta of −$25 and a gamma of zero, and x_2 of the one-year calls, which have a delta of $43 and a gamma of $2,500 per $1,000,000 notional amount. Our swap and other option have a delta of $1,887 and a gamma of −$17,500. We eliminate the delta and gamma risk of the portfolio by setting the delta to zero by the equation

$$\$1,887 + x_1(-\$25) + x_2(\$43) = \$0 \quad \text{(Delta)}$$

and the gamma to zero by the equation

$$-\$17,500 + x_1(\$0) + x_2(\$2,500) = \$0 \quad \text{(Gamma)}.$$

These are simply two equations with two unknowns. The solution is an exercise in basic algebra, but just to make sure you understand, we shall work through it. Rewrite the equations as

$$x_1(-\$25) + x_2(\$43) = -\$1,887$$
$$x_2(\$2,500) = \$17,500.$$

Solve the second equation for $x_2 = 7.00$. Then insert 7.00 for x_2 in the first equation and solve for x_1 to get $x_1 = 87.52$. This means we need to go long 87.52 Eurodollar futures. Round to 88. The solution $x_2 = 7.00$ means that we need to go long 7.00 times the notional amount of $1,000,000 on which the new option's delta and gamma were calculated. In other words, we need $7,000,000 notional amount of the one-year option. These transactions combine to set the delta and gamma of the overall position to approximately zero.[5]

Unfortunately, the use of options introduces a risk associated with possible changes in volatility. Let us take a look at how that risk arises and how we can hedge it.

> A delta and gamma hedge is one in which the combined spot and derivatives positions have a delta of zero and a gamma of zero. The portfolio would then have no gain or loss in value from a small change in the underlying source of risk. In addition, the delta itself would be hedged, which provides protection against larger changes in the source of risk.

TECHNICAL NOTE: Mathematical Foundations of Delta and Gamma Hedging
go to www.cengagebrain.com

Vega Hedging

In Chapter 5, we learned that the change in the option price over the change in its volatility is called its vega. A portfolio of derivatives that is both delta and gamma hedged can incur a gain or loss even when there is no change in the underlying as a result of a change in the volatility. Most options are highly sensitive to the volatility, which changes often. Consequently, it is important to try to hedge vega risk.

Swaps, futures, and FRAs do not have vegas because volatility is not a determinant of their prices. In our example, we need consider only the vega of the three-year call option. Although option pricing formulas often give the vega in its exact mathematical form, we shall estimate the vega by changing LIBOR by one basis point in each direction. Recall that under the initial term structure, the option value is $73,745. If the volatility increases from 0.147 to 0.1471, the new option value will be $73,787, a change of $42. If volatility

---

[5]As a check, we see that the delta is $1,887 + 88(-25) + 7(43) = -12.00$ and the gamma is $-17,500 + 7(2,500) = 0$.

decreases from 0.147 to 0.1469, the new option value will be $73,703, a change of −$42. This is an average change of $42. Because we are short this option, the vega of our portfolio of the four-year swap and this three-year option is −$42.

Now consider the one-year option that we introduced in the last section to use for gamma hedging. It will also have a vega that must be taken into account. Its vega is estimated to be $3.50 for every $1,000,000 notional amount. Our delta- and gamma-hedged portfolio would have $7 million face value of this option, making the vega $24.50. That would make our overall portfolio have a vega of $24.50 − $42, or −$17.50. Thus, we still have a significant risk that volatility will increase, and each 0.0001 increase in volatility will cost us $17.50.

In order to hedge delta, gamma, and vega, we need three hedging instruments. Because of the vega risk, at least one of the instruments has to be an option. Let us use an option on a Eurodollar futures that trades at the Chicago Mercantile Exchange alongside the Eurodollar futures. The option has a delta of −$12.75, a gamma of −$500, and a vega of $2.50 per $1,000,000 notional amount. This leads to the following set of simultaneous equations:

$$\$1,887 + x_1(-\$25) + x_2(\$43) + x_3(-\$12.75) = 0 \text{ (Delta)}$$
$$-\$17,500 + x_1(\$0) + x_2(\$2,500) + x_3(-\$500) = 0 \text{ (Gamma)}$$
$$-\$42 + x_1(\$0) + x_2(\$3.50) + x_3(\$2.50) = 0 \text{ (Vega)}.$$

The first equation sets the portfolio delta to zero, the second sets the gamma to zero, and the third sets the vega to zero. The coefficients x_1, x_2, and x_3 represent quantities of $1,000,000 notional amount that should be established with Eurodollar futures, the one-year option, and the option on the Eurodollar futures. To solve these equations, we first note that the second and third equations can be written as

$$x_2(\$2,500) + x_3(-\$500) = \$17,500$$
$$x_2(\$3.50) + x_3(\$2.50) = \$42,$$

which is simply two equations with two unknowns. Multiplying the second equation by 200 gives us $700x_2 + \$500x_3 = \$8,400$. Then adding the two equations gives $3,200x_2 = \$25,900$, which gives $x_2 = 8.09375$. Inserting 8.09375 for x_2 in either of these equations gives $x_3 = 5.46875$. Thus, we need 8.09375($1,000,000) = $8,093,750 notional amount of the four-year option and 5.46875($1,000,000) = $5,468,750 notional amount of the Eurodollar futures option. We then insert 8.09375 and 5.46875 into the first equation for x_2 and x_3, giving us $x_1(-\$25) + 8.09375(\$43) + 5.46875(-\$12.75) = -\$1,887$. Solving for x_1 gives a value of 86.61. This means that we would buy 87 Eurodollar futures.[6]

A vega-hedged portfolio is one in which the portfolio value will not change as a result of a change in the volatility of the underlying source of risk.

It should be apparent by now that the dealer should not hedge by setting the delta to zero and then attempting to hedge the gamma and vega risk with other instruments. As these instruments are added to eliminate gamma and vega risk, the delta hedge is destroyed. There are two possible approaches to solving the problem, one being the simultaneous equation approach that we followed here. It is guaranteed to provide the correct solutions. Another approach would be to solve the gamma and vega hedge simultaneously, which will set the gamma and vega to zero, but leave the overall delta nonzero. Then the delta hedge can be set with Eurodollar futures, which have a delta but no

---

[6]Because of rounding off to whole numbers of contracts, the overall position is not quite perfectly hedged. The delta is $1,887 + 87(−$25) + 8.09375($43) + 5(−$12.75) = −$3.72. The gamma is −$17,500 + 87($0) + 8.09375($2,500) + 5(−$500) = 234.38. The vega is −$42 + 8.09375($3.50) + 5($2.50) = −$1.17.

gamma or vega. Consequently, adding them to the position at the very end will not change the gamma or vega neutrality.

In spite of a dealer's efforts at achieving a delta-gamma-vega neutral position, it is really impossible to achieve an absolute perfect hedge. The vega hedge is accurate only for extremely small changes in volatility. Large changes would require yet another adjustment. In addition, all deltas, gammas, and vegas are valid only over the next instant in time. Even if there were no changes in LIBOR or the volatility, the position would become unhedged over time if no further adjustments were made. Eventually, the portfolio would become significantly unhedged, so some adjustments might be made to realign the portfolio to a delta-gamma-vega neutral position, possibly as often as once a day.

It is apt to remember a famous expression: *The only perfect hedge is in a Japanese garden.* Any dealer accepts the fact that a small amount of risk will be assumed. To date, however, no major derivatives dealer who has made the effort to be hedged has suffered a significant loss, and most have found market making in derivatives to be a moderately profitable activity with very low risk. This is a testament to the excellent risk management practiced by the major derivatives dealers.

On the other side of the transaction is the end user, the party who approaches the dealer about entering into a derivatives transaction. Most end users are corporations attempting to hedge their interest rate, currency, equity, or commodity price risk. Some will speculate from time to time. Most, however, already have a transaction in place that has a certain amount of risk. They contract with the dealer to lay off that risk. Rarely will the end user engage in the type of dynamic hedging illustrated above. That is because the end user is not typically a financial institution like the dealer. Financial institutions can nearly always execute transactions at lower cost and can generally afford the investment in expensive personnel, equipment, and software necessary to do dynamic hedging. Most end users enter into derivatives transactions that require little or no adjustments. You have, of course, seen many such examples throughout this book. Some end users have, however, suffered losses from being unhedged at the wrong time or from outright speculating. Yet, most end users could have obtained a better understanding about the magnitude of their risk and the potential for large losses had they applied the technique called Value at Risk, or VAR.

Value at Risk (VAR)

Value at Risk, or **VAR**, is a dollar measure of the minimum loss that would be expected over a period of time with a given probability. For example, a VAR of $1 million for one day at a 5 percent probability means that the firm would expect to lose at least $1 million in one day 5 percent of the time. Some prefer to express such a VAR as a 95 percent probability that a loss will not exceed $1 million. In this manner, the VAR becomes a maximum loss with a given confidence level. The significance of a million dollar loss depends on the size of the firm and its aversion to risk. But one thing is clear from this probability statement: A loss of at least $1 million would be expected to occur once every 20 trading days, which is about once per month.

VAR is widely used by dealers, even though their hedging programs nearly always leave them with little exposure to the market. If dealers believe that it is important to use VAR, that should be a good enough reason for end users to employ it, and surveys show that an increasing number of end users are doing so.

The basic idea behind VAR is to determine the probability distribution of the underlying source of risk and to isolate the worst given percentage of outcomes. Using 5 percent as the critical percentage, VAR will determine the 5 percent of outcomes that are the worst. The performance at the 5 percent mark is the VAR.

TABLE 15.4 PROBABILITY DISTRIBUTION OF CHANGE IN PORTFOLIO VALUE

CHANGE IN PORTFOLIO VALUE	PROBABILITY	CUMULATIVE PROBABILITY
−$3,000,000 and lower	0.05	0.05
−$2,000,000 to −$2,999,999	0.10	0.15
−$1,000,000 to −$1,999,999	0.15	0.30
$0 to −$999,999	0.20	0.50
$0 to $999,999	0.20	0.70
$1,000,000 to $1,999,999	0.15	0.85
$2,000,000 to $2,999,999	0.10	0.95
$3,000,000 and higher	0.05	1.00

> Value at Risk, or VAR, is the minimum amount of money that would be lost in a portfolio with a given probability over a specific period of time.

Table 15.4 provides a simple illustration with a discrete classification of the change in the value of a hypothetical portfolio. Note that each range has a probability and a cumulative probability associated with it. Starting with the class with the worst outcome, VAR is found by examining the cumulative probability until the specified percentage is reached. In this case, VAR for 5 percent is $3,000,000. This would be interpreted as follows: There is a 5 percent probability that over the given time period, the portfolio will lose at least $3 million. Of course, VAR can be expressed with respect to any chosen probability. Such statements as "There is a 15 percent probability that over the given time period, the portfolio will lose at least $2 million" and "There is a 50 percent probability that over the given time period, the portfolio will incur a loss" are both legitimate statements of the portfolio's VAR.

Figure 15.1 illustrates the principle behind VAR when the distribution of the portfolio change in value is continuous. The familiar normal, or bell-shaped, curve is widely used,

FIGURE 15.1 Value at Risk for Normally Distributed Change in Portfolio Value with Zero Expected Change

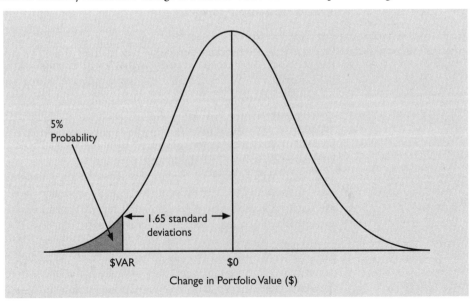

In a normal distribution, a 5 percent VAR occurs 1.65 standard deviations from the expected value. A 1 percent VAR occurs 2.33 standard deviations from the expected value.

although not necessarily appropriate in many cases. Accepting it as legitimate for our purposes, we see where the 5 percent VAR is noted, which is 1.65 standard deviations from the expected change in portfolio value, which in this example the expected change is zero. Of course, not all portfolios have an expected change of zero. In any case, the rule for determining VAR when applying normal probability theory is to move 1.65 standard deviations below the expected value. Beyond that point, 5 percent of the population of possible outcomes is found. For a VAR of 1 percent, you would move 2.33 standard deviations below the expected value.

Calculating VAR in practice is not quite this simple. The basic problem is to determine the probability distribution associated with the portfolio value. This necessitates estimating the expected values, standard deviations, and correlations among the financial instruments. The mechanics of determining the portfolio probability distribution are relatively easy once the appropriate inputs are obtained. The process is the same as the one you might already have encountered when studying investments. Let us take that process a little bit further here.

Assume you have two assets whose expected returns are $E(R_1)$ and $E(R_2)$ and whose standard deviations are σ_1 and σ_2 and where the correlation between their returns is ρ. The portfolio's expected return is a weighted average of the expected returns of assets 1 and 2,

$$E(R_p) = w_1 E(R_1) + w_2 E(R_2),$$

where w_1 and w_2 are the percentages of the investor's wealth that are allocated to assets 1 and 2, respectively. The portfolio standard deviation is a more complicated weighted average of the variances of assets 1 and 2 and their covariance,

$$\sigma_p = \sqrt{w_1^2 \sigma_1^2 + w_2^2 \sigma_2^2 + 2w_1 w_2 \sigma_1 \sigma_2 \rho},$$

where the expression $\sigma_1 \sigma_2 \rho$ is recognized as the covariance between assets 1 and 2. There are three methods of estimating VAR.

Analytical Method The **analytical method**, also called the **variance-covariance method**, makes use of knowledge of the input values and any necessary pricing models along with an assumption of a normal distribution.

The analytical method assumes a normal distribution and uses the expected value and variance to obtain the VAR.

We illustrate the analytical method with two examples. Suppose a portfolio manager holds two distinct classes of stocks. The first class, worth $20 million, is identical to the S&P 500. It has an expected return of 12 percent and a standard deviation of 15 percent. The second class is identical to the Nikkei 300, an index of Japanese stocks, and is valued at $12 million. We shall assume the currency risk is hedged. The expected return is 10.5 percent, and the standard deviation is 18 percent.

The correlation between the Nikkei 300 and the S&P 500 is 0.55. All figures are annualized. With this information, we can calculate the portfolio expected return and standard deviation as

$$E(R_p) = (20/32)0.12 + (12/32)0.105 = 0.1144$$

$$\sigma_p = \sqrt{(20/32)^2(0.15)^2 + (12/32)^2(0.18)^2 + 2(20/32)(12/32)(0.15)(0.18)(0.55)}$$
$$= 0.1425.$$

Now let us calculate this portfolio's VAR at a 5 percent level for one week. First, we must convert the annualized expected return and standard deviation to weekly equivalents. This is done by dividing the expected return by 52 (for the number of weeks in a year) and dividing the standard deviation by the square root of 52, which is 7.21. This gives us 0.1144/52 = 0.0022 and 0.1425/7.21 = 0.0198. Under the assumption of a normal distribution, the return that is 1.65 standard deviations below the expected return is

$$0.0022 - 1.65(0.0198) = -0.0305.$$

The portfolio would be expected to lose at least 3.05 percent 5 percent of the time. VAR is always expressed in dollars, so the VAR is $32,000,000(0.0305) = $976,000. In other words, the portfolio would be expected to lose at least $976,000 in one week 5 percent of the time, or 1 out of 20 weeks.

Let us now calculate VAR for a portfolio containing options. In fact, let us make it an extremely risky portfolio, one consisting of a short call on a stock index. We assume that the call has one month to go before expiring, the index is at 720, the exercise price is 720, the risk-free rate is 5.8 percent, and the volatility of the index is 15 percent. We shall ignore dividends. Inserting these figures into the Black-Scholes-Merton model tells us that the call should be priced at $14.21. Assume that the index option contract has a multiplier of 500, so the total cost is 500($14.21) = $7,105. We shall assume that the investor sells 200 contracts, resulting in the receipt up front of 200($7,105) = $1,421,000. The worst outcome for an uncovered call is for the stock to increase.

Let us look at the 5 percent worst outcomes, which occur on the upside. Using the same information on the index from the previous example, we must first convert to monthly data. The expected return on the index is 0.1144/12 = 0.0095 and 0.1425/3.46 (the square root of 12) = 0.0412. On the upside, the 5 percent tail of the distribution is 0.0095 + 1.65(0.0412) = 0.0775. That would leave the index at 720(1.0775) = 775.80 or higher. If the option expires with the index at 775.80, it will have a value of 775.80 − 720 = 55.80. Thus, our net loss will be 55.80 − 14.21 = 41.59 per option. The total loss will be 200(500)(41.59) = $4,159,000. Thus, the VAR for this short call is $4,159,000 and we can, therefore, say that the portfolio will lose at least $4,159,000 in one month 5 percent of the time. This would be once every 20 months.

Although we calculated an expected value in these examples, it is fairly common to assume a zero expected value. This is because one day is a common period over which to calculate a VAR and the expected daily return is very small. A typical VAR calculation is much more highly influenced by the volatility than by the expected return.

The analytical method uses knowledge of the parameters of the probability distribution of the underlying sources of risk at the portfolio level. Because the expected value and variance are the only two parameters used, the method implicitly is based on the assumption of a normal distribution. If the portfolio contains options, the assumption of a normal distribution is no longer valid. Option returns are highly skewed, and the expected return and variance of an option position will not accurately produce the desired result, the return that is exceeded, say, 5 percent of the time. One approach is the one used here: We identified the critical outcome of the underlying and then determined the option outcome that corresponds to it.

Another commonly used alternative employs the delta, rather than the precise option pricing model, to determine the option outcome. In fact, the analytical or variance-covariance method is also sometimes called the **delta normal method**. Although this method is only approximate, it has some advantages. The delta is a linear adjustment of the underlying price change to the option price change, and linearity is a desirable and simplifying property. When the outcome of a normal distribution is adjusted in a linear manner, the result remains normally distributed. Thus, the delta normal approach linearizes the option distribution; in other words, it converts the option's distribution to a normal distribution. This can be useful, particularly when a large portfolio is concerned. For longer periods, such as the one-month period used here, the delta adjustment is sometimes supplemented with a gamma adjustment.

Another important concern in using the analytical method is that large portfolios can be very complicated to work with. In these examples, we identified only a single source of risk. For large institutions, there are literally thousands of sources of risk. The volatilities and correlations of these diverse sources of risk must be captured and consolidated into a single volatility for the portfolio. This requires massive amounts of information. Fortunately, this information is readily available. MSCI recently acquired the RiskMetrics Corporation, a spin-off of the noted Wall Street firm J.P. Morgan, that previously had provided downloadable data sets, which are updated daily, on the Internet. This information is based on recent historical price behavior and is smoothed via a weighting of current and past volatility. For more information, see www.msci.com/products/riskmetrics. html. While this information is no longer free to the general public, it is widely used by professionals with subscriptions.

The primary advantage and disadvantage of the analytical method is its reliance on the assumption of a normal distribution. The following method gets around that assumption.

Historical Method The **historical method** estimates the distribution of the portfolio's performance by collecting data on the past performance of the portfolio and using it to estimate the future probability distribution. Obviously, it assumes that the past distribution is a good estimate of the future distribution.

> The historical method uses actual data from a recent historical period to determine the VAR.

Figure 15.2 presents an example of the information obtained from a historical sample of daily portfolio returns over approximately one year, 254 trading days in this case. The information is presented in the form of a histogram. The person doing the analysis would choose the most appropriate intervals. In this case, the 13 worst outcomes, which is about 10 percent of the total possible, are shaded. This means that the critical portfolio VAR is a loss of 10 percent. If the portfolio size is $15 million, then the VAR is $15,000,000(0.10) = $1,500,000. Thus, we can say that the portfolio would be expected to lose at least $1.5 million in one day about 5 percent of the time, which is about once per month.

The historical method obviously produces a VAR that is consistent with the VAR of the chosen historical period. Whether this is an accurate method depends on several factors. Obviously, it matters greatly whether the probability distribution of the past is repeated in the future. Also, the portfolio held in the future might differ in some way from the portfolio held in the past. For example, the S&P/Nikkei portfolio, which is currently $20 million in the S&P and $12 million in the Nikkei, could be reallocated. In fact, unless each asset performs identically, the portfolio is automatically reallocated. One asset grows in value at a greater rate than the other, and this changes the portfolio's expected return and standard deviation. This problem, however, can be accommodated by using the historical returns but applying new weights to each asset in accordance with the current weights rather than the historical weights.

Another limitation of the historical method is that it requires the choice of a sample period. The outcome can be greatly affected by how large a sample one selects. Normally, the larger a sample is, the more reliable the estimates obtained from it, but the larger the sample is, the older are some of the data and the less reliable they become.

Another problem with the historical method is that the historical period may be badly representative of the future. For example, suppose the historical period included the stock market crash of October 1987, a day in which the market lost over 20 percent of its value in one day. Is this extreme outcome an accurate reflection of the VAR? Such an

FIGURE 15.2 Histogram of Portfolio Returns for 254 Days

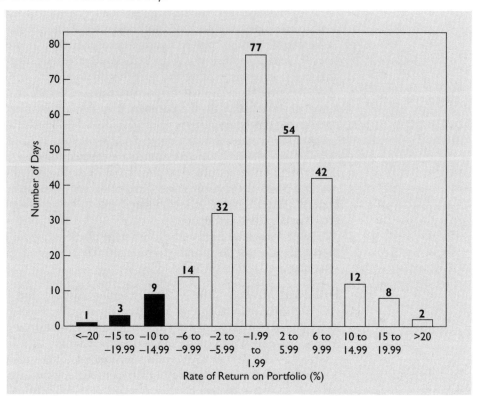

outcome would tremendously bias the volatility. Yet days like that are the very outcomes that risk managers should be worrying about.

The final method combines many of the best properties of the previous two methods.

> To obtain the VAR, Monte Carlo simulation generates random outcomes based on an assumed probability distribution.

Monte Carlo Simulation Method The **Monte Carlo simulation method** is based on the idea that portfolio returns can be fairly easily simulated. Simulation requires inputs on the expected returns, standard deviations, and correlations for each financial instrument. In Appendix 14, we examined one procedure for simulating stock prices called the Monte Carlo method. Essentially the same procedure is used when calculating VAR except that it is necessary to ensure that the portfolio's returns properly account for the correlations among the financial instruments. This means that one cannot simply independently generate returns for, say, the S&P 500 and Treasury bonds. One set of returns can be generated, but the other set of returns must reflect any correlation between the two sets of returns. This is done by making an assumption about the process in which asset returns are generated.

Monte Carlo simulation is probably the most widely used method by sophisticated firms. It is the most flexible method, because it permits the user to assume any known probability distribution and can handle relatively complex portfolios; however, the more complex the portfolio, the more computational time required. Indeed, Monte Carlo simulation is the most demanding method in terms of computer requirements. Nonetheless, the vast improvements in computing power in recent years have brought Monte Carlo to the forefront in risk management techniques.

A Comprehensive Calculation of VAR

Let us illustrate the three methods of calculating VAR by using a comprehensive example. Suppose we hold a very simple portfolio consisting of $25 million invested in the S&P 500. We would like to estimate VAR at 5 percent for one day using each of the three methods. First, we collect a sample of the daily returns on the S&P 500 for the past year. This gives us 253 returns. We obtain the following information, which will be useful in some of the VAR calculations:

Average daily return:	0.0457%
Daily standard deviation:	1.3327%

These numbers equate to an annual return of $0.0457(253) = 11.56$ percent and a standard deviation of $1.3327\sqrt{253} = 21.20$ percent.

First, we estimate VAR using the analytical method. Remember that we are assuming a normal distribution. Based on the above parameters, we obtain the following:

$$0.0457\% - (1.65)1.3327\% = -2.1533\%.$$

Thus, our VAR is

$$0.021533(\$25,000,000) = \$538,325.$$

We might, however, believe that the parameters obtained from the historical data are not realistic. Indeed, a 21 percent standard deviation is somewhat high for the S&P 500. Let us use a more realistic number of 15 percent. This equates to a daily standard deviation of $1.3327\sqrt{253} = 0.9430$ percent. Let us use an expected return of 12 percent, which is a daily expected return of $12/253 = 0.0474$ percent. Then

$$0.0474\% - (1.65)0.9430\% = -1.5086\%.$$

Thus, the VAR is

$$0.015086 \ (\$25,000,000) = \$377,150.$$

Which is more correct? That depends on which input seems more reasonable.

Remember that the analytical method is based on the assumption of a normal distribution. Is this a reasonable assumption? Figure 15.3 shows the distribution of returns for the S&P 500 that was used in this example. We see that the distribution does indeed bear some resemblance to the normal, but it probably does not completely adhere to the normal distribution.

Now let us calculate VAR based on the historical method. This method simply requires that we rank the returns from worst to best. For 253 returns, we have $0.05(253) = 12.65$, telling us that the VAR is the twelfth or thirteenth worst outcome. Let us use the thirteenth worst outcome. If we lined up the returns from worst to best, we would find that the thirteenth worst return would be -2.0969 percent. Thus, the VAR would be

$$0.020969(\$25,000,000) = \$524,225.$$

Now let us try a Monte Carlo simulation, where we have considerable flexibility. We must assume a probability distribution to generate the returns, and we must choose the input values. Although one advantage of the Monte Carlo simulation is that we do not need to adhere to the normal distribution, we shall do so here for convenience and because it is the probability distribution you are most likely to be very familiar with. In using the normal distribution, we must input an expected value and volatility. Let us use

FIGURE 15.3 Historical Returns on S&P 500 for One Year

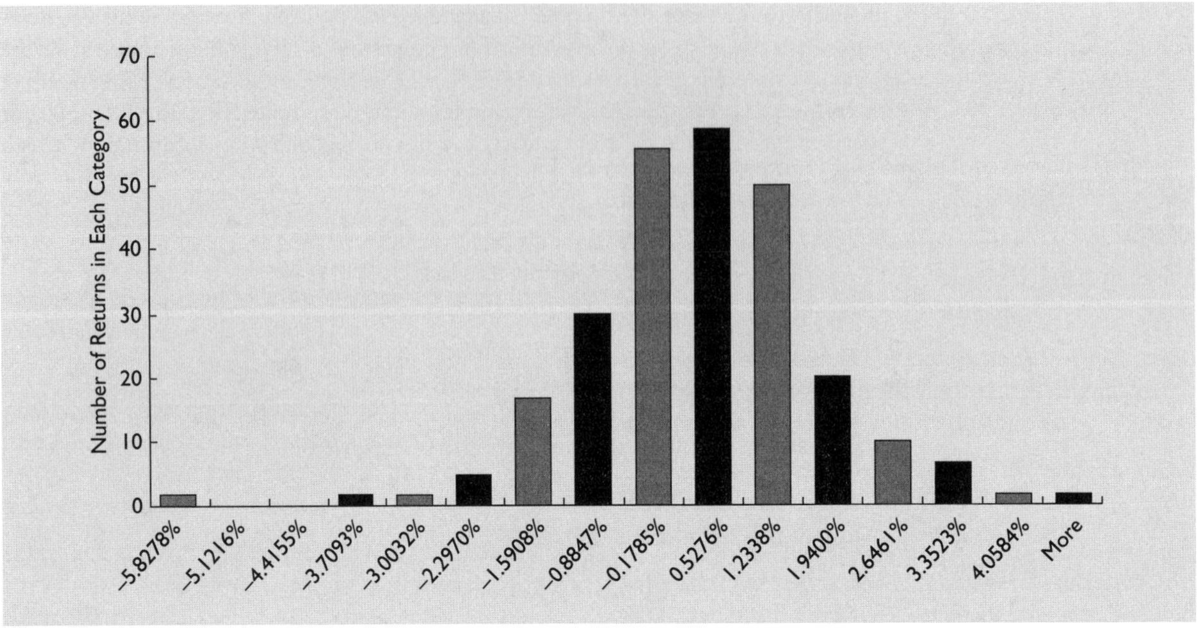

the same 12 percent for the former and 15 percent for the latter that we used in the analytical method. We also have to decide on a time period, which we choose to be one day. In addition, we must decide on the number of outcomes. Normally, many thousands are used, but here we shall use 253, which is about one year and is the number of days over which we collected data. There is no particular reason why we should generate one year's worth of outcomes, and in practice, we would definitely want many more outcomes.

As noted earlier, the exact procedure for a Monte Carlo simulation with a normal distribution was described in the appendix to Chapter 14. Basically, we generate a daily return according to the formula

$$\text{Return} = (\text{Expected Return})(1/253) + (\text{Standard Diviation}) * \varepsilon\sqrt{1/253},$$

where ε is a random number drawn from a standard normal distribution with a mean of zero and a standard deviation of 1.0. Microsoft Excel will generate such numbers with its Analysis ToolPak. Alternatively, a good approximation can be obtained as the sum of 12 random numbers minus 6.0 (rand() + rand() + ... −6.0).

We do this 253 times, thereby obtaining 253 random returns. Once again, we simply sort them from worst to best and obtain the thirteenth worst return. Here, this is −1.3942 percent. Thus, the VAR is

$$0.013942(\$25,000,000) = \$348,550.$$

Of course, different values will be obtained from one simulation to another.

We now have a number of candidates for our VAR:

$538,325 (Analytical Method),

$377,150 (Adjusted Analytical Method),

$524,225 (Historical Method), and

$348,550 (Monte Carlo Simulation Method).

Which is correct? We simply do not know. The methods are so different and the inputs are so critical that this is a common result. In fact, even more variation could be obtained if we collected our data over different time periods or, for example, if we used weekly or monthly data instead of daily data. Or we could run more simulations or perhaps use a nonnormal distribution. The possibilities are almost endless. Moreover, the range of numbers shown here is actually quite small compared to what is frequently found in practice. Most real-world portfolios are far more complicated than this. They usually contain options, which tend to cause larger discrepancies. In short, VAR is a number that is quite sensitive to how it is calculated. That does not mean it is useless or unreliable. Knowing the potential range of VAR is itself useful. Moreover, one should always follow up the calculation with an ex post evaluation. If we settle on a VAR of, say, $400,000 in this example, we should expect that this value will be exceeded no more than 5 percent of the time. If it is exceeded far more or far less than 5 percent of the time, we know that $400,000 was not a good estimate of the VAR.

Assessing the accuracy of VAR systems is an important component of maintaining a quality enterprise risk system. Presently, there are many different procedures for making this assessment, although they are quite technical.[7]

Benefits and Criticisms of VAR

Although widely criticized, VAR has been embraced by the risk management industry. VAR, or some variation thereof, is used by nearly every major derivatives dealer and an increasing number of end users. VAR is perhaps most beneficial in communicating information to nontechnical personnel. To tell a CEO that a firm is expected to lose at least $400,000 in a day 5 percent of the time, meaning about once every month, conveys a lot of useful information that the CEO can easily grasp. The trade-off, however, is that if the number is inaccurate, the CEO will have less confidence in the number and in the person giving him or her the number. Accurate estimation with continuing ex post follow-up is critical in using VAR.

VAR is also widely used in banking regulation. The objective of banking regulators is to ensure that the banking system does not fail and that consumers and savers are protected. Most banking regulators use VAR as a measure of the risk of a bank. A common specification for VAR in this context is ten days with a 1 percent probability.

Likewise, banks and corporations that are engaged in significant trading activities commonly use VAR as a measure to allocate capital. In other words, they set aside a certain amount of capital to protect against losses. The amount of capital set aside is often the VAR.

VAR is also used in the evaluation of the performance of investment managers and traders. The modern approach to performance evaluation is to adjust the return performance for a measure of the risk taken in achieving that performance. VAR is often used in this context as a measure of risk.

Thus, we see that VAR has a variety of practical applications. Nonetheless, VAR must be used carefully. We have barely scratched the surface of VAR, but we have encountered enough to get you started in understanding it. There is much written on VAR; in fact, it is probably one of the most written-about topics of recent years. You will not be able to operate in the risk management world without encountering something written about it.

---

[7]See, for example, Joe H. Sullivan, Zachary G. Stoumbos, and Robert Brooks, "Real Time Assessment of Value at Risk and Volatility Accuracy," *Nonlinear Analysis: Real World Applications*, 2007.

Extensions of VAR

> Stress testing means to estimate how a portfolio will perform if extremely rare events occur.

In addition to estimating VAR, a risk manager will often subject the portfolio to a **stress test**, which determines how badly the portfolio will perform under some of the worst and most unusual circumstances. Consider the portfolio we discussed earlier that consisted of $20 million invested in the S&P 500 and $12 million invested in the Nikkei 300. Let us presume that in a given week, both markets perform terribly, with the Nikkei losing 30 percent of its value and the S&P 500 losing 25 percent of its value. Then the Nikkei would lose $3.6 million and the S&P 500 would lose $5 million, for a total loss of $8.6 million, which is 26.9 percent of the total value of the portfolio. Although such an outcome is extremely unlikely, a risk manager might test the portfolio's tolerance for such a remote possibility. If the performance is tolerable, then the portfolio risk is assumed to be acceptable. Stress testing can be quite valuable as a supplement to VAR and other techniques of risk management. Yet, stress testing has its own criticisms, including the fact that it places a tremendous emphasis on highly unlikely events.

The most important point to remember about VAR and stress testing, as well as any financial statistic, is that these are just estimates and cannot be expected to provide the full picture. Hence, some variations of VAR are widely used as a supplemental source of risk management information. Some risk managers focus on the expected loss beyond the VAR. For example, consider the VAR calculation we did for the S&P 500. Using the historical method, we ranked the outcomes and found that the VAR was 2.0969 percent, or $524,225. If we averaged all of the outcomes worse than −2.0969 percent, we would obtain an average loss of −2.8778 percent, or $719,450. This figure can be interpreted as the expected loss, given that the loss incurred exceeds the VAR. This figure is also sometimes known as the **Conditional Value at Risk**, because it reflects the expected loss conditional on the loss exceeding the VAR.

Value at Risk is a reasonable technique for use by firms that have assets whose values can be measured fairly easily. A financial institution would be one of those types of firms. Many corporations, however, have assets that generate cash flows but whose values cannot be easily determined. Consider for example, a company whose primary business is copper mining. Expenses are incurred in the mining process, and cash is generated to cover those expenses when the copper is sold. Of course in theory, a copper mine has a market value, which would presumably come from discounting the stream of cash flows expected over the life of the mine. In practice, determining that value is difficult. The firm could put the mine on the market for sale, and a buyer would have to determine the value in order to make an offer. But the company could not reasonably expect to put the mine up for sale on a regular basis just to determine its market value. Thus, it would be very difficult to generate a VAR for a copper mine. As an alternative, the firm could use a technique called **Cash Flow at Risk**, or **CAR** (also sometimes known as CFAR). CAR would be defined in terms of an expected cash shortfall. For example, suppose that the copper mine was expected to generate a cash flow of $10 million per year with a standard deviation of $2 million a year. The CAR at a probability of 5 percent would be 1.65($2 million) = $3.3 million. This means that

$$\text{Prob}[10 \text{ million} - \$3.3 \text{ million} > \text{Actual Cash Flow}] = 0.05.$$

In other words, the probability that $10 million − $3.3 million = $6.7 million will exceed the actual cash flow is 5 percent. That is, the probability that the actual cash flow will be less than $6.7 million is 5 percent. Note that CAR is calculated in a slightly different manner than VAR. It is expressed in terms of a shortfall from the expected cash flow. Because deviations from the expected value are on average equal to zero, we calculate the CAR without adjusting for the expected cash flow. In other words, the CAR is simply based on the standard deviation times 1.65 (assuming a desired probability level of 5 percent), because the average deviation from the expected value is zero.

Although CAR can be more applicable to certain types of companies, most of the same issues and problems associated with VAR apply equally to CAR.

Another alternative to VAR and CAR is the concept of **Earnings at Risk**, or **EAR**. For companies that are concerned about shortfalls in earnings per share, EAR can be used to measure the risk. Of course, we know that value and cash flow are far more important than earnings, because the earnings are a reflection of assumptions about accounting methods, and they do not take risk or the time value of money into account.

Regardless of whether one uses VAR, CAR, or EAR, a good risk manager will collect data over the risky time period and evaluate after the fact whether the measure was a good one. For example, if the VAR is $1 million for one day at 5 percent, then the risk manager can expect to see a loss of at least $1 million about one day in a month. Over a period of many months, perhaps even many years, the risk manager can determine whether $1 million is a reasonable reflection of the true risk.

We have now completed our examination of market risk. We next turn to the other major type of risk: credit risk.

> Cash Flow at Risk (CAR) and Earnings at Risk (EAR) are alternatives to VAR that measure expected shortfalls in cash flow and earnings and could be more appropriate than VAR for some types of companies.

MANAGING CREDIT RISK

Earlier in this chapter, we mentioned a party that could borrow at a fixed rate of 10 1/2 percent or at a floating rate of LIBOR plus 1.1 percent. That party issues floating-rate debt and enters into a swap in which it pays a fixed rate of 9 1/4 percent and receives a floating rate of LIBOR, for a net fixed rate of 10.35 percent, a savings of 15 basis points over issuing fixed rate directly.

If the firm had borrowed at a fixed rate, it would have assumed no credit risk. A lender cannot default. If it borrows at a floating rate and swaps it into a synthetic fixed-rate loan, it faces the risk that the swap dealer will default, leaving it owing the floating rate of LIBOR. Perhaps the 15 basis point saving is simply compensation for bearing the risk that the dealer will default.

The risk of default is faced by any party that may receive obligatory payments from another party. This risk, called **credit risk or default risk**, is faced by any lender. We have mentioned it many times earlier in the book, especially in conjunction with over-the-counter derivatives.

> Credit risk is the uncertainty and potential for loss due to a failure to pay on the part of a counterparty.

Because banks are used to making loans, their derivatives business is not taking on a different kind of risk than one they already have years of experience with. Because the notional amount on a derivative is not at risk, however, the credit risk of derivatives is typically much lower than the credit risk of loans. Nonbank end users typically do not make loans. When they become users of swaps, however, they become creditors.

Earlier in the book, we commented on credit risk whenever we discussed over-the-counter instruments. Futures and exchange-listed options are insured against credit risk by the clearinghouse. Because there has never been a default by the clearinghouse, these contracts can be considered credit-risk free. Over-the-counter contracts are subject to credit risk that varies from party to party, from type of contract to type of contract, and from one point in time to another point in time.

In the bond market, credit risk is typically assessed by examining the credit ratings of issuers. Credit ratings are provided by several firms, most notably Standard & Poor's,

Moody's, and Fitch. Although each agency has its own labels, terms such as *Triple-A* and *B-double AA* are used, with the more A's the better. Thus, you would see ratings such as AAA, AA, A, BAA, BBB, BB, B, and so on down to D. Analysts for these companies base their ratings on a variety of factors, most notably the financial health of the issuer, as well as the states of the economy and the issuer's industry.

To gain a better understanding of what credit risk really involves, let us take a look at the issues underlying credit and default. Interestingly, much of what we know about this subject comes from option pricing theory.

Credit Risk as an Option

Let us consider a very simple firm that has assets with a market value of A_0 and a single zero coupon debt issued with a face value of F. That is, the amount F is due when the bonds mature at time T. The debt has a market value of B_0. Thus, the market value of the stock is

$$S_0 = A_0 - B_0.$$

When the debt matures, the firm will have assets worth A_T and will owe the amount F. If $A_T > F$, the firm will pay off the debt, leaving the amount $A_T - F$ for the stockholders. Thus, the value of their claim at T is $S_T = A_T - F$. If the value of the assets is not adequate to pay off the debt, the creditors will receive the assets worth A_T and the value of the stockholders' claim is zero. In other words, the firm's assets are fully paid out in the form of partially repaying the creditors or paying the creditors in full, leaving the remainder for the stockholders. Table 15.5 illustrates these results.

Notice that the payoff to the stockholders is like a call option. In fact, we could write it as

$$S_T = Max(0, A_T - F),$$

which should look like a call option worth S_T at expiration, in which the underlying is an asset worth A_T at expiration and F is the exercise price. Ignoring the difference between the symbols we use here and those used in Part I, it should be easy to see that stock is indeed a call option and could be priced using the Black-Scholes-Merton model. But before we do that, let us take a further look at the nature of these claims.

If stock is indeed a call option, then we should be able to use put-call parity to relate it to some type of put option. Recall from Chapter 3 that put-call parity for standard options is $P_e(S_0,T,X) = C_e(S_0,T,X) - S_0 + X(1 + r)^{-T}$. In the present situation, we shall use the notation S_0 for the current value of the call, F for the exercise price, and A_0 for the asset price, which is the underlying. Thus, put-call parity would look as follows:

$$P_0 = S_0 - A_0 + F(1 + r)^{-T}.$$

TABLE 15.5 PAYOFFS TO THE SUPPLIERS OF CAPITAL TO THE FIRM

		PAYOFFS OF BONDS AND STOCK	
SOURCE OF CAPITAL	MARKET VALUE AT TIME 0	$A_T < F$	$A_T \geq F$
Bonds	B_0	A_T	F
Stock	S_0	0	$A_T - F$
Total	$B_0 + S_0$	A_T	A_T

But what exactly is the put? In general, a put is the right to sell the underlying at the exercise price. It is not apparent what the put represents when the stockholders' claim is viewed as a call option. Let us rearrange put-call parity:

$$S_0 = A_0 + P_0 - F(1 + r)^{-T}.$$

By definition, the value of the assets is the market value of the stock plus the market value of the bonds: $A_0 = S_0 + B_0$. This means that

$$S_0 = A_0 - B_0.$$

Using the previous two equations, we see that

$$B_0 = F(1 + r)^{-T} - P_0.$$

Thus, the market value of the bonds, which are subject to default, is the market value of a risk-free bond and a short put. The bondholders have, in effect, written an implicit put option to the stockholders. So the stockholders' claim is a claim on the assets, minus a risk-free bond, plus a long put.

The implicit put written by the bondholders to the stockholders is just a way to specify the limited liability feature that characterizes the nature of corporate ownership. A corporation can borrow money, promising to pay a given amount. If the corporation is unable to pay this amount, it can discharge its obligation in full by turning over (selling) the assets to the bondholders. The personal assets of the owners are not at risk. Thus, their claims are limited to a value of zero. The right held by the stockholders to default without putting their personal assets at risk is regarded in legal circles as limited liability. In economic terms, this right is a put option written by the bondholders to the stockholders.

Because equity is a call option, it can be valued using the Black-Scholes-Merton model. We insert the asset value as the underlying and the bond face value as the exercise price. The risk-free rate and time to expiration are obvious. The volatility is the volatility of the log return on the assets. The Black-Scholes-Merton model for S_0 is, thus,

$$S_0 = A_0 N(d_1) - Fe^{-r_c T} N(d_2).$$

The Black-Scholes-Merton model can also be used to value the risky bond. Recall that $B_0 = A_0 - S_0$. Thus, the market value of the bond can be found as

$$B_0 = A_0 - (A_0 N(d_1) - Fe^{-r_c T} N(d_2)) = Fe^{-r_c T} N(d_2) + A_0(1 - N(d_1)).$$

We see that the value of the bondholders' claim is equivalent to the value of a partial claim on a risk-free bond paying F at maturity plus a partial claim on the assets. This should make sense in that there is some probability that the bondholder will receive the full face value and some probability that the bondholder will receive some of the assets, which will be less than the face value.

Let us now turn to the question of how credit risk arises in derivatives.

Credit Risk of Derivatives

There are two types of credit risk in derivatives. **Current credit risk** is the risk to one party that the other party is unable to make payments that are currently due. Current credit risk is faced by only one party in a derivatives transaction, the party who holds the contract as an asset. In other words, the amount due to that party is positive, so it is subject to the possibility that the other party will default. The other party currently owes more than is owed to it, so it faces no current risk of default. **Potential credit risk** is the risk that the counterparty will default in the future.

Current credit risk is the risk that the party owing more than the other in a derivatives transaction will default right now. Potential credit risk is the risk that either party will default at any time during the life of the contract.

Both current and potential credit risk of over-the-counter options are faced by the buyer only. Because the buyer pays the premium to the seller and does not have to do anything else, the seller faces no credit risk. The buyer, however, may eventually choose to exercise the option, by which time the seller may be bankrupt. FRAs and swaps have two-way credit risk. Each party is obligated to do something for the other. Holding other things constant, the credit risk of an FRA or interest rate swap is determined by the credit quality of the counterparty, the terms of the contract, and the shape of the term structure. Consider, for example, a five-year plain vanilla interest rate swap. With an upward-sloping term structure, the implied forward rates are rising. These rates can be equated to the floating rates and will equal the eventual floating rates if there is no shift in interest rates during the life of the swap. When the swap is first established, the party paying the fixed rate and receiving the floating rate will initially pay more than it receives, but later the floating receipts will begin to overtake the fixed payments. At any given time, current credit risk is faced by one party only, which is the party to whom the contract has positive value. Potential credit risk will reflect the combined effects of the risk of changes in interest rates and the risk of the counterparty's assets over the remaining life of the contract. Both parties face potential credit risk.

In the case of interest rate swaps, the potential credit risk is largest during the middle of the swap's life. Potential credit risk is low at the beginning of the swap's life because it is assumed that the swap would not be entered into if there were any significant problems on the near horizon. Potential credit risk is high during the middle part of the swap's life because the counterparty has had time to have its financial condition deteriorate. Potential credit risk is low during the latter part of the swap's life because there are fewer payments remaining.

Recall that interest rate swaps do not involve the exchange of principal but currency swaps often do. This also keeps the credit risk low at the end of the life of the interest rate swap but raises it somewhat for the currency swap.

The explicit prices of derivative transactions do not necessarily differ according to the credit risk of the transaction. Many derivatives dealers and end users will transact only with customers of a minimum acceptable credit quality. Thus, counterparties who barely pass the hurdle pay the same as counterparties who are essentially risk free. Assessment of a counterparty's credit risk is done much the same way as when extending credit. Financial statements and ratings are used along with simulations and other statistical techniques. VAR can even be adapted to accommodate credit risk, although it is much more difficult to do. Stress testing is commonly used to assess credit risk by assuming that extreme economic conditions occur and estimating the likelihood of default.

Although qualifying parties pay the same explicit rate on a derivatives transaction, there are some implicit methods of differentiating among parties with different credit risks.

The primary methods of managing derivatives credit risk are limiting exposure to a given party; collateral; marking to market; netting; credit derivatives; and, for some dealers, separately capitalized derivatives subsidiaries.

The primary method used to manage credit risk is to limit the amount of exposure to a given party. The higher the credit quality of the counterparty, the greater the amount of business that can be done with it. This is similar to the principle of diversification. A party spreads out its transactions with numerous end users or dealers. An extreme case of this method is to do no business whatsoever with a counterparty whose credit quality is below a minimum level.

Collateral is commonly used in lending and is becoming increasingly used in derivatives transactions. The two parties might agree that each post collateral by depositing cash or securities with a bank or by providing a letter of credit from another bank. The parties may agree that on any settlement date, the party to whom the derivative value is negative will post collateral equal to a given percentage of the notional amount or the value of the contract. Another type of arrangement is for neither party to post collateral, but if either party's credit is downgraded by one of the rating agencies, that party will post a specific amount of collateral. Some transactions are structured so that a ratings downgrade gives the other party the right to terminate the contract at that point, meaning that the value of the swap is due and payable at that time.

We discussed marking to market extensively when we studied futures markets. Marking to market is designed to reduce credit risk by forcing losing parties to pay winning parties before losses accumulate to a large amount. Some derivative contracts are structured to have marking to market on a periodic basis. For example, a swap that settles semiannually might stipulate that the contracts are marked to market every two months. When the contract is marked to market, the market value is calculated. The party to whom the value is negative owes that full amount in cash to the other party. The fixed rate is then reset to the current market fixed rate. The actual settlement, meaning the exchange of interest payments, proceeds at the regularly scheduled dates, although with a new fixed rate. This procedure forces the party on the losing side to pay up before the accumulated loss is potentially much greater.

One should not always assume that the party with the weaker credit is the dealer. Many dealers are banks whose credit ratings are held down by the possibility of loan losses in their domestic and global banking business. In response to the concerns of some end users, a number of dealers have set up separate subsidiaries that do exclusively swap and derivatives transactions with end users. These subsidiaries are provided a large capital cushion and are not responsible for the debts of the parent company. Consequently, the subsidiary would have a higher credit rating than the parent company and most of these subsidiaries are rated AAA. These types of firms are called **enhanced derivatives products companies** and sometimes **special purpose vehicles** (also known as special purpose entities). When these firms were first created several years ago, they were greeted with much enthusiasm. The amount of business they have generated, however, has been surprisingly small. In fact, many parent companies also maintain derivative groups within the parent company as well as the subsidiary. Most end users were content to do business with the parent company as long as its rating was reasonably high, although not necessarily AAA.

Another procedure widely used to reduce default risk is netting. Because it is used so much and it is so important, we shall devote a special section to it.

Netting

Netting is a term that describes several similar processes that are used to reduce the amount of cash paid from one party to the other by deducting any cash owed by the latter party to the former party. Netting between two parties is called **bilateral netting**, while netting across several parties is called **multilateral netting**. Multilateral netting is effectively what happens when there is a clearinghouse, such as the options or futures clearinghouses we discussed in Chapters 2 and 8.

There are several forms of netting. We have already seen **payment netting**, in which two parties who owe each other money on a given day agree to simply determine the net amount owed and have one party pay the other. As you should remember, this is a fairly standard procedure in interest rate swaps. If party A owes $1,250,000 to party B who owes $890,000 to party A, then party A simply makes a payment of $360,000 to party B. This eliminates the possibility of party B defaulting, at least on this payment.

In **cross product netting**, payments for one type of transaction are netted against payments for another type of transaction. Suppose, for example, that on the date on which party A owes $260,000 to party B, party B also owes A $175,000 as the interest on a loan. If the two parties had agreed to cross product netting, then A would owe B only $260,000 − $175,000 = $85,000. Of course, the two parties might seldom have

---

MAKING THE CONNECTION

What Derivatives Tell Us About Bonds

Here in our treatment of credit risk, we learned that the stock of a firm that has issued debt is like a call option on the assets of the firm. We saw that a bond subject to credit risk can be viewed as a risk-free bond and a short put option on the assets. In other words, the bond-holders have implicitly written a put option to the stock-holders. In legal terms, this put option is the principle of limited liability: The claims of the bondholders cannot be met with the personal assets of the stockholders. The bondholders must accept either the amount owed to them or the value of the assets of the firm. Thus, the stockholders can discharge their liability by effectively selling the firm to the bondholders.

As we saw in this chapter, we can determine the market value of the bonds. Let us work an example. Consider a company that has assets worth 1,000. It has one issue of zero coupon bonds outstanding, which matures in two years. The bonds have a face value of 800. The volatility of the assets is 25 percent, and the risk-free rate is 4 percent. Let us use the Black-Scholes-Merton model to determine the market value of the stock, treating it as a call option on the assets. The following shows how this is done, with calculations obtained using the spreadsheet BSMbin9e.xls.

Black-Scholes-Merton Variable	Variable in Credit Risk Model	Value
S_0	A_0	1000
X	F	800
r_c	r_c	0.04
σ	σ	0.25
T	T	2
$C_0(S_0,T,X)$	S_0	294.17

Plugging in to the Black-Scholes-Merton model, we would obtain a value as indicated above of 294.17. Thus, the market value of the bonds would be

$$B_0 = A_0 - S_0 = 1{,}000 - 294.17 = 705.83.$$

Let us now determine the yield on the bonds. The bonds have a current value of 705.83 and pay off 800 in two years. The continuously compounded yield, y, can be found using the following relationship:

$$705.83 = 800e^{-y2}.$$

Solving for y gives

$$y = \frac{\ln\left(\dfrac{800}{705.83}\right)}{2} = 0.0626.$$

Note that this bond offers a risk premium of 2.26 percent over the risk-free rate. This value is typically called the yield spread. The size of the yield spread reflects the credit risk assumed by the lender.

By varying the inputs, we can observe how the yield spread changes. In the table below, we see how the yield spread varies with the maturity of the bond, holding everything else constant.

Maturity	Value of Stock	Value of Bonds	Bond Yield (%)	Yield Spread (%)
1	247.79	752.21	6.16	2.16
2	294.17	705.83	6.26	2.26
3	334.29	665.71	6.13	2.13
4	369.98	630.02	5.97	1.97
5	402.34	597.66	5.83	1.83

The relationship between a bond's yield (or yield spread) and maturity is often called the credit risk structure of interest rates. In this case, the credit risk structure is increasing out to two years, but then it begins to decrease. This pattern means that over the near horizon, the debt is somewhat riskier. The risk over the longer horizon, however, is smaller, because the firm has more time to improve its financial condition.

The table below shows how the yield spread changes if the amount of the debt increases. In other words, we see below how the yield spread changes if the company has more debt.

Face Value of Debt	Value of Stock	Value of Bonds	Bond Yield (%)	Yield Spread (%)
400	630.91	369.09	4.02	0.02
600	451.23	548.77	4.46	0.46
800	294.17	705.83	6.26	2.26
1000	176.77	823.23	9.73	5.73
1200	100.08	899.92	14.39	10.39

Naturally, the more debt the company carries, the larger the yield spread. Note, however, that the firm could carry debt with a face value of $1,200, which exceeds the value of the assets of $1,000, and not be bankrupt. The debt would have a value, as indicated above, of about $900, reflecting the fact that the debt is not due for two more years and that the company could easily be in better financial condition by that time.

In the table below, we examine how the yield spread changes if the volatility of the assets changes.

Volatility	Value of Stock	Value of Bonds	Bond Yield (%)	Yield Spread (%)
0.05	261.51	738.49	4.00	0.00
0.15	267.75	732.25	4.42	0.42
0.25	294.17	705.83	6.26	2.26
0.35	330.66	669.34	8.92	4.92
0.45	370.91	629.09	12.02	8.02

Note that the more volatile the assets, the riskier the debt, as we might expect.

The Black-Scholes-Merton model can be very useful for evaluating credit risk. For example, the KMV Corporation, which was acquired by Moody's, had a service that provides credit risk information based on the application of the Black-Scholes-Merton model in the manner shown here. This approach is now offered in several products provided by Moody's.

transactions with payments due on the same day. Consequently, cross product netting usually comes into play in bankruptcy or in a takeover involving two parties, each owing the other various amounts arising from different transactions.

If the parties agree to **netting by novation**, the net value of their mutual obligations is replaced by a single new transaction. In our example above, if A owes B $85,000, then the transactions that have an aggregate value of $85,000 to B are replaced by a new transaction with a value of $85,000. Netting by novation is used more often in the foreign exchange markets.

Closeout netting is the stipulation that if default occurs, only the net amount is owed. This greatly reduces the credit risk by reducing the amount of cash owed by a defaulting party by the amount owed to it. Consider the following example:

Company XYZ and dealer FinSwaps are engaged in four transactions with each other. From the dealer's perspective, the market values are as follows:

Swap 1	−$1,179,580
Swap 2	+$1,055,662
Option 1	+$1,495,255
FRA 1	−$ 892,530
	+$ 478,807

XYZ defaults with no closeout netting:
Suppose XYZ demands payments on swap 1 and FRA 1 and refuses to pay on swap 2 and option 1. FinSwaps owes XYZ $2,072,110, the sum of the values of swap 1 and FRA 1. This process is commonly called cherry picking because the bankrupt party selects the attractive transactions and walks away from the others.

XYZ defaults but closeout netting is used:
XYZ owes FinSwaps $478,807.

Netting is the process of reducing credit risk in which amounts owed from one party to the other are netted against amounts owed from the latter to the former to arrive at an overall amount owed by one party to the other.

Today, there is hardly an issue over the use of closeout netting. It is standard in virtually every swap in most countries, and most countries' bankruptcy laws have been revised to recognize the legitimacy of closeout netting.

In the presence of netting, the credit risk of swaps is clearly limited to the net payments, which is less than the present value of the interest payments on a loan of equivalent notional amount. Because of this and the fact that the over-the-counter derivatives market has imposed strict requirements to reduce the credit risk, its record in the matter of defaults is excellent. The default of the London borough Hammersmith and Fulham in 1988 was the result of a legal ruling that permitted it to walk away from losing transactions and accounted for about half of all defaults in the over-the-counter market until that time. The record since that time has been quite good as well. In fact, the derivatives market has established a much better record on the matter of default than has the commercial loan market. Clearly, the concerns expressed by some over the large size of the market (as exemplified by the notional amount outstanding) overstate the real risk.

Credit Derivatives

In the early 1990s, a major innovation in credit risk management appeared on the scene: the **credit derivative**. A credit derivative is an instrument designed to separate market risk from credit risk and to allow the separate trading of the latter. Specifically, it is a derivative or derivative-like instrument with a payoff determined by whether a third party makes a promised payment on a debt obligation. Credit derivatives permit a more efficient allocation and pricing of credit risk. Parties who want to rid themselves of credit risk can engage in credit derivative transactions to pass the credit risk on to another party who is willing to accept it. Ultimately, this transferal of risk greatly benefits those who borrow and lend, as well as those who transact in derivatives that are subject to default, for it helps assure them that the premiums associated with the risk of default are appropriate for that level of risk. Banks, in particular, use credit derivatives both as buyers and sellers. Banks must limit the amount of exposure to a particular borrower, to a particular geographic area, or to a particular industry. They can often provide a loan, thereby servicing the borrower, but can then sell the credit risk using a credit derivative.

Of course, for any party that eliminates credit risk, there must be a party that accepts it. Purchasing credit risk that is unrelated to the risks already in a portfolio can help diversify the portfolio. In addition, speculators could be willing to accept the credit risk, believing that it is less than what is priced into the contract. The primary parties that accept the credit risk transferred through credit derivatives are other banks, insurance companies, and hedge funds.

A credit derivative is an instrument whose payoff is largely determined by the credit of another party. Credit derivatives are used to separate market risk from credit risk and permits the separate trading of credit risk. Each transaction involves three parties: the credit buyer, the credit seller, and the reference entity.

A credit derivative transaction involves three parties. One is the credit derivatives buyer, which is a party that holds credit risk that it wants to eliminate. The second party is the credit derivatives seller, which is the party that is willing to acquire the credit risk. The third party is the party on whose credit the transaction is based. This party is called the **reference entity**. For example, suppose Bank A has made a loan to Company C. Now Bank A has too much exposure to the credit of Company C and wants to sell the credit risk. It finds another company willing to take on the risk, which happens to be a hedge fund called Fund B. Bank A is the credit derivative buyer, Fund B is the credit derivative seller, and Company C is the reference entity. The reference entity is involved in the credit derivative in name only. In fact, it may well be unaware that it is the reference entity in a credit derivatives transaction. It is the right of the party exposed to the credit risk of the reference entity to sell that risk to another party without involvement of the reference entity.

Credit derivatives are somewhat more complex than other derivatives for a variety of reasons. Credit risk is more difficult to measure, and losses from credit events are less frequent than losses from movements in, say, interest rates or exchange rates. Hence, it is more difficult to build historical models of credit losses. Credit derivatives are also less liquid instruments than ordinary derivatives, and they involve complex legal issues related to contract terms and documentation as well as to definitions of what constitutes a credit loss.

For example, there are numerous types of events that might be specified as a credit loss in the contract. These include not making an interest or scheduled principal payment following a reasonable grace period, declaration of bankruptcy, repudiation of a liability, restructuring of the borrower's other debts, or acceleration of payment of another liability. The latter could be caused by a provision in another liability that permits another creditor to require premature payment of a debt. These possible events must be spelled out in the contract.

We should also remember that a credit derivative is itself subject to credit risk. If the party promising to pay in the event of a credit loss is unable to pay, there is a credit loss on a credit derivative. The potential for a default by both the reference entity and the seller is, however, usually very small.

Nonetheless, the credit derivatives market is large and growing rapidly. The Bank for International Settlements surveys that we previously cited have only recently begun documenting the size of the credit derivatives market. Its surveys, however, are limited to only one type of credit derivative (credit default swaps, which we will cover later). As of December 2010, the notional amount of these instruments is estimated at $29.9 trillion, but keep in mind the misleading nature of notional amount as a measure of risk. In the case of credit derivatives, this figure represents the aggregate face value of bonds and loans covered by credit derivatives. The market value of these credit derivatives is estimated at $1.4 trillion. Some other information is available from the United States Office of the Comptroller of the Currency, which regulates federally chartered banks in the United States. Its surveys, obtainable from its website, www.occ.treas.gov, indicate that the notional amount of credit derivatives at these large U.S. banks was $14.1 trillion at the end of December 2010.

Now let us take a look at the various types of credit derivatives. In the discussions that follow, we will use the term *buyer* to refer to the credit derivatives buyer who is the party who wants to eliminate the credit risk and *seller* to refer to the credit derivatives seller who is the party willing to accept the credit risk.

> A total return swap is a type of credit derivative similar to an ordinary swap. The credit derivative buyer pays the credit derivative seller the total return on a bond of the reference entity, while the seller makes interest payments to the buyer. In this way, credit losses on the bond are passed on from buyer to seller.

Total Return Swaps Perhaps the simplest credit derivative is the **total return swap**, which is a swap transaction in which the buyer agrees to pay the total return on a particular reference asset, such as a specific bond issued by the reference entity, to the seller. The seller, in turn, agrees to pay the buyer a rate such as LIBOR plus a spread. As in any swap, these payments are made on a regular schedule, usually quarterly or semiannually. The total return includes any interest payments as well as unrealized capital gains. If the bond incurs a capital loss, the buyer then receives a payment from the seller. The buyer is, in effect, promising to pay the seller the bond's total return and to correspondingly receive an interest payment, thereby ridding itself of the risk of price changes caused by factors

FIGURE 15.4 Total Return Swap

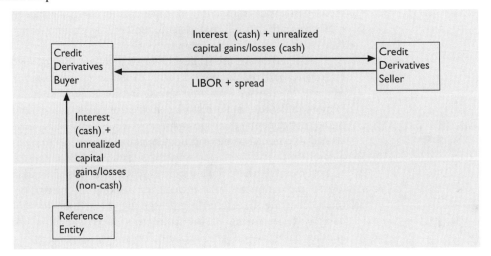

unrelated to interest rate movements. Presumably, such price changes would occur primarily from changes in the reference entity's credit risk. The structure of a total return swap is illustrated in Figure 15.4. Note that unrealized capital gains and losses are non-cash amounts, but the swap requires cash payment for unrealized capital gains and losses.

The total return swap maintains the bond in the possession of the buyer. The seller is seeking the return on the bond without buying the bond. Note that market risk due to interest rate movements is not completely eliminated because those movements are reflected in the LIBOR payment. Incidentally, the LIBOR payment can, alternatively, be a fixed rate or it can be converted from LIBOR to a fixed rate with a plain vanilla swap. Note that the total return swap is much like an ordinary swap, but the interest payment corresponds to that on a specific bond and the unrealized capital gains and losses are paid.

Total return swaps are practical only for reasonably liquid bonds and not for ordinary loans. This is because the parties must be able to identify the total return over the settlement period in order to determine how much the buyer owes the seller. Consequently, there must be a reliable measure of the market value of the bond, which can occur only if there is an actively traded market for the bond or a dealer willing to quote a price for the bond.

A credit default swap is a type of credit derivative in which the credit derivative buyer makes periodic payments to the credit derivative seller, who pays the buyer if and when a credit loss is incurred on the reference entity.

Credit Default Swaps A second type of derivative is the **credit default swap**, sometimes called a **credit swap**. The buyer holds a bond or loan issued by the reference entity and enters into the credit default swap, which obligates it to make a series of periodic payments to the seller. If a credit event occurs to the reference entity, the seller compensates the buyer for the loss. This compensation can take one of two primary forms. In a *cash settlement*, the seller pays the buyer the difference between the amount defaulted less any amount recovered. In *physical delivery*, the buyer simply delivers the reference instrument to the seller. Of course, in earlier chapters, we discussed the use of cash settlement and physical delivery for other derivative contracts. One other type of settlement, *called fixed settlement*, is also used, although infrequently. In a fixed settlement, the seller pays the buyer a fixed amount regardless of the amount of the loss.

FIGURE 15.5 Credit Default Swap

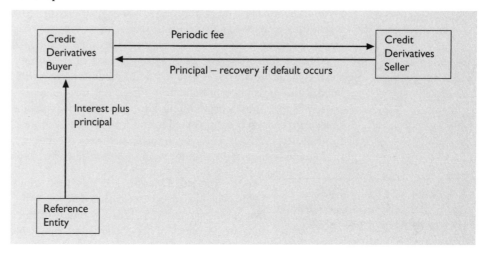

Although a credit default swap is called a swap, it is easy to see why it is essentially an insurance policy.[8] The buyer pays the seller a periodic fee, which is similar to an insurance premium. The seller then compensates the buyer in the event that a credit loss occurs. Credit swaps can be written on a reference entity's bonds or loans. A credit default swap is illustrated in Figure 15.5.

Credit default swaps are probably the most widely used credit derivative, and there are many variants. One of the primary differentiating features is how the reference entity is specified. The type of credit default swap we have been describing is on a single reference entity. There are other credit default swaps in which the reference entity is actually a portfolio of loans or bonds of various reference entities. This portfolio is usually referred to as a basket. For a credit default swap on a basket, the swap is specified to pay off when the nth party to default actually defaults, where n is a contractually specified number. That is, a first-to-default credit default swap will pay off when the first entity in the basket defaults. A second-to-default credit default swap does not pay off until the second default occurs. The payoff is based only on the second default and does not cover losses from the first default. Therefore, n can be any number up to the total number of reference entities in the basket.

The basic idea behind pricing credit default swaps is to determine the amount the buyer would pay the seller to insure against default. Effectively, this procedure means to convert a bond that is subject to default into a risk-free bond. The default-free bond is clearly worth more than the otherwise equivalent bond that could default. Using the notation we specified earlier in explaining how the equity and debt of a firm can be analyzed using the Black-Scholes-Merton model, we find this difference to be the current value of the credit default swap or **CDS premium**:

$$\text{CDS premium} = Fe^{-r_c T} - B_0.$$

---

[8]In the United States, insurance is regulated at the state level. Hence, any product called *insurance* requires regulatory approval from all 50 states before it can be generally offered. Credit derivatives serve much of the same purpose as credit insurance but are private contracts and are not directly regulated by the federal or state governments.

This amount would be paid by the CDS buyer to the CDS seller. As explained above, this premium is usually paid periodically, such as quarterly or semiannually. Finding the premium thus reduces to a problem in time value of money. What series of equivalent payments, called an annuity, has a present value equal to the CDS premium? Regardless of whether the premium was paid all at the start or over time, the CDS premium has a value equivalent to what it would take to eliminate the credit risk, thereby converting a bond with a possibility of default into a default-free bond.

In practice, most corporations have more complex capital structures than just the single zero coupon bond specified in this framework; so more complex models are needed to adequately derive the CDS premium. Nonetheless, the idea is simple: One must determine the amount of money the creditor would pay a third party to eliminate the default risk.

> A credit spread option is a type of credit derivative that is an option on the yield spread of a bond. The option buyer pays a premium to the seller and receives an option. When this option is exercised, the option buyer will receive the difference in the yield spread on the bond and the exercise rate, a specified yield spread.

Credit Spread Options Bonds that could potentially default have yields that are in excess of the yield on otherwise comparable default-free bonds, such as U.S. Treasury bonds of the same maturity. The difference in the yield of the potentially defaultable bond and the Treasury bond is called the yield spread. It fluctuates as credit risk changes. When investors perceive that the potentially defaultable bond has greater credit risk, that bond becomes less attractive than the Treasury bond and its price declines, causing the spread to widen. Hence, the yield spread is a good indication of the credit risk of the bond. A **credit spread option** is an option in which the underlying is the yield spread. It fluctuates with investors' perceptions of the credit risk. Suppose the credit risk of the reference entity currently dictates that it should pay 50 basis points in yield over a U.S. Treasury note of comparable maturity. The buyer might buy a credit spread option with an exercise rate of 60 basis points. At expiration, or early if the option is American style, the option is in-the-money if the credit spread exceeds 60 basis points. Of course, this will occur only if the market perceives that the credit risk has increased. For this right, the buyer pays the seller a premium up front. Thus, this instrument is like an ordinary option, but the underlying is the spread of the bond over the otherwise comparable U.S. Treasury security. This type of credit derivative also requires that the underlying bond be sufficiently liquid such that a reliable assessment of its credit spread can be obtained. An illustration of a credit spread option is shown in Figure 15.6.

Credit Linked Security Another type of credit derivative is the **credit linked security**. This type of instrument appears to be an ordinary bond or note, paying interest and

FIGURE 15.6 Credit Spread Option

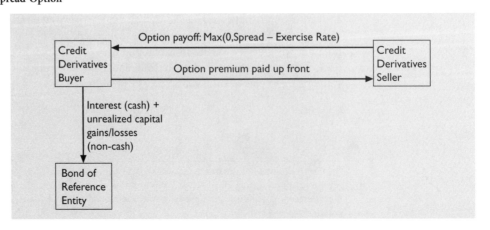

FIGURE 15.7 Credit Linked Security

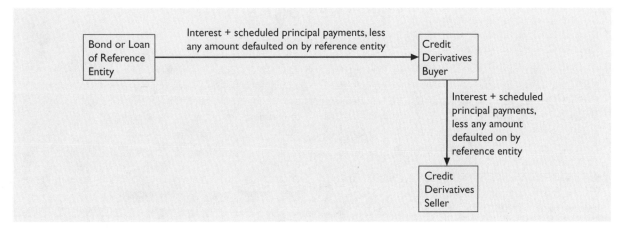

A credit linked security is a type of credit derivative in which a party issues a note or bond in which the principal repayment can be reduced by any credit loss incurred on a reference note or bond.

principal. Underlying the note, however, is the credit quality of the reference entity. If the reference entity defaults on some other specified instrument or obligation, the credit linked security pays back less than its full principal. For example, let us say party A buys a credit linked note from party B. Party B in turn is holding a note issued by party C. If party C fails to pay party B, the latter is then able to reduce its obligation to party A. In this manner, party A assumes some of the credit risk of both parties B and C. Party B, often a bank, is thus able to lay off some unwanted credit risk. Of course, party A receives a higher interest rate on the note as compensation for acceptance of this risk. An illustration of a credit linked security is shown in Figure 15.7.

A synthetic collateralized debt obligation, or synthetic CDO, is a securitized instrument in the form of tranches that represent prioritized claims on a portfolio of credit default swaps.

Synthetic CDOs In Chapter 14, we discussed asset-backed securities. We illustrated how mortgages are combined into portfolios and how claims on the interest and principal from the mortgages are sold in the form of pass-throughs and collateralized mortgage obligations, or CMOs. Recall that in a CMO, claims on the underlying portfolio are divided into prioritized securities called tranches. When the underlying securities are bonds or loans instead of mortgages, this instrument is called a **collateralized debt obligation**, or **CDO**. When the underlying securities are bonds, the instrument is sometimes called a collateralized bond obligation, or CBO. When the underlying securities are loans, the instrument is sometimes called a collateralized loan obligation, or CLO.

These types of instruments have played an important role in the development of credit derivatives. Specifically, credit derivatives themselves are sometimes combined into a portfolio, and claims on that portfolio are sold through credit default swaps. This type of instrument is known as a **synthetic CDO**.[9] In a strict sense, it is not a unique credit derivative, being only a combination and repackaging of existing credit derivatives. But CDOs are so widely used that it is well worthwhile to treat them as a distinct instrument.

With a synthetic CDO, the issuer enters a portfolio of credit default swaps on various reference entities, thereby assuming the credit risk of all of the reference entities. Let us refer to this portfolio as the underlying credit portfolio. The issuer then eliminates the

---

[9]CDOs wherein the underlying is a portfolio of securities are now sometimes called cash CDOs to distinguish them from synthetic CDOs, wherein the underlying is a portfolio of credit derivatives.

MAKING THE CONNECTION

Unfunded Synthetic CDOs

A cash collateralized debt obligation is fully funded, meaning that the tranche purchasers have no obligation to make further cash investments even if credit defaults are widespread. If there is a 100 percent loss on all underlying debts within the CDO, the CDO investors will have lost only their original investment.

A funded synthetic CDO requires investors to provide the equivalent amount of capital to fully fund the potential credit default losses within the synthetic CDO. A fully funded synthetic CDO, however, does not offer the same return potential as a partially funded or unfunded synthetic CDO.

An unfunded synthetic CDO does not require investors to provide capital at the start. Rather, the investors must agree to provide funding as credit losses occur. The unfunded synthetic CDO investor is like an insurance company, receiving periodic premiums in return for guaranteeing losses if they occur.

Clearly, unfunded synthetic CDOs expose investors to future potential payments during a time of financial crisis. Often, during such times, investors are scrambling to find sources of cash to provide for their own funding mandates, such as endowments and pension funds. The unfunded synthetic CDO, although offering considerably higher expected returns, has the untimely consequence of requiring cash payments at the very time many investors are particularly strained for cash.

Therefore, prudent investors in unfunded synthetic CDOs will establish highly liquid, low credit risk investments to provide the potential future required payments should they be demanded from their unfunded synthetic CDO investments. Also, prudent investors in unfunded synthetic CDOs will limit their overall exposure to these types of investments so as to avoid experiencing catastrophic losses at the very time many of their other investments are performing poorly.

credit risk by issuing a combination of credit default swap tranches with other parties. Recall from Chapter 14 that a tranche is a piece of a portfolio that has been ordered with respect to a specified priority in which the portfolio experiences claims or bears losses. In a synthetic CDO, these tranches assume, in a specified order of priority, the credit losses from the underlying credit portfolio. The highest-priority tranche bears credit losses last, with each tranche below it bearing credit losses successively earlier. At least one tranche will probably bear little credit risk because all of the other tranches will assume any losses ahead of it. The lowest-priority tranche will bear the most credit risk, because it will have to assume the first credit losses from the underlying credit portfolio. Other tranches lying between the two extremes bear various degrees of credit risk. Figure 15.8 illustrates a synthetic CDO.

FIGURE 15.8 Synthetic CDO

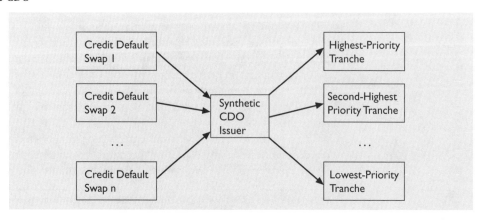

The credit risk assumed is, of course, a major determinant of the pricing of these tranches. Parties purchasing the riskier tranches pay less and have higher expected returns because of the risk. The pricing of credit derivatives is quite complex. The basic idea stems from the notion of default as an option, as discussed earlier, but while the theory is sound, implementing it is difficult. Moreover, the pricing of credit derivatives is complicated by the fact that the payoffs are often contingent on the credit risk of multiple entities. Hence, the correlations between the respective credit risks of the various entities are important and quite difficult to evaluate.

In spite of the complexities of credit derivatives, the market is, as noted earlier, growing rapidly. In fact, credit derivatives have become such a popular instrument that a number of organizations have created indices of the performance of credit derivatives. These indices are useful measures of the general level of credit risk in the economy. In addition, it is possible to buy and sell the indices as one would an ordinary security. Thus, in addition to engaging in direct transactions in credit derivatives, market participants can buy and sell credit risk as though it were a mutual fund.

OTHER TYPES OF RISKS

Although market risk and credit risk comprise the two primary risks, they are by no means exhaustive. The unforeseen circumstances that can occur touch on almost all aspects of running a business.

Operational risk is the risk of a breakdown in the operations of the derivatives program or risk management system. This could include such events as power failures, computer problems such as viruses and software bugs, the failure of staff personnel to monitor and record transactions properly, the failure of staff personnel to have the necessary knowledge of potentially complex transactions, the failure to have proper documentation, and fraud perpetrated by traders or staff personnel. These risks are present in virtually any type of business operation, but because derivatives transactions are generally somewhat complex and usually involve large amounts of money, the need to avoid these problems is critical.

Perhaps the most important part of operational risk is the effectiveness of proper controls. For example, if certain persons are authorized to engage in derivatives transactions, then it is imperative that their activities be monitored by personnel who report to persons higher in the organization. Anyone authorized to trade must be restricted in what contracts and how much that person can trade. Controls must be in place to make sure that these policies are followed. As obvious as that seems, some firms have not done a good job of ensuring that well-established policies and procedures are actually followed. In fact, it is safe to say that many derivatives losses can be traced in part to operational risks. In many cases, unauthorized trades took place. An individual in a company made trades that were inappropriate or exposed the firm to excessive risks that clearly were risks the firm had not authorized its traders to take. Such an individual is often called a rogue trader, trading within the firm but outside its control parameters.

Operational risk is receiving a great deal of attention today. Unfortunately, it is one of the most difficult risks to manage. First, it is difficult to identify and even define. Second, it does not easily lend itself to analysis. Operational risk losses, fortunately, do not occur often. Yet when they do occur, they can lead to tremendous losses. The infrequency of their occurrence leads to two major problems. One is that they are not amenable to analysis by standard statistical techniques. A normal distribution or even other common statistical distributions do not fit the unusual profiles of operational risk losses. Another problem is that little data exists on operational risk losses. When companies incur such losses, they do their best not to reveal this information, for it tends to be embarrassing and suggests sloppiness in their internal systems. The infrequency of past problems and lack of data make it difficult to predict when and where such losses will occur. The risk management industry, however, is beginning to recognize this problem, and some efforts to share data among firms have begun.

Operational risks are more along the lines of risks that are addressed by traditional insurance policies. When an insurance firm provides protection against a singer's voice during a concert tour, it is insuring against an infrequent event of an operational risk nature. When an insurer provides protection against employee fraud, it is insuring against operational risk. It is not surprising, therefore, that insurance companies have begun to look at marketing products for insuring against operational risk in the financial industry and, in particular, in connection with derivatives-related transactions. While there are no derivative contracts that protect against operational risk, some discussion has begun toward creating operational risk derivatives, and they will surely exist in the near future.

Model risk is the risk that in pricing a financial instrument such as a derivative, the firm will use an inappropriate model or a model containing errors (including programming bugs and errors) or use incorrect inputs. This is a critical issue for dealers, because offering derivatives at attractive prices and then managing the risk is their business. It can also be critical for end users, because they are less likely to have the personnel and knowledge to properly price the instruments.

We have learned enough in this book to take a quick look at model risk. Suppose a customer wants to buy a three-year American put option on the S&P 500. Let the index be at 1,450; the exercise price be at 1,450; the risk-free rate be 6 percent; the volatility be 18 percent; the dividend yield be 1.5 percent; and, of course, the time to expiration be three years. Because this is an American option, we should use a binomial tree to properly reflect the early exercise feature. It is tempting, nonetheless, to use the Black-Scholes-Merton model, so that is what we mistakenly do. Using the spreadsheet BSMbin9e.xls, we obtain a value for the call of 88.05. Let us get the correct value, however, using the binomial model. Using 200 time steps, we obtain 111.82. This is an error of over 20 percent. If the customer wanted $1,000,000 of notional amount of this option, we would be losing over $200,000 just in selling the option. Further losses would undoubtedly be incurred in trying to manage the risk by delta, gamma, and vega hedging.

Here is another variation of model risk. Suppose we used the correct model, sold the option at 111.82, and then hedged away the risk with other transactions. Now suppose one year later we needed to assign a value to the option. With two years to go and the same S&P value, the put would be worth 99.56. But suppose we used a volatility of 22 percent. The put would have a value of 122.68. This is a significant difference. Yet volatility variations from, for example, 18 percent to 22 percent are common. One might be tempted not to view this as a form of model risk, but any time the inputs are unknown, model risk exists. With an input as critical as the volatility is to an option, the model risk can be tremendous.

Some major financial institutions have discovered embarrassing errors, even in simple valuation problems such as forward contracts, that have led to significant losses. The best insurance against model risk is knowledge: knowledge of the theories and models.

Liquidity risk is the risk that a firm will need to enter into a derivatives transaction and find that the market for that transaction is so thin that the price includes a significant discount or premium for that liquidity. Anyone making a market in an illiquid instrument will bear significant risk and would charge wide bid-ask spreads or even be unwilling to trade. Most plain vanilla derivatives have little such risk, but exotic transactions can have significant liquidity risk. Liquidity risk is hardly confined to derivatives, however, as was evidenced in the August–September 1998 period when the famous hedge fund Long-Term Capital Management (LTCM) found itself holding positions in very illiquid bonds from around the world. LTCM had sophisticated risk management systems and some of the smartest people in the business, but it misestimated the effects of illiquidity during a global financial crisis where markets around the world were falling in unison. LTCM suffered severe losses that led to a bailout by a consortium of banks that was orchestrated by the U.S. Federal Reserve.

A great deal of research is going on to model liquidity risk or, at the minimum, to think about its effects when managing other types of risks. Some discussion has begun on the creation of liquidity risk derivatives, which would allow parties to buy and sell liquidity risk just like any other form of risk.

Accounting risk is the uncertainty over the proper accounting treatment of a derivatives transaction. Accounting for derivatives has been a significant source of controversy and risk for many years. Users of derivatives have lived with an ongoing concern that the manner in which they account for derivatives will be declared inappropriate after the fact and that they will be required to restate certain transactions with the potential to lower past earnings figures. The significance, timeliness, and critical importance of proper accounting for derivatives is a reason we examine this subject in more detail in the next chapter.

Legal risk is the risk that the legal system will fail to enforce a contract. For example, suppose a dealer enters into a swap with a counterparty that, upon incurring a loss, then refuses to pay the dealer, arguing that the dealer misled it or that the counterparty had no legal authority to enter into the swap. These arguments have been successfully used in the legal system, particularly by local governments. The risk of contracts not being enforced is a serious one for dealers.[10] This risk can effectively turn a swap or an FRA into an option, because the counterparty simply walks away without paying if the market moves against it. Not too surprisingly, no counterparty has ever claimed that it was misled or had no authority to do derivatives after making money on them. Efforts to control legal risk largely arise from having good documentation of all transactions. The industry, through its trade association ISDA (International Swaps and Derivatives Association), has established standards of documentation for various derivative transactions, including contract templates, formal definitions of key terms, and specific provisions that are widely used in over-the-counter derivatives transactions. ISDA has also been instrumental in lobbying and seeking legal opinions before issues become tied up in litigation.

> In addition to market and credit risks, risk managers must consider operational risk, model risk, liquidity risk, accounting risk, legal risk, tax risk, regulatory risk, and settlement risk.

Tax risk is the risk that taxes or the interpretation of tax laws will change unexpectedly. A good example of this was described in Appendix 11 where the tax status of hedging, which had been established almost a half century prior, was called into question. For a period of time, the possibility existed that certain hedging transactions would be taxed in a different manner, rendering them much less attractive. Moreover, the threat that completed transactions will have to be re-taxed always looms. Tax risk has managed to completely eliminate the use of certain transactions, such as the American Stock Exchange's PRIMES and SCORES, which were precursors to the equity-linked debt we covered in Chapter 14. As another example of tax risk, the U.S. Congress has been considering for many years levying a tax on each futures transaction to pay the cost of regulating the futures markets.

Regulatory risk is the risk that regulations or regulatory philosophy will change. Because regulators are appointed by the political party in control, it is easy for a

---

[10]The aforementioned Hammersmith and Fulham case illustrates the dangers of legal risk to the dealer. The case was supported on the doctrine of *ultra vires*, which means to have no legal authority.

regulatory agency to go from a free-market, light-regulation approach to a more direct and heavy-headed approach. Regulatory risk means that certain existing or contemplated transactions can become illegal or regulated.

Settlement risk is commonly faced in international transactions. Let us say that a bank in country A engages in a financial transaction with a corporation in country B in which both the bank and the corporation will be required to pay each other rather than net their payments.[11] The bank and the corporation are 12 hours apart with the bank's day beginning first. On settlement day, the bank wires its funds to the corporation under the assumption that when the markets open, the corporation will wire its funds to the bank. When the corporation's markets open, however, the corporation announces that it is bankrupt and will suspend all payments. Thus, the bank will be out the money and will have to get in line with the corporation's other creditors. This risk is sometimes called **Herstatt risk**, named for the German bank that in 1974 failed under similar circumstances. Settlement risk can arise out of bankruptcy, insolvency, or fraud.

This enumeration of risks does not necessarily cover every possible contingency. Foreign currency transactions, for example, are subject to political risk, meaning that the government of a country may take over the financial system and declare certain transactions null and void or refuse to allow currency to leave the country. The Chicago Board of Trade was forced to suspend operations one day due to a flood in downtown Chicago. Risk managers needing to trade CBOT products had to look for substitutes in other markets. It would be impossible to have every contingency covered, but risk managers need to be aware of as many problems as possible that could occur.

> Systemic risk is the risk that failure of one or more financial institutions will trigger more failures, ultimately leading to a breakdown of the financial system.

There is one final source of risk that is of considerable concern to many people, especially regulators. There is a belief that when one company defaults, it could trigger the default of one of its creditors, which could trigger further defaults. These effects could ripple through the entire financial system, leading to widespread panic and a meltdown of the whole system. This is called **systemic risk**. In modern times, the closest the world's economy has come to such a breakdown was during the stock market crash of October 1987. On a lesser scale, another example is the global financial crisis that occurred in September 1998. As it turned out, while there was a great deal of panic and enormous losses, the markets did not even come close to a total breakdown. Regulators worry, however, that the volume of derivatives transactions, particularly over-the-counter derivatives, is much greater now. While this might be a legitimate concern in an economy in which most financial institutions do not practice risk management, there is little cause for concern today. Nearly every major financial institution in the world practices risk management, and most maintain a relatively hedged position in derivatives. There have been numerous shocks to the financial system in the 1990s, but none has come remotely close to causing a systemic breakdown.

PERSPECTIVES ON FINANCIAL RISK MANAGEMENT

Now that we have finished covering the technical details of various methods for financial risk management, we offer a few qualitative comments. There are two general approaches to managing financial risks, view driven and needs driven.

View-driven risk management is primarily focused on the manager's view of the future. If a particular market risk looks likely, then that risk is mitigated. If a particular market risk looks highly unlikely, then that risk is not mitigated. Remember that in most

---

[11]For example, a currency swap is usually done without netting because the payments are occurring in two different currencies.

cases, hedging is a costly exercise. Thus, the decision to leave a particular risk unhedged will prove profitable if that particular risk does not appear. Clearly, there is great risk to view-driven risk management. In the period you choose not to hedge, the risk might appear, causing great loss. In the period you choose to hedge, the risk might not appear, resulting in costly hedging. Thus, even the act of hedging to eliminate risk is itself taking some risk, the risk that the adverse event will not happen. View-driven risk management appears to be the dominant approach to managing the financial risks of an organization.

Needs-driven risk management is primarily focused on the manager's view of the existing risk exposures. For example, most people purchase automobile insurance or homeowners insurance from the needs-driven perspective. That is, you do not try to determine whether you will have a car accident this month before purchasing automobile insurance. The decision to leave a particular risk unhedged would be based more on your ability to withstand the exposure as opposed to your prediction of the likelihood that it occurs. Bank asset-liability management is an example of needs-driven risk management. The bank's analysts determine the interest rate sensitivities of both the assets and liabilities. Based on this gap analysis, the bank may or may not implement some sort of hedging strategy. Likewise, an airline hedging fuel prices or a food processor hedging commodity prices are both reflections of needs-driven risk management. Fuel and commodities are the raw materials they use to create their services and products.

Ultimately, financial risk management is a unique blend of these two approaches to managing risk. For some entities, the focus will be almost exclusively view driven whereas for other entities, the focus will be almost exclusively needs driven. A risk manager must carefully think through her approach to financial risk management before the major crisis events occur; otherwise, reckless decisions in the storm may very well sink the firm. The view-driven approach is attractive due to the constant high-pressure decisions that must be made almost daily. Nonetheless, the view-driven approach is in some sense a process of making speculative bets, because it arises from having a view of the future. If successful over a long period of time, the view-driven approach would be very profitable. Of course, predicting the future is difficult, if not impossible, so a long-term view-driven approach is unlikely to add much value. Moreover, history has taught many risk managers that those things not seen in history do happen. The more seasoned risk professionals tend to lean more toward needs-driven risk management. That is, they determine the current financial risk exposures the firm is facing. Then they insure the downside risk should adverse events occur. Once insured, the risk manager has very little to be anxious about. Organizations that do this are often simply acknowledging that factors such as interest rates, exchange rates, and commodity prices are factors over which they have no control and no particular ability to forecast. Thus, managing that risk, usually in the form of hedging, makes sense. With the risk of these factors under control, they can focus on doing the things they do best.

Summary

In this chapter, we looked at the concept of risk management; that is, the process of determining a firm's desired level of risk, determining the level of risk a firm currently has, and then taking action to ensure that the former is equal to the latter. We looked at some techniques for managing market risk, including delta, gamma, and vega hedging. We also examined the concept of Value at Risk (VAR), which measures the minimum loss expected over a period of time with a given probability. VAR is becoming widely used in the financial world today. We examined some variations of VAR, including Cash Flow at Risk and Earnings at Risk, and extensions such as stress testing.

We also looked at credit risk, noting how credit risk entails elements of option pricing theory. We learned how current credit risk differs from potential credit risk, and we examined some procedures for reducing credit risk, including the netting of payments owed by parties to each other, and the use of credit derivatives to separate and trade credit risk. We looked at various other types of risks, including operational risk, model risk, liquidity risk, accounting risk, legal risk, tax risk, regulatory risk, and settlement risk. From a broader perspective, we discussed systemic risk, which is the risk of a meltdown of the entire financial system.

Virtually all of what we have learned so far has been of an analytical or quantitative nature. We concluded this chapter with a discussion of two approaches to financial risk management, view-driven and needs-driven risk management.

We should recognize that there is a great deal to know about risk management that is not analytical. Risk management is effective only if people and organizations implement these techniques in an appropriate manner and if the organizational infrastructure is conducive to the practice of risk management. In Chapter 16, we conclude this book with a look at the organizational aspects of risk management.

Key Terms

You should be able to give brief definitions of the following terms:

risk management, p. 533
financial risk management, p. 535
market risk, p. 536
Value at Risk (VAR), p. 543
analytical method/variance-covariance method, p. 545
delta normal method, p. 546
historical method, p. 547
Monte Carlo simulation method, p. 548
stress test/Conditional Value at Risk/Cash Flow at Risk/ (CAR), p. 552
Earnings at Risk (EAR)/ credit/default risk, p. 553

Current credit risk/Potential credit risk, p. 555
enhanced derivatives products companies/special purpose vehicles/Netting/bilateral netting/multilateral netting/ payment netting/cross product netting, p. 557
Closeout netting/netting by novation, p. 559
credit derivative/reference entity, p. 560
total return swap, p. 561
credit default swap/credit swap, p. 562

CDS premium, p. 563
credit spread option/credit linked security, p. 564
collateralized debt obligation (CDO)/synthetic CDO, p. 565
Operational risk, p. 567
Model risk/Liquidity risk, p. 568
Accounting risk/Legal risk/ Tax risk/Regulatory risk, p. 569
Settlement risk/Herstatt risk/ systemic risk/View-driven risk management, p. 570
Needs-driven risk management, p. 571

Further Reading

The following references discuss risk management in general:

Chew, L. *Managing Derivatives Risk: The Use and Abuse of Leverage*. New York: Wiley, 1996.

Coleman, T. S. *A Practical Guide to Risk Management*. Charlottesville, VA: Research Foundation of the CFA Institute, 2011.

Field, P., ed., *Modern Risk Management: A History*, London: Risk Books, 2003.

Gastineau, G. L., and M. P. Kritzman. *The Dictionary of Financial Risk Management*, 2nd ed. New Hope, PA: Frank Fabozzi Associates, 1999.

Haslett, W. V. "Bud," ed. *Risk Management: Foundations for a Changing World*. New York: Wiley, 2010.

Jorion, P. *The Financial Risk Manager Handbook: 2001–2002*. New York: Wiley, 2001.

Kolb, R. W. "Risk Management and Risk Transfer: Distributive Justice in Finance." *The Journal of Alternative Investments* 13 (2010): 90–98.

Lewis, M. *The Big Short: Inside the Doomsday Machine*. New York: W. W. Norton, 2010.

Smithson, C. W. *Managing Financial Risk: A Guide to Derivative Products, Financial Engineering, and Value Maximization*, 3rd ed. New York: McGraw-Hill, 1998.

Smithson, C. W. "Quantifying Operational Risk," *Risk* 17 (July 2004): 57.

The following are good references on credit risk and credit derivatives:

Credit Derivatives: Applications for Risk Management, Investment and Portfolio Optimisation. London: Risk Books, 1998.

Credit Risk: Models and Management. London: Risk Books, 1999.

Derivatives Credit Risk: Further Advances in Measurement and Management, 2nd ed. London: Risk Books, 1999.

Saunders, A. *Credit Risk Measurement: New Approaches to Value-at-Risk and Other Paradigms.* New York: Wiley, 1999.

Value at Risk is widely covered in the literature. Following are two excellent books on the topic:

Dowd, K. *Beyond Value at Risk: The New Science of Risk Management.* Chichester, UK: Wiley, 1998.

Jorion, P. *Value at Risk: A New Benchmark for Controlling Derivatives Risk*, 2nd ed. New York:

McGraw-Hill, 2001. The assessment of Value at Risk as an emerging subject is covered in the following articles:

Berkowitz, J., and J. O'Brien. "How Accurate Are Value-at-Risk Models at Commercial Banks?" *Journal of Finance* 57 (2002) 1093–1111.

Kupiec, P. H. "Techniques for Verifying The Accuracy of Risk Measurement Models," *Journal of Derivatives* 3 (2005): 73–84.

Sullivan, J. H., Z. G. Stoumbos, and R. Brooks. "Real-Time Assessment of Value-at-Risk and Volatility Accuracy," *Nonlinear Analysis: Real World Applications*, 2007.

Concepts Checks

1. How is the practice of risk management similar to hedging, and how is it different?
2. Identify why risk management can be beneficial to stockholders.
3. How is market risk different from credit risk. Are techniques for managing market risk appropriate for managing credit risk? Explain.
4. Identify the three parties involved in any credit derivatives transaction and describe how they differ in their roles and responsibilities with regard to the transaction.
5. If a portfolio of derivatives is delta hedged by adding a position in Eurodollar futures, what other forms of market risk might remain? How can these risks be eliminated?
6. What is the general idea behind determining the CDS premium?

Questions and Problems

1. Identify and explain the primary methods of managing credit risk for derivatives dealers.
2. Identify and explain four forms of netting.
3. Interpret the following statements about Value at Risk so that they would be easily understood by a nontechnical corporate executive:
   a. VAR of $1.5 million, one week, probability = 0.01.
   b. VAR of $3.75 million, one year, probability = 0.05.
4. Critique each of the three methods of calculating Value at Risk, giving one advantage and one disadvantage of each.
5. Comment on the current credit risk assumed for each of the following positions. Treat them separately, that is, not combined with any other instruments.
   a. You are short an out-of-the-money interest rate call option.
   b. You entered into a pay fixed-receive floating interest rate swap a year ago. Since that time, interest rates have increased.
   c. You are long an in-the-money currency put option.
   d. You are long a forward contract. During the life of the contract, the price of the underlying asset has decreased below the contract price.
6. Explain how closeout netting reduces the credit risk for two firms engaged in several derivatives contracts.
7. How does the legal system impose risk on a derivatives dealer?
8. Identify and discuss benefits for managing financial risks.
9. Compare and contrast view-driven risk management with needs-driven risk management.
10. Compare and contrast total return swaps, credit default swaps, and interest rate swaps.
11. Consider a firm that has assets that generate cash but which cannot be easily valued on a regular basis. What are the difficulties faced by this firm when using VAR and what alternatives would it have?
12. How is liquidity a source of risk?

13. Explain how the stockholders of a company hold an implicit put option written by the creditors.

14. Identify the five types of credit derivatives and briefly describe how each works.

15. Suppose your firm is a derivatives dealer that has recently created a new product. In addition to market and credit risk, what additional risks does it face that are associated more with new products?

16. Suppose the periodic payments made by a CDS buyer to a CDS seller are worth $1 per $100 notional value of debt per quarter. Explain how this figure is related to the value of the debt and the value of an otherwise equivalent bond that is default-free.

17. Consider a portfolio consisting of $10 million invested in the S&P 500 and $7.5 million invested in U.S. Treasury bonds. The S&P 500 has an expected return of 14 percent and a standard deviation of 16 percent. The Treasury bonds have an expected return of 9 percent and a standard deviation of 8 percent. The correlation between the S&P 500 and the bonds is 0.35. All figures are stated on an annual basis.

   a. Find the VAR for one year at a probability of 0.05. Identify and use the most appropriate method given the information you have.

   b. Using the information you obtained in part a, find the VAR for one day.

18. Calculate the VAR for the following situations:

   a. Use the analytical method and determine the VAR at a probability of 0.05 for a portfolio in which the standard deviation of annual returns is $2.5 million. Assume an expected return of $0.0.

   b. Use the historical method and the following information for the last 120 days of returns to calculate an approximate VAR for a portfolio of $20 million using a probability of 0.05:

Less than −0%	5
−10% to −5%	18
−5% to 0%	42
0% to 5%	36
5% to 10%	15
Greater than 10%	4

19. The following table lists three financial instruments and their deltas, gammas, and vegas for each $1 million notional amount under the assumption of a long position. (Long in a swap or FRA means to pay fixed and receive floating.) Assume that you hold a $12 million notional amount long position in the three-year call option, an $8 million notional amount short position in the three-year swap, and an $11 million notional amount long position in the FRA. Each derivative is based on the 90-day LIBOR.

Instrument	Delta	Gamma	Vega
3-year call option with exercise rate of 0.12	$40	$1,343	$5.02
3-year swap with fixed rate of 0.1125	$152	−$678	$0
2-year FRA with fixed rate of 0.11	$72	−$390	$0

   a. As described above, you have three instruments currently in your portfolio. Determine your current portfolio delta, gamma, and vega. Describe in words the risk properties of your portfolio based on your calculations.

   b. Assume that you have to maintain your current position in the call option but are free to increase or decrease your positions in the swap and FRA and you can add a position in a one-year call with a delta of $62, a gamma of $2,680, and a vega of $2.41. Find the combination of notional amounts that would make your overall position be delta hedged, gamma hedged, and vega hedged.

20. Suppose you own 50,000 shares of stock valued at $35.50 per share. You are interested in protecting it with a put that would have a delta of −0.62. Assume, however, that the put is not available or is unfairly priced. Illustrate how to construct a dynamic hedge using a risk-free debt instrument that would replicate the position of having the put. Ignore the cost of the puts. Show how the hedge works by explaining what happens if the stock falls by one dollar.

21. Company CPN and dealer SwapFin are engaged in three transactions with each other. From SwapFin's perspective, the market values are as follows:

Swap 1	−$2,000,000
Forward 1	+$1,500,000
Option 1	−$ 500,000
	−$1,000,000

Explain the consequences to SwapFin if CPN defaults with and without closeout netting. In your answer, explain what is meant by cherry picking.

22. (Concept Problem) Suppose you enter into a bet with someone in which you pay $5 up front and are allowed to throw a pair of dice. You receive a payoff equal to the total in dollars of the numbers on the two dice. In other words, if you roll a 1 and a 2, your payoff is $3 and your profit is $3 − $5 = −$2. Determine the probability associated with a Value at Risk of $0.

23. (Concept Problem) A company has assets with a market value of $100. It has one outstanding bond issue, a zero coupon bond maturing in two years with a face value of $75. The risk-free rate is 5 percent. The volatility of the asset is 0.30. Determine the market value of the equity and the continuously compounded yield on the bond. (Use the spreadsheet BSMbin9e.xls for calculations.)

CHAPTER 16

Managing Risk in an Organization

In risk management, you're only as good as your weakest link, and unless you have firm discipline across the business, you get yourself into trouble.

Anonymous former senior executive of Lehman Brothers
CFA Magazine, January–February, 2009, p. 33

CHAPTER OBJECTIVES

- Understand the differences in the practice of risk management by dealers and by end users

- Know the principles that lead to an effective risk management organizational structure

- Understand the basic principles of derivatives accounting as set forth in FAS 133

- Examine some of the incidents in which companies have suffered losses using derivatives

- Learn the important points related to the responsibilities of senior management for a company's derivatives and risk management function

In the first 15 chapters, we studied the use of many types of derivatives to manage risk in a variety of situations. We learned what types of contracts are available and the situations for which each is most appropriate. We also learned that derivatives are powerful instruments that have high degrees of leverage. Moreover, some of these instruments are quite complex. Because of these attendant factors, there is another important component of the process of using derivatives for managing risk: effective risk management requires an effective organizational structure. The use of derivatives for managing risk can be dangerous in the absence of proper personnel, teamwork, controls, and organization. Up to now, we have largely focused on the quantitative aspects of risk management. The concerns of this chapter are mostly qualitative. It is easy to neglect these more subjective factors that lead to good risk management, but they are critically important. In fact, all of the quantitative models for and analytical knowledge about risk management would be wasted if an organization could not implement sound risk management policies.

To understand how risk management is best practiced, we must start with a perspective on the risk management industry and the profession of risk management itself. We need to understand the types of organizations that operate in the risk management industry. Then we shall take a look at how the practice of risk management fits into a typical organizational structure. We shall next turn to the very important requirement of properly accounting for risk management. Then we shall take a look at the accepted recommendations for how risk management should be practiced. Knowing that we can learn as much about how to do things well by studying how to do things badly, we shall conclude by looking at what happens when an organization does not practice good risk management.

THE STRUCTURE OF THE RISK MANAGEMENT INDUSTRY

The risk management industry is made up of **end users**, **dealers**, and other firms, including consultants and specialized software companies.

End Users

End users are generally thought of as firms that want to engage in derivatives transactions to manage their risk. Needing to execute a derivatives transaction, end users contact derivatives dealers, whom we shall discuss in the next section. The end user could be thought of as the party who is purchasing a service while the dealer is the supplier of the service.

The end user community primarily consists of nonfinancial corporations. Other end users include investment firms, which include pension plans and mutual funds. In addition, some financial institutions that are not in the business of being derivatives dealers will still use derivatives to manage their risks. At times, even a dealer, managing its own risk, will take the position of an end user opposite another dealer. Many foreign governments use derivatives. In the United States, state and local governments use derivatives, although somewhat less than corporations. With the exception of certain agencies, such as the postal service, however, the U.S. federal government does not use derivatives. Many private organizations, such as charities, endowments, and universities, use derivatives.

> An end user is a corporation, an investment firm, a financial institution, a government, or a private organization that engages in derivatives transactions with a derivatives dealer.

Obviously, there are minimum firm sizes necessary to justify certain derivatives activities, but risks of as little as a few million dollars can justify over-the-counter derivatives, and even smaller sizes can be managed with exchange-traded derivatives. As one might expect, larger firms use derivatives more and have more organized and sophisticated risk management operations.

In a typical corporation, the treasury department has responsibility for managing the firm's cash. It operates in the financial markets on a regular basis, borrowing cash, repaying loans, and wiring funds to and from domestic and foreign offices. If the firm engages in derivatives transactions to manage financial risk, these transactions are typically executed and managed by the treasury department. Normally, a treasury department is a cost center and not a profit center, meaning that its job is to perform a function at the lowest possible cost and not try to earn a profit. In recent years, however, many corporate treasurers, sometimes responding to pressure placed on them by senior management, have begun using derivatives to speculate and turn a profit. Unfortunately, this has put pressure on some companies to speculate in markets they know little about and has led to some excellent examples of bad risk management.

Some derivatives activities are conducted outside of the treasury. For example, a firm might have a commodity purchasing manager who hedges its exposure to commodity prices. Some firms run highly decentralized derivatives activities. They may have numerous subsidiaries, each of which engages in its own hedging. We shall discuss these types of organizational issues later in this chapter.

End users have shown a preference for particular types of derivative instruments for a given type of risk. Forward contracts are preferred for foreign exchange risk, with swaps being the primary instrument for managing interest rate risk, and futures being preferred for commodity price risk. Stock market risk is primarily managed with options, both over-the-counter and exchange-listed.

Dealers

Dealers, as previously noted, are financial institutions making markets in derivatives. These institutions include banks and numerous investment banking/brokerage firms. They quote prices indicating their willingness to take either side of derivatives transactions. These prices, as we noted previously, are stated in terms of a bid price and an ask price, with the price they are asking being higher than the price they are bidding.

A derivatives dealer is a firm that is in the business of offering to take either side of a derivatives transaction with an end user. The dealer usually hedges its risk and earns a profit from the difference in the prices it bids and offers.

Dealers will not naturally have offsetting positions. Any risk that remains is usually hedged by taking on new and offsetting derivatives, which may be in the form of exchange-traded or over-the-counter contracts. Thus, the dealer is not exposed to market movements and earns a profit off the spread between its buying and selling prices.

Most dealer firms have highly sophisticated derivatives operations. They employ individuals with training in finance, economics, mathematics, physics, computer science, and engineering. Many of their technically trained personnel design new derivatives and risk management strategies and determine how to price them. Dealers also employ sales personnel who call on potential end users, examine their risk management needs, and try to convince the end users to engage in transactions with the dealers. Dealers generally make large investments in computer hardware and software for managing their derivatives positions. Derivatives activities have been a tremendous source of profits for many dealers.

Other Participants in the Risk Management Industry

The growth in risk management has created an industry of firms providing consulting and software services. Consulting services include general risk management consulting, legal and accounting/auditing, and personnel search. The specialized knowledge required to program computers, understand the emerging derivatives law, provide proper accounting and auditing functions, and search for specialized technical personnel has led to profitable opportunities for individuals and firms with these skills.

ORGANIZING THE RISK MANAGEMENT FUNCTION IN A COMPANY

The quality of an organization always starts at the top. This means that senior management and the board of directors must take the initiative for being knowledgeable and aware of the derivatives activities the firm engages in. This does not mean that they must be experts in derivatives, but they should be able to define each of the instruments used by the firm and should know why the firm uses them. Most importantly, they must establish written policies and procedures governing the use of derivatives. These policies must specify a rationale for the use of derivatives, define the circumstances under which derivatives can be used, authorize the appropriate personnel to execute transactions, define trading limits, establish control procedures to ensure that all policies are followed, and address the issue of how the performance of a derivatives/risk management operation will be evaluated.

Senior management is particularly responsible for ensuring that competent personnel with sufficient technical knowledge are employed by the firm when such skills are needed. They must also authorize the expenditure of funds for the necessary hardware and software.

But in order to do these things well, an organization must have a structure conducive to the proper practice of risk management. Risk management can be practiced differently depending on whether the organization is a dealer or an end user.

A dealer organization, which is in the derivatives business to earn a profit, will engage in numerous transactions and naturally should practice risk management at the centralized firmwide level. If there are relationships between movements in interest rates, stock prices, and foreign exchange rates, and there nearly always are, it would be unwise to have separate risk managers monitoring the performance of the bond department, the equities department, and the various international operations. Rather, most dealers have opted for a single risk manager, who often reports to the chief executive officer. The risk manager should have access to all of the necessary financial and statistical information and should have the authority to stop traders from trading and/or force them to unwind positions. It should not be possible for traders or derivatives sales personnel to influence the risk manager. Some dealers use a risk management committee, but in either case, the risk manager's or the committee's responsibility is usually to senior management. In any case, *independent risk management is probably the most important requirement for an effective risk management system.*

> One of the most important organizational considerations in risk management is to have an independent risk management function, meaning that the risk manager has access to necessary information, the authority to take corrective action, and immunity from the influence of traders and sales personnel.

A corporate or end user risk management function can be surprisingly decentralized. Some firms may have purchasing departments that hedge purchases of raw materials. Many firms will have foreign subsidiaries that hedge their own operations. Most corporations delegate domestic interest rate hedging to the treasury department. The treasury's normal responsibility is managing cash and bank loans. In recent years, many corporations have begun to centralize their risk management activities, focusing on risk management of the firm as a whole. This enables the firm to allow certain natural hedges to work. For example, a firm might be exposed long to German interest rates in one division and short in another. If each division hedges separately, unnecessary transactions are done. A centralized risk management function would determine that the risks of two divisions are at least partially offsetting.

MAKING THE CONNECTION

Professional Organizations in Risk Management: GARP and PRMIA

Financial risk management is an excellent career choice, but a difficult career to get into. As usual, experience is important, because few people can go right into a financial risk management position out of school. There are a number of schools with graduate programs in financial risk management or related aspects of financial risk management. The most important requirements, however, are a keen analytical mind, a willingness to work long hours, and a solid understanding of how financial markets work. Financial risk management jobs are found in virtually every medium-to-large bank, many large corporations, and even some nonprofit organizations and government agencies.

Practitioners of financial risk management have formed two professional organizations, the Global Association of Risk Professionals, known as GARP, and the Professional Risk Managers' International Association, known as PRMIA.

As of this writing, GARP (www.garp.org) has about 150,000 members from approximately 195 countries

around the world. GARP's corporate mission is stated as follows:

The Global Association of Risk Professionals (GARP) is a not-for-profit organization and is the only globally recognized membership association for risk managers. GARP's mission goal is to help create a culture of risk awareness within organizations, from entry level to board level. In the areas of financial and energy risk management, GARP sets the global standard in professional designation with the FRM® (Financial Risk Manager) and ERP® (Energy Risk Professional) certifications. Through trusted education and training, media, and events, GARP promotes best practices in risk management and supports ongoing professional and career development for risk managers.

GARP is governed by a group of about 20 trustees and an executive committee of seven. GARP has 57 professional chapters in 40 countries. The chapters conduct meetings that typically include outside speakers.

GARP also holds national and international meetings and conventions. There are several levels of membership, each providing different privileges and having different levels of dues. The highest level of membership costs $195. A student membership is $95. GARP's primary focus is its professional certification programs, including the Financial Risk Manager (FRM) exam, a two-part examination. Part I of the FRM exam consists of about 100 multiple choice questions covering the following:

- Financial Markets and Products
- Foundations of Risk Management
- Quantitative Analysis
- Valuation and Risk Models

Part II of the FRM exam consists of about 80 multiple choice questions covering the following:

- Market Risk
- Credit Risk
- Operational Risk
- Risk Management and Investment Management
- Current Issues in Financial Markets

The second organization, PRMIA (www.prmia.org), consists of about 80,000 members from around 200 countries as of November 2011. PRMIA's objectives are stated as follows:

PRMIA's mission is to provide a free and open forum for the promotion of sound risk management standards and practices globally. To accomplish this our mission, PRMIA's objectives are:

- *To be a leader of industry opinion and a proponent for the risk management profession*
- *Drive the integration of practice and theory and certifying the credentials of professional risk managers*

- *Connect practitioners, researchers, students and others interested in the field of risk management*
- *Be global in focus, promoting cross-cultural ethical standards, serving emerging as well as more developed markets*
- *Work with other professional associations in furtherance of the PRMIA's mission*

PRMIA is governed by a nine-person board of directors, an advisory panel, and various other committees. PRMIA has about 60 chapters worldwide. Like GARP, PRMIA conducts meetings, conferences, and conventions. PRMIA currently assesses no dues, receiving support from sponsoring organizations. PRMIA also conducts its own certification exam called the Professional Risk Manager (PRM) exam. Four different exams must be passed to achieve the PRM designation:

- Finance Theory, Financial Instruments and Markets
- Mathematical Foundations of Risk Measurement
- Risk Management Practices
- Case Studies, PRMIA Standards of Best Practice, Conduct and Ethics, Bylaws

The test is computerized, so results are known immediately. PRMIA has arranged for the exam to be offered in more than 140 countries worldwide. PRMIA quotes the recent pass rate as just over 50 percent. The cost is $195 for each exam, but discounts are available if more than one exam is taken on a given day. The maximum cost is $500 if the candidate takes all four exams in one sitting. PRMIA provides a recommended reading list and sample questions.

There are no clear advantages to one organization or exam over another. Anyone pursuing a career should be a member of one organization, if not both. Student membership is highly encouraged.

Many corporations unfortunately do not provide for an independent risk management function. As previously noted, they sometimes operate their treasury department as a profit center. Instead of attempting to simply manage the firm's cash and bank loans efficiently, treasurers sometimes start trading in the derivatives markets with the objective of earning a profit. It is not reasonable to expect that they can do this effectively over the long run, and unfortunately for some firms, the long run came early in the form of large derivatives losses.

Derivatives dealers have two distinct groups of derivatives specialists. One group is the sales personnel, who call on clients, analyze the clients' risks, and offer the dealer's products and services for the purpose of managing the clients' risks. The other group is made up of traders who execute derivatives transactions for the dealer. Most dealers also have research departments, normally made up of technically trained personnel who conduct research, design and price new products, and provide support for sales personnel and traders.

> A typical dealership operation is divided into two groups: the front office, meaning the trading function, and the back office, meaning the clerical, record-keeping function. Effective risk management requires that these two functions be separate.

Most corporations do not have research departments but may have a few individuals on the staff with trading experience and a high degree of technical expertise.

The derivatives operations of dealers are typically segregated into what are called the **front office** and **back office**. Some firms have an additional layer between the front office and back office, which is naturally called the **middle office**. The front office consists of the traders and their assistants. The back office personnel are the clerks and operations officers whose job is to process the paperwork and generate the necessary reports. It is considered critical by nearly every dealer that the front and back office functions be separate. If they are not, as we shall see later in this chapter in the example of the failure of Barings Bank, the proverbial "fox is guarding the chicken coop." In some firms, the back office may be the only control mechanism. While this is not the optimal structure, at the very least, the back office should not have to report to the front office or feel any pressure from it. The middle office is typically where trade monitoring and risk management is conducted.

All firms should also have a legal department or have access to external legal counsel. The attorneys are responsible for ensuring that all contracts are properly documented and conform to appropriate laws.

Within most firms there is an individual called a compliance officer who is responsible for ensuring that all internal and external regulations are followed.

The accounting function is an important one in all organizations. Although an accounting system is not the same as a risk management system, the two must not be inconsistent. An accounting system also provides for periodic auditing, but does not substitute for risk management. Auditing simply determines whether the financial records have been kept in conformance with the policies established by the accounting profession and the firm. Auditing is a periodic process. Risk management is a continuous process requiring far more than checking financial entries.

Any firm that engages in derivatives and risk management activities should provide for regular evaluation of its performance. It should define its objectives and establish a system that will provide timely and unbiased assessments of the quality of its activities. This is not a simple task because objective performance evaluation is quite difficult to do, but this issue must be addressed nonetheless.

Although there are many effective variations, Figures 16.1 and 16.2 illustrate examples of a derivatives/risk management operation for a dealer and for a corporate end user.

FIGURE 16.1 Example of a Derivatives/Risk Management Operation for a Dealer

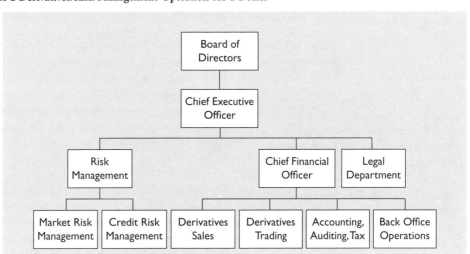

FIGURE 16.2 Example of a Derivatives/Risk Management Operation for a Corporate End User

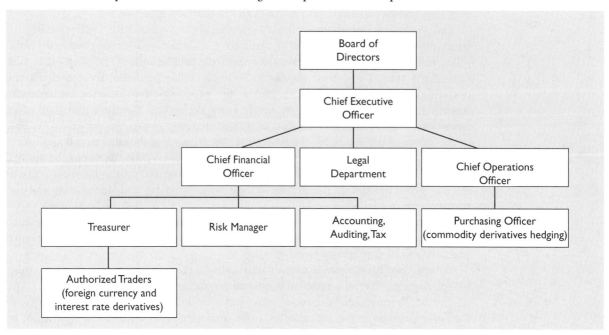

The dealer operation is centralized with an independent risk manager reporting to the chief executive officer. The corporate structure shown here is a little less centralized with derivatives activities undertaken by both a purchasing officer and the treasurer. This firm has established a risk management function that reports to the treasury. It is unlikely, however, that the risk manager has sufficient information to monitor the purchasing officer's hedging transactions or the authority to do much about it if policies are not followed or problems occur.

A new trend in organizing the risk management function within a company is the principle of **enterprise risk management**. Enterprise risk management, sometimes known as firmwide risk management, is a process in which risk is managed in a centralized manner, but in which all risks are integrated into a single function. As an example, many companies integrate their interest rate and currency risk management so that these functions are in the same area of responsibility. A firm still faces other financial risks, which might include exposure to commodity prices and even exposure to equity prices, the latter primarily in its pension fund. An integrated risk management function would bring the management of these risks under control of a single risk management function.

A true enterprise risk management system, however, would consolidate the management of other types of risks. For example, most firms spend a considerable amount of money on insurance, but the management of risks covered by traditional insurance policies is typically done in a separate function. Many risks are managed internally by efforts to avoid the exposure. For example, the risk of fire and dangerous factory work is minimized by using safety precautions. A true enterprise risk management function would bring the management of all types of risks under the same area of responsibility. In fact, the insurance industry is moving into offering financial risk management products. In some cases, financial

Enterprise risk management is a process in which a firm controls all of its risks in a centralized, integrated manner. These risks include not only its traditional financial risks, such as interest rate and foreign currency risks, but also risks traditionally managed by the use of insurance policies and other means.

derivatives are combined with insurance contracts to truly integrate the management of these diverse and seemingly unrelated risks.

RISK MANAGEMENT ACCOUNTING

One of the most controversial issues in the risk management world is the proper accounting treatment of derivatives transactions. Because of the unusual characteristics of many derivatives and the relative newness of many of these instruments, the accounting profession has not, until recent years, begun to catch up with the derivatives world. For many years, derivatives were off-balance-sheet items, meaning that it was difficult, if not impossible, to determine from traditional financial statements what types of derivatives were being used and the effects of those derivative transactions on earnings. Much of the problem stems from the fact that the most widely used and accepted application of derivatives, hedging, leads to considerable complications in accounting. Hedges often generate cash losses and gains, while the transactions they are designed to hedge generate only paper gains and losses. If derivative gains and losses are realized and reflected in income statements while gains and losses on the transactions they are designed to hedge are not realized until later, a hedge, which is designed to reduce volatility, will give the appearance through accounting statements of an increase in volatility.

> Hedge accounting is a method of accounting for derivatives transactions such that gains and losses on the derivatives are tied to gains and losses on the instruments being hedged.

One solution to the problem is to use **hedge accounting**. Hedge accounting permits the firm to defer the gains and losses on the derivative until later when the hedge is completed. For example, a firm that holds a stock and hedges its future sale with a derivative would not recognize the derivative gains and losses until the security is actually sold. Unfortunately, hedge accounting can lead to abuses that mislead users of financial statements. For example, suppose a firm plans to borrow money at a later date. It enters into a derivative to hedge any increase in interest rates. Suppose it incurs a gain on the derivative resulting from an increase in interest rates. Then suppose it ultimately decides not to borrow the money. It records a profit on the derivative and does not take out the loan. Had it incurred a loss on the derivative, it might well have gone ahead and borrowed, imbedding the derivatives loss in the higher interest rate on the loan. Was this even a hedge? Probably not because there was clearly no firm commitment to borrow. Yet hedge accounting was used.

Swaps, forwards, and futures pose an interesting issue in derivatives accounting. They have a zero value at the start and yet gain and lose value as the underlying moves. As the derivative gains value, it effectively becomes an asset; as it loses value, it effectively becomes a liability. Should that asset/liability be shown on the balance sheet? The practice of good accounting suggests that it should. But how?

In the United States, the appropriate methods for accounting are established by the Financial Accounting Standards Board (FASB). A worldwide organization, the International Accounting Standards Board (IASB) attempts to coordinate and standardize accounting principles across countries. Neither of these bodies has any legal authority. They simply represent efforts on the part of the accounting profession to establish acceptable norms. Auditors' reports must indicate whether established accounting norms have been followed. For publicly traded companies, the securities regulators, such as the Securities and Exchange Commission in the United States, require certain standards and prohibit misleading information in accounting statements. Thus, while accounting standards technically carry no legal weight, they effectively constitute a rule of law.

In 1996, the FASB undertook a project to study and establish standards for accounting for derivatives. This culminated in the release in 1998 of Financial Accounting Standard 133, called **FAS 133**, *Accounting for Derivative Instruments and Hedging Activities*.

This controversial document has undergone much scrutiny and criticism but has survived and appears to be the norm to which derivatives accounting will conform. Here we shall look at the important elements of FAS 133, which went into effect for most firms in June 2000. FAS 133 has been amended several times with FAS 137, 138, 149, 155, and 161. The International Accounting Standards Board adopted a similar document, IAS 39, which is somewhat broader in that it applies to all financial assets and liabilities while FAS 133 applies only to derivatives. IAS 39 was adopted in 2001 and implemented in January 2005.

FAS 133 basically takes the position that all derivatives transactions must be marked to market, meaning that the gains and losses incurred from derivatives transactions over the accounting period are determined, regardless of whether the derivative transaction has been terminated, and reported in financial statements. In addition, derivatives must appear on the balance sheet as assets and liabilities. But first, FAS 133 had to define what a derivative is.

> FAS 133 is the policy of the U.S. Financial Accounting Standards Board that specifies appropriate procedures for accounting for derivatives.

Under FAS 133 a derivative has one or more underlyings and one or more notional amounts, which combine to determine the settlement or payoff. It must require either no initial outlay or an outlay that is smaller than would be required for other contracts with similar payoffs. In addition it requires a net settlement or physical delivery of the underlying.

FAS 133 permits some exceptions to the rule. For example, purchases of assets on time are not derivatives. The purchases of assets with payment to occur very shortly are not derivatives. Insurance is not a derivative. Options used in executive compensation are not derivatives, at least not with respect to the regulations prescribed by FAS 133; these instruments do, however, have their own accounting requirements. Certain embedded derivatives may or may not be derivatives. For example, interest-only and principal-only strips are not generally derivatives, but options imbedded in certain floating-rate securities may be considered derivatives and, therefore, may have to be separated and conform to FAS 133.

FAS 133 classifies all derivatives transactions into one of four categories: fair value hedges, cash flow hedges, net investment in foreign currency operations, and speculation.

Fair Value Hedges

A **fair value hedge** is a transaction in which a firm hedges the market value of a position in an asset or a liability. The gain or loss on the derivative is recorded and reflected in current earnings. In addition, the asset or liability is marked to market and its gain or loss is also reflected in current earnings.

> A fair value hedge is one in which the derivative and the instrument being hedged are both marked to market and gains and losses on both are recorded in current income.

For example, a firm holds a security and enters into a derivative transaction to hedge the future sale of the security. At the end of the quarter, the firm is preparing its financial statements and the hedge is still in place. Let us say that there is a loss in value of the security of $100,000. Its derivative, however, incurs a gain of $96,000. It records the following accounting entries:

Debit Derivative (for example, swap, futures)	$96,000
Credit Unrealized Gain on Derivative	$96,000
Debit Unrealized Loss on Security	$100,000
Credit Security	$100,000

Remember that debits increase and credits decrease assets, and debits decrease and credits increase liabilities and capital. Credits increase and debits decrease income. Thus, in the first entry, an asset account (the derivative) is increased and income (the unrealized gain) is increased. In the second entry, income is decreased (the unrealized loss) and an asset (the security) is decreased. The net effect is that both income and assets are decreased by $4,000.

If the hedge is effective, it will have little effect on income and, therefore, on earnings. Otherwise, earnings will fluctuate. Hence, effective and ineffective hedging will be properly reflected in earnings.

To qualify for fair value accounting, firms must maintain proper documentation of every transaction and the hedge must be expected to be effective. The sale of options, however, is ordinarily not eligible for fair value accounting. In addition, bonds that are expected to be held to maturity are not eligible for hedge accounting. Certain anticipated transactions, however, can be eligible for hedge accounting, although many of these will fall under the following category.

Cash Flow Hedges

In a **cash flow hedge**, the risk of a future cash flow is hedged with a derivative. A classic example is a firm planning to take out a loan. It might sell Eurodollar futures or buy an FRA to hedge the risk of an increase in interest rates. Cash flow hedging is somewhat more complicated than fair value hedging and must meet a more stringent requirement.

In a cash flow hedge, the firm marks the derivative to market, thereby recognizing the gain or loss in its value. The derivative will then show up on the balance sheet at its current market value. The firm then records that gain or loss in a separate category called Other Comprehensive Income, or OCI. OCI is not an ordinary income account; it is actually a temporary capital account and appears next to equity in the balance sheet. Thus, gains and losses on derivatives go into capital. Then at the hedge termination date, the underlying transaction, such as the firm taking out a loan, is completed. Then the derivative is removed from the books, and the amount recorded to OCI is moved from OCI; this amount is then used to adjust the value of the underlying transactions as well as the earnings. Thus, derivatives gains and losses do not affect income while the hedge is in place, but instead show up in this temporary holding account, OCI, that appears as a part of capital. Ultimately, the transaction the derivative is designed to hedge is undertaken, and the derivatives gain or loss is moved to income as well as to the underlying transaction. In addition, cash flow hedge accounting requires a separation of a hedge's results into "effective" and "ineffective" components. Most hedging instruments do not exactly match the risk exposure; hence, some portion of the derivative hedge will not match the risk exposure. This slippage is designated ineffective and can be required to be treated as speculation if it is outside a reasonable range, a point we will discuss later.

Let us consider an example of a loan that the firm anticipates. Suppose that six months from now, the firm plans to issue a $1,000,000 one-year zero coupon note. It buys an FRA to hedge against rising interest rates. While the hedge is in place, interest rates go down and the FRA incurs a loss of $10,000. Later, the FRA expires with a loss of $12,000 and the note is issued. The firm issues the note at 7 percent for one year, thereby generating an initial cash inflow of $(1 - 0.07)\$1,000,000 = \$930,000$. With cash flow hedging, there would be an interim transaction of

Debit Other Comprehensive Income	$10,000
Credit FRA	$10,000

with the FRA showing up as a liability. When the loan is taken out, the transactions are

Debit Cash	$930,000
Credit Notes Payable	$930,000
Debit FRA	$10,000
Debit Other Comprehensive Income	$2,000
Credit Cash	$12,000
Debit Notes Payable	$12,000
Credit Other Comprehensive Income	$12,000

The first entry reflects the fact that a note was issued for $930,000 and cash was received. In the second entry, the FRA is removed from the books as a liability and a further $2,000 loss is recorded in Other Comprehensive Income. Cash of $12,000 is expended to cover the payout on the FRA. In the third entry, Other Comprehensive Income is closed out and the note balance is reduced from $930,000 to $918,000. In other words, we have now effectively borrowed $918,000 and will later owe $1 million.

Suppose, however, that this were not a perfect hedge. Assume that at the interim period, the loss was $11,000 but the effective part of the loss was $10,000. Thus, there is an ineffective part of the hedge that resulted in a loss of $1,000. We would record the following entry:

Debit Current Income	$1,000
Debit Other Comprehensive Income	$10,000
Credit FRA	$11,000

At expiration, let us say that the cumulative loss on the FRA is $15,000 and of that amount, $12,000 is effective and $3,000 is ineffective. The first entry above for the $930,000 note is the same. The next two entries become:

Debit FRA	$11,000
Credit Other Comprehensive Income	$11,000
Debit Current Income	$2,000
Debit Other Comprehensive Income	$1,000
Debit Notes Payable	$12,000
Credit Cash	$15,000

The first entry above removes the FRA from liabilities and removes all but $1,000 of the Other Comprehensive Income account. The third entry closes out Other Comprehensive Income and reduces Current Income by $2,000. Notes Payable will go from $930,000 to $918,000, reflecting the loss of $12,000 as the effective part of the hedge. The ineffective part is $2,000, which goes into Current Income and combines with the $1,000 previously added to Current Income in the earlier entry to reflect a $3,000 loss for the ineffective part of the hedge.

As noted, cash flow hedging requires a separation of the effective and ineffective parts of hedging. The effective part is deferred and carried in the equity account, whereas the ineffective part must be recorded immediately into income. The FASB has not prescribed

A cash flow hedge is one in which a future cash flow is hedged. Derivatives are marked to market and gains and losses are recorded to a temporary capital account until the hedge is completed. Hedging gains and losses must be separated into effective and ineffective components.

precisely how the effective and ineffective components are to be separated. Rough rules of thumb have emerged suggesting that an effective hedge is one in which 80 to 125 percent of the gain or loss on the hedged instrument is matched with a gain or loss on the derivative. Nonetheless, the rules are still murky here and cash flow accounting remains somewhat more difficult to use, even though a firm may have no choice in whether it has to use it. In particular, futures, where maturities do not line up perfectly with hedge termination dates, are more likely to be ineffective hedges—at least by FASB rules—and, therefore, could lead to more volatile earnings.

As with fair value hedges, cash flow hedges must be well documented at the start and must be expected to be effective, and firms must specify how they will determine the hedge's effectiveness. Anticipated transactions must be highly likely to occur, and the details of the transaction must be spelled out quite specifically. Generally, written options do not qualify.

Foreign Investment Hedges

Foreign currency hedging had already been treated in Statement of Financial Accounting Standard 52 (SFAS 52), a document released a number of years prior to the release of FAS 133. The primary rules in SFAS 52 were retained. Firms often hedge anticipated currency transactions as well as currency translations of their foreign operations. Currency translations of their foreign operations are an accounting entry to reflect the influence of changes in foreign exchange rates on foreign subsidiaries. These hedges are permitted and qualify for hedge accounting if certain conditions are met. Those conditions are similar to those we previously identified. The hedges must be documented and expected to be effective. Measurement criteria for effectiveness must be clearly specified. Foreign currency hedges not designed to hedge translation can still qualify for fair value or cash flow accounting under the criteria listed above.

Speculation

Trades that do not qualify for fair value, cash flow, or foreign currency hedge accounting must be considered speculation. Derivatives are marked to market, and gains and losses are recorded in current income with no offsetting adjustments to any other accounts.

Some Problems in the Application of FAS 133

FAS 133 made substantial progress in clearing up a great deal of confusion over the proper accounting for derivatives. Nonetheless, it left some problems unresolved and generated some lingering concerns.

For example, FAS 133 does not prescribe what constitutes effective hedging. Thus, there is some fear that restatements of earnings will be required if later it is determined that the effectiveness test used by a firm is not acceptable. FAS 133 also requires that some embedded derivatives be stripped out and valued. This can be extremely complex and is subject to a wide margin of error. FAS 133 does not permit hedge accounting for bonds designed to be held to maturity. It reflects the all-too-common and naive view that as long as a bond is to be held to maturity, any losses in value are ultimately recouped. This ruling overlooks the opportunity cost of holding a bond in an environment of higher interest rates. It reflects, not surprisingly, an accounting view of a transaction rather than an economic view. Under FAS 133, valuation of derivative instruments and the corresponding hedged instrument is critical. Although we have placed a great deal of emphasis on valuation in this book, it is not a simple task for a firm to obtain a reliable value for a derivative or for the hedged instrument. Nonetheless, if FAS 133 forces firms to pay more attention to the market values of their derivatives and their hedged instruments, it probably serves a good purpose.

FAS 133 does not permit macro hedges. In a macro hedge, a firm takes all of its positions into account and hedges the net exposure. For example, a firm could have exposures to a variety of asset classes. Due to correlations among those asset classes, there may be considerable risk reduction. The firm may then choose to hedge only the remaining risk. Yet, such hedges will no longer qualify for hedge accounting. Hedges must be transaction specific.

Disclosure

The U.S. Securities and Exchange Commission requires that publicly traded firms provide qualitative and quantitative disclosures of their derivatives and risk management activities.

Closely related to the issue of accounting for derivatives is the matter of how much information about a firm's use of derivatives is disclosed in annual reports and 10-Ks. In 1997, the U.S. Securities and Exchange Commission ordered that large firms and banks would be required to provide more disclosure of their accounting policies with respect to derivatives; more quantitative and qualitative information about their market risk; and more information about instruments used, positions taken, commitments, and expected transactions. Companies must categorize their derivatives into one of two categories: trading, meaning essentially speculative, and non-trading, meaning essentially hedging.

For their quantitative disclosure, companies must present (1) tabular information on the market values of their derivatives and relevant contract terms categorized by expiration date, (2) sensitivity analysis of potential losses, or (3) the Value at Risk. For their qualitative disclosure, companies must identify their primary exposures and how they manage those exposures.

The SEC's disclosure requirements have been controversial, requiring that firms reveal information that could be useful to competitors. Moreover, the requirement that firms reveal their financial risks and how they manage them overlooks the fact that firms face a variety of nonfinancial risks, which they are not required to disclose. For example, an airline faces the risk of a crash, resulting in catastrophic human and financial loss. Yet, it is not required to disclose how it manages that risk or what the effect of a crash would be on its VAR. Such rules have the potential to penalize users who are prudently managing their financial risks.

Avoiding Derivatives Losses

As we have seen throughout this book, derivatives are highly efficient instruments that can be used to manage risk. Nonetheless, part of the price we pay for such instruments is that they are highly leveraged and can be easily misused. Because every derivative generates a gain that is matched by a loss on the other side of the transaction, someone must lose money. In some cases, those losses have been large and surprising to those who incurred the losses. Large losses also tend to make for good headlines, and consequently, many firms have found themselves embarrassingly portrayed on the front pages of newspapers. The losses have ranged from small amounts to almost unbelievably large sums of money. The types of organizations and derivatives used have run the gamut. Fortunately, the incidence of losses, which seemed to peak around 1994, has decreased in recent years. We now take a look in more detail at four of the most celebrated stories of derivatives losses.

Metallgesellschaft: To Hedge or Not to Hedge?

Our proposed risk management program not only protects the pump profit margins with a minimum amount of risk from the spot market, but also offers us an opportunity for extraordinary upside profit with no additional risk.

Metallgesellschaft's Business Plan
Quoted in Antonio S. Mello and John E. Parsons
"Maturity Structure of a Hedge Matters:
Lessons from the Metallgesellschaft Debacle"
Working Paper, February 1995, Columbia University

The industrial firm Metallgesellschaft A.G. (MG) was the fourteenth largest corporation in Germany in 1993. Founded in 1883, it employed 58,000 people, had 251 subsidiaries worldwide, and was engaged in a variety of businesses primarily related to mining, metals, and energy products. In late 1993 and early 1994, it incurred losses in futures trading totaling about $1.3 billion, which was approximately one-half of its capital at that time. The losses were all the more remarkable due to the fact that MG had traded futures successfully for many years. Although the firm was saved by a $1.9 billion bailout by a consortium of banks, the affair has raised concerns on several counts. If an extremely experienced firm can be nearly bankrupted by trading derivatives, how can less experienced firms expect to use them successfully? And if losses of that size can be generated trading on the highly regulated exchange-listed futures markets, how dangerous can the unregulated over-the-counter markets be? MG's loss was all the more remarkable due to the fact that *it was designed to be a hedge.* Or was it?

The troubles were caused by a U.S. subsidiary of MG called MG Refining and Marketing (MGRM). In 1992, MGRM developed a marketing strategy whereby it would offer to U.S. firms long-term fixed-price purchase contracts on gasoline, heating oil, and diesel fuel. MGRM's customers were able to lock in their purchase prices for up to ten years provided they agreed to buy from MGRM. These transactions were forward contracts at prices $3 to $5 per barrel lower than the spot prices at that time. Because MGRM was committed to delivering the products at expiration, it was short in the forward markets for these various energy products.

To hedge its risk, MGRM entered into long futures contracts on the New York Mercantile Exchange. Its futures hedges accounted for about 40 percent of its commitment, while over-the-counter derivatives contracts covered about 60 percent. Recognizing the illiquidity of all but the shortest futures contracts, MGRM hedged its position primarily in the shortest-term futures contracts for unleaded gasoline, heating oil, and crude oil. Its over-the-counter contracts were also short-term. MGRM also entered into a contract with a partially owned U.S. firm, Castle Energy, to purchase all of Castle's output at fixed margins for up to ten years.

By late 1993, MGRM was long futures contracts for 55 million barrels of various energy products and had swaps in place to purchase at least another 100 million barrels. These quantities were almost precisely the amount of its forward commitments to its customers. In other words, MGRM used what we described in Chapter 10 as "a naive hedge ratio" of one-to-one.

As we have learned, however, a one-to-one hedge ratio is rarely appropriate. If the hedged instrument moves more or less than the hedging instrument, the position may be underhedged or overhedged. Also, because the hedging instruments, futures, had a short maturity, they had to be rolled over as each contract expired. MGRM simply settled up expiring contracts and purchased the next shortest maturity contract. This strategy, called a stack hedge or stack-and-roll hedge, works successfully provided that the markets are in backwardation, meaning, as we covered in Chapter 9, that the more distant futures price was lower than the spot or nearby futures price. Energy markets are often in backwardation, a result of the convenience yield, a concept we also previously covered. We emphasize that while energy markets are *often* in backwardation, they can convert to contango without much notice and that is precisely what they did.

In late 1993, energy prices began falling and over the course of that year fell by almost a third. MGRM's long futures positions began incurring losses, resulting in large margin calls. While the firm was theoretically gaining on its fixed supply contracts, those gains would not be realized until the oil was delivered. As we noted, the delivery commitments were spread out up to ten years in the future. The company's realized losses drained its cash, and its paper gains produced no cash to offset. Soon the company was staggering under the weight of these huge losses. The parent company had to make a decision about unwinding its position or continuing to fund the account. It chose to unwind. In retrospect, that was the worst thing it could have done. In less than six months, energy prices recovered all of their lost ground, meaning that MGRM's now unhedged short forward delivery contracts incurred further losses.

As we noted in the first paragraph of this story, the parent company was bailed out by a consortium of banks, some of which were on its board of directors. The chairman of MG and the head of MGRM's U.S. oil trading operation were both fired and filed suits for conspiracy and defamation against their former employers. MG ultimately reported a loss of over $1.7 billion for its fiscal year ending September 30, 1994.

It is not clear exactly why MGRM's hedge was so poorly balanced. Some experts suggest that MGRM was speculating and knew exactly what it was doing. Others say that MGRM had an effective hedge in place and could have produced the cash to meet its margin calls without liquidating its futures contracts, which, in hindsight, would have recouped its losses less than a year later. The CFTC, exercising a rarely used and somewhat controversial authority, fined MGRM $2.2 million for failing to exercise adequate internal controls and ordered it to demonstrate in the future that such controls were in place.

Orange County, California: Playing the Odds

I am one of the largest investors in America. I know these things.

Robert Citron
Quoted in Philippe Jorion
Big Bets Gone Bad, Academic Press, 1996

Due to my inexperience, I placed a great deal of reliance on the advice of market professionals.... I wish I had more training in complex government securities.

Robert Citron
Testimony before Senate Special Committee
on Local Government Investments, January 17, 1995
Quoted in *Risk,* March 1995

Orange County, California, is one of the wealthiest communities in the United States. Home to Disneyland, the California Angels, and John Wayne Airport, it reported a loss of $1.6 billion in its investment account in 1994 and declared the largest municipal bankruptcy in U.S. history. How this could have happened is not at all a mystery. Orange County's treasurer, Robert Citron, was engaged in a clever investment scheme that turned a low-risk essentially money market fund into a turbo-charged investment account.

The 69-year-old Citron, with 24 years' experience as the county treasurer, operated a fund that invested in short-term, fixed-income securities. The fund not only invested

Orange County funds but also accepted the funds of almost 200 other municipal governments in California. How it did this is not surprising. The Orange County fund had been earning 300 to 400 basis points above the returns earned on a similar fund operated by the state of California. The Orange County fund's market value was almost $7.5 billion. In June 1994, Citron was reelected county treasurer in spite of warnings by his opponent that the portfolio was excessively leveraged.

By late 1994, a series of sharp increases in interest rates, triggered by the Federal Reserve's efforts to control inflation, brought the value of the fund down by a staggering $2 billion. Orange County was forced to declare bankruptcy. Citron and his chief investment officer were arrested. Citron declared that he had been tricked by his brokerage firm, Merrill Lynch, into making these investments, about which he now stated that he knew little. Orange County went into reorganization, cut services drastically, laid off employees, and filed a $3 billion lawsuit against Merrill Lynch.

It did not take long to determine what had gone wrong. Citron had used leverage to purchase additional government securities through reverse repurchase agreements. Recall from Chapter 9 that we introduced the concept of a repurchase agreement. Let us say that another municipality gives Mr. Citron $100 million to invest. Citron purchases intermediate-term U.S. Treasury notes, which have an average maturity of about 4 years and a duration of about 3.5 years. Citron then executes a reverse repurchase agreement with a securities dealer or bank, pledging the $100 million of securities for a loan of almost $100 million, let us say $90 million. He then uses the $90 million to purchase additional similar securities. This can be done several times with the same money. Ultimately, Citron had leveraged the county about threefold, bringing its total invested funds to about $20 billion while its total equity was only about $7 billion. This tripled its duration. Thus, what should have been a fairly low-risk, short- to intermediate-term fund had the risk of a fund of long-term bonds. When bankruptcy was declared and Citron's strategy was revealed, it should have come as no surprise. *The Wall Street Journal* had reported as early as April 1994 that Citron had leveraged the portfolio almost threefold. It was noted that one municipality withdrew about $4 million at that time because it considered the fund too risky. This probably proved to be the best decision of that treasurer's career.

As in any leveraged bond investment, the results are quite good when interest rates are falling. When the 1994 interest rate increases caused the fund to have a series of huge margin calls from their broker, Orange County began dipping into its cash reserves. When it could no longer generate enough cash to meet its margin calls, its lenders began selling the collateral, which amounted to about $10 billion. This sent shock waves into the bond market, and prices tumbled.

It should be noted that the word *derivatives* has not been mentioned in conjunction with this Orange County story. Although there were some derivatives in the portfolio, mostly in the form of structured notes, the damage had little to do with derivatives. Citron had simply used U.S. government intermediate-term notes, combined with the leveraging power of repurchase agreements, to destroy almost 20 percent of the fund's value.

To say that Orange County invested unwisely and did not practice risk management is probably an understatement. There was no risk management whatsoever. Citron was supposed to be monitored by the elected county board, but little monitoring was done. The board trusted the veteran treasurer and let him do what he wanted.

Orange County offered to repay the municipalities and other agencies whose funds it had invested about three-fourths of their money, plus other securities that would be repayable over a long period of time, but most of the payments were contingent on winning the lawsuit against Merrill Lynch. Almost 2,000 of the 15,000 county employees lost their jobs. The county sold nearly $100 million of its assets and proposed a sales tax increase, but the voters overwhelmingly turned it down. The county even tried to sell John Wayne Airport but found that the sale was not permitted by federal law. In 1996, Citron pled guilty to six felony counts and was sentenced to a year in jail and fined $100,000. Orange County was able to issue new debt and to defer repayment of old debt, and by mid-1996 it had emerged from bankruptcy. Eventually, it settled its lawsuit with Merrill Lynch.

Barings PLC: How One Man Blew Up a Bank

Nick Leeson, whom most of you know and all of you have heard of, runs our operation in Singapore, which I want you to emulate.

Ron Baker, Head, Financial Products Group, Barings
Quoted in *Rogue Trader* by Nick Leeson, 1996, p. 143

Barings PLC was a British investment bank that had been founded in 1763. It had played a major role in British history, financing the Napoleonic Wars, and included Queen Elizabeth II among its many well-heeled clients. One weekend in February 1995, Barings was forced to declare bankruptcy, a result of losses of about $1.2 billion, or nearly twice its capital. The losses were attributed to futures trading in its Singapore office by a 28-year-old former clerk named Nick Leeson. Barings was rescued by the Dutch banking concern Internationale Nederlanden Groep (ING), which purchased its assets (approximately $900 million) and assumed most of its liabilities for about $1.61.[1] ING immediately injected about $1 billion in capital. Some of Barings' liabilities, however, were not assumed, and those bondholders suffered big losses.

Leeson had joined the bank in July 1989, having previously worked in London for the American bank Morgan Stanley. As a clerk handling the settling of transactions, he proved to be exceptionally well organized, and his work in Barings' back office impressed his superiors. In March 1992, he requested and received a transfer to the Singapore office, which was actively involved in futures trading in Tokyo and Osaka, Japan, and at the Singapore International Monetary Exchange (SIMEX). Again Leeson proved to be excellent at organizing the back office. All the while, Leeson was learning the ropes of trading futures. Soon he was executing arbitrage transactions, buying Japanese stock index futures in Singapore and simultaneously selling the same contract in Osaka, capturing differences in the prices of the same contract on the two exchanges.

Transactions of this sort should be low risk. One position will gain, and the other will lose a similar amount. The net should be a small profit resulting from slight differences in the prices of the contract on the two exchanges. As Leeson relates the story in his book *Rogue Trader,* in 1992, he began hiding his losses in a special account. Soon it began appearing that Leeson was generating huge profits. Because Leeson was responsible for the back office and his employees were loyal to him, he was able to keep the losses tucked safely away whenever reports were required or auditors showed up. In 1994, he reported profits of about £28 million but had hidden losses of £180 million. From January 1, 1995, to February 24, Barings' last day, Leeson produced profits of almost £19 million and losses of over £600 million, and it was getting increasingly difficult to cover his trail.

Recall from Chapter 7 that we discussed the straddle, a strategy involving long positions in puts and calls with the same exercise price. Leeson was generating more funds by entering into short straddles, a total of almost 20,000 contracts. This meant that

---

[1]Yes, that is one dollar and 61 cents, which at that time was equivalent to approximately one British pound.

Leeson profited as long as the market stayed fairly stable. With high volatility, he would lose big. In late January 1995, Leeson held over 3,000 contracts long of the Japanese Nikkei 225 stock index futures at the Osaka exchange. On January 17, an earthquake struck the Japanese city of Kobe, and the index fell about 13 percent over the next five weeks. Leeson was generating large losses but increased his bets that the market would turn around. Ultimately, Leeson held a $7 billion position that would gain if the market moved up and lose if it moved down. He held about 17,000 contracts in Osaka and over 40,000 in Singapore. He also held huge positions in Japanese government bonds and Euroyen.

The evidence suggests that Barings' executives in London had been warned about Leeson's trading as early as 1992. In 1994, an audit concluded that while Leeson had done nothing wrong, although in fact he had, the potential for wrongdoing was there. It noted that Leeson was running both the front office and back office, although generating large profits with little risk.

Thursday, February 23, was Leeson's last day of work at Barings' Singapore office. He and his wife secretly fled Singapore the next day. They went to several Asian countries before eventually flying to Frankfurt, Germany, where he was arrested by German police a week after fleeing Singapore. Singapore sought extradition while Leeson's British lawyers worked toward having him charged and extradited by England. British authorities were unable to determine that he had violated any of their laws, and in October 1995, a German court agreed to turn him over to Singapore. Leeson returned to Singapore and plea-bargained a potential 14-year prison sentence down to 6½ years for fraud.

The Barings story shocked the financial world. There were concerns that the SIMEX clearinghouse might fail or use customer funds to cover its losses. The Bank of England, which had rescued Barings once in 1890, considered doing so again, but it quickly became apparent that only investors and not customers would lose money over the Barings failure. While the financial system suffered a shock, it showed no threat of widespread failure, the systemic risk that we previously mentioned. When ING purchased Barings about a week after the failure, the market settled down quickly and no further shocks were felt.

Barings is a classic story in bad risk management. It violates virtually every rule. Leeson was in control of both the back and front offices and, hence, had the ability to hide losses for an extremely long time. Barings' risk management system was nothing more than audits and regular reports from Leeson showing his positions and performance. The reports were falsified, and the auditors' examinations were not sufficient to identify the problem, although they did warn of the potential for fraud. It hardly mattered because they were ignored. The London office was under the impression that this 28-year-old clerk with no college degree was earning large profits arbitraging price differences in two markets. It never questioned how unlikely these profits really were.

Barings was a wake-up call to the rest of the financial world. Risk management became of paramount importance.

Procter & Gamble: Going Up in Suds

I've seen things in the market where I scratch my head and can't imagine why people did it. For example, when P&G lost all that money, I couldn't fathom what anyone at that company was thinking when they looked at that formula of the swap and said, 'Yes, that's exactly what I want to put on.'

Anonymous
"Confessions of a Structured Note Salesman"
Derivatives Strategy, November 11, 1995

The Procter & Gamble Corporation (P&G) is one of America's best-known companies. It is also a large multinational corporation with extensive foreign operations and significant interest rate and foreign exchange risk. In late October 1993, P&G entered into an exotic swap with its dealer, Banker's Trust (BT). The payment on the swap was determined by a complex formula relating short-term interest rates to long-term interest rates. In early 1994, P&G entered into another exotic swap, this one linked to the exchange rate on the German mark. This transaction was similar to the range floaters that we discussed earlier. Both parties paid floating rates tied to German interest rates. P&G was betting on Deutsche mark swap rates staying between 4.05 percent and 6.10 percent. Both of its positions were essentially bets that U.S. and German interest rates would not increase significantly. If P&G was correct, it would be locking in an attractive below-market borrowing rate of 40 basis points below the commercial paper rate. If it was wrong, P&G would suffer large losses by being forced to borrow at substantially above-market rates. The transactions also contained option features that allowed P&G to lock in a cumulative gain or loss.

In April 1994, P&G disclosed that it had taken a $157 million pretax charge as a result of those transactions. Effectively, P&G ended up borrowing at 1,412 basis points more than the commercial paper rate. Although the amount lowered its earnings per share only 15 cents, it became a public relations nightmare. P&G's treasurer, Norman Mains, was reassigned. Later in 1994, P&G filed suit against BT for $130 million under four counts: fraud, negligent misrepresentation, breach of fiduciary duties, and negligence. P&G also pursued charges against BT under the federal RICO (Racketeer Influenced and Corrupt Organizations) Act, a law designed to punish organized crime. The RICO Act had been applied successfully in cases not involving organized crime, and it permitted punishment of up to treble damages.

BT argued that P&G ran a sophisticated derivatives operation and was highly experienced in currency and interest rate derivatives. On that point, BT was certainly correct. P&G had many years of successful experience with these types of instruments, some of them being quite leveraged and exotic. So what was P&G's basis for arguing that BT had defrauded it? BT routinely tape-recorded all its conversations with its derivatives clients. P&G got a court order to obtain the tapes and found that BT derivatives personnel had made statements to the effect that P&G had no idea it was being taken advantage of. P&G argued that BT was its adviser and that it had, therefore, relied on BT's advice and that it was fraudulent for BT to have led it into these transactions.

In the summer of 1996, BT's newly appointed chairman, although confident of a victory in court, elected to put the matter behind them by settling with P&G. BT ended up paying about $80 million to P&G. BT had also settled a number of other cases out of court. Regulators fined it and forced it to agree to take various actions to change its derivatives sales and operating procedures.

In response, a number of leading derivatives dealers organized an informal working group to develop self-regulatory procedures. Although these procedures are nonbinding, they represent an effort by the industry to develop standards of practice in derivatives sales and trading. Of particular note was the fact that, unless made specific, all transactions are at arm's length, meaning that the dealer is not an adviser to the end user.

Much can be learned from careful study of historical cases. PRMIA has produced several well-documented derivatives cases. They are available at http://prmia.org/index.php?page=publication&option=caseStudies.

RISK MANAGEMENT INDUSTRY STANDARDS

The experience of many organizations such as those discussed in the previous section has undoubtedly taught several lessons that have saved other organizations from loss and embarrassment. Recognizing these concerns, the risk management industry has made several efforts to identify practices that are consistent with effective risk management. Organizations such as PRMIA and GARP promote professionalism and high standards in the practice of risk management. A number of other organizations have established formal standards, which are called *best practices*. The purpose of such industry standards is to facilitate quality risk management, with the main objective being to help firms avoid unnecessary financial distress. Ultimately, it is vital that senior management understand the wide array of financial risks posed by their current exposures as well as contemplated future exposures. Hopefully, this understanding will provide improved financial decision making that reduces potential future loss.

The first set of standards was identified by the G-30, or Group of 30, a private international organization of economic and financial experts who study and evaluate issues facing the international financial community. Its 1993 report listed 24 standards for best practices by dealers and end users, along with recommendations for legislators, regulations, and supervisors. The report is available only by purchase from the G-30, but the standards can be found at the website of the Risk Institute, http://riskinstitute.ch/136160.htm. The report emphasizes the importance of senior management's involvement in the process of risk management and the necessity for having an effective and independent risk management system. It explicitly recommends the use of such concepts as netting; VAR; delta, gamma, and vega; and the need for market and credit risk management. Although some of this report is outdated, it still remains the gold standard for risk management.

The Risk Standards Working Group is an informal committee of consultants and practitioners from the institutional investment industry, which largely consists of pension funds and endowments. This group's efforts are directed toward improving risk management in the investment management industry. Its 20 recommendations are available at www.cmra.com/risk_standards_working_group.php. These recommendations are similar to those of the G-30 Report but are adapted more to the investment management industry.

RESPONSIBILITIES OF SENIOR MANAGEMENT

A company in which management fails to act in the shareholders' interests and the board of directors fails to adequately monitor management is a fertile ground for corruption and exploitation of shareholders. Such companies are said to have poor corporate governance. In 2001–2002, there were a number of financial scandals that, while largely unrelated to derivatives use, nonetheless brought to attention the problems of poor corporate governance. Several high-profile firms such as Tyco, Enron, Adelphia, HealthSouth, and WorldCom became associated more with reckless management and exploitation of shareholders than with the products and services they provided. As a consequence of these scandals, in 2002, the United States Congress passed the Sarbanes-Oxley Act, known as SOX, which, among other things, emphasized the responsibilities of senior management to properly oversee all operations of the firm.

Although improving risk management is not the explicit intent of SOX, any reasonable interpretation of the Act leads to the conclusion that senior management will be held liable for poor risk management regardless of how low in the organizational structure problems occur. SOX and the growing emphasis on good corporate governance are consistent with risk management industry practices, which in fact predated the problems of poor corporate governance that gave rise to the law. SOX, however, made it a legal mandate that senior management ensure that a firm engage in practices that are beneficial to the shareholders and avoid practices that hurt shareholders. Good risk management is clearly consistent with SOX. But until SOX, good risk management was clearly a desirable objective. After SOX, it has become effectively the law and imposes severe penalties upon senior management if it fails to carry out its responsibilities. In order to do so, senior management must establish an organizational structure and procedures that ensure that the risk management function will be effectively carried out. Of course, senior management is not expected to have detailed hands-on knowledge of risk management. It must, however, provide that responsible personnel are in control of a firm's risk management practices. In this section, we conclude by looking at a few general guidelines that senior management should follow to ensure that the risk management function is under control.

- *Establish written policies.*
  A company should establish in writing its policies with respect to how risk will be managed within the company. These policies should identify the risks to which the company is exposed and discuss its tolerance for risk and its willingness and capacity to bear risk. These policies should identify the objectives of the company's risk management program and define its expectations. They should define how and why derivatives can be used to manage risk. Finally, these policies should provide for and discuss how the policies will be reviewed and possibly adjusted over time.

- *Define roles and responsibilities.*
  As we previously mentioned, the company should have an independent risk monitoring system with clear lines of authority. Senior management must know who within the organization is taking risks. The organization must choose a structure that is clearly centralized or decentralized. The firm must determine whether the risk management system will be an integrative, firmwide, enterprise risk management system, as opposed to a system in which risks are managed separately. Finally, the company must establish checks and balances.

- *Identify acceptable strategies.*
  The organization must identify which risks should be acquired, which risks should be managed, and which risks should be mitigated. It should define the scope of allowable derivatives activities. It should establish trading limits that apply at the overall firm level; the level of a division, group, or portfolio; and also the level of an individual.

- *Ensure that personnel are qualified.*
  Senior management is always responsible for ensuring that personnel have the knowledge, ability, training, and resources to carry out their duties. Senior management will ordinarily focus primarily on senior-level officers and employers, who in turn are responsible for junior-level employees.

- *Ensure that control systems are in place.*

> In carrying out its risk management responsibilities, senior management must establish written policies, define roles and responsibilities, identify acceptable strategies, ensure that personnel are qualified, and ensure that control systems are in place. Senior management is not necessarily directly involved in the day-to-day risk management activities but ultimately bears responsibility.

Senior management is responsible for ensuring that valuation and monitoring software, hardware, and personnel are in place. Again, this system must provide for independent risk monitoring, meaning that the risk manager must be responsible to senior management and not to traders. Control systems must specify limits and restrictions on trading, must be enforceable, must identify how exceptions to the rules can be handled, and must ensure that modern risk management techniques are used. Backup systems and periodic review of the control function must be provided. Senior management must also ensure that performance is evaluated on a risk-adjusted basis and that risk takers are compensated in a manner that does not encourage excessive risk taking.

In summary, we see that senior management is as responsible for the risk management function of an organization as it is for the quality and safety of the products and services a firm provides. Senior management does not have to be involved in the day-to-day risk management activities, but it must ensure that capable individuals are. In short, senior management is ultimately responsible. If anything goes wrong, senior management is and should be blamed.

Summary

This chapter has taken a different look at risk management from what we saw in the first 15 chapters. Until now, we primarily focused on quantitative analysis of risk management tools such as options, futures, forwards, and swaps. But quantitative analysis is not all there is to know about managing risk. There are many qualitative factors that are just as important.

In this chapter, we looked at the risk management industry and saw how it consists of dealers, end users, and a number of other firms providing advice in the areas of law, accounting, software, and general consulting. We examined how an organization structures its derivatives function, noting that some organizations have centralized risk management and some have decentralized risk management. In some cases, companies integrate the management of all the risks within an organization into a single process, called enterprise risk management.

We also looked at the basic principles underlying the practice of accounting for derivatives and risk management. We saw that derivatives are typically accounted for using a process called fair value accounting or cash flow accounting. Derivative transactions that qualify as hedges are accounted for jointly with the underlying on which the hedge is based. We looked at how some firms have suffered tremendous losses using derivatives and how these losses have led to the establishment of industry standards for best practices in risk management. Finally, we looked at the responsibilities of senior management in ensuring that the risk management function is effective.

This book has taken you on a tour of the world of derivatives and risk management. As you probably believe, the subject is a complex one, but you now have the tools to move on to further study of this fascinating subject. When the time comes that you execute your first derivatives trade, we hope that you will ask yourself one simple question: Am I practicing risk management?

Key Terms

You should be able to give brief definitions of the following terms:

end users/dealers, p. 576

front office/back office/
  middle office, p. 581

enterprise risk management, p. 582

hedge accounting/FAS 133, p. 583

fair value hedge, p. 584

cash flow hedge, p. 585

Further Reading

The following books provide information on risk management in general:

Chew, L. *Managing Derivatives Risk: The Use and Abuse of Leverage.* New York: Wiley, 1996.

Coleman, T. S. *A Practical Guide to Risk Management.* Charlottesville, Virginia: Research Foundation of the CFA Institute, 2011.

Fraser, J., and B. J. Simkins, eds. *Enterprise Risk Management: Today's Leading Research and Best Practices for Tomorrow's Executives.* New York: Wiley, 2010.

Gastineau, G. L., and M. P. Kritzman. *The Dictionary of Financial Risk Management*, 2nd ed. New Hope, PA: Frank Fabozzi Associates, 1999.

Haslett, W. V. "Bud," ed. *Risk Management: Foundations for a Changing World.* New York: Wiley, 2010.

Jorion, P. *Financial Risk Manager Handbook: 2001–2002.* New York: Wiley, 2001.

Lam, J. *Enterprise Risk Management: From Incentives to Controls.* New York: Wiley, 2003.

Marthinsen, J. *Risk Takers: Uses and Abuses of Financial Derivatives.* Boston: Pearson Prentice Hall, 2009.

Patterson, S. *The Quants: How a New Breed of Math Whizzes Conquered Wall Street and Nearly Destroyed It*. New York: Crown, 2010.

Smithson, C. W. *Managing Financial Risk: A Guide to Derivative Products, Financial Engineering, and Value Maximization*, 3rd ed. New York: McGraw-Hill, 1998.

Some books covering accounting, legal, and organizational aspects of derivatives are as follows:

Anson, M. J. P. *Accounting and Tax Rules for Derivatives*. New Hope, PA: Frank Fabozzi Associates, 1999.

Gastineau, G., D. J. Smith, and R. Todd. *Risk Management, Derivatives, and Financial Analysis under SFAS 133*. Charlottesville, Virginia: Research Foundation of the Association for Investment Management and Research 2001.

An excellent website on FAS 133 and IAS 39 is maintained by Professor Bob Jensen of Trinity University: www.trinity.edu/rjensen/acct5341/speakers/133glosf.htm

Johnson, P. M. *Derivatives: A Manager's Guide to the World's Most Powerful Financial Instruments*. New York: McGraw-Hill, 1999.

Klein, R. A., and J. Lederman. *Derivatives Risk and Responsibility*. Chicago: Irwin, 1996.

McLaughlin, R. M. *Over-the-Counter Derivative Products: A Guide to Business and Legal Risk Management and Documentation*. New York: McGraw-Hill, 1999.

Modern Risk Management: A History. London: Risk Books, 2003.

Stories of some famous derivatives losses are told in the following books:

Dunbar, N. *Inventing Money: The Story of Long-Term Capital Management and the Legends Behind It*. Chichester, UK: Wiley, 2000.

Fay, S. *The Collapse of Barings*. New York: W. W. Norton, 1997.

Jorion, P., and R. Roper. *Big Bets Gone Bad: Derivatives and Bankruptcy in Orange County*. Orlando, FL: Academic Press, 1995.

Concepts Checks

1. Explain why end users who conduct their risk management operations in the treasury department should not require the treasury department to be a profit center.
2. Distinguish the typical objectives of a dealer engaging in a derivatives transaction from those of an end user.
3. Identify the two primary types of derivatives specialists within a dealer organization.
4. Discuss the advantages and disadvantages of a centralized versus a decentralized risk management operation of an end user firm.
5. Explain the difference between centralized and enterprise risk management.

Questions and Problems

1. Distinguish between the front office and the back office of a derivatives dealer. Explain why it is important to keep the front and back offices separate.
2. Explain why the traditional auditing function cannot serve as the risk management function.
3. Why is hedge accounting used, and how can it be misused?
4. Explain how an organization determines whether a hedge is sufficiently effective to justify hedge accounting.
5. Describe the primary differences between accounting for fair value hedges and accounting for cash flow hedges.
6. Identify the three ways in which U.S. companies can satisfy the SEC requirement that they disclose how they use derivatives to manage risk.
7. Summarize in one sentence how each of the following organizations failed to practice risk management:
   a. Metallgesellschaft
   b. Orange County
   c. Barings
   d. Procter & Gamble
8. What is the purpose of risk management industry standards?
9. What responsibilities does senior management assume in a risk management system?

10. What is the most important component of an effective risk management system?

11. Briefly explain how speculative derivatives transactions are treated from an accounting perspective.

12. One responsibility of senior management is to identify acceptable risk management strategies. Identify three categories of risk, focusing on broad classifications and not on specific types of risks.

13. Identify and discuss five problems with regard to the application of FAS 133.

14. Suppose that a firm engages in a derivative transaction that qualifies for fair value hedging. The firm holds a security and hedges it by selling a derivative. During the course of the hedge, the security increases in value by $20,000, while the derivative decreases in value by $22,000. Explain what accounting entries would be done and how the firm's earnings and balance sheet would be affected.

15. Suppose that a firm plans to purchase an asset at a future date. The forward price of the asset is $200,000. It hedges that purchase by buying a forward contract at a price of $205,000. During the hedging period, the forward contract incurs a paper loss of $15,000. At the end of the hedge, the forward contract has lost an accumulated value of $20,000 and the asset is $20,000 cheaper. Explain what accounting entries would be done and how the firm's earnings and balance sheet would be affected. What would be different if it was not an effective hedge?

16. Explain the advantages for senior management having detailed written policies for financial risk management.

17. Define and explain what is meant by independent risk monitoring. How can senior management improve independent risk monitoring?

18. ACB, Inc., engages in a forward transaction and is applying fair value hedge accounting. ACB holds the underlying instrument and hedges it by selling this forward contract. During the hedge period, the underlying instrument increases in value by $250,000, while the derivative decreases in value by $220,000. Identify the accounting entries required and how ACB's earnings and balance sheet would be affected.

19. Explain the accounting of hedging currency translation of a firm's foreign subsidiary.

20. Explain how cash flow hedge accounting is applied in principle. Specifically, identify how this accounting treatment is different from the typical way cash flow transactions accounting is handled.

A senior derivatives trader, interviewed recently by Risk, was asked how he thought the derivatives market would develop over the next five years. His response was a spin on an old joke—each desk will comprise a sophisticated trading model, a trader, and a dog. The model will make all the trading decisions; the trader acts as a back-up in case the model crashes; and the dog is trained to bite the trader if he or she tries to touch the model in any other circumstance.

Nick Sawyer
Risk, September 2006, p. 6

List of Important Formulas

Intrinsic Value of American Call

$$C_a(S_0,T,X) \geq \text{Max}(0,S_0 - X)$$

Maximum Spread of European Calls

$$(X_2 - X_1)(1 + r)^{-T} \geq C_e(S_0,T,X_1) - C_e(S_0,T,X_2)$$

Maximum Spread of American Calls

$$X_2 - X_1 \geq C_a(S_0,T,X_1) - C_a(S_0,T,X_2)$$

Lower Bound of European Call

$$C_e(S_0,T,X \geq \text{Max}[0,S_0 - X(1 + r)^{-T}]$$

Intrinsic Value of American Put

$$P_a(S_0,T,X) \geq \text{Max}(0,X - S_0)$$

Maximum Spread of European Puts

$$(X_2 - X_1)(1 + r)^{-T} \geq P_e(S_0,T,X_2) - P_e(S_0,T,X_1)$$

Maximum Spread of American Puts

$$X_2 - X_1 \geq P_a(S_0,T,X_2) - P_a(S_0,T,X_1)$$

Lower Bound of European Put

$$P_e(S_0,T,X) \geq \text{Max}[0,X(1 + r)^{-T} - S_0]$$

Put-Call Parity for American Options

$$C_a(S_0',T,X) + X + \sum_{j=1}^{N} D_j(1 + r)^{-t_j} \geq S_0 + P_a(S_0',T,X) \geq$$

$$C_a(S_0',T,X) + X(1 + r)^{-T}$$

Put-Call Parity for European Options

$$S_0 + P_e(S_0,T,X) = C_e(S_0,T,X) + X(1 + r)^{-T}$$

Lower Bound of European Foreign Currency Call

$$C_e(S_0,T,X) \geq \text{Max}[0,S_0(1 + \rho)^{-T} - X(1 + r)^{-T}]$$

Lower Bound of European Foreign Currency Put

$$P_e(S_0,T,X) \geq \text{Max}[0,X(1 + r)^{-T} - S_0(1 + \rho)^{-T}]$$

Put-Call Parity of Foreign Currency Options

$$S_0(1 + \rho)^{-T} + P_e(S_0,T,X) = C_e(S_0,T,X) + X(1 + r)^{-T}$$

Stock Prices in Binomial Model

$$S_u = uS$$
$$S_d = dS$$
$$S_{u^2} = u^2 S$$
$$S_{d^2} = d^2 S$$
$$S_{ud} = udS$$

Call Prices in One-Period Binomial Model

$$C_u = \text{Max}[0,uS - X]$$
$$C_d = \text{Max}[0,dS - X]$$
$$C = \frac{pC_u + (1 - p)C_d}{1 + r}$$

Call Prices in Two-Period Binomial Model

$$C_{u^2} = \text{Max}[0,u^2 S - X]$$
$$C_{ud} = \text{Max}[0,udS - X]$$
$$C_{d^2} = \text{Max}[0,d^2 S - X]$$
$$C_u = \frac{pC_{u^2} - (1 - p)C_{ud}}{1 + r}$$
$$C_d = \frac{pC_{ud} + (1 - p)C_{d^2}}{1 + r}$$
$$C = \frac{pC_u + (1 - p)C_d}{1 + r}$$
$$= \frac{p^2 C_{u^2} + 2p(1 - p)C_{ud} + (1 - p)^2 C_{d^2}}{(1 + r)^2}$$

Value of p in Binomial Model

$$p = \frac{1 + r - d}{u - d}$$

Call Prices in n-Period Binomial Model

$$C = \frac{\sum_{j=0}^{n}\frac{n!}{!j(n-j)!}p^j(1-p)^{n-j}\text{Max}[0,u^jd^{n-j}S-X]}{(1+r)^n}$$

Binomial Probabilities

$$u = e^{\sigma\sqrt{T/n}},\, d = 1/u \text{ when } p = (1+r-d)/(u-d)$$

or

$$u = e^{(\ln(1+r)-\sigma^2/2)(T/n)+\sigma\sqrt{T/n}},$$
$$d = e^{(\ln(1+r)-\sigma^2/2)(T/n)-\sigma\sqrt{T/n}}$$
$$\text{when } p = \frac{e^{\sigma^2(T/n)/2}-e^{-\sigma\sqrt{T/n}}}{e^{\sigma\sqrt{T/n}}-e^{-\sigma\sqrt{T/n}}}$$

Per Period Risk-Free Rate in Binomial Model

$$(1+r)^{T/n}-1$$

Hedge Ratios in Binomial Model

$$h = \frac{C_u - C_d}{uS - dS}$$
$$h_u = \frac{C_{u^2} - C_{ud}}{u^2S - udS}$$
$$h_d = \frac{C_{ud} - C_{d^2}}{duS - d^2S}$$

Sequence of Hedge Portfolio Values in Binomial Model

$$V = hS - C$$
$$V_u = huS - C_u$$
$$V_d = hdS - C_d$$

Black-Scholes-Merton Call Option Pricing Model

$$C = S_0N(d_1) - Xe^{-r_cT}N(d_2)$$
$$d_1 = \frac{\ln(S_0/X) + (r_c + \sigma^2/2)T}{\sigma\sqrt{T}}$$
$$d_2 = d_1 - \sigma\sqrt{T}$$

Black-Scholes-Merton Put Option Pricing Model

$$P = Xe^{-r_cT}[1 - N(d_2)] - S_0[1 - N(d_1)]$$

Call Delta

$$\text{Call } Delta = N(d_1)$$

Call Gamma

$$\text{Call } Gamma = \frac{e^{-d_1^2/2}}{S_0\sigma\sqrt{2\pi T}}$$

Call Rho

$$\text{Call } Rho = TXe^{-r_cT}N(d_2)$$

Call Vega

$$\text{Call } Vega = \frac{S_0\sqrt{T}e^{-d_1^2/2}}{\sqrt{2\pi}}$$

Call Theta

$$\text{Call } Theta = -\frac{S_0\sigma e^{-d_1^2/2}}{2\sqrt{2\pi T}} - r_cXe^{-r_cT}N(d_2)$$

Put Delta

$$\text{Put } Delta = N(d_1) - 1$$

Put Gamma

$$\text{Put } Gamma = \frac{e^{-d_1^2/2}}{S_0\sigma\sqrt{2\pi T}}$$

Put Rho

$$\text{Put } Rho = -TXe^{-r_cT}[1 - N(d_2)]$$

Put Vega

$$\text{Put } Vega = \frac{S_0\sqrt{T}e^{-d_1^2/2}}{\sqrt{2\pi}}$$

Put Theta

$$\text{Put } Theta = -\frac{S_0\sigma e^{-d_1^2/2}}{2\sqrt{2\pi T}} + r_cXe^{-r_cT}(1 - N(d_2))$$

Present Value of a Series of Discrete Dividends

$$\sum_{j=1}^{T}D_j(1+r)^{-t_j}$$

Stock Price minus Present Value of Dividends

$$S_0' = S_0 - D_te^{-r_cT}$$
$$S_0' = S_0e^{-\delta_ct}$$

Sample Estimate of Mean of Continuously Compounded Return

$$\bar{r}^c = \sum_{t=1}^{J}r_t^c/J$$

Sample Estimate of Variance of Continuously Compounded Return

$$\sigma^2 = \frac{\sum_{t=1}^{J}(r_t^c - \bar{r}^c)^2}{J-1} = \frac{\sum_{t=1}^{J}(r_t^c)^2 - \left(\sum_{t=1}^{J}(r_t^c)\right)^2/J}{J-1}$$

Implied Volatility of At-the-Money Call

$$\hat{\sigma} \approx \frac{C}{(0.398)S_0\sqrt{T}}$$

Profit from Call Transaction Held to Expiration

$$\Pi = N_C[\text{Max}(0, S_T - X) - C]$$

Profit from Call Transaction Terminated at T_1

$$\Pi = N_C[C(S_{T_1}, T - T_1, X) - C]$$

Profit from Put Transaction Held to Expiration

$$\Pi = N_P[\text{Max}(0, X - S_T) - P]$$

Profit from Put Transaction Terminated at T_1

$$\Pi = N_P[P(S_{T_1}, T - T_1, X) - P]$$

Profit from Stock Transaction

$$\Pi = N_S(S_T - S_0)$$

Ratio of Calls in Riskless Spread

$$\frac{N_1}{N_2} = -\frac{\Delta_2}{\Delta_1}$$

Price of a Forward/Futures Contract

$$f_t(T) = F(0,T) = S_0(1 + r)^T$$

Value of a Forward Contract

$$V_t(0,T) = S_t - F(0,T)(1 + r)^{-(T-t)}$$

Price of a Futures Contract on Dividend Paying Asset

$$f_0(T) = S_0(1 + r)^T - D_T \quad \text{(Discrete)}$$
$$f_0(T) = S_0 e^{(r_c - \delta_c)T} \quad \text{(Continuous)}$$

Value of a Futures Contract on Dividend Paying Asset

$$V_t(0,T) = S_t - D_{t,T} - F(0,T)(1+r)^{-(T-t)} \quad \text{(Discrete)}$$
$$V_t(0,T) = S_t e^{-\delta_c(T-t)} - F(0,T)e^{-r_c(T-t)} \quad \text{(Continuous)}$$

Price of a Forward/Futures on Foreign Exchange

$$F(0,T) = f_0(T) = S_0(1 + r)^T/(1 + \rho)^T$$

Value of a Forward on Foreign Exchange

$$V_t(0,T) = S_t(1 + \rho)^{-(T-t)} - F(0,T)(1 + r)^{-(T-t)}$$

Price of a Forward/Futures on Commodity

$$F(0,T) = f_0(T) = S_0(1 + r)^T + s$$

Spot Price under Uncertainty and Risk Neutrality

$$S_0 = E(S_T) - s - iS_0$$

Spot Price under Uncertainty and Risk Aversion

$$S_0 = E(S_T) - s - iS_0 - E(\phi)$$

Cost of Carry Futures Pricing Model

$$f_0(T) = S_0 + \theta$$

Cost of Carry Futures Pricing Model with Convenience Yield

$$f_0(T) = S_0 + \theta - \chi$$

Forward/Futures Put-Call Parity

$$P_e(S_0,T,X) = C_e(S_0,T,X) + (X - f_0(T))(1 + r)^{-T}$$

Intrinsic Value of American Call on Futures Contract

$$C_a(f_0(T),T,X) \geq \text{Max}(0, f_0(T) - X)$$

Intrinsic Value of American Put on Futures Contract

$$P_a(f_0(T),T,X) \geq \text{Max}(0, X - f_0(T))$$

Lower Bound of European Call on Futures Contract

$$C_e(f_0(T), T, X) \geq \text{Max}[0, (f_0(T) - X)(1 + r)^{-T}]$$

Lower Bound of European Put on Futures Contract

$$P_e(f_0(T),T,X) \geq \text{Max}[0, (X - f_0(T))(1 + r)^{-T}]$$

Black Call Option on Futures Pricing Model

$$C = e^{-r_c T}[f_0(T)N(d_1) - XN(d_2)]$$
$$d_1 = \frac{\ln(f_0(T)/X + (\sigma^2/2)T)}{\sigma\sqrt{T}}$$
$$d_2 = d_1 - \sigma\sqrt{T}$$

Black Put Options on Futures Pricing Model

$$P = Xe^{-r_c T}[1 - N(d_2)] - f_0(T)e^{-r_c T}[1 - N(d_1)]$$

Implied Repo Rate

$$\hat{r} = \left(\frac{f_0(t)}{S_0}\right)^{1/t} - 1$$

Invoice Price on U.S. Treasury Futures Contract

Invoice price = (Settlement price on position day)
(Conversion factor) + Accrued interest

Spot Price for Justifying Exercise of Wild Card Option

$$B_5 < f_3(CF)$$

Implied Repo on T-Bond or T-Note

$$\hat{r} = \left[\frac{(CF)(f_0(T)) + AI_T + CI_{0,T}}{B_0 + AI_0}\right]^{(1/T)} - 1$$

Implied Repo Rate on T-Bond or T-Note Spread

$$\hat{r} = \left[\frac{(CF(T))f_0(T) + AI_T + CI_{t,T}}{(CF(t))f_0(t) + AI_t} \right]^{1/(T-t)} - 1$$

Implied Repo Rate on Stock Index Futures

$$\hat{r}_c = \frac{\ln(f_0(T)/S_0)}{T} + \delta_c$$

Profit on Short Hedge Held to Expiration

$$\Pi(\text{short hedge}) = (S_T - S_0) + (f_0 - f_T)$$

Profit on Long Hedge Held to Expiration

$$\Pi(\text{long hedge}) = (S_0 - S_T) + (f_T - f_0)$$

Basis Today

$$b_0 = S_0 - f_0$$

Basis at Time t

$$b_t = S_t - f_t$$

Profit on Short Hedge Closed Out Prior to Expiration

$$\Pi(\text{short hedge}) = (S_t - S_0) + (f_0 - f_t) = b_t - b_0$$

Profit on Long Hedge Closed Out Prior to Expiration

$$\Pi(\text{long hedge}) = (S_0 - S_t) + (f_t - f_0) = b_0 - b_t$$

Variance of Profit from Hedge

$$\sigma_{\Pi}^2 = \sigma_{\Delta S}^2 + \sigma_{\Delta f}^2 N_f^2 + 2\text{Cov}_{\Delta S \Delta f} N_f$$

Minimum Variance Hedge Ratio

$$N_f = -\frac{\sigma_{\Delta s \Delta f}}{\sigma_{\Delta f}^2} = -\rho_{\Delta s, \Delta f} \frac{\sigma_{\Delta s}}{\sigma_{\Delta f}}$$

Hedging Effectiveness

$$e^* = \frac{\sigma_{\Delta s}^2 - \sigma_{\Pi}^2}{\sigma_{\Delta s}^2} = \frac{N_f^{*2}\sigma_{\Delta f}^2}{\sigma_{\Delta s}^2} = \rho_{\Delta s, \Delta f}^2$$

Modified Duration of Bond

$$MD_B = \frac{DUR_B}{1 + y_B} \approx -\frac{\Delta B/B}{\Delta y_B}$$

Modified Duration of Futures Contract

$$MD_f \approx -\frac{\Delta f/f}{\Delta y_f}$$

Price Sensitivity Hedge Ratio

$$N_f^* = -\left(\frac{MD_B}{MD_f}\right)\left(\frac{B}{f}\right)\beta_y$$

Stock Index Futures Hedge Ratio

$$N_f = -\left(\frac{\beta_S}{\beta_f}\right)\left(\frac{S}{f}\right)$$

Profit on Intramarket Futures Spread Trade

$$\begin{aligned}\Pi &= [f_t(2) - f_0(2)] - [f_t(1) - f_0(1)] \\ &= [\theta_{t,2} - \theta_{0,2}] - [\theta_{t,1} - \theta_{0,1}] = [\theta_{t,2} - \theta_{0,1}] - [\theta_{0,2} - \theta_{0,1}]\end{aligned}$$

Profit on Intermarket Futures Spread Trade

$$\begin{aligned}\Pi &= [f_t(C2) - f_0(C2)] - [f_t(C1) - f_0(C1)] \\ &= [S_{t,C2} + \theta_{t,C2} - S_{0,C2} - \theta_{0,C2}] \\ &\quad - [S_{t,C1} + \theta_{t,\,C1} - S_{t,C1} - \theta_{0,C1}] \\ &= \{[S_{t,C2} - S_{t,C1}] - [S_{0,\,C2} - S_{0,C1}]\} \\ &\quad + \{[\theta_{t,C2} - \theta_{t,C1}] - [\theta_{0,C2} - \theta_{0,C1}]\}\end{aligned}$$

Futures Contracts Required to Achieve Target Duration

$$N_f = \left(\frac{MD_T - MD_B}{MD_f}\right)\left(\frac{B}{f}\right)$$

Futures Contracts Required to Achieve Target Beta

$$N_f = (\beta_T - \beta_S)\left(\frac{S}{f}\right)$$

Cash Flow to Floating Rate Receiver in Plain Vanilla Swap

$$(\text{Notion Amount})(\text{LIBOR} - \text{fixed rate})\left(\frac{\text{Days}}{360 \text{ or } 365}\right)$$

Price of Eurodollar Zero Coupon Bond

$$B_0(t_i) = \frac{1}{1 + L_0(t_i)\left(\dfrac{t_i}{360}\right)}$$

Value at Fixed Rate Bond

$$V_{FXRB} = \sum_{i=1}^{n} R\left(\frac{t_i - t_{i-1}}{360}\right)B_0(t_i) + B_0(t_n)$$

Value of Floating Rate Bond

$$V_{FLRB} = 1 \text{ (at time 0 or payment date)}$$

$$= \frac{1 + L_0(t_1)(t_1/360)}{1 + L_t(t_1 - t)(t_1 - t)/360}$$

(between payment dates 0 and 11)

Value of Swap

$$VS = V_{FLRB} - V_{FXRB}$$

Fixed Rate on Interest Rate or Equity Swap

$$R = \left(\frac{1}{q}\right)\left(\frac{1 - B_0(t_n)}{\sum\limits_{i=1}^{n} B_0(t_i)}\right)$$

Payoff of Equity Swap to Receive Fixed, Pay Equity

(Notional Amount) ((Fixed rate)q
−Return on stock over settlement period)

Payoff of Equity Swap to Receive One Stock Index, Pay Another

(Notional Amount) (Return on one stock index
−Return on other stock index)

Value of Equity Swap to Receive Equity, Pay Fixed

$$\left(\frac{S_t}{S_0}\right) - B_t(t_n) - Rq \sum_{i=1}^{n} B_t(t_i)$$

Payoff to Holder of Long FRA

$$(\text{Notion Amount})(\text{LIBOR} - \text{agreed upon rate})\left(\frac{m}{360}\right)$$

Payoff on Long (Receive Floating) FRA (Advanced Set, Advanced Settle)

$$(\text{Notional Amount})\left(\frac{(\text{LIBOR} - \text{Agreed upon rate})\frac{m}{360}}{1 + \text{LIBOR}\frac{m}{360}}\right)$$

Fixed rate on FRA

$$F = \left(\frac{1 + L_0(h + m)\left(\frac{h + m}{360}\right)}{1 + L_0(h)\left(\frac{h}{360}\right)} - 1\right)\left(\frac{360}{m}\right)$$

Value of FRA

$$\text{VFRA} = \left(\frac{1}{1 + L_g(h - g)\left(\frac{(h - g)}{360}\right)}\right)$$
$$- \left(\frac{1 + F\left(\frac{m}{360}\right)}{1 + L_g(h + m - g)\left(\frac{h + m - g}{360}\right)}\right)$$

$$\text{VFRA} = \frac{(F_g - F_0)\left(\frac{m}{360}\right)}{1 + L_g(h + m - g)\left(\frac{h + m - g}{360}\right)}$$

Payoff from Interest Rate Call

$$(\text{Notional Amount})\left(\text{Max}(0,\text{LIBOR} - X)\left(\frac{m}{360}\right)\right)$$

Payoff from Interest Rate Put

$$(\text{Notional Amount})\left(\text{Max}(0,X - \text{LIBOR})\left(\frac{m}{360}\right)\right)$$

Interest Rate Option Price (C denotes Black Option Pricing Model)

Interest rate option price $= e^{-F(m/365)}C$

Interest Rate Option Contract Price

Contract premium

$= (\text{Notional Amount})\left(\frac{\text{days}}{360}\right)(\text{Interest rate options price})$

Value of Payer Swaption at Expiration

$$(\text{Notional Amount})\text{Max}(0,R - X)\left(\frac{\text{days}}{360}\right)\sum_{i=1}^{n} B_0(t_i)$$

Value of Receiver Swaption at Expiration

$$(\text{Notion Amount})\text{Max}(0,X - R)\left(\frac{\text{days}}{360}\right)\sum_{i=1}^{n} B_0(t_i)$$

Number of Shares and Puts to Insure Portfolio

$$N = \frac{V}{S_0 + P}$$

Minimum Value of Insured Portfolio

$$V_{min} = \frac{XV}{S_0 + P}$$

Number of Treasury Bills to Insure Portfolio with Calls and Treasury Bills

$$N_B = \frac{V_{min}}{B_T}$$

Number of Calls to Insure Portfolio with Calls and Treasury Bills

$$N_C = \frac{(V - N_B B)}{C} = \frac{V}{S_0 + P}$$

Number of Futures in Dynamic Hedge with Stock Index Futures

$$N_f = \left[\left(\frac{V_{min}}{X}\right)N(d_1) - \left(\frac{V}{S_0}\right)\right]e^{-r_c t}$$

Number of Treasury Bills in Dynamic Hedge

$$N_B = \frac{V - N_S S_0}{B}$$

Number of Shares of Stock in Dynamic Hedge with Treasury Bills

$$N_f = \left(\frac{V_{min}}{X}\right) N(d_1)$$

Value of Asset-or-Nothing Call Option

$$DC_{aon} = S_0 N(d_1)$$

Value of Asset-or-Nothing Put Option

$$DP_{aon} = S_0[1 - N(d_1)]$$

Value of Cash-or-Nothing Call Option

$$DC_{con} = e^{-r_c T} N(d_2)$$

Value of Cash-or-Nothing Put Option

$$DP_{con} = e^{-r_c T}[1 - N(d_2)]$$

Relationship of Asset-or-Nothing Options

$$DC_{aon} + DP_{aon} = S_0 N(d_1) + S_0[1 - N(d_1)] = S_0$$

Relationship of Cash-or-Nothing Options

$$DC_{con} + DP_{con} = e^{-r_c T} N(d_2) + e^{-r_c T}[1 - N(d_2)] = e^{-r_c T}$$

Value of Contingent-Pay Call

$$C_{cp} = \frac{C_e(S_0, T, X)}{e^{-r_c T} N(d_2)}$$

Payoff of Average Price Call

$$Max(0, S_{avg} - X)$$

Payoff of Average Price Put

$$Max(0, X - S_{avg})$$

Payoff of 3-Period Average Strike Call

$$Max(0, S_3 - S_{avg})$$

Payoff of 3-Period Average Strike Put

$$Max(0, S_{avg} - S_3)$$

Payoff of 3-Period Lookback Call

$$Max(0, S_3 - S_{min})$$

Payoff of 3-Period Lookback Put

$$Max(0, S_{max} - S_3)$$

Payoff of 3-Period Fixed-Strike Lookback Call

$$Max(0, S_{max} - X)$$

Payoff of 3-Period Fixed-Strike Lookback Put

$$Max(0, X - S_{min})$$

Value of Equity as Option on Asset

$$S_0 = A_0 N(d_1) - Fe^{-r_c T} N(d_2)$$

Value of Debt Based on Equity as Option on Asset

$$B_0 = A_0 - (A_0 N(d_1) - Fe^{-r_c T} N(d_2))$$
$$= Fe^{-r_c T} N(d_2) + A_0(1 - N(d_1))$$

Credit Default Swap Premium

$$CDS\ premium = Fe^{-r_c T} - B_0$$

References

This compilation of books, articles, and monographs includes items referenced in this book as well as classic references and other useful articles dealing with topics covered in this book. It is not intended as a comprehensive bibliography of derivatives.

Abken, Peter A. "An Introduction to Portfolio Insurance." *Federal Reserve Bank of Atlanta Economic Review* 72 (November–December 1987): 2–25.

Abken, Peter A. "Interest Rate Caps, Collars, and Floors." *Federal Reserve Bank of Atlanta Economic Review* 74 (November–December 1989): 2–24.

Abken, Peter A. "Beyond Plain Vanilla: A Taxonomy of Swaps." *Federal Reserve Bank of Atlanta Economic Review* 76 (1991): 12–29.

Abken, Peter A. "Valuation of Default-Risky Interest-Rate Swaps." *Advances in Futures and Options Research* 6 (1993): 93–116.

Alexander, Carol, and Elizabeth Sheedy, eds. *The Professional Risk Managers' Guide to Financial Instruments. Prmia Risk Management Series.* New York: McGraw-Hill, 2008.

Alexander, Carol, and Elizabeth Sheedy, eds. *The Professional Risk Managers' Guide to Financial Markets. Prmia Risk Management Series.* New York: McGraw-Hill, 2008.

Alexander, Gordon, and Michael Stutzer. "A Graphical Note on European Put Thetas." *Journal of Futures Markets* 16 (1996): 201–209.

Anderson, Ronald W. "The Regulation of Futures Contract Innovations in the United States." *The Journal of Futures Markets* 3 (1984): 297–332.

Anson, Mark J. P. *Accounting and Tax Rules for Derivatives.* New Hope, PA: Frank Fabozzi Associates, 1999.

Arak, Marcelle, Arturo Estrella, Laurie Goodman, and Andrew Silver. "Interest Rate Swaps: An Alternative Explanation." *Financial Management* 17 (1988): 12–18.

Arak, Marcelle, Philip Fischer, Laurie Goodman, and Raj Daryanani. "The Municipal-Treasury Futures Spread." *The Journal of Futures Markets* 7 (1987): 355–371.

Arak, Marcelle, Laurie Goodman, and Susan Ross. "The Cheapest to Deliver Bond on the Treasury Bond Futures Contract." *Advances in Futures and Options Research* 1, part B (1986): 49–74.

Arditti, Fred D. *Derivatives: A Comprehensive Resource for Options, Futures, Interest Rate Swaps, and Mortgage Securities.* Boston: Harvard Business School Press, 1996.

Augen, Jeff. *Trading Options at Expiration: Strategies and Models for Winning the Endgame.* Upper Saddle River, NJ: Pearson Education, 2009.

Austin, Michael. "Index Option Overwriting: Strategies and Results." *Derivatives Quarterly* 1 (Summer 1995): 77–84.

Baer, Herbert L., Virginia Grace France, and James T. Moser. "What Does a Clearinghouse Do?" *Derivatives Quarterly* 1 (Spring 1995): 39–46.

Barone-Adesi, Giovanni, and Robert E. Whaley. "Efficient Analytic Approximation of American Option Values." *The Journal of Finance* 42 (June 1987): 301–320.

Baxter, Martin, and Andrew Rennie. *Financial Calculus.* Cambridge, UK: Cambridge University Press, 1996.

Beckers, Stan. "Standard Deviations Implied in Option Prices as Predictors of Future Stock Price Variability." *Journal of Banking and Finance* 5 (September 1981): 363–382.

Becketti, Sean. "The Prepayment Risk of Mortgage-Backed Securities." *Federal Reserve Bank of Kansas City Economic Review* 74 (1989): 43–57.

Beder, Tanya Styblo. "Equity Derivatives for Investors." *The Journal of Financial Engineering* 1 (September 1992): 174–195.

Behof, John P. "Reducing Credit Risk in Over-the-Counter Derivatives." *Federal Reserve Bank of Chicago Economic Perspectives* 17 (January–February 1993): 21–31.

Bell, Adrian R., Chris Brooks, and Paul Dryburgh. "Interest Rates and Efficiency in Medieval Wool Forward Contracts." *Journal of Banking and Finance* 31 (2007): 361–380.

Berkowitz, Jeremy, and James O'Brien, "How Accurate Are Value-at-Risk Models at Commercial Banks?" *Journal of Finance* 57 (2002): 1093–1111.

Bernardo, Antonio E., and Bradford Cornell. "The Valuation of Complex Derivatives by Investment Firms: Empirical Evidence." *The Journal of Finance* 52 (June 1997): 785–798.

Bernstein, Peter L. *Against the Gods: The Remarkable Story of Risk.* New York: Wiley, 1996.

Bernstein, Peter L. *Capital Ideas Evolving.* New York: Wiley, 2007.

Bernstein, Peter L. *Capital Ideas: The Improbable Origins of Modern Wall Street.* New York: The Free Press, 1992.

Bessembinder, Hendrik. "An Empirical Analysis of Risk Premia in Futures Markets." *The Journal of Futures Markets* 13 (September 1993): 611–630.

Bhansali, Javesh D. "Managing Interest Rate Risk through Caps." *Derivatives Quarterly* 3 (Spring 1997): 39–45.

Bhattacharya, Mihir. "Transaction Data Tests of Efficiency of the Chicago Board Options Exchange." *Journal of Financial Economics* 12 (1983): 161–185.

Bicksler, James, and Andrew Chen. "An Economic Analysis of Interest Rate Swaps." *The Journal of Finance* 41 (July 1876): 645–656.

Billingsley, Randall S. *Understanding Arbitrage.* Upper Saddle River, NJ: Wharton School Publishing, 2006.

Billingsley, Randall S., and Don M. Chance. "Options Market Efficiency and the Box Spread Strategy." *The Financial Review* 20 (November 1985): 287–301.

Black, Fischer. "Fact and Fantasy in the Use of Options." *Financial Analysts Journal* 31 (July–August 1975): 36–41, 61–72.

Black, Fischer. "How to Use the Holes in Black-Scholes." *Journal of Applied Corporate Finance* 1 (Winter 1989): 67–73.

Black, Fischer. "How We Came Up with the Option Formula." *Journal of Portfolio Management* 15 (Winter 1989): 4–8.

Black, Fischer. "The Pricing of Commodity Contracts." *Journal of Financial Economics* 3 (January–February 1976): 167–179.

Black, Fischer, Emanuel Derman, and William Toy. "A One-Factor Model of Interest Rates and Its Application to Treasury Bond Options." *Financial Analysts Journal* 46 (January–February 1990): 33–39.

Black, Fischer, and Piotr Karasinski. "Bond and Option Pricing When Short Rates Are Lognormal." *Financial Analysts Journal* 47 (July–August 1991): 52–59.

Black, Fischer, and Myron Scholes. "The Pricing of Options and Corporate Liabilities." *Journal of Political Economy* 81 (May–June 1973): 637–659.

Black, Fischer, and Myron Scholes. "The Valuation of Option Contracts and a Test of Market Efficiency." *The Journal of Finance* 27 (May 1972): 399–418.

Blomeyer, Edward C., and James C. Boyd. "Empirical Tests of Boundary Conditions for Options on Treasury Bond Futures." *The Journal of Futures Markets* 4 (1988): 185–198.

Blomeyer, Edward C., and Robert C. Klemkosky. "Tests of Market Efficiency of American Call Options." In *Option Pricing,* edited by Menachem Brenner. Lexington, MA: Heath, 1983.

Bluemke, Andreas. *How to Invest in Structured Products: A Guide for Investors and Asset Managers.* West Sussex, UK: John Wiley & Sons, 2009.

Bodurtha, James N., and Georges R. Courtadon. "Efficiency Tests of the Foreign Currency Options Market." *The Journal of Finance* 13 (March 1986): 151–162.

Bookstaber, Richard M. *Option Pricing and Investment Strategies.* Chicago: Probus Publishing, 1989.

Bouzoubaa, Mohamed, and Adel Osseiran. *Exotic Options and Hybrids: A Guide to Structuring, Pricing and Trading.* West Sussex, UK: John Wiley & Sons, 2010.

Boyle, Phelim, and Feidhlim Boyle. *Derivatives: The Tools That Changed Finance.* London: Risk Books, 2001.

Breen, Richard. "The Accelerated Binomial Option Pricing Model." *Journal of Financial and Quantitative Analysis* 25 (1991): 153–164.

Brennan, Michael J. "The Pricing of Contingent Claims in Discrete Time Models." *The Journal of Finance* 34 (1979): 53–68.

Brennan, Michael J., and Eduardo S. Schwartz. "The Valuation of American Put Options." *The Journal of Finance* 32 (May 1977): 449–462.

Brenner, Menachem, and Marti G. Subrahmanyam. "A Simple Formula to Compute the Implied Volatility." *Financial Analysts Journal* 45 (September–October 1988): 80–83.

Briys, Eric, Mondher Bellalah, Huu Minh Mai, and Françoise de Varenne. *Options, Futures and Exotic Derivatives: Theory, Application and Practice.* Chichester, UK: Wiley, 1998.

Brooks, Robert. "Approaches to Valuation Illustrated with Interest Rate Swaps." *Derivatives Quarterly* 4 (1998): 51–62.

Brooks, Robert. *Building Financial Derivatives Applications with C++.* Westport, CT: Quorum Books, 1999.

Brooks, Robert. *Interest Rate Modeling and the Risk Premiums in Interest Rate Swaps.* Charlottesville, VA: Association for Investment Management and Research, 1997.

Brooks, Robert. "The Life Cycle View of Enterprise Risk Management: The Case of Southwest Airlines Jet Fuel Hedging," *Journal of Financial Education*, forthcoming.

Brooks, Robert. "Samuelson Hypothesis and Carry Arbitrage" (November 11, 2010). Available at SSRN: http://ssrn.com/abstract=1568969.

Brooks, Robert, and Miles Livingston. "A Closed-Form Equation for Bond Convexity." *Financial Analysts Journal* 45 (November–December 1989): 78–79.

Brown, Keith C., ed. *Derivative Strategies for Managing Portfolio Risk.* Charlottesville, VA: Institute for Chartered Financial Analysts, 1993.

Brown, Keith C., Van W. Harlow, and Donald J. Smith. "The Empirical Analysis of Interest Rate Swap Spreads." *Journal of Fixed Income* 3 (1993): 61–78.

Brown, Keith C., and Donald J. Smith. "Default Risk and Innovations in the Design of Interest Rate Swaps." *Financial Management* 22 (Summer 1993): 94–105.

Brown, Keith C., and Donald J. Smith. "Forward Swaps, Swap Options, and the Management of Callable Debt." *Journal of Applied Corporate Finance* 2 (1990): 59–71.

Brown, Keith C., and Donald J. Smith. *Interest Rate and Currency Swaps: A Tutorial.* Charlottesville, VA: The Research Foundation of the Institute of Chartered Financial Analysts, 1995.

Buetow, Gerald W., and Frank J. Fabozzi. *Valuation of Interest Rate Swaps and Swaptions.* New Hope, PA: Frank J. Fabozzi Associates, 2001.

Burghardt, Galen, Terry Belton, Morton Lane, Geoffrey Luce, and Richard McVey. *Eurodollar Futures and Options: Controlling Money Market Risk.* Chicago: Probus Publishing, 1991.

Burghardt, Galen, and Morton Lane. "How to Tell If Options Are Cheap." *Journal of Portfolio Management* 16 (Winter 1990): 72–78.

Caks, John, William R. Lane, Robert W. Greenleaf, and Reginald G. Joules. "A Simple Formula for Duration." *The Journal of Financial Research* 8 (Fall 1985): 245–249.

Campbell, Tim S., and William A. Kracaw. *Financial Risk Management: Fixed Income and Foreign Exchange.* New York: Harper Collins, 1993.

Carpenter, Jennifer N. "Current Issues in Accounting for Derivatives." *The Journal of Derivatives* 3 (Spring 1996): 65–71.

Castelino, Mark G. "Minimum-Variance Hedging with Futures Revisited." *Journal of Portfolio Management* 16 (Spring 1990): 74–80.

Celebuski, Matthew J., Joanne M. Hill, and John J. Kilgannon. "Managing Currency Exposures in International Portfolios." *Financial Analysts Journal* 46 (January–February 1990): 16–23.

Chance, Don M. "A Chronology of Derivatives." *Derivatives Quarterly* 2 (Winter 1995): 53–60.

Chance, Don M. "Competition and Innovation in U.S. Futures Markets." *The Journal of Alternative Investments* 11 (Summer 2008): 97–109.

Chance, Don M. *Essays in Derivatives*, 2nd ed. New York: Wiley, 2008.

Chance, Don M. *Managed Futures and Their Role in Investment Portfolios.* Charlottesville, VA: Research Foundation of the Institute of Chartered Financial Analysts, 1994.

Chance, Don M. "Research Trends in Derivatives and Risk Management Since Black-Scholes." *The Journal of Portfolio Management* 25th Anniversary Issue (May 1999): 35–46.

Chance, Don M. "A Synthesis of Binomial Option Pricing Models for Lognormally Distributed Assets." *Journal of Applied Finance* 18 (2008): 38–56.

Chance, Don M. "Translating the Greek: The Real Meaning of Call Option Derivatives." *Financial Analysts Journal* 50 (July–August 1994): 43–49.

Chance, Don M., and Stephen P. Ferris. "The CBOE Call Option Index: A Historical Record."

The Journal of Portfolio Management 12 (Fall 1985): 75–83.

Chance, Don M., and Michael L. Hemler. "The Impact of Delivery Options on Futures Prices: A Survey." *The Journal of Futures Markets* 13 (April 1993): 127–155.

Chang, Carolyn W., and Jack S. K. Chang. "Forward and Futures Prices: Evidence from the Foreign Exchange Markets." *The Journal of Finance* 4 (September 1990): 1333–1336.

Chang, Eric C. "Returns to Speculators and the Theory of Normal Backwardation." *The Journal of Finance* 40 (March 1985): 193–208.

Chang, Eric C., Peter R. Locke, and Steven C. Mann. "The Effect of CME Rule 552 on Dual Traders." *The Journal of Futures Markets* 4 (1994): 493–510.

Chang, Jack S. K., and Latha Shanker. "Hedging Effectiveness of Options and Currency Futures." *The Journal of Futures Markets* 6 (Summer 1986): 289–305.

Chen, Andrew H., Marcia Millon Cornett, and Prafulla G. Nabar. "An Empirical Examination of Interest-Rate Futures Prices." *The Journal of Futures Markets* 13 (October 1993): 781–797.

Chen, K. C., and R. Stephen Sears. "Pricing the SPIN." *Financial Management* 19 (Summer 1990): 36–47.

Chew, Lilian. *Managing Derivatives Risk: The Use and Abuse of Leverage.* New York: Wiley, 1996.

Chicago Board Options Exchange. *Market Statistics 1996.* Chicago: Chicago Board Options Exchange, 1996.

Ching, J. "A Market Perspective on Interest Rate Swap Clearing and Execution." *Futures Industry* (June 2011): 28–34.

Chiras, Donald P., and Steven Manaster. "The Information Content of Option Prices and a Test of Market Efficiency." *Journal of Financial Economics* 6 (June–September 1978): 213–234.

Chriss, Neil A. *Black-Scholes and Beyond: Option Pricing Models.* Chicago: Irwin Professional, 1997.

Christoffersen, Peter F. *Elements of Financial Risk Management.* Amsterdam: Academic Press, 2003.

Chua, Jess H. "A Closed-Form Formula for Calculating Bond Duration." *Financial Analysts Journal* 40 (May–June 1984): 76–78.

Chung, San-Lin, and Mark Shackleton. "The Binomial Black-Scholes Model and the Greeks." *Journal of Futures Markets* 22 (2002): 143–153.

Clarke, Roger G. *Options and Futures: A Tutorial.* Charlottesville, VA: The Research Foundation of the Institute of Chartered Financial Analysts, 1992.

Clarke, Roger G., and Robert D. Arnott. "The Cost of Portfolio Insurance: Tradeoffs and Choices." *Financial Analysts Journal* 43 (November–December 1987): 35–47.

Clarke, Roger G., and Mark P. Kritzman. *Currency Management: Concepts and Practices.* Charlottesville, VA: The Research Foundation of the Institute of Chartered Financial Analysts, 1996.

Clements, Sherwood, Alan J. Ziobrowski, and Mark Holder. "Lumber Futures and Timberland Investments." *Journal of Real Estate Research* 33 (2011): 49–71.

Clewlow, Les, and Chris Strickland, eds. *Exotic Options: State of the Art.* London: International Thomson, 1997.

Clewlow, Les, and Chris Strickland. *Implementing Derivatives Models.* Chichester, UK: Wiley, 1998.

Cohen, Guy. *The Bible of Option Strategies: The Definitive Guide for Practical Trading Strategies.* Upper Saddle River, NJ: Financial Times Prentice-Hall, 2005.

Coleman, Thomas C., and Roger D. Rutz. "Self-Regulation and Government Regulation of Futures and Options Markets." *Journal of Business* 59 (1986): S1–S4.

Coleman, Thomas S. *A Practical Guide to Risk Management.* Charlottesville, Virginia: Research Foundation of the CFA Institute, 2011.

Commodity Futures Trading Commission. *Annual Report,* various years.

Conine, Thomas E., and Maurry Tamarkin. "A Pedagogic Note on the Derivation of the Comparative Statics of the Option Pricing Model." *Financial Review* 19 (November 1984): 397–400.

Constantinides, George M., Michal Czerwonko, Jens Carsten Jackwerth, and Stylianos Perrakis, "Are Options on Index Futures Profitable for Risk-Averse Investors? Empirical Evidence." *The Journal of Finance* 66 (2011): 1407–1437.

Constantinides, George M., Jens Carsten Jackwerth, and Stylianos Perrakis. "Mispricing of S&P 500 Index Options." *Review of Financial Studies* 22 (2009): 1247–1277.

Cooper, Ian, and Antonio Mello. "The Default Risk of Swaps." *Journal of Finance* 46 (1991): 597–620.

Corcoran, Andrea M. "Developing a Risk Management Plan: A System Checklist for Derivatives." *Derivatives Quarterly* 1 (Winter 1994): 10–15.

Cornell, Bradford. "Spot Rates, Forward Rates and Exchange Market Efficiency." *Journal of Financial Economics* 5 (August 1977): 55–65.

Cornell, Bradford, and Mark Reinganum. "Forward and Futures Prices: Evidence from the Foreign Exchange Market." *The Journal of Finance* 36 (December 1981): 1035–1045.

Corrado, Charles J., and Tie Su. "Implied Volatility Skews and Stock Index Skewness and Kurtosis Implied by S&P 500 Index Option Prices." *The Journal of Derivatives* 4 (Summer 1997): 8–19.

Cox, John C., Jonathan E. Ingersoll, Jr., and Stephen A. Ross. "The Relation between Forward Prices and Futures Prices." *Journal of Financial Economics* 9 (December 1981): 321–346.

Cox, John C., and Stephen A. Ross. "The Valuation of Options for Alternative Stochastic Processes." *Journal of Financial Economics* 3 (1976): 145–166.

Cox, John C., Stephen A. Ross, and Mark Rubinstein. "Option Pricing: A Simplified Approach." *Journal of Financial Economics* 7 (September 1979): 229–263.

Cox, John C., and Mark Rubinstein. *Options Markets*. Englewood Cliffs, NJ: Prentice-Hall, 1985.

Cox, John C., and Mark Rubinstein. "A Survey of Alternative Option Pricing Models." In *Option Pricing*, edited by Menachem Brenner. Lexington, MA: Heath, 1983.

Crabbe, Leland E., and Joseph D. Argilagos. "Anatomy of the Structured Note Market." *Journal of Applied Corporate Finance* 7 (1994): 85–98.

Credit Derivatives: Applications for Risk Management, Investment and Portfolio Optimization. London: Risk Books, 1998.

Credit Risk: Models and Management. London: Risk Books, 1999.

Crouhy, Michel, Dan Galai, and Robert Mark. "Model Risk." *The Journal of Financial Engineering* 7 (September–December 1998): 267–288.

Crowley, Paul. "Why and How Fundamental Managers Should Use Options: Part I." *Derivatives Quarterly* 2 (Spring 1996): 52–66.

Crowley, Paul. "Why and How Fundamental Managers Should Use Options: Part II." *Derivatives Quarterly* 2 (Summer 1996): 40–55.

Daigler, Robert T. *Financial Futures Markets: Concepts, Evidence, and Applications*. New York: Harper Collins, 1993.

Daigler, Robert T. *Financial Futures & Options Markets: Concepts and Strategies*. New York: Harper Collins, 1994.

Dawson, Frederic S. "Risks and Returns in Continuous Option Writing." *The Journal of Portfolio Management* 5 (Winter 1979): 58–63.

Dawson, Paul. "Comparative Pricing of American and European Index Options: An Empirical Analysis." *The Journal of Futures Markets* 14 (May 1994): 363–378.

Derivatives Credit Risk: Further Advances in Measurement and Management, 2nd ed. London: Risk Books, 1999.

Derman, Emanuel. *My Life as a Quant: Reflections on Physics and Finance*. New York: Wiley, 2004.

Derman, Emanuel, and Iraj Kani. "The Ins and Outs of Barrier Options: Part I." *Derivatives Quarterly* 3 (Winter 1996): 55–67.

Derman, Emanuel, and Iraj Kani. "The Ins and Outs of Barrier Options: Part II." *Derivatives Quarterly* 3 (Spring 1997): 73–80.

Derman, Emanuel, and Iraj Kani. "Riding on a Smile." *Risk* 7 (January 1994): 32–39.

DeRosa, David F. *Currency Derivatives*. New York: Wiley, 1998.

DiMartino, Dawn, Linda Ward, Janet Stevens, and Winn Sargisson. "Procter & Gamble's Derivatives Loss: Isolated Incident or Wake-Up Call?" *Derivatives Quarterly* 2 (Spring 1996): 10–21.

Dowd, Kevin. *Beyond Value at Risk: The New Science of Risk Management*. Chichester, UK: Wiley, 1998.

Drennan, Ann S. "Keys to Successful Risk Management: Part 1." *Derivatives Quarterly* 1 (Summer 1995): 54–58.

Drennan, Ann S. "Keys to Successful Risk Management: Part 2." *Derivatives Quarterly* 2 (Winter 1995): 46–51.

Drennan, Ann S. "Keys to Successful Risk Management: Part 3." *Derivatives Quarterly* 2 (Spring 1996): 47–51.

Dubofsky, David A. *Options and Financial Futures: Valuation and Uses*. New York: McGraw-Hill, 1992.

Dubofsky, David A., and Thomas W. Miller, Jr. *Derivatives: Valuation and Risk Management*. New York: Oxford University Press, 2003.

Duffie, Darrell. "Corporate Risk Management 101: Why Hedge?" *Corporate Risk Management* 3 (May 1991): 22–25.

Duffie, Darrell. *Futures Markets*. Englewood Cliffs, NJ: Prentice Hall, 1989.

Duffie, Darrell, and Kenneth J. Singleton. "An Econometric Model of the Term Structure of Interest-Rate Swap Yields." *The Journal of Finance* 52 (1997): 1287–1321.

Dunbar, Nicholas. *Inventing Money: The Story of Long-Term Capital Management and the Legends Behind It*. Chichester, UK: Wiley, 2000.

Dupire, Bruno. "Pricing with a Smile." *Risk* 7 (January 1994): 18–20.

Durbin, Michael. *All About Derivatives*. New York: McGraw-Hill, 2005.

Dusak, Katherine. "Futures Trading and Investor Returns: An Investigation of Commodity Risk Premiums." *Journal of Political Economy* 81 (December 1973): 1387–1406.

Eaker, Mark R., and Dwight M. Grant. "Currency Hedging Strategies for International Diversified Equity Portfolios." *Journal of Portfolio Management* 17 (Fall 1990): 30–32.

Eckerdt, Walter L., Jr., and Stephen L. Williams. "The Complete Options Indexes." *Financial Analysts Journal* 40 (July–August 1984): 48–57.

Ederington, Louis H. "The Hedging Performance of the New Futures Market." *The Journal of Finance* 34 (March 1979): 157–170.

Edwards, Franklin R., and Jimmy Liew. "Hedge Funds versus Managed Futures as Asset Classes." *The Journal of Derivatives* 6 (Summer 1999): 45–64.

Edwards, Franklin R., and Cindy W. Ma. *Futures and Options*. New York: McGraw-Hill, 1992.

Einzig, Robert, and Bruce Lange. "Swaps at Transamerica: Applications and Analyses." *Journal of Applied Corporate Finance* 2 (Winter 1990): 48–58.

El-Jahel, Lina, William Perraudin, and Peter Sellin. "Value at Risk for Derivatives." *The Journal of Derivatives* 6 (Summer 1999): 7–26.

Elton, Edwin, Martin Gruber, and Joel Rentzler. "Intra-Day Tests of Efficiency of the Treasury Bill Futures Market." *Review of Economics and Statistics* 66 (1984): 129–137.

Epps, Wake T. *Pricing Derivatives Securities*. Singapore: World Scientific, 2000.

Equity Derivatives: Applications in Risk Management and Investment. London: Risk Books, 1997.

Evans, John, and Stephen H. Archer. "Diversification and the Reduction of Dispersion: An Empirical Analysis." *The Journal of Finance* 23 (December 1968): 761–767.

Fabozzi, Frank J. *The Handbook of Fixed Income Securities*, 4th ed. Homewood, IL: Business One Irwin, 1994.

Fabozzi, Frank J., Anand K. Bhattacharya, and William S. Berliner. *Mortgage-Backed Securities: Products, Structuring, and Analytical Techniques*. Hoboken, NJ: John Wiley & Sons, 2007.

Fay, Stephen. *The Collapse of Barings*. New York: W. W. Norton, 1997.

Fenton-O'Creevy, Mark, Nigel Nicholson, Emma Soane, and Paul Willman. *Traders Risks, Decisions, and Management in Financial Markets*. Oxford: Oxford University Press, 2005.

Ferguson, Robert. "Some Formulas for Evaluating Two Popular Option Strategies." *Financial Analysts Journal* 49 (September–October 1993): 71–76.

Figelman, Ilya. "Expected Return and Risk of Covered Call Strategies." *The Journal of Portfolio Management* 34 (Summer 2008): 81–97.

Figlewski, Stephen. "The Birth of the AAA Derivatives Subsidiary." *The Journal of Derivatives* 1 (Summer 1994): 80–84.

Figlewski, Stephen. "Explaining the Early Discounts on Stock Index Futures: The Case for Disequilibrium." *Financial Analysts Journal* 40 (1984): 43–47, 67.

Figlewski, Stephen. "Hedging Performance and Basis Risk in Stock Index Futures." *The Journal of Finance* 39 (July 1984): 657–669.

Figlewski, Stephen. "Hedging with Stock Index Futures: Theory and Application in a New Market." *The Journal of Futures Markets* 5 (Summer 1985): 183–199.

Figlewski, Stephen. "How to Lose Money in Derivatives." *The Journal of Derivatives* 2 (Winter 1994): 75–82.

Figlewski, Stephen. "What Does an Option Pricing Model Tell Us about Option Prices?" *Financial Analysts Journal* 45 (September–October 1989): 12–15.

Figlewski, Stephen, William L. Silber, and Marti G. Subrahmanyam. *Financial Options: From Theory to Practice*. Homewood, IL: Business One Irwin, 1990.

Financial Derivatives: New Instruments and Their Uses. Atlanta: Federal Reserve Bank of Atlanta, 1993.

Finnerty, John D. "Financial Engineering in Corporate Finance: An Overview." *Financial Management* 17 (Winter 1988): 14–33.

Finnerty, John D. "The Time Warner Rights Offering: A Case Study in Financial Engineering." *The Journal of Financial Engineering* 1 (June 1992): 38–61.

Finnerty, John D. and Pathak Kishlaya. "A Review of Recent Derivatives Litigation." *Fordham Journal of Corporate & Financial Law* 16 (2011): 73–123.

Flavell, Richard. *Swaps and Other Instruments*, 2nd ed. New York: Wiley, 2010.

Francis, Jack Clark, and Avner Wolf. *The Handbook of Interest Rate Risk Management*. Burr Ridge, IL: Irwin Professional Publishing, 1994.

Franckle, Charles T. "The Hedging Performance of the New Futures Market: Comment." *The Journal of Finance* 35 (December 1980): 1273–1279.

Fraser, John and Betty J. Simkins, eds. *Enterprise Risk Management: Today's Leading Research and Best Practices for Tomorrow's Executives.* New York: Wiley, 2010.

French, Kenneth. "A Comparison of Futures and Forward Prices." *Journal of Financial Economics* 12 (1983): 311–342.

French, Kenneth. "Detecting Spot Price Forecasts in Futures Prices." *The Journal of Business* 59 (1986): S39–S54.

French, Kenneth. "Pricing Financial Futures Contracts: An Introduction." *The Journal of Applied Corporate Finance* 1 (1989): 59–66.

From Black-Scholes to Black Holes. London: Risk/ FINEX, 1992.

Froot, Kenneth A., David S. Scharfstein, and Jeremy C. Stein, "Risk Management: Coordinating Corporate Investment and Financing Policies." *The Journal of Finance* 48 (December 1993): 1629–1658.

Furbush, Dean. "Program Trading and Price Movements: Evidence from the October 1987 Market Crash." *Financial Management* 18 (Fall 1989): 68–83.

Fusaro, Peter, ed. *The Professional Risk Managers' Guide to the Energy Market. Prmia Risk Management Series.* New York: McGraw-Hill, 2008.

Gadkari, Vilas. "Relative Pricing of Currency Options: A Tutorial." *Advances in Futures and Options Research* 1, part A (1986): 227–245.

Galai, Dan. "Characterization of Options." *Journal of Banking and Finance* 1 (December 1977): 373–385.

Galai, Dan. "A Convexity Test for Traded Options." *Quarterly Review of Economics and Business* 19 (Summer 1979): 83–90.

Galai, Dan. "Empirical Tests of Boundary Conditions for CBOE Options." *Journal of Financial Economics* 6 (1978): 187–211.

Galai, Dan. "A Survey of Empirical Tests of Option Pricing Models." In *Option Pricing,* edited by Menachem Brenner. Lexington, MA: Heath, 1983.

Galai, Dan. "Tests of Market Efficiency of the Chicago Board Options Exchange." *The Journal of Business* 50 (April 1977): 167–197.

Garcia, C. B., and F. J. Gould. "An Empirical Study of Portfolio Insurance." *Financial Analysts Journal* 43 (July–August 1987): 44–54.

Garman, Mark B., and Steven W. Kohlhagen. "Foreign Currency Option Values." *Journal of International Money and Finance* 2 (1983): 231–237.

Gastineau, Gary L. "An Index of Listed Options Premiums." *Financial Analysts Journal* 33 (May–June 1977): 70–75.

Gastineau, Gary L. "An Introduction to Special Purpose Derivatives: Options with a Payout Depending on More Than One Variable." *The Journal of Derivatives* 1 (Fall 1993): 98–104.

Gastineau, Gary L. "An Introduction to Special Purpose Derivatives: Path-Dependent Options." *The Journal of Derivatives* 1 (Winter 1993): 78–86.

Gastineau, Gary L. *The Options Manual,* 3rd ed. New York: McGraw-Hill, 1988.

Gastineau, Gary L., and Mark P. Kritzman. *Dictionary of Financial Risk Management,* 2nd ed. New Hope, PA: Frank Fabozzi Associates, 1999.

Gastineau, Gary L., and Albert Madansky. "Some Comments on the Chicago Board Options Exchange Call Option Index." *Financial Analysts Journal* 40 (July–August 1984): 58–67.

Gastineau, Gary L., Donald J. Smith, and Rebecca Todd. *Risk Management, Derivatives, and Financial Analysis Under SFAS 133.* Charlottesville, VA: The Research Foundation of the Association for Investment Management and Research, 2001.

Gay, Gerald D., and Robert W. Kolb. "Immunizing Bond Portfolios with Interest Rate Futures." *Financial Management* 11 (Summer 1982): 81–89.

Gay, Gerald D., Robert W. Kolb, and Raymond Chiang. "Interest Rate Hedging: An Empirical Test of Alternative Strategies." *The Journal of Financial Research* 6 (Fall 1983): 1–13.

Gemmill, Gordon. *Options Pricing: An International Perspective.* London: McGraw-Hill, 1993.

George, Thomas J., and Francis A. Longstaff. "Bid-Ask Spreads and Trading Activity in the S&P 100 Index Options Market." *Journal of Financial and Quantitative Analysis* 28 (September 1993): 381–397.

Geske, Robert. "A Note on an Analytic Formula for Unprotected American Call Options on Stocks with Known Dividends." *Journal of Financial Economics* 7 (December 1979): 375–380.

Geske, Robert. "The Valuation of Compound Options." *Journal of Financial Economics* 7 (March 1979): 63–81.

Geske, Robert, and H. E. Johnson. "The American Put Option Valued Analytically." *The Journal of Finance* 39 (December 1984): 1511–1524.

Gibson, Rajna. *Option Valuation.* New York: McGraw-Hill, 1991.

Gombola, Michael J., Rodney L. Roenfeldt, and Philip L. Cooley. "Spreading Strategies in CBOE Options: Evidence on Market Performance." *The Journal of Financial Research* 1 (Winter 1978): 35–44.

Goodman, Laurie S. "Anatomy of the Secondary Structured Note Market." *Derivatives Quarterly* 2 (1995): 39–43.

Goodman, Laurie S. "The Use of Interest Rate Swaps in Managing Corporate Liabilities." *Journal of Applied Corporate Finance* 2 (1990): 35–47.

Gould, John P., and Dan Galai. "Transactions Costs and the Relationship between Put and Call Prices." *Journal of Financial Economics* 1 (1974): 105–129.

Grabbe, J. Orlin. "The Pricing of Call and Put Options on Foreign Exchange." *Journal of International Money and Finance* 2 (1983): 239–253.

Gramm, Wendy L., and Gerald D. Gay. "Scams, Scoundrels, and Scapegoats: A Taxonomy of CEA Regulation over Derivative Instruments." *The Journal of Derivatives* 1 (Spring 1994): 6–24.

Gray, Roger W. "The Search for a Risk Premium." *Journal of Political Economy* 64 (June 1961): 250–260.

Group of Thirty. *Derivatives: Practices and Principles.* Washington, D.C.: Group of Thirty, 1993.

Grube, R. Corwin, Don B. Panton, and J. Michael Terrell. "Risks and Rewards in Covered Call Positions." *The Journal of Portfolio Management* 5 (Winter 1979): 64–68.

Hart, James F. "The Riskless Option Hedge: An Incomplete Guide." *The Journal of Portfolio Management* 4 (Winter 1978): 58–63.

Hartzmark, Michael L. "Luck versus Forecasting Ability: Determinants of Trader Performance in Futures Markets." *Journal of Business* 64 (1991): 49–74.

Hartzmark, Michael L. "Returns to Individual Traders of Futures: Aggregate Results." *Journal of Political Economy* 95 (1987): 1292–1306.

Haslett, Walter V. "Bud," ed. *Risk Management: Foundations for a Changing World.* New York: Wiley, 2010.

Haug, Espen Gaarder. *The Complete Guide to Option Pricing Formulas,* 2nd ed. New York: McGraw-Hill, 2007.

Heath, David, Robert Jarrow, and Andrew Morton. "Bond Pricing and the Term Structure of Interest Rates." *Econometrica* 60 (January 1992): 77–105.

Heath, David, Robert Jarrow, and Andrew Morton. "Bond Pricing and the Term Structure of Interest Rates: A Discrete Time Approximation." *Journal of Financial and Quantitative Analysis* 25 (1990): 419–440.

Heath, David, Robert Jarrow, and Andrew Morton. "Contingent Claim Valuation with a Random Evolution of Interest Rates." *The Review of Futures Markets* 9 (1990): 54–76.

Hemler, Michael L., and Thomas W. Miller, Jr. "Box Spread Arbitrage Profits Following the 1987 Market Crash: Real or Illusory?" *Journal of Financial and Quantitative Analysis* 32 (March 1997): 71–90.

Hentschel, Ludger, and Clifford W. Smith, Jr. "Controlling Risks in Derivatives Markets." *The Journal of Financial Engineering* 4 (June 1995): 101–125.

Herbst, Anthony F., Dilip D. Kare, and Stephen C. Caples. "Hedging Effectiveness and Minimum Risk Hedge Ratios in the Presence of Autocorrelation: Foreign Currency Futures." *The Journal of Futures Markets* 3 (1989): 185–197.

Hicks, John R. *Value and Capital,* 2nd ed. Oxford: Clarendon Press, 1939.

Hieronymous, Thomas A. *The Economics of Futures Trading.* New York: Commodity Research Bureau, 1977.

Hill, Joanne, and Frank J. Jones. "Equity Trading, Program Trading, Portfolio Insurance, Computer Trading and All That." *Financial Analysts Journal* 44 (July–August 1988): 29–38.

Hill, Joanne, and Thomas Schneeweis. "The Hedging Effectiveness of Foreign Currency Futures." *The Journal of Financial Research* 5 (Spring 1982): 95–104.

Ho, Thomas S. Y., and Sang-Bin Lee. "Term Structure Movements and Pricing Interest Rate Contingent Claims." *The Journal of Finance* 41 (December 1986): 1011–1030.

Hodgson, Raphael. "The Birth of the Swap." *Financial Analysts Journal* 65 (2009): 32–35.

Houthakker, Hendrik S. "Can Speculators Forecast Prices?" *Review of Economics and Statistics* 39 (1957): 143–151.

Howard, Charles T., and Louis J. D'Antonio. "The Cost of Hedging and the Optimal Hedge Ratio." *The Journal of Futures Markets* 14 (April 1994): 237–258.

Hsia, Chi-Cheng. "On Binomial Option Pricing." *The Journal of Financial Research* 6 (1983): 41–46.

Hsieh, David A., and Merton H. Miller. "Margin Regulation and Stock Market Volatility." *The Journal of Finance* 45 (March 1990): 3–29.

Hull, John C. *Fundamentals of Futures and Options,* 7th ed. Upper Saddle River, NJ: Prentice Hall, 2010.

Hull, John C. *Options, Futures and Other Derivatives,* 8th ed. Upper Saddle River, NJ: Prentice Hall, 2012.

Jabbour, George, and Philip Budwick. *The Option Trader Handbook: Strategies and Trade Adjustments.* Hoboken, NJ: John Wiley & Sons, 2010.

James, Jessica, and Nick Webber. *Interest Rate Modelling.* Chichester, UK: John Wiley, 2000.

Jarrow, Robert A., ed. *Over the Rainbow: Developments in Exotic Options and Complex Swaps*. London: Financial Engineering, 1995.

Jarrow, Robert A. *Modelling Fixed Income Securities and Interest Rate Options*, 2nd ed. Stanford, CA: Stanford University Press, 2002.

Jarrow, Robert A., and George Oldfield. "Forward Contracts and Futures Contracts." *Journal of Financial Economics* 9 (1981): 373–382.

Jarrow, Robert A., and Andrew Rudd. *Option Pricing*. Homewood, IL: Irwin, 1983.

Jarrow, Robert A., and Stuart Turnbull. *Derivative Securities*, 2nd ed. Cincinnati, OH: South-Western, 2000.

Jha, Siddhartha. *Interest Rate Markets: A Practical Approach to Fixed Income*. New York: Wiley Finance, 2011.

Johnson, Leland L. "The Theory of Hedging and Speculation in Commodity Futures Markets." *Review of Economic Studies* 27 (October 1960): 139–151.

Johnson, Philip McBride. *Derivatives: A Manager's Guide to the World's Most Powerful Financial Instruments*. New York: McGraw-Hill, 1999.

Jones, Frank J. "Spreads: Tails, Turtles, and All That." *The Journal of Futures Markets* 2 (Spring 1981): 63–82.

Jones, Travis, and Robert Brooks. "An Analysis of Single-Stock Futures Trading in the U.S.," *Financial Services Review* 14 (June 2005): 85–96.

Jorion, Philippe. *The Financial Risk Manager Handbook: 2001–2002*. New York: Wiley, 2001.

Jorion, Philippe. *Value at Risk: A New Benchmark for Controlling Derivatives Risk*, 2nd ed. New York: McGraw-Hill, 2001.

Jorion, Philippe, and Sarkis Joseph Khoury. *Financial Risk Management: Domestic and International Dimensions*. Cambridge, MA: Blackwell, 1996.

Jorion, Philippe, and Robert Roper. *Big Bets Gone Bad: Derivatives and Bankruptcy in Orange County*. Orlando, FL: Academic Press, 1995.

Kairys, Joseph P., Jr., and Nicholas Valerio III. "The Market for Equity Options in the 1870s." *The Journal of Finance* 52 (September 1997): 1707–1723.

Kamara, Avraham. "The Behavior of Futures Prices: A Review of Theory and Evidence." *Financial Analysts Journal* 40 (July–August 1984): 68–75.

Kamara, Avraham. "Issues in Futures Markets: A Survey." *The Journal of Futures Markets* 2 (Fall 1982): 261–294.

Kane, Edward J. "Regulatory Structure in Futures Markets: Jurisdictional Competition Between the SEC, the CFTC and Other Agencies." *The Journal of Futures Markets* 3 (1984): 367–384.

Kat, Harry M. "Portfolio Insurance: A Comparison of Alternative Strategies." *The Journal of Financial Engineering* 2 (December 1993): 415–442.

Kat, Harry M. *Structured Equity Derivatives*. Chichester, UK: Wiley, 2001.

Kawaller, Ira G. "A Note: Debunking the Myth of the Risk-Free Return." *The Journal of Futures Markets* 7 (1987): 327–331.

Kawaller, Ira G. "Interest Rate Swaps versus Eurodollar Strips." *Financial Analysts Journal* 45 (September–October 1989): 55–61.

Kawaller, Ira G. "Choosing the Best Interest Rate Hedge Ratio." *Financial Analysts Journal* 48 (September–October 1992): 74–77.

Kawaller, Ira G. "Comparing Eurodollar Strips to Interest Rate Swaps." *The Journal of Derivatives* 2 (Fall 1994): 67–79.

Kawaller, Ira G. "Foreign Exchange Hedge Management Tools: A Way to Enhance Performance." *Financial Analysts Journal* 49 (September–October 1993): 79–80.

Kawaller, Ira G. "Short-Term Interest Rate Hedging: Hedge Ratios Revisited." *The Journal of Financial Engineering* 3 (September 1996): 267–277.

Kawaller, Ira G. "Tailing Futures Hedges/Tailing Spreads." *The Journal of Derivatives* 5 (Winter 1997): 62–70.

Kawaller, Ira G. "The TED Spread." *Derivatives Quarterly* 3 (Spring 1997): 46–54.

Kawaller, Ira G. "Trading and Hedging with Option Calendar Spreads." *Derivatives Quarterly* 1 (Summer 1995): 73–76.

Kawaller, Ira G. "Understanding Structured Notes." *Derivatives Quarterly* 1 (Spring 1995): 29–32.

Keynes, John Maynard. *A Treatise on Money*. London: Macmillan, 1930.

Klein, Robert A., and Jess Lederman, eds. *Derivatives Risk and Responsibility*. Chicago: Irwin Professional, 1996.

Klemkosky, Robert C., and Bruce G. Resnick. "An Ex-Ante Analysis of Put-Call Parity." *Journal of Financial Economics* 8 (1980): 363–378.

Klemkosky, Robert C., and Bruce G. Resnick. "Put-Call Parity and Market Efficiency." *The Journal of Finance* 34 (December 1979): 1141–1155.

Kolb, Robert W. *Financial Derivatives*, 2nd ed. Cambridge, MA: Blackwell, 1996.

Kolb, Robert W. *The Financial Derivatives Reader*. Miami: Kolb Publishing, 1992.

Kolb, Robert W. *Options: An Introduction*. Miami: Kolb Publishing, 1991.

Kolb, Robert W. "Risk Management and Risk Transfer: Distributive Justice in Finance." *The Journal of Alternative Investments* 13 (2010): 90–98.

Kolb, Robert W. *Understanding Futures Markets*, 3rd ed. Miami: Kolb Publishing, 1991.

Kolb, Robert W., and Raymond Chiang. "Improving Hedging Performance Using Interest Rate Futures." *Financial Management* 10 (Fall 1981): 72–79.

Kolb, Robert W., Gerald D. Gay, and William C. Hunter. "Liquidity Requirements for Financial Futures Hedges." *Financial Analysts Journal* 41 (May–June 1985): 60–68.

Kolb, Robert W., and James A. Overdahl. *Futures, Options, and Swaps*, 5th ed. New York: Blackwell, 2007.

Kritzman, Mark. "The Minimum-Risk Currency Hedge Ratio and Foreign Asset Exposure." *Financial Analysts Journal* 49 (September–October 1993): 77–78.

Kritzman, Mark. "What Practitioners Need to Know About Option Replication." *Financial Analysts Journal* 48 (January–February 1992): 21–23.

Kupiec, Paul H. "Stress Testing in a Value at Risk Framework." *The Journal of Derivatives* 6 (Fall 1998): 7–24.

Kupiec, Paul H. "Techniques for Verifying the Accuracy of Risk Measurement Models," *Journal of Derivatives* 3 (2005): 73–84.

Kuserk, Gregory J., and Peter R. Locke. "Market Maker Competition on Futures Exchanges." *The Journal of Derivatives* 1 (Summer 1994): 56–66.

Kuserk, Gregory J., and Peter R. Locke. "Market Making with Price Limits." *The Journal of Futures Markets* 16 (September 1996): 677–696.

Kuserk, Gregory J., and Peter R. Locke. "Scalper Behavior in Futures Markets: An Empirical Examination." *The Journal of Futures Markets* 13 (June 1993): 409–431.

Labuszewski, John. *Trading Options on Futures*. New York: Wiley, 2000.

Lam, James. *Enterprise Risk Management: From Incentives to Controls*. Hoboken, NJ: Wiley, 2003.

Lambert, Emily. *The Futures: The Rise of the Speculator and the Origins of the World's Biggest Markets*. New York: Basic Books (2011).

Latané, Henry A., and Richard J. Rendleman, Jr. "Standard Deviations of Stock Price Ratios Implied in Option Prices." *The Journal of Finance* 31 (May 1976): 369–382.

Leeson, Nick, and Edward Whitley. *Rogue Trader: How I Brought Down Barings Bank and Shook the Financial World*. Boston: Little, Brown, 1996.

Leuthold, Raymond M., Joan C. Junkus, and Jean E. Cordier. *The Theory and Practice of Futures Markets*. Englewood Cliffs, NJ: Prentice Hall, 1989.

Lewent, Judy C., and A. John Kearney. "Identifying, Measuring, and Hedging Currency Risk at Merck." *Journal of Applied Corporate Finance* 2 (Winter 1990): 19–28.

Lewis, Michael. *The Big Short: Inside the Doomsday Machine*. New York: W. W. Norton, 2010.

Levy, Jared. *Your Options Handbook: The Practical Reference and Strategy Guide to Trading Options*. Hoboken, NJ: John Wiley & Sons, 2011.

Lindsey, Richard R., and Barry Schachter. *How I Became a Quant: Insights from 25 of Wall Street's Elite*. New York: Wiley, 2007.

Lintner, John. "The Valuation of Risk Assets and the Selection of Risky Investments in Stock Portfolios and Capital Budgets." *Review of Economics and Statistics* 47 (February 1965): 13–37.

Litzenberger, Robert H. "Swaps: Plain and Fanciful." *The Journal of Finance* 47 (July 1992): 831–850.

Locke, Peter R., Asani Sarker, and Lifan Wu. "Market Liquidity and Trade Welfare in Multiple Dealer Markets: Evidence from Dual Trading Restrictions." *Journal of Financial and Quantitative Analysis* 34 (March 1999): 57–88.

Longstaff, Francis A. "The Benefits and Costs of Dual Trading." *Journal of Financial Engineering* 2 (1993): 51–54.

Ludwig, Mary S. *Understanding Interest Rate Swaps*. New York: McGraw-Hill, 1993.

MacBeth, James D., and Larry J. Merville. "An Empirical Examination of the Black-Scholes Call Option Pricing Model." *The Journal of Finance* 34 (December 1979): 1173–1186.

MacBeth, James D., and Larry J. Merville. "Tests of the Black-Scholes and Cox Call Option Valuation Models." *The Journal of Finance* 35 (May 1980): 285–300.

Mackay, Robert J. "Removing the Major Tax Impediment to Business Hedging." *The Journal of Financial Engineering* 2 (March 1993): 19–26.

MacKenzie, Donald. *An Engine, Not a Camera: How Financial Models Shape Markets*. Cambridge, MA: The MIT Press, 2006.

MacKenzie, Donald. "An Equation and Its Worlds: Bricolage, Exemplars, Disunity and Performativity in Financial Economics." *Social Studies of Science* 33 (December, 2003): 831–868.

MacKenzie, Donald. "Long-Term Capital Management and the Sociology of Arbitrage." *Economy and Society* 32 (August, 2003): 349–380.

MacKenzie, Donald. "Physics and Finance: S-Terms and Modern Finance as a Topic for Science Studies." *Science, Technology, & Human Values* 26 (Spring 2001): 115–144.

MacKenzie, Donald, and Yuval Millo. "Constructing a Market, Performing Theory: The Historical Sociology of a Financial Derivatives Exchange." *American Journal of Sociology* 109 (July, 2003): 107–145.

MacKinlay, A. Craig, and Krishna Ramaswamy. "Index-Futures Arbitrage and the Behavior of Stock Index Futures Prices." *The Review of Financial Studies* 1 (1988): 137–158.

Malkiel, Burton G., and Richard E. Quandt. *Strategies and Rational Decisions in the Securities Options Market*. Cambridge, MA: The MIT Press, 1969.

Managing Currency Risk. Charlottesville Association for Investment Management and Research, 1987.

Manaster, Steven, and Gary Koehler. "The Calculation of Implied Variances from the Black-Scholes Model: A Note." *The Journal of Finance* 37 (March 1982): 227–230.

Manaster, Stephen, and Steven C. Mann. "Life in the Pits: Competitive Market Making and Inventory Control." *Review of Financial Studies* 9 (Fall 1996): 953–975.

Mann, Steven V. "Calls Are Like Air Conditioners; Puts Are Like Heaters." *Journal of Financial Education* 22 (Spring 1996): 61–64.

Margrabe, William. "The Value of an Option to Exchange One Asset for Another." *The Journal of Finance* 33 (March 1978): 177–186.

Marshall, John F., and Vipul K. Bansal. *Financial Engineering*, 2nd ed. Miami: Kolb Publishing, 1993.

Marshall, John F., and Kenneth R. Kapner. *The Swaps Market*, 2nd ed. Miami: Kolb Publishing, 1993.

Marthinsen, John. *Risk Takers: Uses and Abuses of Derivatives*, 2nd ed. Boston: Pearson, 2008.

Mason, Scott, Robert Merton, André Perold, and Peter Tufano. *Cases in Financial Engineering: Applied Studies of Financial Innovation*. Englewood Cliffs, NJ: Prentice Hall, 1995.

McCabe, George M., and Charles T. Franckle. "The Effectiveness of Rolling the Hedge Forward in the Treasury Bill Futures Market." *Financial Management* 12 (Summer 1983): 21–29.

McCabe, George M., and Donald P. Solberg. "Hedging in the Treasury Bill Futures Market When the Hedged Instrument and the Delivered Instrument Are Not Matched." *The Journal of Futures Markets* 9 (December 1989): 529–537.

McDonald, Robert L. *Derivatives Markets*, 2nd ed. Boston: Pearson, 2006.

McIntyre, Michael L., and David Jackson. "Great in Practice, Not in Theory: An Empirical Examination of Covered Call Writing." *Journal of Derivatives & Hedge Funds* 13 (2007): 66–79.

McIver, Jeffrey. "Tree Power." *Risk* 6 (December 1993): 58–64.

McLaughlin, Robert. *Over-the-Counter Derivative Products: A Guide to Business and Legal Risk Management and Documentation*. New York: McGraw-Hill, 1999.

McMillan, Lawrence G. *McMillan on Options*. New York: John Wiley, 1996.

Mehrling, Perry G. *Fischer Black and the Revolutionary Idea of Finance*. New York: Wiley, 2005.

Melamed, Leo. *For Crying Out Loud*. Hoboken, NJ: John Wiley & Sons, 2009.

Merton, Robert C. "The Relationship between Put and Call Option Prices: Comment." *The Journal of Finance* 28 (March 1973): 183–184.

Merton, Robert C. "Theory of Rational Option Pricing." *Bell Journal of Economics and Management Science* 4 (Spring 1973): 141–183.

Meulbroek, Lisa. "A Comparison of Forward and Futures Prices of an Interest Rate-Sensitive Financial Asset." *The Journal of Finance* 47 (March 1992): 381–396.

Midanek, Deborah Hicks, and James I. Midanek. "Understanding Mortgage-Backed Securities." *Derivatives Quarterly* 2 (Spring 1996): 39–46.

Miller, Merton H. "Financial Innovation: Achievements and Prospects." *The Journal of Financial Engineering* 1 (June 1992): 1–13.

Miller, Merton H. "Index Arbitrage: Villain or Scapegoat?" *The Journal of Financial Engineering* 1 (December 1992): 319–324.

Modern Risk Management: A History. London: Risk Books, 2003.

Modest, David M., and Mahedevan Sundaresan. "The Relationship between Spot and Futures Prices in Stock Index Futures Markets: Some Preliminary Evidence." *The Journal of Futures Markets* 3 (1983): 15–41.

Moran, Matthew T. "Taking a Ride on the Volatile Side." *Journal of Indexes* (October–November 2004): 16–19.

Mossin, Jan. "Equilibrium in a Capital Asset Market." *Econometrica* 34 (October 1966): 768–783.

Mueller, Paul A. "Covered Call Options: An Alternative Investment Strategy." *Financial Management* 10 (Winter 1981): 64–71.

Mullaney, Michael. *The Complete Guide to Option Strategies: Advanced and Basic Strategies on Stocks, ETFs, Indexes and Stock Index Futures.* New York: Wiley Trading, 2009.

Musiela, Marek, and Marek Rutkowski. *Martingale Methods in Financial Modelling.* Berlin, Germany: Springer-Verlag, 1997.

Naib, Farid A. "FX Option Theta and the 'Joker' Effect." *Derivatives Quarterly* 2 (Summer 1996): 56–58.

Nance, Deana R., Clifford W. Smith, Jr., and Charles W. Smithson. "On the Determinants of Corporate Hedging." *The Journal of Finance* 48 (March 1993): 267–284.

Nawalkha, Sanjay, and Donald Chambers. "The Binomial Model and Risk Neutrality: Some Important Details." *The Financial Review* 30 (1995): 605–618.

Neal, Robert. "Direct Tests of Index Arbitrage Models." *Journal of Financial and Quantitative Analysis* 31 (1996): 541–562.

Neftci, Salih N. *An Introduction to the Mathematics of Financial Derivatives.* San Diego, CA: Academic Press, 1996.

Neftci, Salih N. *Principles of Financial Engineering.* Amsterdam: Elsevier, 2004.

Nelken, Israel. *The Handbook of Exotic Options: Instruments, Analysis and Applications.* Chicago: Irwin Professional, 1996.

Neuberger, Anthony. "Hedging Long-Term Exposures with Multiple Short-Term Futures Contracts." *The Review of Financial Studies* 12 (Fall 1999): 429–459.

Nielsen, Lars Tyge. *Pricing and Hedging of Derivative Securities.* Oxford: Oxford University Press, 1999.

O'Brien, Thomas J. "The Mechanics of Portfolio Insurance." *The Journal of Portfolio Management* 14 (Spring 1985): 40–47.

O'Brien, Thomas J. "Portfolio Insurance Mechanics." *Journal of Portfolio Management* 14 (1988): 40–47.

Olson, Erika S. *Zero-Sum Game: The Rise of the World's Largest Derivatives Exchange.* Hoboken, NJ: John Wiley & Sons, 2011.

Over the Rainbow. London: Risk, 1996.

Parkinson, Michael. "Option Pricing: The American Put." *The Journal of Business* 50 (January 1977): 21–36.

Patterson, Scott. *The Quants: How a New Breed of Math Whizzes Conquered Wall Street and Nearly Destroyed It.* New York: Crown, 2010.

Pelsser, Antoon, and Ton Vorst. "The Binomial Model and the Greeks." *Journal of Derivatives* 1 (1994): 45–49.

Petzel, Todd E. "How Expensive Is It to Insure Your U.S. Equity Portfolio?" *Derivatives Quarterly* 3 (Spring 1997): 81–83.

Phillips, Susan M., and Clifford W. Smith, Jr. "Trading Costs for Listed Options: The Implications for Market Efficiency." *Journal of Financial Economics* 8 (1980): 179–201.

Pirrong, Craig. "The Clearinghouse Cure." *Regulation* (Winter 2008–2009): 44–51.

Pirrong, Stephen Craig. "Market Liquidity and Depth on Computerized and Open Outcry Trading Systems." *The Journal of Futures Markets* 16 (August 1996): 519–543.

Pirrong, Stephen Craig. "Metalgesellschaft: A Prudent Hedger Ruined, or a Wildcatter on NYMEX?" *The Journal of Futures Markets* 17 (August 1997): 543–578.

Pirrong, Stephen Craig. "The Self-Regulation of Commodity Exchanges: The Case of Market Manipulation." *Journal of Law and Economics* 38 (April 1995): 141–206.

Poitras, Geoffrey. "Turtles, Tails, and Stereos: Arbitrage and the Design of Futures Spread Trading Strategies." *The Journal of Derivatives* 5 (Winter 1997): 71–87.

Pounds, Henry M. "Covered Call Option Writing: Strategies and Results." *The Journal of Portfolio Management* 5 (Winter 1978): 31–42.

Pozen, Robert. "The Purchase of Protective Puts by Financial Institutions." *Financial Analysts Journal* 34 (July–August 1978): 47–60.

Prisman, Eliezer Z. *Pricing Derivative Securities.* San Diego, CA: Academic Press, 2000.

Pryke, Michael, and John Allen. "Monetized Time-Space: Derivatives-Money's 'New Imaginary.' " *Economy and Society* 29 (May 2000): 264–284.

Rao, Ramesh K. S. "Modern Option Pricing Models: A Dichotomous Classification." *The Journal of Financial Research* 4 (Spring 1981): 33–44.

Rendleman, Richard J., Jr. *Applied Derivatives: Options, Futures, and Swaps.* Malden, MA: Blackwell, 2002.

Rendleman, Richard J., Jr. "Covered Call Writing Strategies from an Expected Utility Perspective." *The Journal of Derivatives* 9 (Spring 2001): 63–75.

Rendleman, Richard J., Jr. "Duration-Based Hedging with Treasury Bond Futures." *The Journal of Fixed Income* 9 (June 1999): 84–91.

Rendlemen, Richard J., Jr. "First Derivatives National Bank: A Case Problem in the Management of Interest Rate Risk." *The Journal of Risk* 1 (1999): 63–85.

Rendleman, Richard J., Jr. "Option Investing from a Risk-Return Perspective." *The Journal of Portfolio Management* 25th Anniversary Issue (May 1999): 109–121.

Rendleman, Richard J., Jr. "A Reconciliation of Potentially Conflicting Approaches to Hedging with Futures." *Advances in Futures and Options Research* 6 (1993): 81–92.

Rendleman, Richard J., Jr., and Brit J. Barter. "Two-State Option Pricing." *The Journal of Finance* 34 (December 1979): 1093–1110.

Rendleman, Richard J., Jr., and Christopher Carabini. "The Efficiency of the Treasury Bill Futures Market." *The Journal of Finance* 44 (September 1979): 895–914.

Rendleman, Richard J., Jr., and Richard W. McEnally. "Assessing the Cost of Portfolio Insurance." *Financial Analysts Journal* 43 (May–June 1987): 27–37.

Rentzler, Joel C. "Trading Treasury Bond Spreads against Treasury Bill Futures: A Model and Empirical Tests of the Turtle Trade." *The Journal of Futures Markets* 6 (1986): 41–61.

Resnick, Bruce G. "The Relationship between Futures Prices for U.S. Treasury Bonds." *Review of Research in Futures Markets* 3 (1984): 88–104.

Resnick, Bruce G., and Elizabeth Hennigar. "The Relationship between Futures and Cash Prices for U.S. Treasury Bonds." *Review of Research in Futures Markets* 2 (1983): 282–298.

Ritchken, Peter. *Derivative Markets: Theory, Strategy and Applications*. New York: Harper Collins, 1996.

Ritchken, Peter. *Options: Theory, Strategy, and Applications*. Glenview, IL: Scott Foresman, 1987.

Ritchken, Peter H., and Harvey M. Salkin. "Safety First Selection Techniques for Option Spreads." *The Journal of Portfolio Management* 9 (1981): 61–67.

Ritter, Jay R. "How I Helped Make Fischer Black Wealthier." *Financial Management* 25 (Winter 1996): 104–107.

Roll, Richard. "An Analytic Valuation Formula for Unprotected American Call Options on Stocks with Known Dividends." *Journal of Financial Economics* 5 (November 1977): 251–258.

Roll, Richard, and Stephen A. Ross. "The Arbitrage Pricing Theory Approach to Strategic Portfolio Planning." *Financial Analysts Journal* 40 (May–June 1984): 14–26.

Ronn, Aimee Gerberg, and Ehud I. Ronn. "The Box Spread Arbitrage Conditions: Theory, Tests, and Investment Strategies." *The Review of Financial Studies* 2 (1989): 91–108.

Rubinstein, Mark. "Alternative Paths to Portfolio Insurance." *Financial Analysts Journal* 41 (July–August 1985): 42–52.

Rubinstein, Mark. "Derivative Assets Analysis." *The Journal of Economic Perspectives* 1 (Fall 1987): 73–93.

Rubinstein, Mark. *Derivatives: A PowerPlus Picture Book: Volume 1: Futures, Options and Dynamic Strategies*. Corte Madera, CA: Mark Rubinstein, 1999.

Rubinstein, Mark. "Implied Binomial Trees." *The Journal of Finance* 49 (July 1994): 771–818.

Rubinstein, Mark. "Nonparametric Tests of Alternative Option Pricing Models Using All Reported Trades and Quotes on the 30 Most Active CBOE Option Classes from August 23, 1976, through August 31,1978." *The Journal of Finance* 40 (June 1985): 455–480.

Rubinstein, Mark. "Portfolio Insurance and the Market Crash." *Financial Analysts Journal* 44 (January–February 1988): 38–47.

Rubinstein, Mark. "The Valuation of Uncertain Income Streams and the Pricing of Options." *Bell Journal of Economics* 7 (1976): 407–425.

Rubinstein, Mark, and Hayne E. Leland. "Replicating Options with Positions in Stock and Cash." *Financial Analysts Journal* 37 (July–August 1981): 63–72.

Rubinstein, Mark, and Eric Reiner. "Breaking Down the Barriers." *Risk* 4 (September 1991): 28–35.

Sadr, Amir. *Interest Rate Swaps and Their Derivatives*. New York: Wiley Finance, 2009.

Saliba, Anthony J. *Option Spread Strategies: Trading Up, Down, and Sideways Markets*. New York: Bloomberg Financial, 2009.

Santoni, G. J., and Tung Liu. "Circuit Breakers and Stock Market Volatility." *The Journal of Futures Markets* 13 (May 1993): 261–277.

Saunders, Anthony. *Credit Risk Measurement: New Approaches to Value-at-Risk and Other Paradigms*. New York: Wiley, 1999.

Schachter, Barry. "Swap Pricing and Swap Mispricing." *Derivatives Quarterly* 2 (Summer 1996): 59–64.

Schwager, Jack D. *The New Market Wizards: Conversations with America's Top Traders*. New York: Collins Business, 2005.

Senchak, Andrew J., and John C. Easterwood. "Cross Hedging CDs with Treasury Bill Futures." *The Journal of Futures Markets* 3 (1983): 429–438.

Shafer, Carl E. "Hedge Ratios and Basis Behavior: An Intuitive Insight?" *The Journal of Futures Markets* 13 (December 1993): 837–847.

Shapiro, Alan C. *Multinational Financial Management*, 6th ed. New York: Wiley, 1999.

Sharpe, William F. "Capital Asset Prices: A Theory of Market Equilibrium under Conditions of Risk." *The Journal of Finance* 19 (September 1964): 425–442.

Shastri, Kuldeep, and Kishore Tandon. "Arbitrage Tests of the Efficiency of the Foreign Currency Options Markets." *Journal of International Money and Finance* 4 (December 1985): 455–468.

Shastri, Kuldeep, and Kishore Tandon. "On the Use of European Models to Price American Options on Foreign Currency." *The Journal of Futures Markets* 6 (Spring 1986): 93–108.

Shastri, Kuldeep, and Kishore Tandon. "Options on Futures Contracts: A Comparison of European and American Pricing Models." *The Journal of Futures Markets* 6 (Winter 1986): 593–618.

Sheikh, Aamir M. "Transaction Data Tests of S&P 100 Call Option Pricing." *Journal of Financial and Quantitative Analysis* 26 (December 1991): 459–475.

Shimko, David C. *Finance in Continuous Time*. Miami: Kolb Publishing, 1992.

Shover, Larry. *Trading Options in Turbulent Markets: Master Uncertainty Through Active Volatility Management*. New York: Bloomberg Press, 2010.

Shreve, Steven. E. *Stochastic Calculus for Finance I: The Binomial Asset Pricing Model*. New York: Springer, 2005.

Siegel, Daniel R., and Diane F. Siegel. *Futures Markets*. Hinsdale, IL: Dryden Press, 1990.

Siems, Thomas F. "Risk Management: Turning Volatility into Profitability." *Derivatives Quarterly* 2 (Spring 1996): 22–31.

Silber, William L. "Marketmaker Behavior in an Auction Market: An Analysis of Scalpers in Futures Markets." *The Journal of Finance* 39 (September 1984): 937–953.

Silber, William L. "Technical Trading: When It Works and When It Doesn't." *The Journal of Derivatives* 1 (Spring 1994): 39–44.

Singleton, J. Clay, and Robin Grieves. "Synthetic Puts and Portfolio Insurance Strategies." *The Journal of Portfolio Management* 10 (Spring 1984): 63–69.

Slivka, Ronald T. "Call Option Spreading." *The Journal of Portfolio Management* 7 (Spring 1981): 71–76.

Slivka, Ronald T. "Risk and Return for Option Investment Strategies." *Financial Analysts Journal* 36 (September–October 1980): 67–73.

Smith, Clifford W., Jr. "Corporate Risk Management: Theory and Practice." *The Journal of Derivatives* 2 (Summer 1995): 21–30.

Smith, Clifford W., Jr. "Option Pricing: A Review." *Journal of Financial Economics* 3 (January–March 1976): 3–51.

Smith, Clifford W., Jr., and Charles W. Smithson. *The Handbook of Financial Engineering: New Financial Product Innovations, Applications, and Analyses*. New York: Harper Business, 1990.

Smith, Clifford W., Jr., Charles W. Smithson, and Lee Macdonald Wakeman. "The Evolving Market for Swaps." *Midland Corporate Financial Journal* 3 (Winter 1986): 20–32.

Smith, Clifford W., Jr., and René M. Stulz. "The Determinants of Firms' Hedging Policies." *Journal of Financial and Quantitative Analysis* 20 (1985): 391–405.

Smith, Donald. J. "Aggressive Corporate Finance: A Close Look at the Procter & Gamble-Bankers Trust Leveraged Swap." *The Journal of Derivatives* 4 (Summer 1997): 67–79.

Smith, Donald J. "The Arithmetic of Financial Engineering." *Journal of Applied Corporate Finance* 1 (1989): 49–58.

Smith, Donald R. "A Simple Method for Pricing Interest Rate Swaptions." *Financial Analyst Journal* 47 (May–June 1991): 72–76.

Smith, Stephen D. "Analyzing Risk and Return for Mortgage-Backed Securities." *Federal Reserve Bank of Atlanta Economic Review* 76 (1991): 2–13.

Smith, Tom, and Robert E. Whaley. "Assessing the Costs of Regulation: The Case of Dual Trading." *Journal of Law and Economics* 37 (1994): 215–246.

Smithson, Charles W. *Managing Financial Risk: A Guide to Derivative Products, Financial Engineering, and Value Maximization*, 3rd ed. New York: McGraw-Hill, 1998.

Smithson, Charles W. "Quantifying Operational Risk," *Risk* 17 (July 2004): 57.

Sofianos, George. "Index Arbitrage Profitability." *The Journal of Derivatives* 1 (Fall 1993): 6–20.

Solnik, Bruno H. *International Investments*, 4th ed. Reading, MA: Addison-Wesley, 1999.

Srivastava, Sanjay. "Value-at-Risk Analysis of a Leverage Swap." *The Journal of Risk* 1 (1999): 87–101.

Stapleton, Richard, and Marti Subrahmanyam. "The Valuation of Options When Asset Returns Are

Generated by a Binomial Process." *The Journal of Finance* 39 (1984): 1525–1539.

Stein, Jerome L. "The Simultaneous Determination of Spot and Futures Prices." *The American Economic Review* 51 (December 1961): 1012–1025.

Stoll, Hans R. "Lost Barings: A Tale in Three Parts Concluding with a Lesson." *The Journal of Derivatives* 3 (Fall 1995): 109–115.

Stoll, Hans R. "Principles of Inter-Market Regulation." *The Journal of Financial Engineering* 2 (March 1993): 65–71.

Stoll, Hans R. "The Relationship between Put and Call Option Prices." *The Journal of Finance* 31 (May 1969): 319–332.

Stoll, Hans R., and Robert E. Whaley. "Futures and Options on Stock Indexes: Economic Purpose, Arbitrage, and Market Structure." *The Review of Futures Markets* 7 (1988): 224–229.

Stoll, Hans R., and Robert E. Whaley. *Futures and Options: Theory and Applications.* Cincinnati, OH: South-Western, 1993.

Stoll, Hans R., and Robert E. Whaley. "Program Trading and Expiration Day Effects." *Financial Analysts Journal* 43 (March–April 1987): 16–28.

Stone, Charles A., and Anne Zissu. "The Risk of Mortgage Backed Securities and Their Derivatives." *Journal of Applied Corporate Finance* 7 (1994): 99–111.

Strong, Robert A. *Derivatives: An Introduction.* Cincinnati, OH: South-Western, 2002.

Stulz, René M. "Options on the Minimum or the Maximum of Two Risky Assets: Analysis and Applications." *Journal of Financial Economics* 10 (July 1982): 161–185.

Stulz, René M. *Risk Management & Derivatives.* Cincinnati, OH: South-Western, 2003.

Sullivan, Joe H., Zachary G. Stoumbos, and Robert Brooks. "Real-time Assessment of Value-at-Risk and Volatility Accuracy." *Nonlinear Analysis: Real World Applications*, 2007.

Sun, Tong-Sheng, Suresh Sundaresan, and Ching Wang. "Interest Rate Swaps: An Empirical Investigation." *Journal of Financial Economics* 34 (1993): 77–99.

Sundaram, Rangarajan K. "Equivalent Martingale Measures and Risk-Neutral Pricing: An Expository Note." *The Journal of Derivatives* 5 (Fall 1997): 85–98.

Sundaresan, Suresh. *Fixed Income Markets and Their Derivatives*, 2nd ed. Cincinnati, OH: South-Western, 2002.

Sundaresan, Suresh. "Futures Prices on Yields, Forward Prices, and Implied Forward Prices from Term Structure." *Journal of Financial and Quantitative Analysis* 26 (September 1991): 409–424.

Taleb, Nassim Nicholas. *The Black Swan: The Impact of the Highly Improbable.* New York: Random House, 2007.

Taleb, Nassim Nicholas. *Dynamic Hedging: Managing Vanilla and Exotic Options.* New York: Wiley, 1997.

Taleb, Nassim Nicholas. *Fooled by Randomness: The Hidden Role of Chance in the Markets and in Life.* New York: Texere, 2001.

Tan, C. *Demystifying Exotic Products: Interest Rates, Equities and Foreign Exchange.* West Sussex, UK: John Wiley & Sons, 2010.

Telser, Lester G. "Futures Trading and the Storage of Cotton and Wheat." *Journal of Political Economy* 66 (June 1958): 233–255.

Telser, Lester G. "Why There Are Organized Futures Markets." *Journal of Law and Economics* 24 (1981): 1–22.

Telser, Lester G., and Harlow N. Higinbotham. "Organized Futures Markets: Costs and Benefits." *Journal of Political Economy* 85 (1977): 969–1000.

The Options Institute. *Options: Essential Concepts and Trading Strategies*, 3rd ed. New York: McGraw-Hill, 1999.

Thomsett, Michael C. *Getting Started in Options*, 8th ed. New York: Wiley, 2009.

Toevs, Alden L., and David P. Jacob. "Futures and Alternative Hedge Ratio Methodologies." *Journal of Portfolio Management* 12 (Spring 1986): 60–70.

Tosini, Paula A. "Stock Index Futures and Stock Market Activity in October 1987." *Financial Analysts Journal* 44 (January–February 1988): 28–37.

Trennepohl, Gary. "A Comparison of Listed Option Premiums and Black-Scholes Model Prices: 1973–1979." *The Journal of Financial Research* 4 (Spring 1981): 11–20.

Trennepohl, Gary L., and William P. Dukes. "Return and Risk from Listed Option Investments." *The Journal of Financial Research* 2 (Spring 1979): 37–49.

Trippi, Robert R. "A Test of Option Market Efficiency Using a Random-Walk Valuation Model." *Journal of Economics and Business* 29 (Winter 1977): 93–98.

Tucker, Alan L. "Empirical Tests of the Efficiency of the Currency Option Market." *The Journal of Financial Research* 8 (Winter 1985): 275–285.

Tucker, Alan L. *Financial Futures, Options, and Swaps.* St. Paul: West Publishing, 1991.

Turnbull, Stuart M. "Swaps: A Zero Sum Game?" *Financial Management* 16 (Spring 1987): 15–21.

Veit, W. Theodore, and Wallace W. Reiff. "Commercial Banks and Interest Rate Futures: A Hedging Survey." *The Journal of Futures Markets* 3 (1983): 283–293.

Vignola, Anthony, and Charles Dale. "The Efficiency of the Treasury Bill Futures Market: An Analysis of Alternative Specifications." *The Journal of Financial Research* 3 (1980): 169–188.

Wagner, Wayne, and Sheila Lau. "The Effect of Diversification on Risk." *Financial Analysts Journal* 27 (November–December 1971): 48–53.

Wall, Larry D., and John J. Pringle. "Alternative Explanations of Interest Rate Swaps: A Theoretical and Empirical Analysis." *Financial Management* 18 (1989): 59–73.

Wall, Larry D., and John J. Pringle. "Interest Rate Swaps: A Review of the Issues." *Federal Reserve Bank of Atlanta Economic Review* (November–December 1988): 22–40.

Welch, Robert L., and Louis Culumovic. "A Profitable Call Spreading Strategy on the CBOE." *The Journal of Derivatives* 2 (Spring 1995): 24–44.

Whaley, Robert E. *Derivatives: Markets, Valuation, and Risk Management.* New York: Wiley, 2006.

Whaley, Robert E. "On the Valuation of American Call Options on Stocks with Known Dividends." *Journal of Financial Economics* 9 (June 1981): 207–212.

Whaley, Robert E. "On Valuing American Futures Options." *Financial Analysts Journal* 42 (May–June 1986): 49–59.

Whaley, Robert E. "Valuation of American Call Options on Dividend Paying Stocks: Empirical Tests." *Journal of Financial Economics* 19 (March 1982): 29–58.

Wilmott, Paul. *Derivatives: The Theory and Practice of Financial Engineering.* Chichester, UK: Wiley, 1999.

Wilmott, Paul, Sam Howison, and Jeff DeWynne. *The Mathematics of Financial Derivatives.* Cambridge, UK: Press Syndicate of the University of Cambridge, 1995.

Yadav, Pradeep K., and Peter F. Pope. "Stock Index Futures Arbitrage: International Evidence." *The Journal of Futures Markets* 9 (December 1990): 573–604.

Yaksick, Rudy. "Swaps, Caps, and Floors: Some Parity and Price Identities." *The Journal of Financial Engineering* 1 (June 1992): 105–115.

Yates, James W., Jr., and Robert W. Kopprasch, Jr. "Writing Covered Call Options: Profits and Risks." *The Journal of Portfolio Management* 6 (Fall 1980): 74–80.

Zimmermann, H., and Wolfgang H. "Amazing Discovery: Vincenz Bronzin's Option Pricing Models." *Journal of Banking and Finance* 31 (2007): 531–546.

Zivney, Terry L. "The Value of Early Exercise in Option Prices: An Empirical Investigation." *Journal of Financial and Quantitative Analysis* 26 (March 1991): 129–138.

Solutions to Concept Checks

Chapter 1

1. **(Return and Risk)** Financial markets distinguish the qualities of stocks and bonds by their prices. The markets set the price so that the return expected by investors is appropriate for the level of risk. In competitive and efficient markets, the expected return will vary directly with the level of risk. If one wants to earn a higher return, it is necessary to assume more risk. This is the risk-return trade-off. Investors trade off risk against return.

    The risk-return trade-off will also hold in derivative markets. The risk-return trade-off is a fundamental result of the nature of competition in the marketplace. Attractive low-risk investments will have their prices driven up, and this will lower the expected returns. High-risk investments will have their prices driven down, and this will result in higher expected returns.

2. **(Risk Preference)** An investor who is risk averse does not like risk and will not take on additional risk without the expectation of higher return. Such an individual will try to get the highest return for a given amount of risk or the lowest risk for a given amount of return. An individual who is risk neutral will simply seek the highest return without regard to risk.

3. **(Return and Risk)** The expected return consists of the risk-free rate and a risk premium. The risk-free rate is the return one expects from investing money today and thereby forgoing the consumption that could be obtained. A risk premium is the additional return that one expects to receive by virtue of assuming risk.

4. **(Introduction)** Real assets consist of the tangible assets of the economy; however, for our purposes, we also define them to include such intangible assets as management talent, ideas, and brand names. They are distinguished from financial assets, which are securities. These securities represent claims on business firms, which own the real assets, or on governments.

5. **(Introduction)** Business risk is the risk associated with a particular line of business, whereas financial risk is the risk associated with stock prices, exchange rates, interest rates, and commodity prices. An example would be that a firm might be in the business of manufacturing furniture. Business risk would reflect the uncertainty of the furniture market, whereas financial risk would reflect the risk associated with the interest rates that would impact their borrowing costs. In addition, a business might also be affected by exchange rates. Some of the financial risks can also be business risks. The business risk of a bank, for example, is highly affected by interest rate and exchange rate risk.

Chapter 2

1. **(Exercise Prices)** The goal when establishing the exercise prices is to provide options that will attract trading volume. Most option trading is concentrated within options in which the stock price is close to the exercise price. Accordingly, exchange officials tend to list options in which the exercise prices surround but are close to the current stock price. They must use their judgment as to whether an exercise price is too far above or below the stock price to generate sufficient trading volume. If the stock price moves up or down, new exercise prices close to the stock price are added.

2. **(Market Maker)** Market makers use a variety of techniques to trade options intelligently and

profitably. Many look at fundamentals, such as interest rates, economic conditions, and company performance. Others rely on technical analysis, which purports to find signals of the direction of future stock prices in the behavior of past stock prices. Still others rely simply on intuition and experience. In addition, market makers tend to employ different trading styles. Some are scalpers, who try to buy at the bid and sell at the ask before the price moves downward or after the price moves just slightly upward. Scalpers seldom hold positions for more than a few minutes. In contrast, position traders have somewhat longer holding periods. Many option traders, including some scalpers and position traders, are also spreaders, who buy one option and sell another in the hope of earning small profits at low risk.

3. **(Exercising an Option)** An American option can be exercised at any time up through the expiration date. A European option can be exercised only on the expiration date. An American option is equivalent to a European option with the additional feature that it can be exercised early.

4. **(Listing Requirements)** All options of a particular type—call or put—on a given stock are referred to as an option class. For example, the Apple calls are one option class and the Apple puts are another. An option series is all the options of a given class with the same exercise price and expiration. For example, the Apple September 175 calls are a particular series, as are the Apple October 180 puts. In recent years, many options have been listed on more than one exchange. An options exchange determines whether options of a particular stock will be listed on its exchange. The company itself does not make this decision.

5. **(Options)**
   a. Homeowners insurance is a put option. In the event of a loss, the insurance company pays you a portion of the value of the house. The rest is like a deductible. The premium on the put is the insurance premium.
   b. The guaranteed tuition arrangement is a call option granted to you by the school. If you enroll now, you can "purchase" the education at a fixed price up through the next four years. The premium on the option is the fact that you have to enroll in this particular school for your freshman year. Of course, you do not have to exercise the option by continuing to enroll thereafter.

   c. This is not an option because no one has the opportunity to forgo exercise. It is actually a forward contract. If the lease were cancelable over the period during which the rental rate was fixed, it would be a call option.

Chapter 3
1. **(Entire Chapter)** This tutorial provides a review of the entire chapter.
2. **(Maximum Value of Call)** A call option with zero exercise price guarantees that at the expiration date, you will get the stock. Thus, you have the same claim on the value of the stock at the option expiration as would a person who already owned the stock; so the call is equivalent to owning the stock. Note, however, that we must exclude the possibility of dividends, because the owner of the stock would get the dividends during the option life, while the call option holder would not.
3. **(Effect of Exercise Price)** If both options were deep out-of-the-money, they might have prices of zero. As in the previous question, the two options are expected to expire out-of-the-money.
4. **(Principles of Call Option Pricing)** European call: We know that its price cannot exceed S_0 but must exceed $Max(0, S_0 - X(1 + r)^{-T})$. With an infinite time to expiration, the present value of X is zero (so the lower bound is S_0), and because the upper bound is S_0, the call price must be S_0.

   American call: We know that its price cannot exceed S_0, but it must be at least as valuable as a European call. Thus, its value must also be S_0. Note that if exercised early, it would be worth only $S_0 - X$; so it will never be exercised early.
5. **(Entire Chapter)** An in-the-money call would then have a fixed, guaranteed payoff at expiration and, thus, would be equivalent to a risk-free bond with that payoff at maturity. An out-of-the-money call would have no chance of expiring in-the-money and would, thus, be essentially dead. An in-the-money put would likewise now have a fixed, guaranteed payoff at expiration and would become equivalent to a risk-free bond. An out-of-the-money put would have no chance of expiring in-the-money, so it would be essentially dead.
6. **(General Arbitrage)** The coin tosses are clearly independent. Thus, in some cases, the first coin will come up heads and the second tails, resulting in your earning $10 and paying $5. In some cases, the first coin will come up tails and the second

heads, resulting your earning $5 and paying $9. You could make this an arbitrage only by linking the outcomes so that the $10 and $9 payoffs and the two $5 payoffs occur on the same outcome. An obvious way would be to toss a single coin, but that might not be practical. You could possibly link the payoffs to some type of event with two outcomes, such as whether the stock market goes up or down in a given period of time. Of course, you would still have to find two parties who would accept the odds and payoffs.

7. **(Effect of Time to Expiration)** Ordinarily, the option with the longer time to expiration would sell for more. If both options were deep out-of-the-money, however, they could both sell for essentially nothing. The market would be expecting that both the shorter- and longer-lived options will expire out-of-the-money.

Chapter 4

1. **(Hedge Portfolio)** For a call, a hedge portfolio will consist of n shares of stock and one short call. The shares of stock, n, will be a long position that reflects the next two possible values of the call and stock. The call is short because the call and stock move opposite each other, so a short position in the call is needed to offset a long position in the stock. If the option is a put, a long position in n shares will be hedged by a long position in one put. The number of shares, n, is also a reflection of the next two possible option and stock values. The put is long because it already moves opposite the stock.

2. **(Underpriced Call)** This means that the option is trading in the market for a price that is lower than its theoretical fair value. Consequently, the option is underpriced. An underpriced option should be bought. To hedge the position, one should sell n shares of stock, where n is the hedge ratio as defined in the chapter.

3. **(One-Period Binomial Model)** When we price an option according to its boundary conditions, we do not find an exact price for the option. We provide only limits on the maximum and minimum price of an option or group of options. In the case of options differing by exercise prices or in the case of put-call parity, we can price only the relationship or difference between the option prices. We cannot price each option individually without an option pricing model; however, an option pricing model must provide prices that conform to the boundary

conditions. Because boundary condition rules require fewer assumptions, we can say that they are more generally applicable and are more likely to hold in practice. They are incomplete, however, in the sense that they do not tell us exactly what the option price should be, which is what an option pricing model does tell us.

4. **(American Puts and Early Exercise)** At each point in the binomial tree, the option price is computed based on the next two possible prices, weighted by the appropriate probability values and discounted back one period. If the option can be exercised early, we determine its intrinsic value (i.e., the value it would have if it were exercised at that point). If the intrinsic value is greater, it replaces the computed value. This is done at all nodes. Note that it is quite possible that the option will be exercised at many different nodes.

5. **(One-Period Binomial Model)** A binomial option pricing model enables us to see the relationship between the stock price and the call price. The model shows, in a simple framework, how to construct a riskless portfolio by appropriately weighting the stock against the option. By noting that the riskless portfolio should return the risk-free rate, we can see what the call price must be. We can also understand the forces that bring the call option price in line if it is not priced according to the model. In addition, the model illustrates the importance of revising the hedge ratio. Finally, the model is probably the best way to handle the problem of pricing an American option.

Chapter 5

1. **(Stock Prices Behave Randomly and Evolve According to a Lognormal Distribution)** The familiar normal, or bell-shaped, distribution is a symmetric probability distribution that depends only on the mean and variance. A lognormal distribution is skewed, having more extreme right values. A lognormal distribution, however, is normal in the logarithm. Thus, if x is lognormally distributed, its logarithm, lnx, is normally distributed. With respect to stock prices, the logarithm is of the rate of return. That is, let $(S_1 - S_0)/S_0$ be defined as the return over period 0 to period 1. Then if it is lognormally distributed, $\ln(S_1/S_0)$ is normally distributed. Note what appears to be a slight inconsistency: $(S_1 - S_0)/S_0$ is a percentage return whereas S_1/S_0 is 1.0 plus the percentage return. That does

not matter as we can always shift a normal distribution by adding a constant such as 1.0, and it does not affect the fact that it is normally distributed. It just slides it over.

2. **(Stock Pays No Dividends)** The Black-Scholes-Merton model assumes no dividends, but actually this was just for convenience to allow us to start at the simplest level. If the dividends are appropriately modeled, the Black-Scholes-Merton model handles stocks with dividends with only the minor adjustment that we must remove the present value of the dividends from the stock price before using it in the model. We can do this by subtracting the present value of the stream of discrete dividends over the life of the model or by discounting the stock price by the dividend yield rate over the life of the model.

3. **(BSM Model as the Limit of the Binomial Model)** In a discrete time model, the stock price can make a jump to only one of two possible values. The length of time over which the move can be made is finite. In a continuous time model, the stock price can jump to an infinite number of possibilities. The length of time over which the move can be made is infinitesimal (very, very small). The difference between the two models is perhaps best described in the text as the difference between still photos and a movie.

4. **(Volatility or Standard Deviation)** The variance or standard deviation, sometimes called the volatility, is the most critical variable for two reasons: (1) It is the only variable that is not directly observable and, thus, it must be estimated, and (2) the model is particularly sensitive to the estimate of volatility.

5. **(A Nobel Formula)** The variables in the binomial model are S_0 (the stock price), X (the exercise price), r (the discrete risk-free rate), u (one plus the return on the stock if it goes up), d (one plus the return on the stock if it goes down), and n (the number of time periods). The variables in the Black-Scholes-Merton model are S_0 (the stock price), X (the exercise price), r_c (the continuously compounded risk-free rate), σ (the standard deviation of the continuously compounded return on the stock), and T (the time to expiration). The variables S_0 and X are the same in both models. In the binomial model, r is the discrete interest rate per period. In the Black-Scholes-Merton model, the interest rate must be expressed in continuously compounded form. The annual discrete interest rate (r) is related to the annual continuously compounded rate (r_c) by the formula $r_c = \ln(1 + r)$. Then the binomial rate per period is found as $(1 + r)^{T/n} - 1$. The up and down factors in the binomial model are directly related to σ in the Black-Scholes-Merton model by the formula $u = e^{\sigma \sqrt{T/n}} - 1$ and $d = (1/(1 + u)) - 1$. The time to expiration (T) in the Black-Scholes-Merton model is related to the length of each binomial period by the relationship T/n where n is the number of periods. Thus, all of the Black-Scholes-Merton variables are either equal to or directly convertible to binomial variables.

Chapter 6

1. **(Puts and Stock: The Protective Put)** A protective put establishes a minimum price at which a stock can be sold. In a bear market, the stock will lose value that can be recovered by exercising the put. This makes the put like an insurance policy that pays off in the event of a loss. The premium on the put is like the premium on the insurance policy. If the price of the stock goes up, the insurance is not needed; so the put is allowed to expire.

2. **(Puts and Stock: The Protective Put)** The higher the exercise price, the higher the price at which the stock can be sold. This reduces the overall loss in a bear market, but, of course, will require a higher premium. It is, therefore, like taking a lower deductible in an insurance policy. By forcing the insurer (the put writer) to assume more of the potential loss, the cost of the insurance (the put premium) rises.

3. **(Call (Put) Option Transactions)** Both strategies are indeed bullish. Buying a call gives you the option to buy the stock at a favorable price. Writing a put, on the other hand, gives you the obligation to buy the stock at what might be an unfavorable price. Both the call buyer and put writer will profit in a bull market, but the call buyer will do better in a strong bull market because the profit will be higher the higher the stock price. The put writer's profit is limited to the original premium received. In a bear market, the call buyer will have limited losses, while the put writer will lose more the lower the stock price. All of this makes it sound as though the call buyer does better than the put writer, but this is not necessarily so. The call buyer is paying a premium, while the put writer is receiving a premium. The put writer earns interest on the premium, while the call buyer forgoes interest.

4. **(Buy a Call)** The call with a higher exercise price will be far more speculative, because the stock price must go higher in order to break even; however, the premium on such a call will be lower. A call with a lower exercise price will have a greater chance of expiring in-the-money; however, the premium will be higher. The trade-off is between taking a gamble on the call with a higher exercise price at the cost of a small premium or buying the safer call with a lower exercise price at the cost of a larger premium.

5. **(Different Holding Periods)** When a call is purchased, the buyer pays for both the time value and the intrinsic value of the option. As the call gets closer and closer to expiration, it will lose its time value. At expiration of the call, the holder collects only the intrinsic value. By selling the call prior to expiration, the holder is able to recover some of the time value previously purchased. For a given stock price, this increases the profit or decreases the loss; however, the shorter the holding period, the less time the stock price has to move upward. The trade-off in deciding whether to sell an option early is between cutting the loss of time value and giving the stock enough time to make a substantial move.

Chapter 7

1. **(Option Spreads: Basic Concepts)** Simple long or short positions expose the trader to considerable risk. This is especially true for short positions. By taking an opposite position in another option (i.e., executing a spread), the trader is able to keep the risk to a more manageable level. Combined positions of options and stocks do the same thing—the option serves as a hedge for the stock, or the stock serves as a hedge for the option. A position in both options and stocks, however, is harder to execute because the options and stock trade in different markets. This results in time delays in getting the trades executed. On the other hand, a spread can be executed much faster, with both transactions done almost simultaneously in the same market.

2. **(Bull Spreads)** Because the stock price is closer to the higher exercise price than to the lower exercise price, the short call at the higher exercise price has the greater time value. Therefore, holding the position longer could result in a greater time value decay on the short call than on the long call. This will occur only, however, if the stock price does not

move down. The cross-over point indicated in Figure 7.2 in the chapter is a critical stock price below which the shorter holding period is preferred. If it appears as if the stock price will fall below the cross-over stock price, the position should be closed as soon as possible, but only if the stock price is not expected to turn back around before the options expire.

3. **(Spreads)** Both a straddle and a time spread can be used in this situation. A straddle consisting of the purchase of a put and a call with identical exercise prices and expirations would profit if the stock price moved substantially in either direction. A time spread consisting of the sale of a longer-term option and the purchase of a shorter-term option would also profit if the stock price moved significantly in either direction. This is because a large stock price move will allow repurchase of the longer-term option when it has little time value remaining. Note that this example is the opposite of the one discussed in the text. Also, a butterfly spread that is short the high and low exercise prices and long two of the middle exercise price could be used in this situation, but it would have limited gains if the stock price moved substantially.

4. **(Collar)** A protective put provides insurance against a drop in the stock price below the put exercise price. The put has a cost that can be offset by selling a call. The call exercise price will be above the put exercise price. This forces the investor to be willing to give up gains in the stock beyond the call exercise price. Thus, the stock effectively has a lower limit on its value, which is the exercise price of the put, and an upper limit on its value, which is the exercise price of the call effectively creating a collar.

5. **(Straddle)** First, note that the graph for a short straddle held to expiration is an inverted V. If closed out prior to expiration, a short straddle (which involves the sale of both a put and a call) will require the repurchase of both options. This means that prior to expiration, there will be time values on both the put and the call that will have to be repurchased. These time values are highest if the stock price is close to the exercise price. So the profit if the stock price is near the exercise price is lower the shorter the holding period. The longer the investor can hold the position, the less time value that remains on the options; however, this also gives the stock more time to move substantially and potentially generate a large loss.

Chapter 8

1. **(Introduction)** A forward contract obligates the holder of the long position to purchase the commodity at a future date. A call option grants the holder of the call the right but not the obligation to purchase the commodity at a future date. A put option grants the holder of the put the right but not the obligation to sell the commodity at a future date. A call is more like a forward contract than a put because long positions in the two contracts are bullish. The holder of the forward contract, however, is obligated to buy the good at the future date. The holder of the call can simply let the option expire if the market price of the commodity is less than the exercise price. A call holder pays a premium for the right not to exercise. The holder of a long forward contract does not pay a premium and gives up the right not to exercise.

2. **(Organized Futures Trading)** While both forward and futures contracts are agreements to purchase a good at a future date, a futures contract provides liquidity by having a central marketplace and standardized contract terms. This allows holders of futures contracts to sell them in the market at any time prior to expiration. Futures trading is governed by the formal regulations of the futures exchange. Most important, the losses incurred by futures traders are guaranteed by the clearinghouse, which requires the daily settlement of gains and losses. That is, the holders of profitable contracts do not have to worry about whether their gains will be paid by the holders of losing contracts. Forward contracts, however, are subject to default risk. Forward contracts can be tailored to the unique needs of firms. For example, a firm may need to execute a hedge in which the expiration is a specific date. Futures contracts expire only on certain dates, which may not fit the needs of the firm.

3. **(Development of Options on Futures Markets)** In an option on a futures contract, the underlying is a futures contract. Thus, if the holder exercises a call option on a futures, it creates a long position in a futures contract, and if the holder exercises a put option on a futures, it creates a short position in a futures contract. As in options on assets, an option on a futures requires that the buyer pay the premium up front. There are two expirations, the expiration of the option and the expiration of the underlying futures, although for some contracts, these expirations are the same. In that case, exercise of the option on the futures creates a futures contract that immediately expires, thereby turning into the spot asset and making the option on the futures the same as an option on the asset.

4. **(Daily Settlement)** A: 1,000, OL: 4,200, S: −5,200

	A	OL	S	Change in Open Interest
(a)	500	4,700	−5,200	none
(b)	1,700	3,500	−5,200	none
(c)	1,200	4,200	−5,400	increase by 200
(d)	200	4,200	4,400	decrease by 800

If A trades with OL, one or the other is merely offsetting, and thus, open interest does not change. If A trades with the shorts, both are reducing or increasing their positions; so open interest changes. In other words, if traders trade with others who hold the same positions, open interest will not change. If they trade with those holding opposite positions, open interest will change.

5. **(Organized Futures Trading)**
   a. A centralized trading facility. The exchange is a formal market place for trading the contracts.
   b. Standardized terms. This establishes that certain contracts are identical and, thus, are perfect substitutes for each other.
   c. Rules. The exchange establishes rules and regulations that permit trading to transpire in an orderly manner.
   d. Clearinghouse. The clearinghouse associated with the exchange provides a guarantee that each party to the contract will perform as expected. The clearinghouse also provides the bookkeeping system that keeps track of the transactions and the margin deposits.
   e. Contract development. The exchange continuously monitors economic conditions and develops new contracts designed to meet the changing needs of hedgers and speculators.

Chapter 9

1. **(Value of a Forward/Futures Contract)** Other than the insignificant margin requirement, a futures contract requires no initial outlay of funds. Immediately after buying the contract and before the price changes, the holder of the contract cannot receive anything for selling it. Because you cannot receive anything for it, it has no value. The

spot commodity, however, requires payment, and it can be resold immediately for cash. Thus, it has value equal to whatever price it will fetch in the market, the current spot price. This result applies equally to a forward contract.

2. **(Concept of Price versus Value)** The spot price is affected by the cost of carry and the risk premium. The cost of carry is the cost of storing an asset plus the interest forgone by investing funds in the asset. The storage costs include the actual direct physical costs of storage. The risk premium is the amount by which the expected future price is discounted to compensate the person holding the asset for assuming the risk.

3. **(Forward/Futures Pricing Revisited)** When there is a negative cost of carry, we usually find an explanation in the form of a convenience yield. The idea behind it is that spot prices are unusually high, owing to a greater shortage of the good now than is expected in the future. Thus, there is a "premium" paid to owners of the good, which is called the convenience yield. It is simply an unusually high spot price that rewards holders of the good and discourages storage. Convenience yields are likely to exist on goods with harvests that produce random output and goods that are consumed. In addition, the goods should be storable. They are unlikely to be found on stocks and bonds because their future supplies are fairly well known and they are not really "consumed," although in a minor sense bonds are.

4. **(Forward/Futures Pricing Revisited)** Contango is a market in which the futures price exceeds the spot price. The cost of carry is the difference between the futures price and the spot price. It is positive in a contango market. In contrast, backwardation is a market in which the futures price is less than the spot price. In that case, the cost of carry is negative. A negative cost of carry is usually explained by justifying a convenience yield. In such a market, the spot price is abnormally high as a result of a shortage of the good. The negative cost of carry is a disincentive to store the good. The convenience yield refers to the premium in the spot price that reflects the attractiveness of owning the commodity at a time when it is in short supply.

5. **(Commodities and Storage Costs)** The futures price is the expected spot price of wheat in December. Therefore, traders expect the spot price of wheat in December to be $3.64.

Chapter 10

1. **(Carry Arbitrage and the Implied Repo Rate)** A repurchase agreement (repo) is a type of loan in which the borrower sells a security such as a T-bill with the agreement to buy the security back at a later date. The security serves as a form of collateral. The difference between the price at which the investor purchases the security and the price at which the investor sells it reflects the rate of interest. Most repurchase agreements are short-term, frequently for an overnight period; however, some repos are for as long as two weeks. In pricing futures, the repo represents the cost of financing the spot position. The repo rate implied by the relationship between the futures and spot prices is the implied repo rate. If the implied repo rate exceeds the actual rate on repo financing, the cash-and-carry transaction should be done. Otherwise, the reverse transaction should be done. Of course, transaction costs must be covered.

2. **(Stock Index Arbitrage)** There are several factors that make stock index futures arbitrage difficult. Transaction costs always interfere with the opportunity to earn an arbitrage profit, and because fractional contracts cannot be traded, the arbitrage is only approximate. By far, however, the most difficult part of the transaction is simultaneously buying or selling all of the stocks in the index and the futures contract. Also, at expiration, the arbitrageur must simultaneously reverse the original transaction by selling or buying the stocks in the index.

3. **(Stock Index Arbitrage)** Program trading is the rapid execution of a large number of stock transactions, usually in connection with a transaction such as index arbitrage. All of the shares must be bought or sold simultaneously. It is controversial because if many large investors execute similar program trades at the same time, the prices of the securities could move quite substantially. Thus, many people believe that program trading can increase volatility. The opposing view, however, is that such trading makes the market more efficient by bringing prices rapidly to their true values.

4. **(Carry Arbitrage and the Implied Repo Rate)** Based on carry arbitrage, the futures-spot price relationship is

$$f_0(T) = S_0 + \theta.$$

Assuming no significant storage cost, the cost of carry, θ, is strictly the interest, iS_0. Now the implicit interest cost is

$$\theta = f_0(T) - S_0.$$

Thus, θ is the implied cost of financing expressed in dollars, iS_0. Suppose we express carry cost as a percentage of the spot price, θ/S_0. In this case, the result is just interest, i. We denote this implied interest i as $\hat{r}$ for the purpose of comparing it to the actual riskless interest rate. Therefore, $\hat{r}$ is the implied repo rate. If the cost of financing the position—the actual repo rate—is less than the implied repo rate, the arbitrage will be profitable.

5. **(Determining the Cheapest-to-Deliver Bond on the Treasury Bond Futures Contract)** The Treasury bond contract is based on the assumption that the underlying bond has a 6 percent coupon rate and a maturity or call date of not less than 15 years. Because the contract assumes delivery of a bond with a 6 percent coupon, the delivery of a bond with coupon other than 6 percent would have a different market value. Therefore, an adjustment is necessary in the invoice price. The adjustment is based on the CBOT's conversion factor system. The conversion factor is defined for each eligible bond for a given contract. The conversion factor is the price of a bond with a face value of $1, coupon and maturity equal to that of the deliverable bond, and yield of 6 percent. The maturity is defined as the maturity of the bond on the first day of the futures contract delivery month.

Chapter 11

1. **(Short Hedge and Long Hedge)** The terms *short* and *long* refer to the position taken in the futures contract. A short (long) hedge means that you are short (long) futures. Because a hedge implies opposite positions in the spot and futures markets, a short (long) hedge means that you are long (short) in the spot market.

2. **(The Basis)**
   a. The basis is defined as the difference between the spot price and the futures price.
   b. At expiration, the spot price must equal the futures price, give or take a small differential for transaction costs. Therefore, over the life of the contract, the spot and futures prices will converge and the basis will go to zero at expiration.

c. The basis is the difference between the spot price and the futures price. If the basis is positive and strengthens, the spot price increases more or decreases less than the futures price (or the spot price goes up and the futures price goes down). Because a short hedge is long the spot and short the futures, this is beneficial. Because the long hedge is long the futures and short the spot, this hurts the long hedge.

3. **(Contract Choice)** The most important factor is to have a strong correlation between the spot and futures prices. It is also important that the futures contract have sufficient liquidity. If the contract is not very liquid, then the hedger may be unable to close the position at the appropriate time without making a significant price concession. This weakens the effectiveness of the hedge by making the futures price less dependent on the spot market and the normal cost-of-carry relationship between the two markets. In addition, the contract should be correctly priced or at least priced in favor of the hedger. For example, a short (long) hedger would not want to sell (buy) a futures contract that was underpriced (overpriced) as this would reduce the hedging effectiveness.

4. **(Contract Choice)** The rule of thumb is that the contract chosen should expire as soon as possible after the hedge termination date but not during the month of the hedge termination date. This is because there is sometimes unusual price behavior in the expiration month resulting from a possible shortage of the deliverable good. If the contract expires before the hedge is terminated, the hedger will have to roll the contract into the next expiration. This would incur additional transaction costs. The appropriate expirations are
   a. September
   b. March of the next year
   c. March of the current year
   d. September

5. **(Why Hedge?)** One reason firms hedge is because they can do it more effectively than their shareholders. They are better able to assess the risks, and they have lower transaction costs. Of course, this does not address the question of why the shareholders would want to hedge in the first place, but this may be because they want to find a more acceptable combination of risk and return. Firms also hedge because of tax advantages; because they want to reduce the probability of bankruptcy (which has many costs associated

with it); and because the managers are hedging to protect their own wealth, which is tied so closely to that of the firm.

Chapter 12

1. **(Introduction)** Interest rate swaps are more widely used than currency and equity swaps, because nearly all businesses face some form of interest rate risk. Interest rate swaps are the primary means of managing that risk. Some businesses face currency risk and a few face equity risk, but there is virtually no business that does not assume some form of interest rate risk.

2. **(Structure of a Typical Currency Swap)** Notional amount is often exchanged in a currency swap, because the amounts are in different currencies. These amounts are equivalent at the start of the swap but not likely to be equivalent at the end of the swap. In an interest rate or equity swap, the notional amount is in the same currency, so it would serve no purpose to exchange it. It would be an exchange of equal amounts at the beginning and end of the swap.

3. **(Pricing and Valuation of Interest Rate Swaps)**

   a. In an interest rate swap, the party paying fixed and receiving floating has a position equivalent to issuing a fixed-rate bond (and thus paying interest at a fixed rate) and using the proceeds to buy a floating-rate bond (and thus receiving interest at a floating rate). A similar but opposite argument can be used for the counterparty.

   (Pricing and Valuation of Currency Rate Swaps)

   a. In a currency swap, the party making payments in currency A and receiving payments in currency B has a position equivalent to issuing a bond in currency A and using the proceeds to buy a bond in currency B. A similar but opposite argument can be used for the counterparty.

4. **(Pricing and Valuation of Interest Rate Swaps)** Swaps are similar to forward contracts in that they involve the commitment to make a fixed payment and receive a floating payment at a future date. While a forward contract is a single payment, a swap is a series of payments. Thus, a swap is like a series of forward contracts. Both swaps and forward contracts require no up-front payments, and both are subject to default risk. There are some differences, however, in that in a swap, both sides of the first payment are known. Also, for a swap, all of the fixed payments are the same, whereas in a

series of forward contracts, each contract would be priced separately and would have different fixed rates.

5. **(Some Final Words about Swaps)** There are several ways to terminate a swap. A party can go back to the counterparty and ask for an offsetting swap. The parties effectively create the opposite swap. They then hold opposite positions to each other. They can keep the two swaps in place with each making their series of payments, but there will be credit risk. Alternatively, the parties can cancel the two swaps, with the party owing the greater amount making a cash payment of the net amount owed on the two swaps to the other party. If this method is used, the parties simply agree to accept whatever terms exist in the market at the time the opposite swap is put in place. Another means of canceling the swap is for one party to have already entered into either a forward contract or an option on a swap of the opposite position. This arrangement permits establishment of the terms of the offsetting swap before that swap is needed.

Chapter 13

1. **(Structure and Use of a Typical FRA)** Most interest rate derivatives, specifically swaps and options, pay off later than the expiration or settlement date. For example, at the expiration of an interest rate option, the underlying interest rate is compared to the exercise rate. If the option is in-the-money, it pays off but at a later date. If the underlying rate is, for example, the rate on a 90-day Eurodollar, the payoff will typically occur 90 days later. This arrangement is in keeping with the fact that on a given day, the 90-day Eurodollar rate as of that date implies an interest payment that will be made 90 days later. A similar procedure occurs on the settlement dates of a swap. On an FRA, however, the payoff typically occurs on the expiration date. The amount paid, however, is then discounted to reflect the deferred payment.

2. **(Structure and Use of a Typical FRA)** FRAs are essentially (plain vanilla interest rate) swaps with a single payment. Most swaps have multiple payments. The first floating payment in a swap is known, however, whereas in an FRA, the first floating payment is not known. It will be determined on the expiration date.

3. **(Interest Rate Option Strategies)** An interest rate option requires that you pay a premium up front.

Take an interest rate call, for example. When the option expires, you decide whether to exercise it. In effect, you have the right to receive a floating interest rate and pay a fixed interest rate. You would choose to do that if the floating interest rate were higher. The actual payment you receive occurs at a later date. With an FRA, you pay nothing up front, but agree that on the expiration date, you will make an interest payment at a predetermined fixed interest rate and receive an interest payment at a floating rate. A financial manager might want to buy an interest rate call or FRA to protect against a future interest rate increase. In the case of the interest rate call, the manager can still benefit if rates go down, but that comes at the expense of having to pay a premium up front. With an FRA, the manager will gain if rates go up and lose if rates go down, but pays no up-front premium. So the manager saves the up-front premium by giving up the right to gain if rates fall.

4. **(Interest Rate Option Strategies)** First, let us consider only a single call option in the cap and put option in the floor. A long interest rate call and short interest rate put can be equivalent to a single payment in swap to pay fixed and receive floating. The long call pays off $\text{Max}(0, \text{LIBOR} - X)$, and the short put pays off $-\text{Max}(0, X - \text{LIBOR})$. This means that the combination will pay off LIBOR $- X$ in all cases (i.e., LIBOR $- X$ on the call and 0 on the put if LIBOR $> X$ or 0 on the call and $-(X - \text{LIBOR})$ on the put if LIBOR $\leq X$). If the exercise rate, X, is chosen to be the swap rate, then this combination pays off the same as a single payment in a swap. To replicate the series of payments in a swap, one would need a cap, which is made up of a series of interest rate calls, and a floor, which is made up of a series of interest rate puts.

5. **(Interest Rate Caps, Floors, and Collars)** An interest rate cap provides protection against increases in the interest rate over the exercise rate at the expense of having to pay cash up front. By combining a short position in an interest rate floor, you obtain an interest rate collar, which will provide the same protection, but the firm can pay for it in a different way. When a party buys an interest rate floor, it obtains protection if rates fall below the floor exercise rate. By selling a floor, a firm receives a premium up front as compensation for the possibility that it will have to make payments to the floor holder if rates fall below the floor exercise rate. Thus, if the buyer of a cap sells a floor with a lower exercise rate, the payment received up front from the floor can offset the payment made for the cap. The disadvantage of a collar is that the gains from falling interest rates below the lower strike are forgone. Typically, the exercise rate on the floor is set such that the floor premium precisely offsets the cap premium.

Chapter 14

1. **(Portfolio Insurance)** Insuring a portfolio using stock and puts is the ideal approach. You simply buy the appropriate put and hold the position until the put expiration. The put will protect against a drop in the price below the exercise price. An equivalent result can be achieved by replicating the put through dynamic trading of stock index futures. This type of transaction will only work, however, if the stock price changes are small and the position is revised often. Thus, it is easier to do the transaction with a put—no adjustments to the position are needed. In practice, however, puts are seldom available with the terms and conditions needed or the puts that are available are not sufficiently liquid.

2. **(Structured Notes)** Most structured notes are tailored (i.e., structured) to the specific needs of an investor. A portfolio manager whose portfolio is exposed to loss from falling interest rates over the holding period might purchase an inverse floating-rate note as a type of hedge. If interest rates decrease, the inverse floater will gain, thereby offsetting some or all of the loss on the rest of the portfolio. Of course, the inverse floater will lose if rates rise, thereby offsetting some or all of the gain on the rest of the portfolio.

3. **(Mortgage-Backed Securities)** In an interest-only mortgage strip, as in any instrument, the value of the instrument will be related to interest rates. The strip is a claim on a series of future fixed interest payments. Consequently, its value will fluctuate as interest rates fluctuate, decreasing with rising interest rates and increasing with falling interest rates. The magnitude of the stream of interest payments will vary, however, as homeowners choose to pay off their mortgages early. This typically occurs with falling interest rates. Consequently, the gains from the effects of falling rates are partially offset by the fact that the stream of future payments can abruptly cease. This makes the value of the strip quite volatile; prepayments can terminate the stream. In the example in the book, we looked at

only a single underlying mortgage. In practice, mortgage strips are based on portfolios of underlying mortgages, not all of which prepay at the same time but all of which have the tendency to prepay faster as rates fall. Thus, there are two factors that determine the value of ten strips: one is the effect of discounting, and the other is the prepayment effect.

4. **(Path-Dependent Options)** A path-independent option is one in which the value is determined only by the value of the underlying at the option's expiration. This contrasts to the path-dependent option, in which the value of the option can be affected by how the underlying arrived at its value at the option expiration. An American option, which can be exercised early, is a path-dependent option, whereas a European option, which pays off based only on the expiration value of the asset, is a path-independent option. Other examples of path-dependent options include Asian options, which pay off based on the average underlying price on its way to expiration; look back options, which pay off based on the high or low price of the underlying during the option's life; and barrier options, which can terminate or activate based on the underlying price hitting a specific level during the option's life.

5. **(Path-Dependent Options)** There are a variety of possible situations. Barrier options do not pay off in some states in which ordinary options pay off. Thus, any situation in which an investor thinks a particular state highly unlikely is a candidate for using a barrier option. Another good example is an up-and-out put. An investor might buy a put for downside protection. If the asset price rises, the investor may feel the put is no longer needed. An ordinary put could be sold, but it would be cheaper to have simply bought an up-and-out put in the first place. The investor runs the risk that the asset, having risen sharply, then falls sharply. The investor would then be stuck without the put protection, but the willingness to bear that risk is what makes the up-and-out put cheaper than the ordinary put. Similarly, a down-and-out call will terminate if the underlying asset price falls to the barrier. An investor using such an option would be saying that he or she is willing to bear the risk of the asset price falling, the call knocking out, and then the asset price rising and missing out on a potentially positive payoff at expiration. This makes the down-and-out call cheaper in the first place. Numerous other examples could be constructed, but all should be based on the notion that a barrier option will not pay off in some

states in which an ordinary option would pay off. If investors are willing to bear the risk of those states occurring, then the barrier option will be more appropriate.

Chapter 15

1. **(Benefits of Risk Management)** Hedging is a strategy designed to reduce risk. Risk management encompasses hedging, but goes beyond. It consists of identifying the appropriate level of risk that a firm should have, determining the level of risk that a firm currently has, and adjusting the actual level of risk to the desired level of risk. Obviously, in some situations, this will involve increasing the firm's risk. Risk management is also an ongoing process in which monitoring a firm's risk and making appropriate adjustments continually keep the firm at its desired level of risk.

2. **(Benefits of Risk Management)** Risk management can be beneficial to shareholders because firms can adjust risk levels better than their shareholders, tax advantages can accrue because of the progressive tax structure, bankruptcy costs can be avoided, the underinvestment problem (wherein firms in near-bankruptcy avoid taking on value-creating projects because the benefits go to the bondholders) can be avoided, and risk management can help firms be sure that sufficient cash is available to fund investments.

3. **(Managing Market Risk)** Market risk is associated with movements in interest rates, exchange rates, commodity prices, and stock prices. Credit risk is the risk associated with having a counterparty fail to pay off. Market risk and credit risk are typically managed separately and require different techniques. Market risk is managed by looking at deltas, gammas, vegas, VAR, etc. Credit risk is typically managed by monitoring the extent of activity with a given party and by using credit enhancements such as collateral and marking-to-market. Market risk and credit risk can be related, such as when your counterparty to a swap is in financial trouble but you owe it more than it owes you, in which case you have no credit risk.

4. **(Credit Derivatives)** The three participants are the credit derivative buyer, the credit derivative seller, and the reference entity. The buyer starts with some type of credit exposure to the reference entity. That is, the buyer might be a bank or an investor who has extended credit to the reference

entity through a loan or bond. To eliminate the credit risk, it engages in a credit derivatives transaction with the credit derivatives seller. The seller thereby assumes the credit risk of the reference entity and compensates the buyer if a credit loss occurs. In return, the seller receives compensation, which differs depending on the type of credit derivative.

5. (**Delta Hedging**) The portfolio might contain gamma and vega risk, the former being the risk of delta changing, and the latter being the risk of the volatility changing. Eurodollar futures do not have gammas or vegas, so the addition of them in order to delta hedge does nothing to the gamma or vega. These risks can be hedged only by adding offsetting positions in instruments that have gammas and vegas.

In addition, the portfolio might have credit risk. Eurodollar futures do not have credit risk, but they also do not assist in managing credit risk.

6. (**Credit Derivatives**) The general idea behind determining the CDS premium is that the premium is the amount of money that would be paid by the CDS buyer, who is exposed to the credit risk, to the CDS seller, who is willing to insure the credit risk. This amount of money effectively converts the credit-risky bond to a risk-free bond. The money is typically paid over the life of the bond.

Chapter 16

1. (**End Users**) Treasury departments typically manage the cash of a company. They borrow and invest money and generally ensure that the company has the cash it needs in the right place at the right time but that it does not let its cash sit idle. Treasury departments often use derivatives to manage the risk associated with this activity. Normally, the treasury department is a cost center, generally incurring costs but not attempting to generate revenues that cover its costs. It simply provides support services. If a treasury is operated as a profit center, it would probably have to speculate in the financial markets, and that would entail trading derivatives to attempt to earn a profit. So the treasury department would probably need to speculate by trading derivatives with the objective of making a profit, rather than managing risk.

2. (**Dealers**) The objective of a derivatives dealer is to provide liquidity services to end users. A dealer stands ready to take either side of a transaction (buying or selling). It then hedges the risk it

assumes by engaging in other transactions that pass the risk on to other parties. An end user typically faces some type of risk and seeks out a dealer with whom it can trade to pass on that risk. Neither party wants to assume the risk, but dealers stand ready to take either side of a transaction, while an end user has a specific transaction it needs to do to eliminate the risk.

3. (**Dealers**) Within a derivatives dealer operation, the two primary types of specialists are traders and sales personnel. The former engage in the derivatives transactions that provide risk management services to customers and lay off the dealer's risks. The latter call on customers to sell the company's risk management services.

4. (**End Users**) In a decentralized risk management operation, risk is managed at the micro level. A particular department, group, or division that faces some risk will manage that risk within its own area. In a centralized risk management system, all of the risk of an organization is managed within a single risk management department, group, or division typically located near the top of the organization. A decentralized system has the advantage of having the risk managed at the level at which it is incurred, which can result in more effective risk management, because the individuals have more expertise about the risk. But decentralized risk management results in duplication of efforts. In addition, some risks within a company might offset if managed at a consolidated level. A centralized system can result in significant savings and provides for the use of risk management specialists. It also has the benefit that the company can get a single overall look at its risk.

5. (**Organizing the Risk Management Function in a Company**) Typically, a centralized risk management system manages only a limited number of risks, usually those associated with financial markets. But a company faces many types of risks. Its products may fail, its reputation may be tarnished, and its employees may be injured. These risks are normally managed by insurance and by efforts to avoid the loss (e.g., safety programs for employees) or loss minimization efforts (e.g., sprinkler systems to reduce fire losses). An enterprise risk management system brings the management of these risks under the same area as the management of financial risks. As a result, there can be significant savings and the benefit of being able to get a better overall picture of the company's risk.

Glossary

The number in parentheses indicates the first chapter where the term is noted as a key term. Note that not all terms are key terms; hence, such terms will not have a number. In addition, some terms do not appear in the text at all and are defined here as a convenience for the reader who may encounter these terms in other books or in practice.

Accounting risk (15) The risk associated with improper accounting treatment for a transaction, which may arise when accounting procedures and rulings change or have not yet been established.

Accreting swap A swap in which the notional principal increases through time. See also Index amortizing swap.

Accrued interest The amount of interest accumulated on a bond since its last coupon payment date.

Against actuals (8) See Exchange for physicals.

All or none order (2) An order to purchase or sell a security or derivative in which the broker is instructed to fill the entire order or not fill any of the orders.

Alternative currency option An option in which the payoff is a function of the performance of two or more currencies. The holder has the right to decide which currency will be compared with the exercise price to determine the payoff.

Alternative option (14) An option involving more than one underlying asset whose payoff is determined by either the better performing (max) of the two assets or the worse performing (min) of the two assets. The rate of return of the better or worse performing of the two assets is compared to the exercise rate.

American option An option that can be exercised on any day during its life.

Amortizing swap See Index amortizing swap.

Analytical method (15) A method for estimating the Value at Risk in which knowledge of the input values and a pricing model are used with an assumption about the type of probability distribution associated with the risk. Also known as Variance/covariance method and Delta normal method.

Anticipatory hedge (11) A transaction in which a hedger expects to make a transaction in the spot market at a future date and is attempting to protect against a change in the spot price by trading a derivative.

Arbitrage (1) A transaction based on the observation of the same asset or derivative selling at two different prices. The transaction involves buying the asset or derivative at the lower price and selling it at the higher price.

Arbitrage pricing theory A theory of asset pricing in which the expected return is a function of the asset's sensitivity to one or more underlying economic factors.

Arbitrageur (8) An individual who engages in an arbitrage transaction.

Arrears swap A fixed-for-floating rate swap in which the payment is made on the same day that the floating interest rate is determined. See also Delayed settlement swap.

Asian option (14) An option in which the final payoff is determined by the average price of the asset during the option's life. See also Average price option and Average strike option.

Ask price (2) The price at which a market maker offers to sell a security or derivative.

Asset allocation How an investment portfolio is allocated across asset classes.

Asset-backed security A security providing the holder returns based on the payments from a portfolio of underlying securities.

Asset-or-nothing option (14) An option which, if it expires in-the-money, pays the holder the underlying asset while the holder does not have to pay the exercise price.

Asset pricing theory The study of the economic processes through which prices and expected returns on securities are formulated.

Assigned (2) The chosen writer of an exercised option.

Assignment The procedure in which the holder of a short position in an option is instructed to buy or sell the underlying asset or futures from or to the holder of the long position.

Associated person (AP) (8) An individual affiliated with a firm engaged in any line of futures-related business but excluding individuals who execute trades, manage portfolios or pools, give advice, or perform clerical duties.

As-you-like-it option (14) See Chooser option.

At-the-money (2) An option in which the price of the underlying stock or futures equals the exercise price.

Average price option (14) An Asian option in which the average price of the asset over the life of the option replaces the price of the asset at expiration in determining the option's payoff.

Average strike option (14) An Asian option in which the average price of the asset over the life of the option replaces the exercise price at expiration in determining the option's payoff.

Back office (16) The clerical, record-keeping function in a derivatives/risk management system.

Backwardation (9) A condition in financial markets in which the forward or futures price is less than the spot price. Also known as an inverted market.

Barrier option (14) An option that either does not begin or terminates early if the underlying asset price hits a certain level called the barrier. If the option does not begin or terminates early, the holder might be paid a rebate. See also In-option and Out-option.

Basis (11) The difference between the spot price and the futures or forward price or the difference between a nearby futures or forward price and a deferred futures or forward price.

Basis point A measure commonly applied to interest rates or yields equal to 1/100 of 1 percent.

Basis risk (11) The uncertainty of the basis over the hedge period.

Basis swap (12) A swap in which both parties make payments at different floating rates.

Baskets (14) Single options written on a specified combination of securities or currencies.

Bear (6) A person who expects the market to go down. Sometimes referred to as bearish.

Bear market A market in which prices are falling.

Bear spread (7) An option spread designed to profit in a bear market. Also known as a bearish spread.

Beta A measure of the responsiveness of a security or portfolio to the market as a whole.

Biased expectations A condition in which investor's expectations of a rate, a security price, or a return systematically differ from the subsequent long-run average rate, price, or return.

Bid price (2) The price at which a market maker offers to buy a security or derivative.

Bid-ask spread (2) The difference between the ask price or rate and the bid price or rate.

Bilateral netting (15) Netting between two parties. See also Netting and Multilateral netting.

Binary option (14) See Asset-or-nothing option and Cash-or-nothing option.

Binomial Allows the stock price to go either up or down, possibly at different rates.

Binomial model (4) An option pricing model based on the assumption that at any point in time the price of the underlying can change to one of only two possible values.

Binomial option pricing model (4) See Binomial model.

Black model (9) A pricing model for an option on a forward or futures contract.

Black-Scholes-Merton model (5) A widely used pricing model for an option on an asset.

Black-Scholes-Merton option pricing model See Black-Scholes-Merton model.

Block trade The sale of at least 10,000 shares of stock normally conducted with considerable care so as to minimize the impact on the stock price.

Board broker (2) See Order book official.

Bond option An option to buy or sell a bond.

Boundary condition A statement specifying the maximum or minimum price or some other limitation on the price of an option.

Box spread (7) A risk-free combination of a call money spread and a put money spread.

Breakeven stock price (6) The underlying asset price at which a strategy has a zero profit.

Break forward (14) A forward contract with an upside payoff like a call, but which has a possible negative value at expiration so as to compensate for the fact that it has no initial value.

Broker A person who arranges a financial transaction by bringing a buyer and seller together and usually earns a commission.

Bull (6) A person who expects the market to go up. Sometimes referred to as bullish.

Bull market A market in which prices are rising.

Bull spread (7) An option spread designed to profit in a bull market. Also known as a bullish spread.

Business risk (1) The risk associated with a particular line of business.

Butterfly spread (7) An option transaction consisting of one long call at a particular exercise price, another otherwise identical long call at a different exercise price, and two otherwise identical short calls at an exercise price between the other two.

Buy back A method of terminating a swap in which a party makes or receives a cash payment to or from the counterparty in the amount of the value of the swap. Also called a close-out.

Buying the spread (7) See Debit spread.

Calendar spread (7) An option transaction consisting of the purchase of an option with a given expiration and the sale of an otherwise identical option with a different expiration.

Call (1) An option to buy an asset, currency, or futures. Also refers to the early retirement of a bond.

Call date The earliest date at which a bond can be called.

Callability A feature associated with many bonds in which the issuer is permitted to pay off the bond prior to its scheduled maturity date.

Callable bond A bond that the issuer can retire prior to its maturity date.

Call option (2) See Call.

Cap An option transaction in which a party borrowing at a floating rate pays a premium to another party, which reimburses the borrower in the event that the borrower's interest costs exceed a certain level, thus making the effective interest paid on a floating rate loan have a cap or maximum amount. Can also be used in other cases where the underlying is an asset price, commodity price, or exchange rate.

Capital Asset Pricing Model A model that gives the equilibrium expected return on an asset as a function of the risk-free rate, the expected return on the market, and the asset's beta or systematic risk.

Capital market The financial market in which long-term securities such as stocks and long-term bonds are traded.

Caplet (13) One of the component options of a cap.

Carry (9) The difference between the cash received from holding an asset and the interest forgone or other costs associated with holding it.

Carry arbitrage (10) A theoretically riskless transaction consisting of a long position in the spot asset (hence you are "carrying" it) and a short position in the futures contract (hence you do not have market risk so it is arbitrage).

Carry arbitrage model (9) A model for pricing futures and forward contracts in which the futures or forward price is determined by executing a strategy of buying the asset and selling the futures or forward and in which no arbitrage profits will be earned.

Cash and carry arbitrage (10) See Carry arbitrage.

Cash Flow at Risk (CAR) (15) A measure of the expected cash shortfall from a critical level.

Cash flow hedge (16) A type of hedge in which a future cash flow from an asset or liability is being hedged and which may qualify for hedge accounting. See also Hedge accounting.

Cash market (1) See Spot market.

Cash-or-nothing option (14) An option which, if it expires in-the-money, pays the holder the exercise price.

Cash settlement (2) The feature of certain derivatives that allows delivery or exercise to be conducted with an exchange of cash rather than the physical transfer of assets.

CDS premium (15) The amount of money the creditor would pay a third party to eliminate the default risk. In the case of a single zero-coupon bond, it is the difference between the present value of the face amount of the zero-coupon debt, discounted at the risk-free rate, and the current market price of the bond.

CFTC-SEC accord (2) See Johnson-Shad agreement.

Cheapest-to-deliver (10) Often futures contracts permit the seller the ability to deliver from a variety of instruments; hence, the seller will deliver the lowest cost instrument. See Cheapest-to-deliver bond.

Cheapest-to-deliver bond (CTD) The bond that, if delivered on the Chicago Board of Trade's Treasury bond or note contract, provides the largest difference between the invoice price and the cost of the bond.

Chooser option (14) An option in which the holder decides at a specific time during the option's life whether it will be a put or a call. Sometimes called an as-you-like-it option.

Circuit breaker (8) See Trading halt.

Class All of the options of a particular type (call or put) on a given stock, index, currency, or futures commodity.

Clearing firm (2) A company that is a member of a futures or options clearinghouse.

Clearinghouse (2) An institution associated with an options or futures exchange that guarantees the performance of both parties to the contract, collects margins, and maintains records of the parties to all transactions.

Cliquet option (14) An option that allows an upward resetting of the exercise price as the asset price crosses a series of thresholds.

Closeout netting (15) Netting in which at the termination of a transaction only the net amount is owed.

CMO See Collateralized mortgage obligation.

CMT rate (12) Constant Maturity Treasury rate, the rate on a Treasury security of a given maturity. Often used as a floating rate in a constant maturity swap.

Collar (7) An option strategy in which a position in an asset is hedged by buying a put with an exercise price typically lower than the current asset price with the cost of the put partially covered by the premium from selling a call at a higher exercise price. For interest rate options designed to protect a loan, the put is a floor and the call is a cap. See also Zero cost collar.

Collateral Any type of cash or security set aside as protection for the lender in a loan. Also used as a credit enhancement in a derivative transaction.

Collateralized debt obligation (15) A type of security in which a portfolio of debt obligations are divided into tranches with different payment characteristics, different priorities, and different risks and are passed through, less a service fee, to holders.

Collateralized mortgage obligation (14) A type of mortgage-backed security in which mortgage payments are divided into tranches with different payment characteristics, different priorities, and different risks and are passed through, less a service fee, to holders.

Combination An option strategy involving positions in a put and a call. Sometimes used to refer to any option strategy involving more than one option.

Commercial paper A short-term promissory note issued by a large, creditworthy corporation.

Commission A fee paid by the parties in a transaction to a broker for arranging the transaction.

Commission broker A trader on the floor of a futures exchange who executes transactions for off-the-floor customers.

Commodity Any asset, but more frequently used to refer to an agricultural product or sometimes a metal or natural resource.

Commodity fund (8) See Futures fund.

Commodity futures Any futures contract, but primarily a futures on an agricultural product or sometimes a metal or natural resource.

Commodity Futures Trading Commission The federal agency that regulates the futures markets.

Commodity option (8) An option on a commodity, but more often an option on a futures contract.

Commodity pool (8) A private investment arrangement in which individuals combine their funds and the total amount of funds is used to trade futures contracts, with a cash reserve set aside to meet margin calls.

Commodity pool operator (CPO) (8) The organizer or manager of a commodity pool.

Commodity swap (12) A swap in which two parties agree to make payments to each other with at least one party's payments calculated according to the price of a commodity. The other party's payments can be calculated according to any formula.

Commodity trading advisor (CTA) (8) An individual who specializes in offering advice regarding the trading of futures contracts.

Comparative statics An examination of the effects on a model of changes in the variables that influence the model.

Compound option (14) An option to buy or sell another option.

Conditional Value at Risk (15) A measure of the expected loss of an organization, given that a loss occurs.

Constant maturity swap (12) A swap where one side pays a rate associated with an instrument of constant maturity, which is usually greater than the settlement period of the swap. See also CMT rate.

Contango (9) A condition in financial markets in which the forward or futures price is greater than the spot price.

Contingent-pay option (14) An option in which the premium is paid at expiration and only if the option expires in-the-money.

Contingent premium option An option in which the premium is paid at expiration and only if the option is in-the-money. See also Pay-later option.

Continuous time (5) A characteristic describing a class of option pricing models in which time moves in extremely small (infinitesimal) units. The Black-Scholes-Merton model is a continuous time model. Contrast with Discrete time.

Continuously compounded rate A rate of return in which the asset value grows continuously.

Convenience yield (9) A premium imbedded in the spot price that provides an extra return for those holding the commodity and usually observed during shortages of the commodity.

Conversion (6) An arbitrage transaction consisting of the sale of a call and the purchase of a synthetic call.

Conversion factor (10) An adjustment factor applied to the settlement price of the Chicago Board of Trade's Treasury bond and note contracts that gives the holder of the short position a choice of several different bonds or notes to deliver.

Convertible bond A bond which the holder can convert into a specified number of shares of stock.

Convexity A mathematical relationship between the change in a bond price and the change in its yield, beyond that explained by its duration. Knowledge and use of convexity is helpful in obtaining effective hedge results.

Cost of carry (9) The cost involved in holding or storing an asset that consists of storage costs and interest lost on funds tied up.

Cost of carry model (9) See Carry arbitrage model.

Counterperformativity (5) In the human sciences, when an observed activity is made less consistent with a particular economic model as participants increasingly believe in the model.

Coupon The interest paid on a bond.

Covariance A measure of the association between two random variables.

Covered call (6) A combination of a long position in an asset, futures, or currency and a short position in a call on the same.

Covered interest arbitrage When the combined effects of numerous arbitrageurs pushes the spot rate up and/or the forward rate down until the spot and forward rates are properly aligned with the relative interest rates in two countries.

Credit default swap (15) See Credit swap.

Credit derivative (15) A derivative contract based on the credit risk of a particular party. See also Total return swap, Credit swap, Credit spread option, Credit linked security.

Credit enhancements Any of several means used to reduce the credit risk on a swap or derivative transaction.

Credit event The occurrence of an event related to the credit risk of a party, such as failure to make a scheduled payment, declaration of bankruptcy, repudiation of a liability, or acceleration of payment of another liability.

Credit linked security (15) A security that pays off less than its face value in the event of a default by a third party on a separate obligation.

Credit risk (15) The risk that a party to an over-the-counter derivative contract will not pay off as required. Also known as default risk.

Credit spread (7) An option spread in which the amount paid for the purchased option is less than the amount received from the sold option.

Credit spread option (15) An option in which the underlying is the spread on a credit-risky security over an otherwise comparable Treasury security.

Credit swap (15) A type of credit derivative in the form of a swap in which one party makes periodic payments to the other and the other party makes payments to the first if a particular credit-related event, such as a default or downgrade, occurs.

Cross hedge (11) Involves an additional source of basis risk due to the difference between the asset being hedged and the asset underlying the futures.

Cross product netting (15) Netting in which payments owed for one transaction are netted against payments owed for another type of transaction. Thus, parties could net one type of derivative against another, as well as against loans.

Cross-rate relationship The association among the exchange rates of three currencies.

Currency hedge See Foreign investment hedge.

Currency swap (12) A transaction in which two parties agree to make a series of payments to each other in different currencies.

Currency option See Foreign currency option.

Currency warrants Options on various foreign currencies underwritten by investment banking firms and often trades on the American Stock Exchange.

Current credit risk (15) The risk that a party to a transaction will be unable to make payments that are currently due.

Daily price limits The maximum and minimum prices at which a futures contract can trade. These are established by the clearinghouse and are expressed in relation to the previous day's settlement price.

Daily settlement (8) The process in a futures market in which the daily price changes are paid by the parties incurring losses to the parties making profits. Also known as marking to market.

Day order (2) An order to purchase or sell a security or derivative that is canceled if unfilled by the end of the day.

Day trader (8) A derivatives trader who closes out all positions by the end of the trading session.

Dealer (16) A person or firm engaged in the business of buying and selling securities or derivatives for profit. A dealer stands ready to buy or sell at any time.

Debit spread (7) An option spread in which the amount paid for the purchased option exceeds the amount received from the sold option.

Deductible A concept in insurance representing the amount by which an insurance payoff is reduced as a result of the insured assuming some of the risk.

Deep in-the-money (3) An option that is in-the-money by a significant, though unspecific, amount.

Deep out-of-the-money (3) An option that is out-of-the-money by a significant, though unspecific, amount.

Default risk (15) See Credit risk.

Deferred strike option (14) An option in which the exercise price is not set until a later time during the option's life but prior to expiration.

Delayed settlement swap The standard procedure in an interest rate swap in which the floating interest rate is observed at the beginning of the settlement period and the interest is paid at the end. See also Arrears swap.

Delivery The process in which a futures or forward contract can be terminated at expiration through the sale of the asset by the holder of the short to the long.

Delivery day (8) The day on which an asset is delivered to terminate a futures or forward contract.

Delivery option (10) Any special right or option inherent in a futures contract, held by the holder of the short position and granting flexibility with regard to the item delivered or the timing of delivery. See also Timing option, Quality option, End-of-month option, Switching option.

Delta (5) The ratio of the change in a derivative's price to a given change in the price of the underlying asset or futures.

Delta hedge (5) A transaction in which an asset or derivative is hedged with another asset or derivative in such a manner that the hedge is adjusted so that the effect of small changes in the underlying is removed and the hedge provides a risk-free return.

Delta neutral (5) The condition in which an investor's portfolio is delta hedged and, therefore, unaffected by small changes in the value of the underlying.

Delta normal method (15) See Analytical method.

Derivative (1) A contract between two parties providing for a payoff from one party to the other determined by the price of an asset, an exchange rate, a commodity price, or an interest rate.

Designated primary market maker (2) A firm chosen to provide both buy and sell prices that is not allowed to trade on behalf of customers, must trade solely for its own account, is allowed to hold a lower required margin, and is allocated a minimum share of certain transactions.

Diagonal spread An option spread in which the options differ by both time to expiration and exercise price.

Diff swap (12) A swap in which one party's interest payments are denominated in one currency while the notional principal is stated in another currency.

Diffs Futures contracts based on the difference between two prices, exchange rates, or interest rates.

Digital option (14) See Asset-or-nothing option and Cash-or-nothing option. Same as Binary option.

Discrete time (5) A characteristic describing a class of option pricing models in which time moves in distinct (finite) units. The binomial model is in discrete time. Contrast with Continuous time.

Diversification An investment strategy in which funds are allocated across numerous different assets.

Dividend protection A feature associated with the original over-the-counter options market in which the exercise price was adjusted by the amount of any dividend paid on the underlying stock.

Dividend yield The ratio of the dividend to the stock price.

Dollar return (1) A measure of investment performance, the total dollar profit or loss.

DOT An acronym for Designated Order Turnaround, the New York Stock Exchange's system for expediting stock transactions that is used frequently in program trading.

Down-and-in option An in barrier option in which the premium is paid but the option does not actually begin unless the asset price falls to a specified barrier.

Down-and-out option An out barrier option in which the premium is paid but the option terminates early if the asset price falls to a specified barrier.

Down-option (14) A type of barrier option in which the barrier is below the current level of the underlying.

Dual trading (8) The practice of a floor trader on a derivatives exchange trading for his or her own account as well as for a customer.

Duration (11) A measure of the size and timing of a bond's cash flows. It also reflects the weighted average maturity of the bond and indicates the sensitivity of the bond's price to a change in its yield.

Dynamic hedging (14) An investment strategy, often associated with portfolio insurance, in which a stock is hedged by selling futures or buying Treasury bills in such a manner that the position is adjusted frequently and simulates a protective put.

Dynamic trading (5) Establishing and maintaining a hedge portfolio by constantly adjusting the relative proportions of stock and options.

Early exercise Exercise of an American option before its expiration date.

Earnings at Risk (EAR) (15) A measure of the expected shortfall in earnings from a critical level.

EDPC See Enhanced derivatives products company.

Efficient market A market in which the price of an asset reflects its true economic value.

Electricity derivative (14) A derivative in which the underlying is the price of electricity.

Electronic designated primary market maker (2) Similar to a designated primary market maker, a market participant who operates only on the electronic exchange, not on the trading floor.

Electronic trading A system of trading derivatives or securities in which bids and offers are posted to an electronic medium, such as a computer system or the Internet, and in which transactions then take place by executing orders through the system. See also Open outcry.

Empirical test A procedure in which data are subjected to various statistical measures to determine if a theory, model, or hypothesis is correct.

End-of-month option (10) Either the right to defer delivery on the Chicago Board of Trade's Treasury bond futures contract until the final business days of the month during which the contract does not trade, or any similar right inherent in a futures contract. Can also refer to exchange-listed options whose expirations are on the last business day of the month.

End user (16) A firm that enters into derivative transactions with a dealer for the purpose of managing its risk.

Enhanced derivatives products company (15) A subsidiary established by a bank or swap dealer for the execution of swaps and designed so as to have a higher credit rating than the parent company itself.

Enterprise risk management (16) An approach to managing risk in which all risks in an organization are managed jointly in an integrated manner.

Equity basket A combination of equity securities, otherwise known as a portfolio, but upon which a derivative contract is created.

Equity collar See Collar.

Equity derivative (14) Any type of derivative contract in which the payoff is based on a stock or stock index.

Equity forward (14) A forward contract in which the payoff is based on a stock or stock index.

Equity-linked debt A security that promises a minimum return plus a given percentage of any change in the market above a certain level.

Equity option (2) An option on a common stock.

Equity swap (12) A swap in which two parties agree? to make payments to each other with at least one? party's payments calculated according to the performance?of a stock or index. The other party's payments can be calculated according to any formula.

Euro (2) The currency used in the European Union created as a composite of the currencies of those countries.

Eurodollar A dollar deposited in a European bank or a European branch of an American bank.

Eurolibor/Euribor An interest rate paid on deposits of euros. Eurolibor is based on deposits in London while Euribor is based on deposits elsewhere in Europe. See also Euro.

European option An option that can be exercised only when it expires.

Exchange for physicals (8) A method of delivery on a futures contract in which the long and short agree to delivery terms different from those specified in the futures contract.

Exchange-listed derivative An option or futures that trades on an exchange.

Exchange option (14) An option granting the right to acquire one asset by giving up another asset.

Exchange rate The rate at which a given amount of one currency converts to another currency.

Ex-dividend date A day designated four business days prior to the holder-of-record date after which an investor purchasing a stock does not receive the upcoming dividend.

Exercise (2) The process by which a call option is used to purchase or a put option is used to sell the underlying security, futures, or currency or convert to its cash value.

Exercise limit (2) The maximum number of option contracts that any one investor can exercise over a specific time period.

Exercise price (2) The price at which an option permits its owner to buy or sell the underlying security, futures, or currency.

Exercise rate (13) The fixed rate in an interest rate option, cap, or floor.

Exercise value (3) See Intrinsic value.

Exotic options (14) A family of options with payoff features different from those of standard European and American options.

Exotics (2) Financial derivatives that are out of the ordinary, such as an option that expires if the stock price falls to a certain level.

Expectations theory A theory of the term structure of interest rates that generally implies that the current forward rate is an unbiased predictor of future spot rates.

Expiration date (2) The date after which a derivative contract no longer exists. Also known as the expiration.

Extendible bond A bond in which the holder can choose prior to or at maturity to extend the maturity date.

Face value The principal amount borrowed on a loan.

Fair value hedge (16) A type of hedge in which the market value of an asset or liability is being hedged and may qualify for hedge accounting. See also Hedge accounting.

FAS 133 (16) A ruling established by the U.S. Financial Accounting Standards Board that specifies the appropriate manner for accounting for derivatives transactions.

FCM (8) *See* Futures commission merchant.

Fiduciary call (14) A form of portfolio insurance in which funds are allocated to calls and Treasury bills such that the transaction is equivalent to a protective put.

Financial asset (1) An asset representing a claim of one party on another.

Financial engineering (1) The process of developing, designing, and implementing creative financial contracts, frequently involving derivatives, for the purpose of solving specific risk management problems.

Financial futures (8) Futures on securities, sometimes including futures on foreign currencies.

Financial risk (1) The risk associated with changes in such factors as interest rates, stock prices, commodity prices, and exchange rates.

Financial risk management (15) See Risk management.

Fixed-for-floating rate swap An interest rate swap involving the exchange of fixed interest payments for floating interest payments.

FLEX options Options traded at the Chicago Board Options Exchange that allow the user to specify the strike price, expiration date, and other contract terms in contrast to ordinary CBOE options in which the terms are standardized.

Floating-floating swap See Basis swap.

Floating rate bond A bond in which the interest payments are adjusted periodically to be consistent with current market interest rates. Also in the form of a loan or note.

Floor An option transaction in which a party lending at a floating rate pays a premium to another party, which reimburses the lender in the event that the lender's interest revenues are below a certain level, thus making the interest received on a floating rate loan have a floor or minimum value. It can also be used in other cases where the payoff is tied to an asset price, commodity price, or exchange rate.

Floor broker (2) A trader on the floor of the options exchange who executes trades for others who are off the floor.

Floorlet (13) One of the component options of a floor.

Foreign currency futures A futures contract providing for the purchase of a foreign currency.

Foreign currency option An option providing for the purchase or sale of a foreign currency.

Foreign investment hedge A type of hedge related to transactions in foreign currencies that may qualify for hedge accounting. See also Hedge accounting.

Forward commitment (8) See Forward contract.

Forward contract An agreement between two parties, a buyer and a seller, to buy an asset or currency at a later date at a fixed price.

Forward discount The relationship between the spot and forward exchange rates of a foreign currency in which the forward rate of a currency is less than the spot rate.

Forward market A market in which forward contracts are constructed.

Forward premium The relationship between the spot and forward exchange rates of a foreign currency in which the forward rate of a currency is greater than the spot rate.

Forward price (9) The contractually agreed price stated in the forward contract.

Forward rate The rate agreed upon in a forward contract for a loan or implied by the relationship between short- and long-term interest rates.

Forward rate agreement (FRA) (13) A transaction, similar to a forward contract, in which one party agrees to make a future interest payment based on an agreed-upon fixed rate of interest and receives a future interest payment based on a floating rate such as LIBOR.

Forward-start option (14) An option in which the premium is paid today but the option's life does not begin until later.

Forward swap (13) A forward contract obligating the two parties to enter into a swap at a future date.

Forward value The current market value of an existing forward contract.

FRA (13) See Forward rate agreement.

Free market A market characterized by a high degree of efficiency and little or no regulatory influence.

Front office (16) The trading function in a derivatives/risk management system.

Full carry A condition associated with a futures contract in which the futures price exceeds the spot price by no less than the cost of carry.

Futures commission merchant (8) A firm in the business of executing futures transactions for the public.

Futures contract An agreement between two parties, a buyer and a seller, to purchase an asset or currency at a later date at a fixed price and that trades on a futures exchange and is subject to a daily settlement procedure to guarantee to each party that claims against the other party will be paid.

Futures exchange (8) An organized facility for trading futures, which is governed by a corporate charter with rules and regulations. It may utilize a trading floor or may be an electronic exchange. See also Electronic trading.

Futures fund (8) A mutual fund that specializes in trading futures contracts.

Futures market (1) An organized exchange for trading futures, which are subject to a daily settlement procedure.

Futures option (8) An option on a futures contract.

Futures price (9) The quoted price on a futures contract to deliver some underlying in the future.

Futures spread Strategy involving a long or short position in one futures contract and an opposite position in another.

Futures value (9) The current market value of a futures contract, zero once the position is mark-to-market at the end of each day.

FX swap In the foreign currency markets, a long position in one forward contract and a short position in a forward contract on the same currency but with a different expiration date.

Gamma (5) The rate of change of a derivative's delta with respect to a change in the price of the underlying asset or derivative.

Gamma hedging (5) A hedged position, usually combined with a delta hedge, in which changes in the delta will be unaffected by large movements in the underlying.

Garman-Kohlhagen model A model for pricing European foreign currency options.

Generic swap See Fixed-for-floating rate swap.

Geometric Brownian motion A statistical model based on random movements often used to describe changes in asset prices from which derivative prices can often be obtained.

GLOBEX2 A system of automated trading operated by the Chicago Mercantile Exchange in which bids and offers are entered into a computer and executed electronically.

Good-till-canceled order (2) An order that is in effect until canceled and is used most often with stop orders and limit orders that may take some time to execute.

Grade A measure of a commodity's relative quality.

Greeks A group of measures that provide an approximation of the movement in an option price for a movement in some other variable, such as the underlying or volatility.

Group of Thirty An organization of bankers and economists who conduct studies on various issues important to the efficient operation of international financial markets and systems.

Hedge A transaction in which an investor seeks to protect a position or anticipated position in the spot market by using an opposite position in derivatives.

Hedge accounting (16) A form of accounting for derivatives transactions in which certain transactions, qualifying as hedges, are accounted for in such a manner that the gains or losses from hedges are, to an extent, limited by specified rules, combined with gains and losses from transactions they are designed to hedge, so as to minimize the hedge, so as to minimize? the impact on reported earnings.

Hedge fund A type of mutual fund in which positions are potentially taken in a broad variety of instruments, often including short positions, and often associated with highly speculative trading.

Hedge portfolio (4) A portfolio being hedged, often used in the context of a long stock–short call or long stock–long put in which the hedge ratio is adjusted through time to produce a risk-free portfolio.

Hedge ratio (4) The ratio of derivatives to a spot position (or vice versa) that achieves an objective such as minimizing or eliminating risk.

Hedger (1) An investor who executes a hedge transaction.

Hedging effectiveness (11) A statistical measure of how well a particular hedging strategy works—specifically the percentage of the risk reduced; usually the correlation coefficient squared.

Herstatt risk (15) See Settlement risk.

Historical method (15) A method for estimating Value at Risk that uses historical information on the portfolio's recent performance to estimate its future probability distribution.

Historical volatility (5) The standard deviation of a security, futures, or currency obtained by estimating it from historical data over a recent time period.

Holder-of-record date The day on which all current shareholders are entitled to receive the upcoming dividend.

Holding period The time period over which an investment is held.

Horizontal spread (7) See Calendar spread.

Hybrid (1) An instrument or contract that possesses some of the characteristics of a derivative.

IMM Index The method of quoting the price of a Treasury bill or Eurodollar futures contract on the International Monetary Market in which the price is stated in terms of a discount from par of 100.

Immunization A bond portfolio strategy in which the return is protected against changes in interest rates and is obtained when the duration equals the holding period.

Implied modified duration The duration of the bond underlying a futures contract that is implied by using the futures price as though it were the price of the bond.

Implied repo rate (10) The cost of financing a cash and carry transaction that is implied by the relationship between the spot and futures price.

Implied volatility (5) The standard deviation obtained when the market price of an option equals the price given by a particular option pricing model.

Implied yield (11) The yield on the bond underlying a futures contract that is implied by using the futures price as though it were the price of the bond.

In-arrears swap See Arrears swap.

Index amortizing swap (12) A swap in which the notional principal is reduced according to a schedule that may call for an accelerated reduction the lower interest rates fall.

Index arbitrage The purchase (sale) of a portfolio of stocks representing an index and the sale (purchase) of the corresponding futures contract. The trade is designed to profit from mispricing in the relationship between the spot and futures prices.

Index option (2) An option on an index of securities.

Index swap A swap in which one party's payments are based on an index, such as an equity index. See also Equity swap.

Initial margin (8) The minimum amount of money that must be in an investment account on the day of a transaction. On futures accounts, the initial margin must be met on any day in which the opening balance starts off below the maintenance margin requirement.

In-option (14) A type of barrier option in which the premium is paid but the option does not actually begin unless the asset price crosses a specified barrier. See also Down-and-in option and Up-and-in option.

Installment option (14) An option in which the premium is paid in equal installments. At each payment date, the holder decides whether to continue paying the premium or let the option expire.

Institutional investor A term used to refer to a firm or organization as an investor as opposed to an individual investor.

Instrument (1) The broadest possible term to designate financial securities, financial contracts, and even items (e.g., temperature measurements). For example, derivatives performance depends on how other financial instruments perform.

Interbank market (8) An informal organization of banks that execute spot and forward transactions in foreign currency.

Intercommodity spread A futures transaction involving a long position in a futures on one commodity and a short position in a futures on another commodity.

Interest-only strip (14) A financial instrument providing investors with the interest payments on the portfolio of underlying debt securities, often mortgages. *See also* Principal-only strip.

Interest rate call (13) The right to make a known interest payment.

Interest rate cap (13) A cap in which the payoff is determined by a floating interest rate.

Interest rate collar (13) A collar in which the payoff is determined by a floating interest rate.

Interest rate derivative (13) An option, forward, futures, swap, or other derivative instrument in which the underlying instrument is an interest rate. In some uses, the underlying instrument can be a bond.

Interest rate floor (13) A floor in which the payoff is determined by a floating interest rate.

Interest rate futures A futures contract on a fixed-income security.

Interest rate option (13) An option on an interest rate rather than on a security, commodity, or futures

price. Exercise is determined by whether the interest rate is above or below the strike.

Interest rate parity (9) The relationship between the spot and forward exchange rates and the interest rates in two countries.

Interest rate put (13) The right to receive a known interest payment.

Interest rate swap (12) A transaction between two parties who agree to make interest payments to each other according to different formulas.

Intermarket spread (11) Transactions in which two futures contracts are on different underlying instruments. Also called intercommodity spread.

Internal rate of return (IRR) The discount rate on an investment that equates the present value of the future cash flows with the price.

International Swaps and Derivatives Association An organization of derivatives dealers, a major activity of which is the simplification and promotion of standardized low cost derivatives procedures.

In-the-money (2) A call (put) option in which the price of the asset or futures or the currency exchange rate exceeds (is less than) the exercise price.

Intracommodity spread See Intramarket spread.

Intramarket spread (11) Transactions in which two futures contracts are on the same underlying instruments. Also called intracommodity spread.

Intrinsic value (3) For a call (put) option, the greater of zero or the difference between the stock (exercise) price and the exercise (stock) price. Also called parity value.

Introducing broker (IB) (8) A broker who arranges futures transactions for customers but contracts with another firm or individual for the execution of the trade.

Inverse floater (14) A type of floating rate structured note that pays more interest as interest rates fall and less as interest rates rise.

Inverted market (9) See Backwardation.

IO See Interest-only strip.

ISDA See International Swaps and Derivatives Association.

Johnson-Shad agreement (2) The 1982 agreement between CFTC chairman Phillip McBryde Johnson and SEC chairman John Shad that established the lines of regulatory authority over options.

Kappa (5) See Vega.

Knock-in option (14) See In-option.

Knock-out option See Out-option.

Lambda (5) See Vega.

Law of one price (1) The principle that two identical assets or portfolios cannot sell for different prices.

Lead market maker (2) At the CBOE, if physical "pit" trading exists, a market participant who must maintain a presence in specific trading areas consistent with his or her selected option classes.

LEAPS Long-term Equity Anticipation Securities. Exchange-listed options on individual stocks and indices with expirations of more than one year.

Legal risk (15) The risk that the legal system will fail to enforce a contract. Legal risk is primarily faced by dealers and may arise when an end user loses money in a transaction and claims that the dealer misled it or that the end user had no legal authority to enter into the transaction and the dealer should have informed it of such.

Less than full carry (9) When the commodity has a convenience yield and the futures price is less than the spot price plus the cost of carry.

Leverage The use of debt to magnify investment returns.

Limit down (8) An occurrence in which the futures price moves down to the lower daily price limit.

Limit move (8) An occurrence in which a futures price hits the upper or lower daily price limit.

Limit order (2) A request to purchase or sell a security or derivative that specifies the maximum price to pay or minimum price to accept.

Limit up (8) An occurrence in which the futures price moves up to the upper daily price limit.

Liquidity A feature of a market in which transactions can be quickly executed with little impact on prices.

Liquidity provider (2) A market participant who provides both buy and sell prices for some subset of

contracts offered on the exchange during some specified period of time.

Liquidity risk (15) The risk associated with a thin market for a transaction, as manifested by few dealers and wide bid-ask spreads.

Listing The offering of a security, option, or futures for public trading on an exchange.

Local (8) A trader on the floor of the futures exchange who executes trades for his or her personal account.

Lock-in option (14) An option, when the underlying asset reaches a certain level, allows the holder to set the final payout as the current intrinsic value.

Lognormally distributed (5) A probability distribution of asset returns that is often used to develop option pricing models. An important feature is that the asset price cannot be zero or negative.

London Interbank Offer Rate (LIBOR) The interest rate on certain Eurodollar deposits involving London banks.

Long (8) A position involving the purchase of a security or derivative. It also refers to the party holding the long position.

Long hedge (11) A hedge involving a short position in the spot market and a long position in the futures market.

Lookback option (14) An option granting the right to either buy the underlying asset at its lowest price during the option's life or sell the asset at its highest price during the option's life. Also called a no-regrets option.

Lower bound A value established as the lowest possible price of an option.

Macaulay's duration (11) A version of duration that measures the timing and size of a bond's cash flows, a present-value weighted measure of cash flows.

Maintenance margin (8) The minimum amount of money that must be kept in a margin account on any day other than the day of a transaction.

Managed funds (8) An arrangement in which commodity trading advisors are allocated funds for the purpose of trading futures contracts for a client. Structured as private arrangements, futures funds, and commodity pools.

Margin (2) Funds kept in a margin account for the purpose of covering losses.

Market efficiency (1) A concept referring to a market in which prices reflect the true economic values of the underlying assets.

Market maker (2) A trader in a market who is responsible for buying and selling to the public.

Market-on-close order An order to purchase or sell securities or derivatives that requests the broker to execute the transaction at a price as close as possible to the closing price.

Market order (2) A request to purchase or sell a security or derivative in which the broker is instructed to execute the transaction at the current market price.

Market portfolio The portfolio consisting of all assets in the market.

Market risk (15) The risk that a firm's value or cash flows will be affected by movements in interest rates, exchange rates, stock prices, rates, exchange rates, stock prices, or commodity prices.

Market segmentation theory A theory of the term structure stating that supply and demand forces within each segment of the term structure determine the equilibrium interest rate for that maturity.

Market timing An investment strategy in which the investor attempts to profit by predicting the direction of the market.

Marked to market (8) See Daily settlement.

Master swap agreement A contract form developed by ISDA for simplifying and standardizing swap transactions.

Middle office A component function of a derivatives/risk management system between the front and back office.

Minimum variance hedge ratio The ratio of futures contracts for a given spot position that minimizes the variance of the profit from the hedge.

Min-max option (14) An option involving more than one underlying asset whose payoff is determined by either the higher value (max) of the two assets or the lower value (min) of the two assets. The value of the better or worse performing of the two assets is compared to the exercise price. Also called a rainbow option.

Model (4) A simplified representation of reality that uses certain inputs to produce an output, or result.

Model risk (15) The risk associated with the use of an incorrect or inappropriate model or a model containing errors or incorrect inputs.

Modified duration (11) A version of duration that measures the price sensitivity of a bond to changes in yield, a useful measure in interest rate risk management.

Modified lookback option (14) A lookback option in which the payoff is determined by replacing the exercise price by either the high or low price reached by the asset during the option's life.

Money market The market for short-term securities.

Money spread (7) An option transaction that involves a long position in one option and a short position in an otherwise identical option with a different exercise price.

Monte Carlo simulation (14) A procedure for pricing derivatives that involves the generation of random numbers representing prices of the underlying and calculating the derivative value as an average of the possible derivative values obtained from the simulations.

Monte Carlo simulation method (15) A procedure for estimating Value at Risk using Monte Carlo simulation. Compare with Historical method and Analytical method.

Mortgage-backed security (14) A security providing the holder returns based on the payments from a portfolio of underlying mortgages.

Mortgage pass-through (14) A type of mortgage-backed security in which mortgage principal and interest payments are passed through, less a service fee, to holders of the security.

Mortgage strip (14) See Interest-only strip and Principal-only strip.

Multi-asset option (14) An option whose payoff is based on the performance of more than one underlying asset. See also Exchange option and Min-max option.

Multilateral netting (15) Netting between more than two parties, which is essentially equivalent to a clearinghouse.

Multiple listing The listing of identical options on more than one exchange.

Mutual fund A company whose shareholders' money is pooled and used to purchase securities.

Naked call See Uncovered call.

National Association of Securities Dealers A former organization of firms that served as market makers for stocks traded over-the-counter, now part of FINRA.

National Futures Association An organization of firms engaged in the futures business that serves as the industry's self-regulatory body.

Nearby contract (1) The futures contract that is closest to maturing when compared to other futures contracts on the same exchange and the same commodity.

Needs-driven risk management (15) A risk management approach where the primary focus is on the manager's view of the existing risk exposures and not the manager's view of the future. *See also* View-driven risk management.

Net interest (9) The interest opportunity cost of holding any asset less any cash flow in the form of explicit interest or dividends received.

Net present value The present value of an investment's cash flows minus the initial cost of the investment.

Netting (15) The practice of aggregating all swaps between two parties and determining the net amount owed from one party to the other.

Netting by novation (15) Netting in which the net value of a combination of transactions is replaced by a single transaction.

Non-recombining tree (4) A binomial tree in which an up move followed by a down move does not put you in the same location as a down move followed by an up move.

No-regrets option (14) See Lookback option.

No risk premium hypothesis A theory of futures markets in which the futures price is determined such that a speculator in futures contracts does not expect to earn a risk premium. In this case the futures prices will be an unbiased predictor of the future spot price.

Normal backwardation (9) A condition in which the forward or futures price or rate is less than the expected future spot price or rate at expiration.

Normal contango (9) A condition in which the forward or futures price or rate is greater than the expected future spot price or rate at expiration.

Normal distribution A probability distribution often described as a bell-shaped curve. Also called a standard normal distribution.

Normal probability (5) The probability that a normally distributed random variable will be less than or equal to a given value.

Notice of intention day (8) The second day in the three-day sequence leading to delivery in which the clearinghouse notifies the holder of the long position that delivery will be made the next business day.

Notional amount (1) A measure of the size of a swap or derivative, stated in units of a currency, on which the payments are calculated.

Off-market FRA (13) An FRA in which the fixed rate is not the fixed rate that would produce a zero value at the start.

Offset (2) See Offsetting order.

Offsetting (8) A method of terminating a swap in which a party enters into a new swap with payments occurring on the same dates as the old swap. Both swaps remain in effect. See also Offsetting order.

Offsetting order (2) A derivative transaction that is the exact opposite of a previously established long or short position and cancels the previous outstanding position.

Open interest (2) The number of futures or options contracts that have been established and not yet offset or exercised.

Open outcry (8) A system of trading derivatives or securities in which bids and offers are announced and accepted orally in an open medium such as the trading pit of an exchange.

Operational risk (15) The risk of a breakdown in the operations of a derivatives program or risk management system.

Option (1) A contract granting the right to buy or sell an asset, currency, or futures at a fixed price for a specific time period.

Option class (2) All options of a particular type—call or put—on a given instrument.

Option on futures (1) An option to buy or sell a futures contract.

Option pricing (4) Obtaining the theoretical fair value.

Option pricing model (4) A mathematical equation or procedure that produces the theoretical fair value of an option.

Option series (2) All options of a given class with the same exercise price and expiration.

Options Clearing Corporation (2) The firm that operates as a clearinghouse for the various exchanges that trade options on stocks and indices.

Options exchange An organized facility for trading options, which is governed by a corporate charter with rules and regulations. It may utilize a trading floor or may be an electronic exchange. See also Electronic trading.

Order book official (2) An employee of the Chicago Board Options Exchange who keeps public limit orders and attempts to fill them at the best available price.

Out-of-the-money (2) A call (put) in which the price of the asset, currency, or futures is less (greater) than the exercise price.

Out-option (14) A type of barrier option in which the premium is paid but the option terminates early if the asset price crosses a specified barrier. See also Down-and-out option and Up-and-out option.

Outperformance option (14) An option involving two underlying assets in which the final payout is based on the difference between the values or relative performances of the two assets.

Overnight repo A repurchase agreement with a maturity of one night. See also Term repo.

Overpriced A condition in which a security or derivative is trading at more than its value.

Over-the-counter derivative A derivative created in an over-the-counter market and in which there is no active secondary market.

Over-the-counter market A market for securities or derivatives in which the transactions are conducted among dealers, brokers, and the public off an organized exchange.

Parity (3) See Intrinsic value.

Parity value (3) See Intrinsic value.

Path dependence A characteristic of options in which the payoff of the option is affected by the sequence of prices of the underlying asset as it moves toward expiration. See also Path independence.

Path-dependent option (14) An option where the path followed by the asset during the life of the option has an effect on the option's price.

Path independence A characteristic of options in which the payoff of the option is not affected by the sequence of prices of the underlying asset as it moves toward expiration. See also Path dependence.

Payer swaption (13) A swaption in which the party holding the option has the right to enter into a swap and pay the fixed rate.

Pay-later option (14) An option in which the premium is paid at expiration.

Payment netting (15) Netting in which two parties to a transaction settle the amounts simultaneously owed by having one party pay the other the net amount.

Payoff The amount of money received from a transaction at the end of the holding period.

Percentage return (1) A measurement of an investment's performance computed as the return per dollar invested.

PERCS (Preference Equity Redemption Cumulative Stock) Convertible preferred stock with a maximum payoff, which makes it similar to a covered call.

Perfect hedge A hedge in which the gain on one side of the transaction exactly offsets the loss on the other under all possible outcomes. Rarely exists in the real world.

Performance bond (8) A preferred name for the margin deposit required in futures markets. Makes a distinction between stock market margin, which reflects the borrowing of funds, and futures market margin, which is simply a good-faith deposit.

Performativity (5) In the human sciences, when an observed activity is made more consistent with a particular economic model as participants increasingly believe in the model.

Pit An octagonally or hexagonally shaped, multi-tiered area on the trading floor of a derivatives exchange within which a group of contracts trades.

Plain vanilla swap (12) See Fixed-for-floating rate swap.

Planned amortization class bonds One component tranche of a collateralized mortgage obligation in which an assumed rate of prepayments is embedded into the contract terms. Also called a PAC bond.

PO See Principal-only strip.

Portfolio insurance (14) An investment strategy employing combinations of securities, Treasury bills, or derivatives that is designed to provide a minimum or floor value of the portfolio at a future date.

Portfolio theory The study of the economic processes through which investors' portfolio decisions are made.

Position day (8) The first day in the three-day sequence leading to delivery in which the holder of the short position notifies the clearinghouse of the intention to make delivery two business days later.

Position limit (2) The maximum number of options or futures contracts that any one investor can hold.

Position trader (2) A futures trader who normally holds open positions for a period longer than a day.

Potential credit risk (15) The risk that a party to a transaction will be unable to make payments due in the future.

Preferred habitat theory See Market segmentation theory.

Premium (2) A fee the buyer pays the seller; the option's price.

Prepayment risk (14) In mortgage- or asset-backed securities, the risk to the holder that the underlying mortgage or other underlying securities will be paid off early due to falling interest rates.

Price sensitivity hedge ratio The number of futures contracts used in a hedge that leaves the value of a portfolio unaffected by a change in an underlying variable, such as an interest rate.

Primary market The market for securities originally issued and not previously traded among the public.

Principal-only strip (14) A type of mortgage-backed security in which mortgage principal payments are passed through, less a service fee, to holders. See also Interest-only strip.

Program trading (10) The trading of large blocks of stock as part of a program of index arbitrage or portfolio insurance.

Protective put (6) An investment strategy involving the use of a long position in a put and the underlying asset, futures, or currency to provide a minimum selling price for the asset, futures, or currency.

Pure discount bond A bond, such as a Treasury bill, that pays no coupon but sells for a discount from par value.

Put (1) An option to sell an asset, currency, or futures.

Put-call-forward/futures parity (9) The relationship among the prices of puts, calls, and futures on a security, commodity, or currency.

Put-call parity (3) The relationship between the prices of puts, calls, and the underlying security, commodity, or currency.

Put option (2) See Put.

Quality option (10) The right to deliver any one from a set of eligible bonds on the Chicago Board of Trade's Treasury Bond futures contract or a similar right inherent in any other futures contract.

Quantity risk (11) The risk involved in a hedge in which the hedger does not know how many units of the spot asset he or she will own or sell.

Quanto (14) A derivative in which a foreign currency price or rate is converted to another currency at a fixed rate.

Quanto swap See Diff swap.

Quasi arbitrage (9) An arbitrage transaction in which the holder of an asset sells the asset, replaces it with a futures contract, and then reverses the transaction later when the price converges to the cost of carry price.

Rainbow option (14) See Min-max option.

Range floater (14) A type of floating rate structured note in which the interest payments can change depending on whether a reference interest rate remains in a particular range.

Range forward A forward contract with a limited gain and loss. Also known as a risk reversal and a collar.

Ratio spread (7) A spread transaction in which the number of contracts is weighted to produce a risk-free position.

Real asset (1) A tangible asset such as real estate or equipment.

Real option (2) An option embedded in a corporate investment opportunity.

Receiver swaption (13) A swaption in which the party holding the option has the right to enter into a swap and receive the fixed rate.

Recombining tree (4) A binomial tree in which an up move followed by a down move puts you in the same location as a down move followed by an up move.

Reference entity (15) The party in a credit derivatives transaction on whose credit the credit derivatives transaction is based.

Registered option trader (ROT) (2) An options trader on the floor of the American Stock Exchange who trades options for his or her personal account.

Regulatory risk (15) The risk that regulations or the current regulatory style will change, with adverse consequences for a firm. Regulatory risk may render certain existing or contemplated transactions illegal or hinder the development of new products and solutions.

Repo (10) See Repurchase agreement.

Reportable position (8) The number of contracts that if held by a futures trader must by law be reported to the regulatory authorities.

Repurchase agreement (1) A securities transaction in which an investor sells a security and promises to repurchase it a specified number of days later at a higher price reflecting the prevailing interest rate.

Reset option An option that permits the holder to change the exercise price if the stock price hits a certain level.

Residual tranche One component tranche of a collateralized mortgage obligation entitling the holder to whatever cash remains after all other tranches have been repaid.

Retractable bond A bond in which the holder can choose to redeem prior to maturity.

Return (1) A measure of the increase in wealth from an investment.

Reversal (6) See Offset.

Reverse conversion (6) An arbitrage transaction consisting of the sale of a put and the purchase of a synthetic put.

Reverse floater (14) See Inverse floater.

Rho (5) The rate of change of an option's price with respect to the risk-free interest rate.

Risk (1) In the financial sense, a measure of the variability or uncertainty of a transaction or portfolio.

Risk aversion (1) The characteristic referring to an investor who dislikes risk and will not assume more risk without an additional return.

Risk-free rate (1) The return offered by an investment in an asset with no risk.

Risk management (15) The practice of identifying the risk level a firm desires, identifying the risk level it currently has, and using derivative or other financial instruments to adjust the actual risk level to the desired risk level.

Risk neutral (1) The characteristic referring to an investor who is indifferent toward risk.

Risk-neutral probability (5) The probability that would be assigned to an outcome by a person who is risk neutral (indifferent) to risk. See also Risk neutral.

Risk preferences An investor's feelings toward risk.

Risk premium (1) The additional return risk-averse investors expect for assuming risk.

Risk premium hypothesis (9) A theory of futures markets in which the futures price is determined such that a speculator in futures contracts expects to earn a risk premium for assuming risk, a result of the transferral of the risk premium from hedgers. In this case the futures price will be a biased predictor of the future spot price.

Risk-return trade-off (1) The concept in which additional risk must be accepted to increase the expected return.

Risk reversal See Collar.

Rolling strip hedge A strip hedge with a relatively long hedge horizon in which the longer maturity futures are added as nearby futures expire.

Rolling up A covered call strategy using an out-of-the-money call in which an investor buys back the call when the stock price rises to near the exercise price and sells another out-of-the-money call.

Sale or assignment A method of terminating a swap in which a party makes or receives a cash payment and passes on its swap payment obligations to another party.

Sandwich spread (7) See Butterfly spread.

Scalper (2) A trader on the floor of a derivatives exchange whose trading style involves short holding periods and small profits based on small price changes.

Scratch trade A trade primarily executed to adjust a dealer's inventory and in which no profit or loss is made.

Seat (2) A term used to refer to a membership on a derivatives or stock exchange.

Secondary market The market for assets that were issued previously and are now trading among investors.

Securities and Exchange Commission (SEC) The federal agency responsible for regulating the securities and listed options markets.

Securities Investor Protection Corporation (SIPC) A federal agency that provides investors with insurance against failure of a brokerage firm.

Securitization (14) The process of creating asset-backed securities.

Selling short See Short sale.

Selling the spread (7) See Credit spread.

Series All of the options of a given class with the same exercise price and expiration.

Settlement date (12) The date on which a payment for a swap is made.

Settlement period (12) The period between settlement dates of a swap.

Settlement price (8) The official price established by the clearinghouse at the end of each day for use in the daily settlement.

Settlement risk (15) The risk often faced in international transactions in which a firm exchanges payments with another party and is subject to the risk that its payments may be sent before receipt of the other party's payments, which may not be sent due to bankruptcy, insolvency, or fraud.

Short (8) A term used to refer to holding a short position or to the party holding the short position.

Short hedge (11) A hedge transaction involving a long position in the spot market and a short position in the futures market.

Short sale An investment transaction in which securities are borrowed from a broker and sold to a buyer and, at a later time, repurchased and paid back to the broker.

Selling short (1) Selling an asset that is not currently owned, but borrowed, a position in which the investor benefits if the price falls.

Shout option (14) An option that allows the holder to set the minimum value of the final payout as the current intrinsic value when the underlying asset reaches a certain level.

Simple return A rate of return that is not compounded.

Special purpose vehicle (15) See Enhanced derivatives products company.

Specialist (2) A trader on the floor of an exchange who is responsible for making a market in certain securities or derivatives.

Speculation Investments characterized by a high degree of risk and usually short holding periods.

Speculative value (3) See Time value.

Speculator (1) One who engages in speculative transactions.

Spot market (1) The market for assets that involves the immediate sale and delivery of the asset.

Spot price The price of an asset on the spot market.

Spot rate An interest rate on a loan or bond created in the spot market.

Spread (7) A derivatives transaction consisting of a long position in one contract and a short position in another similar contract.

Spreader (2) A person or institution that engages in a spread transaction.

Stack hedge A hedge in which the hedge horizon is longer than the expiration of the shortest-lived futures contract but due to lower liquidity of longer maturity futures, extra contracts of shorter maturity futures are used. Sometimes called a stack.

Standard deviation A measure of the dispersion of a random variable around its mean, equal to the square root of the variance.

Stock index A combination of stock prices designed to measure the performance of the stocks as a whole.

Stock index arbitrage (10) The purchase or sale of a portfolio of stock that replicates a stock index and the sale or purchase of a futures contract on the index. Occurs when the futures price does not conform to the cost of carry model.

Stock index futures A futures contract on an underlying stock index.

Stock option (2) See Equity option.

Stop order (2) An order to purchase or sell securities or derivatives that is not executed until the price reaches a certain level.

Storage The process in which an asset is held for a certain time period.

Storage cost The cost of holding an asset, including the physical costs of storage and the interest lost on funds tied up.

Straddle (7) An option transaction that involves a long position in a put and a call with the same exercise price and expiration.

Strangle A long put at one exercise price and a long call at a higher exercise price.

Strap An option transaction that involves a long position in two calls and one put, or two calls for every put, with the same exercise price and expiration.

Strategic asset allocation An investment management style reflecting the desired long run allocation of funds across asset classes.

Stress test (15) A method of testing a risk management system in which a portfolio's performance under extremely large changes in the underlying is examined.

Strike price (2) See Exercise price.

Strike rate See Exercise rate.

Strike spread (7) See Money spread.

Striking price See Exercise price.

Strip An option transaction that involves a long position in two puts and one call, or two puts for every call, with the same exercise price and expiration. See also Strip hedge.

Strip hedge A hedge in which a series of futures contracts of successively longer expirations are used to cover a hedge horizon longer than the expiration of the shortest-lived futures contract. Sometimes called a strip.

Stripped treasuries Securities that represent claims on coupons and principal of Treasury bonds. The Treasury bond is purchased and stripped treasuries are sold against the coupons and principal on the Treasury bond.

Structured note (14) A promissory note, usually with a floating rate, in which the coupon has been enhanced by a derivative to provide for an increased or decreased payment.

Swap (1) A derivative transaction in which two parties agree to exchange cash flows calculated according to different formulas. See also Interest rate swap, Currency swap, Commodity swap, Equity swap.

Swap book A swap dealer's inventory of swaps.

Swap dealer A firm that arranges an interest rate or currency swap between two other parties.

Swap option See Swaption.

Swap rate The fixed rate that a swap dealer will pay or receive on a swap.

Swap spread (12) The difference between the fixed rate that a swap dealer will pay or receive and the rate on the U.S. Treasury note of equivalent maturity.

Swaption (1) An option granting the right to enter into a swap. See also Payer swaption and Receiver swaption.

Switching option Sometimes defined as the right to switch bonds in a cash and carry transaction using Treasury Bond futures although this right is a result of the quality option. See also Quality option.

Synthetic call (6) A combination of a long put and long asset, futures, or currency that replicates the behavior of a call. It may sometimes include a short position in risk-free bonds.

Synthetic CDO (15) Credit derivatives that have been combined into a portfolio; claims on that portfolio are sold through credit default swaps.

Synthetic futures contract (9) A combination of a long call and a short put that replicates the behavior of a long futures contract. It may sometimes include a long or short position in risk-free bonds.

Synthetic put (6) A combination of a long call and short asset, currency, or futures that replicates the behavior of a put. It may sometimes include a long position in risk-free bonds.

Systematic risk The risk associated with the market or economy as a whole.

Systemic risk (15) The risk that failure of one or more financial institutions will trigger more failures, ultimately leading to a breakdown of the financial system.

Tactical asset allocation An investment management style in which funds are allocated to various asset classes on the basis of the expected performance of each class over a short period of time, in contrast with strategic asset allocation.

Tail The number of additional futures contracts purchased or sold to complete a wild card or quality option delivery.

Tailing the hedge Adjusting the hedge ratio so that the effects of the interest earned or paid from the daily settlement are taken into account.

Tandem option (14) An option that actually represents a sequence of options, with a new option automatically beginning as soon as a given option expires.

Target beta (11) The desired beta of a stock portfolio.

Target duration (11) The desired duration of a bond portfolio.

Tax risk (15) The risk that tax laws or the interpretation of tax laws will change, with adverse consequences.

TED spread A transaction in which one takes a long position in a Treasury bill or Treasury bill futures and a short position in a Eurodollar or Eurodollar futures or vice versa. Alternatively, the difference between Treasury bill spot or futures and Eurodollar spot or futures rates.

Term repo A repurchase agreement with a maturity of more than one day. See also Overnight repo.

Term structure of implied volatility (5) The relationship between the implied volatility of an option and the expiration of the option.

Term structure of interest rates The relationship between interest rates and maturities of zero coupon bonds.

Theoretical fair price The price of a derivative that permits no arbitrage opportunities. See also Theoretical fair value.

Theoretical fair value (1) The true or appropriate worth of an asset or derivative, which is obtained from a model based on rational investor behavior and the absence of arbitrage opportunities. See also Theoretical fair price.

Theta (5) The rate of change of an option's price with respect to time.

Tick (8) The minimum permissible price fluctuation.

Time spread (7) See Calendar spread.

Time value (3) The difference between an option's price and its intrinsic value.

Time value decay (3) The erosion of an option's time value as expiration approaches.

Timing option (10) Either the right to defer delivery until any acceptable delivery date on the Chicago Board of Trade's Treasury bond futures contracts or any similar right inherent in a futures contract.

Total return swap (15) A type of credit derivative in the form of a swap in which one party agrees to pay the return on a specific security, usually a bond. The other party usually agrees to pay a fixed or floating interest rate.

Tracking error (12) The deviation of the performance of a portfolio from the performance of a derivative used with the portfolio.

Trading halt A rule associated with futures or stock trading in which trading will temporarily cease if prices move by a specified amount during a specified period of time.

Tranche (14) One component of a collateralized mortgage obligation entitling the holder to a specific stream of payments that may differ in characteristics, priority, and risk from another tranche.

Treasury bill A short-term pure-discount bond issued by the U.S. government with original maturities of 91, 182, and 365 days.

Treasury bond A coupon-bearing bond issued by the U.S. government with an original maturity of at least ten years.

Treasury note A coupon-bearing bond issued by the U.S. government with an original maturity of one to ten years.

Triangular arbitrage The foreign currency arbitrage transaction that forces the cross-rate relationship to hold. See also Cross-rate relationship.

Turtle trade An arbitrage spread transaction in which a forward borrowing (or lending) rate is locked in on the Treasury bond or note futures market and a forward lending (or borrowing) rate is locked in on the Treasury bill futures market.

Two-state model (4) See Binomial model.

Unbiased A characteristic of a forecast in which the prediction equals the actual outcome on average over a large number of predictions.

Unbiased expectations theory See Expectations theory.

Uncovered call (6) An option strategy in which an investor writes a call on a stock not owned.

Underlying The asset or instrument on which a derivative's payoff is based.

Underpriced A condition in which a security or derivative is trading at less than its value.

Unsystematic return The portion of a security's return that is related to factors associated with the individual security and not to the market as a whole.

Unsystematic risk The risk of a security related to factors specific to it and not to the market as a whole.

Up-and-in option An in barrier option in which the premium is paid but the option does not actually begin unless the asset price rises to a specified barrier.

Up-and-out option An out barrier option in which the premium is paid but the option terminates early if the asset price rises to a specified barrier.

Up-option (14) A type of barrier option in which the barrier is above the current level of the underlying.

Upside capture (14) The percentage of the market value of an uninsured portfolio earned by an insured portfolio in a bull market.

Uptick An increase in the price of a security or contract equal to one tick.

Utility A measure of satisfaction usually obtained from money or wealth.

Value A monetary measure of the worth of an investment or contract that reflects its contribution to the investor's wealth.

Value at Risk (VAR) (15) A dollar measure of the minimum loss that would be expected over a period of time with a given probability.

Variance A measure of the dispersion of a random variable around its mean, equal to the square of the standard deviation.

Variance-covariance method (15) See Analytical method.

Variation margin (8) Money added to or subtracted from a futures account that reflects profits or losses accruing from the daily settlement.

Vega (5) The rate of change of an option's price with respect to the volatility of the underlying asset or futures.

Vega hedge A hedged position, usually combined with a delta hedge and a gamma hedge, in which changes in the value of the position are unaffected by changes in the volatility of the underlying.

Versus cash (8) See Exchange for physicals.

Vertical spread (7) See Money spread.

View-driven risk management (15) A risk management approach where the primary focus is on the manager's view of the future and not on his or her view of the existing risk exposures. See also Needs-driven risk management.

Volatility The characteristic of fluctuations in price. Usually refers to standard deviation.

Volatility skew (5) The relationship between the implied volatility of an option and the exercise price, which does not form a U-shaped pattern, but is skewed in some form.

Volatility smile (5) The relationship between the implied volatility of an option and the exercise price that forms a U-shaped pattern.

Volatility strategy (7) An option strategy designed to profit from unusually high or low volatility of the underlying asset.

Warehousing The practice in which a dealer holds positions in various swaps in an inventory.

Warrant (14) An option issued by a corporation to buy or sell its stock. Usually has a life of several years when originally issued.

Wash sale A transaction in which a stock is sold at a loss and an essentially identical stock, or a call option on the stock, is purchased within a 61-day period surrounding the sale. Tax laws prohibit deducting the loss on the sale.

Weather derivative (14) A derivative in which the underlying is a measure of the weather.

Wild card option The right to deliver on the Chicago Board of Trade's Treasury bond futures contract after the close of trading in the futures market or a similar right inherent in any other futures contract.

Writer A person or institution that sells an option.

Yield The discount rate on a bond that equates the present value of the coupons and principal to the price.

Yield beta (11) The slope coefficient from a regression of the yield on a spot bond on the yield implied by the futures contract. Measures the relationship between the spot yield and the yield implied by the futures price.

Yield curve The relationship between yields on bonds and their maturities.

Yield to maturity See Yield.

Z statistic (5) A statistic based on a normal distribution. The probability of observing such a statistic is obtained from the normal distribution. See also Normal probability.

Z-bond One component tranche of a collateralized mortgage obligation in which interest accrues but no principal or interest is paid until higher priority tranches are repaid.

Zero-cost collar (13) A collar in which the premiums on the long cap and short floor offset so that there is no premium paid up front.

Zero coupon bond See Pure discount bond.

Zero-plus tick A situation in a financial market in which a trade takes place at the same price as the last trade but the last time a price changed, it increased.

Index

List of Symbols

$$\alpha = \text{alpha, unsystematic return}$$

$$A_0, A_T = \text{market value of firm assets at time 0 and T}$$

$$AI, AI_t, AI_T = \text{accrued interest today, at time t, and at time T}$$

$$b, b_t, b_T = \text{basis today, at time t, and at expiration, T}$$

$$B = \text{market value of bond portfolio}$$

$$\beta, \beta_s, \beta_f, \beta_T, \beta_y = \text{beta, beta of spot asset or portfolio, beta of futures, target beta, and yield beta}$$

$$B_0, B_T = \text{market value of firm debt at time 0 and T}$$

$$B_0(t_i) = \text{price of zero coupon bond observed at time 0, matures in } t_i \text{ days}$$

$$C = \text{(abbreviated) price of call}$$

$$C_1, C_2, C_3 = \text{(abbreviated) price of call for exercise prices } X_1, X_2, X_3$$

$$C(S_0,T,X) = \text{price of either European or American call on asset with price } S_0, \text{ expiration T, and exercise price X}$$

$$C_e(S_0,T,X) = \text{price of European call on asset with price } S_0, \text{ expiration T, and exercise price X}$$

$$C_a(S_0,T,X) = \text{price of American call on asset with price } S_0, \text{ expiration T, and exercise price X}$$

$$C(f_0,T,X) = \text{price of either European or American call on futures with price } f_0, \text{ expiration T, and exercise price X}$$

$$C_e(f_0,T,X) = \text{price of European call on futures with price } f_0, \text{ expiration T, and exercise price X}$$

$$C_a(f_0,T,X) = \text{price of American call on futures with price } f_0, \text{ expiration T, and exercise price X}$$

$$C_u, C_d, C_u^2, C_{ud}, C_d^2 = \text{call price sequence in binomial model}$$

$$\chi = \text{convenience yield}$$

$$CI_t = \text{coupon interest paid at time t}$$

$$Cov_{\Delta S, \Delta f} = \text{covariance of the change in the spot price and change in the futures price}$$

$$Cov_{r_s, r_f} = \text{covariance of the rate of return on the spot and futures}$$

$$\rho_{\Delta S, \Delta f} = \text{correlation of the change in the spot price and change in the futures price}$$

$$CP_t = \text{cash payment (principal or interest) on bond at time t}$$

$$CF = \text{conversion factor on CBOT T-bond contract}$$

$$CF(t), CF(T) = \text{conversion factor on CBOT T-bond contracts deliverable at times t and T}$$

c = coupon rate

CDS premium = credit default swap premium

Δ = delta of an option

$\Delta B, \Delta M, \Delta S, \Delta f, \Delta y_B, \Delta y_f$ = change in bond price, change in market portfolio value, change in spot price, change in futures price, change in bond yield, change in futures yield

$DC_{aon}, DP_{aon}, DC_{con}, DP_{con}$ = value of asset-or-nothing digital call and put, value of cash-or-nothing digital call and put

δ_c = continuously compounded dividend yield

d = (without subscript) $1.0 +$ downward return on stock in binomial model

d_1, d_2 = variables in Black-Scholes-Merton model

D_0, D = present value of dividends to time 0, present value of dividends

D_j, D_t = dividend paid at time j or time t

D_T = compound future value of reinvested dividends

DUR_B = Macaulay's duration

ε = standard normal random variable in Monte Carlo simulation

$E(x)$ = expected value of the argument x

e^* = measure of hedging effectiveness

f_0, f_t, f_T, f = (abbreviated) futures price at time 0, t, and T value of futures position

$f_0(T), f_t(T), f_T(T)$ = futures price or futures exchange rate today, at time t, and at expiration T

$f_0(T)_{(a)}^{\ddagger}$ = critical futures price for early exercise of American option on futures

F = fixed rate on FRAs or continuously compounded forward rate

$F(0,T)$ = forward price for contracts written today 0, expiring at T

FV = face value of bond

g = days elapsed in FRA

Γ = gamma of an option

h = number of days in FRA when originated

h_C, h_S = hedge ratios based on Black-Scholes-Merton model

h, h_u, h_d = hedge ratios in binomial model

i = interest rate for storage problem

J = number of observations in sample

j = counter in summation procedure

K = parameter in break forward contract

k = discount rate (required rate) on stock

LIBOR = London Interbank Offer Rate, a Eurodollar rate

$\ln(x)$ = natural log of the argument x

$L_t(h)$ = h-day LIBOR at t

m = number of days associated with interest rate

M = value of market portfolio of all risky assets

MD_B, MD_f, MD_T = modified duration of bond portfolio, modified duration of futures contract, target modified duration

$$MOS = \text{number of months in computing CBOT conversion factor}$$

$$MOS^* = \text{number of months in computing CBOT conversion factor rounded down to nearest quarter}$$

$$N = \text{total number in summation procedure}$$

$$N_1, N_2, N_3 = \text{quantity of options}$$

$$N(d_1), N(d_2) = \text{cumulative normal probabilities in Black-Scholes-Merton model}$$

$$N_f^* = \text{optimal hedge ratio}$$

$$NPV = \text{net present value}$$

$$N_B, N_C, N_P, N_S, N_f = \text{number of bonds, calls, puts, shares of stock, and futures held in a position}$$

$$NP, NP^{\epsilon}, NP^{\$} = \text{notional principle, euros, dollars}$$

$$n = \text{number of time periods in n-period binomial model}$$

$$\Pi = \text{profit from the strategy}$$

$$P = \text{(abbreviated) price of put}$$

$$P_1, P_2, P_3 = \text{(abbreviated) price of put for exercise prices } X_1, X_2, X_3$$

$$P(S_0,T,X) = \text{price of either European or American put on asset with price } S_0\text{, expiration T, and exercise price X}$$

$$P_e(S_0,T,X) = \text{price of European put on asset with price } S_0\text{, expiration T, and exercise price X}$$

$$P_a(S_0,T,X) = \text{price of American put on asset with price } S_0\text{, expiration T, and exercise price X}$$

$$P(f_0,T,X) = \text{price of either European or American put on futures with price } f_0\text{, expiration T, and exercise price X}$$

$$P_e(f_0,T,X) = \text{price of European put on futures with price } f_0\text{, expiration T, and exercise price X}$$

$$P_a(f_0,T,X) = \text{price of American put on futures with price } f_0\text{, expiration T, and exercise price X}$$

$$p = \text{binomial probability}$$

$$PVBP_B, PVBP_f = \text{present value of basis point change for bond, futures}$$

$$\Phi = \text{risk premium}$$

$$E(\Phi) = \text{expected risk premium}$$

$$q = \text{days/360}$$

$$R = \text{fixed interest rate on swap or bond}$$

$$r = \text{discrete risk-free rate}$$

$$r(a,b) = \text{interest rate over time interval (a,b)}$$

$$\hat{r} = \text{implied repo rate}$$

$$r_h = \text{return on hedged portfolio}$$

$$r_c = \text{continuously compounded risk-free rate}$$

$$r_f = \text{percentage change in futures price}$$

$$r_s = \text{return on stock or spot position}$$

$$r_{Sf} = \text{return on portfolio of stock and futures}$$

$$r_M = \text{return on market}$$

$$r^c = \text{continuously compounded return}$$

$$\bar{r}^c = \text{mean continuously compounded return}$$

$$\rho = \text{foreign interest rate}$$

$$s = \text{storage costs}$$

S_0' = stock price minus present value of dividends

S_{avg} = average stock price during life of option

S_{max} = maximum stock price during life of option

S_{min} = minimum stock price during life of option

S_0, S_t, S_T = stock price (or spot price or spot exchange rate) today, at time t, and at time T

S_T^* = breakeven stock price at expiration

σ = standard deviation or volatility (σ^2 = variance)

T, T_1, T_2 = expiration or time to expiration from the current time

t, t_j = future point in time or time until a particular future date

θ = cost of carry

u = 1.0 + upward return on stock in binomial model

$v_0(T), v_t(T)$ = value of futures contract at time 0 and time t, expiring at time t

$V_0(0,T), V_t(0,T)$ = value of forward contract at time 0 and time t, created at time 0 expiring at time T

V = current value of portfolio

$V_{FLRB}, V_{FXRB}, VS, VFRA$ = value of floating rate bond, fixed rate bond, swap, FRA

V_{min} = minimum or insured value of portfolio

V_u, V_d, V_{ud} = sequence of hedge portfolio values of portfolio in binomial model

YRS = number of years in computation of CBOT conversion factor

y, y_B = yield, yield on spot bond

y_f = implied yield on futures

VAR = Value at Risk

$\sigma^2, \sigma_{r_f}^2, \sigma_1^2, \sigma_2^2, \sigma_p^2$ = variance, variance of return on futures, asset 1, asset 2, portfolio

$\sigma_\Pi^2, \sigma_{\Delta S}^2, \sigma_{\Delta f}^2$ = variance of the portfolio, variance of the change in spot position, variance of the change in futures position

X, X_1, X_2, X_3 = exercise prices or rates

x_1, x_2, x_3 = number of contracts when hedging with option delta, gamma, and theta

w_1, w_2 = weights for assets in portfolio